A Consolidation of Fifty Years of Legal Writings 1938–1988

by Wilbur F. Bowker

WILBUR F. BOWKER
1989

A Consolidation of Fifty Years of Legal Writings 1938–1988

by Wilbur F. Bowker

Compiled and Edited by
Marjorie Bowker
B.A., LL.B., LL.D.
Former Judge
Provincial Court of Alberta
Family and Juvenile Divisions 1966–1983

FACULTY OF LAW
UNIVERSITY OF ALBERTA

First published by
The Faculty of Law
University of Alberta
Edmonton, Alberta,
Canada T6G 2H5
1989

ISBN 0-88864-210-5

Canadian Cataloguing in Publication Data

Bowker, Wilbur F., 1910-
A consolidation of fifty years of legal writings

Includes bibliographical references.
ISBN 0-88864-210-5

1. Law - Canada. 2. Law - Alberta.
I. Bowker, Marjorie Montgomery. II. University of Alberta. Faculty of Law. III. Title.
KE448.B69 1989 349.71 C89-091426-5

Typesetting by The Typeworks, Vancouver, British Columbia

Printed by John Deyell Company, Lindsay, Ontario, Canada

Published with assistance from the Alberta Law Foundation

Dedicated
to
former students
of
Dean Wilbur F. Bowker

Preface

It seems appropriate to assemble in a single collection the legal writings of Wilbur Bowker which extend over a period of five decades.

These writings embrace a wide variety of subjects, from such topics as wills, estates, succession, intestacy and dower, to human rights, anti-discrimination, law reform, medical experimentation, and professional ethics. They mirror the various stages of the author's career, from those of practising lawyer, to graduate student, to law professor, to Director of legal research. They cover historical material, contemporary developments in the law, and possible future trends.

Even while this material is being assembled, Wilbur Bowker is continuing on a long-range project—writing and research relating to Alberta's legal history. With that, as well as with all his previous writings, he has derived inspiration and encouragement from exchanges with colleagues, students and practitioners who have shared his interests. That they and others may in turn derive satisfaction is the purpose of this collection.

MARJORIE BOWKER
Editor

Edmonton, Alberta
July 1987

Contents

Foreword

This collection of legal writings was completed by the editor, Marjorie Bowker, as a personal project and was intended for limited distribution (some fifteen copies in all) to family members, a few libraries, and archives.

By chance, Judge Anne Russell learned of the collection as it neared completion, and asked the Editor for permission to explore the possibility for a wider circulation. She held discussions with several interested persons, and as a result a Committee was formed with the following members:

Mr. L.A. Desrochers, C.R.
Mr. W.H. Hurlburt, Q.C.
Mr. P.M. Owen, Q.C.
Madam Justice E.I. Picard
Judge A.H. Russell
Mr. E.D.D. Tavender, Q.C.
Mr. H.W. Veale, Q.C.
Mr. Justice W.A. Wachowich
Judge W.G.W. White.

Apart from giving their permission, the Bowkers had no part in the publication in its present format and they received no remuneration. It was the view of the Committee that these legal writings and accompanying editorial comments should be published in a special commemorative edition as a tribute to Wilbur F. Bowker, Q.C. who served on the Faculty of Law, University of Alberta for twenty-three years, including twenty years as Dean (1948–1968), and later as first Director of the Institute of Law Research and Reform (1968–1975).

Publication was made possible through a grant from the Alberta Law Foundation.

TIMOTHY J. CHRISTIAN
Dean of Law
University of Alberta

Edmonton, Alberta
December 12, 1988

Acknowledgements

The Publisher gratefully acknowledges a grant from the Alberta Law Foundation which permitted reproduction of these writings in the format of this book.

Permission to reproduce the articles herein has been obtained from the editors of all publications wherein these writings originally appeared.

The commentaries appearing at the top of each article were prepared by the Editor, Marjorie Bowker.

Introduction

by The Honourable
Ronald Martland, C.C.,

Retired Justice, Supreme Court of Canada

I am very pleased to have been asked to prepare an introduction to this volume containing the legal writings of my old friend and former partner, Wilbur Bowker. We had a close association in the law firm now known as Milner & Steer. I admired his careful industry in researching legal problems which he had to consider, and which is manifested in his legal writings.

I am glad that there is included with these writings the excellent article about him written by Professor Trevor Anderson, who was for a time a colleague of Wilbur's on the Faculty of Law at the University of Alberta of which Wilbur was the Dean for twenty years from 1948 to 1968. Professor Anderson's article is a very perceptive study of a man who is a great lawyer and a great teacher. Wilbur's contribution to the Alberta Law School has been immeasurable. At the very outset of his career there at the end of the War, he succeeded in resuscitating the school, when it was at a very low ebb. He assumed a heavy teaching load. During his career at the Law School he not only exerted a great influence over his students in the area of legal education, but also instilled the obligations of a professional lawyer to maintain a high standard of integrity, and not by precept, but by example.

The legal writings included in this book cover a wide variety of subjects. They include, *inter alia,* divorce, studies of the Alberta Dower Act, Civil Rights, evidence, property law, the legal consequences of using volunteers in the testing of new drugs, negligence, book reviews, legal biographies, and historical studies relating to the administration of justice in Western Canada.

As this is an introduction to a book, and not a review of it, I will not attempt to appraise them all. All of them are written in a clear style, without prolixity, and the subjects are dealt with in a logical, orderly manner with a positive statement of the writer's views.

The earliest of them dealt with procedure in divorce actions, and was written in 1937. At this time there was no Canadian Divorce Act. The governing law was the English Matrimonial Causes Act of 1857. The article discussed procedure and contained forms for use in the proceedings. It provided valuable material for practitioners and was of great use to them.

I would like to mention the articles dealing with the Alberta Dower Act. In 1960, the author wrote an article on the Reforms of the Law of

Dower. The Alberta Dower Act gave rise to a large number of cases, and the Act had a somewhat chequered history. This article was a careful and thorough account of the history of the Act and of the decisions of the Courts as to its interpretation.

The article was of great assistance to me in writing the judgment in the case of *Senstad* v. *Makus* (1978) 2 S.C.R. 44, and I was happy to make reference to it in my judgment.

Further reference to the Act was made in a later article in 1982, "Homestead Laws in the Four Western Provinces."

Wilbur was greatly interested in the law relating to civil rights, and there are several articles which deal with this subject. They are dispassionate studies of the problems in this area. Generally, the author did not support drastic general measures to cope with such problems, but prefers, where possible, specific remedies.

He did not favour broadly-drawn declarations of rights, couched in general terms, to be constitutionally entrenched. Writing in 1968 about the proposal for an entrenched Bill of Rights (The Canadian Bill of Rights enacted in 1960 was a federal statute, and its provisions were not entrenched in the Constitution of Canada), the author said:

> "The basic issue is this: To whom do we look for the protection of our basic rights? My answer is Parliament, because we are a democracy. The courts do have a role: they can create benign common law rules and canons of construction of statutes. However, they should not have power to rule that an Act of Parliament is void simply because, in the Court's opinion, the Act infringes a basic right."

I agree with this statement, and, in my view, the mass of litigation that has developed since the enactment in 1982 of the Canadian Charter of Rights & Freedoms has served to support its validity.

Wilbur Bowker has always been a keen student of the legal history of Western Canada. I have enjoyed the biographical sketches of judges and lawyers he has written, which include the articles about Chief Justice Harvey, three Alberta Judges, Arthur Sifton, George Steer, and Malcolm McIntyre.

He has written about the administration of justice in Western Canada in such articles as "Western Style Justice," and "Stipendiary Magistrates and the Supreme Court of the North West Territories." This latter is part of a broader study on Alberta Legal History on which he has been engaged in recent years.

His article on the Sproule case is a fascinating account of a case involving a murder which occurred on Kootenay Lake, B.C. in 1885. The research that went into this article was extensive, and Wilbur and his wife Marjorie visited the scene of the murder on three separate occasions, interviewing people in the area. The case is also of special interest to me because of the description of the unusual developments that occurred in connection with the application to the Supreme Court of Canada for a writ of *habeas corpus*, and the subsequent appeal to the full Court from the decision of Mr. Justice Henry.

I will conclude this introduction by saying how pleased I am that Marjorie undertook the task of assembling and editing her husband's legal writings, which extend over a period of 50 years, and which now appear in this volume.

Ottawa, Ontario
December 9, 1988

1938

Procedure in Divorce Actions in Alberta

Reprinted from
(1938–40) 3 Alberta Law Quarterly
pp. 51–66

At the time this article on Divorce was written (1937), Canada did not yet have its own Divorce Act. That would not come until 1968. Until then, so far as Alberta was concerned, the law governing divorce was the English Matrimonial Causes Act of 1857.

Basically, the only ground for divorce was adultery. Divorce was not very common, and the procedure was not clear-cut, especially in regard to forms. There was no Canadian text on divorce, other than a book by Evans written in 1923.

The editor of the Alberta Law Quarterly *asked Bowker if he would write an article on the subject with guidelines as to procedure and the forms in use.*

Up to the time of publication of Power's book on divorce in the 1940s, this article was the only consolidation of Alberta divorce procedure. Several practitioners indicated they found it useful.

Note: The background for the writing of this article is described in a later article in this collection (see p. 468–469).

The North West Territories Act of 1880, a Dominion Statute, was amended in 1886 to provide that the criminal and civil laws of England as of July 15th, 1870, should be in force in the Territories "insofar as the same are applicable to the Territories." When Alberta was made a Province in 1905, Section 16 of the Alberta Act provided that the laws of the Territories "shall continue" in the province. The Alberta Judicature Act of 1907 set up a Supreme Court but no mention was made of divorce courts. Apparently it occurred to no one prior to 1918 that the Alberta Courts had jurisdiction to grant a divorce but in that year the Appellate Division held that such jurisdiction exists and the Privy Council agreed (Board v. Board 1919 A.C. 956). The ground for the judgment is that the English Matrimonial Causes Act, 1857 (R.S.A. 1922 p. 2977), became part of the law of Alberta under the North West Territories Act and the Alberta Act referred to above, and that as long as it was part of Alberta law the Supreme Court must have jurisdiction to administer it. The 1857 Act effected a drastic change in the law of domestic relations and in its administration. Formerly no Court in England had jurisdiction to grant a divorce "from the bonds of matrimony" though the ecclesiastical courts could grant a divorce *a mensa et thoro,* which was similar to the modern action for judicial separation. Parliament could dissolve a marriage but of course did so very seldom. It is important to note that only the substantive provisions of the Matrimonial Causes Act became part of the law of Alberta and that the procedural provisions did not (Sherman v. King's Proctor, 1936, 2 W.W.R. at p. 154; May v. May, 1934, 3 W.W.R. 471). For example, our Appellate Division held in Wilson vs. Wilson (1920, 3 W.W.R. 535) that an action for judicial separation should be commenced by Statement of Claim rather than by Petition as provided in the Matrimonial Causes Act, and in Board vs. Board (13 A.L.R. at p. 395) it had been held that divorce proceedings should also be commenced by Statement of Claim.

Immediately after the judgment in Board v. Board our Judges drew up rules governing the practice in divorce actions (Consolidated Rules of the Supreme Court, pp. 216 and 217).

The power to amend the Matrimonial Causes Act is of course divided between the Dominion and the Province. Insofar as divorce itself is concerned the Dominion alone has jurisdiction by virtue of Section 91 (26) of the B.N.A. Act. However the Act also provides for actions for judicial separation, restitution of conjugal rights, etc., and insofar as they are concerned the Province has authority to legislate. The Dominion on its part has passed two Statutes by way of amending the Matrimonial Causes Act. They are the Marriage and Divorce Act of 1925, R.S.C. 1927, Cap. 127, and the Divorce Jurisdiction Act, 1930, Cap. 15. The only legislation enacted by the Province is the Domestic Relations Act of 1927 which deals with those parts of the 1857 Act that are within the Province's powers, such as alimony, judicial separation and restitution of conjugal rights. Before this Act was passed the law on such subjects was in a very unsatisfactory state as it was obviously difficult to decide the extent to which the 1857 Act and the decisions thereunder became part of the law of Alberta, and the Act was undoubtedly prompted by the remarks of the judges in various cases.

The 1857 Act permitted a husband to obtain a divorce for adultery but the wife had to prove adultery together with cruelty or desertion. This was amended in England in 1925 to put the wife on the same plane as the husband. This amendment did not of course become the law in Alberta, so in the same year the Dominion passed The Marriage and Divorce Act referred to above which in effect re-enacts the England amendment. The English Matrimonial Causes Act of 1937 enlarges the grounds for divorce to include incurable insanity that has lasted 5 years, desertion for at least 3 years, and cruelty. There is also a provision which says that save in exceptional cases no divorce can be obtained for 3 years after the marriage. The Dominion Senate discussed this Act at the last Session, but it was not enacted as law.

Parties to the Action

In England a husband bringing action must join the adulterer, while in a wife's action the adulteress *may* be joined. In Alberta, however, divorce rule (3) says that "the only parties to the action shall be the husband and wife unless a Judge shall otherwise direct." The former Chief Justice Simmons some years ago advocated a change in the Rules to require the third party to be made a defendant, but no change has been made. Saskatchewan has such a rule. See May v. May, 1934, 3 W.W.R. 471.

Pleadings

Divorce Rule 7 says that "except as provided by these divorce rules, the general rules of procedure shall apply to divorce actions." Thus the action is commenced by Statement of Claim. The essential facts to be pleaded are:

(a) Domicile;
(b) The marriage;
(c) The adultery;
(d) Other material facts, such as children.

Domicile.—The Court will not entertain an action unless the Statement of Claim pleads that the parties are domiciled in Alberta because it is only over such persons that the Alberta Courts have jurisdiction to dissolve marriage and the Statement of Claim must show on its face all facts establishing jurisdiction.

The universal rule, apart from statute, is that the wife takes her husband's domicile and if his is changed hers changes with it and it is impossible for a wife under any circumstances to acquire a separate domicile (Cook v. Cook, 1926, A.C. 444). This rule often works a hardship on a wife who has been deserted and so far as Alberta is concerned there are now two exceptions to the rule.

(i) The Divorce Jurisdiction Act, 1930, Cap. 15 (Canada), which was passed so as to relieve against the rule in Cook v. Cook, provides that "a married woman who . . . has been deserted by and has been living separate and apart from her husband for a period of two years and upwards, and is still living separate and apart from her husband, may in any one of those Provinces of Canada in which there is a court having jurisdiction to grant a divorce *a vinculo matrimonii* commence in the court of such Province having such jurisdiction proceedings for divorce *a vinculo matrimonii* praying that her marriage may be dissolved on any grounds that may entitle her to such divorce according to the law of such Province and such Court shall have jurisdiction to grant such divorce provided that immediately prior to such desertion the husband of such married woman was domiciled in the Province in which such proceedings are commenced."

(ii) The Alberta Domestic Relations Act (1927, Cap. 5) provides by

Section 10 that "after a judgment of judicial separation has been granted... the wife shall during the continuance of the separation... be reckoned as sui juris and as an independent person for all purposes including the acquisition of a new domicile distinct from that of her husband." There may be some doubt as to whether a divorce obtained under the Dominion Act or by a woman whose domicile has changed from that of her husband under the Provincial Act would be recognized in other jurisdictions where the rule in Cook v. Cook still applies. We cannot, however, go into that problem here.

Marriage.—Needless to say, the fact of the marriage must be pleaded. The date and place should be specified, and sometimes the name of the Clergyman is mentioned.

The adultery.—It is not sufficient to plead the bare fact but particulars as to place and time should be given and the name of the adulterer where it is known—otherwise the plea will be that adultery was committed "with a person unknown." Where cohabitation and habitual adultery is relied on rather than an isolated act, it is proper to plead "habitual adultery" between specified dates.

Other material facts.—Where there are children of the marriage the Statement of Claim should so state, together with their names and ages. The Matrimonial Causes Act, Sec. 31, forbids the granting of a divorce where there has been connivance at the adultery, condonation thereof or collusion. It further provides by the same section that in certain cases the Court shall have discretion to refuse to grant a divorce even though adultery is proved, namely, in the case of adultery of the plaintiff, unreasonable delay in bringing the action, cruelty or desertion on the part of the plaintiff, or conduct by the plaintiff conducing to the defendant's adultery. The first group are called absolute bars and the latter discretionary bars. It is customary to plead that the plaintiff has done nothing to constitute an absolute bar. This is correct on principle because, like the allegation of domicile, it is necessary to found the Court's jurisdiction.

As far as the discretionary bars are concerned it has frequently been the practice to plead that the plaintiff has done nothing to raise the discretion against him. As far as Alberta is concerned, however, it seems clear since the decision of our Appellate Division in Sherman v. The King's Proctor, 1936, 2 W.W., p. 152, that no mention need be made of the discretionary bars. Harvey C.J. says at 166:

"There is, however, while no duty, clearly no objection whatever to a plaintiff making the disclosure of such a fact if it existed either in the Statement of Claim or in the evidence at trial if he considers it expedient in his own interest to do so."

McGillivray J., at 174, goes further and suggests that it is improper for a plaintiff to plead that he has committed adultery because at the trial no question directed to this subject may be asked him. In any event the plaintiff should not deny conduct which would raise a discretionary bar if in fact he has been guilty of such conduct. (See remarks of Dysart J. in Boivan v. Boivan, 1937, 1 W.W.R. 125.)

The prayer of the Statement of Claim will ask for dissolution of the marriage, custody of the children and in the case of a wife's action interim alimony and maintenance, costs and interim costs.

The following examples of pleadings and other forms are not set out as models but it is hoped that they cover the essential requirements:

Statement of Claim

In the Supreme Court of Alberta
Judicial District of Edmonton

Between:—

Mary Jones,

Plaintiff,

—and—

John Jones,

Defendant,

Statement of Claim

1. The plaintiff is the wife of the defendant and each is domiciled in the Province of Alberta.

2. The plaintiff was lawfully married to the defendant on January 2, 1925, at the City of Toronto, in the Province of Ontario.

3. The plaintiff and defendant lived and cohabited at the said City of Toronto from the date of the said marriage until the year 1930 and thereafter lived and cohabited in the City of Edmonton, in the Province of Alberta until January 10th, 1936, when the husband deserted the plaintiff. The plaintiff and defendant have since lived apart from each other and both reside at the said City of Edmonton.

4. There are issue of the said marriage the following children, namely:
Alice Jones, aged 10 years;
William Jones, aged 7 years.

5. On the 10th day of June, 1937, the defendant committed adultery with one ________________ (or with a woman at present unknown to the plaintiff) at the __________ hotel in the said City of Edmonton (or since the month of June, 1937, the defendant has lived and cohabited and continually and habitually committed adultery with one _____________ at the said City of Edmonton).

6. The plaintiff has not connived at or condoned the said adultery nor is this action brought in collusion with the defendant or any other person.

Wherefore the Plaintiff claims:

(a) Dissolution of the marriage between the plaintiff and defendant;
(b) Custody of the said children, the issue of the said marriage;
(c) Interim alimony;
(d) Maintenance;
(e) Costs;
(f) Interim costs.

Dated at __________, and delivered, etc.

Issued, etc.

The allegations in paragraph (3) are not strictly necessary but the practice both in England and in the various provinces is to refer to the place or places of residence of the parties since the marriage.

An action for divorce should be taken without undue delay because as mentioned above unreasonable delay raises a discretionary bar, and may be evidence of condonation.

Service

After the Statement of Claim has been issued it must of course be served on the defendant. The only difference between service in divorce actions and in other actions is that in the former the greatest care must be taken to ensure that the person served is actually the defendant. At the time of service it should be remembered that on the application for decree nisi the plaintiff will have to give strict proof of service, so all possible evidence of identity should be obtained. If the person effecting service knows the defendant, so much the better, It is unwise, however, for the plaintiff to effect service as this might give rise to a suspicion of collusion. Frequently the Bailiff or other person effecting service is supplied with a photograph of the defendant and in his affidavit of service the photograph is made an exhibit, and the affidavit states that the person served is the person shown in the photograph. Then when the plaintiff gives his evidence he will identify the photograph as that of the defendant. It is advisable where possible to obtain from the person served a statement that he or she is the defendant and the spouse of the plaintiff, and such admission should be set out in the affidavit. There is also no harm in obtaining the signature of the person served if he will give it. Frequently the person serving the Statement of Claim is instructed to obtain from the defendant an admission of adultery. This practice is, however, to be deprecated.

Ordinarily the defendant will have 15 days in which to file a defence. However, if he is outside the Province at the time, an Order for service ex juris must be obtained. Rule 204 (c) permits service ex juris whenever "any relief is sought against any person domiciled or ordinarily resident within Alberta." This rule was not wide enough to cover cases that might arise under the Dominion Act of 1930, referred to above, so Rule 204 was amended in 1931 to permit an Order for Service ex juris where "a person out of Alberta is a necessary and proper party to an action properly brought by a married woman for a divorce a vinculo matrimonii."

Setting Down for Trial

The great majority of divorce actions are undefended. In actions other than those for divorce the plaintiff may sign judgment as soon as the time for defence has expired if no defence or demand of notice has been filed and where the claim in unliquidated he is obliged to go before a Judge only for the purpose of assessing damages. There are exceptional cases, such as an action for declaratory judgment, wherein the plaintiff must go before the Court even though he has noted defendant in default.

With respect to divorce actions it is fundamental to the principle of The Matrimonial Causes Act that the plaintiff must prove his case. The public is regarded as having an interest in these actions and has a right to be present at the hearing and also if proof before a Judge was not required divorces could be obtained by consent which is contrary to the policy of the Act. Thus Rule 159 of the Rules of Court provides that "No Order for final Judgment of nullity or dissolution of marriage shall be made whether or not there is default of defence until the Judge is satisfied of truth and sufficiency of the facts on which the claim for such Judgment is founded."

Order for Directions

The defendant should be noted in default on the first day after the time to defend has expired. When this has been done the plaintiff applies to a Judge in Chambers for an Order setting the case down for trial. This is really an Order for Directions but it has none of the other provisions usually contained in an Order for Directions. The Order may be in the following form:

(Style of Cause)

Before the Honourable Mr. Justice _____ in Chambers, at Edmonton.	Thursday, the 15th day of December, A.D. 1938.

Upon the application of the Plaintiff, upon reading the proceedings had and taken herein and upon it appearing that the defendant has been noted in default,

It is Ordered that the within action be set down for trial at a sittings of this Honourable Court to be held at Edmonton, at a date to be fixed by the Clerk of this Honourable Court.

____
J.

Entered this _________ day of
_________ A.D. 193____.

In a defended action the Order for Directions is the same as in any other action save for the important exception that no provision may be made for Examination for Discovery. Rule (4) of the divorce rules says:—"The rules relating to Examination for Discovery in the general rules of practice shall not apply to actions for divorce."

Application for Decree Nisi

When the case has been set down for trial the plaintiff applies on the date fixed, for a decree nisi of dissolution of the marriage. This application must of course be made before a Supreme Court Judge. It may not be made in Chambers but must be made in open Court; otherwise both Decree Nisi and Decree Absolute are voidable although not void. (McPherson v. McPherson, 1936, A.C. 179.)

In an undefended case notice of trial need not be given to the defendant (nor in fact need the Decree Nisi or the Decree Absolute be served on the defendant in such cases). On the application for Decree Nisi the proof follows the allegations in the Statement of Claim.

1. *Proof of domicile*.—Usually the plaintiff is present in person on the application for decree nisi. This is not necessarily so, for leave may be given to admit affidavit evidence. Such leave is naturally given more frequently in undefended actions than in defended ones, but even in the former the courts allow it only in exceptional cases (See Bailey vs. Bailey, 1929, 1 W.W. 708, Man. and Emeny vs. Emeny, 1929, 3 W.W. 577 (Alta.), and Grose vs. Grose (Alta.), 1936, 2 W.W. 210, where the Court points out the objections to affidavit evidence.

The plaintiff in proving domicile should testify that the husband lives in Alberta and intends to remain there. Any additional facts, such as the ownership of property and the nature of the husband's business here, should be given. There are of course many cases wherein the question of domicile has arisen and a Court is always reluctant to hold that there has been a change of domicile, but in the average undefended divorce action there is usually sufficient evidence available to satisfy the Court. For a recent Alberta case discussing domicile reference might be made to Corlett vs. Isle of Man, 1938, 3 W.W.R., p. 20.

2. *Proof of marriage*.—The marriage must be strictly proved. Ordinarily the plaintiff will testify as to the place and date thereof and frequently as to the presiding clergyman and the witnesses. Where possible the Marriage Certificate should be produced and identified by the plaintiff, and put in evidence as an exhibit. Where the marriage took place in Alberta the Marriage Certificate is prima facie evidence of the facts thereon stated. (Vital Statistics Act, R.S.A. 1922, C. 24, Sec. 38 (2)). Where the marriage took place outside Alberta it is submitted that the Marriage Certificate is admissible under Sec. 34 (1) of The Alberta Evidence Act, R.S.A. 1922, Cap. 87. Where the marriage took place in a foreign country it is, strictly speaking, necessary to call expert evidence to prove the marriage laws of the country where the marriage took place.

Phipson on Evidence, 7th Ed., pp. 666–692, contains a thorough discussion of methods of proof of marriage.

3. *Adultery*.—It is usually impossible from the nature of the case to obtain direct evidence of adultery but the Court requires at least evidence which raises a strong inference that adultery has been committed. The general rule is that the evidence must be conclusive.

C. v. C., 1919, 1 W.W.R. 982; Leboeuf v. Leboeuf, 1928, 1 W.W.R. 423; Grose v. Grose, 1936, 2 W.W.R. 210.

Admissions of adultery made by the defendant are, of course, admissible and, if the Court is of opinion that the admission was made bona fide, is entitled to grant the divorce on such evidence alone. Robinson vs. Robinson 27 L.J. Probate 91. Gordon vs. Gordon, 1935, 2 W.W.R. 419. Frequently, of course, the genuineness of an admission is questionable and the Court requires additional independent evidence. Admissions are often used as corroboration of other evidence. See Roberts vs. Roberts, 1927, 3 W.W.R. 625: Gowdy vs. Gowdy, 1933, 2 W.W.R. 128.

In proving the adultery, care must be taken not to offend against the rule in Russell vs. Russell, 1924, A.C. 187, which, broadly speaking, is that a plaintiff, in a divorce action, cannot give evidence of non-access if, as a result, a child of the marriage would be shown to be illegitimate. There are various exceptions to the rule and, in fact, they have cut down its effect considerably. For example, it does not apply where the parties are separated under a decree of judicial separation. (Heatherington vs. Heatherington, 12 Probate Div. 112), or under a separation agreement (Mart vs. Mart, 1926 Probate 24.) It might be noted that the birth certificate of a child, of which the defendant is a parent, is admissible to prove that the plaintiff is not the father. Lasko vs. Lasko, 1935, 3 W.W.R. 363.

The rule prohibiting counsel from asking a party to an action questions as to his or her adultery must be remembered (Alberta Evidence Act, Sec. 8). This rule is discussed in the Sherman case (supra) which holds that it may be waived.

Decree Nisi

The form of Order Nisi is set out in the Divorce Rules and would be as follows, in an undefended case:

(Style of Cause)

This Action having come on for trial this day upon hearing the evidence adduced on behalf of the plaintiff, the defendant having been noted in default, and upon hearing counsel for the plaintiff thereon,

1. It is Adjudged and Decreed that the marriage had and solemnized on the ____________ day of ____________ at ______________, between the plaintiff and the defendant be dissolved by reason that since the celebration thereof the said defendant has been guilty of adultery unless sufficient cause be shown to the court why this decree should not be made absolute within three months from the making thereof.

2. It is Further Adjudged that the plaintiff do have custody of the children of the said marriage, Alice Jones and William Jones.

____

Clerk of the Court.

The Decree Nisi should be entered immediately because the practice in Alberta is the three-months period which must elapse before applying for

Decree Absolute does not begin to run until the Decree Nisi is entered. In an undefended action, the Order Nisi need not, of course, be served on the defendant.

Application for Decree Absolute

During the three-months period, the plaintiff should be advised not to do anything that would constitute either an absolute bar or a discretionary bar had it occurred before the Decree Nisi, otherwise the defendant or the King's Proctor or any member of the public might intervene and object to the granting of Decree Absolute. Notice of the application for Decree Absolute need never be given to a defendant unless he has filed a defence or demand of notice (Divorce Rule 6). The application "may be made to any judge sitting in court." This undoubtedly means open court and probably, if the Decree Absolute were not made in open court, the rule in McPherson vs. McPherson would apply and the Decree would be voidable. The notice of the application for Decree Absolute must in all cases be served on the King's Proctor who is always an official in the Attorney-General's Department. He must be served five days before the application is to be made (Divorce Rule 6).

Notice of Motion.—The following form of Notice of Motion may be used:

(Style of Cause)

Take Notice that an application will be made to the presiding Judge of the Supreme Court at a Sittings of this Honourable Court to be holden at the Court House, in the City of Edmonton, in the Province of Alberta, on ____________, the ____________ day of ________________, at the hour of ________ o'clock in the __________ noon, or so soon thereafter as counsel may be heard, for an order that the Decree Nisi made in this action for divorce by the Honourable Mr. Justice __________ on the 15th day of December, A.D. 1938, at a regular Sittings of this Honourable Court held at the City of Edmonton, aforesaid, be made absolute.

Dated at the City of Edmonton, in the Province of Alberta, this ____ day of __________ A.D. 193____.

Solicitors for the Plaintiff.

To: The King's Proctor for Alberta,
Edmonton, Alberta.

Summary of Evidence.—The King's Proctor should, at the same time, be supplied with a written summary prepared by plaintiff's counsel of the evidence given on the application for Decree Nisi. In fact, he occasionally requests a complete transcript of the evidence.

Affidavit of the Plaintiff.—He must also be furnished with an affidavit of the plaintiff in the following, or similar, form:

(Style of Cause)

I, Mary Jones, of the City of Edmonton, in the Province of Alberta, make oath and say:

1. I am the Plaintiff herein and the wife of John Jones, the defendant herein, and as such have a personal knowledge of the matters herein deposed to.

2. That on the 15th day of December, A.D. 1938, I was granted a Decree Nisi for divorce in the within action by the Honourable Mr. Justice ______________ at a Sittings of this Honourable Court held at Edmonton, aforesaid.

3. That since the said 15th day of December, A.D. 1938, there has been no resumption of marital relations between the defendant and myself.

4. I further say that the said Decree Nisi in this action was not obtained by or as a result of any collusion or agreement of any kind between the Defendant and myself or by connivance between myself and the Defendant or any person whatsoever.

5. That I have not condoned the marital offence alleged at the trial of the within action.

Sworn before me at the __________
of______________ in the Province
of__________this ________ day of
________________A.D. 193____.

____

A Commissioner for Oaths.

The above affidavit must be taken after the expiration of the three-months period and, on the other hand, as close as possible to the time of service on the King's Proctor. This affidavit is not referred to in the Divorce Rules but both the King's Proctor and the Court must have evidence that nothing has happened since the Decree Nisi that would give ground for the refusal to grant a Decree Absolute. In most cases the King's Proctor does not appear and notifies the plaintiff's solicitor accordingly. If such letter is written, it should be made an exhibit to the affidavit proving service of the Notice of Motion and of the plaintiff's affidavit.

Affidavit of Search.—Just before the application is made and, on the same day, if possible, the plaintiff's solicitor must search the Court files and take an affidavit in the following form:

(Style of Cause)

I, __________ of the __________ of __________, in the Province of __________, Barrister, make oath and say:—

1. That I did on the __________ day of __________ A.D. 193____, duly search in the office of the Clerk of this Honourable Court at Edmonton, aforesaid, for the purpose of ascertaining if the Defendant had filed a Statement of Defence or Demand of Notice in this action.

2. That I did on the aforesaid date, search in the said office to see if any application had been made by any interested person since the granting of the Decree Nisi herein to show cause why the said Decree Nisi should not be made absolute.

3. No Defence or Demand of Notice has been filed in this Honourable Court and no application has been made at any time or by any person in the within action to show cause why the said Decree Nisi should not be made absolute.

Sworn before me at the ________
of ________, this ________ day
of ______________ A.D. 193____.

____

A Commissioner for Oaths.

Decree Absolute

The plaintiff need not be present on the application for Decree Absolute. His counsel simply refers to the fact that Decree Nisi was given and reads the affidavits mentioned above. If the King's Proctor decides to intervene, he will, of course, appear and oppose the granting of the Decree Absolute. The following is the form of Decree Absolute set out in the Divorce Rules:

(Style of Cause)

Upon application made this day to the Court by the Plaintiff and upon hearing counsel and it appearing that, upon the ________ day of __________ A.D. 19____, it was adjudged and decreed that the marriage had and solemnized on the ________ day of __________ A.D., 19____, at Toronto, in the Province of Ontario, between the plaintiff and the defendant, be dissolved by reason that since the celebration thereof the said defendant has been guilty of adultery, unless sufficient cause be shown to the Court why the said Decree should not be made absolute within three months from the making thereof and no such cause having been shown,

It is Adjudged and Decreed that the said marriage be and the same is hereby absolutely dissolved.

____

J.

Entered, etc.

The Decree Absolute should, of course, be entered at once. The effect of the Decree Absolute is set out in Section 57 of the Matrimonial Causes Act which says:—

> "When the time hereby limited for appealing against any Decree dissolving the marriage shall have expired and no appeal shall have been presented against such Decree or when any such appeal shall have been dismissed or when, in the result of any appeal, any marriage shall be declared to be dissolved but not sooner, it shall be lawful for the respective parties thereto to marry again as if the prior marriage had been dissolved by death. . . . "

It will be seen from the foregoing that the plaintiff should not remarry until the time to appeal has passed. Section 57 is undoubtedly in force in Alberta and was so treated in the McPherson case though the time to appeal would probably be that provided in the Rules, which is twenty days instead of the three-months period provided in Section 55 of the Act itself.

As to the right to appeal from the granting or dismissal of an application for either decree nisi or decree absolute, it is specifically provided for in the Matrimonial Causes Act, but in the Western Provinces certain doubt has arisen. In British Columbia, it is held that there is no right of appeal. Brown v. Brown, 10 W.L.R. 120; Tytler v. Jamieson, 1935, 3 W.W.R. 910. But in Manitoba and Saskatchewan the right is held to exist (Bilsland v. Bilsland, 1922, 1 W.W.R. 718; Henderson v. Henderson, 1927, 2 W.W.R. 473.

As far as Alberta is concerned, that a right of appeal undoubtedly exists seems clear from the Board and MacPherson cases, and moreover the general rules of court, which are applicable to divorce actions, so provide.

1946

Book Review: A Text-Book of Jurisprudence by G.W. Paton. First Edition, 1946.

Reprinted from
(1947) 25 Canadian Bar Review
pp. 931–935

The author of this book, G.W. Paton, was a distinguished legal scholar in Melbourne, Australia.

Though a number of books had been written on Jurisprudence, many are difficult to read because of obscure language. Paton set out to write a book that could be readily understood. He wrote in simple, clear language.

It is a book for general reading: clear, lucid and scholarly. Bowker commends it on its analytical treatment of jurisprudence, though with less emphasis on the philosophical basis of the law.

A Text-Book of Jurisprudence. By George Whitecross Paton, Professor of Jurisprudence in the University of Melbourne. Oxford: The Clarendon Press. 1946. Pp. x, 528. ($6.25)

It is noteworthy that Professor Paton's work is the second of two outstanding works on Jurisprudence written by an Australian within a period of a few months, the first being Professor Julius Stone's *Province and Function of Law.* As Professor Paton points out in his preface, many texts on Jurisprudence are written in a style that is very difficult for students to read. He has aimed at avoiding "the traditional and imposing quadrisyllables which give a superficial impression of learning" and he has succeeded in his object. Teachers of Jurisprudence, searching for a text for students that is not "so bafflingly obscure that it reposes on the shelves unread," will welcome this work. It is clearly and simply written and the propositions are set forth in a lucid and straight-forward manner.

"Jurisprudence" does not indicate the subject matter of a book as precisely as do the titles "Contracts" or "Torts" or "Equity." For example one knows fairly well what ground will be covered before he opens a text book on contracts. But the term "jurisprudence" may cover a variety of things: a study of the philosophy of law, including the natural law, historical, sociological and realistic "schools"; an analysis of legal concepts and principles—the approach of Austin, Gray and Salmond; or a study of law in relation to other disciplines and to everyday life—the sociology of law.[1] Some writers emphasize one or other of these aspects and ignore or minimize the others. Professor Paton has dealt with them all, though not necessarily in the order set out above.

His text is divided into five books. Book I, entitled "Jurisprudence, Law and the State" describes the various schools of jurisprudence (imperative, historical, functional and sociological) and the evolution of law from the primitive community to the modern state. After formulating his definition of law, the author holds that neither a state nor a sanction is essential to a law, though he concedes that they usually do exist in relation to law. He concludes that law is a legal order accepted by the community, which the community considers necessary and is willing to enforce.

His view is that law should not be defined in relation to justice, though later, in discussing the end of law, he shows that law has always been closely related to justice and ethics. His summary of natural law states the conception, originating with the Greeks, that there are immutable eternal rules which must be distinguished from man-made or positive law. However, he deals but briefly with the theories of the scholastics, and does not even mention St. Thomas Aquinas, who premised a Divine Providence which governs mankind and who held that man's reason enables him to discover a portion of this divine law, the portion so discovered being natural law. In view of the tremendous influence of this concept from time to time, including the present, it might have been elaborated further.

In dealing with the extent to which English common law is influenced by the notion of a purpose or ideal in law, the author points out that although English courts (at least since Blackstone) rarely speak of natural law, yet the ethical element is present in the growth of equity and also in the rules restricting the power to contract or make a will on the ground that it is against public policy. The question as to what latitude the courts have in creating new heads of public policy is one aspect of the old problem of a judge's power, or lack of power, to "legislate." There is a Canadian case, *Re Millar,*[2] to which Professor Paton, perhaps understandably, makes no reference, but to which Canadian teachers in discussing the subject of public policy would wish to refer their students. In this case the Supreme Court unanimously upheld a residuary bequest to the woman in Toronto having the greatest number of children during the ten-year period following the testator's death. However, the majority opinion written by Duff C.J., quoting numerous English cases, lays it down that a contract or testamentary disposition will be set aside as against public policy only if it is opposed to the interests of the state or of the people as a whole and if the harm to the public is substantially incontestible and does not depend upon the idiosyncratic inferences of a few judicial minds; and that it is unlikely that a new head of public policy could be discovered at this date. On the other hand, Crockett J. denies vigorously that the power of judges to proclaim new heads of public policy is thus circumscribed.

In Professor Paton's chapter on public law he discusses the relation between courts and administrative bodies. He points out the difficulty of finding a theoretical distinction between the judicial and administrative function. The need of distinguishing the two is particularly important in Canada because the British North America Act says that only the Governor General of Canada can appoint a Supreme or district court judge and, if provincial legislation assigns to an official or board tasks that are similar to those normally performed by a judge, the question arises whether the provincial act is valid. The author mentions the problem as it arises in Canada, but merely says that the test is whether the administrative or quasi-judicial body is asked to do something that was done by a Supreme court judge in 1867. No mention is made of *Toronto* v. *York Township,*[3] which contains a detailed discussion of the problem by the late Chief Justice Rowell.

Book II treats of the source of law—judicial decisions, legislation and legal writings. On the question of *stare decisis,* and the binding effect of precedents, the author suggests that a court of last resort should be given power to correct its own mistakes as long as this power is exercised with great care. In England where the House of Lords is bound absolutely by its own decisions, it does not appear that there are many cases in which the court of last resort has been obliged to follow a previous judgment against its will; and where the law as declared by the House of Lords is unsatisfactory, it is a simple matter for Parliament to amend the law.[4] The Supreme Court of the United States holds itself free to review its own decisions and has avowedly overruled its earlier judgments on many occasions,[5] especially on constitutional questions. The principal reason for this is the great difficulty in amending the United States constitution. Canada has an analogous problem because of the lack of prescribed machinery or settled convention for petitioning the Imperial Parliament to amend the B.N.A. Act. Suppose the Dominion were to amend the Industrial Disputes Investigation Act so as to restore it to its original form, which was held *ultra vires* in *Toronto Electric Commissioners* v. *Snyder,*[6] and were to attempt to apply the act to a nationwide strike such as the current packing-plant strike. Then suppose that the validity of the act were attacked. The Privy Council is not absolutely bound by its own decisions[7] and, although it has frequently made fine distinctions in dealing with its earlier opinions, yet it has not expressly overruled any of them. Is there any possibility that the Privy Council would hold that the subject matter of this act is now within Dominion competence although it was not in 1925? If not, what is the way out of the impasse? The Supreme Court of Canada will normally follow its own decisions, but reserves the right to refuse to follow a previous judgment in exceptional circumstances.[8] This rule seems to have worked better than the one laid down by the English Court of Appeal in 1944.[9] The latter rule is that the court is absolutely bound by its own previous decisions with three exceptions. In the three years that the rule has been in force, the exceptions have been badly overworked with the result that the certainty which the rule was designed to achieve, and which is its only justification, has not been attained.

The chapter on Legislation points out three characteristics of statutory interpretation by the English courts:

(a) the interpretation of statutes critically, rather than sympathetically;
(b) the court's refusal to go behind the face of a statute; that is to say, a court will not examine the proceedings in Parliament leading up to the act, or take cognizance of the intent of members of Parliament as expressed in speeches (the United States Supreme Court has departed radically from this rule);[10]
(c) the binding mass of case law which soon accumulates around a statute.

The work of the Lord Chancellor's Law Revision Committee is mentioned in connection with the problem of law reform and the problem of a closer liaison between the courts, legislature and bodies created to propose reforms is raised. No mention is made however of the work of the commissioners on Uniformity of Legislation in both the United States and Canada.

Referring to text books and other extra-judicial writings as a source of law, the author points out that the former rule that only the books of deceased authors might be cited has been modified and that law review articles are now frequently quoted by the courts, especially in the United States. There is no doubt that writers in legal periodicals are performing an increasingly important function in their critical examination and analysis of all branches of the law.

Books III and IV comprise what seems to this reviewer to be the backbone of the text. The former, entitled "The Technique of the Law," deals with Hohfeld's subdivision of rights into claim, liberty (or privilege), power and immunity, and their correlatives, duty, no-claim, liability and disability. Although this analysis has been criticized, nevertheless it has value, as is shown by its use in the American Restatement of the Law. The latter part of Book III analyzes titles, acts and events.

Book IV is an analysis of Legal Concepts. In connection with the subject of legal personality, note might perhaps have been made of the case of *Leveille* v. *Montreal Tramways* in which a child was held entitled to sue for pre-natal injuries.[11] The various theories of the nature of corporate personality are examined; also the status of associations, such as trade unions. This is of course a vital topic today. The discussion of the theory of contract emphasizes the significance in recent years of legislative interference with freedom of contract.

In discussing the basis of liability in tort, the author observes that "there is no modern decisive authority" on the effect of lunacy as a defence to an action for negligence. The Ontario Court of Appeal has recently dealt with this question in *Buckley & Toronto Transportation Commission* v. *Smith Transport Ltd.*, holding that insanity is a defence.[12] The learned editor of the Dominion Law Reports refers to this as a leading case on the point.

The discussion of the doctrine of *Rylands* v. *Fletcher* will doubtless be re-written in future editions in the light of the decision of the House of Lords in *Read* v. *Lyons,*[13] which appeared after the book went to press.

The author deals then with the adequacy or inadequacy from a social standpoint of the rules of liability in tort. The trend toward compulsory automobile insurance and Contributory Negligence acts shows that the common-law rules of negligence do not always produce socially-desirable results. Mention is made of the English Contributory Negligence Act, 1946, but of none of the Canadian statues which preceded the English act by a number of years. A discussion of unjust enrichment concludes the chapter on tort.

In dealing with the extinction of rights, it is stated that the English rules governing prescription do not give the adverse possessor a full legal title except in the case of easements. It might be noted that under the Canadian Uniform Limitation of Actions Act easements cannot be obtained by prescription and, on the other hand, that one who has obtained a prescriptive title to land may in some provinces at least obtain full legal title.[14]

The chapter on criminal law deals with the theories of punishment, including the question of capital and corporal punishment and juvenile delinquency, the indeterminate sentence and prevention of crime. It might be observed that the Report of the Royal Commission to Investigate the Penal System of Canada[15] contains a careful examination of all these subjects, except that of capital punishment. Book IV concludes with a treatment of property, possession and the law of procedure.

Book V examines the field of law from the standpoint of "interests." This approach, which has been so strongly advocated by Dean Roscoe Pound, is very important in jurisprudence today. Professor Paton divides the principal interests into public and private, and does not employ the category of social interests; this last is used by Pound to include some of those interests classed by Professor Paton as public interests. However, the precise grouping is perhaps unimportant; the value of an examination of law from the standpoint of "interests" lies in its analysis of the rules of law in relation to the wants, claims and desires of persons and of society, the function of law being to effect the best solution of the conflicts between competing interests. This portion of the text is exceedingly brief and might perhaps have been expanded further.

Professor Paton's masterly and comprehensive book has been carefully reviewed in a number of legal periodicals and justifiably praised. With its fair treatment of various controversial topics and its clear exposition of principles and concepts, it is an important and valuable contribution to legal literature. One is pleased to find in a work on jurisprudence frequent reference to judgments of Dominion courts and to the writings of Dominion legal scholars. It would be wrong to criticize the author for restricting the number of citations in a text of this kind. Where in this review reference has been made to Canadian judgments and developments to which the author makes no reference, this has been done simply to indicate the timeliness of the subject matter from the standpoint of Canadian law. A book of this kind stimulates one to think not merely of the separate rules of law but the reasons for them, their relation to each other, their adequacy or otherwise, and contributes toward the building of a better jurisprudence.

Notes

1 This division is used by Professor Jerome Hall in his "Readings on Jurisprudence." His work is divided into three parts of approximately equal length.

2 [1938] S.C.R. 1.

3 [1937] O.R. 177, affirmed by [1938] A.C. 415.

4 For example, The Law Reform (Frustrated Contracts) Act, 1943, passed as a result of the *Fibrosa* case, [1943] A.C. 32.

5 *E.g., Smith* v. *Allwright,* 321 U.S. 649 (1943), in which Mr. Justice Roberts, dissenting, vigorously protested against "the present policy of the court freely to disregard and to overrule considered decisions and the rules of law announced in them."

6 [1925] A.C. 396.

7 *Ontario Temperance* case, [1946] 2 D.L.R. 1 (P.C.).

8 *Stuart* v. *Bank of Montreal* (1909), 41 S.C.R. 516.

9 *Young* v. *Bristol Aeroplane Co.,* [1944] 1 K.B. 718.

10 It is proper to ask whether the English rule which was applied by the Supreme Court of Canada in *Gosselin* v. *R.* (1903), 33 S.C.R. 255 should be modified and, if so, to what extent.

11 [1933] S.C.R. 456.

12 [1946] 4 D.L.R. 721.

13 [1946] 2 All E.R. 471.

14 The Alberta Land Titles Act, R.S.A., 1942, c. 205, ss. 70–71.

15 Known as Archambault Report 1938.

1947

The Law of Evidence: 1923–1947

Reprinted from
(1948) 26 Canadian Bar Review
pp. 246–267

This article appeared in the 25th anniversary issue of the Canadian Bar Review.

That publication had been established in 1923 by the Canadian Bar Association, the purpose being to provide a forum through which lawyers and academics could share their knowledge and experience of the law.

The anniversary issue contains a number of articles on the development of Canadian law during the history of the Bar Review. *Bowker was asked to contribute, and he chose the "Law of Evidence," a subject which he was teaching at the time to law students.*

His article makes reference to the work of the Commission on Uniformity of Legislation (to which Bowker would be appointed in 1952), and efforts then being made to design a Uniform Evidence Act for the provinces. That work would continue for many years, the problem being to design a uniform Act for the provinces which would conform to a federal Evidence Act.

While considerable progress has been made in this direction, it is still in the process of development as of 1987.

Introduction

The law of evidence is the only branch of the whole body of law that enters into every trial, civil and criminal. The entire matter of proof is governed by rules of evidence. The object of a trial is to arrive at the facts in issue and this purpose cannot be achieved without efficient rules. Good rules alone will not ensure a sound finding on the facts, but they are a *sine qua non*.

The common-law rules of evidence have developed over the centuries. On the whole they have doubtless served their purpose well. They are intended to be "practical rules which experience has shown to be best fitted to elicit the truth without causing undue prejudice".[1] The important question is: Are our rules best fitted to elicit the truth? They are legion and they are complicated, sometimes arbitrary and often obscure.[2] What has been sought in recent years is a simplification and a rationalization of the rules. In Canada the Commissioners on Uniformity of Legislation studied the subject for many years, and in 1945 produced a Uniform Evidence Act,[3] which will probably be adopted by the common-law provinces. Parts of it have already been enacted in them all. In the United States, the American Law Institute in 1942 published a Model Code of Evidence. It is much more comprehensive than the Canadian Uniform Act: "its underlying assumption is that no available relevant evidence should be withheld except for the most weighty reasons".[4]

Frequent reference will be made in this article to the Uniform Act and the Model Code, as well as to Thayer's Preliminary Treatise on the Law of Evidence, Wigmore on Evidence (3rd ed., 1940), Phipson on Evidence, (8th ed., 1942), and Cockle's cases and Statutes on Evidence, (7th ed., 1946). For convenience they will be called, respectively, the Uniform Act, the Model Code, Thayer, Wigmore, Phipson and Cockle.

In the past twenty-five years there have been over five hundred reported cases in Canada dealing with questions of evidence. Mention will be made only of decisions on important points. As to the statute law, the Canada Evidence Act[5] and the various provincial acts[6] deal with isolated matters. One good feature is that there is very little controversy as to whether the Dominion Act or a provincial act applies in a given case. This is largely because the Dominion Act makes applicable to proceedings over which the Dominion has legislative authority the laws of evidence in the province in which such proceedings are taken, subject to the provisions of any Dominion statute.[7]

Degree of Proof Required

It is elementary that in a civil case a party must prove his case by a preponderance of evidence,[8] whereas in a criminal charge guilt must be proved beyond reasonable doubt. The latter rule became firmly established about 1800,[9] and a charge to the jury that did not use the phrase "reasonable doubt" in explaining the burden on the Crown would never be upheld.[10] A curious error crept into two Privy Council decisions,[11] in each of which it was stated that a plaintiff must prove his case "beyond a reasonable doubt", but it was soon pointed out in an Alberta case[12] that this "casual observation" could not have been "intended to arbitrarily wipe out a most important and long-standing distinction in the rules of proof in civil and criminal cases".

There is a special rule in criminal cases where the evidence is "circumstantial".[13] In these cases the jury must be told, in accordance with *Hodge's* case,[14] that in order to find the accused guilty they must be satisfied "not only that those circumstances were consistent with his having committed the act, but they must also be satisfied that the facts were such as to be inconsistent with any other rational conclusion than that the accused was the guilty person".

It seems to the writer that the rule in *Hodge's* case is merely an elaborate way of re-stating the rule as to reasonable doubt. Should not a jury acquit in any case where the test of *Hodge's* case is not met? One of the explanations of proof beyond reasonable doubt is that the evidence must demonstrate guilt "in the sense of excluding to a moral certainty all hypotheses (not in themselves improbable) inconsistent with guilt".[15] In other words, where the evidence is circumstantial the direction as to reasonable doubt must be given, and when it has been given must be re-stated in the formula of *Hodge's* case, which hardly seems logical. However, *Hodge's* rule has become so sanctified that failure to state it is misdirection. The precise words need not be used, but it has been held that they are preferable.[16]

One important question still unsettled concerns the degree of proof that must be adduced in a civil case in which the allegation of a party involves the accusation that the opposing party, or the one through whom he claims, has committed a crime. The question commonly arises in the case of a life insurance company defending an action on a policy on the ground that the insured committed suicide. The problem came before the Supreme Court of Canada in 1929 in *London Life Insurance Co.* v. *Lang Shirt Co.*[17] Mignault J., giving the judgment of three members of the five-man court, stated:

> That there is in the law of evidence a legal presumption against the imputation of crime, requiring before crime can be held to be established, proof of a more cogent character than in ordinary cases where no such imputation is made, does not appear to admit of doubt.

His Lordship specifically refrained from deciding whether proof of suicide must be beyond a reasonable doubt, but went on to adopt the statement of Middleton J.A. in the Ontario Court of Appeal that the facts must be inconsistent with any other conclusion than that the evil act was committed, citing *Hodge's* case. In other words, while avoiding the reasonable doubt rule, this case applies the circumstantial evidence rule, which is certainly as strict as the reasonable doubt rule. All the evidence in the *Lang Shirt* case was circumstantial, but even if the rule in *Hodge's* case was properly applied there, which the writer questions, it is submitted that it should not be applied where the evidence is not circumstantial.[18]

An extreme case is *Waselash* v. *Chiscon,*[19] which held that one who denies the making of a promissory note thereby imputes that his signature has been forged, and so must prove the forgery to the degree required by the *Lang Shirt* case. It was decided long ago by the Privy Council that, where a party denies that he has executed a deed, there is no burden on him at all; least of all the burden of proving beyond reasonable doubt that his signature has been forged.[20]

Coming back to the general rule, there are some cases since the *Lang Shirt* decision in which it has been held that only a preponderance is required.[21] On the other hand, *State of New York* v. *Phillips,*[22] a Privy Council appeal from Quebec, seems to say that proof beyond reasonable doubt is required. This was an action for damages for conspiracy to defraud. The trial judge stated "that there was a heavy onus on the plaintiffs, and that it was necessary for them to prove their case as clearly as they would have to prove it in a criminal proceeding". In approving this statement, Lord Atkin said that the defendant's criticism of this statement of the law was ill-founded: "The proposition of the learned judge has been laid down time and again in the courts of this country: and it appears to be just and in strict accordance with the law". Is this to be taken as a rule of general application? The Canadian cases do not support any such broad proposition, nor, according to Phipson,[23] do the bulk of the English cases. The reasons for the stringent rule in criminal cases are the stigma and, in most cases, the loss of personal liberty which result from a conviction. These reasons are not applicable to a civil case.[23A]

Burden of Proof

Fifty years ago Thayer[24] showed that the term, "burden of proof" (or "onus of proof"), is used in two senses: firstly, in the sense that on each issue one party or the other has the duty of showing the affirmative. Thus in an action for breach of contract, plaintiff has the burden of proving the contract and the breach; but if the defendant pleads fraud the burden of that issue is on him. This class of burden never shifts, but remains throughout on the same party, and if, when the evidence is all in, the trier of fact is wholly in doubt as to whether the fact has been proved to the degree required by law, he must find against the person on whom the burden lies. This may be called the burden of persuasion.[25] Usually there is no doubt as to which party carries this burden on a given issue: in cases of dispute it becomes important if no evidence is given at all, or if, after all the evidence has been given, the tribunal finds that it cannot say whether the fact has been proved or not.[26] Thus, in a case where a "statutory onus" to show absence of negligence has been placed on the owner or driver of a motor vehicle, he will be held liable unless he shows by a preponderance of evidence that his negligence did not cause the accident.[27]

Turning to the second sense in which the term burden of proof is used, it is often stated in judgments that the burden or onus shifts from one party to the other during the trial; so that, when the same term is used for a burden that never shifts and for one that does, confusion is inevitable.[28] This second type of burden is sometimes called the burden of adducing evidence.[29] At the start of a trial the plaintiff normally carries the burden in both senses with respect to the facts he must establish. However, if he tenders evidence from which the fact may be found in his favour, then the defendant is faced with the obligation of adducing contrary evidence if he wants to avoid an unfavourable verdict.[30]

The operation of the two burdens is shown in those negligence cases in which *res ipsa loquitur* applies. The burden of persuasion is on the plaintiff but, once he has proved the fact of his injury, the defendant has the burden of adducing evidence.[31]

Chief Justice Duff introduced Thayer's distinction over thirty years ago[32] and it has been applied frequently since in the Supreme Court of Canada.[33] The writer does not know of any Privy Council case, except *Geel* v. *Winnipeg Electric,*[34] that discusses the distinction clearly, though the terms "burden" and "onus" are used over and over again.

In a criminal case, the burden on the Crown to prove guilt is the burden of persuasion. Prior to 1935, juries were sometimes directed that, once the Crown has proved the killing, the accused "has to show" circumstances, such as accident or self-defence, to obtain an acquittal, or provocation to obtain a verdict of manslaughter. In *Woolmington* v. *D.P.P.*[35] the House of Lords held such a direction to be wrong: the Crown must prove the intent as well as the killing. True, intent may be inferred, but it is a different matter to tell the jury that the accused must negative intent. The effect of the incorrect direction is to tell the jury that the accused must give evidence or at least call other witnesses—that he is under a burden, at least that of adducing evidence. The fact is that no burden is placed on him. He need not tender any evidence at all. Certain Canadian cases had anticipated the *Woolmington* case[36] and it has been applied many times.[37]

An observation might be permitted here: in *Woolmington's* case Lord Sankey said, "throughout the web of English criminal law one golden thread is always to be seen, that it is the duty of the prosecution to prove the prisoner's guilt", and his judgment has the effect of bolstering this rule against a threatened encroachment which might easily have been permitted to slip into the law. Much concern is shown today over alleged infringements of civil liberties, and proposals are made for constitutional safeguards in the nature of a bill of rights. Here is an example of an important protection to liberty that did not depend on any statute in the beginning and is preserved by the same arm of the government that originated it, namely the judiciary.

There are exceptional cases, as Lord Sankey pointed out, where the onus is placed on the accused: for example, where the defence of insanity is raised, the rule is that the accused must show by a preponderance of evidence that he was insane.[38] Another exceptional case is where a statute says that the burden of proof on a given issue shall be on the accused. Such provisions are now common both in England and in Canada. In these cases, must the defendant merely create a reasonable doubt, or must he prove by a preponderance or beyond reasonable doubt that he is within the exception? The weight of authority is in favour of the second of these, preponderance.[39]

Presumptions

The term "presumption" has been used in different senses and the phrase, "there is a presumption", may mean either that the presumption *may* be made or that it *must* be made.[40] There are few Canadian cases analyzing these matters and this discussion will be confined to the general rules on the subject and to some of the proposals that have been made to clarify them.

Presumptions are divided into three classes:

(1) Irrebuttable presumptions of law. These are in effect substantive rules of law.[41] A classic example is the rule that a child under seven years of age is incapable of committing a crime.[42] This class of presumption needs no comment and will not be further considered.

(2) Rebuttable presumptions of law.

(3) Presumptions of fact.

As to the last two, Mr. Justice Denning says:

> The distinction is not clearly drawn in the books but it would appear that presumptions of law are presumptions of general application recognized by the law; whereas presumptions of fact are presumptions from the facts of a particular case. The division is unsatisfactory because the line between them is difficult to draw, and it does not connote any difference in the legal effect of the presumptions.[43]

His Lordship proposes to discard the use of the terms, "presumption of law" and "presumption of fact", and to divide presumptions into the two new classes: firstly, those which unless and until rebutted, *must* be drawn when the basic fact on which the presumption rests has been proved; and, secondly, those which *may* be drawn from a fact that has been proved. He terms the former "compelling presumptions" and the latter "provisional presumptions". It is striking that his proposal is very similar to the distinction adopted in the Model Code,[44] though the terminology differs. The Code uses the single term "presumption" in the sense of a compelling presumption[45] and has no synonym for "provisional presumption".

There might still be difficulty in deciding whether a given "presumption" is a true presumption (compelling presumption) or merely a justifiable inference (provisional presumption), but the classification would be an improvement over the existing ones.[46] It will be noted that Denning J. has in several cases used his own classification of presumptions and burdens. These cases,[47] as well as his original proposal, will repay examination.

In the United States much learning has been expended on the subject of presumptions, their relations to burden of proof, the effect to be given them, and the rules for deciding when they have been rebutted. The thorough discussion by S.J. Helman, K.C., in this Review, of the competing American views makes further comment unnecessary.[48]

What is the effect, in Canada, of a compelling presumption? What does the person against whom it operates need to do to rebut it? The writer hesitates to generalize, for Canadian courts have theorized very little on the subject. It is suggested that most courts take the view that the party against whom a presumption operates has the burden not only of adducing evidence but of persuasion, the degree being either a preponderance or, as in the case of the presumption against suicide, to some greater degree.[49]

Before leaving this subject, mention should be made of one case in which some systems of law provide a presumption, but in which the common law provides none, namely, as to the time of death of persons who die in a common disaster where there is no evidence as to which one died first.

The Uniform Insurance Act has created the artificial presumption that the beneficiary died first and the Uniform Commorientes Act, that the older died first.[50]

Judicial Notice

There is no need to catalogue the classes of matters of which the court will take judicial notice.[51] The examples taken from Canadian cases will suffice.

The court takes judicial notice of the law, but not of the law of another country[52] or of another province.[53] The Supreme Court of Canada will take judicial notice of the laws of all the provinces.[54] Section 29 of the Uniform Act provides for judicial notice of statutes of the Imperial Parliament, of Canada and other dominions and of all Canadian provinces, and of a wide variety of ordinances. Notice will be taken of a proclamation in the Canada Gazette bringing into force a Dominion statute,[55] or in a provincial Gazette,[56] but there is considerable authority for saying that, in the absence of provision to the contrary,[57] the court cannot take judicial notice of an order in council unless a copy is actually produced in court.[58]

On the subject of matters of common knowledge or general notoriety, notice has been taken of the two most important events in the period under review, namely, the depression[59] and World War II.[60] Lesser matters have also received recognition: for example, the fact that (in 1938) women wore high-heeled shoes,[61] but not (in 1923) that a "worm" is an article suitable for the manufacture of spirits.[62] Cases involving spirituous liquor and matters of geography are too numerous to mention.

A striking example of the use of judicial notice is seen in the case holding *ultra vires* the Alberta Bank Taxation Act.[63] Duff C.J. computed that, if all the provinces passed similar taxes, they would total 6¼% of the banks' paid-up capital and 12½% of their undivided profits. He then said that it was the court's duty to take judicial notice of the fact that the profits of banking in Canada could not enable banks to pay such a tax; and, being in effect prohibitive, it was *ultra vires*.

It will be noted that there are certain matters of which the court *must* take judicial notice,[64] whereas of other subjects it *may* take notice. Our courts have not discussed this distinction but it is well recognized.[65]

Can evidence ever be given to dispute matters judicially noticed? This has been debated in the United States,[66] but the writer knows of no case in Canada on the point.

Relevancy and Exclusionary Rules

It is elementary that evidence is not admissible unless it is relevant to the facts in issue; unless it has probative value. One rule is that "transactions" (including lawsuits) should not operate to prejudice a third person who is now party to an action. Does this rule apply so that a party to a civil action cannot tender evidence of a conviction for the purpose of proving that the opposite party, or the person through whom he claims, has committed a crime? There were cases both ways when *Hollington* v. *Hewthorn*[67] was decided in 1943. After a thorough examination of the authorities, it was held that the conviction was irrelevant and consequently evidence of it inadmissible. This judgment is of course not binding in Canada. Dr. C.A. Wright has made a most searching criticism of the decision and concludes that it is illogical.[68]

Another exclusionary rule bars evidence of "similar facts",[69] except to show "design"[70] or "scheme"[71] or "a systematic course of conduct"[72] or "intent" where *mens rea* is denied[73] or "identity",[74] or in cases such as incest "to establish guilty relations and that a sexual passion existed".[75]

These many exceptions are hardly satisfactory. It has been suggested that it would be simpler to provide generally for admission of evidence of similar facts unless it is tendered merely to show bad character or a disposition to commit crimes, or unless the probative value is slight.[76]

A similar exclusionary rule bars evidence of character except where it is in issue, as it may be in libel actions, or in rape charges where the bad character of prosecutrix may be shown, or where an accused has given evidence of his good character: apart from such cases, evidence of bad character, *e.g.* of previous convictions, is excluded unless it is within one of the exceptions to the rule against similar facts.[77]

The benefit of this rule has however been whittled away by the effect of section 12 of the Canada Evidence Act, which says that a witness may be cross-examined as to previous convictions. Probably Parliament never intended this section to be used as a means of bringing out character evidence against an accused who testifies, but such has been the effect. It is important to note that, in England, questions to an accused as to previous convictions are forbidden except in specified circumstances.[78] It would have been possible for the courts to hold that, notwithstanding the absolute terms of section 12, questions as to convictions should be asked only if relevant, as provided by the English section, but they have not done so. The effect is to compel an accused who has previous convictions to forego the right to give evidence or to run the risk of being confronted with his past record.[79]

The last class of evidence that is excluded is "opinion" evidence: a witness may not express his opinion of the facts, though it is inevitable that he will include in his testimony inferences that are actually opinion. As far as the writer knows, Canadian courts do not forbid a witness stating inferences he has drawn, unless the court considers the witness incompetent to draw them. The same principle is stated in the Model Code.[80] The important exception to the opinion rule is that an "expert" may testify as to his opinion on facts in issue.[81] The current question in connection with expert evidence is whether the court should not appoint experts instead of leaving it to the parties to call their own. It is notorious that witnesses selected by the parties are generally biased, whether intentionally or not,[82] and extreme divergences of opinion between the opposing experts are commonplace.[83]

Little has been done in Canada to find a better method of obtaining expert evidence, though several proposals respecting expert medical testimony have been made in this Review.[84] In Quebec, the court may appoint an expert to investigate and report and the Supreme Court of Canada, in dealing with the evidence of an expert appointed under the Quebec provision, has pointed out that his testimony, being impartial, is entitled to more weight than that of a party's witness.[85] The Uniform Act does not provide for the appointment of experts by the court. The only improvement it makes is to permit an expert to file a report of his findings, which is preferable to a piecemeal verbal statement given in answer to questions: he may of course be cross-examined on his report.[86] By way of comparison, the Model Code empowers the court to appoint its own experts,[87] who may be examined or cross-examined by the parties.[88] In addition the parties may call their own witnesses.[89] In England also there is provision for a court expert.[90]

Provision is often made for appointment by the court of "referees" to investigate and report,[91] for the appointment of medical examiners in negligence and nullity actions,[92] for the obtaining of expert assistants, such as accountants, merchants, etc.[93] and for the trial of cases by a judge sitting with assessors instead of alone or with a jury.[94] The classic use of assessors is of course in admiralty cases.[95] The writer is unable to say why greater use is not made in Canadian courts of the power to try cases with assessors. It might not be a cure-all, but surely is worth an attempt.

Hearsay

Hearsay is evidence of a statement made by someone who is not under oath and is not available for cross-examination. In these circumstances it is considered that the statement is unreliable and therefore should be excluded entirely.[96] Of course it is possible to tender evidence of a statement made by a party who is not a witness where the question is whether the statement was made, not whether it was true. Such a case is not a true exception to the rule against hearsay.[97]

Sometimes judges seem to consider that the rule is based on fundamental principles of justice. But it is significant that the War Crimes Act[98] contains broad provisions for the admission of hearsay evidence against persons charged under it; and the maximum penalty is death.[99]

The cases in Canada on hearsay are merely applications of the rule[100] and of its many exceptions. In sum these cases create a "conglomeration of inconsistencies".[101] The first group of exceptions has to do with statements made by persons since deceased:—

(a) Dying declarations in homicide cases, where the death of the deceased is the subject matter of the charge and where the declaration concerns the circumstances of death.[102]

(b) Statements against pecuniary interest. Canadian courts apply the rule that the statement is admissible even though only prima facie against interest, and all "incidental facts" are admitted along with the statement against interest.[103]

(c) Statements made in the course of duty.[104]

(d) Declarations as to pedigree made by a member of the family of the person whose pedigree is in question.[105] Doubtless this exception will rarely be invoked in future because registration of vital statistics will render it unnecessary.

(e) Declarations as to public and general rights, such as the boundaries of a village or the existence and location of a public highway.[106] This exception too will become of decreasing importance with the extended use of land registry systems.

(f) Declarations by a testator in relation to his will.[107] The extent to which such declarations are admissible is a complicated question and will not be discussed here.

The second group of exceptions does not depend on the death of the declarant:—

(a) Public documents, registers and records such as admiralty charts,[108] and an order of a railway board,[109] but not every report by a public officer made in the course of duty.[110] A great difference of opinion has arisen recently as to whether a soldier's record of service is a public document.[111]

(b) Evidence given in other proceedings between the same parties or their privies where the witness is not available. The leading case is still *Walkerton* v. *Erdman*.[112]

The recent trend is toward broadening the exceptions. This trend is evidenced by the Model Code[113] and to a lesser degree by the English Evidence Act, 1938.[114] The latter was adopted in 1939 in Manitoba[115] and is a part of the Uniform Act.[116] It is confined to documentary hearsay and is limited to cases where the circumstances in which the document came into being are such as to make it trustworthy. Lord Maugham, who sponsored the Act, has stated that it was felt advisable not to extend it to oral hearsay,[117] though there are others who consider that the extension would be justified.[118] Writing in 1942, Dr. C.A. Wright expressed the fear that the Act would not effect any real improvement,[119] but recent cases show that the English courts are applying it liberally.[120]

Res Gesta

Evidence of what another person said is admissible if it was part of the event or thing or fact or transaction in question. Unlike the exceptions to the hearsay rule, it is not admitted as evidence of its truth, but because it was made. It is a "verbal act".[121] It is hard to define the scope of the term and it has been used as an excuse for admitting almost anything that is more or less contemporaneous[122] with the "events" or "transaction".[123]

Statements showing the declarant's state of mind are sometimes admitted, seemingly as *pars rei gestae;*[124] likewise evidence of complaints made at the first opportunity by a female complainant in sex cases, to show consistency in her story and to negative consent.[125]

Admissions and Confessions

Whether admissions and confessions are exceptions to the hearsay rule is not important. The former are always admissible against the maker and in certain cases against others.[126] Confessions are admissible if shown by the Crown to be voluntary.

The only important problem in connection with admissions is this: When is a statement made in the presence of a party to be treated as involving an admission by him that the statement is true? The effect of *Rex* v. *Christie*[127] is that evidence of the statement need not as a matter of law be excluded where the accused denied it, though the judge may in his discretion exclude it in such circumstances[128] and the statement is evidence against him only to the extent that he adopts it by his words, conduct or demeanour. The *Christie* case has been applied many times in Canada.[129] Mere silence is not an admission unless the statement is made on an occasion when a reply might properly be expected.[130]

With respect to confessions, the writer had intended to consider in detail certain recent cases, particularly *Gach* v. *Rex*[131] and *Rex* v. *Deagle*.[132] However, the whole subject of confessions has been examined thoroughly by T.D. Macdonald and A.H. Hart[133] in recent months and further comment is needless. In deciding whether to admit a confession, the problem is one of striking a balance: on the one hand, exclusionary rules that are too rigid will tend to "sacrifice justice and common sense at the shrine of mercy—or of guilt";[134] and, on the other hand, inquisitional methods, trickery and coercion by police are not to be encouraged. Messrs. Macdonald and Hart[135] propose in effect that these broad principles should govern the admissibility of confessions.

Answers made on oath pursuant to a statute requiring that answers be made are not regarded as confessions and therefore, when the person making such answers is later charged with a criminal offence, the Crown need not show that the answers were voluntary.[136]

Corroboration

(1) *In criminal cases.* Where corroboration is required by statute,[137] the accused cannot be convicted unless there is corroboration "in some material particular by evidence implicating the accused". On the other hand, where the need for corroboration is not mandatory, but is only a matter of practice, as in the case of evidence of an accomplice of the prosecutrix in a rape charge, the jury must be told that it is unsafe to convict on the uncorroborated evidence of the accomplice[138] or the prosecutrix.[139] The proper form of charge is laid down in the leading case of *Vigeant* v. *Rex*.[140] The cor-

roboration must be evidence independent of the person whose evidence needs corroboration,[141] and must implicate the accused.[142] The bulk of case law is huge. A leading text is Graham and Read, *Corroboration in Criminal Matters* (1928). Tremeear's *Criminal Code*[143] contains a thorough digest of the cases.

(2) *In civil cases.* The Uniform Act[144] provides that in actions for breach of promise, actions by or against the representatives of a deceased person, actions by or against lunatics and actions where the evidence is that of a child of tender years, corroboration in some material respect is required. The majority of the common-law provinces have similar provisions.

The same difficulty arises here as in criminal cases, namely of deciding whether the evidence relied on as corroboration is "material". The decisions are too numerous to analyse, but the recent trend is to put a wide interpretation on "material", to hold that corroboration may be "afforded by circumstances" and to treat probabilities and inferences as corroboration.[145]

It has been suggested that it might be better, at least in claims involving estates, to forego the statutory requirement and merely apply the common-law rule of practice which permits the jury or judge to act on the uncorroborated evidence if convinced it is true.[146] Mr. Justice Bergman of Manitoba favours this view,[147] which is still the rule in England in claims against an estate, though in breach of promise cases corroboration has been required by statute since 1869.[148] There are no cases on the need for corroboration in claims by or against lunatics, and very few respecting the evidence of a child of tender years.[149]

Privilege Against Testifying and Incompetence to Testify

Certain of the so-called espionage cases raised points of interest in connection with section 5 of the Canada Evidence Act, which requires a witness to answer incriminating questions but provides that, if he objects to answer on the ground that his answer may incriminate him, the answer shall not be receivable in evidence against him in any criminal trial. Certain witnesses who refused to answer questions before the Royal Commission on Espionage, on the ground that the answers would incriminate them, were found guilty of contempt.[150] To have found otherwise would have been directly contrary to the section. The term "witness" applies to a person called before a royal commission as well as to a witness in court.[151] Moreover the witness is bound to object flatly and to state the proper ground of his objection[152] and the court or other tribunal is not bound to inform him of his right.[153] The course followed by the Royal Commission has been the subject of criticism which will not be considered here.[154]

As to the competence of an accused to testify there is an abundance of cases dealing with the proviso that neither judge nor prosecution shall comment on the failure of accused or his wife to testify. The high-water mark of protection to the accused was reached in *Bigaouette* v. *Rex*.[155] In more recent cases such a remark as "the Crown's evidence is not denied" has been held to be permissible.[156] The statutory provision that a spouse is a competent witness for the accused[157] and in specified cases is competent and compellable for the Crown[158] preserves those exceptional cases in which the spouse might have testified for the Crown at common law. Is a wife compellable in those cases, or merely competent?[159] And is she competent where there is no evidence other than her own against her husband?[160] The protection of communications between husband and wife and the prohibition against questions as to the witness's adultery require no comment.

The abolition of the rule in *Russell* v. *Russell*[161] by statute in nearly all provinces is important.[162] This rule and its exceptions were the subject of an exhaustive and devastating criticism by Dr. C.A. Wright on behalf of the Ontario Commissioners on Uniformity.[163] There is no doubt that this criticism hastened the abolition of the rule.

The privilege given to a witness to refuse to disclose the name of a prosecutor in criminal proceedings needs no comment.

The privilege attaching to communications between solicitor and client has not been extended in Canada to physicians, clergymen, bankers, accountants or others in a confidential relationship, though in *Halls* v. *Mitchell*[164] Duff J. pointed out that eminent judges have stated that there is no logical reason why the privilege should not extend to physician and patient.[165]

Another privilege based on public policy pertains to documents or communications respecting "matters of state".[166] It is not every public document that comes within the protection: there may be nothing in the public interest that requires exclusion,[167] and in a recent Alberta case[168] the trial judge refused a claim of privilege on behalf of the provincial government with respect to the verbal testimony of a policeman and a government official who had obtained statements while investigating an accident.

Duncan v. *Cammell Laird,*[169] a leading case on the question of privilege from production of Crown documents in actions between private persons, has been criticized in a note in this Review.[170] There the House of Lords held that, if the objection is validly and formally taken on the ground that production of the document would be injurious to the public service, the objection by the Ministers of the Crown is conclusive, and the court should not even look at the document. The learned commentator criticized this judgment as giving unfettered discretion to the executive branch to say whether the privilege exists.

The next privilege to be noted is that protecting communications made "without prejudice" in negotiating settlement of a disputed claim, which otherwise would be admissible as an admission. This privilege has been applied to a verbal offer of settlement which the court said was implied without prejudice,[171] and has been extended to the whole of a series of letters,[172] but it has been stated that if a settlement is reached the correspondence is admissible because a new contract has then been made.[173] There is no privilege with respect to articles seized under a search warrant that is invalid or improperly executed.[174]

Conclusion

The importance of a thorough knowledge of the rules of evidence is obvious. Only a fraction of the rulings on questions of admissibility ever reach the law reports. It is sometimes said that in England the barristers know the rules of evidence and realize that the judges know them, and so little time is wasted in unwarranted objections. In the United States it appears that the constant use of objections is a real obstacle to the proper trial of cases.[175]

The need for a continuing critical analysis of the rules of evidence with a view to their simplification and rationalization is pressing. The work of the Commissioners on Uniformity of Legislation in Canada in producing the Uniform Act is encouraging. The searching criticisms by Dr. C.A. Wright in this Review, the work of Wigmore and the writings of E.M. Morgan, some of which have been cited in this article, and the reforms effected by the Model Code should be given the most careful study.[176]

Simpler and more efficient rules of evidence will not only check the tendency to substitute other bodies for courts of law but, more important, will benefit immeasurably the whole administration of justice.

Notes

1 *Thompson* v. *R*, [1918] A.C. 221, *per* Lord Dunedin; quoted in *R*. v. *Barbour*, [1938] S.C.R. 465. The passage refers to the rules of evidence in criminal cases, but is applicable generally.

2 See C.A. Wright, The Law of Evidence: Past and Future (1942), 20 Can. Bar Rev. 714.

3 Proceedings of the Canadian Bar Association, 1945, p. 271.

4 E.M. Morgan, Comments on the Proposed Code of Evidence (1942), 20 Can. Bar Rev. 271.

5 R.S.C., 1927, c. 59.

6 In Quebec, the Code of Civil Procedure.

7 Footnote 5 *supra*, section 35.

8 *R*. v. *Sincennes-McNaughton*, [1928] S.C.R. 84.

9 Thayer, pp. 551 *et seq.;* Wigmore, §2497.

10 *Rex* v. *Labine*, [1937] 3 W.W.R. 214 (Alta.).

11 *McDaniel* v. *Vancouver General Hospital*, [1934] 3 W.W.R. 619, and *Gray* v. *Caldeira*, [1936] 1 W.W.R. 615.

12 *De Paoli* v. *Richardson*, [1936] 2 W.W.R. 183.

13 For a definition see: Smith, Components of Proof (1942), 51 Yale L.J. at p. 562; Wigmore §25; Wills, Circumstantial Evidence (5th ed.), pp. 19–20.

14 (1838), 2 Lewin 227; 168 E.R. 1136.

15 *Clark v. R*. (1921), 61 S.C.R. 608, *per* Duff J. at p. 618; applied in *R*. v. *Findlay*, [1944] 1 W.W.R. 609 (B.C.), *per* O'Halloran J.A.

16 *McLean* v. *R*., [1933] S.C.R. 688; *Fraser* v. *R*., [1936] S.C.R. 1 and 296; *R*. v. *Comba*, [1938] S.C.R. 396; *Cote* v. *R*. (1941), 77 C.C.C. 75 (Can.).

17 [1929] S.C.R. 117: it had been held in *Moretti* v. *Dom. of Can. Guar.* etc., [1923] 3 W.W.R. 1 (Alta.), that the suicide need be proved only by a preponderance.

18 Later cases applying the judgment of Mignault J. are: *McPhadyen* v. *Employers' Liability Assce. Co.*, [1933] O.R. 332; on appeal, p2. 663, the point was

not raised; *Mader* v. *Sun Life Assce. Co.*, [1934] 4 D.L.R. 59 (N.S.); *New York Life* v. *Schlitt*, [1945] S.C.R. 289 (alleged suicide); *Earnshaw* v. *Dom. of Can. Gen. Ins. Co.*, [1943] O.R. 385 (alleged drunken driving).

19 [1945] 1 D.L.R. 497 (Ont.).

20 *Doe d. Devine* v. *Wilson* (1855), 10 Moore P.C. 502, 14 E.R. 581; quoted in *Clark* v. *R.*, footnote 15 *supra*, *per* Duff J. at pp. 616–7.

21 *Italian Realty Co.* v. *Guardian Assce. Co.*, [1935] 2 D.L.R. 425 (N.S.); *Bukowicki* v. *Bukowicki*, [1945] 3 W.W.R. 402 (Alta.); *Davis* v. *Quayle*, [1946] 1 W.W.R. 96 (Alta.).

22 [1939] 3 D.L.R. 433.

23 P.7.

23A With respect to matrimonial causes, a judgment of the English Court of Appeal in *Churchman* v. *Churchman*, [1945] P. 44, at p. 51 states that: "The same strict proof is required in the case of a matrimonial offence as is required in connection with criminal offences properly so-called". This statement had reference to proof of connivance, but has been applied to proof of adultery: *e.g.*, *Ginesi* v. *Ginesi* (1947), 63 T.L.R. 545; *Morrison* v. *Morrison*, [1948] 1 W.W.R. 110 (B.C.). Of the thousands of divorces granted each year in Canada, it would be interesting to conjecture the number in which adultery was proven beyond reasonable doubt.

24 Cap. 9, pp. 353–389.

25 Wigmore terms it "the risk of non-persuasion of the jury", §2485; Phipson calls it "the burden of proof on the pleadings", p. 27; Halsbury (2nd ed., Vol. 13, Evidence, 612 at p. 543) uses the term "burden of proof as a matter of substantive law or pleading"; the Model Code, rule 1(3), says "burden of persuasion of a fact"; Mr. Justice Denning, Presumptions and Burdens (1945), 61 L.Q.R. 379, says "legal burden".

26 *Robins* v. *National Trust Co.*, [1927] A.C. 515, at p. 520; *Harmes* v. *Hinkson*, [1946] 3 D.L.R. 497 (P.C.).

27 *Geel* v. *Winnipeg Electric*, [1932] A.C. 690. In frustration cases, where one party alleges that frustration was brought about by the other party's default, he must prove it: *Constantine Line* v. *Imperial Smelting Co.*, [1942] A.C. 154; discussed by J. Stone, Burden of Proof and the Judicial Process (1944), 60 L.Q.R. 262. In restraint of trade cases the burden is on the covenantee to show that the covenant is reasonable: *Routh* v. *Jones*, [1947] 1 All E.R. 758; *Connors* v. *Connors Bros. Ltd.*, [1939] S.C.R. 162 (on appeal to the Privy Council the point was left open, *Connors Bros.* v. *Connors*, [1941] 1 D.L.R. 81.

28 In *Abrath* v. *N.E.Ry.* (1883), 11 Q.B.D. 440, affirmed by (1886), 11 A.C. 247, Brett M.R. at p. 451 uses the term in the first sense, Bowen L.J. at p. 456 in the second.

29 Phipson, p. 28. The Model Code, rule 1(2), says "burden of producing evidence of a fact". Mr. Justice Denning, footnote 25, *supra*, says "provisional burden"; he has a third class of burden called "ultimate burden".

30 Wigmore §2487, explains this burden in relation to a jury trial. The writer has found his dicussion difficult, and will not attempt to explain it.

31 *Malone* v. *T.C.A.*, [1942] O.R. 453; editorial note to *Scrimgeour* v. *Board of Management of American Lutheran Church*, [1947] 1 D.L.R. 677 (Sask.); G.W. Paton, Note (1936), 14 Can. Bar Rev. 480, and (1937), 15 Can. Bar Rev. 45; *Nystedt* v. *Wings Ltd.*, [1942] 3 W.W.R. 39 (Man.) *per* Dysart J. at p. 50.

32 *Koop* v. *Smith* (1915), 51 S.C.R. 554, at pp. 558–9.

33 *McKee* v. *Philip* (1916), 55 S.C.R. 286, *per* Duff J. dissenting at pp. 299–300; *Smith* v. *Nevins*, [1925] S.C.R. 619, *per* Duff J. dissenting; *Ontario Equitable Life & Accident Co.* v. *Baker*, [1926] S.C.R. 297, at pp. 308–9; *Dillon* v. *Toronto Millstock Co. Ltd.*, [1943] S.C.R. 268.

34 Footnote 27, *supra*.

35 [1935] A.C. 462.

36 *Picariello* v. *R.*, [1923] 1 W.W.R. 1489 (Can.), especially the judgment of Duff J.; *Primak* v. *R.*, [1930] 1 W.W.R. 755 (Sask.).

37 *Manchuck* v. *R.*, [1938] S.C.R. 341,

and *R.* v. *Jackson,* [1941] 1 W.W.R. 418 (Sask.) (provocation); *R.* v. *Philbrook,* [1941] O.R. 352 (self-defence); *R.* v. *Cechetto* (1942), 79 C.C.C. 36 (N.S.) (alibi), and cases quoted in the editor's note to that case; *Taylor* v. *R.,* [1947] S.C.R. 462 (provocation and drunkenness). A leading case on receiving stolen property, which raises similar questions, is *Richler* v. *R.,* [1939] S.C.R. 101.

38 *R.* v. *Clark,* footnote 15, *supra; Smythe* v. *R.,* [1941] S.C.R. 16; *R.* v. *Gibbons,* [1947] 1 D.L.R. 45 (Ont.).

39 *R.* v. *Lobbins,* [1940] 3 W.W.R. 301 (Alta.); *R.* v. *Hellenic Colonization Assn.,* [1942] 1 W.W.R. 810 (Alta.); *R.* v. *Carr-Briant,* [1943] K.B. 607 (Eng.); J.C. Martin (1939), 17 Can. Bar Rev. 37. See also: *Attygalle* v. *R.,* [1936] A.C. 338; *Seneviratne* v. *R.,* [1936] 3 All E.R. 36 (P.C.).

40 Morgan, Some Observations Concerning Presumptions (1931), 44 Harv. L.R. 906; Model Code, pp. 306–312; see generally Thayer, Cap. 8, pp. 313–352.

41 Phipson, p. 661.

42 Criminal Code, s. 17.

43 Footnote 25, *supra* at p. 381.

44 Pp. 306–312.

45 Rule 701.

46 See E.M. Morgan, The Law of Evidence: 1941–1945 (1946), 59 H.L.R. 481, at p. 495.

47 *Emanuel* v. *Emanuel,* [1945] 2 All E.R. 494, at p. 496; *Rowing* v. *Minister of Pensions,* [1946] 1 All E.R. 664, at p. 665; *W.* v. *Minister of Pensions,* [1946] 2 All E.R. 501, at p. 502.

48 Presumptions (1944), 22 Can. Bar Rev. 118.

49 See *Clark* v. *R.,* footnote 15, *supra; N.Y. Life* v. *Schlitt,* footnote 18, *supra.*

50 Both Acts are discussed in a note by G.D. Kennedy in (1946), 24 Can. Bar Rev. 720, which points out that the former has been enacted in all common-law provinces and the latter in all but Alberta.

51 Phipson, pp. 16–23, enumerates them; also Wigmore, § §2572–2582. For a thorough discussion see E.M. Morgan, Judicial Notice (1944), 57 Harv. L. Rev. 269.

52 *Walkerville Brewing Co.* v. *Mayrand* (1929), 63 O.L.R. 573.

53 *Can. Natl. S. S.* v. *Watson,* [1939] S.C.R. 11; noted in (1939), 17 Can. Bar Rev. 755.

54 *Ottawa Electric* v. *Letang,* [1924] S.C.R. 470; reversed on other grounds, [1926] A.C. 725.

55 *R.* v. *St. Peters* (1927), 47 C.C.C. 204 (N.S.).

56 *R.* v. *Wagner,* [1931] 2 W.W.R. 650 (Man.).

57 *E.g.,* Criminal Code, s. 1128.

58 *R.* v. *Kishen Singh,* [1941] 2 W.W.R. 145 (B.C.), *per* O'Halloran J.A. dissenting; *R.* v. *Yee Clun,* [1928] 3 W.W.R. 558 (Sask.); *R.* v. *Rudin & Co. Ltd.,* [1942] 1 W.W.R. 615 (Sask.).

59 *E.g., Mills* v. *Angus,* [1933] 2 W.W.R. 218 (Sask.).

60 *E.g., Saskatoon Mtge & Loan Co.* v. *Roton,* [1942] 2 W.W.R. 219 (Sask.) (that Paris was in enemy-occupied territory).

61 *Gregson* v. *Vancouver,* [1939] 1 W.W.R. 347 (B.C.).

62 *R.* v. *Holmes,* [1923] 1 W.W.R. 34 (Alta.).

63 *Re Alberta Statutes,* [1938] S.C.R. 100; affirmed [1939] A.C. 117.

64 *E.g.,* statutes: s. 29 of the Uniform Act.

65 Wigmore, §2583, at p. 580.

66 Morgan, Judicial Notice, footnote 51 *supra,* at pp. 279–287.

67 [1943] K.B. 587.

68 Note (1943), 21 Can. Bar Rev. 653.

69 *R.* v. *Brunet,* [1928] S.C.R. 375; *R.* v. *Barbour,* footnote 1 *supra; R.* v. *Campbell,* [1946] 3 W.W.R. 369 (B.C.); *Koufis* v. *R.,* [1941] S.C.R. 481.

70 *R.* v. *Baker,* [1926] S.C.R. 92; *Paradis* v. *R.,* [1934] S.C.R. 165.

71 *R.* v. *Hamilton* (1931), 66 O.L.R. 537.

72 *R.* v. *Christakos,* [1946] 1 W.W.R. 166 (Man.); *R.* v. *Stawycnuj,* [1933] 2 W.W.R. 495 (Man.).

73 *R.* v. *Anderson,* [1935] 3 W.W.R. 272 (B.C.); *R.* v. *Pinsk,* [1934] 3 W.W.R. 752 (Sask.).

74 *R.* v. *Lyons,* [1944] 2 W.W.R. 129 (B.C.).

75 *Munro* v. *Krause,* [1931] 2 W.W.R. 685 (Alta.); *R.* v. *Pegelo,* [1934] 1 W.W.R. 573 (B.C.).

76 Dr. Wright, footnote 2 *supra,* at p. 717.

77 *E.g., R.* v. *McLaren,* [1935] 2 W.W.R. 188 (Alta); *R.* v. *MacDonald,* [1939] O.R. 606.

78 Criminal Evidence Act, 1898, 61 and 62 Vic., c. 36, s. 1(f). See *Maxwell* v. *D.P.P.,* [1935] A.C. 309; *Stirland* v. *D.P.P.,* [1944] A.C. 315.

79 See Dr. C.A. Wright's criticisms in a number of notes: (1934), 12 Can. Bar Rev. 519; (1935), 13 Can. Bar Rev. 605; (1940), 18 Can. Bar Rev. 808; (1941), 19 Can. Bar Rev. 219 and 614.

80 Rule 401.

81 As to when a witness is an expert rather than a witness of fact, see: *Buttrum* v. *Udell* (1925), 57 O.L.R. 97; *Leeson* v. *Darlow* (1926), 59 O.L.R. 421.

82 *Brownlee* v. *Hand* (1930), 65 O.L.R. 646. Wigmore, §563, is not too critical; nor Lord Macmillan in his chapter, "The Professional Mind", in Law and Other Things (1934). For a good discussion of the whole subject see H.A. Hammelmann, Expert Evidence (1947), 10 Mod. L.R. 32.

83 *E.g., Powlett* v. *U. of A.,* [1933] 3 W.W.R. 322; varied [1934] 2 W.W.R. 209 (Alta.) (medical experts); *Re Withycombe Estate,* [1945] S.C.R. 267 (real estate valuators).

84 D.E. Robertson, Medico-Legal Evidence (1938), 16 Can. Bar Rev. 185; Dr. Hubert W. Smith, Scientific Proof and Relations of Law and Medicine (1943), 21 Can. Bar Rev. 707; From an English Office Window: Medical Assessors (1944), 22 Can. Bar Rev. 266.

85 *Citadel Brick Ltd.* v. *Garneau,* [1937] 3 D.L.R. 169 (Can.); *quaere,* whether he should be subject to cross-examination by the parties.

86 S. 10.

87 Rule 403.

88 Rule 407.

89 Rule 404.

90 O. 37A, r. 1–11 (1934).

91 *E.g.,* Alberta Rules of Court, 461 and 491–500.

92 *E.g.,* Alberta Rules 259–260 and 663.

93 Alberta Rule 853: Holmstead & Langton, Judicature Act (5th ed.), pp. 901–903.

94 *E.g.,* Alberta Rule 281; Ontario Judicature Act, R.S.O., 1937, c. 100, ss. 64–69, annotated in Holmstead & Langton, footnote 93 *supra,* at pp. 273–281.

95 Halsbury (2nd. ed.), Vol. 1, Admiralty, sec. 214 at p. 133; Courts of Admiralty Act, 1934, S.C.c. 31, s. 30; Supreme Court Act, R.S.C., 1927, c. 35, s. 31. It will be noted, however, that even nautical assessors frequently disagree, and in modern cases in the House of Lords it has been stated that today navigation is mainly a matter of commonsense, so that a judge can decide navigational questions as well as an expert: *S.S. Australia* v. *S.S. Nautilus,* [1927] A.C. 145, and cases appended to the judgment in that case.

96 Phipson, p. 207, gives additional reasons for the rule. See also E.M. Morgan, Comments on the Proposed Code of Evidence, footnote 4, *supra,* at p. 282.

97 *R.* v. *Container Materials Ltd.* (1940), 74 C.C.C. 113 (Ont.); affirmed on other grounds (1941), 76 C.C.C. 18; affirmed [1942] S.C.R. 147.

98 1946, c. 73 (Can.), Schedule, Regulation 10.

99 *Ibid.,* Regulation 11(1).

100 *E.g., National Fire Ins. Co.* v. *Rogers,* [1924] 2 W.W.R. 186 (Sask.) (factory records); *Anthony* v. *Charter,* [1933] 1 W.W.R. 310 (Alta.) (statement by plaintiff as to date of birth).

101 E.M. Morgan, footnote 4, *supra,* at p. 290.

102 *Debortoli* v. *R.,* [1926] S.C.R. 492; *Chapdelaine* v. *R.,* [1935] S.C.R. 53; *Schwartzenhauer* v. *R.,* [1935] S.C.R. 367.

103 *McDonald* v. *Young,* [1934] 4 D.L.R. 172 (N.S.).

104 *Palter Cap Co.* v. *Great West Life Assce. Co.,* [1936] O.R. 341; Dr. C.A. Wright in a Note in (1936), 14 Can. Bar Rev. 688, points out the difficulty in applying the idea of "duty" and proposes that any statement be admissible if made in the ordinary course of work, even though there was no duty to make it in a narrow sense.

105 *Pejepscot Paper Co.* v. *Farren,* [1933] S.C.R. 388; *Sewell* v. *Urquhart,* [1930] 2 D.L.R. 547 (N.B.); *Croft* v. *Wamholt,* [1930] 2 D.L.R. 996 (N.S.); *Re*

Anderson, [1947] 3 D.L.R. 302 (N.B.).

106 *Williams & Wilson* v. *Toronto*, [1946] O.R. 309.

107 *E.g.*, *Walsh* v. *Cruickshank*, [1947] 2 W.W.R. 464 (Alta.).

108 *R.* v. *Bellman*, [1938] 3 D.L.R. 548 (N.B.): compare *R.* v. *Price Bros.*, [1926] S.C.R. 28, where old maps were held to be of little evidentiary value. See also *Fulton* v. *Creelman*, [1931] S.C.R. 221, where the admissibility of an old registry book was doubted.

109 *Littley* v. *Brooks & C.N.R.*, [1930] S.C.R. 416.

110 *Hudson's Bay Co.* v. *Wyrzykowski*, [1938] S.C.R. 278.

111 *Hare* v. *Hare*, [1943] 3 D.L.R. 579 (Ont.), *per* Fisher J.A., *Bell* v. *Bell*, [1945] O.R. 251, and *Elson* v. *Elson*, [1946] 3 W.W.R. 789 (Sask.) hold it is; *contra*, *Stafford* v. *Stafford*, [1945] 1 D.L.R. 263 (Ont.), and *Tomlinson* v. *Tomlinson*, [1945] 1 W.W.R. 371 (Sask.).

112 (1894), 23 S.C.R. 352. Later cases are: *Whimbey* v. *Hyde* (1926), 60 O.L.R. 399; *Shumardo* v. *Tor. Gen. Trusts*, [1940] 2 W.W.R. 564 (Man.); *Richey* v. *Richey*, [1941] 2 W.W.R. 91 (Man.).

113 Cap. VI, Rules 501–531.

114 1 & 2 Geo. VI, c. 28; Cockle, p. 582; Phipson, p. 261.

115 Now R.S.M., 1940, c. 65, ss. 52–54.

116 Ss. 52–56.

117 Lord Maugham, Observations on the Law of Evidence (1939), 17 Can. Bar Rev. 469.

118 *E.g.*, S.J. Helman, The Reform of the Law of Hearsay (1939), 17 Can. Bar Rev. 302.

119 The Law of Evidence: Present and Future, footnote 2, *supra*.

120 *E.g.*, *Andrews* v. *Cordiner* (1947), 63 T.L.R. 299; *Edmonds* v. *Edmonds* (1947), 63 T.L.R. 327.

121 *Cassels* v. *Tor. T.C.*, [1938] O.R. 155; Wigmore, §1745, distinguishes between verbal act and a spontaneous exclamation, which in some jurisdictions is recognized as an exception to the hearsay rule. See also *R.* v. *Deacon* (1947), 87 C.C.C. 271, *per* Bergman J.A. at pp. 320–1; reversed on other grounds (1947), 89 C.C.C. 1 (Can.).

122 Cases on contemporaneity are: *Chapdelaine* v. *R.*, [1935] S.C.R. 53; *R.* v. *Elliott* (1928), 62 O.L.R. 1; *Gollogly* v. *Pritchard*, [1946] O.W.N. 888.

123 "Bedingfield's Case" in Thayer's Legal Essays, p. 206, is a classic discussion. See also Wigmore § §1766–1769.

124 *R.* v. *Wysochan* (1930), 54 C.C.C. 172 (Sask.); *R.* v. *Wilkinson*, [1934] 3 D.L.R. 50 (N.S.).

125 *E.g.*, *R.* v. *Marsh*, [1940] 3 W.W.R. 621 (B.C.).

126 *E.g.*, partners, *Riddell* v. *Botfield*, [1923] 1 W.W.R. 1109 (Man.); and against a principal where made by an agent, *Nagel* v. *C.N.R.*, [1930] 2 W.W.R. 431 (Sask.).

127 [1914] A.C. 545.

128 *R.* v. *Harrison*, [1946] 3 D.L.R. 690 (B.C.).

129 *Hubin* v. *R.*, [1927] S.C.R. 442; *Stein* v. *R.*, [1928] S.C.R. 553; *Chapdelaine* v. *R.*, [1935] S.C.R. 53; *R.* v. *Emele*, [1940] 2 W.W.R. 430 (Sask.).

130 *R.* v. *Keiwitz*, [1941] 3 W.W.R. 693 (B.C.); *R.* v. *Dimetro & Mitchell*, [1946] 1 D.L.R. 286 (Ont.).

131 [1943] S.C.R. 250.

132 [1947] 1 W.W.R. 657 (Alta.).

133 The Admissibility of Confessions in Criminal Cases (1947), 25 Can. Bar Rev. 823.

134 This is a combination of the remarks of Parke B. and Erle J. in *Reg.* v. *Baldry* (1852), 5 Cox. C.C. 523.

135 Footnote 133, *supra*.

136 *Walker* v. *R.*, [1939] S.C.R. 214; *R.* v. *Mazerall*, [1946] O.R. 511, 762; *R.* v. *Lunan* (1947), 88 C.C.C. 191 (Ont.); and see Report of Royal Commission (the Taschereau or "Espionage" Report), Ch. XI, at pp. 671–3 (Ottawa: King's Printer, 1946).

137 *E.g.*, Criminal Code, ss. 1002–1003.

138 *Gouin* v. *R.*, [1926] S.C.R. 539; *Boulianne* v. *R.*, [1931] S.C.R. 621; *Chapdelaine* v. *R.*, [1935] S.C.R. 53.

139 *Mattouk* v. *Massad*, [1943] A.C. 588; *McIntyre* v. *R.*, [1945] S.C.R. 134.

140 [1930] S.C.R. 396. See also *Brunet* v. *R.*, [1928] S.C.R. 375, and *Pitre* v. *R.*, [1933] S.C.R. 69.

141 *Hubin* v. *R.*, [1927] S.C.R. 442.

142 *Baker* v. *R.*, [1926] S.C.R. 92; *R.* v.

Silverstone, [1934] O.R. 94.

143 (5th ed., 1943), pp. 1259–1285.

144 Ss. 13–16.

145 *Cox* v. *Hourigan,* [1941] S.C.R. 251, *per* Kerwin J.; *Ollson* v. *Fraser,* [1945] O.R. 69; *Brown* v. *Rotenberg, [1946] O.R. 363; Szczepkowski* v. *Eppler,* [1946] 3 D.L.R. 641 (Can.) (claims against estates); *Mott* v. *Trott,* [1943] S.C.R. 256 (breach of promise); *Smallman* v. *Moore,* [1946] O.R. 867 (both classes).

146 Phipson, p. 477; *National Trust* v. *Ayton,* [1934] 1 W.W.R. 285 (Man.).

147 Proceedings of the Canadian Bar Association, 1945, pp. 237–8.

148 Evidence Further Amendment Act, 32 & 33 Vict., 1869, c. 68, s. 2.

149 *Cuthbertson* v. *Lethbridge,* [1929] S.C.R. 176; *Robinson* v. *P. Burns & Co.,* [1928] 1 W.W.R. 76 (Alta.).

150 *Re Gerson & Nightingale,* [1946] S.C.R. 538; *Re Gerson,* [1946] S.C.R. 547.

151 *R.* v. *Smith,* [1947] O.R. 378. See also: *R.* v. *Harcourt* (1929), 53 C.C.C. 156 (witness before a provincial securities board).

152 *R.* v. *Smith,* footnote 151, *supra.*

153 Report of Royal Commission, footnote 136, *supra,* at pp. 672–3; *Tass* v. *R.,* [1947] S.C.R. 103.

154 M.H. Fyfe, Some Legal Aspects of the Report of the Royal Commission on Espionage (1946), 24 Can. Bar Rev. 777; Report of Civil Liberties Committee of the Canadian Bar Association (1946), 24 Can. Bar Rev. 697, at pp. 705–708.

155 [1927] S.C.R. 112.

156 *Wright* v. *R.,* [1945] S.C.R. 319.

157 But not compellable: *R.* v. *Arneson,* [1930] 3 W.W.R. 163 (Alta.).

158 Canada Evidence Act, s. 4.

159 Note *R.* v. *Lapworth,* [1931] 1 K.B. 117; J.A. Weir (1931), 9 Can. Bar Rev. 216.

160 Note *R.* v. *Schaefer* (B.C.), unreported; George Murray (1946), 24 Can. Bar Rev. 916.

161 [1924] A.C. 687.

162 Uniform Act, s. 5.

163 Proceedings of the Canadian Bar Association, 1945, p. 250; reprinted in (1945), 23 Can. Bar Rev. 536.

164 [1928] S.C.R. 125, at pp. 136–7.

165 The Model Code extends the privilege to the priest-penitent relationship (Rule 219) and to the physician-patient relationship (Rules 220–223).

166 Thus a chartered accountant who investigated a company's affairs for the Dominion Government could not be compelled to testify: *Lund* v. *Walker,* [1931] S.C.R. 597.

167 *Dufresne Const. Co. Ltd.* v. *R.,* [1935] Ex. C.R. 77, where the documents were excluded on another ground, namely that they were prepared by government officials for the guidance of the Minister of Public Works with respect to suppliant's claim.

168 *Lengyel* v. *Swanson & Calgary Power Co. Ltd.,* [1947] 2 W.W.R. 648.

169 [1942] A.C. 624.

170 (1942), 20 Can. Bar Rev. 805.

171 *Cook* v. *Nova Scotia L & P. Co.,* [1930] 1 D.L.R. 836 (N.S.).

172 *McLeod* v. *Pearson,* [1931] 3 W.W.R. 4 (Alta.).

173 *Fischer* v. *Robert Bell Engine & Thresher Co. Ltd.,* [1923] 3 W.W.R. 320 (Sask.).

174 *E.g., R.* v. *Hawkins* (1923), 42 C.C.C. 305 (Que.); *R.* v. *Kostachuk,* [1930] 2 W.W.R. 464 (Sask.); *R.* v. *Lee Hai,* [1935] 2 W.W.R. 177 (Man.).

175 Wigmore, §8c, especially at pp. 267–269, quoting W. Hearn "I Object".

176 The Model Code has not been adopted in all the States overnight; in fact it may be long before it is generally accepted. See E.M. Morgan, footnote 46, *supra.*

1952

Intestate Succession to Personal Property

Unpublished paper prepared at Yale University during a course on Legal History

Bowker spent a sabbatical year at Yale University in 1952–53.

One of his subjects of study was Legal History. His professor was Sam Thorne who was one of the leading instructors on Legal History in his day. He later went on to Harvard. Bowker got an "A" in his course. He chose this topic for his paper as he taught Wills and Personal Property at the University of Alberta.

The purpose of this paper is to sketch the development of the English law of intestate succession to personal property. The story is one of competing claims—by crown, lord, church, administrators, creditors, and the intestate's family. Until feudal times the family was the main beneficiary. Then for centuries wife and relations were pushed aside. Later the wheel came full circle. The present law is much like that of the Conqueror.

To Glanvil's Time

Before the Norman Conquest life was simple and primitive. Population was small and few were wealthy. An examination of Anglo-Saxon wills shows that testators bequeathed cash, armlets, cups, silver, jewelry, clothes, arms, and livestock.[1] And they devised land. However most persons died intestate. The Anglo-Saxon laws, including rules of succession, were based on the German. The order of succession in German law was (1) sons, (2) daughters, (3) grandchildren. Then came (1) father, (2) mother, (3) brothers, (4) sisters. Ernest Young says, "It cannot be doubted that the order of succession in Anglo-Saxon law was substantially that given above, although there is evidence only for the first two classes." He points out that the laws of William I were like the German, and he discards the laws of Cnut and Henry I as unworthy of credit.[2]

When we speak of "laws" of this period we mean customs or alleged customs, reduced to writing long after.

Cnut's law, of about 1030, says:[3]

> If a man departs from this life intestate, whether through negligence or sudden death, his lord shall take no more from his property than his legal heriot. But, according to his direction, the property shall be very strictly divided among

> his wife and children and near kinsmen, each according to the share which belongs to him.

The heriot is a tribute due to the lord on the tenant's death. Cnut's laws prescribe the heriot for persons of the different ranks. If the tenant "falls before the lord" the heriot is forgiven and the goods are to be divided "justly." Selden says this means the division is made in the common law courts instead of the lord's court. He also says it must be inferred that children rank first in distribution, as German law provides.[4]

The "laws" of Edward the Confessor resemble those of Cnut. They were written by Lambard, and Thorpe says they are not reliable.[5]

The laws of William I say: "If a man dies intestate his children shall divide the inheritance equally among themselves."[6] Unlike Cnut's law and like the German, this excludes the wife, but puts daughters with sons.[7]

Next comes the charter of liberties of Henry I, in 1100. It might be translated thus:[8]

> If any baron or man of mine, being sick, disposes of his property, I concede that this may be done. If, prevented by force or infirmity, he does not dispose of his wealth, his wife or children or parents or lawful men, will divide it for the good of his soul, as to them seems best.

It may be that "or" should be read "and." These mediaeval documents do not have the precision of a modern statute.

The custom of Wessex sets out the order of succession where there are no children—father, and mother, then brother and sister, then aunts, then "whoever is in closest relationship"; and males are preferred to females.[9]

Maitland says: "About the rules of intestate succession which prevailed here before the conquest we know little; they may have been different in the different folks, and at a later time they may have varied from shire to shire." There was as yet no "representation" of the deceased—no one responsible for gathering in and distributing assets, and for payment of debts.[10]

The work known as "Glanvil" was written around 1187, late in the reign of Henry II. It is the first dependable account of English law. By this time military tenures were established. The eldest son was heir to land so held. In other tenures, all sons took, or perhaps the youngest.[11] A freeman not in debt may make a will of his moveables, but from what follows this means that he may bequeath only part—the "dead's part." When he dies intestate, one third belongs to the heir (the editor says this means "children"), one third to the wife, and the remaining third is reserved to himself. This is the only part of which he may dispose by will; and he can no longer will his land. If he has no wife but has children, he may dispose of half of his goods.[12] Executors of wills are mentioned, but the administrator does not yet appear.

In a later passage Glanvil says: "But when anyone dies intestate, all his chattels are understood to belong to the lord." This appears in a section dealing with deceased bastards and usurers,[13] and should not be taken to contradict the general rule. One writer, Mr. Gross, mistakes this for the general rule. His purpose was to show that at this period and even later, an intestate's goods went to his lord (who might or might not be the king). He quotes from numerous town charters to prove the point. However he cannot properly rely on the statement he quotes from Glanvil.[14]

In Glanvil we see the writ *de rationabili parte bonorum:*[15]

> Of the chattels that were of the aforesaid R., I command you that you cause them all to be in peace, so that no part be removed . . . until his debts are entirely discharged, and of the residue there shall be afterwards a reasonable division made, according to the custom of my land.

Fitzherbert explains this writ.[16]

> The writ lieth where the wife after the death of her husband cannot have the third part of her husband's goods after the debts are paid, and funeral expenses performed. For then she may have this writ against the executors of her husband; and it seemeth by the statute of Magna Carta, c. 18, that this was the common law of the realm; and so it appeareth by Glanvil, that after the debts are paid, the goods shall be divided into three parts; one part for the wife, another part for sons and daughters, and the third unto the executors.

This share of wife and children was sometimes called the "legitim," a term used in Roman law. Later the right to this legitim disappeared in parts of the country, or at least could not effectively be set up; and a wife or children wanting to assert it were obliged to allege a local custom.[17]

Fitzherbert ranks sons with daughters, and Lord Hale[18] thinks this was the law, though as already mentioned, some think that sons were preferred.

Maitland points out that there are few cases of the issue of the writ in the thirteenth century. The reason is that this writ was brought against the executor, and the church courts had jurisdiction over wills.[19]

Magna Carta

Chapter 26 of John's charter of 1215, reproduced as chapter 18 of the charter of Henry III in 1225, provides that on the death of the holder of a lay fief, the sheriff shall attach his chattels to the value of the debts, "and the residue shall be left to the executors to fulfil the will of the deceased; and if there be nothing due from him to us, all the chattels shall go to the deceased, saving to the wife and children their reasonable shares."

McKechnie says that this clause was inserted because the sheriffs frequently seized goods worth much more than the amount of the debt to the king, and kept the surplus.[20]

There has been a difference of opinion as to whether the saving clause actually secures to the wife and children their reasonable parts, or whether it applies only where local custom conferred to them a part. McKechnie, relying on Glanvil, takes the first view.[21] Coke takes the second,[22] and says that the writ *de rationabili* lies only where there is a local custom. The first position seems originally to have been the correct one, but by the time of Coke the second had prevailed.[23]

Chapter 27 of John's charter is important.

> If any freeman shall die intestate, his chattels shall be distributed by the hands of his nearest kinsfolk and friends, under supervision of the church, saving to every one the debts which the deceased owed to him.

This chapter deals with the case of an intestacy, while chapter 26 dealt with the case of a will, indicating that even where a man left a will his wife and children were entitled to their reasonable parts.

Chapter 27 was omitted from Henry's charter. Selden says it was included in some manuscripts but omitted from the printed copies and from the confirmation of Edward II.[24]

Chapter 27 was in part a concession to the church but its main purpose was to protect the family of an intestate from "the scramble that often took place for an intestate's chattels."[25] It was a concession by king and barons that they would not attempt to seize an intestate's goods. Maitland comments on its omission from Henry's charter:[26]

> We may guess that it was withdrawn by Henry's counsellors in the interest of their infant king. The thought may have crossed their minds (and John may at times have put this thought into practice) that intestacy was a cause of forfeiture. But this clause though it was deliberately withdrawn seems to have settled the law.

In other words the church continued to supervise the administration of intestates' estates from this time. There is no clear evidence that they had done so earlier,[27] though the charter of Henry I speaks of the division of the property of a baron "for the good of his soul," which may imply church intervention.

Lord Phillimore wrote a puzzling footnote to a case of 1809. He describes the abuses connected with intestate estates in the Norman period, and the statutes later passed in an attempt to remedy them. He then says:[28]

> The 32nd article of Magna Carta extorted from King John expressly provides against them; but it is a curious fact and one which strongly marks the influence of the papal power in England at that period that this article was wholly omitted in the Magna Carta of Henry III.

Clearly he means chapter 27. His explanation of the withdrawal is obviously wrong.

Bracton

Bracton's great work was written around 1260, late in the reign of Henry III. The main passage on intestate succession reads:[29]

> Likewise if a free man has died intestate, and suddenly, his lord shall not meddle with the goods of the deceased, except as regards that alone, which

> appertains to himself, for instance that he may have his heriot, but the executorship of the goods shall belong to the church and to his friends; for a man does not deserve any penalty though he has died intestate.

This passage confirms the role of the church prescribed by chapter 27. Another important point is this. The phrase "and suddenly" implies, as does the charter of Henry I a century and a half before, that the right of his family to his chattels arises only if he died so unexpectedly that he was unable to make a will. The inference is that if he deliberately died intestate his goods might be forfeited. This is surprising, especially when a man could dispose only of the "dead's part" in any event. Moreover Selden says that in the time of Henry III intestacies "questionless were very many."[30]

Yet all other writers accept the view that it was a disgrace to die intestate. A dying man was expected to die confessed, and if he were confessed he would make a will, under the priest's encouragement. Thus dying without a will was linked to dying unconfessed, and so was disgraceful.[31]

The term "executorship" in the above passage of course means "administration."[32] The administrator was not yet known by that name and the word "executor" was used to include administrators.

Having explained that the church and friends have the "executorship," Bracton then tells us who is entitled to the property beneficially. After the debts and expenses have been deducted,

> the whole which remains over, shall be divided into three parts, of which let one part be left to the children of the deceased, if he has male children, the second to the wife, if she survive, and of the third part the testator may have the free disposal.

If there be children and no wife or wife and no children then one half is at the disposal of the deceased. If no wife or child he may dispose of the whole.[33]

Twiss translates "puer" as son and "liber" as child, but others agree that both words should be read to include daughters.[34]

Bracton then explains that the local custom of a town, city, or vill may differ from these general rules. In London for example the wife can claim no more than her dower, and the children can claim no more as of right than their father has left them. When Coke discussed this subject in connection with chapter 18 of Magna Carta (c. 26 of John's) he set out in Latin this passage from Bracton. However he put it forth as the general rule instead of an exception, and on the strength of it stated that the alleged right of the wife and children to their reasonable parts, or legitim, which the husband could not take away from them, was never the common law.[35] His error has been noted by Blackstone, Beale, and others.[36]

A point about Bracton's account of the custom of London that is puzzling and on which I have seen no comment is this: his description of the London custom does not seem to be accurate. We shall see that the common law right of wife and children to their reasonable parts persisted in London longer than in any other part of the realm.

We have mentioned that Bracton's account of "executorship" inferentially confirms chapter 27 of John's charter. This excludes lord or king from seizing the goods. We must take note of some of the views expressed on this subject. Selden refers to a close roll of 7 Henry III (1222) indicating that the king asserted the right to seize an intestate's goods. Selden says this can be justified only on the assumption that the intestate was indebted to the crown.[37]

Hensloe's case, reported by Coke, says:[38]

> Of ancient time, as appears by record, when a man died intestate and had made no disposition of his goods, nor committed his trust to any, in such case the king, who is parens patriae, and has the supreme care to provide for all his subjects, that every one should enjoy that which he ought to have, used by his ministers to seize the goods of the intestate, to the intent that they should be preserved and disposed for the burial of the dead, for payment of his debts, to advance his wife and children if he had any, and if not those of his blood.

Then this care and trust went to the ordinaries, but only by delegation from the king, as Lyndwood, the great ecclesiastical lawyer, acknowledged.

The most interesting case on the relation between crown and church is Dyke v. Walford, a Privy Council case of 1846. A bastard died intestate in the Duchy of Lancaster, and without kin. Bona vacantia of course goes to the crown, but in this case it was argued against the crown that the property went to the Queen as Duchess of Lancaster. In 1377 Edward III granted the Duchy to John of Gaunt and his successors as Duke of Lancaster. Included in the grant were *jura regalia*. The crown argued that the right to intestates' effects was not *jura regalia* in 1377 but instead lay in the church and so did not pass by the grant. The Privy Council rejected this argument.[39]

> The clergy had never at any time in this country by law any beneficial interest in the property of intestates, but merely the right or duty of jurisdiction or administration, and the right of possession for the latter purpose.

The interference of the clergy came as the result of the creation of "pious uses" and neither Magna Carta or the 1285 act (to be noted later) implies that the ordinary was beneficially entitled to the goods. True, it was hard at this time to compel the ordinary to make a satisfactory account.

> Under these circumstances it was to be expected that gross abuses would prevail and that the property would often be misappropriated to the administrators; and so much the more as regard was to be had to the good of the soul of the deceased in the administration of the estate, and this consideration would leave a large discretion to the ordinary. We find accordingly that such abuses did prevail, but they were treated as abuses by both the ecclesiastical and civil authorities, and attempts were made by both to correct and repress them.

Burn, writing in the eighteenth century, had taken a view more favorable to the clergy, though he acknowledged the difference of opinion. He says[40] it is plain by the common law, and before the 1285 statute "the ordinary had the absolute disposal of intestates' effects'' and that the king could claim them only where the deceased was indebted to the crown. He cites as authority Bacon's Abridgement for the proposition that neither wife nor kin had any right to a share, but that the ordinary was to distribute to pious uses and might as a matter of grace allow the wife and children to share. Bacon's authority is the argument of counsel in Palmer v. Allicock[41] and Coke's comments on the 1285 statute. The latter do not support the statement, unless possibly by inference.[42]

Establishment of the Administrator

We have seen that after Magna Carta the control of the church over intestates' effects was strengthened. The dead's part, which was one-third or one-half of the whole, went to "pious uses." Selden says that "the distribution *in pios usus* was the devising them among the next of kin, according to their nearness and want; not an employing them to other uses at the ordinary's arbitrary discretion."[43] However all other writers treat it as meaning what the phrase implies. The goods were to be used for the good of the soul of the deceased, and generally the church kept them. Besides the injustice to kin, creditors went unpaid. The ordinary could not be sued, though by this time an executor could sue and be sued; he was a true personal representative.[44]

We have already referred to the 1285 act—the Statute of Westminster. It provided:

> The ordinary from henceforth shall be bound to answer the debts as far forth as the goods of the dead will extend, in such sort as the executors of the same party should have been bounded, if he had made a testament.[45]

Grazebrook v. Fox, in 1561, quaintly explains the reason for this act.[46] The law had adjudged the ordinary the most proper person to have disposition of an intestate's goods,

> for it was to be presumed that the ordinary who had the care of his soul in his lifetime, would be the fittest to have the care and disposal of his goods *in pios usus* after his death, for which reason . . . the law committed them to the ordinary and therefore the ordinary might seize them and keep them without waste and he might have given them or aliened them, or have otherwise disposed of them at his pleasure, and the money arising from them he was to dispose of *in pios usus,* and if he did not, he broke the confidence and trust reposed in him for which he stood charged in conscience to God: but nevertheless the gift or alienation of the goods by the ordinary was good by the law of the realm . . . and the common law did not make him, being a spiritual governor, subject to temporal suits for such things, and this was a great defect in the common law.

The act enabled creditors to sue the ordinary in the temporal courts. True, opinions have been expressed to the effect that the statute was but an affirmance of the common law.[47]

Blackstone's comment on the act is:[48]

> This was the first check given to that exorbitant power which the law had intrusted with ordinaries. But though they were now made liable to the creditors of the intestate for their just and lawful demands; yet this residuum, after payment of debts, remained still in their hands, to be applied to whatever purposes the conscience of the ordinary shall approve.

The ordinary was the bishop or one *in loco episcopi*. Incidentally, Coke says that the derivation of the word is *ab ordine,* to put the bishop in mind of the duty of his place, and of that order and office that he is called unto.[49] The usual explanation is that the word has reference to ordinary in contrast to extra-ordinary or peculiar jurisdiction. The ordinary was sometimes called "executor legitimus" for he derives his authority from the law instead of from a will.[50] We shall see that the Archbishop issued canons to try to hold the ordinaries to their duties, but the 1285 act was the first check imposed by the temporal power. The ordinary did not always carry out personally his duties and take charge of the assets, but appointed someone to act on his behalf. This person was "bound by the equity" of the 1285 statute, but could not sue.[51]

In 1357, during the reign of Edward III was passed an act which created the modern administrator in name and fact. The ordinary is no longer to have personal charge and responsibility.

> In case where a man dieth intestate the ordinaries shall depute the next and most lawful friends of the dead person intestate to administer his goods.

This new "executor dativus" or administrator may sue and be sued in the king's court in the same way as an executor, and is accountable to the ordinary as an executor is.[52]

Grazebrook v. Fox explains the purpose of the act.[53] The 1285 statute limited the ordinary's liability to goods actually come into his hands and he had no way to compel payment of debts due the intestate. Moreover,

> the ordinary is a spiritual governor, wholly conversant in spiritual causes, to whom it is inconvenient to toil in the temporal concerns of others and therefore the statute has given him the liberty to appoint others to take the trouble of administration, though he could before the act appoint a deputy by the common law.

Holt, C.J., gave a different explanation. He said,[54]

> The ordinary, having the power of distribution, used to dispose of part among the relations, and the other part to charities; but (the 1357) statute took away such right from the ordinary, and fixed the title to the personal estate in the administrator.

The comments of the King's Bench in Carter v. Crawley[55] are not flattering to the church courts: they "anciently grasped at a large jurisdiction," and where there was no will the ordinary had the absolute disposal of the estate. Then the 1285 act forced them to pay debts. Thereupon, their meddling with deceaseds' estates, which was very beneficial before, became very troublesome, and to free themselves from it they were fain to put the administration thereof into third persons' hands, who might give them security to save them harmless from suits.

From these cases, it is clear that the 1285 act was really the death blow to the ordinary's power. The role of "executor legitimus" became more of a burden than a profit. The practice of appointing deputies increased, until Parliament decided that the best solution was to create a true personal representative; and that he should be selected from among those most interested in their property—the nearest relations ("next and most lawful friends") of the deceased.[56]

After the reformation it was popular for judges and writers to stigmatize the church. They spoke as though all the clergy conspired to misappropriate all the property they could get into their hands. This is misleading and unfair. The canons published by Lyndwood in 1432 show that the Archbishops tried to prevent abuses in connection with wills and intestacies.

Most of the relevant canons are those of John Stratford, Archbishop of Canterbury, and issued in 1342. One canon forbids anyone from alienating goods in fraud of Church, king, creditors, wives, or children.[57] Another, in confirmation of an earlier canon of Archbishop Boniface, forbids lords of fees from seizing an intestate's goods and refusing to pay creditors or to distribute the portions belonging to wife, children, and parents, and "that portion which after the custom of the country pertaineth to the dead, otherwise to be bestowed for them at the disposition of the ordinaries."[58] Another directs the bishops, after payment of debts, to dispose of and distribute the goods "In charitable deeds for the soul's health of the dead, and unto such persons as were his servants or neighbours of the dead, or such other, retaining nothing thereof to themselves" except reasonable expenses.[59]

The Statute of 1529 and After

Five years before the Reformation the Parliament of Henry VIII passed a law to regulate fees to be taken on probate of wills. It was passed to stop the ordinaries from exacting exorbitant fees. Included is a section dealing with intestacy. It *requires* the ordinary to grant administration "to the widow of the same person deceased, or to the next of his kin, or to both, as by the discretion of the same ordinary shall be thought good." The ordinary is to take security for good administration. He may appoint one or more when there are several of the same degree of kinship.[60]

Before the act the wife was not eligible, and the ordinary sometimes appointed persons who would be friendly and amenable to the ordinary. According to Carter v. Crawley[61] the act did not at once put an end to such practices. The ordinaries

had a liberty expressly provided to refuse the wife, if they pleased; and if there were many in equal degree of the next of kindred, to grant administration to

> which they please, and refuse the rest, which liberty was a great advantage to their jurisdiction. For they would choose him that was most obsequious to them, and when they called to account upon pretext of bestowing the overplus for the good of the deceased's soul, (a device in those popish times to make profit to the clergy) they disposed of the overplus as their own.

The judgment goes on to say that

> upon the reformation that pretext vanished, but they thought it allowable to distribute the surplus among the kindred, according to the rules of the civil law, *de successoribus ab intestato*. And this was so reasonable that they used this course without blame a great while, and inserted a clause into all their bonds for security to account to the ordinary, that the overplus upon such account should be distributed as the ordinary should appoint.

We must now look at the question: who was beneficially entitled to the property after payment of debts[62] by the sixteenth century? One might think that it is still the wife, children, and a part for the dead but this was not so except where the old rules prevailed as local custom. Holdsworth says:[63]

> In theory no doubt the administrator should have distributed the estate according to the old customary rules. He should have given their shares to the wife and children and have distributed the share of the deceased in pious uses.

The common law courts took the position that their concern with administrators was confined to actions by and against them. The administrator was the legal owner of the assets, and the common law courts took the same position in relation to the next of kin that they took with all *cestuis qui trustent*. It was no concern of theirs that the legal owner committed a breach of faith.[64] The wife and children could go to the church courts for their remedy. For a time the ordinaries succeeded in compelling administrators, who always gave a bond for due administration, to give wife and kin their reasonable parts. But by the middle of the sixteenth century the church courts were no longer potent.[65] Then by the end of the century the common law courts began actively to interfere with the courts spiritual. We have the ironical position that the ordinaries, who in the thirteenth and fourteenth centuries were the villains of the story, are now frustrated in their efforts to secure to wife and children their reasonable parts.

A case of 1625 illustrates the position. The sister of an intestate sued the administrator in the church court to compel him to distribute part of the estate to her as a next of kin. He applied in the King's Bench for prohibition and it was granted. Hutton, J. said that the 1357 act compelled the ordinary to grant administration, and that then he was *functus officio*. The administrator had an absolute interest in the goods.[66]

> Although at the civil law the administrator was accountable as servant to the ordinary, and might be discharged by him, and a repeal might have been of the letters of administration at the ordinary's pleasure, yet at this day, especially after the statute of 21 Henry VIII, the administration being duly com-

> mitted by the ordinary, cannot now be repealed, and if there be a suit to have it appealed, a prohibition lies.

Then in 1666 came Hughes v. Hughes.[67] A son was granted administration and gave the usual bond. His sister asked the Court Christian to compel him to give her a reasonable share by the ancient law. Her brother brought prohibition. She invoked statutes and cases, the law of nature and of nations. The recent prohibitions were improper. The decision is not given but the reporter says: "et puis per act del parl pur melieux settlement des intestates estates fut contrived." This of course refers to the Statute of Distributions. Before examining it we will see what happened to the second part of the common law rule—the restriction on testamentary power to the dead's part.

As early as the fourteenth century, men sometimes made a will of all their personalty. The wife and kin fell between two stools. The common law courts thought such questions were for the church courts, and the latter had no rules of their own on the subject. The writ *de rationabili parte bonorum* existed for the relief of wife and children, but as we have seen it came to be accepted that it only lay where local custom imposed a restriction on testation—for example in London and York.

Holdsworth says:[68]

> It is probable that it will not be possible to give a complete account of the reasons for the disappearance of the older scheme till we know something more of the proceedings of the ecclesiastical courts of the northern and of the southern province.

He suggests that the reasons may be the confusion over jurisdiction, growth of the sentiment that a man should be able to dispose of the property he acquired from his wife on marriage, since she could not, and the absence in many places of a court designed to look after children's interests.[69]

The Statute of Distributions[70]

This landmark statute, passed in 1670, does two things: (1) it enables the ordinary to compel administrators to distribute the effects among wife and children; (2) it specifies who shall take. One third goes to the wife and two thirds to children; if no children one half to wife and one half to next of kin; if no wife, all to children, and if no wife or child, all to next of kin. As Blackstone comments, "It is obvious to observe how near a resemblance this statute of distributions bears to our ancient English law, *de rationabili parte bonorum*."[71] The provisions for computing next of kin, and allowing persons to take by representation, and for taking into consideration amounts advanced to children by way of portion need not concern us.

An important section reads:

> This act or anything herein contained shall not anyways prejudice or hinder the customs observed within the City of London or within the Province of

> York or other places having known or proved customs peculiar to them, but that the same customs may be observed as formerly; anything contained herein to the contrary notwithstanding.

A clause in the Statute of Frauds[72] six years later made it clear that when a wife died the husband is entitled to administration and to her goods beneficially.

Temporarily the first object of the act was achieved. The hand of the church courts was strengthened. But before long the common law courts resumed their policy of obstruction. When the church courts tried to compel debtors of the deceased to pay, prohibition was issued. Action in debt was for the temporal courts.[73] Then the court of chancery came to the attack. It was fitted to handle administrative matters and interfered in the administration of estates. This happened as early as 1688. An administratrix passed her accounts in the ecclesiastical court and obtained a decree for distribution. Chancery ignored these proceedings and decreed an account of the whole estate. "The judgments of the ecclesiastical court are as much subject to the equity of the court of chancery as the judgments at law."[74]

In time the jurisdiction of the church courts was reduced to the granting of probate and administration. When they were replaced by a new Court of Probate in 1857, this court inherited the same narrow powers.[75]

The Customs of London and York

As we have seen the general rule in Bracton's time provided for division of the intestate's goods into wife's part, bairns' part and dead's part; and a man could dispose only of the last of these. We have seen the disintegration of both parts of the rule, and the new provisions for succession laid down in the Statute of Distribution.

We have also seen that the statute recognized and preserved the customs of London and the Province of York. Burn[76] says that since these customs

> comprehend so considerable a part of the kingdom, it is somewhat strange that so few authors have taken any pains to inform their readers or themselves. The civil law acknowledgeth not these customs; nor yet doth the common law and therefore perhaps neither civilians nor common lawyers have judged them a proper subject for their inquiries. And yet the general notion thereof seemeth to have sprung from the civil law, which establisheth what the civilians call the *legitime,* although much different from our customs; and these customs are so ancient, and of ancient times were of such general and almost universal extent, that some of the greatest lawyers have doubted whether they were not part of the common law.

His explanation of the origin of the custom is this. When land held in military tenure came to devolve on the eldest son, then "that the other children might not be destitute, a portion was provided for them out of the personalty, which the father might not give by will, nor the ordinary by distribution in case of intestacy." The custom disappeared in parts of the realm when the Statute of Wills in 1540 permitted the devise of lands. In York military tenures persisted longest because of threats from the Scots; and even when Burn wrote, in 1788, great parts of land could not be devised by will.

We shall make no detailed criticism of this theory. It is plausible, and neither Maitland nor Holdsworth is dogmatic on the subject. Yet the authorities we have examined do not indicate that the right to a reasonable part arose from the fact that land held in military tenure had to go to the eldest son. That right appears to antedate military tenure. Moreover the breakdown of the right seems to have begun before the Statute of Wills.

The old rule survived in York in full vigor until the end of the seventeenth century. However the part of the custom that forbade a man from bequeathing more than the dead's part of his chattels was abrogated by statutes of 1692 and 1704.[77] Thereafter he could will all of them, but if he died intestate the old custom applied until 1856.

Wales was another part of the realm in which a similar custom was "alleged" to exist. A statute of 1695 gave the power to make will of personalty.[78]

The incapacity to leave all personal property by will persisted longest in London. When Parliament conferred the power in 1724 the act[79] recited that merchants refuse to become freemen of London because of the custom restraining such freemen from disposing of their personal estates. The act specifically preserves the custom in case of intestacy.

Although the custom remained in York, Wales and London in cases of intestacy until 1856, the Statute of Distributions operated on the dead's part so that it was distributed pursuant to that statute.[80]

The 1856 act terminated "the special customs covering the distribution of the personal estates of intestates observed in London, York and certain places" and the Statute of Distributions applied universally.[81]

A year later, as we have seen, the powers of the ecclesiastical courts were taken from them and given to a temporal probate court; and incidentally the jurisdiction of the church courts in matrimonial matters was vested in a temporal court. The Judicature Acts created the Probate Divorce and Admiralty Division of the High Court of Justice.[82]

The Present Law

By 1873 when the first Judicature Act was passed the law of intestate succession stood thus. A person could will both land and personal property without restriction (save in the case of a married woman prior to the Married Women's Property Acts). A married man was under no obligation to leave anything to wife or child. If a person died intestate his real property descended to his heir by the feudal rules (modified in some respects by statute). His personal property went according to the Statute of Distributions. The executor and administrator were still *personal* representatives, not *real* representatives. Debts of an intestate were still paid out of personalty, not out of real property.

A series of statutes in the period since the Judicature Acts has radically changed the law in all these respects. The Land Transfer Act, 1897 provides that real property (with minor exceptions) shall devolve on the executor or administrator, and is made available for payment of debts, though the heir still takes on intestacy.[83]

Early in the twentieth century it was widely felt that real property law should be simplified, and that the law of real and personal property including the law of descent should be assimilated so far as possible. In 1925 a number of revolutionary statutes were passed to that end. The act of main interest to us is the Administration of Estates Act.[84] All property devolves on the executor or administrator.[85] The court has discretion as to the person to be made administrator.[86] Descent to the heir is abolished.[87] The scheme of distribution is more elaborate than that provided by the Statute of Distrib1utions. The surviving spouse receives all personal chattels and £1000; also a life interest in all the residuary estate if no issue, or in half the residuary estate if issue. Subject to the spouse's interest statutory trusts are created of all property in favor of issue; if no issue then in favor of parents, next of brothers and sisters, next of grandparents, and next of aunts and uncles.[88]

The last act to be noted is the Inheritance (Family Provision) Act, 1938.[89] If a married person does not make reasonable provision for the surviving spouse, unmarried daughter, or infant son, or for a child incapable of maintaining himself, then the court may make provision out of the estate for the maintenance of such persons.

Conclusion

It is an exaggeration to say that the present law is a reversion to that of the time of Glanvil and Bracton. There is no "dead's part" to be left for the good of the soul. The rights of dependents under the 1938 act is not exactly the same as the rights invoked by the writ *de rationabili parte*.

Yet what we have described is really a cycle. In the Middle Ages the law of land became entirely separate from that of personal property. The divergence of the rules of succession was the main factor in that separation. In the last sixty years the dead hand of feudalism has been lifted from the land laws.

The most significant lesson that one learns from the foregoing outline is that most of the changes in the law of intestate succession to personal property were the by-product of the pressure and influence exerted by competing interests. The interposition of the church tended to protect the family from the claims of king and lord; later the administrator was created to protect the family against the ordinaries; then the ordinaries tried to protect the family from the administrator; and the jealousy of temporal courts frustrated the ordinaries. Parliament came to the rescue of the family in 1670, and then the court of chancery supplanted the courts spiritual as its protector.

Finally, the sketch we have given illustrates the truism that law is a reflection of a culture, including its social and moral views. When Parliament abolished that part of the customs of York and London that forbade a husband from making a will of wife's part and bairns' part it was doubtless influenced by the rise of individualism; and when in 1938 it interposed in favor of dependants who were ignored in a will, it reflected the present trend toward enforcement of moral obligation.

Notes

1 Whitelock, Anglo-Saxon Wills (1930).
2 Young, Anglo-Saxon Family Law, in Essays on Anglo-Saxon Law (1876).
3 Robertson, Laws of the Kings of England from Edmund to Henry I.
4 Selden, Disposition of Intestates' Goods, Works, Vol. III, Pt. II, 1676–7.
5 Thorpe, Ancient Laws, I, 456–57.
6 Robertson, op. cit., note 3, 269.
7 Young, op, cit.; note 2 insists "children" should read "sons," 133.
8 Stubbs, Charters, 118. Swinburne, Wills (1803) says this charter gave birth to the ecclesiastical jurisdiction in England over intestates' estates, II, 776–77, note.
9 Thorpe, op. cit., note 5, 574–75.
10 Pollock & Maitland, History of English Law, II, 255–60, 2 ed. (1905), hereafter cited "P. & M." See also Holdsworth, History of English Law, I, 90–3, 96–97, 3 ed. (1922, 1923), hereafter cited "Holds."
11 Glanvil, Bk. VII, c. 3, 125–28, Beale (ed.).
12 Ibid., Bk VII, c. 5, 133–36, 138.
13 Ibid., Bk. VII, c. 16, 150–52.
14 Gross, Mediaeval Law of Intestacy, 18 Harv. L.R. 120, (1905).
15 Glanvil, Bk. XII, c. 20; also Bk. VII, c. 7, 8.
16 F.N.B. 284–85 (1793).
17 Ibid.
18 Hale, History of the Common Law of England, 313.
19 P. & M., II, 352. For the history of this jurisdiction see Selden, Original of Ecclesiastical Jurisdiction of Testaments, Works, III, 1665.
20 McKechnie, Magna Carta, 322–26, 2 ed. (1914).
21 Ibid.
22 Co. Inst., II, 33; see also Holds. III, 553.
23 The writ in *Y.B. 1 & 2 ed. II (S.S.) 39* (1308) states: ". . . and by the usage of the country the third part thereof ought to remain to the dead man and one part to his wife and one part to his unadvanced children." The judgment is not given, but a note of later date says: "The opinion is that first the husband's debts should be paid and then the testament should be executed, and the wife and children have no action if the husband has devised all his goods. But after debts paid and testament executed, the wife and children take their share by custom and not by the rigour of the law." The writ in *Y.B. 6 & 7 Ed. II (S.S.) 30–31* (1313) invokes Magna Carta: "Seeing that it is provided by the great charter of the liberties of England, that children after the death of their father, are to have their reasonable share of the goods and chattels which he had on the day of his death... and that G. our father had goods to the value of £300 which went into the hands of his executrix, who refused to deliver us £100 for our share... but detained it wrongfully and against the tenor of the great charter of the liberties aforesaid." The writ was abated because it referred to the "executrix of G." instead of to the "executrix of the testament of G."!! In *Y.B. 17 Ed. III (R.B.) 144* (1343) the writ was brought by a woman against the executors of her first husband. It purports to be based on the general law and not on local custom: "Whereas the common custom of the realm was that the wife should have a reasonable part of her husband's goods. . . . "
24 Selden, Works, 1678–79.

25 McKechnie, op. cit., note 19, 327.
26 P. & M., II, 357.
27 Holds. I, 626; Selden, Works, 1676–78.
28 *Earl of Warwick* v. *Greville,* 1 Phill. Ecc. 123.
29 f.60b, Twiss (Ed.), 481.
30 Selden, Works, 1683.
31 P. & M., II, 356; Holds. III, 535–36.
32 Selden, Works 1684–85; Co. Inst., II, 398.
33 f.60b, 61, Twiss (Ed.), 484.
34 e.g. P. & M. II, 350 n4; *Blackborough* v. *Davis,* 1 P. Wms. 41, per Holt, CCJ.
35 Co. Inst. II, 32.
36 Bl. Comm. II, 492–93; Glanvil 135, Beale (ed.).
37 Selden, Works, 1683.
38 9 Co. Rep. 36b.
39 5 Moore P.C. 434.
40 Burn, Ecclesiastical Law, IV, 227 et seq., 5 ed. (1788), hereafter cited "Burn."
41 3 Mod. 59 (1684).
42 Co. Inst., II, 397–99.
43 Selden, Works, 1680.
44 Holds. III, 573–74, 583; P. & M. II, 347.
45 13 Ed. I s.l c.19.
46 11 Plowd, 275. The quoted passage is a dissent but the majority do not disagree on this point.
47 Snelling's Case, 5 Co. Rep. 82b; Hensloe's Case, 9 Co. Rep. 36b.
48 Bl. Comm. II, 495.
49 Co. Inst. II, 398.
50 Holds III, 566.
51 Holds. III, 568.
52 31 Ed. III s.l c.11.
53 Note 48 above.
54 *Blackborough* v. *Davis,* 1 P. Wms. 41 (1701).
55 Sir. T. Raymond 496 (1682).
56 *Dyke* v. *Walford,* 5 Moore P.C. 434 (1846); Hensloe's Case, 9 Co. Rep. 36b.
57 Lyndwood, Provinciale, Bk. III, Tit. 11, 62–63 (1929).
58 Ibid., Bk. III, Tit. 13, c.5, p.66.
59 Ibid., Bk. III, Tit. 13, c.6, p. 68.
60 21 Henry VIII c.5 ss.3.
61 Note 57 above.
62 Creditors were sometimes defrauded by the following device. The kin would find a man of straw and have him made administrator. He handed the assets to the kin without first paying debts. The church courts were unable to put a stop to this practice, so in 1601 a statute was passed. It put an end to this particular fraud; 43 Eliz. c.8.
63 Holds. III, 556.
64 Holds. III, 556–57, 585–95.
65 Holds. III, 557.
66 Fotheby's Case, Cro. Car. 62; also Levanne's Case, Cro. Car. 202.
67 Carter 125.
68 Holds. III, 554.
69 Holds. III, 554–56.
70 22 & 23 Car. II c.10.
71 Bl. Comm. II, 516.
72 29 Car. II c.3 s.25.
73 *Clarke* v. *Clarke,* Ld. Raym. 585 (1707).
74 *Bissell* v. *Axtell,* 2 Vern. 47.
75 20 & 21 Vict. c.77.
76 Burn, IV, 380–81.
77 4 Wm. & Mary c.2; 2 & 3 Anne c.5.
78 7 & 8 Wm. & Mary c.38.
79 11 Geo. I c.18.
80 1 Jac. II, c.17 s.8; Burn, IV, 388–89.
81 19 & 20 Vict. c.94.
82 Holds. I, 638–40.
83 60 & 61 Vict. c.65.
84 15 Geo. V c.23.
85 s.1.
86 s.10.
87 s.45.
88 ss.46, 47.
89 1 & 2 Geo. VI c.45.

1952

Book Review: A Text-Book of Jurisprudence by G.W. Paton, Second Edition, 1952.

Reprinted from
(1953) 31 Canadian Bar Review
pp. 330–332

As already noted, Bowker in 1946 wrote a review of Paton's first edition of his book on Jurisprudence (see above, p. 14).

In the second edition, Paton acknowledged Bowker's letter, written privately following the first edition, pointing out four errors which Bowker did not wish to refer to in his earlier review of the first edition.

Second editions of books do not ordinarily get as long a review as the first, unless there are major changes. Here, the changes were mainly in the arrangement of subject matter.

Bowker wrote this review in 1952 while on a sabbatical year at Yale University.

Books on Jurisprudence are never best sellers. Writers who have come into prominence since Bowker wrote these reviews are Dworkin, Rawls, Fuller and Hart. The emphasis now is more on the "end of law," rather than the analytical approach employed by Paton.

A text-book of Jurisprudence. By George Whitecross Paton. Second edition. Oxford: The Clarendon Press. Toronto: The Oxford University Press. 1951. Pp. xiii, 507. ($4.75)

Professor Paton, who is now Vice-Chancellor of the University of Melbourne, published the first edition of his text on jurisprudence in 1946. It was exceedingly well received and twice reprinted. Now the author has given us a second edition. The main changes are improvement in the arrangement of subject-matter and the addition and re-writing of a number of sections.

The work consists of six books. The first, entitled "Introduction", has chapters on the nature of jurisprudence, the evolution of law and the nature of law. In the second, "The Purpose of Law", are chapters on natural law and law as the protection of interests. Book III, "The Sources of Law", has a new chapter on custom and separate chapters on the judicial method (precedent), statute law, and legal writings and professional opinion.

The last three books, comprising three fifths of the whole, are devoted to what is called "analytical jurisprudence"—the analysis of legal concepts, principles of liability and the main divisions of the law. Book IV, "The Technique of the Law", includes classification, rights and duties, and titles, acts and events, whereas in the earlier edition classification is covered in Book I. The change is for the better. Book V, "Law and the State", has chapters on public law and criminal law, which had been separated in the first edition. Book VI, the last, is similar to Book IV of the original edition, save that the title has been changed from "The Analysis of Legal Concepts" to "Private Law" and the subject of criminal law has been put elsewhere. The chapters here are on legal personality, rights created by a juristic act (agreements), rights directly created by law (mainly torts), remedial rights, extinction of rights, property, possession, and procedure.

Many present-day writers divide jurisprudence into three separate branches: the philosophy of law, which seeks to find the purpose of law in some ideal or other; sociological jurisprudence, which is concerned with law as it operates in a society; and analytical jurisprudence, which examines the principles, concepts and rules of a legal system. As a text of which the greatest part is an exposition of analytical jurisprudence, Professor Paton's book already enjoys a high reputation. Indeed, Roscoe Pound has said that it may well supersede *Salmond,* which for long has been recognized as the leading students' text.

Professor Paton's discussion of the philosophy of law is confined to a short description of various "schools" of jurisprudence in the first chapter and to his account of natural law in Book II. He places natural law with "Law as the Protection of Interests", which he says is really natural law in another form, both being "the attempt to examine the connexion between the needs of man as a rational being". To this reviewer it seems that natural law belongs rather under philosophy of law, for it seeks abstract rules of justice to which man-made law should conform. The interest approach, on the other hand, emphasizes the function of law as a means of satisfying the interests (or wants, demands, claims) of individuals and society, and is a variety of sociological jurisprudence. The leader of the school on this continent is of course Roscoe Pound, who has written extensively on the subject in the last half century. Although he has never attacked the importance of ideals or moral values in law, and unlike some American jurists has never repudiated the usefulness of analytical jurisprudence, yet his great contribution is that he led legal thought in the United States toward a new emphasis on the importance of law as an instrument to satisfy wants and, in the case of conflict, to effect a compromise that produces the least possible friction.

Doubtless Professor Paton, like most lawyers in Canada, thinks mainly in terms of analytical jurisprudence. His treatment of the province and function of law is not nearly as exhaustive as, for example, the works on those subjects by Professor Julius Stone and Professor Friedmann. Yet it is fortunate that a book already widely used in Canada does not ignore them completely.

We in Canada have paid insufficient attention to the interest approach.

Bound by a strict doctrine of precedent and the rule of parliamentary sovereignty, judges in Canada can hardly mould the law to the same extent as in the United States. Yet there are cases where Canadian courts do have a choice; and in these cases it is beneficial to consider the effect of the decision on society, to weigh the interests involved. To do so does not involve the rejection of legal concepts, though it puts emphasis on the facts. It does remind us that concepts are not an end in themselves and that the judicial process is not as much the automatic application of logic as some may think.

To take an example, we decide many important constitutional cases on reference and factual evidence is never or seldom admitted. In *Re Wartime Leasehold Regulations* the Chief Justice of Canada ruled that factums should not contain factual material except on matters of which judicial notice may be taken. Would not the courts find that they can more satisfactorily answer the question asked of them if evidence of the relevant facts were before them?

Again, courts sometimes employ canons of construction as though the purpose is to render statutes ineffective. One time-honoured canon is that criminal laws and taxing laws must be construed narrowly or strictly. But, as Paton says at page 189, "there are welcome signs that a pedantic use of technical rules is falling into disfavour". An example was given in Canada two years ago when the Supreme Court saved from emasculation the amendment to the Criminal Code respecting habitual criminals. A provincial court of appeal had applied the canon of construction in spite of a provision in the federal Interpretation Act that criminal laws are to be deemed remedial and in spite of the fact that its interpretation meant that the only person who could be treated as a habitual criminal was one who had been convicted three times of stopping the mail with intent to rob or search.

The controversy in this Review and elsewhere over the *Nolan* case is related to the same general problem. Ought the courts to adopt a "sociological" approach to statutes and, if so, how far should they go in giving effect to the social purpose? Should we perhaps modify the rule that a court may not look at what Paton calls the "preparatory work" or what Americans call the "legislative history" of a statute—debates in Hansard, reports of royal commissions, and the like?

Another rule which tends to limit the power of courts to modify rules of law to meet new demands is the strict doctrine of precedent. Paton asks whether it is too rigid, and says (page 162), "The answer tentatively suggested is that while it leads to confusion if lower courts do not follow decisions of upper courts in the same hierarchy, the House of Lords should be given power to correct its own mistakes".

Yet again we have the matter of citing books and articles to the court. As Paton says in an interesting chapter on professional opinion as a source of law, English courts have abandoned the old rule that counsel must not cite the works of living authors. Yet the Chief Justice of Canada, if one may judge from statements he has made from the bench, still objects to the citation of articles from legal periodicals.

One of the great virtues of this book is its clarity. Another is the temperate and constructive nature of the criticisms and the absence of dogmatism. If any book can demonstrate that "jusisprudence" can be made palatable, and that a knowledge of the subject is of practical value, it is this.

1954

The Honourable Horace Harvey, Chief Justice of Alberta

Reprinted from
(1954) 32 Canadian Bar Review (2 parts)
pp. 933–981 and 1118–1139

Following the death of Chief Justice Harvey in 1949, his son asked Bowker to write an article on his father's judicial contribution.

There have been very few articles written on Western Canadian judges. Harvey C.J. was a very significant figure in our judicial history, having served as a judge for 45 years (1904 to 1949). Previous to that, he had been Deputy Attorney General for the North West Territories at the capital in Regina.

This article has been often quoted—and more so in recent years with the growing interest in legal history.

"Who is going to run this country, the Chief Justice or the Government?" On July 11th, 1918, an army officer named Major R.B. Eaton put this question to John McCaffary, a deputy sheriff. McCaffary had come to Victoria Barracks at Calgary to execute a writ of attachment against Lieutenant-Colonel Philip Moore for declining to obey an order by way of habeas corpus that directed him to bring before the Supreme Court of Alberta twenty conscripts in his battalion. Colonel Moore had been told by his military superiors at Ottawa to absent himself and the deputy sheriff had been unable to find him. Major Eaton's rhetorical question was really an accusation that Horace Harvey, Chief Justice of Alberta, was trying to obstruct the Canadian government in its prosecution of the war.

This incident requires explanation. In the early years of the First Great War Canada's military forces were raised entirely by voluntary enlistment. By August 1917 the government had decided that conscription was necessary and asked Parliament to pass the Military Service Act, which provided for conscription, but exempted persons in essential occupations. By the spring of 1918 it had become apparent that reinforcements were still inadequate. The cabinet could have asked Parliament to amend the Military Service Act by removing the exemptions, but instead in April 1918, while Parliament was in session, the Governor in Council made two orders in council under the War Measures Act, which gives the Governor in Council wide powers to make orders in the interest of national safety during war. In this case the orders removed exemptions in the Military Service Act and provided that exempt persons could be called for military duty. Both houses of parliament approved the orders. The reason why the government acted by means of orders rather than by amendment to the Military Service Act was that the need for soldiers was urgent and an amendment would have taken considerable time.

One of the persons who had been exempted was an Alberta farmer named Lewis. A few weeks after the orders were made, Lewis found himself in the army at Sarcee Camp near Calgary, training for overseas service. On June 21st, his counsel, R.B. Bennett, K.C., applied to the full court, sitting at Calgary, for his release by way of habeas corpus. Stuart, Beck, Simmons and Hyndman JJ. agreed that there was no power under the War Measures Act to cancel exemptions granted by the Military Service Act. Harvey C.J. dissented on the ground that the War Measures Act confers on the Governor in Council the widest authorization to take measures in the interest of national safety, provided of course that those measures are taken "by reason of the existence of... war".[1]

The judgment ordering the release of Lewis was delivered on June 28th and there is a note by the Chief Justice in his judge's book that the court agreed to a stay for two weeks on condition that Lewis "be not removed from the province". On July 5th the Dominion cabinet responded to the *Lewis* judgment and then reciting the urgent military situation, it directed that the orders of April 1918 be given effect "notwithstanding the said judgment and notwithstanding any other judgment or any order that may be made by any court" and then directed that instructions be sent accordingly to the officers commanding the military districts of Canada.

A conscript named Norton, along with nineteen others at Sarcee Camp, promptly applied by way of habeas corpus for discharge from military custody. Stuart J., before whom the application for habeas corpus came, ordered that they were not to be removed from the province. The application was directed to Lieutenant-Colonel Moore and was returnable on Wednesday, July 10th, before Harvey C.J., Stuart and Beck JJ. Instead of Moore, an army officer named Major Carson appeared on behalf of the Adjutant General and stated that Moore had stayed away on the instructions of the Adjutant General. Counsel for the conscripts thereupon applied for and obtained an order for a writ of attachment against Lieutenant-Colonel Moore.

The next day, July 11th, the sheriff and his officers searched for but failed to find Colonel Moore. It was during this search that Major Eaton put his indignant query to the deputy sheriff. Not only had the authorities at Ottawa instructed Moore to evade the writ but, as the Chief Justice said in court the next day, "the sheriff has been met by armed military resistance in his effort to execute the writ". The situation was descried in vivid detail by a newspaper dispatch of the same day:

> Victoria Park Barracks, headquarters of Col. Phil Moore, Commanding Officer of the First Alberta Depot Battalion, has been turned into an armed camp. The Strathcona Horse has been brought in from Sarcee Camp to guard headquarters. Armed guards have been placed at every vantage point, and the Arts Building in which Col. Moore has his office is patrolled with a strong guard. Partitions have been torn down and two machine guns placed that will sweep the open space in front of the building.

That afternoon James Muir, K.C., applied on behalf of the Minister of Justice for a stay of the habeas corpus proceedings until the Supreme Court of Canada could rule on the validity of the original orders. Counsel for the conscripts was willing to agree to a stay if the government would undertake not to remove them from the province. This was by now the main issue, for Major Carson admitted in court that some of the twenty applicants had already been sent out of the province. In the hope that the government would give the undertaking, the hearing was adjourned until the morning of the next day, Friday, and then again until the afternoon. When the hearing was finally resumed, Mr. Muir read a telegram from the Minister of Justice declining to agree to hold conscripts in their own provinces until the legality of the orders was finally decided. To do so "would paralyze general operations".

Thereupon the Chief Justice delivered judgment in open court. "The military authorities and the executive government have set at defiance the highest court in this province", he said. The court could either abdicate its authority and functions or else continue to perform its duties and not prove false to the oath of office each member had taken. It would be of little use to put Lieutenant-Colonel Moore in jail. Since he refused to produce the applicants, the court must find someone else to do it. "The order should therefore go directing the sheriff to obtain the persons of the applicants or such of them as may be within the jurisdiction of the Court and to bring them before the court and that there they be discharged from military custody without further order". It is clear that the court anticipated that the sheriff would need the aid of a *posse comitatus*.

The judgment added that the court was not unmindful of the urgent need for soldiers but that it should not substitute expediency for law as the basis of judicial decision. "It is also apparent to us that without doubt there is enough might though not right behind the military authorities to prevent this Court's officers from performing their duty, and even to destroy both the members of the Court and its officers, but while the Court remains it must endeavour to perform its duty as it sees it." Then follows the comment that the court had tried, consistent with its duty to the applicants, to do nothing to hinder the army or the government but had "met with little success"—an understatement to be sure.[2]

Excitement was high and the Calgary city council feared violence. Present in court that afternoon was H.P.O. Savary, K.C., representing the council. He asked that the order not issue until noon of the next day, and the court agreed. The same evening Mr. Frank Freeze (who was acting mayor) met with Colonel McDonald, the District Officer Commanding, Major Carson and the sheriff. On his own responsibility Colonel McDonald undertook not to move the applicants from the Calgary judicial district until after twenty-four hours notice to the sheriff. The Chief Justice was invited to the meeting and instructed the sheriff not to execute the court's order unless notice was given. The acting Minister of Militia, Mr. Burrell, wired Colonel McDonald that the Militia Department would honour the undertaking. At last the government had capitulated.

Exactly a week later the Supreme Court of Canada ruled on a similar application for habeas corpus made on behalf of an Ontario farmer, Edwin Gray. The court held valid the orders in council, and so over-ruled *Re Lewis.*[3] The crisis was over. The dissenting opinion of Harvey C.J. on the validity of the orders was vindicated. Yet in the meantime he had enforced the law as his colleagues had declared it. Throughout the crisis he was calm, restrained, anxious to conciliate, and yet unflinching when it appeared that the government of Canada would persist in defying the court's order. For their part the chief military authorities on the spot acted too with restraint, in their dilemma doing all they could to avoid an open clash and the further inflaming of public opinion.

The incident is reminiscent of a similar one that occurred in the United States during the Civil War, but with a different result. President Lincoln suspended the writ of habeas corpus in 1861, though it is doubtful whether he had the power. One of the many alleged sympathizers with the Confederacy taken into custody by the military authorities was a man named Merryman, who was held in a military fort in Maryland. When he petitioned for a writ of habeas corpus, Roger Taney, Chief Justice of the United States, went to Baltimore to receive it. The Chief Justice ordered the army general having custody of Merryman to produce his prisoner. Instead, the general sent an aide, taking the position that he would not obey the order unless the President told him to. The Chief Justice directed a writ against the general, but the marshal was unable to find him. At this point, acknowledging that the force of the military was greater than that of the writ, the Chief Justice took no further step, save to send a copy of his opinion to the President.[4]

Early Career

The *Lewis* and *Norton* judgments are among hundreds that Horace Harvey wrote during his forty-five years on the bench. He delivered his first at Regina on October 18th, 1904, on behalf of the Supreme Court of the North-West Territories en banc. It was a dispute over the right to the "land scrip" the Dominion government issued to half-breeds. This scrip entitled the holder to select a parcel of land. Frequently it was bought and sold, and in this case two persons claimed to be buyers of the same scrip. The judgment is short, confident and a clear analysis of the rights of a holder of scrip.[5] His last judgment was delivered in June 1949, less than three months before his death, when he was almost eighty-six years old. A notorious drug peddler had appealed from a conviction on the ground that Crown counsel had asked prejudicial questions, and the Chief Justice, speaking for a majority of the Appellate Division of the Supreme Court of Alberta, allowed the appeal. This judgment too is clear and convincing.[6]

The forty-five years separating these two judgments mark one of the longest, if not the longest, terms of office of a superior court judge in Canadian history. It was surpassed by the late Chief Justice J.E.P. Prendergast of Manitoba, who was a member of the judiciary for forty-seven years, from 1897 to 1944, but for the first five years he sat as a county court judge.

We propose to attempt an assessment of Horace Harvey's part in the development of the law and the administration of justice in Alberta, but, before doing so, should say something about his early career. Born in 1863 on a farm near Aylmer, Elgin County, in what is now Ontario, he was graduated from the University of Toronto in 1886 and a year later received the degree of Bachelor of Laws. The Law Society of Upper Canada admitted him as a student at law in 1886. At this period Osgoode Hall had no law school, but students did have to pass examinations set by the law society. These covered all basic subjects, the required reading including parts of Blackstone, Story's *Equity, Pollock on Contracts, Best on Evidence, Byles on Bills* and O'Sullivan's *Government of Canada*. A student with a Bachelor of Arts degree had to spend only three years instead of five under articles.[7] On passing the last examinations, Mr. Harvey, in Easter Term 1889, was called to the bar of Ontario and admitted to practise as a solicitor.[8]

He practised in Toronto for four years. In 1893 he was married to Miss Louise Palmer of Toronto. The same year the young couple went west to Calgary where Mr. Harvey became the partner of Peter McCarthy, Q.C. Calgary became a city that year, with a population of 4,000. Indeed the whole population of the North-West Territories was less than a hundred thousand. The great migration of settlers was to take place in the next fifteen years.

The Law Society of the North-West Territories did not yet exist, the rolls being kept by the Lieutenant-Governor in Council. The official North-West Territories Gazette records that Mr. Harvey was enrolled as an advocate on May 22nd, 1893. He was in private practice for three years and his name appears as counsel in two reported cases. In December 1896 he became Registrar of Land Titles at Calgary. Under the Australian (Torrens) system of land registration, which Parliament had established in the Territories in 1886, the registrar is in charge of the government land titles office and is responsible for the issuing of titles and the recording of all charges on the title—good training for a man who as a judge was to decide many problems under the Land Titles Act. This position he held for three years.

In January 1900 the Gazette carried notice of the appointment of "Horace Harvey, Esq. of Osgoode Hall, Toronto, Barrister-at-law and an advocate of the Territories to be deputy of the Attorney-General, *vice* Hugh Amos Robson, resigned". When the Hudson's Bay Company in 1869 ceded its vast territories to Canada, the Dominion created out of them the province of Manitoba and the North-West Territories, both of which came into existence on July 15th, 1870.[9] Until 1888 the Territories were ruled by a lieutenant-governor in council. Orders in council issued under the various North-West Territories Acts of the Parliament of Canada gave the council power to make ordinances on many, but not all, of the subjects that are within the jurisdiction of a province. After 1888 an elected assembly replaced the council as the law-making body. In 1900, when Mr. Harvey went to Regina as deputy attorney-general, the minister under whom he was to serve was Mr. F.W.G. Haultain, who was "premier" as well as attorney-general. Haultain led the movement for provincial status and his part in the creation of Alberta and Saskatchewan was that of a great statesman.

His deputy was of course concerned with administration rather than policy. Although the name "H. Harvey" appears occasionally in the reports as Crown counsel both in civil and criminal cases, his most important work was undoubtedly in the drafting of ordinances. The law-making process had to keep step with immigration and the problems that came with it. In Mr. Harvey's four years as deputy, the legislature passed almost one hundred and fifty public ordinances. Many were amendments or revisions of earlier enactments—on municipalities and schools, regulation of the professions, administration of justice, prairie fires and control of liquor. New acts during his period of office concerned fire and hail insurance, brands, incorporation of companies by registration of a memorandum of association instead of letters patent, succession duties, trustees. Obviously many of the ordinances were borrowed from other jurisdictions, but to say this is not to detract from the magnitude of the task that fell to the early assemblies. There was no time to let the law grow as it did in the older colonies. It had to be transplanted, and in those circumstances the deputy attorney-general probably had a greater responsibility than anyone else for deciding what laws should be introduced, and for settling the details.

After four years as deputy attorney-general, Mr. Harvey was appointed by the Laurier administration a puisne judge of the Supreme Court of the North-West Territories. In this year, 1904, the courts had not been long in existence. They had been established by Parliament in 1876, with stipendiary magistrates as the first judges. The magistrates however had a wider jurisdiction than we should expect today: a stipendiary magistrate, for example, sitting with a justice of the peace and a jury of six, convicted Louis Riel of high treason in 1885.[10]

The year 1886 was an important one for the Territories, because in that year was passed a new organic act, which established the Supreme Court of the North-West Territories with five judges, as well as the act creating the Torrens system. Judicial districts were already in existence. In the same year the assembly also made an ordinance regulating procedure, the forerunner of the provincial rules of court.

In 1887 the administration of Sir John A. Macdonald appointed the first judges: Hugh Richardson, James F. Macleod, Charles B. Rouleau, Edward L. Wetmore and Thomas H. McGuire. The first three had been stipendiary magistrates and Macleod, whose name survives in Fort Macleod in southern Alberta, had been as well a commissioner of the North-West Mounted Police. Wetmore was a barrister from New Brunswick and McGuire a barrister from Ontario. Many years later Horace Harvey made the following comment on the court of 1887:

> . . . In little more than a decade, the Judicial machinery of the Territories had developed from its primitive beginning to become as complete in general character as, and equal in dignity and authority to, that of the Provinces.
>
> Speaking with a personal knowledge of its first members, with all but one of whom I was brought frequently in contact, and with one of whom I was subsequently a colleague, I feel no hesitation in stating that in this respect there was no inferiority to the personnel of the Superior Courts of the Provinces. This is also apparent from a perusal of its reported decisions.[11]

In 1900 Parliament provided that one of the judges should be chief justice and four years later authorized appointment of a fifth puisne judge. It has been said that the Laurier government planned originally to name Haultain as the fifth judge but that he decided to remain in politics to continue the campaign for provincial status. In any case the appointment went, on June 27th, 1904, to Horace Harvey. He joined Chief Justice A.L. Sifton and Justices Wetmore, Scott, Prendergast and Newlands, and was assigned to the Judicial District of Southern Alberta, which meant that he moved from Regina to Fort Macleod. All the judges sat together en banc to hear appeals, usually at Regina though occasionally at Calgary, but from 1904 the judge appealed from could not sit save in exceptional circumstances. When the two provinces of Alberta and Saskatchewan were formed from the Territories in September 1905 the court continued to act for both. In 1906 T.C. Johnstone and C.A. Stuart were added to the court.

Then in 1907 each province created its own Supreme Court. The first Saskatchewan judges were Wetmore C.J., Prendergast, Newlands and Johnstone JJ., and the Alberta judges, Sifton C.J., Scott, Harvey and Stuart JJ. Later in 1907 N.D. Beck, K.C., was added to the Alberta court. The organization of the new provincial courts was like that of the old. In Alberta appeals were heard from the beginning at Calgary and Edmonton. Harvey J. moved from Macleod to Calgary in 1905 and to Edmonton, the new capital, in 1907. At this time court in Edmonton was held upstairs in the Sandison block, which stood on Jasper Avenue immediately east of the MacDonald Hotel. The Court House was built some six years later.

In 1910 Chief Justice Sifton resigned to become premier of Alberta in place of the Hon. A.C. Rutherford, and Horace Harvey was made Chief Justice of Alberta. The vacancy on the court was filled by the appointment of W.C. Simmons. In 1912 William L. Walsh, K.C., was appointed a sixth member of the court. In 1913, the legislature made a change in the constitution of the court, effective in 1914, which Chief Justice Harvey once explained as follows:

> . . . by 1914 it was thought that the inconvenience of completely stopping trial work for sittings in banc and the increase of work called for a change and provision was made for three additional judges, making nine in all, and for an Appellate Division of four, which would sit for the hearing of appeals, the other five continuing as trial judges. The provision called for the judges themselves making the assignment each year for the following year with changes of personnel as desired.[12]

The three members added to the court in 1914 were M.S. McCarthy, W.C. Ives and J.D. Hyndman.

The "Appellate Division", it is to be noted, was not a separate division and it consisted of four members rather than an odd number. Chief Justice Harvey, writing in 1948, said that he still thought that "it is an advantage for a trial judge to have some experience as an appellate judge, as it is for an appellate judge to have experience at trials". He also stated that he had felt "that in the case of judges of co-ordinate jurisdiction, an equal division in the Appellate Division which left the judgment of a trial judge unaffected was fairer than a setting of it aside by a majority of three to two or two to one". He conceded that on this point there was a difference of opinion.[13]

In any event the provincial legislature decided in 1919 to create two distinct divisions. The Appellate Division was to consist of the Chief Justice of Alberta and four justices of appeal and the Trial Division of the Chief Justice of the Trial Division and five other judges. Statutes to this end were passed in 1919 and 1920 and proclaimed as of September 15th, 1921. The Meighen administration, which was in power at the time, appointed Scott J. as Chief Justice of Alberta, and the justices of appeal were Stuart, Beck, Hyndman and J.A. Clarke, the last named being a new appointment to the court. Chief Justice Harvey was made Chief Justice of the Trial Division, the other justices being Simmons, Walsh, McCarthy, Ives and T.M. Tweedie, a new appointee. The constitution of the court remained the same until 1954 when an additional trial judge was provided.

When Ottawa appointed the two chief justices, Harvey C.J. took the position that the statutes creating the two divisions did not in fact abolish the old Supreme Court of Alberta, so that he was still Chief Justice of Alberta, rather than Chief Justice of the new Trial Division. On a reference to the Supreme Court of Canada his contention was upheld but on appeal to the Privy Council in 1923 it was rejected.[14] However, Chief Justice Scott died in July 1924 and Horace Harvey was then made Chief Justice of Alberta. Mr. Justice Simmons became Chief Justice of the Trial Division at the same time.

Contribution to Criminal Law

Although Chief Justice Harvey's decisions extended over the whole of the law, and although he handled with equal care all problems coming before him, he had a particular interest in criminal law and procedure. In this field his judgments came to be regarded as especially authoritative, and it was perhaps here that he made his greatest single contribution to sound development of the law. He had the advantage of an intimate knowledge of the special procedure which the Northwest Territories Act established and the province of Alberta inherited. For example, there never has been a grand jury and the petty jury has always had six members instead of twelve. As the Chief Justice once pointed out, an indictable offence may be tried in Alberta by any one of four tribunals of fact—a jury of six, a Supreme Court judge (if the accused consents), a district court judge under the procedure for speedy trials, and a magistrate. He added that "jury trials are very few; trials by Supreme Court and District Court Judges alone much greater and trials by magistrates probably many times more than all other trials".[15] It may come as a surprise to some persons to learn that the Criminal Code has a special provision, applicable to Alberta alone, which states that a charge of *any* indictable offence may be tried by a Supreme Court judge sitting without a jury, if the accused consents.

Sitting often on appeals until 1921, and continually from 1924 until his death, Chief Justice Harvey was always careful to see that the fundamentals of "due process of law" were observed. For example, he was always scrupulous in insisting that guilt be proved. As he once said, "conjecture and surmise cannot be substituted for legal evidence".[16]

Under the Code an appellate court must decide whether errors made at the trial constitute a "miscarriage of justice". The Chief Justice took the generally accepted position that the verdict stands if the appeal court is convinced that any reasonable jury *must* have found as it did even though no error had been made at the trial. In applying this rule the Chief Justice kept a good balance between extremes. He insisted on fairness to the accused while avoiding the tendency to hold trivial mistakes fatal to the conviction. As he said in one of his last judgments, on an appeal from a conviction for murder:

> . . . careful as a trial Judge may be and as this trial judge was, it would be practically impossible to conduct such a lengthy trial completely free from anything which could be criticized, for Judges like other human beings have limitations, but I am not satisfied that anything to which objection has been taken caused any substantial prejudice to the appellant.[17]

On the other hand, he would order a new trial where he felt the jury *might* have acquitted the accused had the error not occurred.[18]

Several times he spoke out against improper police methods. For example, he quashed a conviction where the accused had been arrested on a blank warrant.[19] In another case he wrote a judgment for the court reversing an acquittal of police officers on a charge of assault. They had treated a prisoner with brutality—an offence which he said was, happily for the respect for law and order, of the rarest occurrence.[20] By the same token he sometimes protested against what he felt were attempts by an accused to abuse the machinery of the criminal law–it is not to be turned into a joke or farce[21] or a game.[22]

He wrote many judgments on other points of criminal procedure, interpreting the statutes and settling the practice. Many of these decisions concerned every-day technical matters of no dramatic interest, but yet of the first importance to the due administration of justice. After all, it is fairness and certainty in procedure as much as anything else that we have in mind in speaking of British justice, a tradition that goes back to Magna Carta.

Many judgments relate to admissibility of evidence. Early in his career, on a reserved case after a conviction for murder, he wrote an important judgment holding admissible a statement of the victim as forming part of the *res gestae,* and a further statement as showing the state of mind of the victim.[23] Frequently he had to rule on the admissibility of confessions. Generally he scrupulously followed the principles laid down in the leading cases, such as *Ibrahim* v. *R.*[24] and *Sankey* v. *R.*,[25] and never fell into the error of treating an exculpatory statement as a confession or subject to the same rules governing admissibility.[26] However, his judgment in *R.* v. *Deagle*[27] in 1947 goes rather far in excluding a confession. The accused was arrested on one charge and, in the course of making a confession, admitted guilt of an entirely different offence. The confession was held inadmissible on the trial of the latter offence. This judgment applied and perhaps extended the well-known case of *R.* v. *Dick* in Ontario.[28]

In two or three instances his judgments in matters of criminal evidence have not prevailed.[29] On the other hand, many others have been followed by courts outside Alberta, and the writer has noted one case in which the Supreme Court of Canada approved one of his decisions as against a judgment of the Court of Appeal of Ontario. The Alberta court had said that a person accused of attempted rape may be convicted of indecent assault as an offence that is included in a charge of attempted rape. The Ontario Court disagreed but on appeal the Supreme Court ruled that the Alberta view was correct.[30]

Before referring to decisions on substantive criminal law, we will mention a series of important cases relating to the power of a superior court on certiorari from a conviction at a trial before a police magistrate. In 1916 the Chief Justice was faced with the argument that the conviction should be quashed if it appears that there is no evidence to support the finding of the magistrate. Stating that he had for several years doubted the sufficiency of this objection to the conviction, he decided "to examine carefully the authorities to settle the point definitely in my own mind as being of value for future cases". He concluded that he might not look at the facts to see whether there was evidence to support the conviction.[31] Some of his colleagues took a contrary view.[32] Then in 1921 came the leading case of *R.* v. *Nat Bell Liquors Limited.* A magistrate had convicted the company for unlawfully keeping liquor for sale contrary to the Liquor Act, 1916, and made an order for forfeiture of the stock of liquor worth $50,000. On certiorari Hyndman J. quashed both conviction and order. The Crown appealed. Harvey J., dissenting, would have restored the conviction and forfeiture. He reiterated that on certiorari the court or judge has no power to weigh the evidence. The other two judges, Stuart and Beck JJ., examined the evidence and held that the conviction was not justified. On the Crown's appeal, the Judicial Committee upheld the dissenting view.[33] In later cases, in which the Chief Justice did not take part, the Alberta court tended to restrict the application of *Nat Bell*.[34] Moreover, some courts have reduced its scope in the judicial review of the decisions of administrative bodies. The noteworthy fact here is that Harvey C.J. anticipated it against the views of most of his brethren.

On substantive criminal law, there is a number of judgments on difficult and important points to note, first on *mens rea*. In one case he held a man guilty of bigamy even though the man thought he had a valid divorce.[35] In two others, the question whether the absence of *mens rea* is a defence under the liquor laws had to be considered. It is an offence, for example, to permit a person apparently under the age of twenty-one to remain in a beer parlor and, further, it is an offence to supply liquor to a person under twenty-one. Must the Crown prove guilty knowledge in these cases? In the former case the answer is yes, in the latter, no; on a charge of permitting the Chief Justice said "knowingly" must be implied, for one cannot "permit" something of which one does not know, but on a charge of supplying, "knowingly" should not be implied. These conclusions were reached after a searching examination of the statute and of cases from England and the other provinces.[36]

The age of the motor car brought new problems for the substantive law. An important case in 1939 involved a charge of having the "care or control of a motor vehicle" while intoxicated. The accused was seated behind the wheel of his car unconscious from drink, with the car keys on the seat. The Chief Justice took the view that in these circumstances the accused could not be said to have the care or control of the car.[37] Judicial opinion in Canada is far from unanimous on this point. Another controversial decision is *R.* v. *Nickle* in 1920. Here the Chief Justice concurred in a judgment of Stuart J. holding the accused, who had been intoxicated and driving his car faster than the legal speed limit, guilty of manslaughter. He had killed the victim in the course of committing unlawful acts and so was guilty of manslaughter whether negligent or not.[38] Then in 1940, in a dissent, he said that *Nickle* was still good law, though the majority held that gross negligence must be shown.[39]

The two world wars gave rise to several noteworthy cases. In World War I the public and the authorities too were most sensitive to anything that seemed to indicate a pro-German sentiment. However understandable this may be, the question for the courts remained whether the statements complained of were seditious. In most cases the accused was a person of German descent who had made some such remark as that he hoped Great Britain would lose or he was glad that the Lusitania had been sunk. In the first case that came before the Appellate Division, *R.* v. *Felton* in 1915,[40] the question arose squarely whether the Crown must prove seditious intent. After a careful examination of the English authorities, which he found difficult to reconcile, the Chief Justice concluded that the Crown need not prove actual intent; the judge or jury may infer it from the words and the circumstances. Stuart J. had misgivings but agreed with the result.

The next year a similar case came before the court in *R.* v. *Trainor.*[41] Harvey C.J. did not sit. The judgment of Stuart J. is a forceful protest against the notion that every bit of irresponsible bar-room talk is seditious. The law does not forbid disloyalty of the heart, nor the utterance of a word or two which merely reveal the existence of such disloyalty. Seeking a test, he used the following words, "... I think something is due to the dignity of the law and that the courts should not, *unless in cases of gravity and danger,* be asked to spend their time scrutinizing with undue particularity the foolish talk of men in bar rooms and shops or a word or two evidently blurted out there impulsively and with no deliberate purpose". In the phrase the writer has put in italics, Stuart J. in effect enunciated a test very close to the "clear and present danger" test which Holmes J. later formulated in the Supreme Court of the United States.

One would like to know whether Chief Justice Harvey agreed with his brother judge. Perhaps not, for his judgment in *Felton* shows that he took a strict view against the accused, and an earlier judgment of his on an analogous charge points the same way. A storekeeper had put up a notice to say that he was selling out and leaving Canada because Americans were not wanted in Canada. The unusual charge of uttering false news was laid against him. The Chief Justice, then sitting in the trial court, found as a fact that the government wanted Americans to settle here and convicted the accused.[42] Perhaps one can agree with Professor F.R. Scott that this judgment "seems to verge on harshness".[43]

The last case of interest in World War I is *R.* v. *Bleiler,* in which the accused was convicted of attempted treason in trying to sell the Kaiser an invention for use in the war. The Chief Justice held that the conviction could not stand because there is no such offence as an attempt to commit treason.[44]

The second world war furnished no reported case on seditious utterance, possibly because the Defence of Canada Regulations, issued under the War Measures Act, had wide provisions making almost every criticism of the war effort an offence and the power to intern without trial could be used to curb seditious statements. The two cases of interest are of a different kind. In the first, escaped prisoners of war were charged with stealing a car; and in the second, prisoners were charged with the murder of a fellow prisoner. In both the accused argued that the Geneva Convention of 1929 as well as the common law permitted them to attempt escape and that anything done during an escape or attempted escape is beyond the jurisdiction of the ordinary courts. The Chief Justice examined the contention thoroughly and rejected it.[45]

We shall now refer briefly to the subject of contempt of court. At common law a superior court has power to punish summarily for criminal contempt. This may take various forms, but the one of particular interest here is comment on pending trials. Courts in this country have adhered generally to the English view that biased comment on a case pending in the courts may influence the result of the trial and hence is unfair to one of the parties and punishable as contempt. The power to punish should of course be exercised "with extraordinary care".[46]

In 1911 a newspaper published an article on a pending civil jury trial, which tended to create sympathy for one of the parties, and the full court imposed a fine. The Chief Justice said: "This subject is a comparatively new one in this province, and the purpose which it is hoped this case will serve is to extinguish in its inception any possible tendency towards what has been termed 'trial by newspaper', rather than to punish purely for the offence committed".[47] The writer of a note in the Yale Law Journal in 1950 cites this as an example of cases in which "judges have sometimes gone to absurd lengths in warding off fancied dangers to justice".[48] We do not propose to debate the point here, but suggest that Canadians who read the leading United States cases[49] may well conclude that Chief Justice Harvey's view is preferable to one that deprives a judge in a state court of power to punish summarily a radio station that has broadcast the most damaging statements against a negro just arrested for a brutal murder.[50]

On such important questions as punishment, juvenile delinquency and rehabilitation of criminals, there is little in the reports, perhaps not surprisingly, to indicate the social views of the Chief Justice. He was generally stern in passing sentence at trials, and on appeal did not readily interfere to reduce a heavy punishment. For example, in upholding a sentence of twenty years and thirty lashes for robbery, he said:

> There is no doubt the sentence is a severe one, but we all know that of late years there seems to have been almost an epidemic of crimes of this character, and under such circumstances we cannot be guided by rules that would be applicable in normal conditions.[51]

He did address himself seriously to the problem of relating sentences to previous convictions, the age of the accused, and the like.[52] Once in discussing suspended sentences he commented that there had been very few cases of the breach of a recognizance, which "speaks well for the principle of suspended sentence".[53]

Constitutional Law

"Constitutional law" in Canada means principally the provisions of the British North America Act as interpreted by the courts. The main problems that come before the courts concern the division of legislative powers between the federal parliament and the provincial legislatures or, to put it another way, the limitations on central and local powers.

During his judicial career, extending over practically the first half of the present century, the Chief Justice had to consider many attacks on legislation, most often on provincial legislation but sometimes on federal. The primary question is whether the statute in issue is *in relation to* one of the heads of subject matter allotted to the legislature enacting it. Chief Justice Harvey decided several cases where an attack on a federal act was met by the argument, sometimes that it was in relation to the "peace, Order, and good Government of Canada", sometimes to the "Regulation of Trade and Commerce", or to "Agriculture" or "Criminal Law". An amendment in 1919 to the Canada Temperance Act, for example, involved the application of the opening words of section 91. Years before, Parliament had passed the Canada Temperance Act, prohibiting the sale of liquor in any municipality that had voted in favour of prohibition. The Privy Council, in *Russell* v. *R.*,[54] upheld the act under the peace, order and good government clause. The 1919 amendment extended the provisions of the act so as to prohibit the importation of liquor into a whole province that voted for prohibition and the Chief Justice, affirmed by the Supreme Court, held it valid too.[55]

Under the commerce clause, the question arose as to the validity of a provision in the Canada Grain Act requiring a grain buyer to take out a licence. The Chief Justice held that the Dominion's jurisdiction over trade and commerce does not permit it to regulate contracts in a particular trade in a province.[56] On the other hand, a later case held valid the Live Stock Pedigree Act, which forbids a person to make a false statement about an animal when he applies to register it. This act relates to agriculture—improving the breed of animals—and is competent under section 95 of the British North America Act.[57] These two cases show what fine distinctions are sometimes drawn in this area. The writer would have thought that the grain trade, by reason of its national and international aspects, is properly a subject for Dominion regulation, even if the legislation incidentally affects contracts that are intra-provincial. Yet the Supreme Court of Canada had in 1925 held not,[58] and the judgment of Harvey C.J. on the Canada Grain Act is merely an application of that decision.

The last important case on Dominion legislation is one in which the validity of a section of the Criminal Code, barring a civil action for assault where the defendant has been convicted of the crime of common assault, was questioned. The Chief Justice pointed out that, two years before, the full court had upheld the section.[59] True, a recent Privy Council decision had held that the federal Industrial Disputes Act was invalid because it was in relation to property and civil rights in a province. Nevertheless, the section in the Code appears to be properly ancillary to valid criminal legislation and, besides, the court should not refuse to follow an earlier decision of its own merely because it thinks that a higher court might decide differently.[60]

By far the greatest number of constitutional cases coming before any provincial court concern the validity of provincial acts. Does the act in pith and substance relate to one of the heads of subject matter that section 92 allots to the provinces or is it, on the other hand, a colourable attempt to invade Dominion jurisdiction? Is the purpose or effect of the act the controlling test? Does the subject matter of the act have a double aspect, so that provincial and federal legislation on the same subject can both stand? Lastly, assuming that a provincial act is within one of the heads of section 92, and so within provincial jurisdiction, does it conflict with valid Dominion legislation, or, even if there is no direct conflict, has Parliament occupied the field?

A few examples from cases in which Chief Justice Harvey took part will show the difficulties. For instance, the province has jurisdiction over solemnization of marriage, but not over the subject of marriage and divorce, which is allotted to Parliament. May a province provide in its Solemnization of Marriage Act that the parents' consent to the marriage of a minor is a condition precedent to the validity of the marriage? The Chief Justice concurred in a judgment of McGillivray J.A. holding that the provision related to capacity to marry and hence is beyond the power of the province; but the Supreme Court held it in relation to formalities of marriages in the province and so valid.[61]

Again, the province passes a prohibition act. Does the statute operate to prevent a wholesale liquor company from exporting liquor from the province? Harvey C.J. and Stuart J. held that the act was in relation to property and civil rights in the province, and so valid, even though it incidentally affected trade and commerce, a head of Dominion jurisdiction. The majority, however, held it invalid to the extent that it prohibited export.[62]

What then of a provision in the Government Liquor Control Act making it an offence to be intoxicated in a public place? The Criminal Code prohibits the making of a disturbance in a public place by being drunk. In one case the accused contended that the provincial enactment in reality created a crime, and moreover a crime already covered by the Code. The Chief Justice, for the majority, held that the province may pass laws respecting the control and use of intoxicants and that the section in question is properly ancillary to that subject. The province has dealt with intoxication in a public place as an aspect of controlling the consumption of liquor, not from the aspect of controlling public morals.[63]

Many cases have arisen over the applicability of provincial laws to railways, banks or the like, or to Dominion companies generally. The British North America Act of course specifically gives the Dominion exclusive jurisdiction over banks and interprovincial railways; "the Incorporation of Companies with Provincial Objects" is a head of provincial power under section 92, but there is no analogous head under section 91 giving the Dominion power to establish companies with Dominion objects. Early in his career Horace Harvey had to face the niceties of interpretation resulting from this constitutional position.

While still deputy attorney-general he had drafted the Prairie Fires Ordinance, which required the taking of precautions to prevent fires, among them the use of proper smoke stacks and the erection of fire guards. In 1905 the Canadian Pacific Railway was charged with a breach of the ordinance.[64] Mr. Harvey was now Mr. Justice Harvey and declined to sit, a note in his judge's book explaining, "I had been interested in this as D.A.G.". The same point came up again in 1907, however, and this time he took part, doubtless considering that the earlier decision upholding the act had altered his position. Was the ordinance in relation to interprovincial railways or not? The Chief Justice thought not, but the Supreme Court of Canada disagreed, holding it invalid as against the railway.[65]

In these cases the statute applied to interprovincial railways. There were other cases in which provincial legislation purported to apply to ordinary trading companies, many of which are incorporated under federal law. Can such companies be required to register before carrying on business in a province? While deputy attorney-general, Horace Harvey had drafted an ordinance of this type. The Massey-Harris Company, a farm-implement manufacturer incorporated under Dominion law, promptly contended that the ordinance could not apply to it. Harvey J. again disqualified himself and the court en banc, sitting without him, upheld the ordinance.[66]

During the next fifteen years or so the implement companies led the attack against laws of this kind, which all the western provinces had. By 1921 the Privy Council had made it clear that a province may not require a Dominion company to register as a condition of carrying on business or bringing action.[67] Then the dispute shifted to the validity of provincial sale of shares acts, which forbade the sale of a company's shares without the permission of a provincial board. In 1929 the Judicial Committee held these statutes, too, invalid as applied to Dominion companies.[68]

The next year Alberta followed Ontario's lead and passed a Security Frauds Prevention Act framed to avoid the infirmities of the Sale of Shares Act. The new act applied to all securities, not merely to shares in companies; securities could be sold only by registered brokers; a special power was given the attorney-general to investigate companies and to apply to the court to enjoin persons who engage in fraudulent acts from trading in securities. The attorney-general immediately investigated a transaction among several Dominion companies. They sued to enjoin him. The Chief Justice ruled the act invalid on the ground that the legislature has but limited power to require Dominion companies to furnish information and therefore cannot delegate to the attorney-general unlimited power. On the attorney-general's appeal to the Judicial Committee, the companies attacked the whole act, including the registration requirement. Some constitutional lawyers, including Mr. Wegenast,[69] thought that the new statute would not be sustained because it could not be distinguished from acts the Privy Council had held invalid. It was an attempt to do indirectly what the province could not do directly. Lord Atkin said, however, that the Security Frauds Prevention Act is legislation in relation to the carrying on of a business within the province. Once this has been decided, it is clear that the act is not invalid merely because it incidentally affects matters within the Dominion's power. The act, to adopt the wording of the earlier cases, does not destroy or sterilize or substantially impair the powers and capacities of Dominion companies, at least of honest ones. Lord Atkin did agree with Chief Justice Harvey that one section of the statute making any fraudulent act not covered by the Criminal Code an offence was invalid as being criminal law.[70] This case ended some twenty years of litigation, and securities acts of this kind are now an integral part of corporate financing throughout Canada.

Another field in which the provinces have found it hard to frame valid statutes is that of taxation. The power they possess is in relation to "Direct Taxation within the Province in order to the raising of a Revenue for Provincial Purposes". Many tax laws have been attacked on the ground that they impose an indirect tax. For example, a succession duty may be indirect because it is imposed on the personal representative of the deceased in the expectation that he will recoup himself from the estate or the beneficiaries. In 1915 the Chief Justice ruled that the Succession Duty Ordinance was free of this vice, that it did not in fact impose liability on the executor for duty, but was a direct tax on the property of the estate.[71] Eighteen years later the Privy Council overruled this case,[72] and the act was then reframed.

A sales tax is usually regarded as indirect, but, where the province imposed on mine owners a tax of two per cent of gross revenue, the Chief Justice held the tax to be direct and so valid. Although the burden of such a tax is usually shifted to the purchaser of the product, it could not be shifted here because of competition in the industry. The Privy Council held the tax indirect: its general tendency rather than its incidence in a particular case is the test.[73]

The next requirement is that the tax must be "within the Province". The province of Alberta at one point claimed income tax on income paid outside the province to a resident who never brought it in. The Chief Justice, dissenting, thought that this tax was on income outside the province and therefore invalid, but the prevailing view of the court was that it was imposed on the person and hence valid.[74]

Not only tax laws but provincial legislation generally must be intraprovincial. For example, an act relating to property and civil rights outside the province is unconstitutional. The leading case is *Royal Bank* v. *R,* which arose out of the difficulties between the government and the Alberta and Great Waterways Railway, a company formed in 1909 to build and operate a railway. At the same time the province passed an act guaranteeing payment of the railway's bonds, which were sold in England and the proceeds paid to the Royal Bank in New York. The bank's head office in Montreal credited the amount of the proceeds to an account in its Edmonton branch, in the provincial treasurer's name. Within a few months public criticism of the government's transactions with the railway brought about the appointment of a royal commission to investigate, and forced the resignation of the cabinet. This was the occasion on which Sifton C.J. resigned to become premier. In the meantime the railway had made default in payment of interest on its bonds, and when the legislature met in special session in November 1910 it passed an act declaring that the proceeds belonged to the province and requiring the bank to pay them over. The bank refused and the province brought action, the issue being whether the 1910 statute was valid.

The Chief Justice upheld the act. It was in relation to property and civil rights in the province, even though it incidentally affected rights outside—in this case the right of the bondholders to sue the bank in Montreal for the return of their money. The Judicial Committee reversed on the ground that, from the moment the 1910 act was passed, the bondholders were entitled to claim from the bank at its head office in Montreal the money they had advanced solely for a purpose which had ceased to exist. Their right was a civil right outside the province and the province could not validly legislate in derogation of it.[75]

During the depression of the thirties various provinces, including Alberta, restricted creditors' rights by requiring a permit to sue, by staying actions for debt, or by reducing the principal. Many mortgages on property in the prairie provinces are payable in eastern Canada, so that one ground of attack on these acts was that they related to property and civil rights outside the province, within the principle of *Royal Bank* v. *R*. As we shall see later, the Chief Justice accepted this argument, though it has always seemed to the writer that the province is not stripped of legislative power over a mortgage on Alberta land merely because the mortgage debt is payable outside the province.

The constitutional cases of greatest importance during the last twelve years of the Chief Justice's life arose out of the legislation of the Social Credit government, which came to power in 1935 when the depression was at its worst. The Social Credit party was anti-creditor, its economic theories calling for "debt-free" money and control of credit by the people. The first few years of its tenure of office were stormy. The legislature extended the Debt Adjustment Act, which required a permit from a board before suing for debt, passed an act to reduce the amount owing on debts, restricted the remedies of mortgagees and vendors of land, enacted various temporary moratorium laws, reduced the interest payable on the bonds of, or guaranteed by, the province, and passed legislation designed to give the province control over banks.

In the six-year period from 1937 to 1943, the Governor-General in Council disallowed eleven statutes or amendments, as compared with one in the preceding thirty-two years of the province's existence.[76] In 1937 the Lieutenant-Governor invoked a power rarely used and reserved his assent to three bills. The province argued that the power of disallowance and reservation no longer subsisted, but the Supreme Court rejected this contention;[77] and, incidentally, the three reserved bills were held ultra vires on a reference.[78]

These issues of course never came before the Alberta courts, but many other important constitutional problems did. In 1936, a Reduction and Settlement of Debts Act reduced the amount owing on large classes of debts, forbade collection of interest, and extended time for payment. Chief Justice Harvey held the act invalid on several grounds. He applied the principle of *Royal Bank* v. *R*. to hold that the province cannot legislate in derogation of civil rights outside the province, and many mortgages on Alberta land were payable in eastern Canada. Then, the Dominion's Bankruptcy Act and

Farmers' Creditors Arrangement Act already covered the matter of relief to distressed debtors. Finally, the provincial act is in relation to interest, a subject reserved to Parliament.[79]

The legislature passed no more acts of this type, but there was already on the statute book a Debt Adjustment Act, which required a permit from a Debt Adjustment Board before actions of debt could be brought. The act had been passed in 1933, but after 1935 the board used its powers to force creditors to agree to reduction of debts and extension of time. The first serious attack on the act was made by the holder of a promissory note. Negotiable instruments are within the jurisdiction of Parliament, and the Bills of Exchange Act gives the holder the right to sue on the note and to recover from any party liable on the note. The Chief Justice concurred in a judgment holding that the province cannot abridge these rights and the Supreme Court sustained it.[80]

In 1941 the Governor in Council referred to the Supreme Court the question whether the Debt Adjustment Act was ultra vires in whole or in part. The ultimate decision of the Privy Council on this reference held the act invalid on the ground that it was an invasion of Parliament's power in relation to bankruptcy and insolvency, and moreover that it interfered with and obstructed actual legislation of Parliament.[81] But before this decision, though after the Supreme Court had ruled the act invalid, the legislature, in 1942, enacted that all actions to which the Debt Adjustment Act applied should be stayed until the Privy Council's decision. Chief Justice Harvey, writing for the majority, held that the act providing for the stay was invalid on the ground that it is for the courts to determine whether the legislature has exceeded its powers, and "the legislature should recognize and observe that determination".[82] This decision was never appealed to a higher court, but its soundness may be doubted in the light of the Privy Council's decision in *Montreal Trust Co.* v. *Abitibi Power and Paper Co.*[83]

Another statute of 1942 amended the Judicature Act by fixing a one-year period of redemption in actions for foreclosure, with power in the court to decrease or extend the period. Harvey C.J. for the majority ruled that this amendment, like the act last discussed, had the effect of nullifying the Supreme Court judgment holding invalid the Debt Adjustment Act. The Supreme Court reversed, sustaining the amendment.[84]

In addition to its many efforts to aid debtors, the legislature took steps to relieve the province of its burden of debt. It did this, in 1936, by enacting statutes that reduced by one half the interest payable on bonds issued or guaranteed by the province. A holder of both provincial bonds and bonds of an irrigation district guaranteed by the province decided to try to enforce payment. The resulting litigation was in the courts for years. The moves and counter-moves were these. The bondholder sued the irrigation district for arrears of interest. The trial judge found that the statute reducing interest was in relation to interest, a head of Dominion jurisdiction, and gave judgment for the bondholder.[85] The legislature responded by enacting that actions on guaranteed bonds could not be taken or continued without the consent of the

Lieutenant-Governor in Council. The effect of this statute was of course to take from the plaintiff the fruits of the judgment. The bondholder started again. In holding the last act ultra vires, Ewing J. said at the trial, "If either the Dominion or the Provinces be at liberty to invade at will the legislative jurisdiction of the other and give practical effect to that invasion by denying the Courts jurisdiction to declare such invasion to be unlawful, then the division of powers as contained in the B.N.A. Act is a futility". On appeal, the Chief Justice stressed the purpose as well as the effect of the act and concluded that it was auxiliary to the statute reducing interest and so, like it, was unconstitutional.[86] The next year the same bondholder brought a petition of right with respect to arrears of interest on provincial bonds. The Chief Justice did not sit when the court held invalid, as being in relation to "Interest", the statute reducing interest on provincial bonds.[87]

On an appeal to the Privy Council from both decisions of the Appellate Division, the judgments below were sustained. Had the legislation only incidentally touched the subject of interest it might have been valid, but it was in pith and substance interest legislation and did not come under any of the heads of section 92.[88] The bondholder's victory was an empty one, however, for the province continued to pay the reduced rate of interest until it refunded the bonds in 1945.

The efforts of the province to interfere with and control banking in the province are largely outside the scope of this article, for few of them came before the Chief Justice. At the peak of the political turmoil in the summer of 1937, a Credit of Alberta Regulation Act and a Bank Employees Civil Rights Act were passed. These remarkable efforts to bring banks under provincial control were disallowed eleven days after their enactment. Two months later a new bank control bill was passed, together with a bill imposing a crushing tax on banks. These were two of the three bills to which the Lieutenant-Governor reserved assent.[89] After a lull during the war, the legislature in 1946 made its last attempt to regulate banks in a statute entitled the Alberta Bill of Rights Act.

Part I of this unusual legislation contained a loosely drawn list of freedoms and economic rights of citizens, together with a declaration of the duty, spelled out in some detail, to be a good citizen. Part II set up an elaborate scheme to implement the act, which included a board to control lending by "credit institutions", a term that covered banks. Chief Justice Harvey delivered the judgment holding Part II to be a measure to control the banking business and so incompetent. He was prepared to sever Part I, but the Judicial Committee held that it must fall with Part II.[90]

This concludes the account of the Chief Justice's important cases on the distribution of powers between Parliament and the provinces. It remains to mention two other possible restrictions on legislative competence: first, in connection with delegation of legislative power; and, secondly, with the appointment of provincial tribunals and boards with judicial functions.

Long ago the Judicial Committee, in *Hodge* v. *The Queen,* rejected the argument that the provincial legislatures may not delegate their powers.

They are in no sense delegates of the Imperial Parliament and their authority is as plenary and ample within the limits prescribed for them as that of the Imperial Parliament.[91] In spite of this decision, however, attacks on legislation are sometimes based on the argument that the legislature has made an improper delegation of its powers, in that it has purported to delegate wider powers than it possesses or that, in delegating, it has abdicated its function. These contentions are usually unsuccessful.[92]

Chief Justice Harvey in his dissent in *Re Lewis,* subsequently upheld by the Supreme Court of Canada in *Re Gray,* supported the widest delegation in wartime by Parliament to the Governor-General in Council, yet, when he came to deal with the power of the Alberta legislature to delegate to the Lieutenant-Governor in Council, he held that a delegation of power to fix fees payable by foreign companies and to require information from them is invalid as applied to Dominion companies. The legislature itself has but limited power over Dominion companies and cannot delegate an unlimited power to the executive.[93]

Again, in 1936, the legislature passed the Reduction and Settlement of Debts Act, already referred to, one provision of which said that the act would not apply to a debt declared by the Lieutenant-Governor in Council to be a debt to which the act did not apply. The Chief Justice held that this provision purported to delegate a legislative function which could not validly be conferred on the executive,[94] a view that seems to be akin to the American doctrine of separation of powers as it stood before the United States Supreme Court modified it by permitting delegation within broad limits. In any event, the Privy Council in 1938 approved a judgment of Chief Justice Martin of British Columbia that is inconsistent with the position taken by Chief Justice Harvey.[95] Indeed, the narrow scope Chief Justice Harvey gave to the province's power to delegate is hard to reconcile with his reasons in *Re Lewis,* even though he sought to distinguish that case on the ground that the statute there was a war measure.

Provincial legislatures frequently seek of course to confer judicial functions on tribunals and boards. Persons attacking the constitution of these agencies contend that they purport to exercise the powers of a superior, district or county court, whereas under section 96 of the British North America Act the judges of superior, district and county courts are to be appointed by the Governor-General.

In 1917, Harvey C.J. considered an act giving justices of the peace jurisdiction over claims for debts up to $50.00 in value. A detailed examination of the history of section 96 and of the various colonial courts in existence at Confederation led him to the conclusion that the B.N.A. Act recognizes tribunals other than those mentioned in section 96 and that a justice's tribunal is outside the section.[96] What then of an act giving magistrates jurisdiction in family matters, such as family maintenance and custody of children? The Chief Justice held such a statute invalid as being contrary to section 96[97] and cases in at least two other provinces followed his opinion;[98] but in 1938 the Supreme Court of Canada disapproved them.[99] A mere increase of jurisdiction does not apparently change an inferior tribunal into a superior court under section 96, though it is hard to say where the precise line between the two is to be drawn.

The proliferation of administrative agencies during recent years gives rise to a similar problem. Here too the party attacking the jurisdiction of the provincial agency frequently argues that it is a court as contemplated by section 96. The decisions of some provincial courts have gone far in upholding this ground of attack, but the Privy Council has tended in the other direction.[100] The Chief Justice had already held that a provincial act giving to a board the power to fix milk prices is valid: the board is not a court under section 96.[101]

The task of passing on the validity of statutes, which of course does not fall to English courts, is one of the most difficult duties of judges under a federal system. So many doctrines have been evolved since 1867 to assist in determining validity, and the distinctions are often so fine, that it is sometimes hard for a judge to know which rules to apply. Certainly if one were to adopt in Canada the popular American practice of keeping a score of a judge's rulings, showing their fate at the hands of higher courts, no trial judge or judge of an intermediate court of appeal would have a perfect record. We do not propose to assess Chief Justice Harvey's contribution to constitutional law on any such basis as this. It can be said that his judgments show a good grasp of principles and an earnest effort to apply them. It has always seemed to the writer that some of his reasons for holding against the province's debt legislation went too far, but this is a matter of opinion, and even here the Supreme Court and Judicial Committee upheld him on a number of important issues.

Domestic Relations

When Mr. Harvey first went to the bench in 1904, the law of domestic relations was still undeveloped; by the time of his death in 1949, a large body of decisions, to which he had made a substantial contribution, and a variety of statutes had brought a great measure of certainty into the law. One of the first important problems was that of the court's jurisdiction to grant a decree of divorce. During the era of the old North-West Territories, and for the first thirteen years of Alberta's existence, no one attempted to bring an action for divorce. It was generally assumed that the courts had no jurisdiction and that the only way an aggrieved spouse could obtain a dissolution of marriage was by a private bill in Parliament.

In 1918, however, there came before the court a petition for divorce. The Chief Justice, in dissent, thought that the court had no jurisdiction. He noted that neither the North-West Territories Act of 1886 nor the provincial act of 1907 creating the Supreme Court of Alberta gave the Supreme Court of the Territories or its successor, the Supreme Court of Alberta, the jurisdiction the English Court of Divorce and Matrimonial Causes had exercised from 1857. He concluded that the omission of any reference to the English

Court of Divorce and Matrimonial Causes in the Dominion and Alberta acts, which did specifically mention the other English courts, was intentional and that "no jurisdiction in matters of divorce was ever conferred on this Court". The majority, on the contrary, were agreed that the court had jurisdiction. Their argument went like this. The Dominion statute of 1886 provided that the laws of England as of July 15th, 1870, were to be in force in the Territories so far as applicable. The Privy Council had held in 1908 that the Matrimonial Causes Act, 1857, in so far as it established a substantive law of divorce, was in effect in British Columbia and this decision was applicable by analogy in Alberta. Once it is accepted that the law of divorce is part of Alberta law, then the Supreme Court of Alberta has jurisdiction to administer it. The Privy Council affirmed.[102]

Soon after, the court had to decide whether the parties to a divorce action must have an Alberta domicile, or whether a Canadian domicile is sufficient, to confer jurisdiction. The Chief Justice laid down the rule, which has been followed ever since, that an Alberta domicile must be shown.[103] He took no part, however, in the leading case of *Cook* v. *Cook,* in which the Privy Council ultimately held that the court of the husband's domicile has exclusive jurisdiction to dissolve the marriage, even though the wife has secured a decree of judicial separation.[104]

On the question of the standard of proof of adultery in divorce actions, he concurred in a decision that the preponderance of evidence rule applies, but that the evidence should perhaps be stronger than in the ordinary civil case.[105] Yet, when the question came up again in 1948, he wrote a dissent in which he stated that adultery must be proved beyond reasonable doubt.[106] Doubtless he was influenced by the English decisions that say the higher standard is necessary. The confusion, and it is a confusion that has prevailed throughout the common-law jurisdictions of the Commonwealth, now appears to have been settled at least for this country by the Supreme Court of Canada. The requirement of the Matrimonial Causes Act, 1857, that the court must be "satisfied" that adultery has been committed means that the standard is the same as in any civil case.[107] If the Chief Justice fell into error, it was out of the great respect he had for English authority and his ever-present desire for uniformity.

Two of his judgments are of interest not only because they settled important questions so far as the province is concerned, but because of the parallel they furnish with later decisions of the highest English court. The facts in the Alberta case of *H* v. *H* differ from those in *Baxter* v. *Baxter,*[108] but in the former the Chief Justice held, like the House of Lords in the latter, that sterility differs from impotence and is not a ground of nullity.[109] In another divorce case[110] the wife obtained a decree nisi, but on her application for a decree absolute the King's Proctor intervened to show cause why the decree should not be granted, producing evidence that she had herself committed adultery. Since the plaintiff's adultery creates a discretionary rather than an absolute bar, the question was whether the discretion should be exercised in favour of a plaintiff who has failed to disclose it. The Chief Justice examined numerous English cases indicating the difficulty of giving a clear-cut answer. The practice in England was to require the plaintiff to disclose his adultery in the pleadings and then to furnish a statement of particulars to assist the court. Although the inference could be drawn that failure to take this course would result automatically in refusal of a decree, the Chief Justice thought that even in England the trial judge must still exercise his discretion as the Matrimonial Causes Act requires him to do. Seven years later the House of Lords in *Blunt* v. *Blunt*[111] addressed itself to the question of the nature and proper exercise of the discretion. The Lord Chancellor, Viscount Simon, confirmed the view that a plaintiff is under a duty to disclose his own adultery, but added that non-disclosure is not necessarily fatal. The difference between the views of Viscount Simon and Harvey C.J. is that in England, unlike Alberta, there remains a duty to disclose. The Chief Justice did not however go so far as McGillivray J.A., who said in the same case that, where both spouses have committed adultery and are anxious to part, it is not in the public interest to keep them together.

A number of miscellaneous, though important, cases on the substantive law of domestic relations can be grouped together at this point. In 1944 came an important case on the subject of collusion. The defendant wife had paid the costs of the husband's action, which was brought under arrangement with her and for her benefit. After a long review of the cases, the Chief Justice held that collusion exists where the suit is procured by agreement or bargain between the parties and rejected certain decisions to the effect that something more is needed—improper motive or dishonest purpose.[112] In another case the wife of a husband who was domiciled in Alberta went to the United States and secured a divorce, not of course recognized here. Then, when the husband died, she claimed a share of his estate as widow. The Chief Justice recognized that the "divorce" did not affect her status as wife but held that, in so far as it was a judgment *in personam,* it bound her and she could not be heard to impugn the jurisdiction of the court she had invoked.[113] In still another case, a "wife" brought an action for alimony and alternatively for compensation for services rendered her "husband", who already had a wife. The majority maintained the action on the latter basis, with the Chief Justice dissenting on the ground that the parties had never contemplated that she would be compensated.[114]

The problem of incapacity to enter into the marriage contract by reason of insanity came before the court in 1929. A husband brought action to annul a marriage on the ground that his wife was insane at the time of the ceremony. Later she became hopelessly insane. The test of *Durham* v. *Durham* was applied: Did she have the capacity at the time of the marriage to understand the nature of the contract and the duties and responsibilities it creates? After holding that the wife had been sane under this test, Harvey C.J. remarked:

> It is, no doubt, a hardship that this plaintiff, a comparatively young man, should be doomed to live without a mate while the defendant lives, but that is

> a matter for the consideration of Parliament, not the Courts, and it may be said it is the second part of the 'better or worse' for which he took her for life.
>
> It must not be overlooked also that as regards policy rather than law a judgment that would bastardize an innocent child for the benefit of the father who had been instrumental in bringing it into the world could have little to be said in its favour.[115]

The last noteworthy case has to do, not with divorce or other actions between the spouses, but with a dispute between a wife and a third party. The question was whether a husband may be joined in an action by or against the wife. There the plaintiff had joined the husband in an action against the wife for slander. The Chief Justice held that a provision in the North-West Territories Act, 1875, meant that the husband was no longer a necessary or proper party.[116] Shortly afterwards the House of Lords held by a bare majority that a similar provision in the Married Women's Property Act, 1882, did not have this effect: although the husband is no longer a necessary party, he is still a proper party to an action in tort against the wife.[117]

Real Property

One of the features of land law in Alberta is the Torrens system of land registration, which we have mentioned earlier in connection with Chief Justice Harvey's position as Registrar of Land Titles at Calgary. The unsettled Territories were well suited to receive the system because the Crown had granted but very small portions of the land in the Territories by 1886, when the Territories Real Property Act was passed, and it was easy to bring under the statute Crown grants made after it came into operation.

The typical land titles act has a number of basic provisions. The registrar issues a certificate of title to every parcel of land and the original title is kept at the land-titles office; all mortgages and other charges are registered against it and have priority according to time of registration; the certificate of title is indefeasible; until registered an instrument creates no interest in the land and knowledge of an unregistered interest is not of itself fraud in a person acquiring the land or an interest in it; and, lastly, an assurance fund is established to compensate persons who have suffered damage through a mistake of the registrar.

It would serve no good purpose to list the large number of the Chief Justice's judgments on these topics. A few important decisions that have helped to shape the province's land law will, however, be mentioned. In 1918 the full court had to decide whether foreclosure of a mortgage extinguishes the debt. A Torrens mortgage, unlike a common-law mortgage, is merely a charge on the land, but a mortgagee obtaining foreclosure acquires legal title. Chief Justice Harvey held that the mortgagee takes title in full satisfaction and the debt is extinguished. The Supreme Court of Canada reversed,[118] but the legislature promptly amended the Land Titles Act to conform to the Chief Justice's opinion.

This was in 1919 and the same year a mortgagee attempted to avoid the result of the judgment. The land was worth $6,500 and the mortgage debt was $20,500. The resourceful mortgagee took action and, instead of applying for foreclosure, asked the court's approval of its offer to buy the land for $6,500 and also a "deficiency judgment" for $14,000. The mortgagor, naturally enough, argued that the sale to the plaintiff was tantamount to a foreclosure order and so extinguished the debt. This case, *Security Trust Co.* v. *Sayre and Gilfoy,*[119] went to the Supreme Court, where the six judges divided evenly, and in the result the opinion of Harvey C.J. prevailed. In his view the order approving a sale to the mortgagee was not the same as a foreclosure, so the deficiency judgment was proper.

After this case, mortgagees whose security was worth less than the debt often followed the same course. However, when the depression came, the value of mortgaged land frequently fell far below the amount of the debt so that many judges felt it unfair to give deficiency judgments, and refused. Then in 1939 and 1940 the legislature put an end to any possibility of obtaining such a judgment by abolishing altogether the right of mortgagees (and of vendors of land) to obtain judgment for the debt. The only remedy left was sale and, if the sale was abortive, foreclosure. This remains the law today, save for minor changes and exceptions in the legislation, the most important being loans made under the National Housing Acts. The continued trend of restricting mortgagees' rights may be contrasted with a comment of the Chief Justice in *Sayre*. He there observed that the various acts to protect debtors had been induced by the special conditions of World War I and that a change might soon be made to restore creditors' remedies. This prediction never came true. The depression, and possibly World War II, caused a further curtailment of a mortgagee's and vendor's remedies, as our brief account has indicated.

The only other cases we shall mention on the Land Titles Act throw light on the Chief Justice's attitude toward the judge's role in interpreting statutes. Over and over again he stated that the courts are not concerned with the fairness or wisdom of legislation and must give effect to it even though the result is unjust. For example, he held in 1914,[120] and the Appellate Division agreed in 1921,[121] that, contrary to general belief and the spirit of the act, the assurance fund provision in the Land Titles Act was not effective to provide compensation to a claimant in all cases where he had been damnified by a mistake or misfeasance of the registrar. In 1937 a claimant against the fund argued for a wider construction of the assurance fund provisions, but the Chief Justice replied that the legislature had had many years' notice of the two decisions and had done nothing; it was unfortunate that the act did not give full protection, but "the responsibility to see that the statute law is just is on the legislature and not on the courts".[122]

Yet he took a different position when he had to deal with the Dower Act of 1917. The nature of that act can be explained in his own words:

> When the Torrens system was introduced into the North-West Territories in 1886 the wife's right to dower as well as the husband's estate by the

> curtesy, was abolished as being in conflict with what was supposed to be an inherent principle of that system as regards freedom of transfer and the ability to ascertain every interest in the land by reference to the face of the current certificate of title. That principle has been departed from in many respects and the Legislature has provided in lieu of the old dower, right to a life estate in a third of all the husband's lands, the right to a life estate in the whole of the homestead. . . . [123]

Moreover, the Dower Act, as it stood in 1939, said that where the husband disposed of the homestead without the wife's consent, given in a prescribed manner, the disposition was null and void. A situation could arise where the wife's consent was given irregularly, or where the husband swore falsely that he had no wife or that the land was not his homestead. Then, after the buyer had acquired title in good faith, the wife, or even the husband, might bring action against him for a declaration that his title was null and void. If the action were successful, the Dower Act would become a device to enable the vendor to escape from an honest bargain, and security of title would be undermined. In a case in 1939 the wife did bring action against the transferee, after the husband had falsely sworn that the land was not his homestead. The Chief Justice felt bound to say that the disposition was null and void as against the wife's possible life interest, but refused to hold that it was entirely void. Then he observed:

> If the legislature intended to give [the section] a different meaning one would have looked for such words as 'absolutely' or 'for all purposes'.[124]

Three years after this decision the legislature took the Chief Justice's hint and provided that a disposition without consent is "absolutely null and void for all purposes". Four years later a case arose in which the husband, in transferring the homestead, falsely swore that he had no wife. The transferee gave a further transfer and both were registered at the same time. The Chief Justice held that, although the first transfer was null and void, the second was not, and the second transferee obtained title free of any claim of the wife.[125] At this point the legislature gave up and passed a new Dower Act, which does not in terms make the disposition null and void. The Chief Justice did not live long enough to help unravel the problems created by the new act.[126]

Important parts of the law of real property remain outside the Land Titles Act. For example, an agreement for sale is not a registerable document, and the right of either party to sue for specific performance and the purchaser's right of rescission are governed largely by the general law. These subjects are of importance in any locality, particularly when prices of land fluctuate rapidly.

In a time of land speculation and rising prices the tendency is for vendors to try to escape from their obligations under contracts of sale, with the result that purchasers' actions for specific performance or damages come increasingly before the courts. When prices fall the trend is reversed, and it is the purchaser who tries to escape from his agreement. In the period from

1910 to 1912 Alberta had a spectacular land boom, which collapsed just before the beginning of World War I. In the next few years the court was occupied with cases in which a purchaser owing the vendor large sums of money on land of little value refused to pay and in some cases repudiated the agreement. Sometimes the purchaser could show that the vendor was merely a purchaser on time from the registered owner and did not himself have title to the land. The cases established that on these facts the vendor could not maintain an action for the purchase price.[127] In other cases the purchaser, casting about for some ground or other on which he could escape from his agreement, found that the vendor did not have the mineral rights or the coal rights. Although the purchaser had probably not had the slightest interest in coal rights when he entered into the agreement, nevertheless he could obtain rescission of the agreement, though in one case the Chief Justice found that the purchaser had waived his right to rescind by accepting a transfer of portions of the land.[128]

The Chief Justice's attitude toward the conduct of a defendant who raised the defence that the vendor did not have title to the minerals appears in a 1926 case:

> I have no sympathy with the act of a purchaser who after years of occupation and use of the lands and after having prevented the vendor from making any other sale out of which he might have secured his full purchase-price takes advantage of something which he never considered of any importance to escape from a contract which has become burdensome by reason of depreciation in land values or some other cause and throw the burden back on his vendor.[129]

In that case an agreement for farm lands was made in 1920 with the purchase price payable over a long period. The buyer took possession and, becoming financially involved in 1925, consulted a solicitor, who discovered by search of the title that the minerals were reserved to a third party. Then the buyer sued for rescission of the agreement. The Chief Justice held the law to be settled that an agreement to sell land entitles the buyer to the minerals, so that when the buyer discovers that the vendor has no title to them, he may rescind and recover the instalments paid the vendor.

Most of the cases on this subject were in the decade beginning in 1915 and not many have arisen since. It is true that prices fell again during the depression, but most purchasers on time in the nineteen twenties did not buy as a speculation but rather because they wanted to settle on the land. It may be, too, that agreements for sale were more carefully drawn than in the early years. In any event the leading cases are still those that arose out of the land boom before World War I.

Torts

As might be expected, the Chief Justice was called upon during his many years on the bench to deal with most branches of the law of torts.

From the period of World War I, negligence actions were frequent. In many of them the plaintiff was a careless driver who was hit by a train or a careless pedestrian struck by a car. He always alleged that the other party had the last clear chance or, on the doctrine of *B.C. Electric Railway Co.* v. *Loach,*[130] that, but for his prior incapacitating negligence, would have had it. Typical of these difficult cases was one in which a man on a bicycle rode over a railway crossing and was hit by a train, which he had seen coming. The Chief Justice, presiding at the trial, thought that if a watchman had been present as required by law the accident might have been prevented. Although the railway's negligence was prior in time to the plaintiff's, it was prior incapacitating negligence within the *Loach* case: the plaintiff's position was like that of the famous donkey in *Davies* v. *Mann.*[131] The Appellate Division agreed, but the Supreme Court reversed on the ground that the plaintiff's contributory negligence was clear and in part at least was the direct cause of the accident.[132] This decision is of interest because Duff and Anglin JJ. both expressed regret that the law did not permit apportionment of responsibility and it was only a year later, in 1924, that Ontario passed the first contributory negligence act in any common-law province.

Alberta did not have the act until 1937, and in the meantime the Chief Justice took part in many cases where the issue was whether the plaintiff's contributory negligence was fatal to his claim. These cases are of historic interest for their fine distinctions and for the lengths to which the judges sometimes went to save a plaintiff from the consequences of his carelessness. We shall not, however, examine them in detail. Most of them were tried by a judge alone, and the Chief Justice sat on the appeal. Sometimes his view prevailed, sometimes not.[133] It seems probable that his decisions were influenced by his concept of the role of an appellate court in reviewing findings of fact. In the early years he considered that an appeal court had no greater liberty to interfere with the findings of fact of a trial judge than with the findings of a jury. Later, in 1921, he pointed out that the more recent authorities hold that, except as to matters in which the trial judge has an advantage derived from observing the witnesses, not only are the judges of the Appeal Court free but they are bound to express their own opinion.[134] For a number of years he freely reversed the finding of fact of a trial judge, but the Supreme Court frequently restored them, and by 1936 we find him saying that an appeal court should not disturb a trial judge's findings unless satisfied that he is clearly wrong.[135]

A special problem that often arises in this era of traffic signals and through highways is whether a car driver having the right of way is entitled to assume that others will yield to him. It is obvious that he is not entitled to run down everyone he sees in his path; but, on the other hand, if he were always obliged to anticipate that others would not grant him his right of way, traffic would scarcely move. This problem came before the court in 1939, when a car came onto a main highway without first stopping as the law required. Analyzing a number of English cases, the Chief Justice, in dissent, said that the driver on the main highway is entitled to assume that other cars will stop before entering the highway. The majority held, however, that he still owed a duty toward the other vehicle and both drivers were to blame.[136]

The Alberta Contributory Negligence Act states that liability shall be proportioned to degree of fault, but in addition has special sections providing that the doctrine of last clear chance shall not be applied against a party unless his negligent act was "clearly subsequent to and severable from" the negligent act of the other party. In the leading case of *Foster* v. *Kerr*[137] a car driver struck a man walking, contrary to statute, on the right side of the road. The court might have decided that the driver had the last clear chance and so was solely to blame. Both parties, however, were held equally to blame and the plaintiff recovered one half of the damages suffered. Harvey C.J. concurred in the opinion of Frank Ford J.A., who said that in deciding whether both parties were at fault the "broad common sense" rule should be applied: the party who is last negligent is not solely to blame unless his negligence is clearly subsequent and severable. This approach to the act means that courts will tend to apportion fault unless, in the words of Lord Tucker in *Sigurdson* v. *British Columbia Electric Railway Company,* "the dividing line is clearly visible".[138] We know of no decision of the Chief Justice tending to whittle down the decision in *Foster* v. *Kerr.*[139]

This is a convenient place to refer to the cases on the "onus" section in the Vehicles and Highway Traffic Act, which puts on the driver or owner of a motor vehicle the burden of proof that the loss or damage did not arise through the driver's negligence. Several provinces, including Alberta, had this provision before World War I, but its full significance does not appear to have been recognized until some time later. For example, plaintiffs continued to plead particulars of negligence and it was not until 1930 that the Appellate Division, with Harvey C.J. concurring, held that a plaintiff need not do so.[140] The main question, however, was whether the section placed on the defendant the burden of persuasion or merely the lesser burden of adducing evidence in the first instance that his negligence had not caused the accident. In 1921 in *Carnat* v. *Matthews*[141] Harvey C.J., without expressly distinguishing the two burdens, indicated in one passage that only the secondary burden need be discharged. In the leading case of *Winnipeg Electric Co.* v. *Geel,*[142] the defendant relied on this passage, but the Judicial Committee held that it did not accurately state the effect of the section: the burden of disproving negligence rests on the defendant throughout. Curiously, the judgment compares the effect of the section to that of *res ipsa loquitur,* as Harvey C.J. had done in the rejected passage. The better opinion is that in cases of *res ipsa loquitur* the burden of persuasion remains on the plaintiff.[143]

These cases on onus are not mentioned for the sake of showing that the Privy Council disapproved a statement in one of the Chief Justice's judgments, but rather because they illustrate the fact that he dealt in a forthright manner with novel issues and, although his opinions did not always prevail, yet they always canvassed the problem carefully and often were accepted in other courts, as was his judgment in *Carnat* before the *Geel* case.

The last interesting problem in motor-vehicle law is also a puzzling one—whether the plaintiff's action partakes of a claim in trespass or on the case. In 1924, in *Burd* v. *Macaulay,* an action against a car driver was brought just under six years after the accident. The Statute of Limitations of 1623 was pleaded, under which actions on the case had to be brought within six years and for trespass, assault and battery, within four years. The Chief Justice at trial examined the old decisions at length, and the Appellate Division sustained his opinion that the action was one of trespass.[144] The point is academic in Alberta to-day, for a one-year period is now provided in the Vehicles and Highway Traffic Act, but in at least two other provinces *Burd* v. *Macaulay* has been recently discussed at length.[145]

In negligence cases generally, the attitude of Harvey C.J. deserves mention because it showed a commendable tendency not to be hasty in finding negligence on the part of the defendant. For example, he once remarked:

> . . . there is a tendency amongst Judges sitting in the calm atmosphere of the Court and looking at the case from behind rather than from before to demand from defendants in negligence actions rather more than should be expected from a reasonably prudent person and to hold them liable unless they have been excessively prudent and have taken precautions which only after-events suggest.[146]

The Chief Justice usually refrained from explicit criticism of the common law, answering the argument that the law is harsh by saying that it is for the legislature and not the courts to change it, but he was by no means lacking in human sympathies. In one case we find him appealing to the defendant's generosity. A fire had broken out in a mine and a workman had been injured in trying to save property when some dynamite exploded. The mine owner was not liable because *Rylands* v. *Fletcher* did not apply and the workman was the author of his own injuries; but, said the Chief Justice, "I cannot avoid expressing the view that since what he was doing was purely and simply the expression of his better nature when he was assisting in trying to save his employer's property, a reciprocal expression on the part of the defendants would be becoming".[147] A measure of understanding and sympathy also appears in a case in which a railway appealed from a jury's award of $27,000 to an employee who had suffered a head injury:

> If it were a Superior Court Judge who had lost a leg which would in no way interfere with his performance of his regular duties and whose pecuniary loss would, therefore, be insignificant, I think that we at least would consider a verdict of $10,000 or $15,000 to err if at all on the side of being too small. It would not be surprising if laymen jurors might consider their pain and suffering of equal worth to that of a Judge, and so long as we recognize the right of juries to determine damages we must attribute to them as much as to Judges the characteristics of reasonable men.[148]

One of the most complicated and uncertain parts of the law of negligence is of course the liability of occupiers of premises to persons injured. There are few reported judgments of the Chief Justice in this field. In one of the few, where a guest after a banquet fell down the shaft of a service-elevator, it was held that he was not an invitee at the time and place of the injury and the defendant succeeded. In the course of his judgment the Chief Justice said:

> The 'impulse of compassion' is no doubt a most commendable attribute on grounds of common humanity but... it is not merely an unsafe, but even a wrong, foundation upon which to base the determination of a legal right.[149]

Later he concurred in a judgment of McGillivray J.A. applying *Addie* v. *Dumbreck*[150] to the case of a child trespasser who was killed by a cave-in of earth at an excavation.[151] In other words, the court adopted the "Draconian" rather than the "humanitarian" view toward the child trespasser.

Another subject on which there has been uncertainty and conflict is the liability of a public hospital for the negligence of its professional staff. In 1926 Harvey C.J. concurred in a judgment relieving a hospital from liability for its nurse's negligence when a patient was burned by a hot-water bottle. The basis of the decision was that a hospital is not liable for its nurse's negligence when it is related to her professional duties. The court purported to follow *Hillyer* v. *St. Bartholomew's Hospital,*[152] but on appeal the Supreme Court of Canada held that *Hillyer* does not apply to a nurse's ordinary duties.[153] As late as 1938 the Chief Justice was still not questioning *Hillyer*. In a case of that year, where the plaintiff had received X-ray injuries through a nurse's negligence, the hospital escaped because the negligence was in the performance of professional duties.[154] More recently the trend, both in England and Canada, has been to make the hospital liable in cases of this kind.

The rule in *Rylands* v. *Fletcher* engaged the attention of Chief Justice Harvey many times. Some judges have tended to expand the doctrine and apply it to cases where the basis of liability ought really to be negligence, but the Chief Justice was not among them. He even held that explosives kept by a coal mine are outside the rule. They are not like water, gas and electric current, which must be kept confined to prevent injury, for without the intervention of some other agency they will not cause injury.[155] Of course a person keeping explosives must exercise great care and therefore negligence is easier to establish in the case of explosives than of ordinarily harmless chattels.[156] A city that drills a gas well under statutory authority is not strictly liable for an explosion,[157] and likewise an irrigation company whose water escapes.[158]

The question of strict liability came up again in the leading case of *London Guarantee and Accident Co.* v. *Northwestern Utilities Limited*. Gas had leaked from a break in the gas company's main into a nearby hotel and caused a fire. At the trial the principal defence was that the main had subsided and cracked because of excavations dug by the City of Edmonton near the main, while the plaintiff's case was that the main was improperly constructed. The defendant was successful on the issue of fact and won in the trial court. On appeal, Harvey C.J. agreed that *Rylands* v. *Fletcher* did not apply because the company had statutory authority to carry gas in its mains;

the company's employees, however, were or should have been aware of the city's activity near the main and, since gas is highly dangerous, the company was under a duty to take steps to protect its main. Thus was a favourable finding of fact at trial turned into a finding of negligence on appeal. The company appealed to the Judicial Committee, but without success. Lord Wright, speaking on behalf of their lordships, agreed that the company was negligent for the reason given by Harvey C.J.[159] The practical effect seems to be that the gas company was in a worse position than it would be under the doctrine of strict liability, for the act of the city was the conscious or deliberate act of a third person, one of the exceptions to liability under *Rylands* v. *Fletcher*.

Turning now from the field of negligence to other torts, we find a number of novel issues, in which the Chief Justice showed a willingness to break new ground, at least in the absence of binding authority. Where there was no precedent in Canada or England he never hesitated to cite and rely on American authorities. One of his favourite American source books was *Lawyers' Reports Annotated*.

On an unusual set of facts he held it defamatory to say of an affianced man that he is married, and he who utters the original slander may be liable for its repetition by another.[160] In another case a woman sued the father of her former fiancé for inducing his son to break the engagement. To the defendant's argument that the law knows no cause of action for inducing a breach of promise to marry, the Chief Justice answered:

> It is urged that there is no precedent to be found for an action for inducing the breaking of a promise of marriage but it may be answered that there never is a precedent until one is made, but one naturally hesitates to make a new legal precedent at this stage of the history of the law on a point of such comparatively common occurrence.

Then, after referring to the principle of *Lumley* v. *Gye*,[161] he continued:

> Though there appears to be no decided case where the principle has been applied to a contract to marry there seems no good reason why it should not be, as it is expressed, absolutely general in its application though the consideration of what would be 'sufficient justification' in such a case might take one over a much wider field than in many other classes of cases.[162]

In yet another case a husband sued a funeral director who permitted an autopsy on the body of the wife after the husband had refused consent. The Chief Justice reasoned that the husband had a duty to bury his wife's body, and hence the custody and control of the body until burial. The defendant's act was an unauthorized interference with these rights, and actionable. Moreover, damages for mental anguish may be awarded in such circumstances. The reasoning may be open to criticism, but the case does show that the Chief Justice did not blindly follow old dogma—in this case the rule that there can be no property in a dead body. This is one of several instances in which he cited and followed an American case.[163]

A case decided in 1930 shows that he could treat the law of tort as a subject to be moulded to the needs of the times rather than as static rules to be applied mechanically. A moving van caught fire and the contents were burned. The owner of the contents sued the van company and recovered. Although the majority of the Appellate Court upheld a finding of negligence, the Chief Justice was inclined to think that the van company was under the strict liability of a common carrier:

> While I would think it not safe on the evidence to hold that the defendant is a common carrier, I am by no means satisfied that it should not be considered subject to the same liability as a common carrier...
>
> ... with the advances made in the last quarter of a century in regard to road motor transportation and the assumption by motor vans and lorries of the ordinary business of common carriers, it is clear that the question is likely to come up for decision in the not distant future. ... [164]

Since that case was decided the legislature has put commercial vehicles in the class of common carriers.

With torts must come to an end this discussion of Horace Harvey's contribution to the substantive law of his province and of his country. One could catalogue in addition a list of cases in which he passed on important points of contracts, insurance law, passing-off, creditors' remedies, fraudulent conveyances, estoppel,[165] and the interpretation of statutes ranging from the Accidental Fires Act, 1774, to those, like the Farm Machinery Act, protecting farmers against importunate salesmen. In administrative law his most important case is *Board of Public Utility Commissioners* v. *Model Dairies,* in which he dealt with the power of a court to review the decisions of an administrative agency. Finding nothing in the proceedings before the board to indicate any departure from the elementary principles of justice, he showed no inordinate zeal to set aside the board's order suspending the licence of a dairy company, and upheld it.[166] In labour law he had to consider the old question of the legal status of a trade union,[167] picketing[168] and the position of a worker who has been expelled by a trade union[169] or dismissed by his employer.[170] But the cases that have been discussed on criminal law, constitutional law, domestic relations, real property and torts will sufficiently indicate his contribution to substantive law and something of his concept of the judicial function.

Practice and Procedure

So far in this article we have given an account of Chief Justice Harvey's early career and of his leading decisions on various subjects—the criminal law, constitutional law, domestic relations, real property and torts. These decisions on substantive law give some indication of his contribution to the jurisprudence. His judgments on matters of practice and procedure, often of equal importance to the administration of justice, help to give a picture of other judicial characteristics and attitudes.

Rules of Court, like statutes, are never exhaustive and the judges must fill in the gaps. It is always most disconcerting to the practitioner when the requirements in procedural matters at trial and in chambers differ from judge to judge. As the Chief Justice said in one case, "What the practice should be seems of less importance than that it should be authoritatively settled".[171] He frequently spoke for the Appellate Division in laying down the practice to be followed in the future. Thus in a case where a question arose as to the proper practice on applications for possession of land under wartime rental regulations, he wrote:

> As it was stated by counsel that the Chamber judges are not following a uniform practice in respect to such applications, we intimated that we would give some direction as to the proper practice so that there might be uniformity,[172]

and he proceeded to do so.

Most decisions on practice concern of course the rules of court. During the Territorial period, the rules were contained in the Judicature Ordinance until 1898, when they were set out separately.[173] On the formation of the province, the same rules remained in force until 1914, when a completely new set was made.[174] Before this the English practice applied where the local rules were silent,[175] but the 1914 rules, which basically remain in force to this day, are an exclusive code, under which the court has been able to develop an independent practice.[176]

In several cases interpreting the 1914 rules the Chief Justice referred to the fact that he had been a member of the commission that drew them,[177] an approach that raises an interesting point of construction. In 1305 Chief Justice Hengham said to counsel, "Do not gloss the statute, for we know better than you: we made it".[178] On the other hand, Lord Halsbury said that the worst person to construe a statute is the one who was responsible for its drafting, because he tends to give effect to what he meant, not what he said.[179] When Harvey C.J. had to construe the 1914 rules he referred to the intention of the framers, including himself.[180] Yet many years later, interpreting the revised rules of 1944, in which he had had no hand, he aligned himself on the side of Lord Halsbury, observing that "it seems to me to be a very unsafe principle on which to interpret a statutory provision or rule by reference to what the framers intended by it".[181]

One of the most important contributions he made to sound procedure was to insist on strict compliance with the requirements of statutes and rules. He would never tolerate careless or inept practices and on at least two occasions, in an effort to prevent the filing of untidy appeal books and factums, he deprived a successful appellant of his costs.[182] He insisted, though perhaps not always with success, that counsel file their factums on time. When they were late he always knew it, because he had the clerk bring them to him as soon as they arrived. Invariably he read them before the appeal came on for hearing and it was obvious from his remarks to counsel that he knew what they contained, grasped the issues and had familiarized himself with the relevant statutes and cases.

He was generally more ready than his brethren to set aside a garnishee summons, bill of sale or caveat because of a defect in the supporting affidavit. The rules of court specify certain information "necessary" in an affidavit in support of a garnishee summons, the Bills of Sale Act prescribes the contents of the affidavit that must accompany a bill of sale or chattel mortgage and the Land Titles Act requires an affidavit of bona fides to support a caveat. In the many cases where these affidavits were faulty the Chief Justice showed little inclination to invoke the "slip rule" or a curative section.[183]

The leading case of *McPherson* v. *McPherson* seems to furnish an exception to his usual strictness in procedural matters. Here a divorced wife sued to set aside the divorce previously granted against her. She alleged, among other things, that the decree nisi had been made in the judges' library and not in open court. The Chief Justice held that the library became in fact an open court when the presiding judge declared it to be so, but that, even if it were not, the decree was not a nullity. The writer listened to the argument on appeal and formed the impression that the Chief Justice was influenced towards his conclusion by the fact that in his early days at the bar and on the bench court had sometimes to be held in a building other than a court house, even in a pool hall, and that he saw no objection to holding it in a library. The Privy Council held, however, that the hearing had not been in open court and the decree was therefore voidable, but that the divorced wife had waited too long to complain.[184]

On matters of practice arising under the rules of court, he helped to settle a number of important principles, for example, on examination for discovery of a company officer,[185] inspection of documents where privilege is claimed,[186] the right to a summary judgment,[187] the striking of pleadings[188] and the amendment of pleadings at trial.[189]

The history of the provisions for jury trial in civil cases is of interest. Before 1914 either party could demand as of right a jury trial in certain enumerated cases, including nearly all common-law actions.[190] Horace Harvey drafted the new jury rules,[191] which allowed a jury as of right in a small number of actions. In other cases the judge had a discretion to direct trial by jury. The members of the court were so far apart on the grounds justifying an exercise of the discretion that in the first case to come before the Appellate Division "no reasons for judgment were ever given because the members of the Court were unable to agree upon any satisfactory interpretation of the rule".[192] They never did agree[193] and so in 1918 the rules were changed to restore the right in almost all cases, save that the judge might direct trial without a jury where the prolonged examination of documents or a scientific inquiry would make this course more convenient.[194] These rules are still in effect. The Appellate Division, and particularly Harvey C.J., remained hesitant to lay down any general rule that a trial judge should exercise his discretion by refusing a jury, for example where medical evidence is to be called.[195] The Chief Justice's own opinion on jury trials appears in the following passage:

> There is no doubt that the training and experience of a Judge aid him to subordinate his sympathies and his other emotions to his judgment and make him a better person than an inexperienced layman to decide most matters that require to be decided in a Court of law, but it does not follow that that makes him a safer or surer person to decide even some of those questions than *six* laymen, and there may even be matters which have to do with the relations of the parties in which the judgment of a layman in their own walk of life may be more likely to be correct than that of a Judge.[196]

Rules of court are a mere framework and the judges must give them content. Whether certainty and efficiency or uncertainty and inconvenience are the result depends peculiarly on the courts. No short summary of practice cases can do justice to the common sense with which Chief Justice Harvey disposed of arguments on the meaning of the Alberta rules. His mark appears clearly on the present practice in the province.

The Doctrine of Precedent

One of Chief Justice Harvey's most strongly held tenets was that courts should follow precedents. In many cases he accepted without question the decisions of the Judicial Committee of the Privy Council or the Supreme Court of Canada even when they were at variance with views he had himself expressed.[197] He followed not only binding authority but, with a few exceptions, the decisions of co-ordinate courts in other provinces, particularly where a Dominion statute was in issue. In one case, for example, where the question was whether a lien note is a promissory note under the federal Bills of Exchange Act, he said:

> If the present case comes within the principle of these decided cases, whatever might be my personal view, I should hesitate to disregard the decisions of the highest courts in three of our Provinces. . . . I have endeavoured to make a distinction on this basis; but after very careful consideration the only conclusion I can come to is . . . that I must therefore hold that the instrument sued on here is not a negotiable promissory note.[198]

Again, he stressed many times the importance of uniformity in criminal procedure, a matter governed by federal legislation.[199] Where Alberta had adopted a statute from another province, which had already been interpreted there, then that interpretation should be followed in Alberta.[200] Often he applied without question the decisions of English courts, though in one case he refused to follow the English Court of Appeal[201] and in another, the Court of Criminal Appeal.[202]

His strong belief in *stare decisis* became apparent when the court en banc[203] had to consider whether it was bound by its own decisions. In 1919 in *R.* v. *Schmolke*[204] he gave the opinion of the full court, following a decision of the full court in Nova Scotia, that a magistrate had jurisdiction under the Inland Revenue Act to try a charge of possession of an unlicensed still.[205] The next year the court, considering the same problem in *R.* v. *Hartfeil,* by a majority of four to one overruled *Schmolke*. The Chief Justice dissented vigorously:

> It must be quite apparent that if the Court does not show respect for its own decisions it can hardly be surprised if no one else does. It throws the door of uncertainty wide open and every counsel not satisfied with a decision can come back and demand a re-argument of the whole question. It leaves a trial Judge in the uncertain position of not knowing whether he should act on his own judgment rather than follow a decision of this division, which this division on appeal from him may itself refuse to follow. . . . [206]

Stuart J., on the other hand, advanced strong reasons for refusing to follow *Schmolke*. It had been decided, not on the merits, but out of a desire for uniformity in the criminal law throughout Canada. He was "extremely pessimistic about the possibility of this being brought about. . . by means of provincial Courts of Criminal Appeal following previous decisions of the Courts of other provinces", and he doubted "if eastern Courts of Appeal will generally be found very ready to bow to decisions from the west". A provincial court should not be expected to follow a decision rendered in any province, even if it is firmly of opinion that the decision was wrong, just because it happens to have been decided first. Beck J. had no qualms whatever about departing from an earlier case: "Sitting as a member of the Appellate Division I repeat what I have said on more than one occasion that I feel bound not to refrain from expressing my real opinion upon questions of substantial importance notwithstanding a decision of this division to the contrary".[207]

Fourteen years later, when the Appellate Division was a separate branch of the court in fact as well as in name, it had to consider whether to follow the British Columbia Court of Appeal, which had held that a particular type of slot machine is a gaming device and so subject to forfeiture. In the course of his judgment Chief Justice Harvey said:

> The criminal law is the same throughout Canada and if respect is to be maintained for the administration of it the Courts of the different provinces should not place different interpretations on it but leave it for the Supreme Court of Canada or Parliament to correct any wrong decision.[208]

The different interpretations of the law on slot machines "has not increased respect for the courts and has confused and complicated and made more difficult the enforcement of the criminal law in this regard". He then took occasion to discuss *Schmolke* and *Hartfeil*. In *Hartfeil* the court had considered itself free to depart from its earlier decision because the Appellate Division was then a mere "voluntary committee" of the court and the decision of one committee was not binding on another committee. But this reasoning could not possibly be applied after 1921, when the Appellate Division became a separate entity. It should now adhere to its own decisions. He then rehabilitated the rule laid down in *Schmolke* that the court should follow decisions from courts of last resort in other provinces on matters of criminal law. It is "a very salutary rule to follow for general purposes though I would not say that like any other good rule there might not be possible exceptions, as if for instance we were satisfied that the other decision is clearly wrong".

In his early days on the bench he had certainly on one occasion at least considered that a wrong decision need not be followed. A few months after his appointment, the Supreme Court of the North-West Territories en banc had to decide the neat question whether a railway conductor who accepts a bribe to allow a passenger to ride without a ticket is guilty of stealing the amount of the fare from the railway. Harvey J. stood alone in saying that he is not guilty of theft, whatever other crime he may be guilty of.[209] Six years later the Supreme Court of Alberta en banc faced the same problem. Horace Harvey was now Chief Justice of Alberta. Although the new court had taken the place of the old, he said,

> it is an entirely different Court, and is not in my opinion bound by decisions of that Court any more than it would be by the decisions of its sister Court of the Province of Saskatchewan which occupies the same relation to the earlier Court that this Court does.[210]

He held the same opinion he had in 1905, and this time two of the four other judges sitting agreed with him and the conviction was quashed.

In spite of his respect for precedent, he was still a "strong" judge, and this is not the only case in which he clung to his opinion. He was not a party, for example, to a frequently cited judgment in which the majority of the court laid down a series of conditions that, if present, precluded a trial judge from refusing to accept evidence in a criminal case[211] and, where he could, he restricted it in later cases, though he did not expressly repudiate it.[212]

Like most judges, he could draw on occasion what may seem to an observer a fine distinction in order to preserve a previous judgment of his own. Where the Supreme Court has handed down a decision that seems to conflict with a judgment of his own in another case, is a provincial judge being any less than human if he tries to reconcile the two when the situation arises again? Here is an example from the judicial career of Harvey C.J. A judgment creditor wants to seize the crop of his judgment debtor and has a seizure made, but the wife claims the crop on the ground that she owns the land. The creditor replies that the husband is the real farmer, and that therefore he, the creditor, is entitled to seize the crop. In 1926 the Appellate Division held in *Standard Trusts Co.* v. *Briggs* that the test is: Who carries on the farming operations, the husband or the wife?[213] On the other hand, in 1927 the Supreme Court of Canada appeared to say in the *Tencha* case, an appeal from Manitoba, that the test is: Who is owner of the land?[214] Then in 1930 a creditor in Alberta seized the crop on land the debtor had transferred to his wife but continued to farm himself. The Chief Justice did not ignore the argument that the Supreme Court had overruled the *Briggs* case, but a close scrutiny of the two judgments enabled him to say that it had not. *Tencha* does not exclude entirely the test that the person in possession or occupancy, rather than the owner of the land, is owner of the crop.[215]

Though Chief Justice Harvey usually insisted on following precedent, sometimes uncritically, and even when it was not strictly binding, yet he was capable of demonstrating what Sir Frederick Pollock once termed "judicial valour".[216] As we have seen, he did not hesitate to break new ground in the law of torts,[217] and, as we shall now see, he did not slavishly apply in Alberta the law of England.

By the North-West Territories Act, 1886, the laws of England as they existed on July 15th, 1870, were declared to be in force in the Territories "so far as the same are applicable" and until repealed or altered by the appropriate legislature. This provision was brought forward by the Alberta Act. Since it is the judges who say whether a particular statute or common-law doctrine is applicable in Alberta, they have in their hands wide power to determine the direction that Alberta law will take. True, the legislature can always change the law as declared, but it seldom does.

The matter of imprisonment for debt is an example. In 1869 the Imperial Parliament had passed the Debtors Act, which generally abolished the imprisonment of debtors, but provided that any person with the means to pay who makes default in payment of a debt or instalment of a debt due from him under a judgment of a competent court might be committed to prison for a term not exceeding six weeks. In 1907 Scott J. committed a debtor to prison under this act and on appeal the debtor argued that the act was not applicable to conditions in Alberta. Harvey J., writing for the majority in a three to two decision, pointed out that, if it were not in force, the more drastic common-law power to imprison would still apply, which he obviously thought would be absurd.[218]

During World War I, as a result of the campaign for women's rights, Alberta appointed a number of women magistrates. An accused who had been tried by one of these women magistrates applied to quash the conviction, arguing that at common law a woman could not hold public office. Scott J. expressed serious doubts whether a woman was qualified to be appointed to the office of police magistrate, but nevertheless refused to quash. Harvey C.J. sat on the appeal, though the judgment of the court was written by Stuart J. After a searching examination of the historical background, the judgment concluded that women were eligible for public office in England in 1870. In any event, "In my opinion, in a matter of this kind the Courts of this province are not in every case to be held strictly bound by the decisions of English Courts as to the state of the common law of England in 1870. We are at liberty to take cognizance of the different conditions here, not merely physical conditions, but the general conditions of our public affairs and the general attitude of the community in regard to the particular matter in question."[219]

Perhaps it was this victory that encouraged the champions of women's rights in Alberta to insist on the right of women to sit in the Senate. The issue involved the interpretation of section 24 of the British North America Act, 1867, which says that "The Governor General shall from Time to Time... summon qualified Persons to the Senate". No woman had ever been summoned, the assumption being that only men are persons for the purpose of the section. In 1927 five Alberta women set in motion a reference to the Supreme Court of Canada on the question, Are women eligible for appointment to the Senate of Canada?

Influenced by the common-law rule that women could not hold public office, the Supreme Court answered the question in the negative. The five Alberta women then appealed to the Judicial Committee. In stating his famous doctrine that the British North America Act is a "living tree capable of growth and expansion", and that women are eligible to sit in the Senate, Lord Sankey used words similar to those of Stuart J. just quoted: "their Lordships do not think it right to apply rigidly to Canada of to-day the decisions and the reasonings therefor which had commended themselves, probably rightly, to those who had to apply the law in different circumstances, in different centuries, to countries in different stages of development".[220]

Although the Chief Justice did not share the readiness of some judges to hold English law unsuitable to conditions in Canada, he never applied it automatically if he genuinely felt it out of harmony. As late as 1927 the court had to consider whether the rule in Shelley's case, which the House of Lords held in 1897 to be still the law of England, is in force in Alberta. Suppose a will provides: "I devise Blackacre to *X* for life and then to his heirs". The words "to his heirs" are words of limitation, not of purchase, and give *X* the fee simple and the heirs nothing, no matter what the intent of the testator or how absurd the result. In the Alberta case, the Chief Justice said that the rule in Shelley's case, like the mortmain laws, rests on reasons affecting the land and society of England, but not applying in a new colony. Even if the rule were introduced, it was abrogated by the Torrens system.[221]

Judicial Traits

Chief Justice Harvey was not unique in his stand that, following of necessity from the doctrine of parliamentary sovereignty, the wisdom and fairness of statutes are a matter for the legislature. Over again he insisted on the duty of the court to give effect to statutes, however harsh the consequences. In the *Nat Bell* case, for example—where the chief witness for the Crown was an informer and the penalty imposed on the company a fine and the forfeiture of over a thousand cases of liquor—Harvey C.J. observed in his dissent:

> Nor is it within our province to consider the wisdom or justice of either the law which it is sought to enforce or the methods by which it is sought to enforce it. The legal aspect only of these is for our consideration and we have no duty or right to deal with legislative or executive functions, whatever our personal opinions may be.[222]

Yet it would be wrong to leave the impression that he always insisted on giving literal effect to the words of a statute. Where it seemed necessary he was prepared to imply words[223] or, conversely, to restrict the literal meaning.[224] We have already seen that he went to some length in upholding a disposition of land which the Dower Act declared to be null and void. For the greater part, his interpretation of statutes was guided by the orthodox canons and rules. His important contribution was insistence on uniform interpretation of Dominion laws and of provincial laws *in pari materia*—a trend which, if generally adopted, will have a healthy effect on Canadian jurisprudence.

As for decisions on matters governed solely by case law, the Chief Justice generally was guided by logic and analogy. One might think from some of his judgments that he considered the duty of a judge merely "to match the colors of the case at hand against the colors of many sample cases spread out upon [his] desk".[225] His belief in the advantages of *stare decisis* may sometimes have led him in this direction. But, though he sometimes decided a point as he would not have done had it been novel, this was the consequence of his concept of the judicial function, not of any notion that rules of law bear no relation to the needs of society.

Much can be said for the emphasis put by scholars like the late Mr. Justice Cardozo and Roscoe Pound on the importance of remembering that rules of law are not an end in themselves and that judges, in reaching decisions, should think in terms of the welfare of society and the accommodation of conflicting interests. There is no reason for thinking that Chief Justice Harvey would have quarrelled with their approach, but he would certainly have said that questions of this sort are in the main to be left to the legislature. He would not have denied that judges may legislate "interstitially", but for him the interstices would have seemed minute: the scope allowed the judiciary to mould the law on "functional" or "sociological" lines is confined within very narrow bounds. In one case at least the Chief Justice specifically referred to the practical implications of any decision the court might make. The dispute arose when an early snowfall prevented a thresherman from completing his contract to thresh a farmer's crop. The thresherman claimed payment for what he had threshed and the farmer counterclaimed for breach of contract. The Chief Justice, speaking for the court, applied the well-known cases on impossibility of performance and held for the plaintiff. Of interest here is his statement that in a province where hundreds of millions of bushels of grain are threshed each year and the threshing season is short, "it is not merely of special interest that each farmer should get his grain threshed but it is of general interest that each thresher should be enabled to use his outfit to its fullest capacity".[226] This observation does not indicate "arid conceptualism".[227]

If a judge is restricted in giving effect to what is socially or economically desirable, it follows that he is similarly limited in giving effect to what seems to him morally just. Chief Justice Harvey had a strong "prejudice" in favour of the sanctity of promises, yet his concept of the role of the courts led him to refrain, assuming the law to be clear, from imposing his own views of what is honourable. In a case that came to the court in 1948, when the Chief Justice was a very old man, a trade union contended that a Dominion order in council permitted it to terminate a collective labour agreement with a coal company in spite of the express terms of the agreement:

> It was urged by counsel [for the company] that the attempt to terminate the agreement is in complete disregard of the [union's] solemn promise. That, of course, involves a question of honour which can enter into consideration by the court only if, and so far as, it can help to determine the question of legality, but is naturally a satisfaction to any judge when he can come to the conclusion that no reflection can be cast on the law as supporting what appears to be not honourable.[228]

Some years earlier he had expressed a similar point of view, somewhat less succinctly, in a case where the former principal of a business college in Calgary sought, on the ground that it was in restraint of trade, to set aside a covenant that he would not compete in Calgary for five years after leaving the college:

> One wonders whether in this day [just after the outbreak of the Second World War] when we are confronted with a situation in which the heads of nations enter into solemn contracts and treaties with the apparent intention of abiding by their promises only so long as they consider them in their interest and repudiating them when they find them of no further value to themselves, which conduct with the spirit underlying it meets with the universal abhorrence of all right-thinking people, the highest Courts or the Legislatures might not properly consider that the preservation of the sanctity of contracts entered into by 'men of full age and competent understanding' is of even greater public interest than any restriction on freedom of trade which might be involved. . . . Fortunately many—perhaps a majority—of our people have such a sense of honour that they would scorn to repudiate their solemn promise on any legal ground of its invalidity but with the example of the tendency and practice we see abroad in high circles that sense of honour may become blunted and give way to the sense of seeming self-interest with disastrous results unless halted by the Courts or the Legislatures.[229]

The Chief Justice's strict sense of probity also found expression when he came to deal with charges of misconduct against barristers and solicitors. Until the year 1922 the Appellate Division was vested with the power of disciplining members of the profession and applications used to be made to the court to strike a practitioner off the rolls or restore him. The function of the court in dealing with these applications he once described in the following words:

> The relationship of solicitor and client is a fiduciary one, involving the utmost confidence on the part of the client, and requiring the strictest honour on the part of the solicitor and the purpose of giving the Court the power which is now sought to be invoked is to preserve that honour inviolate amongst solicitors who are its officers, and it appears to me that that end can only be accomplished by imposing suitable punishment for transgressors committing breaches of trust and honour.[230]

Twice he cited with approval[231] the following passage from an English case:

> We have a duty to perform to the suitors of the Court, and not only to the suitors of the Court but to the profession of the law, by taking care that those permitted to practice in it are persons on whose integrity and honour reliance can be placed.[232]

On applications for reinstatement the Chief Justice tended to require stronger evidence of rehabilitation than did some of his brethren.[233] With a sound instinct for the relevant, he insisted that fitness to practise, not mere punishment, is the test in deciding whether to strike or keep a lawyer off the rolls. The court's concern must be to see that he is a person of such character that the confidence reposed in him will not be betrayed.[234] The Chief Justice did not easily yield to the common desire to give a wrongdoer another chance.

Certainly Harvey C.J. was a "strong" judge, with a trace of iron in his makeup. Once he censured a trial judge he thought had been unfair to a party: "He [the defendant] does resent, however, the strictures and contemptuous references and findings of desertion and of perjury by the learned trial Judge in his reasons for judgment and I think he is justified in so doing, for, in my opinion, they are entirely unwarranted by the evidence".[235] In one case, in which the Chief Justice presided at the trial, his charge to the jury included a castigation of defence counsel for what he considered unjustified aspersions on Crown witnesses;[236] and on the appeal in another he said, mildly enough, that counsel had "spent nearly two days in trying to satisfy us that 'in addition to' meant something different from what anyone would ordinarily think it meant".[237] On rare occasions he paid an express compliment to counsel.[238]

In the first twenty odd years of the province's history the Supreme Court of Alberta had three outstanding appellate judges, Harvey C.J. and Stuart and Beck JJ.A. Occasionally they differed strongly from each other but the combined effect of their work was to give the province in its formative years a body of sound case law. Mr. Justice Stuart was interested in both philosophy and legal history and his scholarly judgments indicate a continual search for first principles. Mr. Justice Beck had a special interest in equity and was inclined to put "justice before precedent"; in the words of the Chief Justice in 1932, "there has never been a Judge in this province more insistent upon the Court according the fullest protection possible to an accused person".[239]

The Chief Justice's own judgments reveal him as a careful and thorough workman, with a highly developed sense of relevancy. His reasons for judgment, though the style is not particularly distinguished, are clearly and succinctly expressed in their statement both of the facts and the law. He examined cases that were not in the factums and the writer knows of only one case in which he overlooked a relevant authority that might have changed his opinion.[240] Usually he avoided extended comment and consequently few of his judgments are long. His practice was to set out the facts, then the relevant cases in an orderly way, and finally to apply the cases to the facts. On occasion he would refer to a law review article or a standard textbook. Always he declined to discuss matters that did not arise on the appeal[241] or that might affect the interests of parties not before the court.[242]

His judgments give an impression of confidence and conviction. It would not appear that he was ever greatly troubled by the possibility that they might be wrong. This is not to imply that he did not recognize the difficulty of reaching a correct decision, but rather that he was philosophical about the possibility that he might be reversed. As he once observed, "That is what a judge is for—to decide difficult questions. If they were easy they would not ordinarily come before him."[243]

Although he often differed from his colleagues, there is never a suggestion of rancour in the pages of his judgments. The same spirit finds expression in a case where a certain judge and members of the legislature had harshly criticized the police magistrate who had presided at the trial:

> It must be apparent to anyone conversant with Courts of law that it is no reflection whatever upon a Judge or magistrate that a higher Court should take a different view of the law or the facts from that taken by him. There probably never was a Judge yet no matter how able, and not being in the highest Court from which there was no appeal, who has not had his judgment reversed by a higher Court with nevertheless, perhaps, a fair prospect of its being restored by a still higher Court. There is room for an honest difference of opinion on most matters which come up for judicial decision, otherwise they would not have to be decided, but when the honesty of the Judge is impugned it is quite a different matter. Of course no one should be entrusted with the power of deciding the questions which come before magistrates and Judges who cannot be trusted to exercise that power honestly.[244]

Horace Harvey would doubtless have agreed with Lord Macmillan that a judgment is not an appropriate vehicle for wit and pleasantry,[245] yet once or twice he did indulge in mild humour, tinged with irony. In one case, the operator of a motion picture theatre was charged with violation of the Lord's Day Act, when he showed a picture on Sunday and placed a collection plate at the door. The act forbade performances at which a fee was charged and the Chief Justice, in dissent, held that the theatre director was guilty of a violation of the act. In the course of his judgment he said:

> The word 'collection' ordinarily suggests a voluntary contribution because that is the kind of collection which is most frequently in evidence. But at a certain time of the year we realize that the collection made by the tax collector has sufficient force behind it. Every large law office also has its collection department contributions to which have little spontaneity or voluntariness.[246]

In one of the many prosecutions under the prohibition law, a druggist who sold a concoction called "Tonic Port" argued that it was so nauseating that no one could possibly drink enough to become intoxicated. A majority of the court agreed, but not Harvey C.J.:

> There is nothing moreover in the evidence of the defendant's expert witnesses to warrant the conclusion that by the exercise of a perseverance which might perhaps be more commendable in a worthier cause the nausea caused when

> one first tries to drink the liquor in question may not wear away and disappear in later efforts. Most smokers of tobacco could probably furnish evidence of such a possibility.[247]

In another liquor case the Chief Justice's humour was vicarious, for he merely concurred in a judgment of Hyndman J. A physician was charged with giving a prescription for forty ounces of whiskey to a man who was not in fact sick, and the evidence showed that the "patient" had told the doctor he was about to go to Banff on a fishing trip. Mr. Justice Hyndman said:

> No matter what our opinions may be as to the virtue of Scotch whiskey on a fishing expedition the Act does not permit it and it is therefore a question for the Legislature to deal with. I am certain it is the judgment of many people that to permit its use on such occasions as a precaution against chills (the great fear of the trout fisherman) would tend to much greater production of fish in these times of scarcity of food.

However, "even if a party fishing at Banff actually took ill, 40 ounces would be much more than he would reasonably need, as Banff is well supplied with doctors and hospitals and I fancy enough whiskey to restore life to any hapless, chilled fisherman".[248]

Chief Justice Harvey's public services were extensive. During his long term of office he sat on several royal commissions and other inquiries, and at various times he was appointed administrator of the province in the absence of the Lieutenant Governor. But his special interest, apart from his judicial work, was undoubtedly in the University of Alberta, of whose board of governors he was chairman from 1918 to 1940.

The University of Alberta was established by provincial statute in 1906, classes were begun in 1908, and in 1910 a new act established the board of governors, most of whom, including the chairman, are appointed by order in council. Chief Justice Harvey was the second chairman. The governors have the main responsibility for the management of university affairs and the office of chairman is an onerous one. A glance at the minutes of the board during the twenty-two years of Horace Harvey's chairmanship reveals the many important decisions and the innumerable matters of detail in which he had a hand. The depression of course put a halt to physical expansion and when the postwar building programme took place he had retired.

As chairman of the board, rather than as Chief Justice, he was interested in a constitutional dispute between the province and the Dominion over the right to Alberta lands which had escheated. When the province was created, "All Crown lands, mines and minerals and royalties incident thereto" were kept by the Dominion. The right of escheat is a royalty and therefore the Dominion was entitled to land in the province that had escheated. In an attempt to secure for itself lands of an intestate who dies leaving no next of kin (heirship having been abolished long before), the province passed an act in 1915 providing simply that all property of the intestate should vest in the province. The Supreme Court held it invalid in so far as it interfered with the Dominion's right of escheat.[249]

Then in 1921 the legislature tried again. A new statute, the Ultimate Heir Act, provided that every person dying intestate with no kin was deemed to have made a will in favour of the University of Alberta. When the Dominion contended that this act too was invalid, as an encroachment on its right of escheat, the province argued that it had power to amend the law of inheritance. The Appellate Division, sitting without the Chief Justice, upheld the act, but the Privy Council in 1928 declared it invalid in so far as it applied to lands.[250] Since he was chairman of the Board of Governors, the Chief Justice had not sat, but it is probable that he thought the act valid. One of the province's main arguments in the litigation was that the distinction between real and personal property disappeared when the law of both the North-West Territories and Alberta assimilated the descent of real property to that of personal property, and the Chief Justice had said in another case that the Territories Real Property Act perhaps changed real into personal property.[251] In any event, in 1930 the Dominion transferred to the province all lands, mines, minerals and royalties. In other words, the right of escheat is now vested in the province and the province may do what it wishes with escheated lands. The important point from the university's standpoint is that the Ultimate Heir Act was never repealed. It still stands in the statute book and over the years has brought to the university property of substantial value.[252]

Among the public inquiries and royal commissions on which the Chief Justice sat were an investigation of possible impropriety by members of the legislature during the railway crisis of 1910, several inquiries into municipal finances and one to determine the cause of a coal mine explosion. In 1932 he investigated for the federal government a charge that the "Gypsum Queen", a schooner alleged to have been sunk by a submarine in 1915, had in fact not been, and that compensation had been improperly paid. He found the charge substantiated and the captain was subsequently convicted of obtaining money from the Crown under false pretences.[253]

One of the greatest public services the Chief Justice performed was as chairman of the War Mobilization Board for Alberta during the last war. This board was responsible for the call-up of draftees and the disposal of applications for deferment and exemption from military service. Although he was seventy-eight when he took the post, he worked tirelessly for over four years, carrying on his judicial functions as well. Those who were associated with him on the board speak in the highest terms of his industry, attention to detail, fairness, and toleration of the views of others. The reputation of the Alberta board for wisdom and impartiality in carrying out its onerous and often delicate task was due in large measure to the Chief Justice's influence.

He received the honorary degree of Doctor of Laws from the University of Alberta in 1917 and from the University of Toronto in 1936. A posthumous acknowledgment of his public services was made five years after his death when in 1954 the Geographic Board of Alberta and the Canadian Board on Geographical Names decided to name various geographic features in Alberta after some of the province's pioneers and builders. Among those honoured was Chief Justice Harvey, the name "Harvey Lake" being given to a lake twenty-one miles north-west of the town of Jasper in Jasper National Park.

The writer cannot speak from a close personal acquaintance, but over a number of years he did observe the Chief Justice on the bench. Of medium height and build, with a fresh complexion, good features and white hair, he had a distinguished, almost benign, appearance. On the bench, his questions and comments kept counsel to the point and discouraged loose and inaccurate statements. At the same time he was—though detached—polite, equable and dignified.

Off the bench he spent most of his time on his judicial work. His main diversions were in growing flowers and collecting stamps. Not a gregarious person, the center of his life was his home, though he did attend many functions, and enjoyed small gatherings. At them he was gracious, congenial, and an interesting conversationalist.

An organization that did hold great interest for the Chief Justice was the Canadian Bar Association. He was a member from its formation in 1914 and shortly before his death was made an honorary member. He attended the annual meetings regularly and was at the meeting, in Ottawa, as late as 1947. He also enjoyed attending the functions of the Law Society of Alberta and until shortly before his death used to come to the annual banquet of the law students at the University of Alberta. If he ever thought any of these gatherings were too boisterous, he gave no sign. As Mr. J.W. Hugill, Q.C., an old friend, says of these occasions, he responded to witticisms even against himself with an "enigmatic smile".

Mrs. Harvey died in May 1948 after a married life of fifty-five years. Their only child, Alan Burnside Harvey, was a Rhodes Scholar from Alberta for 1918. Proceeding to Oxford in 1920, he received the degrees of B.C.L. and M.A. and was admitted to the English bar as a member of the Middle Temple. After his return from England he practised law in Edmonton until 1937, when he moved to Toronto. Mr. A.B. Harvey, Q.C., was editor of the fifth edition of *Tremeear's Criminal Code,* which appeared in 1944, and for a number of years has been Editor of Reports for the Law Society of Upper Canada.

After Mrs. Harvey's death the Chief Justice's health failed, though his last judgments indicate no decline in his faculties. To the end the notes in his judge's book were precise, accurate and formal, and the handwriting firm until the last few months. The last entry was made less than three months before his death, which occurred on September 9th, 1949.

Regrettably his extra-judicial writings were not extensive. He did write one or two articles for the law journals on the early administration of justice in the North-West,[254] but, like many others whose ability, knowledge and experience would enable them to make a contribution to legal literature, he could not find time for both writing and his many duties, and had to choose. The hundreds of his reported judgments remain as a record of his public service. Indeed one might say of the Honourable Horace Harvey, Chief Justice of Alberta, as Lord Wensleydale said of himself, that his biography is found in the pages of the law reports. A long story it is, a story of a worthy contribution to the establishment and development of law in Alberta, and hence to Canadian society.[255]

Notes

1 *Re Lewis* (1918), 13 Alta. L.R. 423, 41 D.L.R. 1, [1918] 2 W.W.R. 687.

2 *Re Norton* (1918), 13 Alta. L.R. 457, [1918] 2 W.W.R. 865. In each report the editor's summary of the facts contains inaccuracies as to dates. The writer has relied on the Chief Justice's judge's book and on newspaper accounts in the Calgary Herald and Edmonton Bulletin from July 10th to 13th, 1918.

3 *Re Gray* (1918), 57 S.C.R. 150, [1918] 3 W.W.R. 111.

4 Fairman, The Law of Martial Rule and the National Emergency (1942), 55 Harv. L. Rev. 1253, at pp. 1278–81; Swisher, Roger Taney (1936) pp. 548–560.

5 *Patterson* v. *Lane* (1904), 6 Terr. L.R. 92.

6 *R.* v. *Byrnes,* [1949] 2 W.W.R. 209, [1949] 4 D.L.R. 39.

7 The requirements appear in various issues of the old Canada Law Journal, *e.g.* (1885), 21 Can. L.J. 202–204.

8 (1889), 25 Can. L.J. 18–19; 392–3.

9 A useful memorandum of statutes, orders in council and ordinances relating to legislative powers and the administration of justice in the Territories from 1867 to 1898 appears in (1885–1893), 1 Terr. L.R. vii–xxiv. See also Harvey, Formerly Rupert's Land, Part II, in Obiter Dicta, 1948, Fall Issue, p. 37, for an account of the courts of the North-West Territories from 1880.

10 *R.* v. *Riel* (*No. 2*) (1885), 1 Terr. L.R. 23, 2 Man. R. 321; leave to appeal refused (1885), 10 App. Cas. 675.

11 Harvey, The Early Administration of Justice in the North West (1934), 1 Alta. L.Q. 1, at p. 15.

12 Harvey, *supra,* footnote 9, at p. 41.

13 *Ibid.*

14 *Scott* v. *A.-G. for Canada,* [1923] 3 W.W.R. 929, [1923] 4 D.L.R. 647, 40 T.L.R. 6 (P.C.); rev'g (1922), 64 S.C.R. 135, [1922] 2 W.W.R. 289.

15 *R.* v. *Joseph,* [1939] 2 W.W.R. 69, at p. 72, [1939] 3 D.L.R. 22, at p. 24.

16 *R.* v. *Constable,* [1936] 2 W.W.R. 273, at p. 277; [1936] 3 D.L.R. 391, at pp. 394–5. See also *R.* v. *Diamond* (1921), 16 Alta. L.R. 302, [1921] 2 W.W.R. 45, 59 D.L.R. 109.

17 *R.* v. *McLaren,* [1949] 1 W.W.R. 529, at p. 538, [1949] 2 D.L.R. 682, at p. 690. See also *R.* v. *Melyniuk,* [1930] 2 W.W.R. 179, [1930] 4 D.L.R. 462, 24 Alta. L.R. 545; *R.* v. *Olstad,* [1943] 1 W.W.R. 565, [1943] 2 D.L.R. 710.

18 *R.* v. *Brand,* [1928] 3 W.W.R. 641, [1929] 1 D.L.R. 815, 24 Alta. L.R. 5; *R.* v. *Barrs,* [1946] 1 W.W.R. 328, [1946] 2 D.L.R. 655.

19 *R.* v. *Bottley,* [1929] 2 W.W.R. 76, [1929] 2 D.L.R. 766.

20 *R.* v. *McDonald,* [1932] 3 W.W.R. 418, at p. 425, [1933] 1 D.L.R. 46, at p. 53, 26 Alta. L.R. 460, at p. 467.

21 *R.* v. *Lombard* (1914), 7 Alta. L.R. 270, at p. 272, 5 W.W.R. 1089, at p. 1089, 15 D.L.R. 613, at p. 614.

22 *R.* v. *Scown,* [1945] 1 W.W.R. 686, at p. 692, [1945] 4 D.L.R. 202, at p. 206.

23 *Gilbert* v. *R.* (1907), 38 S.C.R. 284, 12 C.C.C. 127. Both reports include the judgment of the court en banc and of the

Chief Justice of Canada. In affirming the admissibility of both statements, the Supreme Court held the second admissible on the ground that it was made in the presence of the accused.

24 [1914] A.C. 599.

25 [1927] S.C.R. 436, [1927] 4 D.L.R. 245.

26 *R.* v. *Hurd* (1913), 6 Alta. L.R. 112, 4 W.W.R. 185, 10 D.L.R. 475. See *R.* v. *Mandzuk,* [1946] 1 D.L.R. 521 (B.C.C.A.).

27 [1947] 1 W.W.R. 657, [1947] 2 D.L.R. 659. For criticism of the judgment, see Macdonald and Hart, The Admissibility of Confessions in Criminal Cases (1947), 25 Can. Bar Rev. 823, at pp. 847–849.

28 [1947] O.R. 105, [1947] 2 D.L.R. 213.

29 (1) *R.* v. *Hamlin,* [1929] 3 W.W.R. 258, [1930] 1 D.L.R. 497, 24 Alta. L.R. 296; overruled by *Paige* v. *R.*, [1948] S.C.R. 349, 92 C.C.C. 32. The latter case holds that unsworn evidence of a child cannot be corroborative in a charge to which section 1002 of the 1927 Code applies. Incidentally it approves a judgment of Harvey C.J. in *R.* v. *Whistnant* (1912), 5 Alta. L.R. 211, 8 D.L.R. 468, which says that unsworn evidence of a child cannot be corroborative in a charge to which section 1003 of the 1927 Code applies.
(2) *R.* v. *Searle,* [1929] 1 W.W.R. 491, 51 C.C.C. 128, 24 Alta. L.R. 37, on the effect of an explanation by the accused on a charge of receiving stolen goods. This decision appeared to have the approval of the Supreme Court of Canada in *Richler* v. *R.*, [1939] S.C.R. 101, [1939] 4 D.L.R. 281, but was adversely criticized in *Ungaro* v. *R.*, [1950] S.C.R. 430, [1950] 2 D.L.R. 593. See comment by W.J. Stainton on *Ungaro* (1951), 29 Can. Bar Rev. 885.
(3) *R.* v. *Ambler,* [1938] 2 W.W.R. 225, [1938] 3 D.L.R. 344. Harvey C.J. concurred in a judgment holding that a conviction must be set aside where the trial judge sitting without a jury has failed to declare that he had in mind the rule that it is dangerous to convict on the uncorroborated evidence of an accomplice. He restricted *Ambler* in *R.* v. *Joseph,* [1939] 2 W.W.R. 69, [1939] 3 D.L.R. 22, and in *R.* v. *Kagna,* [1943] 1 W.W.R. 33, [1943] 1 D.L.R. 289. Cases in other provinces which appear to be inconsistent with *Ambler* are cited in Tremeear, Criminal Code (5th ed., 1944) pp. 1273–74. In *Ungaro* v. *R.*, *supra* this footnote, the Supreme Court of Canada found it unnecessary to resolve the conflict. In *R.* v. *Perensky,* [1950] 1 W.W.R. 1090 (Alta.), Boyd McBride J. applied *Ambler* while expressing his disagreement.

30 *R.* v. *Quinton,* [1947] S.C.R. 234, 88 C.C.C. 231. The Alberta case is *R.* v. *Stewart,* [1938] 3 W.W.R. 631, [1939] 1 D.L.R. 233.

31 *R.* v. *Carter* (1916), 9 Alta. L.R. 481, 10 W.W.R. 602, 28 D.L.R. 606; cf. *R.* v. *Clarke* (1918), 13 Alta. L.R. 468, 41 D.L.R. 713.

32 *R.* v. *Emery* (1916), 10 Alta. L.R. 139, 33 D.L.R. 556.

33 [1922] 2 A.C. 128, [1922] 2 W.W.R. 30.

34 *R.* v. *Oakes,* [1923] 1 W.W.R. 1220, 39 C.C.C. 329; *R.* v. *McMicken,* [1923] 3 W.W.R. 879; 41 C.C.C. 156; *R.* v. *Kramer,* [1924] 1 W.W.R. 714, 41 C.C.C. 403. Compare *R.* v. *Fodor,* [1938] 1 W.W.R. 497, [1938] 2 D.L.R. 290. This was a case of a writ of prohibition, and Harvey C.J. took part.

35 *R.* v. *Bleiler* (1912), 4 Alta. L.R. 320, 2 W.W.R. 5, 1 D.L.R. 878.

36 *R.* v. *Stokes,* [1924] 3 W.W.R. 869, [1925] 1 D.L.R. 274, 21 Alta. L.R. 51; *R.* v. *Mainfroid,* [1926] 1 W.W.R. 465, [1926] 1 D.L.R. 1013, 22 Alta. L.R. 17.

37 *R.* v. *Butler,* [1939] 3 W.W.R. 433, [1939] 4 D.L.R. 592. See now Code section 285(4c), enacted in 1951.

38 (1920), 16 Alta. L.R. 1, [1920] 3 W.W.R. 1016, 34 C.C.C. 15. See also *R.* v. *Field* (1928), 23 Alta. L.R. 621, [1928] 3 W.W.R. 757, [1929] 1 D.L.R. 739.

39 *R.* v. *Wilmot,* [1940] 2 W.W.R. 401, [1940] 3 D.L.R. 358.

40 (1915), 9 Alta. L.R. 238, 9 W.W.R. 819, 28 D.L.R. 372. See also *R.* v. *Cohen* (1916), 9 Alta. L.R. 329, 10 W.W.R. 333, 28 D.L.R. 74.

41 (1916), 10 Alta. L.R. 164, [1917] 1

W.W.R. 415, 33 D.L.R. 658.

42 *R*. v. *Hoaglin* (1907), 12 C.C.C. 226.

43 Scott, Publishing False News (1952), 30 Can. Bar Rev. 37.

44 (1917), 10 Alta. L.R. 520, [1917] 1 W.W.R. 1459, 35 D.L.R. 274.

45 *R*. v. *Kaehler,* [1945] 1 W.W.R. 566; [1945] 3 D.L.R. 272; *R*. v. *Perzenowski,* [1946] 3 W.W.R. 678, [1947] 1 D.L.R. 705.

46 *Re Campbell and Cowper,* [1934] 3 W.W.R. 593, [1935] 1 D.L.R. 633, *per* McGillivray J.A. On the distinction between criminal and civil contempt, see *Tony Poje* v. *A.-G. B.C.,* [1953] 2 D.L.R. 785 (Can.).

47 *Hatfield* v. *Healy* (1911), 3 Alta. L.R. 327, at p. 332, 18 W.L.R. 512, at p. 518. In 1915 Harvey C.J. concurred in a judgment holding that the rule on comment on pending cases is not confined to jury trials, for a judge in his anxiety to remain uninfluenced may lean the other way: *Re Whiteside* (1915), 9 Alta. L.R. 232, 9 W.W.R. 846, 26 D.L.R. 615.

48 Note, Contempt by Publication (1950), 59 Yale L.J. 534, at p. 540.

49 *Bridges* v. *California* (1941), 314 U.S. 252; *Pennekamp* v. *Florida* (1946), 328 U.S. 331; *Craig* v. *Harney* (1947), 331 U.S. 367.

50 *Maryland* v. *Baltimore Radio Show* (1950), 338 U.S. 912. The Supreme Court refused to grant certiorari with the result that the decision of the highest Maryland court setting aside a summary punishment for contempt was left standing.

51 *R*. v. *Melyniuk* (1930), 24 Alta. L.R. 545, at p. 551, [1930] 2 W.W.R. 179, at p. 184, [1930] 4 D.L.R. 462, at p. 467. See also *R*. v. *Boardman* (1915), 9 Alta. L.R. 83, 6 W.W.R. 1304, 18 D.L.R. 698.

52 *R*. v. *Scheer* (1932), 26 Alta. L.R. 489, [1932] 3 W.W.R. 555, [1933] 1 D.L.R. 310.

53 *R*. v. *Abbott,* [1940] 3 W.W.R. 289, [1940] 4 D.L.R. 478.

54 (1882), 7 App. Cas. 829.

55 *Gold Seal Ltd*. v. *Dominion Express Company,* [1921] 1 W.W.R. 804, 58 D.L.R. 51, 16 Alta. L.R. 113; aff'd (1921), 62 S.C.R. 424, [1921] 3 W.W.R. 710, 62 D.L.R. 62. See *A.-G. for Ont*. v. *Canada Temperance Federation,* [1946] A.C. 193, [1946] 2 W.W.R. 1, [1946] 2 D.L.R. 1.

56 *Trimble* v. *Capling* (1927), 22 Alta. L.R. 536, [1927] 1 W.W.R. 188, [1927] 1 D.L.R. 717.

57 *R*. v. *Davenport* (1928), 23 Alta. L.R. 525, [1928] 1 W.W.R. 876, [1928] 2 D.L.R. 852.

58 *R*. v. *Eastern Terminal Elev. Co.,* [1925] S.C.R. 434, [1925] 3 D.L.R. 1.

59 *Trinca* v. *Duleba,* [1924] 2 W.W.R. 1177, 20 Alta. L.R. 493.

60 *Dowsett* v. *Edmunds,* [1926] 3 W.W.R. 447, [1926] 4 D.L.R. 796, 22 Alta. L.R. 292.

61 *Neilson* v. *Underwood,* [1934] S.C.R. 635, [1934] 4 D.L.R. 167, rev'g [1933] 2 W.W.R. 609, [1933] 4 D.L.R. 154.

62 *Gold Seal Ltd*. v. *Dominion Express Co*. (1920), 15 Alta. L.R. 377, [1920] 2 W.W.R. 761, 53 D.L.R. 547. In the later case between the same parties, footnote 55 *supra,* the Supreme Court judgment contains dicta supporting the view of Harvey C.J. and Stuart J.

63 *R. v. Osjorm,* [1927] 2 W.W.R. 703, [1927] 3 D.L.R. 1018, 22 Alta. L.R. 582.

64 *R*. v. *Canadian Pacific Railway Co*. (1905), 7 Terr. L.R. 286, 1 W.L.R. 89.

65 *C.P.R*. v. *The King* (1907), 39 S.C.R. 476, rev'g (1907), 6 W.L.R. 126.

66 *R*. v. *Massey-Harris Company* (1905), 6 Terr. L.R. 126, 1 W.L.R. 45, 9 C.C.C. 25.

67 *John Deere Plow Co*. v. *Wharton,* [1915] A.C. 330, 7 W.W.R. 706, 18 D.L.R. 353; *Great West Saddlery Co*. v. *The King,* [1921] 2 A.C. 91, [1921] 1 W.W.R. 1034, 58 D.L.R. 1.

68 *Re Sale of Shares Act,* [1929] A.C. 260, [1929] 1 W.W.R. 136.

69 Wegenast, Canadian Companies (1931) pp. 692–699.

70 *Lymburn* v. *Mayland,* [1932] A.C. 318, [1932] 1 W.W.R. 578, [1932] 2 D.L.R. 6, rev'g (1931), 25 Alta L.R. 310, [1931] 1 W.W.R. 735, [1931] 2 D.L.R. 698.

71 *Re Cust* (1915), 8 Alta. L.R. 308, 7 W.W.R. 1286, 21 D.L.R. 366. In this case Harvey C.J. suggested that a succession duty might not be a tax at all but

an appropriation by the province of a portion of the estate. On this point compare *Re Agricultural Land Relief Act,* [1938] 3 W.W.R. 186, [1938] 4 D.L.R. 28.

72 *Provincial Treasurer of Alberta* v. *Kerr,* [1933] A.C. 710, [1933] 3 W.W.R. 38, [1933] 4 D.L.R. 81.

73 *The King* v. *Caledonian Collieries, Limited,* [1928] A.C. 358, [1928] 2 W.W.R. 417, [1928] 3 D.L.R. 657, aff'g [1927] S.C.R. 257, [1927] 2 D.L.R. 70, rev'g (1926), 22 Alta. L.R. 245, [1926] 2 W.W.R. 280, [1926] 2 D.L.R. 1070.

74 *Kerr* v. *A.-G. for Alberta,* [1938] 3 W.W.R. 740, [1938] 3 D.L.R. 23; aff'd [1942] S.C.R. 435, [1942] 4 D.L.R. 289.

75 *Royal Bank* v. *The King,* [1913] A.C. 283, 3 W.W.R. 994, 9 D.L.R. 337, rev'g (1912), 4 Alta. L.R. 249, 1 W.W.R. 1159, 2 D.L.R. 762.

76 The writer has relied on Schedule 1, R.S.A., 1922, p. 2996, S.A. 1942, p. 337, S.A. 1954, p. 659.

77 *Re Power of Disallowance,* [1938] S.C.R. 71, [1938] 2 D.L.R. 8.

78 *Re Alberta Legislation,* [1938] S.C.R. 100, [1938] 2 D.L.R. 81. The Privy Council declined to consider the validity of two of the bills, the Credit of Alberta Regulation Bill and the Publication of Accurate News and Information Bill, and upheld the judgment of the Supreme Court on the third, respecting the taxation of banks: [1939] A.C. 117, [1938] 3 W.W.R. 337, [1938] 4 D.L.R. 433.

79 *Credit Foncier Franco-Canadian* v. *Ross,* [1937] 2 W.W.R. 353, [1937] 3 D.L.R. 365.

80 *A.-G. for Alberta and Winstanley* v. *Atlas Lumber Co. Ltd.,* [1941] S.C.R. 87, [1941] 1 D.L.R. 625, aff'g [1940] 2 W.W.R. 437, [1940] 3 D.L.R. 648.

81 *A.-G. for Alberta* v. *A.-G. for Canada* (Debt Adjustment Act), [1943] A.C. 356, [1943] 1 W.W.R. 378, [1943] 2 D.L.R. 1, aff'g [1942] S.C.R. 31, [1942] 1 D.L.R. 1.

82 *Re Legal Proceedings Suspension Act,* [1942] 2 W.W.R. 536, [1942] 3 D.L.R. 318.

83 [1943] A.C. 536, [1943] 2 W.W.R. 33, [1943] 4 D.L.R. 1.

84 *Roy* v. *Plourde,* [1943] S.C.R. 262, [1943] 3 D.L.R. 81, rev'g [1942] 2 W.W.R. 607, [1942] 3 D.L.R. 646.

85 *Independent Order of Foresters* v. *Leth. Nor. Irrig. Dist.,* [1937] 2 D.L.R. 109, [1937] 1 W.W.R. 414.

86 *I.O.F.* v. *Leth. Nor. Irrig. Dist.,* [1938] 3 D.L.R. 89, [1938] 2 W.W.R. 194, aff'g [1937] 4 D.L.R. 398, [1937] 3 W.W.R. 424.

87 *I.O.F.* v. *The King,* [1939] 2 D.L.R. 671, [1939] 1 W.W.R. 700, aff'g [1939] 2 D.L.R. 53, [1939] 1 W.W.R. 275.

88 *The King* v. *I.O.F.,* [1940] A.C. 502, [1940] 2 D.L.R. 273. For later unsuccessful efforts by the province to prevent I.O.F. from collecting its judgment against *Leth. Northern,* see [1944] 1 D.L.R. 660 and [1945] 1 D.L.R. 298. Harvey C.J. took part in both these cases, but they are not of constitutional interest.

89 See footnote 78 *supra*.

90 *A.-G. for Alberta* v. *A.-G. for Canada* (Alberta Bill of Rights Act), [1947] A.C. 503, [1947] 2 W.W.R. 401, [1947] 4 D.L.R. 1, aff'g in part [1947] 1 D.L.R. 337.

91 (1884), 9 App. Cas. 117.

92 There is an exception where a province purports to delegate its powers to Parliament. See *A.-G. for N.S.* v. *A.-G. for Can.,* [1951] S.C.R. 31, [1950] 4 D.L.R. 369; but compare *P.E.I. Potato Marketing Board* v. *Willis,* [1952] 2 S.C.R. 392, [1952] 4 D.L.R. 146.

93 *Re Royalite Oil Company Limited* (1931), 25 Alta. L.R. 206, [1931] 1 W.W.R. 484, [1931] 2 D.L.R. 418.

94 *Credit Foncier Franco-Canadian* v. *Ross,* [1937] 2 W.W.R. 353, [1937] 3 D.L.R. 365.

95 *Shannon* v. *Lower Mainland Dairy Products Board,* [1938] A.C. 708, [1938] 2 W.W.R. 604.

96 *Re the Small Debts Recovery Act* (1917), 12 Alta. L.R. 32, [1917] 3 W.W.R. 698, 37 D.L.R. 170. Earlier cases on the same constitutional problem were:

(1) *Colonial Investment and Loan Company* v. *Grady* (1915), 8 Alta. L.R. 496, 8 W.W.R. 995, 24 D.L.R.

176. The court held invalid a statute giving to the master in chambers a jurisdiction as unlimited as that of a supreme court judge in mortgage actions.

(2) *Polson Iron Works* v. *Munns* (1915), 9 W.W.R. 231, 24 D.L.R. 18. The court held valid rules of court conferring certain powers on the master in chambers.

97 *Roskiwich* v. *Roskiwich* (1931), 26 Alta. L.R. 137, [1931] 3 W.W.R. 614, [1932] 1 D.L.R. 135. See also *Kazakewich* v. *Kazakewich,* [1936] 3 W.W.R. 699, [1937] 1 D.L.R. 548.

98 *Clubine* v. *Clubine,* [1937] O.R. 636 (C.A.); *Krassman* v. *Krassman,* [1937] 3 W.W.R. 349 (Sask.).

99 *Re Adoption Act,* [1938] S.C.R. 398, [1938] 3 D.L.R. 497.

100 *Toronto* v. York, [1938] A.C. 415, [1938] 1 W.W.R. 452, [1938] 1 D.L.R. 593; *Labour Relations Board of Saskatchewan* v. *John East Iron Works, Limited,* [1949] A.C. 134, [1948] 2 W.W.R. 1055, [1948] 4 D.L.R. 673.

101 *Board of Public Utility Commissioners* v. *Model Dairies,* [1936] 3 W.W.R. 601, [1937] 1 D.L.R. 95.

102 *Board* v. *Board,* [1919] A.C. 956, [1919] W.W.R. 940, 48 D.L.R. 13, aff'g (1918), 13 Alta. L.R. 362, [1918] 2 W.W.R. 633, 41 D.L.R. 286.

103 *McCormack* v. *McCormack* (1920), 15 Alta. L.R. 490, [1920] 2 W.W.R. 714, 55 D.L.R. 386.

104 [1926] A.C. 444, [1926] 1 W.W.R. 742, [1926] 2 D.L.R. 762, *sub nom., A.-G. for Alberta* v. *Cook.*

105 *Leboeuf* v. *Leboeuf* (1928), 23 Alta L.R. 328, [1928] 1 W.W.R. 423, [1928] 2 D.L.R. 23.

106 *Molnar* v. *Molnar,* [1948] 2 W.W.R. 1165, [1949] 1 D.L.R. 263.

107 *Smith* v. *Smith,* [1952] 2 S.C.R. 312, [1952] 3 D.L.R. 449.

108 [1948] A.C. 274.

109 *H* v. *H* (1927), 22 Alta. L.R. 565, [1927] 2 W.W.R. 366, [1927] 3 D.L.R. 481.

110 *Sherman* v. *King's Proctor,* [1936] 2 W.W.R. 152, [1936] 3 D.L.R. 90.

111 [1943] A.C. 517. For a discussion of the whole subject, in particular of the effect of *Blunt* v. *Blunt* in Canada, see Power, The Law of Divorce in Canada (1948) pp. 67–81.

112 *Shaw* v. *Shaw,* [1944] 2 W.W.R. 243, [1944] 4 D.L.R. 9.

113 *Re Plummer Estate,* [1941] 3 W.W.R. 788, [1942] 1 D.L.R. 34.

114 *Sheaser* v. *Sheaser* (1926), 22 Alta. L.R. 261, [1926] 2 W.W.R. 389, [1926] 3 D.L.R. 196.

115 *Chertkow* v. *Chertkow* (1929), 24 Alta. L.R. 188, at p. 199, [1929] 2 W.W.R. 257, at pp. 266–7, [1929] 3 D.L.R. 339, at p. 348. The judgment was affirmed, [1930] S.C.R. 335, [1930] 1 D.L.R. 137.

116 *Quinn* v. *Beales* (1924), 20 Alta. L.R. 620, [1924] 3 W.W.R. 337, [1924] 4 D.L.R. 635.

117 *Edwards* v. *Porter,* [1925] A.C. 1.

118 *Mutual Life Assurance Co.* v. *Douglas* (1918), 57 S.C.R. 243, rev'g [1918] 1 W.W.R. 690, 39 D.L.R. 601, 13 Alta. L.R. 18.

119 (1920), 61 S.C.R. 109, 56 D.L.R. 463, aff'g 3 W.W.R. 634, 49 D.L.R. 187, 15 Alta. L.R. 17.

120 *Setter* v. *Forbes* (1914), 8 Alta. L.R. 191, 6 W.W.R. 116, 18 D.L.R. 789, *per* Harvey C.J. at trial.

121 *Teel* v. *Forbes,* (1924), 20 Alta. L.R. 559 [1924] 2 W.W.R. 996, [1924] 3 D.L.R. 670. Harvey C.J. did not take part.

122 *Richert Co.* v. *Forbes,* [1937] 3 W.W.R. 632, at p. 635, [1937] 4 D.L.R. 540, at p. 543. The assurance fund provisions were widened in 1935, but the registrar's error in this case occurred before 1935. In 1949 an important restriction was placed on the right to claim against the fund where the mistake relates to minerals. The claimant is entitled only to the amount he paid out plus a maximum of $5,000. In cases arising since the Chief Justice's death some companies have lost oil rights worth many thousands of dollars as the result of mistakes in the Land Titles Office. See *Imperial Oil Co. Ltd.* v. *Turta,* (1954) 12 W.W.R. (N.S.) 97 (Sup. Ct. of Can.).

123 *Re McLeod* (1929), 24 Alta. L.R. 565, [1929] 2 W.W.R. 252, [1929] 4 D.L.R. 659.

124 *Spooner* v. *Leyton,* [1939] 2 W.W.R. 237, [1939] 3 D.L.R. 148. To ap-

preciate fully the judgment, one should examine the history of the section and the earlier decisions on it.

125 *Essery* v. *Essery*, [1947] 2 W.W.R. 1044, [1948] 1 D.L.R. 405.

126 See *Pinsky* v. *Wass*, [1953] 1 S.C.R. 399, [1953] 2 D.L.R. 545; *McColl Frontenac Oil Co.* v. *Hamilton*, [1953] 1 S.C.R. 127, [1953] 1 D.L.R. 721.

127 *Kromm* v. *Kaiser* (1915), 8 W.W.R. 239, 8 Alta. L.R. 287, 21 D.L.R. 700; *Greene* v. *Appleton* (1915), 8 W.W.R. 867, 9 Alta. L.R. 36, 25 D.L.R. 333.

128 *Franco-Belgian Investment Co.* v. *Duggan* (1920), 15 Alta. L.R. 243, [1920] 1 W.W.R. 728, 51 D.L.R. 602.

129 *Stankievich* v. *Armacost*, [1926] 1 W.W.R. 758, [1926] 2 D.L.R. 401, 22 Alta. L.R. 56. See also *Chekaluck* v. *Sallenback*, [1948] 1 W.W.R. 510, [1948] 2 D.L.R. 452. Where the agreement reserves coal, but the title reserves to a third party all coal "and the right to work the same", a special problem arises: see *Fuller* v. *Garneau* (1921), 61 S.C.R. 450, 58 D.L.R. 642; *Knight Sugar Co.* v. *Webster*, [1930] S.C.R. 518, [1930] 4 D.L.R. 343.

130 [1916] 1 A.C. 719; 8 W.W.R. 1263.

131 (1843), 10 M. & W. 546.

132 *Grant Trunk Pac. Ry. Co.* v. *Earl*, [1923] S.C.R. 397, [1923] 2 W.W.R. 123, [1923] 2 D.L.R. 741, rev'g [1922] 3 W.W.R. 406, 69 D.L.R. 436, which affirmed [1922] 3 W.W.R. 27, 66 D.L.R. 401.

133 Principal cases are *Harnovis* v. *Calgary* (1913), 6 Alta. L.R. 1, 4 W.W.R. 263, 11 D.L.R. 3, aff'd (1913), 48 S.C.R. 494, 5 W.W.R. 869, 15 D.L.R. 411; *Critchley* v. *Can. Nor. Ry.*, [1917] 2 W.W.R. 538, 12 Alta. L.R. 522, 34 D.L.R. 245; *Scott* v. *Calgary* (1927), 22 Alta. L.R. 467; *Root* v. *McKinney*, [1930] S.C.R. 337, [1930] 2 D.L.R. 984, aff'g [1929] 2 W.W.R. 340, [1929] 4 D.L.R. 138; *Green* v. *C.N.R.*, [1932] S.C.R. 689, rev'g (1931), 26 Alta. L.R. 49; *Jeremy* v. *Fontaine* (1931), 26 Alta. L.R. 499.

134 *Royal Trust Co.* v. *C.P.R.*, [1921] 2 W.W.R. 712, 16 Alta. L.R. 523, 60 D.L.R. 379; varied [1922] 3 W.W.R. 24, 67 D.L.R. 518 (P.C.) This was a case on quantum of damages, but the Chief Justice's statement applied to findings of fact generally.

135 *Wandeleer* v. *Dawson*, [1936] 3 W.W.R. 478.

136 *Arcand* v. *Kaup*, [1939] 1 W.W.R. 615, [1939] 2 D.L.R. 456. See *London Passenger Transport Board* v. *Upson*, [1949] A.C. 155, where the comments on this point tend to support the view of the majority in *Arcand*.

137 [1940] 1 W.W.R. 385, [1940] 2 D.L.R. 47. The action was under the Fatal Accidents Act. Harvey C.J. stated that, notwithstanding his concurrence in the main with the reasons for judgment of Ford J.A., he did not wish to bind himself to the view that the statute is a complete and exact adoption of the admiralty rule in all respects. The writer is not clear what Harvey C.J. meant by this reservation.

138 [1952] 4 D.L.R. 1 (P.C.). A number of cases in the last five years hold one of the parties solely to blame where one might think that blame might have been apportioned under the statute. In other words, there appears to be a tendency to cut down the scope of the act. See, for example, *Bechthold* v. *Osbaldeston*, [1953] 4 D.L.R. 783 (Sup. Ct. of Can.).

139 *Jones* v. *Shafer*, [1948] S.C.R. 166, [1948] 4 D.L.R. 81, rev'g [1947] 2 W.W.R. 49, [1947] 4 D.L.R. 294, is a case in which the Chief Justice, for the majority, held the defendant solely to blame and the Supreme Court found him not negligent at all. The case is not important on the Contributory Negligence Act.

140 *White* v. *Henton*, [1930] 2 D.L.R. 959, 24 Alta. L.R. 423, [1930] 1 W.W.R. 685.

141 [1921] 2 W.W.R. 218, 59 D.L.R. 505, 16 Alta. L.R. 275; see also *Turpie* v. *Oliver*, [1925] 3 W.W.R. 687; [1925] 4 D.L.R. 1023, 21 Alta. L.R. 508.

142 *Winnipeg Electric Co.* v. *Geel*, [1932] A.C. 690, [1932] 3 W.W.R. 49, [1932] 4 D.L.R. 51.

143 See the comment of Duff C.J. in *United Motor Services* v. *Hutson*, [1937] S.C.R. 294, [1937] 1 D.L.R. 737; also the editorial note to *Scrimgeour* v. *American Lutheran Church*, [1947] 1

D.L.R. 677, [1947] 1 W.W.R. 120.

144 *Burd* v. *Macaulay* (1924), 20 Alta. L.R. 352, [1924] 2 W.W.R. 393, [1924] 2 D.L.R. 815.

145 *Eisener* v. *Maxwell,* [1951] 3 D.L.R. 345, 28 M.P.R. 213 (N.S.C.A.), where *Burd* was not followed; *Mantey* v. *Spanks,* [1952] 3 D.L.R. 783 (B.C.C.A.), where *Burd* was followed.

146 *Turpie* v. *Oliver* (1925), 21 Alta. L.R. 508, at p. 511, [1925] 3 W.W.R. 687, at p. 690, [1925] 4 D.L.R. 1023, at p. 1025; see also *McLean* v. *Y.M.C.A.* (1918), 14 Alta. L.R. 58, [1918] 3 W.W.R. 522.

147 *Strapazon* v. *Oliphant Munson Collieries* (1920), 15 Alta. L.R. 470, at pp. 472–73, [1920] 2 W.W.R. 793, at p. 795, 53 D.L.R. 124, at p. 126.

148 *Jackson* v. *C.P.R.* (1915), 9 Alta. L.R. 137, at p. 140, 8 W.W.R. 1043, at p. 1044, 24 D.L.R. 380, at p. 381.

149 *Knight* v. *Grand Trunk Pacific Development Company* (1926), 22 Alta. L.R. 237, at p. 244, [1926] 2 W.W.R. 557, at p. 562, [1926], 4 D.L.R. 87, at p. 92; aff'd [1926] S.C.R. 674, [1927] 1 D.L.R. 498.

150 [1929] A.C. 358.

151 *Haines* v. *Brewster,* [1938] 2 W.W.R. 285, [1938] 3 D.L.R. 246.

152 [1909] 2 K.B. 820.

153 *Nyberg* v. *Provost Municipal Hospital Board,* [1927] S.C.R. 226, [1927] 1 D.L.R. 969; rev'g (1926), 22 Alta. L.R. 1, [1926] 1 W.W.R. 890, [1926] 2 D.L.R. 563.

154 *Abel* v. *Cooke and Lloydminster and District Hospital Board,* [1938] 1 W.W.R. 49, [1938] 1 D.L.R. 170.

155 *Strapazon* v. *Oliphant Munson Collieries, Limited* (1920), 15 Alta. L.R. 470, [1920] 2 W.W.R. 793, 53 D.L.R. 124.

156 *Pietrzak* v. *Rocheleau* (1928), 23 Alta. L.R. 337, [1928] 1 W.W.R. 428, [1928] 2 D.L.R. 46.

157 *Purmal* v. *Medicine Hat* (1908), 1 Alta. L.R. 209, 7 W.L.R. 437.

158 *Maunsell* v. *Lethbridge Northern Irrigation District* (1925), 21 Alta. L.R. 499, [1925] 3 W.W.R. 202, [1925] 4 D.L.R. 70.

159 *Northwestern Utilities Limited* v. *London Guarantee and Accident Co.,* [1936] A.C. 108, [1935] 3 W.W.R. 446, [1935] 4 D.L.R. 737, aff'g [1934] 3 W.W.R. 641, [1935] 1 D.L.R. 135. For Lord Wright's own discussion, see The Northwestern Utilities Case, in Lord Wright of Durley, Legal Essays and Addresses (1939).

160 *Bordeaux* v. *Jobs,* [1913] 6 Alta. L.R. 440, 5 W.W.R. 481, 14 D.L.R. 451.

161 (1856), 2 El. & Bl. 216.

162 *G* v. *B and B* (1926), 22 Alta. L.R. 126, at p. 130, [1926] 1 W.W.R. 324, at p. 327, [1926] 1 D.L.R. 855, at p. 857.

163 *Edmonds* v. *Armstrong Funeral Home Ltd.* (1930), 25 Alta. L.R. 173, [1930] 3 W.W.R. 649, [1931] 1 D.L.R. 676. See also *Miner* v. *C.P.R.* (1911), 3 Alta. L.R. 408, 18 W.L.R. 476.

164 *Crum* v. *Big 4 Transfer & Storage Co. Ltd.* (1930), 25 Alta. L.R. 35, [1930] 2 W.W.R. 337, [1930] 4 D.L.R. 486. In *Watkins* v. *Cottell,* [1916] 1 K.B. 10, Avory J. held that a carrier cannot be strictly liable, unless the contract so provides or unless he is a common carrier.

165 Estoppel is of course often classed as a rule of evidence, but this is a convenient place to mention it. The interesting point about the Chief Justice's judgments on this subject is that in three important cases he found an estoppel to be raised against a party to the action, but in all these was reversed when the case went to a higher court. See *Home Assurance Co.* v. *Lindal,* [1934] S.C.R. 33, [1934] 1 D.L.R. 497; *Imperial Bank* v. *Begley,* [1936] 3 D.L.R. 1 (P.C.); *Keyes* v. *Royal Bank of Canada,* [1947] S.C.R. 377, [1947] 3 D.L.R. 161.

166 [1936] 3 W.W.R. 601, [1937] 1 D.L.R. 95. See *Re Securities Act,* [1948] O.R. 70, where the court adopted the interpretation of Harvey C.J. of a statutory provision that the board "shall not be bound by the technical rules of legal evidence".

167 *Williams* v. *Local Union 1562, U.M.W.A.* (1918), 14 Alta. L.R. 251, [1919] 1 W.W.R. 217, 45 D.L.R. 150; rev'd in part (1919), 59 S.C.R. 240, [1919] 3 W.W.R. 828, 49 D.L.R. 578.

168 *R.* v. *Reners* (1926), 22 Alta. L.R. 81,

[1926] 2 D.L.R. 236, aff'd [1926] S.C.R. 499, [1926] 3 D.L.R. 669. This case was decided before section 501(g) was inserted in the Criminal Code. Nevertheless it may still be good law on the facts. See *Williams* v. *Aristocratic Restaurants,* [1951] S.C.R. 762, [1951] 3 D.L.R. 769, *per* Kerwin J.

169 *Corbett* v. *Canadian National Printing Trades Union,* [1943] 2 W.W.R. 401, [1943] 4 D.L.R. 441.

170 *Wright* v. *Calgary Herald,* [1938] 1 W.W.R. 1, [1938] 1 D.L.R. 111.

171 *Hayhurst* v. *Innisfail Motors Ltd.,* [1935] 1 W.W.R. 385, at p. 391, [1935] 2 D.L.R. 272, at p. 277.

172 *Hurov* v. *Clyde,* [1943] 2 W.W.R. 470, at p. 472, [1943] 3 D.L.R. 701, at p. 703. See also *Prudential Insurance Co.* v. *Security Trust Co.,* [1942] 3 W.W.R. 494.

173 R.O., 1898, c. 21. The rules are set out in full with the ordinance.

174 The authority for these rules was the Supreme Court Act, 1907, c. 3. This act and the Judicature Ordinance were replaced by the Judicature Act, 1919, c. 3.

175 The Judicature Ordinance, R.O., 1905, c. 21, s. 21.

176 See *Augustino* v. *Canadian Northwestern Railway Co.* (1928), 23 Alta. L.R. 351, [1928] 1 W.W.R. 481, [1928] 1 D.L.R. 1110.

177 For example, *McDougall & Secord Ltd.* v. *Merchants Bank* (1919), 14 Alta. L.R. 564, at p. 566, [1919] 1 W.W.R. 830, at p. 831, 46 D.L.R. 672, at p. 673; *Webster* v. *Solloway, Mills & Co. Ltd.* (1930), 24 Alta. L.R. 632, at p. 633, [1930] 2 W.W.R. 514, at p. 515.

178 Plucknett, A Concise History of the Common Law (4th ed., 1948) p. 314.

179 Maxwell, Interpretation of Statutes (10th ed., 1953) p. 26.

180 *Godfrey* v. *Marshall* (1917), 11 Alta. L.R. 37, at p. 42.

181 *Cummings* v. *Reister,* [1948] 1 W.W.R. 237, at p. 239, [1948] 2 D.L.R. 153, at p. 154.

182 *Duggan* v. *Waldleigh and Rankin* (1912), 4 Alta. L.R. 114, 1 W.W.R. 595, 1 D.L.R. 871; *Chadwick* v. *Stuckey* (1912), 5 Alta. L.R. 145, 3 W.W.R. 549, 8 D.L.R. 357.

183 See, on garnishee summons: *Mohr* v. *Parks, Brown and National Manufacturing Co.* (1910), 3 Alta. L.R. 252, 15 W.L.R. 250, *Beaubier* v. *Lloyd* (1918), 13 Alta. L.R. 47, [1918] 1 W.W.R. 772, 39 D.L.R. 439, *Adams* v. *Adams* (1921), 17 Alta. L.R. 109, [1922] 1 W.W.R. 47, 62 D.L.R. 721, *McParland* v. *Seymour* (1925), 21 Alta. L.R. 525, [1925] 3 W.W.R. 666, [1925] 4 D.L.R. 944, and *Banque Canadienne Nationale* v. *Labine,* [1933] 1 W.W.R. 385; [1933] 2 D.L.R. 432; on bills of sale: *MacKenzie* v. *Royal Bank* (1931), 25 Alta. L.R. 281, [1931] 2 W.W.R. 129, [1931] 3 D.L.R. 884, rev'd [1932] S.C.R. 524, [1932] 2 D.L.R. 12, and *Kendrew* v. *Cushing,* [1946] 3 W.W.R. 571, 27 C.B.R. 272; and on caveats: *Wilkinson* v. *Shackleton* (1930), 24 Alta. L.R. 377, [1930] 1 W.W.R. 721, [1930] 3 D.L.R. 304.

184 [1933] 1 W.W.R. 321, [1933] 2 D.L.R. 244; aff'd for different reasons, [1936] A.C. 177, [1936] 1 W.W.R. 33, [1936] 1 D.L.R. 321. In a later case, where a magistrate had held court in a private room in the R.C.M.P. barracks, the Chief Justice loyally said, "The well-established common-law right of the public to have access to court trials was quite recently emphasized by the Judicial Committee in an appeal from this province, *McPherson* v. *McPherson*", and the conviction was set aside: *R.* v. *Greenwood,* [1948] 1 W.W.R. 322, at p. 328, [1948] 2 D.L.R. 347, at p. 352.

185 *McDougall & Secord, Ltd.* v. *Merchants Bank* (1919), 14 Alta. L.R. 564, [1919] 1 W.W.R. 830, 46 D.L.R. 672.

186 *Webster* v. *Solloway, Mills & Co., Ltd.* (1930), 24 Alta. L.R. 632, [1930] 2 W.W.R. 514.

187 *Talbourdet* v. *Junker* (1927), 22 Alta. L.R. 435, [1927] 1 W.W.R. 495, [1927] 2 D.L.R. 175.

188 *Security Trust Co.* v. *National Trust Co.* (1928), 24 Alta L.R. 11, [1928] 1 W.W.R. 687, [1928] 2 D.L.R. 393.

189 *Russian Mercantile Co.* v. *Sloboda* (1927), 23 Alta. L.R. 1, [1927] 3 W.W.R. 451. [1927] 4 D.L.R. 931.

190 Judicature Ordinance, R.O., 1905, rule 170. The various jury ordinances and

acts do not require notice in this account.

191 He so stated in *Godfrey* v. *Marshall* (1917), 11 Alta. L.R. 37, at p. 42.

192 As Stuart J. said later in *Salter* v. *Calgary* (1916), 9 Alta. L.R. 334. at p. 335, 10 W.W.R. 173, at p. 174, 27 D.L.R. 584, at p. 585.

193 *Godfrey* v. *Marshall* (1917), 11 Alta L.R. 37, [1917] 3 W.W.R. 1097; *Hubbard* v. *Edmonton* (1917), 37 D.L.R. 458, [1917] 3 W.W.R. 732, 12 Alta. L.R. 115; and *Hogan* v. *Northern Construction Co.* (1918), 13 Alta. L.R. 230, [1918] 1 W.W.R. 652.

194 *McIntyre* v. *Alberta Pacific Grain Co.* (1918), 14 Alta. L.R. 373, [1918] 3 W.W.R. 906, 43 D.L.R. 682.

195 *Duxbury* v. *Calgary* (*No. 2*), [1940] 1 W.W.R. 174, [1940] 1 D.L.R. 684.

196 *Godfrey* v. *Marshall* (1917), 11 Alta L.R. 37, at p. 43.

197 *E.g., R.* v. *Greenwood,* footnote 184 *supra; Re Royalite Oil Co.*, [1931] 2 D.L.R. 418.

198 *Frank* v. *Gazelle Live Stock Company* (1906), 6 Terr. L.R. 392, at pp. 394–395, 5 W.L.R. 573, at p. 575.

199 *E.g., R.* v. *John Irwin Co., Ltd.* (1919), 14 Alta. L.R. 600, [1919] 2 W.W.R. 226, 31 C.C.C. 54.

200 *Bennefield* v. *Knox* (1914), 7 Alta. L.R. 346, 6 W.W.R. 737, 17 D.L.R. 398; following *Ward* v. *Serrell* (1910), 3 Alta. L.R. 138. In one case, however, the Chief Justice accepted the argument that, although two provincial statutes were similar in form, the Alberta legislature may not have known of the decision in the other province interpreting its act, or even of the existence of the act, and so he need not follow the decision: *Anderton* v. *Soroka* (1925), 21 Alta. L.R. 100, [1925] 1 W.W.R. 1019, [1925] 2 D.L.R. 488. In another case he held that the rule in *Bennefield* does not apply where the statute of the jurisdiction of origin received no judicial interpretation until after the Alberta act was passed: *Deugau* v. *Morrison,* [1938] 3 W.W.R. 269, [1938] 4 D.L.R. 353.

201 *Re Western Canada Fire Insurance Co.* (1915), 8 Alta. L.R. 348, 7 W.W.R. 1365, 22 D.L.R. 19. The decision, concurred in by Harvey C.J., was delivered by Beck J.

202 *R.* v. *Girvin* (1910), 3 Alta. L.R. 387, 18 W.L.R. 482.

203 From 1914 to 1921 the court en banc was called the Appellate Division.

204 (1919), 14 Alta L.R. 601, [1919] 3 W.W.R. 409, 33 C.C.C. 371.

205 The act gave magistrates jurisdiction only where the amount of the penalty or forfeiture was $500 or less. On a charge of possessing an unlicensed still, the maximum fine was $500, but added to this was a forfeiture of twice the amount of the licence fee. If these two amounts are to be added together to determine jurisdiction, then it is obvious that the magistrate has no jurisdiction on this particular charge.

206 (1920), 16 Alta. L.R. 19, at pp. 21–22, [1920] 3 W.W.R. 1051, at p. 1053, 55 D.L.R. 524, at p. 525.

207 In a previous case he had said, "I have little respect for the maxim *stare decisis . . .* ": *Reventlow-Criminil* v. *R.M. of Streamstown* (1919), 15 Alta. L.R. 204, at p. 219, [1920] 1 W.W.R. 577, at p. 586, 52 D.L.R. 266, at p. 274.

208 *R.* v. *Glenfield,* [1934] 3 W.W.R. 465, at p. 467, [1935] 1 D.L.R. 37, at pp. 38–39.

209 *R.* v. *McLennan* (1905), 7 Terr. L.R. 309, 2 W.L.R. 227, 10 C.C.C. 1.

210 *R.* v. *Thompson* (1911), 4 Alta. L.R. 18, at p. 19, 1 W.W.R. 277, at p. 278, 21 C.C.C. 80, at p. 82.

211 *R.* v. *Covert* (1916), 10 Alta. L.R. 349, [1917] 1 W.W.R. 919, 34 D.L.R. 662.

212 *R.* v. *Morin* (1917), 12 Alta. L.R. 101, [1917] 3 W.W.R. 693, 38 D.L.R. 617; *R.* v. *Nat Bell Liquors Limited* (*No. 2*) (1921), 16 Alta. L.R. 149, [1921] 1 W.W.R. 563, 56 D.L.R. 523.

213 (1926), 22 Alta. L.R. 113, [1926] 1 W.W.R. 832, [1926] 2 D.L.R. 379.

214 *Banque Canadienne Nationale* v. *Tencha,* [1928] S.C.R. 26, [1927] 4 D.L.R. 665.

215 *F. Moyer Boot & Shoe Co.* v. *Moellendorf* (1930), 25 Alta. L.R. 76, [1930] 3 W.W.R. 311, [1931] 1 D.L.R. 360.

216 Pollock, Judicial Caution and Valour (1929), 45 L. Q. Rev. 293. For sub-

sequent references to this theme see Note (1946), 62 L.Q. Rev. 5; *Candler* v. *Crane, Christmas and Co.*, [1951] 2 K.B. 164, [1951] 1 All. E.R. 426.

217 See also, in the law of wills, *Re Mewburn Estate,* [1938] 2 W.W.R. 433, [1938] 3 D.L.R. 459, rev'd [1939] S.C.R. 75, [1939] 1 D.L.R. 257.

218 *Fraser* v. *Kirkpatrick* (1907), 6 Terr. L.R. 403, 5 W.L.R. 287.

219 *R.* v. *Cyr* (1917), 12 Alta. L.R. 320, [1917] 3 W.W.R. 849, 38 D.L.R. 601.

220 *Edwards* v. *A.-G. for Canada* ("Persons"), [1930] A.C. 124, [1929] 3 W.W.R. 479, rev'g [1928] S.C.R. 276, [1928] 4 D.L.R. 98. For an account of the surrounding events, see Sanders, Emily Murphy: Crusader (1945).

221 *Re Simpson Estate* (1927), 23 Alta. L.R. 374, [1927] 3 W.W.R. 534, [1927] 4 D.L.R. 817; aff'd [1928] S.C.R. 329, [1928] 3 D.L.R. 773. The Supreme Court did not consider it necessary to decide the point, because the wording of the will did not bring the rule into play.

222 *R.* v. *Nat Bell Liquors Limited* (*No. 2*) (1921), 16 Alta. L.R. 149, at pp. 154–155, [1921] 1 W.W.R. 563, at p. 567, 56 D.L.R. 523, at p. 544. For other comments to the same effect see *Mayland* v. *Lymburn,* [1931] 1 W.W.R. 735, [1931] 2 D.L.R. 698, 25 Alta. L.R. 310.

223 *Re McLeod* (1929), 24 Alta. L.R. 565.

224 *The King* v. *C.N.R.*, [1921] 1 W.W.R. 1178, rev'd in part (1922), 64 S.C.R. 264, which was aff'd, [1923] 3 W.W.R. 547 (P.C.).

225 Cardozo, The Nature of the Judicial Process (1921) p. 20.

226 *Klein* v. *Sanderson* (1928), 23 Alta. L.R. 467, at p. 469.

227 Another example is *Arcand* v. *Kaup,* [1939] 2 D.L.R. 456, at p. 473, where the *Chief Justice*, in dissent, gave as a reason for holding that the driver on a main highway should be entitled to assume that others will yield to him, the probability that the legislature wanted to protect the traffic on main highways and so encourage the tourist traffic.

228 *Alexo Coal Co., Ltd.* v. *Livett,* [1948] 1 W.W.R. 195, at p. 200, [1948] 2 D.L.R. 34, at p. 38. The Chief Justice, in dissent, held that the agreement remained binding on the union.

229 *Garbutt Business College Ltd.* v. *Henderson,* [1939] 3 W.W.R. 257, at p. 262, [1939] 4 D.L.R. 151, at pp. 168–169. The court unanimously held that the covenant was binding.

230 *Re Harris* (1910), 2 Alta. L.R. 503, at p. 506, 13 W.L.R. 131, at p. 134.

231 *Re Blaylock* (1914), 7 Alta. L.R. 163, 6 W.W.R. 606, 16 D.L.R. 487; *Re V* (1924), 20 Alta. L.R. 585, [1924] 3 W.W.R. 552, [1924] 4 D.L.R. 852.

232 *Ex parte Pyke* (1865), 34 L.J. (Q.B.) 121, *per* Cockburn C.J. at p. 123.

233 *Re Harris* (1914), 7 Alta. L.R. 272, 6 W.W.R. 628, 17 D.L.R. 103.

234 *Re Knox* (1914), 7 Alta. L.R. 409, 6 W.W.R. 1586, 20 D.L.R. 546.

235 *Sheaser* v. *Sheaser* (1926), 22 Alta. L.R. 261, [1926] 2 W.W.R. 389, [1926] 3 D.L.R. 196.

236 *R.* v. *Shandro* (1923), 19 Alta. L.R. 129, [1923] 1 W.W.R. 405, [1923] 1 D.L.R. 722; and the Appellate Division ordered a new trial on that ground.

237 *National Trust Co., Ltd.* v. *Palace Theatre Ltd.* (1928), 23 Alta. L.R. 427, at p. 436, [1928] 1 W.W.R. 805, at p. 807, [1928] 2 D.L.R. 739, at p. 740.

238 *Garbutt Business College Ltd.* v. *Henderson,* [1939] 3 W.W.R. 257, at p. 268, [1939] 4 D.L.R. 151, at p. 174: ". . . I would like to add a word of commendation and thanks to the counsel engaged for the very great assistance rendered the Court in their careful analysis of the difficult questions of law involved in their written and oral arguments".

239 *R.* v. *Scheer* (1932), 26 Alta. L.R. 489, at p. 491, [1932] 3 W.W.R. 555, at p. 557, [1933] 1 D.L.R. 310, at p. 312.

240 In *Frank* v. *Gazelle Live Stock Association* (1906), 6 Terr. L.R. 392, 5 W.L.R. 573, he applied *Kirkwood* v. *Smith,* [1896] 1 Q.B. 582, which had been overruled by *Kirkwood* v. *Carroll,* [1903] 1 K.B. 531.

241 *R.* v. *Glenday,* [1946] 1 W.W.R. 62, [1946] 3 D.L.R. 218.

242 *Corwin* v. *Avery* (1925), 21 Alta. L.R. 95, [1925] 1 W.W.R. 811, [1925] 2 D.L.R. 599; *Canadian Credit Men's*

Trust Association v. *Edmonton* (1925), 21 Alta. L.R. 160, [1925] 1 W.W.R. 747, [1925] 2 D.L.R. 525.

243 *Godfrey* v. *Marshall* (1917), 11 Alta. L.R. 37, at p. 43.

244 *R.* v. *Dominion Drug Stores Ltd.* (1919), 14 Alta. L.R. 384, at pp. 394–395, [1919] 2 W.W.R. 413, at p. 421, 31 C.C.C. 86, at p. 95.

245 Macmillan, The Writing of Judgments (1948), 26 Can. Bar Rev. 491, at p. 493.

246 *R.* v. *Thompson* (1913), 7 Alta. L.R. 40, at p. 41, 5 W.W.R. 157, at p. 157, 14 D.L.R. 175, at p. 176.

247 *R.* v. *Maclean* (1918), 13 Alta. L.R. 244, at p. 248, [1918] 2 W.W.R. 154, at p. 156, 40 D.L.R. 443, at pp. 444–445.

248 *R.* v. *Rose* (1918), 14 Alta. L.R. 118, at pp. 123, 124, [1918] 3 W.W.R. 950, at p. 955–956, 30 C.C.C. 405, at p. 410.

249 *Trusts & Guaranty Co.* v. *The King* (1916), 54 S.C.R. 107, [1917] 1 W.W.R. 358, 32 D.L.R. 469.

250 *A.-G. for Alberta* v. *A.-G. for Canada* (Escheats), [1928] A.C. 475, [1928] 3 W.W.R. 97, [1928] 3 D.L.R. 849, aff'g [1927] S.C.R. 136, [1927] 2 D.L.R. 194, which had reversed in part (1926), 22 Alta. L.R. 186, [1926] 1 W.W.R. 337, [1926] 1 D.L.R. 924.

251 *Re Simpson Estate* (1927), 23 Alta. L.R. 374, [1927] 3 W.W.R. 534, [1927] 4 D.L.R. 817.

252 While Harvey C.J. was chairman of the board another important lawsuit, arising out of injuries to a freshman student during "initiation" proceedings, was brought against the university. The Chief Justice was named by the university as its officer for purposes of examination for discovery. The late A.L. Smith, K.C., of Calgary, one of counsel for the plaintiff, conducted the examination. Needless to say, Harvey C.J. did not sit on the appeal that was subsequently taken. A divided court held the university responsible: *Powlett* v. *University of Alberta,* [1934] 2 W.W.R. 209.

253 *R.* v. *Hatfield,* [1937] O.W.N. 559.

254 Harvey, The Early Administration of Justice in the North West (1934–35), 1 Alta. L. Q. 1, 171; and Harvey, Formerly Rupert's Land, Obiter Dicta, Spring 1948 issue, p. 37, and Fall 1948 issue, p. 37.

255 During the preparation of this article the writer asked various questions of the Honourable Mr. Justice Frank Ford of Edmonton, who recently retired from the Appellate Division after a long career as a leader of the Alberta bar, a member of the Trial Division for ten years and of the Appellate Division for eighteen. The writer is grateful to Mr. Justice Ford for the valuable information he furnished. S.W. Field, Q.C., of Edmonton was exceedingly helpful in supplying the writer with much information about the Chief Justice and his career and in answering innumerable questions. Others who kindly gave information in reply to specific questions were Lt. Col. F.C. Jamieson, Q.C., S.H. McGuaig, Q.C., and Thomas Powell, a retired court reporter, all of Edmonton. J.W. Hugill, Q.C., now of Victoria, B.C., graciously made available his knowledge of the Chief Justice's career, habits and qualities. The Hon. Lucien Maynard, Q.C., Attorney-General of Alberta, kindly gave the writer access to Chief Justice Harvey's judge's book. During the academic session of 1950–1951 the third-year students in the Faculty of Law at the University of Alberta gathered together and summarized the Chief Justice's reported judgments. Alan B. Harvey, Q.C., was good enough to read an earlier draft of the article. Sole responsibility of course remains the writer's.

1954

Book Review: Legal Theory by W. Friedmann. Third Edition, 1953.

Reprinted from
(1954) 11 University of Toronto Law Journal
pp. 313–319

The author of this book Legal Theory *is Wolfgang Friedmann, Professor of International Law at Columbia University, New York.*

In the course of writing this review, Bowker noticed a number of errata in the book. His Review makes reference to only a few of these errors. However, he wrote privately to the author a 4-page letter listing many additional mistakes. In his letter of acknowledgement, Professor Friedmann thanked Bowker for bringing these items to his attention.

Subsequently, when Professor Friedmann published the next (fourth) edition of his book, he stated in the Preface as follows:

> *"I am most thankful to Dean W.F. Bowker of the University of Alberta School of Law for having pointed out to me a considerable number of errata in the third edition."*

Some time later, Professor Friedmann wrote an article in the Journal of Legal Education *on the subject of book reviews and book reviewers, pointing out the frequency of trivial criticisms appearing in many such reviews. In footnote (2) of that article (14* Jo. Legal Ed., *p. 509) he said:*

> *"Even though few of us will live up to the saintliness of a reviewer of a book of mine, who, having published a lengthy and thoughtful review, then sent me privately, four pages of errata."*

Bowker came to know Professor Friedmann very well, and was saddened to learn in 1972 that, after leaving the Law School one night, he was attacked in the subway by young thugs and murdered. As reported in the New York Times *on September 20, 1972, "three youths tried to rob him. He resisted and suffered a fatal knife wound." The* Times *"News of the Week" section (September 24, 1972, p. 6) referred to "the bitter irony of the tragedy: his professional life had been devoted to seeking the 'rule of law' as a path to peace among nations."*

Legal Theory. By W. FRIEDMANN. Third edition. London: Stevens & Sons Ltd. [Toronto: The Carswell Co. Ltd.]. 1953. Pp. XVI, 520. $5.75.

So widely and favourably known is this work in the decade since its first appearance, that a reviewer of the third edition should perhaps set out in the usual perfunctory manner the table of contents, add a sentence to confirm that the work is still a classic, and then stop. In fact some editors seem to think that anything more would be bad taste—an act of supererogation and an insult to the author and the public. At the risk of being told that further observation is to labour the obvious, it seems to this reviewer that a few comments might with propriety be made. If reasons for this opinion are necessary, the following might be given: (1) There may be some who have not read *Legal Theory* and if a reviewer can encourage them, or even a handful of them, to read it, he should do so. (2) Now that the Supreme Court of Canada is our court of last resort, it is timely to give particular thought to legal theory and in particular to the judicial function. (3) It is always profitable to remind ourselves again of the main issues of legal theory, and to look at the practical working of Canadian law in relation to those issues. No attempt will be made to refer one after the other to the main parts of the book. The following comments will be directed to three points, with a view to relating the text to Canadian jurisprudence: legal theory and its practical effects; natural law; and law in relation to society and, particularly, the relation between judicial decisions and economic or social effects.

Legal theory and its practical effects. Professor Friedmann says that the purpose of legal theory is self-reflection, and standing midway between philosophy and political theory, its contribution is to formulate political ideas in terms of legal principles. It is faced with the same problems as philosophy and political theory—Does will direct knowledge or knowledge direct will? Does intellect or instinct guide man? How can stability be reconciled with the need for change? Is the individual to be subordinated to the community or the community to the individual? Is law determined by ideals or material conditions? As he says, "it is still a common practice among lawyers to look upon legal ideology as a useless speculation of theorists, irrelevant to the administration of law."

Not the least value of *Legal Theory* is to demonstrate the falsity of this attitude. Some of the titles (parts III–VI) indicate the subject-matter: "The Individual, the Universe and Community," "The Impact of Modern Social Developments on Legal Thought," "Modern Political Movements and their Legal Thought," and "Legal Theory, Social Ideals and Legal Practice." The breadth of learning reminds one of Roscoe Pound. Most of us find that what we read about Kant and Hegel (to say nothing of Neo-Kantians and Neo-Hegelians) is abstract and difficult. Professor Friedmann succeeds in describing their views of law and the implications of their legal philosophies as briefly and clearly as one could hope for. The social and political movements of the past century or so are described. What does this have to do with law? One's views and preconceptions on these subjects directly affect one's attitude toward law, and in the case of judges and legislatures they affect the law itself. The man who says "you can't legislate morality" is probably a rugged individualist who does not want to be regulated. The man who objects to codification belongs to the "historical school" though he never heard of it. Mussolini's theory of the state was a perversion of Duguit's idea that society is an organism and that the duty of its members is to strengthen the "social solidarity"; and Hitler's theory of the state is a distortion of Hegel's view that (in Friedmann's words) "true freedom is gained only through the individual's integration in this State."

Probably most persons would agree with Professor Friedmann that the principal legal values in a modern democracy are the legal rights of the individual, equality before the law, the control of government by the people, and the rules of law. These concepts of course are broad and not always defined in the same way; but the value of the author's treatment of them is to show their meaning in Anglo-American democracies, the extent to which they are not achieved, the tendencies in law which may conflict with them. For example, some might ask whether there are other values that supplement or compete with those given. The text mentions that Roscoe Pound, who over thirty years ago formulated a group of postulates for civilized society, has in recent years raised the question whether new postulates are emerging, such as the worker's claim to security in his job, the duty of an industrialized society to bear the burden of human wear and tear, and even the postulate that society should bear the risk of all misfortune to individuals. A great value of discussions such as this one is to make us canvass our beliefs, our attitudes to the relation between man and the state, and the role of law in helping to realize and "maximize" the various values once we are agreed upon them. Probably Dr. Friedmann would agree with John Stuart Mill that if we do not re-examine our own beliefs from time to time and pay attention to criticism of them, they will "encrust and petrify" the mind against other influences and will not allow "any fresh and living conviction to get in" but merely "stand sentinel" over the mind and heart to keep them vacant.

Natural law. The text traces the history of natural or higher law theories from the Greeks to Saint Thomas Aquinas and on to its decline and partial revival. Ever since the firm establishment of parliamentary sovereignty in England, judges do not speak of a natural or divine law superior to man-made law. Nor do they often speak of natural rights, which man-made law cannot infringe. Professor Friedmann has rewritten his discussion of natural law in United States jurisprudence where the theory of the constitution is that natural rights do exist and that the people never authorized the legislature to pass laws that abridge these rights. The Bill of Rights declares these natural rights, but a widely held view in the United States is that the legislature could not curtail them even in the absence of a bill of rights. This theory has had a vast effect on the role of the judiciary. It becomes the guardian of the constitution and has a "veto power" over the legislature. Since the "fundamental principles" are stated in broad generalities, it is obvious that judges, like anyone else, will often disagree on the question whether a statute violates fundamental principles of fairness or deprives a person of a constitutional right. This imposes on judges a task that makes their duty political rather than judicial.

As Professor Friedmann says, the British judge "is spared much of the dilemma which constantly confronts the judicial guardian of a written constitution." In Canada the judges are the "guardians" of the constitution to the extent that they say whether a statute is within the powers of the Dominion or of a province; but this reviewer suggests that they are not the guardians in the same sense that the Supreme Court of the United States is. There was, as Professor Friedmann describes, a long period in which that Court condemned statutes that interfered with property rights, economic interests, and "liberties." Efforts of the legislature to remedy social and economic evils were thus often nullified. In 1937 occurred the "revolution" on the Court that marked a change in its opinion. The author says: "The reconstitution of the courts during Franklin Roosevelt's first and second presidency brought a far-reaching and dramatic reversal in the outlook of the Court and in its scale of values." The fact is that Mr. Roosevelt made no appointments to the Supreme Court in his first term and that the change in the direction of its judgments began in March, 1937, without any change in personnel at a time when the President was attempting to enlarge it. Since 1937 the Supreme Court has ceased to hold invalid minimum wage and hours of labour laws and at the same time has expanded the scope of freedom of speech and freedom of religion so that by 1949 they had attained a "preferred position." Various decisions of the Supreme Court have given protection to the negroes, especially in criminal proceedings and against state laws excluding them from voting in primary elections and providing for segregation in transportation and education.

Professor Friedmann points out that any "higher law" philosophy implies a hierarchy of values and that the growth and decline of many constitutional doctrines shows that this hierarchy varies from age to age and from judge to judge. Comparing the position in Canada to that in the United States, he says, "Neither the Australian nor the Canadian constitutions—which are more easily comparable to the United States constitution than any other—contain Bills of Rights, yet the conflict between economic freedom and State regulation, between the freedom of the individual and the power of self-protection of the State, and other basic conflicts have arisen in much the same manner, though in a different legal form."

It seems to this reviewer that although our courts have power to declare a statute ultra vires it can only be on a ground specifically based on the British North America Acts, and there is no power to declare an act invalid because it is harsh, discriminatory of confiscatory or because in the view of the judge it violates natural law or natural rights. Certainly the late Mr. Justice Riddell who wrote much on the subject, was of this view. It is true that one can find cases in which courts have gone to extreme lengths to hold an act invalid on the ground that it is outside the power of the legislature enacting it; and one might suggest in these cases the courts may have in mind a limitation on legislative power that is not expressly stated in the constitution. Instances that come to mind are cases in which the courts have held invalid provincial legislation setting up administrative boards—for example,

Labour Relations Board v. *John East Iron Works Limited*—and provincial legislation interfering with judgments—for example, *Abitibi Power Company* v. *Montreal Trust Company*. In each of these examples the decisions were reversed by higher courts.

It is true that there have been two cases—the *Alberta Press Case* on freedom of speech and the *Saumur Case* on freedom of religion—in which some judges in the Supreme Court of Canada have said that a province may not constitutionally abridge these two freedoms. But in neither case did a majority take this ground.

Professor Friedmann certainly does not himself subscribe to the view that there is an immutable and universal natural law to which man-made laws must conform. With the laws of Nazi Germany still fresh in everyone's memory we can certainly agree in "a desire to establish minimum standards to which a positive law must comply." But as he adds, "as soon as we go beyond generalities such as the condemnation of laws offending human dignity, we feel uncertain of the point where moral indignation produces legal condemnation." Apart however from the question of statutes there are no doubt cases in which prevalent moral views have an influence on courts in reaching judgments. For example, the Supreme Court of Canada refused to recognize a foreign decree confiscating a ship with meagre compensation (*Laane* v. *Estonian State S.S. Line,* [1949] S.C.R. 530). Our rules of public policy, which operate in a negative way to render invalid contracts or testamentary gifts that are contrary to public policy are based on ideas of morals and the public interest.

The text has a helpful discussion of public policy, largely rewritten in the present edition. As the author states, the House of Lords in 1938 in *Fender* v. *Mildmay* indicated a strong reluctance to hold a gift or contract to be against public policy unless it has been so held in the past. Many persons doubtless ask why we should accept the fact that courts in an earlier period could create heads of public policy but that today they are limited to those same heads. The answer is that our strict rule of precedent coupled with the doctrine of parliamentary supremacy means that the proper course for courts to follow is to leave changes to the legislature. This was the view of a majority of the Supreme Court of Canada in *Re Millar,* [1939] S.C.R. 1, while Crocket J. refused to agree that the courts were practically forbidden to create new heads of public policy. In the famous case of *Re Drummond Wren,* [1945] O.R. 778, Mackay J. had no hesitation in holding that in light of present day thought racial covenants are against public policy, but in the later case of *Noble* v. *Wolf,* the Court of Appeal of Ontario overruled this case; and although the Supreme Court ([1951] S.C.R. 64) held the covenant invalid the decision was based on other grounds. Some provinces have passed legislation designed to render void such covenants.

Related to the concept of natural law is that of "natural justice" which has to do with fundamental fairness, particularly in relation to procedure before courts and especially administrative or domestic tribunals. The two rules most frequently cited are, "hear both sides" and "no man shall be judge in his own cause." In the famous case of *Kuyzch* v. *White,* [1950] 2 W.W.R. 193, O'Halloran J.A. says that the common law does not permit a course of conduct within an association which is contrary to natural justice. On the other hand, his colleague Smith J.A. says, "I must say that I do not care for this phrase which seems to me to have little meaning, and that little misleading." The common law has a remedy when its principles are disregarded without calling in aid "any special brand of justice." It remains for each one of us to reflect upon these opposing views and try to decide which is the sounder and which is the more useful in helping to solve legal problems.

Law in relation to society. Professor Friedmann is particularly interested in this subject and has written extensively on it in other works as well as *Legal Theory*. He makes a contrast between, on the one hand, the "positivist and analytical mentality" which dominated English legal thinking in the nineteenth and, to a considerable extent, in the present century and, on the other hand, legal thought which "reveals a deep appreciation of the interdependence between judicial and social and economic ideology." The "nature of the judicial function" is the main concern of many legal scholars. It could hardly be otherwise when it is no longer generally agreed that the common law was always in existence and needed only to be discovered; and when respectable writers remark that the law (or the constitution) is what the judges say it is. Professor Friedmann's criticism of English and Canadian legal thought is that judges and lawyers too often think of the judge's task as one of mechanically applying fixed rules instead of one of shaping decisions that are wise in their adjustment of the social and economic problems that come before the court. It may help to keep separate cases on the common law, cases interpreting statutes, and cases interpreting the constitution.

With regard to the common law, the criticism is that courts do not take the opportunity of deciding cases in a way that will keep the law in step with social conditions, even when it may be necessary to overrule earlier decisions. This reviewer agrees with the author that there have been cases in which a court has adhered to earlier decisions that are not strictly binding on it and which leave the law back in the nineteenth century. It is easy to cite examples from England, on the subject of an occupier's liability for negligence. Yet there are cases on the other hand that show a change—the doctrine of *volenti non fit injuria* still exists but is rarely applied, and frequently a duty is found to exist where none existed in the past. The author, like various United States writers, thinks that courts could do more than they do to mould the common law to conform to the times and in particular to make the law less "individualistic." This reviewer agrees, but would allow narrower scope for judicial modification. Since parliamentary sovereignty has been firmly established, it is only logical to say that changes in the law are for the legislature. This still leaves room for the courts to modify the law in cases where no binding authority exists.

Regarding statutory construction, the author is doubtless correct in saying that very often courts show a resistance to legislation as though it were an improper intrusion on the common law. Certainly the courts in Canada have whittled down to almost nothing statutes which say that the decision of an administrative board shall be final. On the other hand there are signs that courts may abandon the old artificial canons of construction—for example "a statute must be construed so as to preserve common law rights" and "taxing statutes must be construed narrowly." These and other canons can be used to curtail the scope of an enactment; but critics often tend to look at the worst cases and forget the others. Three years ago the Supreme Court of Canada preserved the habitual criminals provisions in the Canadian Criminal Code by reversing a provincial decision which made it a dead letter. As another example, the Supreme Court of Canada in the *Boucher Case* provided a decision that is as good a practical protection to free speech as one can find; yet too often we point to United States decisions on this subject as models. On the one hand, there are cases in the Supreme Court of the United States which give such scope for freedom of speech as to reach absurdity, and on the other hand, there are recent cases which have curtailed the protection given to free speech by Holmes's "clear and present danger" test.

As for constitutional decisions on the validity of dominion or provincial legislation, the author shares the opinion of those who criticize those decisions of the Judicial Committee of the Privy Council which put a narrow construction on dominion powers. Certainly one can argue that the *Snyder Case* in 1952 and some of the decisions in 1937 on the "new deal" legislation justify this criticism; but the decisions are not all one way. It might be suggested that it is proper for the courts to hold that a subject which in the past was merely provincial in scope has on the facts now become national and therefore a proper subject of dominion jurisdiction. In the case of joint efforts by the Dominion and the provinces to regulate the marketing of natural products, the tendency for long was to hold invalid both dominion and provincial legislation because it related to matters outside either jurisdiction enacting it. Thus, in spite of the theory that the dominion and provincial legislatures between them have plenary power, it seemed impossible to frame valid legislation; the result was that regulation was impossible of achievement. However the Supreme Court of Canada in the *Potato-Marketing Case* in 1952 upheld a delegation by the Dominion to a provincial marketing board of the administration of the Dominion Act, with the result that the combined legislation is effective to regulate both intra-provincial and interprovincial trade. And certainly the recent *Winner Case,* decided by the Judicial Committee of the Privy Council after the present edition of *Legal Theory* went to press, must give comfort to those who prefer a broad construction of the Dominion's powers.

Professor Friedmann is doubtless of the opinion that Canadian courts might follow the Supreme Court of the United States in taking political, social, and economic factors into consideration in reaching constitutional decisions. To the extent that they might admit evidence on references from the executive we can agree. In the *Radio Case,* Newcombe J. said, "My trouble with this case is to know the facts," yet in 1950 in the *Wartime Rent Control Case* the Chief Justice re-emphasized that the court's opinion on these references is given without recourse to evidence or factual material in the factums. If evidence were admitted there would be no need to advocate the "Brandeis brief," hundreds of pages in length. This reviewer doubts that there is or should be too close an analogy between the Supreme Courts of Canada and the United States. As the author well recognizes, many United States decisions blocked worthwhile legislation that never met with difficulty here. The absence of a bill of rights means that our Supreme Court does not have the same scope to interject its social and economic views that the Supreme Court of the United States assumes.

In conclusion, one might suggest a comparison between the effort Professor Friedmann makes to induce us to think of law in terms of society and Dean Roscoe Pound's great campaign directed to the same end in the United States. Judicial interference with legislation is not nearly as extensive in Canada as it was in the United States fifty years ago; yet there is still a widespread tendency to look on legislation as something to resist, and to look on legal rules as something to be applied automatically with little concern over the consequences. Professor Friedmann's approach, strengthened by his broad knowledge of continental as well as English law, has much value for Canadians; and the fact that he has been on the staff of a Canadian law school adds to the interest of his writings.

1955

Professional Ethics

Originally published in
"Proceedings of Commonwealth and Empire Law Conference 1955"
and reprinted in (1955–61) 1 Alberta Law Review pp. 65–70

The first Commonwealth & Empire Law Conference was held in London, England in 1955, and every 5 years thereafter in a country of the Commonwealth (1960 Canada; 1965 Australia; 1971 India).

The invitation was extended to the Canadian Bar Association. Wilbur and Marjorie Bowker attended as members of the Canadian Bar Association.

Prior to the Conference, there was a general appeal from the Canadian Bar association for papers on a legal subject of the writer's choosing. Wilbur Bowker was very active in the Canadian Bar at this time, and was on the Uniform Law Conference.

Bowker's contribution was this paper on Professional Ethics. There were not many Canadian papers in the whole proceedings; only three from any country were on Ethics, the other two being from England.

A profession differs from a trade because the main object of a trade is profit while a profession, in Roscoe Pound's words, is "a group of men pursuing a learned art as a common calling in the spirit of public service." A tradesman does not act on behalf of his customer, but the member of a profession does act on behalf of those whom he serves. This special relationship between lawyer and client or physician and patient is one of trust, calling for rules of conduct higher than those which the general law requires of the ordinary citizen. These rules may be called the ethics of the profession.

To explain "ethical conduct" it might help to describe "unethical conduct." The author of a recent American book on Legal Ethics, H.S. Drinker, says that unethical conduct, calling for disciplinary measures, comes under two headings: (1) moral unfitness to advise and represent clients; and (2) unworthiness to continue in the legal profession. This distinction seems helpful, though in some cases improper conduct may come under both headings.

In the legal profession, it is doubtful whether the ethical standards go back as far as the physician's oath of Hippocrates, but certainly in England they began to develop when attorneys and pleaders emerged in the reign of Edward I. The mediaeval attorney took an oath to truly and honestly demean himself in the practice of an attorney, and the sergeant at law swore that he would serve well the King's people, counsel them truly and not defer or delay their causes for his own profit.

Since this paper will deal specifically with professional ethics in Canada, it may help to mention the differences in the organization of the profession in the two countries. In Canada professions are controlled by the provinces and the typical statute creates a law society whose members alone have the right to practise law and who are both barristers and solicitors. They are officers of the court, which an English barrister is not, and disciplinary power rests in the benchers of the society. The union of the two branches renders inapplicable some of the English rules which deal with the relationship between barristers, solicitors and the public. Most discussions of English ethical standards deal with the ethics of advocacy, and the rules which appear from time to time in the *Annual Practice* are opinions of the General Council of the Bar, save for those relating to the retainers of barristers, which were framed jointly by the two branches of the profession. A practitioner in Canada is subject to the rules governing both branches, but after making allowances for the differences in organization in the two countries, it is correct to say that the profession in Canada adopts the English standards. In each province, however, some standards may be found in statutes as well as in judgments and in custom.

Moreover, there exist in Canada written canons of Ethics of the Canadian Bar Association, a voluntary but influential body. In 1919 the association decided to adopt canons based on those of the American Bar Association, and they were approved in 1920.

Some lawyers in Canada objected to the canons on the ground that in England it has not been found necessary to codify the ethics of the profession, and also because there may be a danger that lawyers will treat them like a taxing statute that applies only where the individual comes within the letter of the law. The answer to this last objection is that the canons are not exhaustive, but "should be construed as a general guide and not as a denial of the existence of other duties." As for the first objection, the English rules already mentioned do constitute a partial codification, and in any case there are many differences between the two countries. In Canada there is no counterpart of the Inns of Court, and instead of a small Bar devoted exclusively to counsel work, there are the provincial societies, most of whose members (except in Quebec) are both barristers and solicitors, with divergent educational backgrounds, many of them living in scattered, thinly populated areas, and without the daily contacts with the courts that an English barrister enjoys. It is hard to see how the formulation of the canons could fail to be beneficial. It is true that so far as I have learned, the only law societies that officially adopted them were those of the Western Provinces. A short examination of the canons will show, however, that subject to minor variations they conform to the high standards of the profession in England.

The Canadian canons are grouped under five headings—the lawyer's duty to the State, the court, his fellow lawyers, his client and himself. We do not propose to summarize the canons in order, but think it worthy of note that they are framed so as to emphasize the various duties of the lawyer, which, of course, put limits on each other duty. No lawyer should fall into the error of misinterpreting Lord Brougham's famous statement in Queen Caroline's case "that an advocate, by the sacred duty which he owes his client, knows in the discharge of that office, but one person in the world, that client, and no other." Lord Brougham did not mean that the advocate has no duty to the State, the court, or the profession, but rather that his duty to his client may require him to attack the character of other persons—in Queen Caroline's case, King George IV. However, one sometimes hears lawyers in conversation stress the obligation to the client as though this were the only duty the lawyer owes.

Coming now to the contents of the canons, we shall mention first those relating to criminal cases. The primary duty of the prosecutor "is not to convict, but to see that justice is done" and he should withhold no facts tending to prove either the guilt or innocence of the accused. There is no ground for saying that generally Canadian prosecutors do not observe the English tradition. The law reports disclose but few instances in which the court has reproved Crown counsel for unfairness. The duty to withhold no relevant information has been laid down by the Privy Council, though in 1951 the Supreme Court of Canada held that there is no rigid rule that the Crown must call every person who appears to know something of the facts or to tender him for cross-examination. The Crown has a discretion with which the court will not interfere unless it appears that the Crown exercised its discretion "from some oblique motive."

The canons prescribe the duty to act on behalf of an accused person when asked by the court, and there are many instances in which this is done. However, there is another canon which says that no lawyer is obliged to act either as advisor or advocate for every person who may wish to become his client. He has the right to decline employment. It may be pertinent to note that it is the general practice for the Crown to pay the fees of counsel for the accused in serious cases where he has no funds, and there has been a strong movement toward setting up machinery in the law societies to provide legal aid for needy persons though in most provinces where such provisions exist the aid is confined to civil cases.

In litigation generally, the canons say that the lawyer's conduct should be characterised by candour and fairness, courtesy and respect to the court and courtesy to the witnesses. The obligation not to mislead the court was well put by the late Chief Justice Anglin in 1909. "The court has the right to rely upon him to assist it in ascertaining the truth. He should be most careful to state with strict accuracy the contents of a paper, the evidence of a witness, the admissions or the argument of his opponent. Knowingly to cite an overruled case or to refer to a repealed statute as still in force would be unpardonable, and counsel cannot be too cautious not to make such mistakes unwittingly."

One specific problem that is of great interest as a matter of ethics, though it does not arise often, is this—is counsel obliged to cite adverse authority? Now if the proceedings are *ex parte* it seems clear that he is bound to do so; ordinarily, however, there is counsel on the other side, and in nearly all cases he will have found the cases in his favour, at least those that are binding or that originate in courts whose judgments have high persuasive authority. Assuming, however, that he has not, there is little discussion in Canada on the point, but it seems clear from the English discussions such as those of Lord Macmillan and Mr. Justice Hilbery that although counsel is not obliged to argue the other side's case he should not knowingly remain silent if he knows of a binding decision that is or appears to be unfavourable. There may be more debate if the case is not binding, but if he is asked if there is authority on the point, he must give it.

The other question that laymen never cease to ask: How do you justify the defence of a guilty man? is not really hard to answer. The canons say that counsel should endeavour by all fair and honourable means to obtain for his client the benefit of every remedy and defence which is authorised by law, and also that it is right to undertake the defence of a person accused of crime, regardless of his own personal opinion as to the guilt of the accused.

Laymen, of course, think that this is mere sophistry. Most of us in the profession are satisfied with the justification which Dr. Johnson gave almost two hundred years ago and with the statement of the General Council of the Bar in 1915 on the position of counsel where his client has confessed. In this case, the 1915 ruling says, it is advisable to withdraw if the confession has been made before the advocate has undertaken the defence, but that if it is made during the proceedings, then counsel should proceed, his duty being to see that his client is convicted only upon proper evidence, though, of course, he should not attempt to set up a defence such as an alibi or to blame another for the crime.

Other duties connected with trials are (1) not to offer evidence which the court should not admit; (2) to treat adverse witnesses with fairness; (3) not to express his personal belief on matters of fact in dispute; and (4) not to testify in a case where he is counsel. No comment need be made on the first of these. As for the second, the Canadian canons do not expressly say that counsel should not ask questions affecting the witness's character merely to attack his credibility unless he has reasonable grounds for believing they are true. This is the English rule, and, as far as I know, is understood to be the rule in Canada. As for the third, this is doubtless observed by experienced counsel, though one sometimes hears counsel say: "I think the evidence justifies a finding for the plaintiff," or "I believe my client innocent." As for the fourth, many cases arise in which the lawyer for a party withdraws as counsel where he knows beforehand that he will be needed as a witness.

The subject of fees is of course important. Indeed this is the one area in which the lawyer's interest conflicts with that of his client. The canons require him to charge neither less nor more than reasonable compensation, and where possible to adhere to established tariffs. He is recommended to avoid unseemly disputes over his fees. In England of course a barrister may not sue for his fee but I know of no such prohibition in Canada. The right of a client to tax his solicitor's account is of course a safeguard against exorbitant fees thought the right is not really a help in small matters. Other important canons relating to fees remind him that he must not stir up litigation for the purpose of seeking a retainer and that "he should not, except as by law expressly sanctioned, acquire by purchase or other any interest in the subject matter of the litigation." In England a barrister may not agree that fees shall be paid according to the event: such an agreement is champertous. However, it appears that a solicitor, though he may not bargain for a percentage of the amount recovered, may act for a client on the understanding that his fees will be paid out of the amount recovered. In the United States agreements for fees based on the amount recovered came to be accepted when personal injury cases became common, for many claimants had no funds. In some Canadian provinces there are provisions in statute or rules of court permitting the solicitor to make a written agreement with his client that fees shall be based on a percentage of the amount recovered, though in Ontario this is confined to non-contentious matters, and usually the agreement is subject to approval of the court. In at least one province (Alberta) it is expressly stated that these agreements do not give validity to a purchase by the lawyer of an interest in the suit or to an agreement that he shall be paid only in the event of success.

Most of the other duties are traditional ones owed to the client—not to represent conflicting interests, to settle if possible, and to keep the client's secrets and confidences. Lastly he is obliged to account promptly to his client for moneys received and to keep trust funds separate from his own. In some provinces there are elaborate rules to this end. To compensate clients for their loss where the solicitor has failed to account, some law societies have established an assurance fund from contributions made by the members.

The last canon we shall note is one which forbids the solicitation of business. Though permitting the use of ordinary simple business cards, it deprecates indirect advertising and self-laudation. There may be details which some solicitors include on letterheads, professional cards or "shingles" that would not be approved in England, but generally speaking all these media have been used with restraint and so far as I know the publication of notices indicating specialisation is disapproved of.

The actual ethical standards of the profession can of course not be determined by reading its paper standards but only by knowing the extent to which they are observed.

Having completed our short review of the Canadian canons we will conclude this paper by a consideration of the question—how best to implant, maintain and strengthen the highest traditions of the profession.

A start should be made with the student entering the Law School. Almost everyone planning to enter the profession in Canada attends a law school after two, three or more years of University training. It may be impossible to appraise the character of applicants but tests of aptitude and interest and personal interviews may assist in making selections that will eliminate some who seem to show little promise.

Then, from the time the student enters law school, his instructors can teach him the history of the profession, encourage the reading of biographies of great lawyers and judges, discuss ethical problems as they arise from time to time, and have him study the canons of ethics. It may be too that a course on the subject might be offered as is done in some American schools: certainly the study of one of the several good case books or J.G. Brinker's recent text would be profitable for though they are American they contain English material and as already stated the Canadian canons resemble the American. Many think that the best way to inculcate high standards is to drop the seeds incidentally but it seems reasonable to say that a deliberate and concentrated study of the subject, aided perhaps by special talks from judges and leaders of the bar, will inevitably give the student a greater awareness of the subject and of its importance than he would otherwise receive.

The next step in the training is the period under articles which in most provinces follows law school training though sometimes is contemporaneous with it. It is customary for the Law Society before approval of the articles to require a certificate of character, but the writer knows of only one case where an applicant with the requisite educational qualifications was ever refused, and that was on the ground that he was a Communist.

During the period of articles the student is, of course, under the tutelage of the practitioner with whom he is articled. One cannot deny the profound influence of a good principal who really accepts his obligations as a preceptor of his student. Of course, if the principal does not himself have exacting standards or does not take the trouble to teach the student, or does not have the type of practice that gives the student wide experience, then the period of articles may be of little value; but in most instances this is not the case. The Law Societies could, however, remind the principal of his obligation to impress on the student our ethical standards.

Next comes the ceremony of admission. In most, if not all, provinces, the candidate takes an oath before the presiding Supreme Court justice. In some, the oath is the same as the English solicitors' oath. In several, it is longer, and combines an oath of allegiance with a pledge that in itself is a short code of ethics. Frequently the presiding justice comments on the oath and emphasises the responsibility and obligations that the new practitioner assumes. After his admission to practice, the young lawyer will, of course, meet ethical problems from time to time; but if he is aware of his obligations and conscientiously addresses himself to the problem, he is unlikely to go far astray.

As long as he is in practice he is, of course, subject to the disciplinary power of the Benchers of the provincial law society, and may be reprimanded, suspended or struck off the rolls. The wise exercise of this power is of the first importance. To adapt the words of Cockburn, C.J., disciplinary bodies can properly say:

> We have a duty to perform to the suitors of the Court, and not only to the suitors of the Court but to the profession of the law, by taking care that those permitted to practise in it are persons on whose integrity and honour reliance can be placed.

In preparing this paper it has not been possible to make an examination of all the types of complaints that come before the disciplinary committees. Doubtless these include failing to account for funds, dilatory conduct or neglect in handling of estates, taking collusive divorce actions, and advertising. It is doubtful that there are many complaints for breaches of etiquette in Court for the judiciary can doubtless deal effectively with these, if necessary by exercising the power to punish for contempt.

It would be unsafe, however, to judge the standard of the Bar solely or mainly by the number of complaints. The objective should not be merely to keep out of reach of the disciplinary machinery, but should be much higher. A lawyer might go through life without ever being the subject of a complaint, even though he is one who buys property from his client at an undervaluation knowing that he can make a profit, who draws his client's will with himself as a beneficiary, who assists clients in illegal schemes, who misleads the court, and who never obliges his fellow lawyer.

It is not enough to say that the great majority do not act in this manner, for the public tends to judge the profession by its less worthy members. The principles which the profession in Canada inherits from the mother country will be secured only if every member of the legal profession remembers that he is in a fiduciary position, an officer of the court, and duty-bound to maintain respect for the law and for the courts and to aid in the administration of justice.

1955

History of the Association of Canadian Law Teachers

(Unpublished)

The Association of Canadian Law Teachers (later called The Canadian Association of Law Teachers) was formed in 1947 largely at the instigation of Professor Frank Scott, Dean of Law at McGill University.

Bowker was one of the original members and continued in an active capacity until 1968 when he left the Deanship. He was Secretary in 1954, elected Vice-President in 1955 and became President in 1956, in Montreal.

The writing of this history arose out of his time as Secretary. The Association had no staff or office, and though the period covered was short, the record would have been lost. Later more formal records were kept.

The accompanying history is the only record of those early years, and is now in the Archives of the Association.

In 1952 Professor W.R. Lederman of Dalhousie Law School prepared a short history which appeared in the *Canadian Bar Review* (Vol. 30, p. 608). In addition a report of the 1953 and 1954 meetings appeared in the same publication (Vol. 31, p. 553; Vol. 32, p. 659). At the 1954 meeting the Association directed the executive to arrange compilation of a record or documentary history of the Association with a view to publication. This is the result. It is based largely on documents prepared or furnished by Professor F.R. Scott (McGill) in the early years and by the secretaries in later years.

The Association was conceived on July 7, 1947. Professor Scott wrote the following letter to the deans of each Canadian law school: Gagne J. (Laval), Beaubien (Montreal), Falconbridge (Osgoode), Tallin (Manitoba), Cronkite (Saskatchewan), Harrison J. (New Brunswick), Steer (Alberta), Macdonald (Dalhousie) and Curtis (British Columbia):

> The members of our Law Faculty feel, as I do, that it would be very useful to have an informal discussion on legal education with representatives from all the law schools in Canada. The meeting of the Canadian Bar Association in Ottawa in early September would seem to provide a convenient opportunity where such discussions might first be held. I am therefore writing to you as Dean of the Law School at ____________ to ask whether you agree that such an exchange of views would be useful and whether you will be at the Bar Association meeting, and can take part. Perhaps if you yourself were not going to Ottawa, you could ask some other member of your faculty to act for you in this connection.

> I believe that a conference of this sort would be most helpful to all of us, and I hope you will be able to attend.

On or about September 4, 1947, those teachers who were at Ottawa met in a room in the Chateau Laurier. Professor Scott was chairman. No minutes were kept. Present were Dean LeMesurier (McGill), J.B. Milner (Dalhousie), E. Whitmore (Saskatchewan), G.V.V. Nicholls, Mr. O'Brien of Montreal, W.F. Bowker (and perhaps one or two others. Gilbert Kennedy? Max Cohen?). The discussion was general. Much time was spent in discussing syllabi and case books, and ways of having cases reproduced by one means or another.

After the meeting, Professor Scott wrote to Dean Kennedy (Toronto) to invite his ideas about the possibility of forming some kind of an organization.

Dean Kennedy replied on September 22, 1947 as follows:

> I was very glad indeed to get your letter of September 19th for the simple reason that before the war I sounded out various people about an organization such as you have in mind and got very little support for it. However, I think the time is ripe for something of this nature and we shall be glad to give it all the support in our power. There are some points which need consideration:
>
> (1) I do not think the organization should be called an association of Canadian Law Schools. Such a name would commit each school officially to the proposed activities and would lead to endless difficulties. When I was dealing with this question before, I sounded out Holdsworth, as he had been most active in a similar matter in the United Kingdom and he told me that the best thing to do would be to have a Canadian association of public teachers of law. This would avoid difficulties which they ran into in the United Kingdom when they founded the Society of Public Teachers of Law there. In other words, we would be a voluntary association of law teachers and our activities would not commit the various authorities of the law schools and we would be free from any official connexion.
>
> (2) I do not think that any meeting in connexion with the Canadian Bar Association would be a success. This is a point which I also took up with my previous activities. Many of the teachers are scattered on holidays, either on this continent or abroad and it would not be practical to expect such an organization to be a success if connected with the Canadian Bar Association meetings. In addition, the Bar Association meets all across Canada and there would be little hope, even if all the teachers were in Canada at the time of the Bar Association meetings, to expect anything like a good attendance.
>
> (3) This leads me to the third point and that is that the meetings should be held annually in the Christmas or Easter holidays at some more or less central point—Montreal, Toronto or perhaps Winnipeg. I believe that we would do well to have it here and I could arrange for accommodations. Christmas would be the best time as then it will be possible to get rooms.
>
> Now, these are the three points which present themselves to me and they are the outcome of some considerable correspondence. If you think along

> these lines, I should be glad if you could drop down to see me, if at all possible. At any rate, I am perfectly certain that there is room for such an association, provided that we try to follow the three points laid down. I am most anxious about it, because we have grown in graduate work here for the LL.M. and the D.Jur. to such an extent that we need to discuss the matter with teachers in the other law schools.
>
> I think an organization such as they have in the United Kingdom is our best plan, with an annual subscription and an annual meeting covering two or three days. If we got a "green light" somewhere, I shall be perfectly willing to help you and get the thing under way, as it is one of my dream children and I am more than ever convinced that the time is now riper than ever. I shall await further communications from you with great interest. Please write to Curtis and tell him what I have said. Indeed, it might be possible for you to send him a copy of this letter.

On October 22 Scott sent to each dean a copy of Dean Kennedy's letter and invited comments.

On December 2 he sent out a further letter:

> I have now had replies from six Law Schools regarding the suggestions of Dean Kennedy which I forwarded to you in my letter of October 22nd. There seems to be no clear opinion regarding the proposal that any association to be formed should represent individual teachers of Law rather than the Law Schools themselves. Osgoode and Dalhousie favour Dean Kennedy's views, McGill would prefer an association of law Schools, and Alberta seems to incline this way. The two French Schools favour the idea of periodic meetings but want further discussion before deciding on the best form these should take.
>
> As regards a December meeting, Dalhousie would send a representative and also Alberta though the latter prefers the time of the Bar Association meeting. I had thought I could attend, but now this seems doubtful. I have had no reply from U.B.C. I personally think therefore that we had better not attempt to hold a meeting this month. Further discussion will be necessary to make our next gathering fruitful. If I might make a suggestion of my own, I think we had better meet once more at the time of the Bar Association. At that meeting we can decide both the form of the future association and the most appropriate time for its meeting. This seems to me something that should be discussed among the individual faculties and not decided until we have been able to exchange views across the table.

1948

Prior to the 1948 meeting of the Canadian Bar Association at Montreal, Professor Scott wrote the deans as follows:

> The law teachers attending the Bar Association meeting hope to get together as we did last year for an informal discussion of common problems. We shall probably meet on the afternoon or evening of the first Monday.
>
> I hope you will be present, or someone from your school who can join us.

He prepared an agenda for the meeting which was held in the McGill law school faculty room in Purvis Hall on Monday, August 30. Items on the agenda were:

1. Election of chairman.
2. Introductory.
3. Purpose of meeting.
4. Association of law schools.
   (a) American
   (b) Canadian
5. Survey of legal education.
6. Problems of the curriculum.
7. Legal books and materials.
8. Future meetings.

The report which Frank Scott later prepared and circulated among the teachers tells what happened:

Present:

Dalhousie University	Dean V.C. Macdonald, J.B. Milner, M. Hancock.
University of Montreal	Jacques Perrault, Albert Mayrand
McGill University	Dean LeMesurier, F.R. Scott, Maxwell Cohen, J.L. O'Brien, J.P. Anglin
Osgoode Hall	Bora Laskin
University of Toronto	Jacob Finkelman
University of Saskatchewan	C.B. Bourne
University of Alberta	Dean W.F. Bowker
University of British Columbia	Dean Curtis, F. Read.

The meeting of the Canadian Bar Association in Montreal provided an opportunity for the above named members of the profession engaged in law teaching to meet together to discuss common problems. Dean C.S. LeMesurier, Faculty of Law, McGill University, was appointed chairman. Certain opening remarks were made by Professor F.R. Scott of McGill, who explained the object of calling the meeting. He said that though no members were present from the University of New Brunswick, Laval or Manitoba he had been in touch with these schools and they had all shown an interest in the idea of this gathering, as had Mr. Nicholls of the *Canadian Bar Review*. He reminded members present that a similar though smaller meeting had been held in 1947, in Ottawa. Summarizing the main thoughts that had emerged from the previous sessions, Professor Scott suggested that three ideas seemed to be agreed upon and were, he hoped, accepted by all present:

a) That Canadian law schools have become an important part of the general legal system and should become known as a third branch of the profession having a status corresponding to the Bench and the Bar.
b) That there is need for a common understanding between the Bar and the Schools of the aims of legal education if we are to produce well-trained lawyers for all the purposes of the Bar and public service.

c) That these meetings of law teachers were not in any way designed to impose decisions upon participating schools but solely to develop co-operation on common problems and to exchange information and ideas.

Discussion thereupon was directed toward the desirability of forming an association of Canadian law schools or of law teachers on a more or less permanent basis. Some doubt was raised as to the utility of the proposal but after considerable discussion led by Dean LeMesurier and Professors Perrault and Finkelman it was generally concluded that a useful purpose would be served by some continuous association of this kind among law teachers in Canada. It was felt that the U.S. experience in the Association of American Law Schools was not entirely applicable to the somewhat different situation in Canada, and that Canadian schools would benefit from closer collaboration among themselves. At this stage, however, any formal organization was thought to be both unnecessary and undesirable.

It was eventually agreed that the law teachers should meet annually if possible, and that the most convenient time would be at the annual meeting of the Canadian Bar Association. It was therefore decided that the meeting should take place at Banff in 1949, but on the day before the opening of the Bar meetings so as to allow a full day for discussions.

It was the general opinion that these meetings would be more properly described as meetings of law teachers than of law schools. The teachers present should be considered as individuals and not as representatives of their schools, to avoid any idea of official delegations. A further decision was taken that a report of the present meeting should be sent to all law teachers and heads of faculties or schools. In this connection it was agreed that it would be useful to draw up a list of law teachers, both part-time and full-time, in all the schools throughout Canada. It was felt that the work of the group could be carried out until the next meeting by the Quebec members who might prepare and circulate certain materials for study before the 1949 meeting.

There was considerable discussion with respect to a study of legal education in Canada that was being undertaken by Professor Maxwell Cohen of the Faculty of Law, McGill University. Professor Cohen had sent out a questionnaire to the Deans of the common law schools and Faculties. He explained that he had no copies in French and did not wish to send it to the French-speaking schools unless they were made fully acquainted with the purposes of the study and thereupon felt willing to co-operate in supplying the information desired. It was the consensus of the meeting that such a study would be most useful but that it would be burdensome to answer this questionnaire if at the same time or shortly afterwards the proposed study of the profession by the Canadian Bar Association would duplicate Professor Cohen's inquiries. It was suggested to Professor Cohen that he communicate with Mr. G.V.V. Nicholls of the Canadian Bar Association to find out the facts about the Bar's research program. After checking with Mr. Nicholls, Professor Cohen was to write to all Deans and inform them as to the results of the discussion and, therefore, whether his study was to be proceeded with.

Considerable discussion took place with respect to problems of the law school curriculum. Dean Macdonald said the essential question was, "What are you going to leave out." Professor Finkelman suggested that we could not talk about curriculum problems until we had examined and considered each other's calendars and experience and that perhaps Professor Cohen's paper might provide the data for discussion next year. Dean Macdonald suggested that one possibility for the meeting next year might be for the members to discuss reports to be given by each school with respect to what each is doing in the matter of curriculum, post-graduate work and other pressing law school matters. This suggestion was welcomed by others present. The discussion then turned to the question of "clinical" or practical training and Dean Macdonald declared that in his opinion such training by law schools generally had failed. But there was general agreement as to the need for some such training before students were ready for practice.

Professor Scott suggested that another function of an association of law teachers might be to keep the schools in touch with their common library problems and to provide an exchange of surplus stocks of books among them so as to fill gaps in this way.

Another matter then considered was the possible publishing of case books that would be acceptable to all Canadian law schools. It was pointed out by Dean Curtis and Dean Macdonald that in many courses simple compilation of cases could be used by teachers in probably all law faculties, who would adapt such materials to fit their own teaching requirements. Even in the civil law schools there were courses on federal statutes and constitutional law for which the need of case reports was much the same as in the common law schools. There were mimeographing facilities at U.B.C. and Osgoode Hall and these might be used to publish case books even though the compilation and editing were done elsewhere.

The meeting adjourned with members present generally feeling that it was most desirable for the law teachers to remain in touch with each other and at some time to formalize these relations into an association. In any case it was definitely decided that a further meeting should be held next year at Banff.

1949

In 1949 Professor Le Mesurier, formerly Dean of Law at McGill, wrote to the Deans on July 19 to say:

> Those of you who were in Montreal a year ago will remember that we held a meeting of the law teachers during the Bar Convention and that it was decided to meet again at Banff a day in advance of the meeting of governing bodies. I have therefore taken it on myself to call a meeting of all teachers available for Sunday afternoon, August 28th. I hope that you will be present and will see that all members of your staff are advised of this gathering. We at McGill feel that we all have a good deal to gain from it.

The meeting was held in a room in the Banff Springs Hotel. No minutes were kept. Those present were Professor LeMesurier, Harrison J. (New Brunswick), J.B. Milner (Dalhousie), Max Cohen (McGill), Dean Wright (Toronto), Dean Tallin (Manitoba), Dean Bowker, Alex Smith and G.W. Reed (all of Alberta), and G.V.V. Nicholls. There was no planned programme and discussion was general.

1950

In the spring of 1950 Frank Scott sent out another letter:

> I am planning to call a meeting of the Association of Canadian Law Teachers for June 8th and 9th in Kingston, Ont. at the time of the meeting of the Learned Societies. Mr. Justice Rand of the Supreme Court of Canada has indicated a desire to be with us to discuss general problems of legal education; in his capacity of Director of the Bar Survey on Legal Education he would like to canvass the views of the teachers. Would you kindly let me know what members of your teaching staff are likely to be in Kingston at that time. It is hoped that a representative group will be present on this important occasion.

The meeting was held as planned. This was the first teachers' meeting held with the Learned Societies and at this meeting the organization was given a name—"Association of Canadian Law Teachers."

Later Professor Scott prepared a memorandum of the meeting:

> For the information of those who were not able to attend, I have prepared the following account of the meeting which took place on the morning and afternoon of June 8, 1950, in the Royal Military College, Kingston, Ontario.
>
> Invitations had gone out to all law schools in Canada, and regrets for absence were received from all those which could not be represented. The following teachers were present:
>
> | | |
> |---|---|
> | Dalhousie | Dean Horace Read, W.R. Lederman |
> | McGill | Maxwell Cohen, C.S. LeMesurier, F.R. Scott |
> | Toronto | Dean Cecil A. Wright, Bora Laskin, John Willis. |
> | Osgoode Hall | D.A.L. Smout |
> | British Columbia | Gilbert D. Kennedy |
>
> In addition, Principal N.A. MacKenzie of British Columbia, Professor J.A. Corry of Queens, and Mr. G.V.V. Nicholls, editor of the *Canadian Bar Review,* sat in during our discussions.
>
> The principal purpose of the meeting was to discuss current problems of legal education with Mr. Justice I.C. Rand of the Supreme Court of Canada, Director of Legal Education section of the Survey of the Legal Profession, who attended our morning and afternoon session. A very fruitful exchange of views took place with him on many aspects of the work of law schools. Particular attention was paid to the problem of the practical training of the law students. The nature of such training presently carried on in various provinces was considered, and much concern was expressed over the inadequacy of this branch of legal education. There was a general feeling that a more organized system of training should be established. The McGill representatives outlined the proposals for the fourth year of practical training under university auspices which will begin in Quebec in the autumn of 1951. Representatives of university law schools were unanimous that the basic training in legal principles required the undivided attention of the student for three full years at least, and that the days of concurrent office and university training were numbered.
>
> In the course of the meetings many wider issues were opened up and explored at some length. All the schools recognized that they are in fact training

a number of students who will never practice law, but that this condition cannot be prevented and is, indeed, to be welcomed. Some time was also devoted to a consideration of the proper relationship between the law school and the legal profession, and also of the increasing need for full-time teachers of law.

After Mr. Justice Rand had retired the meeting turned to a discussion of matters of organization, and of available case books and teaching materials. It was decided that we should formalise our association at least to the point of giving it a name, and the "Association of Canadian Law Teachers" was chosen. I was asked to continue to act as chairman and convener for the coming year. It was also decided, in view of the many advantages resulting from our meetings with other academic and learned societies, especially in the way of contact with other social scientists, that we should hold our next meeting in June 1951 when the learned societies will be meeting at McGill. Members pointed out that this would not cut us off from contact with the Canadian Bar Association, since they in fact would attend its meetings also.

In the matter of publications, volumes containing cases and materials on Constitutional Law and Administrative Law were reported as being under way by Professors Laskin and Willis respectively. Professor Laskin undertook to discuss publication of materials with certain law book publishers. Mr. Nicholls initiated a discussion on writing and research for publication in the *Canadian Bar Review*.

Submitted on behalf of the Association of Canadian Law Teachers.

1951

In the spring of 1951 Frank Scott sent out a further circular with the name of the Association:

> In 1948, during the Canadian Bar Association Convention in Montreal, a group of law teachers met at McGill and decided to form an association which would meet annually to discuss problems relating to legal education and teaching methods in Canada. It was felt that there was a need, not filled by membership in the Association of American Law Schools, for the Canadian law teachers to have an opportunity of meeting one another and exchanging views on matters of common interest to them as teachers. At the last annual meeting held in June, 1950, during the annual conferences of the various Canadian learned societies at Kingston, Ontario, it was decided that the name of the association should be the Association of Canadian Law Teachers.
>
> So far the Association has not adopted a formal constitution, but it has agreed upon certain principles. It is not representative of law schools, but of law teachers. It cannot, therefore, adopt any decisions which are binding on the schools or in any way affect their administration. Its purpose is to secure greater recognition of the law teacher as part of the legal profession, and to assist in developing improved standards of teaching and research. Every individual who teaches in any Canadian law school, whether full-time or part-time, is eligible for membership and is invited to the meetings of the Association. There are at present over 200 such teachers in Canada.
>
> It is hoped that all teachers who can possibly attend will be present at the next meetings, which will take place at the McGill Faculty of Law on June 4th–5th, 1951. Out-of-town members may take advantage of the special Uni-

versity accommodation, details of which are given in the enclosed memorandum, and special convention rates are available on the Canadian railways if the enclosed certificate is duly signed and presented. The Agenda for this year's discussions during the two days of meetings will be as follows:—

1. Teaching materials and case books.
2. Graduate work in Canadian law schools.
3. Practical training for the Bar.
4. Comparative law teaching in Canadian law schools.
5. The place and purpose of institutes in the law school.
6. Organization and purposes of the Association of Canadian Law Teachers.

In addition, there will be a dinner meeting on June 4th with a guest speaker. All sessions will be held in Chancellor Day Hall, 3544 Peel Street, Montreal, beginning at 10:30 a.m. on Monday June 4th. To assist in arrangements, kindly inform the Registrar of McGill University as soon as possible if you can be present.

F.R. Scott.
Convenor

P.S. Dean Griswold of the Harvard Law School has just agreed to speak at the dinner on June 4th.

A significant step at the 1951 meeting was the formulation of "general principles for the constitution of the Association"; and for the first time a regular slate of officers was elected for the following year. The Secretary, W.R. Lederman of Dalhousie Law School, prepared the report which was sent to all teachers. It should be noted that the annual membership fee of $3.00 was never put into effect.

This is an account of the discussions and conclusions of meetings held at McGill University Law School on June 4th and 5th, 1951. Nine of the eleven Canadian law schools were represented. This summary will include:

A. List of those present.
B. Topics considered and the main points contributed in the course of discussion.
C. Constitution and purposes of the Association.
D. Plans for the 1952 meeting.

A. LIST OF THOSE PRESENT:

University of British Columbia	G.F. Curtis
University of Alberta	G.W.T. Reed
University of Saskatchewan	W.F. Whitmore
University of Toronto	C.A. Wright
	F.C. Auld
	W. Friedmann
	F.E. LaBrie
	Bora Laskin
	J.B. Milner
	John Willis
Osgoode Hall Law School	D.A.L. Smout
University of Montreal	H.A. Leal
	A. Mayrand
	P. Carignan

McGill University	W.C.J. Meredith
	F.R. Scott
	M. Cohen
	L. Baudouin
	J.C. Cooper
University of New Brunswick	G.A. McAllister
	W.F. Ryan
Dalhousie University	H.E. Read
	W.R. Lederman
	R.G. Murray
	J.M. Hendry
Montreal, Editor—*Canadian Bar Review*	G.V.V. Nicholls

Also, President MacKenzie of the University of British Columbia attended one session, and Dean E.N. Griswold of the Harvard Law School gave the address at the dinner meeting on the evening of June 4th held in the McGill Faculty Club.

B. TOPICS CONSIDERED AND THE MAIN POINTS CONTRIBUTED IN THE COURSE OF DISCUSSION:

All meetings were plenary sessions in the Common Room of the McGill Law School at Chancellor Day Hall. These subjects were considered:

1. Teaching materials and case books.
2. Study and teaching of comparative law in Canada.
3. Graduate work in Canadian law schools.
4. The place of special institutes.

Teaching Materials and Case Books

It was agreed that, at least in the common law schools of the country, great poverty existed respecting Canadian collections of printed or multigraphed teaching materials. To some extent, this was deemed due to small faculties and overloaded law teachers, and to some extent to lack of contact and collaboration between teachers in different schools. Discussion centered on what could and should be done about this. It appeared that a good number of multigraphed case books were in use, quite a number having been produced for example at U.B.C., the University of Sask., and Osgoode Hall. The total sale of case books multigraphed at U.B.C. over the last three years was given as 7,000—about 4,300 to U.B.C. students and 2,300 to other law schools.

The feasibility of the use of the same books by different schools was then discussed. Some considered a case book too individual a product to be useful to teachers other than the compiler. However, it was pointed out that much depended on the subject concerned and the type of collection attempted. Many thought that case books of wide utility were practical in comparatively settled and developed fields like Contract or Tort, whereas this might not be so at all in newer and more amorphous fields such as Labour or Taxation. In particular this would be so respecting the more settled subjects if the compiler of a collection of cases and materials would keep other users in mind and aim to provide in effect a portable library of standard materials in his subject. Even so it was admitted that any collection involved selection, and would thus to some extent inevitably reflect the preferences, views and methods of the author.

On behalf of the civil law schools it was pointed out that much printed teaching material is available and indeed mandatory respecting the law of Quebec, not to mention the Code itself. Nevertheless it was considered that there exist important fields common to all provinces in which there is scope and need for co-operation between civil and common law schools. Examples of subjects where mutually acceptable collections of teaching materials would be welcome were: Constitutional Law, Criminal Law, Taxation, General Legal Philosophy, Corporation Law, Bankruptcy and Bills and Notes.

While it was the sense of the meeting that much could be done to produce widely acceptable collections of teaching materials in some subjects, nevertheless it was felt that to attempt a specific division of labour in this respect at this time would be premature. It was thought better that first much detailed exchange of syllabi and opinions between teachers of the same subjects should take place. It was decided that it would be an important immediate object of the Association to promote such exchange of information and opinion. Accordingly it was agreed that the Secretary should request each law school dean to compose a dozen complete sets of syllabi for the courses given in his school and to despatch one such set to the dean of each other Canadian law school. Thus there would be in each school a complete file from which any teacher could determine in detail how his subjects were being handled in other places. Correspondence between teachers in the same field might well follow, and in general much benefit would ensue for all concerned—whether or not such interchanges in the end made feasible the production of common case books. Further it was agreed that members attending the 1952 meeting be asked to bring full outlines of their courses with them so that most of the time could be devoted to panel discussions by separate small groups of those teaching the same or related subjects. The plans for the 1952 meeting allow for this, and are given more fully in part D of this summary.

The form and the financing of publication of case books was also considered. While there was some disagreement, majority opinion seemed to the effect that case book projects in Canada would have to rely mainly on multigraphing methods of publication and that instances where printing by law publishers was commercially feasible would be rare. Nevertheless it was made clear that the sympathy and assistance of commercial law publishers would be welcome and that books with a wide professional as well as student appeal might well interest them.

The Study and Teaching of Comparative Law in Canada

In the discussions of this topic, important contributions were made by members with extensive European legal experience and training. It was emphasized that Canada has a unique and favourable environment to stimulate the study of comparative law, in that the common law and civil law systems operate in combination as the law of Quebec. Further, in many federal matters (e.g., the drafting of a Canadian Succession Duty Act) both common law and civil law doctrines (e.g., respecting property and succession) must be considered. It was further pointed out that a knowledge of both systems is very practical for counsel appearing before the Supreme Court of Canada. In spite of these factors it was found that little had been done in Canadian law schools to promote comparative law studies. By way of exception though it was mentioned that there has been some outstanding work in this field by Quebec jurists, and that in the Quebec law schools Roman law is taught, and necessarily comparisons between the common law and the civil code run through all teaching.

Certain advantages of the systematic comparison of various national legal systems were mentioned. Principally they seemed reducible to the following:

(1) Comparative law studies would awaken in the student a healthy critical attitude toward his own legal system and thereby enhance his appreciation of it.
(2) Such studies would facilitate the improvement of one's own legal system.
(3) Such studies would promote uniformity of national laws, and in Canada uniformity of laws between the provinces.

One member very much doubted the usefulness of comparing the common law and civil law systems as a whole. Rather he thought effort and attention should be concentrated on comparing statute law in the field of pressing contemporary social problems. Nevertheless many present were of the opinion that more should be done about comparative law in Canadian law schools.

Certain problems of teaching comparative law were then raised, and certain answers were suggested to them:

(1) Should study of this subject take the form of specific classes or of a teaching technique running through other classes? (It seemed agreed that though both approaches were useful, specific classes were needed.)
(2) If specific classes are to be given, should they be offered at the undergraduate or post-graduate level? (There was disagreement here, but the majority who expressed themselves favoured a class or classes at the senior or post-graduate level. The danger of confusing immature students was emphasized.)
(3) What materials are available for comparative law study and teaching and what facility in languages do teachers and students of this subject need? (In this respect the experts present agreed that so far as the student was concerned sufficient source material was now available in English to allow a proper course to be given to persons with only that language. However the teacher was considered to need several languages—at the very least English and French.)

The question of resources for comparative law teaching in Canadian law schools was also considered. It was pointed out that in many schools faculty members were already overloaded with teaching tasks in one legal system, however desirable comparative law teaching might be as a matter of principle. To correct this it was said that most University administrations would have to be persuaded of the need of more financial backing for law faculties. At any rate, some felt that comparative law could be specifically offered at the graduate level at McGill and the University of Toronto. It was further suggested that there was a place in Canada for an institute of comparative law.

Graduate Work in Canadian Law Schools

It was ascertained that so far as those present knew, the degree of Master of Laws was being offered in Canada at the Universities of Toronto, McGill, and Dalhousie. In the first two institutions named the degree has been offered for many years while the Dalhousie degree was first offered in the session 1950–51. The University of Toronto also offers a Doctor's degree, the conferring of which has apparently been quite rare.

Discussion then proceeded on the following points:

(1) What should be the purpose and plan of a Master's course in law?
(2) What type of student is interested and what good would another year of study do him?
(3) Can Canadian schools compete with the graduate schools of the United Kingdom, France and the United States?

The question was asked whether the emphasis for the year of Master's work should be upon set courses designed to broaden the horizons of the LL.B. degree-holder, or upon intensive research and thesis work in one special field. It seemed the consensus that the ideal Master's course would be a combination of these approaches. It appeared that such was the plan in the Canadian graduate schools mentioned. It was further pointed out that graduate work in the proper academic sense was to be clearly distinguished from short refresher courses for practitioners, however desirable and meritorious these latter projects might be.

It was said that prospective graduate students came mainly from three classes of persons:
(1) Those who wished to follow a certain subject or subjects further than was possible during LL.B. work;
(2) Would-be teachers of law; and
(3) Foreigners.

There was disagreement on whether a Master's degree was any use to a man who intended to enter the practice of law. The point was made in this respect that if a good student was set to wrestling with certain fundamental legal problems, some good would come of it whatever form of legal career he thereafter pursued. It was said that it would always be hard to point in advance to concrete advantages accruing to this or that graduate degree-holder. It was reported that there was a tendency in England for lawyers in the civil service to take the Master's degree and that there were some signs of the same trend in Canada. It was also reported by those from McGill and the University of Toronto that a few foreign students were appearing—e.g., some from Latin American countries at McGill.

The fear was expressed by some that the tendency for the better Canadian graduate students to go to the United States, England or France was so well established that Canadian schools would be left with a secondary class of student. It was not considered that this would be entirely true, especially if some attractive scholarships would be offered at home. At any rate the consensus was that it was very desirable that some Canadian law schools should offer graduate work, particularly in fields such as constitutional law where there are peculiar Canadian problems. Members were then asked if it was the practice at their respective schools to encourage good students to take graduate degrees, and if so where did the faculty usually recommend them to go? It appeared that at all law schools represented good students were encouraged to take graduate study and that in advising where to go a considerable preference was shown for the United States, though some were advised to go to England, and in the case of Quebec students, France.

Members present with long experience in law teaching in England, Continental Europe or the United States objected to the Canadian 'inferiority complex' about graduate work and asserted emphatically that it was time to put it aside. They considered that Canadian law faculties could offer graduate work equivalent in merit to that available abroad.

The Place of Special Institutes

Discussion in this respect was started by an outline of the plan of the newly formed Institute of International Air Law at McGill, given by its distinguished director. As this information is available in printed form from McGill University and in the *Canadian Bar Review* for May, 1951, it will not be summarized here.

While interest was shown in the McGill project, there seemed no disposition among those present to favour the institute method of organizing graduate studies in other fields.

C. CONSTITUTION AND PURPOSES OF THE ASSOCIATION:

(a) The following general principles for the constitution of the Association were agreed:

1) Membership is open to all persons engaged in the teaching of law in Canada (whether full- or part-time), and to the editor of the *Canadian Bar Review.*

2) The Association is representative of law teachers and is primarily concerned with their problems and interests. It is not representative of law schools or their administrations as such.

3) There will be annual meetings. At each annual meeting the place and date for the next meeting will be considered and the executive instructed in this respect.

4) The annual membership fee is $3.00.

5) The executive of the Association is to consist of the following: President, Vice-President, Secretary-Treasurer, and a committee of three. All officers and two of the three committee members are to be elected annually. The third committee member is automatically the retiring President.

6) Constitutional changes require a simple majority in plenary session at the annual meeting.

(b) Discussion of the desirable occasion and time for the annual meeting The issue was whether the Association should make a practice of meeting as one of the Learned Societies which convene annually in early June following the National Conference of Canadian Universities, or whether it should meet with the Canadian Bar Association.

The following points were made in favour of meeting as one of the Learned Societies at a university centre:

1) The contact with university colleagues in other fields is valuable.

2) Convention time could all be devoted to the mutual problems of law teachers.

3) Accommodation and other expenses are arranged at a level which is within reach of persons on university salaries.

4) The dates for the meetings of the Learned Societies are suitable for law teachers being in early June just after the closing of law schools.

In favour of meeting with the Canadian Bar Association it was pointed out that it was important for law teachers to maintain close contact with the legal profession as a whole and to take their part in influencing the discussions and recommendations of the Canadian Bar Association in educational matters in particular. Further, it was considered desirable that law teachers should be recognized as a distinct and important branch of the profession, as is the case in the United States and Europe. Nevertheless, the following factors, it was thought, would render a joint meeting with the Canadian Bar Association difficult:

1) The Canadian Bar Association usually meets in late summer or early fall when either law schools have opened or are about to do so. Very few teachers can get away at this time.
(2) Expenses at the Canadian Bar Meetings are much higher than at those of the Learned Societies.
(3) Law Teachers active on C.B.A. committees would have little if any time for separate meetings of law teachers. Indeed, a proper set of meetings for law teachers would be difficult to fit into C.B.A. proceedings.

On weighing the foregoing considerations the conclusion was reached that as a usual thing it would be best for the Association of Canadian Law Teachers to meet with the other Learned Societies at the university chosen for the National Conference of Canadian Universities. However, as there might be times when it was feasible and desirable to hold the annual meeting in conjunction with that of the Canadian Bar Association, it was decided that the place and date of the next annual meeting should be subject to review each year.

It was decided that the 1952 annual meeting of the Association would be held along with that of the other Learned Societies at Laval University, Quebec City.

(c) Elections to the executive for 1951–2:

President:	G.F. Curtis	— U.B.C.
Secretary-Treasurer:	W.R. Lederman	— Dalhousie
Executive Committee:	F.R. Scott (retiring President)	— McGill
	A. Mayrand	— U. of Montreal
	J.B. Milner	— U. of Toronto

It was decided to offer the Vice-Presidency to M. Guy Hudon of the Faculty of Law, Laval University, as it was considered that law teachers there would be interested in the Association and as Laval is the proposed place for the 1952 meeting.

The sincere thanks of those present was conveyed to the members of the McGill law faculty, and to Professor Scott in particular, for excellent arrangements and generous hospitality.

D. PLANS FOR THE 1952 MEETING:

A meeting of the executive was held at 4:00 p.m. on June 5th, and the following conclusions were reached concerning the program for the 1952 meeting:

(1) The Association would meet for three days.
(2) Those present would quickly separate into panels of teachers concerned with the same or related subjects for detailed discussion of mutual problems, including the matter of teaching materials.
(3) To facilitate these panel discussions, members would be asked to bring with them detailed syllabi or outlines of their respective courses.
(4) The following were suggested as suitable panel subjects for those from

both civil and common law schools:

Constitutional Law
Administrative Law
Contracts
Taxation

Other panels would be arranged as desired, even as late as the first day of meeting.

(5) Plenary sessions would be kept to a minimum—but such sessions would be necessary on the opening and closing days. The teaching of international law in Canada was suggested as a possible topic for a plenary session. Also it was felt the matter of teaching materials and publication problems would need another review.

(6) It was agreed that in the evenings general social gatherings would be much preferable to business sessions.

(7) The question of obtaining a special guest speaker was left open, though certain authorities on international law were considered.

It was also decided that a directory of Canadian law teachers should be prepared. Mr. J.B. Milner undertook to see to this, including the tasks of multigraphing and distribution.

1952

This year the notice of meeting was more detailed and formal, now that the Association had a secretary. The notice, dated March 28, 1952, stated that the programme "will follow the lines laid down in Part D of the report of the proceedings of our 1951 meeting." It was circulated to all teachers through their deans. The meeting was held at Laval University, Quebec, on June 2–4, under the Chairmanship of Dean Curtis, President.

Formal minutes of this meeting were not kept though a brief account appears in the article in 30 Can. Bar Rev. 608 (1952). Complete notes were kept by Mr. Reed (Alberta) the relevant parts of which follow.

> The plenary meetings were held in the library of the Faculty of Law at Laval University and the discussions were held in lecture rooms or the library. All Canadian law schools save Manitoba's were represented. In addition, the Editor and the Assistant-Editor of the *Canadian Bar Review,* the President of the Association of American Law Schools, Dr. MacKenzie from U.B.C., and Mr. McWhinney of Yale and Australia were present at some or all of the meetings.
>
> At the opening session Mr. Justice Gagne, the Dean at Laval, welcomed us and informed us that the Law Faculty was one of the original faculties at Laval and was, therefore, celebrating its centennial along with the University as a whole. Mr. Matthews brought greetings from the American Association. He remarked that it was, perhaps, fitting that he should bring greetings from an Association entering its fifty-second year to one commencing its second year of organized existence.
>
> The first plenary session then got underway. It was found that there was no need to discuss the appointment of Professor Friedmann as delegate to the Comparative Law Conference in Cambridge since this was not a

U.N.E.S.C.O. affair as previously thought. It was unnecessary that our organization become affiliated with the United Nations organization in order to be allowed representatives at Cambridge.

The President reported that the executive had not received any suggestions for procedure at this meeting and so had planned the agenda in accordance with the tentative plans made last year; that is, in the form of plenary sessions and panel discussions. The executive was appointed a nominating committee.

Mr. Milner reported on the law teachers' directory which he had prepared and which was at this point distributed. He pointed out that replies were not received from Manitoba or Montreal and that McGill's came in too late for incorporation. He asked that errors be reported to him and also additions since he intended keeping the directory up to date. Mr. Mayrand from Montreal said that their list would be sent in. He also suggested that a list of subjects be prepared showing the names of all the teachers of each subject. This will be done.

Publication of Teaching Materials

Bora Laskin reported that Carswell's had indicated definite interest in publishing case books at low cost. This interest has not been dampened by the production of his own book. Toronto is prepared to facilitate the administration of any proposed publication.

Mr. Pigeon (Laval) said that the primary difficulty for the French-language schools was the lack of *stare decisis*. He pointed out that the decisions of the judges in the first instance had little effect. Great reliance is placed on the civil code. He admitted that it was a little different with regard to Court of Appeal decisions and very different so far as Supreme Court of Canada decisions were concerned, but he said, "We train students for trial and not for appellate courts."

He agreed that, theoretically at all events, it should be different for federal subjects but in fact it was not, because the students were not trained in the common law techniques and moreover there was always the language problem. Laskin, for example, was just too much for the Laval students. In criminal law the students were not expected to digest cases. The instructor gave a summary.

Mr. Mayrand said that reports were expected to be read at Montreal and so too, said Dean Meredith, at McGill.

Dean Curtis remarked that insurance policies were essentially the same in British Columbia and Quebec and he wanted to make use of Quebec decisions but found that the language prevented him from doing do.

Mr. Pigeon pointed out that it was dangerous to use cases from Quebec without a knowledge of the Quebec practice and the techniques of the civil code.

Mr. Laskin then reported that Toronto got a $50,000 grant from Carnegie for the advancement of comparative law in Canada. This money was to be used on a Dominion-wide basis rather than for the purely private use of Toronto.

Dean Meredith reported that the first 900 pages of Professor Beaudoin's comparative study of the law of Quebec, France and the common law was in press. The text is in French.

Professor Matthews said that the training of a student was always a difficult problem but that he thought there was a great advantage to be gained by putting, say, a B.C. student through the intellectual process of the Quebec civil code. It sharpens their wits in respect to their own law. He reported that in a labour law case book on which he and many others were working a typical fact problem is presented and then the solution given according to the law of a number of different countries. He admitted a certain amount of student resistance.

Monseigneur Vandry delivered an impassioned plea for the unity of Canada and the building of a Christian democracy. To this end the cultural organizations and institutions must be dedicated and devoted whether Catholic or Protestant. Laval's policy was to make use of the French culture for the grandeur and enrichment of Canadian civilization and for this purpose Christian charity was necessary.

Afterwards Mr. Pigeon spoke at some length on *stare decisis* in Quebec.

Dean Curtis pointed out that re-runs of mimeographed materials were now as expensive as the original run because of increased costs.

Mr. Laskin stated that the problem was twofold:

1. Someone had to assume the task of preparing material which the remainder would agree to use. Resources were the difficulty. Money was needed to assist in production. It was up to the school to find that money.
2. Scholarship was required, without which the university law schools in Canada have no business functioning in the long run. Here again money was the chief difficulty.

The University of Montreal suggested that students be required to purchase books and that the cost be added to the tuition fees as was done in the medical faculty. This would help meet the production costs. Dean Curtis pointed out that where faculties are overcrowded and students have to be turned away, as in the case with most medical faculties, such a scheme might work but that he did not think it was feasible in the case of other faculties. Mr. Smout of Osgoode Hall said that what is needed is a combined text and case book such as Cockle. Mr. Milner observed, "I'll retire if I thought that I would produce another Cockle!" Professor Matthews pointed out that this raised the old battle between the deductive and inductive processes. In the American law school where the inductive method is used the chief object is to get away from texts except as a reference. The students do not like it because they have to work and think and struggle. Case books are essential for this process. To the practising lawyer they are useless. In his labour law book there was a slight compromise.

It was suggested that teachers interested in a particular subject should meet together to consider the production of a case book in that field. Each school would send in cases and informative material and a general editor would consolidate the results. To this end funds were needed to enable meetings to be held.

The morning session then came to a close.

Monday afternoon was devoted to panel discussions in administrative law and constitutional law, evidence and taxation.

Tuesday morning a plenary session was held on library problems. Dean Curtis opened the discussion with the remark that insufficient attention was paid by university administrators to libraries and to the special claims by law students and teachers to vital library supplies. The claim, he continued, is lost sight of in the expensive and special equipment required by engineering and medical faculties. A canvass of each law school was then taken.

Mr. Murray for Dalhousie reported that the volume of books was large and the money good but that no one could say what the library had pending a reorganization which was forthcoming.

Mr. McAllister speaking for New Brunswick reported a weak library and difficult mental attitude with regard to this situation. He wanted to know what other schools have so that he can have a bargaining weapon to deal with those who should be pushing the library.

Dean Meredith of McGill said that they had both common and civil books but he had no idea just what.

David Smout from Osgoode reported no problem when the Students' and Great Library were taken together save for a weakness in American periodicals.

Bora Laskin (Toronto) reported a good working library at hand when Dr. Wright took over. This has since doubled in size. The main concentration has been on periodicals. Fifteen thousand dollars were spent last year. He suggested that this organization should fix a minimum budget for library needs, the idea being to canvass the various schools in order to set up a minimum which the organization would endorse. The organization would use what weight it had to back schools having difficulties in securing minimum requirements.

Friedmann (Toronto) spoke of Toronto's comparative law section. A good governmental effort was made to bring the section up to date. In the next few years the plan is to expand. The hope is to obtain a good working library particularly in texts and journals and commentaries on the more prominent legal systems as, for example, of France, Germany, Italy, Spain, etc. Law reports are not envisaged. In a year or two there will be sufficient for research purposes.

The situation in Manitoba appeared to be more or less the same as at Osgoode. Considerable progress has been made in periodicals.

Mr. Whitmore reported that Saskatchewan had an adequate teaching library but was nevertheless woefully weak as was the Bar Library in Saskatoon. Annual expenditures now averaged about fifteen hundred dollars. Lack of initiative was the main problem. Mr. Reed gave the Alberta picture but was unable to speak on funds available. Alberta seems to be the only law school with a properly qualified law librarian.

Dean Curtis said that the large number of students at British Columbia created a problem in some respects but also made available considerable funds. A gift of ten thousand dollars last year helped immeasurably. The civil law section is weak but the plan is to overcome the shortage.

Dean Curtis then suggested that each school should put out a catalogue with the idea of lending books to or exchanging with other schools. The catalogue would list reports, reviews, texts and statutes and would indicate those available for exchange, lending, or purchase.

At this stage a lively discussion ensued. It was ultimately concluded that it would be helpful if each school could prepare a list of reports, journals, and statutes (not necessarily texts) for general circulation. Periodical lists of acquisitions should also be compiled and circulated. Broken parts and missing parts would be indicated. There is no obligation to do this.

A panel discussion on library problems including minimum budgets will be held next year. At that time the problem of a catalogue and the necessity of a grant of funds therefor will be considered. A library committee will be named by the executive to prepare for this discussion.

Professor Matthews referred us to the 1951–52 annual proceedings of the Association of American Law Schools for a report on minimum library needs. The Dean at Southern California is the secretary and could give, on request, information on the present requirements.

The morning session concluded with panel discussion on torts, labor law, and contracts.

Tuesday afternoon was devoted to a tour of Quebec City and the Isle of Orleans. After the tour we rendezvoused on the island at a pleasant cottage belonging to Mr. Taschereau. This was followed by a dinner meeting held at the Circle Universitaire. Professor Matthews was the guest speaker. The theme revolved around the inroads being made on freedom under the law in the United States, particularly the hysteria with which communism is regarded. The race problem also came in for discussion, the whole being related to the functions of a law school. He was thanked by Surveyer J., a very old judge of great charm, who gave an excellent speech. His Lordship was a former lecturer at Laval and is apparently very well known at the American Law School meetings which he used to attend regularly.

The discussion in Wednesday's session on the teaching of international law was opened by Charles Bourne of the University of British Columbia. He put his case in the form of questions.

1. Should international law be taught in Canadian law schools?
   The stock objection is that this subject is not a bread-and-butter course but fifty out of one hundred and eighteen members of the American Association of Law Schools have it on their syllabus. It is important in training leaders in the community. Its study is a good training in jurisprudence for it illustrates the growth of a law system. It does, in fact, have practical value, for example, in the fields of radio, shipping, air and business. Bourne's own experience has been that the students feel it must be taken seriously.
2. For what students?
   (a) As an option course?
   (b) Only law students?
   Arts students are included in British Columbia. Although the course is directed to law students, the experience has been that the arts students have found the course most interesting. Different exams are written.
3. What sort of course?
   This depends on the answers to the question in (2). Time makes it impossible to cover all international law at U.B.C. The laws of war and neutrality are not covered. A compromise between substantive law and organs of organization has been effected. The teaching method, so far as law students are concerned, should be the same as for other law courses (i.e., case and discussion). Materials are reasonably plentiful and the bur-

den not too great on the library. U.B.C. spent two thousand dollars last year on the section.

4. Research in Canada and the publication of materials.
5. What is being done in other law schools?

The schools reported as follows:

Dalhousie—two hours a week, one term, optional. Twelve out of fifty-one in third year took the course. They represented the best students in the class. The course took the form of seminars.

University of New Brunswick—not on the syllabus but those present were hopeful.

Laval—twenty compulsory lectures.

Montreal—twenty compulsory hours in the first year.

McGill—compulsory full year course.

Toronto—two-hour course in third year as an alternative to comparative law.

Manitoba—there is no course.

Saskatchewan—twenty-five hours in the second year for one-half term - compulsory.

Alberta—none.

British Columbia—Two hours a week for the whole of second year - compulsory.

Osgoode—none.

At Toronto the course is open to graduate arts students. It is felt that the standard of undergraduate arts students is too low. The graduate students have fitted in well. Professor Friedmann remarked that the bread-and-butter arguments should be treated with contempt. The teaching of international law will not make lawyers but it is part of the vital education for citizenship. Again many law students do not go into practice and of those that do some eventually get into government and international organizations. The course itself should be treated as a tough, problem subject. But it must also be considered a subject of flux. At Toronto the course is in two parts. (a) Labrie takes the traditional course following text lines. (b) Friedmann takes current problems on organizations, etc. Last year this included: (1) importance of the expanding state functions or communities, (2) international war crimes, (3) international legal personalities, for example, The Schumann Plan.

Dean Curtis regards the development of international law as primarily the function and responsibility of the law school despite the fact that in many American universities and at Montreal Political Science departments often run parallel courses.

The consensus of the meeting was that international law was something that should find a responsible place in the law school curriculum.

President Norman MacKenzie of U.B.C., who sat in on the Wednesday morning meeting, expressed concern at the difference in level of standards when arts students were included. Mr. Bourne found that fourth year students were advisable. Dean Curtis remarked that different exams were helpful. President MacKenzie said that U.B.C. is attempting to break down the artificial boundaries of departments and faculties and that whenever an overlapping is found encouragement is given to bring the faculty or departments concerned together for mutual study and development. Bora Laskin said that at Toronto there was a number of demands from other faculties for the services of the law teachers. Toronto had taken the attitude that they cannot allow full-time men to go to other departments for special courses although for common courses the situation is different. It is the responsibility, however, of the faculty to provide instruction for other faculties. President MacKenzie said that international law is based on a law governing the relations of all nations having relations with each other. It presupposes a concept above law and it is at this point that the Iron Curtain enters the picture. Do we assume an all-embracing system for the present not in existence in toto or do we think in terms of a compromise because of the two ideas of law existing at present in the world?

Professor Friedmann said that you cannot teach without the current background. Most texts and case books are isolated and therefore must be linked to current problems. Mr. Smout of Osgoode asked whether it should be an optional subject. He also asked what should we throw out the window?

Mr. Milner asked whether international law has contributed anything in legal thinking which is not covered by jurisprudence, that is, a jurisprudence which rises above the pure analytical concept. Apart from the trust and corporate personality concepts, do we ever rise above any basic concepts not taught in first year? The only answer to Smout is to re-examine the curriculum in the light of the concepts taught. Mr. McWhinney said the only answer is to be found in electives because of non-practising lawyers. Mr. Milner said that basic concepts are important because we cannot afford electives. Mr. Taschereau concluded the discussion by saying the student must learn international law because he is the leader of democracy. You cannot learn it later or perhaps one should say students do not. Therefore they must be taught.

The discussion then shifted to teaching techniques with Mr. Lederman of Dalhousie the lead-off man. He stated he could not make the case system, that is, the discussion of each case, work in a class of twenty or more and so he switched to the straight lecture system with the hope that spontaneous questions would lead to discussion. He does not believe in and will not cross-examine students. What is the case method? To him it is a list or collection of cases which he hopes the students will read but on which they are not cross-examined. He does not believe that fear is a good motive. Moreover, he feels that he has a duty to the moderate student and he believes that his method is best suited to them. He admits that most questions come from the good student.

Dean Curtis raised the problem of teaching statute law.

Mr. Laskin said that the important thing is the objective.

Mr. Lederman replied, "My objective is to teach the students to become independent thinkers. The Socratic method is best suited for this but it is impossible when you have a large student body."

Mr. Laskin said that techniques are subsidiary to objectives. The case method is a technique for raising problems and seeking solutions. The mere imparting to the students of other ideas is to be avoided. The student's interest in problems and their solutions must be aroused.

Mr. Milner said there are three case methods in use: (1) the treatment of cases as building blocks, for example, three cases build up a law step by step; if there is a gap, you leave a hole in the wall (most American law teachers use this method); (2) assume the mysterious existence of the law and treat cases as applicable to a set of facts, that is, as simply giving vitality to the law; (3) the problem approach—here one treats cases as a record of a solution of the problem which is a recurring fact situation. You have a look at what one or a number of judges have done with these recurring fact situations. You must not stop thinking about the problem although the House of Lords may have done so. The trouble here is that more facts than are disclosed by the record are often required to give a proper treatment to this method.

Mr. Smout of Osgoode said that we do not want uniform techniques. The object should be to get students to enjoy the law. The rest will follow of itself. If there is no enjoyment, there is no honor. Otherwise, there is a danger of turning out smart-alecks and not lawyers. Mr. McWhinney said: if you enjoy, how do you improve? Mr. McAllister said his objective is: What is the law, how should it be used, and what are its implications?

Mr. MacKenzie said that he had to leave but before he did so, he wanted the meeting to know that he felt that there was a real value to be gained from these meetings not only for those attending but in the long run because of what those attending brought back with them for the faculty and the institution.

Dean Curtis said that every day a lawyer gets a new problem to which seemingly there is no answer on the books directly in point. This is what we have to meet. This is the advantage of the case book. The student must be made aware of this. On the other hand, the case book breaks down when you attempt to teach legislation.

Mr. Pigeon said that Laval uses the expository system. Principles are taught. The problem is to get them across to the student. The problem method is used in practice in the fourth year. Professor Friedmann said that he favored the expository system plus seminars with the emphasis on trends.

The closing session in the afternoon was a business meeting. Mr. Mayrand of Montreal was elected President. The place for the next meeting was not settled definitely. Some of the learned societies are going to St. Francis Xavier in Antigonish. Others are going to Western, Ontario. We would have gone to Western if they had had a law faculty. Mr. Mayrand invited the Association to Montreal with Montreal serving as the host university. The Law Faculty there is celebrating its seventy-fifth anniversary.

Although the meeting was devoid of any tangible results, the discussion and interchange of views was stimulating.

1953

In 1953 the meeting was held at the University of Montreal. A detailed account of the proceedings, prepared by Mr. Milner, appears in 31 Can. Bar Rev. 553.

The formal minutes were prepared by W.R. Lederman, the Secretary, and circulated to all members.

Minutes of the 1953 Meeting
(June 4, 5 and 6 at the University of Montreal)

A. REGISTRATION DATA:
Members attending from each Law School were as follows:

Dalhousie	—	4	Read, Meagher, Murray, Lederman
U.N.B.	—	2	McAllister, Ryan
Laval	—	1	

McGill	—	5	LeMesurier, Meredith, Cohen, Scott, Baudouin
U. of Montreal	—	12	
U. of Ottawa	—	2	Rodys,
U. of Toronto	—	5	Freidmann, Laskin, Milner
Osgoode Hall	—	4	Smalley-Baker, Leal, Spence
U. of Alberta	—	2	Smith, Bowker
U.B.C.	—	2	Curtis, Herbert
Total		39	

Special Guests:
Professor Charles B. Nutting, President, Association of American Law Schools
Professor Clive Parry, Cambridge University

B. BASIC RULES OF THE ASSOCIATION'S CONSTITUTION:

(1) Membership is open to all persons engaged in the teaching of law in Canada (whether full- or part-time) and to the editor of the *Canadian Bar Review*.
(2) The Association is representative of law teachers and is primarily concerned with their problems and interests. It is not representative of law schools or their administrations as such.
(3) There will be annual meetings. At each annual meeting the place and date for the next meeting will be considered and the executive instructed in this respect.
(4) The executive of the Association is to consist of the following: President, Vice-President, Secretary-Treasurer, and a committee of three. All officers and two of the three committee members are to be elected annually. The third committee member is automatically the retiring President.
(5) Constitutional changes require a simple majority in plenary session at the annual meeting.

C. OUTLINE OF THE PROGRAMME:

Topics Discussed in Plenary Session:

Problems of law school libraries.
The promotion of research, writing and exchange lectures in comparative law in Canada.
Pre-legal education, and the objectives of legal education in general.
Requirements for admission to the Bar in the various provinces, and plans for practical training of students by apprenticeship, and otherwise.
Practice of the Supreme Court of Canada in the giving of judgments.
Research and writing by Canadian law teachers, with particular reference to the needs of the *Canadian Bar Review* and other Canadian law journals.

Separate Groups held Panel Discussions on the Teaching of:

Jurisprudence (Legal Philosophy); Constitutional and Administrative Law; Contracts.

D. DECISIONS MADE BY THE ASSOCIATION:

Comparative Law:

That the standing Committee be continued under the chairmanship of Professor Friedmann, who is to have power to add to his committee.

Law School Libraries:

(a) That the Standing Committee be continued under the chairmanship of Professor Milner, who is to have power to add to his committee.

(b) It was unanimously resolved that in the opinion of the members present it was essential that effective control of law school libraries should be vested in the respective law faculties.

Supreme Court of Canada Judgments:

It was unanimously resolved that it was not desirable that the Supreme Court of Canada should follow the Privy Council practice of issuing only the one judgment in each case. It was further agreed that it was desirable that the existing right of each justice to issue his own opinion should be maintained, but that wherever possible a "judgment of the court" should be issued defining the extent of majority agreement among the justices upon the reason for disposition of the points at issue. It was noted that a committee of the Canadian Bar Association had been constituted to consider this issue, and the President was authorized to draft a submission, in co-operation with the members of his executive, which would convey to that committee the view of the Association.

Requirements for Admission to the Bar:

It was agreed that the Association should arrange for the preparation of a comprehensive synopsis outlining conditions for admission to the Bar in each Province.

E. OFFICERS OF THE ASSOCIATION FOR 1953–54:

President:	B. Laskin, University of Toronto.
Vice-President:	W.R. Lederman, Dalhousie University.
Secretary-Treasurer:	W.F. Bowker, University of Alberta.
Executive Members:	A. Mayrand, University of Montreal (immediate Past-President).
	F.R. Scott, McGill University.
	H.A. Leal, Osgoode Hall Law School.
	L.P. Pigeon, Laval University.

F. THE 1954 MEETING:

Place:

It was agreed to accept the invitation of the President of the University of Manitoba to meet in Winnipeg at the same time as the other university societies.

Date:

It is expected that the meeting will be for three days during the first week of June.

Programme:

It was agreed that the Faculty of the President, under his chairmanship, be requested to accept responsibility for planning the business programme, after appropriate consultation with members of the executive and other faculties.

G. SOCIAL EVENTS:

Thanks were expressed, in particular to the University of Montreal, and also to the editor of the *Canadian Bar Review* and to the McGill Law Faculty for very generous hospitality.

After the meeting, the incoming President prepared a submission on the one-judgment proposal and after it was approved by the executive copies were forwarded to the Minister of Justice, the President of the Canadian Bar Association, and to the Special Committee of the Canadian Bar Association.

Statement by the Association of Canadian Law Teachers on the Propriety of a One-Judgment Rule for the Supreme Court of Canada

At the annual convention of the Association of Canadian Law Teachers held in Montreal on June 4—6, 1953, notice was taken of a pending investigation by the Canadian Bar Association into the question whether the Supreme Court of Canada should deliver only one reasoned judgment. This question, involving the wisdom of the adoption by the Supreme Court of the Privy Council practice, was debated by members of the A.C.L.T. The debate resulted in the unanimous endorsement of a resolution that (1) the A.C.L.T. is opposed to a compulsory one-judgment rule on the lines of the Privy Council practice; (2) the A.C.L.T. respectfully suggests that the Supreme Court adopt a practice of delivering a judgment of the Court (which will record at least the minimum area of agreement of a majority or more of the sitting Judges) subject to a right in any member of the Court to give a concurring or a dissenting opinion.

The historical reasons for the Privy Council practice are well known. They do not, of course, have any application to the Supreme Court of Canada. The relevant inquiry hence is whether the Privy Council practice has, independently of its origin, such merit as to warrant its adoption elsewhere.

1. No appellate court in any common law jurisdiction adheres to the Privy Council practice. The House of Lords in Great Britain, the High Court of Australia, the Supreme Court of South Africa, the Supreme Court of New Zealand and the Supreme Court of the United States all observe the practice, presently followed by the Supreme Court of Canada, which recognizes the right of each Judge to make his individual pronouncement on a case before his Court.
2. It is not unusual for members of a Court to join in one judgment but this is by free choice and not by the compulsion of any statute or rule of Court or even internal administrative disciplines.
3. A compulsory one-judgment rule assumes either that there is only one solution to any problem or, even if there be more than one solution, then logically, there is no particular point in giving reasons for judgment, because the solution, if obvious to the Judges, ought to be equally obvious to lawyers. (It is quite possible, however, that several Judges may reach the same result for different reasons.) If there is more than one solution, the selection of one by a majority of sitting Judges carries no certainty of its superiority over others, though the selection will settle the particular case. The litigants, the legal profession and the public are entitled to know, in the interest of the administration of justice, what alternative solutions commend themselves to Judges of the Court. This has been the common law tradition, which recognizes and expects the personal contribution of an appellate court Judge so that (1) precision may be given to a majority judgment by the recording of reasoned dissents; (2) growth in the law may be stimulated by the reception of conflicting ideas; and (3) direction may be given to practitioners and teachers of law on the judicial absorption of legal arguments made in the case. It is enough to point to

the judicial careers of Justices Holmes and Brandeis in the United States and Lord Atkin as a member of the English House of Lords to emphasize what has just been said.

4. The relation of *stare decisis* to the matter under discussion deserves a brief comment. If the Supreme Court perseveres in an adherence to *stare decisis,* it is all the more necessary to ensure the fullest freedom of utterance for member Judges. A compulsory one-judgment rule in association with *stare decisis* would devitalize our law. It would give us a superficial certainty without the informing considerations which dissenting and concurring judgments point up. The necessary compromises involved in a one-judgment rule would ultimately lead to guesses as to the meaning or reach of a particular decision. In the result we would get either rigid acceptance of earlier decisions or re-interpretation of an abstract kind, because it would be uninformed by any specific emphasis that is a feature of individual judging. This has been the story of much of the Privy Council's work and it should not be forgotten that that body has accepted the authority of the House of Lords (which permits dissenting and concurring judgments) in what may be called, roughly, matters of common law.
5. If the Supreme Court should decide to take a liberal view towards *stare decisis,* or even to abandon the doctrine whenever it sees fit so to do, there is an equally strong case for keeping open the market of judicial ideas for possible future consideration. The history of law shows that no one generation can permanently bottle up the social pressures that determine our legal rules. No collective or even individual wisdom can have eternal validity when we have to contend with changing social conditions and ideas. Rules of law are not matters of divine revelation. They come from humans who articulate them on the basis of many factors, legal, social, economic, psychological, etc., even though they are expressed within the framework of formal legal logic. The value which we place on freedom of utterance finds one of its loftiest justifications in the individual contributions of eminent Judges to our social cohesiveness.
6. The anonymity implicit in a compulsory one-judgment rule is an invitation to individual irresponsibility of Judges as well as being a denial of their individuality. There is no sensible analogy between the collective responsibility of a cabinet and the collectivisation of members of a final Court. We can only justify the appointment of men of high calibre to our Supreme Court if we expect and permit them to give tangible evidence of their influence on the development of our law. It is as unfair to them, as it is to the legal profession and to the public, to require them to pour themselves into a common mould.

The A.C.L.T. repeats its view that it is opposed to a compulsory one-judgment rule for the Supreme Court. It does, however, see merit in an internal administrative practice by which the Supreme Court would deliver a judgment of the Court (as indicated in an earlier part of this memorandum) while leaving members of the tribunal otherwise free to record individual views.

1954

The following formal minutes of the 1954 meeting kept by W.F. Bowker (Alberta), Secretary-Treasurer, were circulated to all teachers:

Minutes of the 1954 Meeting
(June 3, 4 and 5 at the University of Manitoba
and at the Winnipeg Law Courts)

A. REGISTRATION DATA:

The number attending from each Law School is as follows:

Dalhousie	—	3: Dean Read, W.R. Lederman, Lorne Clarke.
U.N.B.	—	2: Geo. McAllister, W. Ryan
McGill	—	1: Frank Scott
U. of Montreal	—	1: Albert Mayrand
U. of Toronto	—	3: Dean Wright, Bora Laskin, J.B. Milner
Osgoode hall	—	1: Allan Leal
U. of Manitoba	—	19
U. of Saskatchewan	—	1: E. Whitmore
U. of Alberta	—	2: Dean Bowker, Alex Smith
U.B.C.	—	1: Dean Curtis
Total	—	34

Special Guests:

Professor Shelden Elliott, President, Association of American Law Schools
Mr. K. Howard Drake, University of London.

B. BASIC RULES OF THE ASSOCIATION'S CONSTITUTION:

These are set out in paragraph B of the minutes of the 1953 meeting.

C. OUTLINE OF PROGRAMME:

All sessions were plenary. Papers were given on the following topics:

The Desirability of Endorsement by the Association of a Statement of Objectives and Minimum Curricular Requirements	— Dean H.E. Read and Mr. H.G.H. Smith
Objectives and Their Achievement, 32 Can. Bar Rev. 762	— Professor Max Cohen (read by Professor F.R. Scott)
The Shaping of the Curriculum	— Mr. H.E. Carey and Mr. J.E. Wilson
Objectives and Curriculum in Other Jurisdictions	
(a) Great Britain	— Mr. Drake
(b) United States	— Professor Elliott
The Work of the Supreme Court	
(a) Civil Law and Common Law	— Professor A. Mayrand
(b) Public Law	— Professor B. Laskin

Texts of the papers given by Professors Cohen, Mayrand, and Laskin are in the hands of the Secretary.

A detailed report of the programme appears in "The Law Teacher's Annual Meeting" 32 Can. Bar Rev. 659 (1954).

D. STANDING COMMITTEE:

Comparative Law:

The meeting agreed to refer to this Committee a suggestion of Professor Elliott that a study of differences between American and Canadian common law jurisprudence would be of profit and that suggestions be made as to areas that would lend themselves to comparative study. The meeting also referred to this Committee a suggestion that the exchange of law teachers be revived and broadened.

Library:

There was considerable discussion as to the desirability and practicability of compiling a catalogue of all law libraries in Canada and of a greater interchange of books between libraries, e.g., old statutes and law reports of each province.

E. REPORT BY PRESIDENT OF ACTION TAKEN BY EXECUTIVE SINCE 1953 MEETING:

(1) The Executive carried out the instructions of the Association that the President's school assume responsibility for the programme.

(2) The Executive prepared and circulated a statement on the one-judgment proposal.

F. DECISIONS MADE BY THE ASSOCIATION:

(1) That the incoming Executive be asked to take steps to prepare and publish a record of all proceedings of the Association, and to accept Carswell's offer to print the record gratis.

(2) That the incoming Executive be authorized to appoint a committee to prepare a statement of objectives and to mimeograph and circulate it before the next meeting.

G. OFFICERS OF THE ASSOCIATION FOR 1954–55:

President: W.R. Lederman, Dalhousie University.
Vice-President: W.F. Bowker, University of Alberta.
Secretary-Treasurer: G. McAllister, University of New Brunswick.
Executive Members: Bora Laskin, University of Toronto (immediate Past-President).
G.P.R. Tallin, University of Manitoba.
R. Comtois, University of Montreal.

H. THE 1955 MEETING:

It was agreed that the Executive determine the place and time of meeting, bearing in mind the differences of opinion over the advisability of meeting with the Canadian Bar Association as against the Learned Societies. As was agreed a year ago, the programme will be in the hands of the school to which the President belongs.

I. SOCIAL EVENTS:

Thanks were expressed to Dean and Mrs. Tallin for the lovely reception at their home; to Mr. K. Martin for lunch at Lower Fort Garry; and to Mr. Nicholls, Editor of the *Canadian Bar Review,* for his reception preceding the Annual Dinner. The address of Chief Justice Williams following the dinner was enthusiastically received. Special thanks were expressed to the Manitoba Law School for their hospitality and, in particular, to Dean Tallin.

1956

Protection of Basic Rights and Liberties

Reprinted from
(1956) 2 University of British Columbia Law Notes
pp. 281–317

At the time this article was written (1956) there was comparatively little writing in Canada on the subject of basic human rights.

What had originally generated Bowker's interest in this field was the Gouzenko case in 1945 involving the cypher clerk who defected from the Russian Embassy in Ottawa. The government investigation which followed led to the arbitrary arrest of several Canadians on the suspicion of espionage. This led to some civil liberties people protesting a violation of basic freedoms and the demand for a Bill of Rights. Further interest in this subject arose from passage in 1948 of the United Nations Declaration of Human Rights.

Partly because of these events, Bowker chose as the topic for his Master's thesis at the University of Minnesota the subject: Civil Liberties in Canada and the United States (degree granted in 1953).

He would later write an article on Basic Rights for the Canadian Bar Review *(see later in this Collection, p. 224).*

These articles, however, were not repetitious in content.

Since the end of World War II we have seen in Canada a new interest in fundamental rights and freedoms. Some of it is manifest in agitation for a Bill of Rights. There are several reasons for this—for example, the curtailment of many rights during wartime, the events involving Jehovah's Witnesses, and the activities of governmental boards and agencies. The deprivation of basic rights in other parts of the world has had an influence too; this has inspired the United Nations to formulate a declaration of Human Rights, and the existence of this declaration has attracted the attention of legislatures and the public.

Some of the opinion on the subject is really special pleading. Many of those who favour a Bill of Rights have some pet interest that may or may not deserve special protection and on the other hand many in opposition are influenced by a complacency that the facts do not warrant. Moreover, there is often a failure to distinguish between statutory or common law protection of basic rights on the one hand, and constitutional safeguards on the other. It seems to me that it will help to clarify our thinking about fundamental rights if we will ask two questions: (1) what are those rights? (2) to what extent are they secured in Canada? It is only when these questions have been answered that we can intelligently proceed to the further question of ways and means of better securing them. The main purpose of this essay is to discuss these questions, and then to mention briefly some of the implications of a constitutional bill of rights on our governmental system.

I shall be content if my comments succeed in reminding readers of our principal rights and liberties, and that we as lawyers have a special concern in seeing that they are safeguarded. In discussing the subject I shall compare the position in this country with that in the United States.

We in Canada are in a peculiar position in that we inherit English law with a heritage of basic rights. In Great Britain however the doctrine of Parliamentary sovereignty means that the legislature can if it wishes, abrogate these rights. Moreover Britain has a unitary as distinguished from a federal form of government with no written constitution in the sense of a framework of government incapable of amendment by Parliament. We have the federal form, and a constitution that is written (at least in part) so that our courts have a power unknown to modern English Courts—that of declaring a statute invalid. In this we resemble the United States, but still there is a fundamental difference in the constitutions of these two countries. With very minor exceptions, the powers of the Canadian Parliament and the provinces are plenary within their spheres, so that we have parliamentary sovereignty side by side with limitations as to subject matter of legislation. In other words, a legislature that keeps within the subject matter which the British North America Act allots to it, can pass a law that infringes any basic right, just as the British Parliament could. In the United States on the other hand, the powers of nation and state are limited not only by each other's powers, but by limitations which the Constitution imposes on *all* governmental power. These limitations appear in the original constitution, but above all in the first ten amendments, known as the Bill of Rights, and in further amendments passed after the Civil War to protect the free status of the negro. These constitutional restrictions on government power exist on the theory widely held at the revolution, and expressed in the Declaration of Independence, that the powers of government cannot properly be used to deprive citizens of fundamental rights; and any law that does so deprive the citizen is invalid. Moreover, it was not long before the Supreme Court assumed the power to decide whether a statute infringes the safeguards of the Constitution. This is of the first importance, for it makes the Court rather than the legislature the principal guardian of basic rights.

With these preliminary remarks, we shall attempt to outline the principal rights and freedoms. Some writers say that rights, freedoms and liberties are synonymous, but it seems helpful to use the term freedom or liberty with reference to any claim to be free from governmental interference, and the term right with reference to a positive claim that is supported by law. For example the "rights" of assembly or free speech and worship are really liberties or freedoms. They protect the subject against state interference. On the other hand the right to compensation for expropriation of land or the right of a negro to eat in a cafe, is not a freedom, but a right. It must be conceded that the terms are often used interchangeably and in some cases it may be hard to characterize a claim as one or the other. Indeed the United Nations Declaration of Human Rights speaks of the "right to freedom."

Coming now to the question, what are basic rights and freedoms, there is no rigid classification. Opinions differ from age to age and often from person to person. To some, natural rights exist as a matter of religious belief; the right to reproduce and the claim to resist vaccination are often put on this ground. To others they may be a matter of political belief—such as the right to "life, liberty and property," but whatever the source of these natural rights, the theory is that the positive law of the state should not curtail, but should protect them. A convenient grouping of the important rights and freedoms by modern democratic standards is this:

(1) freedom of religion;
(2) freedom of press and speech;
(3) freedom of the person from interference, or security of the person;
(4) political rights—naturalization and voting;
(5) the right to equal protection of the laws, including protection from discrimination based on racial or other grounds;
(6) protection of property and economic rights;
(7) due process of law, including fairness in trials and in the proceedings of administrative tribunals.

This list may not be exhaustive. For example the Universal Declaration of Human Rights includes the right to rest and leisure and the right to a standard of living adequate for the well-being of a person and his family.[1]

I Freedom of Religion

Freedom of religion is not of long standing and was scarcely argued before Spinoza and John Locke wrote in favour of religious toleration late in the 17th century. Both in England and Scotland there is still an established church, though adherents of other religions are no longer under disability. Most of the American colonies had a state Church, though as early as the 17th century striking examples of religious toleration are found in Rhode Island, and also in Maryland. In the colonies which later became provinces of Canada, the instructions to the royal governors allowed a degree of toleration unknown at home. In the case of Quebec the great majority were Roman Catholics, and the fairness of the British Government and Parliament toward Roman Catholics helps to explain why the inhabitants of Quebec did not take sides with the Americans in the Revolution and in the war of 1812.

The most important religious issue in this country has had to do with separate schools.[2] Section 93 of The British North America Act gives to the provinces jurisdiction over education but then proceeds to put limitations on their power; a province cannot prejudicially affect any right with respect to denominational schools which any class of persons had at Confederation, and the privileges of Catholic schools in Upper Canada are extended to the dissentient schools in Quebec. Then follows a unique provision giving an appeal to the Governor General in Council from provincial acts or decisions that infringe these rights and privileges, and, providing that if the province does not execute the decision of the Governor in Council, then Parliament may make remedial laws. The important feature of the system protecting dissentient or separate schools is that their supporters do not have to pay taxes to the other schools.

From the small number of reported cases from Quebec we can infer that the system there has worked well.[3] There has been more litigation in Ontario. For example the Privy Council said that the province could require separate school teachers to be qualified to teach in the public schools;[4] and could require separate schools to give instruction in English rather than French[5] but could not withdraw the privileges of a separate school,[6] and could regulate Catholic secondary schools, and give to the common schools grants of money before making an apportionment between common and separate schools.[7]

A bitter struggle occurred when Manitoba was made a province. The Manitoba Act protected denominational schools, but in 1890 the province established a free school system to which all must contribute. The Privy Council held the law valid.[8] The Roman Catholics appealed to the Governor in Council with a view to obtaining a remedial law under section 93, and when the Privy Council confirmed that the Governor in Council could properly intervene,[9] that body ordered the province to restore to Roman Catholics the privileges they had enjoyed prior to the 1890 Act. The province declined to do so, and a remedial bill in Parliament failed of passage. Later the province restored and then in 1916 withdrew again separate school privileges.[10]

When Alberta and Saskatchewan were made provinces in 1905, a sharp issue arose over the inclusion in the organic acts of clauses securing the privileges of separate schools. However in Alberta the system has since worked with little friction, while at times in the past it has been the subject of bitter political issues in Saskatchewan.

When Newfoundland entered confederation in 1949 the terms of union preserved the rights of denominational schools and colleges and provided that they should receive their share of grants on a non-discriminatory basis.[11]

In the remaining provinces, British Columbia and the Maritimes, separate schools have no protected status and their supporters must pay taxes to the public school system even if they send their children to denominational schools.[12]

The special status of denominational schools in some of the provinces is from one standpoint a protection of the rights of the minority against the majority. Perhaps Confederation could not have been achieved without the concession which section 93 grants. However the view that has prevailed in the United States is that state supported denominational schools are unconstitutional. They violate the provision in the Bill of Rights that

"Congress shall make no laws respecting an establishment of religion," a provision that the Supreme Court has in recent times held applicable to the States. Although state-supported denominational schools are not the establishment of a religion in the strict sense, the Court has held that the purpose of the constitutional provision is to establish a "wall of separation between church and state." It upheld a scheme for paying the transportation of students to parochial schools.[13] Then it held invalid the giving of religious instruction in public schools,[14] but later sustained a programme whereby students were released from school for religious instruction.[15] It is clear from the American decisions that the Constitution as interpreted does not permit of anything comparable to the concessions given to denominational schools in half of our provinces.[16]

On the subject of worship itself, as distinct from separate schools, there have been few cases in Canada, the important ones being related to the activities of Jehovah's Witnesses. This zealous sect disseminates its doctrines by distributing religious pamphlets on the street, and by house-to-house calls.

The most significant case involving a Witness is of course *Saumur* v. *Quebec,* which went to the Supreme Court of Canada in 1953.[17] A Witness was convicted of distributing pamphlets in the streets of Quebec City without the prior permission of the Chief of Police as required by by-law. A minority of four justices would have upheld the conviction on the ground that the by-law is a proper subject for municipal legislation. The Witness relied however on Quebec's Freedom of Worship Act, enacted before Confederation. Of the majority, four held that the by-law conflicts with the Freedom of Worship Act and moreover that freedom of religion is beyond the province's power to restrict. It is not a matter of civil rights in the province within section 92 (13) of the B.N.A. Act. The ninth judge Kerwin J. put his judgment on a narrower ground. The right to exercise one's religion is a civil right and so a proper subject for provincial legislation, but the Freedom of Worship Act gives the Witnesses the right to spread their belief, and the by-law does not prevail over the Act. The significance of the judgment lies in the fact that five of the nine judges held that it is within provincial competence to legislate respecting freedom of religion, while the other four held the contrary.

A number of cases in provincial courts deal with charges against Witnesses of selling or distributing pamphlets on the streets or from door to door without a license as required by local by-law. In all of these cases which I have seen the accused was acquitted. The court invariably says that the by-law is intended to apply to commercial sales and not to distribution of religious literature.[18] The inference from these cases and from the prevailing view in *Saumur,* is that a properly worded by-law could extend to the activities of Witnesses.

A decision well worth examination is one of Mr. Wakeling, a police magistrate in Saskatchewan. That province is the only one so far as I know that has a comprehensive Civil Rights Act. This act guarantees freedom of worship. A Witness was convicted of selling a religious pamphlet contrary to a by-law. The judgment holds that apart from the Civil Rights Act the conviction would have been proper, because the common law does not guarantee freedom of religion, but that the Act, until repealed, has the same effect as a constitutional guarantee would have.[19]

In the United States the Witnesses have defied many local by-laws on the ground that these by-laws violated their constitutional right to freedom of worship. In a remarkable series of cases in the five years between 1938 and 1943 the court held that the Witnesses did not have to obtain a permit to distribute literature,[20] nor to solicit money;[21] that they could ignore a prohibition against distributing hand bills;[22] that they did not have to obtain a license fee to sell books;[23] that they could ignore a prohibition against knocking on doors to distribute literature.[24] After the war the protection given to Witnesses in the name of freedom of religion and speech reached a peak when the Court held that the Witnesses could distribute their pamphlets in a company town[25] and a government-owned town[26] although a state law made it an offence to remain on private property after a request to leave; and later when the court held that an ordinance requiring a permit to use loud-speakers in public places could not apply against a Witness who insisted on talking over a loud-speaker in a public park.[27] However the Witnesses did not win all their cases. The Court held them subject to a by-law requiring a license for a parade,[28] and liable to conviction for using words tending to incite a breach of the peace,[29] and subject to a child labour law.[30] The scope of the loud-speaker case was reduced by a decision in 1949,[31] and in 1953 the Court held that where the Witness was improperly refused a permit to speak in a park his remedy was to apply for a mandamus and that he was properly convicted of speaking without a permit.[32]

A bare recital of these cases does not convey an adequate picture of the forceful opinions in support of freedom of worship. We will give but one example—the dissent of Murphy J. in the child-labour case:

> "... the Jehovah Witnesses are living proof of the fact that even in this nation, conceived as it was in the ideals of freedom, the right to practice religion in unconventional ways is still far from secure. Theirs is a militant and unpopular faith, pursued with a fanatical zeal. They have suffered brutal beatings; their property has been destroyed; they have been harassed at every turn by the resurrection and enforcement of little-used ordinances and statutes. ... To them, along with other present-day religious minorities befalls the burden of testing our devotion to the ideals and constitutional guarantees of religious freedoms."[32a]

The last problem related to freedom of religion has to do with laws requiring school children to salute the flag. Everyone knows of the decision of the Supreme Court of the United States holding that an enactment of this type is an infringement of freedom of religion,[33] but it might not be so well known that there were two flag salute cases in Canada. In one from Ontario the court construed the requirement as inapplicable to persons who objected.[34] In the other, from Alberta, the Court held the school board justified in expelling a student who refused to salute[35] but then the legislature amended the School Act to excuse conscientious objectors.[36]

The only serious charges of oppression of any religious group relate principally to Witnesses in the Province of Quebec. From newspaper accounts and allegations made on behalf of the Witnesses it does appear that there have been cases of harsh treatment, but it is impossible for me to form an opinion of their extent.[37]

Before leaving freedom of religion it is appropriate to mention a case having nothing to do with Jehovah's Witnesses. It is *Birks* v. *Montreal,* in which various Montreal merchants challenged the validity of a Montreal by-law passed under the authority of a Quebec statute which enabled the City to require stores to close on Holy-days. The Supreme Court held the statute and by-law *ultra vires.* True the case may have overtones of religious freedom but the decision rests on the basis that the statute and by-law were in relation to criminal law, a subject reserved to Parliament.[37a]

II Freedom of Press and Speech

After the invention of printing, the Church and Crown were jealous of the power that the printing press gave to anyone who might want to spread the wrong views. Hence the state determined who could operate printing presses, and how many presses there could be, and also said that no book or tract could be published without the license or approval of a censor. The Long Parliament abolished the Star Chamber which had regulated these matters, but then promptly imposed a censorship of its own. This impelled Milton to write Areopagitica. Shortly after the Revolution in 1688 the Licensing Acts were allowed to expire. Thus did Parliament's inaction establish a free or unlicensed press. The absence of licensing does not mean that anyone can say what he wishes. If his statements are seditious he may be liable to a criminal charge, and if libelous, to a criminal or civil charge. Hence if the law on these subjects is very strict, a writer will know that although no censor exists to stop him from publishing what he thinks, the state may punish him afterwards. One need only read the life of Thomas Erskine to see that critics of the government were frequently charged with seditious libel for what would today appear to be mild criticism. Since the Napoleonic wars however, charges of seditious libel are almost unknown, though there has been no change in the law.

In Canada, during World War I, such charges were far from unknown. There is a judgment of the Appellate Division of the Supreme Court of Alberta in 1917 that deserves to be much better known than it is, for the court protested against the tendency to charge with sedition every person who made a disloyal utterance.[38] This judgment is in the spirit of the great free speech opinions of Holmes and Brandeis JJ. in the Supreme Court of the United States. There have been few reported decisions on charges of seditious utterance since that time, and I have found none during the period of World War II. It is true of course that the Defence of Canada Regulations made under the War Measures Act contained stringent provisions making it an offence to utter statements calculated to impede the war effort, and in addition the power to intern could be and was used against persons speaking against the war effort.

The most significant case is *Boucher* v. *R.*, where a Jehovah's Witness was charged in Quebec with seditious libel. He circulated a most scurrilous leaflet attacking the Catholic Church and the judiciary. He appealed his conviction to the Supreme Court of Canada. A five-man court ordered a new trial but when the number of justices was increased to nine, a rehearing was ordered, and Boucher was acquitted. Five justices held that the pamphlet, intemperate though it was, came within the saving clause of the Criminal Code respecting statements that point out matters tending to promote hatred and ill-will.[39] There is no doubt that on the older definitions of sedition (which is not defined in the Code) the pamphlet was seditious and it is of great significance that the majority emphasized that to constitute sedition the words must be uttered with the intention of inciting resistance to and disobedience of the law. Rand J. observed: "Freedom in thought and speech and disagreement in ideas and beliefs, on every conceivable subject are of the essence of our life."

One chapter in the history of freedom of speech in Canada that deserves mention is the enactment of section 98 of the Code in 1919 just after the general strike in Winnipeg. It rendered unlawful any association whose purpose was to bring about governmental, industrial or economic change by force, and made it an offence to belong to such association. This enactment was similar to the "criminal syndicalism" laws of many of the United States (where criminal law as such is left to the states), but it remained in the statute book for only seventeen years. It is true that the sections relating to sedition still make it an offence to advocate governmental change by force, but this is not as stringent as the old section 98, which Parliament repealed because of public criticism. In the United States, on the other hand, Congress passed a law in 1940 making it an offence to advocate the overthrow of government by force—the first such national statute in the United States since the old Alien and Sedition Acts expired in 1801. In the well-known case of the eleven Communists, this act was upheld against a vigorous argument that it abridges freedom of speech.[40] Thus we see that a statute of this kind has been upheld in the United States in spite of constitutional protection for freedom of speech, whereas in Canada the counterpart was repealed in 1936, and the sedition provisions still in effect have not been used as the basis of charges against Communists.

Another contrast between the two countries is this. Various laws in the United States require union officials,[41] and sometimes candidates for public office,[42] state[43] and city employees,[44] and university teachers,[45] to take a "loyalty oath." I know of no such requirement in Canada. Moreover there is here no programme for determining the loyalty of federal civil servants comparable to that in the United States.[46] It may be said that loyalty programmes are related to conduct rather than to freedom of speech, but certainly they tend to curb the expression of non-conforming political views. I am not suggesting that the important American cases upholding these oaths and programmes should have been held unconstitutional, as a minority of the justices maintained. It does seem clear, however, that there is a risk that in the climate of opinion surrounding these enactments a person may find himself in jeopardy of his position if he goes about with a copy of *Das Kapital* under his arm, or makes plain his enjoyment of Paul Robeson's singing, or says that he sees nothing cataclysmic in Russia's victory in the recent Olympic Winter games.

The last remarks are not meant to deprecate the strength of belief in and adherence to freedom of speech in the United States. The invalidity of "prior restraints" or censorship is consistently maintained, and the "clear and present danger" test still has considerable influence. For ten or fifteen years ending around 1949, it appeared indeed that freedom of speech, press and religion held a "preferred position" in the scheme of constitutional rights and liberties. This is no longer so in all respects.[46a] Yet freedom of speech or press has been effective to reduce a court's power to punish summarily for contempt,[47] and has been extended to motion pictures[48] and has had an impact on exclusion of literature by customs officials and the post office and on laws against publishing obscene literature. It would be interesting to compare the Canadian position on these subjects with the American but space does not permit.

To return to Canadian problems relating to freedom of speech, one interesting statute in Canada is Quebec's Act to Prevent the Dissemination of Communistic Propaganda, popularly known as the Padlock Law. Its purpose is what the title declares. The Attorney-General has power to order the closing of premises used to circulate Communist literature, but a judge may review the order. The act has been upheld in the provincial court, though the Supreme Court of Canada will probably pass on its validity in the near future.[49]

We must note here a bill passed in 1937 by the Alberta Legislature "To Ensure the Publication of Accurate News and Information." The Lieutenant-Governor reserved his assent and the Supreme Court on a reference held the bill ultra vires.[50] This well-known judgment is often cited for the proposition that a province cannot abridge freedom of the press—in other words, that there is an unwritten bill of rights that limits the provinces, at least in the realm of freedom of speech. An examination of the judgment shows that only two justices, Chief Justice Duff with Mr. Justice Davis concurring, gave reasons that support this suggestion.[50a] The reasoning goes as follows: (1) the British North America Act contemplates the existence of Parliamentary institutions; (2) the right of public debate is indispensable to the functioning of these institutions; (3) the provinces cannot interfere by limiting the right of public debate. Each of these links in the chain of reasoning seems open to criticism. As to the first, it is true that the British North America Act does contemplate parliamentary institutions; yet it does permit a province to amend its constitution except as regards the office of Lieutenant-Governor. The second and third seem to me still more questionable. One can agree that parliamentary institutions function best where public debate is free but it does not follow from this that the British North America Act forbids restriction of public debate. Such restriction may be unwise but that does not make it unconstitutional. Certainly the British Parliament can abridge free speech. The Chief Justice relied on the preamble to the 1867 statute which says that the various provinces have expressed their desire to be federally united into one Dominion "with a Constitution similar in principle to that of the United Kingdom." Now a cardinal principle of the modern British constitution is that of "parliamentary sovereignty." No one could argue that the British parliament is restricted by any limitation such as a Bill of Rights imposes, and the constitution of Canada confers on the national and provincial legislatures sovereignty within the subjects allotted to them. True it can be answered that restriction of public debate is not allotted to the provinces; but if not it is of necessity allotted to the Dominion. On this point Chief Justice Duff does say the Parliament of Canada can legislate to protect the right of public debate; he does not say Parliament could abridge it in a single province. Yet if a province cannot do so it follows that the Dominion could—a rather startling suggestion.

An incidental comment which can be made in connection with this judgment and which is not always stressed is this—the Chief Justice did not base his judgment on the ground that the Alberta bill violated the limitation which he says the constitution imposes on provincial legislatures. He decided against the province on another ground, as did the other judges. Had he actually held as a second ground of his decision that the act is bad as infringing the right of public debate, then he would have differed from Professor Chafee, the great authority on free speech in the United States. Professor Chafee has discussed the wisdom and the constitutionality of acts which provide for a compulsory "right of reply." The main provision in the Alberta bill was one requiring newspapers that have criticized the government to publish a corrective or amplifying statement if required by a government board. Chafee says[51] that Acts of this kind "seem free from constitutional objection", in other words they do not abridge freedom of press and speech.[52]

III Freedom of the Person

Anglo-Saxon law has recognized freedom of the person for longer than it has accepted the principles of a free press and liberty of worship. In other words the law began to concern itself with protecting the citizen against physical interference before it began to accord him liberty of thought and speech. Indeed the seeds of the principle that the subject should be free from arbitrary interference go back to Magna Carta. It is true that English law did not always achieve this ideal—but the writ of habeas corpus existed for centuries before the statute of 1679 made it really effective. The Petition of Right in 1628 protected the subject against arbitrary arrest, even by the

King's command. Then in 1763 came the famous civil actions by John Wilkes and others against Crown officers for trespass and false imprisonment when the Crown officers made arrests and seizures without proper warrant. The actions succeeded and established the illegality of general warrants of arrests and of seizures of papers without a warrant authorized by law.[53]

In Canada today the Criminal Code does not authorize a general warrant and specifically forbids a blank warrant. The provisions governing arrest without warrant, and the procedure for issuing warrants are designed to prevent abuse of the power of arrest.[54] Similarly the provisions for search warrants[55] are designed to give safeguards against unwarranted invasion of privacy. Sometimes provincial acts such as liquor laws provide for searches, sometimes without warrant, but a search of buildings usually requires a warrant.

Generally, a civil action lies for assault or false imprisonment or trespass in case of wrongful arrest or search on the general principles of the English cases. Indeed the judgment of the House of Lords in 1947 affirming the right to sue for wrongful arrest and demonstrating the narrow limits of the right to arrest without warrant, is bound to be of influence in Canada, whether or not it is strictly binding.[56]

There is, however, some concern in Canada at present on this question—are these traditional sanctions effective to prevent police officials from abusing their powers? In one case where the Crown officers seized papers but improperly kept them instead of bringing before the justice, the court condemned their action—

> "It is gravely disturbing at a time when respect for the law much needs to be fostered to find it treated with contempt by officers employed to defend it and to secure obedience to it. Many years ago it was found necessary to declare the rights of a citizen to the undisturbed and private possession of his letters and papers and books of account against intrusion and trespass under colour of a search warrant, and these rights might well have been considered to be sufficiently established . . . "[57]

In an earlier Ontario case, officers boarded and searched a boat for liquor, knowing they had not the authority. A civil action against them resulted in an award of $500 damages.[58] In an Alberta case, the late Chief Justice Harvey, speaking for the Appellate Division convicted a policeman for assault in forcibly taking property from an arrested man. He said, "Happily for the respect for law and order, charges of this kind are of the rarest occurrence."[59]

It is generally held however, that evidence obtained through an illegal search is admissible.[60] The recent Privy Council judgment in *Kuruma* v. *The Queen*[61] has evoked criticism of this rule.[62] If the police were to make a habit of tortious arrests and searches and the threat of civil and criminal proceedings were not an effective deterrent, then the sanction usually suggested is that the evidence be rendered unadmissible. That is the rule in federal cases in the United States,[63] though the Supreme Court has refused to apply it against the states, even though the constitutional protection against unreasonable searches and seizures applies against the states as well as the federal government.[64] A sharp difference of opinion exists in the United States as to whether the evidence should be admitted or not. It was I think Cardozo J. who suggested that an accused should not go free because of a policeman's error, but others have taken the view that the only effective way to prevent police from exceeding their powers is to suppress the evidence obtained by the illegal search. It is worth notice, however, that the Supreme Court has found no ready test for deciding whether a search is unreasonable, within the Fourth Amendment which contains the prohibition against unreasonable searches and seizures.[65]

Some Canadian cases held that the taking of a blood sample as a test of intoxication is like a confession—the Crown must prove it was voluntarily given. Other cases disputed the analogy, and the Supreme Court of Canada in June 1955, held[66] that various facts including blood tests can be put in evidence without proof that the accused consented. Fauteux J. added, "Doubtless the method used to obtain evidence of this kind, might in certain cases, be illegal, and even give rise to civil or even criminal proceedings against those who obtained the evidence, but it is no longer disputed that in these cases the illegality connected with the obtaining of the evidence does not *per se* affect the admissibility of the evidence."

Now if the police were to make a habit of using violent means to obtain blood tests, and if the threat of an action or charge of assault were not a deterrent, then Parliament might have to take other measures. In October 1955, the Supreme Court of the United States heard argument on the same point—admissibility of blood tests taken without consent. The judgment has not yet come to hand, but in a 1951 case,[67] the same Court held inadmissible evidence consisting of narcotic capsules and produced from the stomach of the accused by means of an emetic. The Court applied the analogy of a coerced confession.

Another interesting contrast between the two countries is this. One of the issues that helped provoke the revolution was the use by Crown officials of writs of assistance to seize smuggled goods. A writ of assistance is little less than a general search warrant. In Paxton's case[68] in Massachusetts in 1761 James Otis made his famous argument that the writ was a roving warrant and contrary to fundamental principles of English law. Although the argument failed, it did forcibly express the concept of inalienable rights which a few years later was a battle cry of the revolution. As far as I know writs of assistance are unknown in the United States and would doubtless constitute an unreasonable search and seizure. In Canada on the other hand writs of assistance may still be issued under the Customs Act, the Excise Act and the Opium and Narcotic Drug Act, and wide powers are conferred by Section 136 of the Income Tax Act. The writ under the second last of these acts is a search warrant in wide terms. For example it authorizes entry by day or night of a dwelling house, by force if necessary, to search for narcotics. It also authorizes the arrest of any person committing an offence under the Act. It does not in terms authorize the person to whom the warrant is issued to seize another by the throat to prevent him from swallowing capsules of narcotics. It is interesting to note, however, that in one case, a policeman thrust his hand into the mouth of a suspect to keep him from swallowing capsules. The un-sportsmanlike dope peddler bit the offending hand and was convicted of obstructing a police officer in the course of his duty.[69]

Wire-tapping is a modern form of search or at least an invasion of privacy. The Supreme Court of the United States held admissible evidence which the prosecution obtained by this device, on the ground that there was no search and no seizure.[70] Later, Congress forbade wire tapping and the Court has held the evidence inadmissible.[71] Some states, New York for example, permit wire tapping if a court order is first obtained. A wide difference of opinion exists as to the wisdom of permitting it.[72]

I know of no Canadian statute on the subject and there are few cases. In one instance the Crown obtained a warrant to enter a telephone exchange and to tap the wires. The Court quashed the warrant because it was not within the provision of the Code that authorizes search warrants.[73]

Another aspect of personal liberty is that of freedom to move from place to place. Under the United States Constitution this is a "privilege and immunity" of national citizenship, so that a state may not exclude citizens of another state. As for the position in Canada, the Privy Council once held invalid a British Columbia statute forbidding Chinese from working in coal mines because in depriving them of the right to work it virtually excluded them from the province. The subject matter of the statute was held to be "Naturalization and aliens" which is outside the powers of a province.[74] Then in the recent *Winner* case, Rand J. expressed the opinion that "a province cannot prevent a Canadian from entering it except, conceivably, in temporary circumstances, for some local reason as, for example, health."[75]

The last class of problem has to do with legislation requiring interference with personal liberty. Typical examples are vaccination and sterilization laws. There are some who insist as a matter of religious belief or on their concept of inherent rights that the state cannot subject them to compulsory treatment of this kind. However, even in the United States where the constitutional safeguards give plausibility to such a contention it has not prevailed. The Supreme Court has upheld both compulsory vaccination[76] and sterilization,[77] though in one case a state law providing for sterilization of persons convicted of certain offences was held invalid because the selection of types of offences seemed to lack a scientific basis, and hence those within the act were denied "equal protection of the laws," which a state cannot deny.[78]

In Canada, compulsory vaccination is commonplace: likewise compulsory treatment of venereal disease, and some provinces have sterilization laws. The Alberta Sexual Sterilization Act,[79] for example, has been in force for twenty-eight years, and it is not a dead letter. Consent is required in some cases, though not where the patient is incapable of giving consent.

A new example of a health measure that has aroused opposition is the proposal for fluoridation of water. Whether or not these schemes are accepted, it is obvious that there can be no constitutional objection.

IV Political Rights—Naturalization and Voting

It is elementary that no one can claim a right to immigrate and that the right to expel is a corollary to the right to exclude. When the government exercises these rights, the main question is whether it has followed a fair procedure, and sometimes whether the substantive law itself is fair. Most of the criticism of the administration of the immigration laws of Canada appears to be directed to procedural rather than substantive defects and to rulings in individual cases, both in relation to exclusion and expulsion of aliens, but I am unable to comment on these charges. For several years a committee of the Civil Liberties Section of the Canadian Bar Association has studied the subject and in 1955 made a report which recommended, *inter alia,* an Immigration Appeal Board. The Minister of Immigration has just announced that the Board has been established and will begin to function on March 1, 1956.[80]

The right to exclude does not extend to a Canadian citizen or to a person with a Canada domicile.[81]

An alien once in the country may own real or personal property and he is "triable at law" like a natural-born citizen but cannot claim public office or "rights and privileges as a Canadian citizen."[82]

As to acquiring of citizenship by naturalization there is obviously no right to claim citizenship. I have no grounds for saying that the judges who admit the applicants to citizenship have been unfair in cases of refusal to admit persons to citizenship. Indeed in the past some have doubtless been admitted who by reason of language or other deficiencies should not be.[83] The Canadian Citizenship Act, enacted in 1946, provides that the applicant must satisfy the courts that he has "an adequate knowledge of the responsibilities and privileges of Canadian citizenship".[84] This seems a laudable requirement, though I am not sure what the responsibilities are.

In an interesting group of cases in the United States, the Supreme Court held that the government was entitled to reject an application where the applicant declined to answer "yes" to the question, "If necessary are you willing to take up arms in defence of this country?" A negative answer was an attempted qualification of the oath of allegiance. Later, however, the court overruled these cases.[85] The Canadian application form does not include this question.

As to depriving a citizen of citizenship, a naturalized citizen as distinct from one born a citizen is subject to deprivation on order of the Governor in Council where he obtained citizenship by fraud, or where he has shown himself to be disloyal.[86] Certainly no one can object to this on principle. I do not know whether the government has invoked these powers.

The main difference between Canada and the United States is that in the latter country, the person deprived of citizenship has recourse to the Courts. The Supreme Court of the United States has held that the proof in support of revocation of citizenship must be clear and unequivocal.[87] In Canada, the person is entitled to ask for an inquiry, and the statute seems designed to ensure a fair hearing by a commission presided over by a person who has held high judicial office or alternately by the Superior Court of the province. I do not suggest that in this particular case the citizen's rights are not safeguarded by this procedure as effectively as they would be by judicial review, but this may be one of those types of cases in which it is preferable to allow appeal to the courts from the executive order. Sometimes the exclusion of judicial review is doubtless wise, but one cannot fail to be impressed by the extent to which the Supreme Court of the United States in this and analogous subjects has protected the rights of the person. The existence of judgments, even dissenting judgments, can do much toward ensuring that the statute is fairly administered.

The subject of depriving a person of citizenship cannot be left without mentioning the orders-in-council made under the War Measures Act at the end of World War II respecting deportation of Japanese. Those including British subjects, both naturalized and natural-born, who had requested repatriation were deported and those who had been naturalized were deprived of citizenship; and after investigation into the activities of certain naturalized Japanese, they might be deported even without consent and deprived of citizenship; but the provision that was most drastic provided for deportation of wives and children under 16 years of age of a deported male—and of course these wives and children were in some cases born in Canada and were Canadian nationals. The Privy Council upheld the orders in their entirety.[88] Some four thousand persons of Japanese race out of twenty three thousand were in fact repatriated.[89]

As for rights of citizenship, it is hard to enumerate them. To what extent can a province, for example, pass discriminatory legislation against persons of a given race, even though they are citizens? It has been held that a province may not exclude them from working in coal mines[89a] but may disqualify them from voting, and from employing white women in their business.[89b] In the recent *Winner* case, Rand J. expressed the opinion that a province cannot prevent a Canadian from entering it.[89c]

In the United States the Fourteenth Amendment forbids a state from abridging the privileges or immunities of citizens of the United States. To ascertain these privileges and immunities one must examine the decisions of the Supreme Court. That tribunal has given narrow scope to the clause. There is, however, authority that it embraces the right to assemble to petition for a redress of grievances, the right to a writ of habeas corpus, the right to move from state to state, and the right to use navigable waters.[89d]

Coming now to the right to vote, the Dominion law has been summarized by Professor F.R. Scott as follows: "The franchise is widely extended, without distinction of sex or requirement of property, and it is encouraging to note that most of the racial discrimination which for so long disfigured our Elections Act was removed in 1948. Only the special cases of the Doukhobors and the Native Indians remain".[90] Canadian citizenship does not however confer a right to vote in provincial elections and some provinces have barred members of certain races from the franchise. Over fifty years ago the Privy Council upheld a British Columbia law forbidding citizens of the Japanese race to vote.[91] This disability remained until 1949 when it was removed, along with that of Indians, leaving only Doukhobors unable to vote.[92] I know of no other province that gives the vote to Indians.

It is worthwhile to note the position in the United States, where a post Civil War amendment provided that the right to vote shall not be abridged "on account of race, color or previous condition of servitude". Various schemes have been used in some of the states in the South to keep negroes from voting, such as a poll-tax and literary test. These requirements have been held constitutional,[93] but are no longer widely used. The main device in recent years has been to leave primary elections in the hands of the parties, which exclude negroes from voting in the party primaries. The Supreme Court has held this too invalid,[94] and the practical result is that for the past decade negroes in the southern states are voting in increasing numbers.

V Protection From Discrimination on Racial and Other Grounds

In most areas the common law does not prevent discrimination against an individual or members of a racial, religious or other group. For example a storekeeper need not sell to everyone; barbers, restaurants and taverns need not serve everyone, and employers may select their employees from any racial groups they wish. The main exception is the case of inn-keepers.[95] The common law duty to accept wayfarers obviously does not permit racial discrimination, and this was illustrated in England during the war when Birkett J. awarded to a West Indian cricketer damages against a London hotel for refusing him a room.[96] I know of no Canadian case on the subject. One does hear of incidents in which hotel managers are alleged to have refused to admit coloured persons or to permit them to eat in the hotel dining room, but I have no way of knowing whether these allegations are true. The common law rule does not apply to restaurants nor beer-parlors and actions by negroes for refusal to serve them have failed.[97]

The Ontario legislature in 1951 took an important step by passing a Fair Employment Practices Act—a type of statute that has been before the American Congress from time to time but so far as I know has never been passed. The preamble is worthy of note:

> "Whereas it is contrary to public policy in Ontario to discriminate against men and women in respect of their employment because of race, creed, colour, nationality, ancestry and place of origin; whereas it is desirable to enact a measure designed to promote observance of this principle; and

> whereas to do so is in accord with the Universal Declaration of Human Rights as proclaimed by the United Nations."

The Act proceeds to forbid employers and trade unions from discrimination against any person on these grounds.[98]

In 1953 Parliament passed a similar act in relation to employees under its jurisdiction.[98a] Manitoba[98b] in 1953 and Nova Scotia[98c] in 1955 have done likewise.

In most fields, the subject of discrimination comes within the power of the provinces. The only comprehensive statute is the Saskatchewan Bill of Rights Act which forbids discrimination "because of race, creed, religion, colour, or ethnic or national origin" in six areas—employment, carrying on business, owning land, accommodations in public places, membership in professional and trade organizations, and education.[99]

The last decade has seen interesting developments in the law respecting covenants by a purchaser of land that he will not resell the land to a member of a specified race. In 1945 Mackay J. wrote his famous judgment in *Re Drummond Wren,*[100] holding these covenants to be against public policy. In 1949 however the Court of Appeal of Ontario overruled this case in *Re Noble and Wolf*. True, the Supreme Court of Canada[101] held the covenant invalid but on the ground that it is not of the type that can "run with the land" so as to bind subsequent buyers. A majority also held that the covenant was void for uncertainty. While the case was before the courts both Ontario and Manitoba passed legislation declaring racial covenants to be void.[102] It is clear from the Supreme Court judgment that they are void in the other common law provinces even in the absence of legislation. Mr. Smout has pointed out in his very helpful article on the *Noble* case that Ontario has forbidden discrimination by insurance companies on the basis of race or religion, and discrimination on these grounds in collective bargaining agreements.[103]

Manitoba has an interesting provision in its Defamation Act which the legislature first passed in 1934.[103a] It forbids libels against a race or religious creed, and a member of a race or creed that has been libelled may sue for an injunction. When the Commissions on Uniformity of Legislation were studying a uniform Defamation Act, they included this provision in a draft act in 1943 but omitted it from the final draft in 1944. Illinois has a group libel act that is criminal rather than civil in nature. A person convicted thereunder challenged its validity on the ground that it violated freedom of speech. The Supreme Court in a 5–4 decision upheld the Act.[103b]

The last important statute to note is Ontario's Fair Accommodation Practices Act, 1954.[104] The preamble states "Whereas it is public policy in Ontario that places to which the public is customarily admitted be open to all without regard to race, creed, colour, nationality or place or origin". The operative part says "no one shall deny to any person the accommodation services or facilities available in any place to which the public is customarily admitted" on the bases referred to in the preamble. The act also incorporates an earlier statute forbidding notices that proclaim a policy of discrimination.

Perhaps it will prove difficult for a colored person to establish discrimination. In two cases the court seems to have gone to considerable length in finding that discrimination was not proved.[104a]

In the United States the problem of racial discrimination has received great attention in the legislatures and the courts, and in the news. An important reason is of course the fact that about one-tenth of the total population is coloured and many states have a long history of segregation laws or practices in housing, schools, transportation and public accommodation.[105] Space does not permit me to trace the history of the attempts by Congress to put an end to segregation in the name of "equal protection of the laws". Some early Civil Rights statutes were held *ultra vires,* others appear to be little used, and many bills before Congress, such as Fair Employment Practices bills, fail of passage. On the other hand the Supreme Court has in the last few years delivered a series of important decisions that certainly take a stand against the validity of discriminatory laws and practices. There were two great obstacles in the way of anti-segregation decisions. First, the injunction that no state shall deny to anyone equal protection of the law does not apply to private persons, but only to action on behalf of the state, and second, a doctrine had existed since 1896 that a state affords equal protection to the negro if it furnishes him separate facilities, provided they are equal to those furnished to whites. This put the seal of constitutionality on segregation laws.

In many places, racial covenants on sale of land have been in common use and unless a statute of the state makes them illegal, it is hard to find any state action. Nevertheless the Supreme Court held in 1948 that a decision in the state court enforcing the covenant is state action and a denial of equal protection.[106] The question whether the owner of a housing development which has received financial aid from the state is justified in refusing to accept negro tenants has not been settled by the Supreme Court[107] but in some cases the owners have in fact admitted negroes along with whites.

Turning from housing to transportation, this is the field in which the separate but equal doctrine was established.[108] Recent decisions made inroads on the doctrine, though two leading cases were based respectively on the commerce clause of the Constitution,[109] and on a federal statute[110] and not on the equal protection clause.

It was in the field of education that the doctrine was whittled down and finally discarded. In 1938 the Court held that a state did not furnish equal protection when it paid the negro's expenses to a university outside the state.[111] Then in 1950 the Court found that a separate school within the state did not meet the requirement of equal protection because the facilities were inferior[112] and that a scheme to have the negro sit in an ante-room at lectures and a special seat in library and cafeteria was a denial of equal protection.[113] Finally, in 1953 cases from four different states and the District of Columbia came before the court, in which negroes challenged segregation *per se* in the school system. The court held unanimously in 1954[114] that segregation even with equal facilities is a denial of equal protection. These momentous decisions overruled the separate but equal doctrine and rendered invalid segregation imposed by state law in the field of education. The holding in the District of Columbia case was based on denial of due process, for the equal protection clause applies only against the states. Before the Supreme Court in its present session are appeals raising the question of segregation in public parks and playgrounds and on public golf courses. Another case is a test of state miscegenation laws, which are designed to prevent mixed marriages. I do not know whether the court has handed down decisions in these cases. Many articles in the press have described the problems arising from the segregation cases and it is too early to say whether desegregation will come quickly and without great difficulty.

In any event, the cases on racial covenants, transportation and education show that the Court has made a great effort to establish equality for the negro.[115]

In the field of labour, I have mentioned that Congress has not passed a general Fair Employment Practices Act, though it has enacted a measure against discrimination by railway unions.[116]

New York furnishes a good example of what a state can do to combat racial discrimination. Unlike our provinces the separate states have their own constitutions quite apart from the federal constitution, and in 1938 New York adopted a new one that said "No person shall, because of race, colour, creed or religion, be subjected to any discrimination in his civil rights by any firm, corporation or institution". This prohibition is not confined to state action, but like many enactments designed to protect basic rights, it is not self-executing. It can be made effective only by legislation passed to enforce it. Thus we find that in 1945 the State legislature passed a law to establish a State Commission Against Discrimination. The State Bar Association opposed it "on the ground that it was an unconstitutional infringement of freedom of contract; it would cause business firms to leave the state; it tried to legislate morallity; it could not be enforced and it would actually intensify group hostility and cause 'riots'."[117] The law has now been in force for ten years, and a recent article states "nothing now remains of the arguments so fervidly advanced against the passage of the anti-discrimination law. None of the awesome prophecies of its opponents has been fulfilled" and "There no longer need be speculation as to whether discrimination in employment and in places of public accommodation because of race, creed, colour or national origin can be eliminated and prevented through legislation".[118] All are familiar with the admission of negroes into major league baseball in 1947. Although the credit for this may go to Mr. Branch Rickey and Jackie Robinson rather than to legislation, one writer has said, "It is not depreciative of Mr. Rickey's courage and vision to state that the New York law against discrimination provided him with legal support for his moral conviction and lightened the heavy incubus of possible disapproval of his action."[119]

It may be in order here to comment on the stock objection to anti-discrimination laws—"You can't legislate morality". Now I will readily admit that a law may become a dead letter and this has been true of some anti-discrimination laws. The New York experience however, is not the only one showing that this is not necessarily so. One answer to the argument is this, "Human nature may not be changed by law, but human behavior certainly can be controlled".[120] An anti-discrimination law such as Saskatchewan's or Ontario's does not say to the restaurant owner, "love the negro". It merely says "sell him a meal". Moreover, many legal rules do take cognizance of prevailing moral views. The Criminal Code contains a number of offences "against morality", and a gift in a will may be void if subject to a condition tending to immorality, and a contract made for immoral consideration is unenforceable.

There is indeed a further point though a debatable one. To some extent, law can create morality. A recent article on the subject says that the school desegregation decision is based on the assumption that morality can be legislated. As the authors of this article point out, it may be conceded that no law or judicial decision which does not have its roots in community beliefs has a chance of being effectively carried out: yet to some extent law can give a lead to customs and mores. Many people, presumably the majority, are prepared to obey the law, even when it effects a change in social custom.[121]

VI Protection of Property and Economic Freedom

We start with the proposition that the British North America Act gives no protection to property or contractual rights. Either Parliament or provincial legislatures may interfere to control or abrogate them. For example no serious question arises over the validity *per se* of wages and hour legislation, fixing of rates and prices, licensing of businesses and zoning by-laws. The question then arises: are there no limits whatever to legislation, even if it is patently harsh and oppressive? Checks do indeed exist, though they are not as obvious as the American prohibition against laws depriving a person of property without due process of law or against taking of property for public use without compensation.

All provincial acts are subject to disallowance by the Governor General in Council. Statutes have been disallowed on the ground that they are harsh, oppressive, discriminatory or confiscatory. Sir Lyman Duff once said, "Those who were responsible for the scheme of Confederation deliberately rejected the American system of constitutional limitations. So far as provincial legislation is concerned they adopted the safeguard of investing the Governor in Council with a power of disallowance".[122] However the power of disallowance operates unevenly and is not a satisfactory safeguard.[123]

Another check on drastic legislation is a tendency which the courts sometimes show to construe legislation narrowly. For example a statute says that a provincial board "may" issue a license to taxi drivers. Sometimes courts hold that "may" means "shall" because the legislation interferes with the common law right to carry on a trade and therefore must be construed narrowly. In fact many canons of construction of statutes reflect this attitude—that they are to be construed narrowly where they interfere with common law rights. I do not mean to support this attitude. Indeed most interpretation acts say that all legislation is to be deemed remedial and to be given a wide construction, but the courts do not always give effect to this directive. As Mr. John Willis once wrote, the use of canons of construction like the one I have mentioned do go some distance toward superimposing an unwritten Bill of Rights on the British North America Act.[124]

Sometimes a person attacks economic legislation on constitutional grounds. He cannot argue that a provincial act is invalid because it is unfair or discriminatory so he contends that it is outside provincial competence: for example, that it is in relation to trade or commerce, or (if it imposes a levy) is an indirect tax. If the act sets up an administrative board, he attacks it on the ground that the board has the functions of a superior or district court and hence is invalidly constituted; or if it is confiscatory he may be able to argue that is destroys civil rights outside the province.

Conversely if the statute is an act of Parliament, he argues that its subject matter is solely within provincial competence—such as rent control, or regulation of the marketing of natural products. The court of course often upholds the act, but sometimes does not. In some of the latter cases, courts seem to have gone to some lengths to hold the statute invalid. I do not want to leave the impression that they consciously or deliberately seek a dubious ground for deciding against the statute, but sometimes the decisions seem to go rather far. For example both Dominion and provinces tried for years to regulate the marketing of natural products—livestock, fruit, vegetables and the like. Since the trade in these products is partly intra-provincial and partly inter-provincial, a provincial law on the subject might be held invalid because it is in relation to trade and commerce[125] and a dominion law because it is in relation to property and civil rights within the province.[126] Thus the theory that the national and provincial legislatures can between them make laws on any subject seems difficult to apply in practice, and for a time regulation of marketing of natural products appeared impossible. However, the judgment of the Supreme Court in the *Willis Case*[127] upholds a scheme of cooperative legislation so that the impasse has been broken.

The constitutional position then in theory is that a legislature may pass any act, provided it is within the heads of subject matter which the British North America Acts allots to that legislature. The late Mr. Justice Riddell often expounded this principle in judgments and extra-judicial writings.

> The legislature within its jurisdiction can do anything that is not naturally impossible, and is restrained by no rule, human or divine. If it be that the plaintiff acquired any rights... the legislature had the power to take them away. The prohibition 'thou shalt not steal' has no force upon the sovereign

body. And there would be no necessity for compensation to be given. We have no such restriction upon the power of the legislature as is found in some states.[128]

I realize that not everyone subscribes to this view. A few judgments actually hold that there is an implied limitation on the power of the legislature. For example, there may be a case where the Court has given its decision. The legislature then passes an act declaring the law to be and always to have been different from what the judgment says. Some courts have said that the legislature has no jurisdiction so to declare the law. "It transcends its true function when it undertakes to say that the language used has a different meaning and effect from that given it by the Courts".[129] It seems clear however that this view is wrong.[130]

Innumerable statutes regulate the carrying on of businesses and the use of property. Many of these are an interference with the rights of the individual, and frequently cause him monetary loss. We have price-fixing, regulation of rates, minimum wages and maximum hours, zoning and bill-board laws. Legislation of this kind may not appeal to the rugged individualist, but he cannot hope to attack its validity *per se*.

In the United States on the other hand, the Constitution says that neither Congress nor state shall deprive any person of life, liberty or property without due process of law. At first sight this may seem to put no restriction on legislation affecting business or use of property; it is in fact a modernized version of the famous clause in Magna Carta relating to fairness in legal procedure. Nevertheless the idea grew up after the Civil War that this put a restriction on the legislative branch in relation to substantive matters; that a statute violates this provision if it unfairly deprives a person of liberty or property. Moreover liberty was extended beyond liberty of the person to such liberties as that of contract, and a corporation was held to be a person for the purposes of this clause. Thus grew the concept of "substantive due process", a contradiction in terms to be sure, but one that for about half a century ending just before World War II operated to impose severe restrictions on economic legislation.[131] The underlying theory was that of laissez faire—that generally the state could not regulate business, and that employer and employee could contract on what terms they wish—the labourer had a constitutional liberty to work for 10¢ an hour for 70 hours a week if he wished, and the state must not take away this liberty.

True, the Court did not always rule against the enactment. For example, zoning and building by-laws were the subject of vigorous attack, but the Court upheld them.[132] Yet in many cases the court did hold the legislation to constitute a violation of due process. Here are some: the fixing of railway rates at an unreasonably low figure;[133] any fixing of prices and rates in a business not "affected with a public interest", such as the selling of theatre tickets[134] and retailing of gasoline[135] and the business of an employment agency;[136] the fixing of the weight of loaves of bread;[137] a requirement that drug stores shall be owned by licensed pharmacists[138] and a license to sell ice.[139] One of the most extreme examples of invalidation of social legislation is in the realm of laws fixing maximum hours[140] and minimum wages for workers,[141] and laws designed to protect from dismissal workers who join a labour union.[142] Decisions of this type attracted criticism and were contrary to the philosophy of the New Deal. Early in 1937 President Roosevelt made his proposal to enlarge the court. Although Congress rejected it, the Supreme Court began to adopt a different approach to this type of legislation so that the cases just described have been overruled, or in the euphemistic phrase, "sapped of their vitality", and statutes passed to regulate business and to strike at social evils are now sustained.[143]

Another constitutional limitation on legislation in the United States is that which forbids a state to pass any law impairing the obligation of contracts. Under a series of decisions written by Chief Justice Marshall early in the nineteenth century a wide effect was given to this "contract clause". It was even extended to government grants so that a state could not modify charters it had granted, unless of course power to do so was reserved. Modern cases have gone in the other direction so that the contract clause is not the obstacle to legislation that it once was. During times of depression the states frequently want to protect mortgagors against sale and foreclosure. In 1934 the Supreme Court upheld an act of this type on the principle that the contract clause does not prevent a state in the exercise of its regulatory or "police" power, from making laws it deems vital in the interests of the state. The effect of this and other modern decisions is to reduce the scope of the contract clause.[144] It is perhaps paradoxical that in Canada where there is no contract clause, important provincial laws designed to protect debtors in times of depression have been held invalid. It is very hard to frame such legislation so that it does not relate to interest or bankruptcy and insolvency, which are under federal jurisdiction.[145]

The last point to mention under this head is that of expropriation, or what is called in the United States the power of eminent domain. The Constitution of that country says that private property shall not be taken for public use, without just compensation. Although this applies to Congress only, the due process clause applies to the states and it has a similar effect. In Canada there is in theory nothing to prevent the state from confiscating property, but statutes invariably provide for compensation. It would take too long to compare the decisions in Canada with those in the United States but it seems fair to say that our expropriation laws as interpreted by the Courts give to the subject protection at least equal to that which the American constitution affords.

VII Due Process of Law—Fairness in Procedure in Criminal and Civil Proceedings and Before Administrative Boards

Once again it is helpful to note that in Canada the rules of procedure designed to ensure fairness are found in statutes and judicial decision, whereas in the United States the Constitution as amended has various requirements to the same end. The original Constitution forbids both Congress and states to pass ex post facto laws and bills of attainder, and also bars the federal government from suspending the writ of habeas corpus unless the public safety so requires in rebellion or invasion. These safeguards are substantive rather than procedural but it is convenient to note them here. Criminal trials in federal courts are to be by jury in the state where the crime was committed.

Many of the states felt that further safeguards were necessary and insisted on amendments to the constitution to secure them. The most important are found in the Fifth and Sixth Amendments, being part of the Bill of Rights. These originally applied only to proceedings in federal courts though the Supreme Court has extended some of them to trials in state courts. In brief they require a grand jury on criminal charges; they protect an accused against "double jeopardy", and a witness in a criminal case against self-incrimination, and every person against violation of the right to life, liberty or property without due process of law. They also require that trials be speedy and public, by an impartial jury, and that the accused be informed of the charge against him, that he be entitled to be confronted by the witnesses as against him, that he can compel attendance of witnesses in his favour, and finally that he be entitled to the assistance of counsel for his defence. The Seventh Amendment preserves the right to trial by jury in civil cases if the amount in controversy is over $90.00. The Eighth is borrowed almost verbatim from the English Bill of Rights, forbidding excessive bail, excessive fines, and cruel and unusual punishments.

It is profitable to study criminal procedure in Canada with a view to seeing how our safeguards compare with those which the Bill of Rights affords. Without attempting here to go into detail one can find both differences and similarities. In half the provinces in Canada the grand jury does not exist. Protection against self incrimination means merely that a witness can object to answer a question on the ground that the answer would incriminate him, and having so objected, he must still answer the question but his answer cannot be used against him if he is later charged.[146]

In the United States, the protection has been extended beyond actual criminal proceedings. A Congressional Committee asks a witness "are you a member of the Communist party?" He refuses to answer on the ground that the answer might incriminate him. Two separate issues have arisen from this situation. First, has the witness really abused the purpose of the Fifth Amendment? Second, is it proper to infer that he is in fact a communist? As to the latter there has been wide controversy. As for the first, Congress decided in 1954 that the immunity was too wide and passed a compulsory Testimony Act which is generally like the Canadian statute. I do not know whether the Supreme Court has yet ruled on the validity of the Act.[147] Lest one think that Canada can feel virtuous because it has avoided a controversy parallel to the Fifth Amendment situation in the United States, it might be well to point out that the Canadian statute can operate harshly. The example I shall use is the proceeding before the Royal Commission on Espionage (the so-called Gouzenko affair). Persons arrested under a special order in council were questioned by the Royal Commission. It has long been settled that the tribunal is not under a duty to advise a witness of his rights under the Canada Evidence Act. The Commission did not so advise the witnesses,[148] and where they did not object to answer on the ground that their answers would incriminate them, the answers were used against them when they were later charged with disclosing information under the Official Secrets Act.[149]

In 1946 the Canadian Bar Association recommended that the Evidence Act be amended to protect the witness unless he waives the protection.[150] The Act has not however been amended.

Another interesting contrast is the meaning of "right of counsel". The Criminal Code, like the Sixth Amendment confers this right; but modern American decisions make it mean much more than it does in Canada. Here, the Court cannot refuse the accused the privilege of counsel; whereas in the United States, Supreme Court decisions hold that unless he waives his right, accused who does not have his own counsel is entitled to have counsel appointed for him in all federal cases,[151] in capital cases in state courts[152] and sometimes in charges of lesser state crimes.[153] It is true that in Canada the Crown does as a matter of custom provide counsel in capital cases, but there is no legal obligation to do so. Legal aid schemes in the different provinces may in time furnish counsel in all cases, but in the meantime, right to counsel in Canada does not mean that the state must provide counsel.

As to the right "of confrontation" of witnesses, the Criminal Code does not so provide in so many words but does in effect. The right of accused to be present and to cross-examine is clear. Indeed there is one respect in which it has been held that the right of confrontation in Canada is wider than the constitutional minimum in the United States. In 1949 the Supreme Court of the United States held that an accused is not denied the right of confrontation merely because the court after a plea of guilty and in considering sentence, heard *ex parte* evidence as to the character of the accused.[154] Shortly afterwards the Court of Appeal in British Columbia dealt with the same problem. Said Chief Justice Sloan: "If [the case just mentioned] holds that a convict may be sentenced on damaging information secretly communicated to a trial judge without giving that convict any right to meet it as best he can, then with the greatest deference, I must refuse to encourage the adoption of such a principle as a part of our Canadian system of criminal jurisprudence."[155]

In connection with trial by jury it is hard to make a detailed comparison of the two countries, but in Canada the right of an accused to elect trial by judge alone is extensive. Indeed in Alberta it extends even to a murder charge.[156] In the United States Congress could not abolish jury trial for the Constitution requires it. The states however may do so.[157] Waiver of the right is permissible under the Constitution.[158] An important issue in the United States in recent years has arisen over the method of selecting jurors—for example in some states negroes have been systematically excluded from the jury. The Supreme Court has held that this is ground for setting aside a conviction.[159] No parallel problem has arisen in Canada. Indeed challenges to the array on any ground are rare. The actual workings of the jury system in the two countries would doubtless be of interest. It appears that the selection of juries in the United States proceeds much more slowly than here, and that the actual trials tend to take longer.

As for the other safeguards of the Fifth and Sixth Amendments, their counterparts exist in Canadian law—protection against double jeopardy, the right to a speedy and public trial and the right to compel attendance of witnesses.

Turning now to the right to jury trial in civil cases, this of course depends on provincial law. Generally the right to a jury trial is preserved, but in some provinces at least it is generally waived in practice. In addition power is frequently given to the court to order a non-jury trial, where the nature of the evidence will be such as to render it inadvisable. In the United States the Constitution ensures the right to a jury trial in federal cases where $20.00 or more is involved. One need scarcely say that this is an anachronism—an eighteenth century safeguard that few would want to insist on today.

With respect to the requirement that conviction shall be had only "by due process of law" it is true that judges do not often employ this term, but the statutes and decisions between them do call for high standards of fairness. The Code does say that an appeal shall be allowed if there has been a miscarriage of justice[160] which connotes the same idea as absence of due process of law. The cases say that the appeal should be allowed if there *may* have been a miscarriage of justice.

In the United States the Supreme Court has in recent years frequently set aside convictions where the police have used third degree methods. It is true that the Supreme Court will not always set aside a conviction in a state court as readily as it will do so in a federal case, but this distinction has no counterpart in Canada where there are not two separate systems of courts for trials of criminal cases. Even in cases from state courts however the Supreme Court has held that abusive police methods are a denial of due process of law. It is hard to say what effect these judgments have had on the actual conduct of police officials but certainly it is hard to see how the Supreme Court could do more than it has done to try to check third degree methods.[161]

I shall say nothing about the details of procedural requirements in civil cases or before administrative boards. There is in Canada, doubtless as in the United States, strong adherence to the principle expressed in English cases: that justice must not only be done but should manifestly and undoubtedly be seen to be done.[162] It is frequently said that judicial and administrative proceedings must meet the test of "natural justice". When one asks what does natural justice require, he finds that the usual answer is—"hear both sides" and "no one shall be judge in his own cause". Some writers include other items such as the right to cross-examine, and the duty of the tribunal to give reasons. In a general way it corresponds to the American "due process of law". The question may be asked whether it means anything more than the principles of common law which govern procedure. This is a good subject for debate, and I am content here to refer to the differing views of O'Halloran J.A. and Smith J.A. in *Kuyzch* v. *White.*[163]

There is a practical question which has had much attention in recent years. Should there be a general statute in each jurisdiction comparable to the Administrative Procedure Act which Congress passed in 1946, for the purpose of ensuring fairness in the proceedings of administrative agencies? I do not know the answer, though on principle it seems sound. The one observation I would like to make here is this—that it is profitable to make comparisons of parallel problems in Canada and the United States, such as the one just mentioned. Comparative law is a good pursuit in itself—but in addition a detailed knowledge of the law of other countries can give us ideas for improving our own law and it can also sometimes show us on closer acquaintance that perhaps our own rules are more suitable for our purposes than other rules that seem attractive at first.

Conclusion

The main purpose I have had in mind in this article is to stimulate interest in the subject of basic rights. We have inherited from Britain a strong tradition in their favour, and we are in a good position to benefit from her experience. However we are not an old and tightly-knit nation, but a federation with a small population and huge area. While we can learn much from Britain we can also profit from the experience of the United States with its federal system, and a Bill of Rights, and there are many problems common to the two countries.

I may be incorrect in suspecting that until the post-war period we have perhaps not been as alert to threats to fundamental rights as either the Americans or British. Most Canadians, I am sure, consider that we have a good record and in many respects we doubtless do. There is however a question as to some episodes; for example, the espionage probe and the treatment of Japanese in World War II and in some parts of the country the treatment of Jehovah's Witnesses. Moreover, as a member of the United Nations we have subscribed to the Declaration of Human Rights and it is only fitting that we examine our laws and practices to see how close we approach the ideals of that declaration.

On some, perhaps most, of the heads I have discussed our statutes and decisions may give us as great practical security as a Bill of Rights. Indeed some of the principles of the American Bill of Rights are no more effective than the laws that implement them.

Statutes and judicial rulings of course do not always give a true picture of the actual practices in a society, and research into the effectiveness of the law can be undertaken with profit. A fundamental question is of course whether a Bill of Rights would furnish a better safeguard for individual rights than we now have. I propose here merely to state some considerations on both sides.

The American theory is that government receives its powers by delegation from the people and that they never grant to government the authority to abridge basic rights. Doubtless the American view accords with Lord Acton's that all power corrupts and absolute power corrupts absolutely. There is a fear of "popular despotism" so that legislatures must be kept in restraint. As Professor McIlwain once said, "the fundamental law of the Constitution is an appeal from the people drunk to the people sober." If one state or province does not accept these values which the nation cherishes as a whole, then it may be possible for that state or province to deprive those, or at least some of those, under its jurisdiction of basic rights, and a Bill of Rights is the best safeguard against this risk.

Opponents of a Bill of Rights, on the other hand say that in a democracy, the legislature carries out the will of the people, or at least of a majority, and that no court should have the power to "veto" legislation designed to carry out that will. Another, and quite different objection to a constitutional restriction on legislative power is this. Even though correct in theory, it brings about a mental attitude in which the people look to the Court, rather than to the legislatures and to themselves for remaining alert to see that fundamental rights are not abridged. No court can effectively preserve these rights if the people and their legislatures have abdicated their responsibility.[164]

As Judge Learned Hand once said:

> . . . this much I think I do know—that a society so riven that the spirit of moderation is gone, no court *can* save; that a society where that spirit flourishes no court *need* save; that in a society which evades its responsibility by thrusting upon courts the nurture of that spirit, that spirit in the end will perish.

In conclusion might I refer to a suggestion which Dr. N.A.M. MacKenzie made to the Senate Committee on Human Rights and Fundamental Freedoms in 1950 when invited to express his views:

> Had you thought of having a study made of the rights and freedoms which we now possess, and whether they are set out in statutes, in the common law or are a matter of custom and practice? Then along with this should go a study of the complaints that have been made, or the abuses which exist, together with requests or suggestions for improvements or changes in the existing practices or laws.[165]

In this article it has been my intention to sketch a number of important problems in the hope of encouraging readers to take an interest in this field. No intelligent recommendation for constitutional, statutory or other safeguards can be made until after thorough studies such as Dr. MacKenzie suggests.[166]

Notes

1 See the Universal Declaration of Human Rights, Articles 24 and 25 (1949). 27 Can. Bar Rev. 203. Another set of Draft articles is contained in the Order of Reference constituting a committee of the Senate of Canada to report on the subject of Human Rights and Fundamental Freedoms. The King's Printer, Ottawa: (1950).

2 See Weir, The Separate School Question in Canada (1934) and Miller, National Government and Education in Canada (1940).

3 The only case in the Privy Council from Quebec is *Hirsch* v. *Protestant School Comm'rs of Montreal* [1928] A.C. 200. It held invalid an enactment that persons of the Jewish faith should be treated for school purposes as Protestants.

4 *Brothers of Christian Schools* v. *Minister of Education,* [1907] A.C. 69. The issue in the case was whether the statute did in fact so require: It was not contended that the province could not so require.

5 *Ottawa R.C. Separate Schools Trustees* v. *Mackell,* [1917] A.C. 62.

6 *Ottawa R.C. Separate Schools Trustees* v. *Ottawa,* [1917] A.C. 76: Compare *Re Ottawa Separate Schools* (1917), 41 O.L.R. 259.

7 *R.C. Separate School Trustees* v. *The King,* [1928] A.C. 363.

8 *Winnipeg* v. *Barrett,* [1892] A.C. 445.

9 *Brophy* v. *Attorney General of Manitoba* [1895] A.C. 202.

10 Weir, *op. cit.* note 2, caps. 6 and 8.

11 See Term 17, R.S.C. 1952, p. 6404.

12 *See Maher* v. *Portland* (P.C. 1874) in Lefroy, Leading Cases in Canadian Constitutional Law (1914).

13 *Everson* v. *Board of Education* (1947) 330 U.S. 1.

14 *McCollum* v. *Board of Education* (1948) 333 U.S. 203.

15 *Zorach* v. *Clauson* (1952) 343 U.S. 306.

16 A good critical article on the cases cited in notes 13 and 14 is Sutherland, Due Process and Disestablishment, (1949), 62 Harv. L. Rev. 1306.

17 [1953] 2 S.C.R. 299.

18 *R.* v. *Mustin,* [1940] O.R. 393; *R.* v. *Kite* [1949] 2 W.W.R. 195 (B.C.); *Ottawa* v. *Irving,* (1951) 99 C.C.C. 318; *Hill* v. *Recorders Court of Montreal* (1955) 112 C.C.C. 225.

19 *R.* v. *Naish* [1950] 1 W.W.R. 987.

20 *Lovell* v. *Griffin* (1938) 303 U.S. 444.

21 *Cantwell* v. *Connecticut* (1940) 310 U.S. 296.

22 *Schneider* v. *New Jersey* (1939) 308 U.S. 147.

23 *Murdock* v. *Pennsylvania* (1943) 319 U.S. 105, *Follett* v. *McCormick* (1944) 321 U.S. 573.

24 *Martin* v. *Struthers* (1943) 319 U.S. 141.

25 *Marsh* v. *Alabama* (1946) 326 U.S. 501.

26 *Tucker* v. *Texas* (1946) 326 U.S. 517.

27 *Saia* v. *New York* (1948) 334 U.S. 558.

28 *Cox* v. *New Hampshire* (1941) 312 U.S. 569.

29 *Chaplinsky* v. *New Hampshire* (1942) 315 U.S. 568.

30 *Prince* v. *Massachusetts* (1944) 321 U.S. 158.

31 *Kovacs* v. *Cooper* (1949) 336 U.S. 77.

32 *Poulos* v. *New Hampshire* (1953) 345 U.S. 395: compare *Niemotko* v. *Maryland* (1951) 340 U.S. 268.

32a *Prince* v. *Massachusetts,* note 30 above at p. 176.

33 *West Virginia* v. *Barnette* (1943) 319 U.S. 624.

34 *Donald* v. *Hamilton Board of Education* [1945] O.R. 518.

35 *Ruman* v. *Lethbridge School District* [1943] 3 W.W.R. 340.

36 1944 c. 46 sec. 9 (Alta.)

37 See How, The Case for a Canadian Bill of Rights (1948) 26 Can. Bar Rev. 759. In a case decided by the Supreme Court of Canada around 14 November, 1955, the court held police officers civilly liable for breaking up a religious service of Witnesses in a home. The plaintiff's name is Chaput, but I do not have the style of cause or any details of the facts or judgment. The decision has not yet come to hand.

37a [1955] 3 S.C.R. 799.

38 *R.* v. *Trainor* [1917] 1 W.W.R. 415.

39 *Boucher* v. *The King* [1951] S.C.R. 265.

40 *Dennis* v. *United States* (1951) 341 U.S. 494. Space does not permit a discussion of the "clear and present danger" test which Holmes J. formulated, but the leading cases are discussed in Chafee, Free Speech in the United States, 2 Ed. (1941). It seems safe to say that the Dennis decision modifies the clear and present danger test in favour of the state. See Mendelson, Clear and Present Danger—from Schenck to Dennis, (1952) 52 Col. L.R. 313.

41 See *American Communication Assn.* v. *Douds* (1950) 339 U.S. 382.

42 *Gerende* v. *Board of Supervisors of Elections of Baltimore,* (1951) 341 U.S. 56.

43 *Wieman* v. *Updegraff* (1952) 344 U.S. 183.

44 *Garner* v. *Los Angeles* (1951) 341 U.S. 716.

45 A useful collection of material on loyalty programmes in schools and universities is found in Emerson & Haber, Political and Civil Rights in the United States, pp. 806–908 (1952). An important case upholding New York's law designed to eliminate subversives from the public school system is *Adler* v. *Board of Education* (1952) 342 U.S. 485.

46 This programme is discussed in Emerson & Haber *op cit* note 45 at pp. 528–567.

46a See Covington, The Dynamic American Bill of Rights, (1948) 26 Can. Bar Rev. 638. The author of this article has been counsel for Jehovah's Witnesses in many of their important cases in the United States. I doubt that he would write quite as enthusiastically today about the decisions under the Bill of Rights, at least in relation to freedom of religion and speech.

47 E.g. *Craig* v. *Harney* (1947) 331 U.S. 367.

48 *Burstyn* v. *Wilson* (1952) 343 U.S. 495.

49 See *Fineberg* v. *Taub* (1939) 77 Que. S.C. 233. The case before the Supreme Court is *Switzman* v. *Elbling*.

50 Re Alberta Statutes [1938] S.C.R. 100; the Privy Council declined to hear an appeal because of repeal of the statute creating the Board that was to administer the impugned bill. See *Attorney General for Alberta* v. *Attorney General for Canada,* [1939] A.C. 117.

50a Perhaps the judgment of Cannon J. should be added to that of Duff C.J. He says the bill is in relation to criminal law and in his discussion of that point does say that the provinces cannot curtail free discussion of public affairs. He then goes on to say that Parliament could do so, as a matter of criminal law.

51 Chafee, Government & Mass Communications, Vol. 1 cap. 8 (1946).

52 I could properly have included the right of assembly with freedom of speech and press. The power to declare an assembly unlawful could be abused (Criminal Code secs. 64–68), but I know of no cases on this.

53 *Leach* v. *Money* (1763) 19 St. Tr. 1002; *Entick* v. *Carrington* (1765) 19 St. Tr. 1030; *Wilkes* v. *Wood* (1763) 19 St. Tr. 1154.

54 1953–54 c. 51 secs. 434–448

55 Secs. 429–433.

56 *Christie* v. *Leachinski* [1947] A.C. 573.

57 *R.* v. *Container Materials Ltd.* (1941) 76 C.C.C. 18 at 52.

58 *Fleming* v. *Spracklin* (1921) 50 O.L.R. 289.

59 *R.* v. *MacDonald* (1932) 59 C.C.S. 56.

60 E.g. *Ship* v. *The King* (1949) 8 C.R. 26; and see the cases collected by Frankfurter J. in *Wolf* v. *Colorado* (1950) 338 U.S. 25.

61 [1955] All E.R. 236.

62 Note, (1955) 33 Can. Bar Rev. 721; letters to Editor, *ibid* pp. 984, 1111.

63 *Weeks* v. *United States* (1914) 232 U.S. 383.

64 *Wolf* v. *Colorado,* note 60 above.

65 *United States* v. *Rabinowitz* (1950) 339 U.S. 56.

66 *Attorney General of Quebec* v. *Begin,* [1955] 5 D.L.R. 394.

67 *Rochin* v. *California* (1952) 342 U.S. 165.

68 Quincy, (Mass.) 51 and App. I. An account of the case appears in Bowen,

John Adams and the American Revolution, cap. 13 (1950).

69 *R.* v. *Brezack* [1948] O.R. 888.

70 *Olmstead* v. *United States* (1927) 277 U.S. 438.

71 *Nardone* v. *United States* (1937) 302 U.S. 379.

72 Brownell, The Public Security & Wire-Tapping, (1954) 39 Cornell L.Q. 195; Rogers, The Case for Wire Tapping (1954) 63 Yale L.J. 792; Donnelly, Comments and Caveats on the Wire-Tapping Controversy, ibid., p. 799.

73 Re Bell Teleephone Co. of Canada (1947) 89 C.C.C. 196. Compare *Reliable Toy Co.* v. *Collins* [1950] O.R. 360, where the Court admitted evidence of a conversation recorded on a recording device concealed in a room.

74 *Union Colliery Co.* v. *Bryden* [1899] A.C. 580.

75 *Winner* v. *S.M.T. (Eastern) Ltd.* [1951] S.C.R. 887, varied [1954] A.C. 541 *sub nom* Attorney General for *Ontario* v. *Winner*.

76 *Jacobson* v. *Massachusetts* (1905) 197 U.S. 11.

77 *Buck* v. *Bell* (1927) 274 U.S. 200.

78 *Skinner* v. *Oklahoma* (1942) 316 U.S. 535.

79 R.S.A. 1942, c. 194.

80 Newspaper dispatches from Ottawa, 30 January, 1956.

81 Immigration Act R.S.C. 1952 c. 145 sec. 4.

82 Citizenship Act, R.S.C. 1952 c. 33 sec. 24; Re Kvasnak [1951] 2 W.W.R. (N.S.) 174.

83 See Re Naturalization Act (1928) 34 O.W.N. 183.

84 R.S.C. 1952 c. 33 sec. 10: see also sec. 33.

85 *Girouard* v. *United States* (1946) 528 U.S. 61.

86 R.S.C. 1952 c. 33 sec. 19.

87 E.g. *Knauer* v. *United States* (1946) 328 U.S. 654.

88 *Co-operative Committee on Japanese Canadians* v. *Attorney General of Canada* [1947] A.C. 87.

89 La Violette, The Canadian Japanese and World War II, appendix E (1948).

89a *Union Colliery Co.* v. *Bryden* [1899] A.C. 580.

89b *Quong Wing* v. *The King* (1914) 48 S.C.R. 440.

89c *Winner* v. *S.M.T.* [1951] 4 D.L.R. 529 at p. 559.

89d See *The Slaughterhouse Cases* (1873) 16 Wall. 30; *Hague* v. *C.I.O.* (1939) 307 U.S. 496; *Edwards* v. *California* (1941) 314 U.S. 160.

90 Scott, Dominion Jurisdiction over Human Rights (1949) 27 Can. Bar Rev. 497.

91 *Cunningham* v. *Tomey Homma* [1903] A.C. 151.

92 British Columbia Elections Act Amendment Act, 1949, c. 19 sec. 3.

93 *Breedlove* v. *Suttles* (1937) 302 U.S. 277; *Williams* v. *Mississippi* (1898) 170 U.S. 213; cf. *Guinn* v. *United States* (1915), 238 U.S. 347.

94 *Smith* v. *Allwright* (1944) 321 U.S. 649; *Terry* v. *Adams* (1953) 345 U.S. 461.

95 Common carriers and various public utilities regulated by statute are other exceptions.

96 *Constantine* v. *Imperial London Hotels* (1943) 60 T.L.R. 510.

97 *Franklin* v. *Evans* (1924) 55 O.L.R. 349; *Christie* v. *York* [1940] S.C.R. 139; *Rogers* v. *Clarence Hotel* [1940] 2 W.W.R. 545 (B.C.)

98 1951, c. 24 (Ont.)

98a The Fair Employment Practices Act, 1952–53 c. 19 (Can.)

98b The Fair Employment Practices Act, now R.S.M. 1954 c. 81.

98c The Fair Employment Practices Act; Statutes of Nova Scotia, 1955 c. 5.

99 1947 c. 33 (Sask.)

100 [1945] O.R. 778.

101 [1951] S.C.R. 64, *sub nom Noble and Wolf* v. *Alley*.

102 R.S.O. 1950 c. 68 sec. 21; 1950 c. 33 (Man.)

103 Smout, Racial & Religious Restraints on Alienation, (1952) 30 Can. Bar Rev. 863 at 870–71.

103a The Defamation Act, R.S.M. 1954 c. 60 sec. 20.

103b *Beauharnais* v. *Illinois* (1952) 343 U.S. 250.

104 1954 c. 157. (Ont.)

104a See *Regina* v. *McKay* (1955) 113 C.C.C. 56; *Regina* v. *Emerson* (1955)

113 C.C.C. 69. A good article on these cases has just come to hand. It is Borovoy, The Fair Accommodatio Practices Act: The "Dresden Affair", (1956) 14 University of Toronto, Faculty of Law Review 13.

105 A valuable collection of material on this subject is found in Emerson & Haber, *op cit* note 45 supra, cap. IX.

106 *Shelley* v. *Kraemer* (1948) 334 U.S. 1. *Barrows* v. *Jackson* (1953) 346 U.S. 249.

107 *Dorsey* v. *Stuyvesant Town,* (1951) 339 U.S. 981 Certiorari refused.

108 *Plessy* v. *Ferguson* (1896) 163 U.S. 537.

109 *Morgan* v. *Virginia* (1946) 328 U.S. 373.

110 *Henderson* v. *Southern Railway* (1950) 339 U.S. 816.

111 *Missouri* v. *Canada* (1938) 305 U.S. 337; also *Sipuel* v. *Board of Regents* (1948) 332 U.S. 631.

112 *Sweatt* v. *Painter* (1950) 339 U.S. 818.

113 *McLaurin* v. *Board of Regents* (1950) 339 U.S. 888.

114 *Brown* v. *Board of Education* (1954) 347 U.S. 483. *Bolling* v. *Sharpe* (1954) 347 U.S. 497. See McWhinney, An End to Racial Discrimination in the United States? (1954) 32 Can. Bar Rev. 545.

115 The Report of President Truman's Commission on Civil Rights. "To Secure these Rights" (1948) is a valuable study of the whole subject.

116 See *Steele* v. *La. & Nashville Ry.* (1943) 323 U.S. 192.

117 Berger, The New York State Law Against Discrimination (1950) 35 Cornell L.Q. 747.

118 Carter, Practical Considerations of Anti-Discrimination Legislation: Experiences under the New York Law Against Discrimination (1954) 40 Cornell L.Q. 40 at p. 57.

119 *Ibid.* at p. 44.

120 Carr, Federal Protection of Civil Rights, at p. 195 (1947).

121 Roche and Gordon "Can Morality be Legislated?" New York Times Magazine, May 22, 1955, p. 10.

122 Re Companies Reference (1913) 48 S.C.R. 331 at p. 424.

123 See generally, Kennedy, The Constitution of Canada, 2 Ed. (1937) pp. 415–430; Memorandum on the Dominion Power of Disallowance of Provincial Legislation, Department of Justice, Ottawa (1937); Forsey, The Prince Edward Island Trade Union Act, 1948, (1948) 26 Can. Bar Rev. 1159 at pp. 1168–1181.

124 Willis, Statute Interpretation in a Nutshell (1938) 16 Can. Bar Rev. I at p. 23.

125 E.g., *Lawson* v. *Interior Tree Fruit & Vegetable Committee* [1931] S.C.R. 351.

126 E.g., Re Natural Products Marketing Act, [1937] A.C. 377.

127 *P.E.I. Potato Marketing Board* v. *Willis* [1952] 2 S.C.R. 392.

128 *Florence Mining Co.* v. *Cobalt Lake Mining Co.* (1909) 18 D.L.R. 273 at p. 279, aff'd [1911] A.C. 412.

129 *Beauharnois L.H. & P. Co.* v. *Hydro-Electric Power Comm.* [1937] O.R. 796.

130 *Western Minerals Ltd.* v. *Gaumont* [1953] 1 S.C.R. 345.

131 See Haines, The History of Due Process after the Civil War (1924) 3 Texas L.R. 1; Selected Essays on Constitutional Law 268 (1938).

132 *Village of Euclid* v. *Ambler* (1926) 272 U.S. 365; see also *Berman* v. *Parker* (1954) 348 U.S. 26.

133 *Chicago Milwaukee & St. Paul Ry.* v. *Minnesota* (1890) 134 U.S. 418.

134 *Tyson* v. *Banton* (1927) 273 U.S. 418.

135 *Williams* v. *Standard Oil Co.* (1929) 278 U.S. 235.

136 *Ribnik* v. *McBride* (1928) 277 U.S. 350.

137 *Burns Baking Co.* v. *Bryan* (1924) 264 U.S. 304.

138 *Liggett Co.* v. *Baldridge* (1928) 278 U.S. 105.

139 *New State Ice Co.* v. *Leibmann* (1932) 285 U.S. 262.

140 *Lochner* v. *New York* (1905) 198 U.S. 45.

141 *Adkins* v. *Children's Hospital* (1923) 261 U.S. 525.

142 E.g. *Adair* v. *United States* (1908) 208 U.S. 161; *Coppage* v. *Kansas* (1915) 236 U.S. 1.

143 Jackson, The Struggle for Judicial Supremacy (1939) is an interesting account of the "revolution" in the Court, which began in 1937.

144 *Home Building and Loan Ass'n* v. *Blaisdell* (1934) 290 U.S. 398; *East New York Savings Bank* v. *Hahn* (1945) 326 U.S. 230. For a survey of decisions on the Contract Clause, see also Hale, The Supreme Court and the Contract Clause (1943) 57 Harv. L.R. 512, 621, 852.

145 Re Debt Adjustment Act of Alberta [1943] A.C. 356; Re Farm Security Act of Saskatchewan [1949] A.C. 110.

146 Canada Evidence Act R.S.C. 1952 c. 307 sec. 5. The typical provincial Evidence Act contains a similar provision.

147 The Compulsory Testimony Act 1954, is not available to me, but it is discussed in an article in the Columbia Law Review (1954) 55 Col. L.R. 632. The validity of the act has been challenged by one Wm. L. Ullmann but I do not know whether the decision has been delivered.

148 This seems clear from the discussion of the subject in the Report of the Royal Commission appointed under order in Council P.C. 411 of February 5, 1948 at pp. 672–674.

149 E.g. *R.* v. *Smith* 1947 O.R. 378; *R.* v. *Mazerall* 1946 O.R. 511, 762; *R.* v. *Lunan* 1947 O.R. 201.

150 Proc. Canadian Bar Association (1946) pp. 141–150. See also Fyfe, Some aspects of the Report of the Royal Commission on Espionage (1946) 24 Can. Bar Rev. 777.

151 *Johnson* v. *Zerbst* (1938) 304 U.S. 458.

152 *Powell* v. *Alàbama* (1932) 287 U.S. 45.

153 *Uveges* v. *Pennsylvania* (1948) 335 U.S. 410.

154 *Williams* v. *New York* (1949) 337 U.S. 241.

155 *R.* v. *Benson* (1951) 100 C.C.C. 247.

156 Criminal Code, sec. 417.

157 *Maxwell* v. *Dow* (1900) U.S. 176 U.S. 581.

158 Orfield, Criminal Procedure from Arrest to Appeal (1947) p. 390–396.

159 See *Hermandez* v. *Texas* (1954) 347 U.S. 473. This was a case of discrimination against Mexicans but the cases on discrimination against negroes are applied.

160 Criminal Code, sec. 592.

161 E.g. *Chambers* v. *Florida* (1939) 309 U.S. 227; but compare *Stein* v. *New York* (1933) 346 U.S. 156.

162 *R.* v. *Sussex Justices* [1924] 1 K.B. 256.

163 [1950] 2 W.W.R. 193, rev'd. [1951] A.C. 585.

164 An excellent article in favour of the power of courts to review legislation that may violate the Bill of Rights is Rostow, and the Democratic Character of Judicial Review (1952) 66 Harv. L.R. 193.

165 Proceedings of the Committee at p. 347.

166 I must not overlook Dean Angus' stimulating article, Rights!! in Vol. II No. 3 (1955) of this publication, p. 149.

1958

Succession to Property in the Common Law Provinces

Reprinted from
Canadian Jurisprudence: The Civil Law and Common Law in Canada
Edward McWhinney, ed., Toronto, Carswell (1958)
Vol. 4, University of Toronto Comparative Law Series
pp. 241–267

This article appeared in a book published by Professor Edward McWhinney of the University of Toronto.

Earlier in this collection of writings is Bowker's paper written at Yale University in 1952 on Intestate Succession to Personal Property. That paper differs from this in that it was a historical study, going back to Norman times, and dealt with personal property only.

The article which follows deals with property in all forms, and outlines the current law on the subject. Unlike the first article, which was confined to intestacy, it extends to wills.

The law of intestate succession and of wills is in large measure the same throughout the Common Law provinces. They all took the law of England as of one date or another and so inherited many English statutes. Often a province has re-enacted these statutes, and in that case the local courts usually apply the body of English case law with which the English Acts had invariably become encrusted. When a legislature decides to change the law, it often turns to the enactments of other provinces or to the model statutes recommended by the Conference of Commissioners on Uniformity of Legislation in Canada. Hence the alterations are often similar and indeed identical as between provinces.

The remaining part of the law on this subject consists of decisions applying Common Law or Equity. Our courts have generally accepted English judgments, decided over a period of centuries by courts possessing a special competence in English property law. In addition, rulings of the House of Lords and Privy Council were considered binding before the abolition of appeals to the Judicial Committee in 1949; even subsequent decisions of those tribunals are of the highest persuasive effect. The Supreme Court of Canada too has an obvious unifying influence.

Yet there are substantial variations. These depend on the extent to which the local legislatures and courts have deviated from the English law to bring about rules that they conceive to be more suited to local conditions.

A change that is universal is the one that brings into the hands of an executor or administrator real as well as personal property; another is the abolition of primogeniture, followed in most provinces by the complete assimilation of the rules governing descent of real property and those for the distribution of personal. It is not the intention here to trace these developments historically but if one were to do so he would find that generally the special feudal rules governing inheritance of land did not survive as long in the colonies and Dominions as they did in the motherland.

My purpose is to describe the law of intestacy and then the law of wills in the nine Common Law provinces. To the former we now turn.

The Law of Intestacy

This is one of the first subjects that the Conference of Commissioners on Uniformity of Legislation in Canada studied. In 1920 they found substantial differences as between the provincial laws governing descent and distribution of real and personal property on intestacy.[1] In 1925 they approved a model Intestate Succession Act that was revised in 1950 and amended in 1955 and 1958.[2] This Act, with some variations, has been adopted in British Columbia, Alberta, Saskatchewan, Manitoba, New Brunswick, Prince Edward Island and Newfoundland.[3] It is customary to include a clause in every uniform Act that "this Act shall be so interpreted and construed as to effect its general purpose of making uniform the law of those provinces that enact it". For some reason, Manitoba and New Brunswick have omitted this provision. Ontario's statute is in different form from the uniform Act and is taken from the English Statute of Distributions of 1670.[4] Nova Scotia's statute shows the influence of the old distinction between real and personal property by dealing with them separately though the descent of real property is in great measure similar to that of personal.[5]

The following description of the division of an intestate's estate is of necessity a summary of the statutory provisions. However, it may be the more interesting if the reader asks himself how the statutes compare with his own idea of a fair distribution. The uniform Act assimilates completely the descent of the real property to personal and treats the husband in the same manner as the wife; this should be remembered in the following account.

The Act deals first with the situation where the intestate leaves a wife and children. If there is one child the division is equal; if more than one the wife receives one-third and the children the other two-thirds. If a child died before the testator leaving issue—which by definition includes all lawful lineal descendants—they divide the child's share *per stirpes*.

Where there is no wife but there is issue then the issue divide all the estate *per stirpes*. For example, if the intestate left a son John and a daughter of a deceased daughter Mary and three children of a deceased son of Mary then John would take half; Mary's daughter would take a quarter and her three grand-children would divide the remaining quarter. If the Act said, as it does not, that all issue take *per capita,* then John and Mary's daughter and her three grand-children being the five living issue would each take a fifth. In other words, distribution *per stirpes* is by branches of the family tree, while distribution *per capita* is by the number of persons entitled to share.

These provisions are in effect in the seven provinces that have the uniform Act, save that in British Columbia the widow receives the first $5,000.00.[6]

In Ontario she likewise receives the first $5,000.00. The provision dealing with the residue is in the wording of the Statute of Distributions, which is not as easy to follow as the uniform Act. However, the result as between widow and children is the same under both. However, where the wife dies the husband always receives one-third if she leaves issue.[7] He is not treated quite as liberally as he would be under the uniform Act, and still less so than under the Statute of Distributions, for that Act left intact his right to all of his wife's personalty.[8]

In Nova Scotia a vestige of feudal influence remains in the fact that the children take all the real property. A surviving wife takes only her common law dower and a surviving husband his estate by the curtesy. Sons and daughters divide the real property equally, with a child of a deceased son or daughter taking the parent's share; but if all the issue are grandchildren they share *per capita,* not *per stirpes*. The surviving spouse always receives but one-third of the personal property even if there is only one child. The other two-thirds goes to the issue in the same way as real property.[9]

One criticism could be made of the provisions dividing property between children and surviving spouse. There may be cases where the widow—or even a widower—should have more than the statutory fraction and other cases where the children should have more. Of course, an increase to one party is at the expense of the others. Most provinces have a statute permitting a widow, widower and child to apply to the court for relief against a *will* but these Acts do not extend to cases of intestacy. However, suggestions have been made over the years that the court should have power to give relief to widow or child on intestacy;[10] and in 1949 Saskatchewan amended its Dependants' Relief Act[11] to that end. Alberta followed in 1955.[12] In England the Intestates' Estates Act, 1952[13] made similar provision. Mr. Justice McLelland of New South Wales writing in 1954 and mentioning deficiencies in the New Zealand and Australian statutes, said: "There is no jurisdiction in cases of total intestacy save in New Zealand and in New South Wales in which state, however, the jurisdiction is quite illogically restricted to applications by widows."[14]

The Saskatchewan and Alberta amendments are a significant extension of the principle of legislation permitting wife and children to obtain relief against wills. The court now has jurisdiction to alter the statutory distribution in order to benefit a spouse or child. I have seen no reported cases save one holding that the Saskatchewan amendment is not retroactive.[15]

The next situation is that of a surviving widow but no children. Should she take everything or should she have to share with parents, brothers and sisters or even more remote relations of her husband? The answers to this question as reflected in the different statutes show a great diversity. The uniform Act does not give the widow the whole estate but does at least grant her the first $20,000.00. The balance she shares equally with the next-of-kin no matter how remote. The four Maritime provinces and Ontario all require her to share with the husband's kin in one way or another. New Brunswick has the uniform provisions.[16] So do Newfoundland and Prince Edward Island, except that in these provinces the wife is required to share with the husband's parents, brothers and sisters, nephews and nieces but not with more remote relations;[17] and Prince Edward Island gives her the first $8,000.00 rather than $20,000.00.

In these three provinces the position is the same where the wife dies. Her husband must share with her kin, for as stated earlier the uniform Act works both ways.

Nova Scotia does not have the uniform Act. The wife takes half the land in lieu of dower and half the personalty. The rest goes to the husband's parents or parent, and next to brothers and sisters (with children representing their parent). If the intestate leaves none of these close kin, the wife takes all. In other words, she is not required to share with remote relations of the husband as she is under the uniform Act. Where the wife dies the husband must share with her kin in the same way she would have had to share with his.[18]

In Ontario, a wife who elects not to take her dower rights receives the first $5,000.00 together with two-thirds of the residue. The remaining third goes to the husband's next-of-kin no matter how remote. Where it is the wife who has died, her husband does not fare quite as well. His share is only one-half.[19]

We have seen that all of the eastern provinces make the wife share with her husband's kin. Turning now to the western provinces one might think that they would simply adopt the uniform provision. Generally they have accepted that Act more completely than the eastern provinces have. However, they have rejected the provision that requires a wife to share with her husband's kin. The prairie provinces gave her everything long before the uniform Act and have simply preserved this distribution.[20] Perhaps they have always favoured the wife because they were until recently pioneer communities made up of young couples who came west and built up the husband's estate by their joint effort. The movement for women's rights might have been another influence. British Columbia had the uniform provision until this year. An amendment of 1958 gives the wife everything.[21] Perhaps this is an acknowledgement of the contribution made by women during the province's first hundred years.

I can see little reason why a wife should have to share with her husband's parents or brothers and sisters let alone his more distant relations. In England she must share with her husband's close kin, but even then she receives the first £20,000, the personal chattels and half the residue.[22]

The next case that an intestacy law must cover is that where there is no spouse or issue. Under the uniform Act the property goes equally to the parents or surviving parent. This is in effect in all the seven provinces that have the uniform Act.[23] In Ontario, the parents and brothers and sisters are deemed to be of equal degree, and hence share the estate.[24] In Nova Scotia real property goes to the parents or parent and personal property to the "next-of-kin" who, of course are the parents so they take the whole estate.[25]

We have next the case where both parents are dead. The uniform Act, as one might expect, puts brothers and sisters next after parents and permits children of a deceased brother or sister to take the parent's share. In the original uniform Act, there then came a proviso that where all brothers and sisters are dead, then nephews and nieces take *per capita*. Now apart from this proviso the situation where all brothers and sisters are dead is that nephews and nieces would come behind grandparents and with aunts and uncles, not ahead of them; for nephews, nieces, aunts, uncles are all of the same degree of relationship to the testator. The purpose of the proviso seems to have been to put nephews and nieces ahead of grandparents and aunts and uncles but it did so only by implication. Opinions were expressed that it did not achieve its purpose[26] so in 1950 the uniform Act was amended to provide that if the intestate leaves no widow, issue, father, mother, brother or sister, the estate shall go to nephews and nieces. Under this amendment they clearly come next after brothers and sisters and ahead of aunts and uncles and even of grandparents. Had the new section stopped there then the question might have arisen whether children of deceased nephews can demand their parent's share. To remove any doubt the section says that in no case shall representation be admitted.

The seven provinces with the uniform Act have all adopted the 1950 amendment.[27] Nova Scotia's provisions dealing with this situation are to the same effect. Nephews and nieces take to the exclusion of aunts and uncles.[28] In Ontario there is no provision to put them ahead of aunts and uncles so they rank equally.[29]

At this point, the revised uniform Act ceases its mention of specific kindred and says that if the intestate leaves none of those specifically mentioned in the provisions discussed above, then "his estate shall be distributed equally among the next of kin of equal degree of consanguinity to the intestate and in no case shall representation be admitted". The method of computing degrees of kindred in all nine provinces is that of the civil law—by counting upward from the intestate to the nearest common ancestor and down to the relative. The seven provinces with the uniform Act have all adopted the section just quoted.[30] It is intended to be a clarification of the earlier clause that said the property goes to the next-of-kin "and those who equally represent them, but in no case shall representation be admitted after brothers' and sisters' children". This wording is the same as that of the Statute of Distributions and the Ontario Act.[31] Its true meaning is that where the next-of-kin are more remote than brothers and sisters then the children of the next-of-kin cannot take by representation. This clause, at one time, was in effect in all provinces that have the uniform Act. It gave rise to much litigation and the courts, notably in British Columbia, had difficulty in applying it. Claims that cannot succeed on a proper interpretation are these: by children of deceased nephews or nieces to share with surviving nephews and nieces;[32] by children of deceased aunts or uncles to share with living aunts or uncles;[33] by children of paternal grandparents to share with living maternal grandparents.[34] The 1950 amendments to the uniform Act make clear the law in the sense just described.

This completes our account of the main provisions of the various Acts. Several other matters must, however, be noted. All the provincial Acts,[35] like the Statute of Distributions, provide that where portions of children's shares have been advanced to them by the parent in his lifetime, this shall be taken into consideration in the distribution of the parents' estate. One might think that this would give rise to family disputes, with one child claiming that another had received payments by way of advancement. However, there are few reported cases. Under the uniform Act the burden of proving that a child has been maintained or educated or has been given money with a view to a portion is on the person who asserts it unless the intestate has expressed or the child has acknowledged the advance in writing. Nova Scotia's provision differs in form from that of the uniform Act and extends to grandchildren but the requirement of proof of an advancement is similar.[36] The Ontario Act makes it even harder to prove an advancement for a written statement by the intestate or a written acknowledgement by the child that a settlement of property is in fact an advancement is required; moreover, maintaining and educating a child is not an advancement.[37]

The case of an illegitimate child is specially mentioned in the uniform Act. At Common Law he was *nullus filius*. He did not inherit from either parent on intestacy and no one could take from him except his wife or issue. His property went to the Crown—real property by escheat and personal as *bona vacantia*. In recent times the public attitude toward him has changed. It is not his fault he is illegitimate and there is a strong trend toward placing him in the position of a legitimate child.

The uniform Act says that illegitimate children and their issue shall inherit from and through the mother as if legitimate; and where the illegitimate dies leaving no widow or issue, his estate goes to his mother, or if she is dead, to her children or grandchildren.

Some provinces had provisions of this kind before there was a uniform Act. The earliest I have found is in the Territories Real Property Act of 1886.[38] When it was re-enacted in Saskatchewan the argument was raised that the legislature could not create new beneficiaries so as to interfere with the Crown's right to the estate of an illegitimate. The Supreme Court of Canada rejected this argument.[39] It is clear that if there is no person among those named the property still goes to the Crown.[40]

The uniform provision is in force in the seven provinces that have the uniform Act.[41] In Ontario the Devolution of Estates Act says that an illegitimate child or relative shall not share under the Act[42] but the Legitimation Act permits the child to take from the mother if she had no legitimate children and permits the mother to take from him.[43] Prince Edward Island has in addition a section that so far as I have found is unique. The wife of an illegitimate child who dies without issue receives only the first $8,000.00 and half of the residue, while the rest goes to the mother. If she is dead, it goes to her other children or grandchildren and it is only if there are none of these persons that the widow takes all.[44] Nova Scotia allows the mother to take in the same manner as if the child were born in wedlock[45] but I have found no provision permitting the child to take from her.

These enactments of course do not place the child completely in the position of a legitimate child in relation to his mother. With a view to bringing this about the Commissioners on Uniformity of Legislation in 1958 recommended the following in substitution for the present uniform sections: "For the purposes of this Act, an illegitimate child shall be treated as the legitimate child of his mother". It is, of course, impossible to say whether any province will enact it.

The uniform Act does not attempt to deal with the situation of an illegitimate child and his father. In Alberta, however, an unusual case arose in 1940. A bachelor named Ogal died partially intestate with distant kin in Europe and having admitted parentage of eight illegitimate children in Alberta. At the time he died it is clear that the relations in Europe were entitled but the legislature intervened by amending the Intestate Succession Act to provide that where an intestate who had no widow or lawful issue dies the illegitimate children and their issue shall inherit as if legitimate. As a protection against unfounded claims the enactment requires acknowledgement or else a judicial finding of paternity.[46] It was made to apply to all estates not administered at the time it was passed. Thus, the property was taken from the European kin and vested in the Alberta children.[47]

Another interesting piece of legislation is British Columbia's Destitute Orphans Act of 1877, now included in the Administration of Estates Act. It applies when an intestate leaves surviving a concubine or illegitimate child or children under 16 for which he was providing. The court may order payment for the maintenance of the concubine or any such child, with a maximum of $500.00 for any of these persons and a limit of 10% of the estate.[48] The original Act recited that divers persons died intestate in the province possessed of considerable property and without heirs in the province but leaving concubines and illegitimate children. The typical situation was that of a person who co-habited with a native, but the Act is general in its terms.

"The section though passed originally to meet social conditions which happily no longer generally prevail in this province, has been retained by the legislature,"[49] and applications are still made from time to time.[50]

The uniform Act deprives a wife of a share in her husband's estate if she has left him and is living in adultery at the time of his death. Manitoba is the only province with the uniform Act that omits the provision.[51] The statutes in Ontario and Nova Scotia are silent on this point, but their Dower Acts embody the old rule that a wife who commits adultery forfeits her dower rights. In Nova Scotia uncondoned adultery is sufficient while in Ontario she must leave her husband and continue in adultery in order to be barred.[52] Living in adultery is, of course, different from mere adultery and it is only the former that deprives a spouse of her share under the uniform Act.[53]

By way of conclusion on the subject of intestate succession several miscellaneous points deserve mention.

(1) The Acts are silent on the question—what happens to the share of a beneficiary who renounces? If a child renounces his share, it goes to the other children.[54] Although I have not found any cases dealing with other kin it seems logical that the renunciation should operate in favour of the other members of the class. If no one remains in the class then it should go to those in the next degree.

(2) The Acts do not contain a no-waiver provision but a number of cases deal with the question. A person may contract out of a statute that was passed for his benefit, but not one that was passed for the public benefit.[55] It is sometimes hard for the court to decide the category in which a statute belongs. The few cases in Canada on the Intestate Succession Act hold that there is nothing to prevent a beneficiary from agreeing to forego his rights on intestacy.[56] The common example is where the wife agrees in a separation agreement to surrender her interest in the husband's estate.

(3) Does a person entitled to take on intestacy forfeit his rights if he feloniously kills the intestate? The law is settled in the case of a beneficiary under a will, and there are cases extending this rule to the case of intestacy.[57] On the basis of public policy the courts have written this exception into the statute. A parallel exception in the case of the Statutes of Frauds has long been established. However, it seems to me that a strong argument could be made that the courts should not read this exception into the Act. In at least one American case this position was taken.[58]

(4) It would be interesting to compare in detail the Canadian statutes with the English. Space does not permit this, but one can say generally that the order in which spouse and kin succeed to the estate bears many resemblances to that of the provincial Acts. On the other hand, the scheme of distribution is much more elaborate. In some cases, there are life estates and the property goes to the administrator on a trust for conversion.[59] The Canadian Acts do not specifically create a trust for conversion though usually there are provisions in connection with the devolution of real property providing for sale for purpose of distribution. In addition, statutes such as the Trustee Acts or Infants Acts frequently permit the sale of an infant's share. It is settled that if the beneficiaries are all *sui juris* they may agree to take the property *in specie*.[60]

(5) The special case of the legitimated child and the adopted child has been regulated by statute. All provinces provide for legitimation by subsequent marriage and several for the case of children of certain void marriages, as where a husband has been reported to be dead or a court has made

an order of presumption of death and the wife has re-married. The typical provision says that the child is for all purposes deemed to be legitimate from birth. As for adopted children Dr. Kennedy has discussed most thoroughly the position of the child on intestacy, both in relation to his natural parents and the adopting parents. In most provinces the child may take from both parents. Dr. Kennedy points out many problems that the present statutes raise and advocates new provisions that will sever the child from his natural family and that will put him completely in the position of a child of the new family.[61]

Dower and Estate by the Curtesy

At Common Law the wife did not inherit the husband's real property but from the earliest times was entitled to dower. Whenever he acquired as sole owner a legal estate in fee tail or fee simple in lands and his wife gave birth to a child who might become heir then her right to dower arose. When the husband died the widow could call on the heir or devisee to assign to her for life an estate in one-third of the lands. Other forms of dower were known but that just described is known as dower by the Common Law and is the one that survived to modern times. Dower attached to all the husband's lands and he could not dispose of them unless his wife "barred" or released her dower. This was inconvenient when transactions in land became frequent. Various devices were available to the husband to circumvent dower. In 1833 Parliament simplified the position by permitting the husband to dispose of land in his lifetime or by will free of dower. Henceforth, dower attached only as against the heir. Then in 1925 the sweeping reforms of property law abolished dower altogether.[62]

A husband's estate by the curtesy is the counterpart of dower but at Common Law extended to all of the wife's lands, not merely one third. The Married Women's Property Act, 1882, permitted a wife to dispose of her land as if she were a *feme sole*. Thus, she could dispose of her land or devise it and curtesy did not arise. It remained however if she died intestate. Like dower, it was abolished in 1925.[63]

Both of these estates were firmly established in the older Common Law provinces but never became so deeply rooted in the west. British Columbia did have them for a time but abolished them in 1925.[64] The prairie provinces did away with them almost from the beginning The Torrens system of registration of title to land was established in Manitoba and the Northwest Territories over seventy years ago and the statutes creating that system did away with dower and curtesy. The late Chief Justice Harvey of Alberta once explained the reason.

> "When the Torrens system was introduced into the North-West Territories in 1886 the wife's right to dower as well as the husband's estate by the curtesy, was abolished as being in conflict with what was supposed to be an inherent principle of that system as regards freedom of transfer and the ability to as-

certain every interest in the land by reference to the face of the current certificate of title."[65]

Doubtless the reason was the same in Manitoba. However, the story does not end here. The movement for Women's Rights included in Western Canada at least agitation for changes in the position of married women in relation to their husbands' property. When the movement was in full blossom during World War I, the Alberta legislature was persuaded to enact a new Dower Act. It did not restore Common Law dower but rather gave the wife on her husband's death a life interest in the "homestead", which is the family home—assuming of course the husband owned it when he died. The Act has been changed frequently and in 1948 a re-enactment gave to the husband the same dower right where the wife died owning the homestead—a novel version of tenancy by the curtesy but called dower. The consent of the spouse is required to a disposition *inter vivos*. This requirement has caused the courts great difficulty but is not of concern here. The significance of the Act in the law of succession is that it assures to the surviving spouse a life interest in the home, and it cannot be affected by the will of the owner. A novel provision includes in dower a life interest in certain personal property of the deceased.[66]

Saskatchewan has not revived dower. The Intestate Succession Act retains the provision abolishing it.[67] However, there is a Homestead Act which prevents the husband from disposing of the home without his wife's consent. It does not give her a life interest on his death but at least preserves the home as part of his estate.[68]

Manitoba has revived dower in a form similar to that of Alberta.[69]

Turning to the eastern provinces, Newfoundland, in the Atlantic, like British Columbia on the Pacific, has abolished dower and curtesy[70] but none of the other eastern provinces has.

The first section of Ontario's Dower Act[71] should bring joy to the heart of an antiquarian. It says that "a widow, on the death of her husband, may tarry in his chief house for forty days within which time her dower shall be assigned her, . . . and for her dower shall be assigned to her the third part of all the lands of her husband whereof he was seized at any time during coverture . . . "—a faithful re-enactment of Chapter VII of Magna Carta.

The wife may, of course, bar her dower. Moreover, the husband on acquiring land may, if he wishes, have the grant put in such a form that he can dispose of it by deed or will, immune from the wife's claim to dower. The draftsman of the deed to the husband and of the husband's disposition must be very careful and even in the middle of the twentieth century there is sometimes doubt as to whether he has succeeded.[72]

If the husband disposes by will of land in which the wife has dower rights then if the will shows an intention that benefits given to the wife in the will are in lieu of dower, she must elect. The intention is often hard to determine.[73] Where he dies intestate the widow may elect to take her share under the Devolution of Estates Act[74] instead of her dower. Likewise a husband may elect to take his estate by the curtesy instead of his share under the Devolution of Estates Act.[75]

In New Brunswick there is little modern case law. The wife must elect within six months if she wishes to take her dower instead of her share on intestacy.[76] Tenancy by the curtesy has been abolished.[77]

In Nova Scotia in the case of intestacy and where there are infants the wife's share of real property is her dower; similarly a husband's only interest in his wife's lands is his estate by the curtesy.[78] The Dower Act specifically puts the wife to her election where the husband has died testate and "by his will manifests an intention to dispose of his real property in a manner inconsistent with his wife's right to dower".[79]

Prince Edward Island's provisions for intestate succession recognize both dower and curtesy but permit the surviving spouse to waive the right in favour of a full statutory share of the estate.[80] The Dower Act has a provision permitting the court to bar dower and to set aside for the wife's benefit part of the proceeds of a sale. I have seen no other section in the provinces having Common Law dower that is so broad.[81]

One forms the impression that even in those provinces where dower and curtesy survive that they are not as important as they were in the past. There is perhaps little objection to retaining them if the owner can dispose of his land freely without the wife's consent but this is still not the position in the provinces that have either Common Law dower or the new western form. On the other hand the enactment of modern Family Relief Acts that permit a surviving spouse to obtain relief against the terms of the will renders these ancient interests less justifiable than they were in the past.

Wills

The Conference of Commissioners on Uniformity of Legislation approved a model Wills Act in 1929. Although only Saskatchewan and Manitoba have specifically adopted it,[82] the statutes in the other Common Law provinces[83] are similar to it, and all are based on the English Act of 1837. In 1957 the Conference approved a new uniform Act[84] that makes several important changes. There is no need here to summarize the main provisions of the provincial laws. Rather I shall note those provisions and doctrines that are of special interest.

On the subject of formalities of execution one can generalize by saying that Canadian courts, like the English, are very strict. For example, the two witnesses must sign in the testator's presence. An Alberta case holds that they did not do so when the testator was lying with his back to the witnesses and unable to turn, though they were in the same room.[85] A case from Quebec illustrates the need of exact compliance with the statutory formalities. The Civil Code permits wills in the English form. One witness signed before the second came into the room. Then the testator acknowledged his signature before both witnesses but the first did not sign again. The Quebec Court of Appeal held the will properly executed because there was no suggestion of fraud and the Court thought the spirit of the Code had been observed. The Supreme Court however held that the formalities had not been observed to the letter and rejected the will.[86]

Holograph wills are not permitted under the English Act but the three prairie provinces, like Quebec, permit them. They appear to be usual in civil law countries and are allowed in Scotland. Their introduction into the prairie provinces[87] was not by reason of any civil law influence but because the legislatures decided that it would be a convenience. In remote areas it is sometimes hard to obtain a solicitor or even witnesses. Perhaps the notion of economy, penny-wise to be sure, was a factor.

Where holograph wills are permitted, questions often arise as to whether a letter or written memorandum is intended to be a will. The courts have sometimes admitted to probate letters that are most informal.[88] In one case from Saskatchewan a man pinned under his tractor scratched his will on the fender. It was admitted to probate.[89]

All of the statutes permitting holograph wills say that the will must be wholly in the handwriting of the deceased. This does not include typing[90] nor filling in blanks in a printed form[91] though if a form is used and the written part can be read as a complete will by itself it is good.[92] The wording of the statutes is such that there is doubt whether the will need be signed at the foot or end.[93] A codicil to a formal will may be in holograph form[94] but in Alberta at least, alterations to a formal will must be formally executed and not by holograph.[95] Of course a holograph will is not effective to pass immovables in a jurisdiction that does not recognize such a will.[96]

The problem of mental capacity to make a will frequently arises. Sometimes it is argued that the burden of proof of lack of testamentary capacity is on the person alleging it. This is plausible, but the generally accepted view is that the propounder of the will must prove capacity. However, if those attacking the will show evidence of insanity, or senility, then the court must decide whether the will presented for probate compares with a hypothetical reasonable will that the testator would make if he were normal. The commonest case is that of hallucinations. The court determines whether they have influenced the disposition of the will, and to do this looks at the facts to see how the testator has dealt with those who by personal relationship or otherwise, had claims upon him. In other words, Canadian courts apply the leading English case of *Banks v. Goodfellow*.[97] Ordinarily courts do not compare the provisions of a will with what they think the provisions should have been. They do so where insanity has been established because they can save the will if they conclude the insanity did not affect it.

If the testator's sanity is not in issue, the question whether he has met his moral obligations, or on the other hand, has made inexplicable or eccentric or absurd dispositions is quite irrelevant. For example, a wealthy man left the residue of his estate to the woman in Toronto bearing the largest number of children in the ten years after his death. The neglected relatives made a valiant but vain effort to set aside the residuary gift as contrary to public policy.[98]

Assuming a sane testator it is still possible that the document is not his will. He may have been the victim of fraud or undue influence. Our courts have applied the English rule that the burden of proof is on the person alleging either.[99] A situation that has caused difficulty is that in which the person drawing the will is also a beneficiary. At one time some courts thought that this creates a suspicion of undue influence or fraud so that the propounder of the will has to remove the suspicion; in other words there is a presumption or at least an inference of undue influence or fraud against a beneficiary who drew the will. This view seems reasonable, but it is not the law. True enough there is suspicion—but it is not a suspicion of undue influence or fraud. It merely adds to the weight of the onus that is always on the propounder to show that the document is in fact the will of the deceased.[100]

Revocation of wills requires brief mention. Generally the statutory provisions are taken from the English.[101] The effect of marriage is not the same in all provinces. Newfoundland does not provide for wills made in contemplation of marriage. Prince Edward Island requires that marriage take place within a month after making such a will. In Ontario the surviving spouse is given a year to elect to take under a will made before but not in contemplation of marriage.

The provisions on revocation by destroying and by making alterations have not produced anything new in principle. The judge-made doctrine of dependant relative revocation has been recognized; since it depends in theory on intention, the courts can really only guess as to what the testator's intention would have been had he known that a valid new will would not follow the revocation[102] or that the revocation would not in fact revive an earlier revoked will.[103] Usually the doctrine is invoked where a will has been destroyed with the intention of revoking it and the revocation is either conditional or under a mistake. It can however apply where the revocation is by a subsequent document though it arises infrequently in this case.[104]

Revival of a revoked will by a codicil is specifically provided for, but the codicil must show an intent to revive and it is hard for the court to know whether the codicil in fact does show intent.[105]

There is no need to summarize those provisions in the statutes that lay down what are really canons of construction. One of the most important says that so far as the testator's property is concerned the will speaks from death, unless a contrary intention is shown. Often it is doubtful whether a contrary intention is in fact shown; for example by the use of the phrase "I give the money *now* in my bank account to John".[106] The Wills Acts do not specifically say so but it is settled that reference to persons as distinct from property is of the date of the will unless a contrary intention is shown.[107]

One specific provision in all Acts that is of interest is that which preserves against lapse certain gifts where the beneficiary has died before the testator. The English Act says that where the gift is to a child or other issue of the testator and the child predeceases the testator leaving issue it does not lapse but goes as if the child had died immediately after the testator. Thus, it might go to the child's creditors or beneficiaries under his will and not to his issue at all.

British Columbia, Ontario, Nova Scotia and Newfoundland have adopted the English section but in Alberta, Saskatchewan, Manitoba and New Brunswick the gift takes effect in favour of those who would take from the beneficiary had he died intestate immediately after the testator.[108] In other words, the gift is saved for the benefit of the issue of the beneficiary together with his spouse, if any; under the intestate succession laws of the provinces they are the ones who would take. This seems better than the English scheme and indeed it might be still better to exclude the spouse of the beneficiary and to provide that the property shall pass to his issue. This is what Prince Edward Island enacted in 1956.[109] Three of the provinces, Saskatchewan, Manitoba and Ontario, extend the scope of the section to include gifts to brothers and sisters. It may be debatable whether the testator would prefer this but, of course, he can always put in his will provisions that indicate a contrary intention. The English section does not apply to class gifts; nor do the comparable provisions in British Columbia, Nova Scotia, Prince Edward Island and Newfoundland.

A large proportion of the cases on wills raises questions of interpretation—what did the testator mean by what he said? Many rules of construction exist and a whole book would be required to deal with them. The question of admissibility of evidence is too vast to attempt to put in a nut-shell. Generally, extrinsic evidence will not be admitted to show what a testator meant, because the statute says the will must be in writing. However, there are cases of ambiguity where the court will admit evidence, and I do not think they can all be brought under the heading of latent ambiguity. Frequently the courts say they can put themselves in the testator's armchair and this requires some evidence of circumstances surrounding the execution of the will. Certainly the courts go to some lengths to overcome deficiencies in expression. The benevolent judgment in *Perrin v. Morgan*[110] has had its influence in Canada. Courts of construction sometimes overlook mistakes and inaccurate descriptions.[111] The general rule is that a probate court may strike out words that were inserted by mistake provided the will was not read over to or by the testator. It may not insert the proper words. However, in one unusual case the husband signed the will intended for his wife. The probate court not only struck out the words but substituted others to make the will sensible.[112]

One rule that deserves special mention has to do with a testamentary gift of land. After making his will the testator enters into an agreement to sell the land and dies before the purchaser has fully paid. The theory is that the execution of the agreement operates as a notional conversion of the testator's interest into a claim for the purchase price. Hence he did not have at death an interest in the land, and the devisee is not entitled to the balance of the purchase price. In *Church v. Hill* the Supreme Court of Canada confirmed this rule, but with regret.[113] In a recent case the testatrix made a devise of land. Since she owned the minerals, they went as part of the devise. Later she granted a "lease" of the petroleum and natural gas. It was subsisting when she died. The Court of Appeal for Saskatchewan held that the lease is a sale of a portion of the land so that *Church v. Hill* applied and the devisee did not take any interest in the petroleum and natural gas. The Supreme Court held that the oil lease was not a grant of the fee simple in the oil but rather a *profit à prendre*. The testatrix still owned the oil and petroleum when she died and they passed to the devisee.[114]

The new uniform Wills Act[115] contains a provision designed to do away with the doctrine of *Church v. Hill* and it extends to gifts of personal property as well as real. Whether any provinces will enact it remains to be seen but certainly it does doubtless carry out the testator's intention whereas the present rule does not.

Many difficult problems arise where a gift is so worded that it may have the effect of postponing the vesting of property to a time subsequent to the testator's death. For example, is a remainder after a life estate vested or is it contingent? In the leading case of *Browne v. Moody*[116] a testator gave the income from a sum of money to A and then said "on the death of A I direct that the said sum is to be divided as follows: one-half to B and the other half equally between C, D and E." One might think, as did the Supreme Court, that the remainder is contingent on the remaindermen surviving A. The Privy Council however held that the remainder is vested on the testator's death. Enjoyment is postponed but not ownership of the corpus of the fund. Then if the will provides that in the event of a remainderman's death before the life tenant, the share of the one so dying shall go elsewhere, this is a clause of divestiture.

It is possible, of course, for a testator to word the gift so that the interest of a beneficiary shall vest only if he survives the life tenant, or attains a certain age or meets some other condition.

In many cases where the gift is not by way of remainder but is simply to A if, at, when, as soon as, or provided he attains the age of 25 or 40, the gift will not vest until he attains that age.[117] However, if the gift so worded is followed by a gift over on A's death before attaining the specified age, then the gift to A is held to be vested on the testator's death but subject to divestiture if A dies before attaining the age.[118] Yet there are cases holding that where a devise of land is to A followed by such a phrase as "this gift to take effect when A attains 25" the result is the same as though there were a gift over—the gift is vested subject to divestiture.[119] I have difficulty in seeing why if it vests at death it should be subject to divestiture. Certainly if the testator leaves a bequest of money to A and there is added a provision that it shall be paid to him at $300.00 a month, or that it shall be held and the income accumulated and paid together with the capital when he reaches 40 he can demand immediate payment—provided of course he is of age and the only one interested in the property.[120]

Gifts are frequently made subject to a condition. Usually the reason is that the testator wants the beneficiary to take or retain the property only if the beneficiary conducts himself in a certain way. Canadian courts recognize the distinction between conditions precedent and subsequent and like English courts tend to hold conditions to be subsequent rather than precedent. In other words, the gift is vested immediately but subject to divestiture on breach of condition. Courts require strict proof of breach. More important, the recent trend is to insist that the condition be most definite and precise. If it is uncertain then the court will hold it void. In the result, the beneficiary may have his cake and eat it too. In the leading case of *Sifton v. Sifton*[121] the Judicial Committee held that a condition requiring the beneficiary to reside in Canada was uncertain. Some years before this decision a testator in England had bequeathed property in trust for his daughter on condition that should she marry a person not of the Jewish parentage and faith, the trust should cease. She married a man admittedly not of Jewish parentage or faith and for the time being assumed her rights under her father's will were forfeit. However, the *Sifton* case encouraged her to attack the condition as void for uncertainty and she succeeded.[122] It is clear that the courts do not favour conditions of this type though they do not actually say they are void as against public policy.[123] If the condition is precedent and uncertain then the gift fails.[124] It should not be inferred however that all conditions relating to the religious faith of the beneficiary are uncertain.[125]

The rule against remoteness of vesting, or the modern rule against perpetuities, of course applies in Canada. The only province with a statute bearing on the rule in relation to wills is Prince Edward Island which has enacted that a future interest may vest as late as sixty years after a life or lives in being, in place of twenty-one years.[126] There are not many reported Canadian cases in which a gift was void under the rule. Canadian testators are perhaps not interested in controlling their property for as long after death as the law allows. One case in which a testator deliberately attempted to exclude his living children and any grandchildren by creating an executory interest in favour of a more remote descendant is *Ferguson v. Ferguson*.[127] The testator seems to have had a wry sense of humour. "It please the Lord to give me two sons equally dear to my heart; to give them equal justice I leave all my land to my first great grandson descending from them." This obviously violated the rule and was void.

A gift that will vest only on the death of the last descendant of the testator of course infringes the rule.[128]

The traditional English approach is to construe the will without reference to the rule and then to apply it. The court is not to be influenced by the fact that one of two possible constructions will render the gift void. The recent text of Morris and Leach[129] on Perpetuities calls this the "remorseless construction" and expresses the opinion that the courts might properly lean toward a construction that preserves the will. Mr. Justice Wilson of British Columbia perhaps did this in the case of a gift to grandchildren at 26. Since the testatrix left children surviving her the gift would appear to violate the rule. However, his Lordship said that the gift actually vested in the grandchildren at birth, though subject to divestiture on death before attaining the age of 26.[130]

No Canadian province has legislation comparable to that of England. The Law of Property Act, 1925 says that where the ascertainment of a beneficiary is made to depend on his attaining an age exceeding 21 years and thereby the gift is rendered void for remoteness, the will shall take effect as if the vesting had been made to depend on the beneficiary attaining the age of 21 years.[131] Morris and Leach express the opinion that it is a beneficent provision that cures what was perhaps the most common single cause of violations of the rule.[132] In a recent case the testator made a gift of income to the children of living persons at the age of 30. Whittaker J., in holding the gift remote, said: "It is unfortunate that there is not in this Province any statutory provision corresponding to s. 163 of the English Law of Property Act, 1925."[133]

Examples where the rule works a hardship and which Professor Leach has made famous are the "unborn widow," the "fertile octogenarian" and the "precocious toddler". I have found none of these in the Canadian reports. However, there are examples of his magic gravel pit.[134] The testator directs that a devise of his gravel pit shall vest in his issue living when it is exhausted. At the time of his death it is almost exhausted but the gift is void for there is a theoretical possibility that it might still be producing gravel for over 21 years. The result is the same if he provides that a gift shall vest when his debts, or specified debts, are paid. This has occurred in Canada.[135]

Another rule which the Supreme Court of Canada established in 1903 relates to restraints on alienation. A devise of land was accompanied by a proviso that the land should not be sold or encumbered for 25 years. The Court held that a general restraint was invalid even though limited in time.[136] The principle is that the power to alienate is one of the incidents of ownership that the testator cannot take away, though there are cases upholding partial restraints.

The English Accumulations Act of 1803[137] forbade the accumulation of income for longer than one of four specified periods. The one usually relevant in the case of wills is that which restricts accumulations to a period of 21 years from the death of the testator. The provinces of British Columbia, Ontario and New Brunswick have their own statutes based on the English Act of 1803.[138] The prairie provinces took the law of England as of July 15, 1870 insofar as it was applicable. The Alberta courts have applied the 1803 Act; probably the position is the same in Saskatchewan and Manitoba. Prince Edward Island's Perpetuities Act permits accumulations for as long as its perpetuity period—lives in being and sixty years. In Nova Scotia there is no local statute and the English Act of 1803 does not apply because Nova Scotia received the law of England as of 1758. Apparently the Act of 1803 is in effect in Newfoundland.[139]

In a typical case the testator directs the payment of one or more annuities out of the income from residue. He further directs that the balance of the income shall be added to capital and retained until the death of the last surviving annuitant and then paid over to a charitable institution. No problem arises if the annuitants all die within 21 years, but sometimes one or more is still living. After the expiration of the statutory period the income can no longer be accumulated.

A beneficiary of age can always stop the accumulation apart from the statute where the accumulation is for his benefit and he is the only one interested in the fund. This is the rule of *Saunders v. Vautier*.[140] Perhaps the beneficiary thus defeats the testator's intention but the rule is well settled. Where this is not possible then the Act operates to put an end to the accumulation after 21 years. What happens to the income thereafter? The 1803 Act and those based on it provide that the "released" income shall go to those who would have been entitled to it had the accumulation not been directed. If the income is from a specific fund it falls into residue;[141] if from residue it goes as on intestacy.[142]

Where the twenty-one years have expired, the persons entitled to the capital are sometimes anxious to ask for payment of the capital to them, to prevent the released income from going to others, usually the next-of-kin. The court will refuse if it finds anyone else, such as an annuitant, has a possible interest in the capital. The result is that the next-of-kin receive the income until the time of distribution arrives.[143]

Powers of appointment are perhaps not a part of the law of wills, yet they are sometimes created in wills and exercised by will. The English Wills Act and those based on it define will to include an appointment by will in exercise of a power; and provide that an appointment made by will in exercise of any power must be in the prescribed form of will; and that where a person having a power to appoint property in any manner he thinks proper makes his will, a general devise or bequest includes the property over which he has the power.

The remarkable feature of powers of appointment is that a testator who creates a power of appointment thereby delegates the making of his will to another. If he were to leave property on trust for such objects as A shall select the trust is clearly ineffective (unless charitable) because the testator must specify the object. Yet, if he grants to A a general power of appointment he has disposed of his property without specifying the object. In other words, a testator who creates a general power delegates to another the naming of his beneficiaries—a direct exception to the general rule that a man must make his own will. At least one Canadian writer has suggested that in spite of the fact that powers of appointment are frequently created by will, they may be invalid; the Wills Act contemplates that a person will make his own will.[144]

The most interesting Canadian case on powers is *Re Mewburn*.[145] There the testator left one-third of his estate to pay the income to his daughter for life, and upon her death the capital to go as she might by deed or will appoint. She requested payment of the capital to herself. A majority of the Appellate Division of the Supreme Court of Alberta, while recognizing the cases in her favour, held that the father's intention was to give her the life estate and that no rigid rule of law permitted her to demand the capital. The Supreme Court of Canada held that the testator's manifest intention was contrary to the authority he had conferred upon her, and that she might exercise the power in spite of the testator's intention.

Another question of interest that the Supreme Court has considered is whether a testamentary gift of income coupled with a power in the beneficiary to demand such portions of the capital as he may wish is a general power of appointment. There is English authority that it is but in the Supreme Court there was no clear-cut decision.[146]

The last subject to be noted in connection with wills is that of charitable gifts. A series of notable English judgments hold invalid a gift "for such charitable or *benevolent* purposes as the executors may select"; a purpose may be benevolent without being charitable.[147] In 1954 the Supreme Court had to consider a gift of residue for "charitable, religious, educational or philanthropic purposes". The unanimous judgment applies the English cases.[148] The decision has been the subject of sharp criticism on the ground that the Court should not have considered itself bound by House of Lords' decisions on the subject but should have considered the issue on its merits; and further that there are cogent reasons for upholding the gift.[149]

In another case, the testator left the residue of his estate to trustees to pay the income in perpetuity to charitable objects; then he added that the persons to benefit directly in pursuance of such charitable objects were to be past or future employees of a life insurance company. The Privy Council held the trust invalid. The latter part permits the income to go to employees for educational, religious or other beneficial purposes, as well as for the relief of poverty and the requirement of public benefit is lacking. Had the trust been solely for the relief of poverty of employees then it might possibly have been upheld, for it is not settled whether the requirement of public benefit in such a case is essential.[150]

Some judges and writers have suggested legislation to preserve gifts such as those just discussed and indeed to render more certain the whole subject of charitable gifts.[151] In its 1957 revision of the Wills Act the Conference of Commissioners on Uniformity of Legislation inserted a provision relating to charitable gifts. It does not define or modify in any way the meaning of "charitable" so doubtless the term carries the traditional meaning. The case it deals with is a trust or gift for a charitable purpose that is linked conjunctively or disjunctively with a non-charitable purpose. If the non-charitable purpose is void for uncertainty or for any other cause the charitable trust or gift is valid and operates solely for the benefit of the charitable purpose; if the non-charitable gift is not void, the trust or gift is valid for both purposes and where the will has not divided the property as between the two, it shall be divided according to the discretion of the trustee or executor. So far as I am aware, no province has yet enacted this provision.

Testator's Family Maintenance Acts: Conclusion

The general rule is that a person may leave his property as he pleases, subject to rights of dower and curtesy, if any. There are two exceptions—a binding contract to leave property by will[152] and an agreement not to revoke a joint will or mutual wills where one of the testators has died, and the survivor has taken the benefits of the will.[153] In the first of these the contract may be unenforceable by reason of the Statute of Frauds—for example, a verbal promise to devise land to the promisee. However, the Supreme Court took the sting out of this rule by holding that the promisee who had given consideration was entitled to claim on the basis of *quantum meruit*.[154] Apart from these exceptions, a testator might leave his property to whom he pleased, ignoring even his wife and children.

New Zealand passed the first Testator's Family Maintenance Act in 1900. All the Australian states have similar statutes[155] as has England,[156] and five Canadian provinces—Ontario and those in the west.[157] The basic provision in nearly all the Acts provides: where a testator has not made adequate provision in his will for the maintenance and support for his dependants, the court may order that adequate provision be made out of the estate for them.

Dependants are the surviving spouse and children. In British Columbia and Manitoba the child may be of any age.[158] In the other provinces he must be under a specified age, which varies from under 16 to under 21, or else he must be disabled. In Saskatchewan any allowance to the wife must not be less than she would receive on intestacy assuming there were children.[159] Under the English Act, the payments must be periodical except in small estates. Under the Canadian statutes the award may be a lump sum though very often it is by way of monthly or other periodic payments.

Space does not permit a review of all the cases laying down the principles on which the acts are to be applied. The statutes themselves deal with this to some extent. Leading New Zealand and Australian cases have frequently been quoted and applied,[160] though with caution where the provincial Act differs from the New Zealand or Australian Act.[161] The judgments of Chief Justice Williams of the Court of King's Bench of Manitoba are most helpful on general principles and factors that the court should consider.[162]

One interesting situation that has arisen several times in Alberta is this. A man of substantial means with a wife and young children leaves everything to his wife. This is commonplace, but since the Family Relief Act has been in effect there is a likelihood that an application by the Public Trustee will be made on behalf of the infants and that the Court will set aside a portion of the estate for them.[163] In other words a testator with young children cannot safely leave everything to his wife.

A most significant feature of Canadian judgments is that the courts show readiness to apply the Acts. Remedial legislation that requires an exercise of the discretion of the Court could become a dead letter, but these statutes certainly have not. They represent a significant change in social attitude. In the middle ages, a wife or children had available the writ *de rationali parte bonorum* where the husband had disposed by will of the "wife's part" and the "bairns part" of his personalty. The modern statutes might be called a return to the middle ages; yet they are a step forward.

Notes

1 See 1920 Proc. Cdn. Bar Assn. 358 for a detailed comparison of intestate distribution of property in all provinces. The proceedings of the Conference were included in the proceedings of the Association through 1947. From 1948 through 1956 they were published separately but continued to be bound with the proceedings of the Association. This last practice came to an end in 1957.

2 1925 Proc. Cdn. Bar Assn. 364; Proc. 1950 p. 48; 1955 p. 115; the 1958 proceedings are not yet published.

3 British Columbia: Administration of Estates Act, R.S.B.C. 1948, c. 6, Part IV; am. 1953 c. 2, 1955, c. 2, 1958 c. 2; Alberta: Intestate Succession Act, R.S.A. 1955, c. 161; Saskatchewan: Intestate Succession Act, R.S.S. 1953, c. 119; Manitoba: Devolution of Estates Act, R.S.M. 1954, c. 63, am. 1957 c. 14; New Brunswick: Devolution of Estates Act R.S.N.B. 1952 c. 62, Part II, am. 1956, c. 33; Prince Edward Island: Probate Act R.S.P.E.I. 1951, c. 124 Part IV, am. 1952 c. 35; Newfoundland: Intestate Succession Act R.S.Nfld. 1952, c. 153.

4 Ontario: Devolution of Estates Act R.S.O. 1950, c. 103, am. 1952, c. 21.

5 Nova Scotia: Descent of Property Act R.S.N.S. 1954, c. 69.

6 British Columbia, ss. 109–112; Alberta, ss. 2–4; Saskatchewan, ss, 2–5; Manitoba, ss. 5–7; New Brunswick, ss. 20–22; Prince Edward Island, ss. 96–99; Newfoundland, ss. 2–5.

7 Ontario ss. 2(1), 11, 28 and 29. Section 30 is a special provision divesting the share of a child who survives his father but dies unmarried and intestate before his mother.

8 See *Lamb v. Cleveland* (1892), 19 S.C.R. 78.

9 Nova Scotia, ss. 2, 6 and 7. Section 5 is a special provision divesting the share of a child who dies under 21 and unmarried.

10 Note, C.B. Bourne, 27 Can. Bar Rev. 228 (1949).

11 R.S.S. 1953, c. 121, ss. 2 and 3.

12 Family Relief Act, R.S.A. 1955 c. 109, ss. 2 and 4.

13 15 and 16 Geo. VI and 1 Eliz. II, c. 64.

14 Foreword to Wright, "Testators Family Maintenance in Australia and New Zealand" (1954).

15 *Zilkie v. Thompson* (1950) 2 W.W.R. 941 (Sask.).

16 New Brunswick, s. 23.

17 Prince Edward Island, s. 100; Newfoundland, s. 6. This variation seems to have come about through a slip. The uniform Act was amended in 1950, and through a change in the numbering of the sections, the distant kin were no longer included in those who share with the wife. The Conference corrected the error in the uniform Act in 1955. These two provinces adopted the 1950 amendments but have not made the correction.

18 Nova Scotia, ss. 3, 4, 6 and 7.

19 Ontario, ss. 11, 28 and 29.

20 Alberta, s. 5; Saskatchewan, s. 6; Manitoba, s. 7.

21 1958, c. 2, s. 8.

22 Intestate's Estates Act 1952, c. 64 s. 1, amending s. 46, Administration of Estates Act, 1925.

23 British Columbia, s. 114; Alberta, s. 6; Saskatchewan s. 7; Manitoba, s. 8(1); New Brunswick, s. 24; Prince Edward Island, s. 101; Newfoundland, s. 7.
24 Ontario, s. 29. Children of deceased brothers or sisters take by representation.
25 Nova Scotia, ss. 3, 6 and 7.
26 G.D. Kennedy, Note 26 Can. Bar Rev. 1251 (1948).
27 British Columbia, ss. 115 and 116; Alberta, ss. 7 and 8; Saskatchewan, ss. 8 and 9; Manitoba, s. 8(2) and (3); New Brunswick, ss. 25 and 26; Prince Edward Island, s. 102, am. 1952 c. 35; Newfoundland, ss. 8 and 9.
28 Nova Scotia, ss. 4(2) and (3) and 6.
29 Ontario, s. 29: *Re Bailey,* [1948] 2 D.L.R. 367; [1948] O.R. 127.
30 British Columbia, s. 117; Alberta, s. 9; Saskatchewan, s. 10; Manitoba, s. 9; New Brunswick, s. 27; Prince Edward Island, s. 104; Newfoundland, s. 10.
31 Ontario, s. 29. Nova Scotia, s. 4(4) omits the first part but includes the second part of this clause.
32 E.g. *Re McLean* [1948] 2 W.W.R. 12 (Man.); *Re Gall* [1937] 3 W.W.R. 266 (Alta.); *Crowther v. Cawthra* (1882), 1 O.R. 128; *Re Beaulieu* [1951] 4 D.L.R. 687 (B.C.); Contra, *Re McIver* [1941] 3 W.W.R. 849 (B.C.); In *Carter v. Patrick* [1935] 1 W.W.R. 383 (B.C.) it was held that where brothers or sisters are next-of-kin then not only children of deceased brothers or sisters but children of deceased nephews or nieces can share. This decision is questionable; see *Re McMahon,* [1948] 1 D.L.R. 80 (N.B.).
33 *Re Robinson* [1941] 2 W.W.R. 86 (B.C.); *Canada Permanent Trust Co. v. McKim* [1938] 3 W.W.R. 657 (Sask.); *Re Shaw* [1955] 4 D.L.R. 268 (Ont.); *Re Wilson* [1949] 3 D.L.R. 408 (N.B.).
34 *Re Cran,* [1941] 1 W.W.R. 209 (Sask.).
35 British Columbia, s. 120: *Blakeney v. Seed* [1939] 2 D.L.R. 287 (B.C.); Alberta, s. 12; Saskatchewan, s. 13; Manitoba, s. 12; New Brunswick, s. 30; Prince Edward Island, s. 107; Newfoundland, s. 13.
36 Nova Scotia, ss. 8–13: *Whitford v. Whitford,* [1942] S.C.R. 166.
37 Ontario, s. 27: see *Re Hall* (1887), 14 O.R. 557 as to the meaning of "advancement".
38 R.S.C. 1886, c. 51 ss. 16 and 17 (Can.)
39 *Re Stone,* [1924] S.C.R. 682.
40 *Re Hamilton* (1948), 28 M.P.R. 53 (N.B.); *Re Miller* (1957), 22 W.W.R. 571 (Man.); *Re Carlson* (1957) 11 D.L.R. (2d) 485.
41 British Columbia, ss. 123 and 124; Alberta, ss. 15 and 17; Saskatchewan, ss. 17 and 18; Manitoba, ss. 14 and 15; New Brunswick, ss. 33 and 34; Prince Edward Island, ss. 110 and 111; Newfoundland, ss. 15 and 16.
42 Section 26.
43 Legitimation Act R.S.O. 1950, c. 203, s. 6.
44 Prince Edward Island, s. 112.
45 Children of Unmarried Parents' Act R.S.N.S. 1954, c. 31, s. 35.
46 Alberta, s. 16.
47 *Re Ogal* [1940] 2 D.L.R. 345, [1940] 1 W.W.R. 665 (Alta.).
48 British Columbia, ss. 101–104.
49 *Manson v. Heaslip* [1949] 1 W.W.R. 717 (B.C.).
50 *Re Wilson* [1938] 1 W.W.R. 856 (B.C.); *Re Rosse* (1952), 4 W.W.R. (N.S.) 218 (B.C.).
51 British Columbia s. 126; Alberta s. 19; Saskatchewan s. 20; New Brunswick s. 36; Prince Edward Island s. 114; Newfoundland s. 18.
52 Dower Act R.S.N.S. 1954 c. 75; Dower Act R.S.O. 1950 c. 109 s. 8.
53 *Re Miller* [1928] 3 W.W.R. 643, [1929] 1 D.L.R. 147 (Alta.); *Burns v. Burns* (1938] 3 W.W.R. 477; [1938] 4 D.L.R. 513 (Privy Council).
54 *Re Wilson* (1924), 26 O.W.N. 270.
55 *Hyman v. Hyman,* [1929] A.C. 601.
56 *Re Janes* [1950] 2 W.W.R. 313 (B.C.); *Re Schop* [1948] O.W.N. 338; Re Rist [1939] 1 W.W.R. 518, [1939] 2 D.L.R. 644 (Alta.).
57 *Re Mediani* [1927] 1 W.W.R. 38, [1927] 4 D.L.R. 1137 (B.C.); *Re Noble* [1927] 1 W.W.R. 938 (Sask.); *Whitelaw v. Wilson* [1934] O.R. 415, [1934] 3 D.L.R. 554. A beneficiary who according to the rules of the criminal law was insane when he killed the intestate is outside the rule: *Re Mason* [1917] 1 W.W.R. 329 (B.C.).

58 *Wall v. Pfanschmidt,* (1914), 265 Ill. 180 in Read and MacDonald, Cases on Legislation (1948).
59 Administration of Estates Act, 1925; Intestates' Estate Act, 1952.
60 *Re Harris* (1914), 33 O.L.R. 83.
61 Kennedy, "The Legal Effects of Adoption", 33 Can. Bar Rev. 751 (1955). See now the new British Columbia Adoption Act, 1957, c. 1, s. 10.
62 Administration of Estates Act, 1925, s. 45, which embodies Dr. Kennedy's recommendation.
63 *Ibid.*
64 British Columbia Administration of Estates Act, s. 122.
65 *Re McLeod* [1929] 4 D.L.R. 659; [1929] 2 W.W.R. 252 (Alta.).
66 Dower Act, R.S.A. 1955, c. 90, ss. 2, 9 and 24.
67 R.S.S. 1953, c. 119, s. 15.
68 R.S.S. 1953, c. 111.
69 Dower Act, R.S.M. 1954, c. 65, ss. 3–10 and 12.
70 Information from Legislative Counsel, St. Johns, Newfoundland, October 1958.
71 R.S.O. 1950, c. 109.
72 E.g. *Re Walsh and Sovis* (1956), 2 D.L.R. (2d) 356 (Ont.); *Re Rowe* (1957), 10 D.L.R. (2d) 215 (Ont.).
73 *Re Hill,* [1951] O.R. 619; [1951] 4 D.L.R. 218.
74 R.S.O. 1950, c. 103, ss. 8 and 11.
75 *Ibid,* s. 28(2).
76 Devolution of Estates Act, R.S.N.B. 1952, c. 62, s. 32; The Dower Act is c. 64.
77 Married Women's Property Act, R.S.N.B. 1952, c. 140, s. 8. The cut-off date is April 29, 1916.
78 Descent of Property Act, R.S.N.S. 1954, c. 69, ss. 7 and 16.
79 Dower Act R.S.N.S. 1954, c. 75, s. 1.
80 Probate Act, R.S.P.E.I. 1951, c. 124, s. 109.
81 R.S.P.E.I. 1951, c. 46, s. 11.
82 Saskatchewan, R.S.S. 1953, c. 120; Manitoba, R.S.M. 1954, c. 293.
83 British Columbia, R.S.B.C. 1948, c. 365; Alberta, R.S.A. 1955 c. 369; Ontario R.S.O. 1950, c. 426; New Brunswick, R.S.N.B. 1952, c. 251; Nova Scotia, R.S.N.S. 1954, c. 315; Prince Edward Island Probate Act, Part III, R.S.P.E.I. 1951, c. 124; Newfoundland, R.S.N. 1952, c. 147.
84 1957 Proceedings 135.
85 *Re Wozciechowicz,* [1931] 4 D.L.R. 585, [1931] 3 W.W.R. 283; Notes, C.A. Wright 10 Can. Bar Rev. 55 and M.M. MacIntyre, *ibid* 253 (1932).
86 *Gingras v. Gingras* [1948] S.C.R. 339.
87 Alberta, s. 5; Saskatchewan, s. 6(2); Manitoba, s. 6(2).
88 E.g. *Re Swords,* [1929] 3 D.L.R. 564; [1929] 2 W.W.R. 245 (Alta.); *Dansereau v. Berget* [1951] S.C.R. 822. Compare *Re Gray,* [1958] S.C.R. 392.
89 *Re Harris,* unreported; Note, 26 Can. Bar Rev. 1242 (1948).
90 *Re Bell,* [1955] 3 D.L.R. 521; 15 W.W.R. 615 (Man.).
91 *Re Griffiths,* [1945] 3 W.W.R. 46 (Sask.).
92 *Re Ford* (1954), 13 W.W.R. (N.S.) 604 (Alta.); *Re Laver* (1957), 10 D.L.R. (2d) 279 (Sask.).
93 *Re Moir* [1942] 1 D.L.R. 337; [1942] 1 W.W.R. 241 (Alta.).
94 *Re Richardson,* [1949] 1 W.W.R. 1075 (Man.); *Re Toole* (1952), 5 W.W.R. 416 (Alta.). Contra, *Re Bennie* (1957), 22 W.W.R. 118 (Sask.).
95 *Re Cottrell* [1951] 4 D.L.R. 600; [1951] 2 W.W.R. (N.S.) 247 (Alta.).
96 *Re Landry and Steinhoff,* [1941] O.R. 67, [1941] 1 D.L.R. 699.
97 L.R. 5 Q.B. 549 (1870). *E.g.* will upheld; *Skinner v. Farquharson* (1903), 32 S.C.R. 58; *Re McKenzie* [1946] 4 D.L.R. 225 (Can.); *O'Neil v. Royal Trust Co.,* [1946] S.C.R. 622.
Will not upheld: *Ouderkirk v. Ouderkirk,* [1936] S.C.R. 619; *Leger v. Poirer,* [1944] S.C.R. 152.
98 *Re Millar,* [1938] S.C.R. 1. "Children" was held to mean legitimate children.
99 *Craig v. Lamoureux,* [1920] A.C. 349; *Riach v. Ferris,* [1934] S.C.R. 725.
100 *Re Harmes,* [1946] 3 D.L.R. 497; [1946] 2 W.W.R. 433 (P.C.); cases cited in note 99; Note, C.A. Wright, 16 Can. Bar Rev. 405 (1938).
101 British Columbia, ss. 16–20; Alberta, ss. 15–19; Saskatchewan, ss. 14–18; Manitoba, ss. 14–18; Ontario, ss. 20–24; New Brunswick, ss. 13–17;

Nova Scotia, ss. 15–20; Prince Edward Island, ss. 80–84; Newfoundland, ss. 9–13.

102 *Re Colville,* [1932] 1 D.L.R. 47, [1931] 3 W.W.R. 26 (B.C.).

103 *Re Minshall,* [1939] 3 D.L.R. 793 (Ont.).

104 *Re Teale* (1923), 54 O.L.R. 130; *Ward v. Van der Loeff,* [1924] A.C. 653.

105 *Macdonell v. Purcell* (1894), 23 S.C.R. 101.

106 *Re Forbes* (1956), 3 D.L.R. (2d) 653 (Ont.).

107 *Re Marks,* [1945] 4 D.L.R. 731 (Ont.).

108 British Columbia, s. 31; Alberta, s. 31; Saskatchewan, s. 30; Manitoba, s. 30; Ontario, s. 36; New Brunswick, s. 29; Nova Scotia, s. 30; Newfoundland, s. 18.

109 Prince Edward Island, s. 95 (1956 c. 30, s. 1).

110 [1943] A.C. 399.

111 *Re McPhee,* [1948] 1 W.W.R. 65 (Alta.); *Re Kemp,* [1954] 2 D.L.R. 451, 11 W.W.R. (N.S.) 624 (Man.).

112 *Re Brander,* [1952] 4 D.L.R. 688, 6 W.W.R. (N.S.) 702 (B.C.). Notes, G.D. Kennedy, 31 Can. Bar Rev. 185, 444 (1953).

113 [1923] S.C.R. 642.

114 *Re Berkheiser,* [1957] S.C.R. 387.

115 S. 21(2), 1957 Proceedings 139.

116 [1936] A.C. 635.

117 *Re Waines,* [1944] 4 D.L.R. 149.

118 *Re Barton,* [1941] S.C.R. 426.

119 *Bickersteth v. Shanu,* [1936] A.C. 290; *Re Peter,* [1952] 4 D.L.R. 259 (Sask.).

120 *Wharton v. Masterman,* [1895] A.C. 184; *Re Burger,* [1949] 1 W.W.R. 280 (Alta.). Compare *Re Boxall,* [1946] 3 W.W.R. 413 (Sask.); Note, D.M. Gordon, 24 Can. Bar Rev. 818 (1946); Correspondence 25 Can. Bar Rev. 117 (1947).

121 *Sifton v. Sifton,* [1938] A.C. 656.

122 *Clayton v. Ramsden,* [1943] A.C. 320.

123 *E.g. Re Hurshman* (1957), 6 D.L.R. (2d) 615 at 619 (B.C.). In this case the condition tended to weaken the marriage bond and on that ground was void as against public policy.

See *Noble v. Alley,* [1951] S.C.R. 64. A racial covenant in a grant of land was held void for uncertainty.

124 *Re Going,* [1951] O.R. 147, [1951] 2 D.L.R. 136.

125 *Re Starr,* [1946] O.R. 252, [1946] 2 D.L.R. 489; *Re Kennedy* [1950] 1 W.W.R. 151 (Man.).

126 The Perpetuities Act, R.S.P.E.I. 1951, c. 108.

127 2 S.C.R. 497 (1879).

128 *Re Metcalfe,* [1946] O.R. 882.

129 Morris and Leach, "The Rule Against Perpetuities," c. IX (1956).

130 *National Trust Co. Ltd. v. Elliott,* (1956), 5 D.L.R. (2d) 81 (B.C.).

131 S. 163 (1).

132 *Op. cit.,* note 129, p. 54.

133 *Re Arnold,* [1955] 4 D.L.R. 536 (B.C.).

134 *Op. cit.,* note 129, pp. 70–83. *Re Arnold,* note 133 comes close to both an unborn widower and a fertile octogenarian.

135 *Belyea v. McBride,* [1942] 3 D.L.R. 785 (P.C.); *Re Smith,* [1942] O.W.N. 455.

136 *Blackburn v. McCallum* (1903), 33 S.C.R. 65.

137 Now substantially re-enacted in the Law of Property Act, 1925, s. 164.

138 Accumulations Restraint Act, R.S.B.C. 1948, c. 5; Accumulations Act, R.S.O. 1950, c. 4; Property Act, R.S.N.B. 1952 c. 177 ss. 1, 2.

139 *Op. cit.,* note 129, p. 260.

140 (1841), 4 Beav. 115.

141 *Re Mackey,* [1944] 3 D.L.R. 298 (Ont.): where the income of residue goes to one person and capital to another the released income goes to him who receives the income; *Re Fulford* (1926), 59 O.L.R 440.

142 *Re Hammond,* [1935] S.C.R. 550; *Re Davis,* [1946] 2 D.L.R. 281 (Ont.). See *Re Fasken* [1953] 2 S.C.R. 10, where the testator anticipated the possibility that the accumulation would exceed 21 years and specifically disposed of the released income.

143 *E.g., Re Burns* (1958), 26 W.W.R. 49 (Alta.).

144 Gordon, "Delegation of Will-Making Power," 69 L.Q.R. 334 (1953). Note, 33 Can. Bar Rev. 955 (1955). See also Note, Falconbridge, 19 Can. Bar Rev. 213 (1941).

145 *Re Mewburn,* [1939] S.C.R. 75.
146 *Wanklyn v. M.N.R.*, [1953] 2 S.C.R. 58.
147 *Chichester Diocesan Fund v. Simpson,* [1944] A.C. 341.
148 *Brewer v. McCauley,* [1954] S.C.R. 645.
149 Todd, Note, 33 Can. Bar Rev. 334; Kennedy, Note, *ibid*. 340 (1955).
150 *Re Cox; Baker v. National Trust Co. Ltd*. [1955] 3 D.L.R. 497 (P.C.).
151 Fridman, "Charities and Public Benefit," 31 Can. Bar Rev. 537.
152 *E.g., Re Davidson* (1947), 20 M.P.R. 53 (N.B.).
153 *Re Fox* [1951] O.R. 378; *Re Johnson* (1957), 8 D.L.R. (2d) 221 (Sask.). Compare *Re Creelman* (1956), 2 D.L.R. (2d) 494 (N.S.).
154 *Deglman v. Trusts and Guarantee Co.* [1954] S.C.R. 725.
155 Wright, "Testator's Family Maintenance" (1954).
156 Inheritance (Family Provision Act), 1 & 2 Geo. 6, c. 45.
157 British Columbia, Testator's Family Maintenance Act, R.S.B.C. 1948, c. 336; Alberta, Family Relief Act, R.S.A. 1955, c. 109; Saskatchewan, Dependants' Relief Act, R.S.S. 1953, c. 121; Manitoba, Testator's Family Maintenance Act, R.S.M. 1954, c. 264; Ontario, Dependants' Relief Act, R.S.O. 1950, c. 101. A uniform Act was adopted in 1945 and amended in 1957. Alberta and Manitoba have this Act. The other Acts are similar.
158 See *Walker v. McDermott,* [1931] S.C.R. 94, where a married daughter obtained relief as against her stepmother.
159 S. 8(2); *Shaw v. Saskatoon,* [1945] S.C.R. 42.
160 *Allardice v. Allardice,* [1911] A.C. 730; *Bosch v. Perpetual Trustee* [1938] A.C. 463; *Dillon v. Public Trustee,* [1941] A.C. 294.
161 See *Meyer v. Capital Trust Corp.*, [1948] S.C.R. 329.
162 *Re Lawther* [1947] 2 D.L.R. 510, [1947] 1 W.W.R. 577 (Man.); *Re LaFleur* [1948] 2 D.L.R. 682, [1948] 1 W.W.R. 801 (Man.); *Re Cousins* (1952), 5 W.W.R. (N.S.) 289 (Man.). The judgment of Egbert J. of Alberta in *Re Willan* (1951), 4 W.W.R. (N.S.) 114 is also valuable.
163 *Re Denton,* [1950] 2 W.W.R. 848 (Alta.); *Re Finlan* (1951), 3 W.W.R. (N.S.) 671 (Alta.).

1957

A Statement on Objectives of Canadian Common-Law Schools

Reprinted from
(1958) 36 Canadian Bar Review
pp. 242–246

In 1956 when Bowker was President of the Association of Canadian Law Teachers, the Association agreed it should have a Statement of Objectives, which Bowker was asked to draft.

Though he presented this Statement to the annual meeting in Ottawa in 1957, it was never acted upon or adopted, the membership believing they had more pressing matters to deal with.

The Statement of Objectives was subsequently published in the Canadian Bar Review.

Introductory Comments

Several years ago the Association of Canadian Law Teachers established a committee to prepare a statement on objectives. Later separate committees were set up for common-law schools and civil-law schools. The committee on common-law schools prepared a report in the form of a statement for submission to the 1957 annual meeting. Before it was presented a motion was passed providing in advance for the disposition to be made of the report; that it be received and discussed and that afterwards the chairman of the committee revise the report in the light of the discussion and circulate it to all law teachers. This course was followed.

In the hope that readers of the Canadian Bar Review will find the statement of interest, it is here set out. Much has been said and written on the subject over the years. This statement draws on ideas expressed from time to time in Canada, England and the United States. At the same time it has been framed in an effort to embody the views of Canadian law teachers, and to state Canadian objectives.

It is recognized that not all teachers will put the same emphasis on one or other of the objectives of law schools. It is not the intention of this statement to be dogmatic about any of them or to prescribe rigid and detailed objectives. There is room for differences of opinion, and the statement is drawn with that fact in mind. It is the hope of the Association that it will draw attention to the teachers' obligations and responsibilities and will serve as a guide to schools and teachers in shaping curricula and in determining methods of teaching.

As a preliminary to this statement of objectives one must first set out the Association's understanding of the role of law, and of the lawyer's functions and qualities. The reason is that law-school objectives are obviously related to the role of law and should be framed to equip the future lawyer to carry out his functions, and to develop the qualities he should have.

I. The Role of Law

Law can be considered in different aspects (1) as a body of rules or commands or norms, (2) in relation to its effect on society and society's effect on it, and (3) in relation to its purpose. The last of these bears comment. Some say that its purpose is to secure the various wants or interests that are asserted in a society; others prefer the view that its purpose is to conform to moral values, fairness and justice. Many doubtless hold that these two purposes are combined. In any case the law has a number of functions—to keep the peace, and to provide for enforcement of promises, protection of property and person, to compensate for losses and to control conduct in many ways. At the present time even in democratic countries it tends to regulate business, property and activities. At the same time it has the function of securing various rights that are considered fundamental such as the equal protection of the law, freedom of religion and speech. In addition it often provides affirmatively for physical, material and intellectual wants. It is not the purpose of this statement to weigh the present-day trends nor to say that law should advance all of them. For every current there is a counter-current. In fact law always has its antinomies. What is of importance is to conceive of law in its function of helping society to bring about those things that are considered good, realizing of course that conflicts exist and that there is never unanimity as to how far any good, or interest or value should prevail.

II. The Lawyer's Functions

It is through the legal profession that the role of the law is effected. The lawyer may be an advocate, a solicitor in general practice or specializing in a particular field, a government employee at every level from the city hall to the United Nations, legal adviser to corporations, politician, judge or law teacher. He is also a very active leader in the life of the community. In the present-day world with its new conflicts and problems he bears a measure of responsibility in improving the social order, even in the international sphere. It is a commonplace that he has a special obligation to uphold the law; to initiate legal reform and also to safeguard fairness in procedure and to see that the legal forms are observed. Indeed he has been described as "the trustee of the integrity of the forms of social order".

III. The Lawyer's Qualities

The lawyer must be equipped to give advice on legal problems and also to take the steps to make his advice effective. If he is primarily a solicitor he must be a good conveyancer, and if a counsel he must be able to cross-examine and to persuade. In both cases he must be skilled in the use of language, in sifting facts and in negotiating with others. Of the first importance are ability in legal research and the "know how" to convert an opinion into effective action.

It is now appropriate to state the qualities or traits that he must have. These include above all high character together with scholarship, industry, thoroughness, good judgment, a sense of professional responsibility, concern in reform of the law and its proper administration, and an interest in public affairs.

IV. The Objectives of Law Schools in Training Students

Obvious among objectives is the giving to students of basic information on the most important branches of the law. Related to this is an understanding of the legislative and judicial processes. He must learn as well to solve legal problems. Because the bulk of the law is so vast that the student cannot receive instruction in any but a fraction of the problems that he will afterward encounter, it is essential that he learn the elements of legal reasoning and the art of legal research; and the ability to form a defensible opinion. So equipped he can efficiently cope with new problems.

The student should also learn about the development of law and legal institutions, whether under the label of legal history or not; and it is beneficial to have an acquaintance not only with international law but also with other systems of municipal law. A student of the common law can profit from an understanding of the civil law in Quebec.

He should be exposed to the great currents of legal thought and to great minds and be encouraged to try to formulate and defend his own philosophy of law.

Since law does consist of rules and doctrine, an understanding of them must remain an important part of the lawyer's training together with a grasp of the doctrine of precedent and of what is generally known as analytical jurisprudence. At the same time, recent years have seen a new stress on law as a function of society with emphasis on its role in social change and in meeting the needs of society with less emphasis on what was done last time and more on what should be done this time. Teachers are not agreed on the relative emphasis to put on each of these approaches. It is sufficient here to say that the student should be aware of both.

It is doubtful that Canadian law teachers regard as an objective of law schools the integration of law with other social sciences. On the other hand in an age of social change and social experiments it is helpful for lawyers to know something of the other social disciplines—at least enough to make use of them.

Another objective is to inculcate in the student the qualities and traits he should have as a member of a learned profession. Perhaps the most important could be summed up in the phrase "a sense of professional responsibility''. This includes high ethical standards, together with an interest in the well-being of the profession, and in the improvement of the law. It certainly does include the obligation to do one's work well and promptly.

Special mention should be made of the teaching of the lawyer's skills. A lawyer's training begins before he enters law school and continues after he leaves—indeed, throughout life. Since we are concerned with the role of a law school, it should be noted that in all the common-law provinces, a student is not qualified to practice on the basis of his law-school training alone. A period under articles in a law office is invariably required. Sometimes articles and class-room training go together though usually articles come after. The purpose of articles is to teach the lawyer's skills by actual experience in legal work in both branches of the profession. In view of this it does not seem appropriate to say that it is an objective of law schools to give this training yet this does not imply a strict division between learning and practice. On the one hand it is doubtful that many teachers claim law schools can do everything as well for the student as articles can do. Conveyancing and preparation and conduct of law suits are examples. On the other hand, law-school training is not isolated from practice and there are many lawyer's skills that can be learned in law school. In a measure a student can be taught to apply the principles he has learned and to gain a degree of ''know how''. Many principles can best be understood by placing them in a practical context. Moreover some of the lawyer's skills, such as the technique of ''devilling'' and effective expression, written and verbal, can be learned in law school.

V. Scholarship and Research

The law school should be a community of scholars who give to the profession leadership and guidance. It should take the lead in giving Canadian answers to Canadian problems. It should become a centre of research and a leading source of legal literature, with a view to improving the understanding of law and its operation, and to law reform.

These objectives are of course not in isolation from those analysed above in connection with training of students. They are set out separately because they deserve special emphasis. Teaching, research and writing all support one another and all are to the same end—to build up a stronger profession equipped to deal with its daily tasks and to help solve the larger problems of our society.

1959

Basic Rights and Freedoms: What Are They?

Reprinted from
(1959) 37 Canadian Bar Review
pp. 43–65

In 1959, Monsieur Jean Castel, the new editor of the Canadian Bar Review, *wished to devote an issue to the Diefenbaker "Bill of Rights" which had been before Parliament for some time, and would be enacted in 1960.*

For this special issue, several articles were included dealing with various aspects of the proposed Bill. Bowker was one of the contributors. Others were: Bora Laskin, then on the Faculty of Law, University of Toronto, later appointed to the Ontario Court of Appeal, then to the Supreme Court of Canada and later its Chief Justice; Frank Scott, Professor of Law at McGill; William Lederman, one-time Rhodes scholar and later Dean of Law at Queen's; Louis-Phillippe Pigeon, Quebec lawyer, later appointed to the Supreme Court of Canada, and Professors Albert Abel and Edward McWhinney of the University of Toronto.

In Bowker's article "Basic Rights and Freedoms: What are They?", he analyzes various such rights. His basic conclusion was that we can safeguard rights and freedoms under our system of parliamentary sovereignty without giving power to judges to strike down what Parliament has legislated.

Introduction

In speaking of basic rights and freedoms we think of the individual in relation to the state. He may claim that the state should leave him alone and not interfere with him in certain activities—he demands liberty or freedom. Again, he may claim the assistance of the state in obtaining for him fair treatment from a branch of government or from an individual. He insists on the state securing to him his "rights". These freedoms and rights may be called basic, inherent, natural, human or fundamental; and the claim to them may be based on religion, philosophy, tradition or on current concepts of fairness.

Since Canada inherited British traditions of government and constitutional law, we naturally start by recalling those well-known historical safeguards of the subject—Magna Carta, the Petition of Right, the Habeas

Corpus Acts, the Bill of Rights, the Act of Settlement. These are all landmarks in the struggle of the individual and Parliament for control over the executive, and which concluded in the establishment of parliamentary sovereignty.

Then if we look at the standard English texts[1] we find they discuss these rights in terms of freedom of person and property, freedom of speech, rights of association and public meeting. These rest in large measure on absence of parliamentary restriction. Since there is no written constitution and hence no limitation of Parliament's power, Parliament can restrict them and in emergencies does.

If one accepts the view that man has certain rights, given by God or a social contract, then the state should not restrict them—not even Parliament. It should not be sovereign for that purpose, and if it takes away basic rights then the people as a last resort have the right to revolt.

The British North America Act in creating Canada gave us the principle of parliamentary sovereignty, but at the same time the federal system necessarily put limitations on central and local legislatures. However, the Act does not remove from the legislatures the power to restrict basic rights, apart from the provisions protecting the French language and denominational schools. Such is the orthodox theory of which the late Mr. Justice Riddell was a vigorous exponent. Provided the legislature keeps within its proper subject matter, it has powers as unlimited as those of the British Parliament and any statute is valid no matter what right it infringes.[2] We shall see later that some cases, particularly in recent years, do not fully accept this theory.

Events throughout the world and even at home have created a new interest in the subject of basic rights since the war; and Canada's membership in the United Nations and execution of the Declaration of Human Rights have naturally drawn attention to the question, how do we stand ourselves?[3]

The starting point must be a description of our rights and freedoms. What are they? The answers to this vary from time to time, from country to country and as between persons. We shall here attempt a survey of those that Canadian law recognizes with some brief references to the position of the United States which is examined in greater detail in another article in this issue.

I. Freedom to Communicate Information and Ideas

In the English tradition freedom in these areas consists in mere inaction by the government. As Jennings has said of freedom of speech, "It arises from the tautologous principle that anything is lawful which is not unlawful. There is no more a 'right of free speech' than there is a right to tie up my shoe lace". The important point is that if we believe in free speech we will not make it unlawful.

We do profess the conviction that within wide limits discussion of matters of public interest, including criticism of government and its policies is in the interests of society. When a state is young and weak, and in times of peril, criticism is often forbidden or punished. Around 1800 both Upper and Lower Canada had Alien and Sedition Acts[4] designed for this purpose and resembling the American laws of 1898 that were invoked to stifle criticism of the government of John Adams.

Coming to modern times, World War I saw many charges of sedition; but in an Alberta case in 1916, *R.* v. *Trainor,*[5] Stuart J. protested against the laying of charges of sedition against every German sympathizer; "the courts should not, unless in cases of gravity and danger, be asked to spend their time scrutinizing with undue particularity the foolish talk in bar rooms". This judgment anticipates to some extent the "clear and present" danger test that Holmes and Brandeis JJ. later developed in the United States in cases of this kind.

Then right after the war, when the socialists in both countries were busy with agitation there occurred the Winnipeg general strike. The leaders were convicted of uttering seditious words[6] and Parliament amended the Criminal Code to make illegal any association whose purpose is to bring about governmental, industrial or economic change by force; the Act made membership in, or speaking for such an association, an offence. During the depression, a few convictions were made, but a strong opposition to it developed and Parliament repealed it in 1936.[7]

It resembles in a general way the many state Acts that were so widely used in the United States just after World War I; and indeed the events surrounding the Winnipeg strike are a faint echo of the round-up of socialists in the United States at about the same time.[8] In 1940 Congress passed a statute of the same general type as the one Canada repealed in 1936. It is still in force and has been held valid.[9] The main offence is advocacy of overthrow of the government by force.

Even without a statute of this type the state can stifle attacks on government through the laws against sedition. This was commonplace in England in the eighteenth century. However, belief in the right of criticism will cut down the scope of this crime. In *Boucher* v. *The King* the court made a decision that deserves to be ranked with the great opinions of Holmes and Brandeis JJ. The judgment is not written in terms of "clear and present danger" or constitutional rights. It simply says there is no sedition without an incitement to violence. Rand J. declared:

> Freedom in thought and speech and disagreement in ideas and beliefs on every conceivable subject, are of the essence of our life. The clash of critical discussion on political, social and religious subjects has too deeply become the stuff of daily experience to suggest that mere ill-will as a product of controversy can strike down the latter with illegality.[10]

The later case of *Switzman* v. *Elbling* held Quebec's Padlock law invalid; and although the basis of the judgment was infringement of criminal law, several members of the court expressed views similar to those just quoted.[11]

The next measure of interest here is an Alberta Bill of 1937 to require newspapers to publish corrections of their criticisms of government. The Lieutenant-Governor reserved his assent and the Governor-General referred the Bill, with others, to the Supreme Court. The Bill was held invalid but Duff C.J. uttered his famous dictum that although the provinces have wide legislative power over newspapers, "the limitation is reached when the legislation effects such a curtailment of the exercise of the right of public discussion as substantially to interfere with the working of the Parliamentary institution of Canada".[12]

So far we have spoken of freedom of speech and not of press.

John Milton's famous argument for a free press was a protest against a licensing ordinance that imposed a censorship or prior restraint. It was achieved in England in 1695 simply because Parliament omitted (for no reasons of principle) to renew the Licensing Ordinance. At this time a free press did not mean that newspapers could say what they liked. It merely meant that no government official would prevent publication. Once published, the printed word was subject to the most stringent laws of sedition. Since the Napoleonic wars they have not been invoked, and freedom of press has come to include the right to criticize.

If one can judge from accounts from the United States, "press" seems to have become almost synonymous with the daily newspaper and that organ has invoked freedom of the press to escape various laws of general application, though usually without success.[13] On the other hand, the Canadian Daily Newspaper Association once published a statement that begins:

> Fundamentally it is not a special privilege reserved for newspaper publishers. It is rather a phase of a much larger freedom—the freedom of all men to speak their minds openly and without fear. The press claims no right which should not belong to every citizen in a democracy, but freedom of the press is an all-important part of this larger freedom; because, under modern conditions, the press is the principal agency by which the ordinary man receives the information he needs to judge the actions of his rulers and make up his mind on public issues. Without newspapers, or with only gagged and blindfolded ones, he is in the dark, and helpless. An unfettered press is therefore one of the essential bulwarks of a democratic world.

Freedom of speech and press may come into conflict with other claims; for example the claim of others that their reputation shall not be damaged by false statements. Some newspapers may think freedom of the press justifies them in libelling others with impunity but fortunately our law says that freedom of the press means no such thing.

The clash of freedom of the press with other interests can be shown in connection with contempt of court. The common law on this subject is that one of the forms of contempt is "scandalizing the court" (intemperate criticism of the judiciary); another is comment on pending cases. Now it is generally agreed that courts should be slow to exercise their summary power to commit for the first of these types of contempt,[14] but in the case of pending trials our courts like the English have been strict in punishing comment that might affect the verdict. Trial by newspaper is not to be permitted.[15] In the United States, on the other hand, a series of decisions has practically abrogated the courts' summary power to commit newspapers for contempt of this type.[16] The accused claims a fair trial; the paper successfully claims the right to publish lurid and prejudicial accounts. Sins, if not crimes are still committed in the name of "liberty".

Two important potential restrictions on freedom of speech and press are regulations of the Post Office and Customs. Canada's Post Office Act used to authorize regulations to prohibit obscene or criminal publications. Obviously, the exercise of this power acts as a prior restraint or censorship. The Act has now been amended to permit the Postmaster General to prohibit delivery of mail to or from a person whom the Postmaster General believes on reasonable grounds to be using the mails to commit an offence. The order is an interim one until a Board of Review has made its recommendation and then the Postmaster General may revoke the order or make it final.[17] An order might be made for the exclusion of literature that, in the opinion of the Postmaster General, is obscene or seditious or blasphemous. In other words, there is still a prior restraint but the Act does seem designed to prevent a hasty or ill-judged decision.

As for the Customs Tariff, item 1201 includes among prohibited goods "books, printed paper, drawings, paintings, prints, photographs or representations of any kind of a treasonable or seditious, or of an immoral or indecent character".[18] This leaves the decision in the hands of officials of the department and has been the subject of criticism. In 1958 Parliament amended the Customs Act to give an appeal to the provincial court where the goods have been refused entry under item 1201.[19] Thus the question of the character of the book is now a matter for the court.

In the United States the Supreme Court has from time to time considered actions of the Postmaster General and the customs authorities as possible infringement of free speech. It is hard to compare the position in the two countries for there have been scarcely any reported cases in Canada. This does not mean that we have had no abuse of government power, but simply that these issues do not reach the courts as readily as in the United States. The Supreme Court has from time to time held invalid rulings of post office and customs authorities.[20]

Motion picture censorship exists in some provinces but I know of no litigation on the subject. In the United States motion pictures were originally held to be outside the protection of free speech. In 1952, however, the Supreme Court held that pictures are not mere entertainment, but are a medium for communication of ideas and hence entitled to the protection of free speech.[21] Censorship of the movies is largely based on obscenity, a difficult quality to define. In recent years, there has been much criticism of the English rule, which is based on the tendency of the words to deprave and corrupt, and which has been applied here.[22] In the United States there has been a tendency to liberalize the rule.[23]

In this country, Parliament amended the Code in 1949, to make it a crime to publish "crime comics". A law of this kind would certainly encounter in the United States a vigorous argument that it infringes freedom of the press.

We turn now to freedom of assembly. Originally it was related to the right to petition Parliament, but is now generally agreed to be independent of petitions, and is, of course, cognate to freedom of speech. In England, the right of assembly exists to the extent that the law does not restrict it. There as in Canada, the main restrictions are in the criminal law. The Canadian Criminal Code forbids unlawful assemblies and authorizes the English device of "reading the Riot Act" for the purpose of dispersing a riotous assembly.[24] During the depression a number of meetings held to protest economic conditions were held unlawful.[25] Another means of curtailing the right of assembly is the requirement of local permits. Refusal of a permit is an effective censorship.

In the United States constitutional protection is given to the rights of assembly and petition. The Supreme Court has frequently set aside convictions against the soap-box orator for speaking without a permit. There is a particularly strong view against prior restraints, and the need of a permit is just that;[26] moreover, if the speaker has permission to speak, and makes an inflammatory speech, the Supreme Court has gone to some lengths in saying that even then he is not guilty of breaking the peace.[27]

In our sketch of freedom of speech, press and assembly space has not permitted more than a glimpse at the vast body of case law in the United States. In the last third of a century the scope of these freedoms has been extended by making them applicable against the states through the Fourteenth Amendment which forbids a state from denying life, liberty or property without due process of law. Liberty in modern times means all those liberties that are essential to ordered liberty (whatever they may be) and includes those we have been discussing. Not only do these "liberties" limit the state, but in the view of some judges they are "preferred" as against other competing rights. In other words, many legal requirements are ineffective against a person who can persuade the court that the requirement infringes his freedom of speech. Examples are these: a labour organizer who refuses to register under state law;[28] picketers who refuse to obey an anti-picketing law;[29] persons who object to taking a loyalty oath;[30] or who refuse to answer questions put by a government committee about political beliefs.[31]

The last subject under this heading is freedom of worship. At first sight it might appear to differ from the others which all have to do with communication of thought from one person to another, whereas a person can worship alone. The fact is, however, that worship is usually conducted in association. Moreover, freedom of worship in a broad sense includes the spreading of the gospel to non-believers. Indeed, freedom of speech as well as of worship carries a connotation of the right to try to persuade others. Both Milton and Mill in their famous essays included both secular and religious speech as part of the same freedom.

The concept of liberty of worship is fairly modern in England. For a long period prior to the Revolution of 1688, harsh persecution of heretical and dissenting sects occurred at intervals. One of the best statements in favour of toleration is John Locke's letter published in 1689. It makes effectively two points: that religion is no concern of the state—"the care of souls is not committed to the civil magistrate any more than to other men"; and that no church should force its views on anyone—"No religion which I believe not to be true can be either true or profitable unto me." The gradual relaxation of disabilities against dissenters, Roman Catholics and others required a century and a half in England.[32] Indeed, Jews were not admitted to Parliament until 1858, twenty-six years after their disability was removed in Quebec.[33]

As a rule, toleration was allowed in British colonies to a greater extent than at home. This was certainly true in Rhode Island, Pennsylvania, and for a time in Maryland; and in Quebec, the Roman Catholic faith was respected almost from the beginning.[34] When Lord Durham made his report after the rebellion of 1837 he found that "religious differences have hardly operated as an additional cause of dissension in Lower Canada, and a degree of practical toleration known in very few communities has existed in this colony from the period of the Conquest down to the present time."

The case was different in Upper Canada, where the Clergy Reserves and the issue of sectarian schools as against public schools caused bitterness almost until Confederation. There is no need to go into detail in connection with the provisions to safeguard denominational schools in section 93 of the British North America Act or the later provisions applicable to the prairie provinces and Newfoundland. There has been much litigation and at times hard feeling in Manitoba and Saskatchewan.[35] At present, the supporters of separate schools may pay their taxes to that school instead of to the school of the majority in five provinces. In the others, the position is the same as in the United States. Taxes must be paid to the general school system and persons wanting a denominational school must pay as well the cost of supporting it.

There have been recent Canadian cases holding that children cannot be compelled to submit to religious exercises. The theory is that the right to give one's children the education of one's choice is anterior to positive law;[36] but the contention that children should not have to go to school at all because of their religious belief has failed.[37]

Throughout the country's history, there has been little strife over worship as distinct from education. The Saskatchewan Bill of Rights Act[38] secures it and the pre-Confederation Freedom of Worship Act has been brought forward in Quebec and Ontario;[39] and, of course, the Criminal Code makes it an offence to obstruct a clergyman in his calling or to obstruct a religious service; and blasphemous libel is a crime.[40]

Most of the cases raising the question of freedom of worship have arisen out of the activities of Jehovah's Witnesses. In several provinces they have been charged under by-laws that require a licence or permit for distributing literature. They have usually been acquitted, at least outside Quebec, on the ground that the by-law was intended to apply to commercial sales and not to religious literature.[41] In the famous case of *Saumur* v. *Quebec,* four of the nine judges upheld the by-law as proper regulation of municipal affairs. Chief Justice Kerwin held that the by-law could not prevail over the Freedom of Worship Act, and the remaining four held that freedom of worship is not a mere civil right, over which provinces have jurisdiction. Rand J. said[42] "Strictly speaking civil rights arise from private law; but freedom of speech, religion and the inviolability of the person, are original freedoms which are at once the necessary attributes and modes of self-expression of human beings and the primary conditions of their community life within a legal order". These liberties can be circumscribed to some extent by other rights, but there is no prior or antecedent restraint placed upon them. A by-law of this kind is a form of censorship.

As yet there is no Supreme Court case on which a majority has taken this view but in *Birks* v. *Montreal* three of the judges adopted this ground in holding *ultra vires* a by-law requiring stores to be closed on holydays.[43]

Most of the judges who have said that the provinces are constitutionally incapable of restricting freedom of speech and worship have not clearly said whether they think Parliament is under the same disability. However, Abbott J. has said that it is, at least in relation to speech on public matters.[44] If he is correct, then he must reject the well-settled concept that between central and local legislatures there is a plenitude of power, and must take the position that in these areas there is an unwritten constitutional Bill of Rights binding both federal and provincial governments.

A later case than *Saumur* is *Chaput* v. *Romain*[45] in which a Witness was awarded substantial damages against police officers who broke up a religious service in his home.

Other cases of some importance are those arising out of the refusal of Witnesses' children to salute the flag or sing the national anthem in school. In an Alberta case, the Board was held entitled to expel the children but the legislature promptly amended the School Act to exempt them,[46] and in Ontario the Court of Appeal held that the School Act excused students whose parents objected.[47] These cases do not seem to be as well known as the American decision that held a similar requirement to be an infringement of freedom of worship.[48]

In the United States the Witnesses have won a large number of cases in which they challenged the right of a city or town to require them to obtain a permit and the Supreme Court agreed that such by-laws cannot constitutionally be applied to the Witnesses' activities. The requirement of a permit makes the by-law particularly vulnerable for it is a prior restraint. It leaves in the hands of a local official the decision whether the Witnesses' literature may be distributed. In other cases,a simple prohibition against distributing hand bills (as distinct from the requirement of a permit) met the same fate. True the Witnesses have not always won. A by-law requiring a permit to hold a parade has been held binding on them; and they may be guilty of creating a breach of the peace if their words are very insulting; and they have been held subject to a child labour law.

On the other hand, some of the cases decided when the triumph of the Witnesses reached a peak about ten years ago go exceedingly far. A Witness successfully defied a local ordinance requiring a permit for the use of sound trucks in city parks; the ordinance left too much discretion to the chief of police.[49] Other American cases held that Witnesses could distribute their pamphlets in a company town and a government-owned town notwithstanding a state law making it an offence to remain on private property after a request to leave.[50]

The main interest in the American cases is this—if we have freedom of religion whether by statute or a written or unwritten Bill of Rights, the balancing of this freedom with others is a difficult task. Some of the American cases appear to deprive municipalities of reasonable powers of regulation.

II. Immigration, Deportation, Citizenship and Voting

Aliens outside Canada have no legal claim to enter. When Mr. Mackenzie King said in 1947 "It is not a 'fundamental human right' of an alien to enter Canada: it is a privilege. It is a matter of domestic policy"[51] he stated the obvious, though many may think we have a moral obligation to admit some aliens. The Immigration Act in prohibiting certain classes does not seem unfair and arbitrary though the additional power given to the Governor in Council to exclude persons may be open to criticism.[52] There has been some adverse comment on the administration of the Act in specific cases; for example, for allegedly arbitrary exclusion. The creation of an Appeal Board in 1946 was apparently in answer to the criticism.[53]

The power to deport is, of course, the correlative of the power to exclude[54] but it is obvious that special hardship may occur in the case of a person who has been a long-time resident. Indeed, the Act does exempt aliens with Canadian domicile from a number of the provisions for deportation.[55] The Act gives judicial review when the person has Canadian citizenship or domicile[56] and even in other cases the courts will intervene if the administrative proceedings are not authorized by the Act.[57] A recent writer says:

> The government can point out that deportation is never ordered except after careful inquiry by administrative officers. The Minister himself may intervene to see that justice is done, and that mercy and compassion temper it. Few immigrants are deported; most deportations are for criminal offences, and an immigrant who applies for relief is never, in practice, deported for that reason alone. Nevertheless, the power exists, and it might have pernicious effects even if it were never used.[58]

While an alien is in Canada, the Canadian Citizenship Act[59] gives him the right to hold property that a natural-born citizen has; and he is triable at law the same as a natural-born citizen. This leaves a great deal unsaid: What other rights does he have? Jurisdiction over naturalization and aliens belongs to Parliament and its power over immigration prevails over that of the provinces.[60] In spite of this British Columbia passed a large number of statutes designed to keep out Chinese and Japanese, or at least to make it hard for them to stay. Indeed, twenty-one were disallowed between 1884 and 1908.[61] Among Acts not disallowed, one forbade Chinese from working in coal mines. In *Union Colliery* v. *Bryden,*[62] the Privy Council held the Act invalid as in relation to aliens and naturalization.

On the subject of naturalization, the Citizenship Act provides for the naturalization of aliens. A person who so becomes a Canadian citizen "is, subject to the provisions of this Act, entitled to all rights, powers and privileges... to which a natural-born Canadian citizen is entitled. . . . "[63] However, the Act does not define them. In *Cunningham* v. *Tomey Hamma,* the Privy council upheld a British Columbia Act depriving Japanese of the right to vote.[64] The significant point in the judgment is that although Parliament has jurisdiction over aliens and naturalization, this does not include privileges or consequences that flow from either status. This seems to leave naturalized citizens or aliens at the mercy of discriminatory provincial legislation.

The only judicial pronouncement indicating a contrary view is a dictum of Rand J. in *Winner* v. *S.M.T.*[65] In discussing provincial power to regulate highways he said: "A province cannot by depriving a Canadian of the means of working, force him to leave it... " and "Highways are a condition of the existence of an organized state; without them its life could not be carried on. To deny their use is to destroy the fundamental liberty of action of the individual, to prescribe his participation in that life; render such a law, the exercise of citizenship would be at an end... " and "To prevent a person from engaging in business at a Post Office or a Customs House or a bank by forbidding him the use of the highways, is, so far, to frustrate a privilege imbedded in Dominion law."

Turning now to denaturalization which is provided for in the Citizenship Act we note that one who is not a natural-born citizen loses his citizenship after ten consecutive years' residence outside Canada.[66] Another provision permits the Governor in Council to revoke citizenship of persons not natural-born (1) for failure to return to Canada to face a treason charge and (2) for fraud in obtaining citizenship.[67] During the present session of Parliament, a debate has taken place on a Bill to remove the first of these grounds.[68]

As for voting rights *Cunningham* shows that a province may deprive a citizen of the right to vote. In fact, such deprivation is now rare. The federal Act gives the franchise to every resident British subject of twenty-one years of age. The only exceptions apart from electoral officers and judges, are Indians, convicts in prison, mentally diseased and certain Doukhobors.[69] Most of the provincial statutes exclude Indians, usually with the exception of those who have had war service and those who have given up their rights as Indians. British Columbia, Manitoba, Newfoundland and Nova Scotia do not exclude Indians, though British Columbia excludes Doukhobors.

An examination of the Indian Act shows that Indians are under many disabilities[70] to which other citizens are not subject.[71]

Before leaving the matter of the franchise we might note that most of the provinces gave women the right to vote during World War I and that no electoral Act now excludes them.

In concluding this subject we might note that there is no statute providing for denial of passports comparable to those in the United States,[72] and no general policy of refusing passports to Communists seems to exist.

III. Substantive Protection of Personal Liberty: Security of the Person

The word liberty is, of course, elusive, for it can range from liberty of speech to liberty to make contracts. Here we mean the claim to be left alone and to do what one wishes in non-economic matters.[73]

It is hardly necessary to say that no one can be held in slavery. It never was recognized in the colonies. The Criminal Code formerly included the crime of kidnapping a person with intent to put him into slavery, but the new Code omits the word.[74] In the United States slavery was, of course, abolished after the Civil War, but in some American states up to recent times it has been possible to keep a workman in peonage by paying him in advance and then punishing him under a law making it an offence to accept salary in advance and then fail to perform the work.[75]

The traditional safeguard against wrongful detention or imprisonment is, of course, the writ of habeas corpus. It antedates the statute of Charles II by centuries; the purpose of that statute and a later one of 1816 was to make the writ more effective.[76] In the colonial period in Canada habeas corpus statutes were passed and a number of provinces have their own today. The Supreme Court of Canada has jurisdiction to issue the writ but has declined to use its powers to interfere in the administration of justice in the provinces and generally the writ is not available as an extra appeal from a conviction.[77] It is, however, frequently used to challenge the validity of a deportation order. Of course, in wartime, internment provisions may operate in effect as a suspension of the writ.

Other forms of interference with the person are compulsory vaccination laws, quarantine for contagious diseases, and compulsory treatment for venereal disease. At least two provinces, Alberta and British Columbia, have sexual sterilization Acts. Under both Acts the basis of sterilization is the likelihood that children of the person will be mentally deficient. However, the consent of the person must be given, or if he is incapable, the consent of specified other persons is required. The Supreme Court recently held that a province may compel a person to take a "breathalyser" test.[78] Legislation of this kind often meets objection based on inherent rights of the person, but even if Canada were to give constitutional protection to inviolability of the person it would probably not apply to provisions like these. In the United States vaccination and sterilization laws were upheld long ago.[79]

The next aspect of liberty of the person has to do with unauthorized activities of government officials—the right to be protected against arbitrary arrest and molestation of the person and the home. These rights were established in England two hundred years ago by the cases arising out of the government's attempt to put to silence the irrepressible John Wilkes.[80]

In Canada the Criminal Code is reasonably clear as to the power to arrest with and without warrant, though the new Code seems to leave the power of an ordinary citizen in some doubt.[81] It does embody the rule of *Christie* v. *Leachinsky*[82] that the person being arrested must be told the reason. A blank or general warrant is not authorized. The warrant must name the accused.[83]

As for searches, the Code prescribes the procedure for issue and execution of a search warrant and many provincial statutes authorize searches with and sometimes without warrant.

A special form of search warrant, still authorized under the customs, excise and narcotics laws, is the writ of assistance, issued by the Exchequer Court. It is widely worded and authorizes searches, seizure and arrest.[84] In the United States, "writ of assistance" is an ugly word. Shortly before the revolution when Crown officers applied to the court in Boston for a writ of assistance, James Otis made his famous, and unsuccessful, argument that such writs are void at common law and the statute authorizing them is contrary to fundamental principles of law. Actually Otis's clients wanted to evade customs duties. The memory of experiences with Crown Officers doubtless was a reason why the American Bill of Rights protects citizens against unreasonable searches and seizures. There is a continual stream of cases to the Supreme Court; an accused person argues that federal authorities seized his property—narcotics, counterfeit money, parts of a still—by an unreasonable search. If he can convince the court that the search or seizure was unreasonable, he can have the evidence suppressed. This is the sanction that the court created to check unreasonable searches.[85] What is an unreasonable search is almost impossible to say—at least the division of opinion on the court so indicates.[86] The concern of the court to discourage unlawful seizures goes back to the English common law,[87] but English law does not use the device of making the evidence inadmissible. The main sanction, apart from public opinion, is a civil action for trespass or assault and sometimes a criminal charge. Our judges have on occasion spoken out strongly against high-handed action by the police.[88] Related to this question is that of admissibility of evidence obtained by a blood test, or a forced emetic. By Canadian law it is admissible; by American it may or may not be, depending on the degree of violence used by the police.[89]

Wire-tapping is a form of intrusion on what might be called a right of privacy. There is so far as I know no legislation on the subject, though in one case the court quashed a "search warrant" authorizing the police to enter a telephone exchange and tap the wires; the Code does not authorize such procedure.[90] In the United States, federal law and some state laws forbid wire-tapping and there has been a continuing debate on the wisdom of these enactments.

IV. Racial Discrimination and Equal Protection of the Laws

Discrimination may take the form of legislation, such as Jim Crow laws, or other government action, such as refusal to select negroes for jury duty; or it can take the form of private action, such as the refusal of a theatre of café owner to admit persons of certain races.

The common law requires only common carriers and innkeepers to deal with everyone, and it has been held in Canada that cafés and beer-parlors are not under this obligation.[91]

As for discriminatory legislation, the most conspicuous examples have been in British Columbia. These were attempts to discourage Japanese and Chinese by making it hard for them to work. Today, outside of the few exceptions in the voting laws, very few statutes, federal or provincial, actually prescribe discrimination. Alberta's Communal Property Act[92] which restricts the size and location of Hutterite colonies has met with some criticism. The government is now studying the operation of the Act.

The most significant trend since the war is the growth of an attitude opposed to discrimination. The judgment of Mackay J. in *Re Drummond Wren*[93] in 1945 received wide acclaim. It held invalid as against public policy a covenant by the purchaser of land not to resell to persons of certain races. True his judgment was overruled, though the Supreme Court held these covenants invalid on other grounds.[94] In the meantime, both Ontario and Manitoba passed legislation declaring such covenants invalid.[95]

The only province with a comprehensive Bill of Rights Act is Saskatchewan.[96] Both that province and Ontario have a Fair Accommodation Practices Act[97] forbidding discrimination by persons operating places to which the public is admitted. The first cases under the Ontario Act were rather discouraging, for the restaurant owner was acquitted on evidence that seemed to show discrimination; however, in a later case there was a conviction.[98]

In the field of labour relations Ontario was the pioneer in prohibiting discrimination by unions and employers with a Fair Employment Practices Act in 1951. Since then similar acts have been passed by Parliament and five other provinces.[99] One observation is relevant here; some persons oppose legislation of this type on the ground that "you cannot legislate morality". As a matter of fact, the legislature *can* lead public opinion if it is neutral, or evenly balanced. Moreover, anti-discrimination laws do not tell the café-owner to love the negro but to serve him. Of course it is easy to point to the difficulties in the United States but even there great progress has been made. New York's anti-discrimination law appears to have improved the lot of the negro[100] and the admission of negroes to organized baseball since 1947 is significant.

It is not necessary to examine in detail the removal of disabilities of women. They have equality with men in holding office and voting. Recently, Parliament passed an Act providing equal pay for women,[101] and a number of provinces have similar Acts.

One cannot leave this topic without reference to Canada's handling of the Japanese after Pearl Harbour. It is not fair to criticize the government in wartime for every stringent measure that hind-sight proves to have been unnecessary. On the other hand, thousands of Canadian citizens, many of them born here, suffered great hardship. Perhaps the uprooting and the uncertainty of their future were the worst features. One cannot read the account of their treatment, including the Orders in Council providing for repatriation to Japan without concluding that a main motive was racism. The sale of their Vancouver property, which scarcely seemed necessary to the War effort, can hardly have any other basis.[102]

V. Protection of Property, Contract, and Other Economic Rights

We begin with the proposition that a Canadian legislature acting within its powers can take away the property of one and give it to another; it can regulate contracts, as by enacting laws to establish minimum wages and hours of labour; it can regulate business; and it can pass laws altering the remedies available under contracts. The late Mr. Justice Riddell often pointed this out.[103] His is not only the orthodox view but in the writer's opinion, correct. It flows from the theory of parliamentary sovereignty which was not curtailed by the British North America Act save by the division of powers, and rare exceptions such as legislation relating to education.

However, some statues are held *ultra vires* because they trench on matters outside the jurisdiction of the enacting legislature. Notable examples are provincial statutes designed to relieve debtors during a depression—they may infringe Parliament's powers over bankruptcy or interest;[104] similarly with statutes reducing interest on provincial bonds.[105] A statute may be invalid even though on a subject within provincial power if it creates a board or tribunal that is in effect a court, the judges of which must be appointed by the federal government.[106] Courts can, in fact, use the British North America Act to create what is, in effect, an area in which neither central nor local powers can operate. They do this by putting a narrow construction on the powers of each. Regulation of marketing furnishes an example, though this problem now appears to be in the course of solution.[107]

In construing statutes, courts can use canons of construction to circumscribe the scope of statutes. Sometimes provincial courts have said that the legislature may not declare a statute to mean something other than what the court has previously said it to mean, and also that the legislature cannot deny access to the courts in individual cases. These views are incorrect,[108] though the legislature cannot bar access in order to prevent a test of the validity of a statute.

As for confiscatory legislation, there is no statute which does not provide for compensation for taking of property and indeed the Supreme Court has declined to recognize a foreign confiscatory statute.[109] However, in theory there is no objection.

VI. Procedure in Criminal and Civil Cases and Before Administrative Boards

Whatever else we mean by "the rule of law", we imply fair and even-handed procedure. We have in mind the clause of Magna Carta, that "no freeman shall be taken, imprisoned, disseised, outlawed, or exiled except by the judgment of his peers or the law of the land." The last phrase is obscure but its influence on English law has been profound. So it is with the next clause: "To no one will we sell, to no one will we deny or defer right or justice." The phrase "due process of law" did not originate in the American Bill of Rights but in a statute of Edward III.[110] The actual content of all these terms has varied over the centuries, but they do connote fairness of procedure. What provisions are in our Criminal Code that safeguard the accused in criminal proceedings? The grand jury survives in half the provinces. Jury trial is preserved for serious offences though the accused in most cases may waive it, and a charge against a corporation under the Combines Investigation Act is tried by judge alone. Selection of juries is left to provincial law, but mixed juries are permitted in Quebec and Manitoba. The reported cases indicate few complaints of unfairness in selection of juries. The charge must give sufficient notice of the offence and the court can order particulars if fairness requires it. The accused is entitled to make full answer and defence and he is entitled to counsel. Trial must be held in open court, with narrow exceptions.

No one is to be charged twice with the same offence, and if a witness is asked an incriminating question he may object to answer, whereupon he must answer but the answer shall not later be used against him.

On appeal, the test is whether a miscarriage of justice has occurred. In the United States, convictions are sometimes set aside for breach of constitutional safeguards even where there is no miscarriage of justice. The only substantial difference between American and Canadian practices lies in the meaning of "right to counsel." In capital cases and sometimes in other cases in the United States this means that the state must provide counsel if the accused has none.[111] This is not so in Canada, though in serious cases counsel is generally provided.

We have set out these well-known provisions to show that they give the same general protection as the American constitution gives. Of course, there are many rules not in the Code such as that excluding confessions unless the Crown shows they are voluntary.

As for civil trials, the jury is disappearing in some provinces though in important cases there is a right to it unless the judge decides it is inappropriate to the type of case before him. Generally the law is similar to that in England and as far as the rules are concerned it is not a reckless opinion to say they are fair. As in England the judge is in charge, whereas in some of the states, at least in the past, the judge's role has been reduced.

As for administrative boards, there has been criticism, as in other places, but in spite of privative clauses in statutes, the courts still exercise jurisdiction to see that "natural justice" is preserved. Much has been written on this concept and it shall not be discussed here.

Conclusion

Although a discussion of the scope and constitutional validity of the proposed Canadian Bill of Rights is outside the subject matter of this article, by way of conclusion I would like to make a few short observations on its scheme. The Bill declares in section 2 certain rights and freedoms and in section 3 provides that federal statutes shall be construed so as not to abrogate those rights and freedoms or to deprive a person of certain safeguards that relate to judicial proceedings, and in particular, to criminal charges.

Some critics of the Bill allege that it is too narrow. My criticism is quite different: if our federal law infringes fundamental rights in any particular, or if it omits to preserve them, appropriate legislation should be passed on the subject. Some people take the other view. They think that a list of our rights and freedoms must be collected together in one place. I am not able to disprove the argument that a separate Bill of Rights has some psychological value on the rest of the world or on immigrants. But surely no one is unaware of the secure position of fundamental rights in Britain, a country that has never enacted a "Declaration of the Rights of Man." Its few landmark statutes are practical and deal with particular matters and on many subjects British law protects fundamental rights by remaining silent.

It is likely that immigrants and others concerned with the state of human rights in Canada will be more concerned about the taste of the pudding than its appearance. That Canada should try to meet the obligations of the United Nations' Universal Declaration of Human Rights, so far as they can be reduced to legal form, is undeniable, but a judgment like *Boucher* v. *The King* is worth a dozen declarations of the right of free speech.

Taking the criminal law as an example, the submission here is that our Code and the common-law rules on criminal proceedings compare favourably with those of other countries. There is no wisdom in passing a separate statute that implies otherwise. If however, our criminal law abridges human rights or omits to safeguard them, then let us amend the Criminal Code. For instance, Parliament deliberately refrained from abolishing capital and corporal punishment when it revised the Code in 1952. The Bill on the other hand says that all acts of Parliament shall not be construed to authorize the imposition of torture or cruel, inhuman and degrading punishment. Does this put an end to capital or corporal punishment? It is certainly arguable that it does.

Another example. The Code has a clear provision for holding trials in camera in certain specified cases. The Bill says all Acts shall not be construed to deprive a person of a public hearing. If Parliament wants to do away with trials in camera, which I doubt, the proper way is to amend the Code, and not to do it by a side wind.

Next, there is the right of the individual to protection of the law without regard to race, national origin, colour, religion or sex. Parliament has already provided equal pay for women and forbidden discrimination in labour relations and in recent years has removed unfair legislation from the statute book. If in the areas over which it has jurisdiction Parliament wants to go further, then it should do so by passing laws with definite sanctions. A bald declaration has no teeth. The present Bill would not be effective to compel a restaurant owner in the Northwest Territories (where the Bill clearly will apply) to serve a negro—but an Act like the Fair Accommodation Practices Act of Ontario or Saskatchewan would.

A further point is this. Some seem to think we should be ashamed because we do not have a Bill of Rights—that unless we spell out our rights they are not secure and perhaps we do not value them. My suggestion is that we have much to be proud of—it is not unfair to point out that we have had no loyalty oaths, no loyalty programmes, no elaborate plan to withhold passports, no section in the Criminal Code proscribing advocacy of overthrow of government by force. These are examples of government action that have troubled responsible men like the late Professor Chafee and Professor Gellhorn. As the former once said, schemes like these are a case of "Give me the hammer Suzy, there's a fly on baby's head". We are better off without them and can take satisfaction in having refrained from them.

On the other hand, section 6(5) of the Bill keeps out of its scope regulations under the War Measures Act. Of all the actions the Dominion government has ever taken, some of the measures under that Act are the most open to question. The handling of the Japanese during World War II perhaps comes first and one can include aspects of the general internment programme under the Defence of Canada Regulations, and some aspects of the Espionage investigation. Yet the Bill affirmatively ensures that they might happen again.

Notes

1 Hood Phillips, Constitutional Law (2 Ed, 1957), Part V; Wade and Phillips, Constitutional Law (5 Ed, 1955), Part VIII; Dicey, Law of the Constitution (9 Ed, 1939), Part II; Jennings, The Law and the Constitution (3 Ed, 1943), Ch. VIII; Keeton, The British Commonwealth (1955), pp. 59–73; Holdsworth, History of English Law (3d ed 1938), Vol. 10, 658–705.

2 Riddell, The Constitution of Canada (1920); *Florence Mining Co. Ltd.* v. *Cobalt Lake Mining Co., Ltd.* (1909), 18 O.L.R. 275; aff'd 43 O.L.R. 474.

3 Proceedings of Special Joint Committee on Human Rights and Fundamental

Freedoms (1947–48); Proceedings of Special Committee of the Senate on Human Rights and Fundamental Freedoms (1950). This Committee recommended a constitutional Bill of Rights and as an interim measure a statutory Bill.

4 Doughty and Story, Canadian Constitutional Documents (vol 1, 1918), p. 15; 34 Geo. III, c. 5 (L.C.)

5 [1917] 1 W.W.R. 415 (Alta.).

6 *R.* v. *Russell,* [1920] 1 W.W.R. 624 (Man.).

7 Criminal Code, R.S.C., 1927, c. 36, s. 98; repealed Stats. of Can. 1936, c. 29, s. 1.

8 See Chafee, Freedom of Speech in the United States (1941), Part I.

9 *Dennis* v. *United States* (1951), 339 U.S. 162.

10 [1951] S.C.R. 265, at p. 288; see also *Saumur* v. *Quebec,* [1953] 2 S.C.R. 299, per Rand J., at p. 330.

11 (1957), 7 D.L.R. (2d) 337 (Can.).

12 *Re Alberta Statutes,* [1938] S.C.R. 100. On appeal, the Privy Council did not consider the "Press Bill", see [1939] A.C. 117.

13 Chafee, II Government and Mass Communications (1947), pp. 500–562.

14 *E.g. Fournier* v. *A.G.* (1911), 17 C.C.C. 108 (Que.); *Re Nicol,* [1954] 3 D.L.R. 690 (B.C.).

15 *E.g. Hatfield* v. *Healy* (1911), 3 Alta. L.R. 327; *Steiner* v. *Toronto Star* (1956), 1 D.L.R. (2d) 297 (Ont.); See also McRuer, Criminal Contempt of Court Procedure (1952), 30 Can. Bar Rev. 225.

16 *E.g. Craig* v. *Harney* (1947), 331 U.S. 367; See *Maryland* v. *Baltimore Radio Show* (1950), 338 U.S. 912.

17 Post Office Act, R.S.C., 1952, c. 212, s. 7.

18 Customs Tariff, R.S.C., 1952, c. 60, sch. "C".

19 Stats. of Can., 1958, c. 26, s. 3.

20 See Chafee, I Government and Mass Communications (1947), pp. 242–366.

21 *Burstyn* v. *Wilson* (1952), 343 U.S. 495; *Superior Films* v. *Industrial Commission* (1953), 346 U.S. 587.

22 *E.g. R.* v. *National News Co.,* [1953] 4 D.L.R. 274 (Ont.). See Mackay, The Hicklin Rule and Judicial Censorship (1958), 36 Can. Bar Rev. 1. For a judgment on obscenity of pictures that combines common sense with a touch of humour see *R.* v. *Stroll* (1951), 100 C.C.C. 171 (Que.).

23 See Gellhorn, Individual Freedom and Government Restraints (1956), Ch. 2.

24 Ss. 64–70.

25 *E.g. R.* v. *Beattie* (1931), 55 C.C.C. 380 (Man.); *R.* v. *Stewart* (1934), 61 C.C.C. 217 (Alta.).

26 *E.g. De Jonge* v. *Oregon* (1937), 299 U.S. 353; *Hague* v. *C.I.O.* (1939), 307 U.S. 496; *Kunz* v. *New York* (1950), 340 U.S. 290.

27 *E.g. Beauharnais* v. *Illinois* (1950), 337 U.S. 1: *Cf. Feiner* v. *New York* (1951),340 U.S. 315.

28 *Thomas* v. *Collins* (1944), 323 U.S. 516; *Staub* v. *Baxley* (1958), 355 U.S. 302.

29 *Thornhill* v. *Alabama* (1940), 310 U.S. 88; *cf. Hughes* v. *Superior Court* (1950), 339 U.S. 410 and companion cases.

30 See *Wieman* v. *Updegraff* (1952), 344 U.S. 183; *Speiser* v. *Randall* (1958), 357 U.S. 313.

31 *Watkins* v. *United States* (1958), 354 U.S. 178; *Sweezy* v. *New Hampshire* (1958), 354 U.S. 234.

32 Taswell-Langmead, English Constitutional History (6 Ed, 1905), Ch. 17, IV.

33 (1832), Wm. IV, c. 57 (L.C.); see Sack, The History of the Jews in Canada, (1945) Chs. 7–9.

34 Kennedy, The Constitution of Canada (1937), Chs. 6 & 7.

35 See: Weir, The Separate School Question in Canada (1934); Miller, National Government and Education in Canada (1940).

36 *Chabot* v. *School Commissioners of Lamorandiere* (1958), 12 D.L.R. (2d) 796 (Que.).

37 *Perepolkin* v. *Superintendant of Child Welfare* (1958), 11 D.L.R. (2d) 417. For the position in the United States see *Meyer* v. *Nebraska* (1923), 262 U.S. 390; *Pierce* v. *Society of Sisters* (1924), 268 U.S. 511.

38 R.S.S., 1953, c. 345, s. 3.

39 Freedom of Worship Act, R.S.Q., 1941, c. 307; Rectories Act, R.S.O.,

1897, c. 306.

40 Ss. 161, 246.

41 *R.* v. *Kite,* [1949] 2 W.W.R. 195 (B.C.); *Ottawa* v. *Irving* (1951), 99 C.C.C. 318; *R.* v. *Mustin,* [1940] O.R. 393; *cf. R.* v. *Napier,* [1941] O.R. 30; *R.* v. *Naish,* [1950] 1 W.W.R. 987 (Sask.).

42 *Supra,* footnote 10, at p. 329.

43 [1955] S.C.R. 799.

44 *Switzman* v. *Elbling, supra,* footnote 11, at p. 371 (Can.).

45 [1955] S.C.R. 874.

46 *Ruman* v. *Lethbridge S. Bd.,* [1943] 3 W.W.R. 340 (Alta.); the amendment is Stats. of Alta., 1944, c. 46, s. 9.

47 *Donald* v. *Hamilton Board of Education,* [1945] O.R. 518.

48 *West Virginia* v. *Barnette* (1943), 319 U.S. 624.

49 *Saia* v. *New York* (1948), 334 U.S. 558; *cf. Kovacs* v. *Cooper* (1949), 336 U.S. 77.

50 *Marsh* v. *Alabama* (1946), 326 U.S. 501: *Tucker* v. *Texas* (1946), 326 U.S. 517; *cf. Breard* v. *Alexandria* (1951), 341 U.S. 622.

51 Quoted in *Re Hanna* (1957), 21 W.W.R. (N.S.) 400 (B.C.); Corbett, Canada's Immigration Policy (1957), p. 1.

52 Immigration Act, ss. 5, 61.

53 Corbett, *op. cit., supra,* footnote 51, pp. 80–89.

54 *A.G. for Canada* v. *Cain,* [1906] A.C. 542.

55 S. 19.

56 S. 39.

57 *E.g. Samejima* v. *The King* [1932] S.C.R. 640; *Re Hanna, supra,* footnote 51.

58 Corbett *op. cit., supra,* footnote 51, p. 92; for a discussion of American deportation cases see Gellhorn, *supra,* footnote 23, pp. 29–38.

59 R.S.C., 1952, c. 33, Part V.

60 B.N.A. Act 1867, ss. 91(25), 95. See Mercier, Immigration and Provincial Rights (1944), 22 Can. Bar Rev. 856.

61 Memorandum on Dominion Power of Disallowance of Provincial Legislation (1946), pp. 68–9, 72–3.

62 [1899] A.C. 580.

63 S. 22.

64 [1903] A.C. 151; see also *Quong Wing* v. *The King* (1916), 49 S.C.R. 440.

65 [1951] S.C.R. 887 varied [1954] A.C. 541. For a discussion of privileges and immunities of United States citizenship see *Edwards* v. *California* (1941), 314 U.S. 160.

66 Stats. of Can., 1952–53, c. 23, s. 19.

67 *Ibid.,* 1958, c. 24, s. 2.

68 Edmonton Journal, February 6th, 1959.

69 Canada Elections Act, R.S.C., 1952, c. 23, s. 14.

70 Indian Act, R.S.C., 1952, c. 149.

71 As to Esquimos The Supreme Court has held that "Indians" in s. 91 (24) of the B.N.A. Act includes the Esquimos in Quebec but I doubt that all Esquimos are included in the Indian Act.

72 See *Kent* v. *Dulles* (1958), 357 U.S. 116, holding the statutes did not give to the Secretary of State unlimited discretion to withhold passports.

73 The liberty to move about might be included here but has been mentioned above in connection with rights of citizenship; similarly with the parents' right over education of children, which was included with freedom of religion.

74 S. 233, replacing former s. 297.

75 *Bailey* v. *Alabama* (1911), 219 U.S. 219; *Pollock* v. *Williams* (1944), 322 U.S. 4.

76 The texts cited in footnote 1 all discuss the writ under security of the person.

77 *E.g. Re Sproule* (1886), 12 S.C.R. 140.

78 *Re sec. 92(4) Vehicles Act* (1959), 15 D.L.R. (2d) 225 (Can.).

79 *Jacobson* v. *Mass* (1905), 197 U.S. 11; *Buck* v. *Bell* (1927), 274 U.S. 200; *cf. Skinner* v. *Oklahoma* (1941), 316 U.S. 535.

80 *Leach* v. *Money; Entick* v. *Carrington; Wilkes* v. *Wood,* (1763), 14 State Trials, at pp. 1002, 1029, 1153.

81 Ss. 434–8 and 25. See Wright, Cases on Torts (2 Ed. 1958), pp. 117–8.

82 [1947] A.C. 573, s. 29.

83 Ss. 440(4), 442(1).

84 Customs Act, R.S.C., 1952, c. 58, s. 143; Excise Act, R.S.C., 1952, c. 100, s. 78; Opium and Narcotic Drug Act, R.S.C., 1952, c. 201, s. 22. The writ which is examined here is under the Opium Act.

85 *Weeks* v. *United States* (1914), 232 U.S. 383. This rule does not apply to

state searches—*Wolf* v. *Colorado* (1949), 338 U.S. 25.

86 *United States* v. *Rabinowitz* (1950), 339 U.S. 56.

87 *Miller* v. *United States* (1958), 357 U.S. 301.

88 See *R.* v. *Container Materials Ltd.* (1941) 76 C.C.C. 18, at p. 52 (Ont.); *Fleming* v. *Spracklin* (1921), 50 O.L.R. 289; *R.* v. *MacDonald* (1932), 59 C.C.C. 56 (Alta.).

89 *Attorney General* v. *Begin,* [1955] S.C.R. 593. *Re sec. 92(4) Vehicles Act, supra,* footnote 78; *Rochin* v. *California* (1951), 342 U.S. 165; *Breihaupt* v. *Abram* (1956), 352 U.S. 432.

90 *Re Bell Telephone Co.* (1947), 89 C.C.C. 196 (Ont.).

91 *Franklin* v. *Evans* (1924), 55 O.L.R. 349; *Christie* v. *York,* [1940] S.C.R. 139; *Rogers* v. *Clarence Hotel,* [1940] 2 W.W.R. 545 (B.C.).

92 R.S.A., 1955, c. 52.

93 [1945] O.R. 778.

94 *Noble* v. *Alley,* [1951] S.C.R. 64.

95 R.S.O., 1950, c. 68, s. 21; Stats. of Man., 1950, c. 33; see Smout, Racial and Religious Restraints on Alienation (1952), 30 Can. Bar Rev. 863.

96 R.S.S., 1953, c. 345; An Alberta Bill of Rights Act, 1946, c. 11 was held invalid because the main purpose was a scheme that interfered with banks, and the Privy Council held inseverable those portions that would have been valid by themselves. *Attorney-Gen. of Alberta* v. *Attorney-Gen. of Canada,* [1947] A.C. 503.

97 Stats. of Sask., 1956, c. 68; Stats. of Ont., 1954, c. 28.

98 *R.* v. *McKay* (1955), 113 C.C.C. 56 (1956), 5 D.L.R. (2d) 403 (Ont.).

99 British Columbia, Manitoba, New Brunswick, Nova Scotia, Saskatchewan.

100 Berger, The New York State Law Against Discrimination (1950), 35 Cornell L. Q. 747. Carter, Practical Considerations of Anti-Discrimination Legislation (1954), 40 Cornell L. Q. 40.

101 Female Employees Equal Pay Act, Stats. of Can., 1956, c. 38.

102 La Violette, The Canadian Japanese and World War II (1947) Chs. 9–12. See *Co-op Committee on Japanese Canadians* v. *Att. Gen. of Can.,* [1947] A.C. 87. *Nakashima* v. *The King,* [1947] 4 D.L.R. 487 (Ex. Ct.).

103 Riddell, The Constitution of Canada (1920).

104 *Re Debt Adjustment Act,* [1943] A.C. 356; *Re Farm Security Act,* [1949] A.C. 110; *Canadian Bankers' Assn.* v. *Att. Gen. of Sask.,* [1956] S.C.R. 31.

105 *Rex* v. *I. O. F.,* [1940] A.C. 513.

106 *Toronto* v. *Olympia Edward Rec. Club,* [1955] S.C.R. 454.

107 *P.E.I. Potato Marketing Board* v. *Willis,* [1952] 2 S.C.R. 392; *Re Farm Products Marketing Act,* [1957] S.C.R. 198.

108 *Western Minerals* v. *Gaumont,* [1953] 1 S.C.R. 345; *Montreal Trust Co.* v. *Abitibi Power Co.,* [1943] A.C. 536.

109 *Laane* v. *Estonian S.S. Line,* [1949] S.C.R. 530.

110 28 Edw. III, c. 3; See Radin, The Myth of Magna Carta (1947), 60 Harv. L. R. 1060.

111 *Uveges* v. *Pennsylvania* (1948), 335 U.S. 437.

1959

Book Review: Civil Liberties and Canadian Federalism by F.R. Scott.

Reprinted from
(1960) 38 Canadian Bar Review
pp. 443–445

The author of this book was a famous Canadian, Frank Scott, who was Professor of Law at McGill University and ultimately its Dean. He was also a distinguished poet.

The book being reviewed here contains two lectures which he delivered at Carleton University in 1959. This was at the time when discussions were under way on a proposed Canadian Bill of Rights, which was in fact enacted the following year by the Diefenbaker government.

Frank Scott was very strong on civil liberties, and considered that the courts are the main protector of liberties.

He was Co-Chairman of the Royal Commission on Bilingualism and Biculturalism in the mid-1950s; he was always fond of the French and strong on nationalism.

In 1954 he was appointed Chairman of a Committee on Legal Research established by the Canadian Bar Association to study ways of improving legal scholarship in Canada. Bowker was the only western representative on this Committee. Its report and recommendations were published in (1956) 34 Canadian Bar Review, *p. 999.*

Civil Liberties and Canadian Federalism. By F. R. SCOTT. Alan B. Plaunt Memorial Lectures, Carleton University. Toronto: University of Toronto Press. 1959. Pp. 58. ($2.00)

This volume contains two lectures that Professor Scott delivered in March 1959 at Carleton University. They were the Alan B. Plaunt Memorial Lectures. The subject was "Civil Liberties and Canadian Federalism". The two concepts joined in the title have long been of interest to Professor Scott. For many years he has written, spoken and worked in the interest of civil liberties and the building of a Canadian nation. He once appeared before a Senate Committee and persuaded them we should have a constitutional Bill of Rights, and was successful counsel in the *Padlock Law* case and *Roncarelli* v. *Duplessis*.

The first lecture describes important constitutional developments since Confederation—the consolidation of the whole of British North America in the Dominion (*pace* Professor Scott) of Canada, definition of provincial status, development from colony to nation and the expansion of governmental activities. Though we have no Bill of Rights, the power of disallowance, the canons of construction and the power of the courts to declare that a statute is *ultra vires* are all devices that can be used to safeguard civil liberties.

The second lecture classifies human rights and civil liberties. Then comes a chronological examination of the leading cases, most of them within the last decade, that show a tendency to protect civil liberties by application of common-law principles, interpretation of statutes and restriction of provincial legislation interfering with freedom of speech, press and religion. The concluding part is an examination of the nature of a constitutional Bill of Rights on the one hand, and an ordinary statutory Bill such as the one introduced in Parliament in 1958 on the other.

The author is doubtless correct in saying that the United Nations Declaration of Human Rights of 1948 has done much to arouse thought on the whole subject and that it deserves some of the credit for the new concern in Canada over human rights and for the growing volume of enactments that remove restrictions on civil liberties and add safeguards to them.

Professor Scott's classification of basic rights includes freedom of the person and the right to vote with freedom of speech and religion and places the right to a fair trial somewhere between these and anti-discrimination laws—all rather strange bed fellows. He has one novel category—minority rights. One might question whether this a useful class or group. Some minority rights are certainly protected in any catalogue of fundamental rights but many are not—such as the "right" of a Doukhobour not to send his children to school or the "right" of a polygamist to have two wives.

Like many Canadian champions of basic freedoms, Professor Scott accepts with enthusiasm the famous dictum of Chief Justice Duff in the *Alberta Press* case in 1938. The reasoning can be put this way: The preamble to the British North America Act says the Dominion shall have a constitution similar in principle to that of Britain; such a constitution requires a Parliament; Parliament can function properly only if there is a free discussion of public issues; free discussion of public issues cannot be curtailed by a province. With respect, it seems to me that a constitution like Britain's means that parliamentary sovereignty applies—subject of course to the division of powers–so that there is no more limitation on the power of a provincial legislature to curtail freedom of speech than there is on the British Parliament. Professor Scott of course recognizes this point but is content to accept the judge-made inroads on parliamentary sovereignty. One cannot deny that Chief Justice Duff's dictum has had and doubtless will continue to have, a profound influence toward creating unwritten limitations on provincial power. Professor Scott does not seem to take this reasoning to its logical and startling conclusion—that if the provinces cannot restrict freedom of speech, neither can the Dominion.

He clearly favours a constitutional amendment that will impose limitations on all legislatures and other branches of government. On the other hand, he is doubtful of the efficacy of the proposed federal Bill, fearing that the taking of this first step—which is a mere Declaration—might confuse the issue and discourage people from further effort.

As a believer in constitutional limitations, Professor Scott looks to the courts as the main protectors of our liberties. In some measure they always have been. However, one might suggest that in a democracy it is proper to look to the legislatures to perform this function and to leave to the courts their common-law role of supplemental support. Instead of this Professor Scott takes the traditional American view that the courts should have a "veto" over legislation that they consider to be an abridgement of basic rights and freedoms. His fear of "legislative tyranny" expresses an attitude toward elected representatives that I do not share.

In one area at least the mere striking down of unfair legislation is not enough—that of discrimination. What the racial minority needs is not so much a shield of constitutional protection against discriminatory legislation, but a sword of anti-discriminatory legislation. A mere declaration that all are entitled to equal protection of the laws is not enough, as American experience shows. Anti-discrimination laws with sanctions are needed. They are effective without a constitutional provision but the converse is not true.

This small volume is another of Professor Scott's many contributions to the cause of civil liberties and is certainly to be welcome as an addition to the Canadian literature, none too extensive, on the subject.

1960

Reform of the Law of Dower in Alberta

Reprinted from
(1960) 1 Alberta Law Review
pp. 501–515

This article has been quoted by Trial Judges, the Court of Appeal and the Supreme Court of Canada.

First delivered as a paper at the Annual Meeting of the Law Society of Alberta at Edmonton in 1960, it continues to be distributed to law students at the University of Alberta in connection with courses on Wills and Property.

The main purpose of our Dower Act is to secure to the wife of a married person an interest in the family home by requiring her consent to a disposition and giving her a life estate on the husband's death. At the same time the purpose of our system of land titles is to enable those dealing with the registered owner of land to rely on the title. These two claims or interests often come in conflict. If, as Roscoe Pound says, the purpose of law is one of social engineering—to satisfy as many interests as possible with a minimum of friction—then it is proper to ask whether our Dower Act is good social engineering. When it was revised in 1948 everyone thought that in future no disposition of the homestead would, in any way, be null or void in the absence of consent. To the contrary the decisions now show clearly that every such disposition is entirely void unless, and until, followed by a new title. Consequently a purchaser, lessee or mortgagee may deal in the best of faith with the registered owner and yet acquire no interest in the land at all—and this in a province with a Torrens system. Perhaps one might suggest that we have not been very good social engineers, that we need a new lubricant to reduce the friction. The purpose of this paper is to propose several alternate oils for the machinery.

A passing reference must be made to common law dower—it was the wife's right on her husband's death to have assigned to her for life one-third of the lands he owned at death or had owned since marriage. The husband had a similar right extending to all the wife's land—this was tenancy by the curtesy. The 1833 Dower Act made several changes in the English law. Dower no longer attached to land the husband disposed of *inter vivos* or by will, but only to land of which he died intestate; however, it was extended to equitable estates owned by the husband at death. In 1925 both dower and curtesy were abolished in England.

In Canada all the older provinces but Quebec took the law of England as of their establishment and so inherited the common law rules on this subject. Dower still exists in all but Newfoundland. However, the husband, on purchasing land, can circumvent his wife's claim by one device or another. It is unnecessary to describe them here. Tenancy by the curtesy remains in all the eastern common law provinces except Newfoundland and New Brunswick (which abolished it as of 29th April, 1916) but seems to be of little practical importance.

Mr. Chitty has said of common law dower: "Dower, it may be safely said, is the last relic of feudalism. It is not only an anachronism but it is obsolete. . . the best that can be said of dower is that it has a nuisance value."[1]

In the United States common law dower has been abolished in most states but in many it has been replaced by "homestead" laws. These vary in detail, one from another, but their usual features are: (1) the owner of the home cannot dispose of, or encumber, it without his spouse's consent; (2) the wife or family has the use of it after the owner's death; (3) it is exempt from sale under execution.

The western provinces have all borrowed from the United States laws of this general type. Our "Dower" Act is really a homestead act. As Egbert J. has observed, "There may be some who think that this is an import we could very well have done without."[2] Yet there is an important social policy behind this type of legislation—to furnish a degree of security to the family.

In considering how better to accommodate this policy to that of the Torrens system it will help to look at the jurisprudence of the western provinces since they introduced homestead laws.

Alberta

The Northwest Territories took the law of England, as of 15th July, 1870, insofar as applicable. Thus common law dower as amended by the 1833 Act became part of the law. Then in 1886 Parliament passed the Territories Real Property Act, providing a Torrens system of registration of titles to land. The existence of common law dower has generally been considered inconsistent with a land registration system for it imposes an invisible encumbrance on the title.[3] Hence the 1886 Act abolished dower and curtesy as well. This remained the law when Alberta was created, and indeed until 1915.

In that year the legislature passed the Married Woman's Home Protection Act. In *Overland* v. *Himelford,*[4] Ives, J. explained the reason and effect of the Act as follows:

> "Previous to the year 1915, the people of this province had experienced a land boom, particularly in the cities and towns, with all its attendant speculation. The wives in Alberta said, in effect, to the Legislature, where this speculation affects our homes we want it stopped. We have a home in the morning but it is sold or mortgaged at night. Our husbands may deal with their lands as they please subject only to their duty of providing us with a home

> which shall be placed beyond the risk of their speculation. These representations resulted in legislation in 1915 called *The Married Woman's Home Protection Act,* ch. 4. The name of this Act is very suggestive, although it created no right of property in the wife. It gave her only a right of filing a caveat which forthwith clouded the title, and prevented the husband from dealing with the land, in so far as registration was required, from the moment the caveat was lodged."

In 1917, it was replaced by The Dower Act. This gave her a life estate in the homestead arising on the husband's death and provided that any disposition made without the wife's written consent is "null and void". The requirement of a certificate of acknowledgment by the wife was in the Act from the beginning, and the alternate requiremment of an affidavit by the husband that he is not married or that the land is not his homestead was added in 1919. From 1917 until today the courts and legislature and the legal profession too have wrestled with the question—what is the effect of a disposition of the homestead made without consent, properly given and executed?

In *Choma* v. *Chmelyk*[5] the husband sold the homestead under agreement for sale. The wife did not consent, probably because the parties did not know of the existence of the Act. Shortly after, husband and wife brought suit for a declaration that the agreement was null and void. Scott, J. held that it was not null and void but merely ineffective to put an end to the wife's potential life estate. Subject to this it was a valid and subsisting agreement. He was influenced by the fact that at common law a husband could sell his land, subject to the wife's inchoate dower rights; and he thought that the new "dower" has the same quality as common law dower. His view does not give due effect to the requirement of consent. Such a requirement is intended to give the wife a "veto" power. This decision really ignores that fact, and yet it has influenced profoundly our law on the subject.

Two years later, in *Overland* v. *Himelford,*[6] the husband granted a lease of the home. The wife signed it as though she were lessor, but did not acknowledge her consent as required by the Act. Six months later the spouses brought action to avoid the lease. Walsh, J. held against them and the Appellate Division was equally divided. Stuart and Ives, JJ. thought the Act was intended to secure to the wife the enjoyment of the family home during even the husband's lifetime unless she consented to change it and that the proper interpretation is to hold the lease entirely void because she did not properly acknowledge her consent.[7] This is the generally accepted view in Saskatchewan and Manitoba. Beck, J. with Harvey, C.J. concurring, said that where the husband makes a disposition without the wife's consent her estate is preserved, thus agreeing with Scott, J. in *Choma*. He held further that she might dispose of her dower interest. By signing the lease she had done so and no certificate of acknowledgment is required.

In the meantime, in 1919 the legislature had amended the Act to say that the disposition without consent was null and void only insofar as it may affect the interest of the said wife.[8] Thus the view of Scott, J. clearly became law.

In 1926 the Legislature struck out of the Act the words added in 1919, restoring it to its original form. This left some doubt as to whether a disposition was not entirely null and void.[9] In 1939 came *Spooner* v. *Leyton*.[10] The husband entered into an agreement to sell the homestead and took an affidavit that it was not his homestead. In fact, the wife had refused to consent. She brought action for a declaration that the agreement was null and void and for possession. The Appellate Division held that the agreement was valid but was subject to the wife's possible life estate. The 1926 amendment of the section did not operate to render the disposition absolutely null and void. The judgment of Scott, J. in *Choma* was still applicable. Harvey, C.J. added that if the Legislature intended to make the disposition completely void, "one would have looked for some such words as 'absolutely' or 'for all purposes'."

In 1942 the legislature added these words. Henceforth a disposition without consent was "absolutely null and void for all purposes." The consequence was that a husband wanting to avoid the disposition could set up the absence of consent by resisting an action for specific performance,[11] or by bringing his own action. *Reddick* v. *Pearson*[12] illustrates the operation of the amendment. Pearson gave to Reddick an oil and gas lease of part of his homestead. Mrs. Pearson signed the lease and a commissioner for oaths signed the certificate of acknowledgment. In fact, Pearson was present at the time and his wife did not actually give an acknowledgment. She did, however, admittedly approve of the transaction. Reddick made monthly payments of $100 for seven months. Then the value of the oil rights increased. McLaurin, J. held that the wife's signature to the lease must be acknowledged just as a consent must be, and since the certificate of acknowledgment was untrue, the lease was void.

It is likely that this case was overruled by *McColl-Frontenac Oil Co.* v. *Hamilton*. The facts were very similar. The only possible flaw was the husband's presence when his wife acknowledged. Howson, C.J. believed the evidence that Hamilton was present and held that the wife's consent was ineffective. On appeal, the court was evenly divided, but only on the finding of fact that the husband was present. The Supreme Court of Canada[13] upheld the oil lease, basing its judgment on section 9, a curative provision that so far as I know was never before considered, though it had been in the Act since 1919. It said that where the wife has given her written consent to a contract "for the sale of property" and the consideration has been partly performed by the purchaser, she shall, in the absence of fraud by the purchaser, be deemed to have consented to the sale in accordance with the Act. The Hamiltons did not allege fraud. The Court held that the oil lease was a sale of property and section 9 applied, thus curing the defect in the consent. One welcomes a curative section in these circumstances, but the Supreme Court had to go to some lengths to apply section 9 to an oil lease. There is force in the dissent of Kerwin, J. that it applied only to an ordinary sale that can be followed by a transfer. In any case, section 9 was omitted from the new Act in 1948, obviously because it was considered unnecessary. In light of the decisions since, one might wish we had a much broader curative provision than section 9. Section 6 (3) is the nearest approach to one in the present Act. It permits a judge to authorize registration of a disposition though proof of execution of consent or of the making of an acknowledgment is defective if he finds that the consent was executed or that acknowledgment was made. Its scope is very narrow.

The cases that brought about the repeal of the old Act were *Essery* v. *Essery* and *Tatko* v. *Leifke,* decided together in 1947. In each case the husband sold the homestead and in executing the transfer took the statutory affidavit that he had no wife. In *Tatko* the transfer was registered and later a further transfer was registered while in *Essery* the original transfer and a further transfer were registered together. Even in the latter situation the Appellate Division held that the second transfer was not void and the widow could not set it aside.[14] It might be noted that the curative provision, section 9, was inapplicable here because it applied only to a faulty consent or acknowledgment and not to a false affidavit.

These judgments were delivered on December 11, 1947. My memory is that the Law Society of Alberta or local bar associations or both recommended that the Dower Act be revised to provide that agreements for sale no longer be null and void if made without consent duly given but that on registration of the transfer the wife be given an action against the husband for half the purchase price. I do not recall what recommendation, if any, was made for the case of a mortgage, lease, or other disposition. In any event, a new Act was assented to on March 31, 1948. The explanatory note says:

> "*The Land Titles Act* was passed to give certainty to title to estates in land and to facilitate the proof thereof. The former *Dower Act* partially defeats the purpose of the *Land Titles Act* by giving rise to uncertainty to title by creating an unregistered interest in land which frequently cannot be discovered and which may override a title obtained on reliance upon the register. The courts have had to deal with numerous cases on *the Dower Act,* many of which arose due to the conflict in principle between it and *The Land Titles Act*.
>
> "The reason for the conflict between the two Acts was the provision that a transfer of a homestead made without the wife's consent was null and void for all purposes. The principal change made in the new Act is that the section making such a transfer null and void for all purposes is removed thereby removing the conflict with *The Land Titles Act*.
>
> "In lieu of making such a transfer null and void for all purposes, such a transfer is prohibited under penalty.
>
> "Under the old Act the wife had a right of action to have the land taken away from the first purchaser under such a transfer and revested in her husband, and the first purchaser had a right of action against the Assurance Fund for damages for the loss of the property purchased by him.
>
> "Under this Act the first purchaser obtains a valid title. Accordingly, the wife has no right of action to have the land revested in her husband. Instead of this the wife is given a right of action against her husband for her loss which is

> fixed by the Act at one-half the value of the property transferred without her consent. If the judgment against her husband is unsatisfied she may recover the amount of the judgment from the Assurance Fund."

The important point to note is that the Act still prohibits dispositions without consent and indeed goes further by imposing a penalty on the married person who makes such a disposition. Then it provides that the land ceases to be the homestead when a transfer by the married person is registered and thereupon the transferor is liable to his spouse in an action for damages in the amount of one-half of the consideration or value of the land. If the judgment is not paid recourse may be had to the Assurance Fund. Another change is a provision giving dower rights to a husband where the wife owns the homestead.

It was not long before queries were raised as to the effect of a sale made without a validly executed consent and objected to by the spouse or even by the vendor before registration of a transfer, and as to the validity of a mortgage, lease, oil lease, or easement. It is quite clear that these are all dispositions, but are not followed by the issue of a new title so the spouse never can have an action for half the purchase price.

The cases that have come before the courts are those of an agreement of sale, where the spouse objected before the time came to give a transfer. The first is *Pinsky* v. *Wass.*[15] In one transaction Pinsky agreed to sell his home to Wass and Wass agreed to sell his to Pinsky. Both husbands and their wives signed the document. No proper dower consent was executed by anyone. Soon after they moved the Pinskys regretted the exchange and brought action to have it set aside. It turned out that Mrs. Pinsky was the owner so Pinsky raised the absence of his consent, under the Dower Act. The trial Judge, McLaurin J., held that nothing in the Act suggests that the purchaser's title is infirm because of lack of consent by the vendor's wife: "having regard to the antecedent legislation repealed by this statute it is reasonable to assume that the legislature desired to get rid of the recurring circumstances where a purchaser's title in a *bona fide* transaction was completely bad." Absence of the statutory consent is not a ground for setting the transaction aside. However, he found for the plaintiffs on an "escape clause" in the agreement. On appeal, O'Connor, C.J.A. would have upheld the trial judge but did not find it necessary to consider the Dower Act. W.A. Macdonald, J.A. attached great importance to the prohibition of disposition without consent and to the penal provision. Each disposition was made in violation of a statutory prohibition and hence is unlawful and void and can confer no rights on either party. "In such a case the court leaves the parties in the situation in which it finds them." In this view the result would be that the Pinskys could not have the agreement set aside and Wass could not get specific performance. Parlee, J.A. with Frank Ford, J.A. concurring, agreed with the view of the trial judge that the agreement was not completely bad. He does not specifically say that the Pinskys might have avoided the agreement had they acted otherwise than they did but he so implies, for he says there was either a consent or waiver or estoppel. Clinton Ford, J.A. thought the agreement was invalid but that the Pinskys were estopped from setting up the non-compliance. Since a majority held the escape clause inapplicable the Wass appeal was allowed and specific performance granted. The Pinskys appealed to the Supreme Court, and succeeded under the escape clause. However, the views of Estey, J. (Kerwin J. concurring) on the Dower Act are of interest—"This direct prohibition, together with the provision for a penalty makes the agreement legally unenforceable at the instance of the married person," It is voidable at the instance of the spouse, Pinsky, and on the facts he is not estopped from asserting his rights. Kellock, J. (Locke J. concurring) held that the Pinskys could not invoke the Dower Act because Pinsky contracted as owner, and his wife by signing the document was undertaking to do whatever would be necessary to enable him to convey. In this view, no question of his dower rights is involved. It is perhaps fair to say that this case left remaining doubts as to the effect of the statute.

The second case is *Meduk* v. *Soja*.[16] Mrs. Meduk owned the home and entered into an informal agreement with the Sojas to sell for cash. When the real estate agent asked Meduk to sign he declined, saying it was not his property. He never executed a consent under the Dower Act. The Sojas took possession but a month later Mrs. Meduk notified them she was rescinding the agreement because they had not paid the purchase price. They then tendered the price which was refused. Soon after Mrs. Meduk took proceedings for possession. The Sojas counterclaimed for specific performance and Mrs. Meduk then raised her husband's refusal to sign a consent under the Dower Act. (Her husband was added as a party when the case was in the Appellate Division.)

The trial judge said: "I hold that this was a voidable agreement and that the plaintiff is estopped from denying the validity of the agreement in favour of the defendants, who are innocent purchasers. It would be inequitable to assist the plaintiff in avoiding specific performance of the agreement and her reliance on the Dower Act was a patent attempt to escape liability." Mrs. Meduk's appeal failed and she appealed to the Supreme Court. An unanimous judgment allowed her appeal. There was no contract in existence. Even if estoppel is available to the purchaser, which was not decided, there is no estoppel on the facts. Meduk's various actions indicating assent to the sale do not estop him from saying he did not consent in writing.

This judgment shows that a sale without consent is void. At least it is void until a transfer is registered. The history of the Alberta Dower Act, fortified by the explanatory note quoted above shows that this is not what the legislature intended; and nearly all the Alberta judges[17] in *Pinsky* and *Meduk*, knowing the background declined to hold the sale void. However, the Supreme Court looked at the prohibition against dispositions without consent, supported by a penalty of fine or imprisonment and concluded the disposition is void. It is easy to point out that during the many years when the Act said the disposition was null and void, it was not, and now when the Act no longer says it is, it is. One may perhaps say with the benefit of hindsight that the Act might have been better framed.

The latest case is *Shopsky* v. *Danyliuk.*[18] Shopsky transferred the homestead to himself and the defendant jointly. He took the statutory affidavit that he was not married and the transfer was registered. He and his wife then brought action for a declaration that the transfer was void. Milvain, J., held that it was. He referred to the provisions in the Act giving the wife an action against her husband for damages of half the consideration or value once the transfer has been registered, but held that it did not prevent the wife, and seemingly the husband who has committed perjury, from asserting that the transfer is void. With respect, this appears to give no effect to section 4 (2) which says that land ceases to be the homestead when a transfer is registered. The Act was intended to make the first transfer indefeasible and to convert the wife's right to refuse consent into an action against her husband for damages. Milvain, J., thought that if this was the intention the legislature could have said so. The suggestion made here is that the legislature did say so.

I know of no case under the 1948 Act dealing with a mortgage to which valid consent has not been given. During the many years when the disposition was good except in relation to the wife's potential life estate, it is clear that the mortgage was effective as against the mortgagor.[19] After the 1942 amendment and under the 1948 Act the question properly arises—can the wife obtain a declaration that the mortgage is entirely void?—or even, can the mortgagor himself? Probably a court would go to great lengths to avoid either result, but one cannot be sure. Certainly in *Reddick* the lessor and in *Pinsky* and *Meduk* and *Shopsky* the transferor seemed to have a status to impeach his own transaction. In *Parslow* v. *Moore,*[20] Walsh, J. dealt with a mortgagor's argument that the mortgage was completely void because his wife's consent was defective. (He knew it was for he procured it.) In the strongest language His Lordship said that in the circumstances the husband would be estopped even if the statute said the mortgage was completely void.

Another question is whether a purchaser, prior to registering title, could rescind the agreement. This suggestion may seem startling but if the transaction is void, he should be able to raise want of title in his vendor, unless perhaps he was fraudulent. There is as yet no direct authority on this point nor on the analogous situation of a lease, oil lease or easement.

This summary of Alberta law on the absence of a properly executed consent is designed to show that the effect of the present Act is not what it was intended to be; that the conflict in policy between the Dower Act and the Land Titles Act is unabated: and that the Dower Act should be changed.

It will help at this stage to see what we can learn from the laws of Saskatchewan, Manitoba and British Columbia, since all these provinces (and no others) have "homestead" laws, more or less like Alberta's.

Saskatchewan

Saskatchewan's Homesteads Act was originally passed in 1915. It never has in terms given the wife a life estate in the homestead. An obscurely worded provision (sec. 12) gives her the right to stay in possession or to the rents and profits if necessary for her support.[21]

Apart from this the wife's rights are purely negative—to prevent disposition by withholding consent. Yet it has been held, contrary to the jurisprudence of this province, that if the husband is in possession of a homestead when he makes a disposition without her consent, he is entitled to an order for possession.[22]

The requirements for consent (sections 4 and 5) are similar to those in Alberta except that the wife's consent is called an acknowledgment, and the officer who takes the certificate of acknowledgment is disqualified if he prepared the document or is otherwise interested in the transaction.

The Act has never clearly spelled out the consequences of a disposition made without a valid acknowledgment and certificate. It has never said that it is "null and void" or "invalid". There was for years doubt as to whether it was void or voidable, but the courts have never suggested that it is valid subject to her life estate. As already stated, the Act gives her none. However, one important difference from our law is that since 1948 we have had no curative provision.[23] Saskatchewan's curative section, 7 (3), says that the person taking the disposition is not bound to inquire whether the facts alleged in the husband's affidavit (that the land is not a homestead or that he has no wife or that his wife has not resided in the province since the marriage) or in the certificate of acknowledgment are true, and an instrument purporting to be completed according to the Act is valid and binding save as provided in section 11. Section 11 says that knowledge by the grantee that the land is the homestead of the grantor and that he has a wife whose consent is required but who is not a party to the instrument is fraud, and the wife may have the instrument or title issued thereon set aside.

The cases on the curative provisions can be divided into two groups (1) those where consent or acknowledgment was not properly given; (2) those where a false affidavit was taken.

Irregularities in the consent or certificate, no matter what they be, are almost sure to be cured by section 7 (3) as long as the wife signed her consent and a certificate of acknowledgment was given even though improperly unless, of course, there was knowledge by the grantee. Thus a purchaser has been granted specific performance where the wife gave her consent before a disqualified person.[24]

A more difficult problem faced the court in *Bonkowski* v. *Rose*.[25] The husband gave an oil lease and the lessee procured the wife's acknowledgment in blank. The lessee then obtained the signature of a qualified officer to the certificate of acknowledgment though in fact the officer never saw the wife. Later the lessee assigned the lease to an oil company which had no knowledge of the irregularities.

The question was whether the assignee can invoke the curative provision. Procter, J.A. held that on a proper construction of the relevant sections the curative provision protects only the person who took under the original disposition and not an assignee from him. Space does not permit an examination of this contention but it seems to me to be sound. Proctor, J.A. also held that previous decisions show the disposition to be void rather than voidable so that the assignee is in no stronger a position than the assignor.

However, the majority held that the curative sections extend to the assignee.

In the subsequent case of *Prudential Trust Co.* v. *Forseth* the Supreme Court considered a number of objections to a disposition of minerals, including the argument that the acknowledgment and certificate were not properly given because they did not describe accurately the actual disposition. The Court held that these irregularities did not mislead the wife. The important part of the judgment is that which approves of *Bonkowski* in holding that an assignee can invoke the curative section.[26]

The lesson we can take from these last two cases is this. If a curative provision is desirable it will be important to determine as a matter of policy whether its protection should extend to an assignee and then to frame a provision that leaves no doubt.

The leading case of *Friess* v. *Imperial Oil* deals with a forged consent. The husband gave an oil lease. As his wife was sick, the lessee's agent had the lessor's daughter sign her mother's name and had a Justice of the Peace sign the certificate. He never saw the wife. Three years later when a better offer was made the wife brought action. The lease was set aside. "The authorities establish that the object of the Act is to prevent the husband from alienating the homestead without the consent of his wife and, in my opinion, it is clear that as against a non-consenting wife every transfer, agreement for sale, lease or other instrument intended to convey any interest in a homestead is invalid and void."[27] The court rejected the defendant's argument of estoppel. Assuming the wife could ratify, she did not. The defendant is bound by its agent's knowledge of the facts and this knowledge is fraud under section 11.

Coming now to the second group of cases, where the husband has taken a false affidavit, a number of judgments deal with affidavits that the land was not the homestead. In *Farmer's Mutual Petroleum* v. *Jackson*[28] the disposition was a transfer of minerals. The husband thought "homestead" meant land he had homesteaded. The purchaser's agent knew he was married and even had been in his home. The trial judge found the agent had knowledge it was the home and set the transaction aside. This was sustained on an equal division in the Court of Appeal.

The Supreme Court dealt for the first time with the case of a false affidavit in *Prudential Trust Co.* v. *Olson,* decided at the same time as *Forseth.* The original grantee assigned to Canadian Williston Petroleums, a *bona fide* purchaser. Martland, J. for the Court held the assignee was protected by the curative section.[29]

Manitoba

In Manitoba, common law dower was abolished in 1885, but in time pressure came for a homestead law. Accordingly, the Dower Act was passed in 1918. Like Alberta's it applies equally in favour of husband and wife, but for convenience I shall speak of the wife's rights. She is given a life estate in the homestead, but the Court of Appeal in *Crichton* v. *Zelentisky*[30] said that it is not actually vested in her on the husband's death but only when the executor conveys it to her and in the meantime she may not enter on the land. The same case held that the life interest is not exempt from her late husband's creditors. Certainly the first holding is not correct for Alberta. As for the second, her life interest is protected in Alberta as against executor creditors but seemingly not as against ordinary creditors.[31]

A disposition without her consent "shall be invalid and ineffective" and the requirements of a formal consent and certificate of acknowledgment are much like those of Alberta and Saskatchewan. Similar too, is the requirement that the grantee take an affidavit that he has no wife or that the land is not the homestead. In addition, there is the novel requirement that where the wife consents the husband must take an affidavit that the consenting woman is, in fact, his wife. In other words, an affidavit is needed even when the wife gives her consent. This has no counterpart in Alberta or Saskatchewan.

The curative provisions are, of course, important. A certificate of acknowledgment is conclusive evidence of the truth of the statements therein except as against a grantee with actual knowledge of their untruth, (section 8 (4)) and an affidavit is valid except as against a grantee with actual knowledge of untruth or who is fraudulent, and there is no duty to inquire as to the truth of the affidavit (section 8 (7)). In principle these curative sections are similar to those of Saskatchewan.

There has been a number of cases in which the grantee has invoked these provisions, and where the disposition has been followed by a new title the grantee has the benefit of the various "conclusive" provisions of the Real Property (Land Titles) Act. An early case points out that where the transferor swore the land was not his homestead and the wife later alleged the transferees knew it was, the burden is on her to prove actual knowledge,[32] and the case is the same where a mortgagor swore he had no wife and there was no suggestion that the mortgagee knew he did.[33]

Manitoba, like Saskatchewan, has had to consider the case of a forged consent. The difficult question is whether the wife is bound where the grantee has acted in good faith. In other words, does the rule that a grantee must be sure of the identity of his grantor apply in favour of the wife? In *Chudyj* v. *Canada Permanent Loan Corp.*[34] the husband forged the wife's signature and the commissioner for oaths, who was agent of the mortgagee, quite improperly took the certificate of acknowledgment though the wife had never appeared before him. The mortgagee foreclosed and then the wife brought action. By a majority of three to two the Court of Appeal held that the company was not affected by its agent's fraud because in falsely signing the certificate he was acting as a public official and not as agent. The majority were clearly influenced by the seriousness from a mortgagee's standpoint of holding a mortgage void in these circumstances. One of them, Richards, J.A. said:

> "It should be borne in mind that there was no provision for dower in Manitoba prior to 1918, and that, when the legislation was introduced, the dangers and troubles of it were considered. The Legislature then clearly endeavoured to protect innocent purchasers. In doing so it provided drastic safeguards. The protection given *bona fide* transactions by *The Dower Act* is, in some respects, much greater than is given by The Real Property Act, 1934, ch. 38, which does not protect persons who rely on instruments which are discovered later to be forgeries. The case of *Gibbs* v. *Messer* [1891] A.C. 248, 60 L.J.P.C. 20, and following cases do not apply to *The Dower Act*."

The dissenting judges held that the provision curing defective acknowledgments does not apply where the wife did not sign the consent. They were also prepared to impute the knowledge of the agent to his principal. In this type of case it seems proper to do so; to protect the principal seems unjust.

In Manitoba where the disposition is "invalid and ineffective" the same question can arise as under a statute where it is void—viz. can the grantee invoke the non-compliance as well as the grantor's wife? Considering the purpose of the Act, one is inclined to answer no because the Act is for the benefit of the wife. On the other hand, if the transaction is regarded as void, not merely voidable, then there is no contract and either party can invoke the fact. In *Wall* v. *Dyck*[35] neither party to the agreement for sale thought of the Dower Act. The buyer, wanting to escape, notified the vendor who quickly produced his wife's consent. The Court of Appeal held he was too late. In Saskatchewan, on the other hand, a seller has been allowed time to produce his wife's consent.[36] This seems fair, but if correct, means the transaction is voidable rather than void. A related question is that of a buyer (or seller) who deliberately enters into an agreement knowing the Act has not been complied with and then brings action to have the agreement declared void. Can he be met with the defence that he does not come into court with clean hands? These questions, and indeed the whole scope of estoppel, have not been worked out in any of the prairie provinces.

The Prudential Trust Company has made its contribution to the law of dower in Manitoba as in Saskatchewan. The case is *Brown* v. *Prairie Leaseholds Ltd.*[37] The transaction was of a type now familiar but the farmer and his wife did not wait long to take proceedings. As is so often the case there was a sharp dispute as to the facts. The trial judge believed the plaintiffs and found that the documents were not completely filled out when the wife signed her consent and gave her acknowledgment to the commissioner who was the grantee's agent. The trial judgment seems to say that there was no contract at all because the document indicated a disposition different from the one Brown thought he was making, but the judgment then speaks of the contract being induced by fraud and then holds that the farmer's subsequent acts did not constitute an affirmation.

The violation of the Dower Act was an alternate ground of the decision. The wife signed voluntarily but she did not consent to all the dispositions in the documents; she thought she was consenting to much less and on her part it is *non est factum*. It was found too that she did not sign "apart from her husband" and that this requirement is as strict as the requirements of the Wills Act. The curative clause did not help the company because its agent took the acknowledgment. The company invoked *Chudyj* for the proposition that its agent in so doing was a public officer. The court held that nevertheless he was the company's agent immediately before and after, and his knowledge of untruth of the certificate was the company's knowledge. This seems sound. If a purchaser uses its agent as a commissioner to take acknowledgments, then his knowledge of the untruth of a statement in an acknowledgment should be attributed to the principal. The Court of Appeal dismissed the appeal without reasons[38] and in refusing leave to appeal to the Supreme Court of Canada[39] said that the question of the wife's consent under the Dower Act "is only of academic importance if the said transfer and assignment were fraudulently obtained, as found by both courts."

British Columbia

The last province to examine is British Columbia. Common law dower, as modified by the provisions of the 1833 Act persisted until 1925 when it was abolished. Then in 1948 the Wife's Protection Act was passed. Its most significant feature is that it applies in favour of a wife only after she has filed an "entry" in the Land Registry (Land Titles) Office against the homestead. This entry is analogous to a caveat by a wife under the prairie Acts but differs in that she has no life interest in the homestead without it.

When she has made entry she is entitled to a life estate in the homestead, and every disposition "shall be null and void for all purposes unless made with the consent in writing of the wife." The formalities of consent and certificate of acknowledgment are similar to those of the other provinces. Many of the provisions seem to be taken from the Alberta Act as it stood just before 1948. The curative provision (section 10 (1)) is almost identical with our old section 9 save that it is confined to a "sale of the homestead" (instead of "sale of property") and thus would perhaps not cover an oil lease. Needless to say there is no provision for an affidavit by the husband that he has no wife or that the land is not his homestead. Under British Columbia's scheme such affidavits have no place. The existence of the entry is notice to all that the land is the homestead and that the owner has a wife. To date, most of the cases have been over the issue of removing the entry or dispensing with consent and need not be noted.

In one case the wife made entry after her husband had made an agreement for sale. It was held her entry was too late. The Act renders void dispositions made after entry, not before, so the entry must be discharged.[40] In another case the husband secretly sold the homestead. After the conveyance was registered the wife brought action to have the sale declared void. The buyer had acted *bona fide* so obviously the wife could not succeed.[41] These are the only reported cases where the wife has challenged a disposition. In time cases will doubtless arise where a wife will allege she did not know what she was consenting to, or that her husband was in the room. The curative section will cover these cases.

Conclusion

The question now must be asked—what should the law of Alberta be? In answering this, we should keep in mind these considerations:

1. The importance from a social standpoint of the wife's claim to some form of control over and interest in the home.
2. The principles of the Torrens system and the interests of a grantee.
3. Other things being equal, the desirability of making such changes in a framework for which we, in this province, are accustomed.
4. The desirability of reducing the inconvenience and uncertainties in conveyancing.

The following alternatives emerge:

First: to abolish the need of consent. The main arguments in favour are (1) it would simplify conveyancing, reduce litigation and remove uncertainties; (2) the purpose of homestead laws is largely served by the Family Relief Act. As against this, the Family Relief Act will not protect a widow whose husband has transferred all his property and it does not give her any direct control over the home. There is a growing acceptance of the idea in England that the wife should have some kind of a claim to the home, and New Zealand has a Joint Family Homes Act.[42] We have given the wife homestead rights for forty years and on the balance many consider they should be preserved.

Second: to adopt a plan like British Columbia's that gives homestead rights when the wife files an entry and not otherwise. This certainly is simpler than our system and it gives third parties notice of the wife's claim. The only disadvantage is that wives may not know of their right to file an entry or may be reluctant to file.

Third: to bring our Act into line with those of Saskatchewan and Manitoba. This means that the cumbrous conveyancing remains but that there is a fairer balance between the interests of wives and third parties. A curative section carefully drawn in the light of the decisions in those provinces will reduce almost to zero the possibility that a *bona fide* grantee will find his interest is in jeopardy, though it is no guarantee against litigation on matters of fact.

One might advance as a fourth possibility a return to our law as it stood prior to 1942—that the consent be required but that the only consequence of an improper disposition is to preserve the wife's life interest. This would have the virtue of disabling a grantor from impeaching his own transaction. On the other hand, it reduces the power of his spouse to prevent a disposition and this is one of the main purposes of homestead legislation.

As a fifth suggestion one might propose community of property. I know little of the subject, but am not inclined to exchange known terrors for unknown. We might find that such a drastic change would be equivalent to throwing out the baby with the bath-water.

Assuming we retain a statute basically the same as our own but altered along the lines of British Columbia's or Saskatchewan's and Manitoba's then a number of subordinate questions should be considered. The length of this paper precludes discussion but I shall set out those that occur to me.

1. Should the husband continue to have dower rights? (My opinion is no.)
2. Should dower rights continue to include a life estate in chattels (section 2 (b) (v)?
3. Should a court have power to order partition or sale of a jointly-owned homestead?[43]
4. Should a spouse who has released dower rights without consideration be able to change her mind as at present (secs. 8 and 9)?
5. Should a disposition be void where the consent is annexed to the instrument and the spouse has omitted to sign the instrument though she has signed the consent?[44]
6. Should the spouse's potential life estate be assignable by him or within reach of his creditors? It may be now.[45]
7. Should the vested life estate be exigible under execution or subject to sale for ordinary debts?[46]
8. Should the action for damages by the spouse be retained—and the claim against the Assurance Fund?
9. Should it be possible for homestead rights to exist in more than one home, as at present?

In conclusion I trust that those interested in law reform will be persuaded that any one of my three proposed oils will reduce the squeaks in the social and legal mechanism.

Notes

1 6 Chitty's Law Journal 133 (1956).

2 *Robertson* v. *Robertson* (1951) 1 W.W.R. (N.S.) 183.

3 *Re McLeod* [1929] 3 W.W.R. 241 per Harvey, C.J.

4 [1920] 2 W.W.R. 481.

5 [1918] 2 W.W.R. 382.

6 Note 5, *supra*.

7 Stuart, J. changed his mind in *Johnson* v. *Johnson* [1922] 2 W.W.R. 272.

8 1919 c. 40. This amendment also said that execution by the wife of a disposition is a consent. Perhaps the legislature intended that execution need not be acknowledged as a consent but *Reddick* v.

Pearson [1948] 2 W.W.R. 1144 holds that it must be.

9 In *Re Miller* [1928] 3 W.W.R. 643 Walsh, J. held that the 1926 amendment made a disposition without consent absolutely null and void.

10 [1939] 1 W.W.R. 734, aff'd. [1939] 2 W.W.R. 237.

11 *Dach* v. *Bochan* [1948] 1 W.W.R. 622. That case holds that even an executor can resist an action for specific performance where the widow did not consent.

12 [1948] 2 W.W.R. 1144.

13 [1951] 4 W.W.R. (N.S.) 77, (1952) 5 W.W.R. (N.S.) 1, [1953] 1 S.C.R. 127.

14 [1947] 2 W.W.R. 1044.

15 [1950] 2 W.W.R. 1278, (1951) 2 W.W.R. (N.S.) 49, [1953] 1 S.C.R. 399.

16 [1958] S.C.R. 167.

17 W.A. MacDonald, J.A., in *Pinsky* is the exception. In *Shopsky* v. *Danyliuk,* note 19 *infra,* Milvain, J. thought that every contract expressly prohibited by statute is void and that the "null and void" provision was omitted from the 1948 Act as *surplusage*.

18 [1959–60] 30 W.W.R. 647. An alternative ground of the judgment is that the transferee knew Shopsky was married and therefore her title is tainted with fraud. This is one of the exceptions to indefeasibility under the Land Titles Act, and this ground of the decision is not the subject of my criticism.

19 *Royal Bank* v. *Wallsmith* [1945] 1 W.W.R. 713 at 717.

20 [1930] 2 W.W.R. 340.

21 E.g. *Re Wenet* [1949] 2 W.W.R. 85.

22 E.g. *Audoorn* v. *Audoorn* [1935] 2 W.W.R. 362.

23 Sec. 6 (3) can be ignored. Even the old Sec. 9 (1) applied in *McColl Frontenac Oil Co.* v. *Hamilton* was much narrower than Saskatchewan's Sec. 7 (3).

24 *Lavoie* v. *Marchildon* (1953) 9 W.W.R. (N.S.) 263.

25 (1955) 16 W.W.R. 481.

26 [1960] S.C.R. 210 at 221–23.

27 (1954) 12 W.W.R. 151 at 155.

28 (1956) 19 W.W.R. 625: compare *Re Scott* [1942] 2 W.W.R. 485.

29 [1960] S.C.R. 227 at 232–34.

30 [1946] 2 W.W.R. 206.

31 Compare *Re Conlin* (1914) 7 W.W.R. 187 with *Re Ferguson* (1957) 23 W.W.R. 521.

32 *McKinnon* v. *Smith* [1925] 3 W.W.R. 290.

33 *Reep* v. *Shuckett* (1955) 15 W.W.R. 375.

34 [1937] 2 W.W.R. 225: compare *Friess* v. *Imperial Oil* note 28 *supra*.

35 *Wall* v. *Dyck* [1950] 1 W.W.R. 699.

36 E.g. *Neilsen* v. *Jenewein* [1924] 2 W.W.R. 696.

37 (1953) 9 W.W.R. (N.S.) 577.

38 (1954) 12 W.W.R. (N.S.) 464.

39 (1954) 13 W.W.R. (N.S.) 40.

40 *Linton's Case* (1951) 3 W.W.R. (N.S.) 509.

41 *Rousseau* v. *Rousseau* (1956) 19 W.W.R. 237.

42 See Macdonald, Observations on the Land Law in the Common Law Provinces of Canada, 197 at 220, in Canadian Jurisprudence (ed. McWhinney) (1958); Milner, Beneficial Ownership in the Family Home: Recent Trends in the British Commonwealth, 37 Can. Bar Rev. 473 (1959); Compare *Thompson* v. *Thompson* (1961) 26 D.L.R. (2d) 1 (S.C.C.).

43 *Robertson* v. *Robertson* (1951) 1 W.W.R. (N.S.) 183 says there is no power; contra, *McWilliam* v. *McWilliam* (1960) 31 W.W.R. 480. The latter case holds that an order for sale under the Partition Act is not a disposition under the Dower Act. See also *Fritz* v. *Fritz* [1950] 1 W.W.R. 446, 1105, (1951) 4 W.W.R. (N.S.) 650 (Man.); *Evans* v. *Evans* (1951) 1 W.W.R. (N.S.) 280 (B.C.).

McWilliam went to the Appellate Division which found it unnecessary to decide whether *Robertson* was correctly decided: (1961) 34 W.W.R. 476.

44 In *Reynolds* v. *Ackerman,* 1953. reported (1960) 32 W.W.R. 289, McBride, J. held it is under sec. 5 (5).

45 I have been told of an instance in which the spouse made an assignment for the benefit of creditors and the assignee filed a caveat against the homestead thus rendering difficult a sale by the owner. In *Proskurniak* v. *Sawchuk* (1959–60) 30 W.W.R. 407, Smith, J. held that the ex-

ecution creditor of the spouse may properly file against the homestead a caveat covering the writ of execution. In an unreported judgment the Appellate Division set aside the caveat on the narrow ground that it did not properly set out the interest it purported to protect.

46 At present it is protected against execution creditors but paradoxically not against ordinary creditors: *Re Ferguson* (1957) 23 W.W.R. 521.

1962

Limitation of Actions in Tort in Alberta

Reprinted from
(1962–64) 2 Alberta Law Review
pp. 41–57

This article deals with an area of provincial legislation in which a great deal of uncertainty existed, namely, the time limitation in which legal action can be brought for damages arising out of the wrongdoing of another. As legislation stood at that time, various limitation periods were prescribed for different classes of tort actions, rendering the law neither "ascertainable, definite, simple or fair" (as stated in the conclusion of this article).

It did produce results: new legislation was introduced in 1966—by the addition of a new Part to the Limitations Act—eliminating most of the confusing limitation periods.

It is generally considered that this article gave the initial impetus to concern for the establishment of a law reform body in Alberta. The immediate result was formation by the Alberta bar of a Law Revision Committee. This was a voluntary group (of which Bowker was a member), but no formal work was undertaken. Following this, however, the Benchers of the Law Society pushed for the establishment of a proper Institute, working through the government and the University, resulting eventually in the Alberta Institute of Law Research and Reform coming into being in 1968, with Bowker as its first Director.

The purpose of this paper is to examine the law of Alberta on the subject of limitation of actions in tort; to see whether the law is uncertain or unfair; and if it is, to suggest changes in the statute law.

Until 1935 this province had no general Statute of Limitations.[1] For claims in tort, the English Limitations Act of 1623 applied. Thus, when an action was brought against the owner of a car who ran down a pedestrian, the Appellate Division in 1924 in *Burd* v. *Macaulay*[2] had to decide whether the action was one of battery (four years) or an action upon the case (six years). The Appellate Division held that the claim was in battery and so was barred because the action was brought more than four years after the accident. Indeed this problem still haunts the courts of other provinces where the local statute is based on the Act of 1623.[3]

Statute of Limitations

However, this province in 1935 adopted a general Act[4] recommended by the Conference of Commissioners on Uniformity of Legislation. This was a great step forward. We are not concerned with those parts dealing with claims relating to land or trusts, but solely with Part I, which prescribes the periods for tort actions.

These are:

Section 5(1)...

(c) actions for defamation, whether libel or slander,

(i) within two years after publication of the libel or the speaking of the slanderous words, or

(ii) where special damage is the gist of the action, within two years after the occurrence of such damage;

(d) actions for

(i) trespass to the person, assault, battery, wounding or other injury to the person, whether arising from an unlawful act or from negligence;

(ii) false imprisonment

(iii) malicious prosecution, or

(iv) seduction,

within two years after the cause of action arose;

(e) actions for

(i) trespass or injury to real property or chattels whether direct or indirect, and whether arising from an unlawful act or from negligence, or

(ii) the taking away, conversion or detention of chattels,

within six years after the cause of action arose...

(j) any other action not in this Act or any other Act specifically provided for, within six years after the cause of action therein arose.

The important point to note is that actions in negligence for personal injury must be brought within two years, and actions for injury to real property or chattels within six years, after the cause of action arose.

Actions for assault, false imprisonment, malicious prosecution and seduction do not require examination. As for defamation, it should be noted that the Defamation Act of 1947 does away with the need to prove special damage in any case. In addition it has special provisions requiring notice before action against a newspaper or broadcasting station, and also requiring that action against them be brought within six months after the plaintiff learns of the defamation.[5]

There are several miscellaneous torts not specifically mentioned in section 5, such as injurious falsehood, conspiracy, and inducing breach of contract. It would seem that these may be brought within six years under section 5 (1) (j). The Supreme Court has held that an action for adultery is within this provision.[6]

It is the action for negligence that raises most problems and this paper will deal particularly with that action. In connection with the application of section 5, there are three questions that must be considered:

(1) when does the cause of action arise?

(2) when does the time expire?

(3) what is a cause of action in tort as distinct from one in contract?

(1) Where the tort is complete when the wrongful act is done, as in assault or false imprisonment, it is obvious that the cause of action arises the moment the wrong is committed. However in the case of negligence, the gist of the action is the damage and not the wrongful act. In almost every case, there is some immediate damage, so for practical purposes the action is complete on the day the defendant commits his negligent act, and time begins to run from that day. It is hard to conceive of an ordinary accident in which no immediate damage occurs, but if there were, then time would run from the date when damage first arose. There are other types of case, however, where there is an interval of time between the wrongful act and the damage. For example, the defendant wrongfully removes the support from plaintiff's land in 1956 and the first damage, in the form of subsidence, occurs a year later. This is when time begins to run and successive actions may be brought for successive damage.[7] Another exceptional case is that of an employer who is negligent in permitting dust or fumes to enter the air so that after a time his employee's lungs are infected. In this case time begins to run from the damage, which may be long after the wrongful act. On the other hand the damage may accrue before the employee is aware of the fact. In that case time is running against him before he knows he has a cause of action.[8] This is of course harsh on the plaintiff. However the problem is not likely to arise in Alberta because these claims come under the Workmen's Compensation Act.

(2) As to the expiration of the time for bringing action, the rule is that the last day is the anniversary of the day on which the cause of action arose. Thus, if a personal injury were sustained on January 31, 1960 the writ could be issued on January 31, 1962 and still be in time. One could argue that the last day is January 30 because in theory the plaintiff could have issued his statement of claim on the day of the accident, and the Act says the action must be brought *within* two years. Thus if one were to count the day of the accident, the last day would be January 30. However the day of the accident is excluded and thus the action may be brought on the anniversary.[9]

(3) Turning now to the question whether an action is in contract or tort, this may be important in the case of personal injuries. The period is two years in tort and six in contract. The problem could arise where a person has a contract with another, (e.g. a guest at a hotel, a spectator at a performance, a passenger on a train, or an employee), and is injured through the negligence of that other. As a general rule he can base his claim on contract or tort, but where it becomes necessary to classify his action the cases say that his action sounds in tort because the obligation to take care arises under the common law and not under a provision in the contract. Thus he should bring his action within two years. The problem however has rarely arisen.[10]

In England, Parliament removed any doubt when it amended the Limitations Act in 1954 to provide that all action for personal injuries shall be brought within three years whether the duty arose under a statute or contract or independently of either.[11]

One reason why there are comparatively few cases interpreting the tort provisions in the general Act (in addition to the existence of the Workmen's Compensation Act already mentioned) is the existence of special statutes which are not only considerable in number, but more important, very wide in their scope. On ordinary principles of construction, a special act prevails over a general one, and in Alberta this principle is set out in the Limitations Act itself. It provides:

> Section 5(2). "Nothing in this section extends to an action where the time for bringing the action is by statute specifically limited".

Vehicles and Highway Traffic Act

The first of these special provisions is section 131 of the Vehicles and Highway Traffic Act.[12] It was enacted in 1941 and has its counterpart in Ontario and the other western provinces.

"(1) No action shall be brought against a person for the recovery of damages occasioned by a motor vehicle, after the expiration of twelve months from the time when the damages were sustained".

(2) [lapse of time is not a bar to a counterclaim or third party proceedings in respect of damages occasioned in the same accident]

(3) [repealed]

(4) [the court may extend the time a further twelve months where the action is brought against the registered owner and it later appears that he was not the actual owner]

Is there any good reason for a shorter period in the case of automobile accidents than for negligence actions generally? I doubt it, but will leave the question here.

Three important questions arise under sec. 131:

(1) When does it apply?

(2) When are damages occasioned by a motor vehicle?

(3) Is a plaintiff under disability (from infancy or unsoundness of mind) bound by the section?

(1) This special limitation was first placed in Ontario's Highway Traffic Act in 1923. During the first few years the courts of Ontario tended to construe it narrowly. The Court of Appeal held in 1926[13] that it is confined to actions for the recovery of damages for a violation of the Act and does not apply to a common law action, e.g., where a passenger sued a tax company for injuries when the driver negligently closed the door on her hand. The same court held in 1928 that the section would not apply if the vehicle were

not on the highway.[14] In that case, the plaintiff on a sidewalk was struck by a bale of hay carried on a truck which was on a highway. The court held the section to apply.

The tendency to construe the section narrowly came to an end with *Dufferin Paving Co.* v. *Anger*.[15] The words in the section should be given their natural and ordinary sense. Thus they apply to an action for damage done to a house by vibrations caused by trucks passing along the highway. The case also says by way of dictum that the section would apply where the plaintiff has a contract with the defendant, for example, where the plaintiff is a passenger in a taxicab. In 1959 an Ontario judge held that the section is not confined to accidents on a highway but applies to one on a farm.[16]

In Alberta, the only reported case on this problem is *Northern Alberta Dairy Pool* v. *Strong*.[17] The defendant was a carrier who conveyed by truck a cargo of cheese owned by the plaintiff. A fire broke out en route thanks to a faulty carburetor, and then a second fire of unknown origin. The cargo was destroyed. Action was brought more than a year later. The defendant pleaded section 131. Milvain J. held that the action was against a common carrier on its common law liability and that the section does not apply. He thought it inconsistent that a common carrier using horses would be subject to a longer period than one using a motor vehicle, and distinguished *Dufferin Paving*. The point seems to be debatable. One can think of other cases where the time limitation does vary with the vehicle. Certainly if a carrier of passengers operates a stage coach as well as a motor bus, the periods are different where a passenger brings action for negligence.

(2) The second ground of decision in *Strong* brings us to the second question—when are damages "occasioned" by a motor vehicle? Mr. Justice Milvain held (and this may be the real ground of the decision) that the damage was not occasioned by the motor vehicle but by the fire, and its origin was unknown. With respect, this ground for the decision seems sound.

There are a number of cases from other provinces on the meaning of "occasioned".[18] Damages are not occasioned by a motor vehicle where its owner claims for damages to a vehicle against a person who had left a boulder on the road[19] or who had allowed his horse to get on the road.[20] The defendant cannot successfully invoke section 131. The damages were occasioned not by the car, but by the boulder or horse and were occasioned *to* the car. In several cases the owner of a car had lent it to another who damaged it by running it off the road. In an action by the owner against the driver for the damage to the car, the defendant cannot obtain the benefit of the section;[21] nor can a bailee who has improperly let someone else drive the car and that person is in a collision.[22]

What then is the position where the passenger in a car brings action against the driver who has been in collision with a train? In an early case, Riddell J.A. said that the damages were not occasioned by a motor vehicle at all, but by the locomotive which was enabled so to occasion them by the negligence of the driver.[23] On the other hand the Saskatchewan Court of Appeal has applied the section in similar circumstances.[24] The later view seems preferable. Indeed where the car hits a cow, or train, it seems correct to say that if the owner of the cow or train were to counterclaim against the owner of the car, he could invoke the section as a defence to the counterclaim.

Sometimes it is said that "occasioned by a motor vehicle" means "occasioned by the driver of a motor vehicle". However, the driver cannot invoke this interpretation where the owner of the vehicle brings action against him for damage to it.

(3) The question of disability from infancy or unsoundness of mind is not difficult. Sec. 5(2) of the Limitations Act, already quoted, says

> "Nothing in this section extends to an action where the time for bringing the action is specially limited by statute."

Section 8 says that a person entitled to bring an action for tort under section 5(1) may do so within two years after the disability ceases. Since an action within section 131 of the Vehicles Act is outside section 5(1) of the Limitations Act, it seems clear that section 8 does not apply in favour of a plaintiff whose action is within section 131. Time runs against him immediately. The Court of Appeal of Saskatchewan has so held,[25] and the Limitations Act and Vehicles Act are for present purposes the same in both provinces.

It might be noted that British Columbia's equivalent to sec. 131 has its own disability provision enabling an infant to bring action within a year of reaching twenty-one.[26]

Municipal Acts

In Canada, municipal statutes often give the municipality the benefit of a short period in actions for damages caused by breach of the statutory duty to repair highways. Our City Act imposes a one-year period and expressly extends its benefit to officials, employees and agents of the City. Notice of the claim must be given in sixty days (twenty-one in snow and ice cases), but notice is not required in the case of death of the person injured or where there is both reasonable excuse for failure to give it and no prejudice to the City.[27]

There is a separate section, 695, for negligence claims.[28] It is generally the same as the non-repair section. The main difference is that it does not specifically apply to an action against a servant or official of the City. Yet it says, "no action shall be brought" for injury or damage alleged to be caused by the City, its officials, employees or agents. This raises a nice question in statutory construction. A similar section has been applied in favour of a street car conductor who was joined with the City as defendant.[29] However, in the recent case of *Herdink* v. *Calgary*[30] the Appellate Division held that a bus driver employed by the City and joined as a defendant is not within section 695 and therefore cannot invoke the plaintiff's failure to give notice.

The judgment points out that unless the section were confined to actions against the City, it would literally apply in favour of an employee who is negligent outside the course of his duties.[30a]

The most startling provision in the City Act, and one which was the subject of two decisions in 1961, (sec. 453) will be discussed later in connection with the Public Officers Protection Act.

Under the Town and Village Act, the only special limitation provision is in connection with the duty to keep streets in repair. In that case notice must be given within one month, and action brought within a year after the cause of action arose.[31] The provisions for excusing notice are like those in the City Act. The position of Municipal Districts is the same, save that the action for non-repair must be brought within six months.[32] The Municipal Districts Act applies to counties.[33] This means that actions in negligence, except for non-repair, are within the general limitation act or any other Act that may apply instead. In fact a municipality is a public authority,[34] so where its own Act is silent it is entitled to the benefit of the special provisions of the Public Officers Protection Act.[35] This Act can conveniently be examined now.

Public Officers Protection Act

It provides;

> Section 2(1) Notwithstanding anything in any Act or in the Consolidated Rules of the Supreme Court, where an action, prosecution or other proceeding is commenced in the Province against a person
> (a) for an act done in pursuance or execution or intended execution of his duty as a public officer, or
> (b) in respect of an alleged neglect or default in the execution of his duty or authority as a public officer,
> the provisions of this Act apply.
> (2) An action, prosecution or proceeding mentioned in subsection (1), does not lie and shall not be instituted
> (a) unless it is commenced within six months after the act, neglect or default complained of, or
> (b) where there is a continuance of injury or damage, within six months after the ceasing thereof.
> (7) This Act does not affect any proceeding by a department of the Government against an authority or officer or a city, town, village, county or municipal district.

This Act is based on the English Public Authorities Protection Act of 1893 (repealed in 1954) and is found in a number of the common law provinces. It does not define public authority or public officer and this alone creates grave doubts as to whom it applies. In Alberta a city policeman[36] and a member of the R.C.M.P.[37] have been held to be public officers. In *Halpin* v. *Reginam*[38] a truck driver for a Dominion experimental farm was denied the benefit of the Act. There may however be an implication in the judgment that he was a public officer, for the emphasis is on the fact that he was not engaged in the execution of a public duty when he committed the negligent act. Elsewhere, school boards and teachers, public hospitals and a variety of municipal and Crown officials and servants, even unto a private in the army, whose duties were to drive a truck,[39] all have been held to be within the Act. Our Appellate Division has held that a man working with his tractor on a highway under the supervision of a district engineer of the Department of Public Works is not a public officer.[40] This case suggests that the Act is confined to public officers who exercise a degree of responsibility or control, though in the case of the army private, the English Court of Appeal rejected this test.

A question that has not arisen in Alberta relates to the limitation in an action against the Crown under the Proceedings Against the Crown Act[41] enacted in 1959. That Act specifies no period. In my opinion, the Public Officers Protection Act applies.[42]

Two recent cases from Calgary disclose a curious situation mentioned earlier in connection with the City Act. Part VII of that Act is headed "Public Utilities" and section 438 makes it clear that the City is liable for damage caused by the negligent operation of its utilities. In the first case, *Harvey* v. *Calgary,*[43] the plaintiff was injured when he touched a live electric wire belonging to the City's electric distribution system. His action was commenced within a year, but after six months. The City invoked section 453 which is near the end of Part VII and reads:

> "The City, its officers, agents and servants, shall be deemed to have the like protection in the exercise of its and their respective offices and the execution of its and their duties as public officers have under the laws of the Province."

From this the City argued that the Public Officers Protection Act applies to actions relating to utilities. Milvain J. found for the City on the merits, but went on to express the opinion that section 453 brings the Public Officers Protection Act into play where the action relates to utilities.

In the later case of *McGinn* v. *Calgary,* decided by Cairns, J. on December 29, 1961,[44] the plaintiff was injured by a city bus and the action like Harvey's was brought within the year but after six months. His Lordship held that the limitation provisions in the City Act provide a complete code for negligence actions and that sec. 453 does not override them.

Time does not permit an analysis of the two judgments, but if the view of Milvain J. is correct, sec. 453 should be repealed forthwith.

The foregoing account shows that it is very hard to determine who is a public officer. In connection with school boards and teachers, it is probable that plaintiffs and perhaps school authorities as well overlooked the fact that boards and teachers are public authorities,[45] and this may be the reason why the School Act was amended in 1952 to provide that the board, officers and teachers "shall be deemed" to be public officers.[46]

Even when a defendant is found to be a public officer he is entitled to the protection of the Act only for an act done in pursuance of his duty as a public officer or in respect of neglect in the execution of his duty or authority as a public officer. If the act is not done in pursuance of a duty, but merely in execution of an incidental power then he does not have the benefit of the Act.[47]

Sometimes the action is not for negligence but for some other tort such as assault, or false imprisonment. In these cases the courts refuse to give the defendant the benefit of statutes like our Protection Act if the defendant's act is completely outside his duties or is done in bad faith.[48]

Another feature of the Act is the short period for bringing action—six months. In no other important limitation provision in Alberta is the period less than a year.

Finally, section 2 says, "Notwithstanding anything in any Act or in the Consolidated Rules of the Supreme Court... the provisions of this Act apply." Being a special Act, it would clearly prevail over the Limitations Act even without the "notwithstanding" clause, but serious problems are created when there is another special statute such as the Vehicles Act, and others I shall mention later.

Fatal Accidents Act

The next statute with its own special period is the Fatal Accidents Act which allows one year from death.[49]

The first situation that requires consideration is this. The victim of the wrongdoer's negligence dies *before* his action in negligence had expired under the applicable statute which would be either the Limitations Act, the Vehicles & Highway Traffic Act, a municipal Act, the Public Officers' Protection Act or some other special act. Now if the action under the Fatal Accidents Act is brought before that period has expired, no possible question arises. However it may expire within a year or even a week of death. Does this mean that the defendant can raise as a defence the original statute so that the plaintiff in the Fatal Accidents Act is barred after the period prescribed by the original statute has passed even though the action is brought within a year of death?

In general, the answer is no. As long as the victim's action was not barred when he died, his dependants have the year given them by the Fatal Accidents Act. They had no cause of action prior to death and it would be unreasonable to say that time was running against them before their cause of action arose. The Privy Council so held in *Gentile* v. *B.C. Electric Railway*.[50]

One might argue that a provision such as section 131 of the Vehicles Act, which is very wide in its terms, leads to the opposite result, but I submit it does not. The only Act that might operate as a bar after its original period is gone is the Public Officers Protection Act for it applies "notwithstanding any other Act'' and the six months' period runs from the wrongful act. If this is the effect then the one-year period of the Fatal Accidents Act is seriously curtailed, and indeed it is barred from the beginning where the victim survived over six months.

Next we shall consider the position where the victim's cause of action was barred before he died. In that event the clear inference from *Gentile* is that the Fatal Accidents action is out of time. The Act says action may be brought when death ''has been caused by such wrongful act, neglect or default as would if death had not ensued, have entitled the injured party to maintain an action and recover damages in respect thereof''. It has long been settled that the dependant's action fails if the deceased himself had obtained judgment or given a valid release, and the same applies where his action was barred before he died. Anglin J. stated in *B.C. Electric Ry. Co. v. Turner*—[51]

> ''I find no satisfactory ground of distribution between the extinguishment of the cause of action by the injured man by an accord and satisfaction, evidenced by a release, and its extinguishment by the recovery of a judgment upon it or the expiry of a period of limitation''.

Trustee Act

At common law an action in tort (with an exception not relevant here) came to an end with the death of either victim or tortfeasor. In 1886 Ontario abrogated this rule by an amendment to the Trustee Act that provides for survival of actions in tort. Our Trustee Ordinance of 1903[52] follows the Ontario Act. Until the House of Lords decision in *Rose* v. *Ford*[53] these survival provisions were rarely invoked. Since then they have been used by the representative of a victim mainly in connection with damages for loss of expectation of life—a claim incidentally that is no longer admitted in most provinces.

England followed Ontario's lead in 1934 and now all the common law provinces have provision for survival of actions in tort, most of them on either the Ontario or English model, but with a variety of limitation provisions. At present the Conference of Commissioners on Uniformity of Legislation is in the process of preparing a model survival Act.

In the meantime, section 32 of our Trustee Act says that where the victim dies, action by his estate against the wrongdoer must be brought within a year of his death; and section 33 says that where the wrongdoer dies, the victim's action against his estate must be brought within a year of his death.

One point on which I have found no direct authority, but which seems clear, is that the action does not survive if the claim was barred under the applicable limitation statute at the time of the death, whether it be of victim or wrongdoer.[54]

The question that has caused difficulty is whether the period in the

Trustee Act prevails over that in another statute that *prima facie* applies. Where the law, either common or statutory, provides for survival of right of action and there is no special time limit then the general limitation act applies. If one turns to our Limitation Act, he will find that it does not mention the death of a claimant. In other words time continues to run as though the claimant were still alive. An obvious example is that of an ordinary debt. On the other hand the Act does provide for the case of the death of a person *against* whom a claim exists:

> Section 5(3)—Where a person has a claim against the estate of a deceased person, and the claim was not barred at the date of death of the person under the provisions of this Act *or any other Act limiting the time within which an action could be brought,* an action may be brought to recover the amount of the claim (a) within the time otherwise limited for the bringing of the action, or (b) within two years from the date of death, whichever period is the longer.

This certainly shows a generous policy in favour of plaintiffs who bring action against an estate. It also shows, from the words I have put in italics, that it can apply to other statutes that impose a limitation. Yet I have found no case in which the italicized words have been applied. Section 5(2) quoted earlier says that section 5 does not apply to claims specially limited under other statutes, but surely 5(2) should be read subject to 5(3).

Returning now to the Trustee Act it is clear that its limitation provision in section 33 prevails over those in the general Act. Thus in an action in negligence for starting a fire, and where the wrongdoer died five months later, an action brought against his estate sixteen months after his death was out of time.[55] It is submitted however that had the Trustee Act not contained its own limitation, the italicized words in section 5(3) would have applied and the action would have been in time.

The real difficulty arises where section 32 or 33 of the Trustee Act comes into competition with another special provision. Section 131 of The Vehicles Act is a conspicuous example. Let us consider first the case where the wrongdoer dies and the victim brings action against the estate, and then the converse case, where the victim dies and his estate brings action against the wrongdoer. (There is also the case where both have died and the action is between the two estates. This situation is mentioned at the end of this section.)

(1) In the Ontario case of *Dressed* v. *Glaser*[56] the accident occurred on September 22, 1951. The wrongdoer died on October 16. His administrator was appointed on October 15, 1952 and action was commenced the next day. Needless to say, the defendant relied on the Vehicles Act and the plaintiff on the Trustee Act. In finding for the defendant the Court of Appeal said the Trustee Act "does not have the effect of taking away a defence which the deceased would have had if he had been living at the time of the appointment of the executor or administrator. Thus it does not operate to deprive the executor of the right to set up the defence the deceased would have had by

virtue of [sec. 131 of the Vehicles Act]". The judgment adds that the Trustee Act is general legislation and the Vehicles Act is special.

(2) In the Alberta case of *Scott* v. *Thompson*[57] the Appellate Division had to consider the converse situation. The accident occurred on November 22, 1952. The victim died on November 27. His executor brought action on November 24, 1953. Again the defendant relied on the Vehicles Act and the plaintiff on the Trustee Act. The Court pointed out that the Trustee Act says the victim's representatives may maintain an action for tort or injuries to the person in the same manner and with the same rights and remedies as the deceased would if living have been entitled to. The reasoning then seems to be that had the victim himself been the plaintiff, his claim would have been barred and that his estate is in no better position.

These two judgments do not give effect to the one-year provisions that the legislature specifically placed in the Trustee Act when it provided that tort actions should survive. It is respectfully submitted that it is only by virtue of the Trustee Act that the action can be brought at all, and that when that legislation is invoked its own limitation period accompanies it. This was the reasoning of Lord J. in a British Columbia case.[58]

A similar issue could arise where the representative brings action against a city or a public officer. On the reasoning of *Scott* v. *Thompson,* the City Act or Public Officers Protection Act would prevail, to the defendant's benefit.

As to the possibility of a conflict between the Trustee Act and the Fatal Accidents Act, I have been unable to construct one. The 1960 amendment to the latter[59] puts beyond any doubt the right of the dependants to bring action against the wrongdoer's estate no matter which of the two dies first. It seems clear on the *Gentile* principle that the Fatal Accidents Act governs, and the fact that the wrongdoer has died, whether before or after the victim, is immaterial.[60]

The only problem I can imagine in a case of this kind arises entirely within the Trustee Act. Suppose now victim and wrongdoer are both dead, but that they died at different times. In a claim under the Trustee Act, e.g. for loss of expectation of life, does section 32 apply or section 33? In other words does time run from the victim's death or the wrongdoer's? Of course if the deaths arose out of a car accident then *Scott* v. *Thompson* says the Trustee Act does not apply anyway. Assuming it to apply, the reasonable rule would seem to be that time would begin to run under the Trustee Act from the death of the one who died first.[61]

Medical, Dental and Hospital Acts

The Medical Profession Act says that no physician "is liable to an action for negligence or malpractice . . . unless the action is commenced within one year from the date when the professional services complained of terminated".[62] Apart from verbal differences the Dental Association Act is the same.[63] The notable feature of these Acts, which are not unique to Alberta, is that time runs from the date when the physician's services relating to the matter of the complaint came to an end.

Usually this is the last day on which the physician attended the plaintiff in connection with the complaint that later becomes the cause of action.[64]

These provisions operate harshly against the plaintiff in a case where the negligence is not manifest for over a year after the patient has ceased to attend. This can occur where an object like a sponge has been left in the patient's body after an operation. In an Alberta case the object was not discovered until five and a half years later. However the plaintiff had consulted the defendant about the pain in her abdomen shortly before the discovery, and he assisted in the removal of the object. McLaurin C.J.T.D. held that the action was in time.[65].

It will be noted that these provisions extend to malpractice as well as negligence so it is suggested here that they apply where there is an unauthorized operation, usually called "medical assault".[66]

The Hospitals Act says that actions against an approved hospital must be commenced within one year after the cause of action arose.[67] I know of no reported case on this section. Where the patient has died after an interval of time, a problem could arise as to whether his representative is entitled to one year from the death or whether he is still bound by the Hospitals Act.

One argument, perhaps fanciful, that a hospital (at least a municipal one) might raise is this. A hospital is clearly a public authority and therefore is entitled to the benefit of the Public Officers Protection Act. It is true that Hall, C.J.Q.B. in Saskatchewan has held that hospital legislation is special and prevails over the more general Protection Act,[68] but our Protection Act has its "notwithstanding" clause, and perhaps a hospital could persuade the court to apply it.

The Calgary Hospital Board Act[69] gives to that Board the benefit of the limitation provision in the City Act, including the requirement of notice.

Amendments, Counterclaims, Third Parties

A judge may at any stage of the proceedings allow either party to amend his pleadings.[70] There is no need here to examine in detail the principles on which the courts exercise their discretion to permit amendments. Generally one can say they do so freely. We are concerned solely with the situation where a plaintiff seeks an amendment that sets up a new cause of action and does so at a time after that new cause of action is barred. The leading case of *Weldon* v. *Neal*[71] holds that such an amendment should not be permitted. The defendant should not be deprived of the benefit of the Statute of Limitations.

Sometimes it is hard to determine whether an amendment in fact sets up a new cause of action. Where the action is for damage to a vehicle and an amendment is proposed after the lapse of the statutory period to include a claim for personal injuries,[72] or loss of employees' services[73] or where the plaintiff wants to make an allegation of wilful and wanton misconduct[74] it has been held that all of these set up a new cause of action.[75]

In a number of cases under the Fatal Accidents Act the statement of claim has been defective in not setting out all the facts required to show a cause of action. In Saskatchewan,[76] Manitoba,[77] and England[78] the Court has taken a strict view and refused to permit an amendment after the statutory period. Our Appellate Division took a more lenient position, where the plaintiff had omitted to state that she brought action as administratrix.[79] She was allowed to make the amendment.

Saskatchewan has a provision in the Queen's Bench Act[80] expressly enabling the Court to permit an amendment even though the statutory period has passed, provided the amendment does not involve a change of parties other than one caused by death of one of the parties. I have found no comparable provision in Alberta and mention it because it seems worth considering.

The subject of adding parties, whether plaintiff or defendant, can be dealt with here, because it is often treated as a matter of amendment even though the adding of a plaintiff or defendant is really more than an amendment. The rules of court provide for adding parties,[81] but the cases say they should not be added after the limitation period has expired.[82] The most helpful case on the whole subject is one in our Appellate Division, *Western Canadian Greyhound Lines* v. *Pomerleau*.[83] In that case the statement of claim described Alcide Pomerleau as owner and John Pomerleau as driver. After the defence was filed, the plaintiff sought to amend, because, in fact, Alcide was driver and John was owner. By this time the one-year period laid down by section 131 of the Vehicles Act had passed. The judgment sets out three classes of cases in which an amendment after the statutory period will be refused: (1) where the action is a nullity *ab initio,* (2) where it is sought to add or substitute plaintiffs and defendants and (3) where it is sought to add a new cause of action. The amendment here was not within any of these classes and did not prejudice the defendant and therefore was allowed. *A fortiori* an ordinary misnomer may be corrected.

Coming now to counterclaims, the general rule is that a counterclaim must be brought before the time for bringing action has expired. One can imagine an accident in which two car drivers are instantly killed. The representative of one brings action under the Fatal Accidents Act against the representative of the other after 11 months and 28 days. The latter may wish to counterclaim under the same Act, but after the twelve months have gone by, it is too late.

In the case of the Vehicles Act, however, there is a special provision (sec. 131(2)) which says that where action is brought for damages "occasioned by a motor vehicle" and a counterclaim is made by a defendant in respect of damages occasioned in the same accident, the lapse of time limited by this Act is no bar to the counterclaim. In *Buck* v. *Kinshella,*[84] a defendant, who had counterclaimed, sought to amend the counterclaim to correct an error as to which of the plaintiffs was the driver and which was the passenger.

The Appellate Division held that section 131(2) makes it clear that lapse of time is no bar to a counterclaim and hence is not a bar to an amendment thereof. The court can exercise its discretion on the usual principles.

A question that could arise is this. A defendant who counterclaims joins as a defendant to the counterclaim a person who was not a plaintiff in the original action. Does section 131(2) apply so that the person may be so joined after the lapse of a year? The Rules of Court[85] contemplate that such a person may be added and I see no reason why the Rules should not be applied here.[85a] Whether this result is unjust to the person so added, I have no opinion.

The last major problem has to do with proceedings by a defendant to join some one else as a defendant or third party. The Rules of Court have always provided for both of these, but it will be remembered that third party procedure[86] has traditionally been used to enable a defendant to bring into the proceedings someone who is obliged to indemnify him. It could not be used to claim contribution in tort actions for the simple reason that the substantive law did not allow contribution as between co-tortfeasors. It will be remembered too that the courts are reluctant to enforce a new defendant on the plaintiff.

However the Tortfeasors Act of 1936[87] provides:

> 4. (1) Where damage is suffered by any person as a result of a tort . . .
> (c) any tort-feasor liable in respect of that damage may recover contribution from any other tort-feasor who is, or would, if sued, have been liable in respect of the same damage, whether as a joint tort-feasor or otherwise, . . .

And the Contributory Negligence Act of 1937[88] provides:

> Sec. 9. "Whenever it appears that a person not already party to an action is or may be wholly or partly responsible for the damages claimed, such person may be added as a party defendant".[89]

I doubt that this is often done, at least if the plaintiff objects; and in principle it cannot be done after the period of limitation has passed.

However the defendant often takes third party proceedings against someone he alleges to be partly to blame, hoping that the Court will apportion some (if not all) of the fault against that person.

This raises a question. Suppose the third party proceedings are taken after the expiration of the time within which the plaintiff could have sued the third party? Where section 131 of the Vehicles Act applies lapse of time is no bar, and indeed our Appellate Division has held[90] that the defendant may include in the third party proceedings a claim against the third party for the defendant's own damages. Thus he may in effect bring an action against the third party after the year has passed.

In cases to which section 131 does not apply, real difficulty has arisen as to whether third party proceedings can be taken with a view to obtaining contribution where the plaintiff's right of action against the third party has expired. The most likely case is that where the third party is a public officer. Quite possibly, the action was started more than six months after the accident. Had the public officer been sued in the first place, he would have had a defence. In *Sobble* v. *Mills,*[91] Boyd McBride J. held that in these circumstances the defendant was not entitled to have the public officer joined. He adhered to this view in *Sargent* v. *Canadian Coachways,* but the Appellate Division upheld the third party notice because there was doubt as to the correctness of the view of Mr. Justice McBride and also doubt as to whether the third party was within the Protection Act.[92]

When the case was decided on its merits, the third party was found not to be a public officer, so we do not know what position the Appellate Division would have taken had he been.[93]

Several years later, the English Court of Appeal held, at least by way of dictum, in *Wimpey* v. *B.O.A.C.*[94] that the effect of section 4(1)(c) of the Tortfeasors Act is that a defendant's action for contribution may be brought after judgment against him has been obtained and that therefore, where a defendant seeks contribution through third party proceedings, time does not run in favour of the third party from the date of the accident, but only from the time the plaintiff obtains judgment against the person seeking contribution. In this view third party proceedings against a public officer are on time even though instituted more than six months after the accident. Since the *Wimpey* case Parliament has repealed the Public Authorities Protection Act, so the exact question cannot again arise in England, but there may be similar situations where the third party has the benefit of a short period under some other statute.[95]

If the opinion of the Court of Appeal in *Wimpey* is accepted in Alberta, it will mean that section 4(1)(c) operates to remove from a third party a defence that a special limitation period appears to have given him. On the other hand, the opposing view, that of Boyd McBride J., seems unfair to the original defendant. He cannot compel the plaintiff to take action against him within six months and yet if the action is brought after that period, then it is too late for the defendant to join the public officer as a third party with a view of obtaining a contribution from him.

Conclusion

This concludes our survey of the law. Question of limitations arise continually and it is trite to point out that the law should be ascertainable, definite, simple and fair. This account shows that in too many instances our law of limitations does not meet these tests.

It is relevant to note that in England there was after World War II criticism of the Public Authorities Act and of the short period (one year) under the Fatal Accidents Act.[96] In 1948 the Lord Chancellor appointed a Committee to make recommendations on the subject. The Committee recommended the repeal of the Public Authorities Protection Act and an extension to two years of the period under the Fatal Accidents Act.[97] In 1954 Parliament accepted these recommendations, save that it extended the time under the Fatal Accidents Act to three years.[98] One must be envious of the present simplicity of the English provisions.

The foregoing survey, it is submitted, warrants the following recommendations. Because of the length of this paper, they are made without elaboration and in full knowledge that there may be differences of opinion on some of them.

Recommendations:

(1) Repeal of the Public Officers Protection Act and Rule 651 which repeats the main provision of the Act.

(2) Repeal of the requirement of notice before action in claims under the City Act except in cases of failure to repair streets (including snow and ice).[99]

(3) Repeal of the special periods in the municipal acts and the Vehicles Act, so that the general Act will apply.

(4) Enlargement of the period under the Fatal Accidents Act to two years.

(5) If recommendations 2 to 4 inclusive are not practicable, then at least all periods for tort should be set out in the Limitations Act and special provisions should be included to make it clear which provision prevails in a given case. (This last would be a formidable task for the draftsman.)

Notes

1 The Limitation of Actions Act, R.S.A. 1922 was not a general act.

2 [1924] 2 W.W.R. 395.

3 *Eisener* v. *Maxwell*, [1951] 3 D.L.R. 345 (N.S.); *Mantey* v. *Spanks* [1952] 3 D.L.R. 783 (B.C.).

4 Now The Limitation of Actions Act, R.S.A. 1955 cap. 177.

5 R.S.A. 1955 cap. 78, secs. 13–19.

6 *Fediuk* v. *Lastiwka* [1959] S.C.R. 261.

7 The leading case is *Darley Main Colliery* v. *Mitchell* (1886) 11 A.C. 127.

8 *Cartledge* v. *Jopling* [1961] 3 All E.R. 482. Compare 24 Hals. (3 Ed.) page 223, note (b).

9 *Marren* v. *Dawson* [1961] 2 All E.R. 270. Three cases, all from Ontario, are on a statute providing that no action shall be brought *after* six months. This seems the same as a requirement that the action must be brought *within* six months. *Switzer* v. *Kahn* [1929] 4 D.L.R. 232; *Brown* v. *Croucher* [1931] 4 D.L.R. 219; *Dormer* v. *Sumner* [1934] O.W.N. 45. After this paper was given, two students called my attention to sec. 18(1)(k) of the Interpretation Act, 1958, cap. 32 which puts the rule in statutory form.

10 *Puls* v. *Bulman Bros.* [1933] 3 W.W.R. 485 (Man.); *Stewart* v. *Maritime Electric Co.* [1952] 2 D.L.R. 217 (P.E.I.).

11 Law Reform (Limitation of Actions Etc.) Act 1954 (2 & 3 Eliz. 2, cap. 36, sec. 2(1)).

12 R.S.A. 1955, cap. 356; am. 1959, cap. 93, sec. 36.

13 *Harris* v. *Yellow Cab. Co.* [1926] 3 D.L. R. 254.

14 *Hughes* v. *Watkins* [1928] 2 D.L.R. 176.

15 [1940] S.C.R. 174.

16 *Viane* v. *Neyens* [1959] O.W.N. 29.

17 (1960) 33 W.W.R. 322.

18 For a definition see *Harris* v. *Yellow Cab. Co.*, note 13 at 255.

19 *Lasby* v. *Everall Engineering Co.* [1960] 32 W.W.R. 335 (Sask.).

20 *Bonany* v. *Gratton* (1960) 23 D.L.R. 591 (Ont.).

21 *Biggs* v. *Baker* [1955] 5 D.L.R. 612 (Ont.); *McLennan* v. *Cotter* (1960) 30 W.W.R. 127 (B.C.). *Hockin* v. *Barber* [1950] 2 W.W.R. 303 (B.C.) is wrongly decided.

22 *McCabe Grain Co.* v. *Achtzener* [1958] 24 W.W.R. (Sask.).

23 *Bizeau* v. *C.N.R. and Aziz* [1926] 4 D.L.R. 1066.

24 *Worsley* v. *Hamilton* (1960) 33 W.W.R. 23.

25 Note 24, *supra*.

26 The section appears in *Schartner* v. *Yoski* (1957) 26 W.W.R. 26.

27 R.S.A. 1955, cap. 42, secs. 697–99.

28 Sec. 695.

29 *Clayton* v. *McNeill's Taxi, et al,* [1946] 3 W.W.R. 218.

30 (1962) 37 W.W.R. 74. The judgment was reported after this paper was presented. It reverses the judgment of Edwards D.C.J. at the trial; (1961) 35 W.W.R. 419.

30a The legislature has since amended the City Act (1962 Chap. 7) to bring within the section an employee acting in the course of his duty. Thus *Herdink* v. *Calgary* is no longer law.

31 R.S.A. 1955, cap. 338, sec. 271.

32 R.S.A. 1955, cap. 250, secs. 240, 242.

33 County Act, R.S.A. 1955, cap. 64, sec. 25.

34 *Bradford* v. *Myers* [1916] A.C. 242.

35 R.S.A. 1955, cap. 262.

36 *Kellie* v. *Calgary* (1951) 1 W.W.R. (N.S.) 691.

37 *Cobble* v. *Mills* [1947] 2 W.W.R. 790.

38 (1955) 14 W.W.R. 495.

39 *Reeves* v. *Deane-Freeman* [1953] 1 All E.R. 461.

40 *Sargent* v. *Canadian Coachways* [1950] 2 W.W.R. 1217.

41 1959 cap. 63.

42 The Crown Proceedings Act, 1947 (Imp.) sec. 30(2) said that "nothing in this Act shall prejudice the right of the Crown to rely upon the law relating to the Limitation of time for bringing proceedings against public authorities". This provision was repealed when the Public Authorities Protection Act was repealed in 1954 (note 11, *supra*).

43 (1961) 35 W.W.R. 666.

44 (1962) 37 W.W.R. 34.

45 *Griffiths* v. *Smith* [1941] A.C. 170.

46 R.S.A. 1955, cap. 297, sec. 449.

47 E.g., *Bradford* v. *Myers,* note 34; *Halpin* v. *Reginam,* note 38; *McGonegal* v. *Gray* [1952] 2 S.C.R. 274.

48 *Chaput* v. *Romain* [1955] S.C.R. 834; *Lamb* v. *Benoit* [1959] S.C.R. 321; *Roncarelli* v. *Duplessis* [1959] S.C.R. 121. These cases are under Quebec statutes that either require notice before suit or that shorten the time. For a Saskatchewan case on false imprisonment, see *Beatty* v. *Kozak* [1958] S.C.R. 177.

49 R.S.A. 1955, cap. 111, sec. 5.

50 [1914] A.C. 1034; also *Venn* v. *Tedesco* [1926] 2 K.B. 227.

51 (1914) 49 S.C.R. 470 at 496. See also *Williams* v. *Mersey Docks* [1905] 1 K.B. 804.

52 Now The Trustee Act, R.S.A. 1955, cap. 346.

53 [1937] A.C. 826.

54 In *Airey* v. *Airey* [1858] 2 All E.R. 571 at 578 the English Court of Appeal expressly left the question open.

55 *Snyder* v. *Powell* (1959) 28 W.W.R. 41.

56 [1954] 1 D.L.R. 655.

57 (1957) 21 W.W.R. 283.

58 *Skobel* v. *McDonald* (1959) 29 W.W.R. 236.

59 1960, cap. 31.

60 If this is correct then the result is the same as that reached by Locke and Cartwright JJ., the only members of the Supreme Court of Canada who found it necessary to deal with the point in *Cairney* v. *McQueen* [1956] S.C.R. 555.

61 On further reflection it seems equally reasonable to say that the plaintiff (the victim's estate) should be allowed a year from the death of the one who died last. I know of no case on the point.

62 R.S.A. 1955, cap. 198, sec. 62.

63 R.S.A. 1955, cap. 82, sec. 46.

64 *Town* v. *Archer* (1902) 4 O.L.R. 383.

65 *Gloning* v. *Miller* (1953) 10 W.W.R. 414.

66 *Boase* v. *Paul* [1931] 4 D.L.R. (Ont.) gives some support to this view, per Hodgins and Middleton JJ.A.; contra, *Marshall* v. *Curry* [1933] 3 D.L.R. 260 (N.S.); dubitante, *Winn* v. *Alexander* [1940] O.W.N. 238; *Bonisteel* v.

Bateman [1945] O.W.N. 163.

67 R.S.A. 1955, cap. 147, sec. 19.

68 *MacArthur* v. *Sask. Cancer Comm.* (1958) 27 W.W.R. 152.

69 1954, cap. 7, sec. 4.

70 C.R. 189: rules 189–203 are on the subject of amendments.

71 (1885) 19 Q.B.D. 394.

72 *Visotto* v. *Western Equipment Ltd.* (1959) 30 W.W.R. 523 (Sask.).

73 *Vancouver* v. *Dubois* (1954) 13 W.W.R. 42 (B.C.).

74 *Bodnarchuk* v. *Kalast* (1959) 28 W.W.R. 97 (Sask.).

75 Compare *Dowling* v. *Rud* (1961) 36 W.W.R. 471 (B.C.).

76 *Shtitz* v. *C.N.R.* [1927] 1 W.W.R. 193.

77 *Last* v. *Ashworth* (1954) 14 W.W.R. 177.

78 *Hilton* v. *Sutton Steam Laundry* [1945] 2 All E.R. 425.

79 *Miller* v. *C.P.R.* [1933] 1 W.W.R. 233.

80 R.S.S. 1953, cap. 67, sec. 43(11).

81 C.R. 61, 62.

82 E.g., *Greig* v. *T.T.C.* [1958] O.W.N. 480; *Crozier* v. *O'Connor* [1960] O.W.N. 352.

83 (1955) 15 W.W.R. 182.

84 (1958) 25 W.W.R. 593.

85 C.R. 103.

85a *Haylon* v. *Sayyeu* 1950 O.W.N. 634 gives some support to this view. It also deals with the problem of a counterclaim under the Fatal Accidents Act and Trustee Act. The question is whether such counterclaims are within sec. 131(2) so that they may be brought after the time limited in these Acts. The Senior Master was doubtful as to The Fatal Accidents counterclaim, but held the counterclaim under the Trustee Act was not within sec. 131(2) and was out of time.

86 C.R. 81.

87 Now R.S.A. 1955, cap. 336.

88 Now R.S.A. 1955, cap. 56.

89 *Cubit* v. *Fortin* [1944] 2 W.W.R. 123 prescribes the practice. It might be noted that in Ontario, where there is a Contributory Negligence Act, but no Tortfeasor's Act, a defendant who has been found liable to the plaintiff may not bring a subsequent action against another for contribution. See *Cohen* v. *McCord* [1944] 4 D.L.R. 753; *Rickwood* v. *Aylmer* [1957] 8 D.L.R. (2d) 702.

90 *Patey* v. *Papley* (1956) 20 W.W.R. 289. Much is to be said for the dissenting view of Johnson J.A. that third party proceedings were not intended for this purpose.

91 Note 37, *supra*.

92 [1949] I W.W.R. 305.

93 Note 40, *supra*.

94 [1953] 2 Q.B. 501, [1955] A.C. 169. The House of Lords left the point open.

95 See *Harvey* v. *O'Dell* [1958] 1 All E.R. 657.

96 An outstanding example is the case cited in note 78, *supra*.

97 Cmd. 7740. This report makes an excellent criticism of defects in the law.

98 Note 11, *supra*.

99 In *Herdink* v. *Calgary,* note 30, *supra,* Edwards D.C.J. gives cogent reasons, and the judgment of the Appellate Division does not touch on them.

1963

Legal Liability to Volunteers in Testing New Drugs

Reprinted from
Canadian Medical Association Journal (1963) 88
pp. 745–751

This article was published at the urging of Dr. Walter C. Mackenzie, Dean of Medicine at the University of Alberta (1958 to 1975), after whom the Mackenzie Health Sciences Centre is named.

Back in the early 1960s, medical schools were asked to study methods of improving medical research into drugs, in order to avoid such outcomes as the thalidomide tragedy. (Thalidomide was a drug prescribed to pregnant women which resulted in their babies being born with deformed limbs.)

One of the questions the Deans of Medicine were asked to study was the responsibility of the researcher if harmful effects or side effects ensued during the testing of drugs by patients, the purpose of testing being to ensure that the drugs were safe and effective. In 1962 Dean Walter Mackenzie referred these questions to Wilbur Bowker, Dean of Law. Bowker gave a long written opinion, which apparently so impressed Dr. Mackenzie that he arranged for its publication (in condensed form) in the Canadian Medical Association Journal.

Before the maker of a new drug puts it on the market, he customarily sends it to practising physicians[1] to try on their patients. A conviction is growing, however, that this testing should be done by trained scientists on volunteers. The editor of this Journal has said: "The procedures involved in this type of testing are such that they require the facilities and personnel of a medical school or other institution geared and equipped for the conduct of clinical research."[2] The object is the better ensuring of the safety of the drug before the maker recommends it for general use.

A new drug is one that because of its composition, method of manufacture, dosage, or route of administration "is not generally recognized by persons qualified to evaluate the safety of the drug as safe for the uses for which it is proposed or recommended".[3] If a new drug is ever to be recognized as safe, it must first be tested on humans.[4] The proposed type of testing is scientific experiment. That is to say, its primary object is the advancement of medical knowledge, rather than therapy for the person to whom the drug is given. Thus it differs from the treatment that a physician prescribes for his patient. For this reason I shall refer to the person carrying out the testing as the scientist, and the person who agrees to submit to the testing as the volunteer. This will prevent confusion with the physician-patient relationship.[5]

Since by definition a new drug is one not generally recognized as safe, the volunteer in taking it runs a risk of harm. If the risk materializes, then the question arises: does the volunteer have an action for damages against the scientist? or against his family physician who referred him to the scientist? or against the maker of the drug?

The rules governing liability to an action for damages are not laid down by statute, but by judgments which constitute the common law.[6] However, the common law gives no direct answer to our problem. There is no English or Canadian decision on the subject. In these circumstances we might hope to obtain assistance from American decisions, but there is none. Thus one must make his forecast of what a court would decide, on the basis of general principle, decisions in malpractice cases and medicolegal literature. The Nuremberg Medical Case, though a criminal proceeding, is highly relevant.

The Scientist

In considering the liability of the scientist we assume that he possesses the proper degree of skill and exercises due care and judgment; in other words, that he is not negligent,[7] and that the injury has resulted from risks inherent in the use of a new drug.

In my opinion the scientist is protected from liability if he gives to the volunteer full and candid information as to the nature of the experiment and attendant risks and if the volunteer then gives his consent in full knowledge of the facts and in the absence of pressure, whether direct or implicit.

In setting forth the reasons, we must begin with the principles governing the physician-patient relationship and, in particular, with the question: may a physician experiment in treating a patient?

Therapeutic Experimentation

Generally, a physician should follow accepted practice, and this seems to be another way of saying he should not experiment. Thus an Ontario decision in 1886, after conceding that experiment is necessary for progress in medical science, added the caution that "he who tries the experiment and thereby injures another must take the consequences".[8] On the other hand, an Alberta case of 1924 held that a physician was entitled to use an ultraviolet lamp, even though it was still to a large extent in the experimental stage. However, he was obliged to use great care.[9] Then in an English decision of 1954, one of the judges said by way of comment:

> We should be doing a disservice to the community at large if we were to impose liability on hospitals and doctors for everything that happens to go wrong. Doctors would be led to think more of their own safety than of the good of their patients. Initiative would be stifled and confidence shaken.[10]

Again, in a Scottish case in 1955 the patient complained that the physician had deviated from ordinary professional practice. One of the judges, Lord Clyde, replied that "such a deviation is not necessarily evidence of negligence. Indeed it would be disastrous if this were so, for all inducement to progress in medical science would then be destroyed." Then he adds that deviation gives rise to liability only where "the course the doctor adopted is one which no professional man of ordinary skill would have taken if he had been acting with ordinary care".[11]

It is true that a number of cases in the United States have held that a physician or surgeon experiments at his peril. This is called the no-experiment rule. Here, however, it is relevant to point out that the word "experiment" as used in connection with the practice of medicine does not have a single meaning. It has been employed to include anything from a carefully conducted new treatment by a skilled physician or surgeon to the action of the charlatan who applies carbolic acid to remove smallpox scars. As used in the latter sense, there can be no objection to the proposition that the physician is liable if he experiments. This type of "experiment" is quackery. However, some cases in the United States seem to apply the no-experiment rule to innovations of the first type. Thus in 1902 a Wisconsin court said: "We have little doubt that if the first case of vaccination had proved disastrous and injured the patient, the physician should have been held liable."[12] Recent medicolegal literature in the United States criticizes these cases on the ground that the no-experimentation rule is an obstacle to progress.[13]

Curiously, this so-called rule purportedly has its origin in *Slater* v. *Baker,*[14] an English case of 200 years ago. Baker was the first surgeon of St. Bartholomew's Hospital and was distinguished in his profession. Some time after Slater's leg had been broken his apothecary took him to Baker to have the bandage removed. In treating the leg Baker used an apparatus that extended the leg and in so doing disunited the callus. The court found that Baker must have been trying to experiment with a new instrument, and that he acted ignorantly and unskilfully, contrary to the known rule and usage of surgeons.

The judgment adds, however, that the evidence of expert witnesses at the trial showed that it was improper to disunite the callus *without consent* and in so doing Baker acted contrary to the rule of the profession. In other words, *Slater* v. *Baker* does not lay down a no-experiment rule at all but rather a no-experiment-without-consent rule, which is vastly different. This leads to an examination of the subject of consent to medical treatment.

Consent in the Physician-Patient Relationship

It is elementary that one person may not intentionally invade the bodily integrity of another without his consent. So to do is a battery, which is now usually called an assault. This applies to a physician.[15] However, his touching of a patient in the course of diagnosis and treatment is done with the patient's implied consent. In the case of surgery it is customary to obtain specific consent, which is often in writing.

Where an operation has produced poor results, the patient may say to the surgeon: "You did not tell me this might happen. If you had I would have refused the operation. Now you must compensate me for the bad results." If this is the only basis of his claim it will fail. English and Canadian courts uphold the surgeon in deprecating the risks of surgery.

In a case of this kind in Ontario, Dr. W.E. Gallie, testifying as an expert witness, said that he did not make a practice of outlining all the risks that attend every operation. If he did describe them all, even the infrequent ones, the patient would refuse and would damage himself by waiting to see what would happen. The court agreed that the duty of the surgeon to deal honestly and frankly with the patient does not require him to warn the patient of dangers incident to, or possible in, the operation.[16]

However, a special treatment may carry unusual risks, especially when it is new. X-ray and shock therapy are examples. Some of the forms of consent for these treatments refer to the fact that there are risks and that the patient has been informed of them.[17, 18] One can at least say that the physician's legal position is stronger if he has disclosed special risks. Indeed, in recent years in the United States a number of decisions have emphasized the need of an "informed consent", and in some the physician has been held liable for failure to disclose the risk of shock therapy and radioactive cobalt treatment where harm had resulted to the patient.[19]

It is clear that the physician may protect himself from an action even where the treatment is new provided he candidly explains the position. We assume of course that he is not negligent in administering the treatment.

This is an application of a general rule that one person cannot claim damages for injury caused by the act of another when the person making the claim has consented to the doing of the act—the Latin maxim embodying the rule is *volenti non fit injuria*. To establish it a defendant must show (1) that the plaintiff had full knowledge of the risks and (2) that he accepted them in the sense that he agreed not to look to the defendant to compensate him in the event of injury. In the case of an action by a patient against his physician or surgeon based on injuries resulting from experimental surgery or treatment, the defence of assumption of risk is open to the doctor.[20] A successful defence is directly proportional to the candour of the disclosure of the risk.

Relevance of Consent on Liability of Scientist to Volunteer

The foregoing discussion brings us to the question whether a volunteer may relieve the scientist from liability for inherent risks in the same way as the patient may relieve his physician. On principle the answer must be yes. Admittedly, there is a difference between the two situations: the patient consents to something intended for his benefit while the volunteer consents to help with a scientific experiment. In my opinion the only difference this makes is that a court would require stronger evidence that the volunteer had full knowledge of the risks than it would require in the case of a patient.

Various writers, medical and legal, in the United States and Britain have discussed the subject.[21] One British scientist, Dr. J.M. Mackintosh,[22] poses the question that is the subject of this article: "suppose no negligence has occurred and in consequence of an experiment—the outcome of which cannot be known—a patient suffers a damage or death". His opinion is that in order to protect the scientist from liability the law would require: (1) that the volunteer had been clearly informed of the nature and purpose of the experiment and of any results that it might involve; (2) that the experiment had been carried out not merely without negligence but with every available precaution against disaster; (3) that the person conducting the experiment can confidently be entrusted with the important task he is undertaking.

We need not comment on the second and third of these requirements because the very purpose of the type of experiment under consideration is to meet them. It is the first that is relevant here. I am in respectful agreement with Dr. Mackintosh's statement. However, a crucial question remains—how does the scientist satisfy the requirement that the volunteer be informed "of any results that it might involve"? The difficulty lies in the fact that the risks are unknown, so in the nature of things cannot be specified.

Let us assume that the scientist conscientiously explains results that he thinks might occur—e.g. dermatitis, paralysis, deafness. However, blindness results. In my opinion the scientist would not be protected were the volunteer to bring action. In other words, the scientist is obliged, if he wishes to protect himself, to disclose the fact that there are unknown risks. I doubt that a stereotyped and formal statement is desirable. However, my concept of what is required is expressed in the suggestion that the scientist first explain the known risks and then add a statement embodying the following idea: "It is always possible that some things may happen that I cannot foresee or imagine. Some drugs produce serious even fatal results; that can be the case with new drugs." The scientist might reply that if he must be this frank then he will not obtain any volunteers. I doubt that this is so. Confidence is the basis of the relationship as it is between physician and patient, and one would hope that candour does not destroy it. In any case we are considering the problem of legal liability, not the recruiting of volunteers, and the point we wish to stress is "the greater the disclosure the greater the protection against legal liability."

The Nuremberg Medical Case

As far as I know, the only reported decision of any court on this subject is one that an American War Crimes Tribunal gave in 1947.[23] It is not binding on any Canadian court. However, if the problem of a scientist's liability to a volunteer were to arise in Canada, one would confidently expect the court to attach great weight to the Nuremberg judgment.

In that case 23 Nazi officials, all but three of whom were medical doctors, were charged with war crimes and crimes against humanity. Specifically, they were accused of taking part in medical experiments during World War II without the consent of the subjects of the experiments whereby the defendants in the course of these experiments committed murders, acts of brutality, cruelty, torture, atrocity and other inhuman actions. They had experimented on prisoners in concentration camps. The latter were not volunteers. The experiments included exposure to low air-pressure and low temperatures, drinking salt water and exposure to mustard gas. Others were related to various diseases, and involved the inoculation of the subjects with typhus bacilli and other organisms. Still others were experiments in euthanasia, bone transplantation and sterilization. In many cases the experiments ended in death and sometimes this was intended. Although a few of the scientists took part with some reluctance, most of them showed complete indifference toward the welfare of the subjects and often were utterly brutal.

Their main defences (apart from denials by some) were (1) orders of superior officials and (2) the national interest in wartime. The tribunal rejected these defences and found 16 of the accused to be guilty. Seven received the death sentence and the other nine received terms of imprisonment ranging from life to 10 years.

The real interest of the judgment for our purposes is in the 10 principles that the tribunal formulated for human experimentation.[24] Unfortunately they are too long for quotation here. The first one is the most important for our purposes. "The voluntary consent of the human being is absolutely essential." He should have legal capacity to give consent, free power of choice, and "sufficient knowledge and comprehension of the elements of the subject matter involved as to enable him to make an understanding and enlightened decision". This requires a full explanation of the experiment including "all inconveniences and hazards reasonably to be expected; and the effects upon his health or person which may possibly come from his participation in the experiment."

Various commentators have discussed the Nuremberg principles and have pointed out certain difficulties in their application.[25] There seems to be agreement, however, that in general they provide sound guidance for the scientist. Although they were formulated in criminal proceedings, they have relevance to an action for damages.

It will be noted that the first principle demands a high degree of frankness. Yet it is not completely unambiguous. Perhaps precision is impossible. Certainly it is hard to achieve in this matter of disclosure of risk. For example, the principle uses the phrase "hazards reasonably to be expected" and later "the effects... which may possibly come". These are not synonymous. The second of them seems to be close to the concept that I have been trying to expound. A critic might say "How can you explain the possible effects when some of them are unknown?" The best answer I can give is that set out earlier: that the requirement is met by a statement of the known risks, the fact of unknown risks and even the ultimate possibility of fatal consequences.[26]

Before leaving the question of consent, we should mention the importance of an understanding by the volunteer. There are different ways of trying to ensure that he knows what he is doing. I do not have a firm opinion as to the value of explanatory pamphlets and elaborate consent forms. In the event of a lawsuit they may assist in proving an informed consent, but on the other hand they may be so technical and detailed as to have the opposite effect.

In connection with the voluntary character of the consent, various writers[27] have discussed the propriety of using as volunteers persons who are employees, members of our armed forces and convicts. Opinion is not unanimous, at least in the case of convicts. The only comment I make here is to observe that if a volunteer from one of these groups were ever to bring action (which is doubtful) a court would require stronger evidence that the consent was truly voluntary than in the case of a volunteer who was not in one of these categories.

Minors and Persons of Unsound Mind as Subjects

From the scientific standpoint, the testing of new drugs on children and the mentally ill is desirable. Who then, if anyone, may give a consent that is binding on the minor or the mentally ill?

Dealing first with the minor, it will help once again to look at the position in relation to medical treatment. The requirement of consent to therapy for the minor can be described as follows:

1. Where he is mature and has left home, he can give his own consent, just as an adult can;

2. Where he is mature and living at home, the position is the same as in (1);

3. Where he is "of tender years", the guardian's consent is necessary.[28]

I know of no decision on this point in England or Canada. A leading American text says it is unsafe for the physician to treat any minor child without the guardian's consent, but then adds that a minor in class 1 may give his own consent.[29] Whatever may be the position in the United States, a mature minor under Canadian law may consent to the risk of injury. He may do so even where the risk is that of damage from another's negligence.[30] This being so, he can obviously agree to medical or surgical treatment which is for his benefit. Thus a person in class 1 or 2 may give his own consent.[31] A child in class 3 cannot effectively do so; his guardian's consent is necessary.[32] If the patient seems to be on the shadowy borderline between class 2 and 3 it is safer for the physician to assume he is in class 3 and to secure the guardian's consent.

What then of scientific experiment? Can the mature minor in class 1 or 2 give his consent as though he were of age? Clearly he can. True, the experiment differs from treatment in that it is not primarily for his benefit. However, there are other cases where a person may agree to an invasion of his bodily integrity where it is not for his benefit. Let us suppose, for example, that an 18-year-old boy has donated blood to the blood-bank without his guardian's consent. If such consent were required by law, then the boy could later succeed in an action for battery against the person who took the blood—which is absurd.[33]

Turning now to the child of tender years, he clearly cannot give a binding consent. The difficult question is whether his guardian can. By way of preface it might be noted that medical authorities have given varying opinions on the ethical propriety of experimentation on children: that it is not permissible; that it is permissible if it may benefit the child or (in one view) other children;[34] that it is permissible if the guardian consents;[35] that it is permissible if the guardian consents *and* there is hope of benefit to the child.[36]

Whatever be the prevailing ethical view, my opinion is that legally the guardian's consent is not binding on the child. In this problem the distinction between therapy and experiment is important. A guardian may certainly give consent to medical treatment, but it is hard to find a principle on which he may agree to expose the child to harm in a non-therapeutic procedure and at the same time bind the child not to take action if damage occurs.[37] The guardian's right to consent to medical treatment rests on the fact that it is for the child's benefit. This factor is absent in an experiment, and the body that the guardian is exposing to risk is not his own.

The person of unsound mind, like the young child, cannot be called a volunteer. The question is whether his guardian or custodian[38] may give on his behalf a binding consent. It is clear that experiments on the mentally ill are frequently desirable. Many drugs are made for them and, besides, tests on animals are of little help. It is also apparent that medical writers are of the opinion that it is ethical if the guardian consents.[39]

Now it is clearly desirable that ethical and legal rules be fairly close together. A wide gap is to the discredit of one or other or both. Indeed I have tried to show earlier that in relation to the no-experiment rule no such gap exists. However, in the case of scientific experiments on the mentally incompetent, I cannot express a confident opinion that a court would absolve a scientist were a patient later to bring action for disabilities incurred while he was the subject of tests of a new drug with his guardian's consent. The reason is the same as in the case of a child—that the guardian's power to give consent is confined to matters that are for the patient's benefit, and the experiment in a new drug is not.

The first Nuremberg rule gives support to this opinion, for it requires that the subject be a volunteer with capacity to give an informed consent. American commentators have criticized the rule on this point for the very reason that it excludes experiments on children and the mentally ill.[40]

A possible criticism of my opinion on this point is that experiments, especially on the mentally ill, are therapy and do not lose this character merely because they have scientific value as well. This objection might be valid in the case of electric shock or insulin shock therapy or prefrontal lobotomy. Perhaps it is sometimes valid even in tests of new drugs. I am not competent to express an opinion whether, for example, the large-scale trials of Salk and Sabin vaccine would be classed as therapy. If, however, all scientific experiments with new drugs are therapy, then the distinction between the two vanishes. That the distinction is valid is the premise of the whole of this discussion.

If the present opinion is correct, it is still not a serious obstacle to research. If the research is ethically proper, then the scientist can proceed, but he does so realizing that, if the subject is harmed, there is a theoretical possibility that he may at a subsequent date bring action. In leaving this subject it might not be presumptuous to express the opinion that if one were to consider whether the loss should fall on the scientist (and possibly the maker) or the unconsenting subject, he might well think that it should not fall on the latter. Perhaps society, through the state, should bear the loss because of the worthy object of the experiment. Discussion of that possibility, however, is outside the scope of this article.

Married Women

The only question here is whether the husband of a married woman would have an action against the scientist if the wife were to be harmed by the new drug so that she could not perform her wifely duties. Assuming that the wife gave an effective consent so that she would herself have no action, then the husband has no action. The subordination of the wife to the husband has largely disappeared from our law and there is no basis for saying that a wife must obtain the husband's consent before volunteering.[41] In the special case of a drug that might render the wife sterile, the situation is analogous to that of an operation. I understand that in the case of an operation it is customary to obtain the husband's consent. Regan says it "is desirable", while Lord Nathan thinks "it is doubtful in the extreme" whether the husband has an action where he does not consent.[42] In my opinion he has no action if sterility to the wife results from administration of a new drug, even though there may be some doubt in the case of an operation intended to bring about sterility in the wife.[43]

Concluding Comment

Several factors quite apart from the binding effect of an informed consent reduce the likelihood of an action or serious threat of action.

1. In most cases the risk of serious injury is very slight.

2. The burden is on the volunteer to prove that the drug has caused his disability; and this is often a hard burden to discharge.

3. In most cases the volunteer will be satisfied if those conducting the experiment assume the expense that he has incurred from the harmful effects of the drug.

A final observation might not be amiss. It would be unfortunate if the scientist were to take either of the following attitudes: (1) one of such apprehension of legal action against him that he does not take steps to obtain volunteers or (2) one of such obsession with the importance and value of what he is doing that he does not concern himself about the welfare of the volunteer. The proper approach is midway between these extremes. Complete candour and a voluntary consent remove the risk of an action against him.

The Family Physician

In many cases the family physician will wish to refer a patient to the scientist. If the physician were to take an active part in the administration of the new drug and were negligent, then he would be liable.[44] Again, if the physician persuaded the patient to submit and did not disclose the risks and if the scientist did not do so either, then the physician as well as the scientist would probably be liable in event of injury.

However, my understanding is that the role of the physician is normally much smaller. Assuming that he merely tells his patient of the experiment and refers him to the scientist and exerts no pressure on him to volunteer, then in my opinion the physician is under no liability if harm ensues. The position is analogous to that where he refers his patient to a competent specialist. In that event he is not liable for the negligent or unauthorized act of the specialist.[45]

The Maker of the Drug

The writer enters this topic with diffidence. He cannot visualize all of the steps between manufacture and consumption, and in any case the factual situations vary so much that there would be little point in attempting a sweeping generalization. There is no need to discuss here the liability of a seller to a buyer under the Sale of Goods Acts, for there is no sale by maker to user. One proposition that can be stated with confidence is that the maker is liable to the consumer for negligence.[46] Thus if ground glass or arsenic or too many grains of the drug were put into a capsule and harm resulted, negligence would probably be found. Similarly, misleading or inaccurate information or directions given to the scientist, and resulting in harm to the volunteer, would render the maker liable.[47]

If, however, the maker has been careful throughout and the information he supplies to the scientist is as complete and accurate as possible, what is the maker's position if the patient is harmed? It is important to remember that the maker does not put out the drug with knowledge of its effects. They are as unknown to him as to the scientist. On principle there seems to be no basis for holding the maker liable.[48]

Then there may be a case where the scientist has been negligent or has administered the drug without a proper consent and so is liable to the volunteer. He is then interested in the possibility of obtaining indemnity or at least contribution from the maker. Unless the maker has been negligent, there is no basis for holding him liable, even in part.

Of course the maker and scientist are working toward a common end—to determine the value of the drug. There may be cases where it may seem unfair to the scientist that the whole burden of a judgment in favour of the volunteer should fall on him. Perhaps the solution is to make an agreement with the maker for complete or partial indemnity. Discussion of this possibility, however, is outside the scope of this article.

The writer acknowledges with thanks the very substantial help that Dr. E.E. Daniel, Head of the Department of Pharmacology, University of Alberta, has given him in preparation of this article, and also profitable discussions with Dr. G.R. Macdonald of Edmonton, and with Dr. M.J. Huston, Dean of the Faculty of Pharmacy, University of Alberta.

Notes

1 Hatry, P.: *Clin. Pharmacol. Ther.*, 4: 4, 1963.

2 Editorial: *Canad. Med. Ass. J.*, 86: 838, 1962.

3 Reg. C. 01. 301 under Food and Drugs Act.

4 Reg. C. 01. 307 recognizes this.

5 Beecher, H.K.: *J. A. M. A.* 169: 461, 1959. It is the source of several others cited below. Another very good discussion is Ladimer, I., Ethical and legal aspects of medical research on human beings, *Journal of Public Law,* 3: 467, 1954.

6 Lederman, J.J.: *Canad. Med. Ass. J.*, 87: 216, 1962.

7 Nathan, Lord and Barrowclough, A.R.: Medical negligence, Butterworth & Co., Ltd., London, 1957.

8 *McQuay* v. *Eastwood* (1886) 12 Ontario Reports, 402. In that case the physician omitted to use a new technique and the court held he was justified in so doing.

9 *Baills* v. *Boulanger* (1924) 4 Dominion Law Reports 1083.

10 Roe v. Minister of Health (1954) 2 Queen's Bench Division 66.

11 *Hunter* v. *Hanley*, (1955) Sessions Cases 200.

12 *Allen* v. *Voje* (1902) 89 Northwestern Reporter 924.

13 Cady, E.L., Jr.: *Ann. West Med. Surg.*, 6: 164, 1952.

14 95 English Reprints 860 (1767).

15 *Marshall* v. *Curry* (1933) 3 Dominion Law Reports 78 is an exception to the general rule. There the surgeon was justified in performing an unauthorized operation because the urgency was great (from a medical standpoint) and the patient could not be consulted because he was under anesthetic.

16 *Kenny* v. *Lockwood* (1932) Ontario Reports 141; see also Nathan op cit note 7, 48–57.

17 Regan, L.J.: Doctor and patient and the law, 3rd. ed., C.V. Mosby Company, St. Louis, Mo., 1956, p. 509.

18 Medico-Legal: *Brit. Med. J.,* 2: 370, 1950.

19 Oppenheim, Informed Consent to Medical Treatment. Cleveland-Marshall Law Review, 11: 249, 1962; in *Bolam* v. *Friern Hospital* (1957) 2 All England Reports 118 the physician was held not liable.

20 This defence is hard to establish in an ordinary action of negligence, but the reasons for this do not apply to surgical or medical treatment that is not negligent. See Williams, G., Joint torts and contributory negligence, Stevens, London,

1951, cap. 12 for an analysis of the difference between the two cases.

21 Beecher; Ladimer op cit note 5.

22 Mackintosh, J.M., quoted by Beecher op cit note 5, 475.

23 The official report of the trial is not available to the writer, but a good account is Mitscherlich and Mielke, The death doctors, Elik. London, 1962.

24 *Ibid.*, 353–354. They are also set out and discussed in Beecher, op cit note 5 supra, 472–474.

25 Beecher, *Ibid.;* Report of the National Conference on Legal Environment of Medical Science, 1959, 88–90.

26 Doubtless there are many experiments in which the risk of damage is most remote. If the scientist is confident that no harm will occur and so gives a much milder caution, then no problem will arise if in fact no harm results.

27 E.g., Beecher, note 5, 464–465.

28 The father is guardian under the common law. In some provinces both parents are now guardians. If both parents are dead the court may appoint one. Sometimes a statute names a public official as guardian of wards of the government and of children in institutions.

29 Regan, op cit supra note 17 at 78.

30 In *Miller* v. *Decker* (1959) Supreme Court Reports 624 a 19-year-old passenger in a car failed in his action against the driver because he had assumed the risk of injury from the driver's negligence.

31 Nathan op cit note 7, 171–179 supports this view.

32 The physician's right in an emergency to treat a child without the guardian's consent need not be discussed for it has no bearing on scientific experiments.

33 The Canadian Red Cross accept donations of blood from persons 18 years of age and up to 65, and do not require parents' consent.

34 These opinions appear in correspondence in the *Lancet* quoted by Beecher, op cit note 5 at 469.

35 McCance, R.A.: *Proc. Roy, Soc. Med.*, 44: 189, 1951.

36 Report of National Conference, note 25 supra at 79–81.

37 An American case, *Bonner* v. *Moran,* 126 Federal Reporter (2d) 121, 1941 is against the view here expressed. In that case a physician took from a 15-year-old boy a portion of his skin for grafting. His guardian's consent was not sought. Later the boy succeded in an action of battery against the physician. The judgment says that had the guardian consented the action would have failed. If this is sound law (which the writer doubts) then a guardian should be able to consent on the child's behalf to an experiment, because donation of skin is no more therapeutic than an experiment.

38 Sometimes the court appoints a "guardian of the person" of one who is of unsound mind. However, where he is in a mental institution, the superintendent is usually more properly called a custodian. Hershey, N. in Report of National Conference, note 25 supra at 68–69 says that a guardian may consent to experiment where the risk is small or there is a possibility of benefit to the patient but that a custodian may not.

39 Ivy, A.C.: *Science,* 108: 1, 1948. The Report of National Conference, note 25 supra at p. 81 says that reasonable expectation of benefit to the person of unsound mind is a requisite.

40 Beecher and Report of National Conference, note 25 supra.

41 Regan op cit note 17, 76–77; Nathan op cit note 7 at 179–182 both support this view in relation to medical treatment. The writer knows of no Canadian case on the subject.

42 Regan, *ibid.:* Nathan, *ibid*. At common law the husband has an action against a person who negligently injures his wife and thereby deprives him of his wife's "consortium". In the writer's opinion the basis for such an action is absent in the situation under discussion here.

43 Tallin, G.P.R.: *Canad. Med. Ass. J.,* 87: 207, 1962.

44 In both *Slater* v. *Baker,* note 14 supra and a Canadian case, *Parmley* v. *Yule,* (1945) Supreme Court Reports 635 a patient recovered against the physician as well as against the specialist. In both cases the physician took an active part in the wrongful procedure.

45 Regan, op cit note 17 at 115; Meredith, Malpractice liability of doctors and hospitals, Carswell, Toronto, 1956 at 103.

46 The governing principle is that of the snail-in-the-bottle case, *Donoghue* v. *Stevenson,* (1932) Appeal Cases 562.

47 Hursh, American law of products liability, Lawyer's Co-operative Publishing Co., Rochester, 1961: vol. II, 545–562 discusses a number of American cases that support these propositions. *Gottsdonker* v. *Cutter Laboratories,* 6 California Reporter 320, 1960 is not relevant here. In that case a supply of Salk vaccine contained live virus, and under California law there was a warranty that the vaccine was fit for its intended purpose.

48 This is the opinion of Mr. John A. Bradshaw, Assistant General Attorney for Parke Davis and Company, who kindly made available to the writer a memorandum he had prepared on the subject. Of course a court might say that the loss should fall on the business concern that hopes to make a profit on the drug, but any such decision would be a radical extension of *Donoghue* v. *Stevenson,* note 16 supra.

1963

Anti-Discrimination Legislation

Reprinted from
(1963) Canadian Bar Association Papers
pp. 28–56

This is a paper which Bowker delivered at the Civil Liberties Section of the Canadian Bar Association for the annual meeting held in Banff, Alberta in 1963.

Part of it was reproduced by the Ontario Human Rights Commission in its publication Human Relations, *of December 1963 (No. 8, pp. 1–3), under the title "We Need the Shield and the Sword in Safeguarding our Human Rights."*

The Civil Liberties Section was formed shortly after World War II. W.F. Bowker was Secretary at the time this paper was presented.

Anti-Discrimination Legislation

The purpose of this paper is to examine the subject of legislation designed to prevent discrimination by one person against another on grounds of race, religion or colour in connection with public accommodation, employment and housing. Since this subject is in large measure within provincial competence, we shall consider it mainly at that level, with reference to federal law where appropriate.

We need not consider legislation that is affirmatively discriminatory for I know of no provincial legislation of this kind, excepting disqualification in some provinces of Indians, (e.g. Alberta) or Doukhobors (e.g. British Columbia) from voting. During an earlier period, British Columbia passed many acts designed to prevent Japanese or Chinese from immigrating, working or voting in the province. So far as one can tell from a perusal of the statute book this discriminating legislation has vanished. Some observers have suggested that Alberta's Communal Property Act (R.S.A. 1955 c. 52) discriminates against Hutterites for it regulates the creation, size and location of Hutterite communities. I doubt whether one should consider this act as a Jim-Crow law and in any event shall not examine it here.

As for federal laws, the Indian Act (R.S.C. 1952 c. 149), is in some respects discriminatory. For example the British Columbia Court of Appeal in *Reg* v. *Gonzales* (1962) 32 D.L.R. (2d) 290, held that the liquor provisions in the Indian Act prevail over the Canadian Bill of Rights (1960 c. 44, Can.). This paper, however, does not attempt to examine the special problems of the Indian Act.

The Right to Discriminate at Common Law

Beginning then with the fact that we do not in Canada have statutes *requiring* discrimination, the position is that private individuals or groups *may* discriminate in the absence of a common law rule or a statute *forbidding* discrimination. Thus, a merchant or landlord may sell or rent to whom he pleases and an employer may hire whom he pleases; and the basis of the choice may be race or colour.

The common carrier and innkeeper are the well-known exceptions at common law. We sometimes point with pride to the judgment of Birkett, J. in *Constantine* v. *Imperial Hotels,* [1944] 2 All E.R. 171. The plaintiff was a West Indian cricket-player who recovered five guineas damages against a hotel which refused to provide him a room in World War II.

However the obligation to furnish food and lodging to a properly behaved wayfarer does not extend to a restaurant that is not part of a hotel (*Franklin* v. *Evans* (1924) 55 O.L.R. 349). In Alberta, the Appellate Division held in 1961 that a negro's action against a motel keeper for refusal to provide him a room cannot succeed, for a motel that does not serve food is not an inn (*King* v. *Barclay* (1961) 35 W.W.R. 240). Since that case the Innkeeper's Act has been amended to bring motels within the definition of an inn even though they do not serve food.

Beer parlours, cocktail lounges, taverns and the like are invariably regulated by provincial statute. I know of no Liquor Act with an anti-discrimination provision, and indeed in Alberta the Liquor Licensing Act (1958, c. 38 s. 80(1)) specifically provides that a proprietor may in his discretion refuse to sell liquor to anyone without giving reasons. The purpose may be to give the proprietor power to keep out undesirables, but obviously it could be used to discriminate.

In two reported Canadian cases, negroes brought action for refusal to serve them liquor, and both times failed. The first case, *Christie* v. *York Corporation* [1940] S.C.R. 139 arose in Quebec. In that province it appears that any person in business may deal with whom he wishes. True, a statute called the License Act (R.S.Q. 1941 c. 76 s. 32) forbids persons holding a restaurant license to refuse without reasonable cause to give food to travellers. However the refusal here occurred in a tavern. It was not a restaurant, so the Supreme Court held that the defendant could legally refuse to serve the negro. The dissent of Davis J. rests on the argument that the holder of a tavern license is not like an ordinary merchant. He sells his beer under a special privilege from the government and should not be able to pick and choose his customers. Incidentally, Douglas J. took a similar position in his concurring opinion in one of the sit-in cases that recently reached the Supreme Court of the United States (*Lombard* v. *Louisiana,* 83 S. Ct. 1122 at 1125–30, (1963)).

A few months after the *Christie* decision, the British Columbia Court of Appeal decided *Rogers* v. *Clarence Hotel,* [1940] 2 W.W.R. 545. The plaintiff was a negro who brought action for refusal to sell him a glass of beer in a beer parlour. The majority simply held that *Christie* v. *York* was based on general principles, and on the effect of the Liquor laws, and that these were the same in both provinces. Therefore the plaintiff failed. The operator of a beer parlour has "complete freedom of commerce."

O'Halloran J.A. dissented on three grounds:

(1) it is contrary to the common law to refuse to serve a person because of race or colour; (2) the defendant held himself out to the public as prepared to serve them with beer; and (3) government control of liquor sales has the effect of making the operation of beer parlours a business "affected with a public interest". Thus a proprietor has no discretion based on race or colour to refuse to serve a patron. This last reason is similar to that of Davis J. dissenting in *Christie* v. *York*.

The question of discrimination has also arisen in connection with theatres. In a case in Quebec in 1919 (*Loew's Montreal Theatres* v. *Reynolds,* 30 K.B. 459) a negro brought action because the theatre had refused to sell him a seat in the orchestra though it would have sold him one in the balcony. Lamothe C.J. held that the proprietor could make his own rules and that the plaintiff must submit to them.

Later in *R.* v. *Desmond,* [1947] 4 D.L.R. 81 a negress in Nova Scotia asked for a ticket downstairs. She was sold a balcony ticket but then insisted on taking a seat below. The provincial tax was one cent higher downstairs so a charge was laid against her for failing to pay the tax. She was convicted. The full court held that certiorari did not lie. However, Hall J. said;

> "Had the matter reached the court by some method other than certiorari, there might have been opportunity to right the wrong done this unfortunate woman.
>
> "One wonders if the manager of the theatre who laid the complaint was so zealous because of a bona fide belief that there had been an attempt to defraud the Province of Nova Scotia of the sum of one cent, or was it a surreptitious endeavour to enforce a Jim-Crow rule by misuse of a public statute?"

There is nothing in the judgment however to indicate that the accused could have succeeded in a civil action for refusal to sell her a downstairs seat.

Thus it seems that apart from the two long-established exceptions, the common law gives no right of action to a person whom a businessman refuses to serve. If such refusal is to be actionable, or is to be made an offence, legislation is necessary.

Fair Accommodation Practices Acts

It is now appropriate to see what various provinces have done to secure the individual against discrimination in places of public accommodation. The first legislation was Ontario's Racial Discrimination Act (1944 c. 51). It merely forbade advertisements indicating a policy of racial or religious discrimination. The Alberta Bill of Rights Act (1946 c. 11) need not be considered. Its main purpose was to control banks and the Privy Council held it *ultra vires* (*Re Alberta Bill of Rights Act,* [1947] A.C. 503). In 1947, Saskatchewan passed a Saskatchewan Bill of Rights Act, (now R.S.S. 1953 c. 345). It enacted among other things, that every person shall enjoy the right to obtain the accommodation or facilities of any hotel, victualling house, theatre or other place to which the public is customarily admitted, regardless of race, creed, religion, colour or ethnic or national origin (s. 11). A person who deprives another of that right is subject to fine and injunction (ss. 15, 16).

Ontario passed the first Fair Accommodation Practices Act (1954 c. 28). Besides re-enacting the Racial Discrimination Act it provides that no person shall deny to another person the accommodation or services available in any place to which the public is customarily admitted because of race, creed or colour. The sanctions are fine and injunction. Of importance is the provision for an officer to investigate complaints, and also one for appointment by the Minister of Labour of a conciliation commission. The preamble to this Act declares its purpose in the following terms:

> "Whereas it is public policy in Ontario that places to which the public is customarily admitted be open to all without regard to race, creed, colour, nationality, ancestry or place of origin; whereas it is desirable to enact a measure to promote observance of this principle; and whereas to do so is in accord with the Universal Declaration of Human Rights as proclaimed by the United Nations."

Two years later Saskatchewan replaced the anti-discrimination section in its Bill of Rights Act with an Act having the same title as Ontario's, and much like it (1956 c. 68). In 1959 New Brunswick (1959 c. 6) and Nova Scotia (1959 c. 4) and in 1960 Manitoba (1960 c. 14) all followed with statutes closely resembling Ontario's and with the same title. Manitoba's has a preamble the same as the first clause of Ontario's. Thus half the provinces have statutes, remarkably uniform, designed to bar discrimination in public places.

As for reported cases, the only ones are from Ontario. The complainants in all three cases were negroes in Dresden. In the first two they waited twenty or thirty minutes and their requests for food or drink were ignored while white customers who had come in later were served. The County Court judge who decided both cases found that the Crown had not proved a denial of service, or that the food was available, or that denial was based on colour. Thus he acquitted the accused (*R.* v. *McKay* (1955) 113 C.C.C. 56; *R.* v. *Emerson* 113 C.C.C. 69: see Borovoy, The Dresden Affair, (1956) 14 Fac. of Law Rev. U. of Toronto 13).

The next case involved the same restaurateur as one of the first cases. He not only failed to serve the negroes but closed the cafe on a Saturday afternoon. The County Court judge found the accused guilty and also held the statute *intra vires* (*R.* v. *McKay* (1955) 5 D.L.R. 2d 403). I recall an article in Maclean's magazine reporting that since this case the Dresden cafe owners have served negroes.

Fair Employment Practices Acts

The next area in which Canadian legislatures have attempted to prevent discrimination is that of employment. Here again Saskatchewan's Bill of Rights Act (sec. 8) first spelled out the right to obtain and retain employment without discrimination as to compensation, terms and conditions of employment because of race or creed. In 1951 Ontario passed a Fair Employment Practices Act (1951 c. 24) with a preamble like that later appearing in its Fair Accommodation Practices Act. The Act specifically forbids an employer to refuse to employ or continue to employ any person or to discriminate against him because of race or religion. Then it forbids trade unions to exclude or expel persons on the same grounds. An offender is subject to a fine and injunction and machinery for conciliation is provided.

Two years later Parliament passed the Canada Fair Employment Practices Act (1952–53 C. 19) confined of course to employment in works or business within Parliament's authority. It is in general like Ontario's. In quick succession Manitoba, (1953 2 sess. c. 18), Nova Scotia (1955 c. 5), New Brunswick (1956 c. 9) and British Columbia (1956 c. 16) followed, and Saskatchewan in 1956 took her provision from the Bill of Rights Act and put it in a new statute. All of these provincial acts are very much like Ontario's and have the same title. We now have six provincial acts and a federal act on this subject.

I have found no reported case on any of these Acts. Incidentally Ontario's Labour Relations Act forbids collective bargaining agreements that provide for discrimination, and in Quebec it has been held without any special provision that the Labour Relations Commission acted beyond its power in certifying a wood-workers' union that excluded Indians who made up a third of the workers (*John Murdock Ltee* v. *Commission* [1956] S.C. 30).

Restrictive Covenants

A purchaser of land may make a covenant with his vendor that he will not use the land in a certain way, and equity holds that such a covenant runs with the land. That is to say, a subsequent purchaser is bound by the covenant. Now in some cases the vendor has taken a covenant that he will not sell to a person of the Jewish or coloured race, or perhaps to a "non-Caucasian". Is such a covenant binding, so that a sale by the original buyer to a person of a proscribed race is void?

In the famous case of *Re Drummond Wren* [1945] 4 D.L.R. 674 a buyer who had given such a covenant asked for a declaration that it was not binding. The argument of interest here is that the covenant is against public policy. Undeterred by the many judicial admonitions not to ride the unruly horse, Mr. Justice Mackay, invoking the United Nations and Atlantic Charters, several Ontario Acts that indicate a policy of non-discrimination, Roosevelt, Churchill, de Gaulle, the World Trade Union Congress, the Pan American Congress and the Constitution of the U.S.S.R., concluded the covenant is obnoxious to public policy. If Jews can be prohibited from buying, so can Protestants, Catholics or other groups and if prohibited from one piece of land, then from others.

> "In my opinion, nothing could be more calculated to create or deepen divisions between existing religious and ethnic groups in this Province or in this country, than the sanction of a method of land transfer which would permit the segregation and confinement of particular groups to particular business or residential areas, or conversely, would exclude particular groups from particular business or residential areas."

Then came *Re Noble and Wolfe*. Mrs. Noble owned a lot at a beach resort that had been developed as a tight-knit community. She covenanted that the land would never be sold, rented, occupied or used by any person of the "Semitic, Negro or coloured race or blood," it being the intention of the original grantor to restrict the resort to persons of "the white or Caucasian race." Mrs. Noble wanted to sell to Wolfe, a Jew, and referred to the court the question whether the existence of the covenant meant that she could not give good title to Wolfe. Schroeder J., [1948] 4 D.L.R. 123 distinguished city residential property from a summer resort and in addition disagreed with Mackay, J. Canada's adherence to the United Nations Charter cannot change domestic law. Mackay J. had created a new head of public policy which Schroeder J. declined to do. The Court of Appeal upheld him, [1949] 4 D.L.R. 375. Robertson C.J.O. conceded that goodwill among the races of Canada is desirable, but that it must be based on genuinely-felt sentiments. Then he said:

> "A wise appreciation of the impotence of laws in the development of such genuine sentiments, rather than mere formal observances, no doubt restrains our legislators from enacting, and should restrain our Courts from propounding, rules of law to enforce what can only be of natural growth, if it is to be of any value to anyone."

The Supreme Court, [1951] S.C.R. 64, held the covenant void. Five of the seven judges held that a covenant of this type had nothing to do with the use to which the land may be put and therefore is not of the kind that runs with the land. Four of the judges also held the covenant void for uncertainty. None of the seven held it against public policy.

In the meantime, after the Court of Appeal's judgment, the legislature of Ontario in 1950 had amended its Conveyancing and Law of Property Act to provide that racial covenants are void. (R.S.O. 1950 c. 68 s. 21). Manitoba did the same (now R.S.M. 1954 c. 138 s. 7). As far as I know no other province has such legislation. In Saskatchewan it is possible that the Bill of

Rights Act (ss. 10, 15) in declaring the right of every person to acquire land may have the same effect. In Alberta the two Registrars of Land Titles have informed me that they never remember seeing a racial restrictive covenant. A valuable article by Mr. Smout (1952 30 Can. Bar Rev. 863) suggests that a careful conveyancer could evade the Ontario statute because it is confined to racial *covenants* and there are other restrictive devices.

The final result of *Noble and Wolfe* is that the covenant is void on the ground of uncertainty. In recent years conditions attached to gifts in wills have sometimes been held void for uncertainty when they relate to marriage of the beneficiary to a person of a given race or religion. It seems to me that the courts have gone to extreme lengths to find uncertainty in these cases; that it is scarcely an exaggeration to say that uncertainty has been invoked where the true ground is public policy.

If this is correct, might it not be better to follow the course of Mackay J. and declare the condition to be against public policy? Or better still to enact legislation? A rule of public policy can operate to render void a condition in a will or a covenant. It cannot very well change the common law in matters such as accommodation and employment, though I realize some observers have suggested that it can. If we are in fact opposed to discrimination then legislation is the most effective legal weapon.

Discrimination in Selling Land and in Providing Mortgages

The next problem is this: If racial covenants are now ineffective thanks to *Noble and Wolfe,* should the law go further and forbid the seller of a house from refusing to sell on the ground of race? The Saskatchewan Bill of Rights Act (s. 10) says that every person shall enjoy the right to purchase, own and occupy land without discrimination. The effect of this may be that a vendor could not refuse to sell solely on grounds of race, though a court might require a more specific provision to produce this result. No other province has attempted to enact anti-discrimination laws in this area, though Windsor, Ontario by resolution of the city council, has forbidden racial discrimination on resale of land bought from the city. In the United States a few cities have ordinances forbidding discrimination on sale of houses in private housing projects. I do not have any information on the workability of such laws.

A form of discrimination akin to refusal to sell property is refusal to lend money on mortgage to a negro who wants to build his house. In both Canada and the United States the national government has helped to finance home-building principally by guaranteeing repayment of mortgages and loans. During the hearings before a Special Committee of the House of Commons on the Bill of Rights in July 1960, one of the members, the Hon. Paul Martin, asked a witness this question:

> "Are you aware that at the present time coloured Canadian citizens—six that I know of, in four different cities—have been denied the opportunity of taking

> advantage of the Central Mortgage and Housing legislation because of colour? You are not aware of that?"

The answer was "No." Later when the then Minister of Justice was before the Committee, the Hon. Mr. Martin made reference to the same point, and hoped that the Bill might forbid such discrimination. It does not, and I do not know whether the regulations under the National Housing legislation contain anti-discrimination provisions.

Discrimination in Rental of Housing

Related to the purchase of land, and perhaps a more acute problem, is that of the rental of housing. During the hearings of the Special Committee mentioned above, the Hon. Mr. Martin referred to the case of a coloured civil servant who was refused admission to a high rental project in Ottawa at the time the Committee was sitting.

Until recently none of the provincial anti-discrimination laws extended to this subject. However Ontario two years ago amended its legislation to provide that no one shall deny or discriminate against any person with respect to occupancy of an apartment in any building that contains more than six dwelling units (now 1961–62 c. 93 s. 3).

This subject of discrimination in housing has been a thorny problem in the large rental developments in the United States. The landlord is reluctant to rent to negroes because their presence may force down the rental developments or drive away the other tenants, while if negroes are refused admission they will congregate in areas that tend to become slums.

Ontario's Human Rights Code

We have now covered the main areas of discrimination as they appear to me to exist in Canada, and the legislation designed to reduce them. It is appropriate here to refer to Ontario's Human Rights Code of 1962 (1961–62 c. 93) which consolidates the previous legislation. The Act begins with a preamble similar to those in the earlier Acts. Then it prohibits discriminatory advertising, discrimination in public places, apartment buildings, employment and salaries for female employees. Next is provision for the Ontario Human Rights Commission which replaced the Anti-Discrimination Commission created in 1958. Since many are of the opinion that the educational and conciliatory purposes of laws of this kind are among the most important, it is worth noting the Commission's functions (sec. 8):

> "(a) to forward the principle that every person is free and equal in dignity and rights without regard to race, creed, colour, nationality, ancestry or place of origin;
> (b) to promote an understanding of, acceptance of and compliance with this Act;
> (c) to develop and conduct educational programmes designed to eliminate dis-

criminatory practices related to race, creed, colour, nationality, ancestry or place of origin."

Another part of the Act empowers the Commission to investigate complaints and also for establishment of boards of inquiry. Then follow the provisions for fines, laying of prosecutions and injunctions.

I do not have the information on which to attempt an appraisal of the results of all these Canadian statutes. There are no reported cases except the three on discrimination in the Dresden restaurants and at the moment of preparing this paper I do not have the reports of the governmental authorities who administer the various acts. Indeed, it is doubtless hard in any event to form an opinion on the efficacy of the legislation. It is safe to say that much depends on the attitude and wisdom of those who administer it.

Two points to consider are these:

(1) Is it better to pass a fairly comprehensive code like Ontario's in the first instance or to start with a single subject such as accommodation practices? I do not have a categorical answer but incline to the view that it is better for a province to gain experience in one area and then go on to others as Ontario has done.

(2) What sanctions are the most effective? Here again I offer no clear-cut answer. Sometimes the criticism is made that the authorities lay too few charges. Yet this may sometimes be the wiser course. The provisions for persuasion and conciliation may be the most effective, at least when the legislation is new. As for the right to bring civil action for damages none of the Canadian statutes expressly confers this right, though some American ones do. Of course a common law action has always lain against an innkeeper but I do not offer an opinion as to whether the present legislation implies a right of action. Nor do I have a firm opinion whether a civil remedy is desirable.

A Glance at the United States

Canada has around 20,000 negroes while the United States has 18,000,000—10% of her whole population and a number equal to all of Canada's. In the deep South over 25% are coloured and in the North each large city has its Harlem. Everyone knows of the social tension today and that the negro is on the verge of open rebellion against the abuses he suffers. In the deep South he is the victim of prejudice when he tries to vote or obtain an education or a decent job. Segregation laws and practices govern his life from the cradle to the grave. When he tries to break out of this pattern, the people in power fight to keep him in it.

The post-civil-war amendments to the Constitution were of course designed to prevent the return of the negro to slavery. To that end the Fourteenth Amendment provides that no state shall deprive any person within its jurisdiction of the equal protection of the laws. The Fifteenth Amendment forbids discrimination in voting on account of race or colour. Both amendments give to Congress the power to enforce their provisions by appropriate legislation. Discrimination, however, has persisted, often supported by the state. There are many reasons for this, three of which have to do with the law itself. First the amendments restrict discriminatory action by the state and not by private individuals. Congress tried in 1875 to reduce discrimination in public places by passing a statute called the Civil Rights Act, which forbade discrimination in hotels, conveyances and places of amusement. The Supreme Court in 1883 held it invalid. Congress cannot pass laws directed to private discrimination but only to discriminatory action by the state. Yet a compensating doctrine has emerged in recent years. State action has come to extend far beyond action by the legislative, executive and judicial branches. Thus the discriminatory practices of municipalities and their officials is state action even where they act illegally; likewise the actions of private individuals who have received state aid or who are using state-owned land, and even the conduct of the Democratic party in conducting its election primaries. This expansion of the concept of state action has operated to extend the protection of the Fourteenth Amendment against many forms of discrimination that at first seem to be merely private action.

Second, the Supreme Court held in 1896 in *Plessy* v. *Ferguson* that a state law does not deprive the negro of equal protection of the law even though it provides for segregation as long as the facilities so provided are equal to those provided for whites. This "separate but equal" doctrine put the seal of legal approval on segregation laws in transportation, education, restaurants and public places generally. In a number of important decisions in education and transportation the Supreme Court held that the separate facilities were not in fact equal. These cases in fact cut deeply into the "separate but equal" doctrine and finally in the School Cases in 1954 the Supreme Court rejected it and held segregation laws to be *ipso facto* a denial of equal protection of the laws.

Third, Congress refuses to pass legislation designed to protect the negroes' constitutional right to equal protection of the law. Between the Reconstruction period and 1957 Southern opposition blocked every proposal for civil rights legislation. At the present time observers are speculating as to whether President Kennedy's latest recommendations can overcome the obstacle of a Southern filibuster in Congress.

The Shield and the Sword

As mentioned earlier, discrimination is not as acute in Canada as in the United States. Denial of the right to vote on racial grounds has practically disappeared in Canada. Segregated schools are unknown, and so are laws against mixed marriages. Discrimination is practised in accommodation, employment and housing as it is in the United States but it never has legal support. In other words it is private.

This brings us to an important question. What is the role of a constitutional safeguard and what is the role of legislation? To borrow the metaphor that an American writer, Robert W. Carr, has used, the constitutional enactment is a shield but the victim of discrimination needs a sword as well. The sword is legislation that forbids discrimination.

All that the American constitution does is to bar discriminatory laws (and other government action). This is fine as far as it goes, but to change the metaphor, it lacks teeth. The teeth are legislation that forbids discriminatory acts by individuals or groups.

Even if a constitutional safeguard were in broader terms than the Fourteenth Amendment this would still be true. For example the New York Constitution of 1938 forbids discriminatory practices by individuals and corporations as well as by the State. If this were sufficient by itself then statutes would not be needed as well. The fact of course is that a complex subject like discrimination in employment can be met only with sanctions and machinery for conciliation. Thus New York passed a Law Against Discrimination (in employment) in 1945. The opposition was bitter, but the Act has in fact done much to put the negro in jobs. Indeed it had a role, though perhaps not the principal one, in putting negroes into major league baseball.

One more example of the shield and sword can be found in legislation of the Canadian Parliament. The Canadian Bill of Rights Act of 1960 though an ordinary statute rather than a constitutional restriction on legislative power does have the same general quality—it first proclaims certain rights (sec. 1) and then provides that all Canadian statutes shall be construed and applied so as not to infringe those rights (sec. 2).

In connection with discrimination section 1 says: "It is hereby recognized and declared that in Canada there have existed and shall continue to exist without discrimination by reason of race, national origin, colour, religion or sex, the following human rights and fundamental freedoms, namely. . . (d) the right of the individual to equality before the law and protection of the law." In the three years since passage of the Bill, the Courts have construed it narrowly, as the annual reports to this section demonstrate. For example the Bill has no effect on the provisions in the Indian Act that impose on Indians special restrictions relating to possession of liquor: *Reg* v. *Gonzales,* (1962) 32 D.L.R. (2d) 290. However the restricted scope of the Bill is not really relevant to the point I wish to make here, which is this. The Bill of Rights like the Fourteenth Amendment is essentially negative: a shield. On the other hand the Canadian Fair Employment Practices Act is affirmative—a sword. The repeal of the Bill of Rights would not affect the Fair Employment Practices Act. The latter would stand in full vigour. On the other hand the repeal of the Fair Employment Practices Act would deprive the victim of discrimination of the only real legislative protection he has because the Bill of Rights, to return to our second metaphor, is toothless.

A constitutional safeguard (or quasi-constitutional, as in the Canadian Bill of Rights) is essentially negative. This may serve the purpose when the sole object is to prevent legislative action: e.g., "Congress shall make no law abridging freedom of speech." It is not completely effective by itself to secure equal protection of the laws, but must have the support of legislation.

To conclude the discussion on this point, a person who believes in a constitutional limitation on the legislature to prevent it from denying the right to equal protection of the laws, should support anti-discrimination statutes; while a person who does not so believe can quite consistently support such statutes.

Legislation and Morality

There is of course opposition to these enactments. For example New York's Law against Discrimination, already mentioned, met opposition on many fronts. The executive committee of the New York Bar Association opposed it. They said it was an attempt to legislate morality (and also that it was an improper interference with freedom of contract, it would drive business out of the state and it would increase group hostility). These fears were unfounded and the Act has had a substantial success.

An example closer to home of opposition to this type of law appears in the following resolution passed in November 1961 by an influential organization in this province:

> WHEREAS several well-intentioned groups in Alberta are pressing the Government to introduce Fair Employment Practices (F.E.P.) and Fair Accommodation Practices legislation; and
> WHEREAS F.E.P. legislation is Communist-inspired, having for its purpose the threat of legal blackmail to force subversive agents into positions at present closed to them; and
> WHEREAS this is achieved by making it illegal for an employer to enquire into or give consideration to any question of "race, colour or creed" in assessing the suitability of an applicant for employment; also by inference, making it illegal for a hotel or motel manager to refuse accommodation to any person, however undesirable his conduct may be, if he should happen to be coloured or to be a militant adherent of a particular creed (e.g. Communism); and
> WHEREAS people cannot be legislated into decency and morality;
> THEREFORE BE IT RESOLVED that the Alberta Government be requested to investigate its purpose and implications very fully before giving consideration to introducing so-called Fair Employment Practices legislation; and
> BE IT FURTHER RESOLVED that the Alberta Government be requested to investigate alternative non-legislative action to arouse the public conscience against deliberate and un-Christian discrimination against any of our coloured fellow-Canadians.

One can see from the last paragraph that the resolution in fact opposes discrimination. This being so it is hard to see why it objects to a statute that provides for education and efforts to persuade, which are important features of the Canadian acts. In any case my main purpose is to refer to the preamble. The second and third recitals are of such little weight as to require no comment. The fourth recital invokes the dogma "morality cannot be legislated." My purpose here is to submit that this dogma is not a valid objection to the laws under consideration.

If it means that legislation or common law rules for that matter never effectively deal with matters of decency and morality, it is patently incorrect. Part IV of the Criminal Code which is headed "Sexual Offences, Public Morals and Disorderly Conduct" deals largely with moral offences. Contracts for an immoral consideration, and gifts in wills subject to a condition conducing to immorality are void. There is of course legitimate debate as to the extent to which law should attempt to prohibit conduct considered immoral. The recent controversy in England on the question of continuing to render criminal homosexual acts in private between consenting adults illustrates this. It does not follow that conduct generally regarded as immoral can never be prohibited or at least effectively influenced by law.

Dean Rostow of the Yale Law School has written:

> "Men often say that one cannot legislate morality. I should say that we legislate hardly anything else. All movements of law reform seek to carry out certain social judgments as to what is fair and just in the conduct of society." (The Sovereign Prerogative (1962) p. 79).

If the dogma means that legislation on matters of morals should have behind it the support of a substantial body of opinion, one cannot argue with it. Society always uses pressures, non-legal and legal, to make its members conform in their conduct. Indeed, one of the roles of law is to operate as an instrument of social control. While law will be ineffective if it goes counter to deeply held views of the great majority, it can on the other hand help to lead opinion. Dicey once said that "no facts play a more important part in the creation of opinion than laws themselves" (Law and Public Opinion, 2 Ed. (1914) p. 465).

I cannot claim to speak as a sociologist, but it is my understanding that although one of the early American sociologists, Sumner, gave some support to the dogma, it does not seem to have general acceptance today. If one examines the welter of current newspaper and magazine articles on desegregation in the United States he will see general acceptance (excepting the intransigent segregationists in the South) that laws are necessary to ease the lot of the negro, though they admittedly are not enough by themselves.

Another answer to the dogma is this: an anti-discrimination law does not purport to make the discriminator love the man of different race or colour. It merely tells him to treat him as he would anyone else.

To conclude, the purpose of this paper is to show that if this country really believes in the United Nations Declaration of Human Rights, and the Principles of the Canadian Bill of Rights, it will through its provincial and federal legislatures support the passage and enforcement of legislation to put all humans on the same basis in matters of employment, public accommodation and housing. Opponents of such measures often invoke the right of the businessman to deal with whom he wants. It does not seem to me unfair to put this question. Can a member of a race that suffers from discrimination justifiably ask society through its branches of government to take steps to protect him from the hurt he suffers through refusal by persons in business or trade to treat him the same as anyone else? In my opinion, the answer is yes; and all that is left is to weigh the victim's claim against that of the person who would discriminate and ask the next question, which of the conflicting claims should prevail in our society?

A Short Bibliography

I do not attempt to cite here even a fraction of the literature. The following are particularly helpful. All are American except the last.

Emerson and Haber, Political and Civil Rights in the United States, 2 Ed. (1958) Vol. II Cap. VII, Discrimination.

Berger, Equality by Statute; Legal Controls over Group Discrimination, (1952).

Konvitz, A Century of Civil Rights (1961).

Carter, Practical Considerations of Anti-Discrimination Legislation, (1954–55) 40 Cornell L.J. 40.

MacDonald, P.V., Race Relations and Canadian Law (1960), 18 Fac. of Law Rev. U. of Toronto 115.

Addendum

This paper was submitted at the end of June 1963. Since then I have obtained more information.

The federal law on fair employment practices includes a provision in the Unemployment Insurance Act, (1955, cap. 50, sec. 22 (2)) that National Employment Service in placing workers in jobs shall not discriminate. An order in council requires contractors for construction or supplies to agree not to discriminate.

In connection with the operation of the F.E.P. Act, the Chief of Fair Employment Practices Division of the Department of Labour states that there were thirty-three complaints between 1953 and 1962, and they were settled. The Department carries on an extensive programme of education toward racial understanding—radio and television programmes, motion pictures and literature.

As for litigation under Ontario's F.E.P. law, McRuer C.J. handed down a decision in May in *Trenton Construction Workers Assn.* v. *Tange Company Ltd.* The labour Board had refused to certify the union on the ground that it discriminated against workmen because of creed. McRuer C.J. found that the Union's constitution did not require discrimination and that discrimination in fact was not proved. True the Union required members to support Christian principles but at the same time would accept a member of any creed.

The regulations under N.H.A. were amended in November, 1960, to forbid discrimination by borrowers who are building houses or apartments for sale or rent. Discrimination is a breach of the conditions on which C.M.H.C. insures the loan. (Regs. 57A–57L). The Director of the Loan Insurance Division of C.M.H.C. informs me that "so far as we are aware we have received no formal complaints relating to this Regulation."

In connection with discrimination in housing, Nova Scotia in 1963 passed a Human Rights Act (1963, cap. 5). It replaces the existing acts and in addition forbids discrimination in the letting of apartments in buildings that have more than four units.

The history of discrimination in apartment houses in Ontario is told by Dr. Hill, Director of Ontario's Human Rights Commission, in an article. It is significant that in the mid-fifties cases of refusal to provide housing to coloured people received great publicity; that an unreported case held (quite properly) that the Fair Accommodation Practices did not apply; that strong requests were made to amend the law so as to prevent such discrimination; that the amendment was made in 1961; that conciliation has been effective and that the landlord's fear of losing his other tenants is unfounded.

In general, the reports I have received from Ontario, New York and the federal Department of Labour point to the great value of conciliation and education. The activity of the Commissioners in investigating complaints and in effecting settlement is a principal feature of the administration of the acts. In Ontario the Commission has underway a study of discrimination in housing and employment in Hamilton and Windsor.

Education includes the publication of pamphlets and bulletins. The Commission informs employees, landlords and businessmen of the law and seeks their cooperation. Notices are provided for posting on the premises (this is done in Manitoba too). In the federal government the Department of Labour has a vigorous programme for attacking discrimination. It uses radio, television, films, and literature.

August 30, 1963

1964

The Uniform Survival of Actions Act

Reprinted from
(1964) 3 Alberta Law Review
pp. 197–201

The Uniform Survival of Actions Act was the work of the Uniform Law Conference (formerly called "The Conference of Commissioners on Uniformity of Legislation in Canada").

This Conference was established in 1918 by the Canadian Bar Association, its purpose being to make recommendations to the various provincial legislatures with a view to achieving uniformity in provincial legislation. Its members are appointed by each province through the Attorney General departments.

Bowker was appointed as one of Alberta's three Commissioners in 1952, and continued in this capacity for 23 years (until 1975). He served as President in 1965.

This article deals with an Act which was the result of 4 years of work of the Commission, culminating in 1963, as the "Uniform Survival of Actions Act", and had been sent to the various provincial governments for possible enactment. The Alberta Commissioners had a major role in its preparation.

The Act was designed to make causes of action in tort survive the death of a victim and wrongdoer. At common law, such actions did not survive the death of such parties, and the estate of the deceased victim could not sue the wrongdoer.

As drafted, certain items of damages do not survive to an estate; e.g., the victim's loss of expectation of life, pain and suffering, and loss of future earnings.

Some individuals took the view that even these claims should survive to the victim's estate. Hence the pros and cons were the subject of a discussion at the annual meeting of the Law Society of Alberta in 1964.

Bowker presented the paper (later published in the Alberta Law Review) *in support of the Act as drafted in the sense that it confined compensation to pecuniary losses alone.*

Taking the opposite position was Herbert Laycraft, a practising lawyer in Calgary (and a former law student of Bowker), who would later become Chief Justice of Alberta (1985).

In discussing this subject it is convenient to use the terms "victim" and "wrongdoer". The phrase "survival of action" means survival of a cause of action for the benefit of the victim's estate and also survival against the wrongdoer's estate.

The common law rule on the survival of causes of action in tort is *actio personalis moritur cum persona*. When the victim dies the cause of action never survives. When the wrongdoer dies it survives only where the claim is for the taking of property and it can be traced to the wrongdoer's estate.

It is now necessary to set out a second common law rule. No living person has a cause of action in tort against another who has wrongfully caused the death of a third. It has nothing to do with survival of actions but is often confused with that subject, because both rules come into play when a victim dies.

Legislation has made a great exception to the second rule. The Fatal Accidents Act[1] gives a cause of action to certain specified dependents of the victim. If a plaintiff cannot bring himself within this class his action remains barred by the second common law rule.

The important point to remember is that a statute providing for survival of actions has nothing whatever to do with the second rule. It abrogates the first rule.

The first survival legislation in Canada appeared in Ontario in 1886 as a provision in the Trustee Act. The Northwest Territories borrowed Ontario's Act and Alberta kept it. Thus section 32 of Alberta's present Trustee Act[2] provides for survival where the victim dies and section 33 where the wrongdoer does. The other western provinces have long had similar provisions. England had none until the Law Reform Act of 1934.[3] Later each Maritime province passed a Survival of Actions Act based on the English Act. Newfoundland's survival provisions are in the Trustee Act, and are confined to torts to property.

In the past four years the Conference of Commissioners on Uniformity of Legislation in Canada has been studying the subject and preparing a Uniform Survival of Actions Act. The work is now complete and the Act will appear in the 1963 Proceedings to be published in the spring of 1964.

Since the Uniform Act, if adopted in Alberta, would make one important change and several minor ones in our law it seems appropriate to bring it to the attention of the profession. Before discussing the Act itself I would like to use the occasion to say a word about the work of the Uniformity Conference in general. It has representatives from all provinces and the federal government. Its purpose appears from its name. Established by the Canadian Bar Association it has had an independent existence for forty-five years. In that period it has produced many model or uniform acts. Among those enacted in whole or in part by the Alberta legislature are: Rules of the Road (in the Vehicles and Highway Traffic Act[4]), Evidence,[5] Wills,[6] Intestate Succession,[7] Devolution of Real Property,[8] Family Relief,[9] Bills of Sale,[10] Conditional Sales,[11] and miscellaneous statutes ranging from Legitimation[12] to the Cornea Transplant Act.[13]

The Conference always welcomes the help of the profession in its work of preparing uniform acts. For example, provincial Law Reform Committees could do much to assist the Conference; likewise provincial Law Societies and the Canadian Bar Association. Indeed in the case of the Companies Act, the latter body has been of great help in the attempt to achieve uniformity.

Once the Conference has adopted a Uniform Act, its introduction into the legislature depends on the Cabinet. Nearly all uniform acts have been passed in at least one province and a few in almost all. Of course a legislature may adopt a uniform act with amendments, or having adopted it *in toto* may later amend it. It seems obviously desirable for the profession to know the content of any uniform act that the Cabinet may bring before the Alberta legislature. Of course uniform acts have always been published and the contents of any bill before the legislature are ascertainable. However the profession does not always make a point of examining these sources and it seems proper and desirable to call the profession's attention to proposed legislation—or potential legislation, as one might call a Uniform Act. Hence the following comments on the Uniform Survival of Actions Act.

All the existing acts have a general provision that causes of action survive, as one would expect in a statute designed to provide for survival. However, nearly all of the Acts contain exceptions. In Alberta, the only one is libel and slander. In other Acts one finds one or more of the following: malicious prosecution, false imprisonment, enticement of a spouse, adultery, defamation.[14] In every case these exceptions apply both when the victim dies and when the wrongdoer dies. Yet there is in fact an important difference between the two situations. Where the wrongdoer dies the plaintiff is still alive and his damages are not mitigated in any way by the wrongdoer's death. Therefore, the wrongdoer's death should make no difference. (One can concede an exception in the case of purely exemplary damages, but as the House of Lords recently pointed out in *Rookes* v. *Bernard,*[15] truly exemplary damages are very exceptional in English tort law). For this reason the Uniform Act simply provides[16] that when the wrongdoer dies causes of action against him shall survive. None of the exceptions in the various existing acts is brought into the Uniform Act.

The death of the victim, however, raises different considerations. Torts that cause property damage or any actual loss to the victim's estate should survive in its favour. On the other hand, there are certain damages that a living plaintiff should be able to recover, but that his estate should not be able to. For this reason the section providing for survival of causes of action where the victim dies makes an exception of actions for adultery, seduction and enticement.[17] These can be described as especially personal in nature. (The English Act[18] contains this exception though that Act extends it to the case of the death of the wrongdoer as well as the victim.) In addition the Uniform Act provides that in cases where the action does survive for the benefit of the victim's estate, there is a restriction on the amount of damages that may be awarded.[19] This is the provision that if enacted here would do away with the claim for loss of expectation of life. It provides:

> 6. Where a cause of action survives for the benefit of the estate of a deceased person, only damages that have resulted in actual pecuniary loss to the deceased person or the estate are recoverable and, without restricting the generality of the foregoing, the damages recoverable shall not include punitive or exemplary damages or damages for loss of expectation of life, pain and suffering or physical disfigurement.

(England has a similar restrictive provision but it does not include claims for loss of expectation.)

It is important to point out the reason for the exceptions in section 3 and the restrictions in section 6. It is this. The basis of damages in tort is compensation. Survival of a cause of action for the benefit of the victim's estate should be to enable the estate to recover pecuniary losses but nothing more. The common law rule clearly worked a hardship where the wrongdoer negligently burned down the victim's barn or smashed his car, and by chance the victim died of a heart attack before he could take action and obtain judgment. However, there are some items of damage that are in a different category. Like claims for adultery, seduction and enticement, they are peculiarly personal. Compensation for pain and suffering, disfigurement, and loss of expectation of life and heavy damages for defamation, false imprisonment and malicious prosecution are the main examples. To allow them to the victim's estate as one would allow them to the victim himself is to give to the estate a windfall. The late Professor Winfield once expressed this view:

> "Where it is the tortfeasor who has died, then whether the tort was a personal one or not, his estate ought to be liable. Where it is the injured party who has died there is something to be said for extinction of an action for a personal tort, for it seems consonant neither with justice nor with the law of tort that a man's successors should profit by a wrong which in origin did *them* no harm; if, however, they are in fact harmed, as might well happen in some cases of defamation of their predecessor, then his remedy ought to survive."[20]

Since the claim for loss of expectation is of particular interest in Alberta, and my purpose here is to support the abolition of that claim, it will help to give its history. Although Ontario has had its survival provisions from 1886 and Alberta since Territorial days, I have never found any suggestion of such a claim in any Canadian case or literature until after the English Courts had accepted it under that country's survival legislation of 1934. In 1935 the Court of Appeal considered a case[21] in which the victim was still alive and the evidence showed that because of his injuries he would probably not live as long as he normally would have been expected to. The Court held this is a proper item to consider in awarding damages to the living victim. Then came *Rose* v. *Ford*[22] in which a 22-year old woman died as a result of the defendant's negligence. Her estate brought action under the survival legislation and claimed that since the victim could have claimed for loss of expectation had she lived, the estate may likewise do so even though the shortening of life is no longer an expectation but an accomplished fact. The House of Lords admitted the claim. Four years later in recognition of the impossibility of putting a money value on expectation of life where the victim had died, the House of Lords in *Benham* v. *Gambling*[23] ruled that the damages should be kept low and in effect set the amount at £200. In recent years the amount has risen to as much as £500.

In Canada in the meantime, *Rose* v. *Ford* was the inspiration for many actions by estates where the victim had died after an accident for which the defendant's negligence was responsible. In the next few years all the common law provinces except Alberta and Manitoba abolished the claim for loss of expectation. The courts of those two provinces and the Supreme Court of Canada are still struggling with attempts to put a value on life for the purpose of actions under the Trustee Act. The awards have ranged from $1,000 to $7,500. A common figure nowadays is around $6,500.

In deciding that the Uniform Act should abolish the claim for loss of expectation, the Conference of course knew that all provinces but two have already done away with it as a matter of deliberate legislative policy. This fact taken by itself would not be sufficient reason for following suit. The Conference was of opinion that abolition is sound in principle. The amount of the award is essentially arbitrary. I do not suggest that mere difficulty in assessment is of itself a reason for rejecting a claim. Everyone recognizes the difficulty of determining *quantum* in almost any case of personal injuries, but here it seems no exaggeration to say there is no rational basis at all. The main reason, however, is more fundamental. In the law of negligence the purpose of an award to a plaintiff is compensation for loss he has suffered. Here however the estate has suffered no loss whatever. An award is a simple windfall which it would not be were the victim alive. In that case he would himself receive the money (and incidentally such awards are rare, so far as reported cases show). Supporters of the claim for loss of expectation might argue that the award will benefit the estate. The answer is that it is of no practical assistance to dependents because they have their action under The Fatal Accidents Act.[24] Usually their damages thereunder are greater than the award for loss of expectation and the amount they receive under the Trustee Act[25] is deducted from their damages under the Fatal Accidents Act. Thus the argument that judgments for loss of expectation serve the purpose of helping dependants under the Fatal Accidents Act is not available. The only ones who benefit from the award are beneficiaries who are not dependants, or creditors.

Another argument used by proponents of the claim is that the law should not make it cheaper to kill than to maim. The answer is that we are not in the realm of punishment but of compensation. A serious injury may well result in smaller damages than a less serious one.

It must be remembered that survival legislation does not confer a cause of action for wrongful death. Yet in effect an award for loss of expectation operates to give the victim's estate such an action. Indeed, one Manitoba judge[26] said that this was the purpose of the legislation! There is no need here for an extended discussion of the logic of the claim. The conflicting viewpoints emerge in the Court of Appeal judgment in *Rose* v. *Ford*[27] itself. My submission is that the award in fact if not in form is one for wrongfully causing death—and the Act permits no such claim. Middleton J. so held in Ontario over forty-five years ago.[28]

I am content to support the criticism of Fleming,[29] and Stone,[30] and to adopt the reasons of Dean Wright[31] and of E.R.E. Carter[32] in favour of abolition.

By way of summary, the purpose of survival legislation is to cure defects in the common law. The present submission is that the real harshness of the common law rule disappears once the victim can recover against the wrongdoer's estate, and the victim's estate can recover for loss to the estate. The legislation should not cast its net so wide as to allow the estate of a victim to make a claim that represents no loss whatever to the estate. If the Fatal Accidents Act is too narrow it should be widened; and a Survival Act should not be the vehicle for doing this indirectly, erratically and inefficiently.

By way of a postscript, may I mention the provision for limitation of actions.[33] If enacted it would overcome the decision in *Scott* v. *Thompson*,[34] holding that the period prescribed in the Vehicles and Highway Traffic Act[35] prevails over that in the Trustee Act.[36]

Notes

1 R.S.A. 1955 c. 111.
2 R.S.A. 1955 c. 346.
3 (Imp.) 24 & 25 Geo. 5 c. 41.
4 (Alta.) 1958 c. 93, amending R.S.A. 1955 c. 356.
5 R.S.A. 1955 c. 102.
6 R.S.A. 1955 c. 369 and (Alta.) 1960 c. 118.
7 R.S.A. 1955 c. 161.
8 R.S.A. 1955 c. 83.
9 R.S.A. 1955 c. 109.
10 R.S.A. 1955 c. 23.
11 R.S.A. 1955 c. 54.
12 (Alta.) 1960 c. 56.
13 (Alta.) 1960 c. 19.
14 See Trustee Act, R.S.A. 1955 c. 346, ss. 32–33, 1960 c. 111; Administration Act, R.S.B.C. 1960 c. 3, s. 71; Trustee Act, R.S.M. 1954 c. 273, s. 49; Survival of Actions Act. R.S.N.B. 1952 c. 223; Trustee Act, R.S. Nfld. 1952, c. 166, s. 22; Survival of Actions Act, R.S.N.S. 1954, c. 282; Survival of Actions Act, 1955 (P.E.I.) c. 17; Trustee Act, R.S.S. 1953, c. 123, ss. 52–53.
15 (H.L. (E.)) [1964] 1 All E.R. 637.
16 s. 4.
17 s. 3.
18 *supra*, n. 3.
19 s. 6.
20 14 Can. Bar Rev. 639, 649.
21 *Flint* v. *Lovell* [1935] 1 K.B. 354.
22 (H.L. (E.)) [1937] A.C. 826.
23 (H.L. (E.)) [1941] A.C. 161.
24 *supra*, n. 1.
25 *supra*, n. 2.
26 Adamson J.A., in *Anderson* v. *Chasney* [1949] 4 D.L.R. 71.
27 *supra*, n. 22.
28 *England* v. *Lamb* (H. Ct. Ont. 1918) 42 O.L.R. 60.
29 *Law of Torts* 701–02 (2d ed. 1961).
30 *Province and Function of Law*, 196–97.
31 16 Can. Bar Rev. 193.
32 32 Can. Bar Rev. 713, 760–61.
33 s.10.
34 (Alta. C.A. 1957) 21 W.W.R. 583.
35 *supra*, n. 4.
36 *supra*, n. 2.

1964

The Professional Responsibility of the Lawyer

Text of an unpublished address given to the Law Society of Saskatchewan at its annual meeting in June, 1964 at Waskesiu, Sask.

If the title were not already long enough, I would have been tempted to add "in Saskatchewan and Alberta." Of course one might say a visitor to the Province should not discuss the profession as it exists within the province where he is the recipient of such kind hospitality. However, we recall that Saskatchewan and Alberta are in fact twins, and although even twins may not be identical on approaching threescore years, it may be that there is still between them enough similarity that problems of concern to one may be of interest to the other.

And so I should like to speak to you on Professional Responsibility as one Albertan sees it, and anything that may emerge to indicate he is not always looking through rose-colored glasses will please be taken as not describing the Saskatchewan Scene.

Now it is not only our provinces, but our professions, that have a common origin. The Legal Profession Ordinance established one Law Society, and our early great lawyers were all on its rolls. The prominent men seemed to be concentrated in Moosomin and Fort MacLeod, and they all belonged to the same Society; and our modern Legal Professions Acts stem from the old ordinance; and our law schools are part of sister universities that came into being soon after the provinces were formed. Indeed, *our* first dean was John Weir, a name that ranks close after the Almighty in legal circles in Alberta, and he was a graduate of Saskatchewan (and a Rhodes Scholar from here).

Now as to the subject of my address, it will be convenient to deal with it in three parts. First, to discuss the meaning of "profession"; second, to explain the concept of professional responsibility as applied to lawyers; third, to examine its state and to consider how it may be strengthened.

I. The Concept of a Profession

Many definitions exist, though most of them are rather descriptions of the main features, and no two are alike. Peter Wright in an article in the *Canadian Bar Review* defines a profession as a "self-disciplined group of individuals who hold themselves out to the public as possessing a special skill, derived from training or education, and who are prepared to exercise that skill primarily in the interests of others." A professional person is a member of such a group.

For convenience, and because it is a simpler statement than most, I shall use Roscoe Pound's—"a group of men pursuing a common calling as a learned art, and as a public service." You will see in this three elements: (1) organization, (2) learning, and (3) a spirit of public service. It is generally agreed that historically there were three professions: theology, medicine and law. Sometimes teaching and the military were included. *Organization* is a criterion in all definitions I have seen. Meetings of this kind recognize this need, and clearly they help to foster the professional spirit. A person who belongs to a profession should regard himself as a member of a group, and identify himself with it. After all, we admit a man to membership in the society, and he becomes responsible for its well-being. I sometimes think that one of the great strengths in the English bar is the close association of counsel. The competition in court, and indeed the association not only in the Inns, but in the robing room, helps to strengthen the spirit of kinship. Now as far as the solicitors' branch is concerned, there is no counterpart of the Inns nor of the contests of litigation, and it is therefore easier for them to carry on simply as individuals. I think this is true of provinces like ours with small numbers scattered over large areas; and the obvious way to combat this centrifugal tendency is through strong associations.

The traditional association has two usual features:

(1) membership is compulsory for practice;

(2) the association has powers of self-discipline.

It is not improper, I think, to refer to the experience of the professions in the United States in the 19th century. After the Revolution they were organized, but at the time of Andrew Jackson's presidency a strong movement called Jacksonian swept the country. The idea behind it was understandable, that in a republic there should be no notions of class, or case or of an aristocracy. However, it took the form of an attack on professional status. In its anxiety to afford equal opportunity for everyone to do what he wishes, the country lowered the requirements for practice so that although in theory requirements of competence and good moral character were retained, they disappeared in fact. After the Civil War the harm was recognized, but it was only around 1900 that the medical profession began to succeed in raising standards, and the struggle in our profession continues. It is perhaps hard for us to realize that, until the last few years, state bar associations were completely voluntary, and no practitioner had to belong. He was admitted to practice by the court, and in many instances the educational qualifications were low, and bar exams were often perfunctory; and discipline was of course left to the courts.

Now when the profession began to move toward raising its standards, it is interesting to note that the leaders pointed to the Law Society of Upper Canada as its model. The campaign is called one for an "integrated bar." Perhaps half the states now have such a bar, and in general it is the establishment of a state society with similar status and powers to our provincial governing bodies.

A last point about organization is this: by itself it does not turn a calling into a profession. The mediaeval guilds were organized, and so are modern groups from trade unions to embalmers. We know of the efforts to attain "professional status," and this is usually marked by an effort to procure from the legislature a monopoly on the calling. Now no one can quarrel with the efforts of any group to raise standards and there are doubtless many skilled callings—such as an airplane pilot—which one should not be permitted to follow unless he meets certain standards. The question arises however—for whose benefit is the exclusive right given? If for the benefit of those already in it so as to create a monopoly without any real basis in qualifications, it is not justified. In other words, the test should be whether it is in the public interest. Indeed so far as our own profession is concerned, we claim the exclusive right to practise law because of the claim to special competence, and it is essential to see that we have that special competence, and also that we do not claim the monopoly if we do not have it.

The second characteristic of the profession is *Learning*. Now there are doubtless many degrees of learning. Here we mean a high degree of intellect, knowledge and skill; and not learning in the abstract but learning applied to the practical problems of those to whom the professional man administers. Skill that is manual, rather than intellectual, is not what is meant. True, some professions like that of the surgeon and dentist require a high degree of physical skill, but it is knowledge behind the skill that makes the calling a profession.

The third characteristic is that of *Service*. The old distinction between the merchant or trader, on the one hand, and the professional man on the other, is often used to bring out this characteristic; and we all know that the one has the primary object of making a profit, and the other, that of rendering a skilled service. In modern times the distinction is becoming blurred. It is good when businesses emphasize service rather than profits; when they abandon caveat emptor, and build up a code of ethics. Yet there is often a conflict between the financial interest of the person rendering the service, and the interest of him who receives it. Traditionally in Europe, a professional man could not legally claim his fee. Although we have abandoned that hall-mark of professionalism here, there is a distinction between the salesman and the professional. I sometimes wonder if all the salesmen of services who speak of their "clients" truly feel the obligation to give advice in their clients' interests, rather than their own. If so, they meet at least this one requirement of professionalism.

II. The Nature of Professional Responsibility

This term has become popular in the United States where the American Bar Association and Law Teachers have given much thought to the subject.

They have accepted the proposition that lawyers have a professional responsibility, and the further proposition that both the profession and law schools have an obligation to strengthen the sense of responsibility of members.

Now what do we mean by professional responsibility? In large measure the answer is easy because it flows from the definition of profession that we have examined:

(1) the member feels an obligation to his group;
(2) he is learned;
(3) he is prepared to render competent legal service—at a fair remuneration.

There are, however, further requirements. Some writers say he must be honest, but I protest on insisting on something that is an obligation of everyone—not merely of a professional man. It is better to say that he is in a position of trust, and owes an obligation beyond ordinary honesty—an obligation that arises from his fiduciary position. These obligations appear in his ethical obligations—that he assumes when he takes his oath, and that are embodied in the canons.

It is not my purpose here to go over the obligations in detail. We all recall the headings in the canons—duty to the state, the court, fellow practitioners, client and oneself. For my purpose we can assume agreement on content. Our concern here is in adherence to them.

Up to this point there is really nothing new in the concept. It says in different words what the English have always taught us. However, the phrase implies even more than competence and good ethical standards. What are these additional factors?

(1) that he has an obligation to see that the law is fair as between citizens and state. After all, the leaders of the struggle of the 17th century against the Stuarts were lawyers;
(2) that he has an obligation to see that the law is improved;
(3) that he has an obligation to see that all persons who need legal assistance shall have it.

Lastly, there is sometimes suggested the obligation to take an active part in public life. This is more debatable as an element of professional responsibility.

III. Strengthening the Sense of Professional Responsibility

Now one need not apologize for looking at this subject. If we were perfect, if men were angels, then we would know that everyone accepts his responsibilities, follows the Golden Rule and lives up to all his moral obligations. However, we know that this is not so; and we all are aware that the profession and the law schools too have examined the subject, usually under the heading "Legal Ethics." Indeed the great battle-cry of those who are trying to strengthen the fibre of the profession is a speech by the late Chief Justice Stone of the Supreme Court of the United States made in 1934. The occasion was the dedication of the University of Michigan Law School. After referring to the fact that historically Anglo-American lawyers had, as a group, acted in the public welfare, he pointed out that big business and a changed society had since come into being. The age of specialization arrived, and it drew into its service the best brains of the profession. Then comes this statement:

> "At its best, the changed system has brought to the command of the business world loyalty and a superb proficiency and technical skill. At its worst it has made the learned profession of an earlier day the obsequious servant of business, and tainted it with the morals and manners of the market place in its most anti-social manifestations."

He added that in any case the result is that the profession has become more absorbed in its clients' interests than in meeting new social problems; and that the Bar did not seem to accept its responsibility for the abuses in business, especially corporate management.

More recently, the present American Secretary of Labor, Mr. Wirtz, when speaking at the dedication of Ohio State's Law School in 1960, examined the subject of the lawyer's responsibility. He called attention to four trouble spots; (1) the parasitical fringe of the profession, (2) the failure to supply legal representation to those who need it, (3) acquiescence in segregation, (4) absence of candour; a tendency in members to mislead through silence.

Now the crucial question is: what can the law schools and profession do to raise these standards?

The law school: the most important factor is the quality of the raw material. We can raise standards, as Dean Lang mentioned yesterday. A member of a learned profession should have a general education as well as professional. The more difficult question is whether we can do anything about character. We clearly have the responsibility for the intellectual part of the student's training. What we can do about instilling in students a sense of responsibility is harder to answer.

We do not give intensive courses in Ethics, though the governing bodies have urged it. Perhaps a course on the Legal Profession should be given. Sometimes we are criticized for not teaching students what is done—etiquette, manners, etc.—but it is still hard to know what can be done by precept. Sometimes, too, we are told we should not graduate students who show an absence of a sense of responsibility—but how are we to do this?

As for the *profession*: the system of articling is based on the premise that graduates need practical training, and that practitioners are competent to give it. In my opinion, the system is good as long as the supply of good principals is adequate to the demand of students. A good senior man should be the most important influence on a young lawyer. It is likely that failure of the articling system is due rather to thoughtlessness on the part of the principal than anything else. The simple fact is that he has a special responsibility to his student to teach him not only practical matters, but his professional obligations.

Then of course comes the *role of the Law Societies*: I think we all recognize that they do an excellent job in the difficult task of discipline. Above this, they are not doing more than before in continuing legal education. As for *law reform*: we probably have not taken the lead as we should have, but there are encouraging signs. As for unfair laws, or oppressive executive action, the record is perhaps spotty.

The significant requirement is to be aware of the need to breed into lawyers the sense of responsibility we have been talking about: if the profession feels it, then those preparing to join the profession will acquire it by contact.

Conclusion

By way of conclusion I would like to express this thought: we must help to train young lawyers to become not mere artisans of the law, but architects. Mr. Wirtz in the speech mentioned earlier concluded with the following statement:

You will be familiar with the story of the three masons. When asked what they were doing, their replies were:

I am shaping a stone;
I am earning my living;
I am building a cathedral.

Let us imagine this question being put to three law students. What are you doing?

I am doing my work;
I am preparing to earn a living;
I am preparing to help make a better civilization.

Malcolm Murray MacIntyre: 1904–1964

Reprinted from
(1964) 3 Alberta Law Review
pp. 161–163

This is a tribute to the contribution of Professor Malcolm MacIntyre as a teacher and scholar, written by W.F. Bowker at the request of the Editor of the Alberta Law Review *following MacIntyre's death in 1964.*

He had for several years been a Professor of Law at the University of Alberta, dating back to 1930.

After the article was published, Bowker received a warm letter of appreciation from his widow.

In 1930 Professor MacIntyre came to the Faculty of Law at the University of Alberta, having taken his Bachelor's and Master's degrees in law at Harvard University. For the next twelve years he and the late Dean Weir each taught about fifteen hours a week. Then in June of 1942 Dean Weir died and his colleague succeeded him. Two years later when the student body had shrunk to a handful because of the war, Dr. MacIntyre took a sabbatical leave which he spent in practice at his home town of Sackville, New Brunswick. Circumstances made it impossible for him to return to Alberta in the fall of 1945 so he resigned. After several years in practice he joined the Faculty of Law at the University of British Columbia where he remained until his death this April.

At Alberta he taught Torts, Sales, Jurisprudence, Wills, Evidence, Partnership and Property. The student body, like the faculty, was small and contact between them was close. Certainly Dr. MacIntyre's students were fond of him. He was friendly, completely lacking in condescension and he enjoyed wrestling with them over legal problems. In his early years some students might have been taken aback by his irreverence to black-letter law and his sociological approach. (He had been a student of Roscoe Pound.) As time passed, however, he succeeded in communicating his concern about the human importance of legal rules and his strong sense of injustice. In the beginning, his power of analysis was not yet apparent, for he seemed preoccupied with uncertainties and doubts. "I don't know. Nobody knows" was sometimes a reply to questions. By 1937–38, however, when he spent a sabbatical at the Harvard Law School, working for his Doctor's degree, his critical power had emerged. It was then that he wrote his famous article, *The*

Rationale of Last Clear Chance, which was published in the Harvard Law Review and the Canadian Bar Review.[1] The leading writers in torts invariably cite it as excellent, and in recent years as classic. A great protagonist of Contributory Negligence Acts, Dr. MacIntyre was impatient with the tendency of the courts to continue to apply last clear chance and so to hold one party solely to blame and make the Act a dead letter. This was the subject of an article, *Last Clear Chance after Thirty Years Under the Apportionment Statutes,* that appeared in the Canadian Bar Review.[2] It shows the breadth and depth of his learning in the subject and his power of analysis and criticism. The tone of the article is pure MacIntyre: humorous, ironical and impatient.

To say that he was a distinguished scholar is of course true. More specifically he was a teacher, and perhaps his greatest contribution to legal education was in his influence on students. He would spend hours on the *Loach* case,[3] and again on *Polemis*.[4] After class his door was always open and the discussion continued. He interested himself in students' problems, legal or personal, and would become intensely involved in them. He imparted his own love of law and his concern for logic, workability and fairness.

His other contribution was of course in legal writing, though the volume is not large. There are seven articles in the Canadian Bar Review, and one on *The Rationale of Imputed Negligence* in the University of Toronto Law Journal.[5] To Alberta lawyers Dr. MacIntyre will be remembered as the one who established the Alberta Law Quarterly in 1934 and ran it almost single-handed until publication was suspended near the end of the war after the publication of five volumes.

On becoming Dean in 1942, he made changes in the curriculum that gave recognition to new needs, particularly in public law. Thus he added both Taxation and Administrative Law to the course at a time when many still did not recognize their importance. Generally, however, he was not particularly interested in administration and organization, nor in following the book. Rules never seemed important, especially those applying to students. Indeed there may have been a bit of Irish in him.

Not being an organization man, he never sought positions on committees and councils. However, he did make a stimulating report as Chairman of the Canadian Bar Association's Committee on Noteworthy Changes in the Statute Law in 1944[6] and was Chairman of an important committee of the Association of Canadian Law Teachers on pre-legal education in 1955–56.

His human traits emerged in little things. Once while in practice he defended a harmless inebriate who had accidentally bumped a pedestrian off the sidewalk, and then was charged with assault. "Doctor Mac" threw himself into this task with as much fervour and anxiety as he expended in a successful appeal on a perpetuities question before the Supreme Court of Canada.[7] His students here still recall a number of incidents. One cold night in Edmonton near the University he found a stray pup. Carrying it in his arms, he went from door to door trying to find the owner. Probably he ended by taking it home. One year at Harvard he had traded his two tickets to the Yale Game for a fur coat. He continued to wear it as long as he remained in Edmonton, disreputable though it became. Then at a Convocation in Edmonton when he did not have his Doctor's hood, he borrowed Mrs. MacIntyre's (her degree being in Home Economics from Mount Allison).

Other qualities can be inferred from his writings. In one long article he made an error in the facts of a case, saying that a truck was unlighted. Noticing his mistake he wrote the Editor of the publication "I am very sorry that it occurred because one naturally regrets being in error and as a result of it a reader could hardly be blamed for expecting other errors in the statement of facts of other cases."[8] In another article he set out to criticize certain provisions in a Contributory Negligence Act. He began by saying:

> "I am about to criticize this Act—and harshly. For that I am sorry and I herewith tender my apologies in advance. No disrespect is intended. The other Uniform Acts with which I am familiar are excellent. This one happens to contain provisions with which I disagree, and since my views are minority views they must be stated strongly, if they are to accomplish their purpose which is to raise doubts as to the wisdom of those provisions."[9]

There is a touch of pathos in the fact that Dr. MacIntyre first became seriously ill early in 1957 while returning to Vancouver from Calgary. He had gone to attend the annual meeting of the Law Society of Alberta in order to be present when the law graduates gave to the University his portrait, which is now in the Law Reading Room. Anyone who saw him in the last seven years was bound to notice the effects of his illness and the courage with which he bore it. He died shortly after giving his last lecture this spring.

The generation of Alberta lawyers who are now approaching middle age remember him with respect and affection.

Notes

1 (1940) 53 Harv. L. Rev. 1225; (1940) 18 Can. Bar Rev. 665.
2 (1955) 33 Can. Bar Rev. 257.
3 *B.C. Electric Co.* v. *Loach* (P.C. (B.C.)) [1916] 1 A.C. 719.
4 *Re An Arbitration Between Polemis and Furness, Withy & Co.* (C.A.) [1921] 3 K.B. 560.
5 (1944) 5 U.T.L.J. 368.
6 22 Can. Bar Rev. 670.
7 *Auld* v. *Scales* [1947] S.C.R. 543.
8 33 Can. Bar Rev. 504–05.
9 (1944) 22 Can. Bar Rev. 670, 675.

1965

Three Alberta Judges

Reprinted from
(1962–64) 4 Alberta Law Review
pp. 5–10

This article was written following the recent deaths of three prominent Alberta judges, whose contribution, Bowker felt, should be recorded. One had been a Chief Justice and two were of the Court of Appeal.

The Honourable Frank Ford had been a close friend of members of the Faculty of Law at the University, which is the reason he was dealt with first.

This article (as with the earlier one on Chief Justice Harvey) reflects Bowker's interest in our historical judicial heritage.

Since the publication of the last issue of the Review, the Honourable Clinton J. Ford of Calgary, retired Chief Justice of Alberta, died at the age of eighty-two. His death was followed early this year by that of Mr. Justice Hugh John Macdonald of the Appellate Division, of Edmonton, and whose age was sixty-six. A short time later, the Honourable Frank Ford of Edmonton, retired Justice of Appeal, died at the age of ninety-one.

Each of these three men as a member of his profession and of the judiciary made a valuable contribution to the administration of justice in Alberta. All three were good friends of the Faculty of Law and the University of Alberta generally, each of them holding the University's honorary degree of Doctor of Laws.

It will be convenient first to refer to the Honourable Frank Ford. Born in Toronto in 1873, he received the degree of Bachelor of Civil Law from Trinity University and was medalist in his class. He also attended Osgoode Hall. Later, in 1909, the University of Toronto granted him the degree of Doctor of Civil Laws. After his call to the Bar of Ontario in 1895, he was associated as a junior with a distinguished Toronto counsel, Dalton McCarthy, Q.C. He later served in the Ontario government and then went into practice in Toronto. Coming West in 1906, he was Deputy Attorney-General of Saskatchewan for four years and then came to Edmonton to practise. Three years later, he was appointed King's counsel in Alberta, having already received that appointment in Saskatchewan (1907) and Ontario (1910).

He was in fact as well as in name a leader of the Bar, and had a large practice in Alberta courts and the Supreme Court of Canada. In 1926 he appeared in two cases before the Judicial Committee of the Privy Council. In *Nadan* v. *The King* he succeeded in his argument that the Criminal Code did not effectively exclude the prerogative right of the King in Council to grant special leave to appeal to the Judicial Committee in a criminal case. Of course, the Statute of Westminster 1931 enabled Parliament to abolish all appeals, and Parliament did so in 1949. In the second case, *Attorney-General for Alberta* v. *Cook,* Mr. Ford contended successfully that the Supreme Court of Alberta had no jurisdiction to grant a divorce to a wife who lived in Alberta where her husband had not an Alberta domicile. This is the case that confirmed the rigid rule that a wife's domicile is always that of the husband. It has attracted criticism, and Parliament in 1930 gave some relief from the consequences of the rule by permitting a deserted wife to sue for divorce in the province in which the husband had been domiciled before deserting her.

In 1926 Mr. Frank Ford was appointed to the Trial Division of the Supreme Court of Alberta. As a trial judge, he was meticulous and exacting both as to matters of substance and form. An undefended action for divorce was no perfunctory matter. Undoubtedly, his strictness with young practitioners was in the long run good for them. One had to be careful in his presentation of evidence and to have his documents in order and correct as to form. On one occasion in Chambers, when a practitioner turned to another beside him to swear his affidavit, a spirited discussion occurred between His Lordship and the person administering the oath as to the proper formula to use when the deponent is sworn in the Scottish manner. Several of his judgments set out the correct form for documents, and there is a reported case in 1927 prescribing the formal parts of an Originating Notice of Motion.

Of the many trials he conducted during his ten years on the Trial Division, the Corona Hotel case (*London Guarantee Company* v. *Northwestern Utilities*) is noteworthy. After a lengthy trial on contested facts, His Lordship found the gas Company not negligent; but in finding the City of Edmonton to blame for the subsidence of the Company's gas pipe he made the comment, almost parenthetically, that the Company must have known that the City's operations were going on. The plaintiffs seized on this finding of fact as the main ground of appeal, and succeeded in the Appellate Division and the Privy Council.

Another action that attracted wide attention was one by a divorced wife to have the divorce set aside as having been obtained through collusion. The careful judgment is characteristic of His Lordship (*McPherson* v. *McPherson,* [1933] 2 W.W.R. 513). This is the case in which the decree nisi had been granted in the Judge's library. The issue as to the validity of a decree given elsewhere than in open court ultimately went to the Privy Council, but Mr. Justice Ford had no part in the disposition of that question.

He was especially interested in Conflicts and Domestic Relations and, indeed, had taught these subjects during the early years of the Faculty of Law. His interest in Domestic Relations was, doubtlessly, related to his familiarity with ecclesiastic law.

His appointment to the Appellate Division coincided with the beginning of a stream of cases in which the validity of provincial legislation was in question. This was in the first years of the Social Credit government, and the impugned statutes were designed to protect debtors and to reduce the interest rate on government bonds. Mr. Justice Ford made an important contribution to these decisions. One can say that he resisted the tendency to hold legislation bad merely because it seemed drastic.

Without attempting an analysis of the many judgments he wrote on the Appellate Division, several characteristics appear. He was a strong judge, and not infrequently dissented. Sometimes his dissent has pointed the way, as in his rejection of the "strict" meaning of collusion, and in his holding that a person with a general power of appointment exercisable by deed may exercise it in his own favour. In other cases his dissent, though supported by authority, has not prevailed, as in his opposition to the notion of a "divisible" divorce. (*Re Plummer,* [1941] 3 W.W.R. 288.)

In 1941 he wrote for the Appellate Division an important judgment holding that a corporation may be guilty of a crime that requires mens rea. Five years later, on reading in the *Law Quarterly Review* an article analysing three 1944 English decisions to the same general effect, His Lordship commented "We were ahead of them here." His judgments are not full of long quotations but draw heavily on English and Ontario precedent. Often he referred to cases and principles in a casual manner and elliptically, and he frequently discussed points that he found it unnecessary to decide. He said, for example, in 1940 that he thought an oil lease was a profit à prendre rather than a lease, though it did not matter for the purposes of the decision whether it was one or the other. In later years this question was often before the courts, until the Supreme Court of Canada held in 1957 that the typical oil lease is a profit à prendre.

The Honourable Frank Ford was a great admirer of English legal institutions and valued greatly the association he enjoyed with British judges and barristers. He approved of their traditions, rules of protocol and etiquette, and his own Court was formal—though he was most convivial and animated in social gatherings. He believed that a lawyer's first task is to steep himself in the law, and it is doubtful that he considered it necessary for a good lawyer to be active in public affairs or an authority on all related disciplines. Indeed, he was fond of quoting the remark made of Lord Brougham "If he knew a little law he would know a little of everything."

His Lordship was a prominent Anglican layman and for many years Chancellor of the Diocese of Edmonton. He became proficient in the French tongue. For his interest in French language and culture, Laval University awarded him the honorary degree of Doctor of Laws in 1946. Always closely interested in the University of Alberta, he was Chancellor from 1941 to 1946; and, long before that, had been one of the four or five people who brought about the establishment of the Faculty of Law in 1921. He taught part-time in the first years and was a close friend of the first Dean, John Weir. He always maintained close contact with the Faculty and its students. Indeed, he continued to attend the meetings of the Law Faculty Council as Honorary Professor and also the students' annual banquets until about the time of his retirement from the Bench in 1954, when he was eighty-one.

The next of the three Justices, The Honourable Clinton J. Ford, was not related to the Honourable Frank Ford, though both were from Ontario. Clinton Ford won the Prince of Wales Gold Medal on graduation from the University of Toronto in 1907, and then studied law at Osgoode Hall. He came to Calgary and was admitted to the Alberta Bar in 1910. On his Bar Examinations, he won the prize presented by Chief Justice Harvey. In 1913 he became Calgary's city solicitor, and in 1922 went into private practice. He had considerable counsel work and a respected position as a leading solicitor. His first judicial appointment was to the District Court in 1942. Three years later he was elevated to the Trial Division, and in 1950 to the Appellate Division. In 1957, on the death of the Honourable George O'Connor, he became Chief Justice of Alberta, retiring in 1961 when the age limit came into effect.

As District Court Judge, he had much to do with applications under The Farmers' Creditors Arrangements Act and Wartime Rental Regulations. Then, later, when he became a member of the Trial Division of the Supreme Court, his cases ran the usual gamut. His written judgments invariably have a clear, precise, and often detailed statement of the facts followed by a lucid discussion of the legal issues. He did not quote at length from judgments and had the capacity to formulate principles clearly. His application of rules was marked by great common sense. Sitting on appeal he was not hesitant about dissenting, though of course he often wrote the judgment for the court. As to deportment, he was mild in manner, gentlemanly, kindly, and he had a simple dignity.

A good judgment of His Lordship's is his dissent in the famous *Turta* case in which he held that the exception to indefeasibility in case of a prior certificate of title operated in favour of the C.P.R. True, his dissent was approved by only a minority of the Supreme Court of Canada; but, nevertheless, it remains a strong statement on a difficult issue.

He wrote a substantial number of judgments on the law of property and the law of succession. All of them show a familiarity with the subject and soundness of judgment. The same can be said of his decisions on municipal and motor vehicle law. As for criminal law, he had not had an extensive criminal practice; and, yet, in the decisions he rendered in criminal cases he showed a marked concern to ensure fairness to an accused. Thus, he was willing to permit a change of plea from guilty to not guilty; he insisted on maintaining the distinction between criminal negligence and non-criminal; and he declined to increase a ten-year sentence for manslaughter where the accused had beaten his twelve-year old child and death resulted.

Since he lived in Calgary, his association with the University and the Law Faculty was not as close as that of the Honourable Frank Ford and Mr. Justice Macdonald. Five years ago, he showed his interest in the Faculty by offering the Clinton Ford Award to the two third-year students making the best argument in a Moot Court Final. This annual Competition has produced a high calibre of argument and indeed holds a central place in the activities of the Faculty. In 1961, four years ago, His Lordship presided at the hearing of the final argument. The case was an "appeal" from an English case on mental shock, *Schneider* v. *Eisovitch*. In presiding, the Chief Justice showed to counsel the courtesy and to their argument the care and attention that he always extended.

During his many years as practitioner and judge, he was active in community affairs. He was prominent in the work of the Y.M.C.A. and he was made a life member of the national council. Brought up a Methodist, he was a prominent layman of the United Church of Canada, which he represented at the World Council of Churches at Amsterdam in 1948; and he was Chairman of the Board of Mount Royal College in Calgary.

Mr. Justice Hugh John Macdonald was born in 1898 in Massachusetts of a Cape Breton father. Coming to Edmonton as a boy, he was trained in this province both for teaching and law. His education was interrupted by a period of service in the United States army. After being principal of the Banff public and high school from 1923 to 1927, he came to Edmonton to practice law. During the next seventeen years as a member of an Edmonton firm, he became a busy solicitor acquiring solid experience in insurance law. Though not one of the leaders of the Bar so far as counsel work was concerned, he did appear in court frequently.

From the beginning he kept a Commonplace Book, in which he noted in alphabetic order points of law that he had encountered; and he maintained this book after becoming a judge.

He was appointed to the Trial Division in 1944 and to the Appellate Division in 1957. He continued to sit there until almost the day of his death which came suddenly in March of this year.

He enjoyed great respect as a trial judge and gained a reputation for care, courtesy, patience and fairness. Competent observers have, indeed, compared him to two of our great judges, the late Mr. Justice Walsh and the late Mr. Justice Ewing. He has indeed been described as an ideal trial judge. Interested in young practitioners, he was always helpful; and he was disappointed, though not censorious, when they made mistakes.

In preparing judgments, he worked hard both on the facts and law. Doubtlessly, his training as a school teacher stood him in good stead in framing his judgments. He did not sidestep hard legal issues. There was a tendency to quote lengthy passages from relevant cases rather than to extract the principles and sum them up. Whether or not many of his decisions become leading cases, he made a workmanlike and worthwhile contribution to our jurisprudence.

To illustrate, one can cite two cases that went to the Supreme Court: *Keyes* v. *Royal Bank,* [1947] S.C.R. 377 and *Patterson* v. *Burton,* [1950] S.C.R. 578. These are good examples of his judgments, not because they were upheld, but because they illustrate his care in handling evidence, finding the facts and dealing with difficult issues. In *Keyes* the bank was liable to its customer for mistakenly certifying his post-dated cheque and in *Patterson* shareholders were liable as contributors even though the shares had been sold to them in violation of the Sale of Shares Act.

His fine human qualities and, in particular, a strong sense of responsibility appeared in many forms. His deep interest in the University led him to serve on the Senate, the Board of Governors, and as President of the Alumni Association. At the time of his death, though retired from the Board of Governors after ten years' service, he was Chairman of a special committee that the Board established in 1964 to make recommendations for revision of the University Act.

For almost ten years after the War, he gave an annual talk to the graduating class in law. It consisted of hints and suggestions, kindly and earnestly given, of things to do and to avoid; and his example as well as his precept set high standards. Unfortunately, he had to discontinue these talks after illness in 1956. For the last years of his life he was frequently unwell and in pain, though an observer would not be aware of the fact.

A year before his death, he addressed the Catholic Lawyers Guild of Edmonton at a luncheon following a Red Mass. The subject of his talk was characteristic of the speaker: What Practitioners are Entitled to Expect from Judges.

While in practice, he served as City Alderman for six years and in the provincial legislature for four. Regardless of political differences, his colleagues invariably respected and liked him. It is a not insignificant fact that he was very fond of sports. He had been a fine athlete, playing second base for years on a good baseball team in Edmonton. All his life, he continued to follow baseball, football, and hockey; and attended major league ball games whenever possible.

At his funeral in St. Joseph's Cathedral, a crowded congregation included the Lieutenant-Governor, the Premier, the Mayor, many members of the Judiciary, and hundreds of friends representing a cross-section of the community—a remarkable tribute to the wide esteem he enjoyed.

1965

Ten More Years Under The Contributory Negligence Acts

Reprinted from
(1965) 2 University of British Columbia Law Review
pp. 198–215

This article was part of a memorial issue of the University of British Columbia Law Review *in honor of the late Professor Malcolm MacIntyre, who in addition to his early years with the University of Alberta Law Faculty, served with the University of B.C. Law School for many years until his death.*

Contributions in the form of legal writings for this memorial issue were invited, and Bowker volunteered the accompanying article.

He chose as his subject the field of Contributory Negligence which was of special interest to Professor MacIntyre, and on which he had earlier written a major article. This piece traces developments over the following ten years.

In 1940 Dr. MacIntyre published an article that all writers cite when they discuss contributory negligence. The title is The Rationale of Last Clear Chance.[1] Last clear chance is a concept that plays a part in the common law of contributory negligence. Contributory negligence is a plaintiff's failure to take reasonable care of himself or his property. It may include breach of duty of care to the defendant, but need not do so. It becomes important when a plaintiff has established the defendant's negligence. The defence of contributory negligence may succeed: in that event the action fails completely. The defence may fail: in that event the action succeeds completely. In the nineteenth century the English courts developed three rules which tell whether it is to be all or nothing.

The first rule is a general one: when both parties are at fault the plaintiff fails. Lindley, L.J., explained the reason: "In such case A cannot say with truth that he has been injured by B's negligence; he can only with truth say that he had been injured by his own carelessness and B's negligence." Then his Lordship added this comment: "But why in such a case the damages should not be apportioned I fail to understand."[2] They are apportioned in Admiralty law and also in the civil law, including that of Quebec. Apportionment means the reduction of the award according to the plaintiff's fault.

The second rule is this: if the defendant is at fault the plaintiff fails if, by the exercise of reasonable care, he could have avoided damage in spite of the defendant's negligence. This rule hardly seems necessary for it is bound to follow from the first rule. However it is set out because it is the converse of the third rule.

The third rule: if the plaintiff is at fault he nevertheless succeeds if the defendant, notwithstanding the plaintiff's fault, could have avoided causing the damage by exercising reasonable care. This is the rule of last clear chance, or last opportunity, or the rule in *Davies v. Mann,* the famous donkey case.[3]

The third rule enables a plaintiff to escape from the harshness of the first two. Since the result is always all or nothing, the defendant strives to bring the case within the first rule, while the plaintiff tries desperately to bring it within the third. The plaintiff received great assistance from an extension of the third rule, known as the doctrine of the *Loach*[4] case: even if the defendant in fact did not have the last clear chance he is still liable if, but for his prior incapacitating negligence, he could have avoided the event that caused the damage.

This doctrine could in theory be turned against the plaintiff but in practice it never has been. We can illustrate this by an Alberta case. The driver of a car was driving quickly along an Edmonton street. A woman stepped off the curb without looking and the car hit her. The Appellate Division went through the intricate rules of the *Loach* case and found that the trial judge had properly held the driver liable because his speed prevented him, after he saw or should have seen the plaintiff, from stopping in time to avoid the accident.[5] It seems to the writer that in this case the court could properly say that even though the driver was negligent the plaintiff should have had the last clear chance. She needed only to look and refrain from leaving the curb. The search for *the* cause was like solving the riddle of the chicken and the egg. "In cases of constructive last chance it is . . . a mere fiction that at a particular instant one party could and the other could not put matters right."[6] Dr. MacIntyre's 1940 article shows that the last clear chance and its extension in the *Loach* case are not based on ordinary principles of causation but rather on the assumption that the defendant's fault is greater than the plaintiff's.[7] Another factor that helped the plaintiff to escape the rigour of the first rule is the tendency of juries to find the defendant negligent, the plaintiff not guilty of contributory negligence, or the defendant to have had the last chance. Both before and after the *Loach* decision in 1916, all provincial courts had a steady flow of cases raising these issues. The absent-minded or hurrying pedestrian (or his personal representative) often recovered against the railway or street car company[8] or car driver;[9] likewise the driver of a car or wagon who did not even look on approaching a crossing.[10] True, trial judges sometimes took the case from the jury and granted a non-suit because the plaintiff's contributory negligence within the first rule was obvious; but one could never be sure what the result would be on appeal.[11]

Of course the plaintiff did not always succeed. One day in Edmonton, one Mr. Earl, during daylight, rode on his bicycle over railway tracks where a shunting engine struck him. The Appellate Division agreed with the trial judge that had a watchman been present as required by a Railway Board Order, he could have prevented the accident, and the railway was liable under the *Loach* doctrine. This case became a landmark, not because the Supreme Court reversed the judgment below and dismissed the action, but because three members of the Court, Duff, Anglin and Mignault, JJ., said they wished there were power to apportion blame and hence the damages, as there is under the civil law, in force in Quebec.[12] The date was 3rd April, 1923.

In 1924 Ontario passed the first Contributory Negligence Act and in the same year the Conference of Commissioners on Uniformity of Legislation in Canada adopted a Uniform Contributory Negligence Act. Thirty years later Dr. MacIntyre wrote an article, Last Clear Chance After Thirty Years Under the Apportionment Statutes.[13] His thesis was that last clear chance had merely been a device to help plaintiffs around the barrier of the first rule of contributory negligence and could be justified on the basis of the defendant's greater fault. The Act rendered the rule unnecessary. However the cases of *McLaughlin v. Long,*[14] *Bechtold v. Osbaldeston*[15] and *McKee v. Malenfant,*[16] all in the Supreme Court of Canada, and *Sigurdson v. British Columbia Electric Railway Co.*[17] in the Privy Council had unfortunately preserved the rule. Thus the statute applies to cases within the first rule and so is of assistance to a plaintiff whose action would have failed under that rule. However it is of no help to a defendant who is within the third rule and he remains liable for the whole of the damage. In Dean Prosser's phrase, the Act "becomes jug-handled in favour of the plaintiff".[18]

The writer's purpose is to review briefly the arguments of the proponents of the Acts with a view to seeing whether they intended to abolish last clear chance, and then to examine the decisions of the past ten years to try to determine whether last clear chance remains in full vigour as it did ten years ago or whether the courts have tended to reject it in favour of apportionment.

The Proponents of the Acts and Last Clear Chance

Turning to the first point, the original Acts were silent on the last clear chance. Dean Prosser has suggested that the reason is that the question never occurred to the legislatures at all.[19]

It may be, however, that the persons in the legal profession who were responsible for the movement that brought out the Acts had some views on the point.

It is clear that many of them had principally in mind a case like *G.T.P. v. Earl* in which the plaintiff failed and the intention was to enable him to recover in part. It is also clear that some wanted to do away with the complicated rules and the intricate and confusing directions and questions to juries.

The first advocacy of legislation came in 1917, a year after the Privy

Council judgment in the *Loach* case. M.J. Gorman, Q.C., of Ottawa wrote an article in favour of provincial laws like the Quebec rule or the Admiralty Conventions Act, which the Canadian Parliament had enacted in 1914.[20] In 1922 Anglin, J., in an address to the Canadian Bar Association said:

> The English law excluding all relief where the plaintiff has been guilty of contributory negligence, however slight, has always seemed to me much less equitable than the provision of the civil law that where there is *faute commune* there should be an apportionment of damages according to the degree of blame attributable to each party. This feature of the civil law has been adopted by the English Courts of Admiralty. The day may come when the Imperial Parliament may incorporate it in the law of England and their respective legislatures in the laws of the Provinces of Canada, other than Quebec.[21]

This was some months before his judgment to the same effect in the *Earl* case.

In March, 1923, Francis King, Q.C., of Kingston made a strong plea to the Ontario Bar Association in favour of apportionment.[22] Mr. Angus MacMurchy, Q.C., reached a national audience five months later when he addressed the annual meeting of the Canadian Bar Association and recommended provincial legislation along the lines of the Admiralty and civil law.[23] Like Anglin, J., he stressed the need to "abate the rigour of the rule at common law" whereby the plaintiff failed under the first rule.

The Association immediately recommended to the Conference of Commissioners on Uniformity of Legislation in Canada that preparation of a Uniform Act was desirable.[24] The Ontario Commissioners on the Conference, of whom Mr. King was one, in 1924 recommended adoption of a Uniform Act modeled on the Maritime Conventions Act rather than on the Ontario Act which had been introduced in 1923 and passed earlier in 1924.[25] The basic provision of the Uniform Act is taken directly from the Maritime Conventions Act, substituting "persons" for "vessels".[26]

Professor Glanville Williams says that Ontario's proximity to Quebec may explain why the former was the first province to pass this legislation.[27] In the next two years, British Columbia, New Brunswick and Nova Scotia each passed the Uniform Act. It is perhaps of some significance that these are all maritime provinces. Alberta, Prince Edward Island, and Manitoba (with an act worded differently) followed a decade later, Saskatchewan in 1944 and Newfoundland, together with the Yukon and Northwest Territories, in the fifties. Thus every common law jurisdiction now has a Contributory Negligence Act. Their essential provisions are the same and in form all but Ontario's and Manitoba's are based on the uniform act.

It was apparent soon after the first provincial acts were passed in the mid-twenties that they did not solve all problems. The question that arose almost immediately was this: does the Act abrogate all of the three rules set out earlier? The first rule is clearly within the Act. Nearly everyone would also agree that the *Loach* doctrine should no longer be applied. The real difficulty arose in connection with the third rule—the one that allowed a plaintiff to recover where the defendant had the last clear chance. If the Act applied, this meant the disappearance of the rule. If it did not then the rule remained and the court might still find a defendant wholly to blame even where the plaintiff was at fault.

If one examines the speeches and statements described earlier to look for a clue, he will probably conclude that the proponent has principally in mind the first rule and intended to abolish it so as to allow the plaintiff to recover part of his loss in circumstances where he would have recovered none at common law. Certainly it was not many months before decisions, notably in Ontario, held this to be the purpose of the Act and restricted it accordingly. They preserved last clear chance.

It was not long before some persons expressed concern over this development. In 1926 an Admiralty lawyer, R.I. Towers, Q.C., of Toronto, presenting a paper to the Canadian Bar Association, expressed concern over the fact that "ultimate negligence" (which means last clear chance and usually including the *Loach* doctrine as well) persisted notwithstanding the statute, and he recommended legislation to abolish the concept of ultimate negligence and thus give wider scope to the Act.[28] The next February Anglin, C.J., who had encouraged this legislation, delivered the leading judgment in *McLaughlin v. Long,*[29] a New Brunswick case. He held that a plaintiff's contributory negligence does not affect his right to recover in full unless it is a *cause* of his injuries; and that it is not a cause where the defendant had the last clear chance. Thus the boy on the running board who was pinned between the truck and the tree recovered in full.

Dean Falconbridge, addressing the Canadian Bar Association seven months later, recommended the amendment of the Uniform Act to make it applicable in partial relief of the defendant where his is the ultimate negligence; the Act should not be confined to relief of plaintiffs who would fail under the common law; the search for ultimate negligence should be rendered unnecessary.[30] The Conference on Uniformity studied the problem. The Ontario Commissioners, through Mr. King, reported agreement with Dean Falconbridge's view but concluded that it was impossible to define in statutory form the point where negligence passes from the irrelevant into that which contributes to the result.[31] The subject was still alive in 1931[32] when the Conference invited a committee of the Canadian Bar Association to study it. The committee recommended an amendment to the Uniform Act to the effect that a negligent party should be bound to contribute even though the other party's negligence was ultimate.[33]

The Conference then referred these recommendations to the Nova Scotia Commissioners for study, who reported back in 1934. The report is signed by Mr. Vincent MacDonald. He pointed out that the decisions had made it clear that the Act does not apply to negligence "in sequence". The report does not favour an amendment that would abolish last chance; "the attempt to abolish the doctrine of ultimate negligence is misconceived; it would do away with our principles of causality." However he thought that courts had often been too astute to find last chance when it was not a *clear* last chance. They had forgotten Lord Birkenhead's advice in *The Volute* in which he had said that the rule should not be applied unless a clear line could be drawn. The tribunal should not use a stop-watch to determine whether one ship's negligence is later and hence the sole cause.

The report accordingly recommends an amendment to the Uniform Act to embody the rule of *The Volute*.[34] The proposed section requires that a judge shall put no question to the jury on last clear chance unless in his opinion the negligence in question is perceptibly subsequent to and clearly severable from the negligent act or omission of the other party so as not to be substantially contemporaneous with it. In 1935 the Conference considered this proposal along with other amendments to the Uniform Act but was not prepared to adopt it. However it published the rejected section with the recommendation "that the several Provinces consider its enactment as part of any statute embodying the Uniform Act in view of the opinion of the Conference that it correctly enunciates the law" as declared in *The Volute*.[35]

So far as the writer knows, this was the last attempt to abolish last clear chance by legislation. Four provinces, Alberta, Saskatchewan, Newfoundland and Prince Edward Island, have included the section in their Acts and the first three have added a companion section for non-jury trials. However it has had no practical effect. In the provinces that have enacted it the courts give as little (or as great) effect to it as the courts of the other provinces give to *The Volute*.

To conclude the first of the two parts of this paper, the history of the subject shows that most of those concerned in bringing about the legislation were content to preserve last clear chance, though they hoped it would play a minor role.

The Last Decade in the Supreme Court of Canada

We shall now examine the decisions of the last ten years. Dr. MacIntyre's 1955 article showed that provincial courts in many cases had applied the Act literally. Some had practically abolished last chance until the Supreme Court of Canada pronounced that it remained, notwithstanding the Act. After *McLaughlin v. Long* the two Supreme Court cases that most distressed Dr. MacIntyre were *Bechthold*[36] and *McKee*.[37] These are both cases in which a stationary vehicle created the danger and then a moving vehicle encountering that danger failed to avoid it and an accident resulted. In both, the Court cast all liability on the driver of the moving vehicle, refusing to hold that the other driver had contributed to the damage.

The first two relevant decisions of the Supreme Court in our ten-year period deal with the same general problem. The stationary vehicle was found partly to blame in *Bruce v. MacIntyre*[38] and so damages were apportioned. However last clear chance triumphed again in *Brooks v. Ward*.[39] We shall refer to these cases later in considering generally the question of the parked vehicle and the moving one.

The two most significant decisions since 1954 have nothing to do with highway accidents. The first of these is *Great Eastern Oil Company v. Best*.[40] Best operated a hardware store and service station in St. John's, Newfoundland. The filler pipe to the gasoline storage tank was inside the shop and the person delivering gas had to put the nozzle of the hose through a hole in the wall into the filler pipe. Within ten feet of the pipe was an oil stove. Some years before, a minor explosion had occurred when someone lit a match in the shop and ignited gas vapour. On another occasion gas spilled over the floor when the gas company's employee was filling the tank, but no harm resulted. In March, 1959, Great Eastern's employee, Oakley, delivered a tank of gas to Best. After inserting the nozzle in the filler pipe he went to the truck to open the valve. After the gasoline started to flow the nozzle slipped partly out and gas spilled onto the floor of the shop and flowed toward the oil stove, which was burning at the time. The vapour was ignited and the store burned down.

The trial judge found Oakley negligent in leaving the nozzle unattended. He further found that Best's negligence was prolonged, obstinate and serious. Applying the Contributory Negligence Act he found Oakley 20% to blame and Best 80%.[41] On appeal the Chief Justice disqualified himself. The trial judge and Winter, J., being the only other justices, constituted the Court. The trial judge, in adhering to his original opinion, discussed *The Volute* and the Newfoundland section which directs the court to ignore last clear chance except in obvious cases. He specifically held that Oakley's negligence was not clearly severable from or subsequent to the continuing act or omission of Best. "Both were functioning causally together." Winter, J., held Best solely to blame. He created a grave danger and Oakley's conduct was merely an error in judgment. Even if he were negligent, the dangerous condition, including the hot stove, was a continuing one that came into operation after Oakley spilled the gasoline.

An unanimous Supreme Court of Canada found Oakley solely to blame. Best's conduct was not proximate in the sense of an effective cause. The Court cited *Ellerman Lines v. Grayson*[42] in which a ship owner recovered from a ship repairer who was installing anti-mine equipment in the ship on Admiralty instructions. An employee of the repairer accidentally dropped a red hot rivet onto a bag of jute and a fire resulted. The House of Lords held the employee negligent in handling the rivet in the presence of the exposed jute. The repairers were under a special duty of care. They could have postponed the work or required the plaintiff to close the holds. The latter was not negligent and even if so, the repairers could have avoided the result by the exercise of reasonable care.

It seems to the writer that Best, in asking the Oil Company to deliver gasoline while he maintained an exceedingly dangerous system on his premises, was much more obviously at fault than was the ship owner in *Ellerman*. One might think that on the ordinary meaning of language Best's conduct contributed to the damage. However the Supreme Court specifically held that Oakley's fault was clearly subsequent to and severable from the plaintiff's. Thus the provision in the Contributory Negligence Act designed to prevent the application of last clear chance except in clear cases is inapplicable.

An interesting sequel was an action by Hand who owned a building adjoining Best's. It too was burned in the fire. Hand brought action against both the Oil Company and Best. The trial judge found Best 75% at fault and the Oil Company 25%. Best appealed to the Newfoundland Supreme Court and in the meantime the Supreme Court of Canada had delivered its judgment on the original action. The Newfoundland Supreme Court pointed out that the present action is by an innocent plaintiff and so raises different considerations from an action between the two negligent parties. Notwithstanding this it concluded that the Supreme Court decision covers Hand's action so the Oil Company is liable to him while Best is not.[43]

The Newfoundland Supreme Court clearly would have liked to hold Best partly liable as the trial judge had done. The writer submits that it was open to the Court to do so. There are in fact many cases in which a plaintiff has been held entitled to recover against each of two defendants whose negligence was in sequence.[44] In a well-known negligence case in the Supreme Court of Canada, a passenger was jolted off a street car onto the railway tracks and a train struck her. Both companies were liable.[45] Professor Glanville Williams has shown most convincingly that the peculiar rules of last clear chance are not based on general principles of causation and remoteness at all. The innocent plaintiff may recover against both defendants even though, as between themselves, one or the other had the last clear chance.[46]

The second significant Supreme Court case[47] forms an interesting contrast to the Newfoundland actions. Hobbs were makers of machinery for manufacturing plastics. They sold a machine to a chemical company in Ontario which was wired in a defective way. The task of connecting the machine fell to Shields who was plant electrician of the chemical company. In setting about to connect it, he neglected to "ground" the machine before turning on the current and was electrocuted when he touched it. His administratrix brought action against Hobbs under the Fatal Accidents Act. The Ontario Court of Appeal upheld the finding of the trial judge that both Shields and Hobbs were at fault and, since it was impossible to determine the degree of fault, it should be apportioned equally. Hobbs appealed to the Supreme Court, contending that Shields' fault was clearly subsequent to and severable from the defendant's. Only six months before the Supreme Court had held that Oakley's negligence was subsequent to and severable from Best's, but in the present case a majority held that Shields' negligence was not severable from that of Hobbs. One might suggest that if Oakley had the last clear chance then *a fortiori* did Shields. The fact that Shields (or his representative) was the plaintiff whereas Oakley was a defendant should not make any difference. The two dissenting members of the Court held that Shields' duty to ground the machine was analogous to a duty to inspect, and his failure so to do relieves the defendant from liability. The writer has no quarrel with the decision in *Shields* because it applies the Contributory Negligence Act and eschews last clear chance. The only point he wishes to make is that if we still have last chance, a better case for applying it could be made in *Hobbs v. Shields* than in *Best*.

Some Notable Cases in Provincial Courts

Turning now to decisions in provincial courts, we shall examine only those that clearly raise the problem of last clear chance. Rather than dealing with them province by province as did Dr. MacIntyre, we shall consider them according to subject matter.

First we shall look at three cases in which the court seemed to go to extreme lengths to invoke last chance.

The first is *Peoples Co-op and Miller v. Anderson*[48] from Manitoba. Miller parked his company's unlighted motor vehicle in his private driveway to the east of a street running north and south. He left the rear end protruding over the paved part of the street. The night was not only dark but foggy. The defendant driving south on the street at 25–30 miles an hour "drifted" to the left and struck the plaintiff's parked car. Now if either party had the last clear chance, it would seem reasonable to say that it was the defendant. In nearly every case where a moving vehicle strikes a stationary one this is the finding, unless of course the court is prepared to apportion fault. Yet the trial judge held the plaintiff solely to blame. Since both vehicles were damaged, the plaintiff had to pay the whole of the defendant's loss. This seems to be last clear chance in reverse. On appeal the court was divided equally so the trial judgment stood. The two justices whose view did not prevail would have held the plaintiff merely one-third to blame and the defendant two-thirds.

The next two cases are from Prince Edward Island. In *Milligan v. MacDougall*[49] the defendant was driving a loaded truck northward at 40 miles an hour in daytime. Coming to a bend to the left he reached for a cigarette, allowing his truck to move to the left of the road where it remained for fifty yards. He refrained from putting on his "booster" brakes because he was afraid his load would shift. The plaintiff was driving toward him at 30 miles an hour and the vehicles met head-on. One might think that the plaintiff could possibly escape a finding of any fault because he was faced with an emergency. In the agony of the moment he stayed on his own side. However the majority held not only was the plaintiff negligent but his negligence was clearly subsequent to and severable from the defendant's.

The second case is *Weeks v. Cousins and Nesbitt*.[50] Cousins was driving west after dark on a wet and foggy night. He was probably travelling over 40 miles an hour, and in any event his speed was found to be too fast considering the weather and the fact that he was approaching a small community. On the north side of the road was a church and on the south side was Weeks' service station. On the service station property and off the highway Weeks' tractor and baler were standing. Nesbitt (the third party) coming from the church entered his car which was headed west. Wishing to go east he attempted to make a U-turn in the middle of the block, though he had seen the lights of Cousins' car coming from behind. Cousins saw that a collision with Nesbitt was imminent so he turned his car sharply to the left. It went onto Weeks' property and smashed the tractor and baler. On both trial and appeal Cousins was held solely liable. Although Nesbitt was negligent there was a clear dividing line between his fault and that of Cousins in failing to take steps to avoid a collision. One might think that Cousins' negligence was prior incapacitating negligence within the *Loach* rule and that the *Loach* rule is no longer part of the law. However the court specifically held that "last clear chance includes . . . not only an actual opportunity but a potential opportunity which had been defeated by prior self-created incapacity of the party" and the *Loach* case was cited. The person who turned around in the middle of the block in the face of oncoming traffic was absolved of all responsibility. When a court invokes the *Loach* doctrine it is indeed shunting the Act into the background.[51]

The Moving Vehicle and the Parked Vehicle

We shall now consider cases involving a collision between a moving vehicle and a stationary one standing on the highway. Under the common law, the tendency was to hold the driver of the moving vehicle liable. One might think he has a better excuse at night but generally he failed then too. Indeed, in a 1933 case where a motorcyclist ran into an unlighted horse and cart, Scutton, L.J., said: "if a person rides in the dark he must ride at such a pace that he can pull up within the limits of his vision, and if in those circumstances he strikes something, either he is going too fast or he has not been keeping a proper lookout."[52] This seems to impose an almost strict liability, but a few months later the court upheld a judgment for a motorcyclist who ran into a lorry that was drawn across the road at night.[53] About fifteen years later there was an attempt to turn the tables completely on the unlighted stationary vehicle by contending that it constituted a nuisance. For a moment this argument seemed to have the acceptance of the English Court of Appeal,[54] but the triumph of the moving vehicle was short-lived. In *Maitland v. Raisbeck*[55] nine months later, a differently constituted Court of Appeal held that the earlier case laid down no such proposition. Several years later the Supreme Court of Canada also rejected the idea that a broken-down truck on the highway automatically becomes a nuisance.[56]

It will be remembered that since the Contributory Negligence Acts the Supreme Court has sometimes tended to hold the driver of a moving vehicle solely to blame, as in *McKee*, while in others it has apportioned blame, as in *Bruce*. We shall now examine the provincial cases on these points. The New Brunswick case of *Dugas v. Le Clair*[57] dealt with a night-time collision between a car and an unlighted truck on the travelled portion of the highway. At trial the driver of the moving car was found solely to blame for failing to see a reflector on the back of the truck. On appeal the court held both drivers at fault. More significant is the fact that the judgment recognizes that absence of lights in recent times is often held to be a contributing cause.

"Courts are now inclined to find that the accident has been caused by negligence on the part of both drivers." The court found the blame to be equal.

In the writer's opinion this last decision takes the proper approach to the statute. This does not mean that the driver of the stationary vehicle should always be held partly at fault.[58] On the other hand, it is not realistic in this day of heavy traffic at fast speeds to take the position that the moving driver is always so negligent as to be the sole cause and that the stationary driver does not contribute when he leaves his vehicle on the highway without lights. The unlighted heavy object may be passive in a physical sense (and so is a trap) but it is active every second as a source of danger. In addition, the suggestion that it is always visible in time for a careful driver to avoid it is a fiction. Moreover, the legislatures have forbidden parking on highways and have imposed the obligation to light because of the danger and because drivers may go too fast or may keep an improper lookout. Rand, J., in his judgments in *Bruce v. McIntyre* and *Brooks v. Ward* (a dissent) puts these points most forcefully.[59] If they are borne in mind then we will have fewer decisions in which a person who irresponsibly leaves a dangerous and scarcely visible object in the line of traffic will be able to persuade the court that he is blameless.

An interesting question that arises in these cases is the following: does it make any difference whether the driver of the stopped vehicle is still present and in a position to move it off the highway or turn on the lights or give some other warning, or whether on the other hand he has left the vehicle unattended? In the former case he literally has it in his power to reduce the danger and on orthodox last chance principles his negligence may be said to be continuing and to persist until the collision. On this reasoning his legal position would be much stronger if he simply were to go away. Yet in that case his conduct is in a sense more flagrant than if he stayed. It is true that when he is absent he can do nothing about the dangers of the situation but this does not seem a valid reason to put all the blame on the driver of the moving vehicle. Rand, J., in *Bruce v. McIntyre* probably does not agree with the writer's suggestion. At least his Lordship thought that Bruce's blame consisted at least partly in sitting in the car without moving it or turning on the lights.

The Pedestrian and the Vehicle

The next class of case is that of the pedestrian and the vehicle. It is commonplace for statutes to require a pedestrian to walk facing the traffic rather than on the right hand side with his back to oncoming cars.

In *Harris v. Cohen,*[60] a Nova Scotia case, the plaintiff (a young woman) disregarded this requirement at night. The driver saw her and slowed down. She knew from the lights that the car was behind. Nevertheless the car struck her. The trial judge, Ilsey, C.J., found her "clearly negligent in being there at all with a car coming behind her" and assessed her fault at 80%. On appeal Vincent MacDonald, C.J., speaking for the court, adopted the position that Dr. MacIntyre always criticized. He held that since the defendant knew of the danger and had the ability to avoid it, his failure to do so destroyed the causal efficiency of the plaintiff's negligent conduct and thus reduced it to the status of a *causa sine qua non,* leaving the conduct of the defendant in the face of the known danger and available opportunity as the sole cause.

In contrast to this case, Currie, J.,[61] held a pedestrian in very similar circumstances to be 30% to blame. In this case the defendant did not actually see the plaintiff until the last minute.

The basic question in these cases is whether the plaintiff's conduct in remaining on the road with his back to the traffic is continuing negligence. The cases exculpating him of course say it is not. The writer thinks that it is, particularly at night. It is obviously harder to see him than in daytime, and atmospheric conditions may be such that the driver cannot easily or quickly distinguish him from a patch in the pavement or a shadow. The pedestrian has put himself in the way of danger and at the same time made it more difficult to avoid oncoming traffic, as he could do if he were facing it.

Dean Wright puts the question: "Why is a pedestrian who walks on the prohibited side of a highway 'at fault'? What is the risk or hazard of not being seen by, or not seeing or avoiding, approaching traffic?"[62] The writer would say that it is mainly the latter in daytime, and both at night. In any case, a holding that his breach of the law did not contribute to his damage requires the application of last chance against the driver in circumstances where the pedestrian's negligence continues to the moment of impact.

An unusual case that is not technically one of a pedestrian arose in Ontario. Cudney's car struck the rear of Carroll's unlighted tractor and knocked Carroll to the road. Cudney stopped and went to Carroll's aid and enlisted the aid of another driver to warn oncoming traffic by flashing his lights. Bennett paid no heed to the warning and came on at high speed, striking and killing the recumbent Carroll on the highway. Cudney was held not to blame at all for striking Carroll's tractor and Carroll was at fault. Now when Bennett recklessly came along and hit Carroll on the road, one might think that Carroll's contributory negligence had spent itself and that, on last chance principles, Bennett would be solely to blame for Carroll's death. However, Hughes, J., held that Carroll's negligence in driving the unlighted tractor still operated and combined equally with Bennett's negligence in causing Carroll's death.[63]

The last important problem in connection with pedestrians is that of the person who walks across the street between intersections in violation of statute and is struck by a car. In *Fairweather v. Renton,*[64] the plaintiff was a sixteen year old boy who started to cross a main street in Moncton, New Brunswick, in the daytime. The Motor Vehicle Act required pedestrians to yield the right-of-way to vehicles between intersections. The boy saw the defendant's car approaching from the right when it was over 100 yards away. He did not look again. The defendant slowed as he approached the boy and then speeded up to pass in front of him but struck him. The trial judge divided the fault equally. The Appeal Division, constituted just as it was a year earlier in *Dugas v. Le Clair*[65] when it had approved of the tendency to apportion blame, held that the plaintiff was not negligent at all, and if he was, his conduct was not a proximate and effective cause of his injury. Bridges, J., in dissent, held that no clear line could be drawn between the fault of the two parties. He would have upheld the trial judge.

The Passenger of the Intoxicated Driver

The next category of case is that of the passenger who rides with a drunken driver and is harmed when the driver is careless and has an accident.[66] The question is whether the defendant can succeed on a plea of *volenti non fit injuria* or, alternatively, contributory negligence. Before apportionment of blame was possible, it did not matter which defence applied for each was fatal to the plaintiff's claim. Today the latter is not a complete answer so it becomes important to distinguish the two defences. Three important cases in the Supreme Court of Canada, *Seymour v. Maloney,*[67] *Miller v. Decker,*[68] and *Lehnert v. Stein*[69] show that the defence of *volenti* is possible, but hard to establish because the defendant must show that the passenger has actually agreed with him to take what Professor Glanville Williams calls the "legal risk". In both *Seymour* and *Lehnert,* the plaintiff was not *volens* but was held to be contributorily negligent in re-entering the defendant's car after his ability to drive was patently impaired. In each case the plaintiff's blame was assessed at 25%. Now it has never been suggested by any of the judgments in these cases that the plaintiffs should be able, notwithstanding their fault, to recover in full on the argument that defendant's negligence was clearly subsequent to and severable from theirs. In fact the point has never been considered so far as the writer knows, save by Vincent McDonald, J., the trial judge in *Seymour v. Maloney.* He found that the plaintiff's conduct in remaining in the car contributed to her injuries.

In *Foster v. Morton*[70] in Nova Scotia the trial judge held the intoxicated driver solely responsible, but on appeal the defence of contributory negligence succeeded to the extent of 25%. The court dealt with a further defence: that the defendant was committing a crime under the Criminal Code and that the passenger had "a common intention to pursue an unlawful purpose" within the Code and so was an accessory, and hence was barred under the *ex turpi* rule. MacDonald, J., canvassed this defence thoroughly and rejected it on the facts.[71]

Conclusion

Space does not permit an examination of the Report of the English Law Revision Committee that recommended legislation in 1939, nor of the statute that resulted in 1945. One can safely say however that the Act has been applied readily, and if last clear chance has not vanished, it is scarcely visible. In actions by workmen against their employers, apportionment is commonplace provided the workman was at fault at all. The employer cannot hide behind last clear chance.[72] In collisions between a stationary vehicle and a moving one, the act is applied.[73] The Court of Appeal in *Davies v. Swan Motors*[74] held that the fault of the man on the running board (unlike that of the boy in *McLaughlin v. Long*) contributed to his injury. It also held both drivers to be at fault, so the damage was divided three ways. As to the theoretical survival of last clear chance, or last opportunity, Denning, L.J., holds it has disappeared, but the writer cannot extract the same firm holding from the other two judgments. Lord Evershed indeed says that last opportunity is gone but *Davies v. Mann* is not!

In conclusion, it seems to the writer that it would be preferable to abolish last chance completely, though he realizes that abolition would not solve the difficult practical problems. He agrees with Dr. MacIntyre that it seems impossible at this late date for the courts to hold it no longer part of the law. This means that an amendment to the Act is necessary. Various persons have suggested phraseology to effect this end. May we commend to the reader (in spite of the double negative) the proposal of Professor Glanville Williams: "Damage shall not be deemed not to be caused by the act of any person by reason only of the fact that another person had an opportunity of avoiding the consequences of such act and negligently or carelessly failed to do so."[75]

Notes

1 53 Harv. L. Rev. 1125 (1940); 18 Can. B. Rev. 665 (1940).
2 Mills v. Armstrong, The Bernina, 12 P.D. 58, 59 (C.A. 1887); *aff'd* 13 App. Cas. 1 (1888).
3 Davies v. Swan Motor Co. (Swansea) Ltd., [1949] 2 K.B. 291 (C.A.).
4 British Columbia Electric Rlwy. Co. Ltd. v. Loach, [1916] 1 A.C. 719 (P.C. 1915) (B.C.).
5 Jeremy v. Fontaine, [1931] 3 W.W.R. 203 (Alta. App. Div.)
6 Hart & Honore, Causation In the Law 206 (1959).
7 G. Williams, Joint Torts and Contributory Negligence 236–254 (1951).
8 Ottawa Electric Rlwy. Co. v. Booth, (1920) 63 Can. Sup. Ct. 80; Long v. Toronto Rlwy. Co., (1914) 50 Can. Sup. Ct. 224; 20 D.L.R. 369.
9 Root v. McKinney [1930] Can. Sup. Ct. 337 (1929); [1930] 2 D.L.R. 984.
10 The City of Calgary v. Harnovis, (1913) 48 Can. Sup. Ct. 494, 15 D.L.R. 411; Canadian National Rlwy. v. Clark, [1923] Can. Sup. Ct. 730, [1923] 4 D.L.R. 727; Green & Breckenridge v. Canadian National Rlwy., [1932] Can. Sup. Ct. 689, [1932] 4 D.L.R. 593.
11 Canadian Pacific Rlwy. Co. v. Smith, (1921) 62 Can. Sup. Ct. 134, Canadian Northern Rlwy. Co. v. Prescesky, [1924] Can. Sup. Ct. 2 (1923), [1924] 2 D.L.R. 504.
12 Grand Trunk Pacific Rlwy. Co. v. Earl, [1923] Can. Sup. Ct. 397, [1923] 2 D.L.R. 741.
13 33 Can. B. Rev. 257 (1955).
14 [1927] Can. Sup. Ct. 303 (1926); [1927] 2 D.L.R. 186
15 [1953] 2 Can. Sup. Ct. 177, [1953] 4 D.L.R. 783
16 [1954] Can. Sup. Ct. 651, [1954] 4 D.L.R. 785.
17 [1953] A.C. 291 (P.C.) (1952) (B.C.).
18 Prosser, Selected Topics On the Law of

Torts, 49–50 (1953). Of course there can be cases where the act is jughandled in favour of the defendant, for in this era of collisions between two well-matched heavy vehicles it is purely a matter of chance as to which party is plaintiff.

19 *Id.* at 49.

20 *Negligence—Contributory "Ultimate" and "Comparative" with a Suggested Statutory Amendment,* 37 Can. L.T. 23 (1917): in 1922, encouraged by the article of Lord Justice O'Connor of Ireland, *Contributory Negligence,* 38 L.Q. Rev. 17 (1922), he wrote a further article having in the meantime failed to interest the Attorney-General of Ontario: *Contributory Negligence* 42 Can. L.T. 425 (1922).

21 Anglin, *Law of Quebec and Other Provinces* 1 Can. B. Rev. 33, 49 (1923).

22 1924 Proc. Conf. Commissioners on Uniformity 37.

23 MacMurchy, *Contributory Negligence,* 1 Can. B. Rev. 844 (1923).

24 1923 Proc. Can. Bar Ass'n. 104–119.

25 1924 Proc. Conf. Comm'rs. on Uniformity 34–36.

26 2. Where by the fault of two or more persons damage or loss is caused to one or more of them, the liability to make good the damage or loss shall be in proportion to the degree in which each person was at fault:

Provided that:

(a) If, having regard to all the circumstances of the case, it is not possible to establish different degrees of fault, the liability shall be apportioned equally, and

(b) Nothing in this section shall operate so as to render any person liable for any loss or damage to which his fault has not contributed.

27 Williams, *op. cit. supra* note 7, at 257–8.

28 1926 Proc. Can Bar Ass'n 170 and 37–40.

29 [1927] Can. Sup. Ct. 303.

30 Falconbridge, *Desirable Changes in the Common Law,* 5 Can. B. Rev. 581 (1927).

31 1928 Proc. Conf. Comm'rs. on Uniformity 90.

32 See *e.g.*, Fairty, *Note,* 9 Can. B. Rev. 52 (1931) and *Weir, Davies v. Mann and Contributory Negligence Statutes,* 9 Can. B. Rev. 470 (1931).

33 1932 Proc. Can. Bar Ass'n., p. 152; 1933 p. 253.

34 1934 Proc. Conf. Comm'rs. on Uniformity 52 and 69.

35 1935 Proc. Conf. Comm'rs. on Uniformity 31; also Vincent MacDonald, *The Negligence Action and the Legislature,* 13 Can. B. Rev. 535, 553–63 (1935).

36 Bechtold v. Osbaldeston, [1953] Can. Sup. Ct. 177.

37 McKee v. Malenfant, [1954] Can. Sup. Ct. 651.

38 [1955[Can. Sup. Ct. 251. This judgment appeared just after Dr. MacIntyre completed his article. See *Correspondence,* 33 Can. B. Rev. 504 (1955).

39 [1956] Can. Sup. Ct. 683. The parked vehicle belonged to Brooks (third party) and the collision was between Ward's car and a car owned by the Crown.

40 [1962] Can. Sup. Ct. 118. The facts and decision bear some resemblance to those in Trans-Canada Forest Products v. Heaps, [1954] 2 D.L.R. 545 (Can. Sup. Ct.). Dr. MacIntyre criticized this judgment for failure to apply the Act, but it seems to the writer that the majority absolved the plaintiff on the ground of no fault rather than that defendant had last chance.

41 (1960–61) 45 Mar. Prov. 207. Trial and appeal are both reported here.

42 [1920] A.C. 466.

43 Hand v. Best and Great Eastern Oil Co., (1962) 34 D.L.R. 2d 282. (Nfld. Sup. Ct.).

44 Grant v. Sun Shipping Co., [1948] A.C. 549, is a good example.

45 Winnipeg Electric Ry. v. C.N.R., (1919) 59 Can. Sup. Ct. 352.

46 Williams, *op. cit. supra* note 7, at 247–54.

47 Hobbs Mfg. Co. v. Shields, [1962] Can. Sup. Ct. 716.

48 (1964) 46 W.W.R. (n.s.) 95 (Man. C.A.).

49 (1962) 32 D.L.R. 2d 57 (P.E.I. Sup. Ct.). The dissent of Bell, J., commends itself to the writer. See also Clyke v. Blenkhorn, (1948) 13 D.L.R. 2d 293 (N.S.C.A.).

50 (1964) 44 D.L.R. 2d 316 (P.E.I. Sup.

Ct.). Dean Wright's editorial note is sharply critical.

51 Morrison v. The Queen, (1963) 36 D.L.R. 2d 518 (P.E.I. Sup. Ct.) applied the Act to a collision between a snow plough and a car. It would be wrong to leave the impression that the Prince Edward Island decisions have always shown an astuteness to avoid apportionment.

52 Baker v. Longhurst. [1933] 2 K.B. 461, 468.

53 Tidy v. Battman, [1934] 1 K.B. 319.

54 Ware v. Garston Haulage Co. [1944] K.B. 30, [1943] 2 All E.R. 558.

55 [1944] 2 All E.R. 272, [1944] K.B. 689.

56 Shafer v. Jones, [1948] Can. Sup. Ct. 166.

57 (1962) 32 D.L.R. 2d 459 (N.B. Sup. Ct.). The plaintiff was the widow of a passenger in the car. A recent British Columbia case, Lyons v. Hembrough and Paisley, (1964) 49 W.W.R. (n.s.) 385 shows the same willingness to find both drivers to have contributed.

58 *E.g.*, Mamczasz v. Bruens, (1964) 43 D.L.R. 2d 707 (Can. Sup. Ct.).

59 [1955] Can. Sup. Ct. at 254–5; [1956] Can. Sup. Ct. 687.

60 [1955] 3 D.L.R. 120 (N.S. Sup. Ct.).

61 Lindfors v. Cameron, (1962) 31 D.L.R. 2d 58 (N.S. Sup. Ct.). See also Tuckey v. Dyer (1961) 27 D.L.R. 2d 408 (N.S. Sup. Ct.).

62 Wright, Cases On Torts 583 (3rd ed. 1963).

63 Carroll v. Cudney, (1963) 38 D.L.R. 2d 113 (Ont. H.C.).

64 (1963) 39 D.L.R. 2d 249.

65 (1962) 32 D.L.R. 2d 459.

66 The same problem can arise where the risk arises from other causes, e.g., a defective vehicle or an irresponsible non-intoxicated driver: e.g., Dorn v. Stevens, (1963) 39 D.L.R. 2d 761 (Alta. Sup. Ct.).

67 *Sub nom* Car and General Insurance Co. v. Seymour and Maloney, [1956] Can. Sup. Ct. 322.

68 [1957] Can. Sup. Ct. 624.

69 [1963] Can. Sup. Ct. 38.

70 (1956) 4 D.L.R. 2d 269.

71 *Cf.* Schwindt v. Giesbrecht, (1958) 13 D.L.R. 2d 770 (Alta. Sup. Ct.).

72 *E.g.*, Stapley v. Gypsum Mines, [1953] A.C. 553.

73 Henley v. Cameron, 65 T.L.R. 17 (1949) (C.A.); Harvey v. Road Haulage Executive, [1952] 1 K.B. 120 (C.A.).

74 [1949] 2 K.B. 291 (C.A.).

75 *Op. cit. supra* note 7, at 516 (sec. 24 (2)(b) of a suggested statute). Other examples are found in Prosser, *op. cit. supra* note 18 at 58; 1932 Proc. Can. Bar Ass'n. 155 (two alternatives are given); 1933 Proc. Conf. Comm'rs. on Uniformity 29–33 (two alternatives are given).

1967

Law of Succession (Common Law)

Unpublished

This paper was prepared for the annual meeting of the Canadian Association of Law Teachers, held in Ottawa in June 1967.

It was to be part of a proposed publication which, however, never materialized.

Professor Jean-Louis Beaudoin, a distinguished French law teacher at McGill, wrote a paper dealing with French law on this subject. Bowker volunteered to do one on the law relating to the common law provinces. This article is the result, but was never published.

See also the paper entitled Succession to Property in the Common Law Provinces, pp. 195–219.

The purpose of this paper is to deal with important aspects of the common law of succession in a way that will permit a comparison with the law of Quebec. The common law provinces do not define succession so we can borrow the Quebec definition: "the transmission by law or by the will of man, to one or more persons, of the property and the transmissible rights and obligations of a deceased person."[1]

May I first mention certain transmissions which may seem to be successions but are not, because they are not "entirely dependent for vigour and effect" upon the death of the donor.

(1) An *inter vivos* trust which creates interests arising on the settlor's death. This is not testamentary, though the law is not clear where the settlor reserves a power of revocation.[2]

(2) An ostensible immediate gift over which the donor retains control until death: for example, an executed grant of land which the grantor retains in his safety deposit box until death.[3]

(3) The right of survivorship in jointly owned property. In the case of joint bank accounts the better view is that the right of survivorship is no more testamentary in nature than is the right of survivorship in land.[4] However, the Supreme Court of Canada in *Edwards* v. *Bradley* specifically left this question open.[5] In a proper case the opening of the joint account may create an immediate gift by way of advancement, but in *Edwards* there was a resulting trust in favour of the estate of the person who had opened the joint account.

(4) The benefits under a life insurance policy. They are not even a part of the estate where the insured has designated a beneficiary.[6]

A provision in an agreement for a loan, whereby any balance owing on the death of a creditor would go to X was recently held to be testamentary.[7]

Once the transaction is held to be testamentary it is ineffective unless the formalities of the Wills Act have been met. An example is that of the employee who participates in his company's saving plan. The written agreement provides that on his death moneys to his credit shall go to his wife; but it is not executed like a will. Unless there is a trust in her favour then the direction in her favour is testamentary, for the employee retains control over the fund until death.[8] One is bound to wonder whether there are many similar plans or benevolent society plans or even pension schemes that are vulnerable on this ground.

Before examining the Intestate Succession Acts and the Wills Acts, I shall note four other statutes that have a bearing on succession.

(1) *Legitimation Acts*

The original Uniform Legitimation Act of 1920 provided only for legitimation by subsequent marriage. The Revised Act of 1960, which most provinces have adopted, makes legitimate the children of a voidable marriage; also the children of a marriage celebrated after the first spouse of one of the parties has been judicially declared to be dead or reported to be dead by the military authorities; and also children of what in Quebec is called a putative marriage. This is a void marriage which at least one of the parties reasonably thought at the time to be a valid marriage.

(2) *Adoption Acts*

Adoption as a legal status is modern in the common law. The early provincial legislation did not clearly remove the adopted child from the family of his natural parents and make it for all purposes a member of the adopting family. In recent years the efforts of Dr. G. Kennedy, Deputy Attorney-General of British Columbia,[9] have led to revised adoption laws. They make the adopted child the child of the adopting parents as though he had been born in lawful wedlock, and he ceases to be the child of his natural parents. Some of the new Acts[10] specifically provide that any reference to "children" in a will or other document, whether made before or after passage of the Act, is deemed to include an adopted child unless the contrary intention is expressed. If a court were to give literal effect to this section it would change the result in *Re Gage,*[11] a case from Ontario. In that case the testator made a gift to his daughter's children. After his death she adopted a child. The Supreme Court held that this child was not one of the children. The Ontario Act did not have a section of the kind just described and it had not been passed until long after the testator had died.

(3) *Survivorship (Commorientes) Acts*

At common law, unlike the civil law, there is no presumption of survivorship where two parties die in a common disaster and there is no evidence as to which survived. In the leading English case of *Wing* v. *Angrave,*[12] husband and wife went down in a sailing ship. These multiple tragedies still take place in boats and also in automobile accidents and aeroplane crashes. The Uniform Survivorship Act was adopted in 1939 and all of the common law provinces have it, or at least a similar act. Whereas the presumption provided by the civil law is based on probabilities, the Uniform Act creates a simple and artificial presumption that the younger died first. The present Insurance Acts, on the other hand, provide that the beneficiary is deemed to have died first. In my opinion it is clear that the Survivorship Act does not come into play at all so far as insurance is concerned.[13]

(4) *Dower and Estate by the Curtesy*

Common law dower describes the right of a widow to a life interest in one-third of her husband's lands on his death and estate by the curtesy is the husband's right to a life estate in all of his wife's lands on her death. The latter has either been abolished in all provinces or at least is of no practical importance. Common law dower remains in the Maritimes and Ontario. In Ontario, at least, it seems that dower can easily be barred or avoided. In addition, a widow may be put to her election when her husband has left to her property by his will.[14]

The four Western provinces have all abolished common law dower. However, there is a new type of "dower" borrowed from the United States, which gives to the wife a life interest in the homestead; and in Alberta the husband has the corresponding right where the homestead is in the wife's name. Most of the problems that arise under these Acts have to do with the validity or otherwise of a disposition made by the husband *inter vivos* without the wife's consent. This complicated problem is irrelevant here.[15]

Intestate Succession

The typical act is based on the Statute of Distribution, 1670, but of course now extends to real property. This discussion is based on the Uniform Intestate Succession Act. If an intestate dies leaving issue, his estate is distributed, subject to the rights of the widow, *per stirpes,* among the issue. Thus if there are two children, A and B, they share equally, but if A had died leaving two children they take his share. If in addition B had died leaving six children they would take B's share. One might think that in the last situation where all the beneficiaries are grandchildren they would take *per capita* as nephews and nieces do. However, they do not because the distribution is *per stirpes.*[16]

If there is a widow she shares with the issue to the extent of one-half if there is one child or issue of that child. Her share is reduced to one-third if there are two or more children, or issue thereof. It is when there is a widow and no issue that we find an interesting difference between the statutes. It is commonplace nowadays to give the widow a preferential share which is generally fixed at $20,000. Apart from this preferential share, the Uniform Act and a number of the provincial acts, following the Statute of Distribution, require the widow to share equally with her late husband's next of kin. The four Western provinces, however, give the wife everything. Whether this is because family ties are stronger in the East or because the wife is less of a breadwinner than in the West, I cannot say. It is clear, however, that in the land of Emily Murphy and Nellie McClung, any legislature with the temerity to return to the old distribution would find itself out of power overnight.

Turning now to the case where there is no widow or issue, the property goes to the parents or the survivor of them. Next, it goes to brothers and sisters in equal shares and the children of a deceased brother or sister (but not more remote issue) take the share their parent would have taken. If brothers and sisters are all dead, nephews and nieces take in equal shares, as already noted, "and in no case shall representation be admitted." The word "representation" as used in intestate succession acts means the right of children to step into their parents' shoes. If there are no nephews or nieces, the property goes to the next of kin, and these are computed by counting upward from the intestate to the nearest common ancestor and then downward to the relative; and kindred of the half blood inherit equally with those of whole blood in the same degree. Under some of the earlier acts, there was much litigation as to when representation was admitted, but under the Uniform Act it is excluded except in favour of issue and nephews and nieces. I can see no room for doubt in the application in the provisions of the Uniform Act.

The provisions from the Statute of Distribution which say that the advancement of a portion to a child must be taken into consideration in distributing the estate have been retained in the Uniform Act.

Now we come to the illegitimate child. Under the Statute of Distribution an illegitimate child did not take at all, and no one could take from him save his wife and legitimate issue. As far as I know, Saskatchewan and Alberta were the first provinces to enable the child to take from or through his mother and the mother to take from him.[17] The Uniform Act had similar provisions but *Re Carlson*[18] shows that they were not effective for all purposes. In 1958 the Uniform Act was accordingly amended to provide that "for the purposes of this Act, an illegitimate child shall be treated as the legitimate child of his mother." This amendment has been enacted in several provinces.

Alberta may be unique in permitting an illegitimate child ever to take from his father. The amendment to the Alberta Act came about in this way. Shortly before World War II, an unmarried man died. He was admittedly the father of eight illegitimate children. All of his lawful kin were in Europe. The legislature in 1939 amended the Intestate Succession Act to provide that where a man leaves no widow or lawful issue and has admitted paternity or has been judicially declared to be the father of an illegitimate child, then the child shall take. The legislature made the amendment retroactive so that the estate was taken from the European kin and given to the eight illegitimate children.[19]

There are three points on which the Acts are silent:

(1) What happens to the share of a beneficiary who renounces? There is authority that if a child renounces, his share goes to the other children.[20] What would happen if the closest kin were brothers and sisters and one of

them renounced, having children of his own? They might argue that they should step into his shoes as though he were dead but I doubt they would succeed.

(2) Is it possible to waive the benefit of the Act? This question usually arises when husband and wife enter into a separation agreement and the wife purports to give up her benefits under the Intestate Succession Act. The authorities say that the waiver is binding,[21] because the Statute is for the benefit of the wife, not for society, so therefore it is open to her to waive it.

(3) Does a person entitled on intestacy forfeit his rights if he commits criminal homicide against the intestate? The Canadian cases[22] say that he does; otherwise if he can show that he was insane within the Criminal Code.[23]

Wills

A man's will is his direction as to the disposition of his property on death. It is sometimes said (1), that a will is in its nature revocable and (2), that the making of a will, like entry into matrimony, is something that a person may not delegate to an agent. These statements are not quite accurate. A man may make a binding contract to leave property by will. If the property is land, then of course the agreement must be in writing under the Statute of Frauds.[24] In addition, it is possible for two people to make mutual wills and in so doing to agree not to revoke them. Such an agreement is effective, but peculiarly enough does not become binding until one of the testators has died not having revoked. If the survivor takes benefits under the will of the one who has died, then he may not validly change his will; or rather if he does, the executor under the new will holds the property in trust for the beneficiaries under the mutual will.[25]

As for the second rule, it is generally true. A will made under a power of attorney would not comply with the Wills Act. Not only must a man sign his own will, unless he has someone sign it in his presence and at his direction, but he must make his own dispositions. There are two apparent exceptions to this. If he makes charitable gifts in his will he may leave it to his executor to select the charities. Secondly, he may, for example, give a life interest to his daughter and give her a power of appointment over the property which enables her to designate the person to whom it shall go.[26]

We turn now to the Wills Act. The English Act of 1837 is the basis for all the provincial acts. My references shall be to the Revised Uniform Act of 1957.

In every province a will may be made in what Quebec calls the "English form" with two witnesses and the well-known provision for signing "in the presence." From the beginning the Courts have been rigorous in insisting on compliance with this requirement and a visual test has been applied even for blind testators. Almost anything will do as a signature and the requirement that it must be at the "foot or end" of the will is interpreted literally. The test is this: can the whole of the disposition fairly be read as leading up to the signature?[27]

It is the provision for holograph wills, permitted in the three Prairie Provinces and Newfoundland, that raises difficult problems. The will must be wholly in the handwriting of the testator but the Uniform Act is not clear as to whether the signature must be at the foot or end.[28]

Where a testator uses a printed form it is clear that the will is not holograph, but there are several cases holding it is, provided the testator does such a poor job of filling in the blanks of a printed form that the dispositions constitute a complete testamentary document. In the case of *Sunrise Gospel Hour* v. *Halpenny,* not yet reported, the Appellate Division in Alberta dealt with a will in which the testator used a printed form. He filled in the executor's name in the clause providing for appointment of an executor, and then in the blank part of the form he wrote out all his dispositions, ignoring the printed portions. The majority held that since the written part constitutes a sensible will it is valid, though of course effect cannot be given to the clause appointing an executor. McDermid J.A., in dissent, held that the clause appointing the executor was intended to be part of the will and since it was not handwritten the will could not be said to be wholly handwritten.

Other problems that arise in provinces which permit holograph wills as well as formal wills are the following:

(1) When is a handwritten document a will? Some very inartistically worded letters have been admitted to probate, some of them as informal and casual as the letter in the Quebec case of *Dansereau* v. *Berget*.[29] On the other hand, a letter of instruction to a solicitor is not a holograph will.[30] Perhaps the most bizarre instance of a valid holograph will is the one that a Saskatchewan farmer scratched on the fender of the tractor under which he was pinned.[31]

(2) Is a holograph codicil to a formal will valid? The cases almost uniformly say that it is and certainly there is nothing in the Act to the contrary.

(3) Is a holograph alteration to a formal will valid? There is authority that it is not[32] and the Uniform Act seems clear that it is not. This means that if a testator writes on the face of his formal will a new clause and signs it the important question is whether this new handwritten clause is an alteration or a codicil. What if it is wedged between the original dispositions?[33] or what if it changes in part one of the original dispositions?

All of the Acts permit simple written wills by servicemen "on active service." This phrase has caused difficulty in the past[34] but the revised Uniform Act defined the term in a way that seems to remove doubt.

The Statute is designed not only to require a certain form for a valid will, but to require that a will shall be revoked only in specified ways; namely, by a subsequent will or a formal instrument of revocation or by destruction of the will with intent to revoke. In addition, marriage revokes a will unless made in contemplation of a specific marriage. The main difficulty arises when the testator has done something to the document by way of partial tearing or burning or by cutting out his signature and the question is whether this act to the document is a destruction and hence effective as a revocation.

The Act provides for revocation pure and simple and one might think that this is the only possible kind of revocation. However, the courts have developed a doctrine known as Dependant Relative Revocation.[35] Sometimes the testator ostensibly revokes his will by destroying it or by a subsequent will, but does so while labouring under a mistake or else intending that the revocation be conditional. In these circumstances, if the Court can infer that he would not have revoked had he not been acting under the mistake or had he known that the condition would not be fulfilled, then the Court will say there was no effective revocation at all. In these cases the Court is trying to determine the intent with which an act is done. Sometimes, the conclusion that the testator would rather have had the original disposition than none at all is mere conjecture.

Revival, like revocation, is not to be left to inference. The only way a revoked will can be revived is by a later will or by a codicil showing an intention to revive. There is no uniformity in the decisions, but generally a mere reference to the date of the revoked will is not enough.[36]

The Statute has a number of sections that begin "Unless a contrary intention appears by the will. . . " and then proceed to lay down a rule. Three of the important ones are these: (1) A will speaks from death with respect to the property of the testator. (2) A gift to issue (and in some cases to brother or sister) who dies before the testator leaving issue does not lapse but takes effect in favour of those who would have taken on intestacy had the beneficiary died immediately after the testator. The Supreme Court had held that this section does not create two successions but a single one.[37] Those who benefit are, of course, the issue together with their surviving parent, who is the son-in-law or daughter-in-law of the testator. Under many Intestate Succession Acts that person receives a preferential share such as $20,000.[38] Because of that fact, the Uniform Wills Act was amended in 1966 to provide that the preferential share should be ignored. (3) An illegitimate child is to be treated as though he were the legitimate child of his mother. This section gives statutory support to the rejection of the old rule of construction which says that "child" in a will means legitimate child. The new Uniform Section is worded broadly and does not require that the gift be to the children. Suppose a court had to deal with a bequest "to the mother who has since my death given birth in Toronto to the greatest number of children as shown by the registrations under the Vital Statistics Act." Could a candidate include her illegitimate children?[39]

The Revised Uniform Act 1957 has two important provisions that are intended to do away with harsh rules of law.

(1) The first rule says that a gift of land is adeemed by an agreement for sale. Thus the beneficiary is not entitled to the purchase moneys accruing due at the testator's death.[40] The rule has been extended so that a gift of company shares fails when the testator has later given an option to purchase and

the option is exercised after his death.[41] The new provision gives to the beneficiary whatever interest the testator had in the property at the time of his death, such as the claim to the purchase moneys.

(2) The second rule says that a gift for "charitable or benevolent purposes" is not a valid charitable gift. The sad story of the failure of Mr. Caleb Diplock's attempt to be generous to worthy causes is well known[42] and the Supreme Court uncritically followed the Diplock decision in *Brewer* v. *MacAulay*.[43] The amendment says that where a gift for charitable purposes is linked conjunctively or disjunctively with a gift for non-charitable purposes and the non-charitable purpose is void, the charitable gift is valid. It has been enacted in several provinces. I am not sure that it would apply to a decision like *Re Cox*.[44] In that case the gift was stated to be for charitable purposes but then the will went on to say that it was for the benefit of employees of the Canada Life Assurance Company. The Privy Council held this was not a charitable purpose, so the gift was void.

At this point one might ask, why not try to include in the Act all the important rules of construction? This may come in time, but the reluctance to codify remains strong.

So much for the Statute. Much of the law of wills is outside the Act. The subject of admissibility of extrinsic evidence on application for probate and in interpreting wills is a good example. Since the Act requires a will to be in writing, it would defeat the purpose of the Act to admit evidence as to what the testator meant or intended. However, on application for probate, evidence is admissible to show that a clause or word in a will was inserted by mistake, at least where it appears that the will had not been read over by or to the testator.[45] As a matter of construction there are several typical situations where there is doubt as to the subject matter of the gift or to the identity of the beneficiary. Using the identity of the beneficiary as an example, the gift may be to "my nephew John Brown." If there are two nephews of that name, or if there is only one nephew, whose name is James Brown, evidence of the testator's intention is admissible. It seems, however, that if there is a nephew who answers the description exactly it is very hard, though not impossible, for another nephew, James Brown, to show he was the one intended. There are many cases in which the Court admits evidence, not of intention, but evidence of facts known to the testator when he made the will, for the purpose of determining whom he meant as beneficiary e.g., that he spoke of his nephew as "John Brown," though the name was really "Jonathan." The Court is said to put itself in the testator's armchair. This rule often permits the Court to apply the gift in favour of persons not literally within it at all. For example, in one recent case, a gift to "my grand-nieces and grand-nephews" was held to be a gift in favour of the testator's wife's grand-nieces and grand-nephews.[46] In another, a gift to "children" went to step-children, the testator having none of his own.[47]

As to the canons of construction, they occupy a good portion of any text on wills. Generally they are based on presumed intention and often they serve a good purpose. However, they sometimes become artificial and the

Courts may apply them too rigidly. In recent times, there has been a healthy trend the other way. The Courts emphasize the need to look at the will as a whole and to resist the tendency to follow automatically decisions on wills with similar wording.

Perhaps the most significant of all these cases is *Perrin* v. *Morgan*[48] in the House of Lords. The will made a gift of "all moneys of which I die possessed" to nephews and nieces. There was no residuary clause. A long line of cases had held that "money" means cash and that it extends to assets such as bank deposits and dividends but nothing more. When the testatrix died she had about £1,000 in money as so defined and over £32,000 in bonds and shares. The House of Lords held that the old meaning of money was artificially narrow and often defeated the testator's intention. Thus the beneficiaries received the bonds and shares. The benign influence of this case has spread far beyond its facts. A good illustration is *National Trust Co.* v. *Fleury*.[49] The testator left income to his daughter and then directed that on her death part of the corpus was to go "to such persons as will be entitled thereto according to the Statute of Distribution... as if I had died intestate in respect thereto." On the daughter's death, the question arose as to whether the testator's next of kin were to be determined at the time of the testator's death or of the daughter's death. The rule of construction is that the relevant time is the testator's death unless the contrary intention is apparent from the will. The daughter's representatives invoked this rule, because she was the sole next of kin at the time of the testator's death. The Supreme Court held that the testator's intention would be defeated if the rule were applied. He did not intend her to take the property absolutely, for he had specifically given her the income. In other words, the Court found an implied contrary intention.

Many of the difficulties in interpreting wills (and one might add, in drawing them) arises from the fact that English property law for centuries has recognized future interests of two main kinds—remainders and executory interests. In connection with remainders, it is sometimes hard to know whether the remainder is vested at the testator's death or whether it is contingent on some event such as the remainderman's surviving the life tenant. Where a testator says: "I leave the income from the residue of my estate to my wife for life and direct my Trustees on her death to divide the residue between A and B." When do A and B become owners of the residue? The answer is, at the testator's death.[50] If he had added "If A or B dies in the lifetime of my wife and leaves issue, the issue shall take the share of the one so dying" then the share of the one so dying goes to his issue by way of divestiture from A. If the testator wants to make the interest of the remainderman contingent on his surviving the widow, he must say so.

Executory interests are of two kinds—springing and shifting. An example of the former is this: "I give $5,000 to John if he reaches twenty-five years of age." John has a springing interest which vests in him at twenty-five and not before. However, if the will says "I give $5,000 to John, but if he dies before attaining twenty-five, the $5,000 shall go to William," then

William has a shifting interest which shifts to him if John dies under twenty-five.

It might be noted here that if the gift is worded "I give John $5,000 to be paid to him when he reaches twenty-five," one might think that the $5,000 does not belong to John until he reaches twenty-five. However, the rule in *Saunders* v. *Vautier* says that John can demand payment on reaching twenty-one because on the wording just quoted his interest is vested and no one else has any interest in the subject matter of the gift. His ownership is absolute. To the intelligent layman, this rule must be incomprehensible for it clearly defeats the testator's intention. However, it is a rule of law, not merely of construction.[51] The simplest way to avoid it is to make a gift over "to William if John dies under twenty-five."

The subject of conditional gifts can properly be mentioned here, for the subject of conditions is closely related to that of future interests. A condition may be precedent or subsequent. If the gift is subject to a condition precedent, the condition must be met before the gift vests; if the gift has added to it a condition subsequent, then the gift is vested, and a breach of the condition subsequent will operate to divest it. The law on conditions is complex because a condition may be void, on any of several grounds—because it is uncertain, or because it is against public policy, or because it is impossible of fulfillment, or because it is repugnant to the gift. It becomes important to determine whether the void condition is precedent or subsequent, because with minor exceptions a void condition precedent makes the gift void while a void condition subsequent makes the gift absolute. There is a presumption in favour of early vesting, even in gifts of personalty, and the consequence is to hold conditions to be subsequent if at all possible. Then if the beneficiary can persuade the Court that the condition is void he can, so to speak, have his cake and eat it too. Indeed the courts have been very ready to hold conditions subsequent to be void. In the well-known case of *Re Sifton,*[52] income was left to the testator's daughter with the proviso that if she ceased to reside in Canada her right to the income should come to an end. The Privy Council held that the phrase "reside in Canada" was uncertain so the daughter could reside wherever she wished. The test of certainty is an exacting one.

In the attempt to rule their beneficiaries from the grave, some testators impose conditions relating to the beneficiaries' religious faith, their conduct, and the kind of person the beneficiary may marry. Let us suppose that a testator gives income to his daughter for life and then provides that her benefits under the will shall cease and determine if she shall "contract a marriage with a person who is not of Jewish parentage and of the Jewish faith." One might think that this condition is against public policy, but of course the Courts are reluctant to create new heads of public policy. They can reach the same result by holding the condition to be uncertain, and this is what the House of Lords did,[53] even though the daughter had married a Welsh Methodist.

Here we may conveniently mention the rule against perpetuities which would not be necessary if there were no future estates. The power to create future estate has in the past tempted some testators to provide that an interest shall become vested only at a far distant date. One might give his land to his descendants living in 2300 A.D. Centuries ago the Courts held such a devise would be against public policy. The gift must vest within a reasonable time, and ultimately this was developed into the modern rule against perpetuities which says that an interest must vest if at all not later than the termination of lives in being plus twenty-one years; otherwise the gift is void. At the present time, testators do not try to violate the rule but often do so unwittingly. The policy of the rule is admittedly sound, but as Professor Barton Leach has shown in his famous examples of the unborn widow, the fertile octogenarian, the precocious toddler, and the magic gravel pit, the rule operates to defeat many gifts that in actual fact could not possibly violate the rule, or that in fact become vested very soon.[54] Some legislatures have, in recent years, passed acts to remove the harshness from the rule and, in Canada, Ontario has taken the lead with its recent statute.[55]

Testators sometimes direct that income from the estate shall be accumulated for a period of years. At common law this was permissible provided the accumulation did not extend beyond the perpetuity period. However, the English Parliament in 1803 passed the Accumulations Act which restricted the period during which income might be accumulated. There are four alternate periods but the important one is a period of twenty-one years from the testator's death. The accumulation is valid to the end of that time but income accruing thereafter must be "released." To whom does it go? The person entitled to the corpus argues that the corpus should be given immediately to him while the next of kin argue that they are entitled to the released income. The two leading cases are hard to reconcile. An important Alberta case goes in favour of the next of kin.[56]

I shall conclude this survey by a reference to testamentary capacity and then to undue influence, fraud, and the "suspicion" that is created when the person who draws the will receives benefits thereunder.

There are innumerable cases in which the testator's testamentary capacity has been attacked. The leading case is still *Banks* v. *Goodfellow*.[57] The testator must understand the nature of what he is doing; the extent of the property of which he is disposing; and the claims to which he ought to give effect. Most important, his mental disorder must not be such as to influence his dispositions. In a modern English case, *Re Park*,[58] a wealthy but senile man married the cashier in his club. Later the same day his solicitor had him execute a will which left the bride a small legacy. He died a few days later. The wife successfully attacked his will on the ground that he did not have testamentary capacity. Then the executor of a will made before the marriage propounded it; the executor replied that the marriage was void because the husband did not have the necessary mental capacity. The marriage was held valid. Birkett, L.J., held that a man might well be able to understand the contract of marriage in its simplicity, but might still be mentally incapable of making a complicated will.

Undue influence on the testator is another ground for holding void a will or part of a will. The burden is on him who attacks the will and he must show that the document does not represent that which the testator truly wanted. It is hard to prove, though if the testator is feeble in mind the court is often ready to find that a domineering person who urged the testator to make a new will has, in fact, exercised undue influence.[59]

Fraud on the testator is likewise a ground for setting aside a will, though this ground of attack is infrequent.[60]

There is a special rule dealing with the case of a person who draws a will and who receives substantial benefits thereunder. The rule says that suspicion attaches to the will and the propounder must remove the suspicion. Suspicion of what? One might think that these facts raise a presumption of undue influence, and some cases say so; but the leading cases say that the suspicion is merely that the document is not truly the will of the testator, and can be removed by evidence that the testator knew what he was doing.[61]

Testators Family Maintenance Acts

During the 19th century a man could will his property as he wished, and was under no obligation to leave anything to his wife or children, let alone to anyone else. The New Zealand legislation of 1900 is the model for the various provincial acts which now restrict freedom of testation.[62] Using the Uniform Act as an example, the main section is in two parts. The first part sets out the circumstances in which dependants may apply for relief under the Act and the second part sets out the power of a court to give relief. Application may be made when the will does not make "adequate provision for the proper maintenance and support of the dependants or any of them." A judge may order that "such provision as he deems adequate shall be made out of the estate of the testator for the proper maintenance and support of the dependants or any of them." In other words, the Court must find an inadequacy in order to have jurisdiction and then it has power to remedy it. Some of the acts set out factors that the Court could consider and a long list of cases puts a gloss on the statute.[63] In British Columbia the first limb of the main section is the same as in the Uniform Act but the second limb enables the Court to order "that such provision as the Court thinks adequate, just and equitable in the circumstances shall be made out of the estate of the testator." In *Re Jones,* the Court of Appeal considered that the wording of the British Columbia statute gave the Court wider latitude than does the wording in the other statutes. The test is whether the widow has received a share that is adequate, just and equitable, and in the case of a large estate, this will be more than an amount sufficient for her needs. The Supreme Court upheld this judgment, but I cannot find that the Supreme Court would have given the widow less had the Act been worded as it is in the other provinces.[64] The Ontario Act, in contrast to British Columbia's, emphasizes maintenance in both limbs of the section and the Supreme Court has hinted that this points to a narrow basis for an award.[65]

The cases sometimes emphasize the moral duty of the just but not loving husband and father; at other times they emphasize the applicant's need. The latter emphasis may permit the court to look at the state of affairs of the dependant at the time of application and even to look into his future. A few of the acts define dependants to mean the wife and the children who are below a given age (nineteen in Alberta) or who are mentally or physically disabled. Most of the acts, however, define dependant to include a child of any age. Thus we have the spectacle of married sons and daughters, long emancipated from their parents, applying for relief, often successfully.[66]

In Alberta, it was formerly customary for a married man to leave everything to his wife even though his estate is substantial. The fact is that unless the estate is very small, the Public Trustee acting on behalf of the children under nineteen years of age will make an application for relief and the Courts have been willing to grant it. Thus a solicitor is under the obligation to caution his client that the Court will, in all probability, vary his will if he leaves nothing to his young children.[67]

Alberta is also the source of an interesting case in which a wealthy widower remarried. He gave assets to the value of over one million dollars to the children of his first marriage. Before he died, his wife brought action to have these gifts set aside. The husband died and the wife continued the action against his executor. Riley J. held that the statute gave him no jurisdiction to set aside the gifts.[68] This is clearly correct, but it does raise the question whether the Act should be amended to protect the wife where the husband has denuded himself of his assets. Even if the policy were sound, the draftsman would have to be very sagacious indeed to avoid evils worse than that which he is trying to remedy.

Several provinces now have widened the statute to make it apply in case of intestacy. Thus in Alberta and Saskatchewan, the wife may apply for more than her statutory share at the expense of the children and the children, if dependants, may apply as against their mother. To date there is no reported case to indicate how the courts will exercise this new power.

The last point to note is that several cases say a person may not validly waive or surrender his right to apply under the Act.[69]

Notes

1 Civil Code, art. 596.

2 Not testamentary—*Corlet* v. *Isle of Man Bank* [1937] 3 D.L.R. 163 (Alta. C.A.); testamentary—*Re Shirley* (1965) 49 D.L.R. (2d) 474 (Sask.).

3 *Main* v. *Main* [1939] 1 D.L.R. 723 (Man.); *Carson* v. *Wilson* (1960) 26 D.L.R. (2d) 307 (Ont. C.A.).

4 *Young* v. *Sealey* [1949] 1 All E.R. 92; Bruce, Note, (1955) 33 Can. Bar Rev. 345.

5 [1957] S.C.R. 599.

6 Insurance Act. (Alberta), ss238, 243 (1960 c49, s4, re-enacting the life insurance provisions; these are uniform).

7 *Western Smallware* v. *Bell* (1966) 55

D.L.R. (2d) 193. (Man. C.A.); compare *Re Parke* (1965) 49 D.L.R. (2d) 568 (B.C.).

8 *MacInnes* v. *MacInnes* [1935] S.C.R. 200.

9 Kennedy, The Legal Effects of Adoption (1955) 33 Can. Bar Rev. 751.

10 E.g., Alberta's Child Welfare Act, 1966 c13, s58(3).

11 [1962] S.C.R. 241; see also *Re Clement* [1962] S.C.R. 235.

12 (1860) 8 H.L.C. 183; 11 E.R. 397.

13 Insurance Act (Alberta), s263 (1960 c49, s4) read with s241, says the insurance is payable to the surviving beneficiary, if any, or to the personal representative of the insured. Compare *Re Currie,* (1964) 41 D.L.R. (2d) 666.

14 Macdonald, Observations on the Land Law in the Common Law Provinces, in McWhinney, Canadian Jurisprudence 197, pp. 209–220 (1958).

15 Ibid.; also Bowker, Succession to Property in the Common Law Provinces, in McWhinney, Canadian Jurisprudence 241, pp. 251–254; also Bowker, Reform of the Law of Dower in Alberta, Alta. Law Rev. 6, 501 (Spring, 1961).

16 The rule was the same under the Statute of Distribution; Williams on Executors, 10th ed., vol. 2, p. 1239 (1905).

17 See *Re Stone* [1924] S.C.R. 682.

18 *Re Carlson* (1957) 11 D.L.R. (2d) 485 (Sask. C.A.).

19 In *Re Ogal* [1940] 2 D.L.R. 345, the validity of the amendment was upheld.

20 *Re Wilson* (1924) 26 O.W.N. 270. In that case the widow unsuccessfully claimed one third.

21 *Re Rist* [1939] 2 D.L.R. 644 (Alta. C.A.); and see generally, Laskin, The Protection of Interests by Statute and the problem of "Contracting Out," (1938) 16 Can. Bar Rev. 669.

22 E.g., *Whitelaw* v. *Wilson* [1934] O.R. 415.

23 *Nordstrom* v. *Baumann* [1962] S.C.R. 147.

24 *Maddison* v. *Alderson* (1883) 8 App. Cas. 467.

25 *Pratt* v. *Johnson* [1959] S.C.R. 102.

26 Gordon, Delegation of Will-Making Power (1953) 69 L.Q.R. 334.

27 *Re Moir* [1942] 1 D.L.R. 337 (Alta. C.A.).

28 The enacting Section (s7) merely requires "handwriting and signature," but the curative provision specifically says that a signature to a holograph will does not give effect to a disposition underneath the signature (sec. 83); see *Re Moir,* note 27, supra.

29 *Dansereau* v. *Berget* [1951] S.C.R. 822. The Privy Council held that the Supreme Court had no jurisdiction to hear the appeal; [1953] 2 All E.R. 1058.

30 *Re Gray* [1958] S.C.R. 392.

31 *Re Harris,* unreported; Note (1948) 26 Can. Bar Rev. 1242.

32 *Re Cottrell* [1951] 4 D.L.R. 600.

33 In *Re McLeod* (1964) 47 D.L.R. (2d) 370 (Alta.) a marginal writing was held to be a codicil rather than an alteration.

34 *Re Wingham* [1949] Pr. 187.

35 Warren, Dependent Relative Revocation, (1920) 33 Harv. L. Rev. 337.

36 *Macdonnell* v. *Purcell* (1894) 23 S.C.R. 101.

37 *Toronto General Trusts* v. *Minister* [1958] S.C.R. 499.

38 *Re Meunier* [1963] 1 O.R. 213.

39 *Re Millar* [1937] O.R. 382, aff'd. [1938] S.C.R. 1.

40 *Church* v. *Hill* [1923] S.C.R. 642.

41 *Re Carrington* [1932] 1 Ch. 1.

42 *Chichester Diocesan Fund* v. *Simpson* [1944] A.C. 341; also *Ministry of Health* v. *Simpson* [1951] A.C. 251; Note, Dennis Lloyd (1948) 26 Can. Bar Rev. 1356.

43 [1954] S.C.R. 645; see Notes (1955) 33 Can. Bar Rev. 334, 340, 630.

44 [1955] 3 D.L.R. 497 (P.C.).

45 *Guardhouse* v. *Blackburn* (1866) 1 P. & D. 109.

46 *Re Lupton* (1964) 44 D.L.R. (2d) 535 (N.S.). For the sequel, see *Re Lupton* (1964) 46 D.L.R. (2d) 421 (N.S.).

47 *Re Connolly* (1965) 47 D.L.R. (2d) 465 (N.S.).

48 [1943] A.C. 399.

49 [1965] S.C.R. 817.

50 *Browne* v. *Moody* [1936] A.C. 635.

51 Examples of gifts contingent on reaching a given age; *Re Waines* [1947] 2 D.L.R. 746 (Alta. C.A.); *Fast* v. *Van Vliet* (1965) 49 D.L.R. (2d) 616 (Man. C.A.). Examples of vested gifts with ineffective attempt to postpone payment; *Re Price* (1966) 55 W.W.R. 26 (Sask.); *Re Beres-*

ford 56 W.W.R. 248 (B.C.). Example of vested gift with gift over on death under stated age; *Re Barton* [1941] S.C.R. 426. In that case the beneficiary did not demand payment on attaining 21, but it is clear that the gift over prevented him from doing so. He was held entitled to the income.

52 [1938] A.C. 656.

53 *Clayton* v. *Ramsden* [1943] A.C. 320.

54 Morris and Leach; The Rule Against Perpetuities, 2 ed. (1962).

55 The Perpetuities Act, 1966, c113.

56 *Re Burns Estate* (1960) 25 D.L.R. (2d) 427 (Alta. C.A.). The reasoning is that a named individual had theoretical interest in the income so that those entitled to the corpus cannot say they were the only ones interested. However, the charities to whom one third of the corpus was to go were held entitled to one third of the income because the testator had shown a general charitable intent.

57 (1870) L.R. 5 Q.B. 549.

58 [1953] 2 All E.R. 1411 (C.A.).

59 *Hayward* v. *Thompson* (1960) 25 D.L.R. (2d) 545 (S.C.C.); compare *MacGregor* v. *Ryan* (1966) 53 D.L.R. (2d) 126 (S.C.C.).

60 In *Crompton* v. *Williams* [1938] O.R. 237 a finding of fraud was supplemental to a finding of undue influence.

61 *Harmes* v. *Hinkson* [1946] 3 D.L.R. 497 (P.C.); *Wintle* v. *Nye* [1959] 1 All E.R. 55 (H.L.). In each of three recent cases the propounder failed to remove the suspicion; *Re Moore* (1965) 52 W.W.R. 449 (B.C.); *Re Timlick* (1965) 53 W.W.R. 87 (B.C.); *Re Freeman* (1966) 55 D.L.R. (2d) 736 (N.B.C.A.).

62 Bale, Limitation on Testamentary Disposition in Canada (1964) 42 Can. Bar Rev. 367.

63 E.g., *Re Lawther* [1947] 2 D.L.R. 510 (Man.); *Re Lafleur* [1948] 2 D.L.R. 682 (Man.); *Re Willan* (1951) 4 W.W.R. (N.S.) 114 (Alta.).

64 [1962] S.C.R. 273.

65 *Meyer* v. *Capital Trust Co.* [1948] S.C.R. 329.

66 *Walker* v. *McDermott* [1931] S.C.R. 94; *Re Fraser* (1965) 48 D.L.R. (2d) 334 (B.C.C.A.); *Re Woods* (1967) 59 D.L.R. (2d) 357 (S.C.C.); *Re Parkanski* (1966) 56 D.L.R. (2d) 475 (Sask.).

67 E.g., *Re Finlan* (1951) 3 W.W.R. (N.S.) 671.

68 *Dower* v. *Public Trustee* (1962) 35 D.L.R. (2d) 29.

69 E.g., *Re Rist,* note 21 *supra;* In *Re Chugg* (1966) 52 D.L.R. (2d) 458 (Alta. C.A.) the Court found it unnecessary to decide whether in any circumstances the wife may during the lifetime of her husband effectively renounce her rights under the Act.

1968

A Canadian Charter of Human Rights?

Unpublished

This paper, presented at the annual meeting of the Canadian Association of Law Teachers held in Calgary in June 1968, was written during the early stages of discussions on a possible Canadian Charter of Human Rights. Only a few writers had at that time focussed on objections to such a Charter. This was 8 years after passage of the Diefenbaker "Bill of Rights" in 1960.

Prior to passage of that Bill, Bowker had appeared before a Joint Committee of the House of Commons and Senate in Ottawa, at which he opposed entrenchment.

In this paper he enlarges further on these views, taking the position that human rights and freedoms can be preserved without giving power to judges to strike down legislation as an infringement of fundamental rights.

Outline of Points

The Charter prepared by the Government of Canada for the constitutional conference in February, 1968, proposes a constitutional or entrenched Bill of Rights to guarantee the fundamental freedoms of the individual from interference whether federal or provincial.

The Charter uses five broad categories:

1. Political freedoms (expression, conscience and religion, assembly and association);
2. Legal rights (security of life, liberty and property, due process of law and related safeguards especially to an accused);
3. Egalitarian rights (protection against discrimination);
4. Linguistic rights;
5. Economic rights.

Except for linguistic rights, these correspond generally to the four broad categories of Mr. Justice Laskin, and which Professor Tarnopolsky uses in The Canadian Bill of Rights.

I shall deal with these five headings in relation to federal power. Are these rights well protected now by statute or common law, either negatively or affirmatively? If not, would they be better protected by an entrenched Bill of Rights? My general position is that our law is healthy and that if it is not, change should come from Parliament and not from a judicial pronouncement that a statute, executive action or common law rule is unconstitutional and void.

The basic issue is this. To whom do we look for protection of our basic rights? My answer is Parliament, because we are a democracy. The courts do have a role: they can create benign common law rules and canons of construction of statutes. However, they should not have power to rule that an act of Parliament is void simply because in the Court's opinion the act infringes a basic right.

We can agree with John Locke that the people delegate certain powers to Parliament, the executive and the Courts, and that they do not delegate the power to deprive themselves of basic rights. It does not follow, however, that a Court should have power to say to the democratically elected representatives: "Your law is void because in our opinion it infringes the rights of the people." Most legislation is a resolution or balancing of conflicting claims and the ultimate decision as to where the balance should lie is better left to the judgment of Parliament. Courts can construe legislation benignly or badly; if the legislature accedes to the construction of the Courts, well and good, but the legislature should have the final say.

In the United States, it is popular to acclaim the "activist" judge as a great protector of human rights and to designate the "passivist" as an Austinian. The fact is that the judges of forty and fifty years ago who struck down social and regulatory legislation in the name of due process were just as activist as Mr. Justice Douglas, and that a judge who declines the power to strike down legislation may be just as concerned in human rights as is Mr. Justice Douglas.

1. Political Freedoms

The grouping of freedom of speech and freedom of religion together under the head "political freedoms" is, in a sense, artificial for the two have completely different origins in Anglo-American legal history. However, they are grouped together in the United States' Bill of Rights and I see no practical harm in putting them under one rubric.

The main federal enactments restricting expression are the provisions in the Criminal Code creating the offences of seditious libel, publishing false news, publishing obscene matter, and crime comics. The significant fact is that, both in relation to obscenity and sedition, the Supreme Court's leading judgments have given great latitude to freedom of expression. The judgment on *Lady Chatterley's Lover* in 1962 rejects the Hicklin test of a tendency to corrupt and a 1964 judgment on "girlie" magazines adopts Mr. Justice Freedman's test that obscenity should be judged objectively and by present-day community standards, with a leaning towards tolerance.

The crime comic section has not been the subject of any authoritative decision. One can imagine, however, that if we had a Bill of Rights and this section were judged by American standards it might be held bad because it is not confined to publication of crime comics to young people and might not meet the constitutional requirement of precise standards; it might be void for vagueness. One may not be convinced of the wisdom of this law but it does not follow that the Courts should strike it down.

As for sedition, the law used to be that the crime is complete if there is a vigorous attack on political institutions. However, the great case of *Boucher* v. *The King* holds that the Jehovah's Witnesses' pamphlet "Quebec's Burning Hate", though violent and intemperate, is not seditious because it does not incite to revolt. Mr. Justice Rand's judgment is based on the proposition that "freedom in thought and speech and disagreement in ideas and beliefs, on every conceivable subject, are of the essence of our life."

It will be remembered that in 1917, Mr. Justice Stuart of Alberta protested against the flood of charges of sedition during World War I and himself evolved a skeletal clear and present danger test for these cases, before Holmes and Brandeis JJ. did.

The proposed Hate Literature Bill in Clause 267 B makes if an offence to incite hatred against an identifiable group in a public place where the incitement is likely to lead to a breach of the peace. Truth is not a defence nor is public interest and benefit. If this bill becomes law, and Mr. Boucher were to distribute his pamphlet among a hostile audience, he would be guilty under the proposed section. For this reason one can question the wisdom of this section of the bill. It is true, of course, that the Supreme Court of the United States upheld a group libel enactment in *Beauharnais* v. *Illinois*. It was conceded however that fair comment and truth would be a defence to the charge. No such defence is possible under 267 B.

Publishing false news has produced few cases, though an old decision of Chief Justice Harvey in Alberta is admittedly severe for it finds guilty persons who merely said that Americans are not welcome in Canada. The crime of watching and besetting could conflict with picketing. There are American cases saying the picketing is protected by freedom of speech and for a time it appeared that almost anything done in the name of picketing was protected. The Supreme Court has, however, put a limit on what pickets may do in the name of free speech.

Another piece of Dominion legislation which could be criticized on the ground that it infringed freedom of the press is the amendment of 1956 to the Excise Tax Act, imposing a special tax on certain non-Canadian magazines. The Supreme Court upheld the Act, which had meantime been repealed. Would the Act be invalid if we had a Bill of Rights? The power to tax can be used to suppress a hostile press, but the tax in question had a defensible reason, the protection of Canadian publications against unfair competition.

To show the difficulty in deciding the limits of freedom of speech or press, or indeed of any of the "political freedoms," one can take the subject of contempt of court. Contempt may be punished summarily as a criminal offence under the common law. Many forms of contempt have nothing to do with freedom of speech but those forms known as scandalizing the Court and comment on pending trials clearly do. Section 8 of our Criminal Code preserves the right of a Canadian court to punish summarily for contempt. On the other hand, this power has been stripped from American trial courts by a series of three decisions culminating in *Craig* v. *Harney*. Then when an effort was made to punish a radio station for contempt in broadcasting statements clearly stating that an arrested Negro was guilty of a heinous crime, the court refused *certiorari* over Mr. Justice Frankfurter's objection in *Baltimore Radio Show* v. *Maryland*. He collects the British cases in which summary punishment was imposed for comment on pending trials. He could have added a number of Canadian cases. Trial by newspaper is not tolerated here. Chief Justice McRuer's imposition of fines totalling $14,000 and a sentence of ten days in jail on American publications who published lurid articles on a pending murder trial in 1954 is a good example of the vigour of our law of contempt.

If we were to have a Bill of rights, the courts would not necessarily follow the American decisions—but let us suppose they did. My submission is that the newspaper's claim to comment on pending trials is a travesty of freedom of press when one remembers that the right to a fair trial is also constitutionally protected. Freedom of the press traditionally means freedom from censorship and in modern times it certainly includes the right to criticize. In the United States the commercial press claims as well (though not always successfully) immunity from general statutes, and also claims the right to intrude on the privacy of others, and also to interfere with and disrupt judicial proceedings. The Warren Commission shows the havoc that newspapers and television can wreak in a criminal trial that has attracted great publicity. The sheriff refused to transfer Mr. Oswald to the county jail in secrecy because he felt obliged "to play ball with the press." Another example can be seen from the trial of Dr. Shephard. It will be remembered that the accused was charged with murdering his wife and that many prejudicial statements were made during the trial. The trial judge's summary power to commit for contempt had been stripped by Supreme Court judgments. Shephard was convicted and over ten years afterwards he complained in a federal court that he had been denied due process of law. The Supreme Court agreed and ordered a new trial. The court admonished the trial judge that he should have taken steps to curtail the undue publicity and yet that very court had deprived him of the most effective power, namely that of summary committal for contempt.

Turning now to freedom of worship or religion, I know of no federal statute that infringes this freedom. Indeed, section 161 makes it an offence to interrupt divine service and this provision was used by the Supreme Court in finding policemen civilly liable when they broke up a meeting of Jehovah's Witnesses in a private home.

It will be noted that neither the Canadian Bill of Rights Act nor the Charter proposes the inclusion in our Constitution of a provision like the clause in the American First Amendment which says: "Congress shall make no law respecting an establishment of religion." This clause has been interpreted very widely. The court has borrowed Jefferson's "wall of separation between church and state" so that many programs for Bible reading in schools and the holding of prayers have been held unconstitutional, and a state may not financially aid denominational schools. It is clear that our whole system of separate schools as it exists in Alberta and Saskatchewan and indeed in Ontario and Quebec would fall if we had such a test. Likewise the provision in the Indian Act that the government may enter into agreements for the education of Indian children with a religious or charitable organization. Historically, much of the schooling, at least in Western Canada, has been given by one or other religious denomination. In many instances they have provided a service that no one else could have done and I am not critical of this. The fact is that our separate schools certainly would be a breach in the wall of separation of church and state within the American Supreme Court decisions. The Charter cautions that a Constitutional safeguard against discrimination in education would have to make allowance for separate schools; an admission that they themselves are in a sense discriminatory.

The Lord's Day Act has, of course, been attacked on the ground that it cannot stand with the freedom of religion clause in the Bill of Rights Act. The Supreme Court has rejected this argument. Mr. Justice Laskin criticized this judgment because our Lord's Day Act was originally upheld as being legislation religious in nature, and he agrees with Mr. Justice Cartwright's dissent. In the United States of course state laws of this kind have been upheld as being secular in nature. This shows the difficulty of determining when there is an infringement of freedom of religion. The Weekly Day of Rest Act 1935 was held bad as extending beyond Dominion competence but surely the legislature at some level should be able to require a day of rest without running afoul of freedom of worship.

As to freedom of assembly and association, the provision in the Code dealing with unlawful assembly (s. 64) makes it an offence needlessly and without reasonable cause to provoke other persons to disturb the peace tumultuously. The Charter expresses the opinion that this and the other provisions in the Code "appear to be consistent with freedom of assembly and association so long as they are clearly related to the preservation of public safety and order." The Supreme Court of the United States has had to struggle with the borderline between freedom of speech and assembly on the one hand and incitement to breach of the peace on the other. There is authority that the constitution does not protect "fighting words" but the *Terminiello* case does protect them. There is no simple answer, with or without a Bill of Rights.

It is relevant to note here a provision known as s. 98 of the Code which was passed in 1919 after the Winnipeg General Strike. It created the offence of being a member of a subversive organization. Tim Buck went to jail after conviction for being a member of the Communist Party. The section was repealed in 1936. In the United States, the Smith Act of 1940 created a similar offence and in the course of upholding this provision in the *Dennis* case, the Supreme Court watered down its clear and present danger test. The Act is still on the statute books though the later *Yates* case revives the clear and present danger test. Thus we tried a statute that created guilt by association and then repealed it by the democratic process. In the United States, on the other hand, the statute has withstood constitutional attack. Even if the Smith Act had been held bad, surely it is healthier to get rid of such a statute by repeal than by judicial veto.

Originally the right of assembly was related to the right to petition the government. The judgments of Mr. Justice Rand would create a national right to assemble and to move from province to province, just as this is a right of national citizenship in the United States. I am not clear as to the limits of right of association as distinct from assembly. Frequently both union members and non-union members assert this right in connection with labour legislation, but I doubt that the right of association renders invalid provisions for a union shop or an open shop.

In connection with employment in the federal public service, employees are forbidden from engaging in political activities. This might be said to interfere with freedom of speech and freedom of association though it will be noted that in the United States such legislation was upheld in the *Mitchell* case.

2. *Legal Rights*

The Charter mentions the problem that would arise if we were to adopt the concept of substantive due process which for so long was used in the United States to strike down minimum wage and maximum hour legislation, rate fixing and regulation of businesses not affected with a public interest. In my view, the concept of substantive due process is a contradiction in terms and due process in its original and proper sense imposes the requirement of fairness in procedure.

In Canada I would generalize by saying that our criminal procedure is basically fair and so meets the concept of "due process" or "law of the land" though the terms themselves are infrequently used. They are found in two sources: (1) the Criminal Code, and (2) the common law. When a person has been convicted, the conviction is to be reversed on appeal if there may have been a "miscarriage of justice." To generalize, it seems fair to say that this provision has been fairly applied in favour of convicted persons so that they will be acquitted or given a new trial if not accorded due process unless the denial of due process were not material to the conviction. The real significance of a constitutional due process clause would be this. It would strike down not only judicial doctrines that in the opinion of the court denied due process but would also render void sections in the Criminal Code. My submission is this: if a given statutory provision is unfair, then Parliament should be asked to change it.

It will be remembered that in the United States the basic criminal law is in the hands of the states whereas in Canada it is, fortunately in my opinion, a federal subject. There is no basis in Canada for the opinion of President Taft and the Wickersham Commission that "the conduct of the ordinary State criminal court cases is a national disgrace." It was only beginning in 1932 in the *Scottsboro* case that the Supreme Court began a detailed scrutiny of claims of convicted persons that they had been denied due process. The court has assumed the role of attempting to enforce due process in state trials and in doing so may have gone too far—at least so far as to attract criticism both in the states and in Congress.

I do not want to underestimate the importance of the role of courts over the centuries in safeguarding the rights of the accused. We have many benign doctrines that are judge-made. For example, our law as to confessions as found in *Ibrahim* v. *The King* is completely fair. On the other hand, I do not favour insertion in the Constitution of detailed rules such as the right to counsel before a suspect may be questioned nor the rejection of confessions merely because they are made after some delay. At one time, our Supreme Court did seem to say that a confession was automatically inadmissible if the usual caution were not given. This notion was rejected in the *Boudreau* case in 1949 and, in my opinion, wisely so. Certainly one would not want to see extensive grilling in this country, but the Miranda rule that the accused must be informed of his right to counsel before being asked questions seems to me dubious to say the least. I return to the proposition that our test in the *Ibrahim* case gives ample protection, at least in Canada, whatever may be the position elsewhere.

An example of the kind of provision in our Bill of Rights Act that seems to me to be pointless is the section which says that all trials shall be public. Now our Criminal Code has always provided for trials in camera in certain cases. It seems to me that if we want to do away with these exceptions, we should amend the Code. I realize, of course, that it has been held that the public trial provision in the Bill of Rights Act does not supersede the Code. I would have thought that it does.

Special mention should be made of the subject of self-incrimination. The Fifth Amendment says that no person shall be required in criminal proceedings to be a witness against himself. In this country, we have made great inroads on the common law self-incrimination rule. Section 5 of the Canadian Evidence Act requires a witness to answer questions but if he invokes the section, then his answer may not be used in evidence against him. He receives no immunity from prosecution. In the United States, the 1954 Compulsory Testimony Act does furnish such immunity. Our provision does not apply where a statute has required a person to give information as in *Walker* v. *The King* (1939). Do we want to put a self-incrimination clause in the Constitution and if so will it render void section 5? Will it apply to answers not given under oath? Space does not permit a survey of the American cases on the self-incrimination clause. It gives much wider protection than does section 5.

My point is that we are either satisfied or dissatisfied with section 5. If we are, why superimpose a self-incrimination clause? If not, surely it would be better to spell out what we want than to impose a limitation with unknown boundaries? The Espionage Commission questioned suspects under oath and then their answers were used against them in subsequent criminal proceedings because they did not invoke section 5. The result is, in my opinion, unfair. This could be remedied by a provision requiring the court to inform the witness of his privilege as the Civil Liberties section of the Canadian Bar Association recommended in 1946.

The right to counsel seems simple enough but it is clear that this does not oblige the Crown to provide counsel. It is only recently that the Supreme Court of the United States decided in *Gideon* v. *Wainwright* that this obligation rests on the State even in non-capital cases. There is a widespread feeling that legal aid schemes should be established in all criminal cases, but I am not at all clear as to whether such a provision should be put in the constitution or as to the types of cases to which it should extend. Another perplexing problem has to do with right to counsel prior to trial. As stated above, it is now clear in the United States that an accused must be told of his right to counsel before he may be questioned. *The Queen* v. *Steeves* from Nova Scotia says otherwise in spite of the right-to-counsel clause in the Bill of Rights Act, and *The Queen* v. *O'Connor* in the Supreme Court holds that there is no obligation on the police to tell an arrested man that he has been arrested or to advise him of his right to counsel before giving him a breath test. I find it hard to support *Steeves* in light of the Bill of Rights but would prefer to exclude the answers under the confession rule than to permit the accused automatically to go free. The Charter's proposal for this situation seems similar, though it appears to extend to real evidence as well as verbal and I am not satisfied that our common law rule on real evidence should be changed.

As to *O'Connor*, I find it difficult to agree with a proposal to exclude evidence of a blood test even where the accused has not been told of the cause of his arrest or his right to counsel. I would solve this by making the test compulsory, but as long as it is not, and since there seems to be no sanctions available against the police by way of civil or criminal action, then suppression of the evidence seems justified.

Another troubling problem is that of *Guay* v. *Lafleur* (1965). The Supreme Court held that in an inquiry under the Income Tax Act, the taxpayer was not entitled to counsel because the hearing does not determine rights and obligations of the taxpayer. It seems to me that this is a type of proceeding in which counsel should be permitted. However, it seems better to me to make this clear in the Income Tax Act itself or possibly in an Administrative Procedure Act rather than through a general provision giving right to counsel and contained in a Bill of Rights.

The last important related subject is that of unreasonable searches and seizures. Our law as to warrants in general protects the subject against wanton ransacking but on the other hand all relevant evidence is admissible.

The Charter suggests that "illegally obtained evidence" be inadmissible. This would be just as hard to apply as the American prohibition against "unreasonable searches and seizures." The doctrine of suppression of the fruits of unreasonable search and seizure is impossible to apply with any rationality for there is no litmus-paper test for an unreasonable search and seizure. In my opinion the suppression doctrine produces miscarriage of justice in many cases. Usually the question is whether the police had time to get a warrant or whether the search was incident to a legal arrest. The price society pays in allowing a guilty man to go free (which is the usual consequence of suppression) is out of proportion to the policeman's "unreasonable" search. The strongest case against the police is that of brutality and I suggest that actions in tort and criminal proceedings are an adequate sanction.

In all these matters the problem is one of enforcing the criminal law and at the same time observing due process. In the last few months both Lord Denning and Mr. Justice Black have pointed out the seriousness of crime and the need to support those trying to enforce the law.

3. Egalitarian rights

The purpose is, of course, to render invalid discriminatory laws. If there is to be an equal protection clause in the constitution, it should not be confined to equal protection with respect to race and religion. It should be general as is the American clause. This point is suggested in the Charter. My main objection to the equal protection clause, however, is not because of its phraseology but rather for the following reason. Even in the United States, it is recognized that differentiation may be made between different classes if, in the opinion of the court, there is a legitimate basis. Thus a statute has been upheld forbidding aliens from operating pool halls, forbidding women from working in bars and for permitting only local residents to be river pilots. The conspicuous example that comes to mind in Canada is the Indian Act. It clearly treats Indians in a different manner from others. One could argue that this is based on a theory of guardianship rather than discrimination, though I realize that this argument was rejected in *The Queen* v. *Drybones*. As long as we have the Bill of Rights, then it should not be construed away as was done in the *Gonzales* case which *Drybones* refused to follow. On the other hand, the question of bringing our Indian legislation up-to-date to meet present-day needs seems to me to be Parliament's responsibility and I am not satisfied that the best way of emancipating Indians is to give to the courts the power to strike down sections of the Indian Act one by one. What we need is not a prohibition against discriminatory laws, but affirmative non-discriminatory laws. Parliament already has several of these including the labour provisions, the section in the Public Service Act and regulations under the National Housing Act.

There is one large subject on which I am not clear as to the best way to try to ensure fairness and on which the Charter gives little guidance. It has to do with immigration and the right of aliens to enter and the right to a fair hearing before deportation. In the *Rebrin* case the Supreme Court held that the deportation order did not deprive Miss Rebrin of her liberty except by due process of law. I am not clear as to whether the person applying for status as a landed immigrant is entitled to know of all the evidence in the hands of the immigration authorities. The judgment of the Court of Appeal in the *Rebrin* case indicates not. Should such a right be accorded, even where the refusal is based on security grounds? Once an alien is in Canada, it seems to me proper to spell out such a person's rights, but the Immigration Act does this only in part. However, there are some rights that it seems to be obvious that an alien should not have. The Charter says there should be no discrimination in connection with voting or the holding of public office or entering a profession but surely an alien could not invoke these provisions.

In connection with those who are citizens, we have nothing in the Citizenship Act spelling out the rights of citizens. Mr. Justice Rand has suggested some rights of citizenship and it seems to me to be a worthwhile effort to try to define these rights which a province could not take away. Perhaps this could be done in a constitutional bill, but scarcely with precision. Another subject has to do with deprivation of citizenship. We already have certain grounds for "denaturalizing" citizens, though they are narrower than originally. The point is that it is hard to determine what substantive rights an alien should have or even a citizen with respect to protection against denaturalization. Certainly if the United States furnishes an example it is hard to determine what these rights are, both substantive and procedural.

4. *Linguistic Rights*

Since I have not examined the proposals of the Royal Commission on Bilingualism and Biculturalism with respect to language guarantees, it is difficult to comment. This is obviously a sensitive political problem and my only comment is that the according of special linguistic rights might, as the Charter says, give rise "to serious practical problems of implementation."

5. *Economic Rights*

The Charter considers this heading as including those provisions in the latter part of the Universal Declaration of Human Rights such as the right to work, protection against unemployment, the right to form and join trade unions and the like. I agree with the comment in the Charter that it is difficult to make these effective in a Bill of Rights. May I observe, however, that in the traditional acceptation of "economic rights," they refer to the right of the individual to be free from government interference. This was the basis of the many decisions in the United States on substantive due process in which legislation regulating economic activities was held *ultra vires*. It seems to be generally conceded today that this is a matter of policy and substantive due process has practically disappeared even in the United States. The American Constitution of course has a clause forbidding the impairment of the obligation of contracts but this has not stood in the way of legislation relieving debtors of their obligation during the Depressions. The Charter makes no mention of a contract clause nor does it specifically refer to compensation for expropriation as does the Fifth Amendment of the American Constitution.

Wartime

The Charter refers to this subject and suggests three alternatives:

(1) removing the War Measures Act from the Bill of Rights,
(2) specifying certain rights which may be infringed in wartime, and
(3) leaving the Bill of Rights applicable on the assumption that the court will make allowance in time of crisis.

This subject illustrates my general point that the proper approach is this: to examine what the federal government has done in World War I and, especially, World War II and then to ask the question—What should we have done differently consistent with national safety? This requires an examination of the innumerable regulations and particularly the Defence of Canada Regulations. One of the most troubling facts is that we have had so little concern since World War II as to what actually happened. There may be information as to the numbers interned and as to whether they were treated fairly, but I have not found it. The Defence of Canada Regulations contained internment provisions much like Britain's. My difficulty is in knowing what information the government had and how quickly and wisely it screened those who had been interned. Needless to say, they were not given anything like a trial and I am prepared to accept the proposition that this was inevitable if protection of sources of information was to be preserved. Organizations declared illegal included not only Nazi and Communist groups, but Jehovah's Witnesses. The most stringent regulations and those which should make us reflect to ask whether we would repeat them again are: (1) Orders in Council relating to the Japanese, not only with respect to their uprooting but the sale of their boats and land and then, of course, the deportation and naturalization orders which were continued under the National Emergency Transitional Powers Act and the validity of which was upheld by the Privy Council, and (2) the espionage or Gouzenko Inquiry. It will be recalled that suspects were secretly arrested, held incommunicado and required to answer questions first by the R.C.M.P. and then by a secret Royal Commission. On occasion they were refused counsel. Several of them were later convicted, largely on their evidence before the Royal Commission, while others were acquitted. I am not sure that the problems raised by this case can be solved by a Bill of Rights or even by provisions in the War Measures Act designed to prevent a repetition of the procedure which violated all principles of due process. In 1961, the House of Commons set up a Select Committee on the War Measures Act. One distinguished Member of the House of Commons was not aware that Canada had deported and deprived of citizenship Canadian citizens. The Committee met only twice and was dissolved on prorogation.

Constitutional Limitations on the Provinces

While my position is one of opposition to a Bill of Rights directed against federal power, there is a stronger case to be made for at least some limitations on provincial power. The reason is this. If we assume we have certain values generally accepted across the country, then all parts of Canada are concerned in preserving these values in each separate part or, putting it another way, we are all concerned in infringements on human rights in a particular province. For example, it seems to me that the persecution of Jehovah's Witnesses in parts of Canada a few years ago was a matter in which the whole of Canada had a stake. Mr. Justice Holmes once made a remark to the effect that while he thought little harm would befall if the court were deprived of the power to strike down federal legislation as contrary to the Bill of Rights, he thought otherwise with respect to state legislation. It will be recalled, of course, that the power of reservation and disallowance to an extent gave federal control over provincial legislation that the federal government deemed unwise. In a sense it served the purpose of a Bill of Rights. It is well known, of course, that this power has operated unevenly and few would say that it is today a satisfactory device for that purpose. The federal parliament through such statutes as the Criminal Code can, of course, give some protection throughout Canada and the courts, particularly the Supreme Court of Canada, can give further protection.

1. *Political Rights*

Dealing briefly with political rights, we now have a substantial body of opinion that a province may not infringe freedom of expression. The cases do not, however, define those limits. It was long ago held that a city could control public speeches in a park and it is commonplace to have in municipal statutes power to control parades and the like. In a number of cases wherein Jehovah's Witnesses were charged with infringement of by-laws against circulating literature, or against circulating it without a permit the courts have tended to construe the by-law as not applying to religious literature. On the other hand, a recent judgment from British Columbia, *Hlookoff* v. *Vancouver* holds that the suspension of a license to publish a newspaper does not constitute an infringement against freedom of the press.

In connection with freedom of religion, only four of nine judges in the *Saumur* case held that the province could not infringe freedom of religion. Then there are difficult issues as to whether various enactments such as the amendment to the Freedom of Worship Act in Quebec and the amendment to their municipal laws designed to regulate the dissemination of literature would be an infringement of freedom of religion assuming such freedom to exist as against the provinces. In the case involving the validity of Alberta's Communal Property Act, now *sub judice* in the Supreme Court of Canada, the attack on the statute has failed so far.

The Charter states that existing provincial limitations on freedom of assembly and association "appear to be consistent" with those freedoms "so long as they are clearly related to the preservation of public safety and order." In the case of a regulation that requires a permit to speak, hold a parade or distribute literature, then if we were to follow American doctrine as expressed in the Jehovah's Witnesses' cases then there would be grave doubt of validity as against freedom of speech, religion and assembly because the requirement of a permit is a classical example of "previous restraint" which can of course be applied solely against those with unpopular views.

2. *Legal Rights*

This covers so many substantive and procedural matters that I will not attempt to go into them in detail. Ontario's Royal Commission (The McRuer Commission) on Civil Rights in Report No. 1 consisting of three volumes deals with these matters in a most comprehensive way. Report No. 2 will discuss *inter alia* a Bill of Rights for Ontario but of course that report is not yet out. At the provincial level one hears many criticisms of the working of provincial boards, both with respect to substantive powers and procedures. Whether an Administrative Procedure Act would help to ensure fairness, I am not sure. In connection with the many enactments in the nature of criminal legislation (at least in the sense that penalties are imposed as a sanction) I am sure there are many provisions that could be improved. Many of the powers of search and seizure may be harsh or capable of abuse. Of course the courts have substantial power now in ensuring fairness and a proper exercise of jurisdiction through the power of *certiorari*. My principal point is the same one as I made in connection with federal powers. With the possible exception of freedom of speech, religion and assembly, it seems to me better that the provinces should be allowed to work out their own answers to these problems.

3. *Egalitarian Rights*

As the Charter points out, remarkable steps have been made in Fair Accommodation Laws and fair labour practices in the last twenty years. I understand that Prince Edward Island has now passed an enactment of this kind so that now all the provinces except Newfoundland have legislation in these fields. Ontario's Human Rights Code is of course notable in that it deals with housing and commercial premises and Nova Scotia's covers apartments. One special subject is that of admission to practice. I disagree with the *Martin* case in British Columbia and always have.

4. *Linguistic Rights*

I have no comment on this subject at the provincial level.

5. *Economic Rights*

Using this term in its older sense rather than in the sense employed in the Charter, I would not want to see the development of a doctrine such as that which prevailed in the past in the United States whereby the courts could strike down provincial legislation as a denial of substantive due process. The B.N.A. Act itself, as it now stands, has sometimes been available for that purpose. The person who did not want to be regulated could object that provincial regulation was an infringement of federal powers and that federal regulation was an infringement of provincial. Inroads have now been made into this no man's land and, in my opinion, this was a fortunate trend.

Conclusion

I know that judicial review is often supported as democratic; it is protection against the whims of a passing majority or an appeal from the people drunk to the people sober. In my opinion a democracy should rely on its elected representatives. The courts can certainly play a role through common law rules and through benign construction of statutes. However, when it comes to power to strike down legislation as in infringement of fundamental rights, I share the law of Morris Cohen who said: "It is curious to note that it is those Americans who are at heart distrustful of democracy who speak of the courts as standing between us and dictatorship and yet their arguments are precisely those which the adherents of Hitler and Mussolini use against the frailty of democratically representative or elective government." Max Lerner put it more briefly: "Scratch a fervent believer in judicial supremacy and like as not you will find someone with a bitterness about democracy."

Or in the words of an English writer, Professor Mabbott: "It is not exaggeration to say that the rights of man and the liberty of the individual have stood solidly against every measure of reform and every effort to promote the public welfare. These doctrines were the principal foes of education, vaccination, public health, slum removal, access to mountains, free libraries, fair taxation, factory reform."

The spirit behind the Bill of Rights is essentially the same as that which impelled Chief Justice Marshall to withdraw the power of a state to tax a federal bank. The power might be abused and therefore must be denied completely. We did much better in *Bank of Toronto* v. *Lambe* and the *Alberta*

Bank Taxation case; and today the United States has moved away from Chief Justice Marshall's doctrine. (Another example of fear of democracy is the American Amendment to prevent a President from being elected for more than two terms shortly after the country elected F.D. Roosevelt four times.)

Judge Learned Hand once said: "... a society so riven that the spirit of moderation is gone, no court can save; that in a society which evades its responsibility by thrusting upon the courts the nurture of that spirit, that spirit in the end will perish."

1968

Alberta's Institute of Law Research and Reform

Reprinted from
(1968) 11 Canadian Bar Journal
pp. 341–347

At the time of writing this article, Bowker had left his position of Dean of Law, which he had held for 20 years, in order to become the first Director of the newly-established Alberta Institute of Law Research and Reform.

Since the Institute was only recently founded, there was considerable interest in its structure and operation.

The Canadian Bar Journal *had been set up to provide popular reading for lawyers (in contrast to the more scholarly articles in the* Canadian Bar Review*). However it ceased to publish after a few years.*

At this time, the Board of Directors of the Institute wanted publicity aimed at the general reading public.

A more scholarly article would appear on this subject by Bowker a year later.

Prior to 1964, Alberta had no permanent body whose function was to make recommendations to the government for law reform. In that year, the Benchers set up a Law Reform Committee of eleven members representing the profession, the Attorney-General's Department, the Judiciary and the Faculty of Law. That Committee made one recommendation of substance, on the subject of limitation of actions in tort. The 1966 amendment to the Limitations Act is the result. The Committee also recommended the Uniform Survival of Actions Act, but without the provision abolishing claims for loss of expectation of life. The Legislative Counsel prepared a Bill but it has not been enacted. In addition, the Committee recommended a Perpetuities Act along the lines of Ontario's new Act but this recommendation was made without independent study. There were also recommendations (1) to study Ontario's Personal Property Security Act and (2) for compensation to victims of crimes and violence. The Committee began a study of the subject of occupiers' liability but the work was not completed.

By the end of 1966, the Benchers felt that law reform could not depend on a voluntary and unpaid Committee with no permanent staff. Early in 1967 discussions began between the Benchers, the Attorney-General's Department and the University of Alberta whereby a Law Reform Commission or Institute be established within the University. From the beginning, everyone believed that the Faculty of Law should have an important part in the proposed body and the members of that Faculty enthusiastically supported it.

In November, 1967, a formal agreement was executed between Her Majesty, the University and the Law Society. It provides for the establishment of an Institute of Law Research and Reform with the following objects:

"(a) To conduct and direct research into law and the administration of justice; and
(b) To consider matters of law reform with a view to proposing to appropriate authority means whereby the law may be made more useful and effective; and
(c) To promote law research and reform; and
(d) To these ends, to work in co-operation with the Faculty of Law of the University and with others."

The affairs of the Institute are governed by a Board of nine members. Representing the Crown are J.E. Hart, Q.C. and S. Friedman, Q.C.; representing the Law Society are H.G. Field, Q.C. (who is Chairman of the Board), W. Hurlburt, Q.C. and Mr. J.S. Palmer of Calgary (who is Vice-Chairman); representing the University are Acting Dean A.R. Thompson and Professor D.T. Anderson of the Faculty of Law and Dr. M. Wyman, Vice-President of the University. The ninth member is the Director. His appointment is made jointly by the Board of the Institute and by the Board of Governors of the University and his function is to be responsible to the former Board for the carrying out of the objects of the Institute. His appointment is an academic one within the University as a member of the Faculty of Law. Although the Agreement does not so specify, it is understood that he will remain in close contact with the Faculty of Law and will teach a course or seminar.

As to finances, the government agreed to provide $25,000 a year for five years and the University $50,000 for five years. At present the full-time staff consists of the Director and his secretary. An assistant to the Director has been appointed as of September 1st. He is an English law teacher, Mr. G.R. Bretten, who has high qualifications in teaching and research. The appointment is a joint one to the Faculty of Law and to the Institute and Mr. Bretten will devote two-thirds of his time to the Institute and one-third to teaching in the Faculty.

From the beginning, it was contemplated that the Institute would engage professional help on an *ad hoc* basis and four persons have already been so engaged on specific reform projects.

As to the physical situs of the Institute, it is in the Rutherford Library on the Edmonton campus, in unoccupied offices of the Faculty of Law. However, it will soon move to the Administration Building. When the Law Building is complete (in 1970 or 1971) the Institute will move into it in quarters specifically planned for that purpose. It is vital that the Institute be physically close to the Faculty. The former depends greatly on the Faculty's book collection which has been much improved in recent years. It is now over 40,000 books and the annual budget is some $60,000. Thus the Institute will have available a good research library. In addition, it will have a small library of its own consisting of statutes, digests and material from other law revision bodies.

The Institute came into being on January 1, 1968 and its Board has met monthly since then. In the five meetings to date, the agenda has been long and the meetings have lasted an afternoon. Since March, the Board has had a representative from the Judiciary to act in an advisory capacity. The Chief Justice of Alberta selected The Honourable Mr. Justice Porter of the Appellate Division. His participation in the meetings and the work of the Board has been vigorous, stimulating and helpful.

It will be appropriate to describe what the Board has done to date under (1) law research and (2) law reform. The first of these may not seem to be of direct interest to the profession but it is in reality of the first importance. It will be recalled that in 1956 a Committee of the Canadian Bar Association under the Chairmanship of Professor Frank Scott reported on the state of legal research in Canada and found it in a sorry state. Medical and physical research has always attracted funds while legal research has always been poverty-stricken. Another reason for the lack of legal research in Canada is that law teachers have had, until recently, heavy teaching and administrative loads so that substantial research was hard to carry out.

It is the purpose of the Institute to encourage research by members of the Faculty of Law. The main medium for this is in the form of grants to full-time teachers on the Faculty. For 1968 the budget allows $15,000 for this purpose. This sum is not to be used to augment salary but rather for the engaging of research assistants, travel and clerical expenses. Three grants have been made to date and it might be of interest to describe them.

(1) Acting Dean Thompson has received a grant to study Administrative Practices Governing Disposition of Publicly Owned Petroleum and Natural Gas.
(2) Professor Frank Jones has received a grant to study Tax Appeal Procedure in Canada.
(3) Professor Burke Barker has received a grant to study the Administration of Criminal Justice in Western Canada.

The total of these three grants is over $7,200. It should be emphasized that the Institute wants to encourage this type of research whether it will lead directly to law reform or not. Faculty members must be encouraged to pursue studies that interest them and that are relevant to their teaching. It is possible for the Board to make a grant to a person not on the Faculty but in view of the amount of funds available it is clear that most grants will be to full-time teachers in the Faculty of Law here.

In addition to these grants, the Institute wants generally to encourage interest and participation in research. The graduate programme in the Faculty of Law is still a modest one but graduate students will be encouraged to engage in research and undergraduate law students will be employed from time to time and indeed already have been. The Institute also hopes to attract distinguished scholars to come from time to time under the auspices of the Institute and the Faculty to give lectures and assist in research. We are presently negotiating with a distinguished professor of Planning Law to come during the 1969–70 session. One by-product of increased research will be an increase in published writings.

Turning now to the law reform aspect, the purpose is to select topics that are relevant in Alberta. Federal subjects are not excluded but do not have priority. The first two topics selected by the Board are (1) Compensation for Victims of Crimes; (2) The general Law of Limitation of Actions. The first of these subjects is of great general interest and schemes are now in effect in England, Saskatchewan, New York, California and New Zealand. The Board has engaged an able young graduate to collect and report on all the schemes and literature on the subject and has engaged one of the graduating class to consult with public officials who can throw light on the nature and extent of the problem in this province. This work is now well under way.

As for Limitation of Actions, one might think that the recent amendments dealing with tort would render this unnecessary. However, there are a few gaps remaining in that subject and in addition there are various problems that have nothing to do with tort such as prescriptive title to land and actions on mortgages and agreements for sale and limitations respecting trustees. The Director has prepared for the Board a report on tort and contract while a capable Calgary practitioner is preparing a report on the other topics. In the present state of the law of limitations, one must read a great many cases after examining the statute or statutes and even then there are uncertainties and injustices. The Institute hopes to produce, for recommendation to the government, a code on the subject that will be clear, comprehensive and fair.

The third subject undertaken has to do with the subject of Wills and Trusts. The Board is of opinion that many judge-made rules and canons of construction should be either codified or abolished and has been fortunate in obtaining the services of S.W. Field, Q.C., now retired, to examine this subject.

The last two subjects that have now been undertaken were decided on at the May meeting. They are: (1) Expropriation and (2) Occupiers' Liability.

As to the first of these, the Expropriation Procedures Act has tidied up one aspect of our law but we will examine it and also the many other acts giving power to expropriate and also the difficult subject of basis of compensation. Recent studies have been made of this subject in Ontario, British Columbia and elsewhere and we received suggestions that this is a worthy object of study. The Board agreed. In connection with occupiers' liability, everyone is familiar with the English act. The now defunct committee had started to work on this subject and, of course, the article by two of our own graduates, Mr. David McDonald and Mr. Leonard Leigh, published several years back, provides an invaluable starting point.

It might be of interest to mention other subjects which the Board already has on its list for possible study. They are: Administrative Procedure, Consumer Protection, Contributory Negligence and Tortfeasors, Deeds, Administration of Estates, Evidence, Family Law, Landlord and Tenant, Age of Majority, Mechanics Liens, Misrepresentation, Perpetuities, Personal Property Security and Right to Privacy.

Many of these topics have been the subject of study and legislation elsewhere and, of course, we can get the benefit of this work.

In its approach to any topic, the first task is to ascertain the existing law of this province and to make a comparative study of the law of other jurisdictions. At this stage outside help is frequently obtained. We have not yet reached the stage of preparation of a draft report for consideration by the Board but probably the Director will have a role in preparing it. When the Board has settled on its report, it will be forwarded to the Attorney-General. Prior to making its report, the Board will of course obtain the opinion of interested persons. Whether we will hold public hearings or invite briefs or follow some other course has not yet been settled for we have not yet reached that stage in any of our projects.

The last point I wish to discuss here has to do with the general approach, or to use a more pretentious word, philosophy of law reform. Any proposal for law reform involves a value judgment. A decision must be made first as to whether the law should be changed, and then a harder decision must be made as to what the change shall be.

One important problem is that of timing. Some projects that would have seemed out of the question five years ago, such as a scheme for compensation for victims of automobile accidents, may now be timely. The same applies to anti-discrimination legislation. Until recently, the general attitude in this province seemed to be one of either indifference or hostility and yet we now have on the statute books an important, though still modest, Human Rights Act.

Another point is that we must make use of reform elsewhere. We owe much to the various committees of the Lord Chancellor and to the English Law Commission which recently took the place of the earlier committees. It would be a waste of effort not to make use of their research and recommendations. The same applies to the Ontario Law Commission which has produced many important reports in its three years of existence. At the same time, we should not rubber-stamp anyone else's legislation. Conditions may be different in Alberta and the outside legislation might not furnish a good solution for our purposes.

One important question is whether we should attempt codification of a given subject. English tradition has generally been against codification but our law is now so complex that whether or not there is a statute on a given subject, it is necessary to read innumerable cases to determine what the law actually is. One should be able to find it on the face of a Statute. This is strong medicine for those of us who have spent our lives in devilling law, but nevertheless economy and certainty require it. In England the Law Commission is already talking about the possibility of codifying the law generally. This would certainly be too ambitious for the immediate future here, but on individual subjects we should attempt to put all the law in the Statute. For example, much is to be said for a code of evidence. In the law of Wills, the present Act contains some canons of construction, and our latest revision did away with the iniquitous doctrine of *Church* v. *Hill* and it preserves some charitable gifts that were formerly void.

At the same time, there are many other rules that might either be abolished or codified such as the rule in *Saunders* v. *Vautier* and the complicated rules about future interests. Then there is the homely example from limitations. Time generally runs from the time "the cause of action arose". One must read many cases to determine when this is and it will be worthwhile to attempt to specify the time in the limitations act itself. We tend to be comfortable with that with which we are familiar and a person who has spent years mastering the cases on the rule against perpetuities or the Land Titles Act might not like to see all this learning swept away. However, there can be no doubt that we should at least try to draft statutes so as to eliminate guessing as to the meaning of words and phrases in the statutes, and to render unnecessary the reading of innumerable cases.

One topic much discussed today is as to the implications of computers on legal research. I do not know the answer to this, but at the moment we still must use the old-fashioned methods. And I do not suppose that computers can provide the recommendation for us.

The Institute hopes that the profession will support its efforts both by making suggestions for reform and providing us with information on existing projects. In the limitations study, the Board, through the courtesy of the Law Society, invited members of the profession to send in briefs. Several useful ones have been received.

The Board realizes that the process is a slow one. However, we are confident that with the help of the judiciary, the profession and responsible citizens we will be able in time to make a contribution to the law of Alberta. It will be remembered too that the benefit is not confined to this province. We have already, in Alberta, made much use of original work elsewhere and will doubtless continue to do so. By the same token, we hope to initiate studies that will be of benefit to other jurisdictions. There has been, in the last decade, a great groundswell of interest in law reform. A bill for a Law Reform Commission was introduced in the British Columbia House at the last session and other provinces are studying a similar scheme. Every new agency that is created should mean economy of effort for the others and mutual benefit. It is not too much to hope that in the near future all of the common law provinces will contribute to systematic law reform and we hope that our Institute will play its part.

1969

Organized Law Reform in Alberta

Reprinted from
(1969) 19 University of Toronto Law Journal
pp. 376–390

In 1969, a year after the Alberta Institute of Law Research and Reform was established, Bowker was asked to write this article on law reform generally, with particular reference to the new developments in Alberta. This invitation came from Professor Ronald MacDonald, Dean of Law of the University of Toronto, and editor of that University's law journal. In a sense it was a sequel and enlargement of the previous article in this collection.

It analyzes the role of law reform bodies in furthering the orderly development of the law, and it reviews the history of such bodies in other jurisdictions, and various studies undertaken elsewhere.

It then deals with the Alberta Institute in respect to its structure, function, policies, and subjects of study.

Almost fifty years ago, Mr. Justice Cardozo expressed the opinion that neither court nor legislature by itself could effectively reform private law. 'The duty must be cast on some man or group of men to watch the law in action, observe the manner of its functioning and report the changes needed when function is deranged.' Accordingly he proposed a permanent law reform committee or commission called a ministry of justice. He added that bodies of this kind are commonplace in Europe, and that similar proposals in Britain go back to Bentham.[1]

In 1934, the New York Legislature passed an act to establish the Law Revision Commission, which has a notable record. The present Chairman says it was 'consciously created' in response to Mr. Justice Cardozo's proposal. He adds that there are now similar statutory commissions in at least four other states: Louisiana, North Carolina, California, and Oregon.[2]

In England, the first continuing body was the Lord Chancellor's Law Revision Committee, established in 1934. War brought it to an end and in 1952 the Lord Chancellor established a Law Reform Committee. The work of these committees is well known.[3] The only similar bodies in the Commonwealth, until recently, appear to be New Zealand's Committee, which dates back to 1937, and Victoria's Law Institute.[4] In Canada, sentiment in favour of such ventures grew after the war, stimulated by speeches, round tables, panels, colloquia, and symposia at lawyers' gatherings throughout the country.[5] The visits of Sir Leslie Scarman, Chairman of the English Law Commission, have provided further impetus.[6]

The last five years are notable for the creation by statute of 'ministries of justice' in Cardozo's sense. These mark a new stage in systematic law reform in the Commonwealth. They are much more ambitious than previous efforts, and obviously are intended to improve the process and increase the volume and tempo of reform. In all cases, the Commission is small in number, composed of senior personnel with some or all members serving full-time, and with good research assistance either within or without the commission, or both. The first of these was Ontario's Law Reform Commission in 1964[7] followed by the Law Commission (for England and Wales) and the Scottish Law Commission established by a single statute in 1965[8] and the New South Wales Law Reform Commission in 1967.[9] The reports and the very valuable working papers or research studies emanating from all these commissions are impressive indeed and of high relevance in Alberta and, doubtless, elsewhere.

In the meantime, New Zealand has a new Commission which appears to be non-statutory[10] while Western and South Australia have created committees and Northern Ireland has a Director of Law Reform.

Alberta's Institute of Law Research and Reform, which is the subject of this article, is not a creation of the Legislature or of the executive, like the committees. Rather, it is the indigenous outgrowth of an earlier attempt in Alberta. Around 1955, S.J. Helman Q.C. of Calgary, and one of the Benchers of the Law Society, put forward the idea of a law reform body with headquarters in the Faculty of Law at the University of Alberta which is in Edmonton and is the only law school in the province. Although the Faculty welcomed the general idea, it was not prepared to assume administrative responsibility. Indeed the Dean's view was that the carriage of law reform should be in the hands of the Attorney General or of the Law Society, though the law school should have a role.[11]

In 1964, the Benchers of the Law Society established a Law Reform Committee. The Chairman was one of the Benchers and the other thirteen members were drawn from the judiciary, the profession (including representatives of the Alberta Branch of the Canadian Bar Association and of the Edmonton and Calgary Bar Associations), and the Faculty of Law. The Attorney General provided secretarial services, but there was no full-time appointee and all members served without remuneration. One good practice of the Committee was to meet at least once a year with the Premier who was also Attorney General. Though not a lawyer, he showed an intelligent and sympathetic interest in the work of the Committee.

At its first meeting in September 1964, the Committee settled on an initial project, namely Limitation of Actions in Tort. The main reason for selecting this subject was that some work had already been done by one of the members of the Committee. A list of potential subjects was compiled, including chattel security, the law of consideration, landlord and tenant, occupier's liability, the Dower Act, and control of administrative tribunals.

On the Limitations study, recommendations were made to the Legislature in 1965, and in 1966 the Limitations Act was amended pursuant to the recommendations. Perhaps one can say that this was a major piece of work. At least the subject is of great practical importance, the law was complicated and unfair, and the amendments were designed to make it simpler and fairer.

The Committee examined the Uniform Survival of Actions Act. On a division of opinion, it rejected the provision abolishing claims for loss of expectation of life. It recommended the act apart from this provision, but the government has not brought it into the Legislature, probably for the reason that the only important provision in the act is the one which the Committee declined to recommend.

The Committee never carried through any of its other suggested projects. It did examine Ontario's Perpetuities Act and Personal Property Security Act and recommended both of them. Perhaps it would be more correct to say that the Committee passed them on to the government, because it made no independent study of them. To date, neither has been enacted. Some preliminary work was done on compensation for victims of crime.

By the end of 1966, the Benchers were of opinion that the Committee, as then constituted, could not properly proceed with the work of law reform. The Committee itself expressed the opinion 'that the time is now approaching for the Government to make provision for research into suitable matters of law reform, as it does in Ontario, and probably for a Director of Research, to assist the Committee in its work.' In December, the Committee put before the Premier a proposal to establish a formal permanent research organization. The Premier invited specific suggestions. In February 1967 the Benchers proposed to the government and the University of Alberta a centre for legal research and law reform under the joint management of the Law Society, the provincial government, and the University of Alberta.

Both the President of the University and the Board of Governors were enthusiastic. Lawyers and law teachers are fond of lamenting, often with good reason, the lack of support for legal research.[12] But there has been no complaint over the University's response in this case. It agreed to give the new venture its support, moral and financial, and has done so. The University asked the Faculty of Law to express its opinion on the proposal. At first there was some concern as to whether 'pure research' would be sacrificed to the role of law reform. Once this misgiving was dispelled, the Faculty eagerly supported the proposal in the hope that it would assist in recruiting, help the Faculty's new graduate programme, bring to the campus distinguished legal scholars from elsewhere, and, above all, that it would stimulate research in the Faculty.

During the summer and fall of 1967 the plans went forward and, on 15 November, an agreement was executed between Her Majesty in right of the province, the Board of Governors of the University, and the Law Society of Alberta. The government agreed to pay $25,000 a year for five years and the University $50,000 a year toward the costs of the Institute. In addition, the University agreed to provide space and to handle the Institute's funds.[13]

The Agreement states the objects of the Institute as follows;

> 2 The objects of the Institute are:
>
> (a) To conduct and direct research into law and the administration of justice; and
>
> (b) to consider matters of law reform with a view to proposing to appropriate authority means whereby the law may be made more useful and effective; and
>
> (c) To promote law research and reform; and
>
> (d) To these ends, to work in co-operation with the Faculty of Law of the University and with others.

Provision was made for a governing board of nine, three to be appointed by the Benchers, two by the Attorney General, three by the University (of whom two are to be from the Faculty of Law), and a Director. He is 'responsible to the Board for the carrying out of the objects of the Institute.' His position is full-time and is the equivalent of a Dean's appointment. He is selected by the Board of the Institute and the Board of Governors of the University. It was understood from the beginning that the Director would teach at least one course in the Faculty of Law in order to maintain contact between Institute and Faculty. The writer was appointed as Director early in December and, on 1 January 1968, the appointment took effect.

The full-time staff presently consists of the Director, a secretary, and an assistant to the Director, who has a University appointment with academic rank. The present Assistant has a joint appointment to the Faculty of Law and to the Institute and teaches one course in the Faculty. Apart from this, he devotes his time to the affairs of the Institute and acts as secretary to its Board. The Chairman of the Board, at present, is one of the Law Society's representatives. The Board has met at least once a month ever since the agreement was made. In addition, there is an informal executive committee consisting of the Chairman, the Director, and one of the Law Society's representatives. They meet at luncheon almost every week. The government's representatives on the Board are solicitors in the Attorney General's Department while those of the Law Society are practitioners and those from the University include two full-time members of the Faculty of Law and the University's Academic Vice-President. As the only non-lawyer on the Board, he has given invaluable help, both in moral support and in making available to the Institute all of the facilities and services of the University that the Institute needs.

All of the Board's members reside in Edmonton except for a Calgary practitioner. Apart from the Director, none receives any remuneration. This is a matter to which I shall return later. One might wonder why the judiciary is not represented. The writer's understanding is that there was a sentiment, at least on the part of some members of the judiciary, that it was not appropriate for them to take part in a law reform body. In any event, the Chief Justice was invited to name one of the Supreme Court justices to an advisory capacity and he named the Honourable Mr. Justice Porter of Calgary, who is in the Appellate Division. His Lordship has taken a great interest in the Institute's work and has made many helpful and stimulating suggestions.

A person familiar with the structure of the new statutory commissions might think that the Institute is under a handicap because it is not an official body with a formal relationship to government and legislature. On the other hand, our independence from the government (apart from financial support and the presence of two government solicitors on the Board) gives substantial freedom of action. Besides, the Institute enjoys good relations with the government and, in particular, with the Attorney General.

As to the physical *situs* of the Institute, it is on the campus but separate from the Faculty of Law. Fortunately, this latter feature is temporary. A new law building is to be begun later this year and the plans contain adequate space for the Institute. Ready access to the Faculty's library, which has a good collection of Commonwealth and American material, is important. In the meantime, the University has earmarked for the Institute a gift of $25,000 which the Institute is using to acquire its own small library of material relevant to legal research: digests, statutes, and the working papers and reports of law reform bodies in the Commonwealth and in the United States, as well as two or three basic sets of law reports.

In its short existence, the Institute has tried to acquaint itself with other law reform bodies and to learn something of their structure, policies and procedures. It has had contact with several, all of whom have been most helpful.[14] However, one cannot rely on others to make judgments for him. He must reach his own decisions. A brief account of our first experience might be of interest.

The Institute's First Effort

In its first month of existence, the Institute selected a topic for reform: Compensation for Victims of Crime. Why this? Because the government was interested, though it did not request us to undertake it. Moreover, the subject seemed to be manageable for an initial effort. The first step was to engage a young practitioner to prepare a working paper. He finished it in six months. It covered all existing schemes and also the considerable literature of recent years. However, this document did not tell us the facts in Alberta. Are there any victims of crimes of violence in Alberta? If so, what are the crimes and the circumstances? What type of injury results? What is the kind and extent of damage, physical and monetary? To find the answer, we engaged a recent graduate for the summer of 1968. She was given access to the files of the Attorney General, the Royal Canadian Mounted Police, and the police forces of Calgary, Edmonton, and Lethbridge.

At this point, there was encountered the problem that must face anyone trying to gather social facts—what to look for, what questions to ask, and how effectively to compile all information in useful form. On these items, one of the members of the Department of Mathematics at the University provided valuable help. The object of the fact-gathering was to determine the annual cost of compensating victims; this is important to the government. The Institute found the average annual compensable loss over the past five years to be about $12,000. It may seem strange that the final report gave the opinion that the annual cost would not be more than $75,000. Maybe this shows that the Institute did not have confidence in its own fact-finding but it seemed wise to be on the safe side.

Having received two good research papers, the Institute faced the next hurdle, that of making its recommendations. A decision was made not to circulate the working papers outside the Institute for comment. It would have taken time and would not have been likely to produce any suggestions that were not already before the Institute. Accordingly, the Board set up a committee of three to draft a tentative report. It was circulated to all members of the Board and discussed at two meetings. Searching criticism was offered and all differences of opinion were resolved. Typically, those items which took the longest time were of little practical importance. The Institute has no firm rule that a dissent or reservation is to be excluded but, obviously, unanimity is desirable. It was achieved here.

The next question was whether to draft a bill. Our recommendations followed the New Zealand and Saskatchewan schemes in many respects, but differed from them in others. The Institute had no draftsman either on its Board or available to it. For this reason, it seemed inadvisable to draft a bill, one Board member referring to the old saying that a two-humped camel is the product of a committee. We knew too that the government has competent draftsmen and concluded that the best course to follow was to present our recommendations in clear, complete, and orderly form. This we tried to do.

The next decision had to do with the disposition of the report. The Institute is not obliged, as is the Ontario Commission, to refrain from publishing or releasing its own reports. The decision was made to release the report to the government, the Law Society, and the University and then to issue a press release. Later, copies of the report and of the two working papers went to the Minister of Justice, to every Canadian attorney general, and to other law reform bodies. Subsequently, a number of additional requests have been received. One matter that may seem trivial was to decide how many copies to produce. We tried to be on the safe side, but our supply is almost exhausted already.

One might think that in the first instance, at least, the report should have been submitted to the government alone. The Institute would probably take this course if it felt that the government would be embarrassed by a public release, but in this case, there was no difficulty.

Having submitted its report, the Institute was, of course, *functus officio*. It is, of course, interested in the fate of its recommendations. In March 1969, a bill based on the report received first reading in the legislature. The Board considered what steps, if any, it should take in the event of discrepancies between the report and the bill. Relations with the government are good, and the government invited comments on the bill. The Board found several variations, mostly by way of minor omissions. It pointed out the differences and most of them have been removed. It seems clear that consultation of this kind is valuable but the Institute, having made its report, does not intend to 'lobby' for enactment of its recommendations.[15]

Some Basic Matters of Policy

At this stage of the Institute's existence, it may seem premature and presumptuous to set out one's emerging ideas about basic principles and policies. On the other hand, a law reform body must operate under some guidelines and practices. The following are considerations that appear to me to be important.

A. *Constitution of the Commission, Committee, or Board*

The English committees have had fourteen members, Alberta has nine, and for the commissions a popular figure, which indeed comes from Mr. Justice Cardozo's proposal, is five. The writer favours a small board. Every member must put his opinion behind every recommendation. As the size is increased, more time is required and recommendations may tend to become bland. Soundness does not vary directly with the number of persons making the proposals.

As to the type of person of most value, one cannot be dogmatic. However, a majority of practicing lawyers with representatives from the judiciary and law schools seems to give a balance. Our Board represents the three parties to the agreement that established the Institute. This has worked well, though I would prefer to have a member of the judiciary on the Board and not merely in an advisory capacity.

One might wonder about the inclusion of government solicitors. This arises from the fact that the Crown is a party to the agreement, and the presence of experienced solicitors from the Attorney General's Department has been a great help. I realize that in the modern type of Commission it may be incongruous to include officers of the Crown because the Commission is an independent body making submissions to government. However, we find it useful and it is not anomalous when one recalls that the government is one of the three 'partners' in the Institute.

The question, to pay or not to pay, is important. In the past, committees like England's have been unpaid. In the modern Commissions it is obvious that full-time members will be paid. What about those who serve part-time? The writer has always leaned toward the position of the amateur as has generally been the case in England and, indeed, is so today in the Conferences on Uniformity in the United States and Canada. However, I am now convinced that a practitioner cannot be expected to sacrifice his livelihood, especially when the task is not a casual one but is heavy. I agree with Ontario's policy of an annual fee. In the case of law teachers or anyone else on full salary from another source, my leaning is still to the view that they should not be paid. Some persons disagree. In Alberta, no one is paid save the Director, who is full-time. The Board is canvassing its policy and may recommend to the 'partners' a modification for the future.

B. *Manpower for Research*

I turn now to the problem of obtaining personnel to do the research that is the foundation of any piece of law reform. Some of the commissions retain their own research staff. We have not yet such assistance, though I hope we will in time. In the meantime, we have engaged practitioners whom we have selected for their competence. We insist on paying a fee and so far there has been no problem.

All the law teachers in Alberta are within the same University as the Institute. So far the Institute has engaged none, partly because a policy has not been settled and partly because we have been able to find experienced practitioners. I expect and hope that some law teachers will be engaged soon.

Law students have been employed during the summer, and have done good work.

Thus far, in speaking of research, I have been speaking of legal research. However, it is obvious that on many, and perhaps most, subjects one must discover social facts. How does the law work? What actually happens? One need not be a disciple of the American Realists to agree that these questions are relevant and indeed vital. If I may give a notable recent example, the Ontario Law Reform Commission's study of 'the law in action' in connection with the law of landlord and tenant was indispensable to the bold and forthright recommendations it has just made for changes in the law respecting housing tenancies. The Osgoode Hall examinations of motor accident claims and of compensation for victims of crime are other recent field studies.

In trying to learn the facts, it may be hard to know how far to go. Beyond a point, diminishing returns may result. Let us take the hidden cause of action in personal injury cases and its relation to limitations of action. It took very few cases to impel the Lord Chancellor to set up the Davies Committee, which made recommendations while the leading case was still in the courts.[16] There was no need whatever for the Davies Committee to send a platoon of researchers throughout the land to find the frequency of similar cases. One is enough.

Another problem about factual surveys is that they require a high degree of technical skill. We, in Alberta, are novices and it may be that we will have to use statisticians, sociologists, and others. I still have a fear, which may be unwarranted, that we might be led into a $10,000 or $15,000 sociological study of the facts of life and not receive our money's worth. While law reform is now a business and we must not be penny-wise in carrying out research, we still have a responsibility to disburse our funds wisely.

A stage that we have not reached in Alberta is the selection of an individual, either from the Board or outside, to be director of research. This is obviously necessary on large subjects. So far the Director has acted in this capacity.

C. Selection of Subjects

Unlike some commissions that are established by statute, the Institute is under no obligation to undertake subjects requested by the Legislature or the government, and the government has no veto power over its programme. On the other hand, a law reform body could not be very effective if it consistently rejected requests by the government. In fact, the only valid reason for declining is that the assignment is one which the law reform body is not able, by reason of the magnitude or nature of the task, to undertake.

It is, of course, easy to compile a list of potential subjects. Within two months, the Institute had about twenty-five topics. This has been increased by suggestions from within, from interested practitioners, from a business association and the government. We have not had suggestions from the public as has the English Law Commission. Of course, the population of Alberta is only a fraction of that of England and Wales. It may be too that we could do more to remind the public of our existence. One of the most important sources is the material from other law reform bodies. A study initiated in one place spreads. In some instances, a preliminary examination must be made to determine whether the subject requires examination but there are innumerable ones where the desirability of examination is obvious even though the solution may not be.

Naturally, a provincial body will concentrate on matters within provincial competence, though in a subject like expropriation, where there are federal statutes as well as provincial, it is conceivable that submissions could be made to Ottawa.

Often it is said that the function of a permanent law reform body is to deal with lawyers' law. As Sir Leslie Scarman has pointed out, this is hard to define.[17] Sometimes it is described as private law and sometimes as those subjects which are not of political interest. However, if 'lawyers' law' excludes every matter of public law and every controversial matter that might become a political issue, it is too narrow. True, most law reform bodies seem to have concentrated on private law and certainly some of us feel more at home with it than with other subjects. It is perhaps easier too, to cope with problems of substantive law than with procedure, constitution of the courts, and the administration of justice, even though these may really be more vital to society. In any case, our Institute, even in its short career, has not confined itself to 'lawyers' law' in its narrow definition. For example, we have undertaken the study of a family court, which is not private law, and of expropriation, which, in Alberta at least, is not without political sensitivity.

Perhaps concentration should be on defects in judge-made law. Yet it may be harder to codify a branch of the common law than it is to amend existing statutes, which are often in need of reform. Indeed, two popular subjects everywhere seem to be expropriation and limitations, which are statutory.

Naturally, a law reformer wants to make an impact on a wide front and he doubtless dreams of reforming the whole of contracts or property or family law and, ultimately, of codifying the *corpus juris*. However, he will inevitably find himself with a number of small subjects as well as a few extensive ones. It seems to the writer that in Alberta at least, the factors in determining the subjects to undertake are (1) reforms already made elsewhere and (2) availability of manpower and funds. Theoretically, of course, urgency should be the main factor.

In England, the Law Commission prepared at the outset a vast First Programme consisting of seventeen topics including codification of the law of contract. We did not establish a First Programme, but to date have undertaken a total of eleven subjects. In each case, the decision was based on a variety of factors. Compensation for Victims of Crime has already been mentioned. The other ten, and the reasons for undertaking them, might be of interest.

(i) Limitation of Actions: because although the 1966 Amendments in relation to torts eliminated many defects, there are still loose ends, and because the Benchers wanted an examination of the whole Act and because we have the manpower and also the benefit of other recent studies in several provinces, Scotland and New South Wales.

(ii) Occupiers' Liability: because we concluded that it is too late for the courts to clear away the jungle, and because an Edmonton practitioner had done a valuable study of the subject and was available to bring it up to date.

(iii) Co-tortfeasors and Contributory Negligence: because there appear to be many defects in our Tortfeasors Act and Contributory Negligence Act, ranging all the way from the baleful influence of last clear chance to the identification of a wife and a gratuitous passenger with the negligence of the husband and the driver respectively, and because Professor Glanville Williams has provided many helpful suggestions for reform, and because our research and recommendations (we hope) will be of assistance to the Conference of Commissioners on Uniformity of Legislation which has the subject on its Agenda.

(iv) Expropriation: because we received a request from various sources, particularly in connection with expropriation of rights of way for oil and power lines, and because of the helpful reports of the Ontario Law Reform Commission and the Honourable Mr. McRuer.

(v) Perpetuities: because, although very few problems have come before the courts of Alberta in connection with wills and trusts, there is concern over the application of the rule in commercial transactions, particularly in the oil industry, and because it seemed desirable to examine carefully the new Ontario Act and alternatives from various sources, notably British Columbia and the State of Victoria.

(vi) The Family Court Project: because considerable work has been done and a good report prepared by a committee of the Benchers on a

proposal for an integrated family court and because the government considers further work is needed and has asked the Institute to undertake it.

(vii) The Family Relief Act (similar to Testator's Family Maintenance Act): because the government referred to the Institute requests to deal with the problem of evasion by a testator and because some work has been done by the Uniformity Commissioners on the problem.

(viii) English Statutes in Force in Alberta: because there is uncertainty as to which statutes are in force here, because of the inconvenience in referring to the English Statute book, because an Edmonton practitioner has made an intensive study of this subject and is available, and because the government wants it.

(ix) Public Inquiries Act: because various recent public inquiries in Alberta and elsewhere and the Salmon Report in England indicate that amendments to the Public Inquiries Act may be desirable and because we have available an experienced person who is willing to undertake the basic work.

(x) Miscellaneous Problems in Wills and Trusts: because there appear to be various rules both of substantive law and of construction that deserve examination and because we have available a capable retired practitioner to do the research.

D. *Reaching a Decision*

We now come to the fourth stage at which a choice must be made. Should recommendations be formulated immediately working papers are received, or should they be circulated outside for comment and criticism? One could follow the policy of omitting this step in the confidence that when the Report is in the hands of the government, due publicity will be given after a bill has been laid before the Legislature. However, it seems sound to try to obtain opinions and criticisms from every person who would like to offer them.

Many topics are of primary interest to lawyers. Yet general circulation to the profession is unproductive. On the other hand, invitations to comment that are directed to persons of competence should evoke constructive criticism. Our experience is too limited to show whether my view is optimistic. Some persons are almost cynical on this point.

On some subjects many groups other than lawyers have a vital interest. In the case of expropriation, for example, interested parties include government, municipalities, and other public bodies, companies with power to expropriate, appraisers and farmers. One could hold public hearings, but a body like the Institute is not in a position to do this frequently and, besides, it is sometimes ineffective.

Once the research is complete, then every member of the reform body must digest it. This may seem so obvious that it should not even be mentioned. However, one can think of instances where material is circulated before a meeting so it can be studied ahead of time, and yet it is in fact not looked at. A person with a quick mind may be able to scan a lengthy memorandum and form a sound opinion all while discussion goes on, but for most of us this is not possible. One needs time to study and meditate.

Another point that may seem mechanical has to do with isolation of the main issues. When the time comes to make recommendations, the deciding body must have an agenda setting out the main policy questions. There can be no rule as to the time required for discussion, but there must be a mean between skimping and wasting time. As Mr. Justice Megarry has said 'For intelligent law reform nobody seems to have evolved a better method than the cut and thrust of discussion in committee.'[18]

In preparing a final report, the drafting seems to be a task for one person. However, content as distinct from form must represent the considered recommendation of everyone who puts his name to the report.

E. Drafting of Bills

The next important matter of policy or practice is whether to draft bills for the Legislature. The New York and English commissions do so and sometimes the Ontario Commission does. In Alberta we do not propose to draft bills. The reason is that, although we now have one competent draftsman on our Board, we do not think it fair to put the burden on him. In any case, in his capacity of legislative counsel, he may be asked to draft a bill when the report reaches the government.

Ideally, a bill should accompany the recommendations. Sir Leslie Scarman has said:

> Clearly, a law reform report is infinitely more valuable if it can formulate conclusions and proposals. Indeed, I am inclined to think that, unless a law reform agency can go so far as to formulate the draft bill that it wants, many valuable proposals will never get on to the statute book.[19]

One might suggest too, that even if it does get on to the statutes, there is danger of variation between report and bill. One cannot blame this on the draftsman. It is an inherent difficulty when one person has to express another's ideas. Of course, good liaison between the recommending body and the government draftsman reduces the risk of misunderstanding.[20]

Law reform meets another hazard that neither a good report nor a well-drawn bill can remove. It is what Mr. Justice Scarman has called 'wrecking amendment' in the Legislature.[21] Someone in the government must not only see that the bill is introduced, but must know enough about it to give intelligent support.

A final hazard which arises only after passage of a bill is that of judicial misconstruction. This is discussed in the next section.

Obstacles to Progress in Statutory Reform

(1) The first obstacle is inertia or opposition to legislation, together with misconstruction of statutes.

A devotee of the historical school believes that courts can better interpret the spirit of the people than can legislatures: that the former are the best medium for keeping law abreast of social wants. Generally this position is discredited today. The arguments against it are obvious and resistance to codification, or at least to legislation, is waning. Legislation, in Pound's phrase, is now 'the growing point of the law.'[22]

Yet there are some areas, particularly in private law, where a good case can be made for judicial development. This is particularly true in tort where *stare decisis* never had the justification that it has in contract and property.

One can give endless examples to show that the common law of tort has, in fact, developed as new problems have arisen. It is often said that although the courts can add new rules, they can scarcely abrogate old ones. Yet, in at least one instance, the Supreme Court of Canada has done so.[23] It refused to follow *Searle* v. *Wallbank*[24] on the duty of an owner of animals to take reasonable steps to fence them in. In England, on the other hand, the Law Commission has recommended abolition of the rule in *Searle*.

Thus, in the field of tort, one who is considering statutory reform has to decide whether it might be wiser to leave the task to the court. In connection with occupiers' liability, the late Dean Wright was hopeful that with 'judicial valour' the courts could clear away the categories of visitor and the corresponding duties of care. A number of cases in the Supreme Court of Canada give some encouragement to this argument. The law reformer must decide whether to act or to keep hands off in the uncertain hope that the courts may be able to rationalize the law.

Even in the field of property, one might find cases where the courts could properly reject old rules. The Supreme Court of Canada, for example, might have refused to hold that an agreement for sale of land adeems a devise, or that a gift to charitable or benevolent purposes is void. In fact, the Court applied both rules[25] and the Revised Uniform Wills Act wisely abolished them. The fact is that judicial legislation remains interstitial.

Assuming then that legislation is the principal medium for reform, there arises the question whether a reforming statute should be in the form of a complete code. Although we now favour legislation we do not always attempt to bring the whole of the law within the statute. The Wills Act is far from a codification. Difficult though the task is the advantages are obvious. Let us assume that a statute—The Wills Act, for example—together with the innumerable cases that encrust nearly every section, produce sound law. Surely it is better to try to incorporate the judicial rules into the statute itself, in the interest of both succinctness and ready accessibility. Of course, those who derive the greatest pleasure from finding an obscure case, like a needle in a haystack, may be deprived of their pleasure; but so were the special pleaders when the forms of action were abolished. No one sheds tears for them.

Judges, in interpreting statutes, often construe benignly to overcome errors or lacunae in an act. On the other hand, there sometimes remains the old tendency to approach a statute like an enemy. Our Interpretation acts say that every act shall be deemed remedial and shall be construed liberally. Sometimes, of course, this seems to be overlooked.

An example of the interplay between legislature and court can be found in the case of Alberta's Dower Act. This is an American type of homestead law, first passed in 1917, which requires the wife's consent to a disposition of the homestead. A slight oversimplification might be put this way: (i) for thirty years the legislature said that a disposition without consent is void and even 'absolutely null and void for all purposes,' but the courts refused to hold it void. (ii) In 1947, the legislature gave up and the Act was recast so that the disposition was no longer to be void. However, a trilogy of cases[26] in the Supreme Court of Canada has held a disposition—even a mortgage—completely void. The moral perhaps is that the lawmaker must make his meaning clear to the interpreter and that the interpreter must understand what the lawmaker means.

(2) A second argument sometimes made against an attempt at statutory reform is that reforms should not be made piecemeal. There may be instances in which one segment of the common law or one provision in a statute cannot be changed by itself without affecting others; they may all form a seamless web. However, there are many other cases in which a reform is self-contained and, if urgent, it should be made even though other reforms of the same branch of law may ultimately be desirable. Off-hand, for example, I see no objection to abolishing interspousal immunity in tort without touching other matters related to domestic relations; or to amending a Testator's Family Maintenance Act to prevent evasions without revising the whole act.

Then there is another point. Experience and changed attitudes may bring about, over a period of time, isolated changes in one jurisdiction or another. In due course, it may be profitable to examine the various changes and to select the appropriate ones and add others and so produce a wider comprehensive statute that would never have been thought of had it not been for the miscellaneous small additions made in the past in one place or another.

The Uniform Legitimation Act provides a good example. As adopted in 1920, it provided for legitimation by subsequent marriage. A few years ago, after the war, it appeared that England and various provinces had extended the statute to cover the children of certain void and voidable marriages. The Uniformity Conference studied these various provisions and in 1960 adopted a revised and wider Uniform Act which might have never been attempted had the Conference not had before it piecemeal amendments made in different jurisdictions.

(3) The third deterrent to action is fear of duplication of effort. It operates as a dead hand in the following manner. Province *A* contemplates a study of its expropriation procedures. Then it learns that province *B* is working on expropriation. This gives an excuse to province *A* to do nothing.

Long afterwards province *A* learns that province *B*'s study had nothing to do with procedures at all. In the meantime, province *B* learned that province *A* is studying expropriation and waits for province *A*.

Of course the proposition that every law reform body should take the maximum benefit that it can from studies elsewhere is obvious. However, it does not follow that every jurisdiction should wait until another one has acted. The obsession with duplication seems to assume that the law of every jurisdiction is the same and that, in addition, the proposed remedies will be the same. This is, of course, not so.

Let us take, for example, the subject of dower. Alberta's Dower Act, already mentioned, is in need of reform. At the same time, Ontario's mammoth study of family law goes deeply into the anachronism known as common law dower. Anything said on this subject in Ontario is of no interest in Alberta because common law dower was abolished in 1886 on the Prairies.

I would go further and argue that the fabric of Canadian law would be stronger if every single province worked independently on a problem that is common to all. As an example, may I return to limitations of action in tort. An intensive examination in Ontario of the defects in its law may have only limited relevance in Alberta and, if Alberta is seriously interested in improving its own law, there is no way to avoid the task of a detailed study of Alberta statutes and cases. Within the last three years, Alberta and Manitoba pursued independent courses in attacking this problem. Manitoba's and Alberta's solutions provide good laboratory material for any other province interested in this subject. Ultimately, an aggregate of amendments on the same subject in all the common law provinces will produce something very close to a uniform act which will be much better than those the various provinces originally had.

(4) The next obstacle to effective law reform is, in a sense, the opposite of the two just described. They are excuses for doing nothing. The fourth is the uncritical borrowing of a statute from elsewhere. Admittedly, any new state, province, or country must borrow and we, in Canada, have been very fortunate in being able to borrow from the British parliament. The Maritime provinces doubtless borrowed as well from the United States and the old Legislature of the Northwest Territories borrowed from various provinces. And the Uniformity Conference has borrowed from Quebec and New Zealand, among many.

My point is that, in borrowing it is important to examine the borrowed act and decide whether it is appropriate. Laziness can manifest itself in indiscriminate borrowing as well as in complete inaction. Sometimes there appears to be an assumption that if England or Ontario has enacted a certain provision, then the same provision must be good for Alberta and that it is effrontery to suggest otherwise.

In 1966, the Alberta Legislature declined to borrow a section from an English act. The government received criticism. Recent cases in the Court of Appeal of England point to the wisdom of the Alberta decision. In a judgment dealing with the English statute, Lord Denning said 'This is one more case on this very complicated and obscure Act.'[27]

(5) The fifth and last type of obstacle is largely mechanical and not based on any shortcomings in judgment of the law reform body. It is the difficulty of getting forward with the work. Sometimes the person doing the preliminary research is delayed and then the preparation of the final report itself encounters difficulty and there may even be lack of unanimity in the end. These problems seem inevitable and there appears to be no recipe for eliminating them.

The Institute's Research Activities

So much for observations on Alberta's Institute in its law reform activities. I shall now describe the efforts that have been made to encourage 'pure' research. In its budget, the Institute has some $15,000 available to persons interested in pursuing a given topic whether it is intended to lead to reform or not. The Board must approve the project. It provides funds to cover travel, stenographic help, and student assistance. An applicant need not be a full-time member of the Faculty of Law, but obviously preference is given to them. The research may produce recommendations for amendment in the law, but the Institute neither adopts nor rejects them.

In the spring of 1968, applications were approved on the following topics: (1) oil and gas regulations in the Northwest Territories and Alaska; (2) administration of criminal justice in western Canada; (3) small claims courts; (4) appeal procedures under the Income Tax Act. By the end of the year one report had been finished and in the others interim reports showed that the work was practically done. Various governmental and other groups have shown interest in three of the reports and it could be that they will have an influence on legislation even though not in the form of recommendations by the Institute. In the first two projects, the application was renewed for 1969–70 and a further grant was given.

Recently, a grant was awarded for research into Alberta statutes giving power to arrest and to make searches and seizures. Needless to say, the applicant conceived the idea after reading the McRuer Report.

It is the hope of the Institute that this research will be of benefit not only to the researcher but indirectly at least to his teaching and possibly to improvement in the law or, at least, to wider knowledge. We have not worked out a policy of publishing these reports, but have encouraged the researcher to publish them.

There is one field in which the Institute would like to see research proceed and one in which the ground, not only in Alberta but perhaps elsewhere in Canada, has scarcely been scratched. This is the field of legal history. In Alberta, we need to preserve the story of the reception of English law in the Northwest Territories and hence into Alberta, the establishment and growth of legal institutions, biographies of judges and lawyers, and the history of the bar.

We realize, of course, that the available funds are very modest, but one might hope that research can proceed without huge sums of money. Perhaps the spirit of the amateur can still be found. Indeed some persons say that commissioned work is not as worthwhile as that which the researcher is inspired to do on his own. Certainly many valuable articles and even books have been produced with no assistance. However, we hope that research grants, modest though they be, will provide encouragement, and that acceptance is still consistent with amateur standing.

To date, the Institute has not made an impact on the graduate programme. It has provided a number of summer jobs for undergraduates. The plan to bring distinguished scholars to the campus for extended visits has not yet materialized but we hope it will soon.

Conclusion

In concluding, the writer has no profound truth or Cardozo-like generalization to inspire the reformer. Most persons will agree with much of Pound's teachings about social engineering, even if he is not philosophically a complete pragmatist. One may accept, too, Pound's interests or Lasswell and McDougal's formula for securing all interests or 'maximizing' all values. Perhaps I can suggest as useful qualities for the law reformer, industry, judgment, and, as the late Honourable Mr. Ivan Rand used to say, imagination.

Notes

1 Cardozo, 'A Ministry of Justice,' 35 *Harv. L. Rev.* 113 (1921).

2 MacDonald, 'Legal Research Translated into Legislative Action', 48 *Cornell L.Q.* 401, at 402 and n. 38 (1963). Tennessee can be added: see Sanford, 'The Work of the Law Revision Commission,' 32 *Tenn. L. Rev.* 11 (1964–65).

3 Megarry, 'Law Reform,' 34 *Can. Bar Rev.* 690 (1956); Gardiner, 'The Machinery of Law Reform in England,' 69 *L.Q.R.* 467 (1953); Lord Kilmuir, 'Law Reform,' 4 *J. S.P.T.L.* 75 (1957); law reform issue, *24 Mod. L. Rev.* 3 (1961) (esp. Wade & Hutton); Gardiner & Martin, *Law Reform Now* (1963), chap. 1.

4 *Commonwealth and Empire Law Conference* (1955), at 156, 172.

5 For the state of organized law reform in 1960 see Read, 'The Public Responsibilities of the Academic Law Teacher in Canada,' 39 *Can. Bar Rev.* 232, at 239–42 (1961). For proposals see Casgrain, 'Presidential Address,' 10 *Can. Bar Journ.* 365 (1967); Waters, 'Law Reform and the English Law Commission,' 32 *Sask. Law Rev.* 1 (1967); Megarry, *supra* note 3, at 703–11.

6 Scarman, 'Law Reform by Legislative Techniques,' 32 *Sask. Law Rev.* 217 (1967); Scarman, 'Law Reform: Lessons from English Experience,' 3 *Man. Law J.* 47 (1967). His Lordship's address to the 1968 meeting of the Canadian Bar Association appears in the 1968 Proceedings, at 252.

7 'Ontario Law Reform Commission Annual Report, 1967,' 11 *Can. Bar J.* 122 (1968); Leal, 'The Ontario Law Reform Commission,' 1 *Can. Legal Studies* 124 (1966).

8 Annual Reports 1965, 1966, 1967; Scarman, *'Law Reform: The New Pat-*

tern' (1967); Scarman, 'Law Reform,' 10 *J. S.P.T.L.* 91 (1968); *Martin, Methods of Law Reform* (1967); Kilbrandon, 'The Prospects of Law Reform,' 17 *No. Ire. L.Q.* 484 (1966); Walker, 'Reform, Restatement and the Law Commissions,' *Jurid. Rev.* 245 (1965); Yardley, 'The Progress of Law Reform in the United Kingdom,' 1 *Irish Jurist N.S.* 66 (1966); Sutton, 'The English Law Commission: A New Philosophy of Law Reform,' 20 *Vand. L. Rev.* 1009 (1966–67).

9 *Report of the Law Reform Commission for Year ended 30 June, 1968*.

10 Northey, 'An Administrative Division of the New Zealand Supreme Court,' 7 *Alta. Law Rev.* 62 (1969).

11 This paragraph is based on the writer's knowledge; see Correspondence, 3 *Alta. Law Rev.* 159 (1963).

12 'Report of Legal Research Committee of Canadian Bar Association,' 34 *Can. Bar Rev.* 999 (1956).

13 The above account of the Benchers' Law Reform Committee and of the genesis of the Institute is based on the writer's knowledge.

14 These are the Ontario Law Reform Commission, the Law Commission, and the Scottish Law Commission. In the case of the New South Wales Law Reform Commission, there has been no personal contact, but the reports and working papers of this Commission have been of assistance. The Director of Law Reform for Northern Ireland has also been of help to the Director of the Institute.

15 The Bill was enacted as The Criminal Injuries Compensation Act, 1969, c.23.

16 The Davies Report is Cmnd. 1829 (1962): the enactment is The Limitations Act, 1963, c. 47; the case is *Cartledge* v. *Jopling,* [1963] A.C. 758.

17 Scarman, *Law Reform: The New Pattern, supra* note 8, at 26–30.

18 Megarry, *supra* note 3, at 701.

19 Scarman, *Law Reform: The New Pattern, supra* note 8, at 35.

20 In at least one case, the draftsman rather than the legislature has been the target of judicial criticism. The English Court of Appeal had to consider a section dealing with persons of unsound mind. Danckwerts L.J. said: 'This is such an extraordinary provision that at times it seems to me that the draftsman must have been of unsound mind'; *Kirby* v. *Leather,* [1965] 2 All E.R. 441 at 445.

21 Scarman, *Law Reform: The New Pattern, supra* note 8, at 26 and 37–44.

22 A notable address on the role of the judiciary in law reform is that of the Honorable Roger Traynor, Chief Justice of California, 'The Courts: Interweavers in the Reformation of Law,' 32 *Sask. Law Rev.* 201 (1967).

23 *Fleming* v. *Atkinson,* [1959] S.C.R. 513.

24 [1947] A.C. 341.

25 *Church* v. *Hill,* [1923] S.C.R. 642; *Brewer* v. *McCauley,* [1954] S.C.R. 645.

26 *Pinsky* v. *Wass,* [1953] 1 S.C.R. 399; *Meduk* v. *Soja,* [1958] S.C.R. 167; *British American Oil Co.* v. *Kos,* [1964] S.C.R. 167.

27 *Pickles* v. *National Coal Board,* [1968] 2 All E.R. 598, at 599.

1970

Case Comment: Regina v. Drybones (Supreme Court of Canada)

Reprinted from
(1970) 8 Alberta Law Review
pp. 409–418

The case which gave rise to this Comment arose in the North West Territories wherein Drybones, a native Indian, was charged with being intoxicated contrary to the Indian Act. By way of defence, it was pleaded that the 1960 Bill of Rights rendered inoperative that section of the Indian Act as being a violation of "equality before the law." After numerous appeals through the courts, the Supreme Court of Canada held that the court has power to declare inoperative or ineffective any law which abrogates or infringes rights or freedoms specified in the Bill.

This was the first case where the Supreme Court struck down legislation under the Bill of Rights Act (it did not do so in the later Lavell case involving the marriage of an Indian woman to a white man).

Bowker was asked by the Editor of the Alberta Law Review *to write a case comment on this decision. He was one of the few who did not applaud the decision: the accused had admittedly committed the offence, even though the offence did not apply to non-Indians. Still Bowker felt there was some basis for treating Indians differently; that there was a reasonable basis for this law, because the liquor problem was particularly acute amongst Indians.*

This Case Comment analyzes all of his reasons for holding to this view.

Ever since the Canadian Bill of Rights Act[1] became law almost ten years ago there has been uncertainty as to whether the Bill empowers a court to declare ineffective or inoperative a provision in a law of Canada which in the opinion of the court abrogates, abridges or infringes any of the rights or freedoms specified in the Bill. Most of the decisions pointed to a negative answer. In *Reg.* v. *Drybones,*[2] however, the Supreme Court of Canada has held that the court does have such power.

The Bill of Rights Act in s. 1[3] declares that six fundamental rights and freedoms have existed and shall continue to exist without discrimination by reason of race. One of the rights is "the right of the individual to equality before the law and the protection of the law." The Bill then provides in s. 2[4] that every law of Canada is to be "construed and applied" as not to abrogate the six rights and freedoms or various other rights specified in s. 2 and connected with judicial or administrative proceedings, especially criminal trials. There is however in s. 2 a *non obstante* clause which permits Parliament to include in any law of Canada an express provision that it shall apply notwithstanding the Bill of Rights. Then s. 5(2)[5] provides that "law of Canada" means an Act of Parliament enacted before or after the Bill.

The Indian Act[6] provides by s. 94:

An Indian who

(a) has intoxicants in his possession,

(b) is intoxicated, or

(c) makes or manufactures intoxicants

off a reserve, is guilty of an offence and is liable on summary conviction to a fine of not less than ten dollars and not more than fifty dollars or to imprisonment for a term not exceeding three months or to both fine and imprisonment.

Drybones was intoxicated in a hotel in Yellowknife in the Northwest Territories. Charged under s. 94(b) he pleaded guilty before a Magistrate. On appeal by way of trial *de novo* before Mr. Justice Morrow of the Supreme Court of the Northwest Territories he was allowed to change his plea and to invoke the Bill of Rights Act. His Lordship found that Drybones was an Indian and that he was intoxicated and that he was off a reserve. One argument of the accused was that he could not be off a reserve when there is none in the Territories. This argument failed. The principal defence was that the Bill of Rights Act renders inoperative s. 94 of the Indian Act.

This issue had arisen in British Columbia in *Reg*. v. *Gonzales*[7] and the judgments in the Court of Appeal in that case became the focal point in *Drybones*. Gonzales was an Indian charged with possession of liquor under s. 94(a). He was convicted before a Magistrate. On appeal by way of stated case, Maclean J. dismissed the appeal and Gonzales appealed to the Court of Appeal on the ground that s. 94(a) infringes the right to equality before the law which the Bill declares. The judgment of Davey J.A. is important because the main issue in *Drybones* was whether that judgment is correct. Davey J.A. first considered the meaning of "equality before the law". He was not sure that s. 94 is a denial of equality but assuming that it is he went on to consider whether s. 2 of the Bill renders s. 94 inoperative. He concluded that it does not repeal any legislation in existence when the Bill became law.

> On the contrary, it expressly recognizes the continued existence of such legislation, but provides that it shall be construed and applied so as not to derogate from those rights and freedoms. By that it seems merely to provide a canon or rule of interpretation for such legislation. The very language of s. 2, "be so construed and applied as not to abrogate" assumes that the prior Act may be sensibly construed and applied in a way that will avoid derogating from the rights and freedoms declared in s. 1. If the prior legislation cannot be so con-

> strued and applied sensibly, then the effect of s. 2 is exhausted, and the prior legislation must prevail according to its plain meaning.

Tysoe J.A., with whom Bird J.A. concurred, reached the same result but on a different ground. He pointed out that there are many statutes which treat one class of person differently from all others and he cited the example from the Judges' Act which prohibits all Federal Judges from voting in Federal elections. He concluded that "equality before the law" in s. 1(b) of the Bill means "in the presence of". That is to say, the Bill does not prevent discrimination between groups but only between persons within a group to which special legislation applies. Equality before the law does not mean the same as equal laws for everyone. The appellant's argument would result in invalidation of much of the Indian Act and Tysoe J.A. was not prepared to give to the Bill such an effect.

A second case which played an important role in *Drybones* is *Robertson & Rosetanni* v. *The Queen*.[8] In *Robertson* the accused were convicted of operating a bowling alley on Sunday in contravention of s. 4 of the Lord's Day Act. They contended that the Bill of Rights renders s. 4 inoperative, and specifically that it infringes their freedom of religion which is one of the freedoms declared in the Bill.

In the hearing before the Supreme Court of Canada five judges sat. Ritchie J. wrote the majority judgment in which Taschereau C.J., Fauteux and Abbott JJ. concurred. Ritchie J. held that the Lord's Day Act did not abridge freedom of religion so therefore did not need to consider the question as to whether the Bill renders inoperative a statute which does abridge that freedom. There is, however, an important passage in his judgment which points out that the Bill is concerned with rights and freedoms *that existed in Canada* on passage of the Bill. He had in mind s. 1 which declares that these rights *have existed* and also s. 5(2) which defines "law of Canada" to include existing statutes. Then he proceeded to examine religious freedom as it was understood prior to the Bill, concluding that the Lord's Day Act is not an abridgement of that freedom. This passage might lead one to think that Ritchie J. was saying that no existing statute could ever be in violation of the Bill. We shall see that in *Drybones* he explained that this was not what he meant.

Of great interest is the dissent of Mr. Justice Cartwright who subsequently became Chief Justice. He found, contrary to the majority, that s. 4 of the Lord's Day Act infringes freedom of religion as that term is used in the Bill, and the fact that the Lord's Day Act had been in force for over half a century before the Bill is irrelevant. Thus he was obliged to determine whether the Bill renders s. 4 inoperative. He addressed himself to the reasons for judgment of Davey J.A. in *Gonzales*. After setting out the key passage (which has already been quoted) he said;

> With the greatest respect I find myself unable to agree with this view. The imperative words of s. 2 of the *Canadian Bill of Rights*, quoted above, appear to me to require the Courts to refuse to apply any law, coming within the legisla-

> tive authority of Parliament, which infringes freedom of religion unless it is expressly declared by an Act of Parliament that the law which does so infringe shall operate notwithstanding the *Canadian Bill of Rights*. As already pointed out s. 5(2), quoted above, makes it plain that the *Canadian Bill of Rights* is to apply to all laws of Canada already in existence at the time it came into force as well as to those thereafter enacted. In my opinion where there is irreconcilable conflict between another Act of Parliament and the *Canadian Bill of Rights* the latter must prevail.
>
> Whether the imposition, under penal sanctions, of a certain standard of religious conduct on the whole population is desirable is, of course, a question for Parliament to decide. But in enacting the *Canadian Bill of Rights* Parliament has thrown upon the Courts the responsibility of deciding, in each case in which the question arises, whether such an imposition infringes the freedom of religion in Canada. In the case at bar I have reached the conclusion that s. 4 of the *Lord's Day Act* does infringe the freedom of religion declared and preserved in the *Canadian Bill of Rights* and must therefore be treated as inoperative.

This was the first time after the passage of the Bill that a member of the Supreme Court had held that the effect of the Bill is to render ineffective a provision in a pre-existing Federal Statute. Since his judgment was a dissent it did not affect the result, and the conviction stood.

The *Gonzales* and *Robertson* cases provide the issues in *Drybones*. Morrow J. quoted a statement from Ritchie J. in *Robertson* that the *effect* rather than the *purpose* of a statute must be examined to determine whether it is in conflict with the Bill. He held that the effect of the liquor provisions is discriminatory. Thus he was required to determine the question whether the Bill renders the liquor provisions inoperative. He quoted from *Robertson* the first paragraph of the passage set out above from the judgment of Cartwright J. and applied it. Thus the accused was acquitted.

The Crown applied for leave to appeal to the Court of Appeal of the Northwest Territories, consisting of three members of the Appellate Division of the Supreme Court of Alberta. Mr. Justice Johnson wrote the judgment while Smith C.J.A. and Allen J.A. concurred. In refusing leave to appeal Johnson J.A. specifically preferred the judgment of Cartwright J. in *Robertson* to that of Davey J.A. in *Gonzales*. It is clear that the court was influenced by the existence of the "unless it is expressly declared" clause in s. 2 of the Bill.

As to the reasoning of Tysoe J.A. in *Gonzales,* Johnson J.A. rejected it. It would restrict the Bill so as to permit discrimination between racial groups as long as all those in the group are discriminated against equally. Johnson J.A. answers the illustration of judges' disqualification from voting by saying that the Bill prevents discrimination only on the grounds specified in the Bill namely, race, national origin, colour, religion or sex.

The Crown obtained leave to appeal to the Supreme Court of Canada and the appeal was argued on its merits, the single issue being whether the Bill renders s. 94 inoperative. The appeal was dismissed, six judges to three. Ritchie J. wrote the majority judgment, with Fauteux, Martland, Judson, Hall and Spence, JJ. concurring. On the central issue, Mr. Justice Ritchie disagreed with Davey J.A. in *Gonzales* and quoted with approval the views of Cartwright J. in *Robertson*. Like the Court of Appeal, he emphasized the "unless" clause in s. 2. It must not be treated as superfluous. Section 2 does not repeal s. 94 but makes it "inoperative".

Ritchie J. then explained his comments in *Robertson* which imply that laws existing before the Bill are of necessity consonant with the Bill because of the statement in s. 1 that the enumerated rights had existed. He had not meant to say this: his reference in *Robertson* to existing laws was for the purpose of examining the decided cases to determine the meaning of freedom of religion as it was understood immediately before enactment of the Bill. He had not said that the Bill is of necessity subject to the Lord's Day Act merely because the latter was an existing statute. Such an opinion would have been contrary to s. 5(2) which declares "law of Canada" to include existing statutes of Canada.

Turning to the meaning of "equality before the law" he held it to mean that no group is to be treated more harshly than another under that law; "an individual is denied equality before the law if it is made an offence punishable at law, on account of his race, for him to do something which his fellow Canadians are free to do without having committed any offence or having been made subject to any penalty." Thus s. 94(b) is inoperative.

Hall J. while concurring in the majority judgment added his specific disagreement with the reasons of Tysoe J. in *Gonzales*.

The dissent of Chief Justice Cartwright is notable in that he reconsidered his opinion in *Robertson* and concluded that the view of Davey J.A. which he had rejected in *Robertson* is in fact the better one. If Parliament intended to confer upon the courts the power and responsibility of declaring inoperative a provision in a statute of Canada, then every Justice of the Peace, Magistrate and Judge of any court has this power and responsibility. Had Parliament so intended it would have added in s. 2 some such words as the following: "and if any law of Canada cannot be so construed and applied it shall be regarded as inoperative or *pro tanto* repealed". His own error in *Robertson* was in the statement that the Bill requires the courts to refuse to apply any law of Canada which infringes one of the declared rights or freedoms. In fact the Bill directs the courts to apply a law of Canada, not to refuse to apply it.

Abbott J. took a similar position. The majority view implies a wide delegation of the legislative authority of Parliament to the courts. It would require the plainest words to impute to Parliament an intention to extend to the courts such an invitation to engage in judicial legislation. With respect to existing legislation, s. 2 of the Bill provides merely a canon or rule of interpretation.

The dissent of Pigeon J. puts emphasis on the opening part of s. 1 of the Bill. The reference to existing law gives precision to the broad phrases used to describe the six enumerated rights and freedoms. The British North America Act itself specifically gives Parliament power to enact legislation in relation to Indians. If the Bill renders inoperative all the legal provisions whereby Indians as such are not dealt with in the same way as the general public, then Parliament has indirectly altered the status of the Indian and has required the insertion of a *non obstante* clause whenever Parliament wishes to legislate under s. 91 (24) of the B.N.A. Act. The "construed and applied" clause is one of construction. Pigeon J. faced the fact that the *non obstante* clause provides the strongest argument against his view. He concluded that proper effect can be given to it without using it to strike down legislation already in existence. Inroads on parliamentary sovereignty should not be implied.

Which interpretation of the Bill is justified on the terms of the Bill? The writer sees much force in the view of Davey J.A. and of the three dissents in *Drybones*. On the other hand the injunction in s. 2 that every law of Canada shall be so "construed and applied" as not to abrogate any of the enumerated rights or freedoms, together with the *non obstante* clause, is apt language to justify the opinion of the majority.

It is elementary that a court may not examine committee reports and debates in Hansard as an aid in construing a statute. However a commentator is under no such censorship. The original 1958 draft of the Bill[9] did not clearly confer on the court the power to declare inoperative a provision which in the opinion of the court is in contravention of the proposed Bill. The Bill which Prime Minister Diefenbaker reintroduced on June 27, 1960, had been substantially amended. After debate the House of Commons established a special committee to study the Bill. In the committee the Honourable Paul Martin quoted from a letter from Andrew Brewin of Toronto to the Chairman of the Committee:

> The declaration by Parliament in general terms could not be said to have the effect of repealing or amending any existing statute which might be thought to be inconsistent with it, nor, in my opinion, would it have the effect of preventing Parliament in future passing any enactment inconsistent with the bill of rights.[10]

Later in the Committee Proceedings[11] the Honourable Mr. Martin proposed an amendment to the Interpretation Act. This amendment provided for the repeal of any existing acts which abrogate any of the declared rights or freedoms. The Committee did not vote on the proposal. However after the Committee reported on 29 July the proposed Bill was debated in the House of Commons on August 1–4. The Honourable Mr. Martin then proposed the same amendment.[12] The Honourable E.D. Fulton, Minister of Justice, opposed the amendment on the ground *inter alia,* that it was not necessary; that the draft Bill as it then stood (and as later passed) and particularly the opening part of s. 2 had precisely the same effect as the Honourable Mr. Martin's amendment to the Interpretation Act would have.[13] The amendment was defeated.[14]

Accepting the construction which the majority put on the bill, there is one argument which the Crown advanced both in *Gonzales* and *Drybones* without success but which seems to the writer to have considerable force. It is the argument that the Indian Act including the liquor provisions are protective and not discriminatory. The British North America Act specifically gives Parliament jurisdiction over Indians and Indian lands. At the first session of the First Parliament of the Dominion of Canada in 1868 a statute establishing the office of Secretary of State dealt in large measure with Indian lands. In addition it forbade the sale or gift of liquor to Indians, and the taking of pawns from Indians for liquor.[15]

In 1876 Parliament passed a comprehensive Indian Act. It contained seven sections dealing with intoxicants, two of which include the prohibitions now contained in s. 94.[16] It is unnecessary to trace the various amendments from 1876 to the present time. There has been some relaxation, particularly in the 1956 amendments which provide for proclamations permitting sale of liquor to Indians and possession of liquor by Indians in accordance with provincial law.[17]

It may be that the efforts to keep liquor from Indians have not succeeded in their purpose and that the remaining prohibitions should be repealed. The recent study by the Canadian Corrections Association,[18] and the brief of the Department of Indian Affairs and Northern Development to the Select Committee of the Senate on Poverty[19] indicate that liquor is still a serious problem but that Indians themselves on the whole would prefer the repeal of the special restrictions relating to them. Granted all this, the liquor provisions were in their inception clearly intended to be protective. Is an enactment respecting Indians necessarily discriminatory and a deprivation of equality because it imposes penalties on them for conduct that others may pursue with impunity? Implicit in the *Drybones* decision is an affirmative answer. My submission is that an enactment respecting Indians can still be protective even though it subjects them to penalties. "We are doing this for your own good" can apply to Indians as well as to children who are chastised by their parents. Moreover, lack of wisdom in a policy or ultimate failure of a policy surely does not convert its quality from protective to discriminatory.

It is not clear from *Drybones* as to the vulnerability of all the liquor provisions. Ritchie J. specifically confined his holding to s. 94(b); Morrow J. to the sections dealing with intoxicants; and the Court of Appeal seems to extend its ratio to all the provisions in the Act which restrict Indians. Is s. 32 restricting sale by Indians of natural products open to attack? Or s. 46 giving to the Minister power in specific circumstances to declare void the will of an Indian?

It is interesting to note the position that the Supreme Court of the United States has taken with respect to Indians. Almost from the beginning Congress passed special legislation relating to Indian lands and sale or gift of liquor to Indians. Under the Constitution the only specific power of Congress over Indians is in the Commerce clause, which gives power "to regulate Commerce... with the Indian tribes". Yet an unbroken line of decisions has held that Congress has in addition the power to legislate with respect to Indians because they are in a state of pupillage or wardship, and the decision to abandon its guardianship rests in Congress; the Court will not overrule the judgment of Congress.[20] It is true that over the years Congress has relaxed its control substantially; it is true too that Congress is not bound by the equal protection clause which restricts the States. However, it is bound by the due process clause which has been widely construed in other areas, and it is not insignificant that the Supreme Court has refrained from striking down Acts of Congress dealing specially with Indians.

As for state laws, every state is enjoined by the Fourteenth Amendment not to "deny to any person within its jurisdiction the equal protection of the laws." Although Tysoe J.A. in *Gonzales* thought that equal protection of the laws is different from equality before the law, the writer cannot define any difference.

There is a valuable case from Idaho, *State* v. *Rorvick,*[21] in which the charge was for sale of intoxicating liquor to an Indian contrary to an Idaho statute. The court was divided. The majority judgment gives a valuable survey of legislation respecting Indians. It points out that President Jefferson was concerned with the effect of liquor on Indians. Congress has always assumed the duty "to protect Indians from well recognized weaknesses". Several cases from other states uphold state legislation of this kind. "Sale to Indians was not prohibited because of their copper colored skin" but "because history proves the [liquor] has cursed and demoralized the Indian". Arguments against the legislation should be addressed to the legislature, not the Court.

The suggestion I have been making is that protective legislation is not discriminatory. This is merely an example of a broader proposition that is well established in the United States in connection with the equal protection clause. That clause does not forbid all classifications; a statute may be invulnerable to attack even though it singles out a special class of persons for treatment that may *prima facie* seem to discriminate against them (or for them and against all others). A Michigan statute forbidding women from obtaining a bartender's license except for the wife or daughter of the male owner of the bar was upheld;[22] also a law excluding aliens from operating pool halls;[23] and a Louisiana statute which in effect ensured that only relatives and friends of river pilots could become pilots;[24] and state laws barring aliens ineligible to citizenship from land ownership.[25] The principle reiterated innumerable times is that the test for denial of equal protection is "whether the challenged classification rests on grounds wholly irrelevant to the achievement of a valid state objective."[26] The application of the test rests with the court. At times the court has been quite willing to find no valid state objective: at others it has deferred to the legislative judgment. If our courts are to use the power to declare an act of Parliament to be a denial of equality before the law then surely they will have to evolve some kind of a test that will permit the preservation of some statutes which deal specially with one group or another.

Returning to the Indian Act, I recognize that Parliament could preserve

s. 94, or the whole Act for that matter, by adding a *non obstante* clause; but it is scarcely satisfactory to proceed in this way. One objection to the power which *Drybones* assures to the courts is that the power is essentially negative. We do not satisfactorily deal with Indians by an Act which confers on the court the power to declare inoperative sections of the Indian Act. The Supreme Court (or lower courts subject to appeal) can nibble away at the Indian Act section by section. They can thus create a vacuum but cannot fill it. The device rendered possible by the Bill is not the way to try to solve the "Indian problem", which admittedly is difficult. The responsibility should be that of the legislature.

There is one point that *Drybones* raises which could have implications in future and which could possibly restrict the scope of the Bill. It has been noted that the six rights and liberties in s. 1 are declared to have existed and to continue to exist "without discrimination by reason of race, national origin, colour, religion or sex". This part of s. 1 was given particular emphasis by the Court of Appeal in *Drybones*. Let us suppose that a statute of Canada infringes any of the six basic rights or freedoms—the right to due process of law and equality before the law and the freedoms of religion, speech, assembly and press. However, the infringement is not based on discrimination by reason of race, national origin, colour, religion or sex. In the view of the Court of Appeal such discrimination is not within the protection of the Bill. If this interpretation is correct, which the writer doubts, the Bill is exceedingly narrow in scope. A statute may abridge freedom of press, for example, or due process of law without having anything to do with racial or religious discrimination.

Now that the power of the court is established the main concern is whether the courts will be astute to declare inoperative subsections, sections or whole statutes. As Pigeon J. said in *Drybones* there is a vast difference between the power of a court to construe a statute and a power to declare it inoperative.

Courts often have construed statutes in conformity with the spirit of the rights and freedoms which the court considers fundamental. The Supreme Court in *Boucher* v. *The King*[27] construed seditious intention in a way that protected from prosecution a person who published a bitter attack on the Catholic Church and the Quebec Courts. Since he did not incite others to violence he did not have a seditious intention. This decision makes freedom of speech mean something.

In another area of human rights, that of fairness in criminal procedure, the courts within limits can construe the Criminal Code or the Narcotic Control Act in a way to avoid harshness. *Beaver* v. *The Queen*[28] is an example. In spite of the stringent wording of the Opium and Narcotic Act, the Supreme Court held it did not prevent the accused from showing an absence of *mens rea*.

Decisions like these may be regarded as wise or unwise, right or wrong. Under our traditional system Parliament may be content to leave the statute as it is, or may decide to amend it. However, should Parliament now wish to "reverse" a decision holding that a statutory provision is inoperative because of conflict with the Bill, it must now add a *non obstante* clause.

If one were to go through the statute book he would doubtless find many provisions which *might* be inoperative. Section 16 of the Criminal Code which requires an accused to show insanity by a preponderance of evidence might be a denial of due process or of the presumption of innocence declared in s. 2(f); and the provisions in the Code[29] for trials in camera might be ineffective because of s. 2(f) of the Bill which requires a public hearing;[30] and s. 5 of the Canada Evidence Act might be an infringement of protection against self-incrimination which is declared in s. 2(d) of the Bill.

The device of trying to secure the enumerated rights and freedoms through the power which the Bill accords to the court has three vices: (1) it is essentially negative, (2) it creates uncertainty, (3) it permits Parliament to evade its responsibility.[31]

Notes

1 S.C. 1960, c. 44.

2 (1969) 71 W.W.R. 161, *aff'g* (1967) 61 W.W.R. 370 and (1967) 60 W.W.R. 321.

3 1. It is hereby recognized and declared that in Canada there have existed and shall continue to exist without discrimination by reason of race, national origin, colour, religion or sex, the following human rights and fundamental freedoms, namely,
(a) the right of the individual to life, liberty, security of the person and enjoyment of property, and the right not to be deprived thereof except by due process of law;
(b) the right of the individual to equality before the law and the protection of the law;
(c) freedom of religion;
(d) freedom of speech;
(e) freedom of assembly and association; and
(f) freedom of the press.

4 2. Every law of Canada shall, unless it is expressly declared by an Act of the Parliament of Canada that it shall operate notwithstanding the Canadian Bill of Rights, be so construed and applied as not to abrogate, abridge or infringe or to authorize the abrogation, abridgment or infringement of any of the rights or freedoms herein recognized and declared, and in particular, no law of Canada shall be construed or applied so as to
(a) authorize or effect the arbitrary detention, imprisonment or exile of any person
(b) impose or authorize the imposition of cruel and unusual treatment or punishment;
(c) deprive a person who has been arrested or detained
(i) of the right to be informed promptly of the reason for his arrest or
(ii) of the right to retain and instruct counsel without delay, or
(iii) of the remedy by way of *habeas corpus* for the determination of the validity of his detention and for his release if the detention is not lawful;
(d) authorize a court, tribunal, commission, board or other authority to compel a person to give evidence if he is denied counsel, protection against self crimination or other constitutional safeguards;
(e) deprive a person of the right to a fair hearing in accordance with the principles of fundamental justice for the determination of his rights and obligations;
(f) deprive a person charged with a

criminal offence of the right to be presumed innocent until proved guilty according to law in a fair and public hearing by an independent and impartial tribunal, or of the right to reasonable bail without just cause; or

(g) deprive a person of the right to the assistance of an interpreter in any proceedings in which he is involved or in which he is a party or a witness, before a court, commission, board or other tribunal, if he does not understand or speak the language in which such proceedings are conducted.

5 5(2) The expression "law of Canada" in Part 1 means an Act of the Parliament of Canada enacted before or after the coming into force of this Act, any order, rule or regulation thereunder, and any law in force in Canada or in any part of Canada at the commencement of this Act that is subject to be repealed, abolished or altered by the Parliament of Canada.

6 R.S.C. 1952, c. 149.

7 (1962) 32 D.L.R. (2d) 290, aff'g 130 C.C.C. 400 and 130 C.C.C. 206; see also *A.G. of B.C.* v. *McDonald* (1962) 131 C.C.C. 126; contra *Richards* v. *Cote* (1962) 40 W.W.R. 340 (Sask.).

8 [1963] S.C.R. 651.

9 (1959) 37 Can. Bar Rev. 1.

10 Special Committee on Human Rights and Fundamental Freedoms, p. 648 (1960).

11 *Id.* at 678.

12 Debates, House of Commons, 1960 Vol. VII p. 7474.

The amendment reads:

"The Interpretation Act is amended by adding thereto under the heading of "rules of construction" immediately before section 9 thereof, the following section as section 8(A).

'8(A) 1. Every act of the Parliament of Canada and every order, rule and regulation thereunder in force at the commencement of this section, and all laws in Canada that are subject to be repealed, abolished or altered by the Parliament of Canada in force at the commencement of this section, are hereby amended by repealing or revoking them to the extent that any provision thereof would abrogate, abridge, or authorize the abrogation, abridgement or infringement of any of the rights or freedoms declared to exist in Canada by the Canadian Bill of Rights.'

'2. No act of the Parliament of Canada, passed hereafter, shall, unless it is otherwise expressly stated in it be interpreted to abrogate, abridge or infringe, or to authorize the abrogation, abridgement or infringement of any of the rights or freedoms declared to exist in Canada by the Canadian Bill of Rights.'

'3. No act, order, rule or regulation or law mentioned in subsection 1, and, unless it is expressly otherwise stated therein, no act hereafter passed, shall be construed or have effect to.'"

13 *Id.* at 7475–77.

14 *Id.* at 7482.

15 S.C. 1868, c. 42, ss. 12 & 13.

16 S.C. 1876, c. 18, ss. 79 & 83.

17 S.C. 1956, c. 40, s. 23.

18 Indians and the Law (1967), esp. c. IV.

19 Special Senate Committee on Poverty, No. 14, Jan. 20, 1970, esp. at 92–94.

20 *U.S.* v. *Kagama* (1880) 118 U.S. 375; *Re Heff* (1905) 197 U.S. 488; *U.S.* v. *Sandoval* (1913) 231 U.S. 28; *U.S.* v. *Nice* (1917) 241 U.S. 591; *U.S.* v. *McGowan* (1937) 302 U.S. 535. All but the first of these cases have to do with liquor. The present federal prohibitions against dispensing liquor to Indians are found in 18 U.S.C.A.1154–56, 1161. It may be noted that *Nice* overrules *Heff* on interpretation of an Act of Congress but both cases support the statement in the text.

21 (1954) 277 P. 2d 566. The writer is indebted to Tarnopolsky, *The Canadian Bill of Rights* (1966), 214 for this reference.

22 *Goesaert* v. *Cleary* (1948) 335 U.S. 464.

23 *Clarke* v. *Deckebach* (1927) 274 U.S. 392.

24 *Kotch* v. *River Commissioners* (1947) 330 U.S. 552.

25 *Terrace* v. *Thompson* (1923) 263 U.S. 197; *Porterfield* v. *Webb* (1923) 263 U.S. 225. These cases may be weakened by *Oyama* v. *California* (1948) 332 U.S. 633 and *Takakashi* v. *Fish & Game Commission* (1948) 334 U.S. 410.

26 *Turner* v. *Fouche* (1970) 90 S.C. 532 at 541.

27 [1951] S.C.R. 265.

28 [1957] S.C.R. 531.

29 ss. 427, 428; also 451(j) dealing with preliminary hearings.

30 MacPherson J. in *Benning* v. *A.G. Sask.* (1963) 41 W.W.R. 497 held that the Bill does not supersede the Code.

31 The writer acknowledges with thanks the help he received from a paper *The Indian Act and the Canadian Bill of Rights* by Colin Taylor, a student in second year law at the University of Alberta. He does not associate Mr. Taylor with the views here expressed.

1973

Experimentation on Humans and Gifts of Tissue: Articles 20–23 of the Civil Code

Reprinted from
(1973) 19 McGill Law Journal
pp. 161–194

This article examines the provisions of the Quebec Civil Code (Articles 20 to 23) dealing with experimentation on humans and gifts of tissue. Quebec was way ahead of other provinces in this field of legislation.

Bowker was familiar with Quebec legislation in this field. The McGill Law Journal *invited him to write an article on this topic.*

He analyzes the Quebec provisions and compares them to those in the common law provinces. The latter did have legislation dealing with gifts of tissue (the Uniform Act) but they had no legislation on experimentation.

This article was frequently quoted by legal authorities in Quebec.

Introduction

Experimentation on humans has taken place for centuries. In the last fifty years, however, and particularly since World War II, it has expanded so that today it is almost a special discipline. It was a necessary prelude to the introduction into general use of many valuable drugs and medical procedures that we now take for granted.

A gift by a living person of a part of his body is likewise far from new, but again new developments have made these gifts an important part of today's medicine. One need only mention blood transfusions and kidney transplants.

So it is with the use of organs and tissues from cadavers. The grafting of corneas of eyes taken from cadavers onto the eyes of living persons to restore sight has been followed by the transplantation of hearts and doubtless other parts of the body will be successfully used before long.

These three developments raise legal as well as ethical questions. Thus it is that the new articles 20–23 of the Civil Code are of general interest, for they deal with all three—experiments, *inter vivos* transplants and transplants from cadavers. The purpose of this article is to examine them in turn and to make some comparisons with legal developments in common law jurisdictions.

Genesis of Articles 20–23

The new articles have been enacted as part of a general revision of the Civil Code that has been under way for several years—the first comprehensive review since 1866.[1] To assist in the revision a Code Revision Office was established and given the responsibility for making recommendations to the Legislature. One of the Office's several committees is on Civil Rights and Duties. The Chairman of the Committee is Professor Paul-André Crépeau, who is also Chairman of the Revision Office. The other Committee members are Mr Justice Albert Mayrand and Mr Normand Lepine. In July, 1971 the Committee prepared a report entitled "Report on the Recognition of Certain Rights Concerning the Human Body". This report recommended five articles to provide for:

(1) the right of a living adult to make a gift but not a sale, of part of his body or to submit himself to experiments;
(2) his right to give instructions about his funeral and the disposal of his remains;
(3) the right of his family to give these instructions where he has not given them;
(4) the right of a physician in urgent cases to remove part of a cadaver to save human life; and
(5) prohibition of autopsies unless authorized by law or with consent.

These recommendations were circulated for comment, and in October, 1971 the Revision Office submitted to the Legislature its own report. It followed the Committee's report with one important change. The first proposal, which dealt with experiments and *inter vivos* gifts, was extended to a minor who is "endowed with discernment", provided his parents consent and there is no serious risk to the minor.

A Bill to embody the proposed articles was promptly introduced and on 1 December, 1971 was passed. The recommended provisions became articles 20 to 23, replacing articles that had dealt with British subjects, aliens and naturalized persons.[2] The new articles contain some changes both in content and form from the recommendations of the Code Revision Office. I shall note them at the appropriate place.

Experiments and 'Inter Vivos' Gifts

The recommendation dealing with human experiments and *inter vivos* gifts of human tissue became article 20. As enacted it contains one provision that goes contrary to the recommendation of both the Committee and the Revision Office: article 20 permits the sale, as well as the gift, of a part of the body that is "susceptible of regeneration".

Article 20 provides:

> A person of full age may consent in writing to disposal *inter vivos* of a part of his body or submit to an experiment provided that the risk assumed is not

disproportionate to the benefit anticipated.

A minor, capable of discernment, may do likewise with the consent of the person having the paternal authority and of a judge of the Superior Court, provided that no serious risk to his health results therefrom.

The alienation must be gratuitous unless its object is a part of the body susceptible of regeneration.

The consent must be in writing; it may be revoked in the same way.

In considering this article, it will be convenient first to deal with experimentation and then with *inter vivos* gifts.

Human Experimentation[3]

So far as the writer knows there is no statute in any common law province, or in Britain, or for that matter in the United States (apart from the *Food, Drug and Cosmetic Act*[4]) that deals with experimentation on humans.

Meaning of Experiment

What does "experiment" mean? It is necessary here to distinguish between experimental therapy on the one hand and scientific experiment (or research study or clinical study or clinical research) on the other. Experimental therapy is a new procedure in the prevention, diagnosis or treatment of disease. It may of course provide important information as well and thus have an aspect of research. However, its immediate purpose is the good of the patient.

Scientific experiment on humans can be defined as something done to the person with the principal purpose of finding out what will happen to the person. Its primary object is the acquisition of new knowledge rather than therapy, and the fact that ultimately it may prove to be beneficial to others or even to the subject does not render it therapy. There may be a sham operation to help determine whether the real operation is of benefit.[5] Moreover, experiments are sometimes performed on healthy persons, and so could not possibly be called therapeutic. Illnesses have been induced, including malaria, typhoid fever and hepatitis. Other procedures have been carried out on healthy persons—for example, the insertion of a cardiac catheter.

The testing of new drugs furnishes another good example of the distinction between the two types of experiment. At one time the drug maker asked practicing physicians to try out the new drug on their patients. Remembering that a new drug is one that has not yet been shown to be safe and effective, this practice is neither good therapy nor good scientific experiment. It is generally agreed today that scientific testing of new drugs should take place before they are put on the market for therapeutic use. It is further agreed that some patients should receive the new drug and others should be used as "controls". The controls may receive either an accepted drug, or a "dummy" drug called a placebo, or no drug at all. This procedure leads to a better assessment of the qualities and effect of the new drug.

A common though not a universal method is to conduct "double-blind" tests. For example, of one hundred patients, fifty may receive the new drug and fifty may receive a placebo. To ensure accuracy in observation of the results, neither the investigator who is conducting the test nor the patient knows whether the patient is receiving the new drug or the placebo. After the drug has been administered and observations taken, someone, preferably a neutral person, ascertains who has received the new drug and who has received the placebo. This procedure leads to a comparatively accurate assessment of the new drug.[6]

It is sometimes said that a test making use of a placebo is therapeutic, even if double-blind. The writer has difficulty with this view. It is true that placebos can sometimes have a good psychological effect. However, in a double-blind test not even the physician administering the capsule knows whether it is the placebo or the unproven drug. In these circumstances the procedure would seem to be research rather than therapy. One might say that the borderline between the two appears to be hazy. Sometimes it is. However, the distinction must be recognized, for it is of practical importance, as we shall see.

When an American war crimes tribunal tried twenty Nazi physicians and three others for crimes against humanity in connection with "experiments" on prisoners in concentration camps, the tribunal in its judgment at Nuremberg laid down ten legal rules that, in its opinion, govern scientific experimentation. We shall have occasion to refer to some of these Nuremberg rules later.[7]

In 1964 the World Health Organization, after lengthy study, published the Helsinki Declaration which prescribes *ethical* as distinct from legal guidelines for human experimentation. This document recognizes the distinction between the two types of experiment. It sets out basic general principles and then in separate sections discusses "clinical research combined with professional care", followed by "non-therapeutic clinical research".[8] The ethical principles of the American Medical Association follow this pattern, distinguishing between clinical investigation primarily for treatment and clinical investigation primarily for the accumulation of scientific knowledge.[9] The guidelines of the Faculty of Medicine at McGill University do likewise.[10]

The purpose of the above discussion was to emphasize the distinction between the two types of experiment. It is relevant now to look at experimental therapy and to ask what the liability of a physician to his patient is when the patient is harmed because the doctor in the hope of benefiting the patient has used an experimental procedure—one that is new or at least not generally accepted. In the common law there is no automatic liability; in other words there is not a "no-experiment" rule. In the United States on the other hand there was such a rule for a long time but it has been eroded. The argument in favour of it is that it discourages reckless experimentation. The argument against it is that it deters progress. A middle ground is to permit it in the sense of not rendering the physician automatically liable if something goes wrong, but to require a high degree of care and also disclosure to the patient of the fact that the treatment is new and risky. The latter requirement is related to the concept of "informed consent" which we shall consider later. In my opinion this "middle ground" represents the common law position.[11]

Turning to article 20, what is the meaning of "experiment" as there used? It reads: "a person. . . may. . . submit to an experiment provided that the risk assumed is not disproportionate to the benefit anticipated". The Committee report states that the draft article contains a general principle "applicable to those kinds of operations performed on a person's living body which are outside of the normal context of the doctor-patient relationship". The Code Office Revision Report repeats these words and adds that the article "envisages essentially the cases where a person consents to submit to an incursion upon his physical integrity without himself directly benefiting from what may result"; and both reports say in slightly different words that since such infringements are highly exceptional they may only be permitted to take place if certain special conditions are met. Thus "experiment" in article 20 would seem to refer to scientific or non-therapeutic experiments.

The article permits a person to submit to experiments provided that the "risk assumed is not disproportionate to the hoped for benefit". It seems clear that the appraisal of risk and benefit must be determined at the time rather than subsequently. The language raises the question of what is meant by "benefit". Since in the writer's opinion, the article applies to scientific experimentation, it follows that "benefit" means future benefit to persons other than the one submitting to the experiment.

The problem of weighing benefit against risk is inherently difficult. The anticipated benefit may be great, or it may be slight; the likelihood of achieving the benefit may be high, or it may be remote. On the other hand the risk may be great or it may be slight.

The weighing of risk versus benefit is of course an understandable approach to take, and it is found in various ethical codes. For example, the Helsinki Declaration states that "clinical research cannot legitimately be carried out unless the importance of the objective is in proportion to the inherent risk to the subject". Dr H.K. Beecher in his own Code argues that:

> . . . the gain anticipated from an experiment must be commensurate with the risk involved. Sometimes large risks are to be taken for large gains, but such risks should be taken in almost all cases only when the patient promises to profit directly from the risk involved in needed therapy.[12]

In view of the difficulty in weighing risk against benefit, I would suggest, with some diffidence, that it might have been preferable had article 20 merely said "provided there is no serious risk to his health". In extending article 20 to minors capable of discernment, the Legislature abandoned a risk-benefit criterion and simply permitted the minor to consent "provided that no serious risk to his health results therefrom".

Informed Consent

Article 20 provides that a person may *submit* to an experiment. It does not use the word "consent" as it does in connection with *inter vivos* gifts of a part of the body. I infer, however, that the intent is to require a consent of the same type that is necessary in connection with *inter vivos* gifts. This being so, the question then arises of the amount of information that must be given to the volunteer concerning the nature of the experiment and the attendant risks. It is commonly said that there must be an *informed* consent, which I take to be similar to "le consentement librement donné" or "la volonté librement exprimée"[13] or "le consentement éclairé".[14] This concept probably has produced more discussion than any other topic in connection with human experimentation, and indeed is much to the fore in connection with therapeutic treatment.[15]

When a physician advises his patient about a proposed treatment, must he disclose the risks, so that if he fails so to do, the consent will be ineffective and the patient can say that the physician acted without consent? The physician or surgeon must explain the risks to enable the patient to exercise an intelligent judgment on whether to elect to proceed. In Canada the few cases dealing with this subject allow the physician a wide scope in exercising his judgment, bearing in mind the desirability of not upsetting the patient. The two leading cases are from the Ontario Court of Appeal. In *Kenny* v. *Lockwood*[16] it was argued that the surgeon had not explained the risk of stiffness resulting from an operation on the hand. A prominent surgeon, Dr Gallie, testifying as an expert witness, said that if he outlined every risk, including remote ones, some of which were rather frightening, the patients would decline the operation and would damage themselves by waiting to see what would happen without the operation. The court held that the defendants were not liable for failure to disclose the risks. In the second case, *Male* v. *Hopmans,*[17] the patient was treated with neomycin although it was known that this drug could affect the hearing. The patient did in fact become deaf. One of his allegations of negligence was that the defendant had failed to disclose this risk. The alternative treatments were very complicated and the court held that the defendant was under no duty to explain them. It was said that the patient probably could not have grasped the explanation or made an intelligent choice.

In an English case, *Hatcher* v. *Black,*[18] the operation was for a toxic goitre. There was in fact a risk to the voice, and the surgeon admitted that he had told the patient that there was no risk. In summing up to the jury, Denning, L.J. (as he then was) directed the jury that the little white lie was justifiable. This decision is not consistent with the view of the New Zealand Court of Appeal in *Smith* v. *Auckland Hospital Board.*[19] In that case the patient specifically asked the surgeon whether there was any risk in a diagnostic procedure called aortography. The surgeon replied that there was none. In fact there was a known risk of loss of circulation which could cause gangrene in a leg and require amputation. This risk materialized. The court found a breach of duty. The difficulty was whether the untruthful answer caused the loss of the leg, for one can only conjecture whether the patient would have rejected the procedure had he been told the truth. The court held that there was evidence on which the jury could find a causal connection between the answer and the loss of the leg.

There has been a difference of opinion on whether, assuming an absence of informed consent, the patient's action is based on negligence or assault. In the *Smith* case the claim was based on negligence. It is submitted that this is the proper basis, though some courts take the view that an uninformed consent is no consent, with the result that the operation is an assault.[20] In the United States the concept of informed consent "has achieved a status in the law of medical practice unmatched both in speed of growth and bulk of commentary".[21] A leading case, *Natanson* v. *Kline,*[22] is consistent with the cases just discussed, though in the United States there may be a greater readiness to find that consent is not informed. At least some members of the medical profession are concerned about the difficulty in achieving informed consent. They feel obliged to show the patient a document that tries to explain the procedure with clarity and the risks with candor; the consequence may be that the patient is confused or frightened or both.[23]

Whatever the duty to explain risks in connection with medical treatment, there is no doubt that in scientific experimentation the duty is very high; and if the disclosure is not made the consent is not an informed consent and therefore is ineffective. The first rule of the Nuremberg Code states that "the voluntary consent of the human subject is absolutely essential". It adds that he must have legal capacity to consent and the power of free choice to enable him to make an understanding and enlightened decision. The nature and purpose of the experiment should be made known; and the means of conducting it, and "all inconveniences and hazards reasonably to be expected; and the effects upon his health or person which may possibly come". The Helsinki Declaration provides that:

> Clinical research [which, at least for practical purposes, can be taken as synonymous with scientific experimentation] cannot be undertaken without his free consent, after he has been fully informed.

The definition of "consent" in the Regulations under the United States *Food, Drug and Cosmetic Act,* in connection with the testing of new drugs, requires the most complete disclosure.[24]

There are two important cases in connection with informed consent to scientific experimentation. The first is *Halushka* v. *The University of Saskatchewan*[25] and the other is the disciplinary proceeding in the New York cancer-cell case.[26] In *Halushka,* the investigators advertised for volunteers to take part in a study of a new anaesthetic. The fee was fifty dollars. Halushka was a university student who volunteered. The procedure called for the insertion of a catheter in an arm and on to the heart, and the giving of the general anaesthetic that was being tested. While Halushka was under the anaesthetic, he suffered a cardiac arrest. He was revived but the harm to his health was considerable. He had signed a consent form in which he said: "I understand fully what is proposed to be done." At the trial he testified that he had "skimmed through" the form and had asked what "accidents" meant, and was told it meant such things as falling down at home after the test.

It was agreed that the experiment had been well conducted. Moreover it was assumed that the anaesthetic, not the catheter, had caused the arrest. The doctors did not testify at the trial. The jury found that the plaintiff had not consented to the performance of the test that was made; that the doctors "committed a trespass" and were negligent. Of three particulars of negligence one was "lack of full explanation to the plaintiff of the test at the time of the so-called 'consent'". The defendants appealed, the main issue being the validity of the consent. The Court of Appeal held that in research the duty of explanation is at least as great as, if not greater than, that owed by a physician to his patient.

> The example of risks being properly hidden from a patient when it is important that he should not worry can have no application in the field of research. The subject of medical experimentation is entitled to a full and frank disclosure of all the facts, probabilities and opinions which a reasonable man might be expected to consider before giving his consent.[27]

One of the investigators had told Halushka that a new drug was to be tested but did not inform him that the new drug was an anaesthetic of which he had no previous knowledge, nor that there was risk involved in the use of the anaesthetic. Neither did he tell him that the catheter would be advanced to and through his heart. Halushka said he was given to understand that it would be merely inserted in the vein in his arm.

> While it may be correct to say that the advancement of the catheter to the heart was not in itself dangerous and did not cause or contribute to the cause of the cardiac arrest, it was a circumstance which, if known, might very well have prompted the respondent to withhold his consent.[28]

It will be noted that in this case the basis of the judgment was that of trespass, or assault, though the jury found negligence as well.

In the New York cancer-cell case,[29] a physician distinguished in cancer research was carrying out a proper and important investigation to determine how quickly the human body rejects implanted cancer cells. The experiment had been carried out on a group of healthy persons (inmates in a prison) who rejected the cells quickly, and then on persons with advanced cancer who rejected them slowly. It then was proper to try to determine whether the slower rejection in the cancer patients was because of their cancer or merely because they were seriously ill. A New York hospital for the chronically ill agreed to provide patients for this purpose. Cells were implanted in a number of patients. They were not told that this was being done. There was no informed consent, and in some cases real consent was impossible because of the patient's state of health or the language barrier. Disciplinary proceedings were brought, on charges of fraud and unprofessional conduct. After extensive hearings the New York Board of Regents upheld its committees' findings that the charges were established. One basis was failure to obtain proper informed consent.

Few would deny that the investigator should be candid. In the cancer-cell case he justified his nondisclosure by saying that he did not want to disturb the patients. This is understandable in therapy, but the fact that patients would be disturbed is the very reason for forbidding the experiment in the absence of consent obtained after explanation.

There are difficulties in connection with the securing of informed consent. Known risks can be explained, but as Dr Beecher has said: "frequently the difficulty is that no one knows what the risks or the benefits really will be".[30] Then there is the question of communication. Some explanations are in technical language, and even where they are simplified, it is hard to be sure that the volunteer understands them.

Article 20 does not specifically require informed consent. However the Committee recognized that informed consent is essential:

> . . . according to the general law of contract, the person of major age must be sane, free and capable of understanding the consequences of his act. The doctor or experimentalist has, moreover, the duty to inform him adequately of the effects and dangers to which the gift or experiment may give rise.

Consent by a Minor Endowed with Discernment

It will be recalled that the Committee had recommended that a person submitting to an experiment must be an adult. At that time the age of majority was still twenty-one, though the Committee doubtless knew it would soon be reduced to eighteen.[31] When the Revision Office made its own report, it had received suggestions that the age limit should be moved downward to include minors "endowed with discernment" subject to two safeguards—parental consent and absence of serious risk. This recommendation went forward to the Legislature which adopted it with a further safeguard, namely, the consent of a judge of the Superior Court. What is the age of discernment? In the common law provinces one speaks of a child of tender years, and indeed Parliament has done so in connection with the testimony of children.[32] It may be that a child beyond tender years is the same as a child endowed with discernment. Neither term is precise.

It might help to look at the common law to see when it permits a person to give his own consent to medical treatment. One recent American work states that:

> The general rule is that parents or guardians must consent to treatment on minors. . . . In some instances, however, a minor approaching majority may give a valid consent if he fully appreciates the nature and the consequences of his act.[33]

In the writer's opinion, the common law of England and Canada permits a minor approaching majority to give his own consent. Lord Nathan, writing in 1957 at a time when the age of majority in England was still twenty-one, said:

> It is submitted therefore that there is no rigid rule of law that an infant is incapable of consenting to the administration of medical treatment.[34]

and later:

> It is suggested that the most satisfactory solution of the problem is to rule that an infant who is capable of appreciating fully the nature and consequences of a particular operation or a particular treatment can give an effective consent thereto, and in such cases the consent of the guardian is unnecessary...

In England the *Family Law Reform Act,* 1969, reduced the age of majority to eighteen. However, it included a special section to provide that a minor who has attained the age of sixteen years may give effective consent to medical treatment.[35]

In Canada most provinces have reduced the age of majority but none has yet passed legislation dealing with the age of consent for medical treatment. There is, however, a recent case in the Ontario High Court holding that a twenty-year-old could give his own consent to treatment for facial scars. This was at a time when Ontario's age of majority was still twenty-one. The court specifically accepted Lord Nathan's statement of the law.[36]

If the common law has been in some doubt on the minimum age of consent to medical treatment, it is still more uncertain in connection with the right of a minor to consent to experimentation on himself. An expression of opinion can be little more than a description of what one thinks the law should be. When the age of majority was twenty-one, the writer expressed the opinion that a mature minor might give a valid consent to submit to scientific experiment.[37] Now that it is eighteen in most provinces, the more mature minor of the past is now an adult and the question could only arise in connection with a person of seventeen years of age or younger. I shall not attempt a prediction here. The problem arises again in connection with the capacity of a minor to donate an organ such as a kidney, which will be discussed below.

Quebec's provision is not clear on the lower limit of consent, just as is the common law. However, Quebec has reduced the risk of abuse by the safeguards that article 20 has placed around experimentation on the minor of the age of discernment.

The Minor Below the Age of Discernment

Article 20 does not cover experiments on children below the age of discernment. The inference is that they are forbidden. Does this mean that Quebec law completely forbids scientific experiments on children? Does the child have a cause of action if he has been the subject of an experiment? Does he have to prove damage? The writer cannot even guess the answers to these questions in Quebec law. It is relevant however to look generally at the question of non-therapeutic experiments on children. Sharp differences of opinion exist on the propriety of using children for research, or at least of exposing them to risk. A strict no-experiment rule would not be realistic. As one British writer pointed out, there are experiments such as a minor change in diet or clothing that could not possibly be harmful.[38]

What of procedures that bear a risk of injury to the child? They might either be forbidden or else might be permissible with the informed consent of the parent or guardian. The legal position is uncertain and ethical opinion is far from unanimous. I shall refer first to a number of statements that say or imply that there should be no experimentation on persons who cannot give their own consent, and then to a number that treat it as permissible with the consent of parent or guardian.

In the Nuremberg judgment, the first rule flatly says that "the person involved should have legal capacity to give consent". Further, article 7 of the United Nations' International Covenant on Civil and Political Rights provides that:

> No one shall be subjected to torture or to cruel, inhuman or degrading treatment or punishment. In particular, no one shall be subjected without his free consent to medical or scientific experimentation.

The first sentence of course has its origin in the English Bill of Rights of 1688 and the Eighth Amendment to the United States Constitution. Although it might seem strange to link experimentation with cruel and inhuman punishment, those who framed this article doubtless had in mind the actions of the Nazi doctors. Thus the article treats medical or scientific experimentation that is conducted without the subject's free consent as cruel, inhuman or degrading treatment.[39]

The British Medical Research Council in its 1963 statement on Responsibility in Investigations on Human Subjects stated:

> The situation in respect to minors and mentally subnormal or mentally disordered persons is of particular difficulty. In the strict view of the [English] law parents and guardians of minors cannot give consent on their behalf to any procedures which are of no particular benefit to them and which may carry some risk of harm. Whilst English law does not fix any arbitrary age in this context, it may safely be assumed that the Courts will not regard a child of 12 years or under (or 14 years or under for boys in Scotland) as having the capacity to consent to any procedure which may involve him in an injury.[40]

An American writer has recently said:

> I do not myself believe that there is such a thing as legitimate third-party consent for children or other incompetents to enter without their wills into research that is not even remotely in their behalf medically.[41]

In the same vein, Warren E. Burger, now Chief Justice of the United States, has stated that "no *adult* has the legal power to consent to experiments on an infant unless the treatment is for the benefit of the *infant*".[42]

Contrariwise, the following statements approve of non-therapeutic experimentation on those who are incompetent to give their own consent including children.

The Helsinki Declaration says: "if he is legally incompetent the consent of the legal guardian should be procured". This implies that the consent will render the experiment ethically proper.

The 1966 guidelines of the American Medical Association provide in paragraph 4(c) that:

> Minors or mentally incompetent persons may be used as subjects [in non-therapeutic situations primarily for the accumulation of scientific knowledge] only if:
> i. The nature of the investigation is such that mentally competent adults would not be suitable subjects.
> ii. Consent, in writing, is given by a legally authorized representative of the subject under circumstances in which an informed and prudent adult would reasonably be expected to volunteer himself or his child as a subject.[43]

An American case that has relevance to this question is *Bonner* v. *Moran*.[44] A fifteen-year old boy donated skin without obtaining his mother's consent. His action against the physician failed at trial but the Federal Court of Appeals directed a new trial because the judge had declined to direct the jury that the mother's consent was necessary. The court held that it was and that a minor could not give an effective consent to this type of procedure. The court was not prepared to make an exception for any minor, for the operation was not for his benefit. The significant point in the judgment, however, is the inference by the court that the mother's consent would prevent any recovery by her son. This is the point of principle on which I disagree.

This does not mean that experimentation on children is always unethical. As Dr Beecher states:

> Parents still have the right to decide whether their children will participate in experimentation, even if not for their direct benefit, provided the studies contemplated have no discernable risk and have been approved by a high level review committee as necessary and valuable for human progress and do not unfairly take advantage of the child.

and

> Research that entails discernable risk may not be performed on subjects too young to give mature and informed consent, unless for their direct benefit.[45]

In spite of the fact that the researcher scrupulously follows these guidelines, the child may still be injured in the course of the experiment. The position I have taken permits him to bring an action against the researcher. In other words the parents' consent and any release they give are not binding on the child. Some may object that a procedure that is ethical should never expose the researcher to legal liability, at least in the absence of negligence, and that my proposal will discourage needed research. It is suggested, however, that this position avoids the extreme of a rigid "no experiment on children" rule, and the opposite extreme of permitting a parent to bar his child from claiming damages for harm from a non-therapeutic intervention. If guidelines like Dr Beecher's are followed the risk of harm is slight; but if it materializes the loss should not fall on the child.

The problems just discussed in relation to children are similar to those which arise in connection with the mentally incompetent. Article 20 by inference excludes experimentation on adults who cannot give their own consent. On this issue the common law is no more settled than it is in the case of children. The need to conduct research and yet to show respect for the individual is just as great as in the case of children.[46]

Experimentation with "Captive Subjects"[47]

The last point to be mentioned about consent to experimentation relates to the use of persons who are adults of sound mind but who may nevertheless be thought to be under some form of constraint so that their consent is not truly voluntary. In the United States prisoners in jails are frequently used in experiments.[48] They may be subject to affirmative pressure that is explicit or, more likely, implicit. Some pressure is perhaps inherent in the status of the prisoner, no matter how much the researcher tries to secure a truly voluntary consent. The question is whether the risk of coercion can only be prevented by excluding the use of prisoners completely. A recent statement commends itself to the writer:

> I am one who happens to believe that prisoners have not been and should not be drummed out of the human race. They ought, therefore, not to be excluded in principle from the community of risk-filled human consent to good purposes, even if the needed practical protections for them are so formidable as to prohibit the general use of prisoners in medical research.[49]

Other groups of whom advantage may be taken are students, employees, and those in the armed services. I do not think one can say that they should all be automatically excluded, but it is clear that special care must be taken to avoid coercion. The reports that produced article 20 do not refer to this problem.

Inter Vivos Gifts of Tissue[50]

Article 20 permits a person of full age to make a gift of part of his body. As we have seen, the implication is that he must be of sound mind. There is no provision for consent by a guardian of a mental incompetent. A minor endowed with discernment may likewise make such a gift subject to the consent of his guardian and of the Superior Court, and provided that there is no serious risk.

Article 20 does not permit a person to be a donor if he is below the age of discernment. What does the common law permit? The answer is not clear. However, there have been cases in the United States of donations of a kidney by a minor or a mental incompetent. These cases show how the law is developing in that country.

The first kidney transplants were performed in a Boston hospital in 1954. The parties were adult identical twins. Two years later the same hospital had three more cases of identical twins. However, one set was nineteen years of age and the other two were fourteen. There was no special problem concerning the recipients, for the parents had power to consent to the operation as in the case of any medical treatment for a child. A serious question arose, however, about whether the hospital could rely on the parents' consent on behalf of the donor. The hospital's solicitors gave an opinion that the parent "has no power to give effective consent to an operation which is both hazardous and personally detrimental to this child".[51] In each case the parents then brought a petition in the Supreme Judicial Court of Massachusetts. The three petitions were heard by three different judges. In each case the court held that it had jurisdiction and gave an order approving the transplant. In all these cases the donor was intelligent and received a candid explanation and gave consent. The psychiatric evidence was to the effect that there would be a beneficial emotional result to the donor if he were permitted to give the kidney to his brother. The court accepted this, finding that if the operation were not performed and the sick twin were to die, there was a danger "of serious emotional impact" upon the healthy twin; that because the risk of emotional disturbance would be reduced and the donor enabled to have the continued companionship of his twin, the donor would benefit; and that the operation was necessary to the donor's future welfare and happiness.[52]

It is relevant to note here the comments of Professor W.J. Curran: (1) on the facts the court might have held that each donor was capable of giving his own consent; (2) the "psychological benefit" to the donor is rather "the prevention of possible detriment than it is the conferring of a positive gain".[53]

In a 1969 case from Kentucky, *Strunk* v. *Strunk,*[54] the sick brother, Tom, was twenty-eight years old. The healthy brother, Jerry, was twenty-seven and an inmate of a state institution for the feeble-minded with the I.Q. of a six-year old. He was the only member of the family who was medically acceptable as a donor. The mother applied to the court for authority to proceed. The court gave the order "because Jerry was greatly dependent upon Tommy, emotionally and psychologically, and... his well-being would be jeopardized more severely by the loss of his brother than by the removal of his kidney".[55] An appeal was taken on behalf of Jerry to the circuit court which upheld the original judgment, and then a further appeal was taken to the Court of Appeal. That court upheld the order by a majority of four to three. The prevailing judgment relied on the opinion of the State Department of Health that the sick brother's life was vital to Jerry's well-being and that the Department "must take all possible steps to prevent the occurrence of any ill feelings Jerry would have if Tom were to die";[56] and it held that a court of equity has inherent jurisdiction to take action to protect the mentally incompetent.

The dissenting judgment of Steinfeld, J. points up the issue. The first and last paragraphs of the dissent are as follows:

> Apparently because of my indelible recollection of a government which, to the everlasting shame of its citizens, embarked on a program of genocide and experimentation with human bodies I have been more troubled in reaching a decision in this case than in any other. My sympathies and emotions are torn between a compassion to aid an ailing young man and a duty to fully protect unfortunate members of society.
>
> I am unwilling to hold that the gates should be open to permit the removal of an organ from an incompetent for transplant, at least until such time as it is conclusively demonstrated that it will be of significant benefit to the incompetent. The evidence here does not rise to that pinnacle. To hold that committees, guardians or courts have such awesome power even in the persuasive case before us, could establish legal precedents, the dire result of which we cannot fathom. Regretfully I must say no.[57]

The latest case is *Hart* v. *Brown,*[58] from Connecticut. Again there is an important difference in the facts. The child who required the transplant was just under eight years old and the prospective donor was her identical twin. The parents requested the operation. Without the transplant the sick twin would probably not have survived, and a transplant from the identical twin was more likely to succeed than one from anyone else. A psychiatrist testified that a successful operation would be of immense benefit to the donor "in that the donor would be better off in a family that was happy than in a family that was distressed and that it would be a very great loss to the donor if the donee were to die from her illness." The court held this evidence to be of "limited value", but did attach weight to the opinion of a clergyman that the parents' decision to consent was morally sound. The court held that the parents were entitled to substitute their consent for that of their minor children; and "to prohibit the natural parents and the guardians *ad litem* of the minor children the right to give their consent under those circumstances, where there is supervision by this court and other persons in examining their judgment, would be unjust, inequitable and injudicious".[59] The order was granted.

How would article 20 apply to the three cases we have just described? In the case of the nineteen-year-old twins, they would now be adults in Quebec and so the donor could decide for himself. What about the fourteen-year-old twins? Are they capable of discernment? In the Massachusetts judgment the court said of the donor: "He is a boy of fourteen with good understanding and intelligence. He has been fully informed of and understands the nature of the operation and its possible risks and consequences." This seems to mean that the donor was capable of discernment. Of course the judge in deciding whether to give consent would look carefully into the donor's capacity, as did the Massachusetts court. The difficulty in fixing a minimum age is shown by the difference of opinion at a discussion of kidney transplants. The opinions range from complete prohibition of donations by infants down to permitting them at the age of twelve or thirteen.[60]

The question of risk of harm would also have to be considered. It appears that in the case of a healthy donor this risk is not substantial.[61]

Under article 20 the Strunk donation would not have been permitted because the donor was mentally incompetent and could not give a valid consent. The result would be the same in *Hart* v. *Brown,* because the donor was under eight years of age and by no stretch of the imagination could be said to be "capable of discernment".

Should the law permit the transplant on the facts of *Strunk* and of *Hart* v. *Brown?*

It is submitted that in general persons incapable of making up their own mind should not be subject to harmful procedures that have no therapeutic value for them. It seems somewhat specious to find therapeutic value to the donor in the psychological prevention of harm to him, as was done in the Boston cases. The situation that is most troubling is that of the eight-year old identical twins. The likelihood of saving one twin's life is great and the physical risks to the other twin are not very great. Besides the parents strongly favour the transplant. Should the law permit the donation even on these facts?

Notwithstanding the forceful judgment in *Hart* v. *Brown,* I think not. The taking of the kidney from the healthy twin means that his body has less inviolability than that of anyone else. I think that this is what Lord Kilbrandon had in mind when he asked the question: "What is the ethical basis for a doctor respecting the prejudices of parents if he is convinced that they are inimical to the welfare of the child?" and when he commented that identical twins are two personalities.[62]

Inter Vivos Gifts under the Uniform Human Tissue Act

In the common law provinces there was until recently no legislation governing *inter vivos* gifts of human tissue. By 1970 a committee of the Medico-Legal Society of Toronto had studied this subject and prepared a draft Act. It came before the Conference of Commissioners on Uniformity of Legislation in Canada the same year. That body adopted it as Part One of a revised *Human Tissue Act.*[63] (The original *Uniform Human Tissue Act* of 1965 dealt only with gifts of cadavers which I shall discuss below.) The Uniform Act was amended in 1971 and re-named the *Human Tissue Gift Act,*[64] but Part One was unchanged.[65] The essential provision is section 3(1):

> Any person who has attained the age of majority, is mentally competent to consent, and is able to make a free and informed decision may in a writing signed by him consent to the removal forthwith from his body of the tissue

specified in the consent and its implantation in the body of another living person.

This has much in common with article 20. The donor must be of age, though a later provision validates the consent of a minor where there was no reason to believe that he was not an adult capable of consent. The requirement of writing is present and it will be noted that the phrase "free and informed decision" is used.

One feature of the Act is that tissue is defined to exclude "tissue that is replaceable by natural processes of repair". This seems synonymous with "regenerative tissue" and the result is that Part One is confined to non-regenerative tissue like kidneys. This reduces the scope of Part One and raises the question whether gifts from minors of skin, bone, or blood are by inference prohibited or whether they are permitted and not circumscribed by the safeguards of Part One. Probably it is the latter for section 10 in Part Three forbids the *sale* of tissue or of any part of the body except blood. This implies that parts of the body other than tissue may be *given*.

Three provinces have passed the Revised Uniform Act.[66] It is likely that most of the others will soon enact it.

The Sale of Blood

The Quebec Committee had taken the firm position that no part of the body should be an article of commerce. "The human body cannot be made a marketable commodity or the object of commercial dealing." And again: "Nor would it be desirable to treat human blood, or any other renewable human tissue differently from other parts of the body. It is not readily obvious why, for example, blood should exceptionally be admitted as the object of a sale or a business." Then follows a quotation from Professor Savatier who said that the human body should not be given for money but can be given for love. The Code Revision Office supported this view. "The gratuitousness of the act is essential. The human body cannot become merchandise, an object of commercial transactions."

However, the Legislature must have been persuaded that it is proper to permit the sale of regenerative tissue, for article 20 provides that "the alienation must be gratuitous unless its object is a part of the body susceptible of regeneration". This means that sale of skin or bone, as well as blood, is permitted. There is a similar provision in the *Revised Uniform Human Tissue Gift Act,* 1971.[67] Section 10 of that Act forbids the sale of any part of the body but makes an exception for blood. This is somewhat narrower than Quebec's exception, for the latter includes all regenerative tissue.

Should the sale of regenerative tissue, or even of blood alone, be permitted by law? Perhaps the issue can be stated with reference to a book by Richard Titmuss. Under the cryptic title, *The Gift Relationship,*[68] this book states in a most persuasive way the case for true donations as distinct from sale of blood. There are two main arguments. The first is that the quality of blood or blood product is better. People who come off the street to sell their blood are often derelicts who conceal their medical history and in whom the incidence of such conditions as hepatitis is higher than it is in donors who contribute gratuitously through organizations like the Canadian Red Cross. The second argument is a moral one, that it is healthier for society if its members take an altruistic interest in helping others. This is the gift relationship in the title of the book.

In the United States commercial blood banks are commonplace. Mr Titmuss estimates that they account for almost half of the blood taken from humans. In Canada the Canadian Red Cross Society collected blood from volunteers in World War II for the use of the armed forces. Near the end of the war, hospital associations and provincial Departments of Health asked the Society to continue the service in peace time. Thus a national system, now called the Canadian Red Cross Blood Transfusion Service, came into being. It relies on donors, and the public has supported it. It is "as complete as any in its development and scope. It is said to be unique among similar services in the world."[69] It is disappointing to a Canadian that Mr Titmuss in his thorough examination of transfusion systems throughout the world, makes no mention of Canada, for the writer's impression is that our system meets the ideal of Mr Titmuss as closely as any in the world.

The question remains, however, should blood *ever* be sold? In Edmonton and northern Alberta in 1972 the Red Cross collected 45,408 units of blood, all donated. In addition, however, there is a special program involving a small number of people, less than twenty in number, who have unusual blood that is valuable in the production of serum. It is only the plasma that is needed and the procedure is called plasmapheresis. The donors spend about three hours at a time to go through the process. These people receive an honorarium. The burden on the donors is such that this compensation seems reasonable and a justifiable exception to the principle of donations.

Another reason sometimes given for permitting the sale of blood in Canada is the possibility of a major disaster that would create an urgent and heavy demand that could only be met by the purchase of blood.

The writer's view is that it would be preferable, contrary to article 20 and the Uniform Act, to forbid the sale of any human tissue with an exception for the Red Cross program of plasmapheresis.[70] If an emergency occurs, the public can be counted on to respond.

Gifts of Cadavers: Autopsies[71]

It will be noted that article 20 deals with two of our main topics, experiments and *inter vivos* gifts, whereas article 21 provides for gifts of cadavers, in whole or in part. Article 22 permits the taking of parts of a cadaver with the consent of the spouse or next of kin, and without that consent in urgent cases to save life. Article 23 provides for autopsies. We shall now examine articles 21–23.

Article 21 provides:

> A person of full age may, in writing, determine the nature of his funeral and the disposal of his remains.
>
> A minor, capable of discernment, may do likewise with the consent of the person having the paternal authority.
>
> The consent must be in writing; it may be revoked in the same way.
>
> In the absence of instructions by the deceased, usage is followed.

It combines the Committee's recommendations two and three. The former is unchanged but the latter, which had listed the persons who in the absence of instructions by the deceased, could decide on the funeral and the disposal of the remains, is replaced by the simple provision that "usage is followed".

The report of the Committee and that of the Revision Office say that the first paragraph:

> . . . states a recognized principle of the civil law. It gives to the person of major age the right to specify in advance the ceremonies to take place after his death, as well as that to decide the manner in which his body will finally be disposed of (for example, by burial, cremation or otherwise). This provision is also intended to cover the gift of the whole or of a part of the cadaver for therapeutic or other legitimate purposes.

In other words this brief article confers on a person two important powers: to make binding provisions for his funeral and to make a gift of all or a part of his body after death. In a common law jurisdiction I doubt that the brief first paragraph of article 21 would be adequate to confer authority on a person to donate an organ for therapeutic or scientific purposes. It is clear, however, that the Code Revision Office is satisfied that it is sufficient in Quebec.

What is the common law on these matters? No one could own a dead body and from this consequence grew the rule that a person could not himself make a binding disposition of his cadaver after death. The latter rule is a *non sequitur*. Even if a cadaver is incapable of ownership it should not follow that a living person cannot make binding directions on the disposal of his body after death. However, the rule is firmly entrenched.

It is accompanied by another rule having to do with burial. In Blackstone's words, the executor had a duty "to bury the deceased in the manner suitable to the estate which he leaves behind him".[72] This duty became converted into a right vested in the executor or the family. These rights are hard to define. For example, does the family have a cause of action when an unauthorized autopsy has been performed? An Alberta case, *Edmonds* v. *Armstrong Funeral Home,*[73] held that those responsible for the burial have certain rights over the body. From this the court went on to find that the unauthorized autopsy was an infringement of these rights. In truth the court was seeking a theory on which to found an award of compensation for the family's injured feelings. Prior to the Alberta decision, a Quebec case had reached the same result in an action by the widow.[74]

The paradoxical result of the common law rules was that the executor or members of the family of the deceased had the power of disposal of his body: he himself did not. Another weakness of the common law is that it was uncertain—or at least it seemed so to the person who wanted to dispose of the body[75] or possibly to remove an organ. He might well be in doubt about who could give him authority, and when in doubt the orddinary course is to refrain.

The English *Anatomy Act*[76] of 1832 was passed to put an end to the "stealing" of bodies from graves to sell to physicians for anatomical study. This Act enabled a person having lawful custody of a body to permit an anatomical examination. It also enabled a person in his own lifetime to direct a post-mortem examination on his body. However, this Act showed the same solicitude for the feelings of the family that the common law had shown, for it permitted the spouse or relative to require interment without such examination.[77]

It was only in recent years that the therapeutic use of any organ from a cadaver became feasible. The first tissue that could be successfully used was the cornea of the eye. It is a transparent hard substance that covers the colored portion. When it is damaged sight is affected or lost. Sight can be restored if the damaged cornea is removed and replaced by a healthy one. A cornea from a cadaver is satisfactory provided it is obtained promptly. The *Anatomy Act* did not cover such a use of any part of the body. To deal with this special situation, the British Parliament in 1952 passed the *Corneal Grafting Act*.[78] It permitted a person to request that his eyes be used after his death to restore the sight of a living person. However, the influence of the common law remained, for even with a request the Act still left the decision to the surviving spouse or near relative, who was given the power but not the obligation to authorize removal of the eyes.

The Canadian National Institute for the Blind was of course anxious to have legislation in Canada to permit gifts of corneas. In 1957 New Brunswick passed an Act[79] similar to the English one and in 1959 the Conference of Commissioners on Uniformity of Legislation in Canada adopted a Uniform Cornea Transplant Act on the same lines.[80] It was promptly adopted in most common law provinces.

By this time, it had become apparent that other parts of a cadaver could be used to aid the living. For this reason Britain in 1961 replaced the original Act by a *Human Tissue Act*.[81] It extends to all human tissue for therapeutic, educational or scientific purposes. However, it leaves the final decision to the person lawfully in charge of the body. The common law solicitude for the feelings of the family is maintained.

The Uniformity Conference made use of this Act in adopting a Uniform Human Tissue Act in 1965.[82] However, the Uniform Act took away the need for authorization by the family of the deceased where he himself had authorized the use of his body. In other words the 1965 Uniform Act puts the wishes of the deceased ahead of those of his family and makes them prevail. This might wound the sensibilities of members of the family, but the Conference thought they should give way to the wishes of the deceased. After all, his purpose is humanitarian—to assist the living.

Another change from the English Act of 1961 has to do with the case where the deceased has given no direction. The Uniform Act lists in order of priority by relationship those persons who may give consent, and puts at the bottom "the person lawfully in possession of the body".

Soon after our Uniform Human Tissue Act came into being, and about the time when several provinces were adopting it, the completion of the first heart transplants raised in acute form an issue that did not arise in connection with corneas. In heart transplants the urgency is so great that questions have arisen about whether the prospective donor might be permitted to die sooner than he otherwise would have, in order to make his heart available to someone who is near death. This has led to a widespread discussion of the question of when death occurs. This was one of the reasons why suggestions were made to the Uniformity Conference to make some revisions in the Human Tissue Act. (Another was to provide for *inter vivos* gifts, already discussed.) As a result, a revised Uniform Human Tissue Act was adopted by the Conference in 1970.[83] It underwent minor changes in 1971 including a change in name to the *Human Tissue Gift Act*.[84] For convenience I shall refer to the 1971 version. It contains several provisions that were included because of problems that arise in connection with heart transplants. For example the consent of the spouse or other member of the family does not have to await death. Section 5(1) provides that where the person "is incapable of giving a consent by reason of injury or disease and his death is imminent" the spouse or other designated person may consent. Again, there may be a case where death is imminent and the physician in charge thinks there will be a coroner's inquest. In that event, section 6 permits the coroner, notwithstanding that death has not yet occurred, to give directions for the removal of tissue. The last provision of interest is one dealing with time of death. The Conference was not prepared to define it. Section 7(1) states that "the fact of death shall be determined by at least two physicians in accordance with accepted medical practice". The remaining subsections of section 7 provide in effect that the physicians who determine the fact of death must be independent of the donor and donee except in the case of cornea transplants.

Ontario, Newfoundland and British Columbia have passed the revised Uniform Human Tissue Act either in its 1970 or 1971 form.[85]

The American Uniform Anatomical Gift Act, 1968, which has been adopted, sometimes with variations, in all States except Massachusetts and Nebraska should now be mentioned.[86] Its basic principle is that of our 1965 Uniform Act; that is to say, it gives priority to the wishes of the deceased over those of his family. Where the deceased has given no directions, the persons who may do so in order of priority are almost identical with those in our 1965 Uniform Act.

The American Act does however have some provisions of interest that are absent both from article 21 and our Uniform Act. It spells out the persons and institutions to whom the gift may be made, and provides that a donee need not be specified. In addition it deals with delivery of the document of gift, with the methods of amending or revoking the gift, and acceptance or rejection of the gift.

If legislation of this kind is to be effective, the public should know about it. They should be assisted in making gifts and the fact of the gift should be known immediately on the donor's death. The Canadian National Institute for the Blind has long provided an "eye bank card" which the donor can carry on his person. However the writer knows of no cards that are available in Canada covering parts of the body other than eyes. The American Uniform Act provides in section 4(b) that the document of gift may be a card designed to be carried on the person.

The American Act does not prescribe a form of gift, but the Uniformity Commissioners noted the usefulness of cards and the desirability of standard forms for use by the donor and by the next of kin. Indeed they prepared "suggested forms" which are set out in the note to the Uniform Act.[87] These forms are of course in conformity with the American Uniform Act. It seems to the writer that it would be helpful in Canada to have forms that could be used under the Canadian Uniform Act and under Quebec's article 21.

We have seen that the existing Acts do not define death. The State of Kansas broke new ground in 1970 in providing a definition. Its Act states that a person is dead if there is an absence of sspontaneous respiratory and cardiac function or if there is absence of spontaneous brain function; and if in the absence of brain function attempts are made to maintain or restore spontaneous circulatory or respiratory function and it appears thatt they will not succeed, death will have occurred when these conditions first coincide. There is a further provision that death is to be pronounced before artificial means are terminated and before any vital organ is removed.[88]

Returning to article 21, it is notable for its brevity. It does not attempt to define death or to refer to certification of death by a physician. Directions for disposition must be made in writing. Like the Uniform Act, it does not require testamentary form. However, there is no alternative of oral consent in the presence of at least two witnesses during the last illness, as there is in our Uniform Act.

A last comment on article 21: it permits a person to regulate the style of his funeral. The Code Revision Office Report states that the civil law had always recognized a person's right to specify in advance the ceremonies to take place after his death and whether his body will be disposed of by burial, cremation or otherwise. I know of no comparable legislation in the common law provinces. As the common law stands, at least in Canada, there is no way of enforcing the wishes of the deceased about his funeral. It would seem desirable to make effective the direction of the deceased as Quebec has done, though an enactment to that effect could not appropriately go into the Human Tissue Gift Act.[89]

Gifts by Relatives: Gifts in Emergency

Article 22 provides:

> A physician may remove a part of the remains, if in the absence of instructions by the deceased, he obtains the consent of the consort or nearest relative of the deceased.
>
> This consent is not necessary when two physicians attest in writing to the impossibility of obtaining it in due time, the urgency of the operation, and the serious hope of saving a human life.
>
> The death of the donor must be ascertained by two physicians who do not participate in any way in the removal or in the transplantation.

The first paragraph requires no comment. It is similar in purpose to the Uniform Tissue Gift Act, and simply authorizes members of the family to make a gift of part of the body where the deceased has not done so.

The second paragraph has no counterpart in any of the legislation that has been discussed. It is notable in permitting the use of part of a cadaver where consent cannot be obtained in time, and where the purpose is to save a human life. This provision doubtless contemplates heart transplants, though it applies to any part of the body.

The Committee referred to this provision as highly exceptional, and they justified it on humanitarian grounds. Solicitude for the family's wishes must give way to save a life. The Commission pointed out the moral duty to go to the assistance of another—and the taking of an organ is a form of "rescue" of the person whose life will be saved by the transplant. Once again there has been a weighing of human need against the rights of the family over the cadaver and article 22 comes down on the side of human need.

It is relevant here to note that in Britain there have been proposals to change the scheme of the *Human Tissue Act* of 1961 so as to permit the taking of organs unless the deceased had forbidden it. Lord Kilbrandon once drafted a section which he put forward for consideration:

> In any designated hospital it shall be lawful to remove from a dead person any organ required for medical or scientific purposes unless the hospital authorities have reason to believe that the deceased in his lifetime had forbidden this to be done, provided that such removal shall not disfigure the dead body.[90]

This has been called a "contracting out" provision which is the reverse of the "contracting in" provision of the Uniform Acts and article 21. For the present at least it seems that "contracting out" legislation in Britain is unlikely.[91]

It seems to the writer that the second paragraph of article 22 created an exception to the "contracting in" principle of article 21. That is to say, it permits the taking of a part of the body without consent of the person himself, or of his kin.

Autopsies

The last article is 23 C.C. which provides:

> An autopsy may be performed only in the cases provided for by law or with the written consent of the deceased.
>
> It may be required by the attending physician or by one of the persons mentioned in article 1056.

The persons mentioned in article 1056 are spouse and "ascendant and descendant relations". This excludes brothers and sisters.

When the Committee prepared the draft article it did not include the attending physician. He was added in the Code Revision Office. The article states that the physician or relations may "require" an autopsy. This would seem to imply that it must be held, though it may be that "require" means "request", which would mean that the decision remains with the coroner.

Traditionally autopsies have been linked with investigations and inquests into the cause of death where violence or foul play is suspected. The *Coroner's Act* of Quebec, like those of the common law provinces, specifically permits an autopsy in these circumstances.[92] In addition, however, there is a provision in the *Study of Anatomy Act* which deals with the case of patients dying in a public institution in which they are supported. The superintendent may order an autopsy when it is necessary to determine the cause of death.[93] In the case of the Notre Dame Hospital in Montreal its private Act was amended in 1924 to permit the attending physician or chief house physician to hold an autopsy on the non-paying patients where desirable from a scientific point of view and to establish the true cause of death.[94]

In the common law provinces the Coroner's Act invariably authorizes a post-mortem examination in connection with a coroner's investigation or inquest.[95] The three western-most provinces have, however, gone further. Saskatchewan and Alberta have similar provisions in the case where a person has died in a hospital after an operation. Either the hospital or the next of kin may request an examination, and the coroner may authorize it.[96] British Columbia's provision differs in that it applies only to a request by a hospital, not next of kin, and it specifies that the examination "may be carried out notwithstanding objection thereto by a person entitled to the custody of the body".[97]

Under Quebec's new article 23 a problem would arise when the attending physician "requires" an autopsy and the relatives object. The Act does not deal specifically with this situation. I think the inference is that the coroner could order the autopsy, but in practice he might defer to the wishes of the family. As in the case of transplants from cadavers, sensibilities are involved. Perhaps the public can be educated to accept the idea of post-mortem examinations. They add to our knowledge. At the same time those conducting the examination should try to guard against disfigurement that would cause the family distress.

Conclusion

Sometimes the relations between law and medicine are uneasy. A distinguished Australian judge has spoken of law "marching with medicine, but in the rear and limping a little".[98] To the medical profession the law is often uncertain or unduly restrictive. No lawyer would say that all of the problems that arise in experimentation and transplantation can be solved by a legal code. In safeguarding the human subject and at the same time giving proper scope for medical and scientific progress, there are many non-legal sanctions or controls. They must supplement the law, or perhaps it would be better to say the law should supplement them.

The most obvious of these controls is the ethical code. It does not provide an automatic solution to every problem. However, it is a healthy reminder to the investigator to be solicitous of the person who has submitted to the experiment. An ethical code is not to be read the way Mr Justice Holmes' bad man looked at the law—how far can I go without getting into trouble? It prescribes a minimum of proper conduct, not a maximum, and it encourages one to keep above the borderline.

Another instrument to protect the volunteer is the research committee. It now exists in many institutions;[99] indeed the United States Department of Health, Education and Welfare will make grants only to institutions having one.[100] This committee sets guidelines, and either by itself or through subcommittees reviews each application and approves, rejects or modifies it. Sometimes researchers object to this procedure in the name of academic or scientific freedom. Assuming wisdom and common sense, these committees are in my opinion helpful and the opposition in the name of academic freedom is untenable.

Another sanction that some favour is to persuade professional journals not to publish the results of research unless it is made "unmistakably clear in the publication that the proprieties have been observed".[101]

It is also suggested in discussions of ethics (legal as well as medical) that the most important factor is the character of the members of the profession. Dr Beecher has put emphasis on the prime importance of "an intelligent, informed, conscientious, compassionate, responsible investigator".[102]

These controls should not be regarded as alternatives. Each has its place and reinforces the other. The more effective they are, the less need for legal sanctions.

These observations have had reference to experimentation but to a considerable extent they are applicable to transplants.

A final word in connection with Quebec's provisions: the common law has tended to resist codification whereas a Civil Code like Quebec's is designed to cover the whole body of law. In times of quick development there is a temptation to codify too soon, but on the other hand it is no credit to the law and is frustrating to the medical and legal practitioner if it is uncertain and hard to find. Quebec's new articles are easy to find and remove much, though not all, uncertainty.

One cannot always foresee how any new legislation will work. However, Quebec's new articles have the virtue of stating the main principles without going into undue detail. Moreover, it is manifest from the Report of the Committee and the Code Revision Office that the framers not only have a knowledge of the subject but a compassionate and humanitarian attitude. It is no coincidence that these articles follow immediately articles 18 and 19 which declare the personality and inviolability of every human.[103]

Notes

1 Crépeau, *Centenaire du Code Civil du Québec, (1966) 44 Can. Bar Rev. 389; Baudouin, Le Code Civil Québecois: Crise de Croissance ou Crise de Vieillesse,* (1966) 44 Can. Bar Rev. 391.

2 S.Q. 1971, c.84. This statute includes also new articles 18 and 19, which the Code Revision Office recommended along with articles 20–23. Article 18 confers legal personality on every person and article 19 says: The human person is inviolable. No one may cause harm to the person of another without his consent or without being authorized by law to do so.

3 Of the huge volume of literature since World War II the following texts are both recent and most helpful:

Katz, *Experimentation with Human Beings* (1971).

Freund (ed.), *Experimentation with Human Subjects* (1970), being a revision of *Daedalus,* Spring, 1969, "Ethical Aspects of Experimentation with Human Subjects".

Annals of the New York Academy of Sciences, "New Dimensions in Legal and Ethical Concepts for Human Research" (1970).

Beecher, *Research and the Individual: Human Studies* (1970).

Pappworth, *Human Guinea Pigs* (1967).

The foregoing are all American except Pappworth, which is English. I know of no Canadian text.

Two articles are:

Waddams, *Medical Experiments on Human Subjects,* (1967) 25 U. of T. Faculty Law Rev. 25.

Bowker, *Legal Liability to Volunteers in Testing New Drugs,* (1963) 88 C.M.A.J. 745.

4 21 U.S.C.A. (1972), s.355(i), 471–72.

5 Beecher, *Surgery as Placebo,* (1961) 176 J.A.M.A. 1102, quoted in Katz, *supra,* 686–7.

6 There may be cases where administration of a drug to patients for the first time and without the use of controls is unquestionably proper. The first patients to whom insulin was given would have died and they were eager to receive the drug: see *Reminiscences on the Discovery of Insulin,* (1962) 87 C.M.A.J. 1045. In the testing of Salk vaccine on hundreds of thousands of children throughout the United States, a difference of opinion arose on whether double-blind tests were necessary. In the result, some were double-blind and in the others, the controls were children who received nothing: see Carter, *Breakthrough: The Saga of Jonas Salk* (1966), ch. 10.

7 They are set out in Beecher, *supra,* 227 and in Waddams, *supra,* 52. For an account of the trials, see Mitscherlich and Mielke, *The Death Doctors* (1962); and Katz, *supra,* 293–306.

8 Beecher, *supra,* 277; Waddams, *supra,* 53.
9 Beecher, *supra,* 222.
10 Notes for the Guidance of Faculty Members doing Clinical Research, 10 Feb. 1967.
11 See Bowker, *supra,* 745–46; Katz, *supra,* 526–29.
12 Beecher, *supra,* 290.
13 Baudouin, *La personne humaine au centre du droit québecois,* (1966) 26 R. du B. 66, 67–68.
14 Mazeaud, *Les contrats sur le corps humain,* (1956) 16 R. du B. 157, 167.
15 Katz, *supra,* devotes the whole of Part 3 to the authority of the subject as guardian of his own fate, 523–724. This Part consists of three chapters of material on informed consent.
16 [1932] 1 D.L.R. 507 (Ont. C.A.).
17 (1966), 54 D.L.R. (2d) 502, and on appeal (1967), 64 D.L.R. (2d) 105, 113. The defendant was held liable on another ground.
18 *The Times,* July 2 1954; quoted in Nathan, *Medical Negligence* (1957), 54.
19 [1965] N.Z.L.R. 191, rev'g [1964] N.Z.L.R. 241.
20 Plante, *An Analysis of "Informed Consent",* (1967–68) 36 Fordham L. Rev. 639.
21 Waltz and Scheuneman, *Informed Consent to Therapy,* (1969–70) 64 N.W. L.Rev. 628.
22 350 P. 2d 1093 (1960) (Kan. S.C.).
23 Cf. Oppenheim, *Informed Consent to Medical Treatment,* (1962) 11 Cleve.-Mar. L.R. 249, 261–4; and Irwin, "Now Mrs. Blare, About the Complications" in Katz, *supra,* 393. On the other hand, cf. Glass, *Restructuring Informed Consent,* (1970) 79 Yale L.J. 533 says that the law on informed consent should be reshaped to give more consideration to the patient's viewpoint.
24 F.R. (1967) 8753 in Katz, *supra,* 573–4.
25 (1965), 53 D.L.R. (2d) 436 (Sask. C.A.).
26 The Jewish Chronic Disease Hospital Case, *Disciplinary Proceedings,* reported in Katz, *supra,* ch. 1. Proceedings by a director of the hospital against the hospital to compel disclosure of its records in connection with the experiment are reported in *Hyman* v. *Jewish Chronic Disease Hospital,* 248 N.Y.S. 2d 245, on appeal 21 App. Div. 2d 495, 251 N.Y.S. 2d 818 (1964), final appeal N.Y. 2d 317, 206 N.E. 2d 338 (1965).
27 (1965) 53 D.L.R. (2d) 436, 444.
28 *Ibid.,* 444–5.
29 *Supra,* f.n. 26.
30 Beecher, *supra,* 20. See also Bowker, *supra,* 747 for a similar statement.
31 S.Q. 1971, c.85, ss.3 and 4, amending articles 246 and 324 of the Civil Code.
32 *Canada Evidence Act,* R.S.C. 1970, c.E-10, s.16(1); cf. also the *Juvenile Delinquents Act,* R.S.C. 1970, c.J-3, s.19.
33 Curran and Shapiro, *Law, Medicine and Forensic Science,* 2d ed. (1970), 574–5.
34 Nathan, *supra,* 174–176.
35 1969, 17 and 18 Eliz. II, c.46, s.8.
36 *Johnston* v. *Wellesley Hospital* (1971), 17 D.L.R. (3d) 139 (Ont. H.C.).
37 Bowker, *supra,* 748.
38 Mitchell, *The Child and Experimental Medicine,* (1964) 1 B.M.J. 721.
39 Beecher, *supra,* 247 sets out amendments submitted, issues discussed and the voting on article 7.
40 Quoted in Beecher, *supra,* 265.
41 Ramsay, *The Ethics of a Cottage Industry in an Age of Community and Research Medicine,* (1971) 284 N.E.J.M. 700, 705–6.
42 Burger, *Reflections on Law and Experimental Medicine,* (1968) 15 U.C.L.A. L. Rev. 436, 438.
43 Quoted in Beecher, *supra,* 223.
44 126 F. 2d 121 (1941). The opinion of the solicitors to the Peter Bent Brigham Hospital in connection with a proposed kidney transplant from one minor twin to the other was that the dictum in *Bonner* v. *Moran* probably would not be followed in Massachusetts: see Katz, *supra,* 946–966.
45 Beecher, *supra,* 67–68.
46 See Katz, *supra,* ch. 12, "Experimentation with Uncomprehending Subjects".
47 See Katz, *supra,* ch. 13. I have borrowed his title.
48 For a robust criticism of experiments on

prisoners in United States' jails, see Mitford, "Experiments Behind Bars", *The Atlantic Monthly,* January 1973, 64. For an account of the concern of the Department of Health, Education and Welfare, see Marston, *Research on Minors, Prisoners and the Mentally Ill,* (1973) 288 N.E.J.M. 185.

49 Ramsay, *supra,* 705.

50 Examples of recent literature include: Wolstenholme and O'Connor (eds.), *Ethics in Medical Progress* (1966); Dworkin, *The Law Relating to Organ Transplantation in England,* (1970) 33 M.L.R 353, 354–64; Castel, *Some Legal Aspects of Organ Transplantation in Canada,* (1968) 46 Can. Bar Rev. 345, 345–78; Kusanovich, *Medical Malpractice Liability and the Organ Transplant,* (1971) 5 U. of S.F. Law Rev. 223, 225–38.

51 The opinion is set out in Katz, *supra,* 964–966.

52 See Ktaz, *supra,* 967–72 for an account of one of the cases.

53 Curran, *A Problem of Consent: Kidney Transplantations in Minors,* (1959) 34 N.Y.U. Law Rev. 891, 897–8.

54 445 S.W. 2d 145 (1969) (Ky. C.A.).

55 *Ibid.*, 146.

56 *Ibid.*, 146–7.

57 *Ibid.*, 149, 151 *per* Steinfeld, J., Neikirk and Palmore, JJ., concurring, dissenting.

58 289 A. 2d 386 (1972).

59 *Ibid.*, 391.

60 Wolstenholme and O'Connor, *supra,* 203.

61 *Ibid.*, 19–20, 209–10.

62 *Ibid.*, 39, 203.

63 Proc. Conf. of Comm'rs on Uniformity of Leg'n in Can. (1970). 138.

64 The 1970 revised Uniform Act was recommended by the Ontario Commissioners, but when the Ontario Legislature enacted it in 1971 it made some changes, including the title. The 1971 version of the Uniform Act is virtually identical with the Ontario Act of 1971 (S.O. 1971, c.83).

65 Proc. Conf. of Comm'rs on Uniformity of Leg'n in Can. (1971), 152.

66 *Human Tissue Gift Act,* S.O. 1971, c.83; *Human Tissue Act,* S. Nfld 1971, no. 66; *Human Tissue Gift Act,* S.B.C. 1972, c.27.

67 S.O. 1971, c.83.

68 Titmuss, *The Gift Relationship* (1970).

69 *The Gift of Life,* undated, published by the Canadian Red Cross.

70 As one of the Alberta Commissioners on the Uniformity Conference, the writer queried and then acquiesced to section 10 of the 1971 Uniform Act, which permits the sale of blood. Perhaps it ill becomes him now to criticize that section. The fact is that his misgivings have since increased.

71 See Castel, *supra,* 378–405; and Dworkin, *supra,* 364–76.

72 2 Bl. Comm. 507.

73 [1931] 1 D.L.R. 676.

74 *Phillips* v. *Montreal General Hospital* (1908), 33 C.S. 483.

75 *Hunter* v. *Hunter,* [1930] 4 D.L.R. 255 (Ont. H.C.) held that in a dispute between the executor (a son) and the widow on the place of burial, the executor's wishes should prevail.

76 2 and 3 Will. IV, c.75, ss.7 and 8.

77 *Ibid.*

78 15 and 16 Geo. VI and 1 Eliz. II, c.28.

79 *Corneal Grafting Act,* S.N.B. 6 Eliz. II, c.7.

80 Proc. Conf. of Comm'rs on Uniformity of Leg'n in Can. (1959), 77.

81 9 and 10 Eliz. II, c.54.

82 Proc. Conf. of Comm'rs on Uniformity of Leg'n in Can. (1965), 104.

83 *Supra,* f.n. 63.

84 *Supra,* f.n. 64.

85 *Supra,* f.n. 66.

86 8 Uniform Laws Annotated, Master Edition (1972), 22.

87 *Ibid.*, 31–33.

88 *An Act Relating to and Defining Death,* Sess. Laws Kan. 1970, c.378, reprinted in Katz, *supra,* 1085. Compare Beecher, *supra,* 152–57, 311–18. For an adverse comment, see Kennedy, (1971) 285 N.E.J.M. 946, quoted in Katz, *supra,* 1085. For criticism of s.7 of the American Uniform Act, which provides that a physician shall determine death, see Kusanovich, *supra,* 246–53.

89 The Memorial Society Association of Canada advocates legislation "giving a person the right to decide how his body is to be disposed of after he is dead":

Edmonton Journal, 22 May 1973, 3.

90 Wolstenholme and O'Connor, *supra,* 158.

91 Dworkin, *supra,* 371–72; Zellick, *Organ Transplantation,* (1972) 122 New Law Journal 1078.

92 S.Q. 1966–67, c.19, ss.11, 12 and 18.

93 R.S.Q. 1964, c.250, s.4.

94 S.Q. 1923–24, c.117, s.15, and, as amended, s.20; and see *Ducharme* v. *Hôpital Notre-Dame* (1933), 71 C.S. 377.

95 E.g., *Coroner's Act,* S.O. 1972, c.98, s. 23.

96 *Coroner's Act,* R.S.A. 1970, c.69, s.18(8); *Coroner's (Amendment) Act,* S.S. 1966, c.94, s.6.

97 *Coroner's (Amendment) Act,* S.B.C. 1968, c.11, s.12.

98 Sir Victor Windeyer in *Mount Isa Mines* v. *Pusey* (1971), 45 A.L.J.R. 88, 92.

99 See McGill's Guidelines, *supra.* The University of Toronto's Research Board has for some years had a Human Experimentation sub-committee. The University of Alberta Hospital has a Special Services and Research Committee and the University of Alberta itself recently established a committee structure and guidelines. See Melmon, Grossman and Morris, *Emerging Assets and Liabilities of a Committee on Human Welfare and Experimentation,* (1970) 282 N.E.J.M. 427 and editorial in same volume at 449.

100 Protection of the Individual as a Research Subject, U.S. Gov't Printing Office, 1969.

101 Beecher, *Ethics and Clinical Research,* (1966) 274 N.E.J.M. 1354, 1359–60; see also Editorial, *Ethics of Experiments on Children,* (1973) 288 N.E.J.M. 791.

102 Beecher, *supra,* 1360.

103 The writer acknowledges with thanks the information that he received from Dr D.I. Buchanan, Medical Director at Edmonton of the Blood Transfusion Service of the Canadian Red Cross Society; and the helpful comments of Dr Bernard Snell, Medical Director of the University of Alberta Hospital, who read an earlier draft; and the benefit of discussions with Mrs Margaret Shone, Legal Officer of the Institute of Law Research and Reform, Edmonton, who also read an earlier draft.

1973

Book Review: Human Rights Casefinder: 1953–1969: The Warren Court Era, edited by A.F. Ginger.

Reprinted from
(1973) 11 Alberta Law Review
pp. 415–419

The book being reviewed here is an American publication which is a kind of index to cases dealing with Human Rights which were heard by the Supreme Court of the United States during the era when The Honourable Earl Warren was Chief Justice.

The editor of the Alberta Law Review *asked Bowker to do a review of this book. If he had not been familiar with the jurisprudence of the Supreme Court of the United States, he could not have written this review.*

HUMAN RIGHTS CASEFINDER:
1953–1969: THE WARREN COURT ERA: Edited by A.F. Ginger
Meiklejohn, Civil Liberties Library, California. Pp. XV and 281. $25.00.

The United States produces annually a huge volume of reported cases. To aid in finding them publishers have developed elaborate tools such as West's Key Number Digests and Sheppard's Citations.

The Casefinder is another of these tools, designed to direct one to the cases on Human Rights decided during the "Warren era". This refers to the sixteen-year period when the Honourable Earl Warren was Chief Justice of the Supreme Court of the United States. While the Court has nine members, a total of sixteen justices sat with Chief Justice Warren. At any given time, a majority were among those classed as "activist". The Court acquired this label because it expanded the scope of protection of the individual on many fronts and in the name of one or another of the constitutional safeguards. In other words it struck down legislation and practices that previously had either been free from attack or been upheld. Depending on one's point of view this was either a laudable development in which the Court had to act to protect the individual in the absence of remedial action by Legislature and Executive or else it was an usurpation of power which justified the demand to "impeach Earl Warren".

In describing the Warren Court it is not enough to say that it was activist. At an earlier date the Court earned the same description when it struck down economic and social legislation that offended business interests. The Warren Court, on the other hand, gave its protection to the negro, the poor, the accused and to the protestor.

For example, the Court speeded the process of imposing on the State safeguards in criminal cases that originally applied only at the federal level. One much-discussed case is *Gideon* v. *Wainright* (1963) 372 U.S. 335, holding that even in a non-capital case a state must provide counsel for an indigent accused. Another is *Miranda* v. *Arizona* (1966) 384 U.S. 436, which requires the police to caution an accused person of his right to remain silent and his right to consult his lawyer before asking him questions.

In connection with freedom of speech and assembly, the Court tended to give wide scope to protestors, for example in *Edwards* v. *South Carolina* (1963) 372 U.S. 229 (protest on capitol grounds) and *Cox* v. *Louisiana* (1965) 379 U.S. 559 (protest near court house). *Tinker* v. *Des Moines* (1969) 393 U.S. 503 held that the wearing of black armbands by school children in protest against the Vietnam war was a proper exercise of freedom of speech. It also gave new scope to freedom of the press by restricting the scope of a libel action against a newspaper in *New York Times* v. *Sullivan* (1964) 376 U.S. 255 and by rejecting a claim for damages for breach of privacy brought against a publisher in *Time Inc*. v. *Hill* (1967) 385 U.S. 374.

In the realm of equal protection of the law, the school desegregation case, *Brown* v. *Board of Education* (1955) 349 U.S. 294 is one of the most significant in the Court's history; and the first of the "one man-one vote" cases. *Baker* v. *Carr* (1962) 369 U.S. 186, is another. The Court also gave equal protection to the poor in various ways. It held invalid a state poll-tax in *Harper* v. *Virginia State Board of Electors* (1966) 383 U.S. 663; and a state law requiring an indigent to be a state resident for a year before becoming applicable for public assistance, in *Shapiro* v. *Thompson* (1969) 394 U.S. 618; and required the State to give financial assistance of various kinds to an accused person to eenable him to prepare his defense (*e.g., Griffin* v. *Illinois* (1956) 351 U.S. 12 and *Douglas* v. *California* (1963) 372 U.S. 353).

Outside the heads of protection named in the Constitution, the Court made a beginning toward establishing a constitutional right of privacy, though its precise content is hard to discern. Such a right, in support of the Fourth Amendment protection against unreasonable searches and seizures, was employed in *Katz* v. *United States* (1967) 389 U.S. 347 in holding that the electronic surveillance of a man speaking over the telephone in a public booth was an unreasonable search. Again, in *Stanley* v. *Georgia* (1969) 394 U.S. 557, the court held that the First Amendment in securing free speech, protects the right to receive communications, including obscene films, and that a charge of private possession of the films is not only an infringement of the First Amendment but an unwarranted intrusion on the right of privacy.

The most notable case is *Griswold* v. *Connecticut* (1965) 381 U.S. 479. A state law made the use of contraceptives a criminal offence. In holding it invalid, the nine justices used various reasons, but the majority held that the statute was invalid in invading the right of privacy of married persons.

The Casefinder is not confined to Supreme Court decisions. It includes the reported cases in both State and Federal courts. Moreover the cited cases are not confined to those in the regular law reports. The editor has included a large number which were never reported but which have been collected in the fourteen volumes of a work called the "Civil Liberties Docket" and in a monthly publication called "Meiklejohn Library Acquisitions", and in one or two other collections.

The cases are classified by subject matter, and numbered in a decimal system. Any classification of human rights and liberties is difficult, and no two seem to be precisely the same. The Casefinder, of course, does not attempt to classify the rights and liberties in the abstract but rather in terms of the cases on constitutional rights and liberties that arose in the era of the Warren Court. There are three divisions:

I. Freedom of Expression and Association; embracing speech, press and assembly, religion, and association.

II. Due process and Related Rights; covering procedure in legal proceedings with emphasis on the criminal, searches and seizures, indictments, double jeopardy, self-incrimination, due process, speedy and public trial, right to counsel, confrontation, jury trials, cruel and unusual punishment, and due process for the poor, for the juvenile offender and for the incompetent.

III. Equal Protection (or anti-discrimination); which of course has many and diverse factual settings—elections, jury selection, education (16 pages of cases), housing (almost 5 pages of cases), transportation, and miscellaneous (recreation facilities, dining places, hospitals, government facilities and prisons), family matters (marriage, adoption, custody, *etc.*), employment, and native Indians.

To show the format of the casefinder, I shall take the case in which one Dr. Sheppard, while serving a sentence for murder, brought proceedings in which he alleged he had been denied due process at the trial because of unfair newspaper comment. The reference to this case is as follows: *Sheppard* v. *Maxwell, Warden,* 354.5; X, 42–xiii, 92; 346 F2d 707 (CA 6 1965), *rev'd* and *rem* 384 U.S. 333 (1966); MCLL; ACLU.

The first number shows that the case is listed under heading No. 354, the subject matter of which is due process in connection with "press releases and newspaper coverage". The figure '5' after the decimal point shows that the case is the fifth under the heading. The next two references, each beginning with a Roman numeral, are to volumes and pages in the Civil Liberties Docket. The next item is the citation of the judgment of the Federal Court of Appeals for the Sixth Circuit and then that of the Supreme Court, which reversed the Court below and remanded Sheppard for a new trial. The two sets of initials at the end refer to the Meiklejohn Civil Liberties Library and the American Civil Liberties Union, each of which have material on the case.

It seems clear that this research tool is useful to anyone concerned with learning about the expansion of civil liberties in the United States through judicial decisions in the Warren era. Of what value is it to a Canadian interested in these matters? Leaving aside the value of any comparative study for its intrinsic interest, some of the topics are peculiarly American and have little direct relevance in Canada. The large section dealing with discrimination is an example; the portion dealing with the clause in the First Amendment which prohibits the establishment of religion is another; and the many cases dealing with loyalty oaths and other programs designed to check subversion and which have no counterpart in Canada are another. On the other hand we have some problems such as those relating to denominational schools and arising under section 93 of the British North America Act, that have no counterpart in the United States.

One important difference between the two countries has to do with jurisdiction over criminal law. In the United States the basic criminal law is in the hands of the several states. If abuses occur in the administration of a state's criminal law then the Supreme Court has power by virtue of the Bill of Rights to strike down an offending state law or hold invalid a judge-made rule or the procedure that has been followed in the particular case. The Warren Court was particularly active in scrutinizing state law and imposing on it the Court's concept of due process. Depending on one's point of view, he can regard this as a laudable step in securing to the individual his constitutional rights as against the states, or else he can consider it an unwarranted intrusion into state matters. It is perhaps hard for a Canadian to appreciate the public interest and controversy over many of the decisions. *Gideon* and *Miranda,* already mentioned, furnished examples. So, too, do some of the decisions on searches and seizures, though in *Perry* v. *Ohio* (1968) 392 U.S. 1 the Court upheld the right of a policeman to "stop and frisk" a person suspected of having offensive weapons.

In Canada, of course, criminal law is a federal subject. Many of the American constitutional safeguards are in the Criminal Code and others are part of the common law. In this country there was, until recently, very little discussion of "due process", though one likes to think that as a synonym for fairness, it has in fact been observed in the administration of our criminal law. The passage of Canada's Bill of Rights Act in 1960 declares that every person is entitled not to be deprived of "life, liberty, security of the person and enjoyment of property" except by due process of law. The consequence is that the courts are now frequently faced with assertions that an accused person has been denied due process and our courts are now trying to define its meaning. In so doing they face the difficulties that the American courts have long encountered.

Prior to enactment of the Bill of Rights Act, the phrase "equal protection of the laws" was rarely encountered. The Act declares the right of the individual "to equality before the law and the protection of the law". This clause has been invoked several times. In the important case of *The Queen* v. *Drybones* [1970] S.C.R. 282 the court held that a certain provision in the Indian Act is inoperative because of conflict with the equality clause, and two other provisions of the Indian Act are now before the courts.

In connection with the freedoms of religion, speech, assembly and association, and press, all enumerated in the Act, we had had cases that considered the powers of a province to restrict freedom of religion (*Saumur* v. *Quebec* [1953] 2 S.C.R. 299) and press (*Re Alberta Statutes* [1938] S.C.R. 100) and speech (*Switzman* v. *Elbing* [1957] 7 D.L.R. (2d) 337). Since passage of the Bill of Rights Act federal legislation can be scrutinized under the same heads, as *Robertson* v. *The Queen* [1963] S.C.R. 651 illustrates.

Late in 1972 the Alberta Legislature enacted the Bill of Rights Act based on Canada's, save that the provincial Act omits that portion of Canada's section 2 which deals with particular safeguards in judicial and administrative proceedings.

The existence of the Canada and Alberta Acts will inevitably require lawyers to pay much more attention to the concepts contained in the Acts than they did in the past. This being so, it is inevitable that recourse will be had to American authority. Our Appellate Division, in its first case dealing with due process in connection with a criminal prosecution, quoted from American authorities as to the meaning of that phrase (*Reg.* v. *Martin* (1961) 35 W.W.R. 384). In a recent case on entrapment, Greschuk J. quoted from a judgment of Chief Justice Hughes (*Reg.* v. *Sirois* [1972] 2 W.W.R. 149). Mr. Justice Laskin in his opinions dealing with Canada's Bill of Rights has frequently referred to American doctrines and cases. A notable example is the recent decision in *Curr* v. *The Queen* (1972) 26 D.L.R. (3d) 603. Mr. Justice Laskin discussed at some length American concepts and decisions in connection with the question whether the "statutorily-compelled giving of a breath sample" is an infringement of any of the safeguards in the Bill of Rights Act.

One can confidently predict that references to American doctrine will increase even though our courts will not necessarily accept all of those doctrines as applicable here.

The judge, solicitor or student wanting to pursue American developments in the last twenty years will clearly find the Casefinder of great assistance. This assumes of course that he has access to the American Law Reports, and it will be borne in mind that in Alberta there are few good collections apart from that in the Faculty of Law at The University of Alberta.

1978

Expeditious Justice: Western Style

(Unpublished.) Dinner speech delivered at the annual meeting of the Canadian Institute on the Administration of Justice, held at Edmonton, October 1978.

In 1978 the Canadian Institute on the Administration of Justice held its annual meeting in Edmonton. This is a national association of judges and lawyers for the purpose of improving the operation of the courts. Its headquarters are now in Montreal.

The theme of this particular meeting was Expeditious Justice. Bowker was asked to be the dinner speaker at the closing banquet. He chose as his title "Expeditious Justice: Western Style."

He drew a comparison between Canadian and American historical evolution of law. He credited the R.C.M.P. and such personages as Judge Begbie of British Columbia with providing a level of order and justice quite unlike the vigilante justice to be seen in such communities as Virginia City, Montana before the turn of the century.

This speech was very well received, and many easterners especially found it fascinating.

At various times and places, humans have a tendency to short-circuit the regular judicial system and to avenge serious violent crimes by peremptory means either by taking revenge themselves or by setting up irregular courts to try the alleged offender. This is known as vigilante justice. It has frequently appeared in the *United States* and particularly, though not exclusively, in the Western States. I shall begin by describing the most famous, though certainly not the first example of vigilante justice—that in San Francisco right after the goldrush of '49. Mexico had just surrendered California to the United States. It became a state in 1850 and new legal institutions had hardly taken root. The goldrush brought a horde of adventurers, good and bad. The mining camps were sometimes fairly law-abiding and before legal institutions were established miners' courts settled disputes. In other camps violence was commonplace. In San Francisco itself robberies and killings often went unpunished, so as early as 1851 the merchants and leading citizens organized a vigilance committee to try to put an end to the lawlessness. It operated in semi-secrecy. It was designed and equipped only to deal with serious crime. It had no efficient jail system and the only punishments it inflicted were death, banishment, and whipping. Operating over a short period the vigilance committee convicted one man who had stolen a safe from a merchant, and three for murder. All four were executed. The committee banished many more, most of them to Australia. By the end of the year the work was done so the committee was disbanded.

In the next five years the concern of the citizens of San Francisco was not so much with violent crime. Rather it was corruption, delays and favouritism in the courts, and ballot stuffing, that aroused the citizens again. In November 1855 a thug named Cora killed a U.S. marshal. On Cora's trial for murder the jury was divided. Soon after this, a crusading newspaper editor named King attacked another editor, Casey, as being corrupt. Casey shot him on May 14th, 1856. Casey was charged, and along with him one Ned McGowan who had come out from New Jersey in 1849 and for a short time had held a minor judicial post. On the day King was shot, a leading citizen named Coleman called a meeting to organize a vigilance committee the next day. The meeting was held and the committee was organized. It had an executive committee of 26 and a board of delegates of 108 members and a military force that grew to 6,000 by July. According to Bancroft, the historian who wrote a total of 39 large volumes on the history of the far Western States, British Columbia and Mexico (including two entitled *Popular Tribunals on Vigilante Movements*), and who was pro-vigilante, all of the leaders were able, dedicated men. Many of the political leaders in the State were opposed to the vigilantes, including Governor Johnson who vacillated throughout the 1856 vigilante movement.

The vigilantes demanded and obtained the surrender of Cora and Casey, who were in jail. King died on May 20th and on that day the executive committee put Cora on trial. The proceedings were in secret and the committee refused to allow Cora outside counsel. They provided counsel from among their own members. The committee found Cora guilty. Casey was then tried on the same day with the same counsel and the same result. On May 22nd both were hanged from outside the committee room windows. The committee could scarcely have been more expeditious but one might question its justice.

In the meantime, Ned McGowan, wanted for complicity in the murder of King, hid out for nine months. He worked his way to Sacramento and had the legislature pass an act to change the venue of his trial to Napa, where a friendly jury acquitted him. Then in 1858 he went to the Fraser River where we shall see him again shortly

At this time William Terry came to San Francisco from Sacramento to oppose the vigilance committee. He was a judge of the Supreme Court of California which is the Court of Appeal for that State. He took steps to obtain the release of one Mulligan whom the vigilantes held. He obtained a writ of habeas corpus but the vigilance committee ignored it. On June 2nd and 3rd the governor called up the militia and declared a state of emergency. But this measure was ineffective. Tension mounted and Franklin Pierce, the President of the United States, declined to intervene.

Later in June the vigilance committee seized government arms from a ship. At a confrontation between the committee and their opponents (who called themselves the "Law and Order" group), Terry knifed Hopkins, one of the vigilantes, and the vigilance committee took Terry into custody. They immediately tried him, on 27th June, for the "murder or attempted murder" of Hopkins who was still alive, and also for various assaults and for resisting arrest. They provided him with counsel of their choosing. The trial lasted 25 days, including Sundays, and ended on 22nd July. The executive committee found him guilty of assault only but the larger body, the board of delegates, found him guilty of attempted murder as charged. There was a great difference of opinion as to the disposition to be made of Terry. The upshot was to order his release. The committee smuggled him out of San Francisco and he returned to Sacramento where he resumed his place on the Supreme Court.

During Terry's trial, two men named Heatherington and Brace were arrested for separate murders. The former was tried and convicted by the committee on 27 July and Brace on the 28th and both were hanged on the 29th from a scaffold on a public street. Time does not permit an account of the other actions of the vigilantes or the steps that were taken in the regular courts to bring retribution on them. Considering that its work was done in August, the committee held a ceremonial parade on 18th August and was disbanded soon after. Governor Johnson withdrew his proclamation of emergency on September 20th. Bancroft's judgment is that the vigilantes had cleaned the city of murder, corruption and ballot stuffing and established good municipal government in San Francisco. He states that the rationale of the movement was not revolution but to vindicate government. Man-made laws are subordinate to natural law. Laws are a compact by the majority of the people to provide for government, and the laws are subject to change and annulment. Those who confer power can remove it.

Terry, who was able, personally brave, hot-tempered and given to violence, had further adventures. He became Chief Justice of California in 1857 and at the same time a young lawyer named Stephen Field was elected to the same court. Field came from a distinguished New York family and had arrived in California in the goldrush. He soon made a mark for himself as a lawyer though he had a rather stormy time and on his own statement carried arms during the first few years. The two men were never friendly. In 1859 Terry resigned his Chief Justiceship to fight a duel with a prominent politician named Broderick, then a U.S. senator. Terry killed Broderick and Field succeeded Terry as Chief Justice of California. Six years later President Lincoln appointed him to the Supreme Court of the United States where he sat for 34 years. In the meantime, Terry, after supporting the South in the Civil War, returned to practice in California. In 1883 he acted for an adventuress named Sara Hill who claimed to be the wife of Senator Sharon of Nevada who was worth ten million dollars. Long proceedings began in both federal and state courts over the question of the marriage. In 1886, Sharon having died, Terry married Sara so he now had a wife as well as a client. At that time judges of the Supreme Court of the United States went out on circuit from time to time, and Field's circuit included California. It happened that he sat on an application by Sharon's executors to have the action continued by his estate. Mr. and Mrs. Terry were present when Field made the order. They put on a demonstration in the courtroom. Sara tried to draw a pistol and when the judge ordered her removed Terry drew a knife. A stormy scene followed and Field committed them both for contempt—six months for Terry and one month for Sara. Later Terry made various threats against Field should Field return to California. When he did return in 1889 the U.S. Government against his wishes provided a marshal as bodyguard. He arrived in June. In August he held court in Los Angeles and then took the train for San Francisco. The Terrys got on at Fresno and the train stopped at a little town called Lathrop where passengers could have breakfast at a hotel. Terry sat at one table while Field and his marshal (Neagle) sat at another. As Terry left, he walked behind Field and hit him on the face and head. The marshal shot Terry twice and he died at once. Sara was angry and had both the marshal and Field arrested for murder. The Governor of California withdrew the charge against Field and ultimately the marshal was acquitted.

So much for the vigilantes of San Francisco. They inspired many similar movements in other California centres and in other states and territories in the far West. The tide of miners moved from California to the great Comstock silver lode near Virginia City, Nevada, and then around 1862 to Idaho and Colorado when gold was discovered in those places. Usually the mining camps that mushroomed happened to be in territories that had not yet reached statehood and the judicial machinery was non-existent or ineffective. I shall mention Idaho solely because a man named Plummer was there in 1863 and he left for new diggings in Montana. One important camp was at Bannack which became the temporary capital. The other was at Virginia City, between Butte and Yellowstone. Plummer was a plausible and charming rogue who succeeded in becoming sheriff at Bannack. Before long it was discovered that he was the leader of a gang who robbed the stage coaches of gold and committed a number of murders.

In December 1863, a notorious outlaw named George Ives was tried by a voluntary group, convicted and hanged. This was much like a regular trial in that the crime was proved and Ives was allowed a fair defence. Immediately afterwards the citizens of Virginia City and its neighbour Nevada City organized a formal vigilance movement. It seems to have been on the lines of a fraternal order. Its members vigorously tried to find out who the criminals were. They soon learned of Plummer's role and on the night of 10 January 1864 went to Bannack, arrested Plummer and two confederates and without any pretense of a trial hanged them the same night from Plummer's own gallows. Four days later back in Virginia City, five more outlaws were tried in a most informal way and adjudged guilty by a crowd of miners and hanged forthwith from a beam in a partly-finished building. The roundup continued for a month and the vigilantes executed a total of 21. Many other renegades hurried out of the territory. As best I can tell from the two leading contemporary accounts by Langford and Dimsdale there was nothing approaching a trial except for the two cases mentioned. Yet this vigilance movement is usually cited with approbation. It will be remembered, of course, that the regular courts were not established until a few months later. When they were, Chief Justice Hosmer in addressing the grand jury commended the work of the vigilantes. They continued their operations, especially near Helena, for another year.

Of the many other mining camps that had vigilante activity I shall mention only one—Deadwood in the Black Hills where the goldrush occurred in 1876. This was the site of the invasion by the whites that had prompted Sitting Bull's uprising. Bill Hickok had come to Deadwood from Dodge City a few months before. Legend has it that he was a fearless enforcer of law and an incredible pistol shot. He was playing cards in a saloon when a man named Jack McCall shot him in the back. The miners took McCall and forthwith tried him in an informal miner's court—a scene re-enacted nightly nowadays in Deadwood for the edification of visitors. Surprisingly the miners acquitted him. However, he boasted of his action later and was tried, convicted and executed at Yankton in South Dakota. Visitors to Deadwood reverently go to the little cemetery under the spruce trees where Hickok is buried beside Martha Canary, known as Calamity Jane. Legends tell of their romance. The fact is that there is no clear evidence they ever met. Reluctant though one is to say so, Calamity Jane was completely disreputable, a pathological liar, and she did not look like Jane Russell.

As a sequel to the vigilante activity in Montana in the 1860s there was a remarkable revival twenty years later but this time it was cattlemen, not miners, who took the law into their own hands. Granville Stuart was a leading citizen who had been a miner and indeed been at Virginia City during the troubles there. Later he took up ranching near Lewistown and became one of the state's most distinguished citizens. The ranchers were troubled by horse and cattle thieves, both white and Indian. In 1884 the ranchers proposed to organize a full-fledged vigilance committee. In his *Reminiscences* Stuart says he opposed this. However, some of the ranchers formed a small group of 14 men who set out to eliminate the thieves. They went into the rugged country south of the Missouri River near the mouth of the Musselshell where the thieves were. They burned out a cabin holding eleven men and on the spot or later hanged all but one who escaped. Stuart describes this with approbation though he implies that he did not take part. He does not give the total number who were executed but most writers put it at 35. So far as I know, no charge was ever laid.

Before leaving the American scene may I refer to three incidents which strictly speaking do not represent vigilante justice but, at best, a complete negation of any effort to observe due process of law. I refer to the Lincoln County war in New Mexico in 1878; the Pleasant Valley war in Arizona in 1888; and the Johnson County war in Wyoming in 1892.

By the late 1870s there were large ranches in New Mexico. Two large operators, Murphy and Dolan, did extensive business supplying livestock to the army post near Lincoln in that Territory. They had the support of the Governor, judges and the local sheriff. A man named McSween tried to compete with them, whereupon the Murphy–Dolman men stole McSween's cattle and sold them to the army. The machinery for law enforcement was present but it was inefficient or corrupt. McSween's supporters called themselves Regulators which is a synonym for vigilantes. After several killings on both sides, the Lincoln County war culminated in a five-day battle in the little town of Lincoln during July 1878. The army commander, who did his best to remain neutral, moved in his troops. The net effect was to give the Murphy–Dolan forces the advantage over McSween and they besieged him in his house and burned it. He and several others were killed. Governor Wallace then restored order. The regular court sat the following spring but was ineffective. Only one of the many persons involved came to trial.

Incidentally Billy the Kid was on the McSween side. It was in subsequent months that he became notorious particularly when he escaped from the Lincoln County jail while under sentence of death. In July of that year, Sheriff Garrett, waiting for the fugitive to show up at a ranch house, shot him when he stepped into the darkened room. Both have become legendary heroes and for very little reason.

The Pleasant Valley war in Arizona was a decade after the Lincoln County war. Pleasant Valley is well named for it is in a beautiful area in the eastern part of central Arizona, lying under the Mogollon Rim in the Tonto Basin. The Grahams were leading cattlemen. In the mid-1880s a man named Tewksbury brought in sheep. This produced a feud that lasted for over a year. Nearly every one on each side was killed. The sheriff from Prescott attempted to restore order but without success. A sober account of this episode is entitled *Arizona's Dark and Bloody Ground*. According to the author over twenty persons were killed on both sides. Zane Grey wrote a novel based on these events and called it *To the Last Man*. His account of the main clashes is quite accurate, but he adds a Romeo-and-Juliet love story. When the shooting ended there was in fact one Graham left and one Tewksbury. Graham moved to Tempe, near Phoenix, to farm. In 1892 while driving into town he was shot from ambush. Tewksbury had been seen in the neighbourhood and he was charged with the murder. He was acquitted at trial because the prosecution could not prove that he was the murderer.

The last "war" I shall mention is that in Johnson County in Wyoming in 1892. It is the subject of a scholarly book by Smith called *The War on Powder River*. For years in Wyoming there had been trouble between the large ranchers on the one hand and the small ranchers on the other. The large ranchers accused the others of stealing their calves and branding them, and regarded the small ranchers as rustlers, which some of them were. The legislature and the governor were both on the side of the large ranchers who made up the Wyoming Stock Growers' Association. They succeeded in excluding the small ranchers from each round-up which meant that they could not claim any of the livestock. Tension increased through the 1880s and in 1891 violence broke out. In one episode a rustler and his woman companion were lynched, presumably by the large ranchers. This was nothing to the step that they took next. They hired 22 gunmen from around the town of Paris in Texas for the purpose of invading Johnson County on Powder River on the east side of the Bighorns. A special Pullman took the gunmen to Cheyenne and from there a secret train took them and an equal number of cattlemen, 7 detectives and 6 teamsters up to Casper. From there they rode north toward Buffalo, (the county seat) like a large troop of cavalry although they showed little military skill. Passing by a ranch called the KC where two rustlers were, they besieged the place and finally killed the two men, Champion and Ray. As the invaders advanced toward Buffalo, the citizens of the town came out to stop them. President Harrison authorized the army commander at a nearby post to intervene. He did so and took the invaders into custody. They were taken to Laramie and then to Cheyenne. The Texans were released on bail and were never seen again. The others of the accused were released because Johnson County, which had to bear the expense of prosecuting all the criminal charges, had no more funds. Parenthetically I point out that Wyoming's leading lawyer, Willis Vandevanter, supported the larger ranchers and acted for some of the accused. Later he sat on the Supreme Court of the United States.

May I now turn to the Western Canadian scene. The discovery of gold on the Fraser River in 1858 led the British government to establish the colony of British Columbia. Governor Douglas and Judge Begbie were sworn in on 19th November 1858. Already there was a great influx of miners—nearly all from the States—and many of them acted as though they were still there. Hardly had Begbie arrived when a tense situation developed at Yale which was at the head of navigation. The people there largely represented the San Francisco vigilantes while across the river at a place called Hill's Bar were Ned McGowan and his friends. There was a justice of the peace at each place—Whannell at Yale and Perrier at Hill's Bar. Word reached the governor at Langley Prairie that trouble had broken out. It turned out later that the rumors were exaggerated. The governor sent Begbie and Colonel Moody to investigate. What they found was like the plot of a comic opera. Two Americans, Burns and Farrell, appeared to have assaulted a Negro named Dixon. Whannell imprisoned Dixon to make sure he would prosecute the complaint. He also issued a warrant for the arrest of Burns and Farrell. They were in fact arrested but were taken before Perrier. He asked his constable to bring Dixon before him. This angered Whannell; Perrier then issued a warrant for Whannell's arrest and a warrant to have Dixon brought before him, Perrier. Further, he appointed McGowan and another fugitive from San Francisco as special constables. They seized Whannell and his gaoler. Perrier fined Whannell $25 for contempt of court. When Begbie arrived on the 4th of January he dealt informally with a charge against McGowan and his constable (Kelly) for assault on Whannell and acquitted them though he found McGowan guilty of an unconnected assault. The next day McGowan showed Begbie around the claims at Hill's Bar. Begbie told Governor Douglas that McGowan had been afraid that his enemies at Yale would form a vigilante committee. Begbie's conduct showed him that this would not happen. The events just described are known as Ned McGowan's war. Begbie is given credit for having stamped out the danger of violence and of setting the tone for future mining camps in British Columbia.

Here may I digress to mention a small item in connection with Begbie's visit to McGowan at Hill's Bar. He was accompanied by a Lieutenant Mayne who is quoted in the *B.C. Historical Quarterly* as saying that McGowan "invited us to a collation in his hut, where we drank champagne with some twelve or fifteen of his Californian mining friends." I doubt very much that Begbie would have accepted McGowan's hospitality. My real query, however, has to do with the talk of champagne. This gives me an excuse to mention the many references to champagne in the stories of mining camps. I would like to see a graduate student—in sociology, of course—undertake this thesis: "The consumption of champagne in Western North American mining camps in the second half of the nineteenth century, and its economic, social, and moral consequences." The main problem would be to show that a single case of champagne ever reached a mining camp. It is a long way from Rheims to Yale, B.C. Champagne would never have survived the voyage and besides it was a luxury that miners would not enjoy anyway. Had all the stories of champagne spoken instead of overproof rum, they would be more credible. The rum goes farther, is easier to transport and would not freeze. This subject may have no direct relevance to expeditious justice but it is another example of the myths that have distorted Western history and that have made heroes of Billy the Kid, Wyatt Earp, Jesse James and Bill Hickok.

Following the 1858 rush on the Fraser River the miners went further upstream and on into the Cariboo. Judge Begbie went on circuit and kept order. Moreover, in the early years he acted as an administrator and helped to establish the early mining and land laws. He was hot-tempered and autocratic. When lawyers began to appear in the courts he often quarrelled with them. Bancroft gives Begbie credit for enforcing the law in the British Columbia mining camps which were both in size and personnel comparable to those in the United States. He concludes by saying: "The consequence of it all was that never in the pacification and settlement of any section of America have there been so few disturbances, so few crimes against life or property. And when we consider the clashing elements that came together just as Begbie reached the country, the nature and antecedents of these wild, rough and cunning men, it is wonderful." This has been the general appraisal of Begbie's contribution. On the other hand a writer named Martin Robin, in a history of British Columbia called *The Rush for Spoils,* rejects the accepted opinion. He concedes, "It is doubtless true that the Fraser River and the Cariboo gold rushes presided over by James Douglas and the stern Judge Begbie were less boisterous affairs than the American equivalents; and that vigilantes, posses, desperados and trouble-makers were less free to do their bad thing in British Columbia than in California." He adds however, that "the circumstances were different on the two sides of the border. The Canadian rush followed the American and by then the forces of law had caught up with the wild men." This last passage is completely wrong. The San Francisco troubles were over when Begbie came on the scene, but many more vigilante movements were to follow, as I have described. A recent book called *Strain of Violence* by Richard Brown lists the American vigilante movements. In the far western states alone he names (by my count) 70 of them after 1865, small, medium and large. This excludes Texas which had more than any other single state.

There was a major rush into the east Kootenay in 1864 centering on Wild Horse Creek (now Fort Steele). This was at the same time as the Idaho and Montana rushes and the miners were of the same type. Yet there was no lawlessness. One of the reasons of course was the fact that British Columbia put the miners' customs into statutory form at an early date (1859) and had the wisdom to provide for gold commissioners. They settled many disputes and all historians agree that they were an important institution in the orderly development of British Columbia's mines.

The last Canadian rush of course was that in the Klondike. The fact that it was orderly is not particularly notable because it came at a late date and the Northwest Mounted Police were on the scene. The Shooting of Dan McGrew is a good yarn and Service's rhyme is always fascinating. However, the man from the creeks never did shoot dangerous Dan McGrew in the Malamute Saloon or any place else. They are both imaginary and so is the lady who is known as Lou. On the other hand, in Skagway, Alaska where the ships landed there was an element of lawlessness. One bad man was Soapy Smith, a Colorado gambler and confidence man. He came to Skagway in the summer of 1898 and with his confederates lived by fraud and robbery. Feeling against him produced an incipient vigilante movement. One day in July he went to confront his opponents on the docks and one of them shot and killed him—ostensibly in self-defence. Twice I have heard speakers refer to Soapy Smith being in Dawson City. I can never find any evidence that he ever got over the Chilkoot Pass and I am sure that the NWMP would have turned him back had he tried.

Finally may I say a word about law and order in the ranching world on our prairies. There are many reasons why we had no counterpart of the American experience. We had no aftermath of a terrible Civil War and we never had the struggle over occupation of public land and problems of the fencing of the open range, and the feuds between cattlemen and sheepmen. The basic difference as it appears to me is that we had legal institutions in place and effective before settlement, whereas in the United States settlement came ahead of organized government. There was one bad incident—the Cypress Hills Massacre of 1873. (It is well described in Paul Sharp's *Whoop-Up Country*.) White men, both American and Canadian, having been robbed of horses, made an attack on an Indian encampment just north of the American line and east of what is now the Saskatchewan–Alberta border. They killed a number of Indians. After the massacre they returned to Montana. Two years later the Canadian government failed in efforts to extradite them—and they were cheered as heroes in Helena and Fort Benton.

Later three of them were arrested in Canada and taken to Winnipeg for trial. The evidence was scanty and confused, and the three were acquitted.

The massacre is significant because it stirred Sir John A. MacDonald to establish the NWMP. It is trite to say that they drove out the whisky traders and did a good job of "pacifying the West." An opinion of a Montana rancher is relevant here. I refer to Granville Stuart, whom we saw in connection with the extermination of the Montana rustlers in 1884. In his *Reminiscences* (Volume II, pp. 162–163) he mentions an instance in which Indians from north of the border had stolen horses from Montana ranchers. They asked Major Crozier at Fort MacLeod for NWMP assistance. Stuart says that the accused were promptly arrested and tried before Colonel MacLeod and a jury, and convicted. Sentence was suspended, a decision of which Stuart approved. Then he added, speaking of the Canadian authorities, "their methods of capturing and punishing the thieves and restoring stolen property were both expeditious and effective."

An American author, F.R. Prassel, in his book *The Western Peace Officer* refers to the Canadian West and says: "The Canadian frontier carried with it traditions shared by the United States. By the middle of the nineteenth century, however, the British Commonwealth already recognized the general benefits of central police authority with high standards and relative isolation from political pressure." After describing the establishment of the NWMP he adds: "Within twenty years the Mounties earned and received support of courts and public unmatched by lawmen in the United States. Better law enforcement even contributed to immigration northward to Canada. Settlers preferred the dependable and equitable protection of a central force to local constables or vigilance committees. Indians, outlaws, and ordinary citizens alike came to respect the North West Mounted Police as upholders of the law."

We of course take the "central force" for granted. However, its absence in the United States made effective law enforcement difficult. Even if every local sheriff had been Gary Cooper in *High Noon*—which he was not—he was handicapped by having no authority outside his bailiwick. The U.S. marshals were concerned only in federal offences and the army generally would not intervene in local affairs.

Professor MacLeod of the University of Alberta in his scholarly book *The NWMP and Law Enforcement* points out that for some lesser offences, prostitution, gambling and liquor, the Police did not always prosecute vigorously. As for cattle rustling he mentions that when a great influx of cattle accompanied that of settlers, rustling became serious. He refers to an editorial in the *Calgary Herald* in 1901 complaining that cattle thieving had become so commonplace that "the stockmen were becoming so incensed that one of these fine days we will wake up and find that Judge Lynch has set up his court here." It never happened.

I conclude this account with a reference to the trial of Louis Riel. I realize that he is a hero, martyr and saint to many and a villain to others.

This difference of opinion is understandable and is not my concern. I wish merely to refer to the conduct of the prosecution and to the trial. There was no Supreme Court in the Territories but there were stipendiary magistrates. When joined by a justice of the peace, they had power to try any offence, even treason, with a jury. Thus it was that when the federal authorities charged Riel with treason, the trial was held in the Territories, at Regina which was a small settlement on the railway which had just reached the prairies. The Crown had able lawyers—the Deputy Minister of Justice Mr. Burbidge, Christopher Robinson, and B.B. Osler from Ontario, T.C. Casgrain from Quebec and David Lynch Scott who was the first lawyer on the roll of advocates in the Northwest Territories and who later became Chief Justice of Alberta. For the defence were Charles Fitzpatrick, later Chief Justice of Canada, James Greenshields, a prominent Montreal lawyer, F.X. Lemieux of Montreal, and a capable young Winnipeg lawyer, T.C. Johnstone, who later became a judge in Saskatchewan. In reading the account of any trial it is hard to capture the flavour. However from reading the record, which was recently published in book form, the impression I receive is that Crown counsel were both able and fair. The defence counsel were equally able. There was a remarkable absence of interruptions and only very few objections to the admissibility of evidence. The accused did not attempt to deny the basic allegations concerning the rebellion though he did attempt unsuccessfully to submit evidence to show the provocation that the Metis and Indians had. The main difficulty with the defence was that Riel's counsel wanted to establish that he was not guilty by reason of insanity. He vigorously insisted that he was sane and at one time his counsel were on the verge of withdrawing from the defence. Riel was allowed on two occasions to make a statement and in neither one was he curbed. On my reading of the trial, it is remarkable that in this new country far away from the civilized parts of Canada a trial was held that in terms of the dignity and fairness of the proceedings might well have been held in one of the older provinces or at the Central Criminal Court in London. I am aware that not everyone shares this view. One of our best historians recently wrote an essay on the trial and entitled it "Judicial Murder." The only substantial criticism in connection with the trial was that the defence of insanity did not succeed. The fact is of course, as every lawyer knows, that the defence is a very narrow one. An accused person can be quite irrational on many points but as long as he knows what he was doing and that it was wrong he cannot succeed on the defence of insanity. The main criticism in the essay to which I have referred is really of the Federal Government in failing to commute the death penalty. This of course has nothing to do with the trial. It should be remembered too that Riel appealed to the Manitoba Court of Appeal, and even the Privy Council sitting in London entertained his application for leave to appeal to that body.

May I now close with two texts. Any self-respecting clergyman reads his text at the beginning. I have chosen to do the reverse. My first, which I might describe as an Old Testament text, is the well-known provision in

Magna Carta. "To no one will we sell, to no one will we *delay,* to no one will we deny, right or justice." My second text, which I might call the New Testament one, is a footnote in an article that C.C. McCaul wrote in 1884 when he was still a young lawyer practicing at Fort MacLeod. It is from an article in the *Canadian Law Times* (Vol. 4 at 52). In the article McCaul described the wide jurisdiction of the stipendiary magistrates of the Northwest Territories. He pointed out that each magistrate was assigned to a district but that he had jurisdiction over the whole of the Territories. Attached to this passage is this footnote: "Lt.-Col. Macleod, the Stipendiary Magistrate for the Bow River District, gave me the following vigorous example of the extent of his jurisdiction. He said, 'If I am driving over the prairies in any part of the Territories, and a couple of men should happen to meet me with a dispute to be settled, I can then and there convert my buckboard into a Bench, hear the evidence and give judgment.'"

1980

Book Review: A History of Dalhousie Law School by John Willis.

Reprinted from
(1980) 18 Alberta Law Review
pp. 332–336

This history of Dalhousie Law School was begun by Dr. Horace E. Read, who had been the Dean from 1950 to 1964. Following his death in 1975, it was completed by Professor John Willis. The history is significant, since Dalhousie is the oldest common law school in Canada, dating back to 1883. Bowker's review was the first to come out (book reviews being perennially slow).

One of Bowker's motivating factors in producing the review was his long-standing personal connection with Dean Read, who, though a Canadian, was on the Law Faculty of the University of Minnesota in 1946, and was mainly responsible for Bowker pursuing graduate work there in the summers of 1946–8. Not only did the Bowkers stay at their home in Minneapolis, but continued a lifelong association with them. These personal reminiscences are not referred to in the book review.

A HISTORY OF DALHOUSIE LAW SCHOOL, by John Willis, University of Toronto Press, Toronto, 1979, pp. vi and 302, $20.00.

It is fortunate that John Willis was available to "finish what Horace Read began" (p. vi). The author points out in his preface that Read had completed "a rough preliminary first draft" of the period 1883–1950 before his death in 1975, but that "the finished product is mine alone". He adds that it is not the kind of history he would have liked to write, nor is it the one that Dean Read's would have been.

It must be hard to write a history of an institution. It could easily become a mere chronicle of events and a catalogue of facts and names. More than once Professor Willis explicitly states his aversion to such a narrative, and he has certainly avoided it. His account of the development and character of the school, of problems of finance and staffing, makes good reading. He has given a vivid and authentic picture of the men who built the school.

The story begins with the appointment in 1883 of Professor Richard Weldon to provide both technical training, which the practitioners wanted, and a liberal education, which the University wanted. Thus Weldon included subjects like Constitutional History, International Law and Conflicts. The author takes occasion to contrast this "attempt to make the study of law a liberal as well as a technical pursuit" with the "hard-nosed practitioner's slant" of Osgoode Hall Law School operated by the Law Society of Upper Canada and established on a permanent basis in 1889.

Another favourable factor was the outstanding calibre of the "over town instructors" including John Thompson who was later Prime Minister of Canada, Robert Sedgewick who later went to the Supreme Court of Canada, and Benjamin Russell who became a Nova Scotia judge and author of a text on Bills of Exchange.

Almost from the beginning the Law School was full-time and was housed in parts of the Forrest Building where it remained until 1952. One gathers that those quarters, becoming more crowded as time went on, together with the library, always inadequate because it was starved for funds, in some odd way contributed to the character of the school.

After describing the beginnings of the school, Professor Willis divides the rest of the book into roughly equal parts—"Dalhousie's Little Law School: 1887–1945", and the Post-War Period which is itself divided into two parts. The first of these is entitled "Changing: (1945–1966)" and the second is "In the Weldon Building: (1966–1976)".

Coming through are the dedication and stature of those who shaped the school—the students, the University, the profession and above all, the deans and teachers. I was about to say "full-time teachers" but this would leave out many of the practitioners who taught part-time including Benjamin Russell whose contribution on a "pittance of $1,000 a year" was immense. He continued to teach for almost forty years.

Remaining as dean until 1914, and notwithstanding nine years in Parliament, Weldon was an amazing man. The author concludes that he conferred on his students a "college and clan spirit" and inculcated in them his own idealism.

His successor, Donald A. MacRae, who was dean from 1910 to 1924, made many contributions one of which is of general interest because of its influence on other common law schools. He shaped the Dalhousie curriculum that went into effect in 1915. Five years later the Canadian Bar Association adopted it with virtually no change. When the Faculty of Law was established at the University of Alberta in 1921 it adopted the Canadian Bar Association curriculum and indeed retained it with no change for over twenty years, and with only modest alterations until the coming of the present era of options and seminars.

Until the early '20s the dean was the only full-time teacher though the faculty was fortunate in the great support it received from the Halifax Bar. John Read was appointed full-time in 1920 and Sidney Smith a year later. It was under them that the "case method" of teaching really arrived. In the same period the admission requirement was raised to two years of Arts, Harvard accepted Dalhousie graduates as candidates for the LL.M., and the faculty began to produce legal articles, many of which appeared in the newly established *Canadian Bar Review*.

Professor Willis describes the period 1920–1933 as the Golden Age. This begins with the return of the veterans from World War I as students and embraces the last four years of MacRae's deanship, five of John Read's and four of Sidney Smith's. The last named did not leave until 1934. I think the reason the author did not extend the Golden Age to that year is the fact that he himself came to the school in 1933. John Read had recruited to the faculty Angus L. Macdonald in 1924 and Horace Read in 1925. They each had a crushing teaching load and a low salary. In 1930 Vincent MacDonald replaced Angus L. The author gives a vivid portrayal of these men, all of whom went on to distinguished careers. This section of the book ends with an account of the ceremonies in celebration of the school's fiftieth anniversary in the fall of 1933.

The next period is entitled "1933–1945: The Great Depression and the Second World War". Professor Willis himself had joined the faculty in 1933 for one year, and remained to replace Horace Read who went to the University of Minnesota in 1934. The new Dean, Vincent MacDonald, had three young teachers—in addition to Willis they were George Curtis and George Crouse.

Most intriguing is the author's account of the coming of himself and George Curtis. "These two outsiders, Willis and Curtis—the first non-Maritimers ever to teach at the School—were at the beginning regarded, and justly regarded, as something less than 'finds'. But by the time they left, after what was for Dalhousie Law School an unusually long stay, eleven years each, they would have become—for such is the way of the world—'good old John' and 'good old George'" (p. 222). Later, in describing his own legal writings while at Dalhousie, the author says, "in the eleven years he was at the School Willis published eight articles, one of them an acknowledged classic" (p. 136). This is of course true—it is his "Statute Interpretation in a Nutshell" ((1938) 16 *Can. Bar Rev.* 1). Those that he wrote after leaving Dalhousie are, understandably, not mentioned. However, I think they are relevant because they demonstrate the author's scholarship and his pungent style and complete independence. Here are three examples.

1. Professor Willis wrote a note in the *Canadian Bar Review* criticizing the judgment of the Supreme Court of Canada in *Canadian Wheat Board* v. *Hallett* ([1951] S.C.R. 81). This evoked three hostile letters to the editor. Willis made a vigorous reply ((1951) 29 *Can. Bar Rev.* 296, 572, 573, 580 and 708). On appeal the Privy Council vindicated Professor Willis' position (*sub nom A.G.* v. *Hallett and Carey* [1952] A.C. 427).
2. When the reports of Ontario's Royal Commission inquiring into civil rights (the McRuer Commission) appeared, Willis wrote a robust critique ((1968) 18 *U.T.L.J.* 351 and (1970) 20 *U.T.L.J.* 274).
3. He gave a paper entitled "Trends in Administrative Law" to the Administrative Law Section of the Canadian Bar Association at its 1962 meeting in Halifax (published in 1962 papers presented at C.B.A. an-

nual meeting, page 1). The room was jammed and the audience enjoyed the paper. Many of those present had been students of the speaker at one or other of the law schools where he had taught, and went because they knew they would enjoy the "lecture".

The last part of the book entitled "Changing" begins with developments in legal education in Canada generally, including the drastic changes in Ontario. The first section, "Post-War Revival", covers the five years after World War II. With a large enrolment of students and a full-time faculty consisting of Dean Vincent MacDonald, Moffatt Hancock, James B. Milner, and from 1946, Thomas Feeney, the author describes this period as "a second but smaller golden age" (p. 159). Once again his description of each of these and of William Lederman who came in 1949 ("another potential star") makes fascinating reading. It seems that the "chronic impecuniosity" from which the school had suffered was alleviated by increased grants from the province (the Angus L. money) and liberal gifts from Sir James Dunn. (Gifts from Viscount Bennett, a loyal alumnus, had come earlier.)

The next section covering the period 1950–1958 is called "Innovations". When Vincent MacDonald went to the Supreme Court of Nova Scotia in 1950 Horace Read returned as dean. It was still hard to obtain and to keep teachers. Nonetheless Dean Read made important changes—replacing over-town instructors by full-time staff, increasing public law courses and establishing a Legislative Research Centre and beginning a graduate program. In 1952 the school moved from the old Forrest Building to the main campus. At the end of the eight-year period came more innovations—recognition of the Dalhousie degree in Ontario, the raising of admission standards from two to three years of Arts and the coming of George Nicholls who instituted legal research and writing and spurred the faculty to build up the library.

The next section covering the years 1958–1966 is called "On a New Plateau". This saw the beginning of staff meetings and the assertion of power by the faculty and as well the beginning of "student power". One gathers that the faculty's effort to have a major voice in the selection of a dean to succeed Horace Read in 1964 was not successful.

Speaking of Dean Read, he is of course prominent in the story. Of him, Willis says that he always looked at the School "through a rainbow". Referring to his death in 1975 the author concludes with this observation, "Everybody who knew him, even those who did not particularly admire him, agrees that the School stood always first in his thoughts. An excellent teacher, a first-rate author and an unaffectedly kind man, he will be long and deservedly remembered" (p. 227).

The last part entitled "In the Weldon Building", deals with the decade beginning in 1966. The school became a different place. There was more money and a quick increase in numbers both of faculty and students, student activism and ferment over curriculum and teaching methods which brought an end to the old MacRae curriculum. Andrew MacKay, who had succeeded Horace Read as dean in 1964, left the office five years later. This marked the end "in the long line of traditional deans". The vast increase in size of the School put an end to the old intimate atmosphere as well as to the one-man administration. "In a year or two the dean, to the students, will be a somewhat remote figure in the recesses of the Dean's Office: an associate dean and a host of faculty committees will be doing the academic 'joe jobs' that he used to do; and he will in all matters of importance be subject to what is called faculty control" (p. 218). Major developments under Dean Ronald St. J. MacDonald (who came in 1972) were the establishment of a Legal Aid Service, revival of the graduate program, establishment of the Dalhousie Law Journal and of a centre for Marine and Environmental Law. The explosion in the number of teachers from eight or nine to thirty-six meant a loss of close contact with the students and it brought a proliferation of meetings and paper work but also an increase in the amount of legal writing. Because of the very large student body it was impossible to preserve the intimate atmosphere of the old school though efforts were made to keep some of it. "Academically, the student body of today comes in better qualified, works harder, and does better than it did ten years ago" (p. 234). On the other hand, the student is "pampered or mollycoddled." The author concludes that the Weldon tradition of high academic standards and public service continue, although the open-door policy has had to give way in spite of every effort to preserve it.

The author's research has been meticulous. There are however three small inaccuracies.

1. The text states at p. 86 that whereas Dalhousie in 1924 raised the admission standard to two years of Arts, and MacRae recommended this to the Canadian Bar Association as the standard in all common law provinces, Ontario's Osgoode Hall ignored this recommendation for many years. The report of the Canadian Bar Association's committee on legal education in 1933 says that Ontario lowered the standard from two years to one in September 1932. Legal Education, (1933) 11 *Can. Bar Rev.* 475 at 476).
2. In speaking of Dean Read's establishment of the Master's program in 1950, the author at p. 176 quotes a statement that at this time Dalhousie was the only law school in Canada offering Jurisprudence. It was offered in the Faculty of Law at the University of Alberta from the time of its founding in 1921. I took it from Malcolm MacIntyre in 1930–1931 and taught it for some six years beginning in 1945. It has never left the calendar.
3. At p. 184 is a reference to the Viscount Bennett Scholarship. It says that in 1956 one of the graduating class "was the third Dalhousie graduate to win the premier Canadian award, the Viscount Bennett Scholarship, since it was first awarded in 1951." The first selection was made at the mid-winter meeting of the Council of the Canadian Bar Association in 1945, the winner being R.M. Sedgewick, Jr. of Toronto (1946 *Proc. Can. Bar Assoc.* 176). Chief Justice McRuer in his presidential address in 1947 (1947 *Proc.* at 87) said:

> the income from [the Viscount Bennett] fund has been sufficient to provide post-graduate studies for three students during the last two years.

Arnold Moir, now a member of Alberta's Court of Appeal, won the award in 1947.

These three items are really *de minimis*.

This is a good history and easy to read. It is of interest to anyone concerned with legal education in Canada and it brings to life the many men connected with the School who made a great contribution and by way of public service.

1980

Extra-Judicial Writing: The Alberta Law Quarterly, The Alberta Law Review, and Reviews in General

Reprinted from
(1980) 18 Alberta Law Review
pp. 458–470

This is an address which Bowker gave as guest speaker on the 25th anniversary of publication of the Alberta Law Review, *which was begun with his encouragement in 1955 when he was Dean of Law. Little remembered at the time of this anniversary was the earlier existence of the* Alberta Law Quarterly *which functioned from 1934 to 1945. They were similar in the sense that both were publications by the law students under a faculty adviser.*

After reviewing the work of these two University of Alberta publications, Bowker in his address dealt with the influence of legal writings generally on growth of the law and on judgments of courts—a topic with which he was familiar, from several years of teaching Jurisprudence.

I. Introduction

Thanks indeed. The first thing that comes to my mind is whether I can be heard at the back of the room. At one time, the complaint was not that I could not be heard at the back of the room, but that people in the other room could hear me too and did not particularly appreciate it. But with the passage of time, I think that perhaps I had better rely on the microphone.

Now, Mr. Chairman, as Trevor Anderson[1] was making his most kind remarks, this crossed my mind. Three or four years ago when Mr. Justice Stevenson was president of the Sir Winston Churchill Society, Lord Shawcross was invited to speak and Mr. Justice Stevenson had the perspicacity to bring Trevor back from Winnipeg to introduce him. Some of the local dinosaurs said, "What are they bringing in an import for?". Well, Trevor gave the best introduction of a Churchill speaker that was ever given. I only mention that for this reason: his introduction to Lord Shawcross, I think, took 14 minutes. The one tonight, although I didn't clock him, you know, I think took 16 minutes. I won't say anything about his sense of proportion, except that it is rather flattering to myself.

What I want to do in my remarks tonight is to deal with two aspects of the same subject. The first is legal writing here, through the old *Quarterly* and now the *Review,* and the second is the influence of extra-judicial legal writing on the shaping of the law.

Dr. MacIntyre[2] has been mentioned several times tonight in Trevor Anderson's remarks. He came here in 1930, and we were bewildered by Dr. MacIntyre after having had Dean Weir,[3] a master of the Socratic method, and also Mr. Steer,[4] who laid everything out cold. MacIntyre was full of doubts. I am going to mention two little incidents connected with Dr. MacIntyre because he had a great influence on all of us.

I remember when the decision was made to commission pictures by Grandmaison of Mr. Steer and L.Y. Cairns.[5] We went down to Calgary and Dick Burns,[6] whom I am most delighted to see here tonight, was our Calgary liaison. We had a lovely gathering in his home. One troublemaker there said, "Well, it's all right to have a picture of L.Y. Cairns, but I never liked Mr. Steer, and we've got to have MacIntyre there". So there was a great debate about the respective virtues of Mr. Steer and MacIntyre, and we wound up commissioning a picture of MacIntyre too. You can see all three of them in the lobby up on the fourth floor [of the Law Centre, University of Alberta]. If it had not been for Dick's help and the advocacy of this other chap who wanted MacIntyre there, we would not have had his picture. Somebody out at the Coast did it. I was not particularly happy with the picture at the time, but now I am glad that we have it there.

There is one other comment I want to make about MacIntyre, though I don't think I can do justice to it. I had a chat with Mr. Justice Morrow years ago[7]—and I am pleased that Mr. Justice Morrow is here tonight. I remember, when I expressed some misgivings or deprecations of MacIntyre, Mr. Justice Morrow said; "Well, when he came along I saw for the first time", (and I don't think I can do justice to the way he put it), "that the answers aren't all pat, they don't come out like a syllogism. I saw the light when MacIntyre taught us to see that there are two sides to every problem and we want to try to figure out the solution in the best social way". Of course, MacIntyre had been a student of Dean Pound, and I think that is what Bill Morrow was trying to convey. I think Bill's remark made me appreciate MacIntyre more than I ever had before. He went out to the Law Faculty at U.B.C. later, and when you talked to any student from that law school, you knew that they just thought the world of him. It is true that he spent a month on the *Loach*[8] case and he would bring in the *Loach* case whatever was the topic—he had no sense of timing and no idea of any framework—but I think certainly Mr. Burns and Mr. Justice Morrow and Mr. Corbett,[9] and others here tonight who were students of his, like myself, feel greatly indebted to MacIntyre.

II. Legal Writing in Alberta

Now, Dr. MacIntyre was the man who conceived the idea of the *Law Quarterly*. Dean Weir wasn't enthusiastic, but MacIntyre instituted it. I took a quick look through some of the five volumes and I will say this: they were nearly all student articles and they are a good cross-section of the legal issues that we had in this Province at that time. We were in the midst of the Depression. There was all manner of litigation about the constitutionality of early Social Credit legislation, and you can find case notes and comments on those very important and sometimes bitter issues that we faced in Canada in the mid-thirties. I think there are some hidden nuggets there that are very valuable as part of our legal history.

Now there was one thing I noticed tonight. I never remembered it before in connection with the *Quarterly* and I want to tell you about it now. As soon as it was established, MacIntyre went to the Board of Governors and invited them to make an award for the best student articles in the *Law Quarterly*. MacIntyre got $50 from the Board of Governors. The awards that I saw had to do with the year 1935 and the year 1936. The $50 was split twelve different ways. In the first year I forget who won the top prize of $10; but I can say this, and maybe Mr. Burns will correct me if I am wrong: in the second year, 1936, he, as a recent graduate, got the top prize of $12 for his student effort, and I am sure it set him up in practice and he is still in practice. As to other names there, I think McDermid[10] came in at $8.00, Riley[11] came in at $9.00 or $6.00, and there are some names that you would not recognize so I won't bother naming them. I see Peter Costigan here tonight. I hate to say this, Peter, but your father[12] came in at $3.00. This all appears in the *Alberta Law Quarterly*.[13] I was touched by seeing it because nearly every one of those names turned out to be one of distinction in the years following. We can make fun about that pittance, but it had as much significance then as a much larger award would have today.

There was one type of article which they ran, and I applaud this—articles on English judges and lawyers; tiny little ones, but they are still worth preserving and I am glad we have them. Then there was another kind of article and I can remember three of them, but there might have been more. had to do with practical matters. They included forms and precedents, and the first one was by L.Y. Cairns and Ernest Wilson[14] on foreclosure practice in Alberta.[15] Well, all I can say is this: I did a lot of that work in that period and the article by Cairns was always at my elbow. I learned more about the Rules of Court of Alberta and foreclosure practice from that article than from any other single source.

The second one was on originating notices of motion—that's really an exciting topic, I know—by my classmate Bill Parlee.[16] I am sure that there was a judgment that cited Parlee's note, and it is the only piece in the *Law Quarterly* which was ever cited, to my knowledge. I spent a half-day trying to find it and I wasn't able to find it, but I think you could take my word for it that Parlee's article on originating notices of motion was, in fact, cited.

Now I'm going to come to the third article. I do this with some diffidence because, Mr. Chairman, it was my own.[17] It was on divorce practice in Alberta. Now, those knowledgeable about divorce like Leonard Pollock[18] might understandably ask, "What does this chap know about divorce practice?" Well, the answer is, not very much; but I wanted to learn something about it, so I went to the Committee that we had during the Depression called The Needy Litigants Committee which gave permits to bring actions without any fees. It was a good way for young people to get some experience, and I had several of these. I went to them and said, "Will you give me a divorce case?" and they said, "We don't give a Needy Litigants certificate for divorce cases. These are a luxury and they can pay it on their own". But they made an exception for me and they gave me a case. My client was the most scurvy character who ever asked for a divorce in Alberta. But I did what I could to learn something about the practice and when Jim Wallbridge, one of the boys from the *Law Quarterly,* came to me a short time later (this was around 1937) and said, "Will you write something for the *Quarterly?*" I thought, well, I'll write a piece on divorce practice in Alberta. But there was no Kent Power[19] in those days. I don't want to laud my own piece but several solicitors, particularly in the country, did say they found those precedents useful, and I don't think any judge ever said they were in error.

That little piece of mine once stood me in good stead and I'd like to tell you about it. In 1962, I received an anguished phone call from a Vancouver solicitor. He said, "Will you come out to Vancouver to give expert evidence on the law of Alberta on this point? If one of the spouses, after a decree *nisi* but before the decree absolute, goes through a form of marriage, is that marriage valid?" Now you might say, Mr. Chairman, "why would they ask that question?" We all know it isn't valid. But remember, B.C. took the law of England as of 1858 and the requirement of a decree *nisi* wasn't in the 1857 Matrimonial Causes Act. It was in an amendment that came into effect between 1858 and 1870. We all know that we took the law as of 1870, and *Board* v. *Board*[20] said that our judges had jurisdiction in divorce. I said I would go, and my wife typed out a little memo that night, and I appeared before Mr. Justice Ruttan the next day.

Now, I have a bit of a quiff. I don't like the word *expert*. Everybody who ever proclaims anything on any subject is reported in the newspapers as an expert, and I think it's a word that has become cheapened. But technically I had to be qualified as an expert. And I should perhaps say this, that when that lawyer first phoned me and put this problem to me, I said, "Whichever side you're on, that marriage is invalid and I don't care what you want me to say, that's all I'm going to say". Well, it turned out that was what he wanted me to say. So I went out and when I was being qualified I had to show my credentials and I only had two. The first one was that I had taught Domestic Relations one year; but the real clincher was that I had written an article on divorce practice in Alberta in the *Alberta Law Quarterly*. So there was no question about my qualifications.

If you want to read that case, it is *Rogers* v. *Imperial Life*.[21] It went to the Court of Appeal. It involved an insurance policy and the marriages came into it this way: the lady was an adventuress and she married Husband No. 1 in Alberta, then after the decree *nisi* purported to marry Husband No. 2, then later married Rogers. If the second marriage was good, then she was not married to Rogers; but the fact was, the second marriage wasn't effective because it took place between the nisi and the absolute. Rogers was her husband, and she got the insurance. That was a bit of indirect influence of the *Alberta Law Quarterly*.

Now I want to move to the next era. I won't talk about the demise of the *Alberta Law Quarterly* because I had to preside over its funeral when I came in the fall of 1945. Mr. Justice Stevenson and Dr. Alex Smith have written pieces on the subject. You can read about it in the *25th Anniversary Issue* of the *Alberta Law Review*.[22] The *Quarterly* died at the end of the war, and when I came in September, 1945, all I had was an office full of unmailed issues of the last part of Volume 5 of the *Alberta Law Quarterly*. I'm not going to labour that.

The next phase I want to describe is this. Trevor Anderson was kind enough to refer to my effort to do something in legal writing. I might add that when John Willis wrote his history of the Dalhousie Law School[23] and described their course in legal writing under George Nicholls in the late '50s and '60s, he did make this concession: he said, "Well, there had been a course in Alberta before ours. It was one in legal writing of a sort."[24] Now, you get the innuendo there. But I want to say this: beginning in 1950, going through 1958 (and by this time the *Review* was started), we did have, from students in this law school, nine articles in the *Canadian Bar Review*.[25] No other law school ever came within a mile of that.

I want to say something about these articles, or rather, case notes. They came from the course that Trevor mentioned. There were nine of them, but one was a double article, so there were ten authors. Two of those men have died, Bill Stainton of Edmonton and Bob Neve of Calgary. Three of them are practitioners: Miles Patterson and Gordon Brown of Calgary, and James Enright of Edmonton (who is here tonight). Patterson's case note I shall mention in a moment. Gordon Brown's article predicted the result in the *Berkheiser* case,[26] on the nature of an oil and gas lease. Gordon's comment was on a Saskatchewan case, *Re Sykes*.[27] He said quite correctly that it was dead wrong. I was always very proud of Gordon's article.

The case note by Jimmy Enright was on *Beaver* v. *The King*,[28] on the onus in narcotics cases. I'll say this to you: there may be some here tonight who think that students do not have any scholarship. I point out, and Jimmy may remember this, that his article is the only writing I know of in Canada that cites Lon Fuller's "Speluncean Explorers";[29] and if you don't know what Lon Fuller's "Speluncean Explorers" is, I won't take the time to say.

Most of those articles were on evidence. There was one by Jim Woods, who is now a Provincial Court judge. There were two by Queen's Bench judges. One was by Mr. Justice Stevenson on cars stored at owner's risk, which was an important issue for many years, and one was by Mr. Justice William Egbert. Of the present Court of Appeal, there was a piece by Clifton Prowse that he wrote with Miles Patterson. It was a very learned case note on a judgment of the Saskatchewan Court of Appeal in a case called *Clark* v. *Barrick*.[30] It dealt with the effect of a caveat, ad it was the best piece that has ever been written on the effect of a caveat. But they found the frustration many of us do: they wrote this learned article, waited to see what the Supreme Court would do, and the Supreme Court of Canada finally said, "We don't have to deal with the caveat because the acceptance was too late. The offeree waited too long." So we never had the satisfaction of knowing whether the Supreme Court agreed with this article.

The last individual in this group is Ivan Head. If you don't know who Ivan Head is, I'm not going to take time to tell you. His article was on *Guay* v. *The Sun Publishing Company*[31] and he wrote that as a student. Of course, he and Mr. Justice Laycraft wrote a later article[32] and he has written a great deal more, but the first piece he ever wrote was the case note on *Guay*. Whether or not I have any right to be proud of those articles, I am.

Then the *Review* came along and I remember one article that appeared during the transition, and I see Dick Dunlop[33] here tonight. Maybe he can correct me if I'm wrong. In the period I speak of, George Nicholls was the editor of the *Canadian Bar Review;* and if there ever was an exacting editor, it was George Nicholls. I sent him a couple of pieces, including the ones Trevor Anderson mentioned to you, and I got the blue pencil page after page. None of these student articles got the treatment I did. That shows something about the quality of manuscripts that were submitted to Mr. Nicholls. As I recall, we sent Dick Dunlop's manuscript down. It had to do with an oil and gas development contract. The non-operator alleged that the operator was in a fiduciary relationship to the non-operator and that the operator had been in breach of its fiduciary duties. The Supreme Court of Canada said there was no breach. Dunlop's case note was a scholarly criticism of the majority judgment. It ultimately appeared in the *Alberta Law Review*.[34] I think it was during the transition period. And I was proud of that article—I am glad it came out in our *Review* rather than in the *Canadian Bar Review,* but I recall that Nicholls made constructive comments on the case note and that he said, "I want to encourage young people". If you got past George Nicholls, you were pretty good.

There was one other article. It started off in the same course (Legal Writing) as an article on the law dealing with Hutterites in Alberta. It was by a student by the name of Douglas Sanders, who has become a very outstanding civil liberties lawyer in British Columbia. I thought it would be in the *Alberta Law Review,* but he parlayed it up until it appeared in the *Canadian Law Review*.[35] You can find Sanders' article there, but it had its origin in our course on legal writing.

III. The Influence of Legal Writing Generally

I want to move now to the second part of my talk, which has to do with the influence of writing by scholars on the development of the law. Now, I am no authority on Roman law but this statement seems to be accepted: that in Roman law, and in the modern codes that are based on the Roman law, including Quebec's Civil Code, the writings of scholars have much more weight that the judgment of a court. The writings of scholars are called *doctrine* and the writings of judges are called *jurisprudence,* and it is doctrine that has the weight. If you read a case from Quebec, even today, dealing with the Code, it is going to pay much more attention to these writers with names like Planiol (which is only a name to me) and Ripert. Or, in Quebec, Mr. Justice Mignault, not as a justice of the Supreme Court of Canada but as the commentator on Quebec's Code, had—and still has—much more weight than does a judgment on the interpretation of the Code. Now, in our system, the common law system, it is just the reverse. It's interesting to think about the origin of the common law system. We had to have two elements. We had to have judges who wanted to follow what was done before and we had to have what was done before in available written form. That is where the reporters came in. I'm not talking about the reporters tonight. I did that once to the *Law Review* staff, and it's a fascinating story. We could not have the common law system without reporters. So, as our system grew up, a judge was guided by what had been decided before and not by what some writer said.

If you look at books on jurisprudence, you will find a heading "Sources of the Law". The decisions of judges are a direct source and the writings of scholars are called indirect sources. Blackstone pointed out that there were several writers (I won't name all that Blackstone named but I'll mention the main ones) whose works were accepted as expressing the common law or the law that preceded it. The first one was Glanville in Henry II's time and the next one was Bracton in Henry III's time, and there were a few more like Britton and Fleta but nobody knows who they were. Then you get up to Littleton, and Coke's *Commentary on Littleton,* and Coke's three other volumes that he called *Institutes.* And I'd like to tell you a little event that occurred in connection with *Coke on Littleton.* For awhile after the War we did not have the funds for a library that we have now. I'm proud of our library; we have a wonderful collection and we have wonderful people helping us, and I don't think we know how fortunate we are unless we go to some other law libraries. But in the early years after the War we did not have textbooks, so when a friend of mine from the government phoned over and said, "We're throwing out some second-last editions; will you come over and pick them up?" I was there immediately. There was a second-last edition of *Maxwell on Statutes,* and of *Charlesworth on Negligence.* I took them and they were put in our library. We were glad to have them. Well, one of the volumes was *Coke on Littleton;* it was 1832, a fairly modern edition. So I said to my friend, "Now, look, you really don't want to give that away, do you?" and he said, "Yes, I do". So he knew what he was doing when he gave me *Coke on Littleton.* For the next ten years or so, I kept it in my office along with an edition of *Blackstone* from the 18th century where the *s*'s look like *f*'s. Lovely it is. And I used to take that *Blackstone* in with me when we were reading about the rights of ownership in animals, domestic and wild. Blackstone's passage[36] is simply beautiful and I used to read it to every class. Now, I know those books are in the rare book room and I won't make any cheap joke about having to beat down the door to get the book that I got for the library, because the library staff is very cooperative.

So Blackstone named the four writers I have mentioned: Glanville, Bracton, Littleton and Coke. And, of course, he didn't mention himself. Now, if you read modern books on the question of what works could be mentioned in a court of law as indicating the common law of England, Pollock in 1896 said, "They are called works of authority and they end in 1762 with Foster's *Crown Law*."[37] That excludes Blackstone.

Now, it's interesting to note the position in more modern times. In 1935 the House of Lords decided *Woolmington's* case[38] on the burden of proof when the accused pleads the defence of accident. You will remember Viscount Sankey's famous passage: throughout the web of the English Criminal Law, one golden thread is always to be seen—the presumption of innocence.[39] In holding that the accused did not have to prove the shooting was accidental, Viscount Sankey had to reject a statement in Foster's *Crown Law,* which was a book of authority. On the other hand, in the very same year there was a case in which a convicted person applied to quash an order binding him over to keep the peace, on the ground that there was no jurisdiction to bind him over because his offence had not threatened violence to anyone else.[40] (He had warned bookmakers that the police were coming and had previously been convicted eight times for similar offences.) In rejecting the argument, Mr. Justice Humphreys quoted a passage from Blackstone for the proposition that a magistrate can bind over a person whenever it is likely he will break the law even though no breach of the peace is threatened. And His Lordship added, "That in my judgment is the law, and it is too late, in 1935, to attempt to show that Blackstone was wrong."[41] Now, I mention those two cases because Foster was rejected by the House of Lords in the same year that the Court of King's Bench accepted Blackstone though Pollock had said that Foster is a work of authority and Blackstone is not.

Then, as time moved on, the rule was relaxed. It is stated in different ways but generally it went this way until the present century: some judges would say, "You can't quote anybody before us unless he's dead", and others say, "You can't quote anybody before us unless he's both dead and was a judge". I cannot detect which was the right rule. We know that Lord Justice Fry wrote *Specific Performance,* and Lord Lindley wrote both *Partnership* and *Companies*. They were certainly quotable after they were dead.

Now, there was a well known little "incident", I suppose I should call it, in the same era, '35 or '36, when Lord Wright had to deal with a case where a man who had a fishery in a stream complained that a sugar beet factory polluted the stream.[42] The important legal question was whether the plaintiff's right of action was complete on a showing of interference with his right of fishery or whether he also had to prove pecuniary loss. The court quoted a passage from Sir Frederick Pollock's *Torts* and applied it. In introducing the passage from Pollock, Lord Wright said, "The matter is clearly stated in the work, fortunately not a work of authority, but to which we are all as lawyers indebted. . . ".[43] He was saying in a subtle way that he was glad that Pollock was still alive. However, in the *Law Times Reports* the editor thought that "fortunately" was a slip for "unfortunately", and so "unfortunately" appears in the *Law Times Reports*.[44] I might add that I did not discover this. It is mentioned in every book which deals with works of authority.

In that same era there was a great relaxation in the rule as to whom you could cite. Originally they had to be in this narrow category of works of authority; then any deceased judge; the notable breakthrough came (again in 1935) in *Haynes* v. *Harwood*,[45] the rescue case, when the Court of Appeal cited Goodhart's article[46] and applied it. Goodhart lived for many years after that and so that was quite a breakthrough. Another strong influence in favour of breaking down the old rule came from Lord Denning in his review of the third edition of *Winfield*. He welcomed the writings of academic lawyers and added that the old idea that their works are not of authority until they have died has long been exploded.[47] In an address before the Society of Public Teachers of Law, he made the same point.[48] So even in England the old rule has largely broken down.

There was another custom that I was brought up on. It is that you do not cite *Halsbury*. We had a very learned judge here, the Honourable Frank Ford, and he would not accept a citation from *Halsbury* because it wasn't authentic. Well, you see it every day now. Of course, the passage is just as good as the authority behind it. I don't think I rebel against citing *Halsbury* now, but I am quite sure my memory is correct: Mr. Justice Ford wouldn't permit it. Now, I don't want to deter those of you having moots who want to cite *Halsbury*. It can be very useful.

In Australia on the High Court there were judges like Chief Justice Dixon, Mr. Justice Evatt, and Sir Victor Windeyer. They quoted current articles all the time, including those in the *Canadian Bar Review*. And down in the States, I read somewhere that Holmes once said to Pollock that in Massachusetts the rule used to be strict like the English rule, but that isn't so now. You can pick up any judgment, certainly in the Supreme Court of the United States and find that the judges cite, for example, Professor Paul Freund, who is one of the most learned men there is and he is still alive. They are certainly not bothered by this now and they cite law reviews as well as texts all the time.

Now I come to the position in Canada. This may be well known, Mr. Chairman, but I want to tell it anyway. In 1950, some discontented landlords were unhappy that the wartime control over the amount of rents was still in effect under the National Emergency Transitional Powers Act,[49] so they argued that these regulations were invalid because the war power was gone. In fact, this was a very important subject in the civil liberties section of the Canadian Bar Association at that time. At one meeting, my old friend, Jim Milner, who died in 1969, said to me, "Where are you going to go?" I said, "I'm going to the civil liberties section". He said, "Oh, do you want to hear Willes Chitty and his Landlord Protective Association?" At that time they were more concerned about rent controls than they were about freedom of speech.

The case went before the Supreme Court of Canada[50] and one of the lawyers (I think he must have been supporting the regulations) wanted to cite Vincent MacDonald, who had been Dean of Law at Dalhousie, then became a judge, and was one of our greatest writers in the mid-'30s on constitutional matters. He was much like the present Chief Justice of Canada, and felt that Dominion powers had been whittled down by Privy Council rulings. So this counsel wanted to refer to Vincent MacDonald's article in the *Canadian Bar Review.*[51] You cannot find any reference to this in the judgments but according to the article which George Nicholls wrote in the *Bar Review*[52] (remember, he was the editor), Chief Justice Rinfret made the remark, "The *Canadian Bar Review* is not an authority in this court". When George learned of this, he wrote a lengthy article showing how wrong Chief Justice Rinfret was. If you read that article you can get the whole story of the use by courts of non-judicial writing. Since then I doubt very much that there's been any recurrence of that attitude, and we all know that some of the judges freely refer to articles—current articles—and we must all be glad that they do.

Now I want to say a little more about George Nicholls. He was editor of the *Canadian Bar Review* roughly from 1945 to 1957. The first editor had been Charles Morse, followed by Dean Wright. They were great editors and Dean Wright also had a tremendous influence on legal education. Nicholls succeeded Dean Wright and he raised the stature of the *Canadian Bar Review* to a very high degree, there is no question about it. But as I said earlier, in connection with our student case notes, he was a very exacting editor.

In the case on the validity of the barley regulations that forbade profiteering,[53] the profiteer won in our courts and the Wheat Board had to go to the Privy Council to get the regulations upheld. Well, one of the lawyers who had won in the Canadian courts was angry over a case note by Professor John Willis[54] criticizing the judgment of the Supreme Court of Canada. The lawyer also criticized Nicholls for publishing the case note. He said, in effect, "You have no business writing a case note on a case that is still in the courts." Nicholls replied to that in a very robust way and of course he was dead right; there is no tradition that you cannot make a comment on a pending case. If that were so, we couldn't make some flattering remarks about some of the judgments of judges in this room. All of this appears in the *Canadian Bar Review* of 1951.[55]

Mr. Chairman, I have one other comment about George Nicholls. To show what integrity and maybe stubbornness he had, as years went on, he was so concerned about the calibre of material in the *Canadian Bar Review* that this occurred. Now, I am going on my memory here because I was at these meetings. Though I have not documented it, I think you could from the proceedings of the Canadian Bar Association. One year in the early '50s the Right Honourable Arthur Meighen went to Vancouver and talked to the Bar. He was a man of great stature in political life, whatever one felt about his political views. He gave a talk to the Vancouver Bar; I think it was probably that we had too much government and should get back to private enterprise. They sent this speech of Meighen's to George Nicholls and said, "You have to publish it", and Nicholls' position was, "It's got nothing to do with law. I won't publish it". So there was a great furore over that.

And then, a little while later (and this came close to his resignation), I think he turned down at least one or maybe two presidential addresses of the president of the Canadian Bar Association (which paid his salary) and they couldn't understand this. He stuck to his guns and did retire half under fire in 1957.[56] There was another factor. There was an element, I don't think it was a large element, but it was certainly vocal, that the *Canadian Bar Review* was too erudite and what we needed was a chatty, folksy sort of publication and I think the *American Bar Association Journal* was cited. And I remember one of the proponents of this (and fairly highly placed, too) at a meeting I was at who made an attack on the *Canadian Bar Review* as being far too abstract. He said, "When it comes, I fire it in the wastepaper basket". Now he made this remark about two months after my article on Chief Justice Harvey had appeared.[57] You can imagine how I felt.

IV. Conclusion

Now, Mr. Chairman, I just want to make a few comments in conclusion. I tried to think whether I would have any advice to student editors of a law journal and I don't. I met a few in a couple of other law schools I had contact with, and they were the cream of the cream. Maybe it is well known here, and I hesitate to mention this, but down in places like Yale and Harvard when the big New York firms send their hiring partner up to pick the students their letter invariably says, "Law Review or equivalent". Well, the "equivalent" opens it up a bit, but that is the standard they go by. Now my only hesitation in mentioning it is that I would not want to hint that anybody in this law school ever joined the staff of the *Law Review* so that he could get better articles. I would think he would have a better motive than that, but that is simply the case down there. So I have no comment to editors. There have been a couple of instances where the editor of our *Review* brought a manuscript to me and my feeling was, "Oh, I think you could let it pass". But he turned it down, and I think he was right because it was nothing new, it was perfunctory. I think his standards were higher than mine and I was rather proud of him.

Now I will close, Mr. Chairman, with a couple of observations I have (I won't call it advice) for people who want to write. The first thing I would say is that many of us have gone through life wishing we had written more. Many of us feel we have a valid criticism of a judgment and yet we let it pass. I wish we could just overcome that hesitance or procrastination and write more. Now I know if I were a judge I would probably feel like Vice-

Chancellor Megarry when he referred to a method of teaching law "which treated decisions at first instance as barely worthy of consideration, those of the Court of Appeal as usually wrong, and those of the House of Lords as right, though for the wrong reasons".[58] This was before he was a judge. Of course, he is a great author in his own right.

I think that if a person feels strongly enough about a point he should make it. It doesn't have to be an intemperate criticism of the judges. I have an attitude, and this cannot be generalized, that very often we speak in a strident voice. Now Dean Wright liked to do it, he could excoriate the courts of Ontario and I would say he was dead right every time. However, you can still talk to elderly people connected with law in Ontario who don't smile when you mention Dean Wright's name. He made a great contribution with his writing; but we cannot all adopt what I call "the damn fool" school of writing, and I think that for most of us understatement is a little bit better. I think we do miss a great many opportunities to express ourselves in a temperate way and in a way that would be constructive.

On style, I would be the last one to talk about style. I have told you what George Nicholls did to some of my manuscripts and I sometimes think that many of us who have written opinions and drawn conveyances are probably like John Austin. I am speaking of the author of *Jurisprudence*. In writing to his future wife he said that his experience in drafting led to such a taste "for perspicuity and precision, that I shall hardly venture on sending a letter of much purpose, even to you, unless it be laboured with the accuracy and circumspection which are requisite in a deed of conveyance".[59] Well, I am sure I have fallen into that category. Frank Scott told me more than once, "Make it live". He didn't say *jazz it up a bit* but that is what he meant. Of course, it would be wonderful if we all had the style of Frank Scott or Alex Smith (and anyone who has not read Dr. Smith's book on the commerce power in Canada and the United States, or any of his other writings, should do it for that cause alone);[60] but we are not all gifted that way and we just have to put up with it. My last observation would be this: although we may not all have fine writing styles, we don't want our writing to be drab. Holdsworth was drab and so are a lot of other scholars.

A final comment—we often tend to be too prolix. There is a homely phrase, "You can squeeze a lot of water out of most of these articles", and I think that is so. An English writer or scholar, I don't know who he was, in the period after the War when the paper shortage was still acute in England and the *Law Quarterly* had shrunk to practically nothing, looking at the proliferation, the flood of articles from the United States (articles of up to 100 pages and nothing less than a 15-page case note, where the *Law Quarterly* had about a page), said, "What American legal writing needs most is a paper shortage". Now, maybe, Mr. Chairman, after my comments you might think I need a paper shortage too, but in any event, I am finished.

Notes

1 Of the Faculty of Law, University of Manitoba. Mr. Anderson delivered the Introduction to Dr. Bowker's address on this occasion.

2 Dr. Malcolm M. MacIntyre, Dean of the Faculty of Law, University of Alberta, 1942–1944. *See also* W.F. Bowker, "Malcolm Murray MacIntyre, 1904–1964" (1964) 3 *Alta. L. Rev.* 161.

3 Dean John Weir, the first Dean of the Faculty of Law, University of Alberta (from 1921 to 1942).

4 G.H. Steer, Q.C., Acting Dean from 1944 to 1947.

5 The late Judge L.Y. Cairns, who was for many years a part-time lecturer in the Faculties of Law and Commerce.

6 R.J. Burns, Q.C., of the firm Macleod Dixon in Calgary.

7 The Honourable Mr. Justice William G. Morrow of the Alberta Court of Appeal. His untimely death occurred on August 13, 1980, as this article was going to press.

8 *Loach* v. *B.C. Elec. Ry. Co.* (1915) 23 D.L.R. 4 (P.C.), *affg.* (1914) 16 D.L.R. 245 (B.C.C.A.). Dr. MacIntyre's classic article on this case is "The Rationale of Last Clear Chance" (1940) 53 *Harv. L. Rev.* 1225, 18 *Can. Bar Rev.* 665.

9 John H. Corbett, Q.C., of Corbett, Benkendorf, Hodgson & Lachambre in Edmonton.

10 The Honourable Mr. Justice N.D. McDermid of the Alberta Court of Appeal.

11 The late Mr. Justice Harold Riley of the Trial Division, Supreme Court of Alberta.

12 T.J. Costigan, Q.C., of Blairmore, Alberta.

13 *See* "Special Awards" (1935) 1 *Alta. L.Q.* 168 and (1936) 2 *Alta. L.Q.* 29.

14 The late Mr. Justice E.B. Wilson of the Trial Division, Supreme Court of Alberta. His son William E. Wilson, Q.C., was at the banquet.

15 L.Y. Cairns, "Foreclosure of Land Mortgages in Alberta by Way of Court Procedure" (1938) 2 *Alta. L.Q.* 193.

16 W.O. Parlee, "Originating Notice of Motion" (1940) 3 *Alta. L.Q.* 223. W.O. Parlee, Q.C. is the head of Parlee, Irving, Henning, Mustard & Rodney in Edmonton.

17 W.F. Bowker, "Procedure in Divorce Actions in Alberta" (1938) 3 *Alta. L.Q.* 51.

18 Professor L.J. Pollock, Q.C., of the Faculty of Law, The University of Alberta.

19 This reference is to the author of *Power on Divorce and Other Matrimonial Causes,* who also edited *Power's Western Practice Digest* and the *Western Weekly Reports*.

20 [1919] A.C. 956.

21 *Re Rogers* (*Deceased*) (1963) 42 W.W.R. 200 (B.C.C.A.), *affg.* (1962) 40 W.W.R. 317 (B.C.S.C.).

22 *Alberta Law Review Twenty-Fifth Anniversary Issue* (February 1980), at 38, 45.

23 J. Willis, *A History of Dalhousie Law School* (1979, University of Toronto Press). *See also* W.F. Bowker, "Legal Writing at the University of Alberta" (1959) 13 *U. of T.L.J.* 85.

24 *Id.* at 187. The exact words are "The Alberta Law School had had one of a kind since 1944".

25 The nine articles appearing in the *Canadian Bar Review* are: M.H. Patterson and D.C. Prowse, "Torrens System—*Wilkie* v. *Jellett*" (1950) 28 *Can. Bar Rev.* 456; J.S. Woods, "Evidence—Tests for Alcoholic Intoxication" (1951) 29 *Can. Bar Rev.* 521; W.J. Stainton, "Criminal Law—Receiving Stolen Goods" (1951) 29 *Can. Bar Rev.* 885; W.G.N. Egbert, "Divorce—Standard of Proof of Adultery" (1952) 30 *Can. Bar Rev.* 753; R.R. Neve, "Homicide–*Corpus Delicti*—Circumstantial Evidence" (1955) 33 *Can. Bar Rev.* 603; W.G. Brown, "Oil and Gas Lease—Sale of Minerals" (1956) 34 *Can. Bar Rev.* 730; I.L. Head, "Real Property—Torrens System of Land Registration in Saskatchewan" (1956) 34 *Can. Bar Rev.* 736; W.A. Stevenson, "Bailment—Owner's Risk Clause" (1957) 35 *Can. Bar Rev.* 1100; J.E. Enright, "Opium and Narcotic Drug—Possession" (1958) 36 *Can. Bar Rev.* 562.

26 *Berkheiser* v. *Berkhseiser* [1957] S.C.R. 387.

27 *Re Sykes Estate* (1955) 16 W.W.R. 459 (Sask. C.A.), *affg*. 16 W.W.R. 172 (Sask. Q.B.). *Revd*. [1957] S.C.R. 387.

28 [1957] S.C.R. 531; 26 C.R. 193; 118 C.C.C. 129 (S.C.C.).

29 L. Fuller, "The Case of the Speluncean Explorers" (1949) 62 *Harv. L. Rev.* 616.

30 [1951] S.C.R. 177, *revg*. [1949] 2 W.W.R. 1009 (Sask. C.A.).

31 [1953] 2 S.C.R. 216, *affg*. 5 W.W.R. (N.S.) 97, *revg*. 4 W.W.R. (N.S.) 549.

32 I.L. Head and J.H. Laycraft, "Theories of Ownership of Oil and Gas" (1953) 31 *Can. Bar Rev.* 382.

33 Professor Richard Dunlop of the Faculty of Law, The University of Alberta.

34 R. Dunlop, "Oil and Gas Development Contract—Interpretation" (1960) 1 *Alta. L. Rev.* 466, a comment on *Midcon Oil & Gas Limited* v. *New British Dominion Oil Co.* [1958] S.C.R. 314.

35 D. Sanders, "The Hutterites: A Case Study in Minority Rights" (1964) 42 *Can. Bar Rev.* 225.

36 2 Bl. Comm., c. XXV at 391, 392.

37 Pollock's exact words appear in Pollock, *A First Book of Jurisprudence* (1896) at 236.

38 *Woolmington* v. *D.P.P.* [1935] A.C. 462 (H.L.).

39 *Id*. at 481.

40 *R*. v. *Sandbach* [1935] 2 K.B. 192.

41 *Id*. at 197.

42 *Nicholls* v. *Ely Beet Sugar Factory* [1936] Ch. 343.

43 *Id*. at 349.

44 (1936) 154 L.T.R. 531 at 533.

45 [1935] 1 K.B. 146.

46 A.L. Goodhart, "Rescue and Voluntary Assumption of Risk" (1934) 5 *Camb. L.J.* 192, cited *id*. at 156.

47 (1947) 63 L.Q.R. 516.

48 *The Universities and Law Reform* (1949), *J.S.P.T.L.* 258 at 263.

49 S.C. 1945, c. 25.

50 *Reference re Validity of the Wartime Leasehold Regulations* [1950] S.C.R. 124.

51 V.C. MacDonald, "Constitutional Interpretation and Extrinsic Evidence" (1939) 17 *Can. Bar Rev.* 77.

52 G.V.V. Nicholls, "Legal Periodicals and the Supreme Court of Canada" (1950) 28 *Can. Bar Rev.* 422.

53 *A.-G. Can.* v. *Hallet & Carey* [1952] A.C. 427, *revg*. (*sub. nom. Canadian Wheat Board* v. *Nolan*) [1951] S.C.R. 81, *affg*. (1949) 57 Man. L.R. 1 (Man. C.A.).

54 J. Willis, "Administrative Law—Statute Interpretation—Real Constitution versus Lawyer's Constitution" (1951) 29 *Can. Bar Rev.* 296.

55 *See* "Correspondence" (1951) 29 *Can. Bar Rev.* 572 at 573, 578, 580 and 708.

56 *See Proceedings, C.B.A.* (1957) at 59–76.

57 W.F. Bowker, "The Honourable Horace Harvey: Chief Justice of Alberta" (1954) 32 *Can. Bar Rev.* 933, 1118.

58 (1950) 1 *J.S.P.T.L.* at 346.

59 Sarah Austin, Preface to Austin's *Jurisprudence,* Vol. I (4th ed. 1879) at 4, 5.

60 A. Smith, *The Commerce Power in Canada and the United States* (1963).

1981

Book Review: Aspects of Privacy Law: Essays in Honour of John M. Sharp, edited by Dale Gibson

Reprinted from
(1981) 59 Canadian Bar Review
pp. 599–613

This is a review of a book published in honor of a young Professor at the University of Manitoba Law School, John M. Sharp, who died of brain cancer in his 30s, having shown promise of a brilliant future in law teaching. Because he was very strong on "privacy," the essays in this book relate to the law of privacy, with contributions invited from law teachers throughout Canada. Bowker knew John Sharp who had been a guest in our home.

The book consists of 13 essays. Bowker gave it a favorable review, though recognizing how difficult it is to produce a book of essays which "hang together." On further reflection, he feels he might have been more critical, for though the first part was very good, the second part of the book lacked cohesion.

Nonetheless, Bowker used the occasion to discuss the difficulty of talking about the so-called "right of privacy," when that term is used in so many different senses.

Aspects of Privacy Law: Essays in Honour of John M. Sharp. Edited by DALE GIBSON. Pp. xix, 443. ($46.95)

These essays add up to a good book. The subject is timely and this collection, unlike many volumes of essays, has unity, few gaps and little overlapping. It is an approprite tribute to the late Professor John Sharp. He had written a monograph on *Credit Reporting and Privacy: the Law in Canada and the U.S.A.*,[1] had drafted Manitoba's Privacy Act[2] and at his death was engaged in writing a treatise on the law of privacy.

His colleagues in the Faculty of Law at the University of Manitoba conceived the idea of the *Essays* as a way of completing that treatise. Professor Dale Gibson became editor with an editorial board of Professors D.T. Anderson, J. Irvine and P. Osborne. Professor Anderson's dedication is a sensitive, and indeed moving, tribute to Professor Sharp. Each of the other three contributed an essay. The editor in particular deserves credit for the selection of topics and authors. We have had considerable writing on privacy in Canada in recent years but I know of no single book that covers the subject as does this one.

The book is in four parts: Introductory, with one essay; General Legal Protection, with two; Legislative Protection, with three; and Particular Problems and Solutions, with seven.

The introductory essay written by a professor of philosophy, Arthur Schafer, describes the difficulty of defining privacy and right of privacy. He concludes a useful discussion by saying that privacy can be defined by combining two conditions (1) control over information about one's self and over who can sense us, and (2) non-interference in private affairs. He then discusses privacy as a value in our society and the fact that it may be opposed by other values such as crime detection and freedom of expression.

The section entitled General Legal Protection has an essay by Professor Peter Burns on Privacy and the Common Law and one by Professor Patrick Glenn on the Right of Privacy in Quebec Law. Professor Burns says there is no right of privacy *per se* at common law but goes on to show that privacy is protected at least peripherally by various causes of action—trespass to land, chattels and the person, nuisance, defamation, injurious falsehood, wilful infliction of nervous suffering, breach of contract, passing off, appropriation of personality and breach of confidence. He concludes that although common law and equity have given considerable protection to the interest in privacy, there is no general right and only legislation could provide a coherent body of categories of invasions of privacy that would be actionable.

Professor Glenn's essay centers on article 5 of Quebec's 1975 Charter of Human Rights and Freedoms[3] which says: "Every person has a right to respect for his private life." It appears that two types of conduct have been found incompatible with that right—intrusions on solitude and intrusions on anonymity through dissemination of information. Generally, only intentional invasions have been held wrongful and even then there may be defences. Professor Glenn examines them in turn. The remedy for violation is damages and in a proper case an injunction.

The author next deals with privacy and public law—the control of improper dissemination of information by government and credit reporting agencies. He then considers the problem—an intractable one everywhere—of dissemination within government both vertically and horizontally. The author's conclusion is that the right of privacy is fairly well protected in civil law but there is a greater need for reform in public law.

The next collection of three essays, under the heading Legislative Protection begins with one by Professor Philip Osborne on the Privacy Acts of British Columbia,[4] Manitoba[5] and Saskatchewan.[6] Each creates a statutory tort of invasion of privacy. The author describes the growth of the tort in the United States, beginning with the article by Warren and Brandeis in 1920, and then Dean Prosser's equally famous article of 1960 which concludes there are four unrelated torts—unwarranted intrusion, public disclosure of embarrassing facts, appropriation of the plaintiff's name or likeness for purpose of gain, and publicity which places the plaintiff in a false light in the public eye. The author then turns to Canadian law and concludes that protection of the right of privacy is "fragmentary and incomplete". He analyzes the three provincial Acts. Their weakness lies in uncertainty of application, the heavy burden on the plaintiff, the broad and nebulous defenses and lack of access to the Small Claims Court. However he thinks that since these Acts are drafted in general terms the courts may in time put flesh on their bones so as to give substantial protection from invasions of privacy.

The next essay by Professor Gibson is entitled Regulating the Personal Reporting Industry. It deals with provincial legislation designed to ensure fair reports by credit reporting agencies. The United States Congress passed a Fair Credit Reporting Act in 1970[7] and in Canada seven provinces passed such Acts in the next four years. They vary greatly one from another. In 1977 the Uniform Law Conference adopted a Uniform Information Reporting Act (which Professor Gibson calls a Model Act). It provides for licensing and regulates the collection of information, its storage and reporting and requires notice to the subject of the fact of an investigation of him and gives him the right to ask to see the information and to correct errors. The author points out that the Uniform Act does not deal wtih civil liability and that the general law of defamation applies. He agrees with the Alberta case of *Gillett* v. *Nissen Volkswagen Ltd.*[8] which holds that a commercial credit reporting agency does not have a qualified privilege when its report is libellous. The author concludes that the Uniform Act is an improvement on the existing provincial Acts, although no province has yet passed it.

The last essay under the heading Legislative Protection is by Professor Deutscher on the 1974 amendment to the Criminal Code of Canada which regulates electronic eavesdropping and creates the crime of unauthorized eavesdropping. This essay is entitled The Protection of Privacy Act: Whose Privacy is it Protecting? It covers the history of the legislation, its provisions, the cases interpreting it and the 1977 amendment. The author's opinion is that the provisions as interpreted are loaded in favour of the interceptor and give more "privacy" to the intercepting process than to the person whose conversation has been intercepted.

The remaining seven essays in the volume are headed Particular Problems and Solutions. The first two are the longest in the book. The first is by Professor John Irvine on The Appropriation of Personality which is one of Prosser's four torts. This sprightly essay "dissects" the components of personality and different kinds of appropriation. The argument is that the tort of wrongful appropriation, as distinct from defamation and passing off, should be kept within a narrow compass. Recovery should be allowed only for damage to the plaintiff's material interests or reputation. The author concedes that the latter really belongs under defamation. Then follows a close and eminently readable scrutiny of the case law on appropriation of the plaintiff's name and of features such as appearance or voice. The discussion ends with an analysis of the two Canadian cases *Krouse* v. *Chrysler Canada*

Limited[9] and *Athans* v. *Canadian Adventure Camps Ltd. et al.*[10] His conclusion is a vigorous argument that the plaintiff should succeed only if he can prove material damage.

The next essay by Professor H.J. Glasbeek is entitled Limitations on the Action of Breach of Confidence. A person who has received information in confidence should not disclose it. Common law has long enforced this obligation through an award of damages, and equity through the injunction. The author's thesis is that the courts should maintain the present law and should not propound a new tort of invasion of privacy. He divides actions for breach of confidence into three categories: (1) unlawful disclosure of trade secrets: (2) protection of contents of letters, lectures, manuscripts and the like; and (3) protection of professional relationships such as lawyer-client and doctor-patient. In each of these categories the author gives a detailed and useful analysis of the cases. He concludes that the purpose of the action for breach of confidence is to protect the interests described and that protection of sensibilities and dignity is at most secondary. The author submits it would be unfortunate for the courts to attempt to develop a right of privacy on a case to case basis. The courts cannot build up a rational set of principles by attempting on a case to case basis to weigh the harm to the plaintiff's sensibilities as against the public's right to know.

The concluding part of this essay deals with the privilege that a party may assert when called to produce evidence, such as Crown privilege and the solicitor-client privilege. The author is concerned to keep these recognized categories narrow. Privilege should not be extended to every case where disclosure would be a breach of confidence. He discusses Wigmore's four criteria to determine when privilege should be granted and criticizes *Slavutych* v. *Baker,*[11] saying that the majority in the Supreme Court confused privilege with confidentiality.

The essay by Professor (now Dean) Jack London is on Privacy in the Medical Context. The author is not a strong proponent of confidentiality of medical information. He makes an analysis of eight different interests that may come into play and must be balanced one against the other to determine whether confidentiality should be protected. The doctor may refuse to disclose information on the basis of his ownership of the medical records in opposition to the patient's right to know; he may refuse to disclose to outsiders because his professional responsibility obliges him to observe the Hippocratic oath, but on the other hand there may be excuses for disclosure even without the patient's consent; disclosure might be justified in the interest of maintaining high standards of medical care, for instance for research; there may be third parties who have a legitimate interest in obtaining medical information about another; and in trying to decide whether medical information should be privileged in judicial proceedings, the interest in confidentiality must be weighed against the interest in making available all relevant evidence; and finally there is the patient's interest in privacy as against the public interest in obtaining information about him.

Chapter 10 by Bernard Pinsky is on Telephone Solicitation and

Privacy. This is an interesting discussion of the prankster and of the "drummer" who solicits by telephone, of the technique of telephone solicitation and the public attitude to it. There is a passing reference to the significant Alberta case of *Motherwell* v. *Motherwell*,[12] where the Alberta Court of Appeal held that persistent abusive telephone calls amounted to a private nuisance so that the plaintiffs were entitled to an injunction and nominal damages. After discussing several possible ways to restrain solicitation, the author makes an interesting suggestion, apparently conceived by a California law student, whereby a person whose name is in the telephone book could have it starred. The star means that the subscriber objects to commercial solicitation by phone.

The next essay is by Ronald Coke on Freedom of Information. It describes obstacles to the obtaining of information from government—for example, Crown privilege, lack of status before the courts, and government secrecy. The essay describes the American Freedom of Information Act and then the proposed Canadian Act as described by the Honourable John Roberts at a meeting on March 23rd, 1979. (No mention is made of the report of the Standing Joint Committee on Regulations and Other Statutory Instruments. That report, made on June 28th, 1978 is the basis of the proposed Act outlined by the Honourable Mr. Roberts.) Of course the author did not have available the actual Bill C-43 entitled An Act to Enact the Access to Information Act and the Privacy Act which was introduced on July 17th, 1980. The essay ends with a discussion of drafting problems in framing a Freedom of Information Act. There is an appendix of administrative policy manuals issued in connection with Part 4 of the Canadian Human Rights Act, which is entitled Protection of Personal Information. It will of course be replaced by the Proposed Privacy Act.

The essay by Professor Roland Penner is on Illegally Obtained Evidence and the Right of Privacy. He describes our rules of evidence, which admit testimony or things even though illegally obtained. He says that such evidence is usually obtained by an invasion of privacy. He approves the American rule which excludes evidence obtained by an unreasonable search and seizure. He does not rest his support on the argument that exclusion is an effective deterrent to high-handed seizures, but on the ground that it is essential to "judicial integrity"—that is, its purpose is to guard against the bringing of the administration of justice into disrepute. He regrets *R.* v. *Wray*,[13] which denies to the trial judge any discretion to exclude evidence merely because it was obtained by improper or even highly objectionable means. He argues that the court should have a discretion to exclude such evidence as a means of preserving judicial integrity. A discretion is of course a more moderate change from the present law than an outright exclusionary rule would be. This is a careful well-reasoned argument in favour of a discretion. The author makes an important point near the end, namely that Parliament has already given the judge a discretion to exclude evidence obtained by way of illegal electronic eavesdropping where the admission would bring the administration of justice into disrepute.[14]

The last essay is by Professor Ronald Price, and entitled Of Privacy and Prisons. The first part is on the meaning of privacy and right of privacy, thus returning to the theme of Professor Schafer's essay. Professor Price favours a definition of privacy as "the control over or the autonomy of the intimacies of personal identity". The portion on privacy and the prison describes the invasions of privacy to which inmates are subject. Some are incidental to mass activities but some take the form of surveillance and the most demeaning are "body cavity searches". Even room searches can be offensive.

The author then deals with the inmate's right of association—that is, to have visitors and even to marry. As to censorship of mail, Canadian procedures are less liberal to the inmate than are the American. Next the author considers confidentiality of information about the inmate, especially medical and psychiatric.

Lastly Professor Price deals with abuses in the form of programmes designed to modify the inmate's behaviour and then with the completely different problem of supervision of inmates by one of the opposite sex. In conclusion he makes the plea that inmates should not have to forfeit all their rights of privacy, and invokes the golden rule.

My first observation, which is not a criticism of the subject matter of any of the essays, is that the terms 'privacy" and "right of privacy" have been used in so many senses that they lose all meaning. We have in Canada three provincial statutes which create a statutory tort of breach of privacy. Each is called the Privacy Act. Then when Parliament in 1973–74 proposed an amendment to the Criminal Code to regulate electronic eavesdropping and to create an offence of unauthorized eavesdropping, it called the amendment the Protection of Privacy Act. The new part IV.1 of the Code embodying it is entitled "Invasion of Privacy". Later, when Parliament in 1977 passed an anti-discrimination law under the title of Canadian Human Rights Act, it included as Part IV a number of provisions to protect the confidentiality of information held by the federal government on individuals. It gave them the title "Protection of Personal Information". This title is acceptable though "Confidentiality of Personal Information" would have been better. In any case Bill C-43, introduced on July 17th, 1980 provides that Part IV will be replaced by a Privacy Act, as a companion to the proposed Access to Information Act. While one is glad to see Part IV emerge from its half-hidden location in the Canadian Human Rights Act, the new title gives less of a clue to the subject matter of the Act than did the title to Part IV.

In Ontario the Williams Commission made its *Report* in October, 1980 on *Freedom of Information and Individual Privacy*. Volume 3, entitled Protection of Privacy, principally deals with the confidentiality of information held by the provincial government. This criticism of the title of the Commission and of the title of Volume 3 of its report in no way reflects on the seventeen admirable research publications of the Commission or on its most impressive *Report*. It will be noted that the title of Mr. Justice Horace Krever's

Commission is the Royal Commission of Inquiry into the Confidentiality of Health Records in Ontario.[15]

The distinction between privacy and confidentiality emerges in Professor Glasbeek's essay. It appears too from *Malone* v. *Comm'r of Police (No.2)*.[16] The plaintiff asked for declarations that the tapping of his telephone by the police was illegal. He argued that it was a breach of privacy *and* of confidentiality. Vice-Chancellor Megarry held that there is no general right of privacy in English law and then went on to hold that there was no violation of the plaintiff's right of confidentiality. He did not treat the two as synonymous.

Too often however, the so-called interest in privacy threatens to swallow all the other interests in personality. If one looks at Roscoe Pound's catalogue of individual interests he has three large categories—personality, domestic relations and interests of substance. The interests of personality he divides into five heads: the physical person, freedom of will, honour and reputation, privacy and sensibilities, and belief and opinion. It will be seen that privacy is only one out of five and in his discussion of that right Pound confines it mainly to "the demand made by the individual that his private personal affairs shall not be laid bare to the world and be discussed by strangers", together with the suggestion that this right should protect a person's feeling and sensibilities, concluding with the comment that "the problems are rather to devise suitable redress and to limit the right in view of other interests involved".[17]

Another example to show that privacy is only one of a number of interests in personality is found in Quebec's Charter of Human Rights and Freedoms. It will be recalled that Professor Glenn's essay deals with article 5 which says: "Every person has a right to respect for his private life." The Charter also says that every person has a right to life, and to personal security, inviolability and freedom; a right to the safeguard of his dignity, honour and reputation; the inviolability of his home; and right to non-disclosure of confidential information; and the fundamental freedoms, including freedom of conscience, freedom of religion, freedom of opinion, freedom of expression, freedom of peaceful assembly and freedom of association. This enumeration comes remarkably close to Pound's and, like it, shows that privacy is only one of a number of interests in personality.

We have in Canada no constitutional protection of the right of privacy. Indeed it is not mentioned in the Canadian Bill of Rights Act nor in the proposed Charter of Human Rights. However, the Canadian Bill of Rights Act, which has quasi-constitutional status, declares "the right of the individual to life, liberty, security of the person and enjoyment of property, and the right not to be deprived thereof except by due process of law". One might wonder what this could have to do with privacy. However in the United States the due process clause has been the main basis of Supreme Court decisions which establish "zones of privacy" into which the state may not intrude even by legislation. In the name of the right of privacy, the court has struck down laws that prohibit the sale, use or distribution of contraceptives, even to minors; laws that prohibit or regulate the procuring of abortions in the first trimester of pregnancy or that require parental consent to a minor daughter's abortion, and in some circumstances at least, that require notice to the parents; laws that prohibit the possession of pornographic films in one's home; and laws that impose zoning regulations for family dwellings and exclude grandchildren from the definition of family.

Attempts to regulate the grooming of hair have run afoul of the new constitutional right of privacy in many lower courts, though the Supreme Court has upheld such regulations for policemen. Attacks on laws requiring the wearing of motorcycle helmets and prohibiting the smoking of marijuana have usually failed, though in *Ravin* v. *State,*[18] the Alaska Supreme Court held that the state could not prohibit the possession of marijuana for personal consumption in one's home. In Alaska the right of privacy is spelled out in an amendment to the state constitution. The court's reasoning is the same as that of John Stuart Mill—the state should not legislate so as to interfere with the individual's conduct, for example, in moral matters, unless that conduct affects others.

There are cases asserting a right to "informational privacy", in opposition to state laws providing for the gathering and dissemination of information about individuals, and other cases raise the right to "associational privacy" as a basis for striking down, for example, state laws requiring disclosure of membership lists of an organization. The interest which the individual asserts in each of these cases is far from identical, and each differs from that asserted by the person challenging a law that prohibits or regulates abortion. In the last case the claim is to be able to make a choice as to childbearing, free from interference by government.

Another example where the individual may assert the right to make a choice has to do with the decision to accept or refuse medical treatment. The patient should have this right where he is capable of making an informed choice, though it is hard to see what it has to do with a right of privacy. In any case, the New Jersey court in *Matter of Quinlan,*[19] said of a comatose patient that her right to terminate her existence "was a valuable incident of her right of privacy". The court did not stop there. It held that her guardian could assert that right in her behalf. Then in the "Brother Fox" case[20] the New York Appellate Division held that a competent person clearly can make this decision and then went on to say that when the person is incapable, his representative can exercise the patient's right, subject to control by the court. This judgment says that the essence of the right to privacy is "autonomy over matters of personal integrity", including control over one's body. This of course is vastly different from most of the definitions of that right. Moreover even if one accepts it, I have difficulty in appreciating why a third person should be able to exercise that right.

Is there any likelihood that our courts will invoke the word "liberty" in the Canadian Bill of Rights Act so as to hold inoperative legislation of the kinds that have been struck down in the United States? I think not. The only Canadian case of which I am aware that even touches on the question is

Morgentaler v. *The Queen,*[21] where the accused invoked the American decisions in *Wade*[22] and *Bolton*[23] (the so-called abortion cases). Chief Justice Laskin, who was the only member of the court to deal with the question, declined to apply the American cases, though I read his judgment as leaving open the question whether "liberty" in our Bill of Rights Act could ever include privacy or freedom of choice in connection with such matters as abortion.

I turn now to another question—whether it is desirable for each province to have a statute creating the general tort of invasion of privacy. In view of the vagueness of the term and the breadth and uncertainty of the various defences that would be available, I am not persuaded. My reason is that the tort has no discernible boundary. One can then ask—should the provinces pass an Act that embodies Prosser's four torts? Two of them are really close to defamation—public disclosure of embarrassing facts and publicity which places the plaintiff in a false light in the public eye. The latter certainly has an affinity to defamation. This can be seen in *Burnett* v. *The Queen,*[24] which Professor Burns cites. The plaintiff claimed huge damages for invasion of privacy alleging that the Canadian Broadcasting Corporation has surreptitiously taken pictures of him and used them on television in a broadcast called Connections. The reported judgment merely refused to strike out the statement of claim. As to disclosure of embarrassing facts, if it were desired to give a cause of action to the reformed prostitute whose lurid past is disclosed in the press, then the defence of justification could be removed. I point out, however, that even in the United States where this tort has been recognized, the plaintiff faces a formidable obstacle in freedom of speech and press. This is clear from *Cox Broadcasting Corporation* v. *Cohn.*[25] In that case state law made it an offence to publish the name of the victim of rape. The Supreme Court set aside the conviction of a television station for violating the law. The actual ground was that the victim's name was a matter of public record in criminal proceedings. However the judgment strongly implies that even if the information is not a matter of public record it may be hard for the plaintiff to succeed.

Prosser's third tort is appropriation of another's personality for business purposes. In *Athans*[26] the plaintiff succeeded without a statute to help him. However the plaintiff in that case was not claiming for intrusion on his privacy. Rather he was asking compensation for the appropriation of an asset analogous to goodwill. He wanted all the publicity he could get as long as he received compensation. Almost thirty years ago Judge Jerome Frank spoke of the "publicity value" of a man's photograph and the corresponding "right of publicity". The case was a dispute between two chewing gum companies over the use of the pictures of baseball players for insertion in packages of chewing gum. Frank J. said that "in addition to and independent of the right of privacy" a man has a right in the publicity value of his photograph. He added that this right might be called a right of publicity. "For it is common knowledge that many prominent persons (especially actors and ball-players) far from having their feelings bruised through public exposure of their likenesses, would feel sorely deprived if they no longer received money for authorizing advertisements, popularizing their countenances, displayed in newspapers, magazines, buses, trains and subways."[27]

When the actor Cary Grant brought an action against *Esquire* magazine for running his picture superimposed on the torso of a model, he sued both for breach of his right of privacy and of his right of publicity. In refusing to strike out the statement of claim the court noticed that the action for appropriation of personality can protect two different interests. The reticent person who genuinely objects to the publicity truly makes a claim for breach of privacy whereas the person who likes the publicity and merely wants to be paid for it is claiming for something analogous to goodwill.[28]

Finally, the Supreme Court in *Zacchini* v. *Scripps-Howard Broadcasting Co.*,[29] which Professor Irvine cites, flatly holds that an action for damages arising from the showing on television of Zacchini's "human cannonball" act at a county fair was for infringement of Zacchini's right of publicity.

Professor Irvine argues strenuously that this action should be confined to cases where the plaintiff can show a monetary loss because the defendant has for business purposes appropriated an aspect of his personality. This would certainly keep the action from getting out of hand—but what about the actor Alastair Sim who was offended when the Heinz company engaged an actor to simulate Sim's distinctive voice in broadcasts? Mr. Sim certainly did not object to appearing in public but he was genuinely offended by the simulation of his voice to sell pickles. Then there is the case of the pretty but shy Miss Roberson,[30] who found her picture on advertisements for flour. Each of *Athans, Sim,* and *Roberson* asserts a different interest but it seems to me they all deserve protection against the unauthorized use of name, picture or voice for commercial purposes. If the courts cannot confer an action in all these cases under common law and equity then there should be a statute—and unlike Professor Irvine, I would extend it to *Sim* and even *Roberson*.

The fourth of Prosser's torts is intrusion on solitude. There are many such intrusions that should be the subject of an injunction, and in the proper case, damages. I am not at all sure, however, that a statute is needed to protect them. *Motherwell* v. *Motherwell*[31] was a welcome decision. There are other flagrant intrusions that involve a trespass to land or assault. They are covered by existing torts. Then there may be cases which are doubtful. Let us take the American case of *Galella* v. *Onassis*.[32] There a photographer persisted in hounding the widow of President Kennedy and her children, taking photographs wherever he could. The United States Court of Appeals granted an injunction against this "outrageous" conduct, though the majority, with undue solicitude for freedom of the press, framed the injunction in much narrower terms that the dissenting justices would have done. I agree with the dissent. On similar facts would a Canadian court grant an injunction? Section 381 of the Criminal Code makes it an offence to bring compulsion on another by persistently following him about from place to place or by besetting or watching his dwelling house or the place where he resides, works, carries on business or happens to be. Whether or not such conduct constitutes a nuisance at common law I think the court could properly take cognizance of that conduct and enjoin it. In *Burnett* v. *The Queen*[33] mentioned earlier, plaintiff's counsel invoked section 381 to support his argument that breach of privacy is actionable.

As a final comment on the difficulty with privacy, right of privacy and invasion of privacy, an article by Raymond Wacks, which appeared after the *Essays* went to press, effectively expresses my criticisms.[34]

My comments about the tort of invasion of privacy have had to do with common law provinces. In Quebec the draft Civil Code of 1977, which so far as I can ascertain has not yet been enacted by the Quebec legislature, has as Title One, Chapter III the heading Respect of Privacy. It confers the right to privacy and forbids invasion of the privacy of another without his consent or unless expressly authorized by law. Then there is a catalogue of particular acts that are prohibited. It has the virtue of omitting the two of Prosser's torts which are related to defamation. As for the other items some are covered by existing law. Then there is one which says that "no person may... observe a person's private life by any means". This seems rather wide. In any case, the civil law system may be able to work with a provision like Chapter III but it does not seem to me to be appropriate in the common law system.

There are two remaining matters which I shall mention. The first has to do with information about individuals in government files. I shall use medical records as an example. We should start with the proposition that these records are to be kept confidential. Professor London is less concerned about this than I am. There is even a question as to the extent to which this information should be circulated within government. Part IV of the Canadian Human Rights Act and the new Bill intended to replace it permit use of information for administrative purposes and for compatible uses. It seems to me that this is proper, though there will be problems as to what is a compatible use.

As to disclosure to outsiders the general rule should be that it is forbidden. Information gathered by government about individuals should generally be treated as confidential, unless it is a matter of public record. There may be cases where third parties should have access to information but these should be spelled out. Sometimes proponents of freedom of information seem to be indifferent if not hostile to the concern for confidentiality. This is completely misconceived. The purpose of access to information is to enable the public to know how the government is run and not to enable third parties to pry into information about individuals, and gathered in confidence or under statutory compulsion. Let us take an example. There are widespread claims that women who have been awarded maintenance against their husbands or ex-husbands have difficulty in collecting. Often they cannot even locate the man. Should the woman be able to compel a provincial Health Care Insurance office to disclose the husband's address? In 1978 Ontario enacted a Family Law Reform Act. It deals with support obligations and section 26 empowers a court to order any person or public agency to supply the address of a person against whom an application or order for support has been made, and this section binds the Crown. In Alberta, the Institute of Law Research and Reform made a recommendation along the same lines in its *Report on Matrimonial Support*. This type of provision troubles me though I was a party to the Alberta recommendation. Are we going to move toward a national registration that is public? I hope not. It may be that in the particular case of an elusive husband, the interest in obtaining support for the wife should outweigh the interest in confidentiality. Generally however I do not think that either the government or an employer should give out a person's address, to say nothing of other information, to a member of the public.

There is another problem connected with confidentiality, particularly of medical records and school records of older children. Should they be accessible to the parent? This is an exceedingly thorny area. In the name of family cohesion there is strong objection to any proposal that enables the child to shut off information from his parents. On the other hand a child seeking medical care may want to keep the fact from his or her parents, and there is a strong case for saying that the usual confidentiality should apply. Recently the Australian Law Reform Commission made a tentative proposal that in relation to medical and education records a child of twelve should have the right to object to doctors and teachers making information, claimed to be confidential and personal, available, even to parents or guardians. This proposal attracted a barrage of criticism.[35]

Professor London's analysis of the different interests that are involved in deciding upon the physician's rights, the patient's rights and the right of third parties who might want the medical information is helpful though he does not show as much solicitude for confidentiality as I would. It would have been useful had he examined some of the recent legislation that deals with this subject. For example in Alberta every statute dealing with medical records contains a strict secrecy provision with the right in the Minister to release information for specified purposes, for example, research. It seems to me that this is the proper way to deal with this subject. The *Krever Report,* made public just before New Year's, 1981 contains many helpful recommendations.

My last comment has to do with Professor Penner's essay. He argues in favour of discretion in the court to reject evidence that has been obtained in a manner that is discreditable to our system of justice. I firmly agree with him that we should not use despicable means to find out where the gun is hidden. For a long time I agreed with Cardozo's famous statement that an accused should not go free because of a policeman's error but I am now persuaded that a discretion such as Professor Penner proposes and is found in the electronic eavesdropping provisions in the Criminal Code is warranted. I still do not think however that this is the most effective sanction to curb this type of abuse. The eighteenth century cases involving John Wilkes which give a remedy in trespass for illegal ransacking of a home in a search for evidence of a crime are still part of our law. We have had judgments awarding damages against peace officers for tortious conduct, and convictions for such crimes as assault.

Conduct that is a discredit to the administration of justice will be diminished if everyone connected with enforcement of the criminal law constantly bears in mind:

(1) The elder Pitt's declamation beginning: "The poorest man may in his cottage bid defiance to all the forces of the Crown."[36]

(2) The judgment of the Ontario Court of Appeal in *Fleming* v. *Spracklin*.[37]

(3) The comment of Mr. Justice Hope in *R.* v. *Container Materials Ltd*.[38]

Notes

1 (1970).
2 S.M., 1970, c. 74.
3 S.Q., 1975, c. 6.
4 S.B.C., 1968, c. 39.
5 *Supra,* footnote 2.
6 R.S.S., 1978, c. P-24.
7 Oct. 26th, 1970, P.L. 91–566, 84 Stat. 1114, Tit.6.
8 (1976), 58 D.L.R. (3d) 104.
9 (1974), 1 O.R. (2d) 225.
10 (1978), 17 O.R. (2d) 425.
11 [1976] 1 S.C.R. 254.
12 (1976), 73 D.L.R. (3d) 62.
13 [1971] S.C.R. 272.
14 Cr. C., s. 178.16 enacted by S.C., 1976–77, c. 53, s. 10.
15 His report was made public on Dec. 30th, 1980.
16 [1979] 2 All E.R. 620.
17 Jurisprudence (1959), Vol. III, ch. 14, §83.
18 (1975), 537 P. 2d 494.
19 (1976), 355 A. 2d 647.
20 *Eichner* v. *Dillon* (1980), 426 N.Y.S. 2d 517, aff'd by Court of Appeal (New York Times, April 5th, 1981, p. 8 E).
21 [1976] 1 S.C.R. 616.
22 *Roe* v. *Wade* (1973), 410 U.S. 113, 93 S. Ct. 705.
23 *Doe* v. *Bolton* (1973), 410 U.S. 179, 93 S. Ct. 739.
24 (1979), 23 O.R. (2d) 109.
25 (1975), 420 U.S. 469.
26 *Supra,* footnote 10.
27 *Haelan Lab.* v. *Topp's Chewing Gum* (1953), 202 F. 2d 866.
28 *Grant* v. *Esquire* (1973), 367 F. Supp. 867.
29 (1977), 433 U.S. 562.
30 The name is misspelled on p. 81.
31 *Supra,* footnote 12.
32 (1973), 487 F. 2d 986.
33 *Supra,* footnote 24.
34 The Poverty of Privacy (1980), 96 L.Q. Rev. 73.
35 [1980] Reform 112.
36 The complete quotation may be found in *Miller* v. *United States* (1957), 357 U.S. 301, at p. 307.
37 (1921), 50 O.L.R. 289, at p. 290, per Meredith C.J.C.P.: "If the law is to be respected, and properly enforced, the enforcement of it must never be committed to such persons as the defendant, it must be left to trained, experienced, and impartial officers of the law."
38 (1941), 76 C.C.C. 18, at p. 52 (Ont.): "It is gravely disturbing at a time when respect for the law much needs to be fostered to find it treated with contempt by officers employed to defend it and to secure obedience to it."

1981

Minors and Mental Incompetents: Consent to Experimentation, Gifts of Tissue and Sterilization

Reprinted from
(1981) 26 McGill Law Journal
pp. 951–977

This article was written in response to an invitation to contribute a piece for a special issue of the McGill Law Journal *on legal medical matters, in 1981.*

By this time, Bowker had become very much involved in this field of growing importance involving the professions of law and medicine. His interest had begun with the article he wrote in 1963 for the Canadian Medical Journal *(see earlier in this collection). Now with the rapid expansion of new drugs requiring testing, it became increasingly important that proper consents be given by the persons undergoing the testing—which becomes more complicated where such persons are minors or mental incompetents.*

This article examines "Consent" in relation to three areas in which Bowker had a particular interest, namely, medical experimentation, tissue gifts and sterilization.

Introduction

My concern in this paper is with minors and mental incompetents as subjects of research, as donors of human tissue and as subjects of sterilization. In each case one must ask who, if anyone, can properly give consent, and in what circumstances. The question is both legal and ethical. One must look at the question of consent to these procedures where the subject is a mentally competent adult, but first one must examine the subject of consent to medical treatment.

I. Consent to Medical Care

Medical care or treatment is the diagnosis, prevention and treatment of illness. The term "health care" may seem synonymous with medical care but it is intended to be wider. For example, the World Health Organization says: "Health is the state of complete physical, mental and social well-being and not merely the absence of disease or infirmity."[1] With this definition of health, the administration of contraceptives is probably within health care, whereas it is outside the term "medical care".

In general a competent adult may make up his own mind as to whether to receive medical treatment. Thus the physician should not treat him without his consent or, of course, in the face of a prohibition. It was in the context of a prohibition that Mr Justice Cardozo uttered his oft-quoted statement, that "every human being of adult years and sound mind has a right to determine what shall be done with his own body; and a surgeon who performs an operation without his patient's consent commits an assault, for which he is liable in damages".[2]

Consent may be by conduct or it may be specific, whether verbal or written. Hospitals have their own consent forms and sometimes questions arise as to whether they are too wide or whether the patient actually understood them. This is, of course, a problem that can come up in any document. A consent prepared by a physician or institution should be fair and in simple language. There should be no coercion of the patient to sign it, and every effort should be made to see that he understands it. Today the main question is whether the consent must be an "informed consent". What is the duty of the physician to disclose the proposed treatment and alternatives and the risk of each procedure (or both) in order for the consent to be genuine?

Fifty years ago, the Court of Appeal of Ontario held in *Kenny* v. *Lockwood*[3] that the decision as to disclosure of risks is for the physician on the basis of good medical practice. This was the prevailing rule in the United States until about ten years ago. Critics of that rule said it was too paternalistic or authoritarian; that there should be a partnership between doctor and patient, which is only achieved by complete candor that enables the patient to make an intelligent decision.[4] Since then there have been a number of decisions supporting this thesis. The two leading cases are *Canterbury* v. *Spence*[5] and *Cobbs* v. *Grant*.[6] The *ratio* of *Canterbury* is this: "to enable the patient to chart his course understandably, some familiarity with the therapeutic alternatives and their hazards becomes essential".[7] The physician has a duty of reasonable disclosure of the choices with respect to proposed therapy and the dangers inherently and potentially involved. The patient is not bound by the profession's tradition as to what should be disclosed.

> Respect for the patient's right of self-determination on particular therapy demands a standard set by law for physicians rather than one which physicians may or may not impose upon themselves.[8]

As to the scope of the duty of disclosure, the patient must be given enough information for an intelligent choice. The standard is objective: would the reasonable person be likely to attach significance to the risk or cluster of risks in deciding whether or not to forgo the proposed therapy?

In *Cobbs* v. *Grant* the Court asked whether the doctor's duty to disclose and his discretion to withhold information are governed by medical practice or imposed by law? They are imposed by law. The patient is medically ignorant and is entitled to determine whether to submit to treatment. His consent must be informed and he depends on the doctor to inform him. Thus the doctor has "a duty of reasonable disclosure of the available choices with respect to the proposed therapy and of the dangers inherently and potentially involved in each. . . . The evaluation and decision is a non-medical judgment reserved to the patient alone."[9] But what degree of disclosure is required? Full disclosure is too broad. The doctor need not give a lengthy polysyllabic discourse on all possible complications nor need he discuss "the relatively minor risks inherent in common procedures, when it is common knowledge that such risks inherent in the procedure are of very low incidence."[10] For example, the doctor may be obliged to inquire as to allergies to avoid adverse reactions. Where the procedure is more complicated, the jury should be told that "when a given procedure inherently involves a known risk of death or serious bodily harm, a medical doctor has a duty to disclose to his patient the potential of death or serious harm, and to explain in lay terms the complications that might possibly occur".[11] Then follows this rather vague addition: "beyond the foregoing minimal disclosure, a doctor must also reveal to his patient such additional information as a skilled practitioner of good standing would provide under similar circumstances".[12] The scope of the required disclosure is measured by the patient's need for whatever information is material to the decision.

These two cases and some from other states have caused a stir in the United States, both favourable and unfavourable. A recent text says that eighteen states in 1975 and 1976 enacted statutes that either defined or restricted the application of the doctrine of informed consent in reaction to the crisis in malpractice insurance. The authors add that "most of the statutes attempt, in one way or another, to make it more difficult for a patient to be successful in a suit against a physician for failure to obtain informed consent".[13]

Where do we stand on informed consent in Canada today? The answer is found in the Supreme Court's judgments in *Hopp* v. *Lepp*[14] and *Reibl* v. *Hughes,*[15] both decided in 1980. The first of these cases was from Alberta. The issue was the adequacy of the defendant's answer to the plaintiff's concern about the seriousness of an operation for a slipped disc. The trial judge, Brennan J., found it adequate[16] but a majority of the Court of Appeal[17] held otherwise and found the defendant liable. He appealed to the Supreme Court, which restored the trial judgment. Chief Justice Laskin, speaking for the Court, reviewed the cases on informed consent. After discussing the concept of probable risks (as against the merely possible) and material risks (as against immaterial), and of special or unusual risks, the Chief Justice set out the following conclusion:

> In summary, the decided cases appear to indicate that, in obtaining the consent of a patient for the performance upon him of a surgical operation, a surgeon generally should. . . without being questioned, disclose to him the nature of the proposed operation, its gravity, any material risks and any special or unusual risks attendant upon the performance of the operation. How-

> ever, having said that, it should be added that the scope of the duty of disclosure and whether or not it has been breached are matters which must be decided in relation to the circumstances of each particular case.[18]

This passage shows a move toward the proposition that the consent must be informed.

The second case, *Reibl* v. *Hughes,* follows this trend. The defendant operated on the plaintiff for a "plugged" artery near the brain. A serious stroke resulted. The defendant had not mentioned the risk of a stroke. Haines J. held that if the defendant had told the plaintiff of the risk (4% of dying and a further 10% of stroke) the plaintiff would have refused. Thus Haines J. gave judgment for the plaintiff.[19] The Court of Appeal of Ontario ordered a new trial because the trial judge's statement of risk misunderstood the evidence. No one would put the risks to the plaintiff the way Haines J. proposed. He ignored the risks of not operating. Moreover, the plaintiff failed to show that he would not have consented had the defendant disclosed the risk.[20]

The plaintiff appealed to the Supreme Court. Again Chief Justice Laskin wrote the judgment for a unanimous Court. He dealt at length with the causation question: should the Court use an objective or subjective test in deciding whether the plaintiff would have refused the operation had the defendant disclosed the risk? Earlier cases in the provincial courts had been divided on this issue. The Chief Justice held the objective test to be preferable and added "in saying that the test is based on the decision that a reasonable person in the patient's position would have made, I should make it clear that the patient's particular concerns must also be reasonably based; otherwise there would be more subjectivity than would be warranted under an objective test".[21]

The Chief Justice reviewed the evidence at length and the findings in the courts below. He concluded that the defendant, in merely advising the plaintiff that he would do better to have the operation than not to have it, did not give an adequate disclosure of the risks. The Chief Justice then asked what the reasonable person would have done if the risks had been properly disclosed? He took into consideration that the plaintiff was only a year and a half from his pension, that there was no apparent "neurological deficit", no immediate emergency and yet there was a grave risk of stroke from the operation, whereas the risk of stroke without the operation was in the future. Another factor was that the defendant had not made clear to the plaintiff the fact that the operation would not cure his headaches, whereas the plaintiff thought it would. In conclusion the Chief Justice said that in his opinion "a reasonable person in the plaintiff's position would, on a balance of probabilities, have opted against the surgery rather than undergoing it at the particular time".[22] Thus the Supreme Court restored the trial judgment.

Doubtless these two cases will produce a spate of comment. One can scarcely object to the proposition that the patient should receive enough information to make his own decision. It would be unfortunate, however, if the physician's obligation, as now established, were to force him into a wooden and mechanical recitation of all risks as a defence to the possibility of a complaint that he has failed in his duty of disclosure. I am sure the Chief Justice intended to confine the obligation of disclosure of risks to those that are serious. However, even seriousness is relative. Risks that might be regarded as serious in a cosmetic operation would not necessarily be serious in an open-heart operation. Where the proposed procedure is elective, as it was in *Reibl,* then there should be an obligation to describe the alternatives to the operation and the comparative risks. Where, however, an operation is from a medical standpoint not only desirable but urgent, it seems to me that the doctor should not have to go into details of the risks of the operation and then go on to describe the possibilities of serious harm or death that would occur if nothing were done.

I shall now make four short comments on the state of the law in the light of these two decisions. First, we have had cases holding that in the absence of informed consent the plaintiff's action lay either in battery or negligence or both.[23] Fortunately, *Reibl* has not only put an end to the confusion but has placed the action on its proper basis. Disclosure is part of the duty of care and its breach is actionable negligence. Battery "should be confined to cases where surgery or treatment has been performed or given to which there has been no consent at all or where, emergency situations aside, surgery or treatment has been performed or given beyond that to which there was consent".[24] Later in his judgment Laskin C.J.C. said that "unless there has been misrepresentation or fraud to secure consent to the treatment, a failure to disclose the attendant risks, however serious, should go to negligence rather than to battery".[25] What of the case where the surgeon, through a misunderstanding, removes thirteen teeth instead of two,[26] or operates on the spine instead of the foot?[27] In these cases the judgments point to the possibility of an action in either battery or negligence. It may be that Chief Justice Laskin would classify these cases as battery, though one can argue that the action is in negligence. There is no question, of course, where the patient says, of a proposed anaesthetic, "Don't touch my left arm." The touching is clearly a battery.[28] Likewise an unauthorized biopsy for purposes of research is a battery.[29]

Secondly, both cases confirm that in instances of a nervous or apprehensive patient the surgeon has some latitude in deciding how much information of risks to give. *Reibl* also mentions the possibility of a patient waiving his right to an explanation of risks.

Thirdly, the Chief Justice makes a strong case for the objective test in determining causation. Although some judgments and some writers[30] have argued that it is unfair to plaintiffs, I do not object to it as a general rule. One situation, however, is troubling. It is that of the patient who asks a direct question: for example, "If I have the operation for migraine headaches, what are the risks?" Let us assume that the answer is "None", when in fact loss of the sense of smell is a known risk.[31] Then let us take an even more pointed question: "If I have the eye operation will I have double vision?" Again let us assume a negative answer, although the known risk is in fact substantial.[32] In these cases the patient has shown to the doctor his direct concern. It seems to me that, especially in the second case, a court has a strong indication that whatever the reasonable person would have decided, the plaintiff would have decided against the operation.

Fourthly, there is a point that the Supreme Court did not have to consider. It is this. Let us assume a finding that the patient would not have consented had the risk been disclosed. In order to succeed, must he show that the risk that materialized was the one that should have been disclosed? *Canterbury* v. *Spence* says yes: *Halushka* v. *University of Saskatchewan*[33] says no. Doubtless one could write an essay on the application of *Palsgraf*[34] and *Wagon Mound No. 1*[35] to this question. I merely offer the suggestion that on modern tort principles much is to be said for the position taken in *Canterbury*.[36]

A. *Minors*

A mature minor can give his own consent just as an adult can. There seems to have been a contrary rule in the United States but never in England or Canada. Indeed, Professor Somerville has pointed out that Coke said "an infant may bind himself for his . . . necessary physic".[37] *Johnston* v. *Wellesley Hospital*[38] did much to remove widespread, though unwarranted, doubts. Even with the reduced age of majority there is room for the mature minor who can give his own consent. The problem is that as the age decreases uncertainty as to capacity increases. For this reason there should be legislation.

England has put the age at sixteen.[39] It is fourteen in Quebec.[40] In British Columbia, it is sixteen, but the physician must first try to get the parents' consent.[41] The Uniform Medical Consent of Minors Act[42] also fixes the age at sixteen with the important addition that where the minor is under that age he may give his consent if two doctors are of the opinion that the minor understands the procedure and that the treatment is in his best interests.

In Alberta, the Institute of Law Research and Reform in December, 1975 made a report[43] recommending the age of sixteen, but with a special provision whereby the patient could consent to treatment in connection with communicable diseases, drug or alcohol abuse, prevention of pregnancy, and termination of pregnancy. The Alberta Legislature has not yet passed a statute on the subject. My prediction is that the government will bring in a bill before long that is either based on the Institute's report or on the Uniform Act. In Saskatchewan the Law Reform Commission has recommended a different type of scheme.[44] A minor who has capacity to consent may do so. The court has power to declare whether a minor has that capacity and power to dispense with parental consent where the law requires it. It is hard to say whether the Legislature will act on the recommendation.

Where the plaintiff is too young to give his own consent the common law always recognized the parents' right to give it. Indeed at common law the parent has a duty to look after the child's medical care. Modern child-welfare laws provide that parental neglect or refusal to give medical care is a form of negligence.[45] Problems arise where the parent refuses on religious grounds to permit a certain medical procedure, such as the transfusion of blood. In Alberta there is specific provision that as soon as a child is apprehended the authority who apprehended him may authorize medical care without parental consent.[46]

One provision in the English Act is hard to interpret. It says: "Nothing in this section shall be construed as making ineffective any consent which would have been effective if this section has not been enacted." Does this preserve the mature minor rule for persons under sixteen, or does it permit parental consent for them, or does it refer to emergencies? The Uniform Act and the Alberta recommendations both omit that provision. In my opinion, this is wise. I see no need to preserve the mature minor rule when the general age of consent has been brought down to sixteen and where, in addition, there are provisions permitting consent by the minor himself in specific cases even where he is under sixteen.

The only province that has enacted the Uniform Act to date is New Brunswick.[47] In that province, the definition of "medical treatment" omits "any procedure undertaken for the purpose of preventing pregnancy."

A final comment that I should like to make before leaving this topic has to do with the controversy as to whether minors should be able to arrange for themselves contraceptive measures and, in the case of girls, abortion. There has been a tendency to refrain from meeting this problem directly. The Alberta Report[48] is an exception. This is the most emotion-laden issue in the whole area of medical consent. In the United States the Supreme Court has held unconstitutional blanket requirements for parental consent to abortion,[49] and at present there is a case before that Court challenging a state law requiring mere notice to the parents.[50] The Court has struck down a state law prohibiting the sale of contraceptives to minors.[51] I do not care to see these questions resolved as constitutional issues. Nor do I contemplate with any satisfaction the fact that in some cases the minor refuses to take the parents into his or her confidence, or indeed the sexual permissiveness which makes the problem acute. However, when the minor wishes to exclude the parents from participation in the decision, he or she should have the capacity to decide for himself or herself.

B. *Mental Incompetents*

It is customary to distinguish between the mentally retarded or defective (Blackstone's idiot) and the mentally incompetent (Blackstone's lunatic).[52] They will be treated together here. Neither is necessarily incapable of giving consent, for the retardation may be mild, and the mental incompetent may have lucid intervals. As a general rule, however, someone else must authorize medical treatment for persons in both categories.

In connection with mentally incompetent adults, the *Criminal Code* imposes a duty on everyone to provide necessaries for a mentally ill person under his charge.[53] In Alberta, *The Mental Health Act* provides that the

Board in charge of a facility for such patients "is under a duty to provide such diagnostic and treatment services as the patient is in need of and that the staff of the facility are capable and able to provide".[54] *The Dependent Adults Act* in Alberta permits the court to appoint a plenary guardian or a partial guardian.[55] In the case of a plenary guardian, section 9 says that the guardianship order confers on the plenary guardian power "to consent to any health care that is in the best interests of the dependent adult". In the case of an order appointing a partial guardian, section 10 enables the court to include the power I have just quoted. Section 1 defines "health care" to include "any procedure undertaken for the purpose of preventing pregnancy". (The other parts of the definition are obvious.) The question arises whether the guardian can consent to sexual sterilization of the dependent. I shall deal with this later under "Sterilization".

II. Consent to Research on Humans

Research on humans is doing something to a human being for the purpose of gaining knowledge. The term "experimentation" can be given the same definition, but the difficulty is that it is often used to describe innovative therapy. That is to say the purpose is both to gain knowledge and to help the patient. Every medical procedure was innovative at one time. Until thalidomide and the Kefauver hearings[56] in the United States that led to the amendments to the *Food, Drug and Cosmetic Act*[57] in 1962, it was commonplace for drug companies simply to ask physicians to try out a new drug on their patients. It is now recognized that this is not the proper way to determine the safety and efficacy of the drug. There must be systematic research in which the new drug is compared to an accepted drug or to a placebo (inert substance), or both. To make the conclusions scientifically sound this is usually done, at least in the early stages, on a double-blind basis. Neither the patient nor the person administering the drug knows which substance the patient receives. This procedure is obviously research, not therapy.

When ethical codes or statutes speak of experimentation they may mean experimentation that excludes therapy or they may mean experimentation that includes an element of therapy. For example, the Helsinki Declaration[58] gives guidelines for medical research combined with professional care and other guidelines for non-therapeutic research. However, some recent ethical codes define experimentation or research to include experimental therapy as long as the experimental element is important. Thus the Medical Research Council of Canada has said that the distinction between therapeutic and non-therapeutic research should be abandoned: both should come under the heading of research.[59] Later the National Commission for the Protection of Human Subjects of Bio-medical and Behavioral Research in the United States pointed out that the distinction between research and therapy is blurred because both often occur together. Its report takes the position that radically new procedures should be treated as research because formal research today provides the best method of determining whether the new procedure is safe and effective.[60]

In *Zimmer* v. *Ringrose* the defendant used a silver nitrate treatment to bring about sterility. The plaintiff was not rendered sterile and subsequently became pregnant and had an abortion. The trial judge accepted testimony of an expert that the defendant's procedure was experimental and should have been handled through a clinical trial—that is, treated as research. On appeal the Court of Appeal did not agree with this finding.[61]

Even if there are two accepted procedures but complete disagreement as to which is better, a study to settle the question must be done on a systematic basis as research. In the case of breast cancer there may be utter uncertainty as to whether a radical or simple mastectomy is better in the removal of a tumor of a given size. Is it proper for those trying to find the answer simply to alternate the surgery without telling each patient that the actual operation she received was the result of drawing lots? The answer is no.[62] Today there are studies to compare partial as against complete mastectomies. The fact that the operation is being performed on a randomized basis is clearly explained in the consent forms that have come to my attention.

The basis of all modern statutes and ethical codes is the Nuremberg Rules or the Helsinki Declaration (revised at Tokyo in 1975).[63] They require informed consent. Nuremberg says the consent must be that of the subject, whereas Helsinki permits the substituted consent of the guardian of an incompetent or the parent of a minor.

An example of an effort to ensure that the consent of the subject is informed is the United States *Food, Drug and Cosmetic Act*[64] and the Regulations made thereunder.[65] Where the purpose is solely research, the consent of the subject himself must be obtained. If there is a therapeutic element the consent of his representative must be obtained if the subject cannot consent. The definition of consent is as follows:

> "Consent" means that the person involved has legal capacity to give consent, is so situated as to be able to exercise free power of choice, and is provided with a fair explanation of pertinent information concerning the investigational drug, and/or his possible use as a control, as to enable him to make a decision on his willingness to receive said investigational drug. This latter element means that before the acceptance of an affirmative decision by such person the investigator should carefully consider and make known to him (taking into consideration such person's well-being and his ability to understand) the nature, expected duration, and purpose of the administration of said investigational drug; the method and means by which it is to be administered; the hazards involved; the existence of alternative forms of therapy, if any; and the beneficial effects upon his health or person that may possibly come from the administration of the investigational drug.[66]

Quite apart from the *Food, Drug and Cosmetic Act,* the American Department of Health and Human Services (HHS, replacing HEW) has guidelines governing institutions that receive HHS assistance. They must give to HHS an undertaking or assurance, as it is called, to follow these guidelines. They require that a research committee (called an Institutional Review Board or IRB) must pass on all protocols (research proposals). The definition of informed consent is as follows:

> (c) "Informed consent" means the knowing consent of an individual or his legally authorized representative, so situated as to be able to exercise free power of choice without undue inducement or any element of force, fraud, deceit, duress, or other form of constraint or coercion. The basic elements of information necessary to such consent include:
> (1) A fair explanation of the procedures to be followed, and their purposes, including identification of any procedures which are experimental;
> (2) A description of any attendant discomforts and risks reasonably to be expected;
> (3) A description of any benefits reasonably to be expected;
> (4) A disclosure of any appropriate alternative procedures that might be advantageous for the subject;
> (5) An offer to answer any inquiries concerning the procedures; and
> (6) An instruction that the person is free to withdraw his consent and to discontinue participation in the project or activity at any time without prejudice to the subject.[67]

It will be seen that this definition has much in common with the definition of consent under the *Food, Drug and Cosmetic Act*. An additional requirement was recently made whereby the institution must tell the subject whether it provides compensation in case of injury.[68]

For some time in the United States there has been intensive re-examination of the ethical requirements for research on humans. In July, 1974 an Act of Congress established the National Commission for Protection of Human Subjects of Bio-Medical and Behavioral Research. The Committee worked for four years and produced reports on ethical guidelines for research (Belmont Report), psychosurgery, research on institutionalized mentally infirm, research on the fetus, research involving children, IRBs, and on ethical guidelines for delivery of health care by the federal government. Since these reports came out, Congress has considered a number of bills, and HHS has made a number of proposals for new regulations. They are still in a state of flux. The latest I have is a set of proposed regulations by HHS. The requirements for informed consent include the present ones and several more.[69]

In Canada there is nothing comparable to the HHS guidelines but some research institutions in fact follow them. Of course we have reached the stage where these institutions, including universities, have not only framed their own guidelines but have established a research committee or IRB to pass on proposals for research and to scrutinize the forms of consent to be used. Under Canada's *Food and Drugs Act*[70] there are regulations designed to prevent the sale of new drugs until the manufacturer has filed a submission with the Minister, but the manufacturer may sell new drugs to qualified investigators on complying with the requirements in the regulations. These regulations are far less exacting than those in the United States under the *Food, Drug and Cosmetic Act*.[71]

Apart from the Canadian statute just mentioned, the only legislation of which I am aware on the subject of research on humans is Article 20 of Quebec's Civil Code. It permits a person of full age to consent in writing to submit to an experiment provided the risk assumed is not disproportionate to the benefit anticipated.[72]

In the great expansion of research on humans since World War II, there have been remarkable advances, but at the same time there have been instances of imposition on subjects, including research without consent. An English doctor wrote a book alleging improper research on patients.[73] In the United States research has sometimes attracted wide criticism; for example, the Tuskegee study on blacks inflicted with syphilis[74] and the Willowbrook study in which defective institutionalized children were given hepatitis with a view to finding a way to control it in the institution.[75] Dr Beecher, in his "bombshell" article in 1966, condemned many studies he regarded as unethical.[76] In the New York cancer-cell case the proceedings were disciplinary.[77] There has been very little civil litigation. Indeed, so far as I know, *Halushka* v. *University of Saskatchewan*[78] is the only case. The plaintiff volunteered to take part in the study of a new anaesthetic but was not told that there was risk involved or that the catheter placed in his arm would go to the heart. He suffered cardiac arrest. In upholding the jury's verdict for the plaintiff, the Court of Appeal said that "The duty imposed on those engaged in medical research... to those who offer themselves as subjects for experimentation... is at least as great as, if not greater than, the duty owed by the ordinary physician or surgeon to his patient",[79] and "the subject of medical experimentation is entitled to a full and frank disclosure of all the facts, probabilities and opinions which a reasonable man might be expected to consider before giving his consent".[80]

The particular problem in the case of experimentation is that all the risks cannot be known. Generally, previous tests on animals have helped to eliminate a substantial amount of risk, but the researcher cannot know that the risks of which he is aware are the only ones. Another basic problem that arises both in therapy and in research, but which is particularly acute in the latter, is this, Even if the consent form is completely candid and as lucid as possible, there is no guarantee that the subject who gives consent really does so with knowledge and free will. There can be subtle pressures on him both from the outside and because of his position (*e.g.*, as a prisoner). In addition, by reason of sickness, lack of intellect, or inability to speak English, he may not truly give an informed consent. It is for this reason that many people urge that the institution or its IRB should "monitor" the taking of consents.[81]

Should there be legislation in each province on the subject of informed consent to research on humans? One should not denigrate the attempts in the United States food and drug law, and in the various state laws,[82] and in Quebec's Article 20. I am not sure, however, that, for the present, legislation is as useful as ethical guidelines and IRBs. In addition, it is helpful to remember Dr Beecher's observation:

> One must never minimize the importance of striving for truly informed consent, but the patient's greater safeguard in experimentation, as in therapy, is the skilful, informed, intelligent, honest, responsible, compassionate physician.[83]

A. *Research On Children*

While the "mature minor" rule of the common law or a statute specifying the age at which an older minor may give his own consent to medical treatment is sensible, it is arguable that this should not apply where the procedure is research. None of the common law provinces has legislated as yet and there is no case law. In Quebec, Article 20, to which I have referred, says:

> A minor, capable of discernment, may [submit to an experiment] with the consent of the person having the paternal authority and of a judge of the superior court, provided that no serious risk to his health results therefrom.

A minor capable of discernment is the mature minor. He may agree to take part but only if there is no serious risk and with the further safeguard of parental and judicial consent.

In the common law provinces, what is the situation where the minor is not mature but is a child? Can the parent or guardian properly give consent to the child's participation in research on the same basis, as though he were volunteering himself? Some people think that the substituted consent or permission of the parent or guardian is adequate. I do not agree that the child should be exposed to risk on this basis. Opinion is, of course, sharply divided. If advances are to be made in pediatrics then research must be done on children. I do not think, however, that they should be exposed to risks for the ultimate benefit of others. The child should not be exposed to experimentation that carries anything more than minimal risk. Minimal is, of course, hard to define[84] but it is more protective of the child than is the usual risk/benefit formula. There may be rare cases where slightly greater risks are justified. The testing of Salk vaccine might be an example. I am not sure that the nationwide tests in the United States caused merely minimal risk to the children who were first given the vaccine and yet it turned out to be a boon.

The National Commission, in the United States, has made ten recommendations respecting research on children. They support research on children with the approval of an IRB and prescribed safeguards. The research should not involve more than minimal risk and the permission of the child and the parent should be given. Where the risk is more than minimal but the research may benefit the child himself it may be done if the IRB approves. It may also be done where the risk is more than minimal if the research may in future benefit children with the same disease. (This recommendation was not unanimous.) In other cases where there is a serious problem in children's health the research may be done subject to approval at the national level. There are special protections for children who are wards of the state or in institutions.[85]

The MRC report agrees that research must be done on children and incompetents. It proposes consent by parent or guardian and, if that consent is given, a further consent by an ombudsman or advocate of the child or incompetent. The majority would balance risk and benefit just as is done where the subject is a competent adult. Professor Crépeau refused to expose the minor or incompetent to risk for the benefit of others. The guardian is in a fiduciary position and has no right to expose his ward to the risks of an experiment of no direct benefit to himself. I agree with Professor Crépeau.[86]

B. *Research on the Mentally Infirm*

This category of person is analogous to the child. It is quite possible that in the past drugs have been given and operations (*e.g.*, pre-frontal lobotomy) have been performed in circumstances that would not meet the ethical requirements of today. In an American case, *Wyatt* v. *Stickney,*[87] a class action was brought on behalf of patients in Alabama's two mental hospitals to compel them to improve their facilities and treatment so as to bring them up to constitutional standards. The Court ordered that this be done and laid down the minimum standards. These show a humane concern for the welfare of patients. Two of the standards are relevant here. The first says that the patient has a right not to be subjected to experimental research without his informed consent or that of his guardian and after approval by the institution's IRB and in compliance with HHS's rules, which I have set out earlier. The second says that "patients have a right not to be subjected to treatment procedures such as lobotomy, electro-convulsive treatment, aversive reinforcement conditioning or other unusual or hazardous treatment procedures without their express and informed consent after consultation with counsel or interested party of the patient's choice". In a companion case[88] the Court made a similar order in connection with institutions for the mentally retarded.

The recommendations of the National Commission in its Report on Research Involving Those Institutionalized Infirm[89] are much like those for children though there is provision for research being done over the patient's objection if a court so authorizes.

In Canada I know of no statute dealing with research on mental patients. If research is performed and harm befalls them, then the person doing the research should be legally responsible. Such a case is unlikely to arise but I know of no common law principle which permits the guardian or anyone else to expose a mental patient to risk that does not come within the concept of health care. When *The Dependent Adults Act* was introduced in the Alberta Legislature in 1975, the Honourable Helen Huntley, the Minister sponsoring the bill, in referring to the guardian's power to authorize medical treatment, said this:

> Note that the medical treatment must be in the best interests of the dependent adult as an individual, not the best interests of society. This is not a provision to give effect to consents to experimental surgery or involuntary sterilization.[90]

III. Inter Vivos Transplants

It is helpful to remember that some human tissue is non-regenerative. The principal organ of this type in demand for transplants is the kidney. The gift is not fatal to the donor because he has a remaining kidney. Other tissues are regenerative. The main ones for transplant purposes are blood, bone marrow and skin, although skin grafts from one person to another are not usually successful.

Since transplants are modern, there is little authority as to one's right to make a donation. In the case of a competent adult, the only possible argument against it is that it is a maiming. This is simply not the case where the tissue is generative. There may be a stronger argument in the case of a kidney, but even there the donor is not like the man who cuts off his toes to escape military service, and it is farfetched to suggest that there is anything unlawful in the self-sacrifice of the donor of a kidney. There is of course the real possibility that the donor consents under pressure or without knowing the consequences of his sacrifice.

In Canada there is a Uniform Human Tissue Gift Act[91] which is in effect in seven provinces and the Northwest Territories. Part 1 provides for *inter vivos* gifts of tissue. It is limited however to non-regenerative tissue, which for practical purposes means the kidney. The donor must be of the age of majority and "able to make a free and informed decision". The inference is that his consent must be an informed consent. In my view Part 1 makes no change whatever in the common law in the case of a competent adult, though doubtless physicians like to have legislation that spells out the right to remove a kidney.

Since the Act does not apply to regenerative tissue, the common law must still apply. In other words, such gifts by competent adults are permissible. I have no doubt that any court would require informed consent. As to the mature minor, I know of no authority on the subject. It will be recalled, however, that a mature minor can agree to run the risks of another person's negligence.[92] By analogy one can argue he should be able to consent to run risks of a gift of tissue in the interest of another's life or health. When the age of majority was twenty-one the Canadian Red Cross accepted donations of blood from eighteen-year-old donors.[93] In the United States, on the other hand, where the view that no minor can consent even to medical treatment was at one time widely held, the first marrow and kidney transplants were approved not only by the parents but by a court.[94] One cannot state with confidence the position as to these transplants under the Canadian common law. It is possible that the courts would recognize the capacity to make the donations but would be exacting in the requirement of informed consent. In Quebec, Article 20 permits a minor "capable of discernment" to make a gift of tissue on the authority of both parent and court, and no distinction is made between generative and non-generative tissue.

The Uniform Human Tissue Gift Act does not deal with regenerative tissue, and forbids gifts by minors of non-regenerative tissue. Should it be amended to permit gifts by mature minors? At one time the present writer was opposed but is now of the view that with consent of the parents and approval by a court, a provincial board and adequate representation of the mature minor, such legislation can be justified. One can debate whether the provision should apply to a mature minor (who is like the minor in Quebec of the age of discernment) or whether it should be fixed at a given age. The writer prefers the latter, and would keep the age at sixteen. There is, of course, room for difference of opinion on this issue.

The excellent report of the Australian Law Reform Commission on Human Tissue Transplants is instructive. The basic recommendation is that the donor be an adult of sound mind. However, in the case of minors, there is a recommendation that the transplant may be carried out where the tissue is regenerative, and the minor is of sound mind and agrees to the donation, and a parent consents and an independent doctor has discussed the proposed removal with the minor. In the case of non-regenerative tissue, the majority (four of six) thought it should be lawful when the donor is old enough to consent and the parents agree and the recipient is a member of the family, and a special committee of three has approved. One of the two dissenters was Sir Zelman Cowen, now Governor-General of Australia. He would simply have prohibited the removal of non-regenerative tissue from a minor.[95] Division 3 of the draft Ordinance included in the report embodies the majority's recommendation.

In the Capital Territory, a Transplantation and Anatomy Ordinance embodying the draft Ordinance has been passed with only minor changes. Queensland and the Northern Territory each passed an Act on the lines of the draft Ordinance, but omitting Division 3.[96]

In the United States under the common law it is now generally agreed that the parents cannot give a valid consent to the donation of a kidney by their minor child. The consent of the court is required. In the first case, from Boston in 1957, donor and recipient were nineteen-year-old identical twins. The judge found that the healthy twin understood the proposed operation and had consented. Then he accepted psychiatric evidence that the brother's death would have a grave emotional impact on the healthy twin. He held that the operation was necessary for the healthy twin's continued health and well-being and that the operation would confer benefit on him as well as upon the recipient. In the case of fourteen-year-old twins the same reasoning was applied.[97] Professor Curran's observation was that the "benefit" was more the prevention of possible detriment.[98]

In the Connecticut case of *Hart* v. *Brown*[99] the children were identical twins just under eight years of age. In authorizing the transplant, the Court relied more on the right of the parents to make a substituted judgment than on the theory of psychological benefit. However the Court accepted the opinion that the donor would enjoy a better future life if her ailing sister were kept alive and found "some benefit" for the donor.

In the last case, *Little* v. *Little*[100] from Texas, Anne was a fourteen-year-old girl with Down's syndrome. Her younger brother was threatened with death from kidney failure. On the mother's application the Court authorized the transplant. It did so not on the basis of the "substituted judgment" doctrine,[101] but in view of the psychological benefits that Anne would receive in the preservation of her brother's life and satisfaction in making the donation.

We have been speaking of the minor as a transplant donor. The position of the mentally incompetent adult is analogous. In the United States the leading case is *Strunk* v. *Strunk*.[102] Jerry was twenty-seven years old with the mental age of six. His brother Tommy required a kidney in order to survive. The only donor in the family who was suitable from a medical standpoint was Jerry. The evidence was that he was greatly attached to Tommy and that Tommy's visits were important to Jerry as therapy, so that there was justification for authorizing the transplant. A majority accepted this evidence. One should not overlook the forceful dissent. In two subsequent cases, *Re Richardson*[103] and *Re Pescinsky*[104] the Court refused the order. In the first case, from Louisiana, the Court found that the transplant would not be in the best interest of the proposed donor. In the second case, from Wisconsin, the Court held that it had no jurisdiction to make the order.

As a matter of policy, should there be legislation authorizing the guardian or the court to give permission to the donation of tissue by a person who is incompetent either because of age or mental incapacity? Often the argument is advanced that this is a matter for the parent or guardian and that the courts and legislature should not intervene.[105] This assumes that the parent or guardian will always act in the best interests of the child. This assumption may often be true but certainly not universally. That is why we have child-welfare statutes. The strongest case for authorization of the transplant by a court or other tribunal is in the case of identical twins. From the parents' standpoint one can understand their wish to have the donation made. However, the doctrine of the substituted judgment is questionable and the argument that the donation is in the best interests of the child is hard to accept. The Ontario Bill mentioned earlier[106] (s. 17(3)) permits the representative of a child or mental incompetent to consent to a donation of tissue, both regenerative and non-regenerative, but the approval of a Health Procedures Protection Committee is required. I cannot find in the Bill any criteria to guide the Committee.[107] The idea of a Committee to check abuses is commendable, but particularly in the case of a proposed kidney transplant, one might think that if it is to be permitted at all when the donor has not capacity to give his own consent, it should be restricted to a donation between brother and sister. Indeed I am not persuaded it should be done even in that case.

IV. Sexual Sterilization

Where the person is an adult of sound mind there is nothing in the *Criminal Code* or elsewhere to prevent him or her from undergoing this procedure.[108] The *dictum* of Lord Denning in *Bravery* v. *Bravery*[109] seems to have misled some people. He said that it is illegal even when the person agrees to it. This is simply wrong. However, the operation is, for practical purposes, irreversible, and certainly the physician is obliged to explain this to the patient.

The problem arises in connection with minors and mental incompetents, and particularly with the retarded, whether minor or adult. The early statutes in the United States authorizing sterilization, sometimes without consent, were principally concerned with eugenics. In Alberta *The Sexual Sterilization Act* was along these lines. Enacted in 1928,[110] it was repealed in 1972.[111] As the Act stood just before repeal, a statutory board could authorize sterilization of patients with psychosis, mental retardation, syphilis, epilepsy and Huntington's chorea. The grounds for sterilization were the risk of transmission of disease to offspring and the risk of mental injury to progeny or to the patient. Consent of the patient was required, except in the case of psychosis, where substituted consent of the parent or guardian was permitted, and in the case of mental defectives, where no consent was needed.

The Act attracted criticism on both genetic and procedural grounds. Two geneticists made strident attacks on the Act.[112] The motion to repeal[113] shows that the government relied on them heavily. In moving repeal, Mr King had three grounds—medical, legal and moral. As to the first, the Act was genetically unsound and the Eugenics Board had not the expertise nor the information to make sound decisions. Secondly, the Act was ambiguous and had other flaws (here Mr King relied on Professor McWhirter's opinion that those involved in the procedure were guilty of a crime under the *Criminal Code*). Thirdly, the Act violated the fundamental human right to procreate by permitting the government to order the sterilization of certain people without consent. "It is our view that this is a reprehensible and intolerable philosophy and program for this province and this government", said Mr King. He did not seem troubled about substituted consent, for he said sterilization could still be carried out with parental consent.

Since repeal, sterilization of minors has been performed under Alberta's health insurance plan. In the period 1976–1978 inclusive, a total of seventy-eight hysterectomies were performed, eleven other sterilizations on girls and eight on boys. The reasons given are retardation and birth defects. As best I can gather, the hysterectomies were related to inability of the females to attend to personal hygiene.

In Ontario, which has never had a Sterilization Act, there were in 1976 three hundred and eight sterilizations of minors—fifty of boys and the rest of girls, of which one hundred and nine were hysterectomies.[114]

As to adult mental defectives in Alberta, I do not know the position.

When *The Dependent Adults Act* was introduced, the responsible Minister stated it was not the intention to cover sterilization. The definition of health care includes contraception but, quite apart from the Minister's disclaimer, it would be odd to find that a legislature which repealed *The Sexual Sterilization Act* out of solicitude for the fundamental right to procreate had by a side-wind conferred on the guardian of a dependent adult the power to authorize sterilization in the name of contraception.

Turning now to the common law, can a parent give valid consent to the sterilization of a minor child? Here one must note the common distinction between therapeutic and non-therapeutic sterilization. If an organ is diseased and the operation is a by-product of the removal of the organ, it is obviously therapeutic. Sterilization for genetic purposes, that is to prevent the birth of a defective child, is not considered therapeutic, though one could argue that the birth of such a child might affect the mother's health. Sterilization for simple contraceptive purposes is also non-therapeutic whatever be the motive.

There may be cases where it is hard to classify the sterilization. Frequently a hysterectomy is performed on retarded girls because of inability to attend to personal hygiene. The Ontario Association for the Mental Retarded classifies this as non-therapeutic,[115] whereas at least some physicians tend to regard it as therapeutic.[116]

In many cases the parents seek sterilization of a minor daughter because she is more or less retarded and they fear pregnancy. In England Heilbron J. in *Re D*[117] held this to be non-therapeutic and made the child a ward to prevent the sterilization. The trend of decisions in the United States is the same in the case of the minor and also of the defective adult.[118]

In the latter category there is in Canada an important case now in the courts. It is *Re Eve* from Prince Edward Island. The mother applied to be made a committee of her daughter and for authorization to consent to a tubal ligation. Mr Justice McQuaid concluded that he had no authority to exercise the role of *parens patriae,* much as he sympathized with the mother's worry over the danger of pregnancy.[119] In appeal, this judgment was reversed by a divided Court.[120] Mr Justice Campbell held that the court by reason of its *parens patriae* jurisdiction could authorize non-therapeutic sterilization of a mentally retarded person. He then held that the sterilization would be in Eve's best interest and that her committee should be able to exercise a "substituted right" to choose sterilization. The operation would not cause Eve substantial injury. Finally, Campbell J. held that the decision as to the type of operation, tubal ligation or hysterectomy, should be left to the committee.

Mr Justice Large agreed with the order proposed by Campbell J. After a lengthy review of the evidence, he distinguished the English case of *Re D* on the facts. His conclusion was that the procedure is a medical one. Just as the court could authorize a blood transfusion for a child in the face of parental objection, so it can order the sterilization. It is for her protection.

Mr Justice MacDonald dissented. He held that the proposed operation was not for Eve's benefit, welfare or protection, but rather a deprivation of a basic human right. He said the Court had jurisdiction in exceptional cases to authorize non-therapeutic sterilization but that this was not one of them. He listed fourteen factors that should be considered. After quoting at length from a working paper published by the Law Reform Commission of Canada[121] he concluded that on the facts before the Court the operation was not for Eve's benefit. He expressed a fear that the precedent set in authorizing her sterilization would mean authorization of sterilizations for mere convenience, and that the Court's power might be abused.

One point to note about this case is that the mother did not attempt to have the sterilization performed without judicial authorization, which, as mentioned above, has in recent years been commonplace in the case of defective minors in Ontario and Alberta. In *Re Eve* the courts are at least trying to articulate the principle on which the authorization should be granted. In my opinion this should be provided by legislation. The Law Reform Commission's working paper has a number of useful suggestions. The trend today is to provide for sterilization of minor defectives on the basis of the best interest of the patient, or, in the language of the New Zealand statute,[122] for the good of the patient. This may include reasons that would not be within the phrase "therapeutic sterilization". The difficult problem is to decide whether to leave the statute there or whether to spell out criteria. The latter is preferable but there is always the danger of making them too wide. Any sterilization act, in addition to specifying the grounds for the sterilization, should provide a careful set of safeguards to ensure that the patient's interest will be protected by the court or other tribunal that is making the decision.

Conclusion

In all of the procedures—medical care, experimentation, transplants and sterilization—there is need for special solicitude for those who cannot consent for themselves. Their "best interests" are of some help. The National Commission had three basic ethical principles for research on humans—respect for persons, beneficence and justice.[123] Professor Charles Fried says that in medical care and research the patient has a right to lucidity, autonomy, fidelity and humanity.[124] Dr Paul Ramsey speaks frequently of the "canon of loyalty" which a parent owes to his child, the doctor to his patient, and the investigator to his subject.[125] Although the application of these various principles is not always self-evident—indeed one of them may compete with others—their general acceptance will help to insure against the overreaching of those who cannot consent for themselves.

Notes

1 Preamble to Constitution, quoted in Curran & Shapiro, *Law Medicine and Forensic Science,* 2d ed. (1970), 974.
2 *Schloendorff* v. *Society of the New York Hospital* 105 N.E. 92, 93 (N.Y. 1914).
3 [1932] O.R. 141 (C.A.).
4 See, *e.g.,* Glass, *Restructuring Informed Consent* (1970) 79 Yale L.J. 1533.
5 464 F. 2d 772 (D.C. Cir. 1972).
6 502 P. 2d 1 (Cal. *in banco* 1972).
7 *Supra,* note 5, 781.
8 *Ibid.,* 784.
9 *Supra,* note 6, 10.
10 *Ibid.,* 11.
11 *Ibid.*
12 Ibid.
13 Annas, Glantz & Katz, Informed Consent to Human Experimentation: The Subject's Dilemma (1977), 38: see also Horan & Halligan, *Authority for Medical Treatment* (1980) 22 For the Defence 12, 22.
14 (1980) 112 D.L.R. (3d) 67.
15 (1980) 114 D.L.R. (3d) 1.
16 (1977) 77 D.L.R. (3d) 321 (Alta S.C., T.D.).
17 (1979) 98 D.L.R. (3d) 464 (Alta S.C., App. Div.).
18 *Supra,* note 14, 81.
19 (1977) 16 O.R. (2d) 306 (H.C.).
20 (1978) 21 O.R. (2d) 14 (C.A.).
21 *Supra,* note 15, 17.
22 *Ibid.,* 35.
23 In *Halushka* v. *University of Saskatchewan* (1965) 53 D.L.R. (2d) 436, the Saskatchewan Court of Appeal upheld a jury's findings of both battery and negligence with a single award. In *Zimmer* v. *Ringrose* (1978) 89 D.L.R. (3d) 646 (Alta S.C., T.D.), the Court awarded $5,000 for negligence and $1 for battery: the Court of Appeal, in a judgment of 13 February 1981 ([1981] 4 W.W.R. 75), reversed the finding of battery and upheld the judgment in negligence. In *Lepp* v. *Hopp* (*supra,* note 17), the Alberta Court of Appeal gave an award of $15,000 in both battery and negligence. In *Reibl* v. *Hughes* (*supra,* note 19), the trial judge found the defendant liable in both and gave a single award of $225,000.
24 *Supra,* note 15, 10.
25 *Ibid.,* 11.
26 *Parmley* v. *Yule* [1945] S.C.R. 635.
27 *Schweizer* v. *Central Hospital* (1974) 6 O.R. (2d) 606 (H.C.).
28 *Allan* v. *New Mount Sinai Hospital* (1980) 109 D.L.R. (3d) 634 (Ont. H.C.).
29 In *Cryderman* v. *Ringrose* (1978) 89 D.L.R. (3d) 32 (Alta S.C., App. Div.) this question arose but the Court did not have to decide it. The defendant was liable in negligence for other non-disclosures.
30 See, *e.g.,* Bamberg, *Informed Consent after Cobbs—Has the Patient been Forgotten?* (1973) 10 San Diego L. Rev. 913, 924–6; Annas, Glantz & Katz, *supra,* note 13, 30–1.
31 *Koehler* v. *Cook* (1975) 65 D.L.R. (3d) 766 (B.C.S.C.).
32 *Calder* v. *Gilmour* [1978] 3 A.C.W.S. 57 (Sask.).
33 *Supra,* note 23.
34 *Palsgraf* v. *Long Islalnd Ry* 162 N.E. 99 (N.Y. 1928).
35 *Overseas Tankship (U.K.) Ltd.* v. *Morts Dock & Engineering Ltd. (The Wagon Mound No. 1)* [1961] A.C. 338 (P.C.).
36 The uncertainty as to the law on consent to medical treatment has produced endless commentary in the United States. In Canada there is an excellent study paper in the Law Reform Commission of Canada's "Protection of Life" series, *Consent to Medical Care,* written by Professor Margaret Somerville and published in 1979: unfortunately, she was unable to consider the Supreme Court judgments in *Lepp* or *Reibl.* Among recent Canadian writings, see also Picard, "The Tempest of Informed Consent" in Klar, *Studies in Canadian Tort Law* (1977), ch. 4; Castel, *The Nature and Effects of Consent . . . in the Medical Field: Criminal and Private Law Aspects* (1978) 16 Alta L. Rev. 293; Sharpe, *Informed Consent* (1979); Jazvac, *Informed Consent: Risk Disclosure and the Canadian Approach* (1978) 36 U. of T. Fac. L. Rev. 191; Scaletta, *Informed Consent and Medi-*

cal Malpractice: Where Do We Go from Here? (1980) 10 Man. L.J. 289.

37 Co. Littleton 1722, cited in Somerville, *supra,* note 36, 73: see also Dickens, *Contractual Aspects of Human Medical Experimentation* (1975) 25 U.T.L.J. 406, 414.

38 [1971] 2 O.R. 103 (H.C.).

39 *The Family Law Reform Act, 1969,* 1969, c. 46, s. 8.

40 *Loi sur la protection de la santé publique,* L.R.Q., c. P-35, s. 42.

41 *Infants Act,* R.S.B.C. 1979, c. 196, s. 16.

42 Uniform Law Conference, 1975 Proc. 30 and 162; Consolidation of Uniform Acts, 31–1.

43 *Consent of Minors to Medical Care* (1975).

44 *Proposals for a Consent of Minors to Health Care Act* (1980).

45 See, *e.g., Loi sur la protection de la jeunesse,* L.R.Q., c. P-34, and, in Ontario, *The Child Welfare Act,* S.O. 1978, c. 85, s. 19 (ix).

46 *The Child Welfare Act,* R.S.A. 1970, c. 45 (as am.), ss. 16(2) and 17.

47 *Medical Consent of Minors Act,* S.N.B. 1976, c. M-6.1.

48 *Supra,* note 43.

49 *Planned Parenthood of Central Missouri* v. *Danforth, Attorney General of Missouri* 428 U.S. 52 (1976); *Bellotti* v. *Baird (No. 2)* 443 U.S. 622 (1979).

50 *H.L.* v. *Matheson,* from Utah: see 48 U.S.L.W. 2482.

51 *Carey, Governor of New York* v. *Population Services International* 431 U.S. 678 (1977).

52 1 Bl. Comm. 303, 304.

53 R.S.C. 1970, c. C-34, s. 197(1)(c).

54 S.A. 1972, c. 118, s. 24(1).

55 S.A. 1976, c. 63.

56 See Mintz, *The Therapeutic Nightmare* (1965).

57 21 U.S.C.A. § 355. See Talalay, *Drugs in Our Society* (1964); Landau, *Regulating New Drugs* (1973).

58 World Medical Association, *Declaration of Helsinki* (1964), revised at Tokyo, 1975.

59 *Ethics of Human Experimentation* (1977), 6–7.

60 *The Belmont Report* (1978), 2–4.

61 *Supra,* note 23. Compare the duty of disclosure as laid down by the Court of Appeal with that prescribed in *Cryderman* v. *Ringrose, supra,* note 29. The Court of Appeal upheld the judgment in negligence because of negligent after-care. It also found negligence in the failure to disclose risks but found an absence of causation.

62 See Fried, *Medical Experimentation* (1974), esp. ch. 3.

63 *Supra,* note 58.

64 21 U.S.C.A. § 355.

65 § 130.37, Federal Register, June 20, 1967, p. 8753.

66 *Ibid.,* at 8754.

67 45 C.F.R. § 46.107 (1975).

68 Federal Register, Nov. 3, 1978; see Levine, *Advice on Compensation* (1979) 1 I.R.B. 5.

69 § 46.112 Federal Register, August 14, 1979, p. 47696.

70 R.S.C. 1970, c. F-27.

71 Food & Drugs Regs., Division 8; Consol. Regs. 1978, c. 869 at 6293-6301. In *R.* v. *Kripps Pharmacy* [1980] 6 W.W.R. 579 the accused was charged with selling a new drug without having filed a submission. A County Court judge in British Columbia held the regulation invalid not merely as unauthorized by the Act but as unconstitutional. One might hope the case goes further.

72 See Bowker, *Experimentation on Humans and Gifts of Tissue: Articles 20–23 of the Civil Code* (1973) 19 McGill L.J. 161.

73 Pappworth, *Human Guinea Pigs* (1967).

74 See Annas, Glantz & Katz, *supra,* note 13, 59–61.

75 *Ibid.,* 79–81.

76 Beecher, *Ethics and Clinical Research* (1966) 274 New England J. Med. 1354.

77 See Katz, *Experimentation with Human Beings* (1972), Pt 1, ch. 1.

78 *Supra,* note 23.

79 *Ibid.*

80 *Ibid.*

81 See Gray, *Human Subjects in Medical Experimentation* (1975), 243–56.

82 The most significant state laws are those of New York and California. See King, *Health Policy—Ensuring Informed Consent in Human Experimen-*

tation: A Comparison of the Approaches of Two States (1979) 58 N. Carolina L. Rev. 137.

83 *Research and the Individual* (1970), 25.

84 The National Commission's *Report on Research Involving Children* (1978) defines minimal risk as "the probability and magnitude of physical or psychological harm that is normally encountered in the daily lives, or in the routine medical or psychological examination, of healthy children" (p. xx).

85 *Ibid.*, 1–20.

86 *Supra,* note 59, 30–1.

87 (1972) 344 F. Supp. 373 (D.C. Ala 1972).

88 *Ibid.*, 387, *aff'd sub nom. Wyatt* v. *Aderholt* 503 F. 2d 1305 (5th Cir. 1974).

89 (1978), 1–22.

90 Discussion paper, undated, released 8 July 1975. The passage quoted is at p. 16.

91 See Sugiyama, *Inter Vivos Transplantation and the Human Tissue Gift Act* (1976) 23 U. of T. Fac. L. Rev. 124; Clements, *The Human Tissue Gift Act* (1979) 3 Legal Med. Q. 39.

92 *Miller* v. *Decker* [1959] S.C.R. 624; *Kubbernus* v. *Frost* (1978) 10 A.R. 445 (S.C., T.D.). In these cases minor passengers were held to be *volens* in relation to their driver's negligence.

93 The writer ascertained this from officials of the Red Cross at Edmonton in 1963; see Bowker, *Legal Liability to Volunteers in Testing New Drugs* (1963) 88 Can. Med. Assn J. 745, 748, n. 33.

94 See Baron, Botsford & Cole, *Live Organ and Tissue Transplants from Minor Donors in Massachusetts* (1975) 55 Boston U.L. Rev. 159; Katz, *supra,* note 77, 964–72.

95 The Law Reform Commission of Australia, *Report No. 7* (1977), 50–1 (para. 112).

96 Letters from Mr Justice M. D. Kirby, Chairman of the Australian Law Reform Commission, to the writer, dated respectively 25 March 1980 and 30 June 1980.

97 Katz, *supra,* note 77, 971 sets out the judgment.

98 Curran, *A Problem of Consent: Kidney Transplantation in Minors* (1959) 34 N.Y.U. L. Rev. 891; see also Sharpe, *The Minor Transplant Donor* (1975) 7 Ottawa L. Rev. 84, 96–9.

99 289 A. 2d 386 (Super. Ct 1972).

100 576 S.W. 2d 493 (Civ. App. 1979).

101 For a strong argument in favour of the substituted-judgment doctrine, see Robertson, *Organ Donations by Incompetents and the Substituted Judgment Doctrine* (1976) 76 Colum. L. Rev. 48.

102 445 S.W. 2d 145 (KY 1969).

103 284 So. 2d 185 (Ct App. La 1973), 284 So. 2d 338 (La 1973).

104 226 N.W. 2d 180 (Wis. 1975).

105 See, *e.g.*, Goldstein, *Medical Care for the Child at Risk; on State Supervention of Parental Autonomy* (1977) 86 Yale L.J. 645. At 668–70 the author criticizes *Hart* v. *Brown,* not for the result, but because the Court was not endowed with the capacity to determine what risks to take for someone else's child.

106 *The Child Welfare Act,* S.O. 1978, c. 85.

107 The nearest relative of one not mentally competent to consent to a health care service may authorize that service (s. 8(2)); and he must act in good faith having regard to the best interests of the proposed recipient (s. 12); and health care service means a service provided by a person under *The Health Disciplines Act*. The question remains: is the removal of a kidney a health care service for the donor?

108 See Kouri, *The Legality of Purely Contraceptive Sterilization* (1976) 7 R.D.U.S. 1; Dickens, *Eugenic Recognition in Canadian Law* (1975) 13 Osgoode Hall L. J. 547, 556–62; Wilson, *Voluntary Sterilization: Legal and Ethical Aspects* (1979) 3 Legal Med. Q. 13; Kouri, *Non-therapeutic Sterilization* (1979) 57 Can. Bar Rev. 89, 92–4.

109 [1954] 3 All E.R. 59, 67–8 (C.A.).

110 S.A. 1928, c. 37.

111 S.A. 1972, c. 87. The only other province ever to have a *Sexual Sterilization Act* was British Columbia: enacted by S.B.C. 1933, c. 59 it was repealed by S.B.C. 1973, c. 79.

112 McWhirter & Weijer, *The Alberta*

Sterilization Act, a Genetic Critique (1969) 19 U.T.L.J. 424.

113 Alberta Hansard (31 May 1972), 58–33 to 58–41.

114 Cited in Law Reform Commission of Canada, *Sterilization* (1979), 155, from Zarfas, *Sterilization of the Mentally Retarded* (a speech given to the Ontario Psychiatric Association, 5 October 1978).

115 *Ibid.*, 96–7.

116 This is my understanding from conversations with gynaecologists and pediatricians, and is at least implied by the Ontario Medical Association guideline (c) for the sterilization of mentally retarded persons, set out in the Working Paper, *ibid,* 102–3.

117 [1976] Fam. 185, [1976] 1 All E.R. 326.

118 See Holder, *Legal Issues in Pediatrics and Adolescent Medicine* (1977), 274–80.

119 Reported *sub nom. Re E.* (1979) 10 R.F.L. (2d) 317 (P.E.I.S.C.).

120 (1980, 1981) 115 D.L.R. (3d) 283 (P.E.I.S.C. *in banco*), now in appeal before the Supreme Court of Canada.

121 *Supra,* note 114.

122 *Contraception, Sterilization and Abortion Act,* 1977, (set out in *Sterilization, supra,* note 114, 149; and the relevant section is s. 10).

123 See *The Belmont Report, supra,* note 60, 4–10.

124 Fried, *Medical Experimentation, supra,* note 62, 101–4.

125 See *Patient as Person* (1970), *passim.*

1982

Ethical Issues in the Allocation of Health-Care Resources

Reprinted from
Health Care Resources, University of Calgary Institute on Humanities
Community Seminar No. 2, April 1982

This article is contained in a booklet published by the University of Calgary following a colloquium, sponsored by the Calgary Institute for the Humanities, on Health Care Resources, and in which Bowker was invited to participate.

The material which follows is in two parts: the first (entitled Introduction) includes his comments during the opening session involving a hypothetical case.

The second part is the address he gave on the subject of Right to Health Care—an expression which he finds at times confusing but which he analyzes in its various aspects: moral, legal, legislative (federal and provincial) and confidentiality. He deals with the wide spectrum of concerns in health-care delivery, and the current emphasis on rights.

Part I. Introduction to Case Study No. 1

The ethical obligation of the physician, expressed in the Oath of Hippocrates, goes back some two thousand years. The oath has some elements that may seem odd today. It imposes on the physician an obligation to treat his teacher like a parent, and to teach the teacher's sons as well as his own sons and disciples in the medical art if they shall wish to learn it. The physician then swears to follow a regimen for the patient's benefit, and to abstain from whatever is harmful, and not to give deadly medicine or a pessary to procure abortion; with purity and holiness to practice his art; to act for the benefit of the sick and to abstain from mischief and corruption and from seduction of anyone. Then he makes a pledge of confidentiality—not to divulge whatever he sees and hears in his practice "which ought not to be spoken of abroad."

It has always seemed to me as a layman that that profession on the whole has lived up to the obligations of the Oath. I am quite aware, however, of criticisms even from within the profession. Some weeks ago I went to a meeting in Edmonton to hear a Dr. Mendelsohn from Chicago. He excoriated the profession on many counts, especially in connection with gynaecology. His book, Male Practice, is indeed strident. Then there are Ivan Illich and Thomas Szasz whose heretical views are well known.

One does not need to agree with the strictures of these men to realize that the Hippocratic Oath, commendable and influential as it has been in the past, does not deal with the new ethical problems that have arisen as a result of medical advances in the past century, and indeed since World War II. The same can be said of the Declaration of Geneva (1948) and the International Code of Medical Ethics (1949), both adopted by the World Medical Association. However, the Canadian Medical Association's Guide to Ethical Behaviour speaks of the physician's responsibilities to society to improve the standards of medical services to the community and to share in the profession's responsibility to society in relation to public health education, and legislation affecting the health or well-being of the community.

A few weeks ago a book by Robert Veatch, A Theory of Medical Ethics, was reviewed in the New York Times. The reviewer began by saying that in 1972 a substantial number of the graduating class of Harvard Medical School refused to take the Oath of Hippocrates. "The new doctors explained their action in various ways. The Oath, they said, was arrogant and elitist. Nowhere did it mention the rights of patients. Nowhere did it acknowledge responsibilities to society. Nowhere did it deal with issues of justice, equity, liberty or autonomy." (The book itself criticizes the Oath and argues for ethical principles based on John Rawls' version of the social contract.)

I have referred to the fact that medical advances carry with them new ethical issues. A new discipline has come into being, called Medical Ethics or Bioethics or Biomedical Ethics. There are many institutes in the United States devoted to this discipline, and some in Canada. A huge literature has sprung up. I have examined ten bulky texts or books of readings all published in the last five years. It is a fact too, that institutions engaged in research on humans have (especially since thalidomide) established Ethics Committees to pass on the ethical propriety of proposed research. The table of contents of any recent book indicates the subjects which give rise to current ethical concerns. Since the trial of the Nazi doctors, the New York cancer-cell case and other experiments that have been widely condemned, many codes and guidelines for experimentation have been promulgated, including those of the Medical Research Council. Experimentation on children and the mentally incompetent (and also on students and prisoners) has produced endless (and often inconsistent) opinions. The concept of informed consent is relevant not only to research but to therapy. There has been a strong trend, both ethical and legal, to require that consent be "informed". Recently the Supreme Court of Canada in two cases called *Hopp* v. *Lepp* (from Alberta) and *Reibl* v. *Hughes* (from Ontario) has followed this trend.

Another subject raising new ethical issues is that of human genetics. There is dispute as to whether it is ethical even to do research to repair and alter genes. Genetic counsellors have ethical problems in deciding what to tell potential parents, and the parents have ethical problems in deciding for example whether to arrange an abortion, or to allow a severely deformed baby to die.

At each "edge of life"—the foetus and new-born at one end and the terminally ill at the other—there are ethical questions. *In vitro* fertilization, artificial insemination and the "surrogate" mother all are controversial.

There are also ethical controversies over sterilization of minors and mental incompetents and over the taking of tissue, especially when it is non-regenerative (e.g., the kidney) from such persons.

We have problems about the right of mental patients to receive treatment—and even about their right to refuse it.

Then there is confidentiality. When is the physician relieved of his obligation? This is of course the subject of the most thorough inquiry by Mr. Justice Krever in Ontario.

I have not attempted a systematic or complete catalogue of the problems of bioethics. The point is that current ethical concerns go far beyond those contemplated by the Oath of Hippocrates.

The concept that the health field goes far beyond the traditional patient-physician relationship was advanced by the Hon. Marc Lalonde in 1974 when he was Minister of National Health and Welfare. He published a paper called A New Perspective on Health Care of Canadians. It makes the point that we still tend to take the traditional view that health care is simply the treating of existing illness or injury. The fact, however, is that our health is affected by the environment—e.g., air and water pollution, urbanization and working conditions. Moreover it is affected by "lifestyle". A large proportion of deaths, especially among young males, comes from accidents or suicide. Alcohol, tobacco, drugs, poor habits in diet and exercise, refusal to take safety measures—all these take a heavy toll of health. These problems must be faced. Prevention of accidents and illness across a wide front is essential.

Quite apart from health care at the individual (or 'micro') level we have questions at the 'macro' level. What are the principles of justice that guide society in its distribution of health care? Going back to Aristotle, there is endless literature on distributive justice. One can find its source in natural law, or in utilitarianism or in a social contract. In deciding what is just, we must weigh health demands against others—e.g. education and public works. Then within the health field we must try to determine whether to concentrate more on cure or on prevention and rehabilitation, on care for the acutely ill as against care for the chronically ill, and so on.

We have in Canada a notable study on health care—The Report of the Royal Commission in Health Care (the Hall Report) in 1964–65. It does not go into the philosophical basis of society's concern but does stress the individual's responsibility for his or her own health and also society's interest in that health and in public health. I shall close these remarks by reading the opening part of the Health Charter for Canadians.

"The achievement of the highest possible health standards for all our people must become a primary objective of national policy and a cohesive factor contributing to national unity, involving individual and community responsibilities and actions. This objective can best be achieved through a comprehensive universal Health Services Programme for the Canadian people."

Part II. The Right to Health Care.

I. *Introduction: Health and Health Care*

It will be helpful first to say what we mean by health: the dictionaries say "freedom from disease" and "soundness of body". These phrases refer to physical health. More recent definitions extend to mental health.

Some persons, like Dr. Szasz, have argued that there is no such thing as mental illness. However most would agree that there is.[1] It is deviation from the norm. True, it may be hard to determine what is normal, and what deviations from normality constitute mental illness. Still more recently we have a definition of health that extends beyond the physical and mental. The World Health Organization says: "health is a state of complete physical mental and social well-being and not merely the absence of disease or infirmity." It will be noted that "social well-being" has been added. This is even harder to determine. It comes very close to happiness and is clearly more subjective than physical well-being or even mental.

Whether one takes a narrow or wide definition of health, it is clear that no one has a right to health in the sense that someone else is under a duty to provide it. Health is the result of many factors—heredity, nurture, environment and what is called "life-style", to say nothing of medical care. It is not something that one can demand from others as of right.

Now we come to "health care". While most would agree that there is no "right to health" we often hear of the "right to health care". What do we mean by "health care"? Traditionally it means diagnosis and treatment (therapy) and prevention of illness.

The element of prevention has become more prominent in the past century, with the remarkable development of vaccines and the like to prevent epidemics, from smallpox to polio. Today there is increasing emphasis on measures to prevent illness—abstention from tobacco, alcohol and drugs, and good practices in diet, rest and exercise. Then there are accidents. Industrial accidents alone bring many deaths and injuries. Highway accidents cause many more while drownings and fires add to the toll. Measures to prevent these tragic and costly losses can properly be called health care.

There is still an argument that contraception, most abortions and contraceptive sterilization do not come within health care because they are not the treatment or prevention of illness. However modern statutes and proposed statutes frequently include them. The Criminal Code treats some abortions as therapeutic and provides for the establishment of therapeutic abortion committees in hospitals (s. 251). The Uniform Medical Consent of Minors Act defines "medical treatment" to include "any procedure undertaken for the purpose of preventing pregnancy" (s. 1). In a report of the Institute of Law Research and Reform of this province on the same subject, "health care" is defined to include "procedures for the purpose of preventing pregnancy". (The legislature has not yet acted on this report.) Then in the Dependent Adults Act there is a similar definition of health care (s. 1(h)).

II. *Moral (Ethical) Rights and Duties*

Whatever the scope of health care, the title of this paper is "The Right to Health Care". Before speaking of legal rights I shall mention the concept of a moral right and its correlative a moral duty. It is quite proper to speak of a moral duty, for example to warn another person of an impending danger or to throw him a life buoy. The fact is that our law does not in general convert that obligation into a legal one. It does not require a person to be a good Samaritan. The narrow exceptions need not concern us.[2] A physician is under no duty to stop at the roadside to give aid to a person injured in an accident. In the United States there were a number of cases in which the physician having done so was after sued, sometimes successfully, for negligence. To encourage physicians to stop a number of states passed statutes which either forbade the victim of the accident from suing for negligence or which required him to prove gross negligence against the physician. Alberta's Emergency Medical Aid Act (R.S.A. 1980 c. E-9) is of the latter type. It applies to doctors and nurses and also to lay persons. This Act does not impose a duty to stop but is designed to induce a person to do so.[3]

There are, however, two statutes which impose on a person the legal duty to assist another under pain of a penalty. The first of these is section 233 of the Criminal Code. Subsection 2 says that "one having care of a vehicle involved in an accident, with intent to escape civil or criminal liability fails to stop his vehicle, give his name and address and where any person has been injured, offer assistance" is guilty of an offence.

Then in Alberta we have a similar provision in the Motor Vehicle Administration Act. Section 76(1) says that the driver of a vehicle involved in an accident shall remain and render assistance as well as produce certain information. Failure to do so is an offence.

In general, however, a physician is not under a legal duty to accept a given person as his patient. Putting it the other way a person cannot legally compel a doctor to attend to him. This might be so under some systems but not in Canada. Once the physician has undertaken to tend to a patient, however, the situation is different. If he abandons the patient and harm befalls the patient the doctor will be liable in damages. Moreover he may be subject to disciplinary proceedings by his colleagues for breach of ethics. This is illustrated by a Saskatchewan case.[4] Even short of abandonment, a physician may be in breach of his duty to provide care if he simply does nothing when the circumstances call for steps to be taken.[5]

While ethical rights and duties are not of themselves legal rights and duties, this is not to say they are unimportant. Indeed if men were angels we would not need laws to create legal rights and duties. In medicine we have had the Hippocratic Oath or its modern variations for over two thousand years, setting out the physician's ethical obligations to his patient. However, the amazing scientific and medical advances of the last century have raised innumerable ethical issues which were unknown in an earlier age and the Hippocratic Oath does not touch them. A new discipline called Medical Ethics or Bioethics and Biomedical Ethics has come into being. The American literature in recent years is immense.[6] In addition, institutes or centres devoted to this new discipline have come into being in the United States and Canada.

Examples of the ethical issues that have come to the fore in recent years are: the right of the patient to decide on his treatment or to refuse treatment; the right to such information and explanation as will make his consent an informed consent; the right of access to health care; the right to die, and indeed claims on behalf of defective children of the right not to be born. We hear too of the right to life of the fetus and the right of women to "abortion on demand" (the two being obviously incompatible). The new knowledge in genetics has raised issues as to the ethical duties of genetic counsellors and as to the rights of parents to decide the fate of a defective fetus. There are questions as to the ethical propriety of genetic experimentation whether it be new methods of fertilization or the "surrogate womb", or altering genes.

In connection with experimentation generally there are now many codes on the ethical obligations of researchers, and research institutions have ethics committees. Then there are ethical problems in the removal of human tissue for transplants and in connection with sterilization especially in relation to children and mental incompetents who cannot make decisions for themselves. There are Declarations of the Rights of the Child, Patients' Bills of Rights, Experimental Subjects' Bills of Rights, and Mental Patients' Bills of Rights. All these developments have meant that many persons other than doctor and patient are now involved in these matters. It is trite to say that society as a whole has a deep concern in them. Vast differences remain as to whose ethics should be applied but no longer are all these matters simply between physician and patient.

Much of the emphasis has been on specific problems such as those mentioned above. There are however, some attempts to frame ethical theories to provide the basis for decisions and to help in solving dilemmas. Thus the National Commission for the Protection of Human Subjects of Biomedical and Behavioral Research in the United States had as its basic ethical principles respect for persons, beneficence and justice. A text by R.M. Veatch, *A Theory of Medical Ethics* (1981) has as its basic principle the social contract theory of John Rawls.[7]

III. *Legal Rights and Duties*

At this point it will be useful to look more closely at the meaning of a legal right. A great American legal scholar, Roscoe Pound, said "there is no more ambiguous word in legal and juristic literature than the word right." He went on to give five senses in which the word has been used as a noun.[8] We are all familiar with terms often used synonymously with "right"—power, liberty, freedom, privilege and immunity. Legal scholars have expended much learning defining these terms and their correlatives.[9]

We are concerned here with legal relationships between one person and another. A legal relationship as distinct from one that is merely social or moral is one that is recognized and enforced by the state. Here the word right is used in the narrow sense as the correlative of a duty to another. The one who is under a legal duty is sometimes compelled by law to carry out that duty. More often he is subject to a claim for damages (civil liability) or to a penalty (criminal liability) if he is in breach of his duty.

There is another kind of legal claim a person might assert and which is often called a right but which is better called a freedom or liberty. Let us assume that a dying patient chooses to receive no further treatment and that the law will honour his choice. This is often called the right to die but it is better described as a freedom of choice with which others have no right to interfere. Another example: let us assume that the law of a country says that the state may not interfere with a woman's decision whether or not to have an abortion (as is the position in the United States now in the early stages of pregnancy). She has the freedom of choice. However, does she have a right to an abortion in the sense that a physician or hospital is under a duty to perform it? The answer is simply NO.[10]

The difficulty in converting a "right" to health care into a legal right in the strict sense with a correlative duty in others can be seen in the efforts of the United Nations in its concern to ensure health care. The UN charter declares that the UN shall promote "solutions to health problems" (Article 55); then in 1948 the Universal Declaration of Human Rights lists many rights and freedoms. Some (Articles 1–21) are on the lines of traditional bills of rights in that they declare well-known rights and freedoms, for example, the right to a fair trial and freedom of speech. Others declare the right to social security (Article 22), right to education (Article 26) and the right to participate in cultural life and the arts (Article 27). Of particular interest here is Article 25 which says that "everyone has the right to a standard of living adequate for the health and well-being of himself and his family including... medical care... and the right to security in the event of sickness, disability... or other lack of livelihood in circumstances beyond his control." All of these "rights" are of a different dimension from those in the first twenty-one articles. They are more like desirable political objectives and do not lend themselves to inclusion in a typical bill of rights. If all of these are true rights then someone must be under a corresponding duty and it is hard to see who is under that duty. If anyone it is society represented by the state. And it is hard to see how such "rights" can be enforced.

In the present state of civilization, the state may try to help, as many do, but it is not under a duty in the strict sense.

This difficulty was recognized when the UN came to put the provisions of the Universal Declaration into covenants. It framed an International Covenant on Civil and Political Rights based on the declarations in the first twenty-one articles. Then it framed a separate International Covenant on Economic, Social and Cultural Rights, based on articles 22–27. This latter covenant recognizes the right to work (Article 6), to good working conditions (Article 7), to join unions (Article 8) and to social security (Article 9). Then the covenant recognizes that protection should be given to family, mothers and children (Article 10), and the right to an adequate standard of living (Article 11) and education (Article 13). Article 12 is the relevant one for present purposes. This article provides:

1. The States Parties to the present Covenant recognize the right of everyone to the enjoyment of the highest attainable standard of physical and mental health.

2. The steps to be taken by the States Parties to the present Covenant to achieve the full realization of this right shall include those necessary for:
(a) The provision for the reduction of the still-birth-rate and of infant mortality and for the health development of the child;
(b) The improvement of all aspects of environmental and industrial hygiene;
(c) The prevention, treatment and control of epidemic, endemic, occupational and other diseases;
(d) The creation of conditions which would assure to all medical service and medical attention in the event of sickness.

Canada has signed both of the covenants.

The Canadian Bill of Rights Act, 1960, in general follows those articles of the UN Declaration of 1948 which I have called traditional rights and freedoms. It makes no attempt to incorporate the economic and social rights. Similarly when the present Prime Minister of Canada, as Minister of Justice in 1967, proposed a Canadian Charter of Human Rights as part of the Constitution he recommended the traditional rights and freedoms but again omitted the social and economic rights. He explained their omission from the proposed Charter in the following statement:

> The guarantee of such economic rights is desirable and should be an ultimate objective for Canada. There are, however, good reasons for putting aside this issue at this stage and proceeding with the protection of political, legal, egalitarian and linguistic rights. It might take considerable time to reach agreement on the rights to be guaranteed and on the feasibility of implementation. The United Nations recognized these problems when it prepared two separate Covenants on Human Rights—one on Civil and Political Rights and

> one on Economic, Social and Cultural Rights, thus giving nations an opportunity to accede to them one at a time.
>
> It is therefore suggested that it is advisable not to attempt to include economic rights in the constitutional bill of rights at this time.

The general scheme of the 1967 Charter has been incorporated in part 1 of the Constitution Act 1981, which the British Parliament passed in March, 1982. In other words we have no declaration of these economic and social rights. This is not a criticism. I mention it to show that these rights are rather social objectives which cannot effectively be put in a Charter of Rights any more than a right to happiness could be.

It will be noted that although in its proper sense a Bill or Charter of Rights is a part of a state's constitution, the term is frequently used to describe claims made on behalf of a class of persons—claims that may not even be legal, let alone constitutional. Thus one finds various "Bills of Rights"—of patients, mental patients, children and those who are subjects of experimentation. In all these cases the bill is an assertion of a "right" which is not necessarily recognized by law at all.

IV. *The Role of Parliament in Health Care*

The omission of any reference to health care in our new Constitution does not mean that Parliament and the provincial legislatures ignore it. Society does have wants or demands or claims (which the great legal scholar Roscoe Pound described as social interests). The pressure for some is stronger than for others. When it becomes strong enough it may be recognized by law. That is to say the interest is protected by law and supported by sanctions. Indeed Pound includes as one of his social interests, that of the general health.[11] The social interest in the general health is in fact recognized in Canada in many ways.

Since Canada is a federal state jurisdiction in connection with health care is divided. In large measure the direct power belongs to the provinces. The establishment of hospitals and asylums is specifically given to the Provinces (s. 92(7)) and the general regulation of health comes under Municipal Institutions (s. 92(8)) or property and civil rights in the province (s 92(13)) or else under matters of a local or private nature (s. 92(16)). Parliament has specific power over quarantine (on entry into Canada) and the establishment of marine hospitals. It can legislate to make narcotic trafficking a crime, and to combat a widespread epidemic. It has enacted the Food and Drug Act and the Patent Medicine Act and in the Criminal Code has dealt with abortions.[12]

Canada has had a Department of Health ever since 1919. The original Act recites that "it is expedient for the preservation of the health and the promotion of the social welfare of the people of Canada that a Department of Health be established" not only to administer six acts of Parliament but to effect "cooperation with the Provincial, Territorial and other health authorities with a view to the coordination of the efforts proposed or made for preserving and improving the public health, the conservation of child life and the promotion of child welfare." This Act also provided for a national laboratory for public health and research work and for the collection, publication and distribution of information relating to the improved public health, improved sanitation and the social and industrial conditions affecting the health and lives of the people. The present Act establishes the Department of National Health and Welfare and is basically an elaboration of the 1919 Act.

In the meantime Parliament, as far back as 1935, passed an Employment and Social Insurance Act. Part 4 provided for cooperation with the provinces in plans for providing medical care in cases of ill health. By itself it would not have been invalid but the principal part of the Act, providing for unemployment insurance, was held invalid so Part 4 fell with it because it was "inextricably mixed up" with the invalid part. (The B.N.A. Act was amended in 1940 to give Parliament jurisdiction over unemployment insurance.)

Canada has had a Pension Act for Veterans of the Armed Forces since 1919. After World War II, between 1951 and 1957 Parliament passed three Acts to provide for contributions to the provinces in connection with blind persons, disabled persons and hospital insurance. Then in 1961 came a significant event—the appointment of the Royal Commission on Health Services, commonly known as the Hall Commission from the name of the Chairman who was then the Honourable Mr. Justice Emmett Hall of the Supreme Court of Canada. The Commission produced a monumental two-volume report in 1964–65. The Report begins with a short but most significant Health Charter for Canadians.

> The achievement of the highest possible health standards for all our people must become a primary objective of national policy and a cohesive factor contributing to national unity, involving individual and community responsibilities and actions. This objective can best be achieved through a comprehensive, universal Health Services Programme for the Canadian people,
> IMPLEMENTED in accordance with Canada's evolving constitutional arrangements;
> BASED upon freedom of choice, and upon free and self-governing professions and institutions;
> FINANCED through prepayment arrangements;
> ACCOMPLISHED through the full co-operation of the general public, the health professions, voluntary agencies, all political parties, and governments, federal, provincial and municipal;
> DIRECTED towards the most effective use of the nation's health resources to attain the highest possible levels of physical and mental well-being.

The report is as comprehensive as one can imagine. It covers the state of the national health, the existing "health service complex", the problems and future needs, and health costs.

An important statement of basic requirements elaborates the principle of freedom within the health services (Vol. II c. 1). First is that of the physician. The recommended programmes are based on free, independent, self-governing professions. Payment is principally on the fee-for-service concept. The state does not interfere with the physician-patient relationship though the manner of payment is altered. At the same time the physician has social responsibilities and the state becomes involved in whether the services are available and on what terms and conditions.

Next is the freedom of the patient to seek needed health services. That freedom will be expanded by the elimination of the financial barrier. With his freedom the patient has responsibility. He cannot transfer to the state his obligation to advance his own health.

The third freedom is to carry out research and to innovate.

Parliament and the provinces responded by establishing medicare. The Medical Care Act of 1966–67 authorizes contributions to provincial medical care insurance plans. Another Act passed at the same time, the Health Resources Fund Act authorizes contributions to medical schools and the like. Two years later Parliament passed the Medical Research Council Act which gave statutory authority to the Medical Research Council which had been established just before the Hall Report was published. The first two of these three Acts provided for grants to the provinces based on a cost-sharing formula. However in 1977 this system was changed by the Federal-Provincial Fiscal Arrangements Act, to one of "block grants" and adjustment in income tax "points".

Quite apart from these statutes there have been important Federal documents on health care since the Hall Report. In 1968 a conference of Ministers of Health established a Committee on Costs of Health Care. Those costs had risen so rapidly that there were only three alternatives—to reduce standards, to increase costs or to restrain costs by better operation of the system. The Committee's mandate was to make recommendations for the last alternative. It set up seven Task Forces. Four dealt with hospitals—utilization, operational efficiency, salaries and wages, beds and facilities. The other three dealt with health services—methods of delivery of medical care, price of medical care, and costs of public health services. There is no need here to set out the recommendations of the seven Task Forces. They found a substantial number of economic inefficiencies and made suggestions for their removal.

A significant report for present purposes is that of the Honourable Marc Lalonde in 1974 called "A New Perspective on Health of Canadians". It puts forward a new concept of "the health field". It used to consist solely of medical treatment. This is no longer so. We must think of human biology, environment, lifestyle and the organization of health care. Deaths from car accidents, other accidents and suicides form a high percentage of the deaths of the young, particularly males, from the age of 10 through 34. The causes can be put down to lifestyle and environment. The same is probably true with morbidity. We furnish treatment to people whose death, injury or sickness could be prevented by changes in environment and lifestyle.

The report emphasizes that everyone—health professions, health institutions, the scientific community, the education systems, government at all levels, business and labour, voluntary associations and the public all must participate. The two broad objectives of the government of Canada are to reduce mental and physical health hazards and to improve the accessibility of health care.

In 1979 the Ministers of Health agreed to a review of the state of health services. Accordingly the federal Minister of National Health and Welfare appointed the Honourable Emmett Hall, who had been Chairman of the Royal Commission on Health Services, to report on the extent to which the goals and principles set out in the original report have been achieved and to consider whether there should be other principles and changes in legislation. A prime concern was with costs and the effect of the 1977 changes in the basis of Canada's contribution to the provincial health programmes. He reported in 1980.

The report points out that the 1977 changes in the basis of federal contribution was to give the provinces an incentive to reduce costs, but that the federal grant was higher than anticipated and the provinces did not receive as much benefit from the increased "tax points" as expected. Hall found the main issues to be extra billing and the scale of fees. He remained opposed to extra billing and would prefer binding arbitration in disputes between the medical profession and the governments over scale of fees. As to the charging of premiums and ward fees in some provinces, he declined to recommend immediate abolition but favoured it in the long run.[13]

He supported the policy of the Lalonde document described earlier, with its emphasis on prevention. He was, however, doubtful about the prospects.

> "I heard many submissions that this should be the era of Preventive Medicine but few, if any, concrete workable steps to allay the onset of illnesses arising from our present day "Life-style". I see no change in sight in the present Canadian way of life. We are in the era described by Dr. Waldavsky where some 90 per cent of our illnesses, disabilities or complaints are determined by factors over which doctors have little or no control,—but we go to them and expect them to restore us and keep us well while we pursue the same course.
>
> In this climate, curative health services are the last resort and loom large and almost usurp the fiscal capacity of the nation." (p. 66.)

Mr. Hall also supported wider rehabilitation services and their inclusion as insured services, and widened "community health care" outside hospitals. The chapter on nursing proposals is important. Greater use should be made of nurses and they should be a "point of entry" into the health care system in occupational health care, care for the elderly and chronically ill, and home care. He thinks "more nurses could be prepared for midwifery care in normal, healthy pregnancies", but the inference is that he does not favour lay midwives or home delivery, at least for the present. Nurses have a role, too, in immunization programmes, and also in preventing the "epidemic" of adolescent pregnancies.

In connection with medical services on the frontier and in northern outposts he found improvement in the Northwest Territories but not in northern Ontario and Labrador. He indicated sympathy with many of the Indian briefs supporting native medicine and true preventive health care instead of care of the crisis type. The concluding chapter on Health Professionals favoured wider use of psychologists and optometrists (who are in short supply) and chiropractors. He suggested greater support for prosthetic services but declined to recommend wider facilities for abortions. Indeed he regretted the precedence given to them over "painful elective surgical cases of long standing". He reiterated his support of fluoridation and thought that injuries in professional sports should come under workmen's compensation. There should be more funding for some research, e.g., on rehabilitation. In conclusion he appealed for continued cooperation and uninterrupted consultation between federal and provincial authorities.

Before leaving the federal scene it is proper to note Parliament's concern with children's health. The United Nations has made a declaration of the rights of the child. During 1979, the International Year of the Child, a Canadian Commission made a report entitled Canada's Children—National Agenda for Action. Subsequently the standing committee on health, welfare and social affairs of the House of Commons examined the report just mentioned and itself made two reports to the House. The second one was made on July 7th, 1981. Under the heading Children and Health are recommendations for education in prenatal care, nutrition of children, accidents and suicide and the subject of tobacco, alcohol and drug abuse. The last recommendations on health have to do with native children.

V. *Right to Health Care and Provincial Legislation*

Turning now to the provincial level, one finds here a large volume of legislation directed to health care. Because of the provinces' constitutional power and responsibility they deal much more directly with patient care than does Parliament. In Alberta four government departments are involved in health. Pre-eminent are Hospitals and Medical Care, and Social Services and Community Health. The other two are Occupational Health and Safety, and Advanced Education.

What does our provincial law say about the right to health care? Provincial law includes both acts of the legislature (statutes) and principles laid down in judgements of the courts when there is no statute (common law).

Does an individual have a right as against any doctor to claim his services? In other words is a doctor under a duty to attend "on demand"? The answer is no. Indeed the Health Care Insurance Act, carrying out the recommendation of the Hall Report, says that the Act does not interfere with the patient's right to choose his practitioner or with the right of a practitioner to accept or refuse a patient "subject to humanitarian considerations and the traditions and ethics of the profession of which he is a member" (s. 12).

However a person who is registered under the Act "is entitled to the payment of benefits by the Minister in respect of health services provided to him and his dependants". This language is that of legal obligation, though the Minister can assess the exact amount to be paid (s. 4).

In connection with local boards of health and health units they in fact provide a wide variety of services. I do not regard as important the technical legal question "Does a resident have the right to those services?" because the question is not likely to arise. However, I can find nothing in the Public Health Act or the Health Unit Act to oblige these bodies to provide service to one who requests it.

We have other statutes which provide for assistance to those who need health services. The Family and Community Support Services Act provides for municipal programmes for what used to be called preventive social services.The Social Care Facilities Act provides for licensing of facilities to care for the aged and infirm. The Treatment Services Act empowers the Minister (Social Services and Community Health) to pay the cost of treatment for the blind, disabled and others who are severely handicapped. The Minister may pay for these services but nothing in the Act compels him so to do. So with the Assured Income for the Severely Handicapped Act. The Social Development Act, however, says that a Municipality is "responsible" for the social assistance of employable persons (s. 19) and the Act speaks of the Municipality's "legal liability to furnish social assistance" to such persons (s. 20(2)). This says that an employable person has a legal right against his municipality to social assistance.

Turning to hospitals and nursing homes, there is nothing in the Hospitals Act or the Nursing Homes Act to impose an obligation to admit anyone; and the former Act gives specific power to the hospital board to discharge patients (ss. 48, 49).

In connection with mental hospitals, the Mental Health Act says that two "admission certificates" are authority to the hospital to admit and treat a patient (s. 19). Whether the hospital is obliged to admit the person is doubtful because the Act says that when any person is refused admission he and the person who referred him must be told the reason (s. 12). Section 13 imposes a duty of care: "On the admission of a patient to a facility a board is under a duty to provide the diagnostic and treatment services the patient is in need of and that the staff of the facility is capable and able to provide".

This section gives the patient a right to care in the strict legal sense. It imposes a legal duty on the hospital, though the closing part reduces considerably the scope of the duty. Of course a main criticism of mental institutions in the past has been that they were merely custodial and not therapeutic. Section 13 recognizes the change in role.

In the United States the courts have in several notable cases established a right to treatment, and they have found the right in the Constitution.

In two cases from Alabama in 1972, inmates of mental institutions challenged the state's system of care. After lengthy hearings the judge laid down Minimum Constitutional Standards for Adequate Treatment of the

Mentally Ill. This remarkable pronouncement, which takes up over seven pages in the law reports, reads like a statute. It has twenty clauses on patient care, four on qualifications of staff and ten on individualized treatment. A companion case brought on behalf of the mentally retarded produced Minimum Constitutional Standards for Adequate Rehabilitation of the Mentally Retarded. They occupy twelve pages. The federal Court of Appeals affirmed that both mentally ill and retarded have a constitutional right to treatment, based on a concept called "substantive due process".[14]

This is now generally accepted, thought the Supreme Court has not directly affirmed this ruling.[15] A state law of California, popularly called the Mental Patients' Bill of Rights, spells out those rights in great detail.The provisions include the regulation of psychotherapy and electric shock-treatment and are designed to protect patients.[16]

If a mental patient is entitled to treatment, is he entitled to refuse it? A mentally competent person may refuse it, but in many cases the mental patient's capacity to make an intelligent decision is, to say the least, in doubt.

Yet there is some support for the view that a mental patient has a constitutional right to refuse antipsychotic drugs—that forced medication is unconstitutional, at least in the absence of a judicial determination of incompetency or in emergency. A case from Massachusetts so holding is now before the Supreme Court.[17]

I mention these American cases as a matter of interest. One might hope that we can work out a humane regimen without endless litigation and invocation of the new Charter of Rights.

Returning to Alberta's Mental Health Act, Part 3 is entitled Rights of Patients. Curiously the right to treatment is not found in Part 3 but in Part 2. The rights set out in Part 3 include the patient's right to information about his detention and his right to a hearing before a review panel. Censorship of mail is prohibited and the patient is entitled to visitors. I shall deal later with the right of confidentiality which is included in Part 3.

Once a person has become the patient of a physician or of a hospital then of course the duty to take proper care arises and no statute in needed to create that duty. If the patient suffers damage from negligence or from unauthorized treatment he is entitled to bring action for compensation. Difficult questions arise as to whether anyone is to blame, and if so, who. These large questions are outside the terms of this paper.[18]

There is however a trend that must be noted. In the last few years there has been a change in attitude as to the role of doctors and hospitals in relation to patients. Traditionally it has been paternalistic. "We know best what is good for you". The emphasis today is on the individual's power of decision. The patient should have the power to decide what shall be done to him. This means he must be given the information to make a choice. We are now all familiar with the concept of informed consent. The Supreme Court of Canada in two recent cases established it as the test for a true consent to medical treatment[19] and even earlier the Saskatchewan Court of Appeal had laid down this test for consent to non-therapeutic research on a human.[20] These rules are part of the common law. Alberta has not passed any statute on these subjects. In connection, however, with the donation of non-regenerative tissue by a living person, the Human Tissue Gift Act says he must be an adult who can "make a free and informed decision." (s. 3). In connection with sterilization we had at one time a Sexual Sterilization Act. It was repealed in 1972. At the present time it is clear that an adult of sound mind may choose non-therapeutic sterilization, but there is, to say the least, serious doubt as to whether the guardian of a child or mental patient can give a valid consent. Indeed there is now a case before the Supreme Court of Canada from Prince Edward Island as to the power of a provincial Supreme Court, in the exercise of its general powers over incompetents, to authorize sterilization of such a person.[21]

VI. *The Patient's Right to Confidentiality*

There are of course other legal rights of patients in addition to the right to decide on his treatment and the right to a reasonable standard of care. The right to confidentiality goes back to the Hippocratic Oath. This is of course an ethical obligation. Whether a patient could successfully sue the physician for damages for disclosing a confidence is not clear but on principle he should be able to if he can show damage.[22]

At the present time there are huge quantities of medical information held by government and hospitals. The Alberta legislature has enacted a number of provisions which protect the secrecy of medical information—for example, the Alberta Health Care Insurance Act (s. 13); the Hospitals Act (s. 40); the Alcoholism and Drug Abuse Act (s. 38); the Venereal Diseases Prevention Act (s. 24); the Workmen's Compensation Act (s. 19(8)); the Cancer Treatment and Prevention Act (s. 12); the Social Development Act (s. 5); and the Mental Health Act (s. 37). It would be tedious to set out all these provisions. The basic scheme of most of these Acts is to impose secrecy or confidentiality with narrow powers to release information for specific purposes. The Hospitals Act (s. 40(2)) and the Mental Health Act (s. 37(3)) permit the appropriate minister "for the purpose of assessing the standards of care" and improving facilities and procedures to call for medical records. At the 1982 session the Minister of Social Services and Community Health introduced a bill (Bill 30) to amend the Public Health Act. The proposed amendment contained a provision (s. 32.1(1)) like those in the other two Acts—a completely proper provision in my judgment. Yet that provision caused an outcry that the amendment was an unwarranted breach of confidentiality. The bill was withdrawn. Such is the effect of ill-informed criticism.

A problem related to confidentiality is this: should a patient have the right to see his own file? The Hospitals Act says that the Minister may "with the written consent of a patient divulge any diagnosis, record or information relating to the patient to any person" (s. 40(5)). Does this permit him to show the record to the patient himself? I doubt it. The Mental Health Act by way of contrast specifically gives the Minister discretion to release information to the patient (s. 37(6)(a)). Indeed the ill-fated Bill 30 had a similar provision (s. 32.1(6)(b)).

Recently a most significant case has been in the Courts. It is *D.M.* v. *Lindsay*.[23] The plaintiff asked for a copy of his record at the mental hospital at Ponoka for use in another law suit. The Court of Appeal held that although s. 37(6) of the Mental Health Act is permissive, ss. (7)–(9) show that the Court can order disclosure and can supplant the Minister's ruling. This decision gives a patient the right to production of his own record unless the person resisting disclosure (in that case the Director of the Ponoka Hospital) satisfies the Court that the information should not be disclosed. In that case the Court ruled that the defendant had not discharged that onus.

This contentious issue received much attention from Ontario's Commission of Inquiry into the Confidentiality of Health Information (the Krever Commission). Mr. Justice Krever's Report says that "patient access was one of the most controversial and emotional subjects dealt with in our inquiry" (Vol. III, p. 455). His general position was in favour of access and he expressed approval of the onus section in Alberta's Hospital Act, which is the same as the onus section in our Mental Health Act (p. 488).[24]

Quite apart from the provisions of the statutes just described we have a number of acts which require disclosure of medical information.[25] The Child Welfare Act requires anyone who reasonably believes a child has been physically ill-treated to report to the Director. Physicians are not specifically mentioned but are clearly included (s. 35). The Public Health Act authorizes regulations in respect of "the reporting to the local board by a physician of every person under his treatment for any communicable disease or any disease dangerous to the public health" (s. 6(1)(g)). The Venereal Diseases Prevention Act imposes a duty on physicians and hospitals to report to the Director every case of infection with venereal disease (s. 4).

There are cases where a physician though not obliged to furnish information about a patient may do so. The Motor Vehicle Administration Act *permits* physicians to report to the Registrar information of a patient's condition which may affect the operation of a motor vehicle, and optometrists may report any defect in vision (s. 14(2), (3)). There are many other circumstances in which a physician or hospital may be relieved from the usual obligation of confidentiality. For the greater part these are not governed by any statute in Alberta. In many cases there may be doubt as to the propriety of disclosure and of course this is an ethical problem even more than a legal one.

Just to take random examples: a doctor tends a teen-age girl in connection with contraception or abortion and without her consent tells her parents. A doctor or hospital tends a victim of a gun-shot wound and news broadcasts indicate he is a suspected murderer so the police are notified. There is considerable leeway here. To date we have had little legislation on this. The Krever Committee made many recommendations on these matters (c. 16), and also on informing an employer (c. 30) or a school (c. 29) of illness of an employee or student. Generally he would permit the disclosure when it is in the patient's or the public's interest.

VII. *The Right to Practice*

We have been dealing with patients' rights. I turn now to a completely different matter—who has the right to practice medicine? Under the Canadian system which is much closer to the British than to the American, each of the learned professions is largely self-governing. The two main elements of self-government are control over admission to the profession and the power to discipline. In order to practice, a person must be a member of the professional society. He is subject to its by-laws and ethical code, and the society may impose penalties for unprofessional conduct. The penalties usually range from a reprimand to expulsion. (Some professions, notably in the paramedical field, such as Nursing Assistants and Dental Auxiliaries do not have the same autonomy as the other professions.)

Invariably a profession is governed by a provincial statute. We have the Medical Profession Act, the Dental Association Act, the Dental Auxiliaries Act, the Dental Mechanics Act, the Dental Technicians Act, the Registered Nurses Act, the Psychiatric Nurses Association Act, the Nursing Assistants Registration Act, the Pharmaceutical Association Act, the Optometry Act, the Chiropractic Profession Act, the Naturopathy Act, and the Psychologists Act.

At the present time we have acupuncturists claiming the right to practice and there is some advocacy for lay midwives. The Health Occupations Act of 1980 sets up machinery whereby the Minister of Social Services and Community Health may recommend legislation to designate a health occupation as one to which the Act applies. Some groups have applied but to date no designation has been made by the legislature.

A problem which can arise is that of admission of a physician to the staff or to the privileges of a hospital. The Hospitals Act requires each board to have by-laws governing the conduct of physicians practicing in the hospital and procedures for appointment and dismissal of members of the staff. If a member of the staff is dissatisfied with the board's decision, for example not to re-appoint him or to reduce his privileges, he may appeal to the Hospital Privileges Appeal Board and there is a further appeal to the Court (ss. 32–36).[26] In a recent case the hospital revoked a doctor's appointment without a hearing, which the hospital's by-laws required. The Court held that the revocation was ineffective and awarded $10,000 damages.[27] It is clear today that although the physician cannot claim to obtain or keep an appointment he is entitled to a fair hearing before his privileges are removed.

VIII. *Current Concerns Over Health Care*

One indication of concern over health care is the questions put by opposition members in the legislature to the Minister responsible. Taking Hansard for 1981 and to date in 1982, they cover a wide range. Are there plans for midwives and home delivery? Will there be more education respecting alcohol and drug abuse? Will there be a province-wide ambulance service? Will there be health care for psycho-geriatrics? What is being done about the shortage of nurses and psychiatrists? How can we get uninsured, unlicensed and suspended drivers off the road? Is the nursing home at St. Paul being investigated? Are we moving toward group homes for the mentally handicapped? Will there be a Children's Hospital in Edmonton? What is being done to reduce industrial and farm accidents?

In 1981 there were three significant resolutions by private members. The first asks the government to look into the problem of securing doctors for rural centres and training them for rural practice; the second is a proposal for programmes to train technicians in workers' safety at the post-secondary level. The third asks for a study of the need for human tissue and of means to meet it. We have of course a Human Tissue Gift Act, but the purpose of the motion is to encourage people to give donations of their bodies after death—for example, by completing the universal donor card on drivers' licenses.

The daily newspapers too carry items on health care. Clippings from an Edmonton newspaper in the past several weeks are these: complaints about the proposed amendment to the Public Health Act; home births; needless lab tests; reduction in beds at University Hospital; the need for a "tougher" Clean Water Act; balance billing; complaints about young persons in geriatric centres; seat belts; better services needed for deaf-blind; increase in self-induced sickness; complaints of inadequate care for dying; fear of socialized medicine.

IX. *Regulation of Conduct in Interest of Health*

The last point I wish to consider in connection with the individual's rights is the contention that the state should not interfere with a person's decision in connection with his own health and safety. Prominent examples are legislation requiring safety belts or motor cycle helmets and legislation making criminal the use of marijuana and other drugs. The opponent invariably invokes John Stuart Mill who said the state should not put compulsion or control on an individual except to prevent harm to others. To some extent, but never completely, our law has followed this policy. The simple fact is that a person injured because he did not use a seat-belt or motorcycle helmet, or a person using drugs, is not hurting himself only. The burden falls on society and society is entitled to be protected. Our Highway Traffic Act requires motorcyclists to wear helmets (s. 126). Recently a man was acquitted for failure to wear a helmet on the ground that the Act violated the Alberta Bill of Rights because it is discriminatory. The Crown appealed and the Court of Appeal had no difficulty in upholding the Act.[28] We still do not have seat-belt legislation. Now that the constitutional Charter of Rights is in effect, objections to legislation will become more and more frequent. In my view solicitude for individual rights and freedoms must not be permitted to frustrate society's efforts to prevent accidents and sickness.

X. *Conclusion*

In general our law does not give a right to medical treatment in the sense that a given physician is obliged to treat anyone who demands his services. At the same time patients do have substantial rights—to information that will enable them to make their own decisions, to due care, and to confidentiality. Moreover, the legislation at both levels gives all manner of assistance in making health care accessible. The current emphasis on rights has some healthy aspects, but on the other hand we have urgent need for a greater sense of responsibility on the part of individuals in reducing the causes of injury and sickness.

Notes

1 Szasz, "The Myth of Mental Illness" in Mappes and Zembaty, *Biomedical Ethics* (1981) 222.

2 Ratcliffe, The Good Samaritan and the Law (1966); *Horsley* v. *MacLaren* [1972] S.C.R. 441.

3 The writer's reasons for opposing this legislation appear in the Report of the Manitoba Law Reform Commission on "The Advisability of a Good Samaritan Law in Manitoba", (1973) at 8, 9. That Commission recommended against such legislation as had the Ontario Law Reform Commission in 1971.

4 *Stark* v. *Council of Physicians and Surgeons* (1965) 55 W.W.R. 121; *Wilson* v. *Stark* (1967) 61 W.W.R. 648. The action for damages failed because the paintiff did not show that the doctor's negligence caused the patient's death.

5 *Vail* v. *MacDonald* [1976] 2 S.C.R. 825.

6 Gorovitz, *Moral Problems in Medicine* (1976); Humber and Almeder, *Biomedical Ethics and the Law* (1976); Mappes and Zembaty, *Biomedical Ethics* (1981); Hunt and Arras, *Ethical Issues in Modern Medicine* (1977); Shannon, *Bioethics* (1976); Shapiro, *Bioethics and Law* (1981); Veatch and Bronson, *Ethical and Health Policy* (1976).

7 See also Beauchamp and Childress, *Principles of Biomedical Ethics* (1979), which has four main principles—autonomy, non-maleficence, beneficence and justice.

8 Pound, *Jurisprudence* (1959) Vol. IV, 56–58.

9 Hohfeld, *Fundamental Legal Conceptions* (1923); Hall, *Readings in Jurisprudence* (1938), 442–538; Salmond on *Jurisprudence,* 11 ed. (1957) c. 10; Pound, *Jurisprudence* (1959) Vol. IV c. 21; Stone, *Legal Systems and Legal Reasoning* (1964) c. 4.

10 Appleton, *Beyond the Limits of Reproductive Choice* (1981) 81 Col. L. Rev. 721; Churchill and Simon, *Abortion and the Rhetoric of Individual Rights,* 12 Hastings Center Report No. 1, 9 (1982).

11 Pound, *Jurisprudence* Vol. III, 292.

12. For an account of Parliament's role in the health field, see the brochure published in 1974 by the Honourable Marc Lalonde, then Minister of National Welfare: *A New Perspective on the Health of Canadians,* c. 6.

13 See Report of the National Council of Welfare made in May, 1982 and entitled *Medicare and Private Practice*. It is a strong indictment of extra-billing and of premiums. It supports an accessible, universal and comprehensive Medicare.

14 *Wyatt* v. *Stickney* 344 F. Supp. 373 and 387, aff'd in large part in *Wyatt* v. *Aderholt* 503 F. 2d 1307 (1974). For earlier developments see Symposium, *The Right to Treatment* (1969) 57 Georgetown L.J. 673.

15 In *O'Connor* v. *Donaldson* (1975) 422 U.S. 503, this point arose but the

Supreme Court did not have to decide it.

16 Welfare and Institutions Code at 5000–5404.1: In *Aden* v. *Younger* (1976) 129 Cal. Rptr. 535, patients wanting psychotherapy and shock treatment claimed that the restrictions on such therapy were too severe. They won some of their arguments and the Act was amended.

17 *Rogers* v. *Okin,* 634 F. 2d 650; in the Supreme Court the case is *Mills* v. *Rogers.* See Applebaum, "Can Mental Patients Say No to Drugs?" New York Times Magazine, 26 March 1982, p. 46.

18 Picard, Legal Liability of Doctors and Hospitals in Canada (1978).

19 *Hopp* v. *Lepp* (1980) 112 D.L.R. (3d) 67 (S.C.C.); *Reibl* v. *Hughes* (1980) 114 D.L.R. (3d) 1 (S.C.C.).

20 *Halushka* v. *University of Saskatchewan* (1965) 53 D.L.R. (2d) 436.

21 *Re Eve* (1981), 115 D.L.R. (3d) 283; see Starkman, "Sterilization of the Mentally Retarded: The Eve Case" (1981) 26 McGill L.J. 931.

22 Rodgers-Magnet, *Common Law Remedies for Disclosure of Confidential Medical Information,* Report of the Commission of Inquiry into the Confidentiality of Health Information, (Ontario) Vol. III App. 1.

23 (1981), 26 A.R. 159.

24 Krever Report, Vol. III c. 23, *Access to One's Own Health Information.*

25 See Krever Report, Vol. III c. 28, Mandatory Reporting of Health Information.

26 For an early case see *Andreas* v. *Edmonton Hospital Board* [1944] 3 W.W.R. 599 where the Appellate Division upheld the board's decision to refuse the plaintiff admission to its medical staff; also *M.* v. *Cereal Municipa Hospital District* [1946] 3 W.W.R. 699.

27 *Abouna* v. *Foothills Hospital,* [1978] 2 W.W.R. 130 (App. Div.).

28 *Regina* v. *Pennington* (1981) 34 A.R. 330.

1982

Fifty-Five Years at the Alberta Bar: George Hobson Steer, Q.C.

Reprinted from
(1982) 20 Alberta Law Review
pp. 242–295

The writing of this article on one of Western Canada's leading advocates was a voluntary undertaking by Bowker—in a sense it could be termed a "labour of love" because of the respect and affection he had for the man, but also because he felt that the story of George Steer's career is an important episode in our legal history. Besides this, Bowker knew something at first hand about some of the cases he handled.

George Steer, even though one of the busiest of practitioners, lectured for years to law students at the University of Alberta. Wilbur Bowker was one of those students in the early 1930s; and in 1932 he articled to him, then practised for ten years with his firm.

On Bowker's discharge from the army in 1945 at the end of World War II, it was with George Steer's endorsement that he joined the Law Faculty of the University of Alberta in the post-war crisis, largely because of Mr. Steer's own commitment to legal education and to the future of the Law School.

I. Introduction[1]

George Hobson Steer was born in Hamilton, Ontario.[2] He became a schoolteacher. Enrolling at Queen's University as an extra-mural student, he later was in residence there, obtaining the degree of Master of Arts in May, 1912. The next month he came to Edmonton and entered into articles with C.L. Freeman of the firm of Boyle, Parlee, Freeman, Abbott and Mustard. At that time the period of articles was three years for a student with a degree. After a year Steer's[3] articles were transferred to C.H. Grant of Rutherford, Jamieson and Grant. The head of this firm had been the first premier of Alberta. On October 8, 1915 Steer was admitted as a Barrister and Solicitor before Mr. Justice J.D. Hyndman and soon after his name was added to the firm.

From the time of admission he did counsel work. Near the end of World War I he joined the Tank Corps as an officer and was in England at the Armistice. Soon after returning he left the Rutherford firm and joined in practice with Col. C.Y. Weaver. Weaver was a prominent Conservative while Steer, though never active in politics, was a Liberal. At first they did not have any large clients but did look after some British investments and acted for a good number of veterans. When prohibition came to an end after a plebiscite in the fall of 1923, the Northwest Brewing Company retained Weaver and Steer as its solicitors. At this time they joined Wallace McDonald, a senior practitioner, who acted for two lending institutions and had a good mortgage practice.

The firm of McDonald Weaver and Steer came to an end when McDonald died in 1929 and Weaver in 1930. This was the year in which Steer was appointed King's Counsel. In 1931 his name appeared in the firm of Steer, Jackson and Gaunt, though the writer's impression is that Roy Jackson really had an independent practice and that John Gaunt was an employee of Steer. For a short time in 1932 and 1933 the name of J.A. Matheson was on the letterhead. Near the end of 1933 Steer considered joining S.C.S. Kerr and the firm of Dyde and Becker, but before any arrangement was concluded H.R. Milner invited Steer to join his firm. Milner had come from Nova Scotia in 1912 to join Hyndman and Hyndman, and rose quickly at the bar. However, in 1932 he became president of Northwestern Utilities and its affiliated companies and so was seeking an able counsel. Steer agreed to join the Milner firm and moved to it in March 1934, the firm becoming Milner, Steer, Dafoe, Poirier and Martland.[4] After a number of changes in the firm name, it became in later years simply Milner and Steer, as it now is. Steer retired in 1970. (The firm now has some forty-five names on the letterhead and an office in Calgary.)

In all his years of practice he did much solicitor's work as well as litigation. He never deviated from the general practice of law by taking important directorships or running for office. He was a hard worker, prompt and thorough, and single-minded in his attention to clients' affairs—and he expected others to be the same.

The writer makes no attempt to compare Steer with other leading counsel or to compute his record of wins and losses. He prepared evidence carefully and made effective use of expert witnesses. His legal research was thorough. In cross-examination he did not waste words but "went for the jugular", and though not colourful was forceful and effective. In legal argument he put his case clearly, succinctly and with force. He did not hesitate to advise against bringing or defending an action but once he had decided to litigate he was a fighter and did not easily give up. He was a careful and good conveyancer and knew the Rules of Court. When an issue in a matter of practice arose in the course of a case he did not hesitate to take it before the Chambers Judge or even the Appellate Division;[5] and when he considered that a public official or body had refused to carry out a statutory duty, he was prepared to bring proceedings in mandamus.[6]

In his early years Steer was regarded as an equity and property lawyer, probably because he taught those subjects in the Faculty of Law at the University of Alberta. The fact is that he took every type of civil case and a number of criminal cases. He had many constitutional cases in the late thirties and forties and thereafter a large number of oil and gas actions, where his knowledge of equity and property law was put to use. Though often described as a specialist in property law, in constitutional law, in equity, or in oil and gas law, he was still a generalist.[7]

One might gain the impression that he did nothing but work. It would be more accurate to say that he did not waste time. He followed sports closely. In his younger days he was a good tennis player. Later he took up badminton. In the thirties he would leave the Court House after a busy day, drive (with dispatch) to the Badminton Club and play (so the writer is told) with the same vigour he showed in his work. He was a good golfer though after the removal of an eye comparatively late in life played little. During World War II he took up skiing. For years he lunched at the Edmonton Club where he occasionally played poker. He was not particularly interested in travel and indeed did not spend much time on holidays. However, he did enjoy his cottage on Lake Edith in Jasper National Park.

His first wife (née Helen Cameron) had died in childbirth when their only child, Cameron, was born on September 8, 1919. Steer raised his son. At the beginning of World War II Cameron went overseas as a lieutenant of artillery and served throughout the Sicilian and Italian campaigns. Wounded twice, he attained the rank of major. Returning home in 1946 with his war bride, Cameron spent the next five years at University and won the Gold Medal in law on graduation in 1951. He was articled to his father and in later years frequently appeared with him in court. Steer concealed his feelings but it is certain he was moved on the occasion when he presented his son to his old friend Mr. Justice Frank Ford on Cameron's admission to the bar in May, 1952, and again when Cameron was appointed as a judge of the Trial Division of the Supreme Court of Alberta in December 1974, six months before Steer's death. Cameron died from a sudden illness in December, 1979.[8]

In June, 1938, Steer was married to a long time friend, Mrs. Irma May. She survived him by almost four years. A fine person, of remarkable disposition and a gracious hostess, she was an ideal wife.

II. Cases of the Early Years

In describing Steer's cases, the writer will try to maintain a chronological order and at the same time to group them by subject matter. In several instances there will be a compromise.

Steer's first reported appearance in court came within six months of admission to the bar. He acted for two homesteaders near Lake Wabamun. They owned a team of oxen and a cow. The tethered ox broke loose and the other animals followed. They were all struck by a train of the Grand Trunk Pacific Railway. Judge J.L. Crawford awarded the plaintiffs $225. Neil D. Maclean, another young lawyer from Ontario who was to have a distinguished career as counsel, appeared for the Railway on its appeal. Maclean's argument, that the animals were at large through the fault of the owners, failed.[9]

Six other reported cases in this period had to do with claims of priority as between creditors and claims of fraudulent preference.[10] He won the first two and lost the next four of these cases.

Steer's most significant case at this time was *Consolidated Investments Ltd.* v. *Acres.*[11] There had been a dramatic land boom in Edmonton, as elsewhere on the prairies, around 1910. It collapsed just before World War I. On a rising market buyers naturally want to enforce the agreement for sale and vendors are tempted to try to escape it. On a falling market the situation is reversed. Much of our law governing agreements for sale of land and disposition of mineral rights has been established in this context. In *Acres,* the plaintiff's president had gone to Toronto in 1912 and sold a large number of lots on the western outskirts of Edmonton. He painted a glowing picture to Mr. Acres. One of his representations was that the land was within a four-mile circle of the Edmonton post office. It was in fact a half-mile further away. Two years later the vendor brought the usual action for specific performance. Steer for the defendant argued that his client had rescinded the agreement for misrepresentation and also that the plaintiff did not have title to the land. He lost at trial but on appeal the Court held that there was misrepresentation and that the rescission was effective.

Steer's reported cases in the early twenties are not especially noteworthy. He acted for a company whose controlling shareholder, as the Court found, improperly used funds of another company to buy property;[12] he lost an action for specific performance because the Statute of Frauds was a good defence;[13] and he successfully defended an action for rescission[14] and one alleging a fraudulent preference.[15]

In the same period the Law Society of Alberta used Steer as its solicitor in disciplinary proceedings. Until 1921 disbarment for unprofessional conduct was in the hands of the Court, not the Benchers.[16] In one case where the lawyer's main offence was in ignoring the Law Society's letters, Walsh J. declined to disbar him but ordered him to pay the costs, while commenting that "Mr. Steer's attitude had been most commendable."[17] When the Benchers in 1921 were given power to strike off the rolls, an appeal lay to the Appellate Division, as it still does to the Court of Appeal. On two applications for reinstatement in 1924 the Court found no adequate evidence of rehabilitation, though Beck J.A. would have reinstated the applicants under strict conditions.[18]

Steer's first appearance before the Supreme Court of Canada came in 1926 on behalf of the plaintiff in *Standard Trust Company* v. *Hiram M.D.* The action was to set aside a tax sale because the municipality had not given to the plaintiff (a mortgagee) notice of the sale and of its right to redeem. The question was whether the wide curative section in the Act covered failure to give notice. Mr. Justice John Boyle, at trial, answered in the negative. Thus the plaintiff won, but the Appellate Division reversed the trial judge. On the plaintiff's appeal to the Supreme Court the trial judgement was restored. Failure to give notice was so fundamental that it rendered the proceedings ineffectual.[19]

Steer had a small number of matrimonial cases. In 1924, there was no Domestic Relations Act and considerable doubt as to the law on alimony. Nevertheless, Steer succeeded in an action for alimony. Two judges held that an earlier separation agreement had not negatived the duty to support, two found a resumption of cohabitation which brought the agreement to an end, while Beck J.A., expressing uncertainty as to the law of Alberta, simply concurred.[20]

In another case Steer acted for a woman who claimed veteran's insurance on the death of the man with whom she had been living. The Crown denied she was the lawful wife. However the Exchequer Court held cohabitation created a sufficient presumption of marriage and that the Crown had not rebutted the presumption. On the Crown's appeal to the Supreme Court of Canada, Steer was represented by eastern counsel when the appeal was dismissed.[21]

In 1931 a divorced wife brought action to set aside a divorce, the former husband having died in the meantime. Neil Maclean acted for the plaintiff and Steer for the defendant. Each had recently been made King's Counsel. Steer applied for an order striking out the statement of claim, arguing that the divorce was a judgment *in rem* and was not subject to attack after the husband's death even though the plaintiff alleged fraud. Tweedie J., in one of his rare long judgments, rejected this argument and a divided Appellate Division upheld him.[22] The case never went to trial.[23]

Motor vehicle cases, like those in family law, were not frequent. In the days before we had a Contributory Negligence Act, Steer once acted for the plaintiffs whose car collided with a street car at an intersection. The action failed except for the passengers' claims.[24] Later he acted for passengers in a taxi who sued both the taxi company and the other party to a collision. At that time courts were tempted to identify passengers with their driver's negligence and to allow recovery only against the driver who had the last clear chance. In this case S.B. Woods, a leading counsel of the day, vigorously argued that his client (the other party) was not liable. He failed and on his appeal the court did not call on Steer.[25]

The most important vehicle case was *Jeremy* v. *Fontaine* in 1931. Since a plaintiff failed completely if he were guilty of contributory negligence, the courts developed the doctrine of last clear chance to render the defendant liable. In this case Steer acted for a plaintiff who stepped out onto the St. Albert Trail from behind a parked car. The defendant driving along the trail struck the plaintiff. Although the latter was contributorily negligent, Ford J. found that the defendant's brakes were faulty and that had they been sound he could have avoided the accident. In the language of the day he would have had the last clear chance but for his prior incapacitating negligence. The defendant's appeal was dismissed.[26] Today, of course, the plaintiff's damages would be apportioned under the Contributory Negligence Act.

The last important vehicle case, *George* v. *Brown and Imperial Oil*,[27] a decade later, can be noted here. Brown worked as a salesman and supervisor for Imperial Oil Co. He lived in Edmonton but his work was in the Camrose area. On his way back to the city in his own car he struck George's car. George sued Brown and also Imperial as the employer. The trial was by judge and jury, which even in 1940 was becoming a rarity in civil cases in Alberta. The jury found Brown negligent. The judge had instructed them that if they found Imperial had the right to control Brown on his way to and from Camrose they should find Imperial liable. This the jury did. Steer appeared for Imperial on the appeal and succeeded in obtaining an order for a new trial on the ground that the direction was inaccurate as to the basis of the master's liability for the servant's negligence. The writer's recollection is that the second trial never took place.

In the field of real property law, the number of cases in the twenties and thirties was not large. In one important case in 1923, *Andrews* v. *Sinclair,*[28] Sinclair in Australia gave to Griffith of Edmonton a power of attorney to deal with Sinclair's Canadian assets. The instrument said that Sinclair wanted to give Griffith such powers as were needed to dispose of property "with the same powers and authorities in all respects as if I were personally present". No specific power to mortgage land was included, though there were specific powers to lease and sell. The question was this: did Griffith have power to mortgage the lands? Steer argued that he did, but the Appellate Division held that the power to give a mortgage would have to be explicit and could not be inferred from the instrument. Had Sinclair used the form set out in the Land Titles Act, he would have been reminded to specify the power to grant a mortgage had he wished to confer it.

McLeod v. *Pearson,*[29] in 1931, dealt with another important problem in land law. It had to do with the time limit for suing on a mortgage debt, and on suing for foreclosure. Alberta did not have a comprehensive Limitations Act until 1935. Prior to that we had a short statute which had come down from territorial days. It declared that the English Real Property Limitations Act, 1874, was in force. Steer acted for a mortgagor who brought action for a declaration that the mortgage was no longer a charge on the land because the mortgagee had not brought action within 12 years after the right so to do had arisen. S. Bruce Smith, who was to become a leader at the bar and later Chief Justice of Alberta, appeared for the mortgagee. The mortgagor or his agent had signed three letters, all of which acknowledged the debt and one of which had acknowledged the mortgagee's "title". Thus it would appear that the mortgage was still valid. However, the three letters had been written to the mortgagee's former solicitor after he had written to inquire as to whether the mortgagor was keeping up a prior mortgage. The letter from the former solicitor had been written "without prejudice". Frank Ford J. held that such a letter protects subsequent correspondence on the same subject matter, so the three letters from the plaintiff or his agent were also "without prejudice". Therefore they were inadmissible as an acknowledgement. In the result, Steer succeeded in having the mortgage removed from the title.

An unusual case on real property law is *Canadian Mausoleums Ltd*. v.

Irwin.[30] The Edmonton Cemetery Company had agreed to buy lands from the Hudson's Bay Company and then in 1929 gave to Canadian Mausoleums Ltd. an option "for the perpetual right to use a plot of ground in Edmonton Cemetery... for the purpose of erecting a mausoleum thereon and of disposing of the compartments and private rooms in the same". Canadian Mausoleums took up the option and the mausoleum was largely completed by September, 1930. In the preceding month Irwin had purchased two compartments in the mausoleum for $950. In December, 1931, Steer wrote the Mausoleum company that his client repudiated the agreement on the ground that the company "has not a good title to the lands purported to be sold to our client". The company then sued for the purchase price. Mr. Justice Ford held that the agreement gave Irwin an interest in land, though he left open the question as to the nature of the interest. The company's only right in the land was the perpetual right to use it whereas the company had purported to give Irwin possession of the two crypts. This was a greater right than the company had to give. Moreover the Cemetery Company at the time of the repudiation did not have title to the land or the right to compel the Hudson's Bay Company to grant title. Thus Irwin was entitled to repudiate.

The company's appeal was dismissed without reasons and a further appeal to the Supreme Court of Canada was abandoned.

A real property case, *Cristall* v. *T. Eaton Co.*,[31] which came somewhat later, can be described here. In the fall of 1928 Eaton decided to buy land in downtown Edmonton for a store. Cristall owned desirable property. He gave an option to a real estate agency which was attempting to acquire land for Eaton. A condition of the option was that the property "is being purchased for use in connection with a department store site". Through a subsidiary, Eaton took up the option with the condition included. Eaton did not build immediately. Cristall alleged a verbal covenant to build and claimed $490,000 for breach. G.W. Auxier, the solicitor for Eaton, retained Steer. On a conflict of evidence as to what was said during the negotiations, Ewing J. found a verbal undertaking that Eaton would within a reasonable time use the premises as a department store. However, he found no covenant to build, either written or verbal. Thus he did not have to deal with complicated questions of agency, the parol evidence rule, and the Statute of Frauds, all of which had been minutely examined by counsel on both sides. Not long after the trial, Eaton built on the property a store which it still operates.

The last case in this part has nothing to do with property. In 1931, when appeals still lay to the Privy Council, this question arose. Where a Privy Council judgment is in conflict with one of the House of Lords, which of them should an Alberta court follow? Since abolition of appeals to the Privy Council this question has become academic. However it was not academic in 1931. In *Will* v. *Bank of Montreal*,[32] gamblers lured Will into a poker game in Edmonton. One of them, King, filled in a cheque for $50.00 for Will to sign to cover his loss. Will signed it. Later King, having left ample space for the purpose, raised the cheque to $1,150.00 and through a devious route cashed it. Will brought action against his bank for damages for paying a raised cheque.

The Privy Council had said that a customer does not violate his duty of care towards his bank merely by drawing the cheque with spaces which a forger could utilize to raise the cheque.[33] A later House of Lords decision said the customer owes his bank a duty to take reasonable precautions against forgery.[34] H.A. Friedman, another leader of the bar at the time, argued for the plaintiff that an Alberta court was bound to follow the Privy Council. Steer, who had been retained by the bank's solicitors, contended that the House of Lords' judgment was binding. Mr. Justice Frank Ford enjoyed a problem like this. He reviewed many cases. Specifically quoting and adopting Steer's argument, he concluded that the House of Lords "is the supreme tribunal to settle English law"[35] so that he should follow it. Thus Will, having failed to take reasonable steps to guard against forgery, failed in his action. One might wonder why the plaintiff did not appeal. The writer has always understood that the Bank settled in full.

III. Actions Against the City of Edmonton

In the period shortly before Steer joined the Milner firm, he acted for the plaintiff in each of three actions against the City. The first and most significant, *Clarke* v. *Edmonton,*[36] raised the question of riparian rights on the North Saskatchewan River, which is navigable and non-tidal.

In 1882 a number of large river lots were surveyed on both sides of the river at the Edmonton settlement. Lot 21 containing 163 acres was a quarter of a mile wide and a mile from north to south. The northern boundary was the south bank of the river.[37] In 1924 Clarke obtained title to a comparatively small part of the lot between Dowler's Hill Road and the riverbank. In the preceding fourteen years, thanks to floods and changes in the current, a bench had grown up in the river bed adjacent to the south bank. It varied in depth from thirteen feet at the west to half that depth at the east. From north to south the bench varied in width, with a maximum of eighty feet. Beginning in 1920 the city had deposited refuse on a small area at the east end of the bench. Clarke claimed ownership of the bench by accretion, and in 1925 brought action for trespass. At that time, the original bank was still visible, but the bench had grown up with vegetation and a new bank had been formed at the north side of the bench.

Steer acted for Clarke and J.C.F. Bown, the City Solicitor, for the City. Mr. Justice Tweedie held that Clarke did not acquire ownership of the bench by accretion and so dismissed the action. Clarke appealed. Because of the possibility that the Crown in right of Canada owned the bench, the Attorney General of Canada intervened, and was represented by H.H. Parlee, an eminent counsel. Three of the four judges in the result agreed with the trial judge. The original boundary was visible. Chief Justice Harvey added that the bench had not been formed slowly and imperceptibly by accretion, but rather had been formed by avulsion in a fourteen-year period, so the riparian owner could not claim ownership. Mr. Justice Beck gave a lengthy dissent. He held there was a true accretion and that the bench belonged to Clarke. The judgments referred to the common law rule that a riparian owner owned to the middle of the stream, and confirmed an earlier Alberta decision that this rule did not apply in Alberta.[38]

Clarke appealed to the Supreme Court of Canada. Parlee now represented the City and Eugene Lafleur, the great Montreal advocate, appeared for the Attorney General of Canada.[39] In a unanimous judgment in late 1929, the Supreme Court allowed the appeal, agreeing with Mr. Justice Beck, who had died before the appeal was heard. To decide whether Clarke became the owner, the court looked at the law of England as it existed on July 15, 1870, which was the date when the law of England became the law of the Northwest Territories and hence of Alberta. In England an accretion to the shore of a non-tidal navigable river belonged to the riparian owner. This rule did not depend on the notion of ownership to the middle of the stream. The boundary of Clarke's lot was the river, not the old bank, visible though it was.[40]

This case did not end Clarke's litigation with the City. He lived on his land by the river. Not far away the City had a sewage disposal plant. Clarke brought an action in nuisance for an injunction and damages. Again Steer appeared for him, while G.B. O'Connor, another prominent lawyer and later Chief Justice of Alberta, was counsel for the City. Clarke's case was that the odours from the plant were so frequent and intense as materially to interfere with the enjoyment of his home. The evidence at the trial was conflicting. Ewing J. found the odours constituted a nuisance. The question then was whether he would give an injunction in view of the City's statutory authority to operate the plant. The judge held that the City was bound to maintain the plant. However he found that its method of operation was negligent so that its statutory authority did not protect it. He granted the injunction but gave the City time in which to abate the nuisance. The plant was never shut down. The City improved it so that the odours no longer constituted a nuisance.[41]

Steer's last action against the City was *Carmichael* v. *Edmonton*. The Carmichaels, husband and wife, worked at the Edmonton Club (where Steer was a member). On 22nd December, 1931, Mrs. Carmichael slipped and fell on an icy sidewalk just north of the Club and sustained a broken leg. The City Charter required written notice within 10 days, although want of notice was not a bar if there were a reasonable excuse *and* no prejudice to the City in its defence. She did not consult Steer until long after the expiration of the 10 days. He sent notice of the accident on March 2, 1932. The City denied liability so the Carmichaels sued. Steer had to prove gross negligence as the City Charter required.

The plaintiff's witnesses testified that the icy patch had existed for a long time, while the street cleaning crew testified they had removed all snow and ice (by shovelling it from the sidewalk onto their horse-drawn sleighs) the day before the accident. Mr. Justice Ives accepted the plaintiff's evidence. He found gross negligence and on the question of failure to give timely notice he found reasonable excuse and no prejudice. The City appealed. The Appellate Division found prejudice so allowed the appeal. Steer appealed to the Supreme Court of Canada. He retained J.A. Ritchie, an Ottawa lawyer, to argue his case. The appeal failed. Through his London agents Steer applied to the Privy Council for leave to appeal but it was refused.[42]

IV. Fire Cases: Herein the Northwestern Utilities (Corona Hotel) Case

Steer had a number of lawsuits arising from fires, covering a long time span. By a coincidence, in all of his fire cases Steer acted for the defendant. He invariably pleaded the Fires Prevention (Metropolis Act), 1774.[43] Section 86 of that Act said a person is not liable for damages from a fire which accidentally begins on his premises. It might seem odd that an eighteenth century statute dealing with fires in London could possibly be in effect in Alberta, but it is.[44] However, the writer cannot discern that it affected the result in any of the cases about to be described.

Steer's first fire case was *McDonald* v. *Onyschuk*.[45] At that time (1920) the Prairie Fires Ordinance[46] was still in effect. It set out precautions to be taken to prevent fires from spreading. A person building a fire for the purpose of *clearing* land was obliged to have a fireguard and to have three adults with proper extinguishers to guard the fire. The defendant was *breaking* land. His daughter lit several small piles of roots. The fire spread across the road to two or three farms and then consumed the plaintiff's house. The trial judge held that the defendant was "clearing land" and as he had erected no fireguard, he was liable. On appeal Steer argued successfully that the defendant was not clearing land so the Ordinance did not apply. Our law was already settled that where a fire is made "for purposes of husbandry" the old common law rule of strict liability is replaced by liability for negligence, and a majority found no negligence.

In *Gillespie Grain Co.* v. *Wacowich* in 1932, the defendant was the plaintiff's agent at Opal. He kept the company's money in a shoe box on a shelf in his store. The building burned and the money was destroyed. Both the trial judge and the Appellate Division found Wacowich liable for the loss of the money.[47]

The fire that burned down the Corona Hotel in Edmonton on a cold February night in 1932 gave rise to a lawsuit in which London Guarantee Co. and ninety other plaintiffs sued Northwestern Utilities, a company which had provided gas in Edmonton since 1923.[48] The company had an underground gas main in the east-west lane south of the hotel. The main broke at a weld where the main crossed a City street just west of the hotel. The weld had given way because the pipe had subsided. Gas from the broken main seeped underground until it entered the basement of the hotel. The janitor hearing a strange hiss lit a match to find the source. He escaped but the hotel was destroyed; hence the action against Northwestern. The plaintiffs alleged nuisance, both public and private, the doctrine of *Rylands* v. *Fletcher,* breach of statutory duty and negligence.

The case came on for trial before Frank Ford J. in January 1934 and lasted for 14 days. Out of the many issues, all vigorously fought, the plaintiff's main case was that the gas company was negligent in having laid the pipe without proper support beneath, so that it sagged and broke. The gas company's answer was that the reason for the subsidence and consequent rupture at the weld was the action of the City in excavating under the pipe while installing a storm sewer a year before the fire. For the plaintiffs, S.B. Woods was the leading counsel, along with five others. For the defendant were A.L. Smith, an excellent trial lawyer from Calgary, Milner, Ronald Martland, a young partner of Milner's (and from January, 1958 until retirement in February 1982, a judge of the Supreme Court of Canada), and S.C.S. Kerr. The last named represented the defendant's insurer.

The principal question of fact was the cause of the subsidence and break. Lengthy expert evidence was given on both sides and the cross-examination was skilful. The trial judge found as a fact that the City's excavation underneath the gas company's main was the cause of the subsidence and the break. In other words, he accepted the defendant's version of the cause, and rejected the plaintiffs'. The defendant was not negligent. However, near the end of his judgment, Mr. Justice Ford added, almost as an afterthought:[49]

> . . . I think that the defendant ought to have known even if it did not, that the operations were going on, because of the length of time they were carried on and the conspicuous and public nature thereof. I think however that the defendant had the right to rely upon the City engineer . . . seeing that the work was done in such a way that such result as has happened would not occur.

The plaintiffs appealed. Steer had joined the Milner firm two weeks after the judgment. He appeared on the appeal with Smith, Martland and Kerr. Woods and Friedman, for the appellants, argued strenuously but without success that the trial judge's finding of fact was wrong. They also argued that even if it were correct the plaintiffs should succeed because the gas company knew of the City's activity around the gas main and was under a duty to protect it. Three of the five judges accepted this argument so the appeal was allowed.

The defendant had the choice of appealing either to the Supreme Court or direct to the Privy Council. It took the latter course. Milner instructed his London solicitors, Charles Russell & Co., to retain Wilfred Greene, K.C., an outstanding member of the English bar at the time. This was his last case. Before the Judicial Committee rendered its judgment he was appointed Lord Justice of Appeal. Later he became Master of the Rolls and then a Lord of Appeal in Ordinary. Steer appeared with him, while for the respondents

W.N. Tilley of Toronto, a leading counsel, had with him Woods and an English barrister, Frank Gahan, who had a large Privy Council practice though not yet a King's Counsel.

The argument took five days in the latter part of July, 1935. On the Judicial Committee were the Lord Chancellor, Viscount Hailsham (father of the present Lord Chancellor), Lord Blanesburgh and Lord Wright. The last named delivered the judgment which was handed down on October 24, 1935.

The Judicial Committee absolved the defendant from liability under *Rylands* v. *Fletcher* because it came within two of the exceptions—statutory authority and the independent act of a third party. However, the judgment concurred in the view of the majority in the Court of Appeal. Although the City's conduct caused the break, the defendant, in conveying a dangerous substance like gas through its pipes, was under a duty of care to the plaintiffs.[50]

> If they did not know of the City works, their system of inspection must have been very deficient. If they did know they should have been on their guard. . . . Their duty to the respondents was at the lowest to be on the watch and to be vigilant: they do not even pretend to have done as much as that.

Thus the plaintiffs won on a ground utterly different from that on which they had based their case. As Lord Wright said, the respondents "have failed on the issue which has bulked so largely, whether the breaking of the pipe was due to the fault of the City or of the appellants, and succeed on an issue not raised in the pleadings . . . ".[51] For this reason the appellant was required to pay only two-thirds of the respondents' costs.

This is an important case in the law of negligence. It is cited in all the leading texts on torts—Salmond, Winfield, Street, Prosser and Fleming. The late Dean Wright included it in his Cases on Torts and Lord Wright himself, the author of the judgment, once gave a lecture to Harvard Law School on the case.[52]

The amount of damages to which each of the many plaintiffs was entitled was left until after the Privy Council had determined the question of liability. The claims came to a total of some $300,000. They raised many interesting questions in the law of damages in relation to property. What is the value of a profitable but obsolescent hotel? What is the value of a trinket to which great sentiment is attached? What is the value of a well-worn suit of clothes in a depression? The defendant settled all of the claims. However, two persons who had not joined in the principal action sued separately. It is interesting to speculate as to whether they would have had to prove their case all over again had the defendant denied liability. It is not at all clear that the issue would have been *res judicata*. However, the defendant did not take this course. It settled with one of the two. The remaining case went to trial solely on the question of damages. The plaintiff was a retired geologist who claimed $10,000 for notes, reports and maps he had made almost 30 years before. Mr. Justice Ewing awarded him $646.[53]

After the fire the gas company odorized its gas and in addition developed new techniques for detecting leaks in its pipes. Indeed it was not long before a situation arose in which the company had to heed Lord Wright's admonition to protect its pipes. The company had a main which carried the company's gas from its wells near Viking to Edmonton. The main ran under the highway right-of-way a few miles east of the city. A coal mining company planned to run tunnels across the highway and under the main. Mindful of the Corona case, the company was concerned about the possibility that the mining operations might cause the main to subside and possibly to break. The company asked the government to require the coal company to leave in place sufficient coal to eliminate any risk of subsidence. The coal company alleged that this would require it to leave in place 249,000 tons of coal. It brought action for a declaration that (1) the gas company had no right to require the plaintiff to leave any coal in place and in the alternative (2) that the defendant had no right to require the plaintiff to support the gas company's pipe without paying compensation. Martland appeared for the defendant on its application to strike out the statement of claim on the ground that a declaratory judgment should not be given simply to define the mutual rights of the parties, but only where the defendant had illegally threatened the plaintiff's rights, and that there had been no such threat here. Mr. Justice Ives held that the court had no jurisdiction to give a declaratory judgment in this case. The plaintiff merely wanted the opinion of the court; no right of the plaintiff had been illegally threatened, and no consequential relief could follow any of the declarations prayed for. On the plaintiff's appeal, Maclean and his partner E.W.S. Kane appeared for the appellant while Steer and Martland represented Northwestern. Mr. Justice McGillivray for the majority made a lengthy review of the cases on declaratory judgments and concluded that the court had jurisdiction to deal with the declarations sought by the plaintiff. The writer does not know what happened after this judgment.[53A]

Steer's next fire case, *Mudry* v. *Geary,* attracted none of the interest that surrounded the Corona Hotel case. It occurred around 1936, as best the writer can recall, and is not even reported. The defendant was a bank manager in Leduc. Being about to move out of his house, he lit a fire in the lane to burn rubbish. His evidence was that he took stringent steps to put out the fire. A wind rose and sparks spread to the plaintiff's lumberyard, which was largely consumed. Steer succeeded in his argument that the plaintiff had not proved negligence. The writer always thought the defendant to be extremely fortunate.

The last fire case was *City of Edmonton* v. *W.W. Sales Ltd.*[54] Steer was counsel for the Friedman and Lieberman firm, who acted for the defendant. The defendant had used for storage the basement of the Sheldon Block not far from its store. On a January day in 1940 the manager instructed two employees to clean out the cellar. They did so and burned the rubbish in a steel ash-can in the lane. A wind came up and the fire spread to the nearby Powell Block owned by the City. Howson J. found the employees negligent in burning the rubbish in the lane near the buildings. On appeal, Steer's main argument was that the employees had no authority to burn the rubbish and that such authority could not be implied in the face of a by-law prohibiting such burning. The argument failed in the Appellate Division and again in the Supreme Court of Canada. From hindsight it might seem that the argument was hopeless from the beginning. It may be recalled however that the Ontario courts had accepted a similar argument in *Lockhart* v. *C.P.R.*[55] Unfortunately for Steer, the Supreme Court reversed the Ontario Court of Appeal before our Appellate Division's judgment in *W.W. Sales*[56] and the Privy Council affirmed the Supreme Court in *Lockhart* after argument but before judgment in *W.W. Sales* in the Supreme Court.[57]

An insurance case which arose out of a fire and another which arose from an explosion can conveniently be described here. In early 1932, a week before the Corona Hotel fire, a break in the service pipe on the premises of Empire Marble and Tile Co. resulted in an explosion and fire. That company brought an action in negligence against Northwestern Utilities. Ewing J. found that the defendant had negligently installed the service pipe so that it cracked, and gave judgment for the plaintiff. The trial took place in June 1933, some nine months before Steer joined the Milner firm. Milner and Martland had appeared for Northwestern at the trial and with them was S.C.S. Kerr, who represented Northwestern's insurer.

After the judgment the insurer denied liability and Kerr consulted Steer. When the latter joined the Milner firm, Kerr had no objection to his acting for Northwestern in its action on the policy, so Steer did appear. The case came to trial before Ewing J. The defendant argued that Northwestern's liability to Empire Marble & Tile was outside the coverage of the policy because the break in the service pipe occurred on private property, and the pipe was not part of Northwestern's "plant" which was all the policy covered. The trial judge held that Northwestern's liability in the original action was covered by the policy; and that even if it were not, the insurer by participating in the defence of the original action was precluded from denying liability, at least without having reserved its right so to do.

On the defendant's appeal the court did not call on Northwestern's counsel, Steer and Martland. Three of the judges held that the defendant's participation in the defence of the original action, especially in connection with negotiations for settlement, worked an estoppel. A fourth held the policy covered the loss while the fifth did not concur in the dismissal.

On further appeal, a unanimous Supreme Court held that Northwestern's liability in the original action was within the policy. The Court did not express a definite opinion on estoppel but suggested that inasmuch as the policy gave to the insurer a contractual right to co-operate in the defence, the exercise of that right could hardly give rise to an estoppel.[58]

The second insurance case was *Abasand* v. *Boiler Inspection and Insurance Co.*[59] Abasand was a pioneer in efforts to mine the oil sands, extract the oil and refine it. It had a plant, small by present standards, near Fort McMurray. Its insurance policy gave Abasand compensation of $1000 a day for each day of prevention of business as a result of a boiler explosion. The terms of the policy were rather complicated and created great uncertainty as to liability in the event which occurred.

On 21 November 1941 most of the plant was burned down. Abasand claimed $1000 a day for the maximum period of 100 days while the insurer denied liability. Abasand sued. At trial Steer and Martland appeared for the plaintiff while L.H. Fenerty, and his son, R.L. Fenerty, both of Calgary, were for the defendant. The plaintiff showed through expert evidence that there had been an explosion in the boiler. It damaged the boiler and produced a tongue of flame which lit a wooden beam nearby. The disastrous fire ensued.

One clause in the policy said that the compensation of $1000 a day was payable for prevention of business when "caused solely" by an explosion. Another excluded liability for prevention of business resulting from fire outside the boiler following an explosion. The defendant relied heavily on these provisions. Their interpretation and application to the facts produced a remarkable division of opinion as the case went through the courts.

Mr. Justice Shepherd found for the plaintiff. The defendant's appeal was dismissed in a 3–2 judgment. Its further appeal to the Supreme Court was successful in another 3–2 decision. Space does not permit an analysis of the judgments on each side. They are all persuasive, both on causation and interpretation of the policy. Steer's persistence led Abasand to apply to the Privy Council for leave to appeal which was granted. With Steer on the appeal was Frank Gahan who had been on the opposite side in *Northwestern Utilities*. For the respondent was R.L. Fenerty who had been with his father in the courts below. The appeal was allowed.

V. Contracting Out of the Benefit of a Statute

When a statute restricts the rights of A as against B or when it confers rights on B as against A, may B make an agreement with A whereby B contracts out of the benefit of the statute? If the statute specifically prohibits contracting out, that is the end of the matter, e.g., Pension Acts and Workmen's Compensation Acts. Many statutes contain no such specific prohibition—e.g., statutes restricting the rights of creditors as against debtors (of which there are a number in Alberta) and statutes conferring benefits such as the Intestate Succession Act and the Family Relief Act. The rule is this: B may contract out where the statute is merely for his benefit, but where the statute is in the public interest then B may not do so and thus notwithstanding his purported contracting out, may still invoke the statute.[60] One might add that A cannot enforce a remedy pursuant to B's purported contracting out when the Court lacks jurisdiction to grant that particular remedy. Steer had four cases on these problems. In the first three he contended B could validly contract out and in the fourth that he could not.

In the first two cases, in 1938, the facts were essentially the same. In a separation agreement the wife for consideration purported to give up her rights under the Intestate Succession Act and the Widows' Relief Act (forerunner of the Family Relief Act). In one case Steer argued for enforcement of the agreement and in the other Martland so argued. Howson J. gave judgment in both cases on the same day, holding that the wife could not contract out of either statute. Steer appealed one of the cases. The Appellate Division held that a wife could contract out of the Intestate Succession Act but not out of the Widows' Relief Act. Since the wife in that case was claiming only under the latter Act, the appeal was dismissed.[61] The Testator's Family Relief Act which replaced the Widows' Relief in 1947[62] has a somewhat different basis. Under the first Act the wife could apply if she received under the will less than she would have on an intestacy. Under the Family Relief Act she can apply if she did not receive adequate provision under the will. Our courts have held that the agreement cannot oust the jurisdiction of the court under the Family Relief Act, though of course the agreement can be considered in deciding the amount of the award under the Act.[63]

Steer's third contracting out case, *Mutual Life Assce. Co.* v. *Marks and Levitt*[64] arose just after the first two. The plaintiff had a first mortgage against Levitt's farm. Being badly in arrears, Levitt signed a memorandum consenting to foreclosure and waiving any rights under the Debt Adjustment Act. That Act, in language similar to that of the Statute of Frauds, and the Limitations Act, said "no action... shall be taken, made or continued" without a permit from the Debt Adjustment Board. The plaintiff took the usual foreclosure action and obtained the order nisi for foreclosure. Marks was a second mortgagee. He applied to have the order nisi set aside. Ives J. refused the application and granted an order for foreclosure on 3 November, 1938.

Nineteen days later the Legislature amended the Act to provide that any agreement whenever made purporting to deprive any person of the benefit of the Act should be of no effect unless approved by the Debt Adjustment Board. The amendment was in effect when Marks' appeal came on. At first blush, it seemed to apply to the very situation before the court. However the court doubted that the document Levitt signed was an agreement under the section. In any case, the amendment did not make an agreement void. The court below had jurisdiction to make the order nisi. As to the validity of the foreclosure order, the court considered whether the Act was one passed for the public benefit. The court held it was not passed for the benefit of the public and certainly not of second mortgagees. The Act did not remove the court's jurisdiction to order foreclosure. It could be waived like the Statute of Frauds and the Limitations Act.

The fourth case is *Crédit Foncier* v. *Edmonton Airport Co. and Superstein.*[65] Superstein was the main shareholder in the defendant company which was formed to operate a hotel near Edmonton's International Airport. In February, 1961 the company borrowed $300,000 from the plaintiff to build the hotel on the security of a mortgage on the property. Superstein executed a personal guarantee of the mortgage debt and waived any rights under the Judicature Act. That Act, in a carryover from the depression, forbade a money judgment on a mortgagor's covenant to pay, leaving the mortgagee to his remedies of sale and foreclosure.

The company soon defaulted. The plaintiff brought the usual foreclosure action and also sued Superstein on his guarantee. Steer acted for the defendants at the trial. The McCuaig firm for the plaintiff retained W.G. Morrow who was by this time a leader at the bar and was soon to begin a distinguished career as a judge. The trial was the first round of a long and at times acrimonious battle.

The issue of concern here had to do with the guarantee. Steer argued that Superstein's agreement to waive the Judicature Act meant that the mortgagee could obtain a money judgment against him and in so doing collect on the covenant—something the Judicature Act forbade. Thus a main issue in the case was whether a guarantor was within the protection of the Act and if so whether he could waive it. The other main issues—the validity of Superstein's acknowledgment of the waiver and the validity of the chattel mortgage to secure the mortgage debt—will not be considered here. The courts throughout found for the plaintiff on these issues.

The trial judge, Kirby J., assumed (just as the guarantee itself had assumed) that Superstein, the guarantor, was within the protection of the Judicature Act. He went on to consider the validity of the waiver. Steer argued that the Judicature Act provisions were passed as a matter of public policy and therefore could not be waived. Kirby J. however considered himself bound by an Appellate Division judgment[66] on similar earlier provisions and held the waiver valid. That judgment had cited *Mutual Life* v. *Levitt* as authority for the same proposition. Hence Kirby J. granted the usual order nisi/order for sale.

The defendants appealed and replaced Steer by D.P. McLaws of Calgary. The majority upheld the judgment below, one judge on the same ground and two on a different ground, namely that a guarantor is not within the protection of the Judicature Act.

Mr. Justice Johnson, with whom Porter J.A. agreed, wrote a strong dissent. After a careful review of the cases he concluded that if one party could exact a waiver as a condition of some advantage to the other party, the effect of the statute would be nullified. To prevent this, the waiver should be held to be against public policy.

On the defendants' appeal to the Supreme Court, Steer was back as counsel and with him was the Honourable C.H. Locke of Vancouver who had retired from the Supreme Court in 1962. In a short unanimous judgment the court held the guarantee valid because the guarantor was not protected by the Judicature Act. It protected only the mortgagor. The court left open the question whether a mortgagor could waive the benefits of the Act. In the meantime the legislature enacted that waiver of the benefits was to be against public policy and void.[67]

In subsequent proceedings which were protracted and contentious, Steer continued to act. The plaintiff "bought in" at the sale for $275,000, which was the value of the property, and there was a deficiency judgment against Superstein for some $200,000.[68] The law reports do not show whether he ever paid it. The writer understands that some kind of a settlement was effected.

VI. Agreement Not to Compete and Conspiracy in Restraint of Trade

Covenants by a vendor and by an employee not to compete are commonplace; and so are actions in which the covenantor tries to escape from his covenant. It is trite to say that the covenant will be set aside if it is unreasonable as between the parties or contrary to the public interest;[69] and it is now settled that the burden on the covenantee in attempting to enforce the covenant is heavier on an employer than it is on the purchaser.

In *Garbutt Business College* v. *Henderson,*[70] Henderson had been on the plaintiff's staff since 1917. In 1928 the parties signed a contract making him principal of the college. Henderson covenanted that for five years after expiration of the contract he would not be engaged in a business college in Calgary. He left the plaintiff's employment on May 31, 1938 and the next day opened his own college, which he incorporated. He attracted students and Garbutt's enrolment fell.

Garbutt sued for an injunction and damages. Mr. Justice Howson granted the injunction and awarded damages. When the defendant appealed, his solicitor retained Steer as counsel. The Appellate Division dismissed the appeal. This was the first Alberta case thoroughly to canvass the principles. The judgments of Harvey C.J. and Ford J.A. remain of importance. The Chief Justice was clear and emphatic. He thought little of a person who breaks his contract. He recognized, however, that a covenant in restraint of trade is valid only if reasonable. Sometimes the covenant is too wide. This is often fatal to the whole covenant, whether the "overbreadth" has to do with time, place or scope. In this case, Henderson had covenanted among other things not to "be concerned in or interested financially or otherwise in a business college". The Chief Justice thought that this part of the covenant went too far, but that it was severable from the rest of the covenant not to compete. Subject to this, he upheld the injunction and the award of damages. There was a question as to whether Henderson's company should be liable for damages. The Chief Justice said it should because it committed the tort of interference with contractual relations. In his judgments over a forty-five-year period, the Chief Justice rarely paid a compliment to counsel. Here he said:[71]

> I would like to add a word of commendation and thanks to the counsel engaged for the very great assistance rendered the court in their careful analysis of the difficult questions of law involved in their written and oral arguments.

Ford J.A. referred to the "excellent argument of counsel" on the question: what is the covenantee entitled to protect himself against? His answer was—divulging of trade secrets and confidential information and enticing away of customers. The plaintiff came within this test. Ford J.A. thought that Henderson was more like a partner than an employee so that his covenant should be scrutinized with less stringency. Henderson launched an appeal to the Supreme Court but did not proceed.

Steer's other two cases under the heading "restraint of trade" were, respectively, a civil action for conspiracy and criminal proceedings on charges of unduly restricting competition.

In the year 1933 a doughty English woman, Mrs. Floyd, had a confectionery shop on Jasper Avenue. Ice-cream cones sold for five cents. Mrs. Floyd sold "double headers", to the irritation of other confectioners, notably one Lucas and one Strong, who were also on Jasper Avenue though much further west. Mrs. Floyd alleged that these men together with the Edmonton City Dairy and the Northern Alberta Dairy Pool conspired to injure her trade by refusing to sell ice cream to her over a period of four weeks. She consulted Steer shortly before he joined the Milner firm. He advised her that although the alleged facts, if proved, would establish a conspiracy, the damages were minimal and he advised against action. Mrs. Floyd then consulted the Milner firm, which brought action. Before it came on for trial Steer had joined that firm. He and Martland appeared for the plaintiff. H.H. Parlee and S. Bruce Smith (Parlee's junior partner who by this time was well-established as an eminent counsel) were for the Dairy while C. Becker and H.A. Dyde represented the Pool.

During argument there was a detailed presentation by each side of the leading civil cases on conspiracy, which at the time ended with *Sorrell* v. *Smith*.[72] Mr. Justice Frank Ford found that there was no agreement between the two dairies. Each merely yielded for a few days to pressure from the retailers. He added by way of dictum that had the plaintiff proved a violation of the anti-combine provisions in the Criminal Code, and damage resulting therefrom, she would have succeeded in her civil action. This is of course a point on which there has been a difference of opinion.

This account does not do justice to the animated and at times humorous proceedings. The writer recalls Parlee, in the utmost good spirit, cross-questioning Mrs. Floyd closely on the size of the portions which she and her husband scooped out of the ice-cream can.[73]

The so-called "Tobacco case", involving charges of conspiracy in restraint of trade, came five years after the Floyd case and lasted for years. The writer's memory is that proceedings began when a man with a small grocery business in Edmonton complained that his supply of tobacco was cut off after he sold a pack of cigarettes for less than the going price. In any case, the Imperial Tobacco Company, W.C. Macdonald Ltd., various other manufacturers and a number of jobbers, over thirty in all, were charged on 27 February 1939 under section 498 of the Criminal Code with conspiracy to injure persons engaged in the manufacture, distribution and sale of tobacco. The preliminary hearing took several weeks and all the accused were remanded for trial. In Alberta a charge replaces the indictment by a grand jury, and the accused were accordingly charged after the preliminary.

The Crown retained A.L. "Art" Smith, who had been on the Corona Hotel case. He acted with H.J. Wilson. Wilson had wide experience in criminal and constitutional cases in his many years as a Crown solicitor and later as Deputy Attorney General. For Imperial Tobacco the leading counsel was L.A. Forsyth of the Montreal firm, Brown, Montgomery and McMichael (now Ogilvy, Renault). With him was C. Sinclair of Imperial Tobacco in Montreal. Steer acted for Macdonald. When the accused applied on November 18 to quash the charges Steer did not appear because his client did not join in the motion. It would be tedious to recite the grounds of the application. Ewing J. rejected them all.[74] However, he reserved a case for the Appellate Division although he doubted his right so to do. The Appellate Division held the trial judge had no authority to reserve a case until after trial and that there was no right of appeal from the refusal to quash. This judgment illustrates Chief Justice Harvey's vast knowledge of criminal procedure.[75]

The accused then applied for an order for particulars. On January 16, 1940, this application was heard by A.A. McGillivray J.A., who was most experienced in criminal matters. Steer joined in this application on behalf of Macdonald. The demand for particulars occupies five pages in the Western Weekly Reports. McGillivray J.A. directed the Crown to provide particulars of the conspiracy charged in each count.[76]

The trial began at the beginning of May before Mr. Justice McGillivray and a jury of six. The law reports do not record the trial. The writer's memory is that the trial judge made a ruling that a huge number of documents seized from various defendants were inadmissible, and that the Crown decided it would be most difficult to prove the offences without those documents. In any case the Attorney General filed a stay of proceedings on May 10.

On November 19, the Crown laid charges under the Combines Investigation Act. They alleged the same conspiracy as that outlined in the original charge. The accused applied to quash the indictment and Shepherd J. denied the application. Then the accused made a demand for particulars which the Crown delivered on January 29, 1941. The accused then applied to Shepherd J. for further and better particulars. He held the particulars already delivered to be adequate.[77]

Throughout the proceedings Macdonald had disassociated itself from Imperial. On this second charge Macdonald decided not to be represented at all. Imperial thereupon engaged Steer to represent them, along with Messrs. Forsyth and Sinclair. J.C. McRuer of Toronto, who was then an eminent Crown counsel and later had a distinguished career as a judge, appeared with H.J. Wilson for the Crown.

The day after the new charges were laid, namely on November 20, 1940, a Justice of Peace issued a search warrant authorizing the seizure of documents in the office of Imperial Tobacco Sales Co. in Calgary. Counsel for Imperial applied to Ives J. to quash the warrant. He refused and Imperial appealed. The Appellate Division quashed the warrant on the ground that the information and belief of the informant was based on information from the agent of the Attorney General.[78]

The search warrant was quashed on March 31, 1941. Shortly afterwards the case went to trial before Shepherd J. and a jury. At the end of a trial lasting 55 days the accused were convicted and fined. Macdonald Tobacco was the only one of the accused not to appeal. The argument of the appeal took fifteen days. Among a number of grounds, the appellants relied on section 28 of the Combines Investigation Act. It said no person should be charged under that Act at the same time as he was charged on the same facts under section 498 of the Code. The court held that the charge under section 498, though stayed, remained in existence. Thus section 28 came into play and the conviction could not stand.[79]

Mr. Justice Clarke had died before delivery of judgment. The other four members of the court were unanimous. The Crown applied to stay the entry of judgment and for reargument. Section 32 of the Judicature Act said that when a judge had died the remaining judges might give judgment if unanimous or if the judgment of the dead judge could not affect the result. The Crown argued that Clarke J. might have dissented on a point of law and so have given the Crown a right of appeal to the Supreme Court of Canada, and that section 32 could not validly apply to criminal cases. Chief Justice Harvey reviewed the history of majority judgments. He seemed almost indignant at the suggestion that section 32 did not apply to criminal cases, and he rejected it.[80]

The Crown then in May, 1942, applied to Hudson J. of the Supreme Court for leave to appeal. The application was refused. So ended this lengthy and hard-fought contest.[81]

VII. Constitutional Cases: Alberta's Debt Legislation

This part will include a description of some cases in which Steer did not take part. This is necessary to a coherent account.[82]

In Alberta, legislation to relieve debtors preceded the depression. In World War I the Volunteer and Reservists Relief Act, later called the Soldiers Relief Act, provided for the staying of actions for debt and for enforcement of mortgages until two years after the end of the war, or discharge.[83] Then in 1922, just after the United Farmers of Alberta came to power, the Drought Area Relief Act, as its preamble stated, was designed to enable farmers in the drought area of Southeastern Alberta to maintain themselves until the 1923 harvest, and to protect them against "a multiplicity of actions".[84]

In 1923 this Act was succeeded by the first Debt Adjustment Act.[85] Part I provided for a director whose task was to try to bring about the amicable settlement of farmers' debts. Part II dealt with farmers in the drought area. On the filing of a certificate in court that a farmer was entitled to the benefits of Part II, no action for foreclosure or seizure of property could be brought against him without leave of a judge.

In 1931, early in the depression, a new Act extended to the whole province the provision for filing a certificate in court.[86] The next year the Act was made applicable to merchants.[87] Then, as the depression deepened, the legislature took more drastic action. On 6 March, 1933, it amended the 1931 Act to forbid actions for debt against farmers and against resident homeowners in relation to their homes, without a permit from the director. This prohibition applied only to debts which arose before July 1, 1932.[88] The amendment was a stop-gap. A month later the legislature passed a new Act which embodied the amendment and established a Debt Adjustment Board.[89]

Steer began to look into the question of constitutional validity almost as soon as the 1933 Act was passed. This was his first venture into constitutional law. He was convinced the Act was *ultra vires* and on more than one occasion hoped to test it, and its successor Acts of 1936[90] and of 1937.[91]

Social Credit replaced the U.F.A. as the party in power in 1935. This was the beginning of William Aberhart's stormy eight-year tenure as premier. The legislation passed at the first 1936 session has no relevance to the present account. However, the second session saw a Reduction and Settlement of Debts Act. It said that for "old debts" (those arising before July 1, 1932), the creditor could recover only the balance as of that date, reduced by subsequent payments of principal and interest, with no interest to be payable, and the balance to be paid over ten years. For new debts the creditor could collect only 5 per cent simple interest, less all sums paid.[92]

In a matter of months Ewing J. heard argument in six cases, consolidated for trial. The plaintiffs, who were all creditors, challenged the Act. Counsel were George B. O'Connor, R.D. Tighe, S.W. Field and G.H. Steer all of Edmonton and William McLaws and H.G. Nolan of Calgary. William S. Gray and James Frawley appeared for the Crown. All eight were King's Counsel. A principal attack on the Act was that it was legislation in relation to interest, and of course that subject belongs to Parliament under the B.N.A. Act. The government argued that the scope of the term "interest" was narrow—that it covered only usury legislation, and not legislation dealing with contractual interest generally. Ewing J. accepted the plaintiff's argument. On the Crown's appeal, the main arguments for the respondents were made by S.B. Woods and Steer. Chief Justice Harvey upheld the ruling of Ewing J., and went farther. He held that the Act gave the Lieutenant Governor the function of initiating legislation; that one section was an improper delegation to the Lieutenant Governor of the power to legislate; that the Act conflicted with the Bills of Exchange Act, the Bankruptcy Act and the Farmers' Creditors Arrangement Act; and that in the case of mortgages payable outside Alberta the legislation was bad as relating to civil rights outside the province.[93]

Shortly after this decision, in the fall of 1937, a curious episode occurred. The Lieutenant Governor in Council made three Orders in Council amending the Rules of Court. They were never Gazetted. They forbade a Clerk of the court from issuing a statement of claim which challenged the validity of provincial legislation without the permission of the Lieutenant

Governor in Council. Steer immediately drew a statement of claim in a routine foreclosure action, and included a prayer for a declaration that the Debt Adjustment Act was invalid. Expecting the Clerk of the Court at Edmonton, R.P. Wallace, to refuse pursuant to the Order in Council, he prepared the papers for an order of mandamus. However, the Clerk accepted the statement of claim because according to Rule 5 of the Rules of Court, the amending rule, unless it provided otherwise, was effective fifteen days after Gazetting. Thus the amendment was not in effect and the Clerk quite properly was prepared to accept the statement of claim.

On September 24 a new Order in Council, to the same effect as the amendments just described, repealed them and enacted similar provisions effective the next day, September 25. Two days later, Steer issued a statement of claim in a foreclosure action, adding a prayer for a declaration of invalidity of the Debt Adjustment Act. Pursuant to the new amendments the Clerk declined to file it. Thereupon the plaintiff in the foreclosure action sued the Clerk of the Court for damages of $5000 for refusing to issue the statement of claim. The case came on before Ives J. on October 20. In a thirteen-line oral judgment he found the new Rules to be in effect an amendment to the Judicature Act. "The executive arm of the government cannot do it, it requires the legislature to do it." The judgment was for one dollar damages "as asked for", together with a declaration that the Order in Council was invalid and of no effect.[94]

The summer and fall of 1937 produced other dramatic events. On August 17, 1937 the Governor General in Council disallowed three key statutes.[95] Six weeks later the Lieutenant Governor reserved assent to three more bills.[96] The Province challenged the validity of the powers of disallowance and reservation, but failed.[97] Then, as to the three reserved bills, the Supreme Court held all invalid. On appeal, the Judicial Committee agreed that the Bank Taxation bill was invalid but did not pass on the other two because they depended on the Alberta Social Credit Act,[98] which had been repealed just after the Supreme Court judgment.[99] Steer was not among the battery of lawyers on this case.

Reference has been made to the Debt Adjustment Act. In 1941, in a case from Calgary, the Supreme Court held the Act inapplicable to an action on a promissory note.[100] Steer was not on this case. It did not hold the Act to be invalid. However, its reasoning encouraged attack on the Act and indeed on other provincial legislation which allegedly conflicted with federal statutes.

The Legislature in the spring of 1941 enacted a Debt Proceedings Suspension Act 1941,[101] and an Orderly Payment of Land Debts Act.[102] They were disallowed, along with a Draconic amendment to the Limitations Act,[103] on March 27, 1942.[104] In the meantime, O'Connor J. had held the Orderly Payment of Land Debts Act to be invalid, but the Appellate Division said the problem was not before him.[105]

As to the Debt Adjustment Act itself, mortgage companies were not eager in the early years to attack its validity. The Debt Adjustment Board, in the writer's opinion, administered the Act in a responsible way. The director, W.N. Loree, was able and fair. However by 1940 the practice of the Board was to require the applicant for a permit to agree to a settlement on the lines of the Reduction and Settlement of Debts Act which, as described above, had been held invalid. The writer recalls four cases in October 1940. Each involved a mortgage held by a client of Steer's on an Edmonton home. The mortgagor's taxes were in arrears and the City was in position to take title. On application to the Board for a permit, in each case the Board insisted on an offer of settlement. Thereupon Steer on his client's instructions issued a statement of claim in each case. He was prepared to meet a defence based on the absence of a permit by an allegation that the Act was invalid. However these cases did not test the Act. As best the writer can recall, the debtors began to make payments.

Around the same time a mortgagee represented by the Newell Emery firm brought an action without a permit.[106] The sole defence was absence of a permit. The plaintiff argued invalidity of the Act on six grounds. O'Connor J. rejected five of the grounds but accepted the sixth—the Act was insolvency legislation. His judgment was handed down on March 14, 1941. On the same day the legislature enacted the Legal Proceedings Suspension Act, 1941.[107] It provided for a sixty-day stay of actions challenging the Debt Adjustment Act. In the action just described, O'Connor J. held the legislature could not prohibit or delay proceedings to challenge the validity of its legislation.[108]

One might wonder why this case did not proceed further. The reason is that the Governor General referred to the Supreme Court of Canada five questions respecting the validity of the Debt Adjustment Act.[109] On the argument in June, 1941, Steer was not among the twelve lawyers who took part in the argument on one side or the other. Alberta lawyers were Messrs. Tighe, McLaws, Gray and Frawley. Eastern counsel included Messrs. Geoffrion, Varcoe, Tilley, Leonard, McMichael, and Louis St. Laurent. These men need no identification; nor does J.W. De B. Farris of Vancouver who also appeared.

Chief Justice Duff speaking for six of the seven judges (Crocket J. dissenting) found that the Act struck at the substance of creditors' rights, some of which were conferred by federal legislation—the Bills of Exchange Act, the Bank Act and the Companies Act. Moreover, it attempted to establish authority over banks and federal undertakings and companies incorporated under the Dominion Companies Act. Finally, it brought compulsion on creditors of an insolvent debtor and so was legislation in relation to bankruptcy. The judgment came down on December 2, 1941. On March 19, 1942 the Alberta legislature passed the Legal Proceedings Suspension Act, 1942.[110] It recited the pending appeal to the Privy Council on the Debt Adjustment Act, and it postponed until after the decision actions to which that Act applied. The Lieutenant Governor referred to the Appellate Division the question of its validity. McCuaig appeared for the Alberta Mortgage Loans Association, and Steer for the Canadian Bankers Association, while W.S.

Gray and Wilson defended the Act. In a 3–2 decision the majority held the Act to be an indirect method of keeping in effect an Act which the Supreme Court had held invalid.[111]

As to the Debt Adjustment Act itself, the Province's appeal to the Judicial Committee was argued for eight days near the end of 1942. On February 1, 1943 the appeal was dismissed on the ground that the Act invaded Parliament's power in relation to bankruptcy and insolvency and interfered with Parliament's legislation on those matters.[112]

When the legislature passed the Legal Proceedings Suspension Act, 1942, discussed above, it also amended the Judicature Act[113] to provide for a one-year period of redemption in actions on a mortgage or agreement for sale with power in the court to increase or decrease the period. Steer was not on the case which attacked the amendment. In a 3–2 judgment the Appellate Division held it invalid as another attempt to keep the Debt Adjustment Act alive pending the Privy Council decision. The Supreme Court upheld the amendment in a short judgment.[114]

In 1946 the Alberta legislature made a final effort to control banks in the province. It enacted the Alberta Bill of Rights Act.[115] Part I was innocuous but Part II asserted control over banks in connection with the issuing of credit. The Act itself provided for a reference to the Appellate Division as to its validity. Steer and Alexander Smith[116] appeared for the Attorney General of Canada while E.J. Chambers and Stanley Edwards of Calgary represented the Canadian Bankers Association. The Appellate Division upheld Part I but held Part II invalid as legislation in relation to banking. The Province appealed to the Privy Council and the Attorney General of Canada cross-appealed. On that hearing, Steer had with him David Mundell, an able young lawyer who had been counsel to the Royal Commission on Espionage. The Judicial Committee held the two parts of the Act to be so intertwined that Part I was not severable and since Part II was invalid, Part I fell with it.[117]

VIII. Interest on Provincial and Provincially-Guaranteed Bonds

When Social Credit came to power in 1935, the new government found the treasury to be "empty", in the words of an Order in Council of May 30, 1936. That Order reduced the rate of interest on government bonds and on bonds guaranteed by the government. In general the amount of interest was halved. On 1 September, 1936 a Provincial Securities Interest Act validated the Orders in Council.[118]

A fraternal order named the Independent Order of Foresters (I.O.F.) held a substantial number of provincial bonds and also bonds of the Lethbridge Northern Irrigation District, guaranteed by the province. The I.O.F. presented to the Imperial Bank in Toronto the Lethbridge Northern coupons due on November 1, 1936. The Bank offered the reduced amount which the I.O.F. refused. The I.O.F. retained Steer, who brought action on January 5, 1937 to recover the unpaid interest on the guaranteed bonds. In February,

1937 Ives J., in one of his typical laconic judgments, held the Act to be legislation in relation to interest and gave judgment for the arrears.[119] An appeal by the Crown was abandoned when the legislature replaced the Act by three new ones. These were enacted on April 14, 1937. The first Act (Chapter 11) barred actions on guaranteed bonds without consent of the Lieutenant Governor in Council. The second (Chapter 12) reduced the interest on guaranteed bonds and the third (Chapter 13) reduced the interest on government bonds. The reduction was the same as it had been in the previous Act held invalid by Ives J..

When the I.O.F. went to tax its costs and to issue execution on Mr. Justice Ives's judgment, the government invoked Chapter 11 and the Clerk felt bound to refuse to tax the costs or to issue execution. Then when the next coupons fell due on May 1, 1937, the Bank again refused to pay them in full. Thereupon Steer on behalf of the I.O.F. brought another action claiming payment of the judgment and of the amount of the coupons for May 1, and for a declaration that the two Acts relating to guaranteed securities were *ultra vires*.

Mr. Justice Ewing held that an Act barring, or one like Chapter 11 requiring leave to bring, an action which challenged the validity of a provincial act would nullify the constitution and thus was unconstitutional. Then he went on to hold that Chapter 12 was in relation to interest and that it conflicted with the Interest Act which says that a lender may *exact* the interest agreed upon. The Appellate Division upheld this judgment.[120]

Thus far the actions were confined to the Lethbridge Northern bonds. Alberta had no Crown Proceedings Act at the time, and proceedings against the Crown were by petition of right. The I.O.F. presented a petition for a declaration that Chapter 13 was invalid. Mr. Aberhart, who was Attorney General as well as Premier, signed the fiat "Let right be done." The case came before Shepherd J. on February 11, 1939. He held Chapter 13 to be invalid as interest legislation and also on the ground that it interfered with the right to collect interest outside the province. The appeal was heard in Calgary and dismissed in a short judgment.[121]

At this point the Province, which of course had the carriage of both proceedings, appealed to the Privy Council. The appeals were heard over four days in December, 1939, just after war had broken out. Gray for the Crown had with him D.N. Pritt, K.C., a prominent English barrister, while with Steer was Frank Gahan, who has been mentioned earlier. Both appeals were dismissed.[122]

There was no way to enforce payment of the arrears on the provincial bonds. Over five years later, in July 1945 after "protracted discussions and negotiations" with bondholders' committees, the Government made an offer to bondholders pursuant to an elaborate Debt Reorganization Programme. It covered guaranteed bonds as well as government bonds.[123]

In the meantime, Steer persisted in his efforts to collect the judgments against Lethbridge Northern. The I.O.F. issued execution and garnisheed moneys owing to the judgment debtor. The Province also was execution creditor of Lethbridge Northern in a huge sum—over three and a half million dollars. The Province claimed its share of the monies garnisheed and of the property seized under the writ of execution. Mr. Justice Hugh John Macdonald directed an issue, and after the pleadings were closed the parties agreed to state a special case respecting the right of the Crown to share. This issue came on before Mr. Justice O'Connor in July, 1943. He held that the Crown as guarantor could not compete with the I.O.F., but added a "rider" that the I.O.F. would have to share with other debenture holders.[124] Steer appealed the "rider" and the Crown cross-appealed. Frank Ford J.A. for the Appellate Division dismissed the cross-appeal and allowed the appeal on the ground that the rider was outside the terms of the special case.[125]

The last reported episode in this long story was an attack by the Provincial Treasurer and by Lethbridge Northern on the validity of the plaintiff's garnishee and seizure under the writ of execution. Their argument was that the money and property seized were held by Lethbridge Northern in trust for the Provincial Treasurer. By this time the I.O.F. had recovered a third judgment against Lethbridge Northern for some $61,500. McLaurin J. held that there was no trust and moreover that there was no need for the I.O.F. to sue on behalf of all the bondholders; that the right of the sheriff to satisfy judgments by striking a rate was not the I.O.F.'s only remedy; and finally that nothing in public policy prevented execution against an undertaking like Lethbridge Northern. The defendants' appeal was dismissed.[126]

The constitutional cases on legislation to relieve debtors, to control banks, and to reduce interest on provincial bonds, covered more than a decade. By the time the Privy Council decided the reference on the Bill of Rights Act in 1947, the depression was over, World War II was over and the Honourable Mr. Manning had been Premier for four years. The drastic legislation of the early Social Credit period was a thing of the past and so was the bitter litigation and the unusually large number of disallowances—ten of them between August 1937 and March 1942.[127]

There was, however, a mild revival of the old issues over debt legislation with the passage of the Orderly Payment of Debts Act, 1959.[128] It allowed a debtor to apply to the Clerk of Court for an order consolidating his debts. On the making of the order a creditor with a claim of $1,000.00 or less was bound by the scheme of the Act. The Lieutenant Governor in Council referred to the Appellate Division the question of its validity.[129] The Court appointed Steer to represent creditors or others opposed to the Act. The Appellate Division held that the element of compulsion on creditors made the Act invalid as insolvency legislation. On the Crown's appeal to the Supreme Court of Canada, three sets of reasons reached the same conclusion as that of the Appellate Division. Subsequently, Parliament amended the Bankruptcy Act by adding Part X entitled Orderly Payment of Debts.[130]

IX. Miscellaneous Constitutional Cases

In 1950 Steer had a constitutional case that had no connection with Alberta. It arose out of Newfoundland's entry into Confederation on March 31, 1949. Between 1915 and 1949 twelve Newfoundland statutes granted to

Bowater's Newfoundland Pulp and Paper Mills exemptions from certain taxes and customs duties. These exemptions extended to a date beyond 1949. On December 10, 1949 Parliament amended the Income Tax Act to abolish all these exemptions.[131] The Governor in Council promptly referred to the Supreme Court of Canada three questions which asked whether Bowater's was still entitled to (1) exemptions from duty or tax (2) exemptions from obligations imposed by Parliament respecting duty or tax and (3) exemptions from Acts of Canada requiring a license, permit or certificate for export or import of goods.[132]

The writer's understanding is that Bowater's had originally retained J.R. Cartwright of Toronto and that when he was appointed to the Supreme Court of Canada on 22 December, 1949, Bowater's retained Steer in his stead. In any case, he appeared on the reference and with him were Eastern counsel, C.F.H. Carson and C.G. Heward. The company argued that the content of "Bowater's law" was such that in part it fell under provincial jurisdiction and in part under federal, and that the two were so interwoven that legislation at both the federal and provincial level was necessary to remove the exemptions which Bowater's had enjoyed. Only Taschereau J. agreed with this argument. The majority upheld the federal power.

The next two cases are included here rather than with the oil and gas cases because they are related to the transfer of natural resources from Canada to the prairie provinces in 1930 and so have a constitutional aspect. The first case is *A.G.* v. *Whiteshore Salt Company,*[133] from Saskatchewan. Whiteshore held sixteen leases or licenses for the mining of alkali (sodium sulphate), and granted by the federal government before the transfer of natural resources to the Province. In 1931 the Province, at the Company's request, consolidated the leases into two leases. In 1937 they were renewed for 20 years. The legislature amended the Mineral Resources Act in 1947 to require lessees and licensees to pay such royalties as the Regulations might impose. An Order in Council of the same year increased Whiteshore's royalty. Whiteshore contended that the Province had no power to impose the increase. The trial judge agreed. The original leases had not been surrendered but rather had been renewed, and the agreement for the transfer of natural resources forbade an increase in royalties from subsisting leases. The Saskatchewan Court of Appeal affirmed. On the Province's appeal to the Supreme Court, Steer joined E.C. Leslie, the prominent Regina practitioner, as counsel for Whiteshore. They lost in a 3–2 decision. The majority held that the original leases from the federal Crown were surrendered when the consolidation took place in 1931. The new leases did not purport to be renewals. Thus the Province had power to increase the royalties.

Another case involving royalties is *Huggard Assets* v. *A.G. of Alberta.*[134] In 1913 the Canadian government granted to Huggard's predecessor the oil and gas rights in 1320 acres near Fort McMurray. Huggard acquired title. The grant from the Crown had provided for payment of "such royalty upon the said petroleum and natural gas, if any, from time to time prescribed by regulations". The federal government had never imposed a royalty. The agreement to transfer natural resources in 1930 provided that royalties should go to the province. The province claimed the right to impose a royalty. Huggard then brought action for a declaration that the royalty was not exigible.

At the trial S.W. Field appeared for the company and H.J. Wilson for the Crown. Boyd McBride J. held that the royalty clause permitted only the collection of a royalty which had been imposed at the time of the grant. Therefore the company was free from any imposition by the province. In other words, the court found the words ambiguous and construed them against the grantor in whose favour royalties would be payable. The grantor was the Crown in right of Canada and the Province stood in its shoes.

On appeal, the Appellate Division sat with four members, probably because Chief Justice Harvey had just died. The Court was equally divided so the judgment stood. The Province appealed to the Supreme Court of Canada. At this point the federal government retained Steer. He supported the provincial contention. During argument in May, 1950, the Court raised a new question—is the Statute of Tenures, 1660,[135] in force in Alberta? If so, does it prohibit the imposition of the royalty? A rehearing was ordered to deal with this question.[136] Field, Wilson and Steer were all scholarly. The writer doubts, however, that they ever expected to have to debate the intricacies of mediaeval English law of real property in a case from Alberta in the twentieth century. These new questions sent them scurrying to examine Pollock and Maitland, Coke, Blackstone and Challis.

Just what was this Statute of Tenures (more accurately called the Statute to Abolish Military Tenures)? How could it have anything to do with the law of Alberta, which remained unexplored and indeed undiscovered for almost a century after 1660?

To answer the first question one must look to the land law of feudal England. The main "freehold tenures" were knight's tenure and common socage. The latter lacked the prestige of the former, but the services or payments due to the King (from whom all land was, and still is, held) had the virtue of being certain. Knight's tenure, though more honourable, carried with it burdens including the King's right of wardship and of various "aids" or levies. The amount of these exactions was uncertain. By the time of the English Civil War the feudal age was past, and knight's tenure an anachronism. Thus in the year of the restoration of Charles II, Parliament completed a move which had been started before the Civil War to abolish tenure by knight's service and the other military tenures. The Act recites that the consequences of knight's tenure "have been much more burthensome, grievous and prejudicial to the Kingdom than they have been beneficial to the King". Then the Act, which takes up fourteen pages in the Statutes at Large, abolished knight's tenure and converted estates in land so held into free and common socage. To compensate the King for the loss of revenues, he was empowered to impose various rates and duties.

Ten years later the King granted Rupert's Land to the Hudson's Bay Company "in free and common socage". In return, the company by way of "reddendum" had to make a yearly payment of "two Elcks and two black beavers when and so often as Wee our heirs and successors shall happen to enter" Rupert's Land. The "payment" was made in Winnipeg when George VI visited Canada in 1939. This was pure ceremony because the Company had surrendered Rupert's Land in 1869.[137]

Rupert's Land became part of Canada on July 15, 1870. A portion of it became the Northwest Territories, and in 1905, part of the Territories became the Province of Alberta. The North-West Territories Act 1886[138] provided in section 3 that the laws of England as of 15 July 1870 "shall be in force in the Territories, insofar as the same are applicable to the Territories."

After the rehearing before the Supreme Court in October, 1950, the Province's appeal was dismissed in a 4–3 judgment. The minority held that Huggard received a conditional fee and that the condition (payment of royalty) was clear. The royalty clauses contemplated the possibility of an imposition of royalties at some time in the future. The majority did not disagree with this, but in upholding the judgment below did so on a completely different ground—namely that the amount of royalty was uncertain and therefore void. The Statute of Tenures was in force in Alberta and it required that any "service" (which includes a royalty) to the Crown must be certain. The policy of the Statute of Tenures was to put an end to the evil of allowing the Crown arbitrarily to determine the amount of services to be rendered or payments to be made by a grantee of land.

The province appealed to the Privy Council. Steer did not appear on that hearing. The federal Crown was represented by Frank Gahan who was by now a Queen's Counsel. The Saskatchewan government intervened to support the provincial position and was represented by M.C. Shumiatcher.

The Privy Council reversed the Supreme Court on these grounds. (1) The provision for royalties was probably not uncertain. The "reddendum" in the charter of the Hudson's Bay Company had itself been uncertain in a sense because it was payable only when the monarch came to Rupert's Land, and yet it clearly was valid. (2) The Statute of Tenures was probably not applicable to Rupert's Land. It would seem odd that an Act designed to put an end to the peculiarities of mediaeval land tenure in England was intended to apply to a new and remote colony. In any case, the grant to the Hudson's Bay Company was not in knight's tenure but in free and common socage.

The Privy Council said there were then two questions: (1) is the variable royalty inconsistent with free and common socage? (2) even if it is, has subsequent legislation validated the variable royalty? On the first question, the Judicial Committee held that the variable royalty is probably certain but "rather than plunge into the jungle of learned disagreement"[139] on this point, their Lordships assumed that the variable royalty is not certain. That required an answer to the second question, and the decision was that the Dominion Lands Acts of 1886 and 1908 show that Parliament intended to give power to deal with hard cases in a way that infringes "free and common socage".[140] Thus the variable royalties were valid.

X. Two Criminal Libel Cases: "Bankers' Toadies" and "Babies for Export"[141]

Under the Criminal Code publication of a defamatory libel is a crime.[142] In Canada, this charge is infrequent. Recently in England there has been much publicity over the efforts of Sir James Goldsmith to pursue the publishers of *Private Eye* through both criminal and civil proceedings.[143] The prevailing view is that a defamed person should normally be left to his civil action. There may, however, be cases where the libel is particularly serious so that the person defamed wants to press charges. He becomes a "private prosecutor". Under the Code, consent of the provincial Attorney General to any indictment is required, but if he refuses to consent then the court has power to consent.[144] In England, leave of a judge is required to a prosecution against the publisher of a newspaper, but the leave of the Attorney General is not required to any prosecution for criminal libel.[145]

On two occasions an Alberta judge had held that as a general rule the court would not give consent to a charge of defamatory libel after the Attorney General's refusal, because the Attorney General could always stay the proceedings. Thus the judge's consent would be futile and there would be an unseemly contest between the judicial and executive branches.[146]

When Social Credit came to power in 1935, the Alberta newspapers were generally, if not unanimously, hostile. The government decided to counter-attack. An Order in Council of September 22, 1937 authorized the Social Credit Board[147] to publish literature informing the public how to realize the results of social credit. In charge of this programme were George Powell, a consultant brought from England, and Joseph Unwin, a member of the legislature. Powell sketched a leaflet lampooning political opponents. Unwin inserted the names of certain of those opponents. There was a dispute as to authorship, each man giving the major credit to the other. Unwin sent the leaflet to a commercial printer who made 20,000 copies and on September 28 sent them to the Social Credit League in Edmonton for distribution. Several thousand were circulated and the rest were seized under a search warrant dated October 2.

The leaflet had on one side the heading, "Bankers' Toadies". The nine men so designated were S.W. Field, H.H. Parlee, H.R. Milner, J.F. Lymburn, G.D. Hunt, L.Y. Cairns, G.W. Auxier, W.A. Griesbach and D.M. Duggan. All but Hunt and Duggan were well-known Edmonton lawyers, though Major General Griesbach was perhaps better known for his military record and political activity. The leaflet set out the affiliation of each of these men with the financial world or with the "Peoples (!) League". This was an organization opposed to Social Credit. Below the names was the exhortation: "EXTERMINATE THEM", followed by this remarkable *non sequitur,* "And to Prevent all Evasion, Demand the Result you Want $25.00 A MONTH and a Lower Cost to Live". On the other side of the leaflet under the heading "Bankers' Toadies" were these words:

> My child, you should never say harsh or unkind things about Bankers' Toadies. God made Bankers' Toadies, just as He made snakes, slugs, snails and other creepy-crawly, treacherous and poisonous things. *Never* therefore, abuse them—just exterminate them!

General Griesbach decided to lay a charge of criminal libel, and also seditious libel and counselling murder, though these were dropped. He retained Steer, who caused the search warrant to be issued. The complaints were laid on October 5. The preliminary hearings were held separately before Magistrate Harold Gibson. The evidence showed the authorship, printing and circulation of the leaflet. General Griesbach testified that he was incensed by the leaflet and thought it tended to divide the country. On cross-examination he was asked about his sense of humour and replied that it did not extend to amusement over the leaflet. Each of the accused was committed to trial and was granted bail.

On the arraignment before Ives J. on November 9, the agent of the Attorney General stated that the Attorney General (Premier Aberhart) would not prefer charges but would not obstruct the private prosecution. Since the Attorney General would not consent to the charges, Steer applied to Ives J. for consent. It was granted. Unwin selected trial by jury and Powell by judge alone. The evidence was similar in each case and largely a repetition of the evidence on the preliminary.

Unwin was defended by an able and respected criminal lawyer, Fred Jackson. The defence offered no evidence. The jury found Unwin guilty of publishing a criminal libel knowing it to be false. Mr. Justice Ives sentenced him to three months in prison. In Powell's case, the accused was defended by another experienced defense counsel, Hugh Calais Macdonald. Unwin was called by the Crown and Powell testified. Ives J. convicted Powell and sentenced him to six months in prison.

Both men appealed. Unwin was represented by Jackson's partner J.N. McDonald. Powell's counsel was N.D. Maclean as well as Macdonald. On February 7, 1938, Chief Justice Harvey for a unanimous court dismissed both appeals.[148] Thereupon each of the accused went to jail though he was released after his sentence was half-served. The writer recalls that Mr. Unwin received a vociferous welcome from his Social Credit colleagues when he returned to the House, and that Powell went back to England.

In the second case, ten years later, the persons alleged to have been libelled were the four members of the Child Welfare Commission of Alberta and in particular, Charles Hill, the Director. The charge came about in this way. Around the end of World War II, the Imperial Order of the Daughters of the Empire (I.O.D.E.) in Alberta had a sum of money remaining from their efforts to raise funds during the war. Interested in child welfare, they engaged Charlotte Whitton of Ottawa to advise them. Miss Whitton was an able, vigorous and outspoken person who later became a colourful Mayor of Ottawa. Coming to Alberta, she tried to obtain data from the Welfare officials in the government, with a view to recommendations to the I.O.D.E. The government did not co-operate. She then wrote a lengthy report containing many severe criticisms of the administration of child welfare in the province. The report was made public in August, 1947. The government promptly appointed a Royal Commission to inquire into her charges. The members were Chief Justice Howson, Chairman and two District Court judges, E.B. Feir and J.W. McDonald. James Mahaffy, a Calgary lawyer, was counsel for the Commission while S. Bruce Smith and Horace Johnson represented the Child Welfare Branch. Steer appeared for the I.O.D.E. The Commission sat for months examining documents and briefs and hearing a large number of witnesses, including Miss Whitton. The evidence filled six thousand pages. The Commission made its report on December 3, 1948.[148A]

In the meantime, a Toronto magazine called new Liberty came to the centre of the stage. The publisher was a wealthy young man named Jack Kent Cooke. (Later he went to the United States, obtained an Act of Congress making him a citizen and acquired the Los Angeles Lakers basketball team, the Los Angeles Kings hockey team and the Forum where they play.[149]) A reporter named Harold Dingman wrote an article entitled "Babies for Export", based on Miss Whitton's report. He obtained her consent and that of the I.O.D.E. to quote from the report, and indeed sent to Miss Whitton the manuscript of his article.

It was published in the New Liberty for December 27, 1947, (appearing on the newsstands twelve days earlier) accompanied by five drawings which showed pathetic mothers surrendering their babies and also showing the children being farmed out. The last of the five illustrations showed a disreputable-looking man dozing with a bottle beside him while two emaciated boys lifted a heavy log. (The artist, one Cahen, was to testify that it was a liquor bottle and that the man was "sleeping off a drunk".)

The article began:

> One of the blackest and ugliest chapters in the development of modern governments has been written against the Province of Alberta. It is the unparalleled story of government trafficking in illegitimate babies exporting them to foreign homes; and the further story of unjustifiably harsh and delinquent care of Alberta's very young and very old. At these extremes of life, bureaucracy and tyranny rule.

This is followed by a laudatory description of Alberta and its people and then this:

> Suddenly, out of this unique province has come the disturbing story of maladministration of child welfare, the absence of child protection, of baby exports to such distant points as California and South America and Alaska; of mothers pressured into giving up their babies before they even see them.

Then came a description of and extracts from Dr. Whitton's report.

The Howson Commission was sitting. On December 16 it had the

Clerk of the Court at Edmonton send a wire to each of Cooke and Dingman "inviting" them to appear to show cause why they should not be committed for contempt. They declined. In addition, Mahaffy, as counsel for the Commission, asked the distributors of New Liberty in each of the cities of Edmonton, Calgary, Lethbridge and Medicine Hat not to distribute the issue. They wired Cooke for instructions. His wire in reply said: "We are prepared to distribute notwithstanding attempted ban. Proceed with distribution. We undertake to provide counsel and assume all expenses and fines." The Edmonton distributor, John Michaels, a prominent Edmonton businessman, nevertheless did not distribute the issue, but the other distributors did.

The Crown decided to lay a charge of defamatory libel. There was, however, a difficulty. A charge of libel could not be laid in Alberta because the alleged libellers resided, and New Liberty was published, outside that province. Accordingly the Crown charged Cooke with counselling John Michaels, the Edmonton distributor, to publish a libel. In addition the Crown charged Cooke, Whitton and Dingman with conspiracy to publish a libel.[150]

An Edmonton magistrate issued warrants for the arrest of Cooke and Dingman. The Criminal Code provides[151] that where the accused is in another province, a magistrate in that province is obliged to endorse the warrant, whereupon it can be executed in that province. When the warrants were sent to Ontario for endorsement Cooke and Dingman applied in the High Court for an order prohibiting the endorsement. They were represented by Joseph Sedgwick and G. Arthur Martin, both of Toronto. J.R. Cartwright was one of the counsel for the Attorney General of Alberta. The applicants argued that the informations and warrants were defective. Their main contention, however, was that the accused should have been charged with the substantive offence of defamatory libel, which could have been done only in Ontario. Mr. Justice Barlow refused the application.[152] Cooke and Dingman were not in fact arrested but came voluntarily to Edmonton. Miss Whitton had been given a summons and she too came.

The case attracted wide attention and feeling ran high as it had in the Bankers' Toadies case ten years before. The preliminary hearing began on January 27. It was held in the criminal courtroom in the Supreme Court House rather than in Magistrates Court. The Magistrate was Harold Hawe. Frawley and D.B. MacKenzie were for the Crown, Steer for Miss Whitton with S.H. McCuaig and Clarence Smith of Calgary (a brother of A.L. Smith) for Cooke and Dingman.

There is no need to describe the lengthy arguments over admissibility of various telegrams or the evidence of the persons connected with the publication and distribution of the article. (One witness was Roy Thompson who was Chairman of the board of New Liberty, and later became Lord Thomson of Fleet and the head of a large chain of newspapers.)

The notable feature of the preliminary was the decision of the Crown to call Steer as a witness in an endeavour to show Miss Whitton's complicity in the publication of the article. When he took the stand he was asked a question, put by MacKenzie: "Did your client Whitton give you any document purporting to be signed by Dingman?" Steer refused to answer. Martland appeared as his counsel and took the position that an answer would require a breach of Steer's obligation of confidentiality respecting communication with his client. There was considerable argument between Steer on the one hand and the Magistrate and Crown Counsel on the other. The latter submitted that an answer did not involve any breach of confidence; and the Magistrate pointed out that the question did not ask about conversations with or advice to Miss Whitton. Steer replied that he could not answer without revealing a professional confidence and "I do not propose to do it". The Magistrate then said "I think you can and I make the ruling that you answer the question as it was put to you" and: "Either you have to answer it or we will do something else." The hearing was then adjourned until the next day. After a Court reporter gave evidence from his notes of Miss Whitton's evidence before the Howson Commission, Frawley stated "There is no need to put further questions to Mr. Steer" and that the Crown's case was closed.

The three accused were committed to trial for conspiracy to publish a libel, and Cooke alone on the charge of counselling Michaels to publish a libel. Bail was granted. Milner was surety for Miss Whitton and Hugh Pearson, a prominent Edmonton businessman, for the other two. Miss Whitton said she wanted to go to jail instead of being bailed but "on the advice of her counsel she changed her mind".[153]

The trial began on April 4 before Boyd McBride J. without a jury. Sedgwick came from Toronto to appear for Cooke and Dingman. McCuaig was with him. For the Crown were S.C. Blanchard of Calgary, Frawley and A.W. (Abe) Miller, an experienced Edmonton practitioner. The Crown wanted to proceed first with the counselling charge, which was against Cooke alone. Steer filed a notice of motion for an order that the conspiracy charge be heard first "on the ground that the accused Whitton should be heard on the question whether the words complained of are defamatory". The judge referred to the practice whereby charges are usually heard in the order in which the Crown sets them down, but held that in this case it would be unfair to the accused Whitton if the counselling charge were heard first and that the right asserted by the Crown was an infringement of the independence of the judge.[154] Hence he ruled that the conspiracy charge must be tried first. Thereupon the Crown entered a stay of proceedings on that charge and proceeded against Cooke on the counselling charge.

The evidence was similar to that on the preliminary, and occupied four days. Boyd McBride J. gave judgment on 9 April 1948. The courtroom was packed. The writer recalls that immediately before the judge came into Court to give his verdict, Alfred Simpson, the Clerk of the Court and Sheriff, came into the courtroom and in a stern voice told those present (many of whom were leading members of the I.O.D.E.) that there must be no demonstration, whatever the verdict. The judge then entered the courtroom and delivered judgment. He explicitly refrained from detailed findings of fact and from declaring the principles of law applicable to them. The judgment is cryptic as to the reason for this though the writer conjectures that it was because of the existence of the Howson Commission. The judge set out four questions which he asked himself. Did the accused counsel John Michaels? If so, did he counsel Michaels to publish anything? If so was it defamatory? If so, was it without legal justification? Having put these questions he did not answer them one by one but simply pronounced the accused not guilty.[155] Up to that point one could not tell what the judgment would be. It is reasonable to speculate that Sedgwick was prepared for a finding of guilty and had ready a plea as to sentence. In any case, he rose and said:

> I must not thank a judge for having done his duty, but may I thank you for the great consideration you have given to the case and for your persistent kindness at times when I am sure I was a little tiresome; and my client asked me to say this to Your Lordship, regardless of the result, he wanted to say himself that he had no intention at any time to embarrass the Royal Commission that was sitting or to do anything that would have reflected in any way on their conduct or on the conduct of the citizens of Alberta generally, and that, while it is not necessary for him to say anything, he would not like to leave this province with the feeling in the minds of the citizens that he did at any time intend to malign this province or its people.

The judge thanked Sedgwick and court was adjourned.

As mentioned earlier, the Howson Commission did not report until December 3, 1948.[156] The report says that the many accusations against the Child Welfare Branch turned the proceedings into a personal quarrel. The Commission found some of Miss Whitton's criticisms to be warranted. Others were directed against legislation and so irrelevant to the inquiry. The Commission made recommendations on adoptions, handling of neglected and delinquent children, foster homes and training schools and other topics. The report deals with Dr. Whitton's criticism of placement for adoption outside Canada and particularly in the United States. This is of course the subject that provided the title for the article in New Liberty. While the Commission recommended the discontinuance of cross-border placements, it rejected the suggestion of a "black market" or "traffic" in babies. "Not a shred of evidence was brought in to indicate that any Alberta child had been involved in a 'black market' in babies." There had been no "traffic" in babies in the sense of something shady or illicit. The report does not refer to the article in New Liberty, which was of course an exaggeration of the Whitton report, but it says that the Whitton report itself contained "overstatement" and seemed intended to heap discredit on the Child Welfare Department.

XI. Oil and Gas Cases: Herein Borys and Turta

The discovery of oil at Leduc in February 1947 marked the beginning of intensive exploration for oil and gas and also of large-scale production. However, there had been wells in Turner Valley as far back as 1914, a boom in 1929, and a flurry of activity after R.A. Brown, Sr. of Calgary brought in a well in South Turner Valley in 1936. These developments had produced regulatory statutes and some litigation.[157]

During World War II Steer was counsel for the plaintiff in *Vulcan Brown Petroleum* v. *Mercury Oils*.[158] This was a dispute between the Brown interests and A.H. Mayland of Calgary. Mercury Oils was Mayland's company. His counsel was S.J. Helman. As a result of a "maze of transactions and documents", as Chief Justice Harvey put it, Mercury held an oil and gas lease and Vulcan Brown a sublease from Mercury. Vulcan covenanted to drill a well and then to drill a second well within twelve months after abandonment or completion of the first. The first well was completed on June 20, 1938. Before the year was up an Order in Council under the Oil and Gas Wells Act forbade drilling within 440 yards of a producing well. Thus when Vulcan Brown applied to the Conservation Board for permission to drill the second well the application was refused. In light of the failure to drill, Mercury claimed that Vulcan Brown had abandoned the sublease. Thereupon Vulcan Brown sued for a declaration that it was excused from drilling the well and that there was no abandonment of the sublease. The main issue was whether the plaintiff was relieved from its covenant to drill because of the "supervening illegality" produced by the Order in Council. Shepherd J. held that the covenant to drill was made in light of the law existing at the time and that a subsequent Order in Council rendering performance illegal operated to "repeal" the covenant.

The defendant appealed. Chief Justice Harvey would have allowed the appeal. Vulcan Brown could have provided against the effect of changes in the drilling regulations. The other four judges all agreed to dismiss the appeal but it is hard to put the reasons in a nutshell. They held there was no frustration of the sublease; it was still in existence. By implication the parties had agreed that Vulcan Brown should be relieved if the obligation to drill were rendered illegal, as it was.

Mercury appealed to the Supreme Court of Canada. The writer recalls that when Mr. Steer was preparing his factum he consulted John Weir, the Dean of Law and a close friend. This was in the spring of 1942, some three months before Dean Weir died. He was an authority on frustration of contracts and impossibility of performance.

The Supreme Court upheld the lower courts but took a somewhat different and more direct route. Steer had relied on a general rule that a party is relieved from his obligation by reason of supervening illegality. However the judgment simply referred to the lease and sublease and found the answer there. In the head lease Mercury had covenanted to abide by all statutes and regulations, and Vulcan Brown had covenanted to observe the head lease. Mercury could not complain that the plaintiff defaulted in not doing something contrary to the head lease and the sublease.

The Leduc discovery produced vigorous competition between oil companies in acquiring petroleum and natural gas rights. Just as in the case of a land boom, persons who had granted oil rights frequently wanted to escape the bargain in order to make a better deal. Since oil and gas leases often covered the grantor's homestead, the Dower Act came into play because an oil lease was a disposition under that Act and the wife's consent was necessary. If the consent were not acknowledged by the wife apart from her husband then the whole transaction was open to attack.

Six months after the discovery of oil in Leduc, a farmer named Pearson gave a petroleum and natural gas lease to one Reddick. Pearson was to receive $6000 payable at the rate of $100 a month. After he had accepted seven of these payments, he received an offer of a better deal. He alleged that the lease was void because he had been present when his wife signed the consent under the Dower Act and when the Commissioner for Oaths signed the acknowledgement. There was no pretence that the wife had been misled or did not know the nature of the transaction. Mr. Justice McLaurin accepted Steer's contention that the issue was void.[159] Not long afterwards in another case with similar facts the Supreme Court of Canada found a way to uphold the lease by applying the curative section in the Dower Act. It had not been invoked in Reddick.[160]

The Dower Act was completely recast in 1948 as these cases were in the courts. The new Act was designed to put an end to all the litigation over the Dower Act, but it failed in that object. The first important case under the new Act had nothing to do with a petroleum lease but had implications for such a lease, so the writer will describe it. It involved an agreement between Pinsky and Wass for exchange of homesteads. In it was an unusual "escape" clause. Pinsky brought action for rescission, invoking both the escape clause and non-compliance with the Dower Act. Wass counter-claimed for specific performance. Neil D. Maclean acted for Pinsky and Steer for Wass. The spouses had in fact signed the agreement but not the formal consent required by the Dower Act. The trial judge rejected the plaintiff's argument that non-compliance with the Act rendered the agreement void but he held that Pinsky was entitled to invoke the escape clause. Steer appealed. He won but the reasoning of the judges was remarkably diverse, leading Maclean to remark that the Appellate Division, like Gaul, was divided into three parts—not one of the more memorable utterances. Chief Justice O'Connor in dissent declined to deal with the Dower Act. W.A. Macdonald and Clinton Ford JJ.A. held that non-compliance with the Dower Act makes an agreement invalid, but the latter held that Pinsky was estopped from raising the invalidity. Parlee and Frank Ford JJ.A. held non-compliance with the Dower Act does not render the agreement void. None but O'Connor C.J. would have applied the escape clause.

Pinsky appealed to the Supreme Court. He won, thanks to the escape clause. Two of the five judges thought as well that the agreement was voidable for non-compliance with the Dower Act.[161]

When the Canadian Pacific Railway built the first trans-Canada line, it received from Canada large grants of prairie land, including the minerals. At one time coal doubtless was of greater interest to the C.P.R. than petroleum, but the Leduc discovery changed this. The company had land in many areas which produced oil and gas. In 1906 the C.P.R. had sold a quarter section of land near Leduc to one Borys. When the C.P.R. gave him a transfer in 1918 it reserved "coal, petroleum and valuable stone". It will be noted that the C.P.R.'s reservation did not specifically mention natural gas. Borys' son became registered owner in December 1947, ten months after the Leduc discovery. He contended that he owned the natural gas and that no one else could interfere with it. He brought action against the C.P.R. and also against Imperial Oil Limited which was lessee of the petroleum rights from the C.P.R.[162] Borys asked for a declaration that he owned the natural gas and for an injunction to restrain the defendants from removing it. Imperial's counterclaim asked for a declaration that it owned the gas, and alternatively that it was entitled to remove gas to the extent necessary to produce its petroleum. Steer was counsel for Borys' Calgary solicitors. Helman and R.R. Mitchell acted for the C.P.R. while Nolan and Chambers appeared for Imperial Oil. Chief Justice Howson listened to an array of experts on both sides as to whether "petroleum" includes natural gas. Then after examining definitions he concluded that petroleum means crude oil and does not include natural gas. In the Leduc field some gas was separate from the petroleum and in a "gas cap" above it, while some was in solution in the petroleum. It acted as a "lifting agent". Howson C.J. held that the defendants had no right to possess and use the natural gas at the plaintiff's expense.

On the defendant's appeal, W.A. Macdonald J.A. agreed with the trial judge. Parlee J.A., speaking for the other four judges, agreed that petroleum and natural gas were different substances but held that the reservation of petroleum in favour of the C.P.R. meant petroleum in place underground so that natural gas in solution is included; and further that the reservation meant that the defendants could extract the petroleum provided it were done in a reasonable manner, even if it interfered with and wasted the plaintiff's gas. The reservation of petroleum implied the right to recover it. Thus Imperial succeeded on its alternative counterclaim.

Borys appealed to the Privy Council. The respondents cross-appealed the ruling that gas in the gas-cap was not included in petroleum. The argument occupied eight days in July, 1953 and judgment was delivered the following January. In essence the Judicial Committee agreed with the Appellate Division in its reasons and dismissed the appeal and cross-appeal. This was the last of Steer's five appearances before the Privy Council.The writer's recollection is that the Wimbledon tennis championships were being played at the time and that Steer was able to attend some of the matches through the help of Mr. Theobald Mathew of Charles Russell and Company, Steer's London solicitors.

Before *Borys* reached the Judicial Committee, *Turta* v. *C.P.R.*[163] was in the Alberta courts. When Alberta became a province it enacted its own Land Titles Act on the lines of the federal legislation that had been in effect in the Northwest Territories since 1886. A Land Titles office was established at Edmonton and another at Calgary. From time to time the Registrar made mistakes. Subsequently they were discovered. In the case of mistakes relating to ownership of oil and gas, some turned out to be costly. The consequences might not have been so serious had the Assurance Fund been adequate, but the Land Titles Act gave miserly compensation to a person who lost his minerals through the Registrar's error.

The land involved in the *Turta* action was close to the discovery well at Leduc. In 1901 the C.P.R. had acquired title to both surface and minerals. In 1908 it transferred the land to one Podgorny, reserving coal and petroleum. The new title in Podgorny's name should have conformed to the transfer. However, the Registrar made a mistake and reserved only the coal. The consequence was that Podgorny's title showed him as owning the petroleum. By 1918 Anton Turta was owner of the quarter section, having purchased it. A farmer who did not speak English, he never thought of the minerals but the fact is that the title gave him the petroleum.

During World War II, the Registrar, concerned about the errors, made a special effort to correct them. On January 16th, 1943 he altered Turta's certificate of title to show that petroleum as well as coal was reserved to the C.P.R. and at the same time he purported to restore the C.P.R.'s title to the petroleum. Neither Turta nor the C.P.R. knew of the alterations. In the following year Turta transferred one-half of the parcel to each of his two sons and of course their titles showed the reservation of coal and petroleum. At this point Turta owned nothing so far as the register showed.

Whenever there is a "play" for mineral rights, the interested companies search the title of land in the area. In the five or so years after the Leduc discovery the Land Titles Office in Edmonton was a bedlam. Imperial Oil was of course active. In 1946 it had acquired from C.P.R. an option to lease the oil under the Turta land. Right after the Leduc discovery a solicitor for Imperial Oil made an historical search of the title and discovered the original mistake and its purported correction. The actual lease from the C.P.R. to Imperial Oil was made on March 6th, 1951, after Turta had asserted his claim to the petroleum. He had consulted Steer in March 1950. In essence his claim was that he obtained title as a *bona fide* purchaser in 1918. Since the title did not exclude the petroleum, he became owner of it and nothing in the subsequent events deprived him of that ownership. The C.P.R. of course argued that it had never been deprived of ownership. The case raised fundamental questions as to the basic principles of Alberta's Land Titles Act. Was Turta entitled to "rely on the register" even though he had never looked at it and never intended to acquire the minerals? Was the Registrar entitled to make the corrections in 1943? Could the C.P.R. invoke those provisions in the Land Titles Act which create exceptions to indefeasibility of the current title—specifically, misdescription and prior certificate of title? There was a subsidiary question as to whether, assuming Turta had a cause of action, he had delayed too long in bringing it, and conversely Turta argued that, even if the C.P.R. owned the petroleum, he had acquired title by possession of the petroleum for over ten years. Neither assertion under the Limitations Act played a part in the ultimate result.

The trial judge Mr. Justice Egbert analysed the facts and the law in the utmost detail in a long judgment. He held that the purported corrections, though they would have been good as between the C.P.R. and Podgorny, were a nullity as against Turta because he was a *bona fide* purchaser. He was entitled to rely on the state of the title when he acquired the land. The C.P.R. relied heavily on the two exceptions to indefeasibility mentioned above—prior certificate of title and misdescription. Egbert J. held that the first exception comes into play only when there are two certificates of title in existence at the same time. Here the C.P.R. title had long been cancelled and the purported correction did not restore it. As to misdescription, Egbert J. gave it a narrow interpretation. It applied only where the title includes a parcel that was not intended to be transferred and there was no such situation here.

In essence the Court of Appeal agreed with the trial judge, though Chief Justice O'Connor did so with regret. Mr. Justice Clinton Ford dissented on the ground that the C.P.R. had a prior certificate of title. It had never been properly cancelled.

On a further appeal to the Supreme Court of Canada, a majority of six judges to three sustained the judgments below. The dissenters thought that Turta had acquired title to the petroleum by misdescription. Petroleum came within the definition of land and the petroleum was a different parcel from the surface so the exception as to misdescription applied and the fact that Turta was a *bona fide* purchaser from Podgorny made no difference. The majority in essence agreed with the courts below.

The significance of the decision (quite apart from the fact that one party lost the minerals and another one acquired them through a "million dollar mistake" in the Registrar's office) is that it does a great deal to strengthen the notion that "the title is everything". A serious criticism of the law as it stood at the time was that the assurance fund was liable for only the amount laid out for the minerals and a further sum not exceeding $5000.[164] After the Supreme Court's decision, the government asked the Benchers of the Law Society to establish a committee to make recommendations. The committee made a report and in 1958 a new provision allowing more liberal compensation was enacted.[165] It is the present section 176(1). Also in 1958 the Mineral Interests Compensation Act[166] provided for recovery of damages for old mistakes on the same basis as that provided by section 176(1), with a three-year time limit from April 1, 1958 for bringing action against the Registrar.

One point that emerges clearly from *Turta* is that he succeeded because he was a *bona fide* purchaser. Had he received the land as a gift, he would have failed.[167]

A difficult problem that has come up in cases like these is the effect, if any, of the Statute of Limitations. It is now clear that the action for a simple declaration of title by the person whose title had been taken from him by the Registrar's unauthorized act is not one for possession and is therefore not affected by the ten-year time limit in the Limitations Act.[168] Alternatively, there is a completely different question that can arise: is it ever possible for a person to possess minerals so that after ten years he will have acquired ownership by possession as against the registered owner, as is possible in the case of the surface? The case that deals most directly with this question is *Duncan* v. *Joslin*.[169] In that case Steer acted for the plaintiff, whose claim was basically the same as that of Turta. Thus he was held entitled to the minerals. However the defendant had, through the Registrar's error, been registered as owner of the minerals, paid the mineral tax and given an oil and gas lease to an oil company which had carried out seismic surveys. The defendant argued that on these facts he had possession of the minerals and that such possession had extended over a ten-year period so that therefore he had acquired possessory title under the Limitations Act. Mr. Justice Porter was not sure that a fugacious mineral could be possessed, short of actual physical control, and in any event the acts relied on by the defendant did not support a claim of adverse possession. Mr. Justice Kane and Mr. Justice Macdonald examined the facts to determine whether the defendant had acquired possession of the minerals and concluded that he had not. The defendant failed to prove that he was in exclusive, open, or visible and notorious possession for ten years.

Another case arising out of the discovery of the Leduc field is *Cotter* v. *General Petroleums*.[170] Cotter held a petroleum and natural gas lease in the Leduc field and gave the defendant an option for a sublease, exercisable by August 1st, 1948 by drilling a well. The agreement went further in that the defendant covenanted to exercise the option. In view of dry holes nearby, the defendant did not drill. The plaintiff sued for breach of the covenant to drill. Steer was not on the trial, where McLaurin J. held that the defendant broke the covenant. This left a very difficult question as to the amount of damages the plaintiff suffered from the defendant's failure to drill. Cost of drilling would have been $53,000. The plaintiff claimed this sum and in addition some $45,000 for loss of the chance to discover oil. McLaurin J. fixed the damages at the cost of drilling. On the appeal the defendant retained Steer. Chief Justice Harvey, at the age of 86, presided. This was some three months before his death in the fall of 1949. Steer's main argument, one which had not been raised at the trial, was that the covenant to drill was repugnant to the option and therefore must be ignored. The Court of Appeal accepted this argument and so the action was dismissed. The plaintiff appealed to the Supreme Court. Only one judge, Locke J., agreed with the Appellate Division. The majority held that there was no repugnancy between the option and the covenant. They must be read together and the result was that the defendant had covenanted to drill. However, the plaintiff was not entitled to damages equal to the cost of drilling a well, but only to the $1,000 he had paid to preserve the head lease. This result was the next thing to a win for Steer, but the writer's recollection is that he was just as dissatisfied as though his client had been required to pay the amount awarded at trial.

A case which might not have great legal significance but in which important holdings were at stake is *Perry* v. *Harvey*.[171] Harvey held eight Crown leases of petroleum and natural gas rights in the area west of Wetaskiwin. After lengthy negotiations, Perry thought that he had a contract with Harvey to buy the leases, but Harvey withdrew. Steer acted for Perry in his action for specific performance. He won in the Alberta courts, but in the Supreme Court, the appellant's counsel, J.J. Robinette of Toronto, persuaded the court that there was no contract.

In the post-Leduc era, a number of oil and gas cases have dealt with this situation: the owner of the minerals gives an oil and gas lease for one year. The lessee covenants to drill within the year. However, if he does not do so he may extend the lease for another year by paying $1.00 an acre before the year has expired. The payment is called a "delay rental". Let us assume that at the end of the first year, the lessee (an oil company) wants to extend the lease but is late in making the payment even by one day. The company argues there is a "forfeiture" and invokes the provision in the Judicature Act[172] which empowers the Court to relieve against forfeitures. The landowner argues that there is no forfeiture at all but that the lease simply came to an end when the payment required to extend the lease was not made in time.

This was the basic situation in *East Crest Oil Company* v. *Strohschein*.[173] Steer acted for the owner of the land. The oil company failed to pay the "delay rental" due on September 13th, 1950, so the farmer contended that the lease was terminated. The oil company stated that the failure to pay was due simply to an oversight and tendered the payment, relying on a clause which permitted the lessee to remedy a default within 90 days. The tender was refused. Both the trial judge and the Appellate Division held that there was no default or forfeiture and that the lease was simply at an end. The trial judge said "defendant's counsel [Steer] with some force chose to put the plaintiff in the position of having no more than an option to drill for oil and, having failed to protect his position by making the payment of the delay rental on its due date, the option lapsed". In essence both courts accepted this argument.

Some thirteen years later in *Superior Oil Limited* v. *Kanstrup*[174] Steer acted for Superior, the lessee. It drilled a gas well not on the leased land but on pooled land, and capped it because there was no market. The ten-year term of the lease expired soon after. Superior argued that the drilling of the well preserved the lease, and that in any case payment of the "shut-in" royalty of $100, payable under the lease where gas from a producing well was not sold or used, was only a week late so that the lease was still in existence. The trial judge, the Appellate Division and Supreme Court all ruled against the lessee. On the difficult question of construing the lease, and an amendment providing for pooling, Martland J. for an unanimous court held that the existence of the capped well off the leased land but on the pooled land did not operate to keep the lease alive; and even if it did, Superior did not pay the royalty until a week after expiration of the lease, so *Strohschein* applied.

Another case involving minerals raised an intriguing point. After World War I an ex-serviceman named Jardine acquired from the Soldier

Settlement Board the title to a farm in 1928. Minerals were excluded. He willed all his property to his wife and made her executor. He died in 1938 and she died in 1949, with a will making Royal Trust Company her executor. Around that time the S.S.B. decided to make the minerals available to soldier settlers. The Royal Trust Company, representing Jardine's estate, took up the offer and acquired the minerals. The question then was—did the minerals go to Mrs. Jardine under her husband's will, or did Jardine die intestate as to the minerals? Steer argued that they went with the land—that they were grafted on to the surface or an accretion to it. This argument failed, so the minerals went to the next of kin and not under Jardine's will.[175] A similar point came up later on an appeal from Saskatchewan where the mineral rights had been forfeited before the making of a gift of the land and were later restored to the estate. The Supreme Court held the minerals did not follow the gift. It included only what the donor held at the time, namely the surface.[176] More recently, the same basic problem arose again in Alberta in *Re Timms,* and with the same result.[177]

Another unsuccessful effort to secure minerals for the owner of the surface occurred in *Reese* v. *The Queen*.[178] Steer was counsel for the Brownlee firm for the petitioners. They were soldier settlers on land which had been an Indian reserve near Ponoka. The Board's solicitor told them they could acquire the minerals, but in fact an act of 1919 passed before they bought the land excluded the minerals. The judgment held that nothing had occurred to vest the minerals in the petitioners, so they failed.

XII. Utilities Cases

In 1957 Steer appeared in a British Columbia case, *Prince George* v. *Inland Natural Gas Co.*

West Coast Transmission Company had been granted the right by the federal Energy Board to build a natural gas pipeline from a field in the Peace River country in Alberta through British Columbia and on into the United States at a point near Vancouver. Inland Natural Gas Company had permission from the B.C. government to build tributary lines to points in the interior of British Columbia. Both Inland and the Prince George Gas Company wanted to construct a five-mile spur line from West Coast's pipeline into Prince George and to supply that city with gas. Lengthy hearings were held before the Public Utilities Commission. Steer acted along with two British Columbia counsel on behalf of Prince George and the Prince George Gas Company. Inland was successful before the Commission. Prince George made an effort before the Court of Appeal to obtain leave to introduce further evidence but this failed.[179] Then, on the appeal on the merits, the appeal succeeded in a 2–1 judgment. The court had to deal with intricate statutory provisions, a complicated order of the Commission, the economic factors and constitutional questions. O'Halloran J.A., one of the majority, clearly thought that the order of the Commission was unfair to Prince George Gas Company.[180]

Some two years later a contest occurred in a rate case.[181] It involved the City of Edmonton and three other municipalities against Northwestern Utilities Ltd. The Public Utilities Board had applied in Northwestern's favour an amendment which permitted it in fixing rates to consider the effect of undue delay in the hearing. Moreover, it had ruled that the company could change its rates to reflect the increased cost of purchased gas. The municipalities were given permission to appeal, over Steer's objection that there was no question of jurisdiction or law but merely one of fact. On the appeal, three of the five judges held that the amendment applied to an existing application, while all of them held that the Board could not take into consideration the increased cost of purchased gas.[182] Each side appealed. Steer succeeded on both issues.[183]

The last important utilities case is *Canadian Western Natural Gas Company* v. *Central Gas Utilities*.[184] Central was a small company which distributed propane at Vulcan. In 1953 it needed financial assistance and obtained it from International Utilities, the parent company of Canadian Western, with which Milner had long been associated. In the succeeding years International gave further financial help to Central. By 1958, when natural gas became available, Canadian Western offered to buy the Vulcan operation from Central. Central's shareholders agreed, with International's vote in support, though there was vigorous opposition. The Public Utilities Commission approved the sale and Canadian Western obtained a franchise from the town of Vulcan for the distribution of natural gas. Central and its subsidiary thereupon sued Canadian Western, International Utilities and Messrs. Milner and Maybin (an officer of Canadian Western) for (a) conspiracy to destroy competition and (b) for a declaration that Canadian Western held the franchise in trust for Central. W.A. McGillivray, who is now the Chief Justice of Alberta, was for the plaintiffs. Steer appeared for the defendants, and his son, Cameron, was with him. Both claims failed before Milvain J..

On appeal, the Appellate Division agreed that no conspiracy had been proved, but in a 2–1 judgment found Canadian Western to be in a fiduciary position towards Central so that Canadian Western held its franchise as trustee for Central.

Canadian Western appealed to the Supreme Court of Canada. A unanimous court held that International had carried Central through many years of financial difficulty, and that in its dealings with the town of Vulcan, Canadian Western was not in a fiduciary position towards Central.

XIII. Tax Cases

Steer was always alert to see that his client was not fixed with a tax that should not have been imposed. Many problems arose under the Succession Duty Act, the Corporations Taxation Act[185] and the Unearned Increment Tax Act.[186] These did not reach the stage of litigation so far as the writer is aware.

The first reported tax case is *Great West Garment Company* v.

M.N.R.[187] In 1941 the company fixed its officers' salaries at various amounts free of income tax. In 1942 a Salaries Order forbade an increase in salary rates. The income tax rates were increased in 1942 and 1943 so the amount payable to the officers went up accordingly. The M.N.R. alleged that this was a forbidden bonus. Steer appeared for the company. Gerald O'Connor J. rejected the Minister's argument. The salary was increased, but not the rate. Moreover the employer did not bring about the increase; it was the Income Tax Act that did so.

The next income tax case had to do with the estate of Senator Patrick Burns of Calgary who had died in 1937.[188] His will had directed payment of 60 per cent of the income of his trust estate to named individuals and 40 per cent to be accumulated for the lifetime of his daughter-in-law and added to the corpus of the trust estate. On her death the corpus was to be distributed—67 per cent to named individuals and 33 per cent to the Royal Trust Company for the Burns Memorial Trust. The beneficiaries of the trust were five charities—the Lacombe Home at Midnapore, the Salvation Army at Calgary, a children's shelter in Calgary, the families of Calgary firemen and the families of Calgary policemen. The last three were not yet in existence as charitable institutions.

Not long afterwards the Minister of National Revenue claimed income tax in respect of the income that was accumulating for the benefit of the Burns Memorial Trust. Acting for the Royal Trust Company, Steer argued that the Burns Memorial Trust was a charitable institution and so the income was exempt. He failed in the Exchequer Court on the ground that the accumulated income did not accrue to the Trust.

The executors and the Royal Trust Company appealed to the Supreme Court of Canada. They won a partial victory when the Court held that the proportions of the income to go to the Lacombe Home and the Salvation Army were free of income tax for 1938 and 1939 because there was no adequate charging section applicable to them for those years. On a further appeal to the Privy Council, Steer did not appear. H.G. Nolan represented the appellants. The final judgment upheld the Supreme Court, with the variation that the Lacombe Home and the Salvation Army had an exemption for 1940 as well as for the two previous years.

Parenthetically, we shall mention here another issue that arose in connection with the same will.[189] In 1958, at the expiration of twenty-one years from the death of Senator Burns, the daughter-in-law was still alive. Assuming the Accumulations Act of Great Britain to be in force in Alberta, then income after the expiration of the twenty-one years had to be "released". The difficult question in such a case is—to whom is it released? Steer for the Royal Trust Company argued that his client should receive 33 per cent of the income for the Burns Memorial Trust because 33 per cent of the corpus was ultimately to go to that trust for the five charities. The trial judge directed that all the released income should go as on intestacy.[190]

On appeal the Appellate Division held that since the testator had shown a general charitable purpose in the gift of 33 per cent of the corpus, then 33 per cent of the released income should be distributed for charitable purposes pursuant to a scheme to be approved by the Court. In a notable dissent, Porter J.A. held that the Accumulations Act was not in force in Alberta.[191]

Returning to income tax cases, *Noak* v. *M.N.R.*[192] raised the old problem whether a gain on the purchase and sale of property is income or capital. Miss Noak had worked all her life but over the years made a substantial number of investments, including the purchase of houses which she later sold. Rejecting Steer's argument that the profits were capital gains, the Supreme Court found that Miss Noak's main intention was to make profit on resale so the profit was income.

The last case, *Lethbridge Collieries* v. *The King,*[193] is not strictly a tax case. During World War II the federal government was concerned to keep coal mines in production. In 1942 an Order in Council provided for a subsidy of 35 cents a ton in the Lethbridge area. The company took this as a firm offer and acted accordingly but never received more than 16 cents a ton. It brought a petition of right claiming the difference. Steer represented the coal company. Gerald O'Connor J. thought that it was "entitled" to the full subsidy but went on to say that there was no legal liability enforceable by petition of right. Steer argued that there was a "statutory contract" and as an alternative, that the Crown had made an offer which the company had accepted by producing the coal. This argument failed. The company appealed to the Supreme Court which affirmed the trial judge. There was no firm offer to pay 35 cents a ton. The documents announcing the subsidy made it clear that payment was not to be automatic. The board made no order for payment of a subsidy having the force of law, even if it had power so to do.

XIV. The Last Supreme Court Case

Throughout the fifties Steer had a number of appeals in the Supreme Court of Canada, as already described. Then there was a concentration of appeals in the mid-sixties. In addition to *Kanstrup, Superstein* and *Central Gas,* which have been noted, there were three others.

In each of the first two Steer appeared for the plaintiff/appellant and succeeded. One was an action on a guarantee.[194] The other was a claim to the proceeds of the sale of almost four hundred head of cattle.[195] In the third case, the Alberta courts had ruled that William Hawrelak was ineligible as Mayor of Edmonton because he held 40 per cent of the shares of a company which had sold land to the City.[196] Steer joined J.W.K. Shortreed as counsel for the appellant. The appeal was dismissed in a five-line judgment.

After the six cases in the mid-sixties Steer did not appear again in the Supreme Court until his last case, *Walker & Clark* v. *The Queen,* which was argued in October 1969.[197] It dealt with the right of lessees in Jasper National Park to renew their leases. In 1962 the Government had amended the National Parks General Regulations to restrict the right of renewal contained in leases. The lessees formed an association to protect their interests, and retained Steer. (His cottage on Lake Edith was near the townsite of Jasper.) It was necessary to scrutinize a large number of leases to select two that would provide the strongest test case. Walker's lease was of a cottage lot on Lake Edith, while that of M.E. Clark & Son Ltd. was of a commercial lot in the Townsite of Jasper. Granted in 1924 and 1925, respectively, they were for 42 years. Each lease had two renewal clauses—one said that if the parties could not agree on the amount of rent on renewal, it would be fixed by arbitration. The other said that, assuming the lessee had observed the terms of the lease, he could obtain the renewal with the same renewal provisions that were in the original lease. In other words, the leases gave a right of perpetual renewal to the lessees.

As the leases were about to expire, each lessee, having observed the terms of the lease, applied in proper time for a renewal. The Crown was prepared to grant *one* renewal of 42 years, but no more. Each lessee refused to accept this offer but insisted on a new lease containing the same right of renewal as was in the original lease. Each brought a petition of right in the Exchequer Court for a declaration of the right of renewal.

The issue required examination of seven Acts of Parliament and their amendments, and of the Act of the Imperial Parliament confirming the transfer of natural resources to the prairie provinces in 1930, and of the Alberta Land Titles Act. It also called for scrutiny of twelve Orders in Council dealing with National Parks and Forest Reserves, and of five more dealing with Jasper National Park.[198]

The first question was difficult—what was the authority for the original leases? There were regulations of 1909/1911 covering National Parks and regulations of 1913 covering Forest Reserves. The leases themselves appeared to have been drawn in the light of the 1913 regulations. Steer argued that they applied. It was to his interest so to do because the 1913 regulations provided a stronger case for authorization of the right of perpetual renewal. The trial judge held for the Crown on this question. The 1909/1911 regulations authorized leases "for any term not exceeding 42 years with the right of renewal". The Crown argued that this did not mean "right of perpetual renewal". Gibson J., however, held that it did.

The Crown then argued that nonetheless the renewal clauses were of no effect because Parliament had taken away the right of perpetual renewal by subsequent legislation and regulations; that the regulations of 1962 in force when the petitions were brought did not permit a perpetual renewal and that the leases in question were subject to the current regulations. Gibson J. answered this by quoting section 36 of the Interpretation Act which said that repeal of an enactment does not affect rights acquired under the repealed enactment.

The Crown next argued that the leases themselves said that they were subject to regulations from time to time in force "for the control and management of Dominion Parks". Gibson J. agreed with Steer's argument that this referred only to general police regulations in the Parks and did not apply to the regulations empowering the Minister to grant leases.

In the result Steer won at trial, save that the trial judge ruled that the clause in the original leases providing for settlement of rent on renewal by arbitration was of no effect because there was no authority for it in statute or regulation.

The Crown appealed to the Supreme Court of Canada, and the petitioners applied to vary the trial judgment insofar as it held the provision for settlement of rent on renewal by arbitration to be ineffective. On the argument before the Supreme Court, the Crown repeated its two main contentions in the court below:

(1) The regulations never did empower the Minister to grant leases renewable in perpetuity at the lessee's option;

(2) Even if they did, the current National Parks Act and regulations thereunder forbade the grant of leases with a provision for perpetual renewal.

Speaking for six of the nine judges, Martland J. reviewed the legislation prior to the time when the original leases were granted, and then reviewed the regulations. He held, contrary to the trial judgment, that the terms of the leases showed that the Crown had in mind the 1913 regulations rather than those of 1909/1911, and further that those regulations permitted the leases in dispute and that the Crown could not impugn its own grants. Moreover the clause providing for arbitration to settle the amount of the rent on renewal was not invalid.

On the second argument, the Crown contended that the National Parks Act of 1930 and the regulations thereunder forbade the issue of leases with a covenant for perpetual renewal. Martland J. held that in the absence of clear statutory provisions enabling the Crown to escape its contracts, it was bound by them. The subsequent legislation and regulations did not operate to remove the Minister's authority to grant a renewal pursuant to the original lease.

Then the Crown argued that the leases themselves said that they were subject to the Parks Regulations. This argument was based on the provision in each lease that it was subject to regulations "now in force, or which may hereafter be made from time to time in that behalf". Martland J. upheld the ruling of the trial judge that this did not apply to regulations respecting leases.

Abbott and Judson JJ. in dissent thought that the 1909/1911 Regulations applied rather than those of 1913 and that they did not authorize leases with a right of perpetual renewal. Pigeon J. agreed with the trial judge.[199]

Shortly after this decision Steer retired. Though confined to his home, he retained a close interest in legal matters until his death in 1975.

XV. Contribution to Legal Education

While still under articles in Edmonton, Steer for five months had taught in the night class of the Edmonton Public Schools three nights a week, one and one-half hours per night. This was a prelude to his many years in part-time teaching of law students.

Under the Legal Profession Act, 1907, the Benchers had the responsibility of setting exams for articled students.[200] However, the University of Alberta had a role in the instruction of students-at-law. Dr. H.M. Tory, the first president, thought that the University should conduct examinations and appoint examiners for the professional societies. So it was that a new University Act of 1910 empowered the Senate to make arrangements for those purposes with the Law Society and with other professional associations.[201] An agreement with the Law Society was made in 1912.[202] It provided that the University would conduct the examinations of articled students and would select the examiners, with the Law Society's approval.

This did not end the University's involvement in legal education. Although there was no Faculty of Law until 1921, the University in fact offered an LL.B. degree. An articled student could enroll for the degree. To obtain it he or she had to take and pass extra courses over a four-year period. Lectures for the articled students and those for LL.B. candidates were given in Calgary as well as in Edmonton. They were usually in the Court House with barristers and some judges as lecturers. Steer became one of these lecturers shortly after he was admitted to the Bar. The University calendar for 1917–18 shows him as a lecturer in History of English Law and English Constitutional History.

By 1921 both the Law Society and the University wanted a Faculty of Law—one that would provide a three-year full-time course with at least some full-time professors. In contemplation of this the Legal Profession Act was amended in 1921 to provide for admission of graduates of the proposed new course, provided they spent a year under articles.[203]

Dr. Tory was chairman of an advisory committee to help establish the new faculty. The minutes show an organization meeting in the President's house on Monday, 3 October 1921. Chief Justice Harvey, Chairman of the Board of Governors, and Mr. Justice Stuart, Chancellor of the University, were present. From the University were John Weir, newly appointed professor and soon to become Dean, Professor A.F. McGoun and the Registrar Cecil Race. Representing the Law Society were Frank Ford and H.H. Parlee. Steer and William Dixon-Craig completed the Committee. It adopted the Canadian Bar Association curriculum for the first year of the course.

In the following May, Steer was present when a "Law Committee" and then the Advisory Committee confirmed the examination results for first year and settled the curriculum for the two senior years. The list of courses followed that recommended by the Canadian Bar Association. Among the courses approved were Property II and Equity I in second year and Property III and Equity II in third. Property II covered the Land Titles Act while Equity I was on the subject of Trusts. Property III embraced the law of mortgages and agreements for sale and Equity II dealt with the rules of equity excluding trusts. Steer taught them all from the beginning. Each was a heavy course, with a long and comprehensive case list. Generally Steer gave his lectures in the morning—not at the usual starting hour of 8:30 but at 8:00. He did not ask many questions or encourage lengthy debate. However, he pounded home the principle of a case with lucidity and emphasis. He never injected himself into the lectures. He expounded the decision in cases which he himself had argued and without any reference to himself.

He became a close friend of Dean Weir. When Weir died in June of 1942, Steer helped in the reorganization of the Faculty. Dr. Malcolm MacIntyre, who succeeded Weir as Dean, went on sabbatical leave in 1944–45, and Steer was made Acting Dean. There was no one left in the full-time Faculty

At the same time, enrolment had declined so that in 1945 the graduating class had three students. Nevertheless it was necessary to keep the doors open. Steer had the responsibility for recruiting part-time instructors in larger numbers than ever before. In the late summer of 1945, the Faculty was faced with the prospect of veterans coming in substantial numbers. Dr. MacIntyre found himself unable to return. It was in these circumstances that Steer and Dr. Newton, President of the University, and Mr. Justice Parlee, Chairman of the Board of Governors, made an arrangement whereby the writer would come for a year to lecture full-time.[204] Steer remained as Acting Dean until the spring of 1947. His heavy professional commitments induced him with great reluctance to give up his courses one by one and he had handed over all of them to others by the end of the 1947–48 session. Soon after he was made Honorary Professor. He continued to attend meetings of the Law Faculty Council until the end of 1963, and generally to retain his interest in the Faculty. When the new Law Centre at the University was formally opened on May 4, 1972, Steer attended the ceremony with Mrs. Steer, difficult though it was for him to move about.

His concern in legal education extended beyond the Faculty of Law. He felt strongly that the profession had an obligation to train graduates through providing them with articles. Over a thirty-year period fifteen students (by the writer's count) were articled to him.[205] A number more, articled to other members of his firm, came under his exacting tutelage.

In 1946 and the two following years he was Chairman of the Legal Education Section of the Canadian Bar Association. At the 1946 meeting at Winnipeg the association approved the steps taken to establish the Viscount Bennett Scholarships, which in subsequent years have provided for a good number of graduate students a year of graduate study. The same meeting approved establishment of a committee "to report on what, in their view is the most desirable curriculum for Canadian law schools".[206]

Prior to the 1947 meeting in Ottawa, Steer prepared a statement on legal education which he hoped would receive acceptance. The annual proceedings merely reported progress on the matter of curriculum.[207] The writer's clear recollection is that there was objection to the report Steer had prepared on the ground that it was too radical. The report appeared in the form of an article in the Canadian Bar Review.[208]

Having been a Bencher of the Law Society of Alberta in the period 1934–45 and President in his last year as a Bencher, Steer became President of the Conference of Governing Bodies (now the Federation of Law

Societies) in 1947. At the meeting that year Steer reported on a number of questions—some now forgotten, some now answered and some still current. The items were public relations, automatic membership in the Association, an indemnity fund to protect clients (which only Alberta and Manitoba then had), retirement of Superior Court Judges at 75, control of appointment of King's Counsel, an All-Canada series of law reports and uniform standards of admission.[209] On this last item, Dean Vincent McDonald of Dalhousie University was appointed Chairman of a committee to try to establish uniform standards of admission between the common law provinces.[210]

XVI. Conclusion

The writer has described George Hobson Steer's career as it appears in the law reports and as the writer recalls it. Not all of his cases reached the law reports. The writer has omitted a number of interesting cases because no documentation was available.[211] There were also miscellaneous minor cases. Even as late as the mid-nineteen thirties he took some small debt cases and appeared in Magistrates' Court to defend a person charged with speeding, or assault, or criminal negligence, or procuring an abortion. He prepared these defenses, presented the evidence and cross-examined with the same care which he brought to bear in a Supreme Court case.

It will be apparent from this account that Steer was dedicated to his profession. Were a student to mutter against heavy assignments the rejoinder was clear, "If you expect to practise law you must be prepared to work!" At the same time Steer did appreciate good performance and was in many ways helpful to young practitioners though one would never know it from him. Indeed had he been loquacious or given to moralizing or reminiscing it would have been easier to paint a picture. Peculiarly a private man, he kept personal matters and his thoughts and beliefs to himself.

Without the degree of Bachelor of Laws, he received an honorary degree of Doctor of Laws from Queen's University and also from the University of Alberta. On 25 June, 1971 he was appointed to the Order of Canada and the investiture was made by Lieutenant Governor Grant MacEwan at Steer's home on November 7, 1972.

One might wonder why Steer never became a judge. It is commonly understood that twice he had the refusal of an appointment to the Supreme Court of Canada.

At the funeral in Robertson-Wesley Church in June, 1975 the Rev. Dr. Edworthy read Chapter IV of Paul's Second Epistle to Timothy: "I have fought a good fight, I have finished my course, I have kept the faith."

Notes

1 The writer acknowledges with thanks the helpful comments on an earlier draft by Mr. Justice Ronald Martland and by W.H. Hurlburt Q.C.; and the help of Prof. Maurice Sychuk Q.C. on the oil and gas cases; and that of W.B. Kelly Q.C., Secretary, Law Society of Alberta and of James Steer in reply to various inquiries; and the work done by F.P. Layton, then a law student, in the summer of 1975 in collecting Mr. Steer's cases. This last was made possible by a grant to the writer from the Alberta Law Foundation.

2 The Milner and Steer letterhead gives his birth date as 1886.

3 This article refers to many Alberta lawyers and a number from other provinces. Nearly every one was, or became, a King's Counsel or Queen's Counsel. It is with no disrespect to the many distinguished counsel that the writer omits the "K.C." and "Q.C." He also omits "Mr." The writer has difficulty in so doing because he always addressed, and still refers to many of the lawyers mentioned in this article as "Mister".

4 John R. Gaunt and the writer went with Steer to the Milner firm.

5 On disputes over the right to discovery *see Gillespie Grain* v. *Wacowich* [1932] 1 W.W.R. 916 (App. Div.); *Northwestern Utilities* v. *Century Indemnity Co.* [1934] 3 W.W.R. 139; *Reese* v. *The Queen* [1955] Ex. C.R. 187; *Canadian Utilities Ltd.* v. *Mannix Ltd.* (1959) 29 W.W.R. 289 (App. Div.).

6 *R.* v. *Kamak* (1920) 15 Alta. L.R. 373 (App. Div.); *Re G* (1922) 17 Alta. L.R. 473 (App. Div.); *R.* v. *M.D. of Pembina* (1922) 19 Alta. L.R. 9 (App. Div.).

7 When the directors of a Saskatchewan oil company wanted a "completely independent legal opinion" as to whether a proposed agreement was oppressive of minority shareholders, they went to Steer; *see Farmers' Mutual Oil Co.* v. *U.S. Smelting Co.* (1961) 34 W.W.R. 646 at 651 (Sask. C.A.).

8 Cameron's wife had predeceased him in 1962. He left surviving four children.

9 *Waite & Walker* v. *Grand Trunk Pacific Railway* (1916) 11 Alta. L.R. 260 (App. Div.).

10 *MacKinnon v. Horn* (1916) 10 Alta. L.R. 389 (App. Div.); *Re City Transfer Co.* (1917) 11 Alta. L.R. 83 (App., Div.); *Re Extra-judicial Seizures Act* (1917) 12 Alta. L.R. 141; *Tropox* v. *Droney* (1918) 13 Alta. L.R. 39 (App. Div.); *Clarke* v. *Sutherland* (1917) 13 Alta. L.R. 132 (App. Div.); *Sutherland* v. *Clarke* (1917) 13 Alta. L.R. 330 (App. Div.).

11 (1917) 12 Alta. L.R. 210 (App. Div.).

12 *Northern Creameries* v. *Rossington Produce Co.* (1922) 17 Alta. L.R. 478 (App.Div.).

13 *Mandziuk* v. *Czahley* (1920) 16 Alta. L.R. 68 (App. Div.).

14 *Haste* v. *Goodman* (1922) 18 Alta. L.R. 15 (App. Div.).

15 *Banque d'Hochelaga* v. *Potvin* (1924) 20 Alta. L.R. 121 (App. Div.).

16 Legal Profession Act, S.A. 1907 c. 20 s. 52, as am. S.A. 1921 c. 5 s. 7.

17 *Re X* (1920) 16 Alta. L.R. 542.

18 *Re V* (1924) 20 Alta. L.R. 585 (App. Div.); *Re E* (1924) 20 Alta. L.R. 597 (App. Div.). The Court's power to reinstate, given by section 56, was not affected by the 1921 amendment.

19 [1927] S.C.R. 50, *revg.* (1926) 22 Alta. L.R. 148 (App. Div.). In *Standard Trust Company* v. *Stewart M.D.* (1929) 24 Alta. L.R. 56 (App. Div.). Steer failed in an action to redeem lands after an agreement for sale had been made in tax sale proceedings.

20 *Christofferson* v. *Christofferson* (1924) 21 Alta. L.R. 13 (App. Div.).

21 *Proud* v. *The King* [1926] Ex. C.R. 1; *affd. sub nom The King* v. *Proud* [1926] S.C.R. 509.

22 *Blatchford* v. *Van Ruyven* (1931) 25 Alta. L.R. 404 (App. Div.).

23 Frank Ford J. so stated in *McPherson* v. *McPherson* (No. 2) [1933] 2 W.W.R. 513. Later cases show that a person attempting to set aside a divorce has a hard task: *Bukowicki* v. *Bukowicki* [1945] 3 W.W.R. 402; however the action has sometimes succeeded *e.g.* in

Rivas v. *Rivas* [1977] 2 W.W.R. 345.

24 *Weaver* v. *Edmonton* [1923] 3 W.W.R. 682 (App. Div.).

25 *Macdonnell* v. *Pech* (1930) 25 Alta. L.R. 129 (App. Div.).

26 *Jeremy* v. *Fontaine* (1931) 26 Alta. L.R. 499 (App. Div.); *affg.* [1931] 1 W.W.R. 671.

27 [1940] 2 W.W.R. 65 (App. Div.).

28 (1923) 19 Alta. L.R. 463 (App. Div.).

29 [1931] 3 W.W.R. 4.

30 [1933] 1 W.W.R. 405, *aff'd.* [1933] 3 W.W.R. 224 (App. Div.).

31 [1937] 3 D.L.R. 700.

32 [1931] 2 W.W.R. 364.

33 *Colonial Bank* v. *Marshall* [1906] A.C. 559.

34 *London Joint Stock Bank* v. *Macmillan* [1918] A.C. 777.

35 *Supra* n. 32 at 375.

36 [1930] S.C.R. 137; *revg.* (1928) 23 Alta. L.R. 233 (App. Div.).

37 *See* map in MacGregor, *A History of Edmonton* (2nd ed. 1975) at 96, 97. The footbridge across the river near the Muttart Conservatory is at lot 21, as best as the writer can determine.

38 *Clarke* v. *Edmonton* (1928) 23 Alta. L.R. 233 (App. Div.).

39 This must have been one of his last cases, for he died in April, 1930.

40 *Clarke* v. *Edmonton* [1930] S.C.R. 137.

41 *Clarke* v. *Edmonton* [1933] 1 W.W.R. 113.

42 [1933] S.C.R. 650 *affg.* [1933] 1 W.W.R. 533 (App. Div.); *see also* [1934] S.C.R. vii.

43 14 Geo. III c. 78.

44 *Johnson* v. *Conrow* [1951] 4 D.L.R. 493: Coté, "The Introduction of English Law into Alberta" (1964) 3 Alta. L. Rev. 262 at 286.

45 (1921) 17 Alta. L.R. 314 (App. Div.).

46 N.W.T. Ordinances in Force in Alberta, 1915 c. 87.

47 The judgments on the merits are unreported. This paragraph is from memory.

48 *Northwestern Utilities* v. *London Guarantee Co.* [1936] A.C. 108; *affg. sub nom London Guarantee Co.* v. *Northwestern Utilities* [1934] 3 W.W.R. 641 (App. Div.); *revg.* [1934] 1 W.W.R. 675.

49 [1934] 1 W.W.R. 675 at 685.

50 [1936] A.C. 108 at 127.

51 *Id.* at 128.

52 Lord Wright of Durley, "The Northwestern Utilities Case," *Legal Essays and Addresses* (1939) 124.

53 *Reade and George* v. *Northwestern Utilities* [1938] 1 W.W.R. 647.

53A *Kent Coal Co.* v. *Northwestern Utilities* [1936] 2 W.W.R. 393 (App. Div.).

54 [1942] S.C.R. 467 *affg.* [1942] 1 W.W.R. 375 *affg.* [1941] 2 W.W.R. 329.

55 [1939] O.R. 517, *affd.* [1940] O.R. 140.

56 Actually the Supreme Court judgment in *Lockhart* came down five weeks before that of Howson J. in *W.W. Sales* but presumably was unavailable to him.

57 *Sub nom C.P.R.* v. *Lockhart* [1942] A.C. 591 *affg.* [1941] S.C.R. 278.

58 [1935] S.C.R. 291 *affg.* [1934] 3 W.W.R. 507 and 638 (App. Div.); *compare Home Insurance Co.* v. *Lindal* [1934] S.C.R. 33, where the Court found no estoppel when the insured had been driving while intoxicated.

59 [1945] 3 W.W.R. 49, *affd.* [1947] 1 W.W.R. 61, *revd.* [1948] S.C.R. 315 but restored [1949] 2 W.W.R. 1068 (P.C.).

60 *See* Laskin, "The Protection of Interests by Statute: The Problem of 'Contracting Out'" (1938) 16 Can. Bar Rev. 669.

61 *Jones* v. *Kline* [1938] 3 W.W.R. 65; *Re Rist* [1938] 3 W.W.R. 101, *affd.* [1939] 1 W.W.R. 518 (App. Div.).

62 Testator's Family Relief Act, S.A. 1947 c. 12; now the Family Relief Act R.S.A. 1980 c. F-2.

63 *See e.g., Re Berube* [1973] 3 W.W.R. 180 (App. Div.).

64 [1939] 1 W.W.R. 530 (App. Div.).

65 (1964) 46 W.W.R. 221, *affd.* (1964) 48 W.W.R. 641, *affd.* [1965] S.C.R. 441.

66 *Re Seizures Act* [1943] 2 W.W.R. 133.

67 S.A. 1964 c. 40 s. 3, now Law of Property Act, R.S.A. 1980 c. L-8 s. 41(5).

68 (1966) 55 W.W.R. 734 *affd.* (1966) 56 W.W.R. 623 (App. Div.). Steer argued without success (a) that the valuation was too low and (b) that the moneys spent by the receiver to keep the hotel in business were improper disbursements.

69 Where the covenant is reasonable as between the parties, it is rarely held to be against the public interest; *see*, however, *Baker* v. *Lintott* (1981) 25 A.R. 513 (Alta. Q.B.).
70 [1939] 2 W.W.R. 276, *affd*. [1939] 3 W.W.R. 259 (App. Div.).
71 [1939] 3 W.W.R. 259 at 268.
72 [1925] A.C. 700.
73 *Floyd* v. *E.C.D.* [1934] 3 W.W.R. 326.
74 [1939] 3 W.W.R. 394.
75 [1939] 3 W.W.R. 577.
76 (No. 2) [1940] 1 W.W.R. 124.
77 (No. 3) [1941] 1 W.W.R. 393.
78 [1941] 1 W.W.R. 401.
79 *R*. v. *Imperial Tobacco Co. (No. 4)* [1942] 1 W.W.R. 363.
80 *R*. v. *Imperial Tobacco Co. (No. 5)* [1942] 1 W.W.R. 625.
81 *A.G.* v. *Imperial Tobacco Co.* [1942] 3 D.L.R. 33 (S.C.C.).
82 On the constitutional issues considered in this and the next part *see* Mallory, *Social Credit and the Federal Power in Canada* (reprinted 1976).
83 S.A. 1916 c. 6, as am S.A. 1918 c. 25.
84 S.A. 1922 c. 43.
85 S.A. 1923 c. 43.
86 S.A. 1931 c. 57.
87 S.A. 1932 c. 18.
88 S.A. 1933 c. 11.
89 S.A. 1933 c. 13.
90 S.A. 1936 (2nd sess.) c. 5.
91 S.A. 1937 c. 9.
92 S.A. 1936 (2nd sess.) c. 2.
93 *Credit Foncier* v. *Ross* [1937] 2 W.W.R. 353 (App. Div.) *affg. sub nom Royal Trust* v. *A.G.* [1937] 1 W.W.R. 376.
94 *Steen* v. *Wallace* [1937] 3 W.W.R. 654. It is clear from the judgment that Steer asked for only nominal damages.
95 The Credit of Alberta Regulation Act, S.A. 1937 (2nd sess.) c. 1; The Bank Employees' Civil Rights Act, S.A. 1937 (2nd sess.) c. 2; An Amendment to the Judicature Act, S.A. 1937 (2nd sess.) c. 5.
96 The Bank Taxation Act, 1937 (3rd sess.) Bill 1; The Credit of Alberta Regulation Act, 1937 (3rd sess.) Bill 8; The Accurate News and Information Act 1937 (3rd sess.) Bill 9. These bills appear in S.A. 1937 (3rd sess.) pp. 31–39.
97 *Re Disallowance and Reservation* [1938] S.C.R. 71.
98 S.A. 1937 c. 10.
99 *Re Three Alberta Bills* [1939] A.C. 117, *affg*. in part [1938] S.C.R. 100.
100 *A.G.* v. *Atlas Lumber Co.* [1941] S.C.R. 87, *affg*. *Atlas Lumber Co.* v. *Winstanley* [1940] 1 W.W.R. 35.
101 S.A. 1941 c. 41.
102 S.A. 1941 c. 47.
103 S.A. 1941 c. 62.
104 S.A. 1942 p. 337 lists the disallowances.
105 *Plourde* v. *Roy* [1942] 1 W.W.R. 193 and 696 (App. Div.).
106 *North American Life Assce. Co.* v. *McLean* [1941] 1 W.W.R. 430.
107 S.A. 1941 c. 3 (not to be confused with The Debt Proceedings Suspension Act, S.A. 1941 c. 41).
108 *North American Life Assce. Co.* v. *McLean (No. 2)* [1941] 1 W.W.R. 588.
109 *Re Debt Adjustment Act, 1937,* [1942] S.C.R. 31.
110 S.A. 1942 c. 5.
111 *Re Legal Proceedings Suspension Act, 1942,* [1942] 2 W.W.R. 536 (App. Div.).
112 *Sub nom A.G. for Alberta* v. *A.G. for Canada* [1943] A.C. 356.
113 S.A. 1942 c. 37.
114 *Roy* v. *Plourde* [1943] S.C.R. 262, *revg*. *Plourde* v. *Roy (No. 2)* [1942] 2 W.W.R. 607.
115 S.A. 1946 c. 11.
116 Smith had been articled to Steer in 1941–42 and during the next five years worked closely with him on the constitutional cases. He taught Constitutional Law during this period. In 1947 he joined the Faculty of Law as Professor and so remained until retirement in 1973. His text, *The Commerce Power in Canada and the United States* (1963), is an acknowledged classic.
117 *A.G. of Alberta* v. *A.G. of Canada* [1947] A.C. 503 revg. in part *Re Alberta Bill of Rights Act* [1946] 3 W.W.R. 772 (App. Div.).
118 S.A. 1936 (2nd sess.) c. 1.
119 *I.O.F.* v. *Leth. Nor. Irrig. Dist.* [1937] 1 W.W.R. 414.
120 *I.O.F.* v. *Leth. Nor. Irrig. Dist. (No. 2)* [1938] 2 W.W.R. 194 (App. Div.),

affg. [1937] 3 W.W.R. 424.

121 *I.O.F.* v. *The King* [1939] 1 W.W.R. 700 (App. Div.), *affg*. [1939] 1 W.W.R. 275.

122 *Leth. Nor. Irrig. Dist.* v. *I.O.F.: The King* v. *I.O.F.* [1940] A.C. 513.

123 O.C. 1168–45, July 17, 1945; Alberta Gazette Vol. 41 p. 705; *see Re Ramsey Trust Deeds* [1946] 1 W.W.R. 510.

124 *I.O.F.* v. *Leth. Nor. Irrig. Dist.* [1943] 3 W.W.R. 297.

125 [1944] 1 W.W.R. 206.

126 *I.O.F.* v. *Leth. Nor. Irrig. Dist.* [1945] 1 W.W.R. 121 *affg*. [1944] 3 W.W.R. 49.

127 S.A. 1942 p. 337 lists them.

128 S.A. 1959 c. 61.

129 *Re Orderly Payment of Debts Act, 1959,* [1960] S.C.R. 571 *affg*. 29 W.W.R. 435 (App. Div.).

130 S.C. 1966–67 c. 32 s. 22, now R.S.C. 1970 c. B-3, Part X.

131 S.C. 1949 (2nd sess.) c. 24 s. 49.

132 *Re Bowater's Nfld. Pulp & Paper Mills Ltd.* [1950] S.C.R. 608.

133 *A.G.* v. *Whiteshore Salt Co.* [1955] S.C.R. 43 *revg*. [1952] 4 D.L.R. 51 (Sask. C.A.).

134 *A.G. for Alberta* v. *Huggard Assets* [1953] A.C. 420 *revg*. [1951] S.C.R. 427, *affg*. [1950] 1 W.W.R. 69 *affg*. [1949] 2 W.W.R. 370.

135 12 Car. II c. 24.

136 It is clear that the Supreme Court rejected the reasoning of Boyd McBride J. and held that the royalty clause did literally provide for future royalties. The main question in the rehearing was whether the reservation of royalties was "invalid on the ground of uncertainty or any other ground".

137 The writer's understanding is that delivery of the elk and beaver was made by Sir Ashley Cooper, Governor of the Company.

138 49 Vict. c. 25 (Can.).

139 [1953] A.C. 420 at 443.

140 *Id*. at 451.

141 This part is based on Court files, reported judgments, and to a smaller extent, on the recollection of the writer who had some contact with these cases. In connection with the second case, he is indebted to Wm. Henkel, Q.C., Assistant Deputy Attorney General and William Joyce, Manager, Records and Micrographics for making available the Attorney General's files.

142 Sections 264, 265.

143 *Goldsmith* v. *Pressdram* [1977] 2 All E.R. 557 (Q.B.D.), where leave to prosecute was granted; *Goldsmith* v. *Sperrings* [1977] 2 All E.R. 566 (C.A.), where an application to stay or dismiss the plaintiff's actions was dismissed; *see also* Spencer, "Criminal Libel—A Skeleton in the Cupboard" (1977) *Crim. Law Rev.* 382 and 465.

144 Criminal Code, s. 507 and s. 505(1)(b).

145 *Cleaves* v. *Deakin* [1979] 2 All E.R. 497 (H.L.).

146 *R.* v. *Edwards* [1919] 2 W.W.R. 600: *Maloney* v. *Fildes* [1933] 1 W.W.R. 33.

147 Established by the Alberta Social Credit Act, S.A. c. 10 as am. S.A. 1937 (2nd sess.) c. 3.

148 *R.* v. *Unwin* [1938] 1 W.W.R. 339 (App. Div.): *R.* v. *Powell* [1938] 1 W.W.R. 347 (App. Div.).

148A *See* Rook and Schnell, "Charlotte Whitton and the 'Babies for Export' Controversy of 1947–48" [1982] Winter *Alberta History* 11.

149 These details are set out in an article by Scott Young in the Globe and Mail, June 8, 1976, p. 35. A later note in the Edmonton Journal, of which the writer omitted to mark the date, says that Cooke had sold his Los Angeles interests and bought the Chrysler Building in New York.

150 Parliament promptly amended section 888 of the Criminal Code to say that the charge of conspiring to publish a defamatory libel must be tried in the province where the accused resides or where the newspaper is printed—*see* now section 421.

151 Section 461, formerly s. 662.

152 *R.* v. *Cooke and Dingman* [1948] 2 D.L.R. 254 (Ont.).

153 Edmonton Journal, 31 January, 1948.

154 *R.* v. *Cooke* [1948] 1 W.W.R. 849 at 851–854.

155 *Id*.

156 Report of the Royal Commission appointed to Investigate Certain Charges, Allegations and Reports Relating to the Child Welfare Branch of the Depart-

ment of Public Welfare, Section 11, at 49–54.

157 The validity of the Turner Valley Gas Conservation Act, S.A. 1932 c. 6 had been upheld as early as 1933 in *Spooner Oils Ltd.* v. *A.G. Alberta* [1933] S.C.R. 629. That Act and the Oil and Gas Wells Act, S.A. 1931 c. 46 were forerunners of today's Oil and Gas Conservation Act, R.S.A. 1980 c. 0–5.

158 *Mercury Oils* v. *Vulcan Brown Petroleums* [1943] S.C.R. 37 *affg. sub nom Vulcan Brown Petroleums* v. *Mercury Oils* [1942] 1 W.W.R. 138 *affg.* [1941] 3 W.W.R. 384.

159 *Reddick* v. *Pearson* [1948] 2 W.W.R. 1144.

160 *McColl-Frontenac Oil Co.* v. *Hamilton* [1953] 1 S.C.R. 127.

161 *Pinsky* v. *Wass* [1953] 1 S.C.R. 399, *revg.* 2 W.W.R. (N.S.) 47 and restoring [1950] 2 W.W.R. 1278. The later cases on the Dower Act are not part of this narrative; *see Meduk* v. *Soja* [1958] S.C.R. 167; *Senstad* v. *Makus* [1978] 2 S.C.R. 44; *McFarland* v. *Hauser* [1979] 1 S.C.R. 337.

162 *Borys* v. *C.P.R.* [1953] A.C. 217, *affg.* 4 W.W.R. (N.S.) 481, *revg.*, in part, 2 W.W.R. (N.S.) 145.

163 *C.P.R.* v. *Turta* [1954] S.C.R. 427 *affg. sub nom. Turta* v. *C.P.R.* 8 W.W.R. (N.S.) 609, *affg.* 5 W.W.R. (N.S.) 529.

164 S.A. 1949 c. 56 s. 5: R.S.A. 1955 c. 170 s. 176(1).

165 S.A. 1958 c. 34 s. 10.

166 S.A. 1958 c. 43.

167 *Kaup* v. *Imperial Oil Limited* [1962] S.C.R. 170.

168 *See Re Pogue and Lane* (1951) 3 W.W.R. (N.S.) 97, in which Steer was successful and *C.P.R.* v. *Turta* [1954] S.C.R. 427 at 449, 450 *per* Estey J.; *see also supra* n. 167.

169 (1965) 51 W.W.R. 346.

170 [1951] S.C.R. 154 *revg.* [1949] 2 W.W.R. (App. Div.) and restoring except as to quantum [1949] 1 W.W.R. 193.

171 [1953] 1 S.C.R. 233 *revg.* 4 W.W.R. (N.S.) 660 (App. Div.).

172 R.S.A. 1980 c. J-1 s. 10.

173 (1951) 4 W.W.R. (N.S.) 70 and 553 (App. Div.).

174 *Superior Oil* v. *Kanstrup* [1965] S.C.R. 92 *affg.* 47 W.W.R. 129, *affg.* 39 D.L.R. (2d) 275.

175 *Re Jardine* (1955) 17 W.W.R. 197 (App. Div.).

176 *Blackmer* v. *Guaranty Trust Company* (1972) 28 D.L.R. (3rd) 215 (S.C.C.).

177 Unreported, 16 October 1975, J.D. of Edmonton, S.C. 89545 (Alta. S.C. T.D., Bowen J.); *affd.* unreported, 24 February 1977, S.C. 10689 (Alta. S.C. A.D.).

178 [1957] S.C.R. 794, *affg.* [1956] Ex. C.R. 94.

179 (1957) 9 D.L.R. (2d) 47 (C.A.).

180 (1958) 14 D.L.R. (2d) 247 (C.A.).

181 *Edmonton, Jasper Place, Red Deer & Vegreville* v. *Northwestern Utilities* (1959) 29 W.W.R. 457.

182 (No. 2), (1960) 34 W.W.R. 241 (App. Div.).

183 [1961] S.C.R. 392.

184 [1966] S.C.R. 630, *revg.* (1965) 53 W.W.R. 705 (App. Div.) and restoring (1965) 49 W.W.R. 513.

185 Both repealed S.A. 1962 c. 86.

186 Repealed S.A. 1956 c. 57.

187 [1957] Ex. C.R. 458.

188 *Burns' Executors* v. *M.N.R.* [1950] 2 W.W.R. 1290 (P.C.) *revg.* in part [1947] S.C.R. 132 *revg.* in part [1946] Ex. C.R. 229.

189 Both before and after Senator Burns's death Steer appeared on a number of applications relating to the Senator's estate. Not all are reported.

190 Legislation on these bequests: The Burns Memorial Trust Act, S.A. 1956 c. 64, as am. S.A. 1981 (Bill PR 12); The Honourable Patrick Burns Settlement Act, S.A. 1975 (2nd sess.) c. 91, as am. S.A. 1981 (Bills PR 2, 11).

191 *Re Burns Estate* (1960) 32 W.W.R. 689 (App. Div.), *revg.* in part 26 W.W.R. 49. The Perpetuities Act, S.A. 1972 c. 121, declared that the Accumulations Act does not apply in Alberta.

192 [1953] 2 S.C.R. 137 *affg.* [1952] Ex. C.R. 20.

193 [1951] S.C.R. 138 *affg.* [1950] Ex. C.R. 1.

194 *Weldwood-Westply* v. *Cundy* [1965] S.C.R. 586.

195 *Hurly* v. *Bank of Nova Scotia* [1966] S.C.R. 83, *revg.* 52 W.W.R. 513

(App. Div.).

196 *Hawrelak* v. *The Queen* (1966) 55 W.W.R. 320 (S.C.C.), *affg. sub nom R.* v. *Hawrelak* 53 W.W.R. 257 (App. Div.).

197 The writer is indebted to Prof. Walter Mis, who appeared with Steer in the Exchequer Court for assistance in connection with this case.

198 *See Walker & Clark* v. *The Queen* [1969] 1 Ex. C.R. 419 at 438–440, where the statutes and Orders in Council are listed.

199 *R.* v. *Walker & Clark* [1970] S.C.R. 649 varying *sub nom Walker & Clark* v. *The Queen* [1969] 1 Ex. C.R. 419.

200 S.A. 1907 c. 20 s. 32.

201 S.A. 1910 c. 7 s. 40(2).

202 *See* Johns, *A History of the Faculty of Law* (1977) at 4, 5.

203 S.A. 1921 c. 5 s. 7.

204 Steer's "loan" of the writer's services to the University became permanent.

205 Unless shown otherwise, address is Edmonton. (1931–32) The Honourable Carlton W. Clement, retired from the Court of Appeal, January, 1982; (1932–33) Wilbur F. Bowker, Q.C., retired; (1934–35) H. Lyle Jestley, address unknown (these articles were actually served in British Columbia under a special arrangement); (1935–36) Richard G. Johnson, retired, Toronto; (1936–37) John G. McIntosh, Victoria, B.C., died 1964; (1937–38) Frank P. Layton, Q.C., died 1968; (1938–39) George L. Crawford, Q.C., Calgary; (1939–40) Marjorie Bowker (née Montgomery) Juvenile & Family Court Judge; (1940–41) Colonel John P. Dewis, Ottawa; (1941–42) Dr. Alexander Smith, Q.C., retired, Victoria, B.C.; (1941–42) Michel Dubuc, Clerk of Court and Sheriff, died 1959; (1943–44) Thaddeus Ives, Q.C., Lethbridge; (1947–48) David C.L. Jones, retired, Calgary; (1951–52) Mr. Justice Cameron Steer, Supreme Court, Trial Division, died 1979; (1962–63) Murray Dale.

206 1946 Proc. C.B.A. 68, 174.

207 1947 Proc. C.B.A. 30.

208 Steer, "On Legal Education in Canada" (1947) 25 *Can. Bar Rev.* 943.

209 1947 Proc. C.B.A. 132.

210 The Committee made its final report in 1951: *see* 1951 Proc. C.B.A. 115.

211 The same is true of a federal commission or inquiry of which Steer was a member around the end of World War II. The writer's recollection is that it had to do with the grain trade in Saskatchewan. Then there was an inquiry into the collapse of a span of the Second Narrows Bridge at Vancouver after World War II. The writer is not clear as to Steer's role.

1982

Homestead Laws in the Four Western Provinces

Reprinted from
Matrimonial Property Law in Canada
Bissett-Johnson & Holland, eds.
Loose Leaf Release No. 3, August 1982

This article is part of a loose-leaf service on Matrimonial Property Law in Canada co-edited by Professor Bissett-Johnson of Dalhousie Law School, who asked Bowker to write on Dower Acts of the Western Provinces.

It will be recalled that in 1960 Bowker wrote an article on the Law of Dower in Alberta. That article was historical; this one deals with present-day law in the western provinces. These are the only provinces which have dower legislation, though others are now moving towards what is called "consent to disposition." "Dower" as used here means the necessity for a spouse to give consent to any disposition of the home property.

In the United States, such laws are called Homestead Acts. The system was borrowed from the States; that is, Homestead Acts were originally American, and we in the Prairies copied them.

Bowker's article in 1960 deals with three features of the American Homestead Acts, namely:
1. necessity for the wife's consent to disposition of matrimonial property;
2. the wife's life interest in the home property after the owner's death;
3. exemption of the home from creditors' claims.

The article which follows analyzes Acts of the Western Provinces in operation today, and raises such problems as:
—what constitutes the homestead?
—is a summer home a homestead? In Alberta can a wife have two homesteads?
—where people live above a store, is this a "homestead"?

Most important is the effect of non-compliance with the law, since it could produce horrendous results if such transactions were to be automatically declared void.

These and related matters are dealt with in the following article.

1. Introduction

As used in this title, "homestead" does not mean public lands on which a settler makes entry and ultimately obtains title. It simply means land that a married man owns and on which he lives.[1]

Homestead laws originated in the United States. Though they vary widely from state to state the legislation usually does three things: it protects the home against execution creditors;[2] it requires a wife's consent to a disposition of or encumbrance on the home; and it gives the widow and sometimes children the right to remain in the home after the owner's death.[3]

This kind of protection for the wife differs from common law dower. The latter gave her the right to remain in the dwelling house only during the "quarantine" of 40 days from the husband's death, and then gave her a life interest in one-third of the husband's land. Common law dower antedates the Norman Conquest.[4] It was brought into the eastern common law provinces but never took root on the prairies. Manitoba established a land titles (Torrens) system in 1885 and in so doing abolished common law dower.[5] The next year Parliament did the same for the Northwest Territories.[6] As Chief Justice Harvey of Alberta once pointed out, the reason for abolition was that dower was in conflict with the principles of a land titles system—freedom to transfer and the disclosure of every interest in the land on the title.[7]

When Alberta and Saskatchewan were carved out of the Territories in 1905 each province re-enacted the federal land titles legislation of the Territories so never had common law dower. British Columbia, on the other hand, did. Its Dower Act[8] was modelled on England's Dower Act of 1833. It was repealed in 1925.[9]

At present all western provinces have legislation embodying the three elements of the American-style homestead laws. However in none of these provinces are all the provisions in a single statute and there is a confusing variety of titles. The exemption of the homestead from execution creditors is in the Judgments Act of Manitoba, the Exemptions Act of both Saskatchewan and Alberta, and the Homestead Act of British Columbia. The requirement of consent to disposition is in the Dower Act of Manitoba and of Alberta, the Homesteads Act of Saskatchewan and the Land (Wife Protection) Act, formerly the Wife's Protection Act, in British Columbia. The provision giving the wife an interest in the homestead after the husband's death is in the Dower Act of Manitoba and of Alberta and in Saskatchewan's Homesteads Act, while in British Columbia it is in the Estate Administration Act. This article will compare the statutory provisions in the four provinces and the general scheme will be to deal with them in the following order—Manitoba, Saskatchewan, Alberta and British Columbia.

2. Exemption of the Home from Execution Creditors

All four provinces had legislation to protect the home from execution creditors long before they provided for the other two elements of typical homestead laws. In Manitoba this protection goes back to 1871[10] in Saskatchewan and Alberta to a Territorial Ordinance of 1884[11] and in British Columbia to a Colonial Ordinance of 1867.[12] These exemptions have changed remarkably little since first established.[13]

In Manitoba, the Judgments Act provides that the exemption covers the farmland on which the debtor or his family actually resides, where the area of land is not more than 160 acres, and the actual residence or home of the debtor other than a farmer to the value of $2,500, or where the debtor is a co-owner, $1,500.[14]

Saskatchewan's Exemptions Act covers the homestead if it is not more than 160 acres, and in the case of non-farmland the house and buildings occupied by the debtor and the lot or lots on which they are situate to the extent of $16,000.[15] Alberta's Exemptions Act,[16] like Saskatchewan's, has its roots in the Territorial Ordinance mentioned earlier. The homestead must be "actually occupied by the debtor" and is limited to 160 acres, while for non-farmland, the house must be actually occupied and the exemption extends only to a value of $8,000 for house and lots though it has been said that for two judgment debtors who are co-owners, each is entitled to the exemption.[17]

Sometimes, of course, it is doubtful as a matter of fact as to whether the house is actually occupied or is the actual residence. It is clear that the debtor loses the exemption if he abandons the home[18] or if he sells it voluntarily.[19]

Does the exemption extend after the execution debtor's death? Manitoba speaks of "the debtor or his family" in connection with farmland. This could cover the family after the debtor's death, because it had been held even in the case of non-farmland that the widow is entitled to the exemption of $2,500.[20] However one judgment says the exemption ends with the debtor's death.[21] Saskatchewan (s. 6) and Alberta (s.5) extend the exemption after the debtor's death where the property is in the use and enjoyment of widow or children and necessary for their maintenance and support.[22] In Alberta, however, this extension only applies as against *judgment creditors,*[23] while in Saskatchewan it explicitly applies as against all creditors.

British Columbia's Homestead Act[24] differs from the exemptions legislation of the prairie provinces. To attract an exemption the homestead must be registered as such (s. 3). Even then the exemption is only $2,500. Where the owner is married, his wife (if a resident) must consent to abandonment (ss. 3 and 4). Professor Dunlop says that the Homestead Act is of little practical significance today because of inflation and because very few properties are registered as homesteads.[25]

Does the exemption attach where the debtor lives in part of the building, the rest being used for another purpose such as a business or an apartment house? In Manitoba, the courts have dealt with this problem in the context of the Dower Act rather than in connection with exemptions under the Judgments Act. However the two situations are analogous. In general the courts have tended to look to the chief use or primary function of the building. Thus, if that use or function is business rather than residence, the courts have held that the property is not a homestead.[26] Recent cases however, while recognizing the "primary function" test, show more willingness to hold the property to be the home.[27]

In Saskatchewan, the courts have been quite willing to hold the property to be exempt from execution where the building had a store below and the debtor's living quarters were above,[28] and even where the building was a hotel in which the debtor resided.[29] The Alberta cases likewise show a readiness to hold the premises to be exempt as a home when only part of the building is a residence.[30]

In British Columbia, the leading case is in the context of the Land (Wife Protection) Act and not of the exemption legislation, which as stated earlier is called the Homestead Act. The trial judge held that the living quarters, being one suite out of fifteen, were a mere adjunct to the business premises so that the building was not a dwelling. However, on appeal, the court held that it was.[31]

3. The General Scheme of the Homestead Acts[32]

Two factors produced homestead legislation in all of the prairie provinces during World War I—the land boom which had occurred just before the war, and the demand for women's rights. A third possible factor was immigration from the United States where these Acts originated.

Saskatchewan passed its Homesteads Act in 1915. In the same year Alberta enacted a Married Women's Home Protection Act which authorized a wife to file a caveat against the home. It was the forerunner of the Dower Act of 1917. Manitoba's Dower Act dates from 1918.[33] British Columbia's Wife's Protection Act (now the Land (Wife Protection) Act) came 30 years later.

Although the purpose of the legislation is often said to be the protection of the wife in relation to the home, Manitoba's Act "works both ways" (s. 33) and so does Alberta's (s. 2(*d*)). In those provinces it is more accurate to speak of owner and spouse than of husband and wife, though for convenience this account will on occasion assume the husband to be owner in discussing Manitoba and Alberta law.

In considering the main provisions of the various Acts it would be tedious and unhelpful simply to quote them all. This account will describe the basic provisions in a general way.

(1) Meaning of Homestead

In Manitoba "homestead" is defined (s. 2(*d*)) as a dwelling house occupied by the owner and his wife[34] and the appurtenant lands and premises. For an urban home the maximum is six lots or one block or one acre; for farmland it is a maximum of 320 acres. Saskatchewan defines homestead by reference to the definition under the Exemptions Act except that there is no maximum value placed on a non-farm homestead (s. 2(*a*)). In Alberta the homestead is a parcel[35] of land on which the dwelling house occupied by the owner as his home is situate, with a maximum of four lots or not more than a quarter section of farmland. In British Columbia it will be remembered that homestead rights arise only when a homestead "entry" has been made on the title. A homestead is land of which the husband is owner and on which there is a dwelling occupied[36] by the husband and wife as their residence. There is no prescribed maximum (s. 1).

Sometimes there is a dispute as to whether the owner really lives on the land—whether it is actually his "home place". A summer cottage on the farm is not;[37] nor is a farm on which the owner's wife occasionally slept in a trailer.[38]

Then there are cases where the extent or boundary of the homestead is uncertain. An Alberta case points out that this could be so where the home occupies more than the maximum four lots or is in the centre of a section of land.[39] Where the home is on an 80 acre parcel and the owner farms another 80 acres half a mile away, the latter is not part of the homestead.[40]

Questions also arise where the couple live on the property but where the building on the land is used for business as well as for a dwelling. This has been discussed in connection with exemptions. At one time the trend in Manitoba was to apply strictly a "primary purpose" test but it has been relaxed. In the other provinces the courts have been liberal in construing the premises to be the homestead.

What of condominiums? They do not neatly fit into any of the definitions but they should be treated as homesteads. Manitoba has not specifically included them;[41] Saskatchewan[42] and Alberta[43] have brought them under both the exemptions and homestead statutes; while British Columbia has brought them under the Land (Wife Protection) Act.[44]

(2) Duration of Homestead

One might think that the land ceases to be the homestead when the owner and his wife leave it to live elsewhere. The law, however, is not so simple. In Manitoba it is clear that the wife can have rights in only one homestead. The homestead continues so to be even though the husband has changed his home, unless she consents to the change or gives a release of her homestead rights or consents to a sale (ss. 2 and 3). In Saskatchewan, homestead is defined to include property that has been a homestead at any time (s. 2(*a*)). There can be two or more homesteads. Thus a wife was permitted to file a caveat against each of two former homesteads.[45] In Alberta the Dower Act says that a homestead continues as such notwithstanding the acquisition of another homestead or a change of residence of the married person (s. 3(1)). Thus where a farmer retires to a nearby town and acquires a home there his wife has dower rights in both properties so her consent is needed to a disposition of either. However the provision for dispensing with consent (s. 10(1)) applies. It says that the court may take into consideration the wife's preference as to the homestead. Where there are two homesteads at the husband's death the widow has an election[46] and if she does not elect, the court may designate the homestead (ss. 19 and 20). The fact that a homestead remains such even after the parties have left it is sometimes overlooked. If the couple have left the farm, and even if the house has been burned down, the wife's consent is required to a disposition. Similarly, if the couple have fenced off 20 acres where the home is, a disposition of the remaining 140 acres, as well as of the 20, requires the wife's consent.[47]

(3) The Wife's Rights in the Homestead during the Husband's Lifetime

None of the Acts specifically gives the wife a vested estate in the homestead during the husband's lifetime. However, in Manitoba she can file a caveat "claiming an interest in the land" (s. 27) which prevents the registrar from registering a disposition. Saskatchewan too provides for the filing of a caveat, and the form of caveat is set out (s. 8 and Form D). In Alberta there is no specific provision for a caveat, but it was held long ago that the Act gives the wife a contingent life interest and that this is sufficient to support a caveat.[48] The Act does not, however, confer on her a present right of possession during the husband's lifetime.[49] In Saskatchewan, on the other hand, there is an early case holding that the wife has the right to reside on the land so that where the husband transferred it she was entitled to an order for possession.[50] This case has never been overruled though it does not apply where the parties had left the homestead before the husband made a disposition.[51]

There has been a curious development in Alberta. Let us assume that the homestead is in the wife's name and that the husband is an execution debtor. The Land Titles Act says that an execution creditor may file a caveat against land in which the debtor is "interested beneficially". It has been held that this provision justifies the filing by the execution creditor of a caveat against the homestead, even though the debtor is not the registered owner.[52] In a later case the facts were basically the same except that, subsequent to the filing of the caveat, the debtor (husband) released his dower rights and then was divorced. It is clear that a divorce puts an end to a spouse's homestead rights but one might question whether a debtor can give an effective release of his dower rights to defeat the creditor.[53]

In connection with the effect of divorce, none of the Acts mentions this, but the necessary inference is that divorce terminates the wife's rights in the homestead.[54] However in Alberta, where the Act gives the wife an action for damages against her husband when he has transferred the land without her consent, the Appellate Division was divided equally on the question of whether the divorce terminated the cause of action.[55]

(4) The Meaning of "Disposition"

Since all the Acts require the wife's consent to a disposition it is important to know the meaning of that word. Manitoba's definition (s. 2(*c*)) says it includes "every grant, transfer, agreement of sale, grant of an option to purchase, mortgage (legal or equitable), encumbrance, charge, lien, lease for more than three years and every other disposition of the homestead by Act inter vivos, and every devise or other disposition thereof made by will;. . . " However, the elaborate provisions for consent described below apply only to a disposition *inter vivos* (s. 3(1)).

Saskatchewan does not have a definition, but the substantive provision for consent (s. 3) applies to every "transfer, agreement for sale, lease or other instrument intended to convey or transfer an interest in a homestead to any person other than the wife of the owner, and every mortgage intended to charge a homestead a favour of any such person with the payment of a sum of money . . . ".

Alberta's definition is confined to dispositions *inter vivos* and is much like Manitoba's (s. 1(*c*)).

British Columbia's provisions are much like Alberta's (ss. 1, 3).

It will be noted that an oil lease or other profit a prendre though not mentioned specifically in any of the definitions is a disposition. Indeed a number of the important cases have had to do with oil leases. However in Alberta, if the mines and minerals are contained in a separate certificate of title, then the Act does not apply to a disposition of them (s. 24).

In most cases the husband is registered owner of the homestead either alone or jointly with his wife but this need not be so. For example, where a devisee under a will lives on the land but is not yet registered owner, the land is his homestead and the provisions for consent to a disposition are applicable.[56] Again, if the husband is purchaser under an agreement for sale and the land is the homestead, then a quit claim deed[57] or an assignment by the purchaser of his interest is a disposition.

Then there can be an unusual transaction as there was in a Saskatchewan case. The husband, having left his wife, lived with a woman in a home which they owned as tenants in common. He attempted to change this to a joint tenancy of himself and the woman without his wife's consent. This was held to be ineffective because his wife had not consented.[58]

Where spouses are joint owners and the husband brings an action for partition or sale, is this proceeding a disposition? In Manitoba, one case[59] held that it is a disposition and in Alberta there was a case each way.[60] Manitoba's Law of Property Act now says that consent is not required to a partition action[61] and Alberta's Law of Property Act[62] says it is not a disposition.

Another question that might be asked is this. Is the transfer of the homestead from husband to wife a disposition within the Act so that she must consent to the disposition to herself? On principle one would think that the Acts apply only to a disposition to a third party and indeed Manitoba makes this clear (s. 3(1)(*b*)) and so does Saskatchewan (s. 3(1)). The Alberta Act has no such specific provision but it has been held that the consent requirements do not apply.[63] There is however a related problem. The husband may transfer the homestead to his wife or the spouses being joint owners may transfer the homestead to the wife. This having been done, does the husband retain his dower rights in the land? On principle the answer is yes.[64] This question is important in connection with separation agreements wherein the husband agrees to transfer the homestead to the wife and does so. If the wife wishes to ensure that her husband will not have dower rights in the home the only safe course for her would be to insist on a release by her husband of his dower rights.

(5) The Basic Consent Provisions

These are all rather elaborate.[65] In no two provinces are the provisions and the forms exactly alike. It will help to describe Manitoba's and then more briefly those of the other provinces. Consent must be in the form set out in the statute or to the like effect (s. 5(2) and Forms A and B). The requirement of the written consent does not end the formality. The wife is required to "acknowledge apart from her husband that [the consent] was voluntarily executed by her of her own free will and accord and without any compulsion on the part of her husband, and that she is aware of the nature and effect of the same" (s. 8(1)). This acknowledgment must be made before a person entitled to take affidavits, and in the case of a disposition of minerals, before a barrister-at-law or an attorney-at-law (ss. 8(3) and 9(1)). Then the officer must sign a "certificate of acknowledgment" (s. 8 and Form F). It must be attached (s. 8(3)), and for a disposition to be effective the consent must be filed in the Land Titles Office (s. 5(1)). If the man making the disposition is not married or if the land is not his homestead he must so say in an affidavit. Where the wife is owner and makes the disposition the husband's consent is needed, because the Act "works both ways". However no acknowledgment is necessary (s. 33(1)).

The formalities of consent in Saskatchewan have much in common with those of Manitoba. However, the wife must sign the instrument as well as a "Declaration by Wife",[66] though if the declaration is in the instrument, instead of being annexed thereto, her signature to either disposition or declaration is sufficient (s. 4(2), (3)). The declaration is the equivalent of Manitoba's consent. The requirement of an appearance before an officer (e.g., judge, registrar, solicitor, or notary public) and the contents of his certificate (s. 5(1) and Form B) are much like those in Manitoba.[67] The officer who takes the wife's acknowledgment must not be one who prepared the document or is interested in the transaction (s. 3(1)). The affidavit that the land is not the homestead or that the man making the disposition is not married is like Manitoba's, though there is no affidavit that the woman who has consented is the wife.

In Alberta, the forms were recently removed from the Act to the Statutory Regulations.[68] Consent to a disposition of the homestead is mandatory (s. 2(1)) and the consent states that the wife has signed it to give up her dower rights to the extent necessary to give effect to the disposition (s. 4(2)).[69] The wife need sign only the consent form unless it is in a separate document in which case she must sign the disposition as well (s. 4(5)). The requirement of an acknowledgment before an officer is in a general way like those in the other provinces, as is the content of the certificate which he signs (s. 5 and Form C). The affidavit that the owner is not married or that the land is not his homestead is likewise similar to that in the other provinces (s. 4(*b*) and Form B).

In British Columbia, it will remembered, the wife's rights attach only when a "homestead" entry has been made on the title. This simplifies the conveyancing. However, she must consent to a disposition (s. 3) though there is no statutory form. The only other requirement is that of the Certificate of Acknowledgment taken by an officer (s. 8 and Form B).

(6) Dispensing with Consent

All of the statutes empower the court to make an order dispensing with the wife's consent. The grounds vary from province to province. In Manitoba the order may be made when the wife has been living apart for six months or more, or where she is "mentally disordered", and the court may make a monetary award to her (s. 13).

In Saskatchewan, the order may be made when the wife is living apart under circumstances disentitling her to alimony, or when she is of unsound mind (s. 3(2)).

Alberta's elaborate provision says the owner may apply when the parties are living apart, when the spouse has not since the marriage lived in Alberta, when the spouse's whereabouts are unknown, where there are two or more homesteads, where the spouse has executed a release, or where the spouse is of unsound mind (s. 10(1)). The section goes on to enumerate factors that the court may consider (subs. (4)). The court may make the order "if in the opinion of the court it appears fair and reasonable under the circumstances to do so".

British Columbia's provision (s. 9) is somewhat like Alberta's but without mention of specific factors that the court may consider. Some judgments have pointed out that "it is difficult to enunciate any principle" to guide the court in deciding whether it is fair and reasonable to dispense with consent.[70]

(7) Release of Rights

There are various situations in which it may be appropriate for the wife to release her rights, for example, when a separation agreement is made. There is no immediate disposition to a third party but the release frees the husband to make such a disposition.

In Manitoba, the wife may "for valuable consideration, in writing," release in favour of her husband all her rights under the Dower Act (s. 6 and Form E). The requirements of acknowledgment are the same as for a consent to a disposition (s. 8(1) and (3)). A release is not necessarily final. The spouses may terminate it (s. 6(3)) and in addition the court may make an order terminating it in specific named circumstances and if it is deemed "just and reasonable" so to do (s.6(4)).

Saskatchewan has no provision for a release.

Alberta's provisions are rather elaborate. The wife must take an affidavit that she is aware that she is giving up her dower rights and is doing so voluntarily (Form E), and then she must sign the release (Form D) which can be registered in the Land Titles Office. However, as long as the land has not been transferred to a third party, she can repent and file a caveat which restores her dower rights (ss. 7 and 8).

In addition, she may make an agreement with her spouse (e.g. in a separation agreement) releasing her dower rights. She must make an acknowledgment as in the case of a consent but it must be made before a solicitor who is not acting for the husband (s. 9(2) and Form C).

British Columbia does not provide for a release but does provide for "abandonment" which is similar (s. 11). The wife can sign a simple statement of abandonment (Form D). She must acknowledge it before an officer as she would in the case of a consent, and then application (Form E) can be made to the registrar to cancel the homestead entry that is on the register.

4. The Consequences of a Disposition Made in Contravention of the Statute

This has been the most serious and difficult question under the homestead laws. Their object is to protect the wife against dispositions of the home without her consent. On the other hand, buyers, mortgagees and lessees should be able to count on the validity of dispositions to them. The balancing of these two interests has not been easy. Most of the Acts have a fairly broad curative section but sometimes there is uncertainty as to whether it applies. Questions like these have arisen under one or more of the Acts. Is the disposition voidable, or is it void? If void, is it void only as against the wife's interest or is it totally void? Can the buyer raise the defect? Can the husband, who may have been responsible for the non-compliance, raise it to escape from his transaction? When, if ever, can husband or wife be estopped from raising the non-compliance? This account will describe the relevant provisions in the various statutes and the leading decisions that have had to grope with these questions.

(1) Manitoba

The Dower Act begins by saying that a disposition is "invalid and ineffective" unless the wife consents (s. 3(1)). However there are two curative sections. A certificate of acknowledgment is conclusive except where the person acquiring the interest in the homestead had actual knowledge of the untruth of the statements in the certificate (s. 8(4)). In the case of a false affidavit (e.g. that the land is not the homestead) the disposition is valid unless the person taking under it had actual knowledge of the untruth or participated in fraud (s. 8(7)). The person (usually the wife) alleging such knowledge or fraud must prove it.[71]

In one case, the husband mortgaged the homestead. He forged the wife's consent and then obtained a certificate of acknowledgment from an officer who was also the agent of the mortgagee. A divided court held the certificate to be conclusive. The officer's knowledge of the non-compliance was not to be imputed to the mortgagee. This debatable decision [72] was distinguished in a case where the wife did not know what she was consenting to and did not sign apart from her husband, and the officer who took her acknowledgment was agent of the grantee and his knowledge that the certificate was untruthful was attributed to his principal. The transaction was set aside.[73]

The next case is one in which an agreement for sale of the homestead was made without any pretence of a consent by the wife. A week later the buyer withdrew from the agreement because of the absence of consent. Thereupon the wife purported to consent. The Court of Appeal held for the buyer. He withdrew before the wife consented so the agreement never became valid or effective.[74]

A later case held that an interim agreement for sale was a disposition so, in the absence of the wife's written consent, was void. Her willingness to consent was immaterial. The purchaser should not have to wait to find out whether the wife will execute the consent.[75]

What is the position where the wife signs the consent but never makes an acknowledgment so that there is no certificate of acknowledgment by an officer? A case in 1980 holds that there is no valid disposition.[76] A still more recent case is perhaps surprising because it goes far in the opposite direction. The owner and his wife signed an "acceptance" of an offer to purchase. She never signed the form of consent set out in the Dower Act, and of course there was no certificate by an officer. However the trial judge held that the statutory form of consent is only permissive and that the wife's signature to the agreement was adequate.[77] This case can be better understood in the light of recent cases from Alberta which will be discussed later, though even under those cases a mere signature to the agreement as distinct from the statutory consent would not serve to make the agreement binding.

(2) Saskatchewan

Saskatchewan's Homesteads Act has never spelled out the consequences of a disposition made in non-compliance with the formalities laid down in the Act. Nowhere is it stated that the transaction is null or void or invalid or ineffective. One leading case, however, says "It is clear that as against a non-consenting wife every . . . instrument intended to convey an interest is invalid and void"[78] and her apparent acquiescence in the transaction does not create an estoppel.[79]

On the other hand, Saskatchewan recognizes a situation in which the transaction though not enforceable is yet valid. At least it is not a nullity. In an early case the buyer repudiated an agreement for sale three years after it had been made. He did so only when the vendor brought action on overdue instalments. The trial judge gave the wife 30 days to comply with the statutory requirement. She complied. The Court of Appeal upheld this judgment. Two judges emphasized that the wife was in fact willing to consent at the time of the agreement; thus it was not a total nullity, though it was unenforceable unless she were later to give formal consent. This concept of an inchoate or unenforceable agreement that is not yet a nullity is contrary to Manitoba's law, as described above. In the case just described, the other two judges based their concurrence on estoppel of the purchaser. He had farmed the land for three years and did not raise non-compliance until he was sued.[80]

The concept of an unenforceable but valid disposition was accepted in a recent case.[81]

Assuming that there has been a direct violation of the Act, such as a false affidavit or a false certificate by an officer, then the validity of the transaction depends on two curative sections. The first one (s. 7(3)) says that the person taking under an instrument is not bound to inquire into the truthfulness of an affidavit or of a certificate and if the instrument purports to comply with the Act it is valid "save as provided in s. 11". That section says that knowledge on the part of the transferee, mortgagee, etc. that the land is the homestead and the owner has a wife who is not a party "shall be fraud", and the transaction or certificate of title issued thereon may be cancelled.

There have been a number of cases on false affidavits. Section 11 applies only where the wife is not a party to the instrument. It applies of course to the case of a false affidavit.[82] The result depends on whether buyer or mortgagee or lessee knew the owner was married and that the land was his home.[83] In *Prudential Trust Co.* v. *Olsen*[84] the husband transferred oil rights in the homestead. He swore the land was not his homestead. The transferee assigned the oil rights to a bona fide purchaser. The Supreme Court held that this purchaser was entitled to the benefit of s. 7(3), so the transaction stood.

Several cases have had to do with serious flaws in the officer's certificate of acknowledgment.

A leading case holds the transaction invalid where the certificate was false.[85] A daughter signed the "declaration by wife" and the officer who signed the certificate never saw the wife. Thus the oil lease was a nullity even though the wife did not question the transaction for three years. She was not estopped from raising the fact of the false certificate.

Where the officer was disqualified from taking the certificate, the defect was cured where the purchaser did not know of it.[86] It was cured, too, where the officer who signed the certificate respecting an oil lease had never seen the wife but the lessee later assigned to a company which was bona fide.[87]

There are cases, too, where an otherwise fatal non-compliance is cured by the issue of a new certificate of title so that the indefeasibility provisions of the Land Titles Act come into play, e.g. where the wife signed the declaration but the officer was disqualified from taking the certificate;[88] and where the husband had taken a false affidavit but the transferee had in turn transferred the land to a bona fide purchaser.[89]

A recent case shows the new trend toward upholding the transaction where the wife in fact consented even though the requirements as to formalities were not met. In that case the spouses were joint owners. Both signed an agreement for sale but the wife made no declaration and of course there was no certificate. After a long review of the cases, the court held that the sale was binding on the wife.[90] This case shows the influence of *Senstad* v. *Makus* from Alberta, to be discussed later.

(3) Alberta

There is no need to examine the cases prior to 1948 when the Dower Act underwent a major revision. There had been great difficulty in deciding the effect of a disposition in which there was a false affidavit or no formal consent and acknowledgment. The original Act of 1917 said the disposition was null and void. In 1919 an amendment said it was null and void only so far as it affected the wife's interest. In 1926 the provision was restored to its original form. Then in 1942 an amendment employed the emphatic if redundant phrase, "absolutely null and void for all purposes". Nonetheless the Appellate Division in dealing with a false affidavit held that a subsequent transfer from the original transferee was valid.[91]

There was a curative section which applied to a sale. As long as the wife had given her written consent and the purchaser had performed part of the consideration, the wife was deemed to have consented in accordance with the Act.[92] This cured many defective dispositions but did not cover the case of a false affidavit.

The 1948 Act was clearly intended to abandon any attempt to make a disposition null and void. The explanatory note makes this clear.[93] The new curative section (s. 5(3)) deals only with defective execution of consent or acknowledgment and scarcely qualifies as a curative section.

A completely new provision, and one unique in the western provinces, gives the wife an action for half the purchase price or value when the disposition has resulted in registration of title to the homestead in a third person (s. 11).

The new Act did not abandon the old formalities. They were still required. A disposition without consent was forbidden, and a married person who made a disposition in contravention of the requirement of consent was guilty of an offence (s. 2). Thus the policy was still to require consent. However it is doubtful that the Legislature really considered these questions: What is the status of an agreement for sale prior to the issue of a new title in the purchaser? What is the status of a mortgage or lease or oil lease? Can the wife ever be estopped from raising the fact of non-compliance? Can the husband who made the forbidden disposition be estopped from invoking his own improper act? In the years since 1948 the courts have had great difficulty with all these questions. In the first case to go to the Supreme Court of Canada the transaction was an exchange of homesteads. Neither spouse had given formal consent and of course there was no acknowledgment. Both parties had overlooked the Dower Act. As the case went through the courts there was a remarkable division of opinion as to the effect of the 1948 Act and no conclusive opinion.[94] The next case to reach the Supreme Court was *Meduk* v. *Soja*.[95] The wife was owner and under the 1948 Act the husband had dower rights. She made an agreement to sell the homestead without obtaining her husband's consent. The Supreme Court held that the transaction was prohibited by the statute and was "ineffective". The judgment does not say in words that the agreement for sale was void but such is its effect. Neither the vendor nor her spouse was estopped from raising the statute.

Up to this point there had been no case dealing with a mortgage to which the spouse had not consented pursuant to the 1948 Act. To hold the mortgage a nullity is a drastic sanction to impose on the mortgagee who has advanced the mortgage money. However, the Supreme Court held that where the wife did not give her consent to a mortgage granted by her husband, it was void.[96] The judgment expresses doubt as to whether the wife could ever be estopped from raising non-compliance.

In recent years many vendors have tried to escape from an agreement for sale of the homestead because they could get a better price on a rising market. Too often the Dower Act, like the Statute of Frauds, has been used as an instrument of fraud. A purchaser who raises estoppel, even as against the vendor himself, does not succeed.[97] The only judgment that holds the vendor to be estopped is *Palinko* v. *Bower*.[98]

In referring to the number of cases invoking the Dower Act as a reason for refusal by the vendor to perform, McDermid J.A. said:

> One is usually left with the feeling that the real reason is that on a rising market for real estate the vendor's wife with perhaps the encouragement of the vendor feels that a higher price may be obtained and that the vendor and his wife are 'welshing' on the deal. . . . The remedy for such actions however lies with the legislature and not the courts.[99]

However the Supreme Court of Canada did find a remedy, at least in the situation where the wife signed a consent but never made the acknowledgment before an officer. The Alberta courts had held in these circumstances that a disposition was ineffective; that the certificate of acknowledgment was just as essential as the formal consent.[100] However in the significant decision of the Supreme Court in *Senstad* v. *Makus*,[101] Martland J. carefully analyzed the provisions of the Act and pointed out that the consent provision (s. 4) is quite separate from the one requiring acknowledgment (s. 5) and that it is only a disposition without consent that is prohibited (s. 2). What then is the role of the requirement of acknowledgment? Martland J. answered as follows:

> In my opinion the purpose of the requirement of acknowledgment in the present Act is to prevent the spouse from challenging the validity of his or her consent. If a disposition of the homestead is made, carrying the written consent of the spouse but there is no acknowledgment, or an improper acknowledgment, the validity of the consent and therefore of the disposition is open to attack on the ground that the spouse was not aware of the dower rights conferred by the Act, did not appreciate the effect of the consent, or did not give a free and voluntary consent without compulsion. The written consent is prima facie valid, but it may be attacked on any of these grounds if there is not a s. 6 [now s. 5] acknowledgment.
>
> An acknowledgment, as evidence that the consent was freely and voluntarily given, with knowledge of the rights involved, is required to enable the registrar to register a transfer under the provisions of s. 7 [now s. 6]. In this way he is assured, before registering the transfer, that there has been a consent to the agreement for sale which is not subject to possible attack.

This case has done much to remove the non-meritorious defence of lack of acknowledgment.[102] However *Senstad* does not cover the case where the wife merely signs an agreement for sale and does not sign the consent form.[103]

One point that has arisen in all prairie provinces, and especially in Alberta, in connection with the sale of farmland, is this. An agreement for sale covers the homestead and other land as well. If there is no compliance with the Dower Act the sale of the homestead is ineffective. Can the vendor obtain specific performance of the agreement for sale so far as the other land is concerned, with an abatement of the price? The Saskatchewan Court of Appeal answered in the affirmative many years ago.[104] In Alberta in recent years a similar rule has sometimes been applied.[105] In one case, however, the Appellate Division said that neither party intended the agreement would be enforceable for only part of the lands.[106] In another, the court said specific performance should not be ordered where the land to be transferred would be much less than that covered by the agreement.[107]

What about damages in lieu of specific performance? As far as the homestead is concerned it has been held that the award of such damages would subvert the policy of the homestead legislation.[108] However in connection with other land included in the agreement for sale, it is proper to award damages.[109]

The last point to note on Alberta's Act has to do with the cause of action for damages in the amount of one-half of the purchase price which the Act confers on the wife when the husband has transferred the homestead to a third party without obtaining the wife's consent (s. 11). There have been a few such actions.[110] The Act provides that if the judgment is not paid then the court can order payment from the Assurance Fund (ss. 13–17). A literal reading of the Act is that on the issue of a new title the wife's dower right is converted into an action for half the purchase price. However in one case the husband took an affidavit that he had no wife and transferred the lands to himself and a friend. Just before he died he and his wife brought action to set aside the new title. The action succeeded.[111] Then in a recent case the wife signed the dower consent but did so on the husband's insistence and in his presence and without understanding it. The land was transferred to the buyer and then to the defendants who, as the court found, knew that the original vendor and his wife were living on the land. The wife succeeded in an action to set aside the two transfers.[112] Then there is a case in which the husband had transferred the homestead to himself and another, having sworn he had no wife. The wife obtained judgment against her husband's estate and then when it was not paid she succeeded in an application for payment out of the insurance fund. This is all in accordance with the Dower Act. However the judgment says that the wife had a choice between suing for damages and having the transfer set aside.[113] It is hard to find in the Act any right to elect or to set aside the transfer.

(4) British Columbia

The Land (Wife Protection) Act says that when a homestead entry has been made on the title, every disposition is "null and void for all purposes unless made with the consent in writing of the wife". The curative section (s. 10(1)) is almost the same as Alberta's former section, mentioned above. There is of course no need to provide for an affidavit that the man is not married or that the land is not his homestead. That the man is married and that the land is his homestead is self-evident from the "entry". There have been very few cases in which the wife challenged the disposition. In one case the husband made an interim agreement to sell the land before the wife had the homestead entry made on the register. The interim agreement was a disposition so the subsequent entry was ineffective and the court discharged it pursuant to s. 14.[114] In another case the wife, not having made a homestead entry, brought action to set aside an agreement for sale which her husband had made without her knowledge. Needless to say she failed. The Act, unlike those of the prairie provinces, gives no protection prior to the making of a homestead entry.[115] There is no reported case in which the wife alleged that her consent was not genuine or that the certificate of acknowledgment was false.

5. The Interest of the Widow in the Homestead after the Husband's Death

These provisions vary from province to province. In Manitoba, the Act simply says that the wife is entitled to a life estate in the homestead, just as if her husband had left her a life estate by will.[116] However, an important decision says her interest is less than the statute seems to say. On the husband's death his executor brought proceedings to determine whether (a) the widow's life interest was prior to and free of claims of creditors and (b) whether she was entitled to possess and enjoy a life estate in the homestead without the consent of the executor. The Court of Appeal held against the widow on both questions. The life estate does not vest on death and she has no right to possess the home until the executor permits her.[117] This judgment has attracted criticism.[118]

Saskatchewan, in contrast to Manitoba, has never in terms given the widow a life interest. The Homesteads Act says (s. 12) that the homestead vests in the personal representative but this vesting is subject to the Exemptions Act which, it will be recalled, exempts the homestead from creditors while necessary for the widow's support (s. 6). Under the Homesteads Act the personal representative is deemed to be the owner and the widow to be his wife, so that her consent to a disposition is required just as it was in her husband's lifetime (s. 12).

Although the widow's right to possession is not explicitly set out, it has been held that she has that right as against the personal representative.[119] One judge made this comment: "May I express the hope that the law officers of the Crown will give consideration to the state of the statute law governing the right of widows and children in the homestead and other exempted property. The rights of this important group should be accurately defined and not left to implication as at present."[120]

In Alberta, the Dower Act defines "dower rights" to include "the right of the surviving spouse to a life estate in the homestead of the deceased married person" (s. 1(*d*)(iv)). A devolution on death is postponed to a vested estate for life in the surviving spouse (s. 18). These clear and categorical provisions are an improvement on those in the other two provinces. They have not caused difficulty.[121]

Alberta has had since 1926 a unique provision which gives to the widow a life estate in the personal property of her late husband that is exempt from execution (s. 1(*d*)(v) and s. 23). Chief Justice Harvey once said that this was enacted "in total disregard of the old theory that there could be no life estate in personal property".[122]

As for British Columbia, the Land (Wife Protection) Act says (s. 4) that on the death of the owner of the homestead it becomes vested in the personal representative,[123] but that notwithstanding any testamentary disposition or rule of law, "the personal representative shall hold the homestead in trust for an estate for the life of the married man's wife." This provision has produced no litigation.

6. Conclusion

In the past four years every common law province has passed an Act on the subject of matrimonial property, including the home.[124] In each of the western provinces the main provision dealing with the matrimonial home is one enabling the court to grant exclusive possession to either spouse. This is in addition to and not in derogation of rights under the homestead laws. In

Manitoba the Marital Property Act[125] so states; likewise the Matrimonial Property Act of Saskatchewan,[126] the Matrimonial Property Act of Alberta,[127] and British Columbia's Family Relations Act.[128]

In the eastern provinces however the changes have been much more substantial. Newfoundland has created joint ownership of the matrimonial home[129] while every other eastern province has adopted in principle the main feature of the western homestead laws—the need for spousal consent to disposition of the homestead. Indeed the provisions for consent and affidavits are clearly borrowed from the prairie legislation. In Ontario "no spouse shall dispose of or encumber any interest in a matrimonial home" without the consent of, or a release by, the other spouse or without a court order. The court can set aside a forbidden disposition, unless the curative provision applies. There is also provision for affidavits like those in the prairie provinces.[130] The new statutes in the three Maritime provinces are much the same and appear to be modelled on Ontario's.[131]

An Alberta judge once said of that province's Dower Act, "there may be some who think that this is an import we could very well have done without."[132] Certainly many have thought that the dower rights in Alberta are inconsistent with a system of land titles which that province has always had. Yet they remain entrenched and have spread to eastern Canada, at least in the aspect of consent to a disposition. As long as a fair balance is struck between the spouse's interest in the home and the interests of one who bona fide acquires an interest in the land from the owner, such provisions are entirely in keeping with the trend toward protecting the wife in connection with the matrimonial home.

Notes

1 See *Ost* v. *Turnbull* (1977), 4 Alta. L.R. (2d) 358 at 362–3 (C.A.), for a discussion of these two meanings of homestead; also *Re Barker,* [1946] 2 W.W.R. 543 at 546 (Man. Surr. Ct.).

2 Haskins, "Homesteads Exemptions" (1950), 63 Harv. L. Rev. 1289.

3 40 Am. Jurisp. (2d), "Homesteads", pp. 109–275.

4 Haskins, "The Development of Common Law Dower" (1948–49), 62 Har. L. Rev. 42.

5 Real Property Act, 1885 (Man.), c. 8, s. 24.

6 Territories Real Property Act, 1886, c. 26, s. 8.

7 He also thought that Alberta's homestead law was in conflict with those principles: *Re McLeod,* [1929] 3 W.W.R. 241 at 242 (Alta. C.A.); *Essery* v. *Essery,* [1947] 2 W.W.R. 1044 at 1048 (Alta. C.A.).

8 R.S.B.C. 1924, c. 71.

9 Administration Act Amendment Act, 1925 (B.C.), c. 2, s. 5.

10 Administration of Justice Act, 1880–81 (Man.), c. 37, s. 85.

11 Exemptions Ordinance, 1884, No. 28.

12 Homestead Ordinance, R.S.B.C. 1877, c. 84.

13 See Dunlop, *Creditor-Debtor Law in Canada* (1981), pp. 318 and 331–345.

14 C.C.S.M., c. J10, s. 13.

15 R.S.S. 1978, c. E-14, ss. 2(1) [am. 1979, c. 69, s. 14], 10, 11.

16 R.S.A. 1980 c. E-15, s. 1(*j*), (*k*).

17 *Re Burns and Lock* (1977), 4 Alta. L.R. (2d) 258 (T.D.).

18 *Re Hetherington* (1910), 3 Sask. L.R. 232; *Re Burns and Lock,* note 17, *supra*.

19 *Re Finley* (1977), 4 Alta. L.R. (2d) 47 (Dist. Ct.).

20 *Mymryk* v. *Can. Permanent Trust Co.*

(1968), 63 W.W.R. 313 (Man. Q.B.)

21 *Crichton* v. *Zelenitsky,* [1946] 2 W.W.R. 209 at 242 (Man. C.A.).

22 *Re Conlin* (1914), 7 Alta. L.R. 437 (S.C.).

23 *Re Ferguson* (1957), 23 W.W.R. 521 (Alta. S.C.).

24 R.S.B.C. 1979, c. 173.

25 Dunlop, note 13, *supra,* p. 318.

26 *Re Ripstein,* [1927] 3 W.W.R. 791, affirmed [1929] 1 W.W.R. 788 (Man. C.A.).

27 *Packer* v. *Packer* (1959), 31 W.W.R. 22 (Man. Q.B.); *Seroy* v. *Seroy* (1964), 50 W.W.R. 65 (Man. C.A.); *Re Empey,* [1979] 2 W.W.R. 559 (Man. Surr. Ct.).

28 *Re Skeele,* [1923] 1 W.W.R. 117 (Sask. K.B.).

29 *Caryk* v. *Kiefer,* [1922] 1 W.W.R. 281 (Sask. K.B.).

30 *Re Cherniak,* [1930] 1 W.W.R. 676, affirmed 25 Alta. L.R. 44 (C.A.); *Can. Credit Men's Trust Assn.* v. *Umbel,* [1931] 3 W.W.R. 145 (Alta.).

31 *Read* v. *Read,* [1950] 2 W.W.R. 812 (B.C. C.A.), reversing on this point but affirming on other grounds (*sub nom, re Wife's Protection Act*), [1950] 2 W.W.R. 1275; see also *Price* v. *Price,* [1949] 2 W.W.R. 506 (B.C. S.C.).

32 This section deals with the current Acts in each of the western provinces: The Dower Act, C.C.S.M., c. D100; The Homesteads Act, R.S.S. 1978, c. H-5; The Dower Act, R.S.A. 1980, c. D-38; The Land (Wife Protection) Act, R.S.B.C. 1979, c. 223. In some instances the number of a section has been changed recently so will differ from the number referred to in older cases.

33 This Act is much more than homestead legislation. It provides that the widow has an election between taking under her husband's will and taking her share as on an intestacy.

34 The words "and his wife" were added after *Re Dower Act; Re Rodick and Rodick* (1958), 24 W.W.R. 356 (Man. Co. Ct.).

35 For a discussion of "parcel" see *Ost* v. *Turnbull* (1977), 4 Alta. L.R. (2d) 358 (C.A.).

36 On the meaning of occupancy see *Re Gale and Gale* (1962), 39 W.W.R. 246 (Sask. C.A.).

37 *Nat. Trust Co.* v. *Greengard,* [1929] 3 W.W.R. 363 (Man. K.B.).

38 *Alta. Housing Corp.* v. *Nawrot* (1980), 35 A.R. 53 (Q.B.).

39 *Ost* v. *Turnbull,* note 35, *supra.*

40 *Re Homesteads Act: Re Medynski Caveat* (1954), 12 W.W.R. 368 (Sask. Q.B.); compare *Hyder* v. *Edgar* (1979), 10 Alta. L.R. (2d) 17 (Dist. Ct.), and *Re Barker,* [1946] 2 W.W.R. 543 (Man. Surr. Ct.).

41 See Hughes, "Reform of the Dower Act" (1978–79), 9 Man. L.J. 393 at 396.

42 Condominium Property Act, R.S.S. 1978, c. C-2, ss. 44, 45.

43 Condominium Property Act, R.S.A. 1980, c. C-22, ss. 67, 68.

44 Condominium Act, R.S.B.C. 1979, c. 62, s. 112.

45 *Birkeland* v. *Birkeland,* [1971] 5 W.W.R. 662 (Sask. Q.B.); see also *Audoorn* v. *Audoorn,* [1935] 2 W.W.R. 362 at 368–9 (Sask. C.A.).

46 *Re McLeod,* [1929] 3 W.W.R. 241 (Alta. C.A.), affirming [1929] 2 W.W.R. 252.

47 *Elniski* v. *Herchuk* (1978), 8 Alta. L.R. (2d) 97 (T.D.).

48 *Rigby* v. *Rigby* (1922), 17 Alta. L.R. 1 (C.A.).

49 *Jackman* v. *Jackman* (1958), 25 W.W.R. 131, reversed on other grounds, [1959] S.C.R. 702.

50 *Keller* v. *Schultz,* [1920] 3 W.W.R. 188 (C.A.).

51 *Audoorn* v. *Audoorn,* note 45, *supra.*

52 *Proskurniak* v. *Sawchuk* (1960), 30 W.W.R. 407 (Alta. S.C.).

53 *Heiden* v. *Huck* (1971), 5 R.F.L. 264 (Alta. T.D.).

54 *Anderson* v. *Anderson* (1980), 18 A.R. 308 (T.D.).

55 *Clark* v. *Clark* (1965), 54 W.W.R. 744 (Alta. C.A.). In the result the wife's action failed, for the fifth judge found against her on another ground.

56 *Weinberger* v. *Weinberger* (1975), 20 R.F.L. 150 (Sask. Q.B.).

57 *Clark* v. *Clark,* note 55, *supra.*

58 *Toth* v. *Kancz,* [1975] W.W.R. 90 (Sask. Q.B.). Compare *Earl* v. *Earl,* [1979] 6 W.W.R. 600 (Alta. Q.B.).

59 *Wimmer* v. *Wimmer,* [1947] 2 W.W.R. 249 (Man. C.A.).
60 *Robertson* v. *Robertson* (1951), 1 W.W.R. 183 (Alta. S.C.); *contra McWilliam* v. *McWilliam* (1961), 31 W.W.R. 480, affirmed on other grounds 34 W.W.R. 476 (Alta. C.A.).
61 C.C.S.M., c. L90, s. 19(2).
62 R.S.A. 1980, c. L-8, s. 21(1).
63 *Scott* v. *Cresswell,* [1975] 3 W.W.R. 193 at 222–3 (Alta. C.A.).
64 *Anderson* v. *Anderson* (1978), 18 A.R. 308 (T.D.), indicates that he retains his dower rights but *Delves* v. *Delves,* Alberta Decisions, May 1977, is to the contrary.
65 The forms for the prairie provinces are set out in O'Brien's *Encyclopedia of Forms,* 10th ed. (1971): Vol. 7: "Conveyancing and Mortgages". For Manitoba the forms are #259–260; for Saskatchewan #246–248; for Alberta #228–230.
66 Form A.
67 There is a special provision for an additional certificate by a solicitor where the instrument is a transfer to a mortgagee or is a quit claim deed (s. 5(2)).
68 Reg. 470/81, Alberta Gazette, January 15, 1982, p. 1449.
69 Alberta's is the only Act which has a definition of dower rights (s. 1(*d*)).
70 E.g., *Re Wife's Protection Act* (1962), 40 W.W.R. 315 (B.C. S.C.).
71 *McKinnon* v. *Smith,* [1925] 3 W.W.R. 290 (Man. C.A.); *Reep* v. *Shuckett* [1955], 15 W.W.R. 375 (Man.).
72 *Chudyj* v. *Can. Permanent Mtge. Corp.,* [1937] 2 W.W.R. 225 (Man. C.A.).
73 *Brown* v. *Prairie Leaseholds Ltd.* (1953), 9 W.W.R. 577, affirmed 12 W.W.R. 464 (Man. C.A.), leave to appeal to Supreme Court of Canada refused 13 W.W.R. 40.
74 *Wall* v. *Dyck,* [1950] 1 W.W.R. 699 (Man. C.A.).
75 *Rose* v. *Dever* (1972), 7 R.F.L. 118, affirmed [1973] 6 W.W.R. 672 (S.C.C.).
76 *Vandermeulin* v. *Wieler,* [1980] 4 W.W.R. 164 (Man. Q.B.).
77 *Westward Farms* v. *Cadieux,* [1981] 3 W.W.R. 673 at 681–86 (Man. Q.B.). This case was reversed by the Court of Appeal, [1982] 5 W.W.R. 1.
78 *Friess* v. *Imperial Oil Ltd.* (1954), 12 W.W.R. 151 at 155 (Sask. C.A.).
79 *Guzak* v. *McEwan* (1965), 52 W.W.R. 335 (Sask. Q.B.).
80 *Nielsen* v. *Jenewein,* [1924] 2 W.W.R. 696 (Sask. C.A.).
81 *T.D. Bank* v. *Gordon,* [1981] 5 W.W.R. 235 (Sask. C.A.). The defendant spouses were joint owners. Both signed an equitable mortgage but there was no compliance with the various statutory formalities. The land had been sold under a first mortgage and the dispute was over the surplus remaining. The plaintiff was held entitled to the surplus.
82 *Hulowski* v. *Hulowski,* [1945] 3 W.W.R. 753 (Sask. C.A.).
83 Compare *Re Scott,* [1942] 2 W.W.R. 485 (Sask. K.B.), with *Farmers Mutual Petroleum Ltd.* v. *Jackson* (1956), 19 W.W.R. 625 (Sask. C.A.).
84 [1960] S.C.R. 227.
85 *Friess* v. *Imperial Oil Ltd.,* note 78, *supra.*
86 *Lavoie* v. *Marchildon* (1953), 9 W.W.R. 263 (Sask. Q.B.).
87 *Bonkowski* v. *Rose* (1955), 16 W.W.R. 481 (Sask. C.A.), approved in *Prudential Trust Co.* v. *Forseth,* [1960] S.C.R. 210.
88 *Hulowski* v. *Hulowski,* note 82, *supra.*
89 *Deptuch* v. *Kurmey* (1964), 48 W.W.R. 45 (Sask. Q.B.).
90 *Suppes* v. *Wellings,* [1982] 4 W.W.R. 106 (Sask. Q.B.).
91 *Essery* v. *Essery,* [1947] 2 W.W.R. 1044 (Alta. C.A.).
92 *McColl Frontenac Oil Co.* v. *Hamilton,* [1953] 1 S.C.R. 127.
93 It is set out in Bowker, "Reform of the Law of Dower in Alberta" (1955–1961), 1 Alta. Law Rev. 501 at 505. That article describes the early cases in detail.
94 *Pinsky* v. *Wass,* [1953] 1 S.C.R. 399.
95 [1958] S.C.R. 167.
96 *B.A. Oil Co.* v. *Kos,* [1964] S.C.R. 167.
97 *Martens* v. *Burden,* [1974] 3 W.W.R. 522 (Alta. T.D.).
98 [1975] 1 W.W.R. 756, reversed [1976] 4 W.W.R. 118 (Alta. C.A.), on another ground, and refraining from considera-

tion of this point.

99 *DeJong* v. *Gechter* (1976), 27 R.F.L. 31 at 39–40, reversed [1978] 2 S.C.R. 62.

100 *Senstad* v. *Makus* (1976), 26 R.F.L. 199 (Alta. C.A).

101 [1978] 2 S.C.R. 44.

102 Other Supreme Court cases are *DeJong* v. *Gechter,* note 99, *supra,* and *McFarland* v. *Hauser,* [1979] 1 S.C.R. 337.

103 *Senstad* distinguishes and does not overrule *McColm* v. *Belter* (1975), 18 R.F.L. 191 (Alta. C.A.), where the wife signed a memorandum of agreement for sale but did not sign a consent form. See *Hyder* v. *Edgar* (1979), 10 Alta. L.R. (2d) 17 (Dist. Ct.).

104 *Halldorson* v. *Holizki,* [1919] 3 W.W.R. 83 (Alta. C.A.), affirming [1919] 1 W.W.R. 472.

105 E.g., *Martens* v. *Burden,* [1974] 3 W.W.R. 522 (Alta. T.D.); *Farkash* v. *Henningsen* (1981), 32 A.R. 436 (Q.B.).

106 *Senstad* v. *Makus* (1976), 26 R.F.L. 199, reversed on other grounds [1978] 2 S.C.R. 44.

107 *Ost* v. *Turnbull* (1977), 4 Alta. L.R. (2d) 358 (C.A.). See also *McKenzie* v. *Hiscock,* [1967] S.C.R. 781, from Saskatchewan.

108 *McKenzie* v. *Hiscock,* note 107, *supra; Gostevskyh* v. *Klassen* (1980), 21 A.R. 170 (C.A.).

109 *McKenzie* v. *Hiscock,* note 107, *supra*. This case does not mention the rule in *Bain* v. *Fothergill* (1874), L.R. 7 H.L. 158. On the applicability of that rule compare *Ost* v. *Turnbull,* note 107, *supra,* with *Westward Farms Ltd*. v. *Cadieux,* [1981] 3 W.W.R. 673 at 700 (Man. Q.B.).

110 See *Clark* v. *Clark* (1965), 54 W.W.R. 744 (Alta. C.A.). There the action failed because the parties were divorced before judgment.

111 *Shopsky* v. *Danyliuk* (1959), 30 W.W.R. 647 (Alta. T.D.).

112 *Prpich* v. *Komisar,* [1981] 3 W.W.R. 757 (Alta. Q.B.).

113 *Kromm* v. *A.G. Alta*. (1964), 47 W.W.R. 172 (Alta. S.C.).

114 *Re Wife's Protection Act* (1951), 3 W.W.R. 509 (B.C. S.C.).

115 *Rousseau* v. *Rousseau* (1956), 19 W.W.R. 237 (B.C. S.C.).

116 Section 14(1). She has an election whether to take under her husband's will or to take one-half of his estate together with her life interest in the homestead (ss. 15(1) and 17(1)).

117 *Crichton* v. *Zelenitsky,* [1946] 2 W.W.R. 209 (Man. C.A.).

118 *Re Kusy* (1953), 9 W.W.R. 675 (Man. Q.B.); Hughes, "Reform of the Dower Act: Rights of Widows" (1978–79), 9 Man. L.J. 393 at 396–8.

119 *Re Thomson,* [1942] 3 W.W.R. 46 (Sask. C.A.).

120 *Re Wenet,* [1949] 2 W.W.R. 85 at 93 (Sask. K.B.).

121 See *Proskurniak* v. *Sawchuk* (1960), 30 W.W.R. 407 (Alta. T.D.), for a discussion of the wife's rights both before and after her husband's death.

122 *Re McLeod,* [1929] 3 W.W.R. 241 at 242 (Alta. C.A.). In any case it has never been repealed. Its practical value is hard to appraise. There are no reported cases on this enactment.

123 This is by reference to the Estate Administration Act, R.S.B.C. 1979, c. 114, s. 90(1).

124 McClean, "Matrimonial Property-Canadian Common Law Style" (1981), 31 U.T.L.J. 363.

125 C.C.S.M., c. M45, s. 24. See also the Family Maintenance Act, C.C.S.M., c. F20, s. 32.

126 1979 (Sask), c. M-6.1, s. 16.

127 R.S.A. 1980, c. M-9, s. 28.

128 R.S.B.C. 1979, c. 121, s. 77(7).

129 Matrimonial Property Act, 1979 (Nfld.), c. 32, s. 6.

130 Family Law Reform Act, R.S.O. 1980, c. 152, s. 42. *Bergmann* v. *Burns* (1980), 36 O.R. (2d) 4 (H.C.) indicates that the new Ontario legislation will create problems similar to those experienced in the prairie provinces.

131 New Brunswick, Marital Property Act, 1980, c. M-1.1, s. 19; Nova Scotia, Matrimonial Property Act, 1980, c. 9, s. 8; Prince Edward Island, Family Law Reform Act, 1978, c. 6, s. 42.

132 *Robertson* v. *Robertson* (1951), 1 W.W.R. 183 (Alta.).

1982

A Light Hearted View of the History and Traditions of the Legal Profession of Alberta

Unpublished

This was an address given at a luncheon on the occasion of the annual mid-winter meeting of the Alberta Branch of the Canadian Bar Association held in Calgary in January 1982. It was held in the Convention Centre with a large crowd in attendance.

The organizers asked for something "light and relevant." Generally, the talk deals with anecdotes concerning former lawyers and judges, in particular Art Smith of Calgary and Judge Ives. It went on to deal with territorial judges, though time ran out before that topic was fully covered.

This talk will be in two parts: first, some personal recollections from the early thirties, and second, anecdotes about some territorial and early provincial judges.

Fifty years ago the depression was deepening. While the legislature was passing acts to relieve the debtor (especially the farmer and home-owner) law firms were engaged in collecting debts, foreclosing mortgages and making seizures of goods. Collection agencies were busy. Their routine was this—first a courteous letter beginning "Dear Mr. X." The second was "Dear Sir" scolding the debtor for ignoring the first letter and demanding immediate payment. The third lectured the debtor on the importance of keeping his credit good and then gave hints as to unpleasant consequences and sometimes made a direct threat to sue.

One farmer received the three letters from an Edmonton agency. Replying to the third letter, he described the drought, early frost and 40¢ wheat and added, "You can't get blood out of a stone." The agency replied in these words, "You have the wrong proverb. Remember, no matter how hard you squeeze the lemon there's always another drop."

Another agency had an imposing letterhead. It included the words "Docket number" which doubtless was designed to make the debtor feel the agency had something to do with the criminal court. As if this were not enough, there appeared below the agency's name the following, "We collect—peaceably if possible, forcibly if necessary—but we collect."

Another letterhead belonged to a man who spent his time on behalf of farmers who had applied to have their debts reduced and extended under the Farmers' Creditors Arrangement Act. That Act, passed in 1934, began by describing the depressed state of agriculture, the inability of farmers to pay their debts and the need to keep them on the land in the national interest. It set up machinery, the most important part being a Board of Review for each province, with three members including a Supreme Court Judge as chairman. The Alberta Board was busy until after World War II. There was no need for a debtor to have a lawyer or other representative before the Board of Review, though creditors sometimes had a lawyer. The man to whom I have referred appeared continually in Edmonton for a long period of time on behalf of the farmer. His letterhead said this: "Not a lawyer, but the farmer's friend."

For the remainder of my reminiscence, may I mention one judge, Mr. Justice Ives and one lawyer, A.L. "Art" Smith. I have selected them, not because they came from Calgary but because I think they are interesting figures to all Alberta lawyers.

Ives was appointed to the Supreme Court in 1914 and sat for thirty years, the last two years as Chief Justice of the Trial Division. His father was a rancher near Macleod. He came West as a boy before the railway reached Alberta. At that time the main route was up the Missouri River to Fort Benton and then by muletrain to Lethbridge over the Whoop-up Trail. When Ives was a guest of honour at a dinner of the Law Society in the Palliser Hotel not long before his death in the late 1940s, the Law Society presented him with a writing set which had a fine bronze buffalo on the base. When it was presented to him the demonstration was long and enthusiastic. I am sure Ives was moved but his poker face rarely showed emotion. He stood for some time and then, pointing to the buffalo, said "When we docked at Fort Benton in 1882 the deckhands lassoed a fine male buffalo swimming in the river—this is that buffalo."

Ives took his law at McGill and was admitted to practice in the North West Territories in 1901. He practised in Lethbridge. The newspapers called him "the Cowboy Judge." This was accurate. He used to tell a story of his first cattle drive in the Porcupine Hills. The party came to a place where there was an old cabin. The foreman wanted to use the cabin and asked if there was anyone who could whitewash. Ives boasted "I can" and the foreman replied "Kid, you're elected to whitewash the cabin." The moral of the story is that Ives learned to keep his mouth closed—a lesson he never forgot. He sat on the bench with an impassive expression on his face in a head that looked like a great egg. He did not interrupt counsel and indeed rarely uttered a word during a trial. He rarely reserved judgment but delivered it from the bench at the end of the trial. His judgments were short. There was no long analysis of statutes and decisions. Indeed he used to say that if a lawyer brought more than two books into court he must have a weak case. Ives made clear forthright findings of fact and then gave short reasons.

In one well-known case called *Lindal and Beattie* v. *Home Insurance Company,* Beattie drove his car into a pole on Jasper Avenue and his fiancee Miss Lindal was injured. She sued him. The insurance company defended him but after she won said "We don't have to pay because you were drunk." Beattie and Lindal then sued the Insurance Company. They were represented by two outstanding lawyers, H.H. Parlee and Neil D. Maclean. They argued that there was no proof of intoxication and in any event that the insurance company could not raise it after having defended the original action. Ives gave his judgment from the bench. In a few sentences he found Beattie to have been intoxicated and then simply said "There is no estoppel here." Lindal and Beattie appealed. Chief Justice Harvey took twenty-three pages to say the insurance company was estopped from raising drunkenness. Mr. Justice McGillivray took thirteen pages to support the trial judge. Lindal and Beattie won in a 3–2 judgment. The Supreme Court of Canada, in a fairly short judgment, restored Mr. Justice Ives, with one dissent.

He never showed partiality or indeed any emotion from the bench. He was however interested in encouraging young lawyers. There is an anecdote which goes this way. One of the province's most prominent counsel, A. Macleod Sinclair of Calgary, was appearing before Ives, with a young and newly-admitted lawyer on the other side. Sinclair kept making objections when the young man was trying to put in his evidence. Ives called Sinclair up to the bench and out of earshot of anyone else said: "Sandy, you're a bencher of the Law Society?" Sinclair replied "Yes." (He was a bencher from 1925 to 1939.) Ives then asked "The benchers approved this young man for admission to the Bar?" The answer was "Yes." Ives then said "Then why don't you give him a chance?"

Another incident occurred in Edmonton around 1938. Ives was sitting in Chambers. I came down with a new student who had not been in Chambers before. The object was to give him a chance to make his first application. When his turn came he rose and made the application. Ives asked a question. The student looked at me. I leaned over to whisper the reply. Ives said "You keep quiet" and proceeded to catechize the student. I might add that the student never forgot the lesson. Ives made this remark in his testing of young students: "I don't try to correct the bad habits of older lawyers because they're beyond redemption, but maybe I can do something for the young ones."

If I may make another personal reference, I was admitted to the Law Society by Ives in December 1933. Mr. Steer who presented me made no speech. I do not pretend to remember all the judge said. He made a jocular reference to the optimism I had in entering on the practice of law in bad times, then he spoke of the ethical responsibility of lawyers and said "Don't cut corners."

May I now mention a case called *Powlett* v. *University of Alberta*. Powlett Jr. came from Calgary as a freshman in September 1932. He was subjected to the usual "initiation." Near the end of about a week's hazing, he had a mental breakdown. He and his father sued the University. There were several formidable defences—that the University could not be sued for negligence because it was a Crown agency, and that in any event the University was not liable for harm done to a freshman by student hazing. However the University made an additional defence, namely that the boy was a mental case before the initiation. Ives was the judge. There was no jury, but each side had three psychiatric experts, drawn from Vancouver to Montreal. They sat in the jury box throughout the trial and gave their own expert evidence at the end. After a lengthy trial Ives wrote a nine-page judgment finding the University liable. The University appealed. In judgments occupying sixty-seven pages, the Appellate Division upheld Mr. Justice Ives in a 3–2 judgment but reduced the damages from $50,000.00 to $15,000.00.

This case leads me to A.L. "Art" Smith from Calgary. In the Powlett case he was the leading counsel for the plaintiff. With him he had Ronald Martland who had been admitted to the bar the year before. The cross-examination of the University's witnesses—the Provost, students who had been involved in the initiation and the University's psychiatrists—was vital. I have heard Mr. Justice Martland say that in his opinion the cross-examination by Smith in this case is comparable to the great cross-examination of Lord Birkenhead, Sir Edward Carson and Marshall Hall.

The Provost of the University was a key witness and his evidence was designed to show that the University had not taken responsibility for mishaps during initiation. Smith devastated him. One of the student witnesses testified that he had taken the initiation with Powlett and that he enjoyed it. Smith, who knew the boy, got up for cross-examination and simply asked "Benton, you say you enjoyed all this horseplay?" "Yes." "Have any of these psychiatrists examined you?"

The cross-examination of the University's three psychiatrists was of course vital. The plaintiff's psychiatrists testified that the initiation had induced the mental illness. The evidence showed that the boy had been asked the question "What is the highest form of humanity?" The orthodox answer was "A sophomore." The boy replied "R.B. Bennett." He was "tried" and sentenced to utter a solemn recantation. This was one of the events that precipitated the mental disturbance.

One of the University's psychiatric experts, from McGill, having listened to the evidence about the boy's conduct prior to coming to University gave the opinion that he was already mentally ill. There had been evidence that when he got on the train at Calgary to come to Edmonton he ran along the platform with his shoelaces untied. The doctor did not say that this alone was evidence of mental disease but did think it significant. Smith asked the doctor if he had ever gone to Europe and the doctor said he had. Smith asked, "Weren't you excited?" "No." Smith then said "Well I went to Europe several years ago and I'm sure that I could have run down the station platform with my shoelaces untied."

One highlight of the trial was the evidence for the plaintiff of Leonard Brockington. He knew the boy well and regarded him as a prodigy. His evidence from the witness stand was a speech. When it is remembered that Brockington was regarded as Canada's outstanding orator, one can imagine the impact. Another close friend of the plaintiff was R.B. Bennett. He did not give evidence though the fact did come out that the boy had spoken on the radio in favour of Bennett in the 1930 election when Bennett became

Prime Minister of Canada. He took a close interest in the case and it will be recalled that he was never particularly fond of the University of Alberta.

Another case in Edmonton, in which Smith was the leading counsel at the trial for the defendant, was the Corona Hotel case. It arose out of a fire caused by a leak in the gas company's main. There was a great deal of expert evidence on both sides as to the reason why the pipe subsided and cracked, allowing the gas to escape. Again Martland was with him. I recall Martland saying that at the beginning of the trial the expert witnesses on the other side, having had a glimpse of Smith, thought that he was something of a mountebank and that he could be handled easily. By the time they were through they knew better.

One other example to indicate his skill in cross-examination and ability to go the right distance and then stop: at an inquest arising out of the death of a patient at Ponoka, Smith appeared for the Crown. A medical doctor gave evidence on psychiatric matters. When it came to cross-examination Smith simply asked "Doctor, I understand you are a specialist in women's diseases?" The answer was "Yes." Smith sat down.

He was of fine appearance and commanding personality. He put the utmost effort into his cases but did not take them home with him. He enjoyed the good life and in today's language he would be called a "free spirit." On the last day of the Powlett trial it was agreed to have argument by both sides in the evening at 8:00 p.m. Smith was a guest at dinner of a number of University students and arrived at the Court House late. By the time he came into the court room the judge was already on the Bench and the other lawyers were present. Without being at all abashed, Smith apologized. When it came his turn to present his argument (which was on the facts, while Martland argued the law) he made a most moving and indeed emotional "jury speech," even though there was no jury.

One final little incident: When the Calgary Stampeders won their first Grey Cup—in 1948—the game that turned the Grey Cup into a national event, Smith was in the House of Commons. On the following Monday, the newspapers carried an item which, as I remember it, said that Smith came into the House with a cowboy hat and in some way managed to call the Speaker's attention to the fact of the great victory on the preceding Saturday.

I turn now to the Judges of the Territorial period. It is important to remember that the West did not become a part of Canada until late 1870 and that the new Dominion had to establish law and order in an empty land. I will not describe the Acts of Parliament which set up a Lieutenant Governor and Council to make ordinances and to carry on the executive role. Of interest here is the fact that provision was made for Stipendiary Magistrates and the first ones were appointed in 1876. The first two were Matthew Ryan and Colonel Macleod who soon afterwards was made Commissioner of the Northwest Mounted Police so in that capacity was a Stipendiary Magistrate *ex officio*. This might seem strange today but in the shortage of men fitted to be judges it was necessary. Equally strange is the fact that the Stipendiary

Magistrates were on the Territorial Council and had a hand in making ordinances and in the executive branch of government. This too would be unthinkable today, but these Magistrates, particularly Macleod and Richardson, made a valuable contribution as judges, legislators and administrators in the setting up of our legal institutions. Richardson had been an Ontario lawyer. He was a Magistrate and then a judge until his retirement in 1903, did a great deal of work in drafting ordinances and was responsible for the first revision of the ordinances in 1888. Most people, however, know him only as the Magistrate who tried Louis Riel and sometimes Riel's sympathizers speak of him as though he were a hanging judge. The whole record of the trial is available. The only possible defence was insanity and Riel objected to his counsel raising it. One can read and re-read Richardson's directions to the jury. It would stand muster in any court. His direction to the jury on the defence of insanity was upheld by the Manitoba Court of Appeal and the Privy Council turned down Riel's application for leave to appeal to that body. Lord Halsbury said that there had been no clear departure from the requirements of justice.

May I make an observation on this trial. One writer begins an article on it by saying "The Courtroom was small, unadorned, and primitive in its facilities, located in a building which possessed no symbols of a great tradition, it was the office-block of the Canada-West Land Company." Indeed it was not Osgoode Hall or the Old Bailey. Yet Magistrate Richardson, with the assistance of the best lawyers in Canada, conducted a trial for treason (a rare charge in Canada) in a remote village in a Territory that had been in existence for fifteen years and had a judicial system for nine. This is the most significant state trial in Canada's history. Whether one thinks Riel should have been hanged or not, the amazing fact is that a trial of this level was held at all.

Colonel Macleod was from Ontario, a graduate of Queen's and a member of the bar. His reputation stands high as Commissioner of the Northwest Mounted Police in terms of integrity and fairness to the Indians. One of our great early lawyers, the late C.C. McCaul, said this of Macleod as a judge: "Colonel Macleod did not profess to be a very well-read lawyer. In fact, the nicer distinctions and subtleties of the law did not appeal to his type of mind at all. He possessed however a solid sense of justice and a fund of sound common sense; and, above all, he was a gentleman and very human, the best of all qualities in a judge. His administration of criminal law was eminently satisfactory. Without giving way to sentiment, the prisoner was always sure of a fair, impartial and even sympathetic attitude on the part of the judge." McCaul adds that if Macleod erred in imposing sentence, it was on the side of leniency and further that although neither judge nor advocate wore robes until the Supreme Court was created in 1887, the proceedings in Court before Macleod were always conducted with proper decorum and dignity, and that he effectually enforced the respect due not only to himself, but to the other officials of the Court.

There is a tribute to Macleod from a completely different source. Granville Stuart, a prominent Montana rancher, in his *Reminiscences* mentions an incident in which Indians from the Canadian side had stolen horses in Montana. The Montana ranchers reported the theft to Major Crozier at Macleod. Stuart says the accused were promptly arrested, tried before Colonel Macleod and a jury and convicted. Sentence was suspended. Stuart agreed that this was wise; and speaking of the Canadian authorities said "Their methods of capturing and punishing the thieves and restoring stolen property were both expeditious and effective."

Ryan did not have a happy career. A lawyer from Montreal, he came West in 1875 and was appointed by the Liberal administration to deal with the claims of Metis (half-breeds as they were then called) to land or scrip for land, and was made a Magistrate the next year. He was apparently a contentious man and had great difficulties with Herchmer of the Northwest Mounted Police who was also contentious. After Sir John A. MacDonald returned to power in 1878 he set up a commission of three to look into Ryan's conduct. The report has never been made public but Ryan was dismissed in 1881. He was very bitter. When Sir John A. MacDonald, during a debate on the Riel Rebellion in July 1885, took occasion to refer unfavourably to Ryan, Ryan wrote him a letter demanding an explanation. He ended by saying "At present my feeling is that you did me positive injustice not greater, however, than you did in acting on the private information of that scoundrel Herchmer in 1881." A postscript says "I write with pencil because of the severe cold in my room; ink would really not flow." One thing is clear—he had a bitter quarrel with Herchmer and indeed after he was dismissed tried to show to the Minister of Justice that Herchmer had committed various misdeeds including attempts to fabricate evidence against Ryan.

It was two years before a replacement for Ryan was appointed. It was Judge C.B. Rouleau. He had been a magistrate in Quebec and enjoyed a high reputation in the Territories until his death in 1901. The last of the Stipendiary Magistrates to be appointed was Jeremiah Travis, at Calgary. He had taken law at Harvard and prided himself on his legal knowledge. However he was stiff-necked and from the beginning ran afoul of influential citizens in Calgary, which had been made a town the year before. He was zealous in enforcing the liquor law. He jailed a councillor, a hotel-keeper named S.J. Clarke, for obstructing the Northwest Mounted Police who were attempting to make a seizure of liquor. The editor of the *Calgary Herald,* one Cayley, wrote articles severely critical of Travis. He refused to apologize and Travis sent him to jail for contempt. A third opponent of Travis was Mayor Murdoch. When the civic election was held in January 1886 Travis disqualified Murdoch but he was re-elected anyway. Travis fined Murdoch and suspended him from office and installed his opponent, one Reilly. In March, 1886 Travis was suspended from duty. A Royal Commission found him to have been tactless. In 1887 the Stipendiary Magistrates were replaced by the Supreme Court of the Northwest Territories and Travis was not appointed.

The first judges of the new Court were Richardson, Macleod and

Rouleau with two new ones, Judge Maguire from Kingston and Judge Wetmore from St. John. McCaul says that Wetmore "was quite the strongest member of the court." Later of course he became Chief Justice of Saskatchewan.

As to Rouleau, McCaul says, "He had a good deal of Colonel Macleod's *bonhomie* and common sense... but Judge Rouleau was, above all things, a lawyer" and describes his zealous study of English law and his thorough examination of the authorities before delivering judgment: "He had a remarkable faculty of working out the proper principle of distinction that really governed the point in dispute."

A word about Maguire. He had gone to Queen's University and its records show that he obtained prizes in logic, rhetoric and classics. May I mention one case in which he took part. It is *Emerson* v. *Bannerman*. It originated in Calgary. Bannerman had taken a bill of sale from one Sparrow and the law required him to take an affidavit of good faith. He had to swear that the bill of sale was not taken for the purpose of defrauding "any creditors" of Sparrow. The affidavit which Bannerman took said "the creditors" instead of "any creditors." Emerson, who was a creditor, argued that the affidavit was defective so that the bill of sale was invalid as against him. Judge Rouleau upheld the bill of sale. Emerson appealed and the full court heard the argument. In reply to the argument of E.P. Davis (later a distinguished Vancouver lawyer) on behalf of Emerson, Maguire, J. said this:

> The learned Counsel endeavored to show by syllogistic illustrations that the use of the words "the creditors" entirely changed the meaning of the affidavit, overlooking the fact that in cases of universal negatives the logicians say that both subject and predicate are distributed. I do not know that Mr. Bannerman is a logician, or if so, to what school he belongs; whether to an ancient or a modern school; whether he is to be classed as an Aristotelian, an Epicurean, or a Heraclitic-Protagorean; whether his mind is of the Rhetorico Sophistical, or Spenozistic-Metaphysical, or simply Transcendental-Aesthetic order; or is he, like many in these Territories, a lover of Bacon? The evidence does not enlighten us on any of these points nor do I think the omission material. The power of being able to "divide a hair 'twixt South and South-West side," may be interesting to sophistical rhetoricians who have leisure and taste for such subtleties. I do not think we should avoid a bill of sale by reason of the possibilities suggested here.

I might add that Mr. Justice Wetmore did not agree on this point though he concurred in the result.

When Macleod died in 1894, David Lynch Scott who had been one of the prosecuting lawyers in the Riel case and was the first member on the rolls of the Bar of the Northwest Territories was appointed in his place. Later he became Chief Justice of Alberta.

Maguire resigned in 1903 and was replaced by A.L. Sifton who later became Chief Justice of Alberta and resigned in 1910 to become Premier. Richardson retired in 1903 and H.W. Newlands replaced him in 1904. The same year Horace Harvey was appointed as an additional judge. His career of 45 years as a judge, most of it as Chief Justice of Alberta, is well known. He once said of the first five judges of the Supreme Court of the Northwest Territories, "Speaking with a personal knowledge of its first members, with all but one of whom I was brought frequently in contact and with one of whom I was subsequently a colleague, I feel no hesitation in stating that in this respect there was no inferiority to the personnel of the superior courts of the Provinces. This is also apparent from a perusal of its reported judgments."

I might mention here a comment on Chief Justice Sifton made by the Honourable W.L. Walsh who was one of our most distinguished trial judges. Coming from Ontario via the Yukon in 1904 his first case was at Calgary before Chief Justice Sifton. Walsh said, "The Chief Justice was a great judge of character. He possessed a vast fund of common sense, a wonderful memory and an almost uncanny ability to sift the wheat from the chaff, to distinguish truth from falsehood. His findings of fact were usually quite unassailable. He was not a profound lawyer. His conclusions of law from the facts as found by him were not usually reached as the result of an extensive study of the authorities. His judgments after trial were almost exclusively oral, delivered at the close of the trial and in the fewest possible words."

When Alberta and Saskatchewan became provinces in 1905 the judges of the Supreme Court of the Northwest Territories were: Chief Justice Sifton, Wetmore, Scott, Prendergast (replacing Rouleau who had died in 1901), Newlands (replacing Richardson in 1904) and Harvey. In 1906 T.C. Johnstone and C.A. Stuart were added. The provincial Supreme Court in each province was created in 1907 and the judges went to one province or the other. The first members of the Supreme Court of Alberta were Chief Justice Sifton, Scott, Harvey and Stuart. N.D. Beck was added in the same year. The trio of Harvey, Stuart and Beck sat continuously either at trial or on appeal until Stuart's death in 1926 and Beck's two years later. These three men gave Alberta a remarkably strong bench in its first twenty years. They were different one from the other in many ways. Harvey tended to be legalistic and was a great believer in following precedent. Beck was at the opposite extreme. He was not concerned with what had been done before but what should be done now and he was exceedingly solicitous of the rights of an accused. Stuart was somewhere in between. He had a philosophical mind and a very strong intellect. The three had in common an excellent grounding in law and a fine sense of judicial responsibility.

It has always seemed to me that two judgments of Mr. Justice Stuart for the full court in World War I are among the most notable in our legal history. In the first case, *R* v. *Trainor,* he acquitted a man who had been charged with uttering seditious words and in so doing gave great scope for freedom of speech even in wartime. In the other, *R* v. *Cyr,* he said that women could hold public office in Alberta. This was eleven years before the Privy Council said they could sit in the Senate.

The last case I would like to mention involves all three of them as well as Simmons and Hyndman who were by then on the court. The court ruled that a farmer named Lewis was illegally conscripted and ordered his release. The government directed the military authorities to ignore the judgment. The court made a further order for the release of other farmer conscripts. The government still persisted in its refusal. The colonel in charge of the depot at Calgary, which is now Stampede Park, was ordered to defy the sheriff in his attempt to obtain the farmers' release. Machine guns were placed in front of the barracks. The situation was very grave. In a notable judgment Chief Justice Harvey said that in spite of the Army's superior powers the court would do its duty. He ordered the sheriff to bring the men before the court to be discharged. At this point the Army capitulated. (A few days later the Supreme Court of Canada held the farmers were validly conscripted.)

In conclusion may I say this. We hear much of our heritage. The term is often used to describe our natural resources. I have no quarrel with this but our true heritage is in the work and the example set by our forebears. I become impatient when I listen to people say we have no sense of identity. That sense depends in large measure on a knowledge of one's antecedents—of one's heritage from them. Our legal heritage, the contribution of our early judges and lawyers, is a good one. It behooves us to remember and to foster that heritage.

1984

Confidentiality of Hospital Medical Records

Reprinted from
The Record, Newsletter of the
Alberta Health Record Association
September–October 1984

Bowker was invited by the Alberta Health Record Association to contribute this article to its Newsletter The Record *on the subject of confidentiality in connection with hospital medical records.*

This Association comprises hospital personnel engaged in keeping medical records. This is an important item in hospital administration, and includes not only the keeping of records, but accessibility to the same and their transfer from one hospital to another.

A Commission in Ontario, headed by Horace Krever, on Confidentiality of Hospital Records produced a three-volume Report centering on abuses and deceptions perpetrated upon the Ontario health-care system by persons getting access to records by improper means for improper purposes. Though it dealt with Ontario, the Report does have some relevance here.

The Alberta Hospitals Act and Mental Health Act have tried to spell out terms of confidentiality, but legislation could stand improvement. Some of these matters are raised in this article.

The physician's ethical obligation to keep in confidence information derived from his patient goes back to Hippocrates. It is stated in the Canadian Medical Association's Code of Ethics with the addition that the physician will divulge the information "only with the permission of the patient except when the law requires him to do so". The Principles of Medical Ethics of the American Medical Association (1980) say that "a physician shall safeguard patient confidences within the constraints of the law", and an interpretation of 1984 says "The obligation to safeguard patient confidences is subject to certain exceptions that are ethically and legally justified because of overriding social considerations". Then the example is given of the patient who threatens serious bodily harm to another and there is a reasonable probability that the patient may carry out the threat.

The physician's obligation has its counterpart in other health-care professions. For example, the Code of Nurses of the International Council of Nurses says "The nurse holds in confidence personal information and uses judgment in sharing this information". Then there is the Code of Practice for Safeguarding Health Information, issued by the Canadian Health Record Association (quoted in Rozovsky and Rozovsky, *The Canadian Law of Patient Records* (1984) at 79, 80). It is too long to quote here and besides the reader is doubtless familiar with it.

These obligations are *ethical*. For breach of them a member of the profession is subject to disciplinary measures by the governing body. Are they also *legal* obligations? There are very few decisions of courts on this. However it is clear that a court can grant an order (called an injunction) to forbid disclosure. If the disclosure has been made, the patient in theory has an action for damages but his damages might be very slight.

While the physician is under an obligation to observe confidentiality this does not mean that if he is called as a witness in court he can refuse to testify about his patients' affairs. In Alberta he must testify. In contrast the lawyer, with the same duty to observe his clients' confidences, is entitled, if called as a witness, to refuse to answer. This "privilege", as it is called, is the client's, not the lawyer's.

Historically, medical records meant a ledger kept by a physician. Today, vast records are kept not only by clinics but by hospitals (as the readers of this Newsletter know better than most). Moreover demands for information about patients have multiplied—not only from government and health insurance groups but for a variety of social purposes ranging from research to prevention of disease and accidents to statistics and law enforcement. Some of these demands are justified—but the Krever report disclosed in Ontario a widespread practice of obtaining information from hospitals contrary to law and often by the use of flagrant deception—and those seeking the information ranged from doctors and lawyers to insurance adjusters, private investigators and police.

In addition to the pressure on record-holders to divulge information is the growth in use of computers to store it. It is trite to say that the public is concerned that this will increase the risk of improper disclosure of the individual's private affairs, including medical matters.

There is general agreement that confidentiality and the exceptions to it cannot be left to ethical canons and to occasional judgments. Legislation is needed to provide guidance. It should be fair, clear and comprehensive, though this may be hard to achieve.

Before looking at Alberta's legislation and in particular section 40 of the Hospitals Act and its counterpart section 37 of the Mental Health Act, it will help to point out that the law may forbid disclosure. Where it does not forbid, it may *permit* or it may *require* it. The difference is that between "may" and "shall".

We have in Alberta legislation of both kinds. An example of the first is the Motor Vehicle Administration Act. Section 14(2) says that a physician *may* "without acquiring any liability by so doing, report (to the Registrar of the Motor Vehicles Division) any medical information relative to the health of a person holding... an operator's license when the physician believes that the condition in relation to which the information is given may adversely affect that person's operation of a motor vehicle."

Examples of the second category have existed for years in the Venereal Diseases Prevention Act and the Tuberculosis Act. These are being replaced by a new Public Health Act, passed this year. Although not yet proclaimed to be in force, it can be used as an illustration. Part 4, on communicable diseases, says in section 33(1): "Where a physician, a health practitioner, a teacher or a person in charge of an institution knows that a person under his care... is infected with a communicable disease... he shall notify the medical officer of the local board... " immediately. There are several companion provisions which likewise are mandatory (ss. 33(2) and (3) and ss. 34–38). Another example is the new Child Welfare Act. Section 3 requires any person to report when a child is in need of protective services, even though the information is confidential.

Starting with the general obligation of confidentiality, most people would agree that there are circumstances in which there is a public interest in disclosure that outweighs the interest in confidentiality. The Krever Report gives interesting examples. (Vol. II pp. 79–90). A well-recognized situation is that where the physician thinks his patient is a wanted criminal or where the police seek information in connection with their investigations. Mr. Justice Krever said that under Ontario law these disclosures were forbidden and yet "were morally proper despite the current state of the law" (p. 91).

As already mentioned, the law may give a discretion to disclose or it may impose a duty to disclose. The *Tarasoff* case in California shows the difference. A patient of a psychologist employed by the University of California threatened to kill a young woman. The psychologist tried to have him confined but the campus police released him. He killed the woman. Her parents sued the University on the ground that the psychologist had failed in his legal duty to warn them or their daughter of the danger to her. The Supreme Court of California held him to be under such a duty. Needless to say the decision has disturbed psychotherapists. It is one thing to say the physician may disclose the danger, but to put him under a legal duty to disclose, so that he is liable in damages if the victim is hurt or dies, puts him in a serious dilemma.

In Alberta the present administration came into power in 1971. From the beginning it was concerned to protect the confidentiality of information held by government and by hospitals. Thus we have section 40 of the Hospitals Act, section 37 of the Mental Health Act, section 13 of the Alberta Health Care Insurance Act and section 5 of the Social Development Act, and other provisions too numerous to mention. The object has been to protect confidentiality and at the same time to allow (or more rarely to require) disclosure where it is in the public interest.

Provisions like section 40 may in some respects be hard to understand and apply—but one must remember that, as someone said, a good statute is the hardest thing to construct and the easiest to tear down.

Then there can be incidents like we had in April of 1982. The legislature brought in a bill (Bill 30) to amend the Public Health Act. Clause 32.1 of that bill was along the general lines of section 40 of the Hospitals Act. Specifically it authorized the Minister to call for records in the possession of a local health board for the same reasons he can call for them under section 40—to assess standards of care, to improve services and the like. Some of the information is of course sensitive but it is hard to understand the clamour of protest—by the medical profession, in the newspapers and in the legislature. The bill was withdrawn. However the new Public Health Act has a provision (s. 63) much like the clause in the 1982 bill. It produced no great outcry.

We shall now look more closely at section 40, with its thirteen subsections.

Ss. 1—The hospital must keep a record of diagnosis and treatment.

Ss. 2—The minister can call for records, diagnoses and charts, but only in order to assess standards of care, improve procedures, compile statistics, conduct research or for the public interest.

There seems to be uncertainty as to the meaning of record. It is not defined in the Act beyond the reference to diagnosis and treatment. Doubtless experienced record keepers are able to agree in most cases.

Ss. 3—This is of vital importance because it says information from hospital records is CONFIDENTIAL. However it does not stop there. It says the information shall be used only for the purposes of ss. 2. But it does not stop there. It ends with the direction that the information shall not be disclosed so as to be "detrimental to the personal interests, reputation or privacy of a patient or the patient's attending physician". This last part is puzzling. Since the information is confidential, why is it necessary to speak of disclosure at all? The other feature of the last part is that it protects the physician as well as the patient. It is true that in section 17 of the Medical Profession Act there is a similar provision about information that comes before the council and that concerns a member. However the obligation of confidentiality is generally for the benefit of the patient, not the physician, and I am not clear why the latter is protected.

Ss. 4—Since a requirement of confidentiality without any sanctions for breach is "toothless," or in the view of some is not a law at all, ss. 4 makes it an offence wilfully to disclose information to a person not authorized to receive it. The maximum penalty is a $100 fine, or on default in payment 15 days in jail.

Ss. 5—Had the section stopped at ss. 4 it would have been comparatively simple, but it would not have covered nearly all the cases where disclosure should be permitted. Hence ss. 5 which permits a board, the Minister or a physician to give information with the patient's consent; to give it to the Director of Medical Services under the Occupational Health and Safety Act and to the Workers' Compensation Board, Blue Cross or other hospital insurer, and to another hospital or physician.

These exceptions all seem carefully circumscribed and reasonable. In the case of the patient's written consent I do not know whether problems arise as to the validity of the consent, but I should think the hospital is obliged to make sure that the patient really knows what he is consenting to.

Ss. 6—This is another long series of exceptions to ss. 3. The Minister may give information to and receive it from various government bodies. Then come exceptions applicable to boards. A board may give information for medical research or for training in a health records school.

Most people would agree that disclosure in the interest of research is justified as long as the researcher observes confidentiality. Today's ethical guidelines covering research invariably impose this obligation. For example the Medical Research Council of Canada and the Department of Health and Social Services are both emphatic on this. When a board is asked to give information on research it will doubtless appraise the importance of the research and the responsibility of the researchers and the sensitivity of the information. Some persons resent any intrusion on their "privacy" including questions from a researcher but on balance this exception to confidentiality is warranted.

The remaining exceptions in ss. 6 are clearly reasonable. They have to do with the transfer of patients to another hospital and disciplinary proceedings under the Medical Profession Act.

Ss. 7 and 8—These empower a medical examiner under the Fatality Inquiries Act to obtain information about a patient and provide that the information may be admitted in evidence at the inquiry but the hearing must be in private. There are similar provisions in the Mental Health Act's section 37. It seems that some of the news media have complained that they should have access to this information. The government appointed a task force to look into the matter. The chairman is the Honourable Peter Greschuk, a retired Queen's Bench judge. The report should be made public soon. It will be of interest to record keepers, for my guess is that it will provide a close examination of the whole of section 40.

Ss. 9—This exception gives to a Hospital Privileges Appeal Board the right to call for information, and proceedings are to be in private.

Ss. 10—This most important provision deals with the situation where a Board, or a Minister or a physician is *unable* to divulge information because of ss. 3, or *refuses* to divulge information which he is required to divulge under ss. 5. In either event the patient may apply to the court for an order directing release of the information.

Ss. 11—This merely sets out the procedure for making the application.

Ss. 12—This is of the greatest significance for it says "the onus of showing why the order should not be made for the release of the information" is on the person *refusing* it and not on the person applying for release. The Mental Health Act has provisions almost identical. In *Lindsay v. D.M.* in 1981 an ex-patient at Ponoka applied for access to his hospital chart. The hospital director refused. The Court of Appeal held that he did not satisfy the onus of showing why the information should not be released. The judgment says that the section (like section 40) does not spell out the criteria that the court should apply in reaching its decision, though the reference to something "detrimental to the personal interest, reputation or privacy of a patient or the patient's attending physician" is relevant. The judgment says that the purpose of the legislation was to protect the patient's privacy so the court should be vigilant and demand compelling grounds before permitting access to his records. Where however the patient is the applicant there is no risk to his privacy—and the court clearly agreed with the Krever Report in supporting the patient's right of access to his own records, unless the person refusing access can show that such access would do harm—to physician, or patient, or third parties or the practice of medicine. In this case no such risk of harm was shown.

This judgment shows that when a board is in doubt as to whether it should release information to a patient, it can refuse and await the possibility of an application under ss. 7. If an application is made and it succeeds then the board may be liable in costs as was the medical director in *Lindsay*.

Ss. 13—This defines "legal representative" of a patient.

One general remark about section 40. It does not deal with the type of situation mentioned earlier and discussed in the Krever Report for example, where the board has good reason to think a patient has committed a crime or intends to commit one. Under section 40 the board is not permitted to give the information to police or any one else. Whether boards give it or not I do not know. However my respectful suggestion is that section 40 should allow the board to give such information. The key recommendations in the Krever Report, especially 23 (danger to the patient or others) and 24 (belief that the patient has been a victim or perpetrator of a crime) provide a good model.

The report of the Drewry Task Force to review the Mental Health Act has in Chapter XVII a good discussion of section 37 of that Act. The report supports the patient's right of access to his records. Moreover it favours a change in the law to permit disclosure in the interest of public safety and law enforcement on the lines of the Krever recommendations.

Before leaving section 40, it is important to remember that it applies to hospital records, not to records in a physician's office. The Medical Profession Act has no counterpart of section 40. Maybe it should provide for access by a patient to his records and for disclosure to others for specified purposes as does section 40. That however is a large subject outside the scope of this article.

A final question—what is the effect of the new Charter of Human Rights? I do not attempt here to guess. One can hope however that if the legislation strikes a fair balance between confidentiality and access to medical information then it will stand up under attack.

1985

Legal Education

Reprinted from
The Canadian Encyclopedia, 1st ed. 1985
Edmonton, Hurtig Publishers, pp. 995–996

The three-volume The Canadian Encyclopedia *produced by Hurtig Publishers in 1985 is Canada's first national encyclopedia.*

Bowker was asked by the Editor to write an article on Legal Education in Canada. Extensive research was involved, which was accomplished with the help of other deans of law throughout Canada.

It was essential to draw a distinction between the system of legal education in the common-law provinces and that of Quebec.

Legal Education: Because all provinces but Québec inherited the English Common Law, legal education in Canada—training for the practice of law—was in the beginning modelled on that in England. In England, however, the profession was and is divided into 2 mutually exclusive branches—barristers and solicitors. Solicitors deal with clients, but if there is to be a trial in the High Court a barrister must be retained to act as counsel. Barristers, who have the exclusive right to represent a party at a trial or on appeal, are the "senior" branch of the profession, but until very recently the educational qualifications were very low. Although most barristers have a university degree (not necessarily in law) it is not obligatory, and students can still become barristers without having ever been in court. Solicitors, however, must be articled clerks to practising solicitors and must pass examinations. The basic period was recently changed from 5 years to 4, which can be reduced to as little as 2 if the candidate passes certain qualifying examinations and has a university degree.

In Canada (except Québec) the division of the profession into 2 mutually exclusive branches has not occurred; today a legal practitioner in the common law provinces is invariably both a solicitor and a barrister, though in practice many act in the capacity of one or the other.

Before the establishment of the modern law school, the typical provincial Act governing the legal profession provided that applicants had to spend 5 years under articles and to write periodic examinations, though if they held a university degree the period was reduced to 3 years. When modern law schools were established, the articling period was usually reduced to one year after graduation. In Ontario and Manitoba it was once possible to combine part-time law school with part-time articles, but now these provinces have the same system as the others.

In Canada, as in the US and unlike England, students do not come directly from high school to law school. The usual minimum is 2 years of university education and most successful applicants have a degree.

The story of the common-law schools can be divided into 2 periods—from the founding of the Dalhousie Law School in 1883 to 1945, and from 1945 to the present. Dalhousie established a full-time 3-year course soon after the school was founded. It had always had links to Harvard Law School and at the end of WWI its curriculum resembled that of Harvard. Following the recommendations of the Canadian Bar Association in 1920, this curriculum was widely accepted by other common-law schools.

In Ontario the Law Society created its own law school, Osgoode Hall, in 1889. Later the universities of New Brunswick, Manitoba, Saskatchewan, Alberta and BC established law schools.

Shortly after WWII the Law Society made Osgoode a full-time school, but it did not give complete recognition to other schools in Ontario until 1957. In 1966 the society gave up its school and Osgoode Hall became a part of York University. By that time there were 6 faculties in Ontario—at the universities of Ottawa, Toronto, Western Ontario, Windsor, Queen's and York—and in other provinces law schools were also established at the universities of Victoria, Calgary and Moncton, and a common-law course was begun at McGill. By 1984 the number of full-time teachers had risen from about 20 to 600 and student enrolment is now in the thousands. Most law schools impose a quota on admissions. One notable postwar trend has been the marked increases in women students and in women law teachers.

The standard curriculum of 1920 remained virtually unchanged until 1945. In 1957 the Law Society of Upper Canada prescribed the courses it would require of "approved" schools, making amendments in 1969. As all the common-law schools are approved, it is clear that the Ontario prescription has influenced the curriculum in all common-law schools. There are 25 subject-areas, with 6 compulsory "core subjects." The object is to provide a general education that permits a degree of specialization. In some law schools there is special emphasis on specific topics, eg, taxation or oil and gas law.

The teaching method in common-law schools was originally based on the "case method" created in the 1870s by Dean Langdell at Harvard Law School, who believed that law was a science composed of principles that could be learned from reading decisions of appellate courts. Formal lectures were replaced by discussions in class of assigned cases and by questioning of the Socratic type. By the 1920s, all common-law schools in Canada employed one or other variation of the case method.

Since WWII, the use of the case method, at least after the first year of law school, has been criticized on the grounds that it is unproductive and gives a misleading view of law in action. Legislation tends to be ignored in the reading of cases, although its pre-eminent place is now being recognized. There has been emphasis as well on problem solving and legal writing, and on public law as compared to private. Courses in Constitutional

Law were always fundamental, but now courses on Administrative Law, taxation and Labour Law are also important. Another trend is the linking of law with other disciplines, eg, economics, history, psychology and sociology; and to answer the criticism that law school study ignores pressing social needs, there are courses in Property Law, Women and the Law, and Civil Liberties. There has been an effort to strengthen courses on legal theory, the philosophy of law and sociology of law, usually under the rubric of Jurisprudence. Efforts have been made as well to teach ethics and professional responsibility.

The development of these new subjects is not always strong and has to face competition with other subjects. As a result of criticism that law schools fail to teach skills necessary in legal practice—drafting documents, writing opinions, preparing for trial and cross-examination, interviewing and negotiating—there has been increasing emphasis on clinical training. Considerable effort has been made to meet this demand, usually with the help of practitioners and judges. Like every innovation, however, its place in the law school has been debated.

The production of legal journals has conspicuously increased. These journals usefully provide scholarly articles and a forum for criticism and for proposals for reform. In addition, the use of computers is constantly increasing and may soon be indispensable in both law teaching and practice.

The recent report of the Arthurs Committee on Legal Education, *Law and Learning*, states that law schools are "eclectic" and still overemphasize training for the professional rather than the academic. The report advocates research at a high level to help the development of a "scholarly" discipline that will not be shunted aside from professional training. The report specifically recommends an expansion and intensification of graduate study (a number of schools give a master's degree and a few offer a doctorate) with a view to the education of future law teachers and researchers, and recommends that these programs should concentrate on those subjects in which the school is strong. Support for graduate research is hampered, however, by the shortage of funds for scholarships.

The advent of the law school did not mean an end to the system of articles. The purpose of articling is to provide "practical" training, ie, an introduction to practice which the law school has not provided. The success of articles depends on the "principal" and the student. The principal is under a duty to see that the student receives instruction in the basics of practice, but there is little or no supervision to this end. For many years after WWII, the business expansion created a demand for students and good articles were comparatively easy to obtain. In recent years, the number of graduates has been more than the market can easily absorb and the adequacy of the articling system has come into question. To supplement articles, most law societies have established a Bar Admission Course. The most notable is that of Ontario, begun in 1957. When students have finished the year of articles they are required to attend a 6-month course in matters such as rules of procedure, forming companies, handling estates, and real-estate transactions.

This course is described in a handbook published by the Law Society of Upper Canada. The other provinces, except for PEI, have each provided in legislation for a bar admission course. However, these courses are less ambitious than Ontario's and vary a great deal. Some are given throughout the period of articles while others are offered near the end of the articling period, the length of the course varying from one week to 6.

In the US, the requirement of articles is virtually nonexistent. In theory, admission to practice is a matter for the state supreme court. The court in fact delegates its function to bar examiners who set comprehensive exams for those seeking to practice, and who conduct character checks. Another difference between the 2 countries is that the American Bar Association publishes a list of approved law schools, though some unapproved schools still exist; the Canadian Bar Association has no such role and there is no category of unauthorized law schools. Finally, the Canadian type of provincial law society, with statutory control over admission and discipline, is quite different from the type of law society in the US.

Once an individual has been admitted to practice it is important to keep up to date. Legal journals and special lectures and meetings of bar associations are helpful but provide uneven coverage and do not always reach those most in need. In recent years there has been a call for a greater and more systematic program of continuing legal education. In 1978 the Federation of Law Societies of Canada held a Conference on Quality of Legal Services and in 1980 held a workshop on the same subject. It concluded that continuing legal education should be fostered but it was not prepared to recommend mandatory continuing legal education. Organized efforts at programs of continuing legal education are in fact increasing in most provinces.

The legal profession (outside Québec) has never recognized specialties, as does medicine, though in some provinces practitioners may now announce a preferred area of practice. The significant fact is that the "practice of law" is not homogenous, and the variations go far beyond the differences between barrister and solicitor. In addition, lawyers work not only in private practice but also in government and business.

In Québec the legal profession is divided. Advocates form the Barreau de Québec while notaries, governed by their own statute, are somewhat like solicitors. An individual cannot belong to both branches. The course leading to a degree in law in Québec takes 3 years, and the prelegal requirement is a diploma equivalent to an arts degree. If law students wish to become notaries, they must declare so by 1 Dec of their third year. Up to that point, the courses are the same for both branches, with emphasis on the Civil Code. In many other ways the Québec schools have gone through the same experiences and problems as the common law schools. The first faculty of law was established in 1848 at McGill, which now gives a common law as well as a civil law degree (just as does U of O). Laval's law faculty was founded in 1852 and that of U de M is over 100 years old. Other law schools exist at Sherbrooke and U de Québec at Montréal.

Practical training occurs after graduation. For advocates there is an 8-

month "formation professionelle" (similar to a bar admission course), followed by a "stagiaire" (similar to articles) of 6 months, and finally a bar exam. Graduates who wish to be notaries must attend an additional year in notarial practice at a civil law school; finally, they take a notarial examination.

1985

Arthur Sifton

Reprinted from
The Canadian Encyclopedia, 1st ed. 1985
Edmonton, Hurtig Publishers, p. 1695

This is the second article requested from Bowker by the editors of The Canadian Encyclopedia.

He was instructed "to give a picture of the man and keep it to 250 words." "An utter impossibility" said Bowker—but he did it.

This is the result. It is a further example of his interest in personages in our legal history.

Sifton, Arthur Lewis, judge, politician, premier of Alberta (b at St Johns, Canada W 26 Oct 1858; d at Ottawa 21 Jan 1921). Firm, stoical and politically astute, Sifton was one of the most outstanding figures in the political life of the early West. He practised law in Brandon, Man. 1883–85 (with his brother Clifford), in Prince Albert in the North-West Territories 1885–88, and in Calgary after 1889. In 1899 he was elected to the territorial legislature for Banff and from 1901 served on Haultain's Executive Council. He was an early and strong advocate of provincial status. In 1903 Laurier appointed him territorial chief justice, and in 1907 he became the first chief justice of Alberta. As a trial judge he was excellent; he said little and gave short, sound and prompt judgement. In 1910 he resigned and became Liberal premier of Alberta, succeeding A.C. Rutherford. Sifton held together a divided party and was an effective premier, a strong leader and skilled administrator. He pressed for the transfer of natural resources, finally accomplished by J.E. Brownlee in 1930. In 1916 women were given the vote and 2 were made magistrates. During the Conscription crisis of 1917, PM Borden invited leading Liberals, including Sifton, to join a Union government. Though not conspicuous in the Commons, Sifton was valuable in Cabinet and as a delegate to the Paris Peace Conference. In 1919 he became minister of public works and secretary of state, and in 1920 was named an imperial privy councillor.

Reading: L.G. Thomas, The Liberal Party in Alberta (1959).

1985

Medicine and Law: Two Solitudes?

Unpublished text of an address to
the College of Physicians and Surgeons of Alberta
at Calgary on October 3, 1985.

Bowker was invited to be the luncheon speaker at the annual meeting of the Alberta College of Physicians and Surgeons held in Calgary in October 1985.

It is indicative of the increasing interest of the medical profession in medical-legal problems, such as those dealt with in this speech. It also demonstrates Bowker's continuing interest in this branch of law. From all reports, it was well received.

1. Introduction

A great Australian judge once referred to law as "marching with medicine but in the rear and limping a little." The case had to do with a claim for illness resulting from nervous shock. The plaintiff had been an eye-witness to a gory accident caused by the defendent's negligence. He claimed damages for illness resulting from the nervous shock. At one time the courts had said the plaintiff could not obtain damages for such illness, but the judge went on to point out that in more recent times the law recognized that mental illness was just as real as physical, adding that the law "has to-day come a long way."[1]

2. English Law—Common Law and Statutes

The judge was speaking of the English common law. It consists of principles laid down by judges in deciding actual cases. These principles are binding in future cases. They can be rejected by a higher court and the decisions of the highest court are binding on all courts below. The common law system is general throughout the Anglo–American legal world. It differs from that of countries whose law is based on the Roman Code of Justinian such as most European and Latin countries and also Quebec with its Civil Code. Those codes purport to be all-embracing whereas the common law goes from case to case. The common law has its critics—it is hard to find, the principles are not always clear or else they are unsound. Yet on the whole the common law has been a remarkably good institution. Its principles and rules are formulated in actual disputes between person and person rather than by academics sitting around a table, and this has kept it in touch with reality. Moreover it has the capacity to grow with the times. However, if it does become out of date or is unfair, the legislature can always change it by legislation (called acts or statutes) and often does. Yet even when this has happened the judges interpret the legislation. In general they do this faithfully, but courts may give a different interpretation than the legislature intended, for even legislation is not always clear and unambiguous.

This explanation has been given for the purpose of defining the word law in the title. It has many meanings but for our purposes it consists of rules laid down by the state (whether by legislature or courts) and governing the conduct of people.

There is one Canadian institution that deserves note. It is the Uniform Law Conference, made up of lawyers from all provinces and territories and the Federal Government. Its purpose is to prepare statutes in the hope that they will be adopted by all provinces, or at least the majority. Alberta's Human Tissue Gift Act is a uniform act. Nearly every province has adopted it. Another uniform act is the Medical Consent of Minors Act, which only New Brunswick has adopted. The Conference has just undertaken a Uniform Mental Health Act.

We have seen that law consists of the common law and of statutes and that statutes can change the common law. That fact flows from the doctrine that parliament is sovereign. However there is a new factor—the Charter of Rights and Freedoms. It gives to the courts the power to rule that an act or provision in an act is in violation of one of the rights or freedoms set out in the Charter. The final decision rests with the Supreme Court of Canada but in the beginning any provincial court judge in Canada may strike down a statute. Although that judgment is not binding elsewhere it tends to cause ripples all across the country.

An example of the kind of issue that can arise is this: section 37 of the Medical Profession Act permits a judge to order a member of the College to produce his records when a disciplinary complaint has been made against him. The member argues that this procedure is an unreasonable seizure and so forbidden by the Charter. This argument came before Mr. Justice D.C. McDonald and he wrote a lengthy judgment. He felt bound to say there was a seizure because a Court of Appeal judgment had so indicated. However he then held that the seizure was reasonable.[2] Of course a ruling like this can be appealed to the Court of Appeal and then to the Supreme Court of Canada. In the meantime the law will be uncertain. It is inevitable in the beginning that there be a rash of cases but one must hope it will subside soon and that when the law is settled it is settled in a way that does not cripple the power of the legislature.

3. Medicine—Definition of Health

A word about the meaning of medicine. Traditionally it is diagnosis, treatment and prevention of disease. However, the W.H.O. has defined health as "a state of complete physical, mental and social well-being and not merely the absence of disease or infirmity." If this definition of health is accepted then health care is widely extended. The influence of this wide definition can be seen in some modern definitions of health care. For example the definition in our Dependent Adults Act says that it includes "any provision undertaken for the purpose of preventing pregnancy." Preventing pregnancy is not within the traditional definition of medicine. (Another point about this definition—it illustrates the fact that statutes are not always unambiguous. The question here is: does the definition cover a sterilization for contraceptive purposes?)

The common law produced a number of principles and rules relating to medicine. There are now a number of statutes of interest to the medical professions—for example, the Hospitals Act, the Health Care Insurance Act, the Mental Health Act, and at the federal level the Criminal Code. I would like here to describe some legal rules, both judge-made and statutory, that are of interest to physicians. I have chosen those that deal with consent—consent to medical treatment, to experimentation, to gifts of human tissue, to sterilization, and particularly to those situations where the person cannot give his own consent.

4. Consent to Treatment—Informed Consent

We begin with the proposition that except in emergencies, a competent adult must give consent. If he does not, then an operation or other procedure that involves invasion of his body is an assault or battery. The rules on this subject are still in the realm of common law for we do not have any statute on the subject. In many cases consent is given by conduct. The patient holds out his arm for an injection or opens his mouth to have a tooth extracted. In some cases the practice is to ask for a written consent, as in the case of surgery. The main question is this: what should the patient be told in order for his consent to be proper?

For long the leading case was one in Ontario in which the plaintiff complained that she had not been told of the risk that after an operation on her hand it would be stiff and contracted. The case holds that the patient must be able to trust the surgeon to give a clear explanation of the operation and its usual outcome, but that he need not disclose all the dangers inseparable from any operation.[3] Then in a later case, where the doctor had failed to warn the patient that neomycin might cause deafness, the court held that the doctor had not failed in his duty to disclose. An explanation of alternatives would have been bewildering and the patient was not in a position to make an intelligent choice.[4]

Then came two Supreme Court cases, the more important one being *Reibl* v. *Hughes*[5] where the surgeon omitted to tell the patient of the risk of a stroke. The judgment, following recent American cases, says that the surgeon should disclose the nature of the operation, the material risks and special or unusual risks. It rejects the earlier cases which left the extent of disclosure to professional judgment. That is to say, the patient must give an informed consent. However, common risks need not be disclosed. Moreover the patient may be in a bad emotional state so the surgeon is said to have a "therapeutic privilege" not to disclose risks to the patient. Besides, the patient may waive his right to be informed. Assuming a failure to disclose, then the patient must show that he would not have consented to the operation had there been proper disclosure. Here we are in the realm of speculation. The court must try to decide what the reasonable person would have done.

Since this case there have been many alleging an inadequate explanation after something has gone wrong. The great majority have failed. The court found the disclosure to be adequate or else that the patient would have consented even had he received the information to which he was entitled.[6]

If I were asked my opinion, it would be that the principle of informed consent is sound. The patient is autonomous and is entitled to determine what shall be done with his body. However, I think that more weight should be given to professional opinion than the *Reibl* case permits. In England a case recently arose in which the patient was not told that the operation would involve some risk of damage to the spinal cord. The damage occurred and the patient brought action. She relied heavily on *Reibl* and the American cases on which it is based. In the House of Lords (the highest court), one of the judges would have followed *Reibl* and a second would have gone part way but the other three judges supported the principle that the degree of disclosure of risks and of alternate procedures that might be followed was a matter of professional judgment.[7]

One good point about *Reibl* is that in some cases in recent times it has been held that if there is not proper disclosure then the consent is to be treated as though it were never given and the result is that the surgeon has committed a battery. This never made sense and one can welcome the ruling in *Reibl* that where the consent is not informed it is a case of negligence and not of battery.

One might wonder what effect *Reibl* has had on the actual practice of surgeons and physicians in relation to disclosure. A law professor sent out a questionnaire to 1,000 surgeons and received 620 responses. Not all the surgeons had heard of the judgment and some were not clear as to what it said. Others said that since *Reibl* they have made more detailed disclosure of risks than formerly. The author's conclusion was that the rule had had slight impact on surgeons' practice.[8]

A question arises—would it be wise to try to legislate on this subject? In the U.S. about 30 states have done so in reaction to cases like *Reibl*. Some of these acts call for informed consent but the majority of them require only what is in accordance with standard medical practice and in most of the acts a signed consent is conclusive unless there is fraud.[9] I am not at all sure that it would be wise to legislate. This might lead to a stereotyped consent form "that both the physician and patient come to regard as unnecessary red tape, and consequently do not engage in the dialogue envisioned by the doctrine. . . . Each procedure has its own unique risks, and each patient is in some manner unique. Only by going through the difficult task of tailoring information to fit the procedure and the patient is it likely that either individual autonomy or rational decision-making will be promoted. If neither of these functions is furthered, the process becomes meaningless.''[10]

5. Consent for Minors

The next problem that brings law and medicine into close contact is that of consent to the medical treatment of minors. Until recently there was no legislation so the common law applied. The problem with the common law is that there were very few cases on the point in England and Canada but notwithstanding the paucity of decisions it was generally understood that a mature minor could give his own consent to medical treatment.[11] This raised the question, what is the test of maturity? When the age of majority was 21 the question would usually arise in connection with a 20-year-old, a 19-year-old or possibly an 18-year-old. Now, however, with the age of majority at 18 the question arises when the patient is 17 or 16 or perhaps younger.

In recent years there has been widespread demand for legislation to make the law certain. In 1969 an English act fixed the age of consent at 16. However, Parliament added a provision saying that ''any consent which would have been effective if this section had not been enacted'' is still effective. This vague provision raised questions. For example: could a public health authority prescribe contraceptive measures to girls under 16? The government advised the local authorities that they could, at least if the girl insisted on confidentiality from her parents. A Mrs. Gillick, with five daughters under 16, was apprehensive lest any of them might seek contraceptive advice or measures. She asked the health authority to assure her that the daughters would not be advised or treated without her knowledge or consent while they were under 16. The authority refused so she brought action. The trial judge rejected her claim for these reasons. A doctor is not a party to the crime of unlawful sexual intercourse with a girl under 16; and the fact that the girl is under 16 does not automatically mean that she cannot give consent. She can if she is mature, though only in exceptional cases should the parents not be consulted.

The mother appealed and the three judges in the Court of Appeal unanimously reversed the court below. The parent has custody and hence the control of the child up to majority and the girl under 16 can give no valid consent. The doctor advising or providing contraceptives infringes the parents' rights. The court acknowledged the argument that persons under 16 might simply refuse to seek medical care if they knew their parents would become involved; but it did not prevail against the risk of undermining parents' efforts to bring up the child and the fact that the doctor does not know the girl's history and that his action might further a harmful association that the girl had begun. In rare cases, however, the doctor may be entitled to act in spite of the parents' wishes.[12] A case is on its way to the House of Lords but there is no report of a judgment as yet. This case is not binding in Canada but it could have influence. Under our Domestic Relations Act and Child Welfare Act the parents or guardian have custody until the child is 18. I have assumed that even with the reduction in the age of majority, a mature minor might give his/her own consent. However the reasoning of this case is that since the child is in custody of parent or guardian until reaching majority it is the parent or guardian who has the power to consent to medical treatment for the child (subsequently reversed, on or about Oct. 17, 1985).

Over ten years ago the College sought legislation to try to provide certainty. The government asked the Institute of Law Research and Reform to make recommendations. These recommendations were made after wide consultation, particularly with those in the health professions. The report of the Institute recommended 16 as the age of consent. Then came a difficult problem. Should the law provide that a person under 16 could ever give his or her own consent? Assuming this to be desirable then there are two possible ways to legislate. One is to provide that the consent of a person under 16 is valid if two practitioners say that the minor can understand the treatment and that the treatment is in the best interests of the minor's health. The other one is to specify the cases in which a person under 16 could give consent—for example, contraception, abortion, venereal disease and drug addiction. The Institute took the second alternative and subsequently the Uniform Law Conference took the first. The legislature has not acted on the Institute's Report. My guess is that the special provisions for those under 16 are the stumbling block. If this is so then the Uniform Law Conference's alternative seems warranted. I do not wish to underestimate the difficulties. Maybe a flat age of 16 is best or perhaps 14 as Quebec provides. The fact would have to be faced that if this is done some youngsters under the prescribed age might simply go without treatment.

While on the subject of medical care of children, it is relevant to note the general role of the court in protecting the interests of children and also of mental incompetents. Long before there were Child Welfare Acts and Mental Health Acts, the King's Courts exercised on his behalf the power of *parens patriae*—father of the country. Usually they did so to protect the property of the minor or incompetent but were entitled to intervene in other matters when in the best interest of the child. This is why children were made wards of court and our child welfare acts are really an outgrowth of this power. Alberta's new Child Welfare Act, like its predecessor, provides for children in need of protection. One ground on which the court may order protection is that the parents have failed to provide medical care. This frequently arises and then there is the special case of families like Jehovah's Witnesses who refuse to permit transfusion to their child on religious grounds. The Child Welfare Act has machinery for compelling the transfusion notwithstanding the parents' objection.[13]

Another type of case is that of the new baby who has Down's syndrome and also an intestinal blockage. The latter is operable and without the operation the baby will die. However, the parents refuse to consent to an operation. In an English case, the child was made a ward and the Court of Appeal ordered the operation. "It is not for the Court to say that life [of a Down's syndrome child] ought to be extinguished."[14]

In Canada, the B.C. case of Stephen Dawson is well known. He was blind, partly deaf and unable to stand, walk or talk at age seven. Fluid on his brain was drained by a shunt. It needed "revision" but the parents refused consent. Hence he was apprehended. The family court judge supported the parents' position and ordered the child returned to them. On appeal, Mr. Justice McKenzie rejected the proposition that Stephen would be better off dead. "That would mean that his life was not worth preserving and many disabled persons would be in jeopardy." He placed the child in the custody of the Superintendent of Child Services and ordered that the operation be done.[15]

The same problem has arisen many times in the United States, as shown by the recent Baby Doe cases. The President's Commission in 1983 made a report on the subject of deciding to forgo life-sustaining treatment. It puts emphasis on the responsibility of families, professionals, and institutions, with recourse to law only when the law requires it or there is disagreement. On April 15 of this year the U.S. Government published final rules under the Child Abuse Prevention and Treatment Act.[16]

The object of the Act and rules is to balance the protection of disabled infants against the avoidance of undue interference with parental responsibility and the practice of medicine. The rules impose an obligation to provide treatment with three exceptions: (1) where the infant is chronically and irreversibly comatose, (2) where the treatment would merely prolong dying, and (3) where the treatment would be virtually futile for survival and be inhumane. One commentator says these rules are a compromise with little impact on decision making.[17]

6. Withdrawing or Withholding Treatment From Adults

A related question is that of withdrawing, or refraining from, treatment of other patients who cannot make their own decision or are permanently unconscious. The President's Commission's report emphasized the responsibilities of families, professionals and institutions with recourse to the courts only when the law requires or there is disagreement (just as it had done in the case of babies).

The report also deals with the situation where there has been a cardiac arrest and the question is whether the procedure for resuscitation should be set in motion. As I read the recommendations in Chapter 7 they are much like those approved by the CMA, CHA, and CNA. I am not able to make any helpful comment on these guidelines, for it is hard for a layman to judge whether they strike a balance between the preservation of life when warranted and the cessation of life where warranted. The procedural guidelines are obviously well thought out.

7. The Mental Health Act

Before leaving the subject of legislation relating to consent to medical treatment it is relevant to note the Mental Health Act. That Act does authorize a hospital to provide treatment for the patient. A case arose[18] in which the hospital asked to have a guardian appointed under the Dependent Adults Act so there would be someone to consent to an operation for a hernia on a patient in the hospital. The public guardian wanted more powers than the hospital thought he should have and the case came on for trial in the Queen's Bench. In a lengthy judgment it was held that the hospital had a duty to provide medical care but that in relation to non-mental illness consent was needed. Thus if the mental patient was not capable of giving his own consent he needed a guardian to provide it. The judgment points out that we do have a provision (section 20.1 of the Dependent Adults Act, formerly section 3 of the Emergency Medical Aid Act) that deals with adults who are incapable of giving consent. It says that if two physicians are of opinion that the adult is in need of treatment, then it may be provided without the consent of any person. However the judgments holds that section 20 does not satisfy the patient's "need" as well as would a guardian under the Dependent Adults Act, though it "may still be useful in urgent situations where there is not time to have a partial guardian appointed."

Assuming this judgment to be correct then the result is that whenever treatment for a physical illness is necessary and the patient is not competent to give it, a guardian has to be appointed with the possible exception for emergencies. It would seem to me to be preferable to have the Mental Health Act make provision for the treatment of physical ailments of the patient. Indeed the Saskatchewan Law Reform Commission has just made tentative recommendations that are worthy of examination.

8. Sterilization of Minors and Incompetent Adults

One topic on which there is no legislation in any Canadian province is that of sterilization of minors and mental incompetents. We had a Sexual Sterilization Act from 1928 to 1972, when it was repealed largely on the grounds that the eugenic basis was unsound and that in the case of mental defectives the Act took away the right to procreate without consent of the person or his parent or guardian. I have mentioned that our Dependent Adults Act permits a guardian who has authority over health care to arrange for contraceptive measures.

Bearing in mind the repeal of our Sexual Sterilization Act in 1972 I cannot conceive that the legislature intended to confer on guardians, even with the approval of the Court, the power to authorize sterilization of incompetents. Moreover, when the Dependent Adults Act was introduced the minister in charge said it did not cover sterilization. Yet judges have in several cases approved non-therapeutic sterilizations under the Act. If this procedure is to be permitted under Alberta law for persons who cannot consent for themselves then we need guidelines set out in legislation. There is no such legislation in Canada at present. The situation is analogous in the case of a minor. Can a parent give a valid consent to the non-therapeutic sterilization of a minor child? In the United States the general position is that the parent cannot do so and in England a judge in 1976 forbade the sterilization of an eleven-year-old girl with Sotos syndrome.

In a recent B.C. case[19] the mother said her retarded ten-year-old daughter had a phobic aversion to the sight of blood and she sought the court's approval to a hysterectomy before the onset of menstruation. The trial judge held that the phobic reaction was not proved. He thought the girl could be desensitized. Thus he refused the order. The mother appealed and the Court of Appeal authorized the hysterectomy. All three judges emphatically disagreed with the trial judge. Indeed one of them thought the case should never have come before the court.

Then there is the case of the adult who is retarded and whose parent or guardian wants her sterilized for fear of pregnancy. A Prince Edward Island case, *Re Eve*[20] is still in court. In that case the mother sought appointment as guardian so she could approve the sterilization. The trial judge rejected the application on the grounds that he had no jurisdiction. The mother appealed. All three judges on the appeal found they had jurisdiction under the general power of the Superior Court (the *parens partiae* power) to make the order if in the best interest of the mentally retarded person. Two out of three thought that the sterilization was in Eve's best interest. They even authorized a hysterectomy, which is puzzling. The third judge thought that permission should be granted only if it were made clear that the sterilization would be in Eve's best interest and there was not enough evidence before the court to show that it was. Some of the unanswered questions were these: could she give her own consent? is she fertile? is she likely to become pregnant? would other forms of contraception do? He felt the court simply did not have enough evidence. Eve's representative appealed to the Supreme Court of Canada. The case has been argued but the judgment not yet handed down. Just a few days ago one of your members kindly provided me with a press release announcing the CMA's Medical Guidelines for Sterilization of the Retarded. These guidelines are helpful and show concern for the best interests of the incompetent. The release says the CMA is awaiting the judgment of the Supreme Court of Canada in *Re Eve* before preparing step-by-step procedural guidelines.

9. Experimentation

Problems of consent also arise in connection with experimentation on humans. We do not have any statute governing it. However, rules were laid down in the trial of Nazi doctors at Nuremberg. These rules say that "the person involved should have legal capacity to consent." Taken literally, this excludes any research on a child or mental incompetent. This cannot be right. The many ethical codes that have been formulated, particularly in the post-thalidomide period, have recognized the need to do research on these people, but there has been a wide difference of opinion on the question of safeguards. One view is that the parent or guardian can make up his mind whether to consent after knowing the risks and weighing them against the benefits. The other view, short of forbidding such research, is that the research should be done only if the risk is minimal. This was the test laid down by the National Commission in the United States. Its guidelines recommended that allowance be made for greater risk where the research might benefit the child, and also for "a minor increase over minimal risk" where the research is on the disorder the child has; and the recommendations for research on the institutionalized mentally infirm were similar.

In Canada a working group of the MRC examined these matters. The majority thought there should be the usual weighing of risks and benefits with substituted consent. However, Professor Crepeau thought that there should be no experimentation on the incompetents where the research could be of no direct benefit.

10. Gifts of Human Tissue

Problems also arise in connection with donations of tissue. Alberta has a Human Tissue Gift Act, which is a Uniform Act. Part I deals with *inter vivos* gifts. It says that "any adult person who is mentally competent to consent" may make a gift. This excludes minors and the mentally incompetent. However, the Act applies only to *inter vivos* gifts of non-regenerative tissue so if the question were to arise of a gift of regenerative tissue such as bone marrow, skin or blood by a minor or incompetent we would have to resort to the common law. It gives little guidance. (In the United States the general position is that the consent of parent or guardian is not valid but that recourse must be had to the court. This is shown by the cases involving kidney donations by children and incompetents.) There has been criticism of these provisions in our Act largely because they are confined to non-regenerative tissue, and there is uncertainty as to whether a minor or incompetent can ever make a gift, for example, of skin, bone marrow or blood.

Part II of our Act dealing with *post mortem* gifts is worthy of note, for it shows that legislation can bring the law up to date. The common law said that the person did not own his own body. Then came another rule that said one's executor or family had responsibility for burial, and this was converted into a right in the nature of a limited ownership over the body. Thus it was that the family was held to have a cause of action against a doctor and funeral director when an unauthorized autopsy was performed. In other words the common law gave to third persons the power to dispose of the body and their wishes prevailed over the wishes of the deceased. This never made sense. Yet when the British Parliament passed the Anatomy Act in 1832 it preserved the family's right to override the wishes of the deceased who had wanted to give his body for anatomical study. Then when Parliament passed a Corneal Grafting Act in 1952 and replaced it by a Human Tissue Gift Act in 1961 it followed the same policy. A person could make a gift of a part of his body for purpose of a transplant but if he did the final decision rested with the person in possession of the body.

In Canada the Uniform Law Conference in 1959 produced a Corneal Transplant Act. It was a copy of the English one. Then when the Conference looked at England's Human Tissue Act, it concluded that gifts made by the person should be binding and should not be subject to the decision of anyone else. This was made clear in the Uniform Act of 1965 and it has been preserved in Part II of the Uniform Act which Alberta has. In 1968 the American Uniform Law Conference in its Anatomical Gift Act adopted exactly the same principle.

Yet some people still think that the family can override a valid donation made under the Act, though I am confident that the Task Force is under no such illusion. Indeed the great issue today in connection with *post mortem* gifts is whether the law should go further than it does and permit the taking of human tissue unless the person in his lifetime has indicated an objection or unless his family objects. Such a proposal is called an opting-out or contracting-out scheme which is the reverse of our present contracting-in system. The object of course is to procure more organs and tissue. We already have a small opting-out provision because a medical examiner who orders an autopsy may permit removal of the pituitary gland. Indeed in Saskatchewan the same is the case with the cornea.

I do not want to anticipate the recommendations of the Task Force but the prevailing opinion seems to be that, although opting-out may come sometime, the public are not ready for it and it will be better to concentrate on trying to persuade people to make donations and above all to try to obtain the consent of families where no donor card has been signed. In New York recently a law has been passed requiring hospitals to make a request to the family to agree to the donation of organs.

In connection with this topic the huge increase in demand for organs from cadavers has caused concern that an organ might be taken from someone who is still alive. This has led to many efforts to find a suitable definition of death and put it in a statute. Some of these were premature and have been criticized. However I should think that the report of the Law Reform Commission of Canada and the American Uniform Definition of Death Act deserve consideration. This is another case where a difference of opinion exists. Do we need a statutory definition of death and if so what should it be?

The last comment I wish to make in connection with the Human Tissue Gift Act is the prohibition against sale of body parts. When a man offered $5,000.00 for a kidney from a live donor a few months ago the impression I received was that many people were not aware of this prohibition. As to the wisdom of permitting sale, the shortage of organs has led to suggestions to provide for sale either *post mortem* or *inter vivos* or both. My position is simply that of Mr. Titmuss, who made the strongest case for donations as against sale. In our Act and also in Quebec the only exception to this prohibition against sale has to do with blood. The fear is that in an acute shortage it might be necessary to buy it.

11. Conclusion

To conclude, may I suggest that the first measure to help law keep in step with medicine is to have general agreement on all the ethical problems that new advances have created. In many cases this is sufficient. In other cases I suggest the courts can be trusted to give great weight to ethical standards and in some (but not all) cases legislation is desirable. It is significant to note that the Do-not-resuscitate (DNR) Code is the Product of the CMA and the CHA, in co-operation with the Canadian Bar Association. Medicine and law, one hopes, may be marching in step after all.

Notes

1 *Mount Ada Mines* v. *Pusey* (1970–1971) 125 C.L.R. 383 at 395.
2 *Reich* v. *College* (1984) 53 A.R. 325.
3 *Kenny* v. *Lockwood* [1932] O.R. 141.
4 *Male* v. *Hopmans* [1967] 2 O.R. 457.
5 [1980] 2 S.C.R. 880.
6 Picard, Legal Liability of Doctors and Hospitals (2 ed. 1984) p. 107.
7 *Sidaway* v. *Bethlem Royal Hospital* [1985] 1 All ER 643 (H.L.).
8 Robertson, Informed Consent in Canada (1984) 22 Osgoode Hall L.J. 139.
9 Making Health Care Decisions (President's Commission) vol. 3, pp. 204–245.
10 Annas, Glantz and Katz; "Informed Consent to Human Experimentation" p. 42.
11 *Johnston* v. *Wellesley Hospital* [1971] 2 O.R. 103.
12 *Gillick* v. *West Norfolk Health Authority* [1985] 1 All ER 533.
13 *Re D.* 30 R.F.L. (2d) 277 (Alberta).
14 *Re B.* [1981] 1 W.L.R. 1421.
15 *Re S.D.* (1983) 42 B.C. L.R. 153.
16 45 C.F.R. part 1340: Fed Register Apr. 15, 1985 p. 14878.
17 Murray, The Final Anti-climactic Rule on Baby Doe (1985), 15 Hastings Center Report No. 3, June 1985 p. 5.
18 *Re Osinchuk* (1983) 45 A.R. 132.
19 *Re K.* [1985] 3 W.W.R. 204, reversed [1985] 4 W.W.R. 724, (see also 757 re Supreme Court of Canada).
20 (1979) 10 R.F.L. (2d) 317, reversed (1981) 115 D.L.R. (3d) 283.

1986

The Sproule Case: Bloodshed at Kootenay Lake, 1885

Reprinted from
Law and Justice in a New Land
Edited by Louis A. Knafla, 1986 Toronto: Carswell
pp. 233–266

This article relates to a murder which took place on Kootenay Lake, B.C. in 1885, arising out of a disputed mining claim. Sproule, an American citizen, was tried in Victoria and convicted before a Judge of the B.C. Supreme Court, following which he brought a "writ of error" before the full court, and later took habeas corpus *proceedings before a Judge of the Supreme Court of Canada (Henry J.). The latter declared the proceedings null and void, and ordered the accused freed, whereupon the Province of British Columbia asked the full court of the Supreme Court of Canada to review the ruling of Henry J. The latter ruling was reversed, the conviction restored, and Sproule was hanged, despite continuous pressure from the United States government against the conviction and sentence because of his U.S. citizenship.*

The judgment of the Supreme Court of Canada (1886), being 110 pages in length, is perhaps the leading case in Canada on habeas corpus*. Bowker's interest in this subject dates back to 1951 following a casual inquiry from Professor Paul Freund of Harvard University as to cases in Canada on* habeas corpus*. This sparked an interest, and Bowker made a point, intermittently over the years, of reading all cases on* habeas corpus *in Canada (though he never published anything on this subject). In the course of reading these cases he came across the Sproule case, which he found fascinating from the standpoint, as well, of early justice in western Canada.*

Over the years, the Bowkers visited the actual scene of the murder on Kootenay Lake on three separate occasions, talked to people in the area, and mentally re-enacted the events leading up to the murder, and the escape of the accused.

Following this, Bowker did extensive research in the archives in Victoria and in the National Archives in Ottawa, each of which has a bulky file. He came to view the Sproule case as one of the most interesting in our early legal history, equal in a way to that of Louis Riel.

In 1985 Bowker was asked to speak at a Conference in Calgary on Western Canadian Legal History, for which he chose this topic, and was later asked to prepare it for inclusion in a book entitled Law and Justice in a New Land *published by Carswell in 1986.*

Correspondence received since its publication would suggest that the article has made an impact on all who have read it.

The flamboyant title may lead the reader to think that this is a story of multiple killings on the lines of the clash between Vigilantes and the Plummer Gang at Virginia City in Montana in 1863–64, or the Lincoln County War in New Mexico in 1878 involving Billy the Kid, or the Graham-Tewksbury feud between sheepmen and cattlemen in Arizona in the mid-1880s or the Johnson County War in Wyoming in 1892. The fact is that the only physical violence was the killing of Thomas Hammill which led to the murder charge against Robert Even Sproule. The killing and subsequent legal proceedings produced judgments totalling 110 pages in the Supreme Court of Canada Reports, brought about the intervention of the respective governments of the United States and the United Kingdom, and reveal the interplay of lawyers, judges and administrators in the shaping of law and procedures in a young colony.

Discovery of Minerals on Kootenay Lake

The Kootenay country is a right-angle triangle in the southeast corner of British Columbia. Its base of some 140 miles is the American border; its perpendicular is the valley of the Columbia River where it comes down from the Big Bend through the Arrow Lakes and on into the United States, and its hypotenuse is the Great Divide which forms the British Columbia/Alberta boundary. East Kootenay is the valley bounded on the east by the Great Divide and on the west by the Purcell Range. Kootenay Lake is in West Kootenay between the Purcells and the Selkirk Range. Almost 100 miles long, narrow and deep, it is shut off from the outside by mountains and rugged terrain.

A century ago Kootenay Lake was almost inaccessible. True, the Dewdney Trail had been cut in the mid-sixties from Hope on the Fraser to Wild Horse Creek near the present Fort Steele in East Kootenay, but it had become overgrown. The mountains were a barrier to Donald and Farwell (now Revelstoke), towns on the line of the Canadian Pacific Railway, which was completed in November 1885. One could go along the Outlet or West Arm to the Columbia River near Castlegar, but it was not navigable. A few boats plied the Columbia upstream through the Arrow Lakes to Farwell or downstream into the United States. The only feasible route to and from the lake was from Spokane Falls (now Spokane) in Washington Territory and Sand Point in Idaho Territory, 65 miles northeast of Spokane. Each was on the railway. From Sand Point a 35-mile trail led northward to Bonners Ferry, on the Kootenay River just south of the Canadian border. The river was easily navigable for the short distance to the south end of the lake.

Until 1880 Indians had Kootenay Lake to themselves. It had of course been explored earlier. It was the hope of finding gold that finally brought men to the lake just as it had been the reason for the founding of the colony of British Columbia in 1858. The story of the gold rush on the Fraser River and on to the Cariboo and even more remote places is well known. In 1864 there was a short-lived gold rush in East Kootenay at Wildhorse Creek. The colony passed ordinances dealing with gold and placer mining in particular, for it is gold dust that brings about a rush.[1] There was also legislation dealing with quartz mining of gold and the mining of coal. In 1869 the Governor in Council made an ordinance to facilitate the working of minerals other than gold because "it is expedient to develop the resources of the colony by affording facilities for the effectual working of silver, lead, tin, copper, coal and other minerals". However, that ordinance was "not calculated to develop the mineral resources of the province", as the legislature recited in its Mineral Act of 1877.[2] A consolidated Act of 1882[3] was disallowed because section 6 gave to Gold Commissioners the functions of a judge appointed by the Governor General under section 96 of the British North America Act, 1867.[4] A re-enactment of 1884 remedied this defect.[5]

In general the law of B.C., like that of California and Australia, was based on the custom of miners. However, the Gold Commissioners were a B.C. institution. Dr. Ormsby points out that most of them were Irish and the rest English. While they were often unorthodox and sometimes made mistakes, "they were a group of men peculiarly well adapted to frontier service".[6] Important provisions in the legislation of 1882 provided that only a person with a free miner's certificate could locate or work a claim, and hard-rock claims were 1,500 by 600 feet. A claim had to be registered within three days with provision for extension and it had to be "represented and *bona fide* worked by the owner or his agent". The Gold Commissioner could declare a closed season, during which the miner need not work his claim. It was said to be "laid over". Absence from the claim for 72 hours constituted abandonment unless the Gold Commissioner gave permission to be absent.

Kootenay Lake never produced a gold rush for it has no placer gold and indeed no gold quartz. It is, however, rich in other minerals: lead, zinc and sometimes silver. Not long before 1840, a trader for the Hudson's Bay Company named Archibald McDonald was in charge of Fort Colville in Northeastern Washington. He discovered on the shore of the lake an outcrop of minerals—the very one that is part of this story. A prominent American mining man, George Hearst, father of William Randolph Hearst, went to the same spot on the lake in the early 1870s. However, the prospector who enticed him there had "salted" the lead-zinc ore with silver. When Hearst discovered this he lost interest.[7]

The outcrop was called the Big Ledge. It was marked by iron stains that indicate the presence of lead and zinc and perhaps silver. It was at the southern end of the blunt peninsula or "stubby promontory" on the east side of the lake five miles north of the present-day ferry landing at Kootenay

Bay. The promontory protrudes about one quarter of a mile into the lake and is a mile from north to south. Sketch 1 (drawn in 1885) shows the promontory with Galena Bay on the south and North Bay on the north. The indentation on the shore line just west of Sproule's cabin is a pretty and small cove called Bluebell Bay. The sketch does not show the sharp knob or hill to the south of Bluebell Bay, covering much of the Kootenay Chief claim and the southern part of the Bluebell. It is a larger and higher hill than the one shown in the sketch. The trail running eastward from Sproule's cabin is between the two hills. It still exists, and at the eastern edge of the Bluebell claim merges into Fowler Street in Riondel.[8]

Sketch 2 (also drawn in 1885) shows the whole of Kootenay Lake. The promontory is identified by the word "mines", and Galena Bay is shown. The man who rediscovered the Big Ledge there was Robert Evan Sproule. When he came to the lake in 1882 (or possibly 1881), he was about 45 years of age. A native of Maine who had lived in Washington Territory for years, he was credited with developing a coal mine near Tacoma. However, he had some trouble with the law. He was indicted for burning two barns near Tacoma. For some reason he never came to trial, and there were suggestions that he was a fugitive from justice. Always on the move, in the 1880–82 period he was in Idaho, Washington, Montana, England, and South America. These eccentric and sudden moves were characteristic of the man. A friend of Sproule's named Dick Fry of Bonners Ferry told him of the possibility of minerals on Kootenay Lake. He located the Bluebell on 31st July 1882. It is not clear when it was recorded in the Gold Commissioner's office at Wildhorse Creek. A great problem of course was that the round trip to Wildhorse Creek by the only convenient route via the Kootenay River was 480 miles. This lengthy and difficult journey meant that the miner was bound to be away from his claim much longer than the maximum of 72 hours.

The Mining Dispute

Sproule was not left in solitude for long. The wealthy Ainsworth brothers—John of Oakland and George of Portland—had men on the scene almost as soon as Sproule. They established a camp across the lake at the Hot Springs, which are still called Ainsworth. (Later they built two cabins on Galena Bay; one is marked as Hammill's cabin on Sketch 1.) Thomas Hammill, a Cornishman of about 27 years of age, was in charge for the Ainsworths. Two other Ainsworth men were Blasdel (Blaisdell) and Woodbury. On 5th October 1882, Hammill located the Kootenay Chief on behalf of Blasdel. The next day he located the Comfort on behalf of Woodbury. Thus the Bluebell was sandwiched between the two Ainsworth claims as Sketch 1 shows. From the Ainsworth camp across the lake, Hammill kept an eye on Sproule's movements. Indeed his diary notes them and a description of Sproule's cabin.[9] Sproule absented himself from time to time, and he left on 25th October instead of staying until the 31st, which was the end of the open season. He had asked the Gold Commissioner for leave of absence but had not had time for a reply. He posted a notice that he was leaving for ill health and to get provisions. The moment he left, however, Hammill crossed the lake and took up the ground for himself.

At this period, over the winter of 1882–83, Sproule aligned himself with two other Americans, Colonel Hudnut and Jesse Hunley (Hunly). Another associate was W.A. Bailie-Grohman (hereinafter "Grohman"), an English entrepreneur who later told of his years in the Kootenay.[10] He agreed to help the other three in their clash with the Ainsworths in return for a share in the claims. Over the winter both Grohman and Sproule were in Victoria to oppose the granting of a concession to the Ainsworths.[11] The concession was supported by the British Columbia Board of Trade because it would develop an area that had been of no value, would connect it with the settled parts of the province, and would attract settlers.[12]

In the spring of 1883, on 25th May, which was a week before the end of the closed season, Hunley purported to relocate the Kootenay Chief under the title of the Lucy Long. When Blasdel came to the mine on 1st June Hunley was in possession. In the case of the Comfort, one of Sproule's associates named Meyers (Myers) on 25th May purported on behalf of Hudnut to relocate most of that claim which he called the Gem. Thus when the season opened on 1st June all three claims were in dispute. The Ainsworth agents brought action in the Gold Commissioner's court, asserting their right to each of the three claims. The Commissioner was E. Kelly, who came from Wildhorse to the mines for the hearing which began on 31st August. Grohman explains that Kelly lodged in Sproule's cabin and ate his meals at Hammill's because the Ainsworths had more grub. He allowed the dispute to range over a wide area. The trial lasted seven weeks including some adjournments. It is hard to tell who acted for the Ainsworths. It appears to have been A.E.B. Davie, Q.C., the Attorney General. The other side had attempted to get another lawyer who is not named, but who was probably Theodore Davie, the Attorney General's younger brother. Theodore was not available so Grohman, although not a lawyer, represented Sproule and his associates.

Without giving reasons, the Gold Commissioner dismissed all the actions. In other words, he found against the Ainsworth agents and in favor of Sproule and his associates on the dispute over each of the three claims. (There was a fourth action by Woodbury against Meyers for trespassing on the Comfort. That action was of course dismissed because if Hudnut was properly in possession then Meyers was not a trespasser.) The net result of the decision was that Sproule's claim was good and Hammill was a claim jumper, while Hudnut and Hunley were not claim jumpers. Their relocation respectively of the Comfort and the Kootenay Chief was valid.

The Kootenay Mining Appeals

The Ainsworths appealed to the Supreme Court of British Columbia. That court had five judges. They all took trials and three or all five sat on

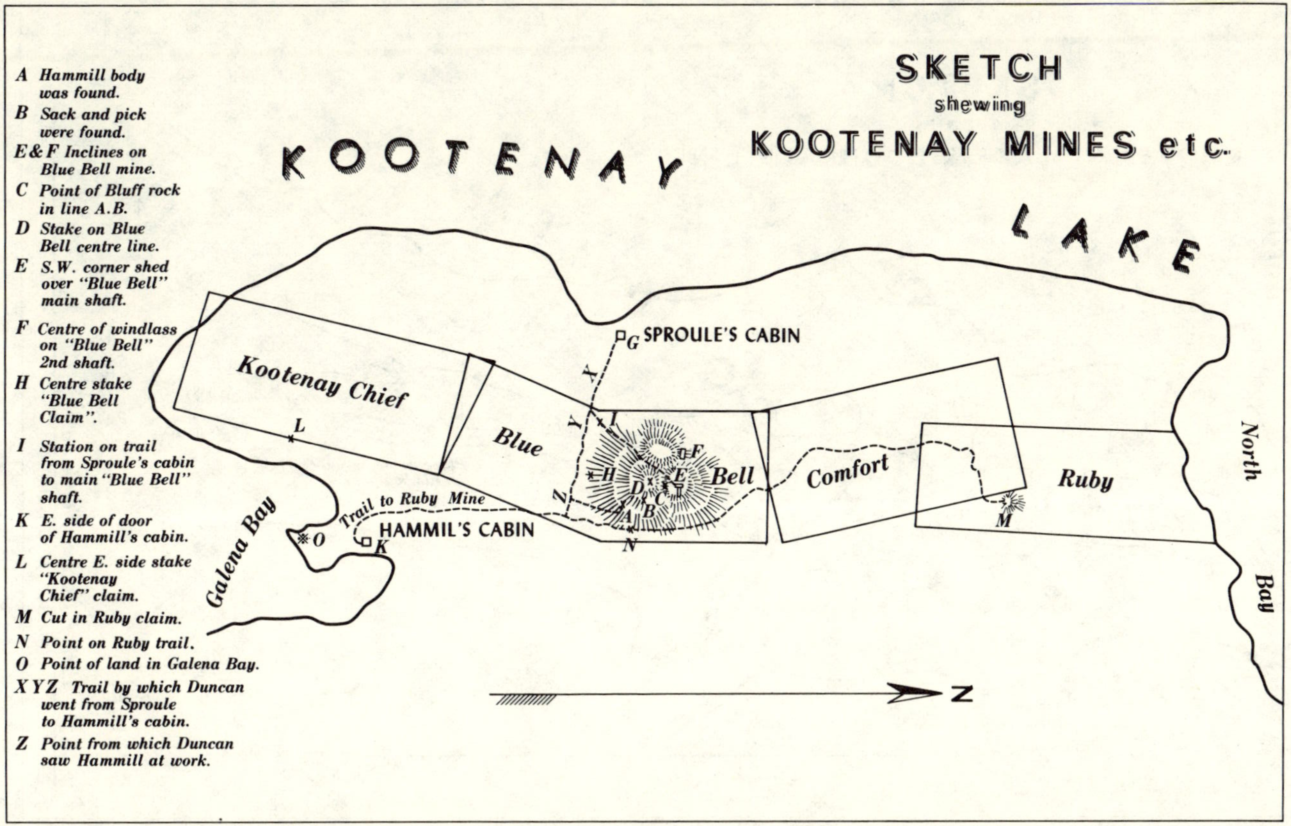
SKETCH
shewing
KOOTENAY MINES etc.
KOOTENAY
LAKE
SPROULE'S CABIN
Kootenay Chief
Blue
Bell
Comfort
Ruby
North
Bay
Galena Bay
Trail to Ruby Mine
HAMMIL'S CABIN
Z
A Hammill body was found.
B Sack and pick were found.
E&F Inclines on Blue Bell mine.
C Point of Bluff rock in line A.B.
D Stake on Blue Bell centre line.
E S.W. corner shed over "Blue Bell" main shaft.
F Centre of windlass on "Blue Bell" 2nd shaft.
H Centre stake "Blue Bell Claim".
I Station on trail from Sproule's cabin to main "Blue Bell" shaft.
K E. side of door of Hammill's cabin.
L Centre E. side stake "Kootenay Chief" claim.
M Cut in Ruby claim.
N Point on Ruby trail.
O Point of land in Galena Bay.
XYZ Trail by which Duncan went from Sproule to Hammill's cabin.
Z Point from which Duncan saw Hammill at work.

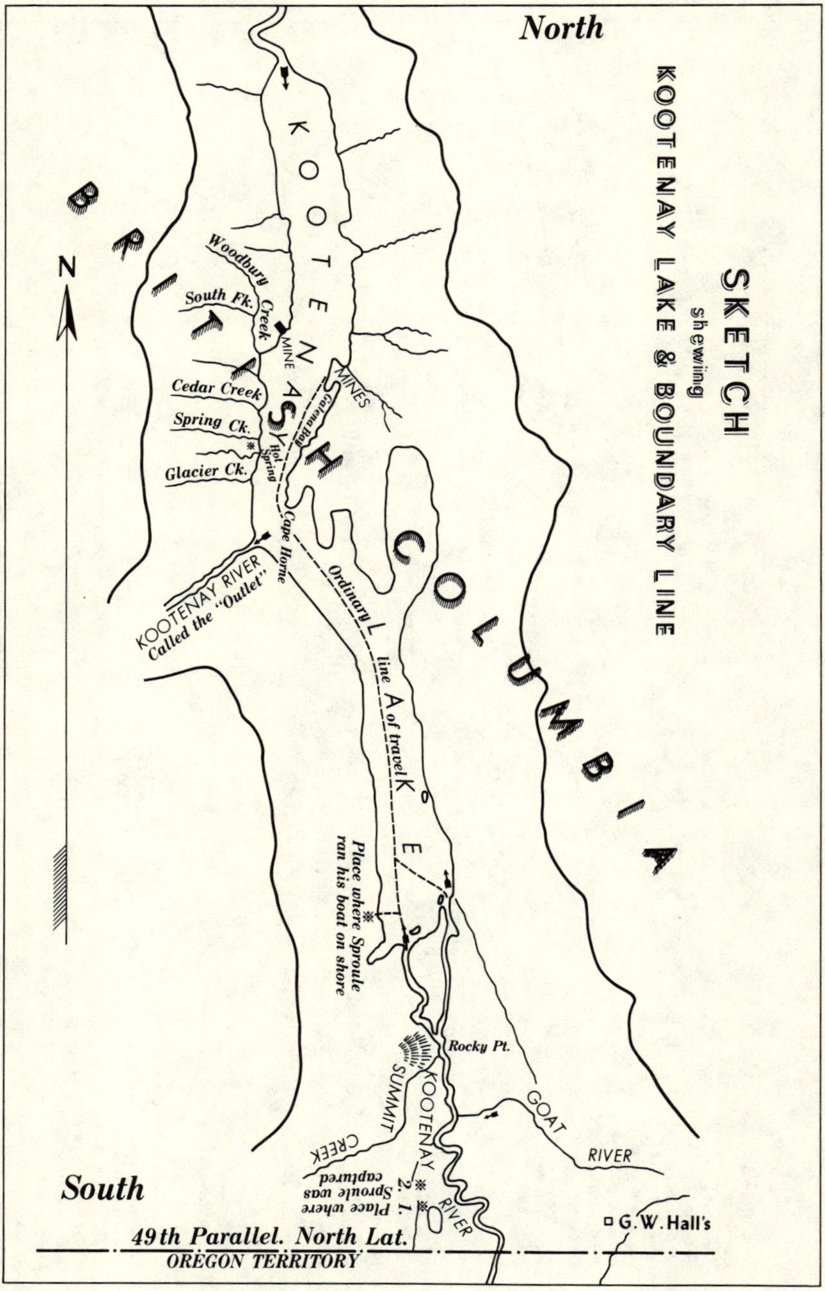

North
SKETCH
shewing
KOOTENAY LAKE & BOUNDARY LINE
BRITISH COLUMBIA
KOOTENAY LAKE
N
Woodbury Creek
South Fk.
MINE
MINES
Galena Bay
Cedar Creek
Spring Ck.
Glacier Ck.
Hot Spring
Cape Horne
KOOTENAY RIVER
Called the "Outlet"
Ordinary line of travel
Place where Sproule ran his boat on shore
Rocky Pt.
SUMMIT CREEK
KOOTENAY RIVER
GOAT RIVER
2. 1. Place where Sproule was captured
G. W. Hall's
South
49th Parallel. North Lat.
OREGON TERRITORY

appeals. Chief Justice Begbie is one of the noted figures in the colony's history.[13] He had been an English barrister who came to British Columbia as its first judge when it was made a colony in 1858, and as its first Chief Justice when it became a province of Canada in 1871. Over the years he had clashed with the legislature and the provincial executive when he thought they were improperly interfering with the authority of the judges.[14] In a famous murder case in 1880,[15] he engaged in an undignified quarrel with J.F. McCreight who appeared for the Crown.

The judge second in seniority was H.P.P. Crease.[16] Like Begbie he had been an English barrister and was the first one in British Columbia. He had a major role in bringing the colony into Confederation in 1871 and soon after was made a judge. The third judge was John H. Gray from New Brunswick.[17] He was a member of the first Canadian Parliament, representing Saint John. He was appointed directly to the British Columbia Court in 1872. At first the Chief Justice was unhappy with the appointment because he did not care for lawyers from the colonies, but later he worked in harmony with Gray. J.F. McCreight came from the Irish Bar by way of Australia to Victoria in 1860, and was made a judge in 1880. Judge Watts says "he knew his law probably better than any previous judge in British Columbia", though his "excessive desire to do justice led to vacillation".[18] His early antagonism to Begbie seems to have disappeared in later years. George Walkem came to British Columbia in 1862 from Lower Canada.[19] Begbie refused to permit him to appear as counsel and would not enroll him as an advocate until ordered by the Governor. Walkem had two terms as Premier and was appointed to the Court in 1882. His political career was turbulent and he was never popular, but during his 22 years as a judge he had a creditable record.

On the appeal of the Ainsworth interests from the judgments of the Gold Commissioner, Begbie, Crease and Walkem sat. The Attorney General appeared for the Ainsworths while M.W.T. Drake, Q.C. and C. Wilson represented Sproule and his associates. The appeal was argued on 25th March and judgment delivered three days later.[20] The Chief Justice began by noting the difficulty that miners had in knowing the mining laws, with no copies available and no Gold Commissioner nearby. Then he ruled on the cases one by one. Taking the Comfort first he found that Woodbury had not abandoned it. It seems that the Commissioner, William Fernie, came into the area on the day Woodbury located it, and granted to him leave of absence for sickness, the leave extending over the closed time. On the same occasion Fernie recorded the Comfort and Kootenay Chief. Hudnut alleged that Woodbury was not really sick, but Begbie pointed out that Hudnut had never taken steps to have the leave of absence cancelled. In these circumstances Hudnut's attempted relocation on 25th May was simply a trespass. Moreover, Hudnut was not a free miner on that day. He did not obtain his certificate until 4th June. In Woodbury's action against Meyers, the latter was of course found to be a trespasser and he had to pay damages of $1.

As to the Kootenay Chief, the Chief Justice found that after Hammill located it for Blasdel on 5th October, more work was done on the claim than the Gold Commissioner required. Moreover, the building of a cabin near the claim must be treated as legitimate mining work, for "the houses are just as useful for working the mines, as the pumps and furnaces with which the water is removed or the ore roasted."[21] It is true that the work ceased more than 72 hours before the end of the open season but this was not fatal. Blasdel had no opportunity to apply to the Gold Commissioner for leave because he was too far away. Since Blasdel still was entitled to the claim when the closed season began, Hunley in attempting to relocate the claim in May was simply a claim jumper. It appears that a man named Gay Reeder (Reader), an associate of Sproule's, had located a claim called the Mogul on the site of the Kootenay Chief before Blasdel had located it. However, Reeder did not assert any interest in the property and Hunley did not purport to claim through him.

Turning to the dispute over the Bluebell, the Chief Justice thought that in October 1882 Sproule had not been spending all his time working the Bluebell as he was supposed to. There was evidence that he had been representing (that is, occupying) and working on, Reeder's claim. If a miner tries to represent two claims then he fails to represent either. "A miner might as well attempt to go to sleep in two bunks."[22] However, the Chief Justice gave Sproule the benefit of the doubt and held that he was representing the Bluebell. It is true that he left the claim from time to time and finally departed in his boat on 25th October. He had applied for leave of absence but there had been no time for a reply. The Chief Justice said that Hammill had been watching Sproule's movements from across the lake, and that he moved over to the Bluebell as soon as he saw Sproule leave. He took it upon himself to decide that Sproule had abandoned his claim, and relocated it in the name of the Silver Queen. In the result the court upheld Sproule's claim to the Bluebell but found against Sproule's associates on the other two claims. Before ending his judgment Begbie observed

> that the whole of this wearisome, expensive, and mischievous litigation has been caused and fostered by the unauthorized intrusion of a stranger, who seems to have succeeded, before the Gold Commissioner, in raising such a cloud of irrelevant statements and controversies, as to entirely obscure that officer's view of the few material facts in each case.[22a]

His interference was entirely illegal, even though he was impelled by the highest motives. The reference clearly is to Grohman. The latter's account of the litigation omits any reference to his castigation and says that he became a good friend of Begbie.

It is frequently said that Sproule lost his law suit. This is utterly wrong. However, his victory was turned into a partial defeat. The reason is that he had assigned a one-third interest in the Bluebell to Hudnut. Hudnut did not pay the costs assessed against him so Woodbury issued execution. The only convenient asset was Hudnut's interest in the Bluebell. By the summer of 1884, some four months after the judgment of the full court, there was a

Deputy Sheriff on Kootenay Lake named George Johnston (Johnson). He advertised the sale of Hudnut's one-third interest in the Bluebell. He sold one sixth for $802.25 and another one sixth for $769.84.[23] Hammill was the purchaser of both. Sproule was more embittered than ever against the Ainsworths when he found that Hammill had acquired an interest in the Bluebell. During this period he uttered various threats against Hammill should he set foot on the claim. His anger was directed too against Grohman. According to the latter, Sproule twice tried to murder him—once on the trail to Sand Point and once on a train outside Sand Point.[24] The date is not fixed but it must have been during the winter of 1884–85. In November 1884, Sproule purported to assign the whole of the Bluebell to the Kootenay Mining and Smelting Company, owned by an American Dr. W.A. Hendricks (Hendryx), in return for 120 shares in the Company. Hendricks engaged Sproule to work on the claim in 1885.

The Murder of Hammill[25]

In Idaho, Sproule hired three American laborers to come with him to the mine at the opening of the 1885 season. Two were brothers, Charles and Adam Wolf (Wolfe, Woolf). The third was Charles Howes (Howse, House). By that time there was a constable, Henry Anderson, at the Ainsworth camp on the west side of the lake. Sproule spent the night of 31st May on the west shore having gone to see Anderson about recording some claims. He returned to his cabin on the east side early on the morning of 1st June. He set his men to work cutting logs for "lagging" which was used to prop up shafts. They then took the lagging uphill to the shaft that had been started. Sproule himself spent some time sharpening a saw. Then he had a talk at his cabin with a miner named John Duncan who was staying with Hammill. His movements during the morning are not at all clear, but he knew that Hammill had come to work on the Bluebell. Sketch 1 shows where Hammill was working, on the slope of the knob just north of the trail from Sproule's cabin. Sproule's workers thought he was going across the lake to the west shore, but they found a note from him saying that he had to go out and would increase their salaries from $40 a month to $45. The note ended with the admonition "don't give up the mine boys, don't give up the mine".

The evidence of Sproule's workers was not always clear or consistent. They said they heard no shot. However, Duncan, who had returned to Hammill's cabin, did hear a shot around 10 a.m. as did a man named Velnoweth (Belnouf) who was working the Ruby claim (north of the Comfort) for the Ainsworths. When he was about to go to the Hammill cabin for lunch he passed by the place where Hammill had been working and found him dying of a gunshot wound. Hammill did not know who had shot him. Velnoweth summoned Duncan and they took the wounded man to his cabin where he died shortly. In the meantime word was sent to Constable Anderson across the lake and he came in the early afternoon. It was then noted that Sproule had gone. Anderson held an informal inquest in the cabin, assisted by six of the miners who were present. They found that Hammill "came to his death by a rifle bullet fired by a person or persons unknown". Hammill was buried not far from his cabin. A wooden marker contained the words "Thomas Hammill assassinated June 1 1885 age 30 years".[26]

When Anderson learned that Sproule had left by boat he went back to the west shore and early in the evening started southward in pursuit. At the outlet he changed to a fast canoe. Accompanied by a miner named Molson and an Indian he paddled all night. The next morning at about 4 a.m. they saw Sproule in his boat ahead of them. When they were within a mile Sproule lowered the small sail and landed on the west shore. His landing place is shown on Sketch 2. It was a poor spot for a landing and the boat was not well secured. Sproule went into the woods. Anderson and Molson remained in the area overnight, and in the morning moved toward the border hoping to intercept Sproule. On 3rd June they had no success. On the evening of 4th June, toward dark, one of the Indians who was assisting Anderson shot at a bear. Sproule heard the shot and emerged soon after. He had few supplies and seemed exhausted. He hesitated a moment, and then gave his rifle to Anderson, who tied his wrists and took him into custody. Sproule did not ask and Anderson did not give the reason for the arrest. Anderson took the prisoner to the Canadian Customs Post where Rykert was in charge. Then he brought Sproule back by a small steamer to the Hot Springs where he was held in custody. Later in a written statement on 14th February 1886, Sproule made detailed complaints of Anderson's harsh treatment of him.

The Stipendiary Magistrate, Arthur W. Vowell, came to the lake and held a preliminary inquiry at the Hot Springs on 22nd June. The witnesses were the men who had been on the scene on 1st June—Anderson, Velnoweth, Duncan, Howes, the Wolf brothers, Molson, and two miners who testified to threats by Sproule against Hammill (Spence Smith and Gay Reeder). Sproule cross-examined some of the witnesses. The magistrate gave him the usual invitation to speak, with a caution. His reply: "I wish to reserve my statement until the time of trial when I may be able to secure some counsel". The magistrate then committed Sproule for trial "at the next court of competent criminal jurisdiction to be held in the Kootenay. . . . " The Attorney General decided to move Sproule to New Westminster because there was no proper lock-up in the whole of the Kootenay. Besides, a trial at the coast would be more convenient for everyone and there were enough eligible men to form both grand and petty jury. An assize was held at Donald in July 1885, with the Chief Justice presiding. The experience was an arduous one. Paulus Aemilius Irving, the Deputy Attorney General, was at the Donald assize and instructed Vowell, the Stipendiary Magistrate who had committed Sproule for trial, to have Sproule taken to New Westminster. Vowell ordered Constables Anderson and Miles to escort the prisoner. The route was by way of Farwell, Shuswap Lake and Kamloops. Sproule was lodged in the New Westminster jail sometime in September.

The only logical place to hold the trial was New Westminster or Victoria. The Crown preferred the latter on the basis of convenience and expense. On 9th October the Attorney General arranged to have the New Westminster gaoler bring Sproule to Victoria. The prisoner and Theodore Davie, who had agreed to act for him, were present when Irving applied on 13th October to the Chief Justice for an order for a change of venue from the Kootenay district to Victoria. The Criminal Procedure Act of 1869 provided that when justice required, the trial of a person charged with felony be held in a district, country of place other than that in which the offence is supposed to have been committed; and the court could then make an order so providing.[27] Such an order is called an order for change of venue. Section 11 said that "such orders shall be made upon conditions as to the payment of any additional expenses thereby caused to the accused as the Court or Judge may think proper to prescribe". This commendable provision protected the prisoner against the possibility that the trial would be moved to a place so remote that his witnesses could not afford to attend. It played a central role in Sproule's case.

For long it had been the general opinion that British Columbia was only one district and no order for change of venue was ever necessary. However, a Sheriff's Act had been passed in 1873, setting up various "shrievalties".[28] In 1885 another murder was committed in the Kootenay District but was tried in the Kamloops District without an order. Theodore Davie, who acted for the accused Malott, argued that the conviction was a nullity because no order for change of venue had been made. On 21st January 1886, sixteen days after Sproule had been sentenced, the full court upheld Davie's argument and ordered a new trial.[29]

When Irving applied before the Chief Justice on 13th October for an order changing the venue, Davie made no objection. The gaoler was anxious to return to New Westminster so Irving hurriedly drew the order. The statute said (section 11(3)) that the order was sufficient warrant to the sheriff for the handing over of the prisoner. Chief Justice Begbie's Bench Book has an entry saying that Theodore Davie pointed out that the proper place of trial was in the Kootenay and that the witnesses for the prisoner were there. The order as written in the Bench Book says: "Crown undertaking to abide by such order as the Judge who tries this case may think just to meet the equity of the Statute of Canada 1869 Chapter 29 section 11, trial to take place at assizes here 23/11." However, the document drawn by Irving failed to include the words just quoted.[30]

Sproule's Murder Trial

In British Columbia at this time the criminal courts were modelled on those of England and in many ways unlike those of today. There were "Courts of Assize and Nisi Prius, and of Oyer and Terminer and General Gaol Delivery". In England the Crown issued a commission, usually to a Queen's Bench Judge, to hold an assize or sitting to hear and determine (oyer and terminer) trials of major offences and to insure that all those in gaol were tried and not left languishing (gaol delivery). The commission named the Commissioner and fixed the date of the assize and the county or counties it was to embrace.

By the time of Sproule's trial, the province had passed several acts that had a bearing on the constitution of its criminal courts. In 1879 the Judicature Act said that they "may be held with or without commissions at such times and places as the Lieutenant Governor may direct."[31] Four years later the Jurors Act set up districts from which grand and petit juries were to be drawn. The Victoria district was basically the same as that of the Sheriff of Vancouver Island—that is, the part of the island south of the 49th parallel excluding the Sooke District.[32] This Act also set out the qualifications of jurors and the list of those exempt from jury duty. Then in 1885 the Assize Courts Act said that these courts should be held at specified places and times, and at Victoria the court was to be held on the first Monday of April and the fourth Monday of November.[33] But in spite of the Judicature Act the McLean case in 1880 had held a commission to be necessary. Thus it was that on 3rd September 1885, the Lieutenant Governor issued a commission to all the judges to hold assizes in the province.[34] Mr. Justice Gray was assigned to the Victoria Assize which was convened on 23rd November. A grand jury of sixteen members was summoned. They indicted Sproule. The indictment had in the margin the words—"British Columbia, to Wit", but the body of the indictment did not say where the crime had been committed.[35] The trial was adjourned twice on the request of Theodore Davie in order that Dr. Hendricks could come to Victoria from Idaho.

The trial began on Wednesday, 2nd December. Attorney General A.E.B. Davie was in charge of the prosecution while his brother Theodore represented Sproule. On the selection of the petit jury, Theodore challenged one juror for cause and sixteen peremptorily, while the Crown had one juror stand aside. The Attorney General's opening speech outlined the evidence the Crown would offer in connection with the killing, and also in connection with the dispute between Sproule and Hammill over the mining claims. The first witness was Nicholas Velnoweth, who described how he found the dying man while on his way from the Ruby claim to Hammill's cabin. Hammill, though dying, appeared to say that he did not know who had shot him. He died just after Velnoweth and Duncan had carried him to the cabin. The witness described how Duncan went to the west shore to summon the constable, told of the inquest held in the cabin, of the inquiry as to Sproule's whereabouts and of the preparations for the pursuit. The second witness was Adam Wolf, one of the two brothers who worked for Sproule. He said that a pick handle found with a gunny sack up the hill near the place whence the shot was fired was like those Sproule had. He also said that Sproule had borrowed his rifle around 10 a.m., left his cabin around 11 a.m. and entered his boat, carrying his own rifle and looking angry. Later Wolf noted that his rifle had been returned having been used. He also mentioned the note Sproule left. Adam was followed by his brother Charles, whose evidence was very imprecise as to times and details but damaging to Sproule. He described the note Sproule left as saying: "I am going out on business. Stay here and do the best you can. Your wages from this [sic] will be $45 per month. Stick by the mine, boys, stick by the mine. R.E. Sproule".

Other witnesses included three American miners who described threats that Sproule had made against Hammill. Then John Duncan testified that Sproule had spoken angrily of Hammill during their talk on the morning of the murder. On cross-examination, Theodore Davie, for whatever reason, tried to bring out from the witness the fact that Hammill had an unprepossessing appearance. Duncan said Hammill had a very light mustache, but denied that he had a retreating chin or turned-up nose. (The photo in the Nelson Museum makes him look presentable.) Duncan had also found him to be a pleasant man without any enemies but Sproule. Jesse Hunley, who had been defendant in the action involving the Kootenay Chief, described the sheriff's sale to Hammill of Hudnut's one-third interest in the Bluebell, and said that Sproule had uttered threats against Hammill on learning of the sale. George Johnston, who was acting as Sheriff on Kootenay Lake in the summer of 1884, testified that he had a writ of execution against Hudnut, and that he seized Hudnut's interest in the Bluebell by virtue of the writ and sold it to Hammill. The Deputy Attorney General, Irving, then told of his efforts to procure the attendance of Charles Howes at the trial. Howes had said that he was unable to come. Gay Reeder, who had been involved in the location of the Bluebell mine and an associate of Sproule, described Sproule's uncertain habits and sudden movements in and out of the country.

The next major witness was Charles Molson. He spent the night of 31st May with Sproule on the west bank. On that occasion Sproule uttered threats against Hammill should he appear on the Bluebell, and the next morning crossed the lake to the Bluebell. Around noon Duncan came to the west shore to tell Molson that Hammill had been shot. They both returned at once to the east shore. Hammill was lying dead in his cabin. Molson examined the site of the shooting. He identified the pick handle as being of the type that only Sproule possessed. He then returned with Anderson to the west side to prepare for the pursuit of Sproule, which he related as that given in the preliminary examination. While Molson was not present when the arrest was made, he testified to two little incidents. On the way back to the mines Sproule asked Molson to have a man named Lundy pull his boat up on the shore because he "did not pull it up very good and I'm afraid it will get away". Sproule was not handcuffed until he had been brought back to the Warm Springs, and when Molson handcuffed him he expressed the fear of being lynched. On cross-examination, Theodore Davie tried to show that Molson's evidence was much more damaging to Sproule than it had been in the preliminary. Davie also attempted through Molson and other witnesses to show that there was a trail along the west side of the lake southward from the point where Sproule had landed. The witnesses denied this. Davie also tried to show through cross-examination that Sproule landed because he had a weak arm that impeded rowing and because his boat was leaking.

The next Crown witness was T.R. Manning, who was engineer on the steamer that took Sproule back to the mines. He testified that when Sproule came aboard he tried to give a message to a man named Rice to take to Dr. Hendricks. The note criticized Anderson for having been in league with Hammill. It expressed the fear that the property of the Kootenay Mining and Smelting Company would be seized, and added that more men were needed to work the claims.

The Constable, Henry Anderson, recounted that on 31st May Sproule had come to the west side to see him. Hammill was present but left when Sproule came. Sproule's discussion with Anderson had to do with the re-recording of some claims. Sproule stayed the night. He mentioned that he did not intend to go to Sand Point but intended to stay and work the claims. Anderson's account of his investigation of the murder was succinct: "I was informed the next day of the murder, made investigation and started in pursuit of Sproule from the Hot Springs." Anderson testified that there was no trail where Sproule had landed on 2nd June, but the trail began fifteen miles south beginning at Rocky Point (which is shown on sketch 2). He also testified that when Sproule walked into the camp after an Indian fired a shot at a bear, he said to Sproule: "I have been waiting for you, Mr. Sproule, throw down that gun!" The witness continued: "he stood moving the rifle backwards and forwards in an undecided manner, when I ordered him a second time to throw his rifle aside whereupon he did so saying, 'All right, then'". He tied Sproule's hands. Sproule had enough food for a day or two but no blankets. Nothing was said by either one about the reason for the arrest. Anderson took $89.15 from Sproule, and Sproule asked him to pay $62.50 to the customs man for duty.

On the morning of 7th December, Theodore Davie made his opening address to the court and jury. He described the differences between Sproule and the Ainsworths, and their oppression. He argued, however, that after Sproule had turned over his interest in the Bluebell to the Kootenay Mining Company in return for shares, any motive that Sproule might have had disappeared. He emphasized the danger of convicting on circumstantial evidence. There were discrepancies in the evidence of the key Crown witnesses. Moreover, the testimony of the Wolf brothers at the preliminary hearing had been much less damaging to Sproule than it was at the trial.

The first witness for the defence was James Hobkirk, a miner from Colorado who said that he had known Hammill there around 1880, and that Hammill was a notorious claim jumper. Dr. Hendricks testified that Sproule had transferred the Bluebell to him in return for shares in 1884. The court would not permit Davie to ask him about a general belief in the existence of a trail at the point where Sproule had landed. Jacob Meyers, who had been a defendant in one of the law suits over the mining claims, described Sproule's erratic movements—on Kootenay Lake in 1881, to a ranch at Bonners Ferry, to Missoula intending to go to Cape Town, to New York and next to Liverpool. From there he went to South America rather than South Africa. In May 1882 he was back at Sand Point, and in the winter of

1882–83 he went to Victoria to oppose the legislation sought by the Ainsworths. Then came the Crown's evidence in rebuttal. Wootton was recalled to testify that the claim jumper in Colorado was not the deceased Thomas Hammill but another man named Hamel. It will be noted that Sproule did not testify on his own behalf. At that time, unlike the present, an accused person was not a competent witness.

Theodore Davie's closing address as reported in the *Daily Colonist* was shorter than his opening one and was free of high-flown oratory. He stressed that the evidence was circumstantial. It was dangerous to convict on such evidence, especially in a capital case. His closing words: "let it not be said of the prisoner as of Henry Blake [in a case quoted], that he was another who went to swell the list of the many victims of circumstantial evidence."[36]

The Attorney General's address defended the change of venue from Kootenay Lake to Victoria which Theodore Davie had criticized. He reviewed all the evidence that pointed to Sproule's guilt and added: "before, however, you convict him you must be satisfied that the facts are incapable of any other hypothesis than that of the prisoner's guilt." This is a good statement of the rule in *Hodge's* case. In his peroration he invoked the Deity and urged the jurymen to do their duty no matter what the consequences. "Do it with due regard to the prisoner—with due regard to society, and you will give a verdict which will have the approval of that great judge who presides at that highest of all tribunals—the Judgment Seat." Then he concluded by assuring them that they will have discharged their duty, and "fulfilled the sacred oath upon which you swore to try this case."[37]

On the following morning, Wednesday, 9th December, Justice Gray charged the jury. He read over to them the whole of the evidence, a task that took five hours. The *Colonist* described the care that he had displayed throughout the trial and his solicitude to ensure that the jury could detect no bias. "The strict impartiality displayed in the charge was a matter of general comment upon the adjournment of the court."[38] Justice Gray concluded: "I cannot define any other theory by which this crime could have happened than that adduced by the Crown". Then in describing Sproule's departure and subsequent arrest he observed, "it seems as if everything had been brought about by some higher power than an earthly one." He ended by saying that "the interests of society are in your hands on the one side and the life of the prisoner at the bar on the other, and I do hope that you will be able to come to a conclusion which will be consistent with what is right between God and man."[39]

After the jury retired at 4:40 p.m., Theodore Davie asked the judge to provide to the jurymen some of the depositions taken on the preliminary. The judge refused. The jury returned at 9:45 p.m. to announce that they were unable to agree. The judge urged them to make a further effort. The jury retired again and returned at 11 p.m. with a verdict of guilty, accompanied with a recommendation to mercy, adding the cryptic statement that they had reason for so doing. Davie then asked that the jury be polled but the judge refused, saying that he was satisfied that the jury was unanimous.

At this juncture Davie asked the judge to "reserve" two points before passing sentence. In other words, he wanted to advance reasons why sentence should not be passed. This practice came from England, but in that country a Court of Crown Cases Reserved had been established in 1848. There was no such court in British Columbia so Mr. Justice Gray asked the other four judges to sit with him as assessors (advisers) while he heard the argument for the defence. It took place on 4th January 1886. The first point was that the court should have admitted evidence to show that Sproule believed in the existence of a trail at the point where he went ashore. The second point was the judge's refusal to poll the jury. Davie contended that in England this was an absolute right though in the United States the rule varied from state to state. His argument made good use of decisions and textbooks, and was forceful though candid in acknowledging the doubt that existed. He invited a dissent so that he might take the point to the Supreme Court of Canada. The Attorney General relied on American authority that the polling of a jury is not compulsory. It only occurs when the court is in doubt whether the jury were agreed. As to questions about the existence of a trail he argued that this was simply hearsay because the witnesses had no first-hand knowledge. The court reserved its decision until the next day.[40]

All the judges were present when the court opened. Justice Gray addressed Sproule. He said that all the judges fully agreed with him, and that he saw no reason to depart from his rulings at the trial. He paid a compliment to Theodore Davie, saying that he had brought his points before the court with extreme clearness, employing good and solid argument and had given good support and assistance to the accused. The Attorney General then moved that sentence be passed. The judge asked Sproule whether he had anything to say. Sproule denied the crime and said that the Crown witnesses were prejudiced:

> There has been a conspiracy in that camp against me since I was there, and upon the part of one of your members and also by men from San Francisco, who never located a mine in their lives other than going into camp and acquiring claims through fraud; one of these men was named Blaisdell [Blasdel].

The judge pointed out that he had no power to hear new evidence. "But I again ask you is there anything you have to say—any legal objection to urge—why sentence should not be pronounced upon you?" Sproule replied by saying that he could show the evidence against him was partly false, and the judge replied that he could not consider that now.

The judge explained to Sproule that he had succeeded in the mining dispute, and yet he had then taken the law into his own hands.

> I wish it to be understood that while every American citizen who may come into this country will be as welcome as you yourself were, we desire to impress upon them that when they come here they cannot bring with them that looseness and laxity of administration which obtains in their own country—to impress upon them that the divine as well as the human law is observed here—that he who takes human life his life shall be required of him.

. . . .

It is true no human eye saw you, no human hand was near; but the shadow of a mightier power followed you, and was around you; whose step was on the water and whose voice was on the wind. . . .

The judge concluded:

I have to pronounce upon you the sentence of this court that you be taken to the place from whence you came and from thence on the 6th March to the place of execution where you shall be hanged by the neck till dead; and may the Lord have mercy on your soul.

He said that he would transmit to the Queen's representative the jury's recommendation to mercy. Finally, he spoke of the efficiency of Constable Anderson and the others who made the arrest and brought the prisoner to justice.[41]

Where a prisoner had been sentenced to death, the trial judge was required to report to the Governor General. Justice Gray wrote his report on 7th January, two days after passing sentence. "The trial lasted for seven days. The evidence was entirely circumstantial but formed in my opinion an unbroken chain that left no possible doubt of the prisoner's guilt. The prosecution was conducted with great fairness and the prisoner was well and ably defended." Referring to the recommendation for mercy, the judge speculated on two possible reasons. The jury might have thought that Sproule had nursed his feelings of hostility against Hammill for so long that he had become "monomaniac on the subject", or the jury might have objected to capital punishment. Then he hinted at his own views in the following words:

It is a question whether it may not sometimes be conducive to the administration of justice to give consideration to these influences and mitigate the extreme penalty of death to imprisonment for life rather than not get a conviction at all. These matters are for the consideration of His Excellency.

He added two comments:

It would have been impossible for the prisoner to have had a fairer trial. Indeed I strained many points in his favor and whenever there was a doubt gave him the full benefit of it. . . . There is a much greater disregard for human life, and much less hesitation in taking it, in these western mining countries than there is with you in the older settled portions of Canada and the United States.[42]

Writ of Error Before the Full Court[43]

There was no appeal in the sense that there is today, but British Columbia had adopted an English procedure known as a Writ of Error. The writ was brought for an error, however trivial, on the face of the record, but not for wrongful admission of evidence or misdirection of the jury.[44]

Theodore Davie, in an elaborate factum, alleged seven errors. One of his points was that the document drawn pursuant to Chief Justice Begbie's order for change of venue said nothing about the payment of additional expense caused to the accused and that this omission was fatal. On reading this, the Attorney General drew up a second document.[45] This second document stated, while the original one had not, that the alleged murder was at Kootenay Lake. More important, it recited: Mr. Irving "now undertaking on behalf of the Crown to abide by such order as the judge who may preside at the trial may think just to meet the equity of the 11th section of 32–33 Victoria Chapter 29... such being the conditions which I think proper to prescribe". The document then, like the first one, provided that the trial should be proceeded with in Victoria. It bore the same date, 13th October 1885, the Chief Justice signed it, and it was made part of the record in place of the first document. It will be noted that the added wording was in fact in complete accord with the conditions the Chief Justice had made and noted in his Bench Book.

Argument on the Writ of Error came before the court on 15th February. The judges present were the Chief Justice and Justices Gray and Walkem. Theodore Davie said he intended to argue that the substitution in the record of the second document for the first constituted a "diminution of the record", which is defined as "incompleteness of the record of a case sent up from an inferior to a superior court". His argument was that the record originally contained the first document, but that the record now before the court on the Writ of Error contained the second, and that this constituted a diminution of the record. He asked for an adjournment to 19th February so that the point could be argued before all five justices. The Crown did not object and the court agreed.

Before adjourning, however, Justice Gray expressed his condemnation of material that had appeared in the newspapers against the prisoner and also publications in his favor. He referred to two items in the *Colonist* two days before (13th February). One of them was a long letter from J.A. Gandy, Justice of the Peace in Washington Territory. He had committed Sproule for trial at Puyallup near Tacoma in 1878 on a charge of arson in the burning of two barns. He went on to say that he did not really think Sproule guilty. He described his good character. The second item was an affidavit taken on 8th February by Charles Howes, Sproule's laborer, who had not appeared at the trial. He denied that Sproule had borrowed Adam Wolf's gun on the day of the murder, and said that Constable Anderson had offered him money to provide evidence against Sproule. This affidavit had been obtained by Davie, who accepted responsibility for its publication. His object was to counteract the effect upon the public mind of the unfair attacks that had been made against Sproule.[46]

On the argument before the five judges on 19th February, Davie first dealt with his attack on the second document (or second order, as he called it). He argued that Sproule had been tried and convicted under the first order and that order did not include any condition about the expenses of witnesses. He argued further that even the second order did not comply with the 1869 statute. His main point, however, was that an order for change of venue could be made only upon condition that the Crown attend to the extra expenses, and that therefore the first order was a nullity and hence the trial and conviction were of no effect. Justice McCreight said that the order for the change of venue was not necessarily part of the record, and the Chief Justice referred to the contents of his Bench Book in connection with the expenses of witnesses quoted earlier. Davie then made his second argument on diminution of record; namely, that the judge's refusal to poll the jury should appear upon the record, which did not mention it. The court rejected both arguments. The second document, set out in the record, "was the order made by the Chief Justice, and the question of the prisoner's right to poll the jury was not a matter to be dealt with on a Writ of Error."[47] Having failed to persuade the court that there was a diminution of record, Davie went on to his submission that there had been seven errors.[48] The first two were combined in the argument and the judgments speak of six.

The first argument attacked the constitution of the grand and petty juries because they were not picked from the whole of the bailiwick of the Sheriff of Vancouver Island. As mentioned earlier, the Jurors Act excluded the Sooke District. The jury should have been drawn from the whole area south of the 49th parallel. The second point had to do with the wording of the indictment. It did not mention the venue or place of the alleged murder. True, it had the words "British Columbia to wit" in the margin, but Davie argued that the absence of any venue in the body of the indictment was fatal. The third point, and the one that was to loom largest of all, was the one that had been argued on the complaint of diminution of record, namely that the order for change of venue was void because the document which the Chief Justice had signed on 13th October was not a valid order.

In his fourth and fifth points Davie attacked the commission which the Lieutenant Governor had signed on 3rd September, authorizing the judges to hold Courts of Oyer and Terminer and Gaol Delivery. This commission was mentioned earlier. Davie argued that the Lieutenant Governor had no power to issue such commissions. Only the Governor General could do so. Moreover, the commission in question authorized the summoning of jurors from the whole of the province instead of the district where the commission was sitting. Then he contended that the commission should have named the districts where the court was to be held, and that once a single court had been held under the commission the commission was exhausted. The sixth and last point was that the Jurors Act was *ultra vires*.

The Attorney General responded by asking the court to find no error. The argument took place on 20th, 22nd and 23rd February. Sproule was in attendance and was also present when judgment was given on 27th February. The judgment was unanimous in rejecting all of the alleged errors. The Chief Justice dealt first with the argument that the order for change of venue was void. He simply said that the provision as to costs was adequate. He did not mention the fact that the document in the record had only been executed after the writ of error had been granted. He dismissed a subsidiary point

Davie had raised, namely, that an order for change of venue could not be made until a grand jury had indicted the accused. This argument was patently wrong on the wording of section 11 of the Criminal Procedure Act. As to the attack on the indictment for failing to show the place of the alleged crime, the Chief Justice pointed out that it appeared elsewhere in the record. He must have been referring to the fact that the second document, unlike the first, had stated that the alleged murder was committed "at Kootenay Lake, in the district or bailiwick of the sheriff of Kootenay", and the definition of indictment in the Act included the record. Moreover, that Act had a curative provision (section 23) which said that want of venue is not fatal to an indictment. Next, he rejected Davie's attacks on the commission under which the court had been held, giving a discourse on the old English commissions. Finally, he dealt with Davie's sixth argument, and found no constitutional flaw in the Jurors Act. Davie had argued that the provisions for summoning jurors and setting out qualifications for and exemptions from jury duty were matters of criminal procedure and thus for Parliament. The Chief Justice said they had to do with the constitution of criminal courts and were therefore within section 92(14) of the B.N.A. Act. He ended by referring to section 32 of the Criminal Procedure Act, which was a broad curative provision. It was intended to restrict

> the trivialities and unfounded quibbles and objections which have long defaced the administration of criminal law; whose forms, humanely intended to protect innocence and insure a fair trial by insisting on full accurate proof of guilt, have too often been perverted and applied for perplexing the innocent and insuring impunity to criminals.[49]

Then he quoted Lord Penzance: "The picture of law triumphant and justice prostrate, is not, I am aware, without admirers. To me it is a sorry spectacle."[50] The Chief Justice concluded by saying that none of the alleged errors embarrassed the prisoner's defence or gave undue advantage to the prosecutor. All of the complaints now raised should have been made before the prisoner pleaded.

Two of the judges, Crease and Walkem, simply concurred. Justice Gray, like the Chief Justice, pointed out that the objections now taken were not taken before trial. Had they been, they might have been corrected. They came within the curative provisions of the Criminal Procedure Act. Gray followed the six points of argument in an orderly fashion and rejected them all. Justice McCreight did the same.

In the meantime, Sproule's friends had been busy trying to show that he was innocent, or at least that his sentence should be commuted. Colonel R.J. Stevens, the United States Consul at Victoria, worked hard on the prisoner's behalf. An affidavit of 13th February by Mary Clark of Seattle stated that she had married Sproule in 1871 and divorced him in 1877. He was always affectionate and kind. His only fault was his roving disposition. The ground for divorce was non-support. Sproule's brother Andrew, who had lived in San Francisco for 30 years, came to Victoria. On 2nd March he wrote a long and well expressed letter to a Senator from California, J.P. Jones, asking him to intercede with the Secretary of State to try to secure a pardon or commutation. Of more significance was a joint affidavit of two of the jurors, Peter Corr and James Boyd, who swore they had consented to a verdict of guilty, being assured in their own minds that the prisoner would not suffer capital punishment. Another juror, William Mann, took a like affidavit. A final interesting document was a letter of 27th April from Mrs. Meyers, wife of Jacob Meyers, a defendant in the mining lawsuits and a witness for Sproule at the murder trial. The addressee was the Governor General. She made a touching appeal for clemency or a new trial, and enclosed extracts from letters Sproule had written her shortly before. They criticized Davie for poor handling of the defence, declared the Crown witnesses to be perjurers, and described the dishonesty of the Ainsworths.

As soon as the full court had rejected the Writ of Error, Col. Stevens, the American Consul, sent his clerk W.G. Kellogg into the Spokane, Sandpoint and Bonners Ferry area. Disguised as a miner, his object was to gather evidence discrediting the Crown witnesses and supporting Sproule, and in trying to discover the real murderer. In a report of 20th March and a further report of 24th April, Kellogg described at length all his efforts. He did gather a number of affidavits and plied a number of people with liquor, but on his own account it was almost a comic opera of futility. The U.S. government's efforts did not stop with the Consul at Victoria. At that time President Cleveland's Secretary of State was Thomas F. Bayard. Colonel Stevens kept Bayard informed of all the information in Sproule's favour that he had gathered. On 17th February 1886 Bayard appealed to Sir Lionel Sackville West, the British Minister at Washington, to appeal for clemency for Sproule:

> While disclaiming any intention or desire to criticize the course of judicial proceedings in British Columbia, there are circumstances connected with the case which make it appear not improper that I should bring it to your attention in order that nothing that might justly mitigate the sentence of the court may be permitted to pass without due consideration.[51]

After the judgment of the full court, Theodore Davie concentrated on furnishing material and soliciting support in the hope that the Governor General would accept the jury's recommendation to mercy. However, on 18th March John Thompson, the Minister of Justice, recommended against it. On 3rd April the Governor General in Council, having examined Justice Gray's report and the petition asking for commutation of the sentence, ordered "that the law be allowed to take its course."[52]

Bayard nevertheless continued his efforts. On 14th April he wrote Sackville West again. A week later Stevens wrote to Clement Cornwall, the Lieutenant Governor of British Columbia, sending to him the bundle of affidavits "which go to prove perjury, malevolence and subornation of witnesses for the prosecution. . . . "[53] The most significant of the documents was an affidavit taken by Charles Wolf on 14th April in the U.S. He swore that he gave evidence at the trial under threats by Constable Anderson, and that he testified falsely at the trial through fear of being implicated in the crime. He said that when he and his brother and other witnesses for the prosecution had reached Victoria at the time of the trial, they were taken to the Gorge Hotel, where they agreed on their testimony in order to convict Sproule. He concluded by saying that the affidavit was made "solely in the earnest hope of being able to undo some of the terrible injury done by the said deponent and other witnesses to the said Robert Evan Sproule."[54] Shortly after appealing to the Lieutenant Governor, Stevens made a similar appeal to the Governor General, the Marquis of Lansdowne, sending him all the affidavits.

Application for Writ of *Habeas Corpus* to Mr. Justice Henry

At this point it would seem that Theodore Davie had exhausted all possibility of saving Sproule from the gallows. Davie, however, was far from through. He could not appeal to the Supreme Court of Canada because section 49 of the Supreme and Exchequer Courts Act[55] provided that no appeal should lie "where the court affirming the conviction is unanimous". Wanting to leave no stone unturned, Davie then examined section 51 of the same Act. It said:

> Any Judge of the Supreme Court shall have concurrent jurisdiction with the Courts or Judges of the several provinces to issue the writ of Habeas Corpus *ad subjiciendum,* for the purpose of an enquiry into the cause of commitment in any criminal case under any Act of the Parliament of Canada. . . .

Davie applied to Justice W.A. Henry on 3rd May 1886. The choice of judges was good from Davie's standpoint. The Supreme Court had already faced a difficult and important question as to the scope of its power in *habeas corpus*. Could it be used as a kind of appeal from a conviction in a provincial court? A woman had been convicted by a magistrate in Ottawa of vagrancy and sentenced to fifteen months' imprisonment. Thereupon she applied for a writ of *habeas corpus* before Chief Justice Ritchie. He found that the magistrate had jurisdiction so that no matter what the merits, a judge of the Supreme Court could not set aside the conviction by *habeas corpus*. The prisoner then appealed to the full court. All of the judges except Henry agreed with the Chief Justice. The *habeas corpus* provision could not be used to review convictions by magistrates throughout the Dominion. In his dissent Justice Henry invoked an Ontario statute which provided for *habeas corpus*. He felt strongly that justice required that the Supreme Court exercise its power to go behind a conviction to see whether the party had been legally convicted.[56]

When Davie made his application to Justice Henry on 3rd May, he was not present, but was represented by a distinguished Toronto lawyer, Dalton McCarthy, Q.C. The judge ordered the sheriff for Vancouver Island, J.E. McMillan, to show cause why the *habeas corpus* should not be issued.[57] At this stage the Deputy Minister of Justice, George Burbidge, Q.C. had been giving all possible assistance to the Attorney General of British Columbia. When the order to show cause came before Henry on 25–26 May, Burbidge and Mr. Gormully, who was agent for the Attorney General of British Columbia, appeared for the Crown. Both McCarthy and Theodore Davie appeared for Sproule. Justice Henry took one month before making his order and decreed on 25th June that a writ of *habeas corpus* should issue to the sheriff, commanding him forthwith to have before the judge at Ottawa the body of Sproule together with the day and cause of his detention.[58]

Justice Henry held that he could look only at the question of the jurisdiction of the court in which the prisoner was tried. If the court had no jurisdiction the prisoner was entitled to his discharge. The judge described the order for a change of venue and said that if that order was defective then the trial of Sproule was without authority. Then he referred to the first document, which of course had no reference to the matter of the expenses of witnesses. He pointed out that the second document was not in existence until after the trial and sentence. "There can be no reasonable doubt that two orders were in fact made, the one last referred to, as I think, being intended to supply what was considered a fatal defect in the previous one." This statement was to arouse the indignation of Chief Justice Begbie. Having found the first order defective, Henry concluded that the trial was improperly and illegally removed to Victoria. Then he added that even if the second document had been made before the trial, it would not have been valid because it did not in its terms actually provide for payment of the additional expense. The record was not conclusive and the court had no jurisdiction. Finally, he accepted Theodore Davie's argument that the Lieutenant Governor of a province had no authority to issue a commission of Oyer and Terminer or Gaol Delivery. This was a matter of criminal procedure and was for the Governor General. He did not rule on the argument that the indictment was invalid because it merely said "British Columbia to wit" and failed to mention any place within the province as the site of the alleged crime. He declined, too, to deal with the argument that the trial judge's refusal to poll the jury was fatal to the conviction.[59]

When Chief Justice Begbie learned of Justice Henry's order of 25th June, he made no public utterance. However, he wrote to Burbidge the same day. He did not yet have Henry's reasons, but he described the chaos that would result from the judgment, and the appalling consequences of the proposition that the Lieutenant Governor's commissions were invalid. Then, after receiving the reasons for judgment, he wrote to the Minister of Justice on 24th July a handwritten letter of sixteen pages. His greatest indignation was directed to the statement quoted earlier, that a second order was made to remedy a fatal defect in the first. This was "a terrible accusation", and "I certainly feel the imputation so galling that I am surprised at the calmness with which I am addressing you." He described in detail the making of the order on 13th October. He added that on the argument before the full court, Davie had withdrawn his objection. The Chief Justice submitted that the federal executive had the responsibility to select between the two decisions.[60]

The Attorney General, like the Chief Justice, was incensed by this interference with the administration of justice in British Columbia. He drafted a return or answer in the name of the Sheriff. Dated 19th July, it referred to the conviction and its affirmation by the full court.

> I hold the prisoner accordingly, and humbly submit that such affirmed conviction and sentence is paramount to the within writ. I have not received or been tendered any expenses of the conveyance of the prisoner. For the above reasons I respectfully decline to produce the prisoner.[61]

On the following day Theodore Davie gave notice that he would apply to Justice Henry on 2nd August through his Ottawa agent A.F. McIntyre for an order that the Sheriff's return to the writ was insufficient and that the prisoner be discharged. In the alternative he asked that the Sheriff be attached for disobedience to the writ. On the argument, Burbidge and Sinclair represented the Crown while McIntyre appeared for Sproule. On 6th August Henry gave his ruling.[62] He pointed out that he had considered whether to discharge the prisoner or to commit the Sheriff for contempt. The judge was clearly angry with the return. He thought that it had been made by someone else who seemed to think that a sheriff could refuse to execute the Queen's writ. He concluded that he had the power to order the prisoner's discharge and did so. The formal order dated the same day, 6th August, recites the various proceedings before Justice Henry and concludes with these words: "I do order that the said Robert Evan Sproule be forthwith discharged out of custody."[63] What could the Crown do now? The Attorney General and Burbidge decided that an appeal lay to the Supreme Court of Canada. Chief Justice Ritchie was on holiday in New Brunswick. Burbidge arranged with him to call a special session on 1st September.

The Judgment of the Supreme Court

Five judges sat on the argument before the Supreme Court. The sixth, Justice Gwynne, was absent. McCarthy and Theodore Davie and McIntyre were for the prisoner, while Christopher Robinson and Gormully appeared with the Attorney General of British Columbia for the Crown. The application was to quash the writ of *habeas corpus* as having been issued improvidently. The argument occupied the first four days of September.

During the argument there was much discussion about the two documents that the Chief Justice had signed. The *Toronto Mail* for 2nd September reported that Justice Strong asked Robinson: "Were two orders for a change of venue made?" Robinson's reply was "Yes sir, one was made and signed, but when the writ of error was taken out, for some reason the judge made a second order which formed the record as made up". Justice Strong then said:

> In a capital offence the action of the judge in making a second order as in this case is a gross impropriety, and if this circumstance were brought before me, although *de hors* the record, I should have struggled hard also to issue the writ of *habeas corpus,* and at any rate it is a circumstance which ought to weigh for the prisoner. It is a dreadful thing to do, after a man has been tried and sentenced, that an order should be altered, and if I had done it I should think I had laid myself open to impeachment. It seems hard that the prisoner should not get the benefit of what seems to be a grossly improper act.[64]

The newspaper account was accurate, as the Attorney General confirmed in his report to the Lieutenant Governor.[65]

Chief Justice Begbie wrote a second letter to the Minister of Justice on 1st October. He returned to the statement of Henry in reference to the two orders:

> The charge against me is that I . . . with the intent to remedy the defect [in the first document] concocted a second, a spurious order, antedating it so as to appear as if made before the trial: in fact that I forged the document with the intent of sending to the gallows a man who I well knew had never been legally tried at all—a judicial murder.

Then he referred to the statement of Justice Strong described above:

> Mr. Justice Strong . . . is reported . . . to have given vent to an outburst of fury against me individually, and to have declared that I ought to have been impeached for having signed the second document. [He added that Henry was incapable of understanding the effect of his own words, and that Strong was] of such uncontrollable irritability of temper that no person in court can venture to remonstrate with him.

(Some British Columbia lawyers might have made a like remark about the Chief Justice.) Begbie's chief concern was that observations like those of Henry and Strong would discredit the administration of justice in the province and encourage crime and disorder. True, the Chief Justice had expressions of support from several men in high places, including Sir John A. Macdonald, but they would not cure the public mischief. He thought the Supreme Court should publicly state that the accusations were "utterly unmerited and unfounded."[66]

Judgment was pronounced on 13th September. The court reversed Henry by a 3–2 majority with Henry and Fournier dissenting. Henry questioned the authority of the Chief Justice to convene the court. On the merits he adhered to his two previous judgments. Fournier dissented on the narrow ground that the court had no jurisdiction to review the actions of Henry. Chief Justice Ritchie thought it quite wrong to say that each of the six judges of the Supreme Court of Canada was in effect a separate court with power to issue a writ of *habeas corpus* in a case like the present. If he had such power it would be broader than that of the judges of British Columbia. His actions would be uncontrollable by any court. The writ of *habeas corpus* is issued out of the Supreme Court and is necessarily subject to the control of the court if improvidently issued. The Chief Justice thought that section 51, giving to every judge of the Supreme Court concurrent jurisdiction with provincial judges in *habeas corpus,* did not apply to a murder case because murder was an offence at common law, and not under a statute of the Canadian Parliament. Therefore Henry had no authority to issue the writ.

Then, assuming his last point to be wrong, the Chief Justice considered the fundamental question whether Henry was justified in issuing the writ and ordering Sproule's discharge. The Chief Justice did not find it necessary to deal with the question whether the Lieutenant Governor or the Governor General could issue a commission for the holding of an assize because the provincial legislation made adequate provision for holding such a court. The British Columbia courts had jurisdiction, and their judgments and sentences were final and conclusive. Part of the record was, of course, the second document signed by the Chief Justice and dated 13th October 1885. He added that even had the second document not been in existence, the first document gave adequate authority for the trial to be held in Victoria, at least in the absence of any objection by the accused, and there was none. Had the trial been in an inferior court, then maybe on *habeas corpus* it would have been possible to go behind the record, but this was not possible where the trial was in a superior court. He was clearly appalled by the thought that a single judge of the Supreme Court, or of a provincial court, could on *habeas corpus* set aside a conviction and a judgment of the full court.[67]

Justice Strong's reasons were much like those of the Chief Justice. He made no criticism of Chief Justice Begbie, and indeed no reference to the substitution of the second document for the first, as he had done during argument. Justice Taschereau held that section 51 did not apply to a murder charge because it was a common law offence. Since the writ was issued without authority the Supreme Court had power to quash it.

After the Supreme Court Judgment

Theodore Davie remained tireless to the end. Back in May he had written Justice Gray to solicit his support for a commutation in light of Charles Wolf's recantation. The judge replied on 18th May that Wolf's letter, written by a person outside the jurisdiction of the court, should receive no consideration. However, he thought that "on the ground of expediency—and on expediency alone—a commutation can be, and for myself I should be glad that it should be, to imprisonment for life".[68] He gave Davie permission to place the letter in the hands of the Minister of Justice. Davie did not do so at once, but after the argument for the Supreme Court, he wrote the Minister on 6th September to urge clemency, enclosing the letter of Gray: "Anticipating the possibility of Judge Henry's action being vacated by the Supreme Court, I seek the consideration of the Executive."[69]

On 21st September Davie wrote the Attorney General asking him to send to Ottawa a report as to Sproule's sanity:

> He wanders in his ideas and at times treats as present and existing facts which have long since transpired. He is firmly impressed so far as I can judge with the impression that I, who have been doing the utmost in my power to save his life, am in league with his enemies to encompass his death.

The Attorney General replied that it was not his responsibility to look into the question of the prisoner's insanity, and that he would take no steps. Davie immediately renewed his request and again without success.[70] However, the *Colonist* reported that a medical examination had been held by two doctors who found Sproule to be sane.[71] The Attorney General in his report to the Lieutenant Governor on 23rd November said: "I am informed that the prisoner's counsel requested Drs. Milne and Harrison to examine the prisoner and that they reported he was sane."[72]

The last hope lay in an appeal to the Privy Council. Davie drafted a petition for leave to appeal. This document, dated 18th September, was served on the Attorney General the same day. It described the different stages in the criminal proceedings. Then it asked for leave to appeal from the judgment of the full court of British Columbia on the polling of the jury, and on the refusal to accept the argument as to diminution of the record. The petition also asked for leave to appeal from the judgment of the Supreme Court of Canada.[73] Davie sent a copy to the Minister of Justice. On 14th October Burbidge on behalf of the Canadian government sent a cable to its London solicitors Bompas, Bischoff, Dodgson & Coxe. It instructed the solicitors to oppose the granting of leave to appeal on the ground that it would paralyze the administration of criminal justice in Canada.[74] Indeed, the submission is that the Privy Council should not entertain any criminal appeal from Canada, though a few months before it had heard an application for leave to appeal in the case of Louis Riel.[75] Even in later years (though prior to the Statute of Westminister, 1931) when Parliament attempted to abolish appeals in criminal cases, the Privy Council held that such legislation did not remove the prerogative power of the Privy Council to entertain appeals.[76] In any case, Sproule's attempt never reached the Privy Council for a ruling. Bompas cabled Burbidge on 14th October that the Privy Council office had no information on the case.[77]

It will be remembered that the date originally fixed for carrying out the death sentence was 6th March. Because of the legal proceedings, six respites of a month each were ordered by one or other of the British Columbia judges, the last being to 16th September. The judgment of the Supreme Court on 13th September produced a flurry of activity by the U.S. authorities. On the next day, Thomas Hotchkiss, the U.S. Consul at Ottawa, asked the Minister of Justice for a further month's respite so that U.S. government could determine what steps to take on behalf of Sproule. The minister yielded to the extent of asking British Columbia's Attorney General to arrange a respite to 1st October and to inform Sproule "that the law will then be allowed to take its course."[78]

The U.S. government applied pressure on London as well. On 25th September, Lord Stanhope, the Secretary of State for the Colonies, sent a cable to Lord Alexander Russell, who was acting as administrator in the absence of the Governor General. The cable quoted a telegram from Bayard to the U.S. Minister to the United Kingdom. The telegram asked for a respite so that an appeal could be taken to the Privy Council. The cable ended with this: "Her Majesty's government hope the request of the United States government will receive all proper attention."[79] Stanhope then cabled the administrator to ask the "nature of Sproule's offence and grounds for refusing to delay execution". Burbidge replied the same day through the Governor General's secretary, explaining the various stages of the criminal proceedings and concluding: "No grounds for further respite. Sentence to be carried out on 1st October."[80]

On 29th September the acting U.S. Secretary of State, James D. Porter, wrote to Sackville West urging a further respite on the ground that an appeal was being launched to the Privy Council, and that a "full compendium" of Sproule's case was on its way to the British government. Both Sackville West and Lord Stanhope appealed to the administrator to meet the American request.[81] When this request reached Ottawa, the Clerk of the Canadian Privy Council wrote to the Governor General's secretary asking that the following telegram be sent to the Colonial Secretary with a copy to Sackville West.

> In deference to the request from Her Majesty's government, my government advise me direct sentence death passed on Sproule to be respited until October 29th but protest against any foreign government impugning our judicial proceedings or in any way interfering with administration of justice here.[82]

On 14th October Stanhope sent a cable to the administrator in Ottawa. It said that the "compendium" furnished by the U.S. government "contains statement which, if information is accurate, deserves consideration". The cable continues by saying that Her Majesty's government had asked Sackville West to send the compendium to the Canadian government. (That government of course knew everything that was in the compendium.) At the end comes a sentence, headed "secret and confidential". It says: "Referring to telegram 29th September am disposed to give support to protest but shall wait conclusion of case."[83] The Canadian government yielded to the pressure to give a respite to 29th October.

On 27th October, two days before the date fixed for the execution, Stanhope sent a cable to the administrator at Ottawa. It refers to the urging of Mr. Phelps, the American Minister to Great Britain, and says that the British government presume that the Canadian Privy Council "fully considered documents sent from Washington upon which representations of United States government are founded". On the same day the Canadian government replied through the Governor General's secretary: "My government have fully considered documents sent from Washington".[84] Two days prior to this, the government asked the Governor General's secretary to send the following telegram to the Colonial Secretary: "My council have decided to allow law to take its course. Execution to take place on date determined".[85] The Canadian government had indeed paid attention to the "compendium" submitted by the U.S. government. On 20th October Burbidge had prepared a 21-page memorandum answering the American allegations.

At the last moment a petition signed by about 600 people, many more than had signed the early petition, was submitted to the Governor General.[86] It referred to the recommendation to mercy, the various reprieves, the fact that the evidence was circumstantial and that the jury and presiding judge had recommended mercy, the recantation of Charles Wolf, the holding of the trial 600 miles from the scene of the homicide, and the opinion of many that a miscarriage of justice had taken place. The execution took place on 29th October. The *Colonist* carried a touching and detailed account of the proceedings.[87]

Postscript

Chief Justice Begbie survived all criticism. Justice Walkem in opening the Lytton assize on 11th October made an indignant rebuttal of Strong's criticisms of the Chief Justice.[88] The *Colonist* carried an editorial saying that there was no need to acknowledge Justice Strong's insult "to one of the purest men who wears the ermine", and "Neither Mr. Justice Strong nor the whole bench of Canada could damage the Chief Justice in the opinion of the people of this province".[89] Then, in opening the Victoria assize on 22nd November, Justice Crease described the matters to come before the grand jury, and continued:

> I come now to a still more important matter which affects the administration of justice to its very foundation. In the remarks I am about to make I speak only for myself and without either consent or communication with my brother judges. This is the first opportunity of defence I have had. I refer to the charges brought by Mr. Justice Strong and Mr. Justice Henry, two judges of the Supreme Court of the Dominion, against all of the five Supreme Court judges of British Columbia. I say all the five, for the attack on the Chief Justice applies to every one of us and I for one, repel it.
>
> The absolute faith of the people in the honesty and impartiality of the supreme judges of the province, in doing justice according to the best of their ability, is the very life of satisfactory administration of the law. The whole fabric has been rudely shaken by the action of the two learned judges at Ottawa.
>
> To those who know us these charges, however gross, fall from us like water from a duck's back, but all the rest of the Dominion don't even know our names, nor do our neighbours in the United States, whose good opinion we have, for thirty years, enjoyed and valued.
>
> Those charges, sprung upon us in the *now* notorious Sproule case, if true, would be destructive of our reputations as judges, as well as to our good name

> as men and citizens (the only heritage which British Columbia judges, necessarily poor, can leave to their children)—throwing a stain upon the grand and petit juries of the country. . . . [90]

If any justification is needed for telling this story, it is to illustrate the problems of legislature, executive and courts in a new land, remote and under-populated. The efforts to establish courts and to apply English law and procedure in a new colony and then in a Dominion, in which legislative and executive powers are divided, is a significant part of our legal history.

Notes

The writer acknowledges with thanks the help of James Whalen and the staff of the Public Archives of Canada; of the late Dr. Willard Ireland and of John Bovey, Archivist of British Columbia, and the staff of the Archives of British Columbia; of Leigh McBride, then a solicitor for Cominco; of Jasper Stanyer, former caretaker of the Bluebell Mine; and Professor Hamar Foster of the University of Victoria.

1 For the early proclamations and the Gold Mining Ordinance of 1867, see *Martin's Mining Cases,* vol. I, pp. 537, 538 and 551.

2 Consolidated Statutes, 1877, c. 126. The next year a much more detailed *Mineral Act,* 1878, c. 13, was passed.

3 Mineral Act, 1882, c. 8.

4 *Memorandum on Dominion Power of Disallowance* (1946), p. 68.

5 Mineral Act, 1884, c. 10.

6 Margaret Ormsby, *British Columbia: A History* (Vancouver, 1964), pp. 180–81.

7 "The Bluebell Story", *Cominco Magazine* No. 4 (1970) 14–16.

8 Plan 5803 in Land Registry Office, Nelson.

9 Provincial Archives of British Columbia: GR 485, vol. 1 [cited hereafter as PABC].

10 Baillie-Grohman, *Sport and Life* (2nd ed. 1907), chapter X.

11 The concession was granted by the Columbia and Kootenay Railway and Transportation Company Act, 1883, c. 25. It gave the Company a grant of 750,000 acres on Kootenay Lake, and required it to operate steamboats on the lake and the Columbia River, and to build a railway from the lake to the river along the outlet.

12 *British Columbia Sessional Papers* (1883) [cited hereafter as *B.C.S.P.*].

13 See David R. Williams, "*. . . The Man For a New Country: Sir Matthew Baillie Begbie*" (Sydney, 1977).

14 *Sewell* v. *B.C. Towing Co.* (*the "Thrasher" case*) (1882), 1 B.C.R. Pt. I 153.

15 *R* v. *McLean and Hare* (unreported): see Foster, "The Kamloops Outlaws and Commissions of Assize in Nineteenth-Century British Columbia", in David H. Flaherty, ed., *Essays in the History of Canadian Law* (1983), II, p. 308.

16 Watts, "Sir H.H.P. Crease", *Advocate* 25 (1967), p. 5.

17 Watts, "Mr. Justice J.H. Gray", *ibid.,* at p. 59.

18 Watts, "Mr. Justice J.E. McCreight", *ibid.,* at pp. 103–104.

19 Watts, "Mr. Justice G.A. Walkem," *ibid.,* at p. 178.

20 *Woodbury* v. *Hudnut: Woodbury* v. *Meyers; Blasdel* v. *Hunley; Hammill* v. *Sproule* (1884), 1 B.C.R. Pt. II 39.

21 *Ibid.,* at 41–42.

22 *Ibid.,* at 43.

22a *Ibid.,* at 44.

23 PABC, No. 50/85.

24 *Supra,* note 10 at 241–49.

25 The material in this part is based on the transcript of evidence at the trial (see note 23, *supra*), and on the account of the trial in the Victoria *Daily Colonist*.

26 It is now in the Nelson Museum and has been replaced by a monument erected by Cominco.
27 32–33 Vict., c. 29, s. 11.
28 36 Vict., c. 7.
29 *R.* v. *Malott* (1885), 1 B.C.R. Pt. II 207 and 212.
30 *Re Sproule* (1886), 12 S.C.R. 140 at 142–43.
31 42 Vict., c. 12, s. 14.
32 46 Vict., c. 15.
33 48 Vict., c. 6.
34 1 B.C.R. Pt. II at 224–25.
35 1 B.C.R. Pt. II at 226.
36 *Daily Colonist,* 9th Dec. 1885.
37 *Ibid.*
38 *Daily Colonist,* 10th Dec. 1885.
39 *Ibid.*
40 *Daily Colonist,* 5th Jan. 1886.
41 *Daily Colonist,* 6th Jan. 1886.
42 Public Archives of Canada [cited hereafter as PAC] RG 13: C-1, vol. 1423.
43 *Sproule* v. *R.* (1886), 1 B.C.R. Pt. II 219.
44 O'Halloran, "Right of Appeal in Criminal Cases", *Canadian Bar Review* 27 (1949) 153.
45 Both appear in *Re Sproule* (1886), 12 S.C.R. 140 at 142–44.
46 *Daily Colonist,* 16th Feb. 1886.
47 1 B.C.R. Pt. II 219 at 233.
48 *Ibid.,* at 234.
49 *Ibid.,* at 241.
50 *Ibid.*
51 PAC RG 13: C-1, 1423.
52 *Ibid.*
53 *Ibid.*
54 *Ibid.*
55 38 Vict. c. 11.
56 *Re Melina Trepanier* 1 (1885), 12 S.C.R. 111.
57 *Re Sproule* (1886), 12 S.C.R. 140 at 145–46.
58 *Ibid.,* at 169–70.
59 The reasons appear at 12 S.C.R. 146–70.
60 PAC RG 13: C-1, 1424.
61 12 S.C.R. at 171.
62 *Ibid.,* at 171–175.
63 Vol. 49, Cases in Supreme Court of Canada: *R.* v. *Sproule,* 12 S.C.R., insert after p. 250.
64 *Toronto Mail,* 2nd Sept. 1886.
65 Report of Attorney General to Lieutenant Governor, PABC, 50/85 p. 47.
66 PAC RG 13:C-1, 1424.
67 12 S.C.R. at 200–203.
68 PAC RG 13: C-1, 1423.
69 *Ibid.*
70 Report, *supra,* note 65 at pp. 58a–58f.
71 *Daily Colonist,* 28th Sept., 1886.
72 Report, *supra,* note 65 at p. 61.
73 PABC, 50/85.
74 PAC RG 13: C-1, 1424.
75 *Riel* v. *R.* (1885), 10 App. Cas. 675.
76 *Nadan* v. *R.,* [1926] A.C. 482.
77 PAC., *supra,* note 74.
78 *Ibid.*
79 *Ibid.*
80 *Ibid.*
81 *Ibid.*
82 *Ibid.*
83 *Ibid.*
84 *Ibid.*
85 *Ibid.*
86 *Ibid.*
87 *Daily Colonist,* 30th Oct. 1886.
88 *Daily Colonist,* 13th Oct. 1886.
89 *Daily Colonist,* 14th Oct. 1886.
90 *Daily Colonist,* 23rd Nov. 1886.

1986

Our Earliest 'Homestead' or 'Dower' Act

Reprinted from
(1986) 24 Alberta Law Review
pp. 522–529

In the course of some general reading, Bowker came across a footnote in a book by L.H. Thomas which alerted him to explore an early Act of the Canadian Parliament which may have been lost to history.

The Act in question was passed in 1878, and though called The Homestead Exemption Act, it resembled and anticipated later Dower Acts.

In other words, at that early date, the Parliament of Canada passed an Act modelled on the American Homestead laws, which in turn were a forerunner to the Dower Acts of the Western Provinces. (See description of these in the earlier article by Bowker in this collection, entitled "Homestead Laws in the Four Western Provinces," 1982.)

Thus, while Homestead acts on the Prairies came into effect around World War I, it is not accurate to say they were the first such, in view of this earlier Act.

This is not an earth-shaking discovery, but is of some historical interest to a scholar.

I. Introduction

This title refers to the American-type of homestead law that usually has three features—it exempts the home from writs of execution, it requires the wife's consent to a disposition of the home and it gives the wife, and sometimes minor children, an interest in the home after the owner's death. The western provinces all have legislation of this general type, though invariably the exemption from writs of execution is in a separate statute.[1]

The writer had long assumed that the dower or homestead legislation of the prairie provinces going back to World War I was the first in Canada. However, he recently noticed a footnote in a book on the political history of the Northwest Territories. That footnote refers to an Act of the Parliament of Canada called the Homestead Exemption Act, which was enacted for the Northwest Territories.[2] It was passed in 1878, eleven years after Confederation and eight years after the Territories became part of Canada. The title of the Act is misleading because it is more than an Exemption Act. It has all the three main features of an American homestead law.

Why did Parliament pass such an Act? Because at that time it exercised in the Territories the powers which the legislatures exercised in the provinces, except those it had delegated to the Territorial Council. It had reserved to itself control over public lands and by the Dominion Lands Act of 1879 established a system of survey for the Territories and provided for free grants of farm land called homesteads. This word unfortunately has more than one meaning and it does not mean the same in the Dominion Lands Act[3] as it does in the Homestead Exemption Act. The Dominion Lands Act provided the framework for settlement of the empty prairies. Then in 1886 the Territories Real Property Act[4] established a system of registration of titles to land—a Torrens system.

The Northwest Territories Act of 1875[5] gave to the Territorial Council and its successor the Assembly specific powers which were narrower than those of a province, and Territorial ordinances could not be inconsistent with federal legislation. It gave the Council six specific powers—taxation for local purposes, property and civil rights, administration of justice, public health, matters of a local or private nature and punishment for breach of ordinances.[6] Two years later Parliament replaced this provision by one enabling the Governor General in Council to confer on the Territorial Council any power not exceeding those of a province under s. 92 of the British North America Act.[7] An Order in Council of May 11, 1877 granted certain powers. They were slightly wider than those of 1875.[8] A new allotment of powers made on June 26, 1883 was almost identical with that of 1877.[9] Then on July 7, 1886 power over direct taxation and incorporation of companies was added.[10]

Parliament's wide legislative power over the Territories is illustrated not only by the statutes described above but by subjects included in the various Northwest Territories Acts. The 1875 Act covered descent and grants of real estate, wills and property rights of married women[11] and by 1886 the Act still dealt with the last two.[12] In short, Parliament had much wider legislative power than it had in relation to a province, and could claim to be the proper body to enact the Homestead Exemption Act.

II. Enactment of the Homestead Exemption Act

On March 7, 1878 the Honourable David Mills, Minister of the Interior in the Liberal government of Alexander Mackenzie, moved first reading of the Homestead Exemption Bill and outlined its main provisions.[13] The second reading was on March 29.[14] The Minister said that legislation of this type was prevalent in the United States and had been a boon in the recent depression. Its extension to the Territories would be of benefit to its people. It recognized the family as the unit of society and sought to protect that unit. A certain amount of the family property should to some extent be protected against adverse fortune. The exemption proposed was $4,000.00. The Bill gave to the wife a life estate in the home and on the death of husband and wife gave to minor children an interest in the home during minority.

Sixteen members took part in the debate. From both sides of the House there was general approval in principle though the exemption of $4,000.00 was thought to be too high. The lending of money and extending of credit would be discouraged if too much protection was given to debtors. Donald Smith, later Lord Strathcona, and member for the riding of Selkirk in Manitoba, thought there should be an exemption like Manitoba's, that went back to 1871.[15] In Manitoba, however, there was no maximum amount and Smith thought there should be, but $4,000.00 was far too high. He did not want settlers to escape from debts incurred before coming into the Territories. That would simply be a premium on dishonesty, and the Territories would be filled up with the idle and indolent.

Another member, the Honourable J.B. Robinson of Toronto West, thought there should be an exemption for homes in every province. Then he gave the precise amount of the exemption in each of thirty-three states and Washington Territory.

The Bill was amended in committee and passed.[16] Section 1 permitted the owner of land in the Territories with a dwelling house occupied by him to register as a homestead eighty acres in a rural locality or a lot in a city, town or village, in the office for the Registry of Titles to Lands. Section 2 made the registered homestead exempt from seizure or sale under execution if the value was under $2,000.00 (one half of the amount originally proposed). Section 3 provided for an affidavit by the owner that he was married, whereupon the Registrar was required to enter the wife's name on the certificate of title and she thereupon became the owner of a life estate, though this life estate was cancelled in the event of her adultery and separation from her husband. Section 4 forbade alienation of the homestead by the owner "except the transfer be executed by his wife, joining with him". Section 5 gave to the wife a life interest in the homestead on the husband's death, and on her death an interest to minor children until they reached majority. The next section was an elaborate provision to cover the case where the homestead was or might be worth more than $2,000.00 Then ss. 7 and 8 provided the machinery for registering a homestead.

Although s. 5 gave to the widow a life estate in the homestead, s. 9 said that where the husband died without a will the widow had to elect between her life estate in the homestead and the share of her husband's property which descended to her by the law of the Territories. What was the property that descended to her? The Northwest Territories Act of 1875 gave detailed provision for the descent of real property. It never descended to the widow but her right to common law dower was preserved. That Act did not deal with succession to personal property, and the writer's guess is that the Statute of Distributions applied.[17] Section 10 said that where the husband died with a will the widow had three choices—her share on an intestacy or the property devised to her in the will or her life estate in the homestead. Section 11 is notable because it makes the Act "work both ways". The Act applied where the woman was the owner. In other words Parliament was more equality-minded than some modern legislatures.

III. Confusion over Registries of Deeds and of Titles

Certain phrases in the Act might puzzle one. Section 1 speaks of "the office for the Registry of Titles to Lands", s. 3 of the "certificate of title" and s. 8 refers to "all the lands embraced in any certificate of title granted under the Registration Act". There was in fact no Registry of Titles, no certificate of title and no Registration Act. These terms crept into the Homestead Exemption Act because the Minister of the Interior had introduced at the same session a Land Titles Act (or Registration Act). The two Acts were companions. However the Minister withdrew the Registration Act because of opposition and the draftsman of the Homestead Exemption Act overlooked this fact. Mr. Justice McGuire in *Re Claxton*[18] said "Parliament had... in 1878, passed an Act dealing with the subject of homestead exemption, but because the provisions of that Act were framed with reference to a Real Property Bill, which was at the same time before Parliament, but did not become law, the Homestead Exemption Act became practically inoperative.... " Incidentally, when the statutes were revised in 1886 the reference to the Registration Act was dropped from the Homestead Exemption Act, and when the Real Property Act came into effect on January 1, 1887, the phrase "registry of titles to lands" and "certificate of title" made sense.

As early as 1875 Parliament had made provision for a Registrar of *Deeds* of land in the Territories.[19] This was replaced by more elaborate provisions in 1880.[20] These in turn were amended in 1884.[21] Then the Territories Real Property Act, passed in 1886, repealed these provisions[22] because the Registry of Deeds was replaced by the Registry of Land Titles. In the meantime the Territorial Council pursuant to the federal legislation on registration of deeds had in 1879 provided by ordinance for the mechanics of registration of deeds though the ordinance carried the misleading title, Registration of Titles.[23] It was repealed by the revised Ordinances of 1888 because the Real Property Act of 1886 had replaced the provisions for a Registry of Deeds with one for a Registry of Titles.[24]

The Real Property Act of 1886 did not explicitly repeal the Homestead Exemption Act but s. 140 said that "all... Acts... relating to... interests of land in the Territories, so far as the same are inconsistent with this Act, are hereby repealed." It is at least arguable that the Homestead Exemption Act was inconsistent with the Real Property Act. Yet on April 1, 1893 Parliament amended that Act so must have assumed that it was still in force. The amendment changed the maximum size of a rural homestead from eighty acres to 160.[25]

IV. A Decade of Difficulties Over Homestead Exemptions 1884–1894

We come now to an account of the sparring between Parliament and the Governor General in Council on the one hand and the Territorial Council and its successor, the Assembly, on the other, in relation to exemption of the homestead from writs of execution. It will help first to mention the Manitoba statute and the Territorial ordinances on the subject of exemptions. At its first session in 1871 the Manitoba legislature created an exemption of homesteads up to 160 acres with no reference to a maximum value.[26] In the Territories the original Exemption Ordinance of 1879 was confined to chattels but in 1884 an exemption for homesteads up to eighty acres was provided.[27] This Ordinance was disallowed on August 15, 1885—not because of the exemption for homesteads but because of a section which forbade the enforcement of judgments against a settler for six years after his arrival in the Territories.[28]

The Territorial Council re-enacted the ordinance in 1885 omitting the section that provoked the disallowance. At the same time the exemption for a homestead was raised to 160 acres and there was a second exemption, presumably for town lots, of the house and buildings occupied by the defendant to the extent of $1,500.00 and the lot or lots on which they were situated. These two exemptions were known as paragraphs nine and ten of Ordinance No. 8.[29]

When the Minister of Justice the Honourable John Thompson scrutinized the 1885 ordinances, his report of 28 April 1886 to the Governor General in Council made no mention of the 1885 Exemptions Ordinance. However, on November 3, 1886 he sent to Lieutenant-Governor Dewdney this telegram: "On looking again at Ordinance No. 8, of 1885, I think I should advise government to disallow it, unless paragraphs 9 and 10 of section 1 are repealed, as ample provision appears to have been made by 41 Victoria, chapter 15. [Homestead Exemption Act] Please Answer."[30]

In reply, Lieutenant Governor Dewdney on 11 November sent to the Minister a report of a subcommittee of his Council. The stipendiary magistrates formed the subcommittee. He also sent a resolution of the Council.

The report, signed by Hugh Richardson as chairman of the subcommittee, states that the Homestead Exemption Act would be in operation prior to the coming into force of the Real Property Act on January 1, 1887. Until that date there was no "office for the registry of titles to lands" and no provision for certificate of titles or memorials, and even after the new Act came in force "it will be impossible for parties generally throughout the North-west Territories to take advantage of its provisions"; and finally, few copies of the 1878 Act were to be found in the Territories and its provisions were "but little known by the general public".[31]

The resolution of the Council stated that settlers, animated with the hope of good crops, and the desire to improve their lands, were induced to buy large quantities of agricultural implements on credit; that because of bad crops their hopes had been disappointed and large numbers of judgments had been obtained against settlers. If not protected by clauses similar to those objected to, hardship would be entailed and they would be compelled to leave the country or else be unable to take advantage of good seasons.[32]

On March 14, 1887, George W. Burbidge, the Deputy Minister of Justice, wrote to Dewdney to tell him that the Minister of Justice "is of opinion that this Ordinance should be repealed at the next session of the council of the North-west Territories".[33] He added that "the objection taken to this repeal by the Civil Justice Committee, that the Homestead Exemption could not be effectively applied until the 1st January 1887, has now no force." In answer to the objection that the Homestead Exemption Act was not well known, the Council should see that it was made known by publication.

The letter ended:[34]

> I am to add that so much importance is attached to this matter by the Minister that, unless the repeal is made by the Council of the North-west Territories, he will probably be obliged to introduce a bill on the subject into the Dominion parliament. The necessity for action in the matter by Parliament is to be deprecated, as it will give great prominence to the exceptional exemptions, which have been sought for by the people of the North-west Territories.

The Council met in October of 1887 for its last legislative session before it was replaced by the Assembly. The Council did not yield to the threat. Nor did the Assembly when it first met in 1888 under a new Lieutenant-Governor, Joseph Royal. One of the first acts of the new Assembly was to consolidate all of the ordinances, and the offending provisions remained in the Revised Ordinances of 1888.[35] These provisions remained to the end of the Territorial period and beyond. In Alberta today the exemption for a farm homestead is almost identical with that in paragraph 9 of the 1885 Ordinance. The exemption for an urban homestead stems directly from paragraph 10, though in 1984 the amount of the exemption was increased from $8,000.00 to $40,000.00.[36]

After the Council and Assembly had weathered the criticisms from Ottawa, the exemption for homesteads came under the scrutiny of the Territorial Court in 1890. One Claxton had acquired a homestead under the Dominion Lands Act. When he received a patent he was an execution debtor. The Registrar was prepared to issue to him a certificate of title under the Real Property Act, but asked the Court whether the writs of execution should appear against the title.[37] Claxton argued that they should not. In a careful examination of the Dominion Lands Act and of the registration provisions in the Real Property Act, Wetmore J. concluded that the executions must appear against the title. Then he dealt with the argument that the Exemptions Ordinance came into play. He concluded that it was *ultra vires*. An ordinance could not be inconsistent with an Act of Parliament even though it was in relation to property and civil rights. Here, the Homestead Exemption Act gave an exemption of eighty acres with a maximum value of $2,000.00 whereas the Ordinance gave an exemption of 160 acres with no monetary limit. Thus there was an inconsistency. The Homestead Exemption Act itself did not apply because the land was never registered as a homestead.

Mr. Justice McGuire gave a similar judgment. He pointed out that in the Ordinance, "homestead" had a completely different meaning from that which it had in the Dominion Lands Act. Later he turned to the validity of the Ordinance. It was *prima facie* a matter of property and civil rights. The question then arose whether the Ordinance was inconsistent with the Homestead Exemption Act. He thought the question "by no means an easy one", but concluded that the Ordinance was inconsistent with the Act and hence, invalid. The remaining three judges, Richardson, MacLeod and Rouleau JJ. simply concurred.

In the spring of 1893 Parliament made an extension to the scope of the Homestead Exemption Act by increasing the maximum acreage to 160. This did not satisfy the Territorial Assembly. On September 13, 1893 it prepared a memorial asking the Governor General in Council to submit to Parliament a new Homestead Exemption Act so as to place the farmers of the Territories upon the same footing in regard to exemptions from seizure and sale as those of Manitoba. The memorial makes no mention of the Territories Exemptions Ordinance. Rather it is directed to weaknesses in the Homestead Exemption Act as compared to Manitoba's exemption provisions. The memorial makes four points: (1) In Manitoba the exemption extended to 160 acres the settler used for cultivation or grazing even though he did not live on them, and to lots up to a half-acre; in the Territories on the other hand the settler must have registered his homestead for the exemption to operate. (2) Under the Homestead Exemption Act a homesteader could not register until he had received a patent for his land, yet the creditor might issue execution against the land, defeating the apparent object of the Act. (3) The wife's consent was needed to alienation of the registered homestead. (4) Because of these objections and because the Act was cumbersome only one registration had taken place in the Territories although the Act had been in force for a period of sixteen years.

The memorial concludes: "the present Homestead Exemption Estates Act is ineffectual and should be replaced and. . . an Act should be submitted to parliament similar in effect to the Manitoba Act dealing with the same subject."[38]

Parliament responded. In the 1894 session the Honourable T. Mayne Daly, Minister of the Interior, introduced a Bill. It did not provide for a new Homestead Exemption Act. Rather it proposed the repeal of that Act, so as to leave the matter of exemptions of real property to the Territorial Assembly. The Minister said the Territories Real Property Act was in conflict with the Homestead Exemption Act. Then he mentioned the 1888 Exemption Ordinance and the fact that the court of the Territories had held it to be *ultra vires*. The solution was for Parliament to give to the Territorial Assembly the authority to pass legislation like the 1888 Ordinance. "It is in order to carry into effect the wishes and desires of the people as expressed by their representatives in the Territorial Assembly, that this Bill is introduced." Then in reply to a question, "the whole matter will be entirely in the hands of the Territorial Assembly." When the Minister moved second reading he said that so long as the Homestead Exemption Act remained on the statute-book the Territorial ordinance would be *ultra vires*. To meet the wishes of the people, the Homestead Exemption Act would be repealed, leaving the law as passed by the assembly of the Northwest Territories in force. The Bill was passed.[39]

The repealing Act went further. It specifically gave validity to the Territorial exemption provisions.[40] As we have seen, those provisions have had not only validity but longevity for in essence they remain after a century as part of Alberta law.

V. Conclusion

The repeal of the Homestead Exemption Act meant that there was no provision in the Territories, or later in Alberta, requiring the wife's consent to a disposition of the home or giving her an interest in the home after her husband's death. This situation continued until World War I. The writer has written elsewhere about the Married Women's Home Protection Act of 1915 and its successor the Dower Act of 1917 which we still have.[41]

In the western provinces today the law does exempt the home from writs of execution, require the wife's consent to a disposition of the home, and give the wife an interest in the home after the husband's death. Thus, it has the three features of the American-type of homestead law.

Recent years have seen an intense growth of interest in Matrimonial Property law generally and particularly in improving the wife's position. Many proposals are designed to protect the wife's interest in the home. Indeed provinces that never had a homestead law are moving in that direction, at least in relation to the need for the wife's consent to a disposition.

The Homestead Exemption Act lasted for only sixteen years and in its short existence was of little use except to render invalid a Territorial exemption ordinance. However its existence illustrates the problems in governing a huge empty territory and in providing a legal framework for the settlers. The writer thought it worthwhile to call attention to a little-known chapter in the legal history of Alberta.[42]

Notes

1 W.F. Bowker, "Homestead Law in the Four Western Provinces" in Bissett-Johnson and Holland, *Matrimonial Property Law in Canada,* Release No. 3, Aug. 1982 at I–43.

2 L.H. Thomas, *Struggle for Responsible Government* (2nd ed. 1978) 75, n. 12. The Act is 41 Vict., c. 15.

3 42 Vict., c. 31. It was a consolidation of previous Acts. A homestead under this Act was a quarter-section of public land to which a settler became entitled on performing certain services while in the Homestead Exemption Act a rural homestead was 80 acres with a dwelling owned and occupied by any person.

4 49 Vict., c. 26; R.S.C. 1886, c. 50.

5 38 Vict., c. 49.

6 38 Vict., c. 49, s. 7.

7 40 Vict., c. 7, s. 3.

8 1 Terr. L.R. at xiii.

9 *Id.* at xv.

10 *Id.* at xix.

11 38 Vict., c. 49, ss. 14–53.

12 R.S.C. 1886, c. 50, ss. 26–40.
13 *House of Commons Debates,* 1878 at 802–03.
14 *Id.* at 1512.
15 Administration of Justice Act, C.S.M. 1880–81, c. 37, s. 85.
16 *Supra* n. 13 at 2006. See n. 2 for citation.
17 *Re Steidel* (1902) 5 Terr. L.R. 303 seems to infer this though the judgment is not clear.
18 (1890) 1 Terr. L.R. 282 at 294.
19 38 Vict., c. 49, s. 54.
20 43 Vict., c. 25, ss. 63–70.
21 47 Vict., c. 23, s. 1.
22 49 Vict., c. 26, s. 140.
23 Registration of Titles Ordinance No. 9 of 1879, amended No. 3 of 1881; amended No. 16 of 1883; consolidated No. 2 of 1884.
24 The Registrar under the Real Property Act had to take cognizance of instruments filed under the Ordinance: *Re Land Titles Act and CPR* (1899) 4 Terr. L.R. 227.
25 56 Vict., c. 19, s. 1.
26 *Supra* n. 15.
27 1884 No. 28, s. 1(9), (10).
28 Orders in Council on the subject of Dominion and Provincial legislation 1867–1895 at 1242–43.
29 1885 No. 8, s. 1(9), (10).
30 *Supra* n. 28 at 1245.
31 *Id.* at 1245–56.
32 *Id.* at 1246.
33 *Id.*
34 *Id.*
35 R.O. 1888, c. 45, s. 1(9), (10).
36 Exemptions Act, R.S.A. 1980, c. E-15, s. 1(j), (k) as am.
37 *Re Claxton, supra* n. 18.
38 Journals of the Legislative Assembly, 1893 at 76–79.
39 *House of Commons Debates,* 1894 at 2289–90 and 4590–91.
40 57–58 Vict., c. 29, s. 2.
41 W.F. Bowker, "Reform of the Law of Dower in Alberta" (1955–61) 1 *Alta. L. Rev.* 501.
42 The writer acknowledges with thanks the helpful comments of W.H. Hurlburt, Q.C. on an earlier draft and also the continual assistance of Neil Campbell, Reference Co-ordinator of the Law Library, University of Alberta, in obtaining for the writer various works not readily available.

1988

Stipendiary Magistrates and the Supreme Court of the Northwest Territories, 1876–1907

Reprinted from
(1988) 26 Alberta Law Review
pp. 245–286

In early 1987 when a national conference on Law in Canadian History was being planned by Carleton University in Ottawa, Bowker received an invitation to attend and to present a paper on a choice of subjects. He chose to deal with the judiciary of the Northwest Territories in the period from 1886 to 1907.

A three-day conference was held in June 1987, at which Bowker presented a paper on this subject. The article which follows is a substantially revised version of that paper. It is part of a broader study on Alberta legal history on which he has been engaged in recent years.

The author discusses the office and role of the early Stipendiary Magistrates in the North-West Territories and their effect on establishing judicial institutions.

I. Introduction: The Hudson's Bay Company Period, 1670–1870

When the North-West Territories became part of Canada on 15 July, 1870, it had no judicial institutions, apart from those in the district of Assiniboia (also known as the Selkirk or Red River settlement). Its centre was upper Fort Garry, now Winnipeg. The Hudson's Bay Company had established trade routes and maintained a measure of order. "But agricultural and surveyed lands, an educational system, municipal and judicial institutions constituted no part of the Company's legacy to the Dominion."[1]

True, the Hudson's Bay Company's Charter of 2 May, 1670 gave power to the Company to create courts. However, it had created none by 1800. When one Lamothe killed King in a dispute over furs near the present Elk Point on the Saskatchewan River in Alberta in 1802 there was doubt as to the jurisdiction of Canadian courts to try him.[2] This incident stirred the British Parliament in 1803 to enact that crimes in Indian Territories could be tried in Lower Canada, or if more convenient, in Upper Canada.[3]

In the next seventeen years the clashes between the North West Company on the one hand and the Hudson's Bay Company and Selkirk settlers on the other produced a spate of trials, civil and criminal, in both Upper and Lower Canada. Doubt remained as to whether Indian Territories included Rupert's Land, so when the Company and the North Westerns made peace in 1821, Parliament passed an Act that said (s. 5) that the 1803 Act applied to the Company's territories. It authorized the appointment of Justices of the Peace with power over non-capital cases and civil cases. The Upper Canada Courts still had jurisdiction and the Company's power to establish courts was preserved.[4]

The Justices of the Peace were never appointed but the Company established a Council in Assiniboia to act both as a primitive court and a legislature. Then after Lord Selkirk's heirs surrendered the settlement in 1836 the Company established courts with a Recorder. The first Recorder was Adam Thom who came in 1839. There was always argument as to whether the Assiniboia Court could try capital cases or whether they had to go to Upper Canada. However, Thom tried an Indian in 1839 and another in 1845. Both were acquitted but a third Indian was tried, convicted and hanged in 1845.[5] In 1848 one Calder was brought to Assiniboia, charged with murder on the Peace River outside of Rupert's Land. Recorder Thom wrote a lengthy judgment to show the Assiniboia Court had jurisdiction.[6] Calder was let out on bail and there is no record of the disposition of the charge. The Company's enemies insisted that the Company had no power to try capital offences in Assiniboia and some members of the Select Committee of the House of Commons inquiring into the Company's affairs in 1857 took this view.[7]

The surrender of Rupert's Land so it could become part of Canada was a slow process. The BNA Act (s. 146) contemplated the admission of Rupert's Land and the North-West Territories into the Union. In 1868 the British Parliament authorized the surrender and also an Imperial Order in Council to declare the admission of Rupert's Land to Canada. The British Parliament further authorized the Canadian Parliament to make laws and constitute courts, but existing courts were continued in the meantime.[8] Because of Louis Riel's Red River Rebellion, an Order in Council was not made until June 23, 1870. It fixed the date at July 15, 1870. On that date, the North-West Territories became part of Canada while the province of Manitoba, much smaller than it is now, was carved out of the Territories.

The Canadian Parliament in anticipation of the transfer had, in 1869, passed an Act for the Temporary Government of the Territories. Though skeletal and imprecise, it enabled the Governor in Council to appoint a Lieutenant-Governor and to authorize him to provide for the administration of justice and to make laws for the peace, order and good government of the Territories.[9] The Governor in Council could also appoint for the Territories a Council of not more than fifteen nor less than seven "to aid the Lieutenant-Governor in the administration of affairs, with such powers as may be from time to time conferred upon them by Order in Council" (section 5). This was replaced by a similar Act in 1871.[10]

II. The First Five Years, 1870–75; Creation of the North-West Mounted Police

The first Lieutenant-Governor of Manitoba was Adams Archibald, appointed 15 May, 1870. On the assumption that the tasks of the Lieutenant-Governor of the North-West Territories would be light, Archibald was given that role as well. On 4 August, 1870 he received instructions to make contact with the Indians and also to report on the state of the laws in the Territories, "together with a full report as to the mode of administering justice, the organization of the courts, the number and mode of appointment of Justices of the Peace, the police arrangements and the means adopted for keeping the peace, etc. etc.". He was also to report on the system of taxation and licensing and municipal organization; also on the state of the Indian tribes, the nature and amount of currency, the land desirable for settlement, and on all subjects connected with the welfare of the Territories.[11]

When Archibald took up his duties at Winnipeg he did not even have a copy of the statute under which he was appointed as Lieutenant-Governor of the Territories. Faced with a serious small-pox epidemic in the valley of the Saskatchewan and south to the United States border, he purported to appoint a Council of three. On 22 October, 1870 he reported this to Ottawa and also reported on the epidemic with a copy of an Ordinance of the same date to prevent the spread of the small-pox.[12] This measure was effective, but on 17 November Joseph Howe, the Secretary of State, wrote Archibald to point out that the latter had no power to appoint the Council and to imply that the Ordinance was passed without authority. The ensuing correspondence shows the difficulty Archibald had in knowing his powers. He urged the appointment of a Council but Ottawa did not act until 1873.[13] However the Lieutenant-Governor's hand in dealing with the small-pox was strengthened by an Order in Council of 3 August, 1871 that authorized him to make laws necessary to prevent the introduction of any epidemic and its spread in the Territories.

As to reporting on the condition of the country, Archibald took prompt steps. A British officer, Captain William Francis Butler, had come to Red River in the summer of 1870 as an Intelligence Officer attached to the Wolseley expedition that brought an end to the rebellion of 1869–70. On 10 October Archibald gave him instructions to go to the Territories to report on disorders, the need for troops and "to state your views on what may be necessary to be done in the interest of peace and order." He was also to deal with the small-pox epidemic and report on the Indians and the fur trade.[14] Butler left Fort Garry on 25 October and returned on 20 February, 1871. His amazing journey up the Saskatchewan as far as Rocky Mountain House and back in the coldest winter weather is told in his remarkable account, *The Great Lone Land*.[15]

As to law and order he reported: "The institutions of Law and Order, as understood in civilized communities, are wholly unknown in the regions of the Saskatchewan, insomuch as the country is without any executive organization, and destitute of any means to enforce the authority of the law." And later, "robbery and murder for years have gone unpunished; Indian massacres are unchecked even in the close vicinity of the Hudson's Bay Company's posts, and all civil and legal institutions are entirely unknown".[16] He gave a graphic account of the epidemic, which was worst at St. Albert, Edmonton and Victoria. He also described the Indian tribes. Then he mentioned the traders at Fort Benton in Montana and their trade in whiskey and arms, even on the Canadian side. He predicted that if trade outward along the Saskatchewan River was neglected it would go to Fort Benton. Finally came his recommendations for bringing about order, establishing the authority of the Dominion, the promoting of colonization in the fertile belt, and prevention of an Indian war. First, there should be a civil magistrate or commissioner to hold court, assisted by local magistrates. Second, a force of 100 to 150 mounted men should be organized for service on the Saskatchewan. Third, there should be government stations at Edmonton and at the junction of the North and South Saskatchewan Rivers with a view to extinguishing Indian title to land along the river so as to make it available for settlement.

Elaborating on his recommendations, Captain Butler thought the commissioner would represent "a commencement, as it were, of civilization in these vast regions". He added that the civil government had to be backed by a "material force".[17] He ended with an eloquent plea that if a powerful nation were to arise across the continent then "surely it is worthy of all toil of hand and brain, on the part of those who today rule, that this great link in the chain of such a future nationality should no longer remain undeveloped, a prey to the conflicts of savage races, at once the garden and the wilderness of the Central Continent."[18]

Butler added in an appendix a list of persons he recommended for appointment as commissioners or justices of the peace. Besides six named individuals, he recommended "all HBC officers in charge of posts", a tribute to the stature of those in charge of the forts. He also listed crimes committed in recent years on the Saskatchewan—five murders and an attack by Crees on Blackfeet as they left Fort Edmonton in April 1870.[19]

To return to the Territorial government at Winnipeg, Archibald was succeeded as Lieutenant-Governor by Alexander Morris in December 1872. Morris had been Chief Justice of Manitoba before he became Lieutenant-Governor of both Manitoba and the Territories. On 12 February, 1873, an Order in Council appointed the first Territorial Council with eleven members. Only two lived in the Territories. The same Order in Council empowered the Lieutenant-Governor in Council "to make provision for the administration of justice in the said Territories, and generally to make and establish such ordinances as may be necessary for the peace, order and good government of the North West Territories." However no ordinance was to come into effect until approved by the Governor General in Council except in case of emergency, and the power of disallowance was imposed as well.[20] In the following August an oath of office was prescribed but it enjoined secrecy for all matters.[21] Secrecy was not intended to apply to legislative matters, so on 1 October another Order in Council made this clear.[22] The secrecy was confined to executive functions.

In March 1873 the Council at its second meeting noted that the immediate appointment of Justices of the Peace was of urgent importance for the repression of crime. It passed an "Act" (or ordinance) authorizing the appointment of 21 men at places scattered between Mackenzie River and Fort Francis. The great majority, if not all, were Hudson's Bay Company factors. Oliver points out that in the old regime, factors were regarded as magistrates. "The Company's officers were still the fittest agents for the administration of justice as Justices of the Peace or Local Magistrates."[23]

When this "Act" came under the scrutiny of Sir John A. Macdonald as Minister of Justice he said the Act was valid but "until the settlement of the country shall have reached a more advanced stage it will be inexpedient to allow the Act to go into operation". However, he thought the justices of the peace should be appointed. Accordingly an Order in Council of 13 October accepted the recommendations and on 23 December appointments were made—not only of the twenty-one but fifteen more.[24]

Parliament gave some attention to the affairs of the Territories in the same year by the enactment of four statutes.

(1) The appointment of the eleven councillors had exhausted the power to appoint, so the 1871 Act was amended to permit the Governor in Council to appoint additional councillors up to a maximum of twenty-one.[25]

(2) The 1871 Act was vague in assigning legislative powers to the Lieutenant-Governor and his Council, so an amendment made it clear that laws for the administration of justice and for peace, order and good government were to be made by the Lieutenant-Governor in Council rather than by the Lieutenant-Governor himself. These laws could be disallowed within two years and matters outside the power of the Territorial Council were vested in the Governor-General in Council. In addition, a large number of Acts of Parliament dealing with criminal law and procedure were made applicable to the Territories.[26]

(3) An Act to fix the rate of customs chargeable on goods brought into Manitoba and the Territories included the significant prohibition of importation of spirits into the Territories, and also forbade the manufacture of spirits in the Territories except by permission of the Lieutenant-Governor. The penalties for contravention included forfeiture of the liquor.[27]

(4) Of the utmost significance was an Act, urgently needed, to bring order to the Territories. In essence it met Butler's recommendation for courts and a police force.[28] Assented to on 23 May, 1873, it authorized the appointment of one or more Stipendiary Magistrates to hold office at pleasure. They had the jurisdiction of two Justices of the Peace. They could try offences like petty theft and assault without a jury. For offences carrying a maximum of seven years' imprisonment, two Stipendiary Magistrates or a Manitoba Queen's Bench judge could try the case in the Territories without

a jury. Where the crime was punishable by death or imprisonment in the penitentiary the trial was to be in the Manitoba Queen's Bench and Manitoba's jury laws applied.

This same Act responded to the request for a police force. It authorized the creation of a Mounted Police Force. While the Bill was before Parliament the Cypress Hills massacre of Indians by whites on May 4 and 5 had shown the urgent need for such a force. The actual creation took the form of an Order in Council of August 30. The force was then organized and the march west began on July 8 1874. Colonel Macleod's occupation of Fort Whoop-up and the establishment of Fort Macleod in the fall are well known.[29] The United States authorities refused to extradite the perpetrators of the Cypress Hills massacre, but three were caught on the Canadian side and tried at Winnipeg in 1876 before Chief Justice Wood of Manitoba and a jury. Though acquitted because of lack of proof, the fact of a trial had a favourable effect on the Indians.[30]

The actual appointment of Territorial Stipendiary Magistrates did not come about overnight. On 8 September 1873 the Territorial Council resolved that "the future welfare of the North West Territories greatly depends upon the prompt and efficient administration of justice"—specifically the need to remove to Manitoba for trial those charged with serious offences would be so expensive as to render the law of no effect. The Territory should have its own judges.[31] Sir John A. appointed none and the Liberals acted only at the end of 1875.

The 1873 Act creating the Mounted Police made the Commissioner and every Superintendent an *ex officio* Justice of the Peace (s. 15) and an amendment the next year gave the Commissioner the powers of a Stipendiary Magistrate while the Assistant Commissioner and Inspectors were *ex officio* Justices of the Peace.[32] The same amendment (section 19) in expanding the duties of the force gave the widest power to search buildings (including wigwams) and conveyances (including canoes) for intoxicating liquor and to destroy it.

Throughout the Territorial period, officers of the Police did in fact try cases and in the early years handled most. The first Stipendiary Magistrates were appointed on November 15, 1875 as of January 1, 1876. They were Matthew Ryan and Colonel James F. Macleod.[33]

Early in 1875, Parliament had passed a new Act to consolidate and amend the previous laws.[34] Marking a new stage in constitutional development, it established a Council that was not connected to Manitoba. It had only five members including Stipendiary Magistrates, their maximum number being three.[35] The Lieutenant-Governor in Council had legislative power over six subjects including administration of justice but not appointment of judges. Provision was made for electoral districts when the population warranted. The creation of municipalities and schools was tied to those districts. Professor Lewis H. Thomas has criticized these provisions and also the uncertainty as to the relationship of council to Lieutenant-Governor in both legislative and executive capacities.[36] The Act however did look forward to the eventual replacement of the Council by a legislative assembly (s. 13).

Several provisions deal with matters that the provinces are given by s. 92 of the BNA Act—descent of land, wills, property of married women and registration of deeds. In the administration of justice, the Lieutenant-Governor could appoint Justices of the Peace and the Council could create judicial districts and the Lieutenant-Governor could provide for civil and criminal courts. In criminal cases the Stipendiary Magistrates were to sit with a Manitoba Queen's Bench judge, without a jury in less serious offences, a jury of six in the more serious, and a jury of eight in capital cases (s. 64). In those cases an appeal lay to the Manitoba Court of Queen's Bench (s. 65). The Stipendiary Magistrates were given jurisdiction in civil cases as well as criminal. They had co-ordinate civil jurisdiction with judges of the Court of Queen's Bench of Manitoba. In larger cases either party could demand a jury of six (s. 71), and in those cases an appeal lay to the Manitoba Court of Queen's Bench.

This Act was not proclaimed until October 7, 1876.[37] Within six months Parliament made important amendments.[38] The powers of the Council were removed from the Act and assigned to the Governor General in Council, doubtless to provide flexibility as changes were warranted. An Order in Council of 11 May 1877 allotted nine heads of power, not as extensive as those of provinces.[39]

The 1877 amendment increased the size of the Council to six, including the Stipendiary Magistrates as *ex officio* members (s. 2). Another provision made it clear that ordinances were to be made by the Lieutenant-Governor sitting with the Council (s. 3). As to the courts, a new degree of independence was granted in both criminal and civil cases by ending the role of the Manitoba courts except for appeals (ss. 7 & 8).

III. The Stipendiary Magistrates

Mention has been made of the appointment of Ryan and Macleod as of 1 January, 1876. Macleod had been Assistant Commissioner of the Mounted Police but was relieved of those duties on becoming Stipendiary Magistrate. However Commissioner French resigned and Macleod was appointed in his place on July 22, 1876. He held that position until 1 October 1880. As Commissioner he had the powers of a Stipendiary Magistrate. During this four-year period he "performed the duties of Stipendiary Magistrate in the Bow River judicial district... in addition to his duties as Commissioner of Police."[40]

On the day Macleod was made Commissioner, an Order in Council appointed Hugh Richardson of Ottawa as Stipendiary Magistrate.[41]

Then when the 1875 Act came into effect on 7 October 1876 Ryan and Richardson were given new appointments as of that date, at a salary of $3,000.00 each.[42] It is hard to say when they first took up their duties. Ryan had come west in 1875 in connection with claims of half-breeds to the allotment of lands in Manitoba pursuant to s. 31 of the Manitoba Act. Instructions for an investigation into the claims were issued on 26 April 1875 and on 5 May J.M. Machar of Kingston and Matthew Ryan of Montreal, Barrister, were appointed as Commissioners. They visited parishes throughout the province to hear claimants and take proof of entitlement. They finished their work within a year and Colonel Dennis the Chief Surveyor said:[43]

> It is gratifying to know that the Commission has effected so much work within the time; and that the duties appear to have been administered well, and with great satisfaction to all classes in the province, not a single complaint, so far as I am aware, having been made of the manner in which the Commissioners have conducted their investigations.

Early in 1876 Archbishop Taché pointed out to the federal government that many half-breeds had moved to the Territories from Manitoba. The government accordingly appointed Ryan in June 1876 to investigate their claims. The Order in Council described him as "Stipendiary Magistrate at Swan River" and directed him to take evidence there and at other places where his duties took him. His authority was to extend over two years. He had not finished by that time and a Dominion land agent was appointed to complete the work.[44]

As to the precise residence of Ryan and Richardson it seems that both were at Swan River. The NWMP had a post called Fort Livingstone on Swan River near the HBC's Fort Pelly. At the time, this locality was of importance on the route west, though it soon became a back-water. Battleford was designated as the capital on 7 October 1876 and the new commission to Ryan and Macleod on the same date directed "that the said Matthew Ryan shall until further order reside at Fort Pelly and the said Hugh Richardson shall until further order reside at Battleford." However, the buildings at Battleford would not be complete for another year and Richardson was still at Swan River when the Council held its first meeting at Fort Livingstone in March 1877.[45]

IV. The Second Territorial Council Established, 1876

It is relevant to note the work of the new indigenous Council because the Stipendiary Magistrates, Ryan and Richardson were *ex officio* members. Colonel Macleod was not a Stipendiary Magistrate though as Commissioner he had the powers of one. The federal government wanted him on the Council so he was appointed as a member on 4 November 1876.[46] Thus these three men had a major role in the making of laws and in assisting the Lieutenant-Governor in his executive capacity. Indeed in the beginning they were the only members of the Council though before long they were joined by other appointed members and from 1881 by elected members. As long as the Council existed, and even after it was replaced by the Assembly in 1888, the judges, and notably Richardson, had a major role in the drafting of ordinances and indeed in shaping their substantive content. Many ordinances were based on legislation elsewhere, especially Ontario, and it was Richardson who selected the provisions that seemed appropriate for enactment in the Territories.

At the first session of the Council the Honourable David Laird of Prince Edward Island, who had been Minister of the Interior, presided as the new Lieutenant-Governor.[47] The two Stipendiary Magistrates and Colonel Macleod were present. Macleod had been married a few days after he became Commissioner, and brought his wife with him. He had to go from Fort Macleod to Chicago to meet her. They proceeded by train to Fargo, North Dakota, by stage to Winnipeg, by cutter to Portage la Prairie and then by dog team in frigid weather to Swan River. A recent article describes the large barracks of sixteen buildings at Fort Livingstone.[48] "There was no guard of honour as the provisional government of the new territory assembled, no booming of guns, no aides, merely four unassuming men seated around a table in a small room in the governor's dwelling."[49]

V. Matthew Ryan's Career as Stipendiary Magistrate

Biographical information on Ryan is scanty. Born at St. John's, Newfoundland in 1810, he was a journalist there. In 1842 he went to Montreal. After working at the *Times* and then the *Pilot* he studied law and was admitted to the bar on 5 May 1849.[50] That period was a stormy one in Canadian politics. The administration was led by Baldwin and Lafontaine of the Reform or Liberal party. They appointed Ryan in 1849 to the Civil Service where he remained until 1858. Thereafter he presumably practiced in Montreal until appointed to enumerate the Manitoba half-breeds in 1875.

From the time of his appointment as Stipendiary Magistrate, Ryan had difficulty in dealing with other officials. At the Council meeting at Fort Livingstone he showed hostility to Macleod and Richardson. The former wrote "There are three members, Richardson, Ryan and myself. The two first do not speak to each other and Ryan does not speak to me! I have proposed a triangular duel to settle the matter".[51]

From the beginning Ryan had difficulty with W.M. Herchmer of the Mounted Police, a brother of Lawrence Herchmer who became Commissioner in 1886. W.M. Herchmer was stationed at Swan River as Inspector until his headquarters were moved to Shoal Lake (now in Manitoba) in 1878.[52] Ryan and Herchmer quarrelled continually. As early as 26 March 1878, Lieutenant-Governor Laird at Battleford wrote this cryptic but ominous note to Ryan at Swan River: "Heard disquieting rumours a week ago, but believe them either false or greatly exaggerated".[53] Complaints about Ryan went to the Department of the Interior and early in 1880 were passed to the Minister of Justice, the Honourable James McDonald. He brought them before the Cabinet. An Order in Council of 3 March 1880 recites that some of the charges were trivial but others more serious and "that these charges taken as a whole appear [to the Minister of Justice] to show such an unsatisfactory state of the administration of justice in the district presided over by Mr. Ryan, as to call for immediate investigation." Three Commissioners were appointed to make enquiry—Edgar Dewdney (who was Indian Commissioner and later Lieutenant-Governor), Joseph Taillefer and James Aikins, a young Winnipeg lawyer who later attained great prominence. Ryan was granted leave of absence. As best the writer can tell, he did not attend meetings of the Territorial Council from this time. The Commissioners reported in 1881. The report has never been made public but it resulted in his dismissal.[54]

Ryan was bitter. He collected and sent to the Minister of Justice statements of various persons to show Herchmer's shortcomings—drunkenness and disorderly conduct, rudeness, attempts to persuade witnesses to tell the Commission that Ryan had been a Fenian, and to persuade one witness to deny he had bought an old NWMP wagon from Herchmer. He also sent a statement from the inhabitants of Minnedosa regretting the enquiry.[55]

Several years later his name came up in a full-dress debate in the House of Commons on the causes of the 1885 rebellion. On July 6, 1885 Edward Blake gave a lengthy and detailed account of the problems of half-breeds and settlers over land. His purpose was to show the neglect and procrastination by the Conservative government from their return to power in October 1878. In reply, Sir John A. Macdonald described in detail the neglect by the Liberal administration of 1873–78 in dealing with the half-breeds' complaints. He criticized the appointment of Ryan and Machar as enumerators. The Liberal government had appointed them only to discredit the Conservatives and "for the purpose of finding employment for their hungry followers". He called the two men "incompetent enumerators".

Some time later, on 20 February 1886 Ryan wrote from Winnipeg to Sir John A. to take issue with the criticism and to ask for an explanation. He ended by saying, "At present my feeling is that you did me positive injustice no greater, however, than you did in acting upon the private information of that scoundrel Herchmer in 1881." He added a post-script. "I write with pencil because of the severe cold in my room; ink would really not flow."[56] He died in 1888 at Winnipeg.

VI. Colonel Macleod's Career as Stipendiary Magistrate

Colonel James F. Macleod, the second of the two original appointees, was born on the Isle of Skye in 1836 and came as a child to Aurora near Toronto. He attended Upper Canada College and entered Queen's College (now Queen's University) in Kingston at age 15, receiving his B.A. in 1854.[57] He was articled to Alexander Campbell of Kingston and was admitted to the bar of Upper Canada in 1860. He practiced at Bowmanville. In 1870 he went as Brigade Major with the Wolseley expedition to the Red River. Though bloodless, it was arduous. Samuel Steele at an old timers' banquet said "The first man in our brigade to shoulder a 200 pound barrel of pork was our brigade major, Lieutenant Colonel Macleod, who carried it over the longest portage on the route and set an example to us in everything."[58] He was made a Companion of St. Michael and St. George and was mentioned in dispatches.

Macleod was always more interested in a military career than in the practice of law. After the Red River expedition he practiced but little, and was in Britain, thinking he might stay, when Sir John A. offered him an appointment as Superintendent in the new Mounted Police. He accepted and became Assistant Commissioner on 28 May 1874 before the march west.[59] His role in leading the force after Commissioner French went back to Swan River and in establishing Fort Macleod is well-known. As has been mentioned he resigned as Assistant Commissioner on January 1, 1876 when appointed Stipendiary Magistrate but on July 22 was appointed Commissioner. As such he still had the powers of a stipendiary magistrate. He was stationed at Macleod and the Mounted Police records show that he tried a good many cases.

In 1877 Colonel Macleod was called on to exercise all his skill. Around the beginning of the year, Sioux Indians under Sitting Bull, having retreated northward after the Battle of the Little Big Horn in June 1876, crossed the border and camped at Wood Mountain just north of the line and about 100 miles east of Fort Walsh. The total number of Indians who came over a period of time was more than 5,000. The Sioux remained for over four years. During all that time Colonel Macleod and Major Walsh handled them with tact and firmness. After long negotiations between Canada and the United States, most of it by way of the British government, the Sioux returned to the United States, and Sitting Bull surrendered to the Americans on 21 July, 1881.[60]

A second major event of 1877 was the signing of Treaty No. 7 with the Blackfoot Indians under Chief Crowfoot at the Blackfoot Crossing on the Bow River in September. Over 100 Police were present to accompany Lieutenant-Governor Laird and Colonel Macleod who were Commissioners to sign the treaty. The comptroller reported, "Not a single casualty occurred, nor yet was there disturbance of any kind amongst the Indians or traders, which was very remarkable when the large number of Indians of different tribes camped so close together is taken into consideration."[61] The Lieutenant-Governor said Macleod "was indefatigable in his exertions to bring the negotiations to a successful termination".[62]

The annual reports of the Commissioner provide a picture of the criminal cases. In 1878 the report for the southern district shows that Colonel Macleod with Inspector Crozier and a jury of six tried a man on three separate charges of stealing a horse. He was convicted and given three years of hard labour. He had to be taken all the way to Manitoba because there was no penitentiary in the Territories. The remaining 13 cases were tried either by Colonel Macleod as Stipendiary Magistrate or by one of the Mounted Police officers as a Justice of the Peace. The report shows that justice was tempered with mercy. The Commissioner's remarks were "Case dismissed for want of evidence", "charge withdrawn and prisoner released", "prisoner cautioned and released", "prisoner discharged; no proof of felonious intent". When the accused was found guilty the fine was very small.

Colonel Macleod added: "In addition to the cases contained in the list, there was an immense number of cases of assault amongst the Indians, generally rising out of disputes about women, which were settled by sending an officer to the camp; indeed, in many instances both parties make for the fort, each trying to be the first to submit his case. In such matters I think it much better not to issue the usual process."

His report adds that he held two civil courts, one at Fort Macleod, and the other at Fort Walsh. The cases were all "matters of account".

The 1879 report of Colonel Macleod says that he held several civil courts both at Fort Walsh and Macleod and that "claims for over $8,000 have been entered and adjudicated upon."[63]

The 1879 reports from the various superintendents show:

(1) From Fort Saskatchewan, Superintendent Jarvis reported that an Indian had been convicted of murder and executed. A more detailed account by Turner says the Indian was Swift Runner, of good character, mild and trustworthy, a considerate husband and exceedingly fond of his children. However he became deranged, believing that a spirit was urging him to cannibalism. While living with his family near the mouth of the Sturgeon River close to Fort Saskatchewan his wife and children disappeared. Good work by Inspector Gagnon showed that Swift Runner had killed his wife and children and engaged in cannibalism. He was tried before Hugh Richardson and a jury on 8 August and convicted. He was hanged on 20 December.[64]

(2) From Fort Macleod Superintendent Winder reported that a starving Indian had killed a cow and offered a horse in payment. The relentless owner laid a charge and Colonel Macleod ordered the Indian to pay $20, the value of the animal. Another man was arrested for horse stealing, "the prisoner, being armed, showed fight; he was secured and brought to Macleod", convicted by Colonel Macleod and sentenced to one year's imprisonment with hard labour.

(3) From Wood Mountain, Superintendent Walsh reported that Sioux on the Canadian side had stolen ten horses and one mule on the American side and brought them to Canada. Walsh with a scout and three men tracked down the horses and returned them to the owner.

(4) From Fort Walsh, Superintendent Crozier reported that "many disputes and difficulties were settled to the satisfaction of justice without going through the legal process".

(5) Superintendent Walker at Battleford reported the pilfering and killing of settlers' animals by Sioux. He called a meeting of the "headmen" of the bands on November 4th. "I. . . cautioned them against intruding themselves on the settlers" and "I told them also, that our great Mother's laws were very just; if a white man stole any of their property, or killed any of their stock he would be punished and if an Indian committed depredations he would certainly be treated in the same manner. . . I also told the headmen

that they must caution their young men against doing anything wrong, as the illegal acts of one or two men would bring discredit on the whole band." (6) From Shoal Lake, Superintendent Herchmer reported four men undergoing sentence and two arrests for smuggling liquor.

The list of charges in the various districts shows that most were for importing or possessing or selling liquor, theft and assault. Many of the accused were acquitted. Of those convicted, most were fined and a few received prison sentences. Except for horse stealing they were short.

In 1880 Colonel Macleod was relieved of the duties of Commissioner as of 1 October, and received a new commission as Stipendiary Magistrate with precedence from 7 October 1876.[65] Like the Commissioners before and after him, he received some criticism and Sir John A. thought he should be relieved in spite of his excellent record. The main complaint against him was of extravagance. Professor Macleod suggests that Macleod's opposition to political appointments to the force was another factor.[66]

Irvine succeeded Macleod as Commissioner. By this time the Sioux were beginning to return to the United States though Sitting Bull remained. Irvine's report for 1880 points out that the disappearance of the buffalo would be harmful to the Indians and that there was a risk of clashes between Indians and settlers, who "unaccustomed to the Indian manner and habits, do not make due allowances and exhibit that tact and patience necessary to successfully deal with Indians".[67] The reports of the superintendents all show concern for the Indians and traffic in liquor. Superintendent Crozier at Wood Mountain described the problems arising from the stealing of horses on one side of the line by Indians who then took them across the border. The police were generally able to recover horses stolen in the United States and to return them there. The American system for returning stolen horses to Canada was not as efficient.

Superintendent Herchmer in reporting from Battleford described his arrest of two Indians at Frog Lake. "I tried them at Fort Pitt, sentenced them, and brought them on to Battleford." This double role of the police of course attracted criticism.

The 1881 report of Commissioner Irvine shows that the taking of stolen horses across the border each way was still a problem. The Mounted Police had returned American horses while "horses stolen by American Indians are, almost without exception, never returned".[68] Superintendent Crozier gave a detailed account of his efforts in restoring a large number of horses belonging to Americans. He pointed out that it was an offence under Canadian law to bring stolen property into Canada and that Indians had been found guilty of this offence. "The Court, however, taking into consideration that the Indians had not heretofore been punished under this Act, and that what they had done was not considered by them an offence in this country, deferred sentence and, after a caution, allowed them their liberty."[69]

The 1881 report also gives an account of the arrest and trial of the Indian charged with the murder of Constable Graburn. He had been murdered in the Cypress Hills in November 1879. (His grave can still be seen on the road from the Cypress Hills to Fort Walsh.) The trial was held before Colonel Macleod and Superintendent Crozier with a jury of six. The accused was found not guilty because after nearly 24 hours' deliberation, the jury had doubts. The report adds that the accused "received a fair and impartial trial, such as is afforded to the humblest of Her Majesty's subjects in every portion of the realm."[70]

In connection with the reports of the bringing of stolen horses across the border, it might be thought that the statements of the Mounted Police were scarcely objective and were self-serving. However favourable opinion of the work of the NWMP comes from a respectable Montana source, Granville Stuart, a prominent rancher in the Judith Basin. In his Reminiscences he refers to the theft by Canadian Indians of horses owned by one Harrison in Montana (the same incident mentioned in the 1881 report). Stuart describes Harrison's request for assistance from the Police, and the prompt arrest, trial, conviction and suspended sentence of the Indian thieves. Stuart adds that "their method of capturing and punishing the thieves and restoring stolen property as both expeditious and effective." He goes on to describe the difference in Montana where inaction by the government led to the formation of the stockgrowers association, some of whom became vigilantes and killed a number of alleged thieves.[71]

One modern American writer speaks in the most complimentary terms of the efficiency of the Police and of the merits of a centralized force. He concludes by saying:[72]

> Within twenty years the Mounties earned and received support of courts and public unmatched by lawmen in the United States. Better law enforcement even contributed to immigration northward to Canada. Settlers preferred the dependable and equitable protection of a central force to local constables or vigilance committees. Indians, outlaws, and ordinary citizens alike came to respect the North West Mounted Police as upholders of the law.

In 1888 Stuart on behalf of the Montana Stockgrowers Association and the Territorial Board of Stock Commissioners, wrote to Commissioner Herchmer to set out a resolution giving a vote of thanks to the officers and men of the NWMP and also the Canadian authorities generally for assistance given to many of the citizens of Montana in recovering horses stolen from Montana.[73]

Sometimes the American authorities reciprocated. Superintendent Antrobus in his 1888 report from Maple Creek described the action of Colonel Otis of Fort Assinboine in the United States. Three horses had been stolen from Blood Indians on the Canadian side and taken as far as Belknap in Montana near the Idaho border. Colonel Otis had them brought back to the boundary and turned them over to the NWMP. Antrobus said, "I would beg to request that my appreciation of the assistance and courtesy I have at all times received from Colonel Otis, of Fort Assinboine, U.S.A., and his officers to be placed on record. They have been the means of our recovering government property taken to Montana by deserters, and it has afforded me much gratification to render them like assistance in a couple of cases."[74]

In 1888 and 1889 the list of crimes was much longer than it had been in earlier years. The more serious cases were tried by judges who had formerly been Stipendiary Magistrates and were now judges of the Supreme Court of the North West Territories.

In 1885 the Minister of Justice called on Colonel Macleod to settle an unseemly dispute between officials of British Columbia and the Dominion. As early as 1869, Parliament had passed an Act for the Preservation of Peace on Public Works.[75] The Governor in Council could proclaim the Act in force where a railway, canal or other public work was under construction. While the proclamation was in force, arms and liquor were banned from the area and could be seized. A commissioner was appointed to administer the Act in the locality where it was in force. He had power to hear cases arising under it. In the Spring of 1885 the Act was in force on the railway belt of the CPR near Farwell (now Revelstoke),[76] also known as the West or Second Crossing of the Columbia River.

On 18 April, 1885 George Johnston was appointed as Commissioner. On 28 May George Burbidge, the Deputy Minister of Justice, made a memorandum to say that the province was granting liquor licences and was enforcing the provincial liquor laws in the railway belt. He was concerned lest the province would challenge the validity of the Public Works Act. During the next month the Secretary of State, J.A. Chapleau, had correspondence with Lieutenant-Governor Cornwall and Premier William Smithe of B.C. over the clash of authority that had arisen. The Premier asserted that the Public Works Act was poorly enforced so that the province was obliged to keep peace and order. He asked the federal government not to interfere. Ottawa refused to withdraw the Public Works Act. The dispute, however, was not settled. Johnston had at Farwell 24 special constables including one Ruddock and later about 20 Mounted Police. On the provincial side were Stipendiary Magistrate Sproat, an official named John Kirkup and one constable. This small force was later augmented by volunteers.

As best I can interpret the events from Johnston's reports to Ottawa, the trouble began in late May. Johnston's Constable Ruddock seized liquor possessed by the holder of a provincial license. Johnston fined the possessor and confiscated the liquor. Then Sproat had Ruddock arrested, seemingly for theft of the liquor. Johnston found the arrestor guilty of assault in arresting Ruddock. Then Sproat laid charges against Johnston, Ruddock and one Orchard for obstructing the provincial police and for rescuing Ruddock from lawful custody.

On 28 August Johnston sent to the Honourable John Pope, Minister of Railways and Canals, a wire setting out the events just described and continuing with the following account. When the charges against Johnston and his two men came on before Sproat, Johnston demanded a seat on the bench as Commissioner of Police. Sproat refused. Johnston then stated "I heard the evidence for the prosecution and dismissed the case". Johnston then ordered Ruddock to leave and Sproat had Ruddock arrested. "He resisted on my instructions." Two days later, on 30 August Johnston again wired to Pope to say that he and Ruddock and Orchard were arrested the night before by the Provincial Police. Johnston ordered his men to stay quietly in the barracks. Two B.C. policemen were under arrest for assaulting Dominion Police.

On 30 August, the same day that Johnston sent his second wire, Sproat wrote to the Attorney General of B.C. his account of the events. It was printed in full in the *Daily Colonist* for 6 September. It describes the action of Johnston and his special constables:[77]

> "They defied the law and the court, rescued a prisoner from lawful custody, assaulted and imprisoned two provincial policemen, pursued another one, assaulted and imprisoned an innocent messenger. . . ; threatened to arrest myself and every officer connected with the province, and marched into the chief streets of this town like cowboys on a raid.
>
> Recognizing that this was civil war and that the situation created was military, I arranged to take the barracks with an overwhelming force of police and volunteers under my personal command, at an early hour on Saturday morning; but having fortunately succeeded by a dash, during the night, in capturing the ringleaders Johnson, Rhodes [Ruddock?] and a man called Fane, the necessity for an attack did not seem immediate though two provincial policemen are still imprisoned."

He adds that he is "awaiting events", and "In the meantime the Dominion policemen are practically confined to their barracks. Yet when messengers went to the barracks on a peaceful mission federal police assaulted and imprisoned one of them and threatened a second messenger who went to the barracks armed with a white flag." He concluded by observing: "This tinges the affair with the burlesque."

Ottawa acted quickly. Burbidge wired Colonel Macleod on 3 September—"Go to West Crossing and straighten it out" adding that the Dominion government selected him as "an officer of experience and judgment". On the same day, the government also provided him with a Commission under the Preservation of Peace Act and another Commission under Canada's Police Act of 1868.

He arrived at Farwell in time for the trial of Johnston and his cohorts on 23 September. Sproat asked Macleod to sit with him on the bench at Johnston's trial because he thought it improper that he alone should try Johnston. The charges against him were for obstructing two provincial special constables and with aiding the rescue of Ruddock from lawful custody. At this point "the defendant withdrew his plea of not guilty, and pleaded guilty and made submission to the court." Kirkup who was chief of the provincial police in the area, speaking on behalf of the three provincial constables who were the complainants, said they did not wish a vindictive penalty but only that the position might be made clear. Sproat said "I am glad. . . to have associated with me a distinguished judge from a sister territory on the other side of the mountains''. Then he set out his views of the law on obstruction of peace officers. The original charges were serious but in view of the conciliatory position taken by the complainants and the plea of guilty and because Johnston ''acted throughout on erroneous legal advice'', the Magistrate said ''It would be beneath the dignity of the court to inflict a vindictive penalty.'' He fined Johnston $10.00 on each of the three charges against him. Colonel Macleod then retired from the bench and Magistrate Sproat disposed of the other cases, remitting the mounted policemen to their own officers for trial.

The last item is in the *Daily Colonist* for October 7, being a dispatch from Farwell on September 30. It says ''Colonel Macleod, Canadian Commissioner to report upon the late troubles here, left on the 24th. The result of his inquiries may be inferred from his sitting on the bench with Mr. Sproat when the offending Commissioner of Police, Mr. Johnston and others, (some in mounted police uniform) pleaded guilty and made submission to the court. The somewhat startling action of the Magistrate and the authority of this court are thus memorably and completely vindicated. It is understood that diplomatically, Colonel Macleod (who won golden opinions here) and Mr. Sproat got on very well''.

It is hard to say why Johnston capitulated. Probably the federal government in its anxiety to avoid a worse confrontation with the British Columbia authorities, ordered him to plead guilty. The Preservation of Peace on Public Works Act seems to have come off second best in its competition with provincial laws. However the last spike in the C.P.R. was driven by Lord Strathcona on 7 November at a point just west of Farwell so there was no longer any need for the special protection of the railway line.

VII. Hugh Richardson, the Third Stipendiary Magistrate

Hugh Richardson was born in London, England on July 21, 1826 and at the age of five came to Toronto with his parents. He was admitted to the Upper Canada bar in 1847 and was a successful practitioner at Woodstock from 1852 to 1872 having been Crown Attorney from 1856 to 1862. In 1872 he joined the civil service of Ottawa as Chief Clerk in the Department of Justice. When the NWMP were about to move west in June 1874, Richardson ''arrived from Ottawa, and held the last conference with the Commissioner. He also brought the final instructions from the government.''[78] He has been credited with drawing the 1875 North West Territories Act.[79]

He held the rank of Lieutenant Colonel in the militia and organized the Oxford Rifle Regiment. During the Fenian raids he served at La Prairie in 1864–65 and at Sarnia in 1866.

As mentioned earlier, he was appointed on 22 July, 1876 as a Stipendiary Magistrate and received a new Commission on 7 October. It assigned him to Fort Battleford. It is hard to say when he came west. It was probably late in 1876. Certainly he was at Fort Livingstone early in 1877 where he stayed for the time being because buildings at Fort Battleford were not ready. In February he applied for leave of absence to go to Ottawa to bring out his family. Edward Blake, the Minister of Justice had "very great hesitation in recommending any leave of absence" but did so. Two months' leave was granted by Order in Council of 3 April, 1877.[80]

The move took far longer. Richardson went to Ottawa to bring out his ailing wife and three daughters. They left Ottawa in early July and went by train to Prescott, Sarnia and Duluth. They had to hire a "strong wagon and two horses" for the trip on to Winnipeg. Heavy rain kept them there twenty days. On August 3 they continued by horse and wagon by way of Portage La Prairie, Fort Ellice, Touchwood Hills and Fort Carlton. There they had to wait while their house was being completed at Battleford. They reached that place on 29 September. It is no wonder that the expenses came to $4,976.94 and that the Minister of Justice wanted details of the enormous cost.[81]

The plans for the house show a spacious four-bedroom dwelling but it was not comfortable. Richardson wrote the contractor at Winnipeg that the house had been drafty and bad for his invalid wife. "Everything was freezing within three feet of a hot stove." A letter, written to Richardson just after his arrival, from Thomas Scott, the chief architect in the Department of Public Works at Ottawa asked: "let me know if you wish to be among the redskins and on the prairie or in civilized society (but not in Ottawa)." Travel from Battleford to other places where Richardson held court was tedious. To explain a large account for a journey to Fort Pitt, Victoria and Edmonton in December 1877 soon after his arrival he wrote, "there are no such places in this country as hotels by the way. Consequently unless one strikes a HBC Post, where the officers in charge are always hospitable and put one up for the night, a trip of this sort is camping out". He added, "you hire horses where you can" and observed that it was unsafe to travel in winter without two men and spare horses.

Almost as soon as the Richardson family arrived in Battleford one of the sub-constables named Elliott fell in love with one of Richardson's daughters whose name seems to have been Luders. Richardson learned of this and forbade Elliott to come to the house which he had done to bring the mail. Elliott wrote Richardson on 18 February 1878: "having heard that you had issued an order to the effect that I was not to convey the mail to your house as heretofore, I beg to state that it gives me great pleasure in giving up so arduous an undertaking, and that prior to this date I had made up my mind to discontinue the carrying of your mail, as only one construction can be put upon the meaning of your order".

On February 25, Elliott and three other constables—Marshall, Balfe and Davis went to Richardson's home and in spite of parental objection took the daughter away. She and Elliott were married that day by a Presbyterian minister, the Reverend Straith. It is hard to tell what happened next but the inference is that her parents took her back home. On the following day Elliott wrote Mrs. Richardson. He was grieved that she was unhappy. He loved her daughter and she returned that affection. They thought they could not obtain sanction from her parents, and being of age, were married the day before, a few minutes past three—honorably married in sight of God and man. "Let my wife come to me Mrs. Richardson... I do not wonder at the treatment I received last night for well I know your hearts are nearly broken. I hope you will forgive us."[82]

At the same time Elliott wrote Colonel Richardson agreeing to "propositions" that Richardson had made through Amedee Forget who was secretary to the Lieutenant-Governor. He does not say what the propositions were, and concluded "my actions... will be strictly honorable."

On the evening of the wedding Superintendent Walker who was in charge at Battleford wrote Richardson to say "the men you mention are not on duty this evening but... will require to be back here by 9:30... I will endeavour to keep Elliott employed for a few days so that he may not give you any trouble."

On March 2 Walker wrote Richardson to say that Elliott was confined to barracks, adding, he might try to "get your daughter out" by way of a ladder at a window.

On the same day Richardson wrote a letter to Walker enclosing criminal charges against the four members of the force under Walker's command and requesting that they be brought before Walker without delay. He gave a list of seven witnesses and asked Walker to let him know the time, because he wanted to be present and give evidence.

Colonel Richardson made three formal complaints. The first alleged that Elliott and Marshall "feloniously and fraudulently allured one Luders Richardson out of the possession and against the will of this informant, her father, she... being under 21 years of age and having a certain contingent interest in the real and personal estate of this informant, with intent her, the said Luders Richardson to cause to be married to the said Elliott... "[83]

The next complaint was made under the Act to establish the NWMP. The Act contained a lengthy list of offences by members of the force. One of them was "disgraceful, profane or grossly immoral conduct."[84] This information charged Elliott and Marshall with disgraceful conduct in having solicited the clergyman to perform the marriage ceremony, falsely representing the parties to be of full age and that the consent of the bride's parents could not be obtained; and in having on the night of 25 February attempted unlawfully and forcibly to enter the house of Richardson.

The last information is against the other two constables, Balfe and Davis, for disgraceful conduct in that on the night of 25 February they had been present when Elliott and Marshall entered the dwelling house of Hugh Richardson and neglected to arrest Marshall and Elliott as in duty bound to do as peace officers.

The next day, March 3, Balfe wrote to Richardson to say "you have defamed me and I am made a prisoner" and asked Richardson to agree with Balfe's allegations or Balfe would see his legal adviser.

On the night of 4–5 March, Elliott, Marshall and Balfe deserted, taking with them Deschamps, a prisoner.[85] Two of the horses were the goverment's, one was Major Walker's and one was Marshall's. Four saddles were missing. Marshall wrote a letter to Walker to say they were obliged to go, and were sorry to do so, and that they had no fault to find with him as he had been a good officer. Apparently they intended to go to Montana. Walker sent out a search party but the melting snow destroyed the tracks and the searchers turned back at the Red Deer River. On 9 March a trader named Gunn provided the fugitives with food on the South Saskatchewan. The four went on toward the Cypress Hills.

In September Elliott surrendered at Fort Walsh. Brought back to Battleford, he was charged with theft of government property and tried on 23 December at the police barracks. A large number of spectators were present. Richardson and W.J. Scott, a Justice of the Peace, presided with a jury of six. Walker was the prosecutor (and also a witness) while Hayter Reed, the Indian agent at Battleford and also a lawyer, defended Elliott. According to the careful account of the evidence in the Saskatchewan Herald for 30 December the evidence was presented in a competent manner while Reeds's cross-examination was skilful.

The only defence witness was Sub-inspector French who had been in charge at Battleford in the autumn of 1878 during Walker's absence. Reed called him to try to show that Elliott had already undergone punishment for the offence now being tried, since he had been incarcerated between 12 September and 12 November. The court refused to permit this question. Then "Mr. Reed delivered an affecting address to the jury, in which he referred pathetically to the feelings of the prisoner's widowed mother, of whom he was the sole support." The newspaper account next says this: "The Stipendiary Magistrate charged the jury at some length and very strongly against the prisoner, after which the jury retired. After about five minutes deliberation they returned a verdict of not guilty."

Three days later Elliott was brought up before the Stipendiary Magistrate on the remaining charges, namely stealing Major Walker's horse and aiding Deschamps to escape. Walker asked for an "enlargement" because of new evidence. He could not fix a definite date because the roads were bad. Elliott was released on his own recognizance of $400. The writer does not know whether Elliott was ever brought to trial on these charges.

Shortly after this the Herald carried a note of the death at Battleford of Richardson's wife and another of the death of his mother at St. Thomas, Ontario, both on 2 February 1879.

Richardson had a large part in the framing of Ordinances. The new Council that came into being on 7 October 1876 inherited practically none for very few of those passed by the old Council came into effect.[86] Indeed the Minister of Justice a week later reported that he had not had time to go through the resolutions of the late Council and he recommended that the new Council should deal with them.[87]

As mentioned earlier, the new Council began its first and only session at Swan River on 8 March 1877. In two weeks the Council made 13 ordinances. The titles show the topics that were of concern to the Council—infectious diseases, protection of buffalo, master and servant, fences, prairie fires, licences and gambling. In addition, there were some technical subjects—administration of justice, exemptions from seizure, assignment of debts, registration of deeds, short forms of deeds and the transfer of real estate by women.

These ordinances were ill-fated because the 1877 Act, passed on 28 April five weeks after the session ended, provided that the powers of the Territorial Council be allotted by the Governor General in Council, as mentioned above.[88] The new Minister of Justice, the Honourable Rodolphe Laflamme, seemed to think that the change in the Act rendered the ordinances of no effect—a rather odd opinion, considering that the 1875 provision was still in force when the ordinances were passed. A memorandum made in 1881 says "none of the ordinances of the Northwest Territories passed prior to 1878 are in force. Those of 1877 were pronounced *ultra vires* by the then Minister of Justice, and were never printed. At the suggestion of the Minister they were repealed and re-enacted since, excepting numbers five and twelve" which provided for protection of buffalo and assignment of debts.[89]

The council moved to Battleford for the 1878 session which opened on 10 July. The Council was reminded of its new list of powers under the Order in Council of May, 1877 and of the new Oath of Secrecy, confined to executive matters.

The Council repealed the 1877 Protection of Buffalo ordinance, which the half-breeds had requested, though Ottawa disallowed it anyway. The 1877 ordinances were re-enacted and new ordinances dealing with brands, and stallions running at large were passed. As a start in establishing judicial machinery a Civil Justice ordinance was passed and it included Rules of Court, making use of the Ontario rules and forms and it set up a system of judicial districts. Originally there were three—Saskatchewan, Bow River and Qu'Appelle.[90] Other ordinances dealt with constables, notaries public and limitation of actions.

These ordinances had a better fate than those of 1877, for they were not disallowed. In 1879 the session began on 28 August and lasted a month. The subject matter was much the same as it had been—infectious diseases, lunatics, ferries, prairie fires, master and servant, licencing and gambling, administration of justice including exemptions, and registration of deeds.

In 1880 the Northwest Territories Act was consolidated. It enabled the Lieutenant-Governor in Council to exercise such powers as the Governor General might confer just as the 1877 provision had done. However section 95 repealed the 1875 and 1877 Acts. The Council had not met in 1880 but met on 26 May 1881. On that date no Order in Council had been made conferring powers under the new Act.

Richardson on June 7 wrote a memo pointing out these facts. He concluded the Lieutenant-Governor in Council had no legal power to make ordinances. He recognized that section 95 of the 1880 Act said that the repeal of the earlier Acts should not affect duties accrued and rights acquired under the earlier Acts. He did not think however that this operated to preserve the Order in Council of 11 May 1877. He added that he had prepared the ordinances but could not aid in making them law.[91] The other members of the council were not deterred by his opinion. Neither was the federal cabinet, because none of the ordinances were disallowed. Everyone but Richardson assumed that the Order in Council of 1877 was still in effect and indeed it was not replaced until a new Order in Council of 26 June 1883 which conferred the same powers.

The 1881 ordinances dealt with stray animals, fences, sheep, driving off of horses and cattle, bulls running at large and ferries. Other ordinances provided for security by public officers, and amendments to the Registration of Titles ordinance, chattel mortgages, marriage and the sale of medicine.

At this period the Council still had the three Stipendiary Magistrates though Ryan was on the verge of dismissal. I doubt he attended the 1881 meeting. Professor Thomas says of the Ordinances of 1878, 1879 and 1881: "The legislation seems to have been carefully prepared, as indeed it should have been with three judges among the councillors."[92] Edgar Dewdney succeeded Laird as Lieutenant-Governor on 31 October 1881. The Council did not meet in 1882. By the time it met in August 1883 Regina had been made the capital and Richardson had moved there.

In the six years Richardson was at Battleford he covered a large area holding court. He was hardly settled in the fall of 1877 when he went on a circuit in December that took him as far as Edmonton, travelling by sleigh. Court was held in any available building such as the Police Orderly Room. When he came to Edmonton in December, 1881, the situation was described as follows in the Edmonton Bulletin: "It was intended that the new school house should be placed at the disposal of the Court, but as the chimney was not quite finished and the stove could not be lighted, it could not be used. Mr. Hardisty then offered the use of the sales room of the Hudsons Bay Company in the Fort for the purpose, and was accepted".[93]

When the Lieutenant-Governor was concerned about establishing electoral districts so that members could be elected to the Territorial Council, his secretary, A.E. Forget on 25 November 1882 asked Richardson to determine if the Edmonton District had the requisite population of 1,000. The district was 30 miles from north to south and 42 miles from east to west and included St. Albert and Fort Saskatchewan. The letter to Richardson said, "You will serve a public interest in providing a report showing the result of your inquiries". With the help of Superintendent Gagnon of the N.W.M.P. and Father Leduc and of one S.D. Mullins, Richardson took a very careful census and on 6 February 1883 wrote Lieutenant-Governor Dewdney to say "While in Edmonton in December 1882 I made the most exhaustive inquiries within reach and have arrived at the conclusion that this District possesses the right to an elected representative under the Act".[94] In the election for Edmonton, Frank Oliver was elected and so began a long and turbulent career in politics. Between the investigation of Ryan and the appointment of Rouleau, Richardson and Macleod were the only Stipendiary Magistrates in the whole Territories. Sometimes prisoners had to await trial for lengthy periods. In February 1881 an editorial in the Bulletin criticized Richardson for not holding court at Edmonton. It added that in the winter of 1876 two Indians died in confinement and in 1877 three prisoners were confined for trial until the middle of December.[95] One might suggest that the criticism is unfair because during much of that period Richardson was engaged in moving his family west. At the time the Bulletin made this criticism, the Lieutenant-Governor on 28 January 1881 asked Richardson to go to Qu'Appelle to try prisoners who had been awaiting trial for nearly six months because Ryan was "absent or incapacitated from performing his duties".[96]

The Courts Lists for 1883[97] give an idea of Richardson's activity at that time. He was alone in the Eastern part of the Territories until Rouleau was appointed late in the year. Civil sittings were separate from the criminal and involved actions in debt, account, replevin, partnerships and torts. The sittings were at Prince Albert in January and May, at Regina in April, August and October, and at Fort Qu'Appelle in April and August, and at Edmonton in July. The lists were lengthy. Sometimes lawyers appeared. Many cases were withdrawn or settled.

From time to time Richardson received letters setting out a complaint against someone or asking for help. He invariably replied promptly. After pointing out that he could not advise or help the person, he outlined the course that the person should follow. On one occasion Father Andre at Duck Lake wrote an indignant letter complaining that Inspector Herchmer and one Owen Hughes had broken down fences around the Roman Catholic Mission and had opened a road across a field. Richardson replied to explain that redress could be had only through the District Court which would sit in Prince Albert in October. Not long after he received a letter from Hughes asking if Richardson could get the Lieutenant-Governor to keep the old trails open. Hughes complained that he could not go anywhere without breaking down someone's fence.[98]

Early in 1882 at Edmonton a number of squatters had settled on land owned by others. The leading citizens of the community formed a vigilance committee with a view to stopping this practice. One Bannerman had erected a house on land he did not own at the top of the river bank near the present Convention Centre. The vigilance committee pushed it over the bank and Bannerman had the leading members charged with malicious destruction of property. After a preliminary before Inspector Gagnon the trial came on before Richardson on June the 17th. The accused were leading citizens—Frank Oliver, D.R. Fraser, Laurence Garneau and Matthew Macaulay. The jury after a short absence found them not guilty.[99]

In August, 1883 Richardson was involved in an incident connected with Nicholas Flood Davin, the colourful and contentious newspaper editor and lawyer from Regina. While en route home from the East by train, he was seen in the corridor at night with his trousers off. Herchmer and his wife were on the train. Herchmer charged Davin with illegally bringing liquor into the Territories. Richardson tried him at Regina on 8 September. He asked Davin if he denied the charge. By way of inducing the judge to impose a light penalty, Davin said it was a small amount such as was usually brought into the Territories by travellers, and that the custom of the police had been to spill the liquor on the frontier and not to prosecute. He said he had not intended to violate section 90(3) of the N.W.T. Act 1880, which prohibited the importation of liquor without special permission. Richardson imposed a $50 fine. The Deputy Minister of Justice asked Richardson to comment on Davin's bitter complaints against Superintendent Herchmer and Inspector Steele. Richardson replied as follows: "During six years residence in the country and frequent travel over a considerable portion, charges of grave misconduct either collectively or individually against Officers of the Force have not come to my notice".[100]

VIII. Ryan's Replacement—Charles Borimee Rouleau

Though Ryan was dismissed in July 1881 no new magistrate was appointed until 28 September 1883. Charles Borimee Rouleau was selected to replace Ryan. He became an *ex officio* member of the Council and was stationed at Battleford and later at Calgary. Born in Lower Canada in 1840 he taught school at Aylmer and then was inspector of schools. Turning to law, he was admitted to the bar in 1868. In 1876 he was appointed Stipendiary Magistrate for the district of Ottawa and seven years later came West.

Soon after Louis Riel returned from Montana in 1884, Dewdney wrote Rouleau to ask particulars of the half-breeds' agitation. A lengthy reply of 5 September 1884 urged that the government settle the half-breeds' claims at once. The Grits used the agitation for their own political ends; the longer the agitation continued the harder it would be to allay; settlement would take away Riel's ammunition; the half-breed agitation meant that the Indians would agitate; once the half-breeds were quiet the Indians could be controlled. Rouleau added that the crops were a failure and the government must give the Indians help or there would be misery and starvation.[101] This perceptive advice came from a man who had been in the Territories for only a year.

Rouleau lived in a house on the south side of the Battle River where the main settlement then was. The Mounted Police Fort was on the north side. Probably his house was the one built for Richardson. Right after the clash at Duck Lake, a large number of Indians including Poundmaker's surrounded the town and its inhabitants took shelter in the Fort. Rouleau moved his family out to Swift Current. Colonel Otter's force, coming from Swift Current, reached Battleford on April 23rd. This ended the looting and burning by Indians. As the troops approached they saw clouds of smoke. "The smoke the troops saw was the result of the Indians' last defiant act at Battleford, the burning of Judge Rouleau's substantial home".[102]

IX. Jeremiah Travis, the Additional Stipendiary Magistrate

In 1885, Ottawa yielded to requests for a fourth Magistrate and Parliament amended the Northwest Territories Act to authorize this.[103] Jeremiah Travis was appointed on 30 July, and assigned to the Alberta district with his seat at Calgary. Born at Saint John, New Brunswick in 1830 he obtained an LL.B. from Harvard in 1866, and had written a book on Canadian Constitutional Law. It was a rather intemperate criticism of decisions of the Privy Council, the Supreme Court and the Provincial Courts.[104] He was in Winnipeg at the time of his appointment, having tried without success to receive an appointment to the Manitoba Court of Queen's Bench. He came to Calgary right after his appointment. In letters to Lieutenant-Governor Dewdney on 11 September and again on 19 September he said he was pleased with his reception by the Calgary Bar and looked forward to working with Dewdney on the Territorial Council.[105] He was in error in thinking that he would automatically be a member of Council because unlike the other three Stipendiary Magistrates, he was not made an *ex officio* member.[106] In the next three months Travis clashed with Mayor George Murdoch, the Calgary Herald and the "whiskey ring".[107] The strict liquor law was unpopular and often violated. The Mounted Police in trying to enforce it were not always popular. Travis was a zealous teetotaller. A councillor S.J. Clarke, who was also a hotel owner, resisted a search by the police for liquor. On 11 November Travis found him guilty of obstructing or assaulting a police officer in the course of duty and sentenced him to six months at hard labour. In his last letter to Dewdney written 3 December, 1885 Travis conceded that "a reaction has set in". He described his sentence of Clarke as moderate. A public meeting condemned Travis. He ruled that Hugh Cayley, editor of the Herald, was guilty of contempt and fined him. Cayley refused to pay and went to jail on or about 6 January. After loud protests on his behalf he was released on 27 January.

The next episode involved municipal affairs. At the year's end an election was held for mayor and councillors for 1886. One mayoral candidate, James Reilly, was anti-liquor, while the incumbent George Murdoch was in the "whisky ring". He and his followers were easily successful, much to the indignation of Travis. He ruled that Murdoch and his followers were disqualified from office by reason of irregularities in the election. He went further and declared James Reilly and his supporters to be elected. The result was chaos. The town was divided into pro- and anti-Travis groups. Protests were made to Ottawa over Travis's actions. He was suspended and a commission was appointed under Judge Taylor of Manitoba. He reported in June 1887. The report was not published. The Commission recommended dismissal because Travis had not been prudent. The problem was solved when the Stipendiary Magistrates were replaced by the Supreme Court of the Territories on 18 February 1887. Travis was not appointed to the new court.

With this background it is no wonder that the Territorial Council passed an ordinance at its 1886 session calling for an election to end the deadlock in Calgary's municipal affairs. It recited that "doubt has arisen concerning the personnel of the mayor and councillors... for the year 1886, and various persons have claimed and are claiming the positions of mayor and councillors... " and that "by reason of the said rival claims, vexatious delays and litigation have ensued, involving great loss and inconveniences to the property holders... and it is at present doubtful if a legal council exists".[108]

One episode involving Travis is not as well known as those just described. While the investigation was under way, Travis wrote to George Burbidge, Deputy Minister of Justice, on 28 August, 1886.[109] The letter begins by saying that members of the Whisky Ring had organized meetings and petitions against Travis because they knew they could not force him to support them in their crime: "Had I been like one of my colleagues (I state nothing but what I am prepared any minute to sustain) lying day after day drunk here at one of the hotels (the Royal) with parties and witnesses kept waiting here from day to day to get him sober enough to hold a court, the opposition and petitions would have no more followed in my case than they have done in his. Likewise as to the action of the government. I should think the government must soon be alive to the fact that if ever there was a time here when a judge was required to administer the law according to his oath (without fear, without favour and without malice), that this is the time."

Burbidge checked to try to identify the judge mentioned by Travis and found that the only one who had sat in Calgary besides Travis was Rouleau. Not wanting to leave Travis's letter on file without giving Rouleau a chance to respond, Burbidge wrote Rouleau on 2 September. After quoting the allegations, Burbidge said "the Minister of Justice has not thought it necessary to ask for a formal report through the Secretary of State. However, he is unwilling to file Mr. Travis' letter without giving you an opportunity for making any explanation which you desire to make." On the same day Burbidge wrote Travis telling him of Burbidge's letter to Rouleau.

On 8 September Rouleau wired Burbidge: "Please send copy of Travis' libelous letter. Intend to prosecute him unless he be sent to asylum. Will answer letter." His answer of the same day said that the accusation was false in every particular and that Rouleau had called a meeting of the Calgary advocates, numbering 12, to lay Burbidge's letter before them in order to give the Department of Justice a unanimous protest against such a vile and malicious accusation. However he explained that Travis came to him and admitted the charge was a falsehood so far as Rouleau was concerned. He asked Rouleau not to let the lawyers see the contents of Burbidge's letter and Rouleau agreed. Travis wrote Burbidge the same day to say he made no charges against Rouleau and did not have him in mind in his first letter. However, he added this curious conclusion: "the statements in my letter of the 8 August were nevertheless literally true, and can be established by incontrovertible testimony whenever that becomes necessary".

On 8 October Burbidge wrote Travis to point out that Travis could have meant no one but Rouleau even though not naming him, but that it now appeared that Travis was not speaking of his own knowledge. On the same day Burbidge wrote Rouleau to explain why he had notified Rouleau of Travis's original letter and Burbidge put a memo in the file the same day "As it appears Mr. Travis' charge of drunkenness against one of his colleagues was not made from his own knowledge but from hearsay, it is not thought necessary to take any further action thereon".

On 14 October Travis wrote a letter making a feeble attempt to justify his original letter to Ottawa. Then he referred to the Reverend John McDougall and James Reilly, Mayor of Calgary, as being persons cognizant of the facts. He concluded the letter by saying that when he came to Calgary conditions were bad with illicit liquor sale, drunkenness and prostitution. He added that he had improved things and that "had government supported me the marked improvement would have been permanent, instead of all having been thrown back as it has been." He concluded by saying that the Northwest was divided into two great classes—the respectable, supporting Travis and the criminal, his opponents.

After his short experience as Stipendiary Magistrate, Travis never returned to public life. He remained in Calgary, amassing some wealth in real estate. He died there in 1911. His unhappy tenure produced some criticism of the government for appointing outsiders, but fortunately the next two appointments of outsiders were excellent.

To sum up the work of the Stipendiary Magistrates, Ryan and Travis were unsatisfactory but neither functioned for long. The other three covered the Territories and dealt with all the important civil and criminal cases for over a decade. They did not produce lengthy written judgments. One group of trials, however, must be noted—the trials for the capital offence of high treason, for the less serious crime of treason felony, for murder, for arson and for theft, all arising out of the Riel Rebellion.

X. The Riel Rebellion of 1885: Trials Before Richardson and Rouleau

The main events of the rebellion are well-known. The Metis on the South Saskatchewan near Batoche persuaded Riel in 1884 to return from Montana to help them with their complaints against the government of Ottawa. Tension increased from month to month. The Metis clashed with a band of Mounted Police and volunteers at Duck Lake on 26 March, 1885. In the following weeks Indians of various tribes threatened Battleford. This was when they burned Rouleau's house and other buildings. Big Bear's Crees massacred nine whites at Frog Lake on 2 April. A few days later the Police abandoned Fort Pitt and the Crees occupied it on 15 April. The main Canadian force under General Middleton marched from Qu'Appelle to the Batoche area. His troops fought an inconclusive battle with the Metis at Fish Creek on 24 April. Colonel Otter's troops marched from Swift Current to Battleford and moved on to Cutknife to attack Poundmaker's Crees on 2 May. The attack was a failure. A week later came Middleton's decisive victory over the Metis at Batoche. Then on 15 May Riel surrendered. Big Bear moved northward from Fort Pitt and after a confrontation at Frenchmen's Butte on 28 May and a final encounter with Major Sam Steele's pursuing force at Loon Lake on 3 June, Big Bear finally surrendered at Fort Carlton on 2 July.[110]

Louis Riel's trial has been called the greatest state trial in Canadian history. On the other hand it has been criticized. Lewis H. Thomas has described it as "judicial murder".[111] This is most unfair to Richardson who presided with a Justice of the Peace and a jury of six. Perhaps Riel's sentence should have been commuted but that was a matter for the executive. While it is hard to recapture the atmosphere of a trial from the printed page, the record shows that Richardson acted with dignity, spoke little and did not demonstrate hostility to Riel, though one can guess that he felt it. Twice he allowed Riel all the time he wanted to make a long speech. The greatest problem Riel's counsel had was with their client who objected to their submission that he was insane—the only possible defence. Richardson's direction to the jury on the defence of insanity was completely in accord with the law of the day. It will be remembered that Riel appealed to the Manitoba Court of Appeal and lost and then applied to the Privy Council for leave to appeal. This was refused.[112]

Many charges were laid against some seventy or eighty Metis and Indians and indeed a few whites in connection with the rebellion. All were tried before Richardson at Regina or Rouleau at Battleford. The trials went on throughout the summer of 1885 and until late October. Some persons thought Rouleau was more lenient than Richardson while others believed he was more harsh.[113] It is hard to generalize but on the whole the trials show an effort by the two Stipendiary Magistrates, and the Crown as well, to be fair. Poundmaker and Big Bear were found guilty of treason felony and sentenced to three years in the penitentiary. Each was released after some seven months at Stony Mountain. A number of Indians were charged with murder for the killings at Frog Lake and two near Battleford. Eight of them were found guilty and were hanged in one "drop" at the Mounted Police barracks at Battleford on 26 November.[114]

XI. Establishment of the Supreme Court in 1887; the Judges' Role in Legislation

In the wake of the Riel rebellion Parliament in 1886 passed three statutes. The North-West Territories Representation Act (c. 24) gave the Territories four members in the House of Commons. Since the British North America Act, 1867 had not provided for representation from the Territories, the Imperial Parliament validated the legislation.[115] The second Act, which had been proposed as early as 1878, was the Territories Real Property Act (c. 267). It provided a system of land titles (the Torrens system), similar to the one Manitoba already had. It was much easier to establish in a territory where nearly all the land was still in the hands of the Crown than in a settled community.

The third Act (c. 25) amended the North West Territories Act and the amendments were included in the revised statutes of 1886 as c. 50. It was of such significance in Alberta's constitutional development that it was published with other Canadian and some Imperial statutes as late as the 1955 Revised Statutes of Alberta. Section 3 declared the laws of the Territories to be those of England as of 15 July, 1870 "insofar as the same are applicable to the Territories" and insofar as they have not been or might be repealed or changed by legislation of the United Kingdom or Canada or the Territories. Sections 4, 5 and 6 established a Supreme Court of five judges (without a Chief Justice). Those eligible were provincial Superior Court judges, the Stipendiary Magistrates and barristers of ten years' standing. The appointment was during good behaviour. Section 14 gave to the court the general powers of a Superior Court of civil and criminal jurisdiction. Judicial districts were to be created (s. 17) and each judge was assigned to one of them, though every judge had jurisdiction throughout the Territories (s. 8). For appeals the court was to sit "in banc" at the "seat of government" which was Regina (s. 15). The Lieutenant-Governor in Council was given jurisdiction over administration of justice in the Territories just as the provinces had under section 92(14) of the B.N.A. Act (s. 27).

This Act came into force on 18 February, 1887.[116] Five judicial districts were created by Dominion Order in Council—Eastern and Western Assiniboia, Southern and Northern Alberta and Saskatchewan.[117] The centenary of this momentous step in the development of legal institutions in the Territories was, so far as the writer knows, scarcely noticed and not observed.

Except for Travis, the Stipendiary Magistrates were all appointed to the new Supreme Court and on 17 September were appointed as members of the Council for its last session.[118] Richardson was the senior judge followed by Macleod and then Rouleau. Before describing the two new judges, Wetmore and McGuire, it is relevant to note that when the Council was replaced by an Assembly in 1888, the statute (s. 2) provided that judges to a maximum of three could be appointed as legal experts.[119] They were to be appointed by the Governor General and became members of the Assembly. They could take part in debates but not vote. The three former Stipendiary Magistrates were appointed on 23 October 1888.[120] There was opposition to the presence of the judges in the Assembly and in 1891 the position of legal expert was abolished.[121]

Mention has been made of Richardson's role in drafting ordinances. When the new Lieutenant-Governor, Joseph Royal, opened the first session of the Assembly on 30 October 1888 he announced that he had appointed Richardson and A.E. Forget, the Secretary to the Lieutenant-Governor, to revise and consolidate the Ordinances. The revision was effective 1 March, 1889. It is in one volume of 526 pages. The longest ordinances were for municipalities, civil justice and schools. Others had to do with government and administration, some with commercial matters, debtor and creditor, and many were related to agriculture—livestock, noxious weeds and prairie fires. There is no doubt that Richardson was the main architect of this revision as he had been of the Ordinances of the previous 10 years. The consolidation shows a creditable performance in the making of laws at a time when the Council's powers were both uncertain and restricted. Many of the Ordinances of course were borrowed, at least in part from legislation of the provinces or of England but many of them were original. Both as to substantive content and draftsmanship they were creditable. The new Assembly had a good foundation on which to build.

The revision came under the scrutiny of the Minister of Justice, John Thompson. He thought some of the provisions in the Municiipalities Ordinance might deal with subjects under Parliament's control, and that the Companies Ordinance in dealing with bills and notes of a company might infringe on Parliament's jurisdiction over negotiable instruments; and that the Schools Ordinance did not give to separate schools the safeguards that section 14 of the North West Territories Act (R.S.C. c. 50) required. However he did not recommend the disallowance of any of the Ordinances. The Minister added that "care seems to have been taken in the revision and that the legislation as a whole is remarkably free from any attempt to usurp authority in respect to subjects that are exclusively within the jurisdiction of the Dominion Parliament."[122]

At the first session of the Assembly Richardson drew rules to govern procedure in the Assembly. These seventy-two rules were much more elaborate than the old ones of the Council. He made a number of motions. The Assembly sought his opinion on the right of the Assembly to hold a plebiscite on prohibition. He replied that it could do so only if the matter were one of a local nature and prohibition was not in that category.[123]

The first nine years of the Assembly's existence marked the struggle led by Frederick Haultain for responsible government. The successive steps—Advisory Council, Executive Committee and finally in 1897 an Executive Council providing the traditional type of Cabinet government—are outside this account.[124] However, the judges still had an important role in connection with federal legislation. The Dominion government looked to them for help in amending the Territories' Real Property Act 1886.

When a Senate bill proposed to remove from the judges their power to deal with examination and adjustment of disputed titles to land, Richardson wrote on 29 December 1892 to the Department of the Interior to say that while this change would relieve judges from the most important of their duties under the Real Property Act, "the judges do not object to performing such duties". He proceeded to give cogent reasons: there had never been an appeal from a judge's decision, there had been no conflicting decisions of the judges, the public had become conversant with the system and the change would give to the Registrar the powers of a judge though he had a less important status.[125]

The judges made recommendations when the Real Property Act was replaced by the Land Titles Act in 1894 and later made suggestions as to amendments.[126] An examination of the numerous reported judgments on land titles matters, including the leading case of *Wilkie* v. *Jellett*[127] shows real concern with making the system work. The writer's generalization is that the rulings were sound and fair. When new problems arose there was sometimes uncertainty and differences of opinion, but no persistent disagreement.

The other federal legislation that required close attention from the Territorial judges consisted of a group of statutes enacted in 1869 to specify various crimes and deal with criminal procedure.[128] The North West Territories Act had special provisions for criminal procedure. In 1891 when Parliament was preparing the Criminal Code that was enacted the next year, the Territorial judges thought that the federal government planned to repeal the special provisions for a jury of six and the power in the judge to select the jury in a peremptory way. Mr. Justice Wetmore drew up a memorandum which Richardson adopted. On 8 June 1891 he sent to the Deputy Minister of Justice a letter saying:

(1) the number of jurors should be kept at six because there were few eligible people at some judicial centres and no accommodation for more.

(2) Section 71 of the North West Territories Act which permitted the judge to summon the jurors should be kept because

(a) it produced a better class of juror and

(b) it expedited the trial and saved expense and time and

(c) the system had worked.

(3) The requirement that a Justice of the Peace must sit with the judge in jury trials should be abolished. The Justices did nothing relating to admission of evidence or charging the jury, and in imposing punishment were likely to do more harm than good.

(4) The number of challenges to a juror (which was smaller than that provided in the Criminal Procedure Act) should be retained.[129]

The recommendations must have had effect because amendments made in September 1891 did away with the need of a Justice of the Peace in jury trials and left the other provisions as they were.[130]

To complete the description of the role of the judges in connection with the content of legislation, it is necessary to note the 1898 Consolidated Ordinances. In February, 1897 the Lieutenant-Governor in Council commissioned Richardson and Mr. Justice Wetmore and C.C. McCaul, the great advocate, to prepare another consolidation of the Ordinances. The resulting consolidation of 1898, twice as large as that of 1888, was a most creditable piece of work. The Ordinances were organized by subject matter—those on government, on administration of justice, relating to real property, mercantile law, special relationships, professions and trades, companies, municipalities, schools and irrigation districts, then agriculture, stock and game, protection of persons and property, intoxicants and miscellaneous. A schedule traces the history of each ordinance from the time it was passed up to the consolidation. Another schedule lists the Ordinances repealed by the consolidation and a third schedule lists those that were left unrepealed but not included in the consolidation. These were nearly all in the nature of private bills including a number creating municipalities. The consolidation ends with a detailed index. The whole format is most useful to the user of the consolidation.

Bearing in mind the role of the judges as members of the Council, and for three years as members of the Assembly, and as draftsmen of the Consolidated Ordinances of 1888 and 1898, one can properly say that the good achievement in the enactment of ordinances from 1877 onwards owes much to the Stipendiary Magistrates and Supreme Court judges, and in particular to Hugh Richardson.

XII. The Members of the Supreme Court

To return to the original members of the Supreme Court: in addition to the three who had been Stipendiary Magistrates there were two new judges—Edward L. Wetmore and Thomas H. McGuire. The former was born at Fredericton, New Brunswick in 1841. In 1856 he went to King's College (now the University of New Brunswick) on a scholarship of £15 a year. He graduated in 1859 and honours were conferred on him for the handsome manner in which he had acquitted himself at his degree examination. At that time it was possible for a person to become an attorney (solicitor) without becoming as well a barrister-at-law. Wetmore was admitted as an attorney in June, 1863 and as a barrister a year later. He practiced with a Fredericton firm and became a Queen's Counsel in 1881. He was Mayor of Fredericton for 2 years and a Commissioner for consolidating the New Brunswick statutes and an MLA from 1883 to 1886.

Stern yet fair, a stickler for form, he was in Mr. Justice Robson's words "in all aspects a satisfactory man".[131] The great counsel, C.C. McCaul, in speaking of the first members of the court said "it is perhaps not an odious comparison to state that Judge Wetmore was quite the strongest member of the court".[132]

A particular contribution of Wetmore, beyond his judgments on substantive law, was a huge number of rulings in matters of civil procedure. The Judicature Ordinance[133] included Rules of Court based on those of England and in some cases of Ontario and Manitoba. In Volume III of the Territories Law Reports, pages 132–477 are almost exclusively practice rulings of Wetmore—by my count seventy-eight of them. One cannot over-estimate the value of these rulings in helping to shape the practice. Wetmore complained in one case: "I must again express my regret that in forming my judgment with respect to the questions of law involved in this case I have had to rely largely on textbooks and digests. Now I have not even the benefit of a library at Regina. I do not suppose that there is a Superior Court in the Dominion of Canada so awkwardly placed in this respect as the Supreme Court of the Territories."[134]

In one case the defendant applied to set aside a statement of claim because it did not contain the material that the rules called for. Wetmore said:[135]

> As a rule I am not disposed to encourage applications on mere technical grounds when no injustice has been done, and when the party complaining has not been in any way misled, and when the application would appear to be made either for delay or for the purpose of obtaining costs. And I would I think be disposed when some trifling inadvertence was taken advantage of to support such application while I granted the application to refuse costs. But I think in this case the proceeding is such a very casual way of following the

practice, that it either shews gross ignorance or gross carelessness on the part of the practitioner and ought to be marked. I will therefore allow the defendant his costs...

Thomas H. McGuire was appointed two months after Wetmore. Born in Kingston, he entered Queen's University in 1866. During the next four years he won four scholarships and won prizes in classics, rhetoric, mathematics, logic, botany and zoology, natural philosophy, metaphysics and chemistry. On graduation in 1870 he led all the graduates in Bachelor of Arts.[136]

He qualified as a barrister in Ontario and practiced in Kingston. Mr. Justice Robson has suggested it could only have been the spirit of adventure that led him to come west.[137] Robson added that McGuire "was a fine-looking man, tall and of a pleasant face, with a fine beard". He was "a proficient writer and a man of general legal experience."

A reading of his judgments shows an excellent style and happy turn of phrase, including some Latin. He was particularly interested in doing what he could to keep the Justices of the Peace in line and to see that they did not go astray. Robson says, and the records show, that he wrote numerous judgments on review or *certiorari*. Indeed he wrote a handbook of seventy-nine pages for Justices of the Peace. This useful little manual explained their role in connection with summary convictions and indictable offences.

His correspondence with Richardson shows a close relationship between them. They worked much together in connection with the Real Property Act and its successor the Land Titles Act and in making recommendations for amendments. He addressed Richardson as "My Dear Chief" though Richardson was not Chief Justice. In one letter from Prince Albert he said "It is swelteringly hot and has been about 100 degrees in the shade for a couple of days past and the sigh of the bard comes to me 'oh for a lodge in some vast wilderness! Some boundless contiguity of shade".[138]

In one case a man named Sparrow gave the defendant a bill of sale of a stack of oats. The plaintiff was a judgment creditor of Sparrow and made a seizure of the oats. He argued that the bill of sale was deficient because the Bills of Sale Ordinance required the defendant to take an affidavit that the bill was not executed for the purpose of protecting the goods against *any* creditors of the vendor.[139] The defendant's affidavit used the phrase "the creditors" instead of "any creditors". The plaintiff argued that "the creditors" could mean "some creditors" and was not the same as "any creditors". Mr. Justice McGuire reviewed cases holding that slight variations do not vitiate the affidavit. Then he said:[140]

> The learned Counsel endeavored to show by syllogistic illustrations that the use of the words "the creditors" entirely changed the meaning of the affidavit, overlooking the fact that in cases of universal negatives the logicians say that both subject and predicate are distributed. I do not know that Mr. Bannerman is a logician, or if so, to what school he belongs; whether to an ancient or a modern school; whether he is to be classed as an Aristotelian, an

> Epicurean, or a Heraclitic-Protagorean; whether his mind is of the Rhetorico-Sophistical, or Spenozistic-Metaphysical, or simply Transcendental-Aesthetic order; or is he, like many in these Territories, a lover of Bacon? The evidence does not enlighten us on any of these points nor do I think the omission material. The power of being able to "divide a hair 'twixt South and South-West side," may be interesting to sophistical rhetoricians who have leisure and taste for such subtleties. I do not think we should avoid a bill of sale by reason of the possibilities suggested here.

Mr. Justice Wetmore did not agree that the two phrases were the same but agreed in the result. Richardson, Macleod and Rouleau all concurred with McGuire.

As for the organization of the court, each judge sat as a trial judge in the district to which he was assigned, though he had jurisdiction throughout the Territories. The court *en banc* sat twice a year at Regina and in the later years sometimes in Calgary. In the beginning a judge could sit on an appeal from his own judgment but after 1894 the trial judge could not do so unless needed for a quorum.[141]

The practice and procedure on appeals seemed to be much like it is today. Appeal books were printed and so were the factums. As the Senior Judge, Richardson was president of the Court. The transcript of evidence was probably taken down in long hand by the judge or a clerk. The questions were often omitted but the answers seem to be complete.

As for the administration of the Court, this was in Richardson's hands. There were continuous problems over Court House space in every judicial centre and also over the inadequacy of lock-ups. Libraries were inadequate, particularly after the Court House fire at Regina in the spring of 1895. There was even a problem at this time over the supplying of judge's books and the payment for them.

It is fortunate that many important judgments have been preserved in the seven volumes of the Territories Law Reports. The original editor was N.D. Beck of Edmonton. Various memoranda at the beginning of Volume 1 are most useful to the historian. Beck was the editor for the first six volumes, aided by T.D. Brown of Regina in Volume 3 and by Brown and O.M. Biggar of Edmonton in Volume 6. By Volume 7 T.D. Brown had succeeded Beck.

The seven volumes cover the twenty years of the court's existence. They give an impresion of high competence, a diligent concern over correctness in interpretation of statutes and application of the common law, fairness and good exposition in the written judgments. Those of Wetmore and McGuire are particularly striking. Each was independent but neither was a chronic dissenter. Rouleau and Richardson frequently wrote judgments on points of law but Macleod did not. His virtues were those of a trial judge.

One writer attempts to make an incompetent out of Rouleau by attributing to him this tired old yarn: after finding an accused to be guilty of theft and sentencing him to six months in jail Rouleau added (according to the story) "if I *really* thought you were guilty I would have given you six years''.[142] The fact is that in criminal cases Rouleau was in the mould of N.D. Beck and Emmett Hall. He was especially solicitous of accused persons and more likely than his brethren to acquit. On a charge of theft of cattle he directed the jury to acquit. The jury ignored him and he was dissatisfied with the guilty verdict. However the full court upheld the conviction.[143] In two other cases of cattle theft he dissented from his brethren all of whom upheld the conviction.[144]

Then there were offences against the liquor laws. The North West Territories Act 1886, had strict provisions to prohibit liquor traffic though there was provision for a permit to import to be issued by the Lieutenant-Governor.[145] Professor Macleod has described the serious liquor problem after settlers began to arrive. Many resented the strict enforcement that had rid the Territories of the whiskey trade. In Prince Albert as well as Calgary strife arose between the police and an element of the public. Macleod says that two decisions of Rouleau J. rendered difficult the enforcement of the liquor provisions. He held that police could not search a saloon without a warrant and in 1889 that once liquor was imported under a permit legal possession was not restricted to the permittee. Macleod adds that the decisions ''were reversed before long''.[146]

Under the Liquor Licence Ordinance of 1891–92 it was an offence for a hotel-keeper to sell liquor after hours. In two cases he acquitted the accused because the Crown did not show that the accused had a licence under the Ordinance.[147]

On a subject far removed from criminal law, Rouleau again anticipated the spirit of Mr. Justice Beck. Each was more interested in doing justice in the case before him than in strict adherence to precedent. In *Pacific Investments* v. *Swan*,[148] the plaintiff knew that certain receivers were to collect monies and pay them out to the defendant. Fearing that the defendant would obtain the monies and that they would be out of the plaintiff's reach should he obtain judgment, Rouleau granted an injunction against the payment to the defendant or the receipt by him of the monies. Mr. Justice Scott set the injunction aside. On the plaintiff's appeal, all three judges were agreed that the plaintiff's material was inadequate to justify an injunction. However, Rouleau differed from Wetmore and Richardson on the question of the Court's jurisdiction to grant an injunction. Wetmore said it could not be granted. The law was clear in England that no such injunction was possible. Rouleau was not concerned about the position in England. ''The conditions in the North-West Territories are entirely different.'' In the Territories a debt could be attached or garnisheed before judgment. These procedures were not available here because the monies to be paid to the defendant were not a debt. He held however that the Court with its capacity to enforce the rules of equity had jurisdiction to grant an interim injunction.

> I am not concerned to seek whether or not any reported case can be found in which the Court of Chancery has interfered in the manner in which this Court may interfere here in a case and under circumstances similar to the present. It may be that there is none, but it is of little consequence that it should be so. It

> may be indeed that to the respondent is due the unenviable reputation of having been the first to design and contrive the peculiar phase of fraud which he rests upon as his defence to the plaintiff's claim; *crescit dolus,* but as fraud increases and extends its ramifications the remedial power of the Court of Chancery to prevent its consequence and to give ample and effectual redress extends also. It matters not how gigantic are its proportions or how new and uncommon the shape which it assumes, the remedial power of the Court rises and becomes equal to the occasion.

This passage shows that Rouleau was of the same mind as Lord Denning who said "Equity is not past the age of child-bearing".[149] Indeed Rouleau's position is analogous to that of Lord Denning when he was instrumental in establishing the Mareva[150] injunction. He was prepared to grant before judgment an injunction that would freeze assets within the jurisdiction in a proper case. "The Mareva injunction is the product of judicial creativity".[151] In Canada the typical Judicature Act has the same provision as the English one that was the basis for the Mareva injunction and Mareva is now widely accepted in Canada.[152]

In connection with Rouleau's interests outside his judicial work, he was a convivial person and enjoyed a poker game.[153] He was also something of a speculator.[154] At one stage, probably when he was stationed at Battleford, he bought three-quarters of a section of land south of the Battle River and one-quarter to the north. He hoped the railway would pass nearby but when built it ran on the far side of the Saskatchewan River.

In July 1890, after Rouleau had moved to Calgary, he sent to one Gauvreau a quantity of half-breed scrip that was good for 240 acres. He explained that he had formed a club to buy the scrip. Gauvreau selected land west of Edmonton. It is now well within the city limits, in Jasper Place.[155]

Six years later Rouleau began to acquire land on either side of the Saskatchewan River about 30 miles west of Calmar and 10 or 12 miles southeast of Tomahawk.[156] His purpose was to wash the gravel for gold and the property was called "Judge Rouleau's Mine". He purchased equipment for dredging but as far as one can tell no gold was ever produced. After Rouleau's death in 1901 the estate had difficulty in disposing of the machinery and it is not clear whether anything was realized from it. Rouleau's only assets were $10,000 in life insurance and the lands just described and a good library. All the assets apart from the insurance were valued at $2,000 while debts were $16,000. It took many years to settle the estate.

To sum up on the first five judges of the Supreme Court, Wetmore was the most outstanding. McGuire too was a strong judge. Richardson did not write so many judgments. He has been described as "dry" and "a bit ponderous" but was still a good judge. Of Macleod, C.C. McCaul said he "did not profess to be a very well-read lawyer. In fact the nicer distinctions and subtleties of the law did not appeal to his type of mind at all. He possessed, however, a solid sense of justice and a fund of common sense; and above all, he was a gentleman and very human, the best of all qualities in a judge. His administration of criminal law was eminently satisfactory."

As to Rouleau, McCaul says he was of a different type. He had a good deal of Colonel Macleod's bonhomie and common sense, and they were very good friends, but Judge Rouleau was, above all things, a lawyer. McCaul speaks most highly of his mastery of English common law and equity and his faculty for working out the principles at issue in the case before him.[157]

Then Chief Justice Harvey said this of these five judges:[158]

> Speaking with a personal knowledge of its first members, with all but one of whom [Macleod] I was brought frequently in contact and with one of whom [Wetmore] I was subsequently a colleague, I feel no hesitation in stating that... there was no inferiority to the personnel of the Supreme Courts of the provinces. This is also apparent from a perusal of its reported decisions.

The opinions of Chief Justice Harvey and C.C. McCaul should suffice, one hopes, to bury for good such a calumny as this: "Two of the five judges of the Supreme Court weren't lawyers. It was difficult to find anyone who had even a smattering of legal training".[159]

The seven volumes of the Territories Law Reports show a substantial body of judgments by the original five members and D.L. Scott. They testify to a grasp of legal issues, good research (especially in the absence of adequate libraries), a sense of responsibility, and as far as one can discern from the judgments, an absence of cliques or animosities.

XIII. Death of Macleod and Appointment of Scott

The first of the original judges to die was Colonel Macleod in 1894. One sign of the esteem in which he was held came almost a decade before he died. Early in 1885, when he was stationed at Macleod as Stipendiary Magistrate, some eighty-five Calgarians sent a petition to Ottawa to ask that Macleod be assigned to Calgary because that place had no resident Stipendiary Magistrate and arrested persons were kept in jail too long. (This was shortly before the ill-fated appointment of Travis.) The residents of Macleod in an undated counter-petition replied that their interests were at least as important as Calgary's; that Macleod was personally known to almost all the residents of Fort Macleod "and that as a judge his impartiality has won our admiration and as a citizen and a neighbour he has endeared himself to all".[160]

Macleod was not moved to Calgary until shortly before his death in 1894. An Order in Council of May 21 recited that Rouleau was overworked while there was comparatively little business at Macleod and the two judges agreed that both should reside at Calgary and both be assigned to North and South Alberta. (Macleod was the judicial centre for South Alberta and Calgary for North.) Macleod's health was bad by this time but he continued his judicial duties until just before his death at Calgary on 5 September.[161] Condolences poured in from all over Canada.[162] An account of his work in the west, written much later by another original member of the North West Mounted Police, Sir Cecil Denny, gives a good description of Macleod.[163]

> His tact and knowledge of human nature, coupled with great forbearance and patience, enabled the North-West Mounted Police to establish law and order

in a hitherto wild and lawless territory. By his skilful handling of the savage and warlike Indian tribes, he gained their complete confidence. The main secret of his success was that when he made a promise it was scrupulously kept, as the Indians learned. While commanding the force later as Commissioner, he also carried out the duties of stipendiary magistrate. His dealing with the turbulent element was based on stern justice, and although he handed out many severe sentences, he retained the respect and confidence of all classes of the white population, including the criminals themselves.

Upon leaving the force, he was appointed judge of the Supreme Court of the Territories, a position he occupied until his death, and in that responsible office no higher praise can be given than that he was an upright and just judge. He died a poor man. Although he had many opportunities to acquire wealth, he took advantage of none.

Macleod was replaced by David Lynch Scott. Born at Brampton in 1845 he was admitted to the bar of Ontario in 1870. He practiced in Orangeville and was mayor of that town. Moving to Regina in 1882 he was the first mayor. He had been active in the militia during the Fenian threat of 1866 and during the Riel rebellion at Regina organized a volunteer corps. He was the only local advocate among the four who prosecuted Louis Riel for treason felony in 1885. He also appeared in the trials that followed—of Poundmaker, Big Bear, the Indians responsible for the Frog Lake massacre and a number of others. Subsequently he often represented the Crown, and from 1 July, 1887 he was legal adviser to the Lieutenant-Governor.[164]

When appointed to the court he was assigned to Calgary. His judgments though not long were well written and careful. Just after his appointment he was asked by R.B. Gordon, clerk of the Assembly, for his views on the qualification of Justices of the Peace. His reply of 10 January 1895 said:[165]

> I doubt the advisability of an examination. It is not done elsewhere, though this is no agrument against it. The appointment is one of honour and the matter should be looked at as a case of the position seeking the man and not the man seeking the position. If an examination were prescribed it would be only those who sought the position that would present themselves and though perhaps well versed in the duties do not always make the most desirable justices, some of them desiring it for the purpose of making an income out of the fees and for that purpose are inclined to encourage the bringing of cases before them.
>
> I am afraid that if an examination were required, those who would make the most satisfactory justices would not present themselves—that is men of good standing and reasonable education who do not covet the position but who have been appointed even without any knowledge of the duty, would soon acquire it and having no ends to serve would perform the duties in an impartial manner. Given a reasonable education I think the standing and worth of the appointee is of far more importance than the knowledge he may possess of the duties at the time of the appointment.

This letter not only throws light on Scott but deals with a very important institution in the establishment of law in the Territories—that of Justices of the Peace. Problems of selection (with patronage sometimes a factor) and paying the costs of the system, supplying the justices with statutes and other necessary information were all formidable but the system worked.[166]

XIV. The Later Appointees to the Supreme Court

This account will conclude with a short description of the appointments made after that of Scott in 1894. In 1900 Parliament provided for a Chief Justice and four puisne judges.[167] One might have thought the appointment of Chief Justice would go to Richardson, but it went to McGuire in February 1902. He resigned after a year and A.L. Sifton, a Calgary lawyer and brother of Sir Clifford, was appointed in his stead in January 1903. The reaction to this appointment is described in the Canadian Annual Review.[168]

> The appointment was variously received. The Manitoba *Free Press* described Mr. Sifton as "one of the most competent members of the Territorial bar" and declared that the fact of his being a brother of the Hon. Clifford Sifton should not be a barrier to his advancement. Some regret was expressed, as the Regina *Leader* put it, that Mr. Justice Richardson had been again passed over, but as a whole the appointment was approved by the Liberal press. It was, however, strongly disapproved by the Conservative papers. The Regina *West*, for instance, called it nepotism, the sacrifice of judicial honour, treachery toward Judge Richardson and the turning of the Judiciary into a part of the political machinery.

Richardson retired in November 1903. Rouleau had died in 1901 and was succeeded by J.E.P. Prendergast in 1902. W.H. Newlands replaced Richardson in 1904 and in the same year Horace Harvey was appointed a fifth puisne judge.[169] Two additional appointments were made in 1906—C.A. Stuart and T.C. Johnstone.[170] Thus the Court in the last few months of its existence had a Chief Justice and seven puisne judges.

Before leaving the Territorial judges, it is relevant to note their salaries. The Stipendiary Magistrates had received $3,000 a year.[171] The Supreme Court Judges originally received $4,000 each.[172] In 1901 a salary of $5,000 was provided for the Chief Justice and $4,000 for the other four.[173] In 1905 the Chief Justice was given $7,000 and the seven puisne judges, $6,000 each.[174]

XV. The New Provincial Supreme Courts: The Lawyers: Conclusion

The provincial Supreme Courts replaced the Territorial Court on 16 September 1907. Those who went to the Supreme Court of Alberta were Chief Justice Sifton with Scott, Harvey, Stuart and N.D. Beck, a new appointee. For Saskatchewan, Wetmore was made Chief Justice with Prendergast, Newlands, Johnstone and a new judge J.H. Lamont.

By way of an aside, it is relevant to mention the lawyers of the Territories. McCaul has given a good account of the migration westward of lawyers to Winnipeg and on to the main towns in the Territories.[175] Many lawyers came in the '80s and '90s and distinguished themselves. It is beyond the scope of this article to set out even a list of them, but one can safely say that even before any legislation was passed to regulate the profession, able and responsible lawyers, many from Ontario, had come to the main centres of the Territories. The first Legal Profession Ordinance was made in 1885 (No. 18) just after the Riel Rebellion. It did not provide for a Law Society but did set out qualifications for admission. The judges had the responsibility of seeing that each applicant had the qualifications for admission to practice, and also had power to discipline an advocate for non-payment of monies received by him as advocate. The Lieutenant-Governor kept the roll of advocates. The Law Society of the Territories was established in 1898 (Ord. No. 21). It provided for Benchers to govern the society. They had control over admission to practise though the main power to discipline members remained in the judges. The Territorial Society like the Territorial Court survived the creation of the provinces by two years and then it was replaced by the two provincial societies.[176]

The writer offers the opinion that the Territories bequeathed to each of the two new provinces an efficient and well-organized court with able judges and a sound body of jurisprudence. Indeed the new provincial Supreme Courts were in large measure a continuation of the Territorial Court in personnel and structure.

Notes

This is a revision of a paper given at a Conference at Carleton University, Ottawa, on Canadian Law in History in June 1987. The writer is indebted to W.H. Hurlburt, Q.C. of Edmonton and to Dean Trevor Anderson of Winnipeg for helpful comments on an earlier draft. He extends thanks too, to the staff of the Law Library, University of Alberta, the Alberta Archives (Edmonton), Glenbow Archives (Calgary), Saskatchewan Archives Board (Regina) and the Public Archives of Canada (Ottawa) for guiding the writer to relevant material. The writer also acknowledges the fine work of Desmond Brown in gathering biographic material on the Stipendiary Magistrates and judges some time ago. The Alberta Law Foundation provided a grant which made possible the help of Dr. Brown and which covered part of the costs of the archival research. Two small points: "Northwest Territories" and "North West Territories" and "North-west Territories" were all used at different times, the last being the general spelling; (2) the term "half-breed" was used in the early statutes. "Metis" is a preferable term today.

1 Oliver, 19 *Canada and Its Provinces,* (1914) 148.

2 Morton, *A History of the Canadian West to 1870–71* (2 ed., 1973) 513, 514.

3 Canada Jurisdiction Act 1803 (U.K.), 43 George III, c. 138.

4 Act for regulating the Fur Trade and establishing a Criminal and Civil Jurisdiction within certain Parts of North America, 1821 (U.K.), 1 & 2 George IV, c. 66.

5 Stubbs, *Four Recorders of Rupert's Land* (1967) at 12–15; Gibson, *Substantial Justice* (1972) 30, 31.

6 *In the Case of James Calder* (1848) reported in 2 Western Law Times 1

(1891).

7 Report from the Select Committee on the Hudson's Bay Company (1857): Christy at qns. 5517–5524, 5894, 6010–6017; Roebuck at 5887–5891.

8 Rupert's Land Act, 1868 (U.K.), 31–32 Vict., c. 105.

9 32–33 Vict., c. 3, extended by the Manitoba Act s. 36.

10 34 Vict., c. 16.

11 Oliver, *The Canadian North-West*, Vol. 2 (1915) 974, 975.

12 *Id*. at 975–979.

13 *Id*. at 979–988.

14 Butler, *The Great Lone Land* (1968) at 353–355.

15 *Id*. His formal report is at 355–386.

16 *Id*. at 357 & 367.

17 *Id*. at 383.

18 *Id*. at 385, 386.

19 *Id*. at 388.

20 O/C Dept. of Int. Vol. 1 at 289.

21 *Id*. at 395.

22 *Id*. at 457.

23 *Supra* n. 11 at 997.

24 *Supra* n. 20 at 507.

25 36 Vict., c. 5.

26 36 Vict., c. 34.

27 36 Vict., c. 39.

28 36 Vict., c. 35.

29 Official Report N.W.M.P., 1874 at 3–28, 57–67 in *Opening up the West* (1973); Denny, *The Law Marches West*, Chapters 3–5 (2 ed., 1972); Macleod, *The N.W.M.P. and Law Enforcement 1873–1905*, Chapters 2 & 3 (1976); Turner, *The N.W.M.P. 1873–93*, Vol. 1 (1950), chap. 4.

30 Sharp, *Whoop-up Country*, c. 4 (1955).

31 *Supra* n. 11 at 1003, 1004.

32 37 Vict., c. 22, s. 15.

33 O.C. 19 June 1880 reciting Macleod's appointment in O/C Dept. of Int. Vol. 3 at 353.

34 38 Vict., c. 49.

35 *Id*., ss. 3 and 61.

36 Thomas, *The Struggle for Responsible Government in the North-West Territories, 1870–97* (2 ed., 1978) 73–90.

37 1877 Statutes, p. liv.

38 S.C. 40 Vict., c. 7, assented to 28 April 1877.

39 O/C Dept. of Int. Vol. 2 at 607.

40 *Supra* n. 33.

41 O/C Dept. of Int. Vol. 2 at 487.

42 *Id*. at 527.

43 Sessional Papers (No. 9) 1876 at 8.

44 Sessional Papers (No. 116) 1885 at 17.

45 O.C. 3 April, 1877, granting him 2 months' leave "from the date at which he may start from Swan River", in O/C Dept. of Int. Vol. 2 at 585.

46 Richardson Papers, Saskatchewan Archives Board, Regina—85, I 5(e).

47 *Supra* n. 36, c. 4 for an account of Laird's tenure of office.

48 *Norquay North Star* 1987 Tourist Edition at 11; see also *Western People*, June 12, 1986 at 6, 7 and MacLaren, *Braehead* (1986) 155, 156.

49 Turner, *Supra* n. 29 at 310.

50 The batonnier of the Montreal bar has confirmed this but has no other information. (Letter 29 July 1976 to the writer.)

51 Turner, *supra* n. 29 at 310; see also MacLaren, *supra* n. 48 at 156.

52 Commissioners Report 1878 p. 24 in *Opening Up the West, supra* n. 29.

53 Laird Letter-Book, File No. AL144, Sask. Archives Board, Regina.

54 *Saskatchewan Herald*, 18 July 1881.

55 Public Archives of Canada, RG 13 A-2, vol. 55 No. 136/83.

56 Macdonald Papers, Public Archives of Canada Vol. 325 Item 13.

57 Letter 26 July 1976 from Rose Mary Gibson, Assistant Archivist, Queen's University.

58 Glenbow Alberta Institute Archives, James Farquharson Macleod M776 No. 11.

59 MacLaren, *supra* n. 48 c. 5 & c. 9.

60 *Opening up the West, supra* n. 29: 1877 App. D.; 1878 App. D.; 1879 at 11–16; 1880 at 14, 15; 1881 at 3, 4.

61 *Id*.: 1877 Report at p. 21; also Denny, *supra* n. 29, Chapters 11 & 12.

62 Denny, *supra* n. 29 at 116.

63 1878 Report at 26, in *Opening up the West, supra* n. 29.

64 Turner, *supra* n. 29 at 500, 501.

65 O.C. 19 June 1880, *supra* n. 33.

66 Macleod, *supra* n. 29 at 40, 41; MacLaren, *supra* n. 48 at 171–174, 198, 201, 202.

67 1880 Report in *Opening up the West, supra* n. 29, at 6.

68 1881 Report in *Opening up the West, supra* n. 29 at 14.

69 *Id*. at 16.

70 *Id*. at 25.
71 Stuart, *Reminiscences,* Vol. 2, 162, 163.
72 Prassel, *The Western Peace Officer* (1972) 216.
73 1888 Official Report at 8 & 65, in the New West (1973).
74 *Id*. at 119.
75 32–33 Vict., c. 24.
76 The following account is based on items in the *Victoria Daily Colonist* and in James Farquharson Macleod, *supra* n. 58 no. 5, and on microfilm.
77 Johnston's wires of 28 and 30 August to Joseph Pope, Minister of Railways.
78 Denny, *supra* n. 29 at 15.
79 This is from the *Saskatchewan Herald* in a clipping in Richardson Papers in the Saskatchewan Archives.
80 *Supra* n. 45.
81 *Supra* n. 46, R-85 I 9.
82 Saskatchewan Archives R-85 I 10.
83 The Offences Against the Persons Act, 32–33 Vict., c. 20, s. 54 made it an offence to abduct an heiress against the will of her father: this provision came from the Imperial Act of 1861; earlier statutes are the Abduction Act, 9 Geo. IV, c. 31 and 4 & 5 Philip & Mary, c. 8 (1558).
84 38 Vict., c. 50, s. 1.
85 From this point the account of Elliott's trial is from the *Saskatchewan Herald,* 23 September and 30 Decermber 1878.
86 *Supra* n. 36 at 67, fn. 89.
87 The Order in Council is dated 25 October 1876.
88 *Supra* n. 38 and 39.
89 Orders in Council on Dominion and Provincial Legislation 1867–1895 at p. 1236.
90 For an account of the sittings of the court in each judicial district under the 1878 ordinance, see McCaul, "Constitutional Status of Northwest Territories" (1884) 2 *Canadian Law Times* 49 at 57–61.
91 Journals of N.W.T. Council 1881.
92 *Supra* n. 36 at 93.
93 *Edmonton Bulletin,* 17 December, 1881.
94 *Supra* n. 46, I 2.
95 *Edmonton Bulletin,* 7 February, 1881.
96 *Supra* n. 46 I 7.
97 *Supra* n. 46 I(1)(c).
98 *Supra* n. 46 I 3 and I 5(a).
99 This account is taken from articles in the *Edmonton Bulletin* of 11 and 18 February, 4 March, 25 March, 17 and 24 June.
100 *Supra* n. 46, I 5(b).
101 Glenbow Archives: *Dewdney Papers,* M 320 Vol. VI at 1402.
102 Beal and Macleod, Prairie Fire at 240 (1985).
103 48–49 Vict., c. 51, s. 126.
104 *See* J.S. Ewart's sarcastic review in (1884) 1 *Man. Law J.* 120; (1885) 2 *Man. Law J.* 28 and Travis's defence at 41.
105 *Supra* n. 101 at 1687, 1691.
106 *House of Commons Debates,* 27 April, 1886 p. 889 col. 2.
107 See Peter Ward's unpublished thesis, University of Alberta, "The Administration of Justice in the North-West Territories 1870–1887" (1966) at 81–85 and Foran, the "Travis Affair", (1971) 19 *Alta. Hist. Rev.* No. 4 p. 1.
108 Ordinance re Municipality of Calgary, O.N.W.T. 1886, No. 1.
109 Saskatchewan Archives, Regina. S.H.S. 188.
110 See Stanley, *Louis Riel* (1963); Morton, ed., *The Queen* v. *Louis Riel* (1974); Beal and Macleod, *supra* n. 102. The last of these has an excellent bibliography at 367–372.
111 This is the title of an account by Dr. Thomas of the trial of Riel, written in 1975.
112 *Regina* v. *Riel* (No. 1) (1885) 1 Terr. L.R. 20; *Regina* v. *Riel* (No. 2) (1885) 1 Terr. L.R. 23; 10 App. Cas. 275.
113 *Supra* n. 102 at 100, 331.
114 For an account of all the trials, see Beal and Macleod, *id.,* Part 3.
115 B.N.A. Act 1886, 49–50 Vict., c. 35 (U.K.).
116 North West Territories Act Amendment Act, 49 Vict., c. 25.
117 1887 Statutes CLIII: previously Ordinances of 1878, 1883 and 1884 had created judicial districts—3 then 4 then 3.
118 O/C, Dept. of Int., No. 9 at 593.
119 51 Vict., c. 19.
120 O/C, Dept. of Int., No. 10 at 499.
121 54–55 Vict., c. 22, s. 2.
122 O/C 27 Jan., 1890, in Orders in Council

on Dominion and Provincial legislation *supra* n. 89 at 1249–51.

123 Journals of Assembly 1888.

124 *Supra* n. 36 c. 7–9, gives a good account of these developments.

125 *Supra* n. 46, III 18.

126 *Id.*, II and III 18 contain bulky material on the Real Property Act and the Land Titles Act. Richardson and McGuire had the main carriage of this work.

127 (1895) 2 Terr. L.R. 133, affg. [1896] S.C.R. 282.

128 32–33 Vict., c. 18–24, 27, 29, 30: these were made applicable to the Territories by 38 Vict., c. 49 Schedule B.

129 *Supra* n. 46, III 8.

130 54–55 Vict., c. 22, s. 67.

131 Robson, "Edward Ludlow Wetmore" (1944) 22 *Can. Bar Rev.* 442 at 446.

132 McCaul, "Precursors of the Bench and Bar" (1925) 3 *Can. Bar Rev.* 25 at 39.

133 R.O. 1888 c. 58.

134 *Allen* v. *Pierce* (1895) 3 Terr. L.R. 319 at 329: the library had been destroyed in a fire on 1 April 1895—see Richardson Papers, *supra* n. 46, III 11.

135 *Clarke* v. *Brownlie* (1893) 3 Terr. L.R. 194 at 196.

136 Queen's College Calendars 1866—1870, made available through the kindness of Rose Mary Gibson, Assistant Archivist, Queen's University, 21 July 1976.

137 Robson, "Hon. Thomas Horace McGuire" (1945) 23 *Can. Bar Rev.* 139.

138 *Supra* n. 46, II(1).

139 R.O. 1888, c. 4, s. 5.

140 *Emerson* v. *Bannerman* (1890) 1 Terr. L.R. 224 at 230. For another example of McGuire's invocation of the rules of logic see *Lamont* v. *CPR* (1900) 5 Terr. L.R. 60 at 63.

141 57–58 Vict., c. 17, s. 4.

142 MacDonald, *Court Jesters,* (1985) at 120. The same author on the same page has Rouleau as a trial judge engaging in repartee with an unnamed Judge of the "Court of Appeal". There was no Court of Appeal. All Judges took trials and sat on appeals. There is nothing in the Territories Law Reprots to support any suggestion of animosity between Rouleau and his brethren.

143 *Reg.* v. *Brewster* (No. 2) (1896) 2 Terr. L.R. 377.

144 *The Queen* v. *Collyns* (1898) 3 Terr. L.R. 82; *The Queen* v. *Forsythe* (1900) 4 Terr. L.R. 398; see also Macleod *supra* n. 29 at 67. Rouleau's charity toward accused persons appears also in *Re Nettleship* (1899) 4 Terr. L.R. 148. See *R.* v. *Mellon* (1900) 5 Terr. L.R. 301 for his insistence on the need to prove mens rea.

145 R.S.C. 1886, c. 50, ss. 92–100.

146 Macleod *supra* n. 29 at 139; also Commr. Herchmer's 1888 Report at 11 and 1889 Report at 22, both in The New West (1973). One of Rouleau's decisions is *Reg.* v. *Whitebeck* (1888) 24 *Can. Law J.* 478.

147 *The Queen* v. *Henderson* (1899) 4 Terr. L.R. 146; *The Queen* v. *Davidson* (1900) 4 Terr. L.R. 425.

148 (1898) 3 Terr. L.R. 125.

149 *Eves* v. *Eves* [1975] 3 All E.R. 768 at 771.

150 *Mareva Compania* v. *International Bulk Carriers* [1980] 1 All E.R. 213.

151 2 Current Law Statutes Annotated 1981, annotation to Supreme Court Act 1981, c. 37.

152 The Alberta provision is s. 13(2) of the Judicature Act. Its counterpart in Rouleau's time was s. 10(8) of the Judicature Ordinance, R.O. 1898, c. 21. Rouleau did not mention this provision. For a recent note see Erickson, The Mareva Injunction Comes to Alberta (1987) 25 Alberta L.R. 305.

153 McLaren *supra* n. 48 at 262.

154 The following account is based on the Short Ross Selwood papers, B.F.S. 559 in the Glenbow Archives.

155 Of this parcel, 160 acres form a square between 92nd and 96th avenues from south to north and from 156th street on the east to 163rd street on the west. The remaining 80 acres are between 92nd and 94th avenues and between 163rd and 170th streets.

156 The property was in a number of small parcels in sections 9, 10, 16 and 35 in Twp. 50, R4, W5 and one parcel in section 2 of Twp. 51.

157 *Supra* n. 132 at 38, 39.

158 Harvey, "The Early Administration of Justice in the North West" (1934) 1 *Alta. L.Q.* 1 at 15.

159 *Supra* n. 142 at 122. Each of the five had been members of a provincial bar.
160 Glenbow Archives, *supra* n. 58, M776, No. 7; MacLaren, *supra* n. 48 at 263 puts this event at 1893.
161 *Id*. at 266, 267.
162 *Supra* n. 58, M776 No. 10.
163 Denny, *supra* n. 29 at 286.
164 O/C, Dept. of Int., No. 11 at 629.
165 Saskatchewan Archives, Regina NWT M41.
166 Unpublished thesis of Thomas M. Reynolds, "Justices of the Peace in the North West Territories, 1870–1905" (University of Regina, 1978) in Sask. Archives Regina R-E 1742. This is a very useful study.
167 63–64 Vict. c. 44.
168 Canadian Annual Review, 1903 at 195.
169 Authorized by 3 Edw. 7, c. 27, s. 2.
170 Authorized by 4–5 Edw. 7 c. 31, s. 4.
171 O/C 22 July, 1876 appointing Richardson, in O/C, Dept. of Int. No. 2 at 487.
172 49 Vict., c. 25, s. 10.
173 1 Edw. 7, c. 39.
174 4–5 Edw. 7, c. 31, s. 4.
175 *Supra* n. 132 at 34, 37, 38.
176 Legal Profession Act (Alta.) 1907, c. 20: Legal Profession Act (Sask.) 1907, c. 19. A good study of the Territorial and Alberta Law Societies is an unpublished thesis of Peter M. Sibenik in 1984 in the Dept. of History, University of Calgary, entitled *The Doorkeepers: The Governance of Territorial and Alberta Lawyers 1885–1928*.

1988

Metaphors and Other Notable Passages in Judgments

Unpublished

On March 19, 1988 Bowker was guest speaker at the banquet for the graduating class in Law, held in the Four Seasons Hotel in Edmonton. It was attended by some 400 persons, including graduands, spouses, children, parents and relatives.

His talk revolved around some amusing passages in judgments as recorded over the years.

The piece which follows is a revised and expanded version of that talk.

Introduction: Style In Judgments

A person who has spent years drawing documents and pleadings—a good conveyancer—tries to be clear and accurate but is not likely to engage in stylish or colourful language. Indeed John Austin wrote to his future wife: "I shall hardly venture on sending a letter of much purpose, even to you, unless it be laboured with the accuracy and circumspection which are requisite in a deed of conveyance."[1]

Legal documents are not as prolix today as in Austin's time, though the objective is the same. Army pamphlets are not noted for their light touch but in World War II one manual of instruction for staff officers sending messages said this: "Imagine you are a miser sending a prepaid telegram to a fool." This is good advice for one giving a legal opinion and may apply to judgments too. Some great judges had no outstanding style—Sir George Jessel, for example.[2] Others like Benjamin Cardozo are famous for their use of English: "The risk reasonably to be perceived defines the duty to be obeyed"[3] and "Danger invites rescue. The cry of distress is the summons to relief."[4]

The writer has been tempted to suggest that the Honourable Samuel Freedman, retired Chief Justice of Manitoba, is a Canadian Cardozo, but helpful friends have pointed out that while Cardozo's style is "magisterial," Freedman's is informal, and his judgments are marked by simplicity. Fortunately they have been collected and published.[5]

Some great judges may on occasion be obscure. Mr. Justice Rand made a notable contribution to our jurisprudence. Of a philosophical bent, he was sometimes abstract. Where a soldier contrary to orders fired a tracer bullet at a barn and the barn burned down, the owner sought to hold the

Crown liable. The Exchequer Court judge, Mr. Justice Gerald O'Connor (from Edmonton), found for the petitioner. On appeal to the Supreme Court, the judgment was reversed by a majority speaking through Rand J. He held that the failure of the officer to prevent the soldier from firing was not a breach of duty to the petitioner.

> "Failure in relation to a duty undertaken or assumed directly toward the injured person becomes affirmative action in the obverse of actual conduct modified by the failure, and the actual conduct may be mere persistence in inaction... "[6]

The writer has been told that Mr. Justice O'Connor pointed out this passage to Rand J. and invited an explanation. The answer has not been recorded.

Lord MacMillan said "While it is quite fitting to mitigate the austerity of a judgment by employing the arts and graces of literary composition, restraint should be exercised in doing so. Elegance of expression, aptness of illustration, well-chosen metaphors and an occasional happy literary quotation are both legitimate and desirable. But a judgment is not an appropriate vehicle for wit and pleasantry at large."[7]

Some Amusing Judgments

In *Lord Advocate* v. *Young,*[8] a case from Scotland, Young shot a rabbit on his farm and was charged with using a gun without a license in violation of the Gun License Act, 1870. He relied on a proviso that an occupier of land could use a gun to kill vermin and argued that a rabbit was vermin. Lord Robertson held it was not, and invoked the Ground Game Act of 1880 which treated rabbits as game, even though it permitted their killing. "This is the darkest hour in the legislative history of the rabbit but his fortunes are still linked with those of the hare" and later "I own to finding it inconceivable that the Legislature should have shown all this ceremony toward the rabbit in 1880 if he had already been cast out among the vermin."

In an English case of late 1987,[9] the Court had to construe a reservation of the exclusive right of "hunting shooting fishing coursing and sporting" over certain lands in respect of "all game woodcocks snipe and other wild fowl hares rabbits and fishing." A dispute arose as to whether this wording covered deer. In a careful judgment Mr. Justice Harman concluded it did not. In the course of his reasons he had occasion to say that in 1921, when the reservation was made, "no gentleman (or even a lawyer) would speak of 'hunting' feathered game... because that is a purely American usage and not used in England in 1921." It seems the proper term was "shooting." He said that the taking of deer by shooting would not in 1921 be appropriately called "hunting deer" except perhaps by Americans. The normal and correct term was "stalking." Later he observed parenthetically that rabbits "are not usually recognized as game save in the Ground Game Acts." He did not say whether they were usually recognized as vermin.

On the question whether one "hunts" or "shoots" feathered game,

Lord Justice Harman (not to be confused with Mr. Justice Harman) in 1968 dealt with a case[10] in which a married couple lived near Red Deer, Alberta. The wife's departure for England is described in these words: "In November, 1967, when her husband was away on what Canadians are pleased to call a "hunting" trip, though we should perhaps call it a shooting holiday, she took the children without his knowledge or consent and removed them to England... " In the same case, Lord Justice Russell referred to the wife's excuse that she took the children back to England because she had nowhere else to go. His Lordship replied: "That, of course, cannot be correct. Red Deer, Alberta, is not a one-horse town."

A Tennessee case of 1902[11] dealt with the word "animal." A statute said that the crew of a train must blow the whistle and apply the brakes whenever an animal or obstruction appeared on the tracks, to prevent accidents. Three of Davis's geese got on the track and were killed. The trial judge held the act applied and awarded Davis $1.50, being their value. On the company's appeal the court held that the geese were not animals or obstructions within the act. "It is true, a goose has animal life and in the broadest sense is an animal; but we think the statute does not require the stopping of trains to prevent running over birds that may be kept for pleasure or profit. Birds have wings to move them quickly from places of danger, and it is presumed that they will use them (a violent presumption perhaps, in the case of a goose, an animal which appears to be loath to stoop from its dignity to even escape a passing train). But the line must be drawn somewhere and we think that the goose is a proper bird to draw it at."

In connection with wandering cattle, the House of Lords in 1947 held that the centuries-old rule—no duty on the owner to fence them in—persists today.[12] Later, the same problem arose in an Ontario case[13] where the Supreme Court refused to follow the House of Lords and upheld Ontario's Court of Appeal.[14] In that court Roach J.A. ended his judgment with this:

> It is now over 200 years since Thomas Gray wrote his famous lines descriptive of rural England at eventide, "the lowing herd winds slowly o'er the lea." The lea no doubt included such highways as then traversed the landscape. As I read the modern English cases the herd may still wander along those same highways without the owner being subject to civil liability for the injuries they may cause. No longer in this Province does "the ploughman homeward plod his weary way." He goes now in his tractor, oft-times along the highway. The farmer whose lands adjoin the King's Highway can in this modern era scarcely know the meaning of "the solemn stillness" of which Gray wrote. No longer can he be conscious of the beetle wheeling his droning flight. What he hears, instead, is the whir of motor cars wheeling their way at legalized speed along the adjoining highway. The common law of England may have been adequate in Gray's day. The Courts in England have held that it is still adequate, but surely it must be apparent that to-day in this Province it is not.

An English case having nothing to do with rabbits, game, geese or cattle is *Re Marquise Footwear*.[15] A maker of ladies' footwear applied for a trademark, Oomphies. The Registrar refused to register the trademark, one ground being that it was a salacious or erotic word. Mr. Justice Evershed allowed the appeal. The word could be used as a trademark, though the judge's opinion of it appears from the following:

> The word which has been the subject-matter of the argument is "Oomphies," and in speaking of it as a word, as one must, one is, I think, paying it a compliment, because it barely deserves an appellation which makes it part of articulate speech, which is said by some to be the only distinguishing feature, if any, between the human race and brute beasts. However, it must be regarded as a word. It owes its origin, according to the evidence, to a cinematograph actress, Miss Ann Sheridan, and, as I understand it, after being particularly applied to her, it has achieved a significance—how widespread I cannot say—meaning those qualities, particularly associated with Miss Sheridan, which have been described variously and of which I can use the expression "sex appeal." In that sense it has apparently a precursor in the word "It," which, beginning by particular reference to Miss Clara Bow, achieved a certain wide significance until it was supplanted by the present word. The present word may possibly have the advantage over the former that it may be of onomatopoeic significance. That being the origin of the word the applicants have added to it the suffix "ies" and have produced the word "oomphies," and Mr. Lloyd-Jacob has said, with justice, that that word, at any rate, is new in the sense that—so far as I know—this is the first occasion on which it has ever been used as a word.

While on trademarks, mention might be made of a recent English case in which a defence was entered in an action for infringement of the trademark "Dry Sack." The plaintiff applied to strike out the defence. The defence was partly bad but the defendant argued that it remained partly good. The argument failed. Lord Templeman said "My lords, I decline to dine on this curate's egg. The trademark's action . . . must be either wholly good or wholly bad."[16] The story of the curate's egg comes from Punch in 1895. The curate was dining with his bishop. The latter said "I'm afraid you've got a bad egg, Mr. Jones." The curate replied, "Oh no my Lord, I assure you! Parts of it are excellent!"[17]

Striking Phrases and Metaphors

Frequently one encounters a short passage, even a single phrase, that is expressed in striking language. One case that law students of the early thirties used to read in Trusts is *Dougan* v. *Macpherson*.[18] The action was brought by one James Dougan against his trustee for having taken advantage of him. The statement of facts says: "It appears that James Dougan had been for many years in a state of chronic impecuniosity"—much more elegant than "was always flat broke" or even "never had any money." This became a by-word among the law students at the University of Alberta, probably because it could be applied to most of them.

One can find many similes or metaphors—Lord Macmillan quoted a simile that he attributed to Lord Davey: "the appellant's case is as full of holes as a colander."[19] A metaphor making the same point goes this way: "the chain of reasoning is full of missing links." The writer does not know the source.

Metaphors can of course be overdone—and they can be more misleading than helpful. A recent article discusses the "penumbra" metaphor that Mr. Justice Douglas of the Supreme Court of the United States used to establish a constitutional right of privacy in *Griswold* v. *Connecticut,*[20] and shows the difficulties with it. The author quotes Cardozo: "Metaphors in law are to be narrowly watched, for starting out as devices to liberate thought, they end often by enslaving it."[21]

Mr. Justice Robert Jackson

American judgments provide endless examples of striking phrases and metaphors. This article will mention but three in judgments of Mr. Justice Robert Jackson of the Supreme Court of the United States. He was always forthright and hard-hitting. In one case the Court had set aside a ruling of the Securities and Exchange Commission[22] which then recast its ruling without changing its essence. When the case reached the Supreme Court a second time the majority upheld the second ruling.[23] Mr. Justice Jackson, who dissented, could not understand the Court's shift in position. "I give up. Now I know what Mark Twain meant when he said 'The more you explain it, the more I don't understand it.'"

In dealing with the disestablishment clause of the First Amendment which says, "Congress shall make no law respecting an establishment of religion . . . ", and which now applies to the several states, the Court had held, in the words of Thomas Jefferson, that the clause built "a wall of separation between church and state." Many cases in the past forty years have shown the difficulty in deciding when legislation has breached the wall. In the first case involving "released time" in school for religious classes,[24] Jackson concurred in striking down the provision. However he feared the Court would be involved in endless cases with no guidance as to where the secular ends and the sectarian begins. He ended by saying "we are more likely to make the legal 'wall of separation between church and state' as winding as the famous serpentine wall designed by Mr. Jefferson for the University he founded." The reference is to the University of Virginia at Charlottesville. The serpentine wall, or at least part of it, remains today.

Soon after, in *Terminiello* v. *Chicago*[25] the accused had made a very inflammatory Nazi-type of speech that produced violence from opponents. He had been convicted of making a disturbance in breach of the peace. In acquitting the accused the Supreme Court ruled that the judge should not have told the jury that speech in breach of the peace included speech which produces anger, invites disputes or brings about unrest or creates a disturbance.

In other words, the Court said that such speech was protected by the First Amendment. Jackson, who had recently been counsel at the Nuremberg trials, wrote a vigorous dissent. If a state or city could not keep order in streets and public places, there would be neither order nor liberty of speech. His conclusion: "The choice is not between order and liberty. It is between liberty with order and anarchy without either. There is danger that if the Court does not temper its doctrinaire logic with a little practical wisdom it will convert the constitutional Bill of Rights into a suicide pact."

Viscount Sumner, Viscount Sankey and Lord Atkin

Each of these members of the House of Lords uttered notable metaphors, some of them in Canadian constitutional cases in the Privy Council. *Re Sale of Shares Act*[26] dealt with a Manitoba statute that forbade Dominion companies from selling shares without the permission of a provincial board. In holding the Act *ultra vires,* the Judicial Committee, through Viscount Sumner, said:

> The general effect of these provisions remains. An artificial person, incorporated under the powers of the Dominion with certain objects, invested by these powers with capacities to trade in pursuit of those objects and with the status and capacities of a Dominion incorporation, is under these Acts liable in the most ordinary course of business to be stillborn from the moment of incorporation, sterilized in all its functions and activities, thwarted and interfered with in its first and essential endeavours to enter on the beneficial and active employment of its powers, by the necessity of applying to a Provincial executive for permission to begin to act and to raise its necessary capital...

In 1930 students taking constitutional law at the University of Alberta had to read this case after the *John Deere*[27] and *Great West Saddlery*[28] cases. *Lymburn* v. *Mayland*[29] which upheld Alberta's Securities Act was in the future. The students were struck by the cadence of this passage and in particular with the "stillborn. . . and sterilized" metaphor. Indeed it became a part of their vocabulary. Of course a quibbler will ask—how can anything be both stillborn and sterilized? The answer is simple: "If it's good enough for Viscount Sumner, it's good enough for us."

Still on the Canadian Constitution, Lord Sankey in the "Persons" case[30] said "The British North America Act planted in Canada a living tree capable of growth and expansion within its natural limits." Not long after, Lord Atkin in striking down federal Weekly Rest, Minimum Wages and Hours of Work legislation that was part of Prime Minister R.B. Bennett's New Deal, said "While the ship of state now sails on larger ventures and into foreign waters she still retains the water-tight compartments which are an essential part of her original structure."[31] One writer has referred to Lord Sankey's "arboreal metaphor" in contrast to Lord Atkin's "marine metaphor."[32]

One must not leave Lord Sankey without mention of his much better-known metaphor when he was Viscount Sankey, Lord Chancellor. In *Woolmington* v. *D.P.P.*[33] he said "Throughout the web of the English criminal law one golden thread is always to be seen"—the duty of the prosecution to prove the prisoner's guilt. Doubtless the "golden thread" has added to the impact of Viscount Sankey's statement of the rule.

Lord Atkin too made other memorable utterances. Probably his "neighbour" test in *Donoghue* v. *Stevenson*[34] has been quoted more than any other passage in recorded judgments—but the passage of interest here is in the dissent of Lord Buckmaster who rejected the cases on which Lord Atkin based his judgment. "So far... as the case of *George* v. *Skivington* and the dicta in *Heaven* v. *Pender* are concerned, it is in my opinion better that they should be buried so securely that their perturbed spirits shall no longer vex the law."

In two later cases Lord Atkin himself referred to spirits of the dead. In rejecting an old rule that held the mere commencement of an action operated as an election not to proceed with an alternative cause of action, he said "When these ghosts of the past stand in the path of justice clanking their mediaeval chains, the proper course for the judge is to pass through them undeterred."[35] Later in *Perrin* v. *Morgan*[36] the House of Lords in construing a gift of "moneys" in a will rejected the narrow meaning that had long been accepted. In the result the beneficiaries of the gift of moneys received over £33,000 instead of £840. Lord Atkin said "I anticipate with satisfaction that henceforth the group of ghosts of dissatisfied testators... who wait on the banks of the river Styx to receive the judicial personages who have misconstrued their wills will be considerably diminished. It will be a relief to the whole legal profession that at last... a blot on our jurisprudence has been removed."

Lord Atkin's castigation of his fellow judges in *Liversidge* v. *Anderson*[37] is well known. He was the only law lord who held the court could consider whether the Home Secretary had in fact reasonable cause to intern a person in wartime under the Defence Regulations. The others all held that the Secretary's statement that he had reasonable cause was conclusive. Lord Atkin said: "I view with apprehension the attitude of judges who, on a mere question of construction, when face to face with claims involving the liberty of the subject, show themselves more executive-minded than the executive." Later came this: "I have listened to arguments which might have been addressed acceptably to the Court of King's Bench in the time of Charles I." Finally he said that the construction put upon the words by the majority could be justified only on the basis of Humpty Dumpty's statement to Alice that a word meant what he chose it to mean.

Professor Heuston has described the tempest that arose. The Lord Chancellor, Viscount Simon, invited Lord Atkin to modify his language, and after the judgment was published, Lord Maugham, one of the majority, wrote a letter to the Times.[38]

Lord Denning

Lord Denning has produced more quotable quotes than any judge.[39] One can go to the All England Law Reports from 1944 through 1982, pick almost any volume and find at least one of his judgments. Many are conspicuous for the striking description of facts, or for the legal doctrine put forward, or both. Many of his propositions break new ground. He insisted that the Court of Appeal is not bound by its own decisions or even by the House of Lords, and that the courts should act when the executive or even Parliament has failed to act. He urged his brethren to be bold and insisted in standing by his beliefs.

In *Candler* v. *Crane Christmas,*[40] the majority rejected a claim for damages resulting from reliance on the defendant's negligently prepared report because the defendant was not under contractual obligation to the plaintiff. Lord Justice Denning in his notable dissent, later adopted in *Hedley Byrne* v. *Heller,*[41] described two categories of judge. "On the one side there were the timorous souls who were fearful of allowing a new cause of action. On the other side there were the bold spirits who were ready to allow it if justice so required." In reply Lord Justice Asquith said he was not defending the law but merely saying what it was. "If this relegates me to the company of timorous souls I must face that consequence with such fortitude as I can command."

Shortly before retirement Lord Denning had occasion to lament that the law on damages for personal injuries was uncertain and unsound. Parliament had not acted and the judges said they could do nothing. "It makes me wring my hands with despair. I would say to the judges 'Ye fearful saints, fresh courage take.'"[42] This line is from William Cowper's hymn, "God moves in a mysterious way."

In one case he rejected the concept of the unity of husband and wife, but he was outdone by Sir George Baker who said that to base a judgment on unity is akin to basing a judgment on the proposition that the earth is flat.[43]

Another case of Lord Denning's illustrates his opposition to the strict doctrine of precedent. He confessed he had been wrong in an earlier case. He added that it was decided *per incuriam* but even if it was not "I am going to risk the disfavour of the House of Lords and say under my breath that we are not bound by our previous wrong decision, reminding myself of what Galileo said when he was likewise condemned for heresy, 'and yet it does move.'"[44]

One could continue indefinitely with fascinating passages from Lord Denning's judgments. In some instances they must be read with the judgments on appeal to the House of Lords.[45] This account will mention only one more—*Air Canada* v. *Secretary of State* (No. 2).[46] It was decided on 24 September, 1982, five days before Lord Denning retired. The case involved the scope of the Crown's claim of the privilege not to disclose documents because of "public interest immunity." This claim had been upheld during World War II in *Duncan* v. *Cammell Laird*.[47] In his judgment in *Air Canada*

Lord Denning described his continuing battle against this claim and he did so by the use of military metaphor. He and two other judges in the Court of Appeal had launched an attack on this claim of privilege. They were called the three musketeers. "Our attack made good progress. We shot down one certificate [issued by a Minister to claim the privilege] after another for some reason or other. We were much helped by some good marksmen from the Commonwealth.[48] But then we suffered a reverse." This is a reference to *Conway* v. *Rimmer*[49] where Lord Denning dissented in the Court of Appeal. "I fought hard but the other two [neither of whom was one of the musketeers] brought up their reserves. They held that they were bound by *Duncan* v. *Cammell Laird*. The three musketeers were driven back. I was taken prisoner. But then from over the hill, there came, most unexpectedly, a relief force." This was the judgment of the House of Lords in *Conway* v. *Rimmer*. Lord Denning had finally won the battle.

Lord Diplock

Lord Diplock sometimes made interesting asides. In cases dealing with constructive desertion by a husband, the statement had been made that the husband's misconduct must be "grave and weighty." Lord Justice Diplock observed: "I await with some philological excitement, an example of conduct which is 'grave' without being 'weighty.'"[50] Then in dealing with an unreported case on limitations he said "The law reporters... exercised a wise discretion in consigning it to the limbo of unreported cases."[51] On one occasion he disagreed with a direction to a jury given by Macnaghten J. in an earlier case and said "No disrespect is intended to that eminent judge and former head of my old chambers if I say that his reputation is founded more on his sturdy common sense than on his lucidity of legal exposition."[52]

Some Equitable Metaphors

In connection with the law of equity several striking phrases have appeared in recent years. In one case a woman claimed an interest in the home of a man although they were not married. Lord Denning said this: since she is not the wife, "a few years ago equity would not have helped her. But things have altered now. Equity is not past the age of child-bearing. One of her latest progeny is a constructive trust of a new model. Lord Diplock brought it into the world and we have nourished it."[53]

In another case the question was whether the charterer of a ship who is sued for the freight can claim a set-off for a shortage in the cargo delivered, it being too late for the charterer to sue for the shortage. Ever since the Judicature Act 1873 the courts, including courts of equity, had never allowed a set-off. Lord Simon of Glaisdale said: "Equity did not bark at all at a claim for freight during this century-long night."[54]

The reference to not barking at night has its origin in Conan Doyle's story, Silver Blaze. A race horse named Silver Blaze was taken out of his stable at night. The dog that was kept in the stable did not bark when the horse was removed, so Sherlock Holmes deduced that the culprit was known to the dog. In other words it was an inside job.[55]

A third case, *Re Gonin,*[56] was an action on a verbal agreement to transfer land. The defendants did not raise the absence of a memorandum but later wanted to amend the defence to plead such absence. Snell on Equity, in its latest edition, had said this was not possible, but the cases cited ended in 1891. Mr. Justice Walton disagreed with the statement and said: "Snell is well-known... as being a work of uncommon accuracy: In this instance, however, I fear that Homer has more than merely nodded, he has snored, and since he has obviously been asleep since 1891 that is perhaps not surprising."[57]

"Bons Mots" in Recent House of Lords' Cases

Very recently the House of Lords has had to wrestle with "impossible attempts" in the criminal law.

A judgment of 1973 in *Haughton* v. *Smith,*[58] had held that an accused could not be guilty of attempting to handle stolen goods when in fact they were not stolen even though he thought they were. Lord Hailsham was a party to that judgment. Then in 1981 Parliament passed the Criminal Attempts Act which was intended to change the law. However, in *Anderton* v. *Ryan,*[59] where the accused bought a video recorder believing it to have been stolen but the Crown did not prove it was stolen, the House of Lords held she could not be guilty of the attempt. Then in *R.* v. *Shivpuri,*[60] the accused thought he was handling heroin or morphine but the substance was harmless vegetable matter.If he was to be found guilty of attempting to handle a dangerous drug, then *Anderton* v. *Ryan* had to be overruled. Lord Hailsham sat on the appeal to the House of Lords. He said he had hoped the 1981 Act would relegate his judgment in *Haughton* v. *Smith* "to the limbo reserved for the discussions of mediaeval schoolmen." Then, like Lord Atkin, he spoke of ghosts of the past. "It was therefore with something like dismay that I learned that the ghost of my speech had risen from what I had supposed to be its tomb and was still clanking its philosophical chains about the field, and that the new Act had formed a tilting yard for a joust of almost unexampled ferocity between two of the most distinguished professors of English criminal law in the United Kingdom." In the same case Lord Bridge referred to an article by Glanville Williams and said: "The language in which he criticizes the decision in *Anderton* v. *Ryan* is not conspicuous for its moderation, but it would be foolish on that account not to recognize the force of his criticism and churlish not to acknowledge the assistance I have derived from it." In the result, *Shivpuri* overruled *Anderton* v. *Ryan*.

Lord Hailsham can be quite blunt in disagreeing with others. On the question whether duress affords a defence to a murder charge, *Lynch* v. *DPP*[61] had held it does where the person is accused of aiding and abetting the murder. Then in *Abbott* v. *The Queen,*[62] the Privy Council held that the defence of duress was not available to the one who did the actual killing. Finally in *R*. v. *Howe,*[63] the House of Lords recanvassed the two earlier cases and overruled *Lynch*. However Lord Hailsham insisted that there was a valid distinction between *Lynch* and *Abbott* and that "those academics who see no difference between [the facts of *Abbott* and *Lynch*] have parted company with a full sense of reality."

Then in *Re B (A Minor),*[64] a sterilization case, he made a similar remark about the judgment of the Supreme Court of Canada in *Re Eve*.[65] He said that to talk of the basic right to reproduce of one who has no understanding of procreation "appears to me wholly to part company with reality."

In the still more recent *Spycatcher* case, involving the injunction to prevent the publication in newspapers of extracts from the book by Peter Wright, the House of Lords in a 3–2 decision upheld the Crown's claim to an injunction pending trial of the action. The two dissenters thought the injunction futile because the book had been published in other countries, and besides the injunction encroached on freedom of speech and press. Lord Ackner, one of the majority, quoted Lord Sankey: "Amid the shifting sands and cross-currents of public life the law is like a great rock on which men may set their feet and be safe." Then he said "For the word 'rock' the appellants [the newspaper publishers] would have your Lordships now read 'jellyfish'!" On the other hand Lord Oliver in dissent said: "Your Lordships are now being asked to beat the air and to interfere with an essential freedom for the preservation of a confidentiality that has already been lost beyond recall."[66]

The latest *bon mot* in House of Lords cases appears in *C.B.S. Songs* v. *Amstrad Consumer Electronics*.[67] The plaintiffs hold copyright in many musical works while the defendants make electronic equipment. The buyer of such equipment, e.g. for home use, often infringes copyright in using the equipment to make copies of the songs. The plaintiff's case was that the defendants were themselves infringers of copyright in that they encouraged the buyers of their equipment to engage in infringement. The House of Lords agreed that the statement of claim should be struck out as disclosing no cause of action. The passage of interest here is near the beginning of Lord Templeman's judgment (or speech, as the reasons for judgment in House of Lords cases are called). He explained that each industry is dependent on the other. "Without the facilities provided by the electronic equipment industry, the entertainment industry could not provide entertainment in the home, and could not, for example, maintain orchestras which fill the air with 20th century cacophony or make gratifying profit from a recording of a group without a voice singing a song without a tune." Presumably Lord Templeman is not a devotee of rock bands.

Lord Simon of Glaisdale

As Sir Jocelyn Simon, Lord Simon[68] had been appointed President of the Probate, Divorce and Admiralty Division in 1962 and went to the House of Lords in 1971. While at the bar he wrote a series of articles in the *Law Quarterly Review* on English Idioms from the Law.[69] They show a vast knowledge of literature, history and language. His judgments, too, reflect his erudition.

In one case, a wife applied for an increase in alimony and the husband argued that she should not benefit from his improved income because their life together had been unhappy and had it continued he would not have been successful. Sir Jocelyn Simon's reply:[70] "I am far from persuaded that domestic infelicity necessarily precluded worldly success—it may even rather stimulate it. Socrates achieved considerable success, Xanthippe notwithstanding; Louis VII of France and Henry II of England each made a mark on their age, though they were married in succession to Eleanor of Aquitaine; the turmoil of Coke's second marriage was a public scandal; and Doctor Proudie achieved the bishopric of Barchester."[71]

In *Lynch* v. *DPP*[72] Lord Simon dissented. In rejecting the defence of duress to a charge of aiding and abetting murder, he spoke of the concept of the free human will. "Even the most devout predestinarian puts off his theology when he puts on his legal robe. The law may be an ass, but it is not Buridan's ass."[73] Later he pointed out that the majority had rejected the opinion of all the great writers, and continued: "My only misgiving is that such an impressive muster should be sent packing so ignominiously. Poor Hale, poor Blackstone, wretched Russell and Kenny; poor, poor Lord Denman." Lord Simon then mentioned Stephen, the framers of Commonwealth Codes and Americans too. They had likewise rejected the defence. "They are like the denizens of the first circle of Hell,[74] who for all their wisdom and virtue lived in such benighted times as to have forfeited salvation. So, too, these great lawyers are too eminent to go altogether unacknowledged, but their words are lost in the gale of juristic change." In *R.* v. *Howe*[75] Lord Hailsham referred to this "eloquent and agonized passage." It is fair to say Lord Simon's dissent in *Lynch* was vindicated in *Howe*.

In *Miliangos* v. *Frank Textiles*[76] the question was whether the House of Lords should adhere to the long-established rule that a judgment should be in pounds sterling even where the contract provided for payment in a foreign currency. When the pound was strong this was of benefit to the plaintiff. Now, however, the pound was weak and the plaintiff asked for judgment in the foreign currency. The majority agreed to overrule the cases establishing the old rule. Lord Simon dissented. He thought that government departments and commercial interests should have a voice in deciding whether the old rule should be changed. "Of course a judge will say: 'I know nothing of such matters. What are they to me in any case? *Fiat justitia ruat libra!*'" This parody of *fiat justitia ruat coelum* says (if the writer's guess is correct) "let justice be done though the pound sterling fall." Lord Simon did not think the new rule would "advance the totality of justice." Later came a striking description of the judge's role. After saying that an expert committee would be able to decide whether the change in the rule would on balance be wise, he continued:

By contrast, the training and qualification of a judge is to elucidate the problem immediately before him, so that its features stand out in stereoscopic clarity, But the beam of light which so illuminates the immediate scene seems to throw surrounding areas into greater obscurity: the whole landscape is distorted to the view. A penumbra can be apprehended, but not much beyond; so that when the searchlight shifts a quite unexpected scene may be disclosed. The very qualifications for the judicial process thus impose limitations on its use. This is why judicial advance should be gradual. "I am not trained to see The distant scene: one step enough for me" should be the motto on the wall opposite the judge's desk. It is, I concede, a less spectacular method of progression than somersaults and cartwheels; but it is the one best suited to the capacity and resources of a judge. We are likely to perform better the duties society imposes on us if we recognise our limitations.

The "motto" is doubtless taken from Cardinal Newman's hymn, "Lead kindly light," but Lord Simon altered the wording. The hymn goes "I do not ask to see the distant scene." Still later in the same judgment Lord Simon, continuing his protest against the action of the majority in overruling earlier cases, said: "... even if sterling veers to every passing breeze, is that any reason why the law should do so? Is it not one of the functions of law in society to give a gyroscopic stability to the ship of state as the weather shifts and the seas mount?"

Where a statute forbade discrimination on the ground of national origin, and the alleged discrimination was based on nationality, Lord Simon pointed out the difference by saying there is today no Scottish or English or Welsh nationality but there still is a Scottish, an English and a Welsh national origin. Here are his words.

Scotland is not a nation in the eye of international law; but Scotsmen constitute a nation by reason of those most powerful elements in the creation of national spirit—tradition, folk memory, a sentiment of community. The Scots are a nation because of Bannockburn and Flodden, Culloden and the pipes at Lucknow, because of Jenny Geddes and Flora Macdonald, because of frugal living and respect for learning, because of Robert Burns and Walter Scott. So, too, the English are a nation—because Norman, Angevin and Tudor monarchs forged them together, because their land is mostly sea-girt, because of the common law and of gifts for poetry and parliamentary government, because (despite the Wars of the Roses and Old Trafford and Headingly) Yorkshireman and Lancastrian feel more in common than in difference and are even prepared at a pinch to extend their sense of community to southron folk. By the Act of Union English and Scots lost their separate nationalities, but they retained their separate nationhoods; and their descendants have thereby retained their separate national origins. So, again, the Welsh are a nation—in the popular, though not in the legal, sense—by reason of Offa's Dyke, by recollection of battles long ago and pride in the present valour of their regiments, because of musical gifts and religious dissent, because of fortitude in the face of economic adversity, because of the satisfaction of all Wales that Lloyd George became an architect of the welfare state and prime minister of victory.[77]

Random Canadian Cases

Two Manitoba cases must not be overlooked. One is the famous judgment of Dysart J. in *Mitchell* v. *Martin*. When a young couple having a party in a tent by the Red River were arrested, his sympathy was clearly with them and his ironic description of the actions of the police chief and the magistrate is a well-known masterpiece.[78]

The second case is *R.* v. *Myrrmidon*.[79] The accused kept his business open on Remembrance Day in contravention of Manitoba's Remembrance Day Act. Mr. Justice Scollin clearly thought little of the argument that the Charter of Rights and Freedoms bars a province from forbidding commerce on Remembrance Day. The accused argued that the Manitoba act violated freedom of expression which is protected by section 2(b) of the Charter, and invoked *R.* v. *Big M Drug Mart*.[80] That case had struck down Canada's Lord's Day Act on the ground that it infringed freedom of conscience and religion which are protected by section 2(a). The judge thought freedom of expression could not be substituted for freedom of conscience and religion. "This sort of substitution presumes the existence of an inventory of interchangeable philosophic spare parts. It is an utterly impermissible method of argument, quite unsuited to the discussion and appreciation of distinct, if related, fundamental freedoms." Later he said "Unlimited rights or absolute freedoms may not have been the order of the day even in the caves of the Neanderthals and certainly modern democratic society is founded on the acceptance of inevitable limits." And again, "Basic rights and freedoms are not two brilliant stars suddenly discovered in 1982 in the far reaches of the legal universe." In connection with the weighing of conflicting interests he declared: "Much depends of course on the balancing of fundamental interests and changing ideals. We must not fossilize the reasonable. The wars of this century and their ravages may vanish from the mind of future generations and the dead of Vimy and Dieppe may then be as mute and forgotten as the fallen of Agincourt and Waterloo." Finally, in reply to the argument that the renting of cassettes is a performance (which is outside the Act), he said, "The reasoning is the handiwork of a linguistic prankster. The argument floats weightless, free of the gravity of relevance."[81]

It seems that Mr. Justice Scollin is one of those judges who "occasionally employ their wit in a controlled fashion to adorn their reasons for judgment."[82] Professor Harvey has given a number of examples from Mr. Justice Scollin's judgments.[83]

A passage that should appeal to one's sense of humour is a lengthy ironic discussion of schools of logic in a judgment of McGuire J. in our old Territorial Supreme Court almost a century ago. The case is *Emerson* v. *Bannerman*.[84] The passage has been published twice so will not be included here.[85]

In a British Columbia case, *Brownlee* v. *Partridge*[86] Mr. Justice John Wilson (later Chief Justice of the Supreme Court of British Columbia) indulged in irony to show his low regard for both parties. The plaintiff was a male (twice married and once divorced because of his adultery) who sued

Mrs. Partridge (a widow) for breach of promise of marriage. The judge said (doubtless with tongue in cheek) that the defendant had promised to marry the plaintiff and that because of her promise the plaintiff agreed to cohabit with her. He was seduced under promise of marriage. The judge observed that this "ineffable couple" had managed to get the better of both worlds. He had claimed married status for income tax purposes. She had claimed a mother's pension yet passed herself off as the plaintiff's wife. The judge concluded that it would be against public policy to enforce the contract. He ended with the observation that if he had found for the plaintiff, the sum of $5.00 damages would have been "ample balm for his wounded feelings."

Another British Columbia case in which the judge thought little of either side is *Soon* v. *Jong*.[87] The plaintiff operated a service station. He was discourteous to Mrs. Jong. She returned with her husband and an altercation took place. Mr. Justice Seaton said:

> The plaintiff addressed her in a manner somewhat different than service station attendants address people on television commercials. He called her a "stupid bitch." She responded as best she could with the limited time for reflection by calling him an "assified chinaboy." She then turned to leave, exposing that part of her person best suited as a target for Mr. Soon's boot. He was accurate. Mrs. Jong responded to this escalation by throwing a bucket of water at the plaintiff.
>
> When asked about his wife being excitable, Mr. Jong said that she was lovable. I would conclude that a woman who throws both bucket and water is not exclusively of lovable character. I am not called upon to decide the characteristics of a woman who merely throws the contents and leave that question for an appellate tribunal.
>
> At this point, Mr. Jong joined the conflict by striking the plaintiff on the face. The plaintiff's friend joined the fray by seizing Mr. Jong while Mr. Soon pulled Mr. Jong's hair. Mrs. Jong effected the release of her husband by scratching Mr. Soon across the face. Mr. Soon got a lid from a barrel as a shield and weapon and the battle continued. Peace was only restored by the arrival of the police.

The result was a stand-off. The Court awarded Soon $100 against the defendants, and awarded Mrs. Jong $100 against the plaintiff.

In an earlier British Columbia case, Chief Justice Wendell Farris, in describing a series of misdeeds by patrons of a cabaret, said of one of them, a woman: "While dancing with one of her men friends she proceeded to slap him on the face. He, being the perfect gentleman and not wishing to receive a present of this kind from a lady, promptly returned it."[88]

The last British Columbia case to be noted here is *Vander Linden* v. *Kellett*.[89] The plaintiff hired a saddle horse from the defendants. The horse reared and threw him to the ground, injuring him. The plaintiff's action was for negligence and in the alternative for breach of warranty that the horse was safe to ride. In dismissing the action, Mr. Justice Smith said:

> The horse in question, which labours under the unusual appellation of "No Name", is still alive, if not kicking, and has annually up to and including this past summer, patiently borne her share of tourist equestrians without incident

> or complaint. The picture that emerges from the whole of the evidence, as I view it, is of an animal tranquil to the point of inertia, and of a docile and benevolent disposition. Despite my sympathy for the plaintiff, whom I found to be refreshingly candid and uncomplaining, I cannot regard this single momentary aberration in the long and otherwise placid life of this horse as indicating any breach of duty in law on the part of the defendants.

In a Saskatchewan case, *Chapman* v. *Kopitoski,*[90] the buyer of land sued to enforce the agreement for sale. The defendant argued that the agreement was unenforceable because there was not a memorandum in writing as required by the Statute of Frauds, an English statute of 1677. Mr. Justice Disbery, delivering judgment in 1972 said:

> Five years hence the tercentenary of this statute should be celebrated by the bar in grateful recognition of the cornucopia of litigation with consequential costs which the statute has showered upon successive generations of deserving counsel. In such a lengthy period an overabundance of often unreconcilable precedents can be found and the opportunity is now mine to add to the muddying of the waters of this pool of precedents fed by the *Statute of Frauds*.

He found there was not an adequate memorandum and dismissed the action. (Various law reform commissions are to-day considering the abolition or modification of this legislation from the reign of Charles II.)

Three Alberta Cases in World War I

This account will conclude with three cases all decided by Alberta's Appellate Division (the court en banc) in World War I. They are described not for elegant English or striking metaphor or irony or humour, but because they deserve to be remembered for their substance.

The first is *R.* v. *Trainor.*[91] The accused was in a drug store at Strathmore on 7 May, 1915 when word came of the sinking of the *Lusitania* by a German submarine. He expressed joy at the news and when the druggist remonstrated with him, he justified the killing of innocent women, children and non-combatants by the Germans. He was convicted of uttering seditious words. On his appeal, Mr. Justice Stuart, speaking for three of the four judges, dealt with the only serious question—were the words seditious in the circumstances? He began by saying: "I think it is about time that the distinction between entertaining disloyal and unpatriotic sentiments and giving utterance to them in a chance expression on the one hand, and the crime of uttering seditious words on the other, should be adverted to."[92] He then examined England's draft Criminal Code (never enacted), based on Stephen's, which had five categories of seditious utterance. Stuart J. examined four of them.[93] The words must (1) bring into hatred His Majesty or the government or constitution, or (2) excite people by unlawful means to attempt to alter any matter by law established, or (3) raise discontent and disaffection, or (4) promote feelings of ill-will between different classes. Stuart J. could not find that Trainor's words brought him within any of these categories. He should not be jailed simply because he was a German sympathizer. Then came this passage:

> There have been more prosecutions for seditious words in Alberta in the past two years than in all the history of England for over a hundred years and England has had numerous and critical wars in that time. The Napoleonic crisis occurred during that period. I do not wish to say anything which would repress the patriotic zeal of our public officials, but we all have great confidence in the stability and safety of our institutions and of the certain victory of our cause. In the circumstances I think something is due to the dignity of the law and that the Courts should not, unless in cases of gravity and danger, be asked to spend their time scrutinizing with undue particularity the foolish talk of men in bar rooms and shops or a word or two evidently blurted out there impulsively and with no apparent deliberate purpose.
>
> It may be asked, are men evidently traitors to be allowed to go around the country making such remarks as were made by the accused? The answer is that when a case is presented in which the accused is shown to be going around saying such things in a persistent, systematic or habitual way then we shall have a different case to be dealt with according to different facts.
>
> What I fear in this case is that the accused is being punished for his mere opinions and feelings and not for anything which is covered by the criminal law.

Trainor's appeal was allowed.

In the United States one Schenck was charged with obstructing recruiting in the armed forces in 1917 just after the United States entered World War I. He printed over 15,000 pamphlets that opposed the draft, and many were mailed, some to draftees. Schenck invoked freedom of speech, protected by the First Amendment. Speaking for the Court, Mr. Justice Holmes rejected this defence and upheld the conviction. At the same time he formulated the "clear and present danger" test. "The question in each case is whether the words are used in such circumstances and are of such a nature as to create a clear and present danger that they will bring about the substantive evils that Congress has a right to prevent."[94] Such danger existed here.

May one suggest that Mr. Justice Stuart, without using the precise formula of Holmes J., anticipated the same general principle? What is more he applied it—and he applied it at a time when Canadian casualties were heavy and the military outlook was gloomy and the public's tolerance for German sympathizers was low. Yet this case is scarcely known.[95] In the United States the clear and present danger test became well established. However in *Dennis* v. *United States*[96] (the case of the twelve communists who were convicted of conspiring to overthrow the United States government by force), the Supreme Court abandoned the test.[97]

Now that we have a Charter of Rights with its guarantee of freedom of expression, it behooves us to be familiar with our own earlier jurisprudence—and *Trainor* should be recognized as a landmark.

The second case is *R*. v. *Cyr*.[98] Alberta had given the vote to women by enacting an Equal Suffrage Act[99] in 1916, weeks after Manitoba and Saskatchewan had each passed a similar Act.[100] These were the first provinces in Canada to confer the vote on women.[101] Parliament did not follow with a general enfranchisement until 1920.[102] Right after Alberta gave women the vote, the government appointed two women to the office of police magistrate—Emily Murphy of Edmonton in June and Alice Jamieson of Calgary in December. Mrs. Murphy is said to have been the first woman appointed to judicial office in the British Empire. Soon after Mrs. Jamieson's appointment she convicted Lizzie Cyr of vagrancy. Cyr applied to Scott J. to quash the conviction on the ground (among others) that a woman was not qualified to be a magistrate. The judge had doubts but held Cyr could not raise the point on an application to quash.

Cyr appealed to the Appellate Division.[103] The appeal was heard by a strong court—Harvey C.J. and Stuart, Beck and Walsh JJ. In delivering judgment for the court, Stuart J. did not take the narrow ground of Scott J. It was necessary to decide whether a woman could be a magistrate, because the two women in Alberta frequently made convictions.

Stuart J. cited instances in which women in England had held public office as far back as the Middle Ages. He recognized however that in the nineteenth century the pendulum had swung. A number of cases had held that women could not vote for members of Parliament or become members of a county council, and there were statements that a woman could not hold public office or exercise any public function. Stuart J. went on to make two bold points: (1) the statements just described were probably inaccurate for England and (2) even if they were correct, they did not apply in Alberta. We took the laws of England as of 15 July, 1870 "insofar as the same are applicable." Many changes had been made in the status of women, and when it was desired to exclude them from voting or holding public office, the legislation was specific. Besides women had been admitted to the professions.

Here is his conclusion:

> I therefore think that applying the general principle upon which the common law rests, namely that of reason and good sense as applied to new conditions, this Court ought to declare that in this province and at this time in our presently existing conditions there is at common law no legal disqualification for holding public office in the government of the country arising from any distinction of sex. And in doing this I am strongly of opinion that we are returning to the more liberal and enlightened view of the Middle Ages in England and passing over the narrower and more hardened view, which possibly by the middle of the nineteenth century had gained the ascendancy in England.
>
> I think therefore that Mrs. Jamieson is not disqualified from holding the office of police magistrate.

A decade later five Alberta women procured a reference to the Supreme Court of Canada on the question—are women qualified to sit in the Senate? Section 24 of the B.N.A. Act said: "The Governor General shall . . . summon qualified persons to the Senate. . . . " No woman had ever been summoned. The federal government, supported by Quebec, took the position that they were not eligible. The judgment of the Supreme Court was unanimous—women were not eligible. The women, supported by the Alberta government, appealed to the Privy Council and won. Viscount Sankey in applying his "living tree" metaphor, mentioned above, held women were eligible.[104] This was an important step in the establishment of equality for women in the political life of the country, but its significance can be exaggerated. The statement is frequently made that women in Canada were not persons until the Privy Council said so. This is a gross distortion. Women always were persons (just as minors are) but they were under a disability. Along with exaggeration of the scope of the judgment in the Persons case is a widespread failure to appreciate the significance of the *Cyr* case.[105]

Cyr was decided in June 1917 when women were only beginning to acquire the vote. It took a lot more courage and foresight in 1917 to say they could hold public office than it took in 1929 to say they could sit in the Senate. Mr. Justice Stuart speaking for Alberta's Appellate Division anticipated Viscount Sankey's living tree by twelve years and nourished it when most people denied its existence.

The third case is *Re Lewis*[106] coupled with *Re Norton*.[107] In 1917, when casualties were heavy in World War I, Parliament passed the Military Service Act. It provided for conscription but those in certain categories, including farmers, could apply for exemption. Then in April, 1918, when Germany was making its last desperate effort to break the Allied line, the Governor General in Council made an Order-in-Council under the War Measures Act to authorize the conscription of persons who had been exempt. So it came about that some twenty Alberta farmers who had been exempt found themselves at the military depot in Calgary. It was at Victoria Park, now the Stampede Grounds. Lewis, represented by R.B. Bennett, applied to the Appellate Division by way of *habeas corpus*. He argued that the Order-in-Council could not repeal the Military Service Act. All the judges but Chief Justice Harvey agreed. Thus on 28 June the Court ordered Lewis's release though the Court agreed to a stay for two weeks provided Lewis was not removed from the province. The government responded with a new Order-in-Council directing the military to ignore the judgment. At that point Norris, another farmer, along with a number of other farmer-conscripts, applied by way of *habeas corpus,* returnable on 10 July and directed to Lt. Col. Moore, the commanding officer. He declined to appear, on instructions from the Adjutant General. The next day, counsel for the Minister of Justice applied for a stay until the Supreme Court of Canada could rule on the validity of the Order-in-Council of April—however, the Minister of Justice would not undertake to hold the conscripts in Alberta in the meantime. At this point, the danger of a physical clash between the civil and military authorities was "clear and present." On July 12 Chief Justice Harvey, notwithstanding his dissent over the validity of the Order-in-Council, delivered the judgment of the Court. The Court could either abdicate its function or perform its duty. There could only be one choice—an order directing the sheriff to bring the applicants before the Court and that they be discharged from military custody.

> In deciding to pursue its proper functions this Court is not unmindful of the fact which the Minister of Justice desires to press on us that the need of Canada for soldiers is very great and urgent, but it is apparent that to allow such a consideration to be our guiding principle would be to substitute expediency for law as the basis of the judicial decision. It is also apparent to us that without doubt there is enough might though not right behind the military authorities to prevent the Court's officers from performing their duty, and even to destroy both the members of the Court and its officers, but while the Court remains it must endeavour to perform its duty as it sees it.

The government of Canada capitulated, at least to the extent of agreeing not to remove the conscripts from the province until after twenty-four hours' notice to the sheriff. A week later the Supreme Court in a case from Ontario[108] overruled *Re Lewis* and upheld the validity of the Order-in-Council.

Every law student knows of Sir Edward Coke's confrontation of James I in the name of the law when the King abused his prerogative, and its significance in our constitutional history, but too few are aware of the courageous stand of our Alberta court on basically the same issue three hundred years later.

Conclusion

Most of this article has been concerned with striking, ironic or humorous passages and metaphors. The reader may well agree with Lord MacMillan's comment quoted near the beginning.[109] The three Alberta cases from World War I have a deep significance that rests on their substantive content, not their style. The writer suggests that they all deserve a place of honour in any catalogue of great Canadian cases. One hears much talk of the Canadian identity. We must foster it, but as Lord Simon has shown in listing factors that constitute a nation—tradition, folk memory, a sense of community—identity depends on knowledge and appreciation of past events. The writer hopes that the law students to whom this paper was originally addressed will cherish these cases as part of our Canadian legal heritage.

Notes

The passages quoted in this piece are ones the writer remembered or noted down on reading them. The following works contain many more examples: Megarry, *Miscellany-at-Law* (1955) and *A Second Miscellany-at-Law* (1973); Blom-Cooper (ed.), *The Language of the Law* (1965); Lord Simon of Glaisdale, *English Idioms from the Law,* 76 L.Q.R. 283 and 429: 78 L.Q.R. 245: 81 L.Q.R. 52; Lord Elwyn-Jones, *The Law as Literature* (1982–83) 47 Sask. L. Rev. 341; Harvey, *Legal Wit and Whimsy* (1988)

Chapter VI. The writer has not attempted to search for cases to quote. Doubtless there are many more Canadian judgments that are noteworthy, to say nothing of British and American ones. The writer is indebted to Mr. Justice W.A. Stevenson of the Alberta Court of Appeal and Dean Trevor Anderson of the Faculty of Law, University of Manitoba, for comments on an earlier draft.

1 Austin, *Lectures on Jurisprudence* (1879) Vol. 1 p. 5.
2 Stubbs, *Sir George Jessel, Master of the Rolls* (1951) 29 Can. Bar Rev. 147. The writer does not imply that Jessel's judgments were not clear.
3 *Palsgraf* v. *Long Island RR* (1928) 162 N.E. 99.
4 *Wagner* v. *International Ry* (1921) 133 N.E. 437.
5 Harvey (ed.), *Chief Justice Samuel Freedman: a Great Canadian Judge* (1983).
6 *The King* v. *Anthony* [1946] S.C.R. 569 at 573.
7 MacMillan, *The Writing of Judgments* (1948) 26 Can. Bar Rev. 491, 493.
8 (1898) 25 R. 778: MacMillan, n. 7 at 494 describes this case. Compare *Re Brocklehurst* [1978] 1 All E.R. 767, 772 where Lord Denning said "They left any game . . . but took the rabbits away with them."
9 *Inglewood Investment* v. *Forestry Commission* [1988] 1 All E.R. 783.
10 *Re T. (Infants)* [1968] Ch. 704 (C.A.). Dean Trevor Anderson called the writer's attention to this case.
11 *Nashville & K.R.* v. *Davis* (1902) 78 S.W. 1050. This case is included in Read & MacDonald, *Cases and Materials on Legislation* (1948) at 1030.
12 *Searle* v. *Wallbank* [1947] A.C. 341.
13 *Fleming* v. *Atkinson* [1959] S.C.R. 513.
14 [1956] O.R. 801.
15 (1946) 62 T.L.R. 641.
16 *Williams and Humbert* v. *W & H Trademarks* [1986] 1 All E.R. 129 at 135 (H.L.). See also *A-G* v. *Guardian* (No. 2) [1988] 2 W.L.R. 805 (the Spycatcher case). The trial judge, Scott J., after describing the numerous applications that preceded the trial, said at 812 "The consequences of this litigious history are, like the curate's egg, good in parts."
17 For this account of the origin of the curate's egg, the writer is indebted to Dr. Juliet McMaster of the Department of English, University of Alberta.
18 [1902] A.C. 197.
19 Macmillan, *supra* note 7 at 494.
20 (1965) 381 U.S. 489. This case struck down a Connecticut statute that forbade the use of contraceptives. Douglas J. found a constitutional right of privacy in the "penumbras" of specific rights contained in the Bill of Rights. It has since been invoked in many contexts—the right to abortion is protected by it, at least in the early stages of pregnancy, but the right to commit sodomy in private is not: see *Bowers* v. *Hardwick* (1986) 106 S.Ct. 2841.
21 Henly, *"Penumbra": The Roots of a Legal Metaphor* (1987) 15 Hastings Const. L.Q. 81. In contrast is an article by McIntosh, *A Poetic for Law: Constitutional Theory as Metaphor* (1987) 30 Howard L.J. 355. The writer found this 80-page article hard to grasp. For misuse of a metaphor, see "Frankfurter J. concurring" in Harvey, *Legal Wit and Whimsy* (1988) at 44–49. The metaphor was "Plimsoll line of due process."
22 *SEC* v. *Chenery Corp.* (1943) 318 U.S. 80.
23 *SEC* v. *Chenery Corp.* (1947) 332 U.S. 194, 214.
24 *McCollum* v. *Board of Education* (1948) 333 U.S. 203.
25 (1949) 337 U.S. 1.
26 *A-G Manitoba* v. *A-G Canada* [1929] A.C. 260.
27 *John Deere Plow Co.* v. *Wharton* [1915] A.C. 330.
28 *Great West Saddlery Co.* v. *The King* [1921] 2 A.C. 91.
29 [1932] A.C. 318.
30 *Edwards* v. *A.G. Canada* [1930] A.C. 630, 641.
31 *A.G. Canada* v. *A.G. Ontario* [1937] A.C. 326, 354.
32 McWhinney, *Judicial Review* 4th ed. (1969) at 51, 52.
33 [1935] A.C. 462, 481.
34 [1932] A.C. 562.
35 *United Australia* v. *Barclay's Bank*

[1941] A.C. 1, 29.
36 [1943] A.C. 399.
37 [1942] A.C. 206.
38 See Heuston, *Liversidge* v. *Anderson* in Retrospect (1970) 86 L.Q.R. 33.
39 Among the many articles on Lord Denning's judgments are Southin, *Lord Denning* (1970) 5 U.B.C. L. Rev. 1; Schmittoff, *Lord Denning and the Contemporary Scene* (1974) 6 Man. Law Jo. 11; Harvey, *It All Started With Gunner James* (1983) 17 Law Soc'y of U.C. Gazette 279. See also Jowell and McAuslan, (eds.) *Lord Denning: the Judge and the Law* (1984).
40 [1951] 2 K.B. 164.
41 [1964] A.C. 465.
42 *Croke* v. *Wiseman* [1981] 3 All E.R. 852, 856: see also *Nothman* v. *Barnet* [1978] 1 All E.R. 1243.
43 *Midland Bank* v. *Green* [1981] 3 All E.R. 744, 751; see also Lord Denning in *Routhan* v. *Arun D.C.* [1981] 3 All E.R. 752.
44 *Shell* v. *Gibbs* [1982] 1 All E.R. 1057 at 1063, 1064.
45 E.g., *Broome* v. *Cassell* [1972] A.C. 1027; *Miliangos* v. *Frank (Textiles) Ltd.* [1976] A.C. 443; *Gouriet* v. *Post Office* [1978] A.C. 435; *Duport Steels* v. *Sirs* [1980] 1 All E.R. 529 (H.L.).
46 [1983] 1 All E.R. 161, 179.
47 [1942] A.C. 624.
48 Among the good marksmen were the judges of the Supreme Court of Canada in *Reg.* v. *Snider* [1954] S.C.R. 479.
49 [1967] 2 All E.R. 1260, rev'd. [1968] A.C. 910.
50 *Hall* v. *Hall* [1962] 3 All E.R. 518, 526. Lord Denning was one who had used the phrase that offended Lord Diplock: see *Timmins* v. *Timmins* [1953] 2 All E.R. 187, 191 (C.A.).
51 *Thompson* v. *Brown* [1981] 2 All E.R. 296, 299.
52 *Royal College of Nursing* v. *DHSS* [1981] 1 All E.R. 545, 567 (H.L.). The earlier case was *R.* v. *Bourne* [1938] 3 All E.R. 615, where the accused was acquitted on a charge of unlawfully procuring an abortion.
53 *Re Eves* [1975] 3 All E.R. 768, 771. This metaphor has an earlier origin: see Megarry, *Miscellany-at-Law,* (1955) at 141, 142.
Jones quoted it at length in *The Law as Literature* at 347, 348.
54 *Aries Tanker* v. *Total Transport* [1977] 1 All E.R. 398, 407.
55 The writer is not a Baker Street Irregular so was not familiar with the dog that did not bark at night. W.H. Hurlburt, Q.C. and Dr. Keith Smillie guided him to the story.
56 [1977] 2 All E.R. 720.
57 The latest edition of Snell (the 28th edition in 1982) acknowledged that the previous editions did not state the law in accordance with recent cases (p. 582).
58 [1975] A.C. 476.
59 [1985] A.C. 60.
60 [1986] 2 All E.R. 534.
61 [1975] A.C. 653.
62 [1977] A.C. 755.
63 [1987] 1 All E.R. 771.
64 [1987] 2 All E.R. 206, 213.
65 [1986] 2 S.C.R. 388.
66 *A.G.* v. *Guardian* [1987] 3 All E.R. 316 at 363, 376.
67 [1988] 2 W.L.R. 1191.
68 Not to be confused with Viscount Simon, who was Lord Chancellor 1940–45.
69 See first (unnumbered) note on page 754, *supra*.
70 *Sansom* v. *Sansom* [1966] P. 52, 57.
71 Doctor Proudie and his wife were characters in Trollope's Barchester novels.
72 *Supra* n. 61 at 689 and 695.
73 Buridan's ass was hungry but it was placed exactly between two haystacks and starved to death because there was no motive why it should go to one or the other. Buridan was a French philosopher of the 14th century who spoke of a man of indecision. Hence Buridan's ass. The writer is indebted to Dr. Rowland McMaster of the Department of English, University of Alberta for the account of Buridan's ass in *Brewer's Dictionary of Phrase and Fable*.
74 See Dante's Inferno, Canto IV. The first circle of Hell was at its border. In it were many distinguished persons. They had not committed any grievous sin but had died unbaptized and so had no hope of seeing God.
75 *Supra* n. 63.
76 [1976] A.C. 443 at 481, 482.
77 *London Borough of Ealing* v. *RRB* [1972] 1 All E.R. 105 (H.L.).
78 [1925] 1 W.W.R. 500. Lord Elwyn- and the leading case of *R.* v. *Boucher* [1951] S.C.R. 265 was in the future.

79 [1987] 6 W.W.R. 204.

80 [1985] 1 S.C.R. 295.

81 Compare *R.* v. *Panel on Take-overs* [1987] 1 All E.R. 564, where Sir John Donaldson, MR said of the Panel—it "is a truly remarkable body . . . it oversees and regulates a very important part of the United Kingdom financial market. Yet it performs this function without visible means of legal support." (Professor Fred Laux of the Faculty of Law, University of Alberta, called the writer's attention to this passage.)

82 Harvey, *Legal Wit and Whimsy* (1988) at 149.

83 *Ibid.* at 149–154. Another has just appeared: *Parasiuk* v. *Canadian Newspapers* [1988] 2 W.W.R. 737.

84 (1890) 1 Terr. L.R. 224 at 230. The judge rejected the argument that "the creditors" in an affidavit of *bona fides* meant something different from "any creditors," which was the phrase required by the Bills of Sale Ordinance.

85 Robson, Hon. Thomas Horace McGuire (1945) 23 Can. Bar Rev. 139, 142: Bowker, *Stipendiary Magistrates and Supreme Court of the North-West Territories 1876–1907* (1987) 26 Alta. Law Rev. 245, 279.

86 [1947] 2 W.W.R. 805.

87 (1968) 70 D.L.R. (2d) 160.

88 *Lehnert* v. *Nelson* [1947] 2 W.W.R. 25, 27.

89 (1971) 21 D.L.R. (3d) 256.

90 (1972) 31 D.L.R. (3d) 479.

91 (1916) 10 Alta. Law Rev. 164.

92 Seditious words and seditious intention were not defined in the Criminal Code of Canada R.S.C. 1906 c. 146 s. 133,

93 He omitted the third—"to incite persons to commit any crime in general disturbance of the peace."

94 *Schenck* v. *U.S.* (1919) 249 U.S. 47.

95 Gray, *Talk to My Lawyer* (1987) at 75–79 describes it.

96 (1951) 341 U.S. 394.

97 For subsequent cases see Emerson, Haber and Dorsen, *Political and Civil Rights in the United States,* 4th ed. (1976) Vol. 1 Chapter IIB and C; Lockhart, Kamisar & Choper, *Constitutional Rights and Liberties,* 5th ed. (1981) Chapter 4 secs. 1 and 2.

98 (1917) 12 Alta. Law Rev. 320.

99 S.A. 1916 c. 5.

100 The date in Manitoba was 28 January, in Saskatchewan 14 March and in Alberta 19 April.

101 See Cleverdon, *Woman Suffrage Movement in Canada,* 2d ed. (1974).

102 Dominion Elections Act, 1920 c. 46 s. 29.

103 It was not then a separate division but was the court *en banc* under a new name.

104 *Supra* n. 30 rev'g., *Re Persons* [1928] S.C.R. 276.

105 There are exceptions: e.g., Stone, *Canadian Women as Legal Persons* (1979) 17 Alta. Law Rev. 331 and Gray, n. 95 at 74, 75.

106 (1918) 13 Alta. Law Rev. 423.

107 (1918) 13 Alta. Law Rev. 457. For a more detailed account see Gray, *supra* n. 95, Chapter 3; Bowker, *The Honourable Horace Harvey, Chief Justice of Alberta* (1954) 32 Can. Bar Rev. 933–937.

108 *Re Gray* (1918) 57 S.C.R. 150.

109 *Supra* n. 7.

Appendices

1976

Wilbur Fee Bowker: In Appreciation

by D.T. Anderson

Reprinted from
(1976) 14 Alberta Law Review
pp. 199–221

The Editor concludes this collection with an article published in the Alberta Law Review *following Bowker's retirement in 1975.*

It is a tribute presented at a dinner given in his honor by a group of Edmonton lawyers. This speaker (and writer of this article) was Professor Trevor Anderson, who had been on the Faculty of Law at the University of Alberta when Bowker was Dean, and on the Board of the Institute of Law Research and Reform when Bowker was Director. Anderson later became Dean of Law at the University of Manitoba.

Wilbur Fee Bowker was born February 18, 1910, in Ponoka, Alberta, one of the most attractive of the pleasant little villages in the rich farming land south of Edmonton. He has ever since retained close connections with his home town, and will point it out from the highway, with more affection than irony, as "the Vale of paradise".

I know little of Wilbur's boyhood.

However, it seems evident that his upbringing in this small village left him three legacies of enduring value. He came to know the true democracy of the Canadian West, which values a man for what he is, how he uses his talents, and how he treats his neighbour. To this I attribute, in part, the extraordinary range and vitality of Wilbur's many friendships. Second, he was fortunate in his family. His father, I think, must have been a remarkable man, with a genius for encouraging the developing interests of a curious and intelligent boy. He furnished him with books, enduring bullion from which good coin may still be struck, and, in an era and circumstances when travel was limited, took his son to interesting places and made him aware of the wider world. A father does this at cost to himself, knowing it must in time take the boy away from home to other places and larger experiences. I suspect Wilbur also inherited from his father his half-bemused, somewhat ironic, view of material progress and its confusing mechanical products. Finally, the Dean was privileged (as I think) to be born at such a time that he could view authentic survivals of the early West, and yet share in his own lifetime in the extraordinary economic, social and political evolution of this province, unequalled in Canada for variety (and, indeed, sometimes peculiarity) and colour, in this century.

To give some historical perspective, perhaps I should recall here that Ponoka, a small settlement near major Indian communities, had been garrisoned (in a little blockhouse, sometimes called "Fort" Ostell) during the 1885 rebellion. By 1901, it had a population of 151—a statistic recalling Bob Edwards' earlier description of Wetaskiwin as "287 souls plus three total abstainers"—at which time the population of what is now Edmonton was 4,176 and that of all Alberta only 73,000. The Dean was born in the midst of the first great influx of new settlement, in Clifford Sifton's era, from Eastern Canada and all quarters of the globe, which raised Alberta's population to 185,412 by 1906, and led to the fevered land speculations which by 1912 raised some Edmonton land prices to $6,000 an acre. Then came the Great War, and the extraordinary emotions it engendered. Transportation was changing, as the automobile joined the train and replaced the horse: the first recorded automobile trip between Edmonton and Calgary was in 1906, but although by 1918 Alberta had only 9,700 cars, by 1919 there were 34,000.[1] From boyhood perceptions have come, I think, the Dean's love of history, and his appreciation of the achievements, splendid if not spectacular, of those who in lawful and orderly ways peopled and built the Canadian West.

Happily, there existed, in the University of Alberta, a school that could respond to the intelligence and curiosity of such young men. It had been founded by the foresight of Premier Rutherford only about twenty years before Wilbur entered as a freshman, at a time when the customs of higher education were little enough known that one student asked the President whether gowns were worn with or without trousers. That remarkable man, the first President, Dr. Tory, had from the outset seen the contribution which the University could make to the new Province: while educating the public to see the University staff not as civil servants but as "independent scholars and thinkers who are to bring us into an appreciation of higher things," he reminded the professors that the University would be "the prophet of the people," from which "would come forth the men who are to make their laws, who shall expound the principles of government, who shall soundly conceive the responsibility of the people," a mandate later to be amply fulfilled by Dean Bowker in his own career. Tory knew the strength of the early University would be in its teachers; if he could not induce the famous scholars in the established seats of learning to abandon their great libraries and comfortable common rooms, he would choose his staff from "young men of talent, learning and promise." So wisely did he make his choices—bringing together men like Alexander (Classics), Broadus (English), and later MacEachern, Sonet, John Macdonald, A.L. Burt—altogether a remarkable constellation—that the new University was soon able to furnish its charges a rich, and liberating, education.

So large and prosperous is this University now, that it is hard for us to see it as it must have appeared to Wilbur when he came up, in 1927 or 1928, at just about the time Dr. Tory was leaving for the National Research Council. The University buildings were the old Arts Building, the power plants, St. Stephen's College, the University Hospital, the old residences, and that lovely crescent of Professors' houses, since vandalized to make a concrete parkade. These were about all that had been accomplished of the extraordinary master plan devised by Dr. Tory and his architects before the War ("damn good plan," he once said, when exasperated by critics), and had been built only with difficulty: the first University building was done with money never properly authorized by the legislature to be spent, and in 1915 the banks had stopped the University's credit, leaving the Arts Building without a roof, while the contractor (an American firm) itself financed the completion of construction.[2]

The relations between the University and the community were close. Prominent citizens, including many lawyers and judges, were involved in the University's government and teaching. Faculty lectured to public meetings throughout the province. (Dr. Tory was once asked to talk to a convention of morticians on "What the undertakers can do to promote the prosperity of Alberta.") Interested members of the public attended open lectures on the campus. Across the river, in the city (reached on the "Toonerville trolley" that crossed the High Level Bridge) student pranks and editorials in the *Gateway* were the subject of comment, outraged or amused. Altogether, the people took a lively interest in the University, and the students enjoyed a splendid vantage point from which to observe the extraordinarily exciting politics of this Province in the Twenties and Thirties.

Within the University, classes were small, many of the students lived in residence, there was a lively range of sporting and extracurricular activities (including debating of a high order) and in the French Club or History Club or like Societies, students and teachers met (often in the professors' homes) for good talk. It was a community, in which the student could combine hard study and the usual undergraduates' earnest discussions of the mysteries of the universe with much innocent fun. Sometimes, the activities were thought to get out of hand, and after the *Powlett* case (a local *cause célèbre* which gripped the attention of the University and public) the custom of "hazing" freshmen was proscribed.[3] However, when our distinguished guest matriculated, it was in force. Indeed, in his first weeks Wilbur Bowker won the attention and affection of the University when, wearing a beanie, he came onto the stage of a local theatre thronged by students in a manner that has been described as that of "a pterodactyl doing Swan Lake," and sang a song which those present (whose memories, like those of the independent witnesses described by Mr. Justice Macnaghten, "as the years go by, become more and more certain and less and less accurate") recall as either *I'm a lonely little petunia in an onion patch* or (as I like to believe to be true), *I'm a little prairie flower, growing wilder by the hour*. In that moment was revealed the dramatic talent that was later to make immortal, among generations of students and the Uniformity Commissioners of Canada, the Dean's rendition of *Casey at the Bat*. Less fortunately, perhaps, there was also released the singing voice still recalled (with somewhat less pleasure) by those who were to hear it daily in his fraternity house (one of the earliest on campus) where he shared an attic room.[4]

University was a rich and happy experience for Wilbur Bowker. He came prepared and ready to learn, and found provided the nourishment he sought and needed. In all his activities–dining in residence with chums, visiting in the homes of friends, enjoying fraternity life—he early showed that genius for friendship we all know.

Between terms, he did various jobs. One experience worth recalling is a summer spent in the Northwest Territories as a deckhand on a river boat, used as an itinerant court by an Edmonton Judge doing Northern duty. I believe that glimpse of the circumstances of frontier justice helped him later to recreate the early career of Chief Justice Harvey.

In 1929, Wilbur Bowker entered the Faculty of Law, thus coming within the charge of the second of those I believe most to have influenced the course of his life, Dean John A. Weir.

The University had from 1913, by agreement with the Law Society, organized lectures and administered examinations for articling students (a "Mr. G.H. Steer of Hamilton" was in the first group); but the real foundation of the Faculty dates from 1921 when legislation recognized the three-year degree programme, 1922 when the young John Weir was appointed a sessional lecturer (on the recommendation of several of his distinguished teachers at Oxford), or 1926 when he became Dean.[5] In the early years, he was ably assisted by Mr. Kleven and later Sigvald Neilson, by the sessional lectures of a group of remarkably able practitioners (including Mr. Steer, Mr. Justice Frank Ford, W. Dixon Craig, H.H. Parlee, H.A. Dyde, L.Y. Cairns, and Mr. S.W. Field), and of course, by Dr. Malcolm MacIntyre, whose still-developing analytic powers and awareness of the social purposes and consequences of law (both nurtured at Harvard, under Dean Pound) had a lasting, liberating effect on students—as described by Dean Bowker himself in a charming memoir.[6] However, it is fair to say that until 1942, when he died, still a young man, for most students the Law School was Weir.

It is impossible for those who did not know him as a teacher fully to understand, or explain, the remarkable dedication, respect and affection this man evoked from the students and the profession. We know that he was very young; that he carried a teaching burden that no one today could tolerate; that his scholarship was exact, and that no matter how great the range of courses he taught, he seemed master of each subject. We have been given pictures of him at his work. Outside the classroom, with strangers or local dignitaries, he is said to have been extremely shy and ill-at-ease; in the classroom, he was a man transformed, at home with his subject and his students, beaming genially at some good answer, gently planting some seeds of healthy doubt whenever students thought the law too certain or too clear, absently rubbing his stomach as he reflected on some question, unfolding from some familiar textbook pages of notes and citations he had inserted on a particular point. Mr. Justice Johnson once told me that if "Johnnie" Weir had asked someone to lay down and be a door mat, every student would have volunteered; and only ten years ago, I knew a discussion to be concluded by the simple assertion that on the point in issue Dean Weir held a particular view. The influence of a great teacher must always be something of a mystery, lying just beyond measurement or explanation, but we may be certain that many of the traits we all admire in Wilbur Bowker as a man and teacher he in his day saw in John Weir, and that it is no idle courtesy, but a carefully considered judgment of great value, when anyone of that era says (as they do) that in Wilbur Bowker the Law School found a fitting successor to this reserved but beloved and powerful man.

In 1932, Wilbur Bowker received his LL.B. degree and entered articles. In Western Canada, that was not an auspicious time to begin the practice of a profession. Many of his classmates found little opportunity; I believe one, later to have an outstanding career as a geologist and executive, used his periods of enforced idleness actually to pan for gold in the North Saskatchewan. Many established lawyers had their savings wiped out by the Depression, and others either did not have work or were not paid for what they did. The prospects for a young man must have seemed pretty bleak, and some of the work there was to be done, such as farm foreclosures, must have been unpleasant indeed for the kindly youngster. There is, in such circumstances, not too much consolation to be found in Daniel Webster's encouraging words, "There is always room at the top!"

In the result, however, whatever its financial rewards, the practice of law proved to be for Wilbur Bowker a tremendous experience. He had found a great calling, and counted himself fortunate in his circumstances. He could work in courts of a quality which still astonishes me, when one considers the size and resources of the Province then, and with a small Bar containing leaders of great ability and some of very colourful personality. He found himself, by happy chance or otherwise, in a firm (after 1934, Milner and Steer), which by reason of its size and the stature and interests of its senior members, was deeply involved in the legal aspects of the great political events that then convulsed the Province—the fall of the U.F.A., the rise of Social Credit, the *Bankers' Toadies* case,[7] some of the challenges to the radical legislation of the new government—and which dealt, on both the solicitors' and barristers' sides, with some fascinating questions of private law. To give but two examples, Wilbur Bowker had much to do with the development of mortgage proceedings in this Province (as protective legislation was attempted), and did much of the staff work in preparing the appeal to the Judicial Committee on the famous case, still cited in the torts textbooks, the "Corona Hotel Case."[8] (Indeed, he used for many years in the Faculty, when teaching the case, a scale model of the situs that had been prepared for use by Mr. Martland in briefing Sir Wilfrid Greene.) Anyone who has ever glanced at Bentwich's *Privy Council Practice,* with a sigh of relief that he need now never read it in earnest, will know what a training in painstaking accuracy preparation of such an appeal afforded a young lawyer. Those were exciting times, made more pleasant by the fact that they were enjoyed in the congenial atmosphere created by colleagues, such as Mr. Martland,[9] who combined hard work and high talents with companionship and good humour in a mixture entirely matched to Wilbur's own chemistry.

Above all, there was Mr. Steer, who perhaps of all those I may mention most helped to shape the pattern of Wilbur's professional life. It is impertinent to me to speak of one whom I only occasionally met, but no account of Dean Bowker's career could be given without reference to Mr. Steer.

Having come West after graduation from Queen's University and read law in offices here, George Steer early established himself, by ability, enormous industry and force of personality, as a leader of the Bar, a status that he retained through the whole of his long and useful life. His concentration was intense and immediate; he wasted no time recalling past accomplishments, but always looked forward to each new challenge. In Churchill's phrase, "he had the root of the matter in him," and relied on native analytic power, sound sense, and a comprehensive grasp of basic principle, to resolve problems, finding later in the catalogue of specific rules and precedents support for his view. He was quick, thorough, immensely demanding of himself and others. A gruff manner hid a sometimes unsuspected sentimentality: he could never think without the deepest emotion of the early loss of his friend, Dean Weir, and he took great pride in the career of his son and in the professional attainments of his former students, as we saw when Alex Smith published his work on constitutional law, and he had a sense of humour that emerged in terse and ironic comment; but these softer qualities were sometimes well concealed, and probably were not very apparent immediately to a beginning law student. When Wilbur became his pupil, Mr. Steer's powers were entering their full maturity; he was known with respect in the Supreme Court and the Judicial Committee, and in Alberta his counsel was sought in matters of great significance. He was an outstanding teacher and principal, revered ever after by Wilbur and later Alex Smith as their "Master in the Law."

But Wilbur, for his part, was an apt pupil, soon "graduating" from a student to the status of respected member of the firm. His colleagues of those years testify to his ability and sound sense as a lawyer, his good humour and reliability as a colleague and his complete integrity in all capacities. He seemed settled for a long and busy career in the practice of law.

However, then came the War. Wilbur, who retains a simple admiration for modest men of valour, tends to speak in wry self-deprecation of his military career, but it is all of a piece with his character. Although well established in practice, and not long since married, he enlisted in the ranks, spurning the opportunity of a commission, threw himself wholeheartedly into the mundane details of basic training, served well as duty required, and rose to the rank of Captain. In the Army, as in all phases of life, he made some good and lasting friendships.

During the late years of the War, the Faculty of Law was reduced almost to extinction. Dean Weir died in 1942; and the helm was taken briefly by Dr. MacIntyre, who carried on with the aid of sessional lecturers. By 1945, however, the student population had shrunk to nine, and that year Dr. MacIntyre left to join his father in practice in the Maritimes. The future of the School must have seemed very uncertain, just at the time when immediate measures were needed to prepare to serve those who would soon be returning from the War to resume their interrupted studies.[10]

Mr. Steer took matters in hand, assuming the duties of Acting Dean. On his nomination, Wilbur Bowker was appointed a full-time teacher. In 1947, Alex Smith, who had served as a sessional lecturer in the War years, was made an Associate Professor, and Mr. Hawco joined the staff as a lecturer. Wilbur Bowker was named Acting Dean in 1947, and in 1948 he became the Dean, assuming the title by which he shall always be known to all those associated with the School in the years that followed.

Although Wilbur has never admitted to this, I suspect every law teacher thinks occasionally of what life would be like if he had continued in the practice of law. There can be no doubt Wilbur would have been a distinguished solicitor, respected for honour and competence, and a progressive force in the profession. Had he been made a Judge, he would have combined with scholarship and a powerful sense of justice, dignity and courtesy. However, I count it to the great fortune of this Province that his services were claimed for legal scholarship. The office and the man were well matched.

The immediate challenge that had to be met, with no opportunity to regroup forces, was to meet the needs of classes soon to be swollen by returned soldiers. Can you now imagine, sympathetically, the plight of one discharged from the services, a dozen years from his own graduation and three years away from practice, having within days to face classes in a range of subjects? And these were no ordinary students; these were men, seasoned by experience, anxious to get on with their lives, expecting efficient organization and competent instruction. The University was overcrowded, and the large classes, swollen by 1950 to 142, were far beyond the capacity of the little reading room in the Arts Building or of any single classroom. However, burning the candle at both ends (and aided by skilful notes prepared by his wife) the Dean—and the students—made it through triumphantly. Those were tough years for the Dean and Alex Smith—though their burden was lightened when Bill Reed[11] joined them as a valued colleague—but they had great regard and affection for the veterans' classes ("good boys," as the Dean calls them, even now) and look back on those strenuous days with pleasure.

Alex Smith, having several times been mentioned, should now be brought to centre stage, the next of those deserving a special place in the story of Wilbur Bowker. Having done some part-time teaching while in practice with Mr. Steer, he joined the Faculty full-time and served it until his retirement in 1974. His scholarship, developed through his teaching and his doctoral studies at Stanford, was massive and exact; his expression was both elegant and precise; both qualities show to advantage in his book on the

Commerce Power.[12] In the opinion of students, and also of colleagues who between them shared experience of most of the great law schools of the common law, he was one of the master teachers of his time. The atmosphere in his classroom was charged with excitement. All his students will recall the skilful design and sequence of his questions, his insistence that they "wrestle with the angels," his impatience with slovenliness or neglect, his warm endorsement of work well done, his infectious and ever-renewed enthusiasm for the challenges of the law. Sometimes the lightning would flash and the thunder roll, but when the sun shone, it warmed the room. His students first feared, then loved him. He pried open their minds, and gave them glimpses of the infinite. Like the Dean, he knew his role was to help the students make themselves into lawyers in the grand tradition, and with Wilbur he shared interests in literature and history. Often agreeing on questions of professional values and educational purpose, different in style and temperament, they enjoyed for over twenty years an association which, while it must have had its occasional strains and tempests, proved a happy and productive partnership. For years, much of the business of the School was done in the doorway between their offices, and a visitor joining them at their habitual sandwich luncheon in Alex's room was treated to fascinating talk that roamed the intellectual universe. It was the good fortune of the Dean to have this learned and stimulating coadjutor, and thinking of the School, we recall them both.

The creative middle years of the Bowker deanship began, one might suggest, in the early Fifties. The urgent demands of the immediate post-war period had been met. Enrolment, which had been swollen to record numbers by the returning veterans, fell to more normal levels and thereafter, for some while, increased only slowly. The transition is marked by the opportunities the Dean had twice to escape the immediate demands of his office for periods of reflective scholarship, taking his LL.M. degree at Minnesota and spending a stimulating term as a Sterling Fellow of the Yale Law School. Brought into close touch with the active and exciting world of American legal scholarship, he made good new friends and learned much, including a detailed and balanced knowledge of American constitutional doctrine that I daresay could be matched by few American lawyers.

Fully to appreciate the achievements of these years, we must remind ourselves of the condition of the School and of legal education in Canada as the Fifties began. The University budget was still stringent. In, say, 1952, the teaching staff was small: Mr. Hawco had left; A.B. Weston[13] had come; that year Alex Smith was on leave at Stanford and Andy Thompson,[14] newly joined, was reading for his LL.M. at Toronto. The library was soon moved from the old Reading Room, long taxed far beyond capacity, to the new Rutherford Building but the collection, although good, was small and the funds needed for its development were not forthcoming until the more opulent days of the mid-Sixties.

On the national scene, while some schools were of age, others, now well established, had not been born or, if alive, were undergoing painful change. Dalhousie was long established; U.B.C. was just coming into being; Manitoba had still a part-time law school, with a few teachers using morning lectures offered over a four-year period to apply some veneer of scholarship to articling students. In Ontario, the Law Society was beginning to feel the pressures to relinquish its monopoly of legal education and to recognize University law degree programmes. To the practitioner, the professional law teacher was still an unfamiliar and somewhat suspect figure; when the Canadian Association of Law Teachers first met formally, in 1951, 24 persons were in attendance. Works of Canadian scholarship—or even basic materials for teaching law—were few.

But if the challenges were formidable, and resources few, the circumstances of the day also provided (I think) the optimum conditions for a man of the Dean's personality and unique qualities as an educator. These, in the smaller school, could be felt full strength. Later, in altered circumstances, they were necessarily somewhat diluted. In the middle and late Sixties, vastly increased enrolments—jumping from 107 in 1959 to 170 in 1965 to over 300 in 1969—made it necessary to divide classes into sections, which not every teacher could meet. More formal procedures and complex regulations reduced the discretion of Deans in many decisions. It became much harder for the Dean to get to know the students, and though he strove mightily to maintain the close relations of an earlier day, less frequent contact in the classroom, his own natural reserve and what may have appeared somewhat old-fashioned manners and sense of propriety made it harder for the students to come to know the Dean, whom they might see only in his official capacity, and to appreciate the colourful personality and progressive attitudes thus somewhat concealed. In a much larger faculty, necessarily mixing ages and experience and subject to more frequent change, a much greater variety of personalities and outlooks had to be accommodated, and frequent committee meetings and formal procedures began to succeed the earlier, informal means by which consensus was reached on school policy. Rapid growth created budgetary and space problems, and in the vast expansion of the University from a small institution to one of the largest in Canada, it became necessary to treat with new and unknown persons in formal and unfamiliar procedures, with much more assiduous attention and a more aggressive spirit. The Dean never saw the internal affairs of the University as a political process. If he did, he lacked the thrusting and guileful manner that some came to expect of the proconsuls of the new academic empire in asserting claims to greater shares of available resources. The Dean's practice was to measure his immediate requirements carefully, state them succinctly, and trust to those making decisions to do the right thing by him. To their credit—even when new styles of dress and haircuts might have suggested to the careless observer that the young were rejecting older values—the students still saw in the Dean an example of simple and straightforward virtues worth their respect, and their testimony of affection and regard on the occasion of his retirement is a treasured memory.

In early and simpler days, however, these standards could be more directly impressed upon the students.

In University matters, the Dean was dealing with old friends, familiar to him and acquainted with the School. Within the Faculty, things were worked out quite informally with colleagues in daily discussions. The Dean, conscientious though he was in the discharge of any duty, was not a master of office management—his own examination papers were always late, rushed to the students with the ink still wet, and he would not have loved the flow charts and computer forms that fill administrators' in-baskets today. He made no deliberate use of techniques, common in large organizations today, to project an image or promulgate a policy. Happily in those simpler days, there was time and occasion to meet and know his colleagues and students, and, by just being himself, to influence them greatly.

For the great influence exerted by the Dean was achieved without being designed, and by example, not precept or exhortation. Under him the school was governed, not by decrees, proscriptions and discipline, but by expectation. Students and colleagues knew that the Dean himself lived by high personal and professional standards; his example made those standards valid for them; and they willingly undertook the obligation to try to live up to his expectations, and felt keenly the desire to avoid the injury he would feel if they were to fall short.

They were made to feel members of a community, and a tradition, to which they had their own special responsibility. To come to class unprepared, for example, was not a purely personal option; it was default on the obligation to assist the class in its common pursuit.

In dealing with students individually, whether in his office or more informally at student parties or sporting events, the Dean showed great understanding and sympathy. He is a perceptive judge of character. His kindliness and discretion tend to conceal how shrewd and penetrating his assessments of persons are; in friends and students, he forgives almost every part but cruelty and double-dealing. In a simpler era, when Deans were entrusted with some discretion, and their decisions not minutely governed by regulations and subject to innumerable appeals, Wilbur Bowker rightly saw in many applicants and students, with unpromising records, the stuff of which good lawyers could be made, and showed them how to use it. I do not think he was often disappointed. When he was, it hurt deeply.

But it is as a teacher in the classroom, not as an official of the University, that graduates will recall the Dean.

Those great performances, as entertaining as they were instructive, have often been imitated. They began quietly, with the calling of the roll, in a soft, almost weary, voice—last names only, except for the women students, who were "Miss" or "Mrs." in those days when to any scholar "Ms." meant only "manuscript." Then, volume rising, there would be a brief recapitulation of the last day's discussion, or the introduction of a new topic. Then, the first of many questions to the class. The starting questions would be gentle and straightforward; the supplementaries, testing the student's initial views in varied hypothetical applications, more penetrating. While listening to answers, or giving his own views, the Dean was always in motion: chewing ruminatively on a cough drop, flipping his piece of chalk (they are said one day to have been interchanged by accident), using the same chalk to trace and retrace his initials on the lectern (what started as a Napoleonic "N" always eventually was reduced to a modest "W"), performing series of mysterious manoeuvres with pointers and map books. Perhaps Wilbur felt that one could say of the teacher what Lord Lyndhurst said of the Judge, that it was his duty "to make it disagreeable for counsel to talk nonsense,"[15] but his questioning was gentle, and serious efforts in reply received genial approbation. Teaching something to each Year, meeting each Year as a class, he came to know the quality of mind of each student, and used his Socratic skills adroitly to suit each case, encouraging the timid or challenging the dogmatic. Occasionally, frustrated by a series of inept or unprepared answers, the Dean would let forth a bleat of exasperation. In turn the students drew forth from him guidance and information, never ceasing to marvel at his incredible recollection of principles and cases, and the fund of legal history, philosophy, and amusing but relevant legal anecdotes which enlivened and enriched the lectures. By the middle of the hour, he would be in full volume—and even down the corridor one could hear in his stentorian tones the elaborate but ordered paragraphs in which he speaks (contrasting so strongly with the simple and declaratory style of his writing), the phrases interrupted by meditative pauses.

How is the impact of a great teacher to be explained? The root of Wilbur's success, I think, was the respect he showed his students, his subject, and his profession. Only direst necessity ever stopped him from meeting a class. He prepared carefully for every class as if it were his first, constantly reviewing the law and seeking new ways to present it. He cared deeply for accuracy in every point. He never glided over any tough problem of importance, but struggled with it, and insisted that the students join him in the effort. He was never dogmatic, and did not seek to make disciples. His object was to help the students make themselves into lawyers who were skilled, rational, sensitive and responsible. He entertained seriously all their views, even from freshmen, and never hesitated to review and then either change or justify his own opinions. He was entirely without the arrogance or pedantry which are so often the vices of the teacher. He was enthusiastic about the law, delighting in the work however hard, and his students caught this infectious spirit. "Gladly wolde he lerne, and gladly teche."

Dean Bowker saw the law in a full perspective, deepened by his knowledge of history and theory, sharpened by his years in practice, focussed on the purposes and utility of rules and institutions. With Holmes, he appreciated that[16]

> . . . a body of law is more rational and more civilized when every rule it contains is referred articulately and definitely to an end which it subserves, and when the grounds for desiring that end are . . . ready to be stated in words . . .

and while realistic in his view of the conservative conventions of the courts and profession, he knew that in the long run, as Lord Mansfield once said, "The reason and the spirit of cases make law; not the letter of particular precedents."[17] Thus, while presenting rules clearly and even canonically, he had a clear view of inconsistencies and inelegancies, a sound sense of which rules were doomed to obsolescence and which contained the seeds of growth, and, without adopting any informal scheme, a clear set of criteria, of human values and interests, by which to assess the law. In the students of such a teacher, the Province has been given a profession capable of apt and creative response to the changing needs of its community.

Ultimately, a community, however soundly conceived its law, must depend upon the ministers of that law and their ethical quality. Professional responsibility is not established by preaching homilies. The young will attach to such matters only such importance as they probably have in the actual life and work of the leaders of the profession whom they respect. Wilbur Bowker provided that example in his teaching, his scholarship, his treatment of students and colleagues, of complete integrity. It was clear to all who knew him that ethics were as essential to his life, or that of the profession, as oxygen is to existence.[18]

Wilbur Bowker believed, and taught us all to believe, in Bacon's credo: "I hold every man a debtor to his profession, from the which as men do seek to receive countenance and profit, so ought they of duty to endeavour themself by way of amends to be a help and an ornament thereto."[19] When a man has several professions, these duties are multiplied.

Wilbur Bowker is the sort of friend who will do three days' solid research to answer a casual inquiry for assistance. He is not like the fabled Sergeant Waller, called "Index," whom fellow lawyers went to only for lists of authorities, which they then took to lawyers of more intelligence, if frailer memory, for an opinion.[20] Wilbur's friends seek his wisdom as well as his learning. His replies to such requests have influenced arguments, articles, statutes and judgments. The trail may be partly followed through acknowledgments in the prefaces and footnotes to the writings of others, but we shall never know the full extent of his service and influence through these friendly offices.

Wilbur Bowker gave his distinguished service to the University, beyond his own Faculty. He was unfailing in his attendance at council and committee meetings. At these, he rarely spoke, but his interventions, though infrequent, had impact—whether in earlier days to give a timely reminder of a student's right to due process, or in later times to suggest that unwieldy procedures should not block effective decision-making. He would give "curbstone advice" on legal points occasionally, but typically would venture no opinion on a point of importance until he had fully "addressed his mind" to it. Outside of council, colleagues from every faculty sought his informed and sagacious judgment. He never sought an office nor declined an assignment. In 1960, he chaired a committee to review the 1942 University Act; its report, largely his work, was done promptly, and formed the basis for all later studies. In 1964, he was, as a member of another committee, the person who (in the opinion of former President Dr. W.H. Johns) "deserves the credit for being the chief contributor to the report of 1965, which was the document on which the new Universities Act of 1966 was based."[21]

Successive governments of Alberta have sought Dean Bowker's counsel on matters of public law, and he has been an adviser to the Province's delegation to federal-provincial constitutional conferences.

His known services to the legal profession are almost too many to recount. A long-time member of the Canadian Bar Association, he served its Council and the Scott Committee on Legal Research.[22] In this Province, he has presented papers or organized panels for many meetings of the Law Society or continuing education programmes.[23] He was an indispensable member of the old Law Reform Committee.[24] He served as co-ordinator of the Special Committee of the Benchers[25] to review the Land Titles Act following the *Turta*[26] case. He was an unfailing source of help to the Society in matters of professional education and qualification, and of course served on the Board of Examiners in Law, delegate of the Universities Co-ordinating Council.

As a law teacher, he was one of the earliest members of the Canadian Association of Law Teachers, later serving as its historian and, in 1955–56, as its President. Twice he had the pleasure of being host to its annual meeting, in Edmonton in 1958 and in Calgary in 1968.

His occasional talks to various professional and community groups are beyond number, and the range of subjects is extraordinarily various. I recall one, to a Librarians' meeting, on early law reporters.

Nationally, he is perhaps best known for his outstanding service to the Conference of Commissioners on Uniformity of Legislation of which, as an Alberta Commissioner, he was a member from 1952 until this year. Through that period, as any review of the *Proceedings* of the Conference will disclose, the Alberta Commissioners on the civil side did a fair, a more than proportionate, share, of the work of the Conference,[27] and they all would wish to acknowledge the leadership and service of the Dean in the preparation of their reports. In 1965 Dean Bowker was President of the Conference. He worked hard at the job, canvassing all Provinces for suggestions to make the Conference more efficient and productive, and examining closely the procedures of its American counterpart, the National Conference of Commissioners on Uniform State Laws. Dean Bowker took (or perhaps made) the opportunity to deliver a Presidential address, and I in turn welcome this occasion to draw attention to that very important, but now rather neglected, statement.[28] To many concerned with legal research and reform, the production of the Conference, although valuable, is disappointingly limited and spasmodic. The explanation, one suspects, lies in problems of funding, organization and procedure. In Dean Bowker's speech is to be found a clear, modest, and (I think) workable prescription for improvement, which must not be overlooked.

Nor were Dean Bowker's services, anymore than his interests, wholly confined to the Law. He has been, and is, a concerned and active citizen, helping church, social service, and fraternal groups. To mention but two activities of many, he has been involved in the organization of the debating programme sponsored by the Churchill Society, and he is a loyal and long-time member of a service club.

Those who have been privileged to work closely with Wilbur in these varied enterprises enjoyed, as could his Faculty colleagues, the delight of his informal conversation, in relaxed moments over lunch or at the close of a meeting. It is as amusing as it is instructive. No matter the subjects over which the talk might range—law, literature, history, travel, sport—the Dean, intermittently re-lighting his cigar, supplies from his extraordinarily capacious memory a flow of anecdotes, apt questions, curious facts, all encouraged by his eager auditors and cast in a distinctive elaborate sequence or structure of sentences built up of plain words, enlivened by some adroitly adapted legal or literary term or some pithy expression redolent of the earlier West.[29]

These many public and professional services, valued though they must be in their own right, seem to me to have another and larger, significance. I see in Wilbur Bowker's career an outstanding example of the role to be played by academic lawyers in their profession and community. His able and selfless service has done much to establish the status of the law teacher in the legal world, and so to enlarge our opportunity for creative service.

Substantial though this list of accomplishments may be, given in even this abbreviated form, it is the more impressive considered against the background of his principal work as dean, teacher—and scholar. Wilbur Bowker is not a facile writer—his research it too thorough, his concern for accuracy too great—but from 1947 on, the Canadian Bar Review, the Alberta Law Review (to which he has in other ways given constant support), and other learned journals—including some in disciplines other than law—have contained a fairly steady flow of articles, notes, and reviews from his pen. These include reports of panels conducted or organized by him at Bar meetings, on subjects such as wills,[30] expropriation,[31] and commercial law,[32] perceptive memorials of early judges;[33] constructive and informed reviews of books on topics from jurisprudence to jury trials.[34] His *magnum opus,* perhaps, is his outstanding biographical article on Chief Justice Horace Harvey.[35] Not only does it bring to life a man who (it seems fair to say) did not have a colourful personality easily revivified for later generations, but it served as a medium to portray the entire evolution of the courts, legislation, social attitudes and jurisprudence of Alberta. Bowker's article on the law of dower[36] now has the stature of a classic. In 1962, he was one of the first, perhaps the first, Canadian writer to treat fully some long neglected basic issues in the laws of governing the limitation of actions;[37] he has argued for a more rational approach to claims based on death caused by tortious injury;[38] and he has reviewed carefully the law of contributory negligence.[39]

To assess the Bowker archive, or even to catalogue it, would require another essay. Here, however, three features of his legal writing, whether articles or law reform reports, may be noted.

First, perhaps the most striking quality is the plainness of the style—simple words and short, declaratory sentences in logical order. Bowker's articles are mainly meat, with little in the way of sauce or garnish. Occasionally he paints a vivid picture—such as that in the Harvey article[40] of the dramatic conflict between the military authorities and the Alberta courts in 1918, when Lewis, a conscript, sought *habeas corpus*[41] (a curious local analogue to the case of Wolfe Tone in Ireland more than a century earlier).[42] Very rarely does the Dean when writing permit himself the ironic humour that enhances his conversation and his informal letters. There is a touch of it in the Harvey article: "The Chief Justice did not easily yield to the common desire to give a wrongdoer another chance."[43] Sometimes the austere style can give peculiar emphasis to the ludicrous or unusual, as many a funny story is best told dead-pan; the history of the interpretation of the Alberta Dower Act is well put in this way.[44] Generally, however, the Dean's written work, lucid and readable as it is, does not reflect the variety and richness of his lectures or conversation. His great performances are given *viva voce*.

However, on examination, this terse style proves to have been deceptive. One soon appreciates that what in the orderly march of his sentences appears so clear, almost elementary, was largely unperceived or unresolved before it fell under his analysis. His articles, the substance reduced by hard work and frequent revision, go to the root of an issue. I cannot fully illustrate this now (and, were I to do so, would select illustrations from his teaching of torts on which, curiously, he has written relatively little), but will give some modest examples. In his article on dower,[45] criticizing then quite recent legislation, the Dean exactly anticipated the problem of the improperly executed mortgage that soon arose in *Kos* v. *Kos*.[46] In 1948, in a general survey of the law of evidence,[47] Dean Bowker expressed the view that the so-called "rule in *Hodge's* Case"[48] was only an elaborate way of restating the rule as to reasonable doubt, in cases where the evidence is circumstantial, and he deprecated the tendency of the Canadian courts to require it to be specifically stated as an independent direction to be put in almost canonical form. Now, consider the words of Lord Morris of Borth-y-Gest, speaking for the House of Lords in 1973:[49]

> . . . here in the home of the common law *Hodge's* case has not been given very special prominence. . . . *Hodge's* case was reported not because it laid down a new rule of law but because it was thought to furnish a helpful example of one way in which a new jury could be directed in a case where the evidence was circumstantial . . . the abstract, and therefore necessarily vague direction that a jury must be satisfied beyond reasonable doubt is the only restriction which in ordinary cases English criminal law imposes on the discretion of juries in pronouncing on the sufficiency of evidence . . . the form of any particular direction stems from the general requirement that proof must be established beyond reasonable doubt. I consider that the form in which this general requirement is emphasized to a jury is best left to the discretion of a judge without his being tied down by some new rule that would likely have the effect that a stereotyped form of words would be deemed necessary . . .

The third feature of these writings worthy of remark, is their positive tone. The merits of others' works or views are fully acknowledged, and when deficiencies in the law are exposed it is with the object of promoting reform. The article on limitations,[50] for example, makes a strong plea (effective, I believe, for a while, until municipalities resorted again to their deplorable habit of seeking special immunities) for the abolition of special periods and the consolidation of all provisions in one clear and accessible statute. The piece on dower,[51] in model fashion, by setting out clearly the purposes to be served by the Dower Act and the Land Titles Act clearly depicts the conflict between the two statutes and suggests balanced measures for their reconciliation.

Two areas in which Bowker has made himself particularly knowledgeable are civil liberties and the legal aspects of medical research and practice, although he did not teach a course in the former subject until after his resignation as Dean, and was led into the latter field indirectly, when asked at various times to lecture to nursing and medical students, to advise members of the University's research departments on the legal and ethical implications of experimentation, and to assist in the study of breathalyzer legislation, and when either or both of the provincial government and Uniformity Commission considered solution of problems concerning blood donations by minors and others, compulsory transfusions, and the donation of human tissue.[52] Very recently, he has been making a detailed study of some of the grave problems that may arise in the course of genetical research and engineering. These various subjects require not only a sound knowledge of law and craftsmanship and perception in the application of old principles to novel circumstances, but an appreciation of medical procedures and the methods and ethics of scientific research. Some indication of the Dean's knowledge and sensitivity in these matters is to be found in his excellent commentary on relevant proposed sections of the Quebec Civil Code.[53]

The Dean's interest in civil liberties, as both scholar and citizen, goes back many years. It predates, but certainly was stimulated by, his studies in the United States. I myself believe that his broad, comparative knowledge of the law and appreciation of the knotty underlying philosophic problems and conflicting interests in this area fully equal (or exceed) those of others better known for their writings on the subject. He has not written as extensively on these matters as one might have wished, although he is the editor of a useful casebook[54] and has written several good articles,[55] of which one, *Basic Rights and Freedoms: What Are They?,* was an early—and is still a very helpful—analysis of the entire subject; with admirable concision, it defined and related the elements of the topic and surveyed the related law. That the Dean has not written more is no doubt explained by the many other demands of a busy life, but one suspects there is another reason for his reticence. Appreciating the range and validity of the various interests to be served and reconciled, seeing these questions in the full perspective of history and philosophy, constrained by a judicial cast of mind and a strong sense of responsibility, he has never been able to commit himself to any simple solution to truly complex issues, and so has had to struggle hard to see his way through the thickets. (As instances of this, one might mention his recognition, in a comment on the *Drybones* case,[56] of the respectability of the argument that the liquor provisions of the Indian Act, whether wise in policy or not, may be defended as protective legislation adopted for a valid purpose if applied equally and without discrimination to all within the protected class;[57] and also his concern about the threat to free expression carried by too broad a legislative sanction against hate literature, repugnant though such vicious trash is to him.) This in my view gives the greater weight to the conclusions he reaches, but necessarily has restricted both the number and the style of his writings. In matters so difficult, another's views can be summarized only at the risk of caricature and injustice, but some account of the Dean's opinions should be given.

Before attempting that, however, one should recall the Dean's personal service to the cause of civil liberty. He is what I call a "limited joiner," uncomfortable in large associations with broadly defined objects which purport to speak on a wide diversity of subjects in the name of their members (he used sometimes to be upset when media reports suggested a majority vote in the last minutes of an ill-attended Bar Association meeting represented the opinion of the Canadian legal profession); for this reason he has not been known as an active member of various civil liberties activist groups, but has chosen to act in an individual capacity or with others on a particular matter. Because some of his interventions have been privately made, in advising lawyers or recommending legislative or procedural change to public authorities, not all his contributions can be measured. At the same time he has always held in great admiration those such as Mr. W. Glen How who have fought the issues in the courts and the public forum, and has taught his students to admire, as exemplars of the best traditions of their future profession, those lawyers who in duty have put popularity and income to hazard by undertaking the representation of unpopular clients or causes. With concern, he has studied the record of the Gouzenko inquiry and the wartime dislocation of Japanese-Canadians, and prepared recommendations for Parliamentary review and control of the powers and procedures then used. (I believe that as a solicitor he had had first-hand experience, in the early part of the War, of the application of special regulations, when he represented some interned persons.) In the cold war period (or "McCarthyite" phase of it), the Dean strongly resisted the notion (which gained some ground elsewhere) that lawyers be subject to some form of loyalty test or excluded from practice for communist beliefs,[58] and at a time when even in the Universities there were authorities who barred certain speakers from addressing students, I believe that he once personally took the chair at a student meeting to ensure a full hearing for a Communist leader.

Dean Bowker from an early date has maintained that discrimination can be limited, and eventually public attitudes altered, by progressive implementation of aptly designed human rights legislation, initially aimed most effectively at improper practices in public accommodation and employment, clearly identified and made subject to an appropriate and flexible range of remedies designed first to secure voluntary compliance but ultimately enforceable by effective sanctions. While acknowledging the limits of the law in shaping common morality (was it Ring Lardner who said, "Prohibition is better than no liquor at all"?), he has effectively argued that the Legislature can lead public opinion and that, in any event, the acts fulfill the immediate purpose of controlling discrimination.[59] I believe it was in part under his persuasion that Alberta adopted accommodation practices legislation, now subsumed under broader measures.

However, Dean Bowker does not favour drastic and comprehensively general measures to deal with abuses that are not widespread and are susceptible to specific remedies. To take one example, he has not favoured the exclusion of illegally obtained evidence as a means for controlling improper police conduct, believing that probative evidence should not be suppressed to the advantage of the criminal when appropriate police behaviour should be (and largely is) secured by a public attitude that requires respect for individual dignity, traditions of responsibility and ethics in the force, an effective internal police discipline, and civil remedies. This is not an absolute position, but one to be reviewed regularly in the light of actual experience; if abuses of power are not being effectively controlled, then it may be necessary to resort to other measures including those (such as the suppression of evidence) that incidentally may in particular cases let the criminal escape justice. The community should be astute to notice any abuses, or failures of existing measures to remedy such wrongs, but should not without proved cause resort to the broader and more drastic measures.

Nor does Dean Bowker favour broadly drawn declarations of rights, whether constitutionally entrenched or only having peculiar status as interpretation acts, that subject both legislative and administrative measures to review by appointed courts. In his view, which he has argued urgently but moderately with full regard for opposing views,[60] it has not been established that sweeping declarations will provide stronger safeguards for liberty than informed and tolerant public attitudes and a tradition of responsible conduct by public officers, supported when occasion requires by specific remedies aimed at identifiable abuses; in view of the confusion and harm that such declarations may cause, the necessity for them must first be established. In his judgment, founded on an extensive knowledge of the current law, that need is not now shown. Broad measures may inadvertently compel the elimination of defensible and useful specific laws (such as those providing for *in camera* proceedings in certain kinds of matters) or preclude public discussion and parliamentary settlement of major issues (such as capital punishment, if held to conflict with prohibitions against "cruel or unusual punishment"). In any event, such Bills typically exempt from their operation many of the very matters that require frequent and close control, such as the regulations under the War Measures Act that provided cover for the Japanese-Canadian removals, general internments, and the espionage inquiry. Above all, bills of rights with the necessary concomitant of judicial review, are inconsistent with our tradition of parliamentary democracy,[61] in which the legislative authority has been left to experiment in working out realistic and acceptable solutions to difficult problems involving the complicated adjustment of competing values and interests. In applauding the goals of the recent decisions of the American Supreme Court in extending human rights, we must not forget that in other eras that same court invalidated a series of humane social and economic measures, nor that in some other countries without charters and judicial review, those very rights are as fully, or better, secured in practice than in the United States. These views were summed up by the Dean in an address (as I recall, to the Law Teachers in Calgary) which ended with the ironic reminder that the American people, having elected one man to the Presidency four times, then changed their constitution to prevent themselves from ever again being able to exercise their judgment in that way.

In 1968, resigning as Dean of the Faculty of Law, Wilbur Bowker was appointed Director of the Institute of Law Research and Reform, when it was created by agreement between the University, the Law Society and the Provincial Government.[62] He brought to this new career extraordinary credentials in both legal research and law reform. Indeed, curiously, he had once himself, in an open letter in the Alberta Law Review, proposed the establishment of some form of permanent committee charged with the continuous supervision and amendment of the law.[63] In retrospect, his whole earlier life in the practice, teaching, and critical study of the law may be seen as preparation for this great opportunity. The appointment was universally applauded, and the subsequent performance of the Institute has met, indeed exceeded, all expectations.

The Institute differs from many law reform commissions in two respects: it has complete freedom to select its law reform projects, and its reports thereon are to the public at large, not to the Government or legislature; and it has a mandate, not only to promote law reform, but to encourage general legal research. It has been faithful to both duties, and enjoyed outstanding success in law reform. Starting without experience, and with only limited resources, the Institute has to date made 17 Reports, and in almost every instance where it has proposed change, the Legislature has acted promptly; now, more fully funded and with an increased permanent staff, it has in train many more projects, some of very large size and difficulty (among them, revision of the Land Titles Act and of companies legislation, and review of the large realm of family law, including property divisions and court jurisdiction and procedures).[64]

Dean Bowker will be the first to insist that full recognition be given to the members of the Board which Fate (in the unlikely guise of the Law Society and the Government of Alberta) has given him to work with, particularly the successive Chairmen, Mr. H.G. Field, Q.C., Mr. W.H. Hurlburt, Q.C., and Judge W.A. Stevenson. He will wish me to note particularly the imaginative and immensely efficient work of Mr. Hurlburt, first as Chairman and later as Associate Director. It gives Wilbur pleasure, and all of us confidence for the future, to know that Mr. Hurlburt will succeed him.

The Board, in their turn, will require that I speak (as indeed, I can from my own knowledge as a member of the first Board) of the enormous, indeed indispensable, contribution of the Director. This new position brought into play all of his scholarly and lawyerly virtues. His massive knowledge of the law enabled the Board to choose projects and plan programmes; his knowledge and industry improved and enlarged every research paper, however good; his sound practical sense averted many possible false steps; his good humour, and sense of reasonable compromise, gave meetings a pleasant tone, no matter how controversial the subject; and his great gifts of logical organization and clear expression gave the finished Reports clarity and impact. In a lifetime in universities, I never took part in seminars more truly educative than the meetings of the Institute Board.

Virtually nothing in law is assured permanence. Today's reforms may be tomorrow's problems. However, I believe that in leaving this office, Wilbur Bowker leaves a lasting legacy, not only in the statute books, but in the example he has given of progressive, reasoned, effective reform.

Wilbur Bowker's solid virtues and achievements have not gone unnoticed. In 1951 he was made Queen's Counsel, and in 1972, in an extraordinary recognition of one of its own sons, the University of Alberta awarded him (along with Mr. Justice Bora Laskin, as he was then, and Lord Diplock) the honorary degree of Doctor of Laws. When he resigned the Deanship in 1968, an issue of the Alberta Law Review was dedicated to him, and his students and the Bar joined *en masse* to tender him a dinner in testimony of their affection and gratitude. This year, at his last attendance at their Conference, the Uniformity Commissioners recognized his outstanding service in a most unusual and apt way, by presenting him a memento of the legendary "Casey at the Bat," whose sad epic he often recounted at their enthusiastic request.

He now enters his formal retirement. It is purely nominal. He proposes to work still on the major Institute projects, has two articles in preparation, wants to write the full account of the extraordinary case of *Re Sproule,*[65] and then, with those details out of the way, to prepare what will be a *magnum opus,* a book that really only he can do, the legal history of Alberta.

We join in wishing him the continued vigour and enthusiasm these works will require. At the same time, selfishly though we may urge their completion, as friends we want him to have the leisure to enjoy fully life with his family, now enriched by grandchildren. For I have left to this moment to mention the greatest event of his life, his marriage in 1940 to Marjorie Hope Montgomery. His home life with Mrs. Bowker and their three children has been the stable centre of a busy life, and in all his work he has enjoyed the companionship and support of a remarkable woman, who in her own right and with his full encouragement, enjoys a distinguished career in voluntary public service and the Law.[66]

That is the formal history of our guest, spanning three distinguished careers in Law. It alone justifies our gathering here to honour him. But you know, as do I, that there are other ties that bind us to Wilbur Bowker.

We love the man for himself—for his warm human qualities, his companionability, his loyalty, his sense of fun, the colour of his personality, and even for his various frailties and eccentricities. We have been fortunate enough to know him well, and to have penetrated that reserve which shyness and a "sense of the proprieties" sometimes (though only briefly) raise as a barrier in the presence of strangers. We, as friends and former pupils—and there is no distinction, for no one has ever known Wilbur Bowker without being in some sense his pupil—know him for the most clubbable of men, the most loyal of friends, an enthusiastic appreciator of the variety of human character and affairs. To us all, he has been an abundant source of life, a creator who has made his friends partly what they are.[67] He is an original, of a distinctive type and tone. To all of us, he is a friend and mentor, and all of us probably will ever see the Law and our professional duty in the lights he has exposed.

There is a theory that men may be judged by their heroes. I don't know about that. We do know the kinds of people and accomplishment Wilbur admires. We have heard him speak with respect of men with outstanding records in military or civil service, who in other spheres disclaimed all recognition of that service; with some contempt, of those who mistook social standing for personal merit; with disappointment, of graduates culpable of some unethical or incompetent conduct; with grief, of a confidence misplaced or a trust violated; with pride, of a graduate who did some particularly creditable work or in the best professional tradition took on some unpopular or difficult cause. He cared about these things, and we have seen in him the qualities he admires in others. Once, speaking of a work of history, he regretted its tendency to exaggerate the flamboyant and notorious, at the expense of "the quiet, dependable, dedicated, ethical types of builder" in the profession. No one should be condemned out of his own mouth, but that phrase of his own seems to me to catch the essence of the man, not least because it is too modest.

In a recent book[68] by a former clerk to Mr. Justice Powell of the U.S. Supreme Court (like Wilbur, a great fan of baseball), the author tells how the Justice once regretted he could not have been a major league player. The clerk argued that it was much better to be a judge: no injuries, no training camp, and a no-cut contract. "Perhaps," said Mr. Justice Powell, "but they never retire your number."

When Wilbur retires, the number is retired.

It is altogether appropriate that his friends in the profession should honour him tonight. In this company, one may recall words once spoken by an English barrister of his Circuit:[69]

> There are welded, if we will, honour, generosity, tolerance, liberality, promptness to recognize the merit of a rival, to praise with alacrity, to censure

with respect; and to learn to prize that salutary clash and criticism betwixt whose endless jar good nature resides.

These seem to me to have special meaning, as we join to recognize one who has proved, what Holmes said, that a "man may live greatly in the Law."[70]

Notes

1 These miscellaneous (and probably irrelevant) historical details are taken from J.G. MacGregor, *A History of Alberta,* esp. pages 145, 156, 174, 194, 226, 243, 258.

2 A good account of the early days of the University is to be found in E.A. Corbett, *Henry Marshall Tory—Beloved Canadian,* from which some of the foregoing has been taken.

3 *Powlett* v. *University of Alberta* [1934] 2 W.W.R. 209 (Alta. App. Div.).

4 Some recollections of the Dean's student days are to be found in a *liber amicorum,* published privately on his retirement in 1975 by the staff of the Institute for Law Research and Reform.

5 These, and other facts concerning the development of the Faculty, are to be found in Dr. W.H. Johns, *A History of the Faculty of Law,* a pamphlet published by the University of Alberta, Edmonton, in 1972.

6 Bowker, *Malcolm Murray MacIntyre, 1904–1964,* (1964) 3 Alta. L. Rev. 161.

7 *See R.* v. *Unwin* [1938] 1 W.W.R. 339 (Alta. App. Div.) and *R.* v. *Powell* [1938] 1 W.W.R. 347 (Alta. App. Div.), rare cases of criminal libel.

8 *Northwestern Utilities* v. *London Guarantee and Accident Co.* [1936] A.C. 108 (P.C.).

9 Later, and now, Mr. Justice Martland of the Supreme Court of Canada.

10 *See* Johns, *supra,* note 5.

11 Mr. G.W. Reed, later Vice-Chairman of Appeals, Ontario Workmen's Compensation Board.

12 Alexander Smith, *The Commerce Power in Canada and the United States.*

13 Later to be of the Faculty of Law, Dar-es-Salaam.

14 Andrew R. Thompson, LL.B. (Man.), LL.M. (Tor.), J.S.D. (Columbia), an outstanding member of the Faculty of Law from 1950 to 1969, a leading authority on petroleum law, and now Professor of Law at the University of British Columbia and Chairman of the British Columbia Energy Commission. In his years in Alberta, he gave great impetus to the development of the library, the institution of graduate studies in law, and the planning for the new Law Centre. He was a founder of the Petroleum Law Foundation. In 1970–71, he was President of the Canadian Association of Law Teachers.

15 Lord Lyndhurst L.C., quoted in Campbell, *Lives of the Lord Chancellors: Lyndhurst,* Ch. 5.

16 O.W. Holmes, *The Path of the Law* (1897) 10 Harvard Law Review 457, reprinted in Holmes, *Collected Legal Papers* (1920), 167. The quotation appears at page 186 of the latter work.

17 Lord Mansfield C.J., *Fisher* v. *Price* (1762) 3 Burr. 1363, 1364.

18 Dean Bowker, in his quiet way, is a man of deeds—one of those, admired by Holmes, who takes on a job, hammers it out as best he can and leaves it unadvertised. He has not often written in general terms about his views on legal education. For these, one must look to the work he did. Perhaps it may also be said that he subscribed (and may still, in large part, accept) the report of a committee of the Association of Canadian Law Teachers, published in (1958) 36 Canadian Bar Review 242, as *A Statement of the Objectives of Canadian Law Schools,* of which he was a principal author. If that is so, it may be said (in gen-

eral terms) that he recognized that law in society serves many functions. Being purposive, whether serving moral ends or some more pragmatic calculus of interests, it must be studied in terms of these purposes. He appreciated that lawyers—as a profession, or individually —play many roles; they have opportunities for creative work with social impact. Law schools cannot provide knowledge of all laws relevant to each social end or professional function. They can (and should) strive to foster an understanding of the purposes of laws, give an appreciation of the nature of legal institutions and processes, provide a knowledge of the basic principles of the law in its main branches, and develop the aptitude of the student to resolve problems by proper analysis, research, and argument. These points may now seem well-established, but there was a time when they amounted to staking a contested claim for the academic study of law and a rejection of the spurious antithesis sometimes drawn, to the intended disadvantage of one or the other, between "practical" and "academic" education. I believe Dean Bowker agreed with the view of the late Dean C.A. Wright in a wise address in 1950: I do not believe there is any clash between these objects [vocational and educational], provided that we do not make the mistake of translating "professional" as mere expertise in existing technique. . .

It is this mistaken narrow professionalism that now and then cries out at the law schools for being academic, impractical and theoretical. In that connection, it may be wise to remember the gibe of Disraeli that 'the practical man is the man who practises the errors of his ancestors.' Personally, I have no hesitation in throwing in my lot with the statement of Holmes that 'Theory is the most important part of the dogma of the law, as the architect is the most important man who takes part in the building of a house. . . . theory is not to be feared as impractical for to be competent it simply means going to the bottom of the subject. C.A. Wright, *The University Law Schools,* (1950), 28 Can. Bar Rev. 140, 143.

In some quarters, in 1950, those were still fighting words. The quotation of them will bring back to some a whiff of the cordite and echo of the cannons of the struggle to establish elsewhere the place of the University law schools. Such a battle did not have to be fought in Alberta, thanks to the foresight and accomplishments of Dr. Tory and Dean Weir, and to the attitudes of a profession that appreciated the value of a sound foundation in legal principle. In 1947 Mr. Steer, then Chairman of the Legal Education Training Section of the Canadian Bar Association, had written that in none of its aspects "is the life of a lawyer without public importance," that "the lawyer, more perhaps than the member of any other learned profession, owes a duty to society to equip himself as a policy maker," and that accordingly the teaching of law was not a matter of a slavish adherence to precedent and existing practice, but a learned study to be conceived in appreciation of the "importance of the political, historical and sociological views" of lawyers and judges: G.H. Steer, *On Legal Education in Canada* (1947) 25 Can. Bar Rev. 942 at 944, 948.

As Dean, Professor Bowker took an undogmatic view of legal education. His principal concern was never the formal structure of the curriculum, but was actually done, for and to the student, in the programme. He ensured that all the main subjects were represented and supported by steady library growth so far as the resources of the school allowed. General courses in Jurisprudence and Equity were preserved. He had reservations about the trend, in the 1960's, towards "optionalization" of the curriculum, fearing both that teaching talents might be spread too thin and that the broad, foundational, education required by students might be restricted. However, he gave warm support to any well-conceived proposals from colleagues for experimental teaching methods intended to make learning more effective. Indeed, before the "problem method" was commonly discussed, he had introduced it into his own teaching. In his pioneering legal research and writing course, the general purpose of which he modestly stated to be to teach the student "to write a defensible opinion," a distinctive requirement was the writing of thorough case notes, of which some ten or twelve were published in the Canadian Bar Review between 1950 and 1960: *See* W.F. Bowker, *Legal Writing at the University of Alberta* (1959) 13 U. of T. L.J. 85.

19 Francis Bacon, *Maxims of the Law: Preface*.

20 Roger North, *Life of Lord Keeper Guilford,* Vol. 1, 24 (1826).

21 Quoted from the Contribution of Dr. Walter H. Johns to the *liber amicorum, supra,* note 4.

22 *See The Thirty-sixth Annual Meeting of the Canadian Bar Association* (1954) 35 Can. Bar Rev. 994, 998–999.

23 *See* notes 30, 31, 32, *infra*.

24 A committee of the Law Society, discontinued on creation of the Institute of Law Research and Reform, as to which *see* note 62, *infra*.

25 A Committee of the Benchers of the Law Society of Alberta, appointed at the invitation of the Provincial Government at a Convocation of the Law Society held in January 1955, to give special study to legislation which might be enacted with respect to settling equities of persons in regard to minerals in respect of errors respecting ownership of or claims to such rights on the Land Titles Office and the establishment of a special assurance fund for such rights, and generally to consider other matters deemed relevant. The Report of the Committee is published in 1 Alberta Law Review 185.

26 *Canadian Pacific Railway and Imperial Oil Ltd.* v. *Turta et al.* [1954] S.C.R. 427 (S.C.C.).

27 Contributions by the Albertan Commissioners included reports on the Survivorship Act (1954, 1956), a report and draft statute on legitimation (1958), a recommendation for a study of the law of domicile (1957), various reports and draft legislation concerning bulk sales (from 1957 to 1967), a report on bills of sale and conditional sales (1958, 1959, 1962) a report and draft legislation on survival of actions (1961, 1963), a report on an aspect of the enforcement of maintenance orders (1963), a report on the application of rules of the road to private property (1964), reports on a human tissue act (1964) and a draft act (1965), a report on aspects of family relief legislation (1965), a report on the last clear chance rule under the Contributory Negligence Act (1967), a report on contributory negligence and joint tortfeasors (1967, 1974), reports and draft legislation on adoption (1967, 1968, 1969), reports on limitation of actions (1967, 1968), a report on the application of the Survivorship Act to life insurance (1968), reports and draft legislation on the rule against perpetuities (1970, 1971, 1972), reports and draft Acts on the interpretation and form of statutes (1970, 1973), a report on *Hollington* v. *Hewthorn* (1974). Dean Bowker also strove regularly and eventually successfully for the restoration of a uniform construction section in each uniform Act: *Proceedings,* 1967, page 27.

28 "President's Address," *Proceedings of the Forty-Seventh Annual Meeting of the Conference of Commissioners on Uniformity of Legislation in Canada,* (1965), 16. In 1971 the Alberta Institute of Law Research and Reform submitted to the Uniformity Conference a statement of ways in which law reform organizations and the Conference could productively work together, *Proceedings,* 1971, 129.

29 One (unsatisfactory) attempt to describe the warm character and appeal of the Dean's conversation is made by Anderson in the *liber amicorum* referred to, *supra,* in note 4.

30 *See The Drafting of Wills* (1956) 2 U.B.C. Legal Notes, 381.

31 *See Panel Discussion on 'Expropriation Procedure and Compensation,'* (1962) 2 Alta. L. Rev. 76 (introductory text prepared by W.F. Bowker).

32 *See Panel on Bills of Sale, Chattel Mortgages and Conditional Sales Agreements,* 1 Alta. L. Rev. 273.

33 W.F. Bowker, *Three Alberta Judges* (1965) 4 Alta. L. Rev. 5.

34 *See, inter alia,* reviews in (1960) 38

Can. Bar Rev. 443 (Scott, *Civil Liberties and Canadian Federalism*), (1947) 25 Can. Bar Rev. 931 (Paton, *A Textbook of Jurisprudence*).

35 W.F. Bowker, *The Honourable Horace Harvey, Chief Justice of Alberta* (1954) 32 Can. Bar Rev. 933, 1118.

36 W.F. Bowker, *Reform of the Law of Dower in Alberta,* (1961) 1 Alta. L. Rev. 501.

37 W.F. Bowker, *Limitation of Actions in Tort in Alberta* (1962) 2 Alta. L. Rev. 41. *See* also J.P.S. McLaren, *The Impact of Limitation Periods on Actionability in Negligence* (1969) 7 Alta. L. Rev. 247, esp. footnotes, 1, 99, 142.

38 W.F. Bowker, *The Uniform Survival of Actions Act* (1964) 3 Alta. L. Rev. 197. For another view, *see* J.H. Laycraft, *Survival of Claims for Loss of Expectation of Life* (1964) 3 Alta. L. Rev. 202.

39 W.F. Bowker, *Ten More Years Under the Contributory Negligence Acts* (1965) 2 U.B.C. L. Rev. 198.

40 *See Bowker,* (1954) 32 Can. Bar Rev. 933–937.

41 *Re Lewis* (1918) 13 Alta. L.R. 423, 41 D.L.R. 1, [1918] 2 W.W.R. 687 (Alta. S.C., Full Court); *Re Norton* (1918), 13 Alta. L.R. 457, [1918] 2 W.W.R. 865; and *see Re Gray* (1918), 57 S.C.R. 150 (S.C.C.), a similar case in which the Supreme Court of Canada held the orders-in-council in question to be valid, and so overruled *Re Lewis*.

42 *The Case of Wolfe Tone* (1798), 27 St. Tr. 614. *See* R.F.V. Heuston, *Essays in Constitutional Law* (1961), 34 *et seq.* Dean Bowker, at page 937 of his article, refers to the case of Merryman, an alleged Confederate sympathizer in the American Civil War, in which an order of *habeas corpus* issued by Chief Justice Taney was involved.

43 *Supra,* note 35, at 1132.

44 *Supra,* note 36.

45 *Supra,* note 36.

46 *B.A. Oil Co. Ltd.* v. *Kos,* [1964] S.C.R. 167 (S.C.C.).

47 W.F. Bowker, *The Law of Evidence: 1923–1947* (1948) 26 Can. Bar Rev. 246, 247–248.

48 *Hodge's Case* (1838), 2 Lewin 227, 168 E.R. 1136.

49 *McGreevy* v. *D.P.P.* [1973] 1 All E.R. 503 (H.L.), 508, 510.

50 *Supra,* note 37.

51 *Supra,* note 36.

52 *See supra,* note 27.

53 W.F. Bowker, *Experimentation on humans and gifts of tissue: articles 20 and 23 of the Civil Code* (1973) 19 McGill L.J. 161. *See* also: Bowker, *Legal Liability to Volunteers in Testing New Drugs* (1963) 88 Canadian M.A. Jo. 745.

54 W.F. Bowker, *Cases on Civil Liberties*. Revised edition. Faculty of Law, University of Alberta, 1972.

55 W.F. Bowker, *Basic Rights and Freedoms: What Are They?* (1959) 37 Can. Bar Rev. 43; *Protection of Basic Human Rights and Liberties* (1956) 2 U.B.C. Legal Notes 281; and *see* (1963) Canadian Bar Papers 58.

56 *R.* v. *Drybones* [1970] S.C.R. 282 (S.C.C.).

57 *Bowker*, (1970) 8 Alta. L. Rev., 409, 414, criticized, Marx, (1972) 37 Sask. L. Rev. 101.

58 *See Martin* v. *Law Society of B.C.* [1950] 3 D.L.R. 173 (B.C.C.A.).

59 *See* the articles referred to in note 55, *supra*.

60 Such as those of E.V. Rostow, *The Sovereign Prerogative,* Yale University Press, 1962.

61 Perhaps he might agree with the view that a democracy that continues to look to judicial review for protection is not unlike an evangelized primitive society that accepts the new deity but as insurance continues to honour its other gods. As Edward S. Corwin once said, "Judicial review represents an attempt by the American Democracy to cover its bet": (1942) 56 Harv. Law Rev. 437.

62 For accounts of the genesis and early operation of the Institute, *see* Bowker, (1968) 11 Can. Bar Jo. 341 and (1969) 19 U. of T. L.J. 376.

63 W.F. Bowker, letter, (1964) 3 Alta. L. Rev. 159.

64 The recent history of organized law reform in Alberta deserves a note. In 1964 the Law Society established a Law Reform Committee with membership drawn from the profession, the judiciary,

and the Faculty of Law. Working without full-time members, supporting staff, or funds, it prepared a set of recommendations concerning limitation of tort actions which were enacted in 1966 as Part 9 of the Limitations Act (now R.S.A. 1970, c. 209), drew the notice of the government to acts recommended elsewhere concerning personal property, security, survival of actions, and perpetuities, and began a preliminary study of the law relating to occupiers' liability. It was soon recognized by the Committee and the Benchers that as constituted the Committee would not be sufficiently effective as a law reform agency. The University of Alberta and the Provincial Government were receptive to suggestions that a better-funded and more permanent research body should be established. On November 15, 1967, the Province, the University and the Law Society signed an agreement establishing the Institute of Law Research and Reform. The agreement has since been amended twice, on December 1, 1969, and on August 30, 1971. The original agreement covered the period January, 1968, to March 31, 1973. The 1971 agreement extended the period to March 31, 1977.

The Institute has several distinctive features, not common to all law reform bodies: it is constituted by agreement rather than by statute; it is independent of government, with freedom to select its reform projects and present its proposals in formats of its own choice; and its objects include not only matters of law reform, but the promotion of general legal research.

The Institute is funded by the Province and the University. The University provides accommodation in the Law Centre, proximate to the Faculty of Law and the Law Library. The institute has a Board of eight members, with power to add an additional member. Each party to the founding agreement appoints one member; two members, the Director and the Vice-President (Academic) of the University, are on the Board *ex officio;* these members appoint the remaining members. The Vice-President (Academic) is not a lawyer, and generally restricts his participation to matters of planning and finance, and other questions of interest to the University. Under practices followed to date, the Board as a whole sets the research programme of the Institute and considers and approves reports recommending reform. It meets at least a full day twice each month, with a smaller Executive Committee meeting weekly to handle continuing business. It has the power to appoint advisory committees. Serving the Institute, under the supervision of the Director, are the Board's Counsel (Mrs. M.A. Shone) and Legal Research Officers. Each summer the Institute engages a number of senior law students to conduct research assigned by the Director. The Board may engage outside lawyers, practising or academic, to conduct research and prepare papers on various reform projects, but the more recent trend has been to do more research "in house." As the Institute progressively acquires greater experience, and takes on a greater volume and variety of projects, it seeks to vary and improve its methods of selecting projects, scheduling work, supervising research, and soliciting relevant public opinion.

Professor Bowker was Director of the Institute from its inception to his retirement in 1975. He is now succeeded by Mr. W.H. Hurlburt, Q.C., an original member of the Board and for a while its Chairman, who served in 1974 and 1975 as Associate Director. The successive Chairmen of the Board have been Mr. H.G. Field, Q.C., Mr. W. H. Hurlburt, Q.C., and (currently) His Honour Judge W.A. Stevenson.

Special mention should be made of the part played in establishing the Institute by Dr. Max Wyman, who as Vice-President (Academic) of the University served on the Board and later, as President, gave it constant support. I believe it was at his suggestion that the University Governors made possible the creation of a working library for the Institute by directing the application for that purpose of substantial moneys from the Charles E. Merril Trust.

Although the Institute has given most of its attention to its law reform work, it has not neglected its more general mission to encourage legal research. In 1968 and 1969, and again in 1974 and 1975, it funded research projects conducted by professors at the University of Alberta. In 1971 and 1972, it sponsored research studies by summer students, including a survey of powers of search, seizure and arrest under various provincial statutes and an analysis of the legal position of "British subjects" under provincial legislation. In response to inquiries or suggestions from private groups, the Institute initiated several research studies, including one on the law governing cremation in Canadian provinces and another on restrictions on the use of land, particularly rural land. The Institute also established the J.A. Weir Memorial Lectures; in March 1972, the Rt. Hon. Sir Victor Windeyer, a distinguished member of the High Court of Australia, gave two lectures on "Some Aspects of Australian Constitutional Law" (later published by the Institute in a booklet) and a third lecture, "History in Law and Law in History," since printed in (1973) 11 Alta. L. Rev. 123.

In law reform, the Institute has developed from modest beginnings to become one of the most productive and successful such agencies in Canada. As of the date of its 1974–75 Annual Report in July 1975, it has issued 17 formal reports. The legislature has taken action on all of the first 13 subjects (except the Guarantees Acknowledgment Act, as to which the Institute recommended only some amendments); the other Reports were then under consideration by the Cabinet or Government Departments. The Reports have varied greatly in length and subject matter as is shown by the following table:

Number and Title of Report

No. 1—Compensation for Victims of Crime (1968)
No. 2—Powers of Personal Representatives to Grant Options (1969)
No. 3—Occupiers' Liability (1969)
No. 4—Age of Majority (1970)
No. 5—Guarantees Acknowledgment Act, R.S.A. 1970, c. 173 (1970)
No. 6—Rules Against Perpetuities (1971)
No. 7—Joinder of Divorce Proceedings with other Causes of Action (1971
No. 8—Assignment of Wages (1971)
No. 9—Rule in *Saunders* v. *Vautier* (1972)
No. 10—Powers of Maintenance and Advancement (1972)
No. 11—Common Promisor and Promisee: Conveyances with a Common Party (1972)
No. 12—Expropriation (1973)
No. 13—Judicature Act, section 24 (1974)
No. 14—Minors' Contracts (1975)
No. 15—Validity of Rules of Court (1975) (to be published Aug. 1975)
No. 16—Rule in *Hollington* v. *Hewthorn* (1975)
No. 17—Small Projects (1975)

Legislation

Criminal Injuries Compensation Act, R.S.A. 1970, c. 75
Wills Act, R.S.A. 1970, c. 393, s. 30
Devolution of Real Property Act, R.S.A. 1970, c. 109, s. 13
Occupiers' Liability Act, 1973, c. 79
Age of Majority Act, 1971, c. 1.
Perpetuities Act, 1972, c. 131
Rules of Court, (Alta. Reg. 315/71)
Wage Assignments Act, 1974, c. 61
Trustee Act Amendment, 1973 c. 13, s. 12
Trustee Act Amendment, 1974, c. 65, s. 9
Common Parties Contracts and Conveyances Act, 1974, c. 20, amended 1975, c. 5 (2 sess.)
Expropriation Act, 1974, c. 27
Judicature Act Amendment, (1974), c. 65, s. 5(2)

The latter report, "Small Projects," dealt with a miscellany of small defects in the Alberta law.

As of June 30, 1975, the Institute had some fifteen other projects, some of them very large, well underway. Among them are review of the decisions of administrative tribunals, a revision of the Alberta companies legislation, confidentiality of government documents, exemptions from execution and garnishment, the Alberta labour law, revision of the Land Titles Act, the law as to residential tenancies, a complete examination of the Limitation of Actions Act, consent of minors to medical treatment, legislation governing partition of concurrent property interests, the law governing sale of goods and services, a review of the Statute of Frauds, and the liability of vendors for defects in houses sold. An excellent working paper on the Contributory Negligence Act and Joint Tortfeasors Act has now been published. A series of very important reform projects are being conducted under the general heading of "family law." Research is well advanced on the Family Relief Act, the law as to support, guardianship, custody and wardship of children, the status of illegitimate children, and miscellaneous topics such as actions for seduction, and the status of "common law" spouses. In 1972, the Institute published a Working Paper proposing a family court supported by necessary counselling services and unifying various powers and procedures now dispersed between different courts; this has been followed by further reports and experimental projects by law reform agencies elsewhere. A major component of the Family Law studies has been a study of the law of matrimonial property. A survey to ascertain community attitudes was conducted, and a working paper, outlining different possible approaches, was widely circulated in 1974 and followed up by a series of meetings with interested groups throughout the Province. The final Report, making definite recommendations, will have been published by October, 1975.

In recent summers, students have been engaged to do research relating to these projects, or on other topics, such as the admissibility of extrinsic evidence in the interpretation of statutes.

Perhaps a law teacher may be permitted to mention the general benefit provided to legal studies by the Institute's thorough and scholarly reports. Its studies of perpetuities, occupiers' liability, covenants with a common promisee, infants' contracts, and family property law have become texts of use to many students outside, as well as within, Alberta.

65 *Re Sproule* (1887), 12 S.C.R. 140 (S.C.C.).

66 Her Honour, Judge M.M. Bowker, received her LL.B. in 1938 and articled thereafter with Mr. George H. Steer, Q.C. She married W.F. Bowker on October 12, 1940; they have three children, Blair, Lorna, and Keith. Among many volunteer activities Mrs Bowker has been Parliamentarian for the National Conference of the Y.W.C.A. (1965), a member of the National Council of Girl Guides of Canada, a member of the Vanier Institute, and a trustee of the University of Alberta Hospital. In 1967 she presented an important brief on mental retardation to a Committee of the Alberta Legislature considering preventive health services; and in 1965 wrote a supplemental or independent report by a Committee considering adoption in Alberta. She will be particularly remembered with gratitude by foreign students she met and helped through the University Women's Club. In 1967 (with Margaret Mead) she received the honorary degree of Doctor of Laws from Ewha Women's University, Korea. Mrs. Bowker was made a Judge of the Alberta Juvenile and Family Court in 1966, and since has achieved national recognition for her leadership in developing the Family Court Conciliation Project; *see Reader's Digest,* September, 1975.

67 A phrase by Noel Annan. of another, in *Maurice Bowra,* 1974, at 48.

68 J.H.Wilkinson, *Serving Justice: A Supreme Court Clerk's View,* 1974, at 113.

69 Quoted by Leonard W. Brockington, (1948) 26 Can. Bar Rev. 1399 at 1409.

70 O.W. Holmes, jnr., *The Profession of the Law,* lecture to Harvard undergraduates on February 17, 1886, *Speeches* (1913), 22.

Biographical Sketch of Wilbur F. Bowker

Born Ponoka, Alberta, 1910

Academic and Professional

Schooling to Grade XI—Ponoka

University of Alberta (1926–1932); B.A. 1930; LL.B. 1932

Admitted to Alberta Bar 1933

Law Practice (1933–1942)
- initially with George H. Steer; later an associate in Milner, Steer

Canadian Army (1942–1945)
- Private (infantry) to Captain
- later posted to N.D.H.Q. Ottawa

Faculty of Law, University of Alberta
- Lecturer (1945–6)
- Associate Professor (1946–7)
- Acting Dean (1947–8)
- Dean of Law (1948–1968)

Master of Laws Degree (LL.M.)
- University of Minnesota
- (3 summer semesters 1946–8)

Yale University Sabbatical Leave 1952–3

Institute of Law Research and Reform
- Director of the Institute 1968–1975
- Member of Board of Directors 1975–1984

Honors

Yale University Sterling Fellowship 1953
Honorary Degree, Doctor of Laws, University of Alberta 1972
Honorary Bencher, Law Society of Alberta 1976
Honorary Professor, Faculty of Law, University of Calgary 1977
Honorary Life Membership, Canadian Bar Association 1979
Paul Harris Fellow, Rotary Club 1980
Bowker Building (Alberta head office for Attorney General's Department) 1981

Bowker Inn (Chapter of Phi Delta Phi, an international legal fraternity established at the University of Alberta) 1985

Personal

Married 1940 to Marjorie Montgomery, lawyer and later Judge of the Juvenile and Family Court (1966–1983)
Children:
Blair Montgomery Bowker, M.D. (b. 1948), internist and endocrinologist, North Bay, Ontario
Lorna Ethel Bowker Pennie (Mrs. Ross Pennie) (b. 1950), social worker, Ottawa
Keith Wilbur Bowker (b. 1952), technician at University Hospital, Edmonton
Seven grandchildren

Chronological List of Writings of Wilbur F. Bowker

1937 Procedures in Divorce Actions in Alberta
(1938–40) 3 Alta. L.Q. 51

1947 Book Review: Paton on "Jurisprudence"
(1947) 25 Can. Bar Rev. 931

1948 Law of Evidence
(1948) 26 Can. Bar Rev. 248

1952 Intestate Succession to Personal Property
(Unpublished; written while a graduate student at Yale University)

1952 Book Review: Paton on "Jurisprudence", 2d ed.
(1952) 31 Can. Bar Rev. 330

1954 Hon. Horace Harvey, Chief Justice of Alberta
(1954) 32 Can. Bar Rev. 933 & 1118

1954 Book Review: "Legal Theory" by W. Friedmann
(1954) 11 U.T.L.J. 383

1955 Professional Ethics
(1955) 1 Alta. Law Rev. 71

1955 History of the Association of Canadian Law Teachers
(Unpublished; in the Archives of the Association)

1956 Protection of Basic Rights and Liberties
(1956) 2 U.B.C. Law Notes 281

1958 Succession to Property in Common Law Provinces
University of Toronto, Faculty of Law, Comparative Law Series

1958 A Statement of Objectives of Canadian Common-Law Schools
(1958) 36 Can. Bar Rev. 242

1959 Basic Rights and Freedoms: What Are They?
(1959) 37 Can. Bar Rev.

1960 Book Review: "Civil Liberties and Canadian Federalism" by F.R. Scott
(1960) 38 Can. Bar Rev. 443

1960 Reform of the Law of Dower in Alberta
(1960) 1 Alta. Law Rev. 501

1962 Limitations of Actions in Tort in Alberta
(1962–64) 2 Alta. Law Rev. 41

1963 Legal Liability to Volunteers in Testing New Drugs
(1963) 88 Can. Medical Assoc. Journal 745

1963 Anti-Discrimination Legislation
Papers at Can. Bar Assoc. Meeting 1963, p. 28

1964 Uniform Survival of Actions Act
(1964) 3 Alta. Law Rev. 197

1964 The Professional Responsibility of the Lawyer
(Unpublished; Address to the Law Society of Saskatchewan)

1964 Malcolm Murray MacIntyre
(1964) 3 Alta. Law Rev. 161

1965 Three Alberta Judges
(1965) 4 Alta. Law Rev. 5

1965 Ten More Years Under the Contributory Negligence Acts
(1965) 2 U.B.C. Law Rev. 198

1967 Law of Succession (Common Law)
(Unpublished; Address to the Association of Canadian Law Teachers, Ottawa, June 1967)

1968 A Canadian Charter of Human Rights
(Unpublished; Address to Association of Canadian Law Teachers, Calgary, June 1968)

1968 Alberta Institute of Law Research & Reform
(1968) 11 Canadian Bar Journal 341

1969 Organized Law Reform in Alberta
(1969) 19 U.T.L.J. 376

1970 Case Comment: R. v. Drybones (Canadian Bill of Rights; Indian Act; Irreconcilable Conflict, Equality Before the Law)
(1970) 8 Alta. Law Rev. 409

1973 Experimentation on Humans and Gifts of Human Tissue
(1973) 19 McGill Law Journal 161

1973 Book Review: Human Rights Casefinder: 1953–1969: The Warren Court Era
(1973) 11 Alta. Law Rev. 415

1978 Expeditious Justice: Western Style
(Unpublished; Address to the Canadian Institute on the Administration of Justice)

1980 Book Review: "A History of Dalhousie Law School" by John Willis
(1980) 18 Alta. Law Rev. 332

1980 Extra-Judicial Writing: The Alberta Law Quarterly, The Alberta Law Review, and Reviews in General
(1980) 18 Alta. Law Rev. 458 (An Address on the 25th Anniversary of the Alberta Law Review)

1981 Book Review: "Aspects of Privacy Law: Essays in Honour of John M. Sharp," edited by Dale Gibson
(1981) 59 Can. Bar Rev. 599

1981 Minors and Mental Incompetents: Consent to Experimentation, Gifts of Tissue and Sterilization
(1981) 26 McGill Law Journal 951

1982 Ethical Issues in the Allocation of Health Care Resources
University of Calgary Institute on Humanities, Community Seminar No. 2, April 1982

1982 Fifty-Five Years at the Alberta Bar: George Hobson Steer, Q.C.
(1982) 20 Alta. Law Rev. 242

1982 Homestead Laws in the Four Western Provinces
"Matrimonial Property Law in Canada," Bissett-Johnson & Holland, eds. Loose Leaf Release No. 3, August 1982

1982 A Light-Hearted View of the History and Traditions of the Legal Profession of Alberta
(Unpublished; Address to the Alberta Branch of the Canadian Bar Association)

1984 Confidentiality of Hospital Medical Records
"The Record," Newsletter of the Alberta Health Record Association, September–October 1984

1985 Legal Education
"The Canadian Encyclopedia," 1st ed. 1985 Edmonton, Hurtig, p. 995

1985 Arthur Sifton
Ibid., p. 1695

1985 Medicine and Law: Two Solitudes?
(Unpublished; Address to the College of Physicians and Surgeons of Alberta, Calgary, October 3, 1985)

1986 The Sproule Case: Bloodshed at Kootenay Lake, 1885
In "Law and Justice in a New Land," edited by Louis A. Knafla, 1986, Toronto, Carswell, p. 233

1986 Our Earliest 'Homestead' or 'Dower' Act
(1986) 24 Alta. Law Rev. 522

1988 Stipendiary Magistrates and the Supreme Court of the North-West Territories, 1876–1907
(1988) 26 Alta. Law Rev. 245

1988 Metaphors and Other Notable Passages in Judgments
(Unpublished; expanded text of a speech given to graduating Law students, March 1988)

Additions by the Editor

1976 Wilbur Fee Bowker: In Appreciation
by D. T. Anderson
(1976) 14 Alta. Law Rev. 199

Biographical Sketch of Wilbur F. Bowker

Index

Writings Not Included In This Collection

Thesis for Master's Degree, University of Minnesota, entitled "Basic Rights in Canada and the United States" (2 personal copies only)

Various Reports of the Alberta Commissioners to Uniform Law Conferences, 1953–1975

Panels for the Law Society of Alberta, Annual Meetings (in which W.F. Bowker was a major participant) on the following topics:

(a) Bills of Sale and Chattel Mortgages, reported in (1955–61) 1 Alta. Law Rev. 273
(b) Expropriation Procedure and Compensation, reported in (1962) 2 Alta. Law Rev. 76
(c) The Drafting of Wills, reported in (1954) 2 U.B.C. Law Rev. 381 (W.F. Bowker as Chairman)

We Need The Shield and the Sword in Safeguarding Our Human Rights "Human Rights" (Ontario Human Rights Commission) Vol. 4, No. 8 (1963).

Address to Alberta Magistrates Association, Jasper, Alberta, 1971 on "Due Process of Law"

Alphabetical Index of Subject Matter